Blues Who's Who

Sheldon Harris

A Biographical Dictionary of Blues Singers

A DA CAPO PAPERBACK

Library of Congress Cataloging in Publication Data

Harris, Sheldon.
Blues who's who.

(A Da Capo paperback)
Reprint. Originally published: New Rochelle, N.Y.: Arlington House, c1979.
Bibliography: p.
Includes indexes.
1. Blues (Songs, etc.)—United States—Bio-bibliography. I. Title.
[ML102.B6H3 1981] 784.5'3'00922 [B] 81-7873
ISBN 0-306-80155-8 AACR2

First paperback printing—August, 1981
Second paperback printing—January, 1983
Third paperback printing—January, 1985
Fourth paperback printing—January, 1987
Fifth paperback printing—March, 1989
Sixth paperback printing—November, 1991
Seventh paperback printing—January, 1994

This Da Capo Press paperback edition of *Blues Who's Who: A Biographical Dictionary of Blues Singers* is an unabridged republication of the first edition published in New Rochelle, N.Y. in 1979, supplemented by author emendations as of November, 1993. It is reprinted by arrangement with Arlington House Publishers.

Published by Da Capo Press, Inc.
A Subsidiary of Plenum Publishing Corporation
233 Spring Street, New York, N.Y. 10013

Manufactured in the United States of America

Contents

INTRODUCTION 9
FORMAT 13
ABBREVIATIONS 17
ACKNOWLEDGMENTS 21
BIOGRAPHIES 27
SELECTED BIBLIOGRAPHY
Books 599
Periodicals 605
Magazines in Print 606
Record Companies 607
FILM INDEX 611
RADIO INDEX 617
TELEVISION INDEX 621
THEATER INDEX 629
SONG INDEX 635
NAMES & PLACES INDEX 699

To the memory of Dr. Marshall W. Stearns,
a gentle and inspiring man

Introduction

BLUES WHO'S WHO is a collection of 571 biographies of selected blues singers, a work that took nearly 18 years of research, not only by myself, but by dedicated writers and contributors the world over. Its scope ranges through various periods and styles roughly covering the years 1900 through 1977.

This is a pioneering effort that attempts to present a detailed listing of each singer's career credits in chronological order, while consolidating the present body of blues knowledge into an accessible and concise reference source.

Each entry has been condensed to the bare facts, without embellishment. They have been gathered from personal interviews and correspondence, a variety of books from many fields, magazine articles, old newspapers, current news items, record album liner notes, bibliographies, discographies, filmographies, publicity information, scrap books, library files, private collections, unpublished material and other sources.

Despite the many thousands of facts to be found here, it should not be assumed that this book is the definitive and final compendium or that all who have ever sung blues have been included. To be certain, many problems had to be faced during the long course of preparation.

Black American blues has a long and colorful history, having existed in commercial and non-commercial form for at least 70 years. During that time it served mostly as a socio-ethnological minority music, surfacing sporadically into the white mainstream as a special style or occasional fad. Its activities were rarely noted by the mass press until well into the 1940s with the emergence of rhythm & blues and later, rock 'n' roll. With the rediscovery of some older singers during the 1960s, blues gradually became recognized as the important and highly influential secular music it is.

Like any other living art form that has subtle and ethereal "rules" that are often changed at will by the artist, it is difficult, if not impossible, to define this mode of singing. Most musicians, singers, fans, writers, critics, collectors and others in the field today profess to know a blues singer "instinctively" when they hear one. But when blues dares to encroach on other musics or assume influences outside the hard-core of a specific blues style, its boundaries become vague and so do most definitions. When a singer is asked to define blues, he usually resorts to the lyric content or an emotion to explain the music. On the other hand, a critic may try to express himself in comparative, technical, historical or racial terms.

Back in the 1940s, blues, to the average fan or collector, usually meant pre-WW2 women singers (considered "classic" blues at the time) while other styles were conveniently slipped into such categories as folk, swing, modern, rhythm & blues and others. Outside of some jazz history books, a limited number of jazz and collector magazines and some specialized folk-blues recordings and field trips, there were few solid biographical facts available on blues singers.

During the 1950s this writer was serving in a volunteer capacity as secretary of the Institute of Jazz Studies in New York City, a non-profit organization devoted to encouraging the study of jazz and related music. The late Dr. Marshall W. Stearns was executive director. Inquiries to the IJS only reaffirmed the lack of available blues information, and consequently a small note pad was used to jot down passing references. By about 1960 the raw data had grown, so serious effort was given to develop it into some kind of index or reference source. As popular interest in blues grew during the 1960s, the notes exploded into a large set of loose-leaf books eventually containing information on well over 1500 singers. Even though the IJS was later transferred to Rutgers University in Newark, N.J., this effort continued as a part-time labor of love until 1974.

The recession that year finally had its personal toll. After 30 years as an advertising executive, this writer was separated from the position. What better time, then, to wrap up the notes for publication? It was not a simple decision. It took four years of frantic full-time work to bring it to its present somewhat organized form.

Among the many problems over the years, one of the most difficult was the range and selection of singers. Limiting the choice only to blues *singers* was an early decision. Reasoning that blues is basically a vocal art and consequently its principal exponents have generally been singers, it was felt that opening the pages to non-singing blues musicians and others would be beyond the intent of this work. As the book enlarged it was also found necessary to eliminate many singers with little or no biographical data in order to keep the entries factually meaningful and the book within bounds.

The problem of exactly who qualified as a blues singer was the most frustrating. Obviously, not everyone who sang blues was a blues singer, per se, and some kind of benchmarks were needed.

1. *Blues singers vs. singers of blues.*
   As there is no accepted definition of a blues singer (nor, for that matter, most any other kind of singer in American music), some distinction of categorization had to be noted, often where none actually existed. For example, some early so-called blues singers were in truth vaudeville entertainers who sang and recorded blues as an accommodation to the times, whereas their general work was non-blues ballads and show tunes. Also, many older "songsters" were quite familiar with hokum-dances (black- or minstrel-inspired early popular music), white country music and popular Tin Pan Alley songs of the day as well as blues. And then, just what kind of folk music did a folk singer sing, especially when he also sang blues? (There are sources that consider them synonymous.) There were also the religious singers, band singers, torch singers, club singers, white country singers, hot-mama singers, rock singers, soul singers and many others who sang blues or

blues-type songs. The point is that the so-called "authenticity" a singer brings to the blues is indeed a nebulous quality.

2. *The blues sound, form and content.*
   Historically, blues are based on the black experience and heritage which include various factors. African influences, southern black language patterns, free expressiveness within recognized bar structures, church music, blue notes and social-personal lyric subject matter are among the considerations. The judgment here is probably the ear itself, admittedly subjective.

3. *Reputation, acceptance and weight of blues work.*
   The expertise and importance of peer acceptance, in addition to critical writings, opinions, discographical listings and total blues work was, with discretion, taken into consideration.

These general guides or tests were applied to a broad range of singers within the many regional and related blues forms, as well as folk, white country, vaudeville, jazz, trad, rhythm & blues, rock and other areas in an attempt to select the most pertinent and recognized blues artists. With such a fractionalized field, there still was no clear-cut recognition standard in all cases and some apparent exceptions to the guides may be noted. While admittedly vague, the bottom line seems to be that the determination of blues singing rests with the performers' interpretation and artistry, and the listeners' acceptance of such.

The final selection of singers and entry facts for each was entirely my own. Whether there should have been more or possibly less choice discretion is certainly debatable. Any oversights, sequential or factual inconsistencies or outright errors are entirely conceivable but, assuredly, wholly unintentional. All substantiated additions or revisions are welcome, so that possible future editions may be more inclusive and complete.

Sheldon Harris
New York
April 1978

Format

The many entry facts in this book were obtained from numerous sources over a long period of time. Their accuracy, of course, is solely contingent on the reliability of those sources. In the case of personal interviews, most details have been accepted as truth unless verified contradictions are found or stronger evidence points otherwise. When an informant could not pin-point or confirm specific time events or places, an approximation was noted. As for secondhand reports, the reputation of the writer, musician, singer, researcher, interviewer or other source was taken into account. As a general rule, faced with contradictory or varying information, preference was given to first-person, eye-witness, after-the-fact reports. Probable facts, when known, are so noted. Most unspecified, incomplete or suspect details have been omitted. With few exceptions, advertisements or publicity promos of forthcoming events were not used, for obvious reasons.

It should be pointed out that the sum total of facts for any one singer may be inconsistent with his actual work, popularity or influence. While some performers received comparatively more notice and press coverage, many talented singers were (and in some cases still are) overlooked by the black as well as white media and the facts are just not available. While every effort was made to be all-inclusive, no assumption should be made that completeness has been achieved or that a brief biography or even a credit period gap necessarily represents musical inactivity. All biographies, at the very most, should be considered representative. It should also not be assumed that all credits are necessarily blues performances, or for that matter, even singing performances.

In addition to career data, outside work and other non-musical sequential events are noted, when known. New careers in related creative fields are carried to their optimum as a legitimate extension of a singer's entertainment and/or musical work.

Biographies list information in the following order. Where facts were unavailable or did not exist, pertinent sub-captions were eliminated.

Name: Most biographies are listed under the singers' true, given name (as known) and include nicknames, titles and other descriptive name appendages. If a singer also used a pseudonym while retaining a true name, the listing will be found under the true name with pseudonyms noted below that name and cross-referenced within the body of the book. If a singer is well known by a professional, legal, married or abbreviated name other than his true name, it is considered for the purposes of this book to be a common alias and the biography will be found under that alias. In such cases, true name (if known) is listed within the body of the text. Unknown maiden or partial names are indicated by ———.

Birth/Death: Whenever possible, facts on birth and death have been confirmed by interview, reports and/or official records. Some singers have been evasive regarding their true birth dates and places. Approximated or unconfirmed information has been so noted.

Instruments: All known instruments played by the singer are listed alphabetically.

Biography: Bio facts are listed mostly by work credits. When applicable, a single credit consists of an event/location/year. While listing credits sequentially assures their chronology, all attempts have been made also to list different same-year credits in their proper order as well. Unfortunately, the use of such an extremely large number of varying, unspecified and undated facts has not always made this possible and some caution should be used in interpretation. A credit signifies at least one appearance during the calendar year, but could also possibly include multiple appearances and returns. Residencies, where known, are so noted. A certain amount of condensation was necessary for brevity, particularly when citing consecutive-year credits for the same club, concert tour or record label. An original recording date is listed as a simple credit (label/location/year) and may also include multiple sessions during any one year. Reissues are not listed. No attempt was made to duplicate existing discographies and reference should be made to those sources for further recording details. Sideman activities in recordings, clubs, bands, sit-ins, etc., are generally not pursued in depth.

Note: Whenever a pertinent question or some detail requires emphasis, it is so listed here.

Personal: Family affiliations, relationships, name similarities and other non-credit facts are so listed.

Billings: All known professional or recording billings are listed but not cross-referenced. While billings are usually coupled with the singer's name, they are not so listed here.

Books: All known books, pamphlets and folios written by or about the singer and his work are listed. These may include biographies, song collections, reference, instructional or other subject material.

Songs: Selected songs, whether lyrics, melodies or both, written by the singer in total or part, are listed alphabetically. A co-author is not listed unless he is also a blues singer in this book in which case the song will be listed for both singers. Sources for composer credits are from phonograph records, sheet music, personal interviews or other, but due to the common intermingling of this music (multiple titles, assumptive credits, buy-out rights, use of PD [public domain] material and questionable copyright procedures), some discretion is advised. Songs usually associated with, but not written by, the singer are not listed.

Awards/Honors: All known awards, citations, honors, recognitions and other achievements are noted. Gold records and other commercially successful recordings have not been listed.

Influences: The prime source for influences has been the singer himself and all are cross-referenced. It should be noted that some influences are instrumental as well as vocal and are often considered interchangeable. Also, in the case of some better known, later-day singers, there seem to be a greater number of "influenced by" names given and it is entirely possible that these may actually be only hand-shake credits.

Quotations: A cross section of opinions representing the general pertinence, style, effect or position of the singer or his work within the blues field is so noted. Outside critiques have been brought into the book to offer a wider range of thought. While selected quotes may not necessarily represent this author's view, they were chosen on the basis of their relevancy, clarity and positiveness, with no controversial intent or detailed analysis intended.

References: Suggested published sources for further study are so listed. References may include detailed and personal interviews or articles, anecdotes, criticisms, remembrances as well as general color and background. The references cited do not necessarily mean they are the source for the entry itself or that there are no others equally as informative.

Photographs: The photographs in this book have been gathered from many collections and are used with the kind permission of the photographers or owners of the pictures as indicated. No illustrations may be reproduced without permission of these owners. While every attempt has been made to trace and credit proper owners, holders of some historic, publicity and other photographs are not known. I wish to extend my apologies to any copyright holder whose photo may be uncredited or inadvertently miscredited.

Abbreviations

For the sake of brevity, the following abbreviations have been used:

ABC	American Broadcasting Company
acc	accompanied/accompaniment/accompanist
AFN	Armed Forces Network
AK	Alaska
aka	also known as
AL	Alabama
ANTA	American National Theater & Academy
app	appeared/appearances
AR	Arkansas
A&R	Artists & Repertoire
ARC	American Record Company
Assoc	Association
AZ	Arizona
b	born
BA	Bachelor of Arts
BBC	British Broadcasting Corporation
Bio	Biography
BMI	Broadcast Music Incorporated
Bros	Brothers
BS	Bachelor of Science
c	circa
CA	California
Can	Canada
CBC	Canadian Broadcasting Corporation
CBS	Columbia Broadcasting System
CCC	Civilian Conservation Corps
CO	Colorado
Co	County
Col	College
Corp	Corporation
CT	Connecticut

C&W	Country & Western
d	died
DC	District of Columbia
DE	Delaware
Demos	Demonstration records
Den	Denmark
Dept	Department
DJ	Disc Jockey
DOA	Dead on Arrival
Ed	Editor
Eng	England
ep	episode
FL	Florida
FM	Frequency Modulation
Ft	Fort
GA	Georgia
Ger	Germany
GI	Government Issue (US Army Enlisted Man)
HI	Hawaii
HS	High School
IA	Iowa
ID	Idaho
IL	Illinois
IN	Indiana
Inc	Incorporated
Infl	Influenced
Inst	Instrument
IWO	International Workers Organization
JATP	Jazz At The Philharmonic
Jr	Junior
KKK	Ku Klux Klan
KS	Kansas
KY	Kentucky
LA	Louisiana
LC	Library of Congress
Ltd	Limited
MA	Master of Arts
MA	Massachusetts
MC	Master of Ceremonies
MD	Maryland
ME	Maine
MI	Michigan
MN	Minnesota
MO	Missouri
MS	Mississippi

Mt	Mount
MT	Montana
NAACP	National Association for the Advancement of Colored People
NAIRD	National Association of Independent Record Distributors
NATRA	National Association of Television Recording Artists
NBC	National Broadcasting Company
NC	North Carolina
NCO	Non-commissioned Officer
nd	no date
ND	North Dakota
NE	Nebraska
NH	New Hampshire
NJ	New Jersey
NM	New Mexico
NV	Nevada
NY	New York
NYC	New York City
OD	Overdose
OH	Ohio
OK	Oklahoma
OR	Oregon
Orch	Orchestra
OWI	Office of War Information
PA	Pennsylvania
Par	Parish
PBS	Public Broadcasting Service
por	portion
POW	Prisoner of War
PR	Puerto Rico
Prof	Professor
Qt	Quartet
R&B	Rhythm & Blues
rec	recorded
rel	released
Rev	Reverend
RI	Rhode Island
RKO	Radio-Keith-Orpheum
SA	South America
SC	South Carolina
SD	South Dakota
Sr	Senior
ST	sound track
TN	Tennessee
TOBA	Theater Owners' Booking Association
TV	Television

TX	Texas
UCLA	University of California, Los Angeles
UK	United Kingdom
Univ	University
US	United States
USA	United States of America
USIA	United States Information Agency
USO	United Service Organization
UT	Utah
VA	Virginia
VOA	Voice of America
VP	Vice President
VT	Vermont
w	with
WA	Washington
WI	Wisconsin
WV	West Virginia
WY	Wyoming
YMCA	Young Men's Christian Association

Acknowledgments

Fortunately, in extended works such as this there are always special persons who step forward with valuable information, assistance, material and support, willing to contribute to that which they feel part of. Without a doubt, their deep concern for American music has, over the years, been a factor in the growth and support of blues.

At the top, I wish to particularly thank these friends who put up with my demands of their time over unforgivably long periods. Their responsibility and constant interest while incurring costs at their own expense are more than cause for this special appreciation.

Bob Eagle, Australia
David Griffiths, Great Britain
Norbert Hess, Germany
Robert Javors, Brooklyn, NY
Amy and Jim O'Neal, Chicago, IL

I also owe a great debt of gratitude to the following fine singers, musicians, noted contributors, photographers and other friends of blues who generously offered whatever I asked. Their unhesitating help and support, their dedication to blues and wanting to participate, consequently now benefits us all.

Alex Albright
May Alix
Ann/Walter C. Allen
Richard B. Allen
William Arnold
Louisa Barker
Clyde Bernhardt
Eubie Blake
Travis Blaylock
E. Lorenz Borenstein
Jack Bradley
Arne Brogger
John Broven
Clarence Brown
Lawrence Brown
Olive Brown
Roy Brown
Beulah Bryant
Alden Bunn
Jean Cameron
Jeanne Carroll
Sharon/Dennis Chalkin
Bea/Irving Chalkin
Rina/Dr. Marc Chalkin
Peter Chatman
David Chertok
John Chilton
Lawrence Cohn

Ada/Jay Cole
Virginia Curtiss
Helen/Stanley Dance
Barbara Dane
Diana Davies
Jimmy Dawkins
Frank Driggs
John Earl
Dave Edwards
William R. Ferris
Ray Flerlage
Doug Fulton
Jeanne Gherson
Manuel Greenhill
Bill Greensmith
Phyllis Haar
Merrill Mills Hammond
Rex Harris
J. S. Hartin
Katherine Henderson
Beverly Hill
John Lee Hooker
Pug Horton
Helen Humes
Alberta Hunter
John Jackson
David A. Jasen
Daisy Johnson
Dr. Helen Armstead Johnson
Tad Jones
Pleasant Joseph
B. B. King
Andy Kirk
Jean Kittrell
Bert Korall
Barbara Kukla
Len Kunstadt
Natalie Lamb
Carol Leigh
Ella Louise Lenoir
John Levy
Isabelle Loonin
Kip Lornell
Pete Lowry
Victoria Lucas
James M. Lynch
Mona MacMurray
Rhoda Mattern
Tom Mazzolini
Mack McCormick
Judith McCulloh
Helen Merrill
Clarence Miller
Mike Montgomery
McKinley Morganfield
Susan Page
Dave Patrick
Terry Pattison
Barbara Phillips
Tom Pomposello
Kerry Price
Mary Prioli
Yank Rachell
Jimmy Reed
Pauline Rivelli
Al Rose
Bob Rusch
Otis Rush
Jimmy Rushing
Tony Russell
Guy Schoukroun
Frank Scott
D. Shigley
W. D. Shook, III, M.D.
Jon Sievert
Dan Singer
Marge Singleton
Al Smith
Carrie Smith
Charles Edward Smith
David Smith
George Smith
Harrison Smith
Julie Snow
Ron Soderberg
Lucille/Otis Spann
Victoria Spivey
Jean/Dr. Marshall W. Stearns
Tom Stern
Mary/Derrick Stewart-Baxter

Chris Strachwitz
Eva Taylor
Jim Taylor
Emma Terry
Blanche Thomas
Rufus Thomas
Bob Thompson
Robert Tilling
Jeff Todd Titon
Steve Tomashefsky
Dietrich v. Staden
Eddie Vinson
Dotty/Dr. Al Vollmer
Aaron Walker
Cliff Warnken
Viola Wells
Ann Wender
Leigh Whipper
Josh White Jr.
Princess White
Big Joe Williams
Spencer Williams
Edith/Millard Wilson
Marjorie Wilson
George Winfield
Andrew P. Wittenborn
Dan Woskoff
Mama Yancey

These organizations were most helpful in their cooperation:

Center for Southern Folklore, Memphis, TN
Classic Jazz Society of Southwest Ohio
Institute of Jazz Studies, New York, NY/Newark, NJ
Lincoln Center Public Library, New York, NY
New York Public Library, New York, NY
Popular Culture Library, Bowling Green State University, Bowling Green, OH
Schomburg Center for Research in Black Culture, New York, NY
Tulane University Library, New Orleans, LA
plus various publicity agents, personal managers and representatives.

I also acknowledge these respected individuals who, through their work in the field, have indirectly added to this book:

Herb Abramson
Edmond G. Addeo
George Adins
Clas Ahlstrand
Chris Albertson
Ian A. Anderson
Ron Anger
Bob Atkinson
Kristin Baggelaar
Cary Baker
Whitney Balliett
Adams Barnes
Bo Basiuk
Bruce Bastin
John Bentley
William Bentley
Chuck Berk
Rudi Blesh
Donald Bogle
Ernest Borneman
Mike Bourne
Perry Bradford
Don Branning
John Breckow
Harold Brenner
Bruce Bromberg
Michael Bromberg
Josh J. Broven
Ron Brown
Yannick Bruynoghe
Dennis Buck
George H. Buck Jr.
John Burks
Stephen Calt
Robert Cappuccio
Jeff Carlson
Samuel B. Charters
Gilbert Chase
Marcel Chauvard
Pete Clayton
A. M. Cohen
Anthony Connor
Pat Conti
Bruce Cook
Gillian Cook
Carol Coy
Alex Cramer
Pete Crawford
Thomas J. Cullen III
Tony Cummings
Lou Curtiss

ACKNOWLEDGMENTS

David Dalton
Bill Daynes-Wood
Jim De Koster
Virgile Degand
Charles Delauney
Jim Delehant
Robert M.W. Dixon
Richard M. Dorson
Harry C. Duncan
Chris Ellis
Ralph Ellison
Philip Elwood
David Evans
David Ewen
Leonard Feather
J. B. Figi
Tom Fiofori
Iola Flerlage
Ray Flerlage
Dick Flohil
Charles Fox
Michael Frank
Ron Freeberg
Phyl Garland
Paul Garon
Richard M. Garvin
Gilbert Gaster
Robert Gear
Karl Gert zur Heide
Martha Gilmore
Ralph J. Gleason
Henry Glover
Tony Glover I
Dave Godin
John Godrich
Joe Goldberg
Albert Goldman
Kenneth S. Goldstein
Pierre Gonneau
Laurraine Goreau
Roy Greenberg
Bob Groom
Stefan Grossman
Louis Guida
Peter Guralnick
Bob Groom
Richard Hadlock
Douglas Hague
Bob Hall
Barret Hansen
Michael Haralambos
Dave Harrison
Ronold P. Harwood
Peter Hatch
Don Heckman
Tony Heilbut
Erwin Helfer
Nat Hentoff
Chris Hillman
Bob Hite
George Hoefer
Robert Holmes
John Holt
Carter Horsley
Tom Hoskins
Langston Hughes
Mark Humphrey
Bruce Iglauer
Bruce Jackson
Graham L. Jackson
Jorgen Jepsen
John Jeremy
Mike John
Nettie Jones
Le Roy Jones
Max Jones
Peter Keepnews
Charles Keil
Don Kent
Fred Kirby
Barry Kittleson
Joe H. Klee
Curtis Knight
Bob Koester
Eric Kriss
Steve La Vere
Eddie Lambert
Iain Lang
Doug Langille
Allen Larman
Ray Lawless
Mike Leadbitter
Ed Leimbacher
Willy Leiser
Jacques Lemetre
Julius Lester
Frank Lieberman
John B. Litweiler
Nick Logan
Alan Lomax
John A. Lomax
Tom Lord
John Lovell Jr.
John Lucas
Michael Lydon
Rich Mangelsdorff
Dave Mangurian
Woody Mann
Chris May
John McDonough
Joe McEwen
Don McLean
Richard McLeese
Mezz Mezzrow
John Miller
Grayson Mills
Donald Milton
Roger Misiewicz
Charles Mitchell
George Mitchell
Carman Moore
Alun Morgan
John P. Morgan
Marcelle Morgantini
Dan Morgenstern
Ed Morris
Robert Morris
Charles Sharr Murray
Doug Murray
Simon A. Napier
Robert Neff
Edmund Newton
Richard Noblett
Herb Nolan
John Norris
Giles Oakley
Justin O'Brien
Paul Oliver
Bengt Olsson
Dr. Harry Oster
Robert Palmer
Hugues Panassié
Neil Paterson
George Paulus
Sharon A. Pease
Nick Perls
Henry Pleasants
Wesley Race
Frederic Ramsey Jr.
Lawrence N. Redd
Jacques Roche
Dr. Hans Rookmaaker
James Rooney
Arthur Rosenbaum
Mike Rowe
Lillian Roxon
Bill Russell
Ross Russell
Brian Rust

Robert B. Sacre
Patrick William Salvo
C. Chris Sautter
Dave Sax
Bob Scheir
Duncan Schiedt
Jack Schiffman
Hammond Scott
Pete Seeger
Bob Shad
Nat Shapiro
Robert Shelton
Robert Sherman
Peter Shertser
Dick Shurman
Paul Siber
Jerry Silverman
Larry Skogg
Neil Slaven
Willie "The Lion" Smith
Dr. Edmond Souchon
Eileen Southern
Purvis Spann
Richard K. Spottswood
Irwin Stambler
Tony Standish
John Steiner
Norman Stevens
Alan Stewart
John Stiff
Darryl Stolper
Richard M. Sudhalter
Lynn Summers
Frank Surge
Sandy Sutherland
Billy Taylor
Keith Tillman
Eric Townley
Ray Townley
Tony Travers
Dean Tudor
Bez Turner
Barry Ulanov
Martin Van Olderen
Guido van Rijn
Carl Van Vechten
Paige Van Vorst
Mike Vernon
Steve Voce
Barry Von Tersch
Gayle Wardlow
Tim Weiner
Ronald Weinstock
Pete Welding
Jann Wenner
Martin Williams
Valerie Wilmer
Alan Wilson
John S. Wilson
Kellogg Wilson
Wilson Winslow
Bob Woffinden
Karl Michael Wolfe
Sally Ann Worsfold
Pat Wyn
Henrietta Yurchenco

Thanks are due also to my editor, Kathleen Williams, for her many considerations; to copyeditor Lillian Krelove for her diligence; to Betty Herman for typing this lengthy manuscript; and to Joseph G. Palladino and Maria Dostis for their conscientious indexing. And finally, I wish to thank my parents, Ruth and Lawrence Harris, for their long and continuing encouragement, and my wife, Gladys, who patiently waited years for this seemingly endless work to be completed.

Biographies

A

ADAMS, JOHN TYLER *"JT"*

Courtesy Cadence Magazine

Born: Feb 17, 1911, Morganfield (Union Co), KY
Inst: Guitar

Father was singer/musician; father taught him guitar at 11 years of age; worked mostly outside music through 20s/30s; moved to Indianapolis, IN, 1941; worked outside music and frequently worked w Shirley Griffith/Scrapper Blackwell/others at local parties/clubs/taverns in Indianapolis area into 50s; rec w Shirley Griffith, Bluesville label, Indianapolis, 1961; mostly inactive in music into 70s; worked Univ of Iowa, Iowa City, IO, 1973

Personal: Married. Has children. Not to be confused with R&B singer Johnny Adams

Songs: "A" Jump/Bright Street Jump/Indiana Avenue Blues/Naptown Boogie

Infl by: Blind Lemon Jefferson

Quote: "JT brought with him from Kentucky a rough and appealing way of singing the old country blues . . ."—Arthur Rosenbaum, Bluesville album 1077

Reference: Cadence magazine, Sept 1977, p 10

ADAMS, WOODROW WILSON

Born: Apr 9, 1917, Tchula (Holmes Co), MS
Inst: Guitar/Harmonica

Moved to Minter City, MS, where he picked up some guitar with friend LC Green as child; worked outside music with occasional local party work in area of Minter City through 30s; moved to Robinsonville, MS, where he occasionally worked w Robert Lockwood Jr/Robert Nighthawk/Sonny Boy Williamson (Alex Miller)/others in area from c1940; worked w Joe Martin in Howlin' Wolf Band, Robinsonville area, late 40s to 1952; app w Joe Martin, WDIA-radio, Memphis, TN, early 50s; rec w Three B's, Checker label,

Photo by Marina Bokelman. Courtesy Dave Evans

Memphis, 1952; rec Charly label, Memphis, 1952; rec w Boogie Blues Blasters, Meteor label, Memphis, 1955; rec Home of the Blues label, Memphis, 1961; continued occasional recording dates early 60s; worked outside music with occasional club work w own trio (including Joe Martin), Robinsonville, MS/West Memphis, AR, areas into 60s; rec Flyright label, Robinsonville, 1967

Songs: Baby You Just Don't Know/Pretty Baby Blues/The Train Is Coming/Wine Head Woman

Infl by: Howlin' Wolf

Reference: Blues Unlimited magazine (UK), Jul 1968, pp 7-8

AGEE, RAYMOND CLINTON *"Ray"/"Roy"*
(aka: Ray Egge/Little Ray/Isom Ray)
Born: Apr 10, 1930, Dixons Mills (Marengo Co), AL

One of 17 children; suffered from polio from age of 4 incurring permanent disability; moved to Los Angeles, CA, mid-30s; formed family Agee Brothers Gospel Quartet working local churches in Los Angeles area from 1937; reportedly worked outside music, Los Angeles area, through 40s into 50s; rec Modern/Aladdin/Queen/Hollywood/RK labels, Los Angeles, 1952; rec Elko label, Los Angeles, 1954; rec Rhythm & Blues label, Los Angeles, c1955; rec Spark/Ebb labels, Los Angeles, 1955; rec Cash label, Los Angeles, c1956; rec RGA label, Los Angeles, late 50s; worked w Bobby Bland, Regal Thea, Chicago, IL, 1960; rec Mar-Jan label, Chicago, 1960; rec Check label, Oakland, CA, 1960; rec Veltone label, Oakland, c1963; rec Shirley/Celeste labels, Los Angeles, 1963; rec RGA label, San Francisco, CA, 1963-9; rec Prowlin' label, Los Angeles, c1965; rec Krafton/Highland/Brandin labels, Los Angeles, late 60s; rec Romark/Watts Way labels, Los Angeles, c1972; rec Solid Soul label, Los Angeles, c1973

Songs: Boy and Girl Thing/Brought It All on Myself/Can't Find My Way/Count the Days I'm Gone/Do You Believe?/Drifting Apart/Faith/Hard Loving Woman/Hard Working Man/I Am the Gambler/I Feel So Good/I'm Not Looking Back/I'm Out to Get You Baby/It Was Your Love/It's a Helluva Thing/It's Hard to Explain/Keep Smiling/Leave Me Alone/Let's Talk About Love/Love Bug/Love Is a Cold Shot/Love Is a Gamble/The Love of Life/The Monkey on My Back/Mr Clean/My So Called Friends/Peace of Mind/Real Real Love/Roll On, Baby/Somebody Messed Up/Soul of a Man/That's the Way It Is/These Things Are True/'Til Death Do Us Part/Tragedy/Watch Where You Step/We're Drifting Apart/You Are My Trophy/You Hit Me Where It Hurts/You Messed Up My Mind/Your Precious Love/Your So Called Friends/Your Thingerma-do

Quote: "One of the most prolific of all the West Coast based R&B vocalists"—Bob Eagle, *Blues Unlimited* magazine (UK), Aug 1973, p 9

Reference: Blues Unlimited magazine (UK), Aug 1973, p 9

Photo by Darryl Stolper. Courtesy Peter B Lowry

ALEXANDER, ALGER *"Texas"*
(aka: Kine Oliver)

Courtesy Living Blues *Magazine*

Born: Sep 12, 1900, Jewett (Leon Co), TX
Died: Apr 16, 1954, Richards, TX

Father was Sam 'Ernie' Alexander; mother Jennie Brooks; worked outside music in Leona, TX into 20s; entertained at local parties/picnics in area from c1923; worked w Blind Lemon Jefferson in Buffalo, TX, early 20s; rec w Lonnie Johnson/Mississippi Sheiks/others, OKeh label, NYC, NY/San Antonio, TX, 1927-30; worked w Lightnin' Hopkins, Rainbow Theater, Houston, TX, c1927; rec w King Oliver, OKeh label, NYC, 1928; worked in local blues contest, Ella B Moore Theater, Dallas, TX, 1928; worked as itinerant singer at picnics/suppers/streets through Texas into 30s; rec Vocalion label, San Antonio/Fort Worth, TX, 1934; worked frequently w Lightnin' Hopkins in streets for tips in Houston through 30s; worked country suppers in Waxahachie, TX, area, mid-30s; toured w Howlin' Wolf, working odd gigs through Texas, late 30s; toured w Lowell Fulson working juke-joints through western Oklahoma/Texas, 1939-40; served time for murder of wife, Paris, TX, prison c1940-5; frequently worked w Lightnin' Hopkins on streets/busses, Houston, 1945 into 50s; rec w Benton's Busy Bees, Freedom label, Houston 1950. Died of syphilis. Buried Longstreet Cemetery, Grimes County, TX

Personal: Was cousin of Lightnin' Hopkins

Songs: Awful Moaning Blues/Bell Cow Blues/Blue Devil Blues/Boe Hog Blues/Broken Yo-Yo/Corn-Bread Blues/Death Bed Blues/Evil Woman Blues/Farm Hand Blues/'Frisco Train Blues/Gold Tooth Blues/Levee Camp Moan Blues/Long Lonesome Day Blues/Mama, I Heard You Brought It Right Back Home/Mama's Bad Luck Child/Ninety-Eight Degree Blues/Penitentiary Moan Blues/Range in My Kitchen Blues/Rolling and Stumbling Blues/Sabine River Blues/She's So Far/St Louis Fair Blues/Tell Me Woman Blues

Infl to: Lowell Fulson/John Hogg/Lightnin' Hopkins/Little Son Jackson

Quotes: "Texas Alexander was unique among commercial recording artists: He sang the rough blues shout and field hollers . . . the purest form of the blues tradition"—Mack McCormick, SOME OF THE PEOPLE, CBS-Radio, c1965

"One of the great blues singers who was known all over Texas"—Chris Strachwitz, *Arhoolie* album 2007

". . . in his most characteristic blues there was a rich imagery and a melodic expressiveness derived from one of the root sources of Texas music, the work songs and prison chants"—Samuel B Charters, *The Bluesmen*, Oak Publications, 1967

Reference: The Bluesmen, Samuel B Charters, Oak Publications, 1967

Agram album AB 2009

ALEXANDER, DAVE
Born: Mar 10, 1938, Shreveport (Caddo Parish), LA
Inst: Drums/Piano

Father was musician who frequently worked local weekend hoedowns and parties; born Dave Alexander Elam; moved to Marshall, TX, at 6 months of age; taught self piano c1945; frequently sang/played piano in local church, Marshall, 1950-2; attended Pemberton HS where he frequently played in school band, Marshall, early 50s; occasionally worked local house parties, Marshall, from 1952; worked Dreamland Inn, Kilgore, TX, 1954; frequent club dates, Longview, TX, 1954; served in US Navy (stationed in San Diego, CA), working occasionally w Bobby Hebb in local bars, 1955-6; frequently worked Bethel Missionary Baptist Church, Oakland, CA, 1957; worked w LC Robinson Band/Big Mama Thornton/Jimmy McCracklin/Lafayette Thomas or solo at Rhumboogie

Dave Alexander
Courtesy C Strachwitz, Arhoolie Records

Club and other piano bars/clubs, Oakland area, late 50s through 60s; worked Cotton Club/Ho-Ti Supper Club, Portland, OR, late 60s; rec World Pacific label, Los Angeles, CA, 1969; worked Ann Arbor Blues Festival, Ann Arbor, MI, 1970; Berkeley Blues Festival, Berkeley, CA, 1970; Fillmore West, San Francisco, CA, c1971; Col of Marin, Kentfield, CA, c1971; San Jose State Col, San Jose, CA, c1971; Univ of Wyoming, Laramie, WY, c1971; rec w LC Robinson, Arhoolie label, San Francisco, 1971; rec (under own name) Arhoolie label, San Francisco, 1972; worked Univ of California Extension Center, San Francisco, 1973; Minnie's Can-Do Club, San Francisco, 1973-5; w Nina Simone, The Troubadour, Los Angeles, CA, c1973; Lion's Share, San Anselmo, CA, 1973; Community Music Center, San Francisco, 1973; Monterey Jazz Festival, Monterey, CA, 1973; The Boarding House, San Francisco, 1973-5; San Francisco Blues Festival, Golden Gate Park, San Francisco, 1973-4; The Bratskellar, San Francisco, 1974; frequently contributed articles to *Living Blues* magazine, 1974; app on BLUES BY THE BAY, KPOO-FM-radio, San Francisco, 1974; worked Marine World, Redwood City, CA, 1974; The Exploratorium, San Francisco, 1974; Berkeley Blues Festival, Berkeley, CA, 1975; Slat's Club, San Francisco, 1975-6; San Francisco Blues Festival, McLaren Park Amphitheater, San Francisco, 1975; Rhythm 'n Motion Festival, Alameda, CA, 1975; The Keystone, Berkeley, 1975; Santa Cruz Blues Festival, Santa Cruz, CA, 1975; app on PERSPECTIVE, KGO-TV, San Francisco, 1975; worked West Dakota Club, Berkeley, 1975; Family Light School of Music Blues Festival, Sausalito, CA, 1975; Cromwell's Restaurant, San Francisco, 1975; Reunion Club, San Francisco, 1975-6; Blue Dolphin, San Francisco, 1976; Green Earth Cafe, San Francisco, 1976; American River Col, Sacramento, CA, 1976; Winterland Auditorium, San Francisco, 1976; Monterey Jazz Festival, Monterey, CA, 1976; Berkeley Square, Berkeley, 1977; Golden Grommet, San

Francisco, 1977; Slat's, San Francisco, 1977

Personal: Married. Used name Omar Hakim Khayyam from 1976. Not to be confused with Dave Alexander ("The Black Ivory King") or David Alexander ("Little David")

Songs: Blue Tumbleweeds/Cold Feeling/Dirt on the Ground/Fillmore Street/Good Home Cooking/Good Soul Music/Highway 59/The Hoodoo Man/I Need a Little Spirit/It's 1984/The Judgement/Lonesome Train Blues/Love Is Just for Fools/The Rattler/Strange Woman/There Ought to Be a Law/13 Is My Number

Infl by: Albert Ammons/Charles Brown/Ray Charles/Floyd Dixon/Meade Lux Lewis/Jimmy Yancey

Quotes: "Alexander is a creator of meaningful songs filled with the hardship of urban existence and loss of rural simplicity, but he is at his best when singing about women, his poignant phrases satirizing relationships and love"—Tom Mazzolini, *Living Blues* magazine, Mar 1976, p 4

". . . one of the most individual and satisfying blues performers in action today [1974]"—John Norris, *Coda* magazine (Canada), Feb 1976, p 18

"A young master craftsman of the blues"—Harry C Duncan, *Downbeat* magazine, Apr 24, 1975, p 35

References: *Living Blues* magazine, Winter 1973 pp 4, 14

Lightnin' Express magazine, #3, pp 40-1

Black Music magazine (UK), Apr 1974, p 43

ALEXANDER, TEXAS
(see Alexander, Alger)

ALIX, MAY *"Mae"*
Born: Aug 31, 1902, Chicago (Cook Co), IL

Born Liza May Alix; won second prize in local talent contest, Dreamland Cabaret, Chicago, IL, 1920; sang/danced acc by Ollie Powers, Dreamland Cabaret, Chicago, 1920-2; worked w Jimmie Noone Orch, Edelweiss Club, Chicago, 1922; Plantation Club, Chicago, 1922; w Duke Ellington Orch, Cotton Club/Hollywood Club, NYC, NY, 1923; Small's Paradise, NYC, c1925; w Carroll Dickerson Orch, Sunset Club, Chicago, 1926; rec w Louis Armstrong Hot Five, OKeh label, Chicago, 1926; worked Florence Mills Memorial Benefit, Alhambra Theater, NYC, 1927; rec w Jimmie Noone Orch, Vocalion label, Chicago, 1929; worked w Eddie South Band and others, in residence, Plantation Cabaret/Music Box Club/others, Paris, France, 1929; worked local night clubs, Los Angeles area, c1930; app in BIG MOMENTS Revue, Lafayette Theater, NYC, NY, 1931; frequently worked Connie's Inn, NYC, 1931-32; app in CONNIE'S INN 1932 REVUE, Apollo Theater, NYC, 1932; app w Louis Russell's Orch, BILLY BANKS REVUE, Lafayette Theater, NYC, 1932; app in KNOCKOUTS OF 1933 REVUE, Lafayette Theater, NYC, 1933; worked Harlem Opera House, NYC, 1933; app in VARIETIES OF 1934 REVUE, Lafayette Theater, NYC, 1933; app in EASTER PARADE REVUE, Apollo Theater, NYC, 1934; worked w Chick Webb Orch and others, Harlem Opera House, NYC, 1935; Swingland Club, Chicago, 1938; Panama Club, Chicago, c1940; It Club, Chicago, c1940; Mimo Professional Club, NYC, c1941; retired from music c1941; worked outside music with occasional work as singing barmaid in later years, Chicago

Personal: Not to be confused with Edmonia Henderson/Edna Hicks/Alberta Hunter who used this name as pseudonym

Billing: The Queen of the Night Clubs

Quote: "May Alix had one of those fine strong voices that everyone would also want to hear"—(Louis Armstrong) Nat Shapiro/Nat Hentoff, *Hear Me Talkin' to Ya*, Rinehart & Company, Inc, 1955

Reference: *Who's Who of Jazz*, John Chilton, Bloomsbury Book Shop, 1970

ALIX, MAY *"Mae"*
(see Hicks, Edna)
(see Hunter, Alberta)

ALLEN, GEORGE
(see Smith, George)

ALLEN, MAYBELLE
(see Johnson, Edith North)

ALLISON, LUTHER SYLVESTER
Born: Aug 17, 1939, Mayflower (Faulkner Co), AR
Inst: Guitar/Harmonica

Father was Grant Albert Allison; mother Elizabeth Larkin; interested in music at early age; toured in The Southern Travellers (family gospel group) working churches through South, late 40s; moved to Chicago, IL, to attend Farragut HS where he learned guitar from 1951; dropped out of school to sit-in w brother Ollie Lee Allison Band, 708 Club, Chicago, 1954-7; together w brother Grant Allison formed The Rolling Stones (later renamed The Four Jivers) to work The Bungalow, Chicago, 1957-8; worked briefly w Jimmy Dawkins Band in local clubs, Chicago, 1957; worked Earl's Place, Argo, IL, 1958; frequently worked w Freddie King's Band and others, Walton's Corner, Chicago, 1958-63; worked Peppermint Lounge, Chicago, c1960; Figaro's, Chicago, c1960; frequently worked outside music with sideman gigs in bands of Magic Sam and others, Chicago, from 1963; worked north side white clubs, Chicago, 1965; worked 1815 Club, Chicago, 1966; rec Delmark label, Chicago, 1967; formed The Tornados, working Birdland, Peoria, IL, 1967-8; worked Back Door Club, Ventura, CA, 1968; Red Velvet Club, Los Angeles, CA, 1968; Golden Bear Club, Los Angeles, 1968; rec w Shakey Jake, World Pacific label, Los Angeles, 1968; worked w Shakey Jake, Playa Del Ray, Los Angeles, 1969; L&A Lounge, Chicago, 1969-70; Tom's Musicians Lounge, Chicago, 1969-70; Chicago Blues Festival, Chicago, 1969; rec Delmark label, Chicago, 1969; State Univ of New York, Albany, NY, 1969; Union Club, Madison, WI, 1969; w own group at Nitty Gritty Club, Univ of Wisconsin, Madison, 1969-71; Univ of Michigan, Ann Arbor, MI, 1969; Ann Arbor Blues Festival, Ann Arbor, MI, 1969-70; w own band at North Park Hotel, Chicago, 1969; Washington Blues Festival, Howard Univ, Washington, DC, 1970; The Main Point, Bryn Mawr, PA, 1970; Philadelphia Folk Festival, Schwenksville, PA, 1970; Berkeley Blues Festival, Berkeley, CA, 1970; w own Blue Nebulae Revue, Oberlin Col, Oberlin, OH, 1970; toured college circuit working concert dates, 1970; worked Univ of Minnesota, Minneapolis, MN, 1970-1; The Matrix, San Francisco, CA, 1970; Whiskey A-Go-Go, Los Angeles, CA, 1970; Fillmore West, San Francisco, 1970-1; Fillmore East, NYC, NY, 1971; w own quartet, Festival of American Folklife, St Helens Island, Montreal, Can, 1971; Boston Univ,

Luther Allison
Courtesy Living Blues *Magazine*

Boston, MA, 1971; worked Coq D'or, Toronto, Can, 1971; Alice's Revisited, Chicago, IL, 1971; rec Gordy label, Detroit, MI, 1972-4; Ann Arbor Blues Festival, Ann Arbor, MI, 1972-3 (por 1972 concert rel Atlantic label); Silver Dollar Club, Minneapolis, MN, 1972; Siena Col Blues Festival, Memphis, TN, 1972; Capitol Theater, Montreal, Can, 1973; The Kove, Kent, OH, 1973; toured w own group working one-nighters through Midwest, 1973; El Mocambo Tavern, Toronto, Can, 1973; Quiet Knight, Chicago, 1974; Univ of Miami, Coral Gables, FL, 1974; Joint Bar, Minneapolis, MN, 1974; The Minstrels, Chicago, IL, 1974; Ann Arbor Blues & Jazz Festival, Windsor, Can, 1974; Sandy's Concert Club, Boston, MA, 1974; Shaboo Inn, Mansfield, CT, 1974; Toronto Blues Festival, Olympic Island, Toronto, Can, 1974; In Concert Club, Montreal, Can, 1974; Tomorrow Club, Youngstown, OH, 1974; Smiling Dog Saloon, Cleveland, OH, 1974; The Sting, Burlington, VT, 1975; Univ of Vermont, Burlington, VT, 1975; The Bottom Line, NYC, 1975; Southern Illinois Univ, Edwardsville, IL, 1975; Cafe Campus, Montreal, Can, 1975; rec Motown label, NYC, 1975; worked Mickell's, NYC, 1975; Univ of Nebraska, Lincoln, NE, 1975; Zoo Bar, Lincoln, NE, 1975; The International Amphitheater, Chicago, 1975-6; Grand Valley State Col Festival, Allendale, MI, 1975; Liberty Hall, Houston, TX, 1975; Antoine's, Austin, TX, 1975; Charlotte's Web, Rockford, IL, 1975-7; The Vibes, Chicago, 1975-7; Amazingrace, Evanston, IL, 1976-8; My Father's Place, Roslyn, NY, 1976; Max's Kansas City, NYC, 1976; rec ST for film COOLEY HIGH, 1976; worked North Sea Jazz Festival 76, Congress Centre, The Hague, Holland, 1976; Mickell's, NYC, 1977; Red Creek Bar, Rochester, NY, 1977; Second Chance, Ann Arbor, MI, 1977; Colonial Tavern, Toronto, Can, 1977; toured Europe working concert dates, 1977; app on SOUNDSTAGE, PBS-TV, 1978

Personal: Married Fannie Mae ———; one child. His brother Ollie Lee Allison was musician

Songs: Bad News Is Coming/Bloomington Closer/Into My Life/Let's Have a Little Talk/Love Me Mama/ Luther's Blues/Ragged and Dirty/Why I Love the Blues

Infl by: BB King/Albert King/Freddie King/Magic Sam/Otis Rush

Quotes: "Luther's blues . . . has all the electronic energy and emotive intensity of the current decade"—Doug Langille, *Coda* magazine (Canada), Sept 1975, p 18

"I believe Luther Allison to be one of the most original exponents of modern blues"—Bob Koester, *Blues Unlimited* magazine (UK), Sept 1971, p 3

References: *Living Blues* magazine, Autumn 1973, pp 23-4

Jazz & Blues magazine (UK), Mar 1972, pp 20-1

Guitar Player, Mar 1976, pp 14, 32

AMERSON, RICHARD MANUEL *"Rich"*
Born: c1887, Livingston (Sumter Co), AL
Died: (unknown)
Inst: Harmonica

Born and raised on farm; illiterate and worked outside music as farmer from childhood; learned harmonica as youth and frequently worked local parties/dances/ breakdowns, Livingston, AL, area, into 50s; rec Library of Congress label, Livingston, 1937/1940 (with some film footage); rec Folkways label, Livingston, 1950; whereabouts unknown thereafter

Personal: His sister Earthy Anne Coleman is recorded singer

Infl to: Vera Hall

Quote: "We feel that Amerson is a folksinger of rare ability and remarkable memory"—Fred Ramsey, *A Guide to Longplay Jazz Records*, Long Player Publications Inc, 1954

AMES, TESSIE
(see Smith, Trixie)

AMOS
(see Easton, Amos)

ANDERSON, PINK
Born: Feb 12, 1900, Laurens (Laurens Co), SC
Died: Oct 12, 1974, Spartanburg, SC
Inst: Guitar

Father was John Anderson; mother was Evelene Irby; moved to Spartanburg, SC, where he was raised from childhood and sang in streets for pennies; taught self guitar and toured as musician/comedian/dancer w Doc WR Kerr's Indian Remedy Company Medicine Show/Frank Curry Show/Emmet Smith Show/WA Blair Show (and other travelling shows) through southeastern US c1915-45; occasionally worked picnics/parties w Blind Simmie Dooley in Spartanburg, SC, area from 1918; rec w Simmie Dooley, Columbia label, Atlanta, GA, 1928; formed own trio working

Pink Anderson *Photo by Kip Lornell. Courtesy Living Blues Magazine*

parties/picnics/suppers/jukes in Spartanburg, SC, area c1945-57; rec Riverside label, Charlottesville, VA, 1950; frequently toured w Chief Thundercloud Medicine Show working carnivals/picnics/streets/fairs through South, 1950s; mostly inactive in music due to poor health from 1957; rec Bluesville label, NYC, NY, 1960-2; app with his son in documentary film THE BLUES, 1963; settled in Jonesboro, SC, and mostly inactive due to illness from 1969; worked Salt Coffeehouse, Newport, RI, 1973; Folklore Center, NYC, 1973; Yale Univ, New Haven, CT, 1973; Harpur Col, Binghamton, NY, 1973; Kirkland Col, Clinton, NY, 1973; suffered heart attack and DOA at Spartanburg General Hospital; buried Lincoln Memorial Cemetery, Drayton, SC

Personal: Married. Had children

Songs: South Forest Boogie/Travelin' Man

Infl by: Simmie Dooley

Infl to: Roy Bookbinder/Andy Cohen/Paul Geremia/Arthur Jackson

Quotes: "In Pink Anderson's blues there is the melancholy and sadness of the Carolina blues at their best"—Samuel B Charters, Prestige-Bluesville album BV 1038

"His blues . . . have the gentle, comtemplative and slightly plaintive sound that typifies the blues of the Piedmont"—Bruce Bastin, *Crying for the Carolines*, Studio Vista Ltd, 1971

"His is a folk voice, and his versions of traditional material have all been tempered and changed by time and personal experience"—Kenneth S Goldstein, Riverside album RLP-148

References: Prestige-Bluesville album BV 1038
Crying for the Carolines, Bruce Bastin, Studio Vista Ltd, 1971

ARCHIBALD
(see Gross, Leon T)

ARCHIE BOY
(see Gross, Leon T)

ARMSTRONG, SHELLEY
(see Easton, Amos)

ARNOLD, BILLY BOY
(see Arnold, William)

ARNOLD, JAMES *"Kokomo"*
(aka: Gitfiddle Jim)
Born: Feb 15, 1901, Lovejoy (Clayton Co), GA
Died: Nov 8, 1968, Chicago, IL
Inst: Guitar

Interested in music early and learned some guitar from cousin John Wigges at age of 10; raised and worked on farm through teens; moved to Buffalo, NY, to work outside music from 1919; occasionally worked small clubs in Buffalo area from 1924; worked w Willie Morris in local clubs, Glen Allen, MS, late 20s; moved to Chicago, IL, 1929; worked mostly outside music with occasional gigs in local clubs/joints in area, 1929 through 30s; rec Victor label, Memphis, TN, 1930; rec Decca label, Chicago, 1934-5; rec Decca label, NYC, NY/Chicago, IL, 1936; believed rec acc w Oscar's Chicago Swingers, Decca label, Chicago, 1936; worked 33rd Street Club, Chicago, 1937; rec Decca label, Chicago, 1937/NYC, 1938; worked Club Claremont, Chicago, 1939; Ruby's, Chicago, c1940; worked mostly outside music in Chicago area from 1941; worked Gate of Horn, Chicago, 1962; suffered heart attack at home and DOA at Provident Hospital; buried Burr Oak Cemetery, Worth, IL

Personal: Name "Kokomo" from title of his 1934 song "Old Original Kokomo Blues" (Kokomo is a coffee brand)

Songs: Back Door Blues/Bad Luck Blues/Big Leg Mama/Big Ship Blues/Biscuit Roller Blues/Bo Weavil Blues/Broke Man Blues/Buddy Brown Blues/Bull Headed Woman/Chain Gang Blues/Cold Winter Blues/Crying Blues/Down and Out Blues/Front Door Blues (32-20 Blues)/I'll Be Up Some Day/Laugh and Grin Blues/Lonesome Road Blues/Milk Cow Blues/Mister Charlie/Monday Morning Blues/My Well Is Dry/Old Black Cat Blues (Jinx Blues)/Old Original Kokomo Blues/Policy Wheel Blues/Red Beans and Rice/Rocky Road Blues/Sissy Man Blues/Wild Water Blues/You Should Not a' Done It (Gettin' It Fixed)

Infl by: John Wigges

Infl to: Elmore James/Robert Johnson/Fred McMullen/Sam Montgomery/Curley Weaver

Quotes: "Arnold was one of the great post-Depression bluesmen"—Dave Harrison, Saydisc album SDR-163

"Arnold is one of the greatest blues singers ever recorded"—Hugues Panassié, *Guide to Jazz*, Houghton Mifflin Company, 1956

References: Blues Unlimited magazine (UK), Feb 1970, p 14

Jazz Monthly magazine (UK), May 1962, p 10

ARNOLD, WILLIAM *"Billy"/"Billy Boy"*

Courtesy Living Blues *Magazine*

Born: Sept 16, 1935, Chicago (Cook Co), IL
Inst: Guitar/Harmonica

One of 16 children; frequently worked outside music from 9 years of age; taught self harmonica, 1947; frequently worked w Bo Diddley Washboard Trio in local streets/parties, Chicago, IL, c1950-1; rec Cool label, Chicago, 1953; frequently worked w Johnny Temple Band/Johnny Shines Band/Otis Rush Band/others in local club dates from 1953; worked w Bo Diddley Band, Stardust Trail Lounge/Castle Rock Lounge/others, Chicago, 1953-5; formed own band to rec VJ label, Chicago, 1954-5; worked Apollo Theater, NYC, NY, c1954; Kid Riviera's Barrelhouse Lounge, Chicago, 1955-6; Ricky's, Chicago, 1955; Pepper's Lounge, Chicago, 1955; worked w Earl Hooker Band, Chicago, 1956; Club Alibi, Chicago, 1956; Jive Club, Lawton, OK, 1956; w Howlin' Wolf/Muddy Waters, Silvio's, Chicago, 1957; Zanzibar Club, Chicago, 1957; w Kid King's Combo, Nashville, TN, 1957; Happy Home Lounge, Chicago, 1958; 708 Club, Chicago, 1958; Club Columbia, Chicago, 1958-9; Rock 'n' Roll Club, Chicago, 1959-60; w Little Walter, McKies Lounge, Chicago, 1959; w Joe Young Band, The Green Door, Chicago, 1959; Steve's Chicken Shack, Gary, IN, 1961; Club Arden, Chicago, 1962; Fickle Pickle, Chicago, 1963; rec Bluesville-Prestige label, Chicago, 1964; worked Big Johns, Chicago, 1965; frequently worked outside music with occasional dance/club work, Chicago, from 1965; rec w

Louis Myers/Moose Walker, Vogue label, Chicago, 1970; worked Stardust Lounge, Chicago, 1971; frequently worked Theresa's, Chicago, 1971-4; frequently sat-in at Louise's and others, Chicago, 1972-6; toured w American Blues Legends 75 working concert dates through England/Europe, 1975; worked 100 Club, London, Eng, 1975 (por rel Big Bear label); toured w Rhythm & Blues: Roots of Rock Show working concert dates through Europe, 1975; worked New 1815 Club, Chicago, 1976 (por shown THE DEVIL'S MUSIC—A HISTORY OF THE BLUES [ep: Sticking with the Blues], BBC-1-TV, Eng); Elsewhere Club, Chicago, 1976-7; Kingston Mines, Chicago, 1976-7; Raven & Rose Tavern, Los Angeles, CA, 1977; toured Germany/Holland/England working concert dates/radio shows, 1977; rec Red Lightnin' label, London, Eng, 1977

Personal: His brothers Jerome and Augustus "Gus" Arnold (Julio Finn) are musicians

Songs: Billy Boy's Blues/Blues on Blues/Diddley Daddy/Don't Stay Out All Night/Evaleena/Hello Stranger/Here's My Picture/I Ain't Got No Money/I Love You Only/I Wish You Would/I'm Gonna Move/Kissing at Midnight/My Heart Is Crying/Oh Baby/School Time/Troubles/Two Drinks of Wine/You Better Cut That Out/You Don't Love Me No More/You're My Girl

Infl by: Little Walter/Aaron "T-Bone" Walker/Jr Wells/John Lee "Sonny Boy" Williamson

Quotes: "A singularly expressive blues singer and a highly gifted blues harmonica player as well"
—Pete Welding, Prestige-Bluesville album 7389

"A very talented musician and vocalist"
—(Dick Shurman) Mike Leadbitter, *Nothing But the Blues*, Hanover Books, 1971

References: Blues Unlimited magazine (UK), Sept/Oct 1977, Nov/Dec 1977, Jan/Feb 1978

Nothing But the Blues, Mike Leadbitter, Hanover Books, 1971

AUNT JEMIMA
(see Wilson, Edith)

AUSTIN, CLAIRE
Born: Nov 21, 1918, Yakima (Yakima Co), WA
Inst: Piano

Parents were Swedish-American; born Augusta Marie———; sang in local church choir as child; studied piano at age of 10; studied voice/drama at Whitmire Studio, Seattle, WA, 1935-6; after graduat-

Photo by Andrew Wittenborn

ing high school worked the Oasis Club, Seattle, 1936; Davenport Hotel, Spokane, WA, late 30s; Clover Club, Portland, OR, late 30s; toured w Chuck Austin Band working US Army camps across US, early 40s; frequently worked Primrose Country Club, Cincinnati, OH, early 40s; settled in Sacramento, CA, working mostly outside music with frequent local gigs, mid-40s through 40s; worked w Turk Murphy Band in residence, Venetian Room at Italian Village, San Francisco, CA, 1952; rec w Turk Murphy Band, Good Time Jazz label, Los Angeles, CA, 1952; worked w Turk Murphy Band, 606 Club, Chicago, IL, 1952; Flamingo Club, Chicago, 1952; app w Turk Murphy Band, local TV, San Francisco, CA, 1952; worked Tin Angel, San Francisco, 1954; rec w Kid Ory Group, Good Time Jazz label, Los Angeles, 1954; worked frequently w Turk Murphy Band at local concerts/riverboats, New Orleans, LA, 1955; rec w Bob Scobey group, Contemporary label, Los Angeles, 1955-6; continued outside music work, Sacramento, CA, through 50s; worked w Muggsy Spanier Band, Squire Girshback's Dixieland Jubilee, Memorial Auditorium,

Sacramento, CA, 1959; settled in Seattle, WA, to work mostly outside music through 60s; worked Golden Nugget, Toronto, Can, 1965; rec w Excelsior Jazz Band, GHB label, 1966; w Gene Mayl's Dixieland Rhythm Kings working local dances, Cincinnati, OH, 1974; toured w Gene Mayl's Dixieland Rhythm Kings working jazz club concerts through Connecticut/Massachusetts, 1975; rec w Gene Mayl's Dixieland Rhythm Kings, Jazzology label, Atlanta, GA, 1976; worked Maggie's Opera House, Cincinnati, OH, 1976-7; weekly residency w Tom Hyers Jazz Band/Trio, Arnold's Club, Cincinnati, 1977-8

Personal: Married Chuck Austin (musician). 3 children

Infl by: Bob Moseley

Infl to: Kerry Price

Quotes: "Her style shows an intelligent absorption of the early blues traditions with a timbre recalling Bessie Smith"—Leonard Feather, *The New Encyclopedia of Jazz,* Horizon Press, 1960

"Her blues are as always definitive and provocative"—George H Buck Jr, Jazzology album J-52

References: The New Encyclopedia of Jazz, Leonard Feather, Horizon Press, 1960

B

B B JR
(see Odom, Andrew)

BABY BLUES
(see Brown, Ida G)

BABY DOO
(see Caston, Leonard)

BABY DUKE
(see Caston, Leonard)

BABY FACE
(see Foster, Leroy)

BABY FACE LEROY
(see Foster, Leroy)

BAKER, FANNIE/FANNY
(see Brown, Lillian)
(see Hegamin, Lucille)

BAKER, McHOUSTON *"Mickey"/"Guitar"*
(*aka:* Mickey/Ed McHouston)
Born: Oct 15, 1925, Louisville (Jefferson Co), KY
Inst: Guitar

Ran away from home as child and spent youth in various orphan homes where he learned music in school bands c1937-40; ran away from homes to hobo north and settled in NYC, NY, where he worked outside music from c1940; began playing jazz guitar c1945; often worked at local dances with a calypso band, NYC, 1948; frequently worked way across US as sideman at odd gigs, late 40s into 50s; worked as guitar instructor in NYC, early 50s; rec w own band/solo/or as session man for Nappy Brown and others, Savoy label, NYC, 1952-3; frequently worked w Earl Warren in early 50s; rec as sideman w Sonny Terry/Jack Dupree/Amos Milburn/Ruth Brown/Ray Charles/others, Victor/King/Aladdin/Atlantic labels, NYC, 1953; teamed w Sylvia Vanderpool to rec R&B songs, Cat label, NYC, 1953; rec solo, Groove label, NYC, 1954; rec w own House Rockers, Rainbow label, NYC, 1955; toured w Sylvia Vanderpool as "Mickey & Sylvia" working night clubs/theaters/TV

Photo by Guy Schoukroun. Courtesy Living Blues *Magazine*

shows, 1955-61; rec as "Mickey & Sylvia," Rainbow label, NYC, 1955; rec acc to Sonny Terry/Big Maybelle/others, Savoy label, NYC, 1955; rec Vik label, NYC, c1955; rec Groove label, NYC, 1956; toured as "Mickey & Sylvia" on Alan Freed Rock & Roll Extravaganzas working concerts across US c1957; toured as "Mickey & Sylvia" on Jocko & his Rocketship Rock 'n' Roll Stars package show working theaters across US c1957; extensive tours as "Mickey & Sylvia" on Ray Charles/Joe Turner Universal Attractions Rock & Roll package shows (with frequent club work) across US, 1957-61; rec Vik label, NYC, NY, 1957-8; worked as "Mickey & Sylvia" in local theater dates, NYC, 1958; rec Victor label, NYC, 1958; rec w Kitty Noble (and solo), Atlantic label, NYC, 1959-60; rec w Sylvia Vanderpool, Victor label, NYC, 1960-1; formed own Willow label to rec, NYC, 1961; moved to Europe settling in Paris, France, working local jazz clubs and rec as session guitarist from 1961 into 70s; app in Belgium film short COLEMAN HAWKINS QUARTET, 1961; rec Versailles label, Paris, France, 1962; rec w Sylvia Vanderpool, Victor label, NYC, 1964-5; frequently toured England/Europe working concert dates, late 60s into 70s; rec acc to Memphis Slim, International-Polydor label, Paris, France, 1967; rec w Jack Dupree, Vogue label, Paris, 1968; rec w Jack Dupree, Crescendo label, Paris, 1971; rec acc to Jimmy Dawkins, Vogue label, Paris, 1971; worked Big Bear Concerts, London, Eng, 1972; rec w Willie Mabon, Big Bear label, London, 1973; rec Black & Blue label, Paris, France, 1973-4; rec Blue Star label, Paris, 1973; worked Jazz Festival, Krizanke, Yugoslavia, 1974; Hot Club of France Concert, Paris, France, 1975 (por rel Flame label); rec Roots label, Austria, 1975; rec Kicking Mule label, England, 1977; worked R&B Festival, Groningen, Netherlands, 1978

Books: *Fun with Guitar Chords,* Mickey Baker, Charles Colin Publishers
Easy 9 Chord Guitar System, Mickey Baker, Charles Colin Publishers
Mickey Baker's Analysis of the Blues for Guitar, Mickey Baker, Charles Colin Publishers, 1960.
Mickey Baker's Guitar Method, Mickey Baker, Lewis Publishing Company, 1960
Mickey Baker's Jazz Guitar, Mickey Baker, Lewis Publishing Company, 1960
The Mickey Baker Jazz Book (no. 1, 2), Mickey Baker, Lewis Publishing Company, 1955

Songs: Animal Farm/Baker's Dozen/Do What You Do/Greasy Spoon/Guitar Mambo/Hey Little Girl/Lazy Daisy/Love Is Strange/Love You Baby/Midnight Midnight/Milk Train/My Dog/Night Blue/Riverboat/Seety Cat/Shake Walkin'/Side Show/Steam Roller/Take a Look Inside/Trouble Is a Woman/Whistle Stop

Infl by: Charlie Christian/BB King

Quote: "Mickey is a guitarist of an incredible ability and proficiency . . ."—Robert B Sacre, *Living Blues* magazine (UK), Jul 1975, p 2

References: *Crazy Music* magazine (Australia), Sept 1975, pp 13-17
Guitar Player magazine, Jan 1976, pp 10, 36-37, 40

BANJO BOY
(see Nash, Lemoine)

BANJO JOE
(see Cannon, Gus)

BANKSTON, DICK

Photo by Marina Bokelman. Courtesy David Evans

Born: 1899, Crystal Springs (Copiah Co), MS
Died: (unknown)
Inst: Guitar/Violin

Learned violin from father as child; moved to Lombardy, MS, 1910, then Drew, MS, 1911; learned guitar from Willie Brown/Charley Patton as youth; worked outside music in area with frequent work w Willie Brown/Tommy Johnson/Charley Patton/Jim Holloway/Cap Holmes/others at dances/parties/picnics on Webb Jennings' Plantation, Drew, MS, and elsewhere from 1916; formed own string band w brother Ben Bankston touring dances in area through

50s; moved to Memphis, TN, to work mostly outside music from 1962

Infl by: Willie Brown/Ben Maree/Charley Patton

Infl to: Tommy Johnson

Reference: Blues Unlimited magazine (UK), Feb 1968, p 14

BARBECUE BOB
(see Hicks, Robert)

BARBEE, JOHN HENRY

Photo by Stephanie Wiesand. Courtesy Norbert Hess

Born: Nov 14, 1905, Henning (Shelby Co), TN
Died: Nov 3, 1964, Chicago, IL
Inst: Guitar

Father was Becker Tucker; mother was Cora Gilton; born William George Tucker; raised on farm working outside music from childhood; taught self guitar working local country suppers in Henning, TN, area as youth; left home to work outside music with occasional street work for tips through South during 30s; occasionally worked w John Lee "Sonny Boy" Williamson in South c1934; worked w Sunnyland Slim and others in local juke joints through Mississippi Delta area from mid-30s; left Luxora, AR, after shooting incident (assuming name John Henry Barbee) and moved to Chicago, IL, to work mostly outside music c1938 into 40s; rec Vocalion label, Chicago, 1938; frequently worked for tips w Moody Jones group in Maxwell Street area, Chicago, early 40s; served in US Army, early 40s; continued outside music work in Chicago through 40s into 60s; rec Spivey label, Chicago, 1964; toured w American Folk Blues Festival working concert dates through England/Europe, 1964 (por Musikhalle Concert, Hamburg, Ger, rel Fontana label); rec Storyville label, Copenhagen, Den, 1964; returned to US due to illness and was subsequently involved in auto accident; while waiting in jail for disposition of case, suffered heart attack and DOA at Cook County Hospital; buried Restvale Cemetery, Worth, IL

Songs: Early (in the) Morning Blues/God Knows I Can't Help It/Hey Baby/I Ain't Gonna Pick No More Cotton/I Heard My Baby/Miss Nellie Gray (Nelly Grey)/No Pickin' No Pullin'/Six Weeks Old Blues

Infl by: Bill Broonzy

Reference: Storyville album 171

BARKER, LOUISA *"Blue Lu"*
(*aka:* Lu Blue)
Born: Nov 13, 1913, New Orleans (Orleans Parish), LA

One of 2 children; interested in music early and began singing blues at local concerts/club halls/parties from 7 years of age; frequently worked (mostly as dancer) w Merry Makers entertainment group at local events/clubs, New Orleans, LA, 1924-30; moved to NYC, NY, where she was inactive in music, 1930-8; rec (as "Lu Blue") w Erskine Butterfield Trio, Vocalion label, NYC, 1938; rec w Danny Barker Fly Cats and others, Decca label, NYC, 1938-9; worked w Danny Barker at occasional local one-nighters/concerts/clubs in NYC area c1938 through 40s; rec w Danny Barker Sextette, Apollo label, NYC, 1946; worked Stuyvesant Casino, NYC, 1948; Central Plaza, NYC, 1948-9; rec Capitol label, Los Angeles, CA/New Orleans, LA, 1948-9; mostly inactive in music in NYC through 50s into 60s; worked Celebrity Club, NYC, 1964; moved to New Orleans, 1965; worked New Orleans International Jazz Festival, New Orleans, 1965; Preservation Hall, New Orleans, 1965; Southern Illinois Univ, Carbondale, IL, 1967; rec Goodtime Louisiana & New Orleans Jazz label, New Orleans, 1967; inactive in music, New Orleans, 1967-73; worked Gulf Coast cruise

Courtesy Frank Driggs Collection

ship *The Viking Sea* touring the Gulf of Mexico, 1974; w Danny Barker's Jazz Hounds, Jazz & Heritage Festival, New Orleans, 1974-5; New Orleans Jazz Festival Concert, Marriott Hotel, New Orleans, 1974; Blanche Thomas Memorial Concert, Grand Ballroom, Royal Sonesta Hotel, New Orleans, 1977

Personal: Married Danny Barker (1930-), 1 daughter

Songs: Don't You Make Me High/Lu's Blues

BARNER, JUKE BOY
(see Bonner, Weldon)

BARNES, FAE/FAYE
(see Jones, Maggie)

BARRELHOUSE SAMMY
(see McTell, Willie)

BARRELHOUSE TOMMY
(see Dorsey, Thomas)

BARRON, ED
(see Bernhardt, Clyde)

BARTON, TIPPY
(see White, Joshua)

BAT THE HUMMINGBIRD/HUMMING-BIRD
(see Davenport, Charles)
(see Robinson, James)

BATES, DEACON L J
(see Jefferson, Lemon)

BATTS, WILL
Born: Jan 24, 1904, Michigan (Benton Co), MS
Died: Feb 18, 1956, Memphis, TN
Inst: Guitar/Mandolin/Violin

Father Miles Batts and mother Irene Gillis were both sharecroppers who moved frequently through area; father was musician who worked in own string band at local country picnics/suppers in area; one of 8 children; taught self violin at about 8 years of age; frequently worked in father's string band at local country suppers from 9 years of age; worked outside music in Moscow, TN, 1914-18; settled in Memphis, TN, to work outside music with occasional street work for tips from 1919; worked w Jack Kelly's Jug Busters on local streets/parties/suppers/white country clubs, Memphis area, from 1925; rec w Beale Street Sheiks, Victor label, Memphis, 1929; rec w Jack Kelly's Memphis Jug Band (Jug Busters), Banner/Vocalion label, NYC, NY, 1933; rec under own name, Vocalion label, NYC, 1933; formed own Batts South Memphis Jug Band working dances/parties/weddings/conventions, Memphis area, from 1934 with frequent tours through Mississippi/Arkansas/Indiana into 50s; rec w Will Batts Novelty Band, Flyright label, Cleveland, OH (?), 1954; suffered stroke and died at John Gaston Hospital; buried Mt Carmel Cemetery, Memphis, TN

Personal: Married Mary ——— (1921). 5 children. His son Will Batts Jr was musician (died 1967)

Reference: Memphis Blues, Bengt Olsson, Studio Vista Ltd, 1970

BAUM, ALLEN
(see Bunn, Alden)

BEAMAN, LOTTIE
(*aka:* Jennie Brooks/Lottie Brown/Clara Cary/Lottie Everson/Martha Johnson/Lena Kimbrough/Lottie Kimbrough/Mae Moran)
Born: c1900, Kansas City, MO (unconfirmed)
Died: (unknown)
Inst: Guitar/Piano

Born Lottie Kimbrough; reportedly raised in Kansas City, MO, during teens; frequently worked as enter-

Courtesy Sheldon Harris Collection

tainer in local clubs/taverns in Kansas City through 20s; rec Paramount label, Chicago, IL, 1924; rec duo w brother Sylvester Kimbrough, Merrit label, Kansas City, 1925; rec Gennett label, Richmond, IN, 1928; rec Brunswick label, Kansas City, 1929; whereabouts unknown thereafter

Personal: Married William Beaman (early 20s). Had 1 child. Her brother Sylvester Kimbrough was recording artist

Billing: The Kansas City Butterball

Songs: Mama Can't Lose/Wayward Girl Blues

Quote: ". . . though she did not rival the greatest of the 'classic singers,' she had a full voice and used moaning and humming choruses to good effect"—(Paul Oliver) McCarthy/Morgan/Oliver/Harrison, *Jazz on Record*, Hanover Books Ltd, 1968

BEATTY, JOSEPHINE
(see Hunter, Alberta)

BELL, CAREY
Born: Nov 14, 1936, Macon (Noxubee Co), MS
Inst: Bass/Drums/Guitar/Harmonica

Mother sang gospel songs in local church; born Carey Bell Harrington; raised and worked on farm from childhood; interested in music early and taught self harmonica at 8 years of age; ran away from home to work outside music with occasional local gigs with a hillbilly band at Bobby Shore's Tavern, Meridian, MS, c1950-1; worked with stepfather Lovey Lee's C&W group in local clubs, Meridian, c1951-5; moved to Chicago, IL, 1956; worked w Lovey Lee Band, Rickey's Show Lounge, Chicago, 1956; frequently worked outside music with occasional street work on Maxwell Street, Chicago, for tips, 1956 into late 60s; worked Cadillac Baby Bar, Chicago, late 50s; w Little Walter, Club Zanzibar, Chicago, c1960; w Big Walter, Drummer's Lounge, Chicago, early 60s; app in film AND THIS IS FREE, 1963; frequently worked w Johnny Young at Pete's Lounge/I Spy Club/J&C Club/Kelly's Blue Lounge/others, Chicago, c1964-6; Centaur Club, Chicago, 1965; worked Ray's Place, Chicago, mid-60s; worked outside music, Chicago, 1966; w Eddie Taylor band in local clubs, Chicago, 1967; toured w Earl Hooker Band as sideman, working clubs through Kentucky/Indiana/Illinois/New York, 1968; rec w Earl Hooker Band, Arhoolie label, Chicago, 1968; rec Delmark label, Chicago, c1969; toured w John Lee Hooker working concert dates through England/Europe, 1969; worked Royal Albert Hall, London, 1969 (por rel CBS label); Duke's Place, Chicago, 1969; Jo Jo's, Chicago, 1969; toured w American Folk Blues Festival working concerts through England/Europe, 1969; w Hound Dog Taylor, Big Duke's Flamingo Lounge, Chicago, 1970; w Eddie Taylor, Wisconsin Blues Festival, Beloit Col, Beloit, WI, 1970; toured w Jimmy Dawkins group working concert dates through Europe, 1970; frequently toured w Muddy Waters and others, working concerts through Europe, 1970; worked Florence's Lounge, Chicago, 1970-1; White Rose Cafe, Chicago, 1970; Ann Arbor Blues Festival, Ann Arbor, MI, 1970; Tom's Musicians' Lounge, Chicago, 1970; app on WFXM/WNUS-radio, Chicago, 1970; app on MADE IN CHICAGO, WTTW-TV, Chicago, c1970; worked Stardust Club, Chicago, 1971; Notre Dame Blues Festival, South Bend, IN, 1971; Univ of Miami Blues Festival, Silver Springs, FL, 1972; John's Lounge, Chicago, 1972; 1815 Club, Chicago, 1972; The Post, Chicago, 1972; rec w Walter Horton, Alligator label, Chicago, 1972; Ann Arbor Blues Festival, Ann Arbor, MI, 1973; toured extensively w Willie Dixon's Chicago Blues Stars working concerts/colleges across US, 1973-6; worked El Mocambo, Toronto, Can, 1973; Festival of American Folklife, Washington, DC, 1973 (por shown in videotape, BORN IN THE BLUES); Grendel's Lair, Philadelphia, PA, 1973; Joe's Place, Boston, MA, 1973; rec w Bob Riedy's Blues Band, Rounder label, Chicago, 1973; rec BluesWay label, Chicago, 1973; worked Flor-

Photo by D Shigley. Courtesy Living Blues Magazine

ence's Lounge, Chicago, 1974; rec w Bob Riedy Blues Band, Flying Fish label, Chicago, 1974; toured w Willie Dixon's Chicago Blues All-Stars working concerts through Australia/New Zealand, 1974; worked Urban Blues Festival, Auditorium Theater, Chicago, 1974; w Chicago All-Stars, Toronto Blues Festival, Olympic Island, Toronto, Can, 1974; rec Spivey label, Brooklyn, NY, c1974; app in film SINCERELY THE BLUES, 1975; worked w Chicago All-Stars, Univ of Oregon, Eugene, OR, 1975; Eddie Shaw's Place, Chicago, 1975; w Willie Dixon's All-Stars, My Father's Place, Roslyn, NY, 1976; The Bottom Line, NYC, NY, 1976; w Bob Riedy Band, Wise Fools, Chicago, 1976-7; Golden Ram, Chicago, 1976; Big Duke's Flamingo Lounge, Chicago, 1976; w Bob Riedy Band, Biddy Mulligan's, Chicago, 1976-7; The Bayou, Washington, DC, 1976; Zoo Bar, Lincoln, NE, 1976-7; Black Swan, Ottawa, Can, 1977; Just Angels, Harvey, IL, 1977; rec TK label (unissued), Chicago, IL, 1977

Personal: Married Dorothy Strozier (1953-66). His son Lurrie Bell is musician. Married Dorothy West (1970-). Father-in-law was pianist/singer Charlie West. Has total of 10 children, 3 of whom are musicians. Stepfather is Lovey Lee, musician

Songs: I Feel Bad, Bad, Bad/Rocking with Chromanica

Infl by: Walter Horton/Little Walter/Wayne Raney/Sonny Terry/Sonny Boy Williamson (Alex Miller)

Infl to: Charlie Musselwhite

Quote: "His [harmonica] modulations and nuances are of all his own development—almost harpsichordic in effect and a real refreshing innovative aural experience"—Len Kunstadt, Spivey album LP-1016

Reference: Crazy Music magazine (Australia), Sept 1974, pp 15-17

BELL, EDWARD *"Ed"*
Born: c1905, (Lowndes Co) AL (unconfirmed)
Died: 1960, Greenville, AL (unconfirmed)
Inst: Guitar

Raised in Greenville, AL, where he learned guitar as youth; worked outside music with frequent work w Joe Dean/Billie Bolling at frolics/parties in area as youth; rec Paramount label, Chicago, IL, c1927; rec Columbia label, Atlanta, GA, 1930; inactive in music working as preacher at Pigrest Baptist Church, Greenville, AL, from early 30s

Billing: The Weird Guitar Player

Quote: "Two singers who came from Alabama to Atlanta, Georgia, were Barefoot Bill and Ed Bell . . . and they had a hard, shouted tone in their singing"—Paul Oliver, *The Story of the Blues*, Chilton Book Company, 1969

Reference: Living Blues magazine, Winter 1972, p 31

BENDER, D C *"Wine Head"*
(*aka:* Bobby Dee/DC Washington)
Born: Jun 19, 1919, Arbala (Hopkins Co), TX
Inst: Guitar

Raised on farm in Polk County, TX; learned guitar from Hardy Gibson, a local musician; left home to hobo through Texas/Louisiana working streets/clubs through 30s/40s; rec Gold Star label, Houston, TX, 1949; teamed w Big Son Tillis working Los Angeles, CA, early 50s; rec w Big Son Tillis, Elko label, Los Angeles, 1953; frequently worked w Lightnin' Hopkins/ Smokey Hogg/ Luther Stoneham in local clubs/ streets, Houston, TX, from 1955; frequently rec acc to other bluesmen on various labels, Houston, through 60s; worked George's, Houston, 1967; Jewish Community Center, Houston, 1967; frequently w Ivory Semien Band in local gigs, Houston, from 1967 into 70s; worked C&P Lounge, Houston, 1970; Irene's, Houston, 1970; Hollywood Lounge, Houston, 1970

Personal: First cousin of Lightnin' Hopkins. Given names are initials only

BENTLEY, GLADYS ALBERTA
Born: Aug 12, 1907, Pennsylvania
Died: Jan 18, 1960, Los Angeles, CA
Inst: Piano

Father was George Bentley, mother was Mary ———; moved to NYC, NY, c1925; worked as entertainer/singer/pianist/male impersonator at The Clam House/Connie's Inn/Cotton Club/Theatrical Grill/others, NYC, mid-20s into 30s; rec OKeh label, NYC, 1928-9; rec w Washboard Serenaders, Victor label, NYC, 1930; owned/operated/performed at Exclusive Club, NYC, early 30s; worked Kings Terrace, NYC, 1933; app w own KINGS TERRACE REVUE, Lafayette Theater, NYC, 1934; frequently worked The Ubangi Club, NYC, 1934-7; app in own UBANGI CLUB REVUE, Lafayette Theater, NYC, 1934; Harlem Opera House, NYC, 1934; Rockland Palace, NYC, NY, 1935; Tondelayo's, NYC into mid-40s; rec

Gladys Bentley *Courtesy Frank Driggs Collection*

Excelsior label, Hollywood, CA, 1945-6; rec Top Hat label, Los Angeles, CA, late 40s; occasionally worked Roseroom Club and others, Los Angeles, through 50s; died at home of pneumonia; buried Lincoln Memorial Park, Los Angeles, CA

Billing: Broadway's Queen of Song & Jazz

Quote: "An amazing exhibition of musical energy, a large, dark, masculine lady, whose feet pounded the floor while her fingers pounded the keyboard, a perfect piece of African sculpture, animated by her own rhythm"—Langston Hughes, *The Big Sea*, Alfred A Knopf, 1940

BERNHARDT, CLYDE EDRIC BARRON
(*aka:* Ed Barron)
Born: Jul 11, 1905, Gold Hill (Rowan Co), NC
Died: May 20, 1986, Newark, NJ
Inst: Trombone

Father was Washington Barnhardt; mother was Elizabeth Mauney, a school teacher; born Clyde Barnhardt; one of 6 children; moved to Richfield, NC (1907-14); Badin, NC (1914-19); Harrisburg, PA (1919); Badin, NC (1919-21); then Harrisburg, PA, to work after school while taking trombone lessons from local musician Joe Vennie, 1921-2; moved to Columbus, OH, to work outside music, 1922-6; worked as sideman w Odie Cromwell Band in local roadhouses/club dates, Battle Creek, MI, 1926; w Tillie & Her Toilers Band, State Theater, Harrisburg, PA, 1927, then brief tour; toured w Charles C Grear Original Mid-Nite Ramblers Band working white ballroom dances through Midwest, 1927; w Mid-Nite Ramblers, Oasis Ballroom, Michigan City, IN, 1927; worked w Henry McClain Band, Huntington, WV, 1928; moved to NYC, NY, 1928; worked w Herb Cowens Orch, Cotton Club, NYC, 1928; frequent gigs w Luckey Roberts Band and others, NYC, 1928; worked in pit band of Whitman Sisters SPIRIT OF 1929 musical comedy revue, Lafayette Theater, NYC, 1928, then toured theaters down East Coast through 1929; worked w Honey Brown's Band (later renamed Willie Wilkins Band), Bamboo Inn, NYC/Phinx Inn, NYC/Quogue Inn, Quogue, NY, 1929-30; w Ray Parker's Orch, Shadowland Ballroom, NYC, 1930-1; worked as sideman/singer w King Oliver & His Harlem Syncopators Orch, NYC, 1931, then toured ballrooms across US (with frequent local radio remotes) through 1931; toured w Marion Hardy's Alabamians working dances on college circuit/hotels through northeastern US, 1931-2; app w Marion Hardy's Alabamians on untitled show, WEAF-radio (NBC-Network), 1932 (remote from airplane over NYC); worked w Billie Fowler Band, NYC area, 1933; w Ira Coffey's Orch, Tibet's Walkathon, Convention Hall, Atlantic City, NJ/Airport Inn, Camden, NJ, 1933; long residency w Vernon Andrade Orch, Renaissance Casino, NYC, 1934-7; w Edgar Hayes Orch working Apollo Theater/Savoy Ballroom/Roseland Ballroom/others, NYC area, with frequent tours between NYC/Chicago, 1937-42; rec w Edgar Hayes Orch, Decca label, NYC, 1938; toured w Edgar Hayes Orch working hotels/dances through Europe, 1938; brief tours w Horace Henderson Orch/Hot Lips Page Orch/Stuff Smith Orch, 1941-2; brief tour w Fats Waller Band working Royal Theater, Baltimore, MD/Howard Theater, Washington, DC, 1942; frequently w Dave Nelson Band/Franz Jackson Band/Jay McShann Band, Savoy Ballroom, NYC, 1942; toured w Jay McShann Band working one-nighters down East Coast, 1942-3; worked w Jay McShann Band, Tick Toc Club, Boston, MA, 1943; in residence w Cecil Scott, Ubangi Club, NYC, 1943-4; w Luis Russell Orch, Savoy Ballroom, NYC, 1944; toured w Luis Russell Orch on Lil Green's package revue working one-nighters, 1944; w Claude Hopkins Orch, Zanzibar Club, NYC (with frequent radio remotes), 1944-5; w Dud Bascomb Orch, Savoy Ballroom, NYC, 1945; rec w Leonard Feather's Blue Six, Musicraft label, NYC, 1945-6; formed The Blue Blazers working Elks Rendezvous, NYC; Savoy Ballroom, NYC, 1946; Greymore Hotel, Portland, ME, 1946; rec w The Blue Blazers, Sonora label, NYC, 1946; rec True Blue label, NYC, 1947; frequently worked Savoy Ballroom/Smalls Paradise, NYC, and occasional tours w Luis Russell Orch to 1951; rec Decca label, NYC, 1948; rec w Kansas City Buddies, Blue Note label, NYC, 1949; extensive on-off work w Joe Garland's Orch in local club dates, NYC, 1949 into 60s; rec Derby label, NYC, 1951; rec Ruby label, NYC, 1953; worked mostly outside music, with occasional local gigs, Newark, NJ/NYC, NY area, 1960-71; rec Saydisc label, NYC, 1971-2; worked occasional gigs w local musicians in NYC area from 1971; worked Connecticut Traditional Jazz Club concert, Meriden, CT, 1972; worked club dates outside London, Eng, 1972; rec w Clyde Bernhardt/Jay Cole Blues & Jazz Band, 400 W 150 label, NYC, 1973; worked Overseas Press Club, NYC, 1974; Connecticut Traditional Jazz Club concert, Meriden, CT, 1975; toured w A Night in New Orleans Revue working concert dates through England/Europe, 1975-6; rec Barron label, NYC, 1975; worked w own Harlem Blues Band, Harbor Island Park, Mamaroneck, NY, 1975-6; Philadelphia Folk Festival, Schwenksville, PA, 1976; app on WBAI-FM-radio, NYC, 1975; interviewed on THE PHIL SCHAAP Show, WKCR-radio, NYC, 1976;

Courtesy Clyde Bernhardt

toured w own Harlem Blues & Jazz Band working dances/concerts/clubs through Europe, 1976-8; worked Oude Stijl Jazz Festival, Breda, Holland, 1977; toured w New Orleans Train Jazz Band working jazz club dates through Belgium, 1977; app on NEWARK AND REALITY, WOR-TV, NYC, 1978; worked Sticky Wicket Pub, Hopkinton, MA, 1978; app on THE GOOD DAY SHOW, WCVB-TV, Needham, MA, 1978; toured internationally w Legends of Jazz into 80s; suffered fatal cerebral hemorrhage; buried Rosehill Cemetery, Linden, NJ

Book: I Remember: 80 Years of Black Entertainment, Big Bands and the Blues, Clyde Bernhardt & Sheldon Harris, University of PA Press, 1986

Songs: Barron Boogie/Cracklin' Bread/Chattanooga Woman/Daisy Mae/Don't Tell It/Gate You Swing Me Down/Good Woman Blues/Hey Miss Bertha/It's Been a Long Time Baby/It's So Good This Morning Blues/Lay Your Habits Down/Red River Blues/So Long Blues/Triflin' Woman Blues/When I'm Gone/Without You

Quote: "He [sings] in the true tradition of the Jimmy Rushings and Joe Turners of the profession."—Gilbert Gaster, *Storyville,* Dec 1972, p 54

References: Storyville magazine (UK), Dec 1972, p 54-70

BERRY, CHARLES EDWARD ANDERSON
"Chuck"
Born: Jan 15, 1926, San Jose (Santa Clara Co), CA
Inst: Guitar/Piano/Sax

Father was Henry Berry, a carpenter; mother was Martha ———; one of 6 children; moved to St Louis, MO, as child where he was raised and frequently sang in local gospel quartet and Antioch Baptist Church choir; attended Simmons Grade School then Sumner HS where he studied guitar, late 30s; frequently worked school glee club/school revues/church functions/houseparties, St Louis, MO, late 30s into 40s; worked briefly w Ray Banks Orch, St Louis, from 1942; served time for robbery in local reform school, St Louis, c1944-7; worked outside music with night-school studies, Poro School of Beauty Culture, St Louis, c1947 into early 50s; formed Chuck Berry Combo working Huff Gardens, E St Louis, IL, 1952; Moonlight Bar, St Louis, MO, 1952; Crank Lounge, St Louis, 1953; Cosmopolitan Club, E St Louis, IL, 1953-5; Stage Lounge, Chicago, IL, 1955; rec extensively, Chess label, Chicago, IL, 1955-64; worked Gleason's, Cleveland, OH, 1956; toured w Alan Freed Presents the Big Beat package show working theaters across US, 1956; toured w Super Attractions Big Show of Stars R&B package show working concert/theater dates across US, 1956-8, then continued extensive tours through US/Canada/Hawaii/Australia/Mexico/England/Europe into mid-60s; worked Paramount Theater, Brooklyn, NY, 1956; app in film ROCK ROCK ROCK, 1956; app in film MISTER ROCK AND ROLL, 1957; worked Newport Jazz Festival, Newport, RI, 1958 (por shown in film JAZZ ON A SUMMER'S DAY); app on Dick Clark's AMERICAN BANDSTAND, ABC-TV 1958; owned/operated Chuck Berry's Club Bandstand (as well as a publicity/recording company), St Louis, MO, 1959-62; app on DICK CLARK'S SATURDAY NIGHT BEECHNUT SHOW, ABC-TV, c1959; app in film GO JOHNNY GO, 1959; toured Mexico working concert dates, 1959; worked Five-Four Ballroom, Los Angeles, CA, 1961; served time on morals charge in Federal Penitentiary, Terre Haute, IN, 1962-3; settled in Berry Park, Wentzville, MO, c1963; worked Civic Auditorium, Santa Monica, CA, 1964 (por shown in film THE TAMI SHOW—UK titles: Gather No Moss/Teenage Command Performance); toured

Courtesy BMI Archives

England/West Germany working concert dates, 1964; worked Beat City, London, Eng, 1964; app on HOLLYWOOD A-GO-GO, syndicated TV, 1965; worked New York Folk Festival, Carnegie Hall, NYC, NY, 1965; toured England working concert dates, 1965; rec Chess label, London, Eng, 1965; worked Olympia, Paris, France, 1965; Village Theater, NYC, NY, 1965; Cafe A Go-Go, NYC, 1965; Memorial Auditorium, Dallas, TX, 1965; Carnegie Hall, NYC, 1966; rec Mercury label, Wentzville, MO, 1966-9; toured France working concert dates, 1966; worked International Jazz Festival, Comblain-la-tour, Belgium, 1966; Fillmore Auditorium, San Francisco, CA, 1967 (por rel Chess label); Academy of Music, Brooklyn, NY, 1967; app on FROM THE BITTER END, WOR-TV, NYC, 1968; worked The Generation, NYC, 1968; toured England working club/concert dates, 1968-9; app on UPBEAT, WNEW-TV, NYC (syndicated), 1968; worked Village Gate, NYC, 1968; Anderson Theater, NYC, 1968; worked clubs/concerts, Vancouver, Can, 1968; Miami Pop Festival, Hallandale, FL, 1968; Hunter Col, NYC, 1969; w Elvin Bishop group, Fillmore East, NYC, 1969; Central Park Music Festival, NYC, 1969; Whiskey A Go-Go, Hollywood, CA, 1969; Fillmore West, San Francisco, 1969; Toronto Pop Festival, Toronto, Can, 1969 (por shown in film, SWEET TORONTO/short film version as KEEP ON ROCKIN'); Seattle Pop Festival, Duvall, WA, 1969; Stone Park Show, Chicago, IL, 1969; frequently rec Chess label, Chicago and elsewhere, from 1969 into 70s; frequently worked Rock & Roll Revival Show, Felt Forum, Madison Square Garden, NYC, 1969-73 (with frequent tours with show across US into 70s); app on DICK CAVETT Show, ABC-TV, 1970; app on MIKE DOUGLAS Show, CBS-TV, 1971; worked Auditorium Theater, Chicago, 1970; Man and His World Concert, Montreal, Can, 1970; The Palladium, Hollywood, 1971; Onondaga Memorial Concert, Syracuse, NY, 1971; The Forum, Los Angeles, CA, 1971; Ohio Valley Jazz Festival, Cincinnati, OH, 1971; The Arena, Long Beach, CA, 1971; frequent hotel dates as headliner, Las Vegas, NV, 1972; Montreux Jazz Festival, Montreux, Switzerland, 1972; Lanchester Arts Festival, Lanchester, Eng, 1972 (por rel Chess label); app on SOUNDS FOR SATURDAY, BBC-2-TV, London, Eng, 1972; worked Villageast, NYC, 1972; toured England/Australia working concert dates, 1973; app on DICK CLARK PRESENTS THE ROCK & ROLL YEARS, ABC-TV, 1973; app in film LET THE GOOD TIMES ROLL, 1973; rec ST for cartoon film HEAVY TRAFFIC, 1973; app on SONNY AND CHER COMEDY HOUR, CBS-TV, 1973; app on SALUTE TO THE BEATLES, ABC-TV, 1975; app on MIDNIGHT SPECIAL, NBC-TV, 1975; app on DON KIRSHNER'S ROCK CONCERT, WNEW-TV, NYC (syndicated), 1975; worked Rock & Roll Spectacular Show, Madison Square Garden, NYC, 1975; app on SAMMY AND COMPANY, NBC-TV, 1975; worked Sportsman's Park, Chicago, 1975; toured England/Australia working concert dates, 1975-6; film clip shown on OMNIBUS (ep: The Friendly Invasion), BBC-1-TV, London, Eng, 1975; app on DINAH!, CBS-TV, 1976; app on DONNY & MARIE Show, ABC-TV, 1977; app on SATURDAY NIGHT, NBC-TV, 1977; app on AMERICAN BANDSTAND 25th ANNIVERSARY, ABC-TV, 1977; app on MERV GRIFFIN Show, WNEW-TV, NYC (syndicated), 1977; toured Europe working concert dates, 1977; worked Sportsman's Park, Chicago, 1977; Rock & Roll Spectacular, Madison Square Garden, NYC, 1977; app on DON KIRSHNER'S ROCK CONCERT, WNEW-TV, NYC (syndicated), 1977; app on AMERICAN MUSIC AWARDS, ABC-TV, 1978; app on SHA NA NA, NBC-TV, 1978; app on TODAY Show, NBC-TV, 1978; app on CHUCK BARRIS RAH RAH SHOW, NBC-TV, 1978; app in film AMERICAN HOT WAX, 1978; app on MIKE DOUGLAS Show, CBS-TV, 1978; app on MERV GRIFFIN Show, WNEW-TV, NYC (syndicated), 1978; app on DICK CLARK'S LIVE WEDNESDAY, NBC-TV, 1978

Books: *Easy Guitar,* Chuck Berry, ARC Music, 1974
Chuck Berry R'n'R Poet, Isalee Music, 1979
Chuck Berry: Autobiography, Chuck Berry, Harmony, 1987

Songs: A Deuce/After It's Over/Aimlessly Driftin'/All Aboard/Almost Grown/Anthony Boy/Around and Around/Away from You/Back in the USA/Back to Memphis/Beautiful Delilah/Betty Jean/Bio/Bordeaux in My Pirough/Bound to Lose/Brenda Lee/Broken Arrow/Brown-Eyed Handsome Man/Butterscotch/Bye Bye Johnny/Carol/Childhood Sweetheart/Christmas/Chucks Beat/Club Nitty Gritty/Come On/Concerto in "B Goode"/Dear Dad/Deep Feeling/Diploma for Two/The Downbound Train/Drifting Heart/Every Day We Rock & Roll/Feelin' It/Festival/Fillmore Blues/Fish & Chips/Flyin' Home/Go Bobby Soxer/Go Go Go/Good Looking Woman/Got It and Gone/Guitar Boogie/Gun/Havana Moon/Have Mercy Judge/Hello Little Girl, Goodbye/Hey Good Lookin'/Hey Pedro/His Daughter Caroline/I Do Really Love You/I Got a Booking/I Got to Find My Baby/I Love You/I Want to Be Your Driver/I Will Not Let

You Go/I'm a Rocker/I'm Just a Name/I'm Talking About You/Instrumental/It Don't Take But a Few Minutes/It Wasn't Me/It's My Own Business/It's Too Dark in There/Jaguar and the Thunderbird/Johnny B Goode/Jo Jo Gunne/Laugh and Cry/Let It Rock/Let's Boogie/Let's Do Our Thing Together/Little Marie/Little Queenie/Little Star/London Berry Blues/Lonely School Days/The Man and the Donkey/Maybellene/Memphis Tennessee/Merrily We Rock & Roll/My Ding-A-Ling/My Dream (poem)/My Little Love-Light/My Mustang Ford/My Woman/Nadine/Night Beat/No Money Down/No Particular Place to Go/Oh Baby Doll/Oh Carol/Oh Louisiana/Promised Land/Put Her Down/Rain Eyes/Ramona Say Yes/Reelin' and Rockin'/Right Off Rampart Street/Rock 'n' Roll Music/Rockin' and Rollin'/Rockin' at the Fillmore/Rockin' at the Philharmonic/Rocking on the Railroad/Roll Over, Beethoven/'Round and 'Round/Run Around/Run Rudolph Run/San Francisco Dues/School Days/She Once Was Mine/Some People/The Song of My Love/Still Got the Blues/Stop and Listen/Sue Answer/Surfin' USA/Surfing Steel/Sweet Little Rock and Roller/Sweet Little Sixteen/Talkin' About My Buddy/Things I Used to Do/Thirteen Question Method/Thirty Days/Together We Will Always Be/Too Late/Too Much Monkey Business/Trick or Treat/Tulane/Vacation Time/Viva Rock & Roll/The Way It Was Before/Wee (Wee) Hours (Blues)/Welcome Back Pretty Baby/Why Should We End This Way?/Woodpecker/You Can't Catch Me/You Never Can Tell/You Two/Your Lick

Awards/Honors: Won *Billboard* magazine Triple Award for Number 1 on R&B/C&W/Pop Chart for 1955 ("Maybellene")

Won *Blues Unlimited* magazine (UK) Readers Poll for Best R&B Singer, 1973

Won Rock Music Award "Hall of Fame," CBS-TV, 1975

Won American Music Conference National Music Award, 1976

Infl by: Walter Brown/Nat Cole/Fats Domino/Louis Jordan/Aaron "T-Bone" Walker

Infl to: Beach Boys/The Beatles/Eddy Clearwater/Jimi Hendrix/Rolling Stones

Quotes: "Berry's music, like the earlier rhythm and blues, was based in the traditional, earthy Negro blues, but he had colored them with a wry, zesty good humor, a sense of joyous affirmation and a rhythmic power . . ."—Pete Welding (source unknown)

"A master of the unpretentious, hard driving type of body music"—Arnold Shaw, *The World of Soul*, Cowles Book Company, Inc, 1970

"One of the enduring legends of rock 'n' roll, and its single most influential figure"—Nick Logan/Bob Woffinden, *The Illustrated Encyclopedia of Rock*, Hamlyn Publishers, 1976

References: Encyclopedia of Pop, Rock, and Soul, Irwin Stambler, St Martin's Press, 1974

Rock Folk, Michael Lydon, The Dial Press, 1971

Blues Unlimited magazine, Collector's Classic #3 (UK), Apr 1964

BEY, IVERSON
(see Minter, Iverson)

BIG BILL
(see Broonzy, William)

BIG BLOKE
(see Oden, James)

BIG CHIEF
(see Ellis, Wilbert)

BIG ED
(see Burns, Eddie)

BIG FOOT
(see Burnett, Chester)

BIG JOE
(see McCoy, Joe)
(see Williams, Joe Lee)

BIG MACEO
(see Merriweather, Major)

BIG MAMA BEV
(see Hill, Beverly)

BIG MAYBELLE
(see Smith, Mabel)

BIG MOOSE
(see Walker, John)

BIG VERNON
(see Turner, Joseph)

BIG VOICE
(see Odom, Andrew)

BIG WALTER
(see Horton, Walter)
(see Price, Walter)

BIG WILLIE
(see Mabon, Willie)

BIGEOU, ESTHER

Courtesy Frank Driggs Collection

Born: c1895, New Orleans (Orleans Parish), LA
Died: c1936 (unconfirmed)

App as singer/dancer/recitalist in Irvin C Miller's BROADWAY RASTUS Revue, Standard Theater, Philadelphia, PA, 1917; Lafayette Theater, NYC, NY, 1917; Orpheum Theater, Baltimore, MD, 1917; toured in DARKTOWN FOLLIES Revue working theaters in Pennsylvania/New Jersey, 1918-20; toured in Perin & Henderson's road show working theaters through South, 1920; rec OKeh label, NYC, NY, 1921; worked Lincoln Theater, NYC, 1921; worked w Bob Slater's Minstrel Maids at The Opera House, Sayville, NY, 1921; worked Renaissance Theater, NYC, 1921; Standard Theater, Philadelphia, PA, 1921; Booker T Washington Theater, St Louis, MO, 1922; Grand Theater, Chicago, IL, 1923; rec OKeh label, NYC, 1923; worked w Lucille Hegamin, Frolic Theater, Birmingham, AL, 1923; toured w Billy King Company working TOBA circuit, 1923; toured as single, working theaters in Pittsburgh, PA/Chicago, IL/New Orleans, LA/Dallas, TX/elsewhere, 1923-5; rec OKeh label, NYC, 1926; continued touring theater dates in Baltimore, MD/Chicago, IL/Dallas, TX/New Orleans, LA/Pittsburgh, PA/Birmingham, AL/elsewhere, 1927-30; reportedly retired to settle in New Orleans, LA, c1930

Personal: Married Irvin C Miller. Reportedly married Sam Grey. Was a cousin of musician Paul Barbarin

Billings: The Creole Songbird/The Girl with the Million Dollar Smile

Songs: Panama Limited Blues/Tee Pee Valley Blues/You Ain't Treatin' Me Right

BILL
(see Broonzy, William)

BIRMINGHAM SAM
(see Hooker, John Lee)

BLACK ACE
(see Turner, Babe)

BLACK, FRANKIE
(see Blackwell, Francis)

BLACK JR
(see Johnson Jr, Luther)

BLACKWELL, FRANCIS HILLMAN *"Scrapper"*
(*aka:* Frankie Black)
Born: Feb 21, 1903, Syracuse, NC (?) (See note below)
Died: Oct 7, 1962, Indianapolis, IN
Inst: Guitar/Piano

Father was Payton Blackwell, a country fiddler; mother Elizabeth Francis; family was of Cherokee Indian heritage; one of 16 children; moved to Indianapolis, IN, 1906; interested in music early and made own cigar box instrument, 1909; taught self guitar working local parties as teenager; frequently worked between Chicago, IL/Indianapolis, IN, from early 20s; often worked outside music through 20s; teamed w Leroy Carr, 1928; rec w Leroy Carr or as single, Vocalion label, Indianapolis/Chicago, 1928-32; rec w

Francis "Scrapper" Blackwell
Courtesy Frank Driggs Collection

Chippie Hill, Vocalion label, Chicago, 1929; rec w Georgia Tom/Teddy Moss/Leroy Carr, or solo, Gennett label, Richmond, IN, 1930; rec w Robinson's Knights of Rest and others, Champion label, Richmond, IN, 1930-1; worked extensively w Leroy Carr in local clubs/theaters, St Louis, MO area, early 30s; worked w Leroy Carr, Booker T Washington Theater, St Louis, c1931; Jazzland Club, St Louis, c1932; rec Vocalion label, St Louis, MO/NYC, NY, 1934; rec Bluebird/Champion-Decca labels, Chicago, 1935; after death of Leroy Carr retired from music to settle in Indianapolis to work outside music with occasional local party/tavern/lounge/concert work, 1935 through 50s; worked w Jack Dupree, Cotton Club, Indianapolis, c1940; worked occasional Indianapolis Jazz Club concerts, Indianapolis, 1955; 1444 Gallery, Indianapolis, 1959 (por rel 77 label); rec acc to Brooks Berry, Bluesville label, Indianapolis, 1959/61; worked Indianapolis Jazz Club concert, Indianapolis, 1960; rec 77 label, Indianapolis, 1960; rec Prestige-Bluesville label, Indianapolis, 1961; was fatally shot in a back alley on the west side; buried New Crown Cemetery, Indianapolis, IN

Note: Most sources give Syracuse, NC, as place of birth but maps of that time list no such town. In all probability his birth was Syracuse (Darlington Co), SC

Personal: Married. Many of his songs written in collaboration w Leroy Carr or his late sister, Mae Malone. Name "Scrapper" given him by grandmother as child

Songs: A Blues/Back Step Blues/Blue 'n' Whistling/Blues Before Sunrise/E Blues/George Street Blues/Goin' to Jail About Her/Leaving You Blues/Naptown Blues/No Good Woman Blues/Sally in the Alley Blues/Shady Lane Blues/Soft Blues/The Truth About the Thing

Infl to: Leonard Caston/Shirley Griffith/Johnny Shines

Quotes: "Scrapper was a self-taught blues artist of the first rank. Taste and dramatic impact ran through even his most casual performances"—Duncan Schiedt, 77 album LA 12-4

"Scrapper's voice is not as clear and confident as it was in the old days, but has taken on a new dimension of depth and intensity of feeling. His blues are less direct and accessible but are more subtle and personal; their meaning has grown more profound over the years"—Arthur Rosenbaum, Prestige-Bluesville album 1047

Reference: Prestige-Bluesville album 1047

BLAND, ROBERT CALVIN *"Bobby"/"Bobby Blue"*
Born: Jan 27, 1930, Rosemark (Shelby Co), TN
Inst: Guitar/Jew's Harp/Tenor Saxophone

Father Leroy Bland; sang gospel as child; learned guitar at about 5 years of age; often sang/entertained on streets/store fronts into 40s; dropped out of school to move to Memphis, TN, mid-40s; formed and worked w The Miniatures (gospel group) in local churches, Memphis area, late 40s; worked briefly w Adolph Duncan Band, Memphis, 1949; together w Johnny Ace/Roscoe Gordon/Willie Nix/BB King/others formed The Beale Streeters working local gigs, Memphis, 1949; app w Beale Streeters, WDIA-radio, Memphis, 1949; frequently worked outside music (as valet/chauffeur to BB King), early 50s; won first prize in amateur show, Palace Theater, Memphis, 1951; frequently worked in Johnny Ace Revue in Memphis area, early 50s; served overseas in US Army Special Services, 1951-4; rec Modern label, Memphis, 1952; rec w Roscoe Gordon Band, Chess label, Memphis, 1954; frequently toured w Little Jr Parker in Blues Consolidated package show working clubs/theaters across US, 1954-61; worked Club Matinee, Houston,

Robert "Bobby" Bland
Courtesy Sheldon Harris Collection

TX, 1955; rec Duke label, Houston and elsewhere, 1955 into 70s; formed own band touring one-nighters/concerts/dances/theaters across US from late 50s; worked Regal Theater, Chicago, IL, 1960; w Jr Parker Band, 5-4 Ballroom, Los Angeles, CA, 1960; Ashland Auditorium, Chicago, c1961; Longhorn Ranch, Dallas, TX, 1962; formed own revue touring one-nighter concerts across US, from 1962; frequently worked Apollo Theater, NYC, NY, from 1963; worked Both/And, San Francisco, CA, 1967; Harlem Cultural Festival, Mount Morris Park, NYC, 1967 (por shown HARLEM CULTURAL FESTIVAL, WNEW-TV, NYC [syndicated]); worked Paladium Ballroom, Houston, TX, 1968; Groove Yard, Vancouver, Can, 1968; Regal Theater, Chicago, 1968; Plugged Nickel, Chicago, 1969; Fillmore East, NYC, 1969; Weequahic Park Love Festival, Newark, NJ, 1969 (por shown on WEEQUAHIC PARK LOVE FESTIVAL, NBC-TV); Apollo Theater, NYC, 1970; Burning Spear, Chicago, 1970-1; High Chaparral, Chicago, 1970; Ann Arbor Blues Festival, Ann Arbor, MI, 1970; Massey Hall, Toronto, Can, 1970; Man and His World Exhibit, Montreal, Can, 1970; Loser's Club, Dallas, TX, 1971; Memorial Auditorium, New Orleans, LA, 1971; Ann Arbor Blues Festival, Ann Arbor, MI, 1972 (por rel Atlantic label); app in ATOMIC MAMA'S WANG DANG DOODLE BLUES Show, WNIB-FM-radio, Chicago, IL, c1972; worked Colonial Tavern, Toronto, Can, 1973-4; Ruthie's Inn, Berkeley, CA, 1973-5; Max's Kansas City, NYC, 1973; rec ABC-Dunhill label, NYC, 1974; rec w BB King, ABC-Dunhill label, Los Angeles, CA, 1974; worked w Mellow Fellows group, High Chaparral, Chicago, 1974-5; Bijou Cafe, Philadelphia, PA, 1974; International Blues Festival, Louisville, KY, 1974; Continental Showcase, Houston, TX, 1974; London House, Chicago, 1974; Newport Jazz Festival, NYC, 1974; Toronto Blues Festival, Olympic Island, Toronto, Can, 1974; Winterland, San Francisco, CA, 1974; Whiskey A Go-Go, Los Angeles, CA, 1974; app on MIDNIGHT SPECIAL, NBC-TV, 1974; app w BB King, SOUL TRAIN, WNEW-TV, NYC (syndicated), c1975; worked The Back Door, San Diego, CA, 1975; Monterey Jazz Festival, Monterey, CA, 1975 (por on KEST-radio, San Francisco); The Boarding House, San Francisco, 1975; The Auditorium, Richmond, CA, 1975; Balmoral Racetrack, Chicago, 1975; Temple University, Ambler, PA, 1975; Concerts at the Grove, Los Angeles, 1975; w own revue, Cotillion Ballroom, Wichita, KS, 1975; Municipal Auditorium, New Orleans, LA, 1975; International Amphitheater, Chicago, 1975-6; The Stingrey, Chicago, 1975-7; Great American Music Hall, San Francisco, 1976; Newport Jazz Festival, NYC, 1976; Electric Ballroom, Atlanta, GA, 1976; Beacon Theater, NYC, 1976; toured extensively w BB King working concert dates across US, 1976; w BB King, Concerts at the Grove, Los Angeles, 1976 (por rel ABC-Impulse label); rec w BB King, ABC-Dunhill label, Los Angeles, 1976; worked Ed Howard's Club, San Francisco, 1976; Kool Jazz Festival, The Astrodome, Houston, TX, 1976; New Orleans Jazz & Heritage Festival, New Orleans, LA, 1976; Civic Auditorium Music Hall, Omaha, NE, 1976; Louisville Gardens, Louisville, KY, 1976; app w BB King, SOUNDSTAGE (ep: Together in the Blues), PBS-TV, 1977; Shea's Buffalo Theater, Buffalo, NY, 1977; Kola Shannah Club, San Bernadino, CA, 1977; Jones Hall, Houston, TX, 1977; The Old Waldorf, San Francisco, 1977; The Burning Spear, Chicago, 1977-8; El Mocambo, Toronto, Can, 1977; Trojan Horse, Seattle, WA, 1977; Melody Fair, Buffalo, NY, 1977; Radio City Music Hall, NYC, 1977; Rosy's, New Orleans, LA, 1978

Billing: The Soul Man

Songs: Drifting from Town to Town/Good Lovin' (Love You, Yes I Do)/Love My Baby

Awards/Honors: Won *Cashbox* magazine R&B Artist of the Year Award, 1961
Won NAACP Image Award, 1975

Infl by: Johnny Ace/Roy Brown/Lowell Fulson/Roscoe Gordon/BB King/Little Jr Parker/Ira Tucker/Aaron "T-Bone" Walker/Jimmy Witherspoon

Infl to: Sugarcane Harris/Bee Houston/Little Milton/Andrew Odom/Johnny Taylor

Quotes: "Bland's style . . . built out of an amalgam of gospel, blues and ballads, has made him one of the biggest names of the last decade in black music"—Jim O'Neal, *Living Blues* magazine, Winter 1970-1, p 15

"For Bobby, the blues are individual pieces of music, many shapes and hues, whether savage, swinging, pensive, plaintive, shouted or softspoken, or an undercurrent which can swell to swamp a ballad"—JB Figi, *Downbeat* magazine, Aug 7, 1969, p 17

References: *Living Blues,* Jul-Aug 1978, pp 8-16
Living Blues, Winter, 1970-1, pp 10-18
Downbeat, Aug 7, 1969, pp 16-17

BLANKS, BIRLEANNA *(Berlina/Berleanna/Birlianna/ Birilannia/Berlevia)*

Courtesy Marge Singleton

Born: Feb 18, 1889, Iowa
Died: Aug 12, 1968, New York, NY

Father was Addison Blanks; mother was Amanda Billups, a full-blooded Indian; moved to E St Louis, IL, where she was raised from childhood; attended local schools/colleges and later worked outside music as schoolteacher c1912; teamed w sister Arsceola Blanks, as "Blanks Sisters," touring as singing/dancing act on vaudeville circuit, late teens; app in Billy King's musical comedy OVER THE TOP, Lafayette Theater, NYC, NY, 1919; app in musical comedy THEY'RE OFF, Lafayette Theater, NYC, 1919; app in musical comedy EXPLOITS IN AFRICA, Lafayette Theater, NYC, 1919; app in musical comedy THE NEW AMERICAN, Lafayette Theater, NYC, 1921; app in musical comedy A TRIP AROUND THE WORLD, Lafayette Theater, NYC, 1921; app in musical comedy DERBY DAY IN DIXIE, Lafayette Theater, NYC, 1921; formed The Three Dixie Songbirds (w Hilda Perlina/Amanda Randolph) to work local club dates, Chicago, IL, c1922; worked as single, Paradise Cafe, Chicago, 1922; worked frequent theater dates, Chicago, 1922-3; app in FROLICERS Revue, Lafayette Theater, NYC, 1923; rec w Fletcher Henderson, Paramount label, NYC, 1923; app w Mae Barnes in LUCKY SAMBO Revue, Colonial Theater, NYC, 1925-6, then Columbia Theater, NYC/ Empire Theater, Newark, NJ/Hurtig & Seamon's Theater, NYC, 1926/Majestic Theater, Jersey City, NJ/Lafayette Theater, NYC, 1927; retired to work outside music in NYC from c1928; entered Florence Nightingale Nursing Home where she died of cancer; buried Woodlawn Cemetery, Bronx, NY

Personal: Married Chesley Cunningham, a baseball player. Her sister Arsceola Blanks married Leonard Harper to work as team ("Harper & Blanks") on vaudeville circuit during teens/20s

Quote: "She had a very deep contralto voice, very expressive"—Marge Singleton (personal interview)

BLAYLOCK, TRAVIS L
(*aka:* Harmonica Slim)

Courtesy Sheldon Harris Collection

Born: Dec 21, 1934, Douglassville (Cass Co), TX
Inst: Harmonica

Raised in Texarkana, TX, area and took early interest in music, learning harmonica at 12 years of age; frequently worked w The Sunny South Singers gospel group in local churches and app with them on KCMC-radio, Texarkana, from c1943; moved to Los Angeles, CA, 1949; toured w Lowell Fulson in package R&B shows working theaters mostly in Houston, TX, area c1950-3; frequently toured as single working one-nighters, 1954-5; worked Club Alabam, Birmingham, AL, c1955; Royal Peacock, Atlanta, GA, c1955; The Matinee, Houston, TX, c1955; Downbeat Club, Houston, TX, c1955; The Auditorium, Galveston, TX, c1955; Crown Propeller, Chicago, IL, c1955; worked frequently as session musician for local recording dates, Los Angeles, CA, 1956; rec Aladdin label, Los Angeles, 1956; rec Spry label, Los Angeles, c1956; rec Vita label, Los Angeles, 1957; frequently toured South working club dates, late 50s into 60s; worked club dates in Los Angeles area through 60s; w Aaron "T-Bone" Walker, Shelly's Manne-Hole, Los Angeles, c1968; w Percy Mayfield, Fillmore Auditorium, San Francisco, CA, c1968; w George Smith, Golden Bear, Los Angeles, 1969; w Harmonica Fats, Daisy Maes, Los Angeles, c1969; w Lowell Fulson, Old Dixie Ballroom, Los Angeles, 1969; w BB King, Five-Four Ballroom, Los Angeles, c1969; rec Blues-Time label, Hollywood, CA, 1969; returned to Texarkana, TX, to work occasional local club dates from 1971

Songs: Do What You Want to Do/Drop Anchor/Going Back Home/Hard Times/I'll Take Love/Lonely Hours/Love/Mary Helen/My Girl Won't Quit Me/Thought I Didn't Love You/You/You Better Believe It

Infl by: Martin Fulson/Aaron "T-Bone" Walker

Infl to: Harmonica Fats

Reference: BluesTime album BTS-9005

BLIND ARTHUR
(see Phelps, Arthur)

BLIND BLAKE
(see Phelps, Arthur)

BLIND BOY FULLER NUMBER 2
(see McGhee, Walter)

BLIND DOGGIE
(see McTell, Willie)

BLIND GARY
(see Davis, Gary)

BLIND SAMMY/SAMMIE
(see McTell, Willie)

BLIND WILLIE
(see McTell, Willie)

BLOOMFIELD, MICHAEL BERNARD *"Mike"*

Courtesy Tom Mazzolini

Born: Jul 28, 1943, Chicago (Cook Co), IL
Died: Feb 15, 1981, San Francisco, CA
Inst: Guitar/Harmonica/Piano

Father was Harold Bloomfield; mother was Dorothy Klein; raised in Chicago, IL; was playing guitar in Chicago, late 50s, occasionally sat in with local blues/rock bands in small clubs/lounges, Chicago, c1960; worked Pepper's Lounge, Chicago, c1962; frequently worked Limelight Theater, Chicago, from 1962; promoted/performed blues concerts, Fickle Pickle Coffee House, Chicago, 1963; frequently worked w Big Joe Williams in local clubs, Chicago, early 60s; rec acc to many blues/folk singers in Chicago, early 60s; rec acc to Yank Rachell, Delmark label, Chicago, 1963-4; rec acc to John Estes, Delmark label, Chicago, 1964; formed The Group working Big John's, Chicago, 1964-5; Magoo's, Chicago, 1964-5; rec acc to Bob Dylan, Columbia label, Chicago, 1965; worked w Paul Butterfield Blues Band, Newport Folk Festival, Newport, RI, 1965 (por shown in film FESTIVAL); rec w Paul Butterfield Blues Band, Elektra label, Chicago, 1965; frequently worked w Paul Butterfield Blues Band in local club dates, Chicago, 1966-7; app w Barry Goldberg Blues Band, WBBM-TV, Chicago, 1966, rec acc Eddie Vinson, BluesWay label, NYC, NY, 1967; formed The Electric Flag (1967-8) working International Pop Festival, Monterey, CA, 1967; Golden Bear Club, Huntington Beach, CA, 1967; scored/rec ST for film THE TRIP, 1967; produced/orchestrated recording for James Cotton, Verve label, NYC, 1967; worked Fillmore Auditorium, San Francisco, CA, 1967 (por rel Columbia label); toured w The Electric Flag working concert dates across US, 1968; rec w Al Kooper, Columbia label, Chicago, 1968; worked Fillmore East, NYC, 1968-9; Fillmore West, San Francisco, 1969-71; w Muddy Waters, Super Cosmic Joy-Scout Jamboree, Auditorium Theater, Chicago, 1969 (por rel Chess label); rec w Muddy Waters Band, Chess label, Chicago, 1969; worked Keystone Korner, San Francisco, 1970-1; The Matrix, San Francisco, 1970; app in film BONGO WOLF'S REVENGE, 1970; frequently toured w Al Kooper, early 70s; worked The Auditorium, Long Beach, CA, 1971; Ash Grove, Los Angeles, CA, 1971; rec ST for film STEELYARD BLUES, 1973 (por rel Warner Bros label); rec w John Paul Hammond/Dr John, Columbia-CBS label, NYC, 1973; rec local TV commercials, Chicago, 1973; briefly reformed Electric Flag group, 1974; app w Muddy Waters, SOUNDSTAGE, PBS-TV (syndicated), 1974; scored ST for film short HOT NASTY, 1975; worked Family Light School of Music, Sausalito, CA, 1975; rec w KGB group, MCA label, Chicago, 1975; worked Newport Jazz Festival, NYC, 1976; San Francisco Blues Festival, McLaren Park, San Francisco, 1976 (por rel Jefferson label); Winterland Auditorium, San Francisco, 1976 (por shown in film THE LAST WALTZ, 1978/por rel Warner Bros label); rec Guitar Player label, Saratoga, CA, 1977: worked w Big Joe Turner, The Palms, San Francisco, 1977; Old Waldorf, San Francisco, 1977; Univ of Oregon, Eugene, OR, 1977; rec Takoma label, San Francisco (?), 1977; worked New Orleans Jazz & Heritage Festival, New Orleans, LA 1977; rec Rounder label, Woodstock, NY, 1977; worked Bottom Line, NYC, 1978; toured clubs into 80s; died of drug OD, buried Hillside Memorial Park, Los Angeles, CA

Book: Me and Big Joe, Mike Bloomfield/S E Summerville, 1980

Songs: Can't Wait No Longer/City Girl/Death Cell Rounder Blues/Death in My Family/Hey Foreman/If You Love These Blues/It's Not Killing Me/Me/My Old Lady/The Train Is Gone/WDIA/Working Man/You're Killing My Love

Infl by: BB King/Muddy Waters/Aaron "T-Bone" Walker/Sonny Boy Williamson (Alex Miller)

Quote: "Bloomfield is regarded as being up there with the great blues guitarists—Eric Clapton, Jimi Hendrix and Johnny Winter"—Lillian Roxon, *Rock Encyclopedia*, Grosset & Dunlap, 1969

Reference: Encyclopedia of Pop, Rock & Soul, Irwin Stambler, St Martin's Press, 1974

BLUE, *"Little"* JOE

Photo by Norbert Hess

Born: Sept 23, 1934, Vicksburg (Warren Co), MS
Died: Apr 22, 1990, Reno, NV
Inst: Guitar

Father was Abraham Fields; mother Willie Hodges; born Joseph Valery Jr; moved to Tallulah, LA, where he was raised from early age; worked outside music in Tallulah area through 40s; moved to Detroit, MI, to work outside music, 1951-3; served in US Army in Korea theater of operations, 1953-6; worked outside music, Detroit, from 1956; frequently worked local talent shows with some sit-in gigs in local bands, Detroit, through 50s; formed The Midnighters to work Apex Club/others, Detroit, late 50s; frequently worked with own band in local bars/clubs, Reno, NV, early 60s; moved to Los Angeles, CA, to work outside music from 1961; worked occasionally at Mo's Swing Club/Tropicana/Skylock Club/Perkins Club/others, Los Angeles, into 60s; rec Nanc label, Los Angeles (?), c1961; rec Kent label, Los Angeles (?), 1964; worked Club Savoy, Richmond, CA, c1964; rec Movin' label, Los Angeles, 1966; rec Checker label, Los Angeles, 1966; frequently toured with various R&B package shows working clubs/theaters through South, late 60s; rec Checker label, Chicago, IL, c1968; rec Jewel label, Shreveport, LA/Hollywood, CA/Los Angeles, CA, 1968-72; worked Fillmore West, San Francisco, CA, 1968; Ann Arbor Blues Festival, Ann Arbor, MI, 1970-1; rec Space label, San Diego (?), CA, 1971; worked Berkeley Blues Festival, Berkeley, CA, 1971; rec Soul Set/Miles Ahead labels, San Francisco (?), early 70s; frequently worked bars/clubs in East Bay area, San Francisco, 1972; worked Continental Club, Oakland, CA, 1973; Ruthie's Inn, Berkeley, CA, 1973; Fergie's, Goleta, CA, 1973; Topanga Corral, Los Angeles, 1973; San Francisco Blues Festival, Golden Gate Park, San Francisco, 1974; Stardust Lounge, San Francisco, 1974-5; Playboy Club, Richmond, CA, 1974-5; Joe's Melody Room, Vallejo, CA, 1974; toured one-nighters through South, 1974; worked Berkeley Blues Festival, Univ of California, Berkeley, CA, 1975; Uptight Club, San Francisco, 1975; Club Shalimar, Berkeley, 1975; app on BLUES BY THE BAY, KPOO-FM radio, San Francisco, 1975; toured w American Blues Legends 75 working concert dates through England/Europe, 1975; worked 100 Club, London, Eng, 1975 (por rel Big Bear label); Club Long Island, San Francisco, 1975; Boston Club, Sacramento, CA, 1975; toured w James Brown Revue working theaters across US, 1975; worked Green Earth Cafe, San Francisco, 1976; Club la Veek, Houston, TX, 1977; worked clubs/festivals across US into 80s; San Francisco Blues Fest working concerts in Europe, 1982; International Jazz Fest, Barcelona, Spain, 1986; club dates in CA/TX through 80s; died of cancer; buried Sierra Memorial Gardens, Reno, NV

Infl by: Louis Jordan/BB King/Joe Liggins/Roy Milton/Mr Bo/Lafayette Thomas

Quote: "His manner is based upon the ever-influential BB King, yet his voice is naturally clear, and his diction is excellent"—(Keith Tillman) Mike Leadbitter, *Nothing But the Blues*, Hanover Books, 1971

Reference: Blues Unlimited magazine (UK), Jul 1975, pp 8-9

BLUE, LU
(see Barker, Louisa)

BLUES BOY
(see Odom, Andrew)
(see Seward, Alec)

BLUES BOY BILL
(see Broonzy, William)

BLUES KING
(see Seward, Alec)

BLUES MAN, THE
(see Sykes, Roosevelt)

BO DIDDLEY
(see McDaniel, Ellas)

BOBBY DEE
(see Bender, D C)

BOGAN, LUCILLE
(*aka:* Bessie Jackson)

Courtesy Sheldon Harris Collection

BOGAN

Born: Apr 1, 1897, Amory (Monroe Co), MS
Died: Aug 10, 1948, Los Angeles, CA

Born Lucille Anderson; moved to Birmingham, AL, at early age where she was raised; rec OKeh label, NYC, NY/Atlanta, GA 1923; moved to Chicago, IL, late 20s; rec Paramount label, Chicago, 1927; rec Brunswick label, Chicago, 1928-30; rec Banner label, Chicago/NYC, 1933-35; rec ARC label group, NYC, 1934-35; reportedly returned to Birmingham, AL, mid-30s; managed Bogan's Birmingham Busters group, Birmingham, late 30s; moved to West Coast, 1948; died at home of coronary sclerosis; buried Lincoln Memorial Park Cemetery, Los Angeles, CA

Personal: Married Nazareth Bogan. 2 children.

Songs: Alley Boogie/Don't Mean You No Good Blues/Down in Boogie Alley/Jim Tampa Blues/Lonesome Daddy Blues/New Way Blues/Pay Roll Blues/Sweet Man, Sweet Man/Tricks Ain't Walking No More/War Time Man Blues/Women Won't Need No Men

Quotes: "Ma Rainey, Bessie Smith, Lucille Bogan—the big three of the blues . . ."—Ernest Borneman, *A Critic Looks at Jazz*, Jazz Music Books, 1946

"Tough-voiced and uncompromising, she did not venture . . . into a kind of popular song form but stayed essentially a blues singer"—Paul Oliver, *The Story of the Blues*, Chilton Book Company, 1969

Reference: Living Blues, #44 (1979), pp 25-28

BOGAN, THEODORE R *"Ted"*

Born: May 10, 1910, Spartanburg (Spartanburg Co), SC
Died: Jan 29, 1990, Detroit, MI
Inst: Bass/Guitar

Father was David Bogan; mother was Cornelia Knuckles; taught self guitar, 1929; frequently worked local parties/picnics/suppers in area, 1929-30; toured w Dr Mines Medicine Show through North Carolina, 1930; app on WSPA-radio, Spartanburg, SC, c1930; moved to Knoxville, TN, 1930; worked w Carl Martins' Four Keys String Band at local dances/picnics/weddings/taverns in area, Knoxville, 1930-2; app WOPI-radio, Bristol, TN/WROL-radio, Knoxville, early 30s; occasional tours w Carl Martins' Four Keys working gigs through West Virginia, early 30s; rec w Four Keys (as Tennessee Chocolate Drops), Vocalion label, Knoxville, 1930; worked w Carl Martin in local gigs, Kalamazoo, MI/South Bend, IN, 1932; moved to Chicago, IL, 1933; frequently worked w Carl Martin in local streets/stockyards/parties/theaters, Chicago area, 1933-7; frequently worked w Jimmy Hazeley/Jimmy Dudley/Les Paul/others, Chicago, 1937 to early 40s; served in US Army, early 40s; worked mostly outside music with occasional small gigs w Carl Martin, Chicago, mid-40s to 1965; returned to music to work as single in local folk clubs/coffee houses/lounges, Chicago, from 1965; worked Festival of American Folklife, Washington, DC, 1970; Philadelphia Folk Festival, Schwenksville, PA, 1971; frequently worked w Carl Martin quartet in local club dates, Chicago, 1972-4; worked Univ of Chicago Folk Festival, Chicago, 1972; rec Rounder label, Chicago, 1972; worked Smithsonian Blues Festival, Washington, DC, 1972; Mariposa Folk Festival, Toronto, Can, 1972; rec Rocky Road label, Chicago, c1972; worked Earl of Old Town, Chicago, 1973-4; toured w Martin, Bogan and The Armstrongs group working colleges in Chicago area, 1973-4; rec Flying Fish label, Chicago, 1973; worked Binghamton Folk Festival, Binghamton, NY, 1974; National Folk Festival, Washington, DC, 1974; Mendota Jazz Festival, Minneapolis, MN, 1974; toured w Martin, Bogan and The Armstrongs quartet on "Music of the People—USA" tour working concert dates through Central and

Photo by Jeff Titon. Courtesy University of Illinois Press

South America under auspices of US State Department, 1975; worked Portland State Col, Portland, OR, 1975; Univ of Oregon, Eugene, OR, 1975; Oregon State Univ, Corvallis, OR, 1975; Philadelphia Folk Festival, Schwenksville, PA, 1975-6; Mariposa Folk Festival, Toronto, Can, 1975; San Diego State Univ Folk Festival, San Diego, CA, 1975; Art Park Theater, Lewiston, NY, 1975; Univ of Notre Dame, South Bend, IN, 1975; Juicy John Pink's Club, DeKalb, IL, 1975; Vegetable Buddies Club, South Bend, IN, 1976; Bobby McGhee's, Cleveland, OH, 1976; Kent State Folk Festival, Kent, OH, 1976; Winnipeg Folk Festival, Winnipeg, Can, 1976; Northwestern Univ, Evanston, IL, 1976; Sylvester's, Chicago, IL, 1976; NAIRD Convention, O'Hare Motor Inn, Chicago, 1977; John Henry Folk Festival, Camp Virgil Tate, Princeton, WV, 1977; Charlotte's Web, Rockford, IL, 1977; Northern Illinois Univ Folk Festival, DeKalb, IL, 1977; toured US working clubs/festivals through 80s; app in film LOUIE BLUIE, c1985; died of heart disease at home; buried Lincoln Memorial Park, Mt Clemens, MI

Song: Ain't Doin' Bad Doin' Nothing

References: *Folk Scene* magazine, Jul/Aug 1975, pp 12-14

Mississippi Rag magazine, Mar 1974, p 5

BOLL WEENIE BILL
(see Moore, Willie C)

BOLL WEEVIL BILL
(see Moore, Willie C)

BONDS, *"Brownsville"/"Brother"* **SON**
(*aka:* Son)
Born: Mar 16, 1909, Brownsville (Haywood Co), TN
Died: Aug 31, 1947, Dyersburg, TN
Inst: Guitar

Father was Aaron Bonds, mother Hattie Newbern; born, raised and worked outside music in Brownsville, TN, area entire life; worked w Hammie Nixon on local streets for tips, Chicago, IL, 1934; rec Decca-Champion label, Chicago, 1934; rec w Hammie Nixon (as Hammie & Son), Decca label, Chicago, 1934; rec Decca label, NYC, NY, 1938; rec w Delta Boys, Bluebird label, Chicago, 1941; was accidentally shot while sitting on Hammie Nixon's front porch and died of wounds; buried St Peter Cemetery, Brownsville, TN

Personal: Married Mary ———

Songs: A Hard Pill to Swallow/Come Back Home

Quotes: "He was a good guitarist and his voice had the usual rural Tennessee nasal sound"—Samuel Charters, *Sweet as the Showers of Rain*, Oak Publications, 1977

BONNER, WELDON H PHILIP *"Juke Boy"*
(*aka:* Juke Boy Barner)
Born: Mar 22, 1932, Bellville (Austin Co), TX
Died: Jun 29, 1978, Houston, TX
Inst: Cymbals/Drums/Guitar/Harmonica

Father was Emanuel Bonner, a sharecropper; mother was Carrie Kessee; one of 9 children; parents died early and he was raised by another farm family, becoming interested in music at 6 years of age; sang in small local gospel group while still in elementary school; taught self guitar at 12 years of age; dropped out of school to work outside music with occasional gigs at local dances/church suppers in Bellville/Brenham, TX, area, 1945-7; moved to Houston, TX, to work outside music from 1947; won first prize at Trummy Cain's talent show, Lincoln Theater, Houston, TX, 1948; app on KLEE-radio, Houston, 1948; worked frequent club/lounge/bar dates in Houston area to 1954; moved to West Coast to work juke joints through California, 1954-7; rec Irma label, Oakland, CA, 1957; returned to Houston, TX, 1957, to work as one-man band in local bars/clubs, then on road working jukes/clubs/bars through Louisiana/Alabama/Tennessee/Arkansas into 60s; rec Goldband/Storyville/Jan & Dill labels, Lake Charles, LA, 1960; worked Bell's Bar, Kenner, LA, c1965; worked Family Inn, Houston, TX, 1966-7; contributed poetry to *The Forward Times* newspaper, Houston, 1966; worked Hayes Lounge, Houston, 1967; Jungle Lounge, Houston, 1967-8; frequently worked clubs/bars/dances/community centers in Houston area, 1967 into 70s; rec Blues Unlimited/Flyright labels, Houston, 1967; rec Arhoolie label, Houston, 1967-70; toured w American Folk Blues Festival working clubs/radio/TV/concert dates through England/Europe, 1969; worked Royal Albert Hall, London, Eng, 1969 (por rel CBS label); rec Liberty label, London, Eng, 1969; worked Ash Grove, Los Angeles, CA, 1970-1; San Diego Folk Festival, San Diego, CA, 1970; Berkeley Blues Festival, Berkeley, CA, 1970; C&P Lounge, Houston, TX, 1970; Koret's Lounge, Houston, 1970; Ann Arbor Blues Festival, Ann Arbor, MI, 1970; Liberty Hall, Houston, TX, 1971; worked club dates in Oakland/Richmond, CA, area, 1971; rec Sonet label, Berkeley, CA, 1972; worked Univ of Chicago Folk

Weldon "Juke Boy" Bonner

Courtesy C Strachwitz, Arhoolie Records

Festival, Chicago, IL, 1972; toured England working club dates, 1972; worked Sinkkasten Club, Frankfurt, Germany, 1972; Grand Central Discotheque, Houston, TX, 1974; Down Under Club, Houston, 1974; worked w Bukka White in local club dates, Austin, TX, 1974; Liberty Hall, Houston, 1974-5; rec Home Cooking label, Houston, 1975; worked Montreux Rock/Blues Festival, Montreux, Switzerland, 1975; toured Europe working concert dates, 1976-7; mostly inactive due to illness from 1977; worked Miller Outdoor Theater, Houston, TX, 1978; died of cirrhosis of liver; buried Rest Lawn Cemetery, Houston, TX

Personal: Married (1950-divorced). 5 children. Named "Juke Boy" as youth as he frequently sang in local bars accompanied by juke box music

Billing: One Man Trio

Songs: A Distant Feel/A Woman's Mind/Bad Breaks/Belfast Blues/Blues for Tomorrow/Blues River Rising/Call Me Juke Boy/Can't Hardly Keep from Crying/Can't Let Your Troubles Get You Down/Can't Win for Losin'/Don't Cry on My Shoulder/Funny Money/Goin' Back to the Country/Going Crazy over You/Hard Luck/Houston the Action Town/How Well I Remember/If You Don't Want to Get Mistreated/I'm a Bluesman/I'm Getting Tired/I'm in the Big City/I'm Not Jiving/It Don't Take Too Much/Jumpin' with Juke Boy/Just a Blues/Just Got to Take a Ride/Let's Boogie/Life Is a Nightmare/Life's Highway/Lonesome Ride Back Home/Lovin' Arms/My Blues/My Time to Go/No Place to Run/Real Good Woman/Rock of Gibraltar/Running Shoes/Sad Sad Sound/Six over Ten/Stay Off Lyons Avenue/Struggle Here in Houston/Texas Turnpike/Tryin' to Keep It Together/The Winds Came/Yakin' in My Plans

Infl by: Jimmy Reed/Sonny Boy Williamson (Alex Miller)

Quotes: "Weldon Bonner is first a writer, then a composer and then a performer"—Larry Skogg, Arhoolie album 1036

"He's one of the most interesting blues poets to come along in years"—Samuel B Charters, Sonet album 634

References: The Legacy of the Blues, Samuel B Charters, Calder & Boyars Ltd, 1975

Jazz Journal magazine (UK), Apr 1975, pp 6-8

Blues Unlimited magazine (UK), Dec 1970/Jan 1971

BOOGIE BILL
(see Webb, Bill)

BOOGIE JAKE
(see Jacobs, Matthew)

BOOGIE MAN
(see Hooker, John Lee)

BOOGIE WOOGIE RED
(see Harrison, Vernon)

BOOKBINDER, PAUL ROY

Photo by Mike Joyce

Born: Oct 5, 1943, New York (New York Co), NY
Inst: Guitar

Father is David Bookbinder; mother is Selma Hofrichtor. Served in US Navy early 60s; briefly attended college, mid-60s; worked Mouth Piece Coffee House, Providence, RI, 1965; worked local hootenannies, NYC area, from 1965; rec Blue Goose label, NYC, late 60s; interested in blues and frequently toured as companion to Blind Gary Davis from 1966; toured w Larry Johnson/Big Boy Crudup/Homesick James/others working concert dates through England, 1970; rec Adelphi label, Silver Spring, MD (?), 1970; frequently worked folk club circuit into 70s; toured England working concert dates, 1972; worked New Jersey Folk Music Society Festival, NJ, 1973; teamed w Fats Kaplan (fiddler) to tour clubs/concerts from 1973; worked Salt Coffee House, Newport, RI, 1973; rec Blue Goose label, NYC, 1975; worked Mariposa Folk Festival, Toronto Island, Can, 1977; toured England working concert dates, 1978

Song: Travelin' Man Blues

Infl by: Pink Anderson/Gary Davis

Quote: "Both his voice and style have been accorded an acclaim uncommon among white blues artists . . ."—Kristin Baggelaar/Donald Milton, *Folk Music: More Than a Song*, Thomas Y Crowell Company, 1976

References: Folk Music: More Than a Song, Kristin Baggelaar/Donald Milton, Thomas Y Crowell Company, 1976

Cadence magazine, Feb 1978, pp 16-22, 28

BOOKER, CHARLIE
Born: Sept 3, 1919, Moorhead (Sunflower Co), MS
Died: Sept 20, 1989, South Bend, IN
Inst: Guitar

Father Lucius Booker; mother Eliza Shaw; born between towns of Moorhead and Sunflower, MS; raised in area working outside music from childhood; occasional local work at parties/picnics in area, late 30s; moved to Leland, MS, early 40s; worked w Willie Love Jr, Casa Blanca Club, Greenville, MS, 1947; Harlem Club, Arcola, MS, late 40s; Matinee Club/49 Club, Drew, MS, late 40s; frequently worked juke joints/poolrooms/dance halls/clubs/others in Greenville, MS, area through 40s into 50s; app on WGVM-radio, Greenville, MS, 1948; rec w Houston Boines, Blues & Rhythm/Modern labels, Clarksdale, MS, 1952; moved to South Bend, IN, to work mostly outside music from 1953; entered St Joseph Medical Center where he died of kidney disease; buried Highland Cemetery, South Bend, IN
Reference: Blues Unlimited magazine (UK), Feb 1973, p 12

BOOKER, *"Little"* JAMES CARROLL

Photo by Norbert Hess. Courtesy Living Blues Magazine

Born: Dec 17, 1939, New Orleans (Orleans Parish), LA
Died: Nov 8, 1983, New Orleans, LA
Inst: Piano

Father, James Carroll Booker II, was minister who played piano; raised in Bay St Louis, MS, learning classical piano, 1943-53; frequently worked local recitals from c1946; returned to New Orleans, LA, to attend local high school, 1953-7; formed own school band, Booker Boy and the Rhythmaires, and app frequently on WMRY-radio, New Orleans, from 1953; rec Imperial label, New Orleans, 1954; worked w Hawketts R&B group at local hops, New Orleans, c1954; rec Chess label, New Orleans, 1956; frequently worked w Cosimo Studio house band on session dates for Ace Records, New Orleans, from mid-50s; rec Ace label, New Orleans, 1958; frequently worked/recorded as sideman for Joe Tex/Lloyd Price/Wilson Pickett/BB King/Aretha Franklin/King Curtis/others, late 50s into 60s; toured w Shirley & Lee working theater dates c1958; toured w Huey Smith's Band working club dates c1959; pickup work in local groups, French Quarter area, New Orleans, 1959; briefly attended Southern Univ, Baton Rouge, LA, 1960; toured w Phil Upchurch group working clubs through South, 1960; rec acc for Jr Parker/Bobby Bland/others, Peacock label, Houston, TX, 1960; rec under own name, Peacock label, Houston, 1960; worked as sideman on Roy Hamilton Show, 1962; w Lloyd Price group, 1963; rec Stax label, 1963; served time for drug use,. Parish Prison, New Orleans, LA/Angola State Prison, LA, mid-60s; rec w Fats Domino and others, New Orleans, late 60s; worked outside music in NYC, NY/Nashville, TN, early 70s; toured concert dates through Europe, 1971; toured w Lionel Hampton Orch c1972; residency at local cocktail lounge, Downingtown, PA, c1972; rec acc to Charles Brown/Sonny Thompson/T-Bone Walker/others, early 70s; lost left eye due to drug use, 1973; worked New Orleans Jazz & Heritage Festival, New Orleans, 1975-80; toured w R&B Festival on concert dates through Europe, 1975; worked 100 Club, London, Eng, 1976; app on HONKY TONK Show, BBC-radio, London, Eng, 1976; rec Island label, New Orleans, LA, c1976; toured concert dates through Eng/Europe, 1977-8; rec Amiga label, Leipzig, Ger, 1977; worked Dortmund Jazz Life Festival, Dortmund, Ger, 1977; rec ST for film PRETTY BABY, 1978; worked Monterey Jazz Fest, Monterey, CA, 1979; residency at Maple Leaf Bar, New Orleans into 80s; rec Rounder label, New Orleans, 1983; died of intestinal bleeding

Infl to: Dr John/Allen Toussaint

Quote: "His two-fisted, syncopated keyboard style was a major influence on New Orleans Rhythm and Blues in the 1950s and 1960s"—Jon Pareles, *NY Times,* Nov 10, 1983

References: Living Blues, Spring 1984, pp 36-37
Blues & Soul magazine (UK), Nov 30, 1976, pp 12-13

BOOKER, JOHN LEE
(see Hooker, John Lee)

BOOZE, BEATRICE *"Wee Bea"*
Born: May 23, c1920, Baltimore (Baltimore Co), MD
Died: 1975 (unconfirmed)
Inst: Guitar

Reportedly born Muriel Nicholls; rec Decca label, NYC, NY, 1942; worked Kelly's Stable, NYC, c1943; reportedly toured w Louis Armstrong Orch working dance/club dates through South, 1943; rec Decca

Courtesy Harrison Smith

label, NYC, 1944; toured w Andy Kirk Band working dance dates through South/Southwest, 1944; worked w Andy Kirk Band, Gypsy Tea Room, New Orleans, LA, 1944; extensive touring as single, working one-nighters in NYC, NY/Indianapolis, IN/Atlantic City, NJ/Cleveland, OH/Detroit, MI/Washington, DC/and elsewhere from 1944 into 50s; rec Harlem label, NYC, 1946; worked Jimmy Ryan's, NYC, c1949; rec 20th Century label, NYC, late 40s; rec w Larry Johnson Band, Apollo label, NYC, 1950; reportedly inactive in music from mid-50s settling in Baltimore, MD, then Scottsville, NY, into 70s; rec w Sammy Price, Stardust label, NYC, 1962

Personal: Married ——— Jeffries

Billings: Queen Bea of Blues Singers/See See Rider Blues Girl

Quote: "Bea Booze, supposedly Decca's answer to Lil Green, will always be remembered for her "See See Rider," arguably the ultimate version"—Derrick Stewart-Baxter (correspondence)

William "Willie" Borum
Courtesy Sing Out *Magazine*

BORUM, WILLIAM *"Willie"*
(*aka:* Memphis Willie B/Willie B)
Born: Nov 4, 1911, Memphis (Shelby Co), TN
Inst: Guitar/Harmonica

Father was a musician; interested in music early and learned some guitar from father and Jim Jackson as child; frequently worked w Jack Kelly's Jug Busters in local streets/parties/suppers, Memphis, TN, area, late 20s; worked w Memphis Jug Band in Church's Park (WC Handy Park)/parties/clubs/dances/along Beale Street, Memphis, with frequent tours south to work Mardi Gras in New Orleans, LA, late 20s into 30s; learned harmonica from Noah Lewis and worked in many local jug bands on streets of Memphis through 30s; frequently worked/toured with many bluesmen including Sonny Boy Williamson (Alex Miller)/Robert Johnson/Willie Brown/Garfield Akers/others through area during 30s; rec Vocalion label, NYC, NY, 1934; worked juke joints along Mississippi levee towns with Son Joe and others, mid-30s; frequently worked w Will Shade/Joe Hill Louis in gambling houses/streets/jukes of W Memphis, AR/Memphis, TN, area, early 30s; served in US Army in North Africa/Sicily/Italy theaters of operation, 1943-6; settled in Memphis, TN, to work outside music with occasional party/picnic/dance/club work in area, 1946 into 70s; occasionally toured w Frank Stokes out of Memphis into northern Mississippi area, late 40s; app on KING BISCUIT TIME, KFFA-radio, Helena, AR, late 40s; mostly inactive into 60s; rec Bluesville label, Memphis, 1961; app in documentary film THE BLUES, 1963; worked w Gus Cannon/Fury Lewis at New York Univ and other gigs, NYC, 1963; rec Albatros label, Memphis, TN, 1978

Songs: Car Machine Blues/Dying Mother Blues/Funny Caper Blues/Good Potatoes/Hard Working Man Blues/Honey Maker Blues/I Have Found Somebody/L&N Blues/Lonesome Home Blues/P-38 Blues/Uncle Sam Blues/Wine Drinking Woman

Reference: Memphis Blues, Bengt Olsson, 1970

BOYD, EDWARD RILEY *"Little Eddie"*
(*aka:* Ernie Boyd)
Born: Nov 25, 1914, Stovall (Coahoma Co), MS
Inst: Guitar/Kazoo/Organ/Piano

Father was William Boyd, a local guitarist; born on Frank Moore's Plantation outside Stovall, MS; raised/worked on Stovall Plantation, Stovall, into teens; interested in music from 13 years of age; ran away from home to work outside music while travelling through Arkansas/Mississippi/Tennessee/Missouri from 1928; frequently worked in local country dance band in local jukes, Woodstock, TN, early 30s; taught self guitar/piano and worked jukes/bars back into Mississippi, early 30s; worked The Hoskins Juke, Clarksdale, Mississippi, early 30s; settled in Memphis, TN, 1936, to work as soloist in Beale Street dives/barrelhouses into 40s; formed The Dixie Rhythm Boys to work Pee Wee's/Jody Farney's/The Big Four and other barrelhouses/parties, Memphis, TN, from 1937 with frequent tours into Tennessee/Arkansas to 1941; to Chicago, IL, to work outside music from 1941; w Johnny Shines Trio, Big Jerry Johnson's Cozy Corner Club, Chicago, IL, 1941; frequently worked w Memphis Slim in local south side clubs/bars, Chicago, early 40s; frequently worked w John Lee "Sonny Boy" Williamson, Triangle Inn, Chicago, 1942-6; worked Club Georgia, Chicago, 1942; frequently w Muddy Waters working west side club dates, Chicago, c1943; rec acc w John Lee "Sonny Boy" Williamson, Victor/Bluebird labels, Chicago, 1945; worked w John Lee "Sonny Boy" Williamson, Van's Hot Spot, Gary, IN, mid-40s; formed own band to work frequently at The Flame Club, Chicago, 1946-8; rec w JT Brown's Boogie Band (others), Victor label, Chicago, 1947-8; rec Aristocrat label, Chicago,

Courtesy Eddie Boyd/Living Blues Magazine

1947-8 (unreleased); rec Victor label, Chicago, 1949 (unreleased); rec Regal/Herald labels, Chicago, 1950; rec JOB label, Chicago, 1951-2; rec Chess label, Chicago, 1951 (unreleased); worked Harmonia Hotel, Chicago, 1952; rec Chess label, Chicago, 1952-7; frequently toured Midwest/South working one-nighters, 1952-7; toured w Little Walter working clubs/halls through Texas, 1953; worked Circle Club, Flint, MI, c1953; McKie's Ballroom, Chicago, 1954; continued outside music work through 50s into 60s; rec JOB/Oriole labels, Chicago, 1958; rec Chess label, Chicago, 1959 (unreleased); rec Bea & Baby/Keyhole labels, Chicago, 1959; rec Esquire label, Chicago, 1960; rec Mojo label, Memphis, TN, 1960-1; rec LaSalle label, Chicago, 1961; toured w Jimmy McCracklin working concert dates, 1962; rec Art-Tone/Push labels, Oakland, CA, 1962; rec Palos label, Big Spring, TX, 1963/Chicago, IL, 1964; worked local coffeehouses, Chicago, 1964; rec Decca label, Chicago, 1965; toured w American Folk Blues Festival, working concert dates through England/Europe, 1965 (por Hamburg, Ger/London, Eng, concerts rel Fontana label); rec acc to Big Mama Thornton, Arhoolie label, London, Eng, 1965; worked Fairfield Hall, London, Eng, 1965; toured as single working concert dates/clubs/lounges through Europe, 1965; frequently worked w Lonnie Graham/Robert Jr Lockwood/others in local clubs, Chicago, through 60s; toured w John Mayall's Bluesbreakers working concerts through England, 1967; rec Philips label, Hilversum, Holland, 1967; rec London-Decca/Blue Horizon labels, London, Eng, 1967; toured concert dates through England/Europe, 1968; rec Blue Horizon label, London, Eng, 1968; rec (in concert) Storyville/Blue Beat labels, Thayngen, Switzerland, c1968; rec Heco label, Berlin, Ger, late 60s; settled in Paris, France, working Trois Mailletz Club, late 60s; extensive tours working concerts through Europe, 1969-70; rec Love label, Helsinki, Finland, 1970; settled in Finland working clubs/concert halls from 1971; rec Sonet label, Stockholm, Sweden, 1973-4; worked concert dates in Helsinki, Finland, 1973; toured w American Blues Legends working concert dates through Europe, 1974; rec FBS label, Chicago, IL, 1974; worked North Sea Jazz Festival 76, Congress Centre, The Hague, Holland, 1976; rec Bluebeat label, Helsinki, Finland, 1976; sat-in w Sunnyland Slim, Elsewhere Lounge, Chicago, 1977; worked Jazz Artdur, Gothenburg, Sweden, 1978

Personal: Married Georgia Mae ———; ——— Graham; Leila ———. Half brother of Memphis Slim and first cousin of Muddy Waters

Songs: Ain't Doin' Too Bad/All the Way/Baby, What's Wrong with You?/Back Beat/Backslap/Be Careful/The Big Bell/The Big Question/Blue Coat Man/Blue Monday Blues/Blues Is Here to Stay/Brotherhood/Came Home This Morning/The Cannonball/Chicago Is Just That Way/Come On Home/Coming Home/Cool Kind Treatment/Dedication to My Baby/Denmark/Do Yourself a Favor/Don't/Drifting/Early Grave/Eddie's Blues/Empty Arms/Five Long Years/Four Leaf Clover/Got to Know/The Guff/Hello Stranger/Hotel Blues/Hush Baby Don't You Cry/I Cried/I Cry/I Got a Woman/I Got the Blues/I Had to Let Her Go/I Love You/I'll Never Stop (I Can't Stop Loving You)/I'm a Fool/I'm a Prisoner/I'm Coming Home/I'm Pleading/I've Been Deceived/It's a Mellow Day/It's Miserable to Be Alone/It's Too Bad/Just a Fool/Just the Blues/Kilroy Won't Be Back/Kindness for Weakness/Let It Be Me/Letter Missin' Blues/Life Gets to Be a Burden/The Loser/Lovesick Soul/Mr Highway Man/My Idea/My Lady/The Nightmare Is Over/Nothing/Nothing But Trouble/Operator/Picture in the Frame/Praise to Helsinki/Praise to My Baby/Rack 'em Back/Real Good Feeling/Reap What You Sow/Rock the Rock/Rosa Lee Swing/Save Her Doctor/She Is Real/She's Gone/She's the One/Steak House Rock/The Story of Bill/Talkin' to the Operator/Tell the Truth/Ten to One/Thank You Baby/That's When I Miss You/Third Degree/The Tickler/Too Bad/Tortured Soul/The Train Is Coming/Tunnel of Love/24 Hours/24 Hours of Fear/Unfair Lovers/Vacation from the Blues/What Makes These Things Happen to Me?/Where You Belong/When the Cuckoo . . ./Why Did She Leave Me?/You Are My Love/You Got to Reap!/Zip Code

Infl by: Big Maceo/Gordon Cakehouse/Leroy Carr/Roosevelt Sykes

Quotes: "A pianist and singer of great standing"—Mike Vernon, London-Decca album LK-4872

"Eddie Boyd was one of Chicago's most popular blues artists in the early and mid-1950's, a strong vocalist, unspectacular but solid piano player, leader of one of the best blues combos of the era, and writer of many memorable, well-crafted songs . . ."—Jim O'Neal, *Living Blues* magazine, Nov/Dec 1977, p 11

References: Living Blues magazine, Nov/Dec 1977, pp 11-15; Jan/Feb 1978, pp 14-23; Mar/Apr 1978, pp 6-17

London-Decca album LK-4872

Blues Unlimited magazine (UK), Dec 1971/Jan 1972

BOYD, ERNIE
(see Boyd, Eddie)

BOYD, ROBERT
(see Byrd, Roy)

BRACEY, ISHMON

Courtesy Sheldon Harris Collection

Born: Jan 9, 1901, Byram (Hinds Co), MS
Died: Feb 12, 1970, Jackson, MS
Inst: Guitar/Piano

Father was Richard Bracey; interested in music early and learned guitar style from Rubin Lacy and others as youth; frequently worked outside music in Byram, MS, area through teens; served as guide/travelling companion for Blind Lemon Jefferson working streets/picnics through Delta area of Mississippi into 20s; frequently worked in local blues bands w Rubin Lacy/Son Spand/Tommy Johnson/others at parties/picnics/suppers, Jackson, MS, area from mid-20s into 30s; worked w Tommy Johnson/Walter Jacobs, Crystal Springs, MS, area c1927; rec Victor label, Memphis, TN, 1928; rec Paramount label, Grafton, WI, 1930; frequently toured w Tommy Johnson working in Dr Simpson Medicine Show and other travelling shows at parties/dances/picnics/fish fries/jukes through South, early to mid-30s; settled in Jackson, MS, to work mostly outside music c1935 through 40s; ordained a minister and served in local churches in Jackson from c1950; suffered unknown illness at home and DOA at University Hospital; buried Willow Park, Jackson, MS

Personal: Married Annie McLaurin

Songs: Bust Up Blues/Left Alone Blues/Pay Me No Mind/Saturday Blues/Suitcase Full of Blues/Trouble-Hearted Blues/Woman Woman Blues

Infl by: Rubin Lacy

Infl to: Shirley Griffith

Quote: "Bracey's voice was intentionally nasal and his singing was direct and unembellished, relying on a marked vibrato for its character"—(Paul Oliver) Albert McCarthy/Alun Morgan/Paul Oliver/Max Harrison, *Jazz on Record,* Hanover Books Ltd, 1968

BRADLEY, VELMA
(see Cox, Ida)

BRAGG, DOBBY
(see Sykes, Roosevelt)

BRANCH, WILLIAM EARL *"Billy"*

Photo by Norbert Hess

Born: Oct 3, 1951, Great Lakes (Lake Co), IL
Inst: Harmonica

Moved to Los Angeles, CA, where he was raised from c1955; taught self harmonica at 11 years of age; went to Chicago, IL, to attend Univ of Illinois, Chicago Circle Campus, 1969 into 70s, receiving BA in political science; settled in Chicago to work outside music with some sit-ins with local blues bands in south side clubs, from c1969 into 70s; occasionally rec as sideman, Chicago, from 1973; teamed w Arvella Gray working streets for tips, San Francisco, CA, 1974; rec acc to Oscar Brown Jr, Atlantic label, Chicago, 1974; rec Barrelhouse label, Chicago, 1975; sat-in w Muddy Waters group, Quiet Knight, Chicago, 1975; w Jimmy Walker Trio, Elsewhere Club and others, Chicago, from 1975; worked w Willie Dixon in Chicago with frequent US tours from 1976; worked w Tin Pan Alley Band in north side clubs, Chicago, from 1976; worked Berlin Jazz Festival, Berlin, Ger, 1977; Quasimodo Club, Berlin, Ger, 1977; Joe's Bierhaus Club, Berlin, Ger, 1977; rec w Tin Pan Alley Band, Mirage label, Chicago, 1978; active in Illinois Arts Council Educational Blues Programs, Chicago, 1978

Song: Billy's Boogie

Infl by: Little Walter/Sonny Boy Williamson (Alex Miller)

Reference: Living Blues magazine, Jul 1975, pp 10-11

BREWER, "*Blind*" **JAMES** "*Jimmy*"/"*Jim*"
Born: Oct 3, 1921, Brookhaven (Lincoln Co), MS
Died: Jun 3, 1988, Chicago, IL
Inst: Autoharp/Guitar/Piano

Father Walter Brewer; mother Ardella Stewart; born almost totally blind; taught music by father; frequently worked streets/stores for tips, Brookhaven, MS, from c1930; frequently worked dances/parties/suppers/churches in Brookhaven area through 1930s; moved to St Louis, MO, to work street cars/streets/taverns in area for tips from early 40s; to Chicago, IL, to work w Arvella Gray on streets and in Maxwell Street area from mid-50s; turned to religious music, 1956; rec Heritage label, Chicago, 1960; worked Blind Pig, Chicago, 1961; Northwestern Univ, Evanston, IL, 1962; frequently worked No Exit Cafe, Chicago, 1962-74; formed The Church of God in Christ group to work Maxwell Street area (or with other street preachers) for tips from 1964; worked Lake Forest Col, Lake Forest, IL, 1964; Mandel Hall, Univ of Chicago, Chicago, 1964; rec w Fannie Brewer (wife), Testament label, Chicago, 1964; worked

Photo by Ray Flerlage (Kinnara Collection). Courtesy Sing Out Magazine

Chances Are Club, Chicago, 1965; Poor Richard's, Chicago, 1966; frequently app on local radio/TV shows in Chicago area/East Coast area, late 60s into 70s; rec ST for UK film BLUES LIKE SHOWERS OF RAIN, 1970; app on MADE IN CHICAGO, WTTW-TV, Chicago, c1970; worked Philadelphia Folk Festival, Schwenksville, PA, 1970; Alice's Revisited, Chicago, 1970; Washington Square Church, NYC, NY, 1970; Bulls, Chicago, 1972; Green Planet, Chicago, 1972; Ratso's, Chicago, 1972; frequently worked Juicy John Pink's Folk Center, DeKalb, IL, 1974-7; Kirkland Col, N Ferrisburg, VT, 1974 (por rel Philo label); Biddy Mulligan's, Chicago, 1974; The Spot, Chicago, 1974; Milwaukee Summer Festival, Milwaukee, WI, 1975; toured w Court Dorsey working Midwest club dates, 1976; worked coffeehouses/festivals/clubs into 80s; died of hardening of arteries; buried Burr Oak Cemetery, Worth, IL

Songs: I Don't Want No Woman If She Got Hair Like Drops of Rain/I Want to Know Why/Liberty Bill /Rocky Mountain/She Wants to Boogie/Why Did He Have to Go?

Infl by: Bill Broonzy/Tommy Johnson

Quotes: "Jim's repertoire is broad and stylistically varied . . . [he] represents a cross section of the musical culture of several generations from Mississippi to Chicago"—A M Cohen, Philo album 1003

"As a blues guitarist he must be considered one of the best in Chicago"—Clas Ahlstrand, *Blues Unlimited* magazine (UK), Dec 1967, p 11

Reference: Blues Unlimited magazine (UK), Dec 1967, p 11

BRIM, GRACE

(*aka:* Mrs John Brim)

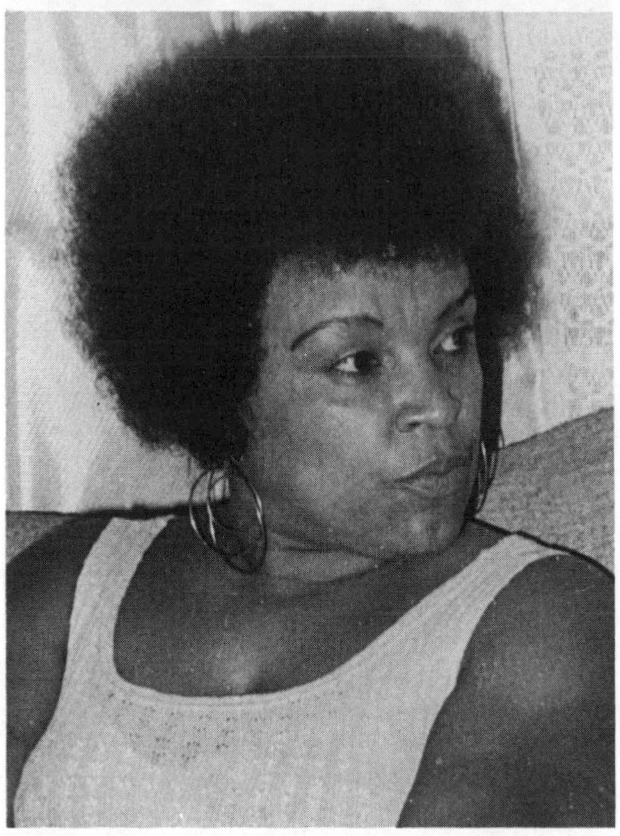

Photo by Amy O'Neal. Courtesy Living Blues Magazine

Born: c1924
Inst: Drums/Harmonica

Joined John Brim group to work local clubs in Chicago, IL/Gary, IN, 1948 into 50s; worked w Big Maceo's Band, Detroit, MI, c1948 into early 50s; rec w John Brim Combo, Fortune label, Detroit, c1950; rec w Roosevelt Sykes, Random label, Chicago, 1951; rec w Sunnyland Slim, JOB label, Chicago, 1952; worked w John Brim Gary Kings in local club dates, Gary, IN, from 1952; rec w John Brim Stompers, Parrot label, Chicago, 1953; rec w John Brim Gary Kings, Chess label, Chicago, c1953-5; continued working local club dates w John Brim group, Chicago, IL/Gary, IN, through 50s/60s; worked as single or with other groups from 1964; worked club dates, Gary, 1969 into 70s; worked w John Brim, Elsewhere Lounge, Chicago, 1975

Personal: Married singer/musician John Brim (1947-64). Her sons Ernest and John Jr and daughter are musicians

BRIM, JOHN

Photo by Jim O'Neal. Courtesy Living Blues Magazine

Born: Apr 10, 1922, Hopkinsville (Christian Co), KY
Inst: Guitar/Harmonica

Parents were farmers; born on farm and taught self guitar as child; was playing blues from 1935 working local parties; moved to Indianapolis, IN, 1941, then Chicago, IL, 1945; frequently worked w John Lee "Sonny Boy" Williamson/Eddie Boyd/Willie Mabon/Muddy Waters/other groups in local clubs, Chicago, 1946-7; formed John Brim and His Gary Kings (including Jimmy Reed) working Club Jamboree, Chicago, IL/Pulaski Lounge, Gary, IN, and other clubs, 1948 into 50s; rec Fortune label, Detroit, MI, c1950; worked w Big Maceo in local clubs, Detroit, c1950; rec Random label, Chicago, IL, 1951; rec

JOB label, Chicago, 1952; rec w own Stompers, Parrot label, Chicago, 1953; rec w Gary Kings, Checker-Chess label, Chicago, 1953-5; rec w own trio, JOB label, Chicago, 1954; rec Chess label, Chicago, 1956; frequently worked/rec as sideman w Jimmy Reed/Sunnyland Slim/Rosevelt Sykes/Big Maceo/Little Walter/others in local clubs, Chicago, through 50s into 60s; worked w own band, Club 99, Joliet, IL, 1962; frequently worked outside music in Gary, IN, early 60s; worked w Jimmy Reed group in local clubs, Chicago, from 1964; frequent outside music work, Chicago, late 60s; worked Rose & Kelly's, Chicago, 1970; formed/rec own BB label, Chicago, c1972; worked Univ of Chicago, Chicago, 1974; Elsewhere Club, Chicago, 1975-7; Chicago Blues Festival, Jane Addams Theater, Chicago, 1975; Kingston Mines, Chicago, 1975-6; Festival of Arts Concert, Univ of Chicago, Chicago, 1976

Personal: Married singer/musician Grace ——— (1947-64). His sons Ernest and John Jr and daughter are musicians

Songs: Be Careful/Ice Cream Man/Rattlesnake/Tough Times/You Got Me

Infl by: DeFord Bailey/Bill Broonzy/Tampa Red

Quotes: "Brim's recording [of 'Rattlesnake'] . . . is one of the great moments of Chicago blues"—Mike Rowe, *Chicago Breakdown*, Eddison Press Ltd, 1973

"[His] recordings [are] noted for a relaxed yet forceful rhythm and beautifully tough character . . ."—Pete Welding, Chess album LP 1537

Reference: Blues Unlimited magazine (UK), Dec 1971, pp 13-14

BRIM, MRS JOHN
(see Brim, Grace)

BRIMMER, SON
(see Shade, Will)

BROOKS, JENNIE
(see Beaman, Lottie)

BROOKS, LONNIE
(*aka:* Guitar Jr)
Born: Dec 18, 1933, Dubuisson (St Landy Parish), LA
Inst: Guitar

Father was Lee Baker Sr; mother Lillie Thomas; born Lee Baker Jr; moved to Garland, LA as infant; encouraged to play music by grandfather who was banjo

Courtesy Living Blues *Magazine*

player; moved to Port Arthur, TX, to work mostly outside music from c1952; occasional small local gigs w Clifton Chenier's Band and others from 1955; rec w own band, Goldband label, Lake Charles, LA, 1957-9; toured South working club dates, late 50s; moved to Chicago, IL, working outside music from 1959; rec acc to Jimmy Reed, VJ label, Chicago, 1960; rec Mercury label, Chicago, 1960; toured South w Jimmy Reed Band, 1960; worked many local clubs as sit-in sideman, Chicago, from early 60s; worked w own band in local clubs in Chicago, IL/E Chicago, IL/Gary, IN, areas, early/mid-60s; frequently rec as sideman on Chicago blues/R&B/soul sessions from mid-60s; rec One-der-ful label, Chicago, mid-60s (unreleased); rec USA/Palos labels, Chicago, 1965; rec Chess label, Chicago, 1967; worked w own band in Rush Street entertainment district, Chicago, c1967-70; rec Chirrup label, Chicago, 1968; rec Midas label, Chicago, late 60s; rec Capitol label, Los Angeles, CA, 1969; worked residencies, Avenue Lounge, Chicago, 1969-74; rec USA label, Chicago, 1972; app on ATOMIC MAMA'S WANG DANG DOODLE BLUES Show, WNIB-FM-radio, Chicago, c1973; worked Ego's Penthouse Lounge, Chicago, 1974; White Stallion, Chicago, 1974; Pepper's Hideout, Chicago, 1974-6; Green Bunny Lounge, Chicago,

1975; toured w Chicago Blues Festival working concert dates through Europe, 1975; rec Black & Blue label, France, 1975; worked w Mack Simmons Band, International Amphitheater, Chicago, 1975; Ratso's, Chicago, 1976; Biddy Mulligan's, Chicago, 1976-8; Zoo Bar, Lincoln, NE, 1976; Zorba's, Cicero, IL, 1976-7; Wise Fools Pub, Chicago, 1977-8; rec TK label, Chicago, 1977 (unreleased); rec Alligator label, Chicago, 1978 (unreleased)

Personal: Married twice. 2 children. Not to be confused with Luther Johnson Jr who also used pseudonum "Guitar Jr"

Songs: All of My Life/Bingo/Broken Hearted Rollin' Tears/Family Rules/The Flip/The Frog/Good Soul Lovin'/The Hoss/Knocks Me Out/Let It All Hang Out/Love Me Love Me/Now You Know/Please/Roll Roll Roll/Tell Me Baby/The Train

Infl by: Gatemouth Brown/Fats Domino/BB King/Little Richard/Jimmy Reed/Aaron "T-Bone" Walker

Infl to: Phillip Walker

Reference: Blues Unlimited magazine (UK), Jan 1976, p 11

BROOMSLEY, BIG BILL
(see Broonzy, William)

BROONZY, WILLIAM LEE CONLEY *"Big Bill"*
(*aka:* Big Bill/Bill/Blues Boy Bill/Big Bill Broomsley/Chicago Bill/Slim Hunter/Big Bill Johnson/Little Sam/Little Son/Natchez/Sammy Sampson)

Courtesy Frank Driggs Collection

Born: Jun 26, 1893, Scott (Bolivar Co), MS
Died: Aug 15, 1958, Chicago, IL
Inst: Guitar/Mandolin/Violin

Father was Frank Broonzy, mother was Mittie Belcher, both parents born into slavery; one of 17 children; moved to Pine Bluff, AR, where he worked outside music (as farm hand) from childhood; interested in music early and learned violin on home-made instrument from uncle Jerry Belcher as child; worked as violinist in local churches, Scott Crossing, AR, 1903; worked as country fiddler at local parties/two-way picnics, Scott, MS, area, 1907-12; worked mostly as itinerant preacher in Pine Bluff, AR, 1912-17; served in US Army, 1918-19; worked as violinist in local clubs, Little Rock, AR, 1919-20; moved to Chicago, IL, to work outside music from 1920; worked occasional gigs w Papa Charlie Jackson in local clubs, Chicago, from 1924; learned guitar and rec as accompanist to many blues singers, Chicago, late 20s into 40s; rec Paramount label, Chicago, 1927-8; continued outside music work with frequent rent party dates, Chicago, into 30s; rec Perfect/Banner labels, NYC, NY, 1930; rec Gennett/Champion labels, Richmond, IN, 1930; rec Paramount label, Grafton, WI, 1931; rec Banner label, NYC, 1932; rec Champion label, Richmond, 1932; worked Regal Theater/Savoy Theater/Indiana Theater/Morson Hotel/Ruby Gatewood's Tavern/Johnson's Tavern/1410 Club/others, Chicago area, from c1932; toured w Memphis Minnie working club dates during 30s; rec Bluebird label, Chicago, 1934-5; rec Banner label, Chicago, 1934; rec ARC label group, Chicago, 1934-7; rec Vocalion label, Chicago, 1938-40; rec Columbia label, Chicago, 1938; worked From Spirituals to Swing concerts, Carnegie Hall, NYC, 1938-40 (por 1939 concert rel Vanguard label); rec OKeh label, Chicago, 1939-42, app in film SWINGIN' THE DREAM, 1939; worked Cafe Society Downtown, NYC, 1939-40; rec w John Lee "Sonny Boy" Williamson, Bluebird label, Chicago, 1939-42; worked w Memphis Slim, Ruby Gatewood's Tavern, Chicago, 1940; Town Hall, NYC, 1940; frequently worked Village Vanguard, NYC, 1940-5; toured w Lil Green road show working dance dates in Chicago, IL/Detroit, MI, and through South, 1941-2; toured club/concert dates through Texas during early 40s; worked w Memphis Slim, Cozy Corner, Chicago, 1942; app in film short BIG BILL BROONZY c1942; worked Million Dollar Theater, Los Angeles, CA, early 40s; rec Hub label, NYC, 1945; worked Apollo Theater, NYC, 1945; Hollywood Rendezvous, Chicago, c1945; rec Columbia label, Chicago, 1945-7; worked Purple Cat, Chicago, c1945; Sylvio's, Chicago, c1945-9; Harmonia Hotel, Chicago, 1946; Blues at Midnight Concert, Town Hall, NYC, 1946; rec w John Lee "Sonny Boy" Williamson, Victor label, Chicago, 1947; rec Bluesman label c1947; rec (as Natchez) United Artist label, NYC, 1947; Music at Midnight Concert, Town Hall, NYC, 1947; worked Gatewood's Tavern, Chicago, 1948-9; rec Mercury label, Chicago, 1949; worked w own Laughing Trio, The Bee Hive, Chicago, 1949; worked mostly outside music (as janitor), Iowa State Univ of Science & Technology, Ames, IA, 1950-1; frequently worked in Studs Turkel's I COME FOR TO SING concert series, Blue Note Club, Chicago, early 50s (por shown remote on local TV); Miss King's, Chicago, c1951; frequently toured England/Europe/South America/Africa/Australia working concert/club dates, 1951-7; rec Vogue/Jazz Society labels, Paris, France, 1951-2; rec Melodisc label, London, Eng, 1951; rec Mercury label, Chicago, 1951; app in concert, Salle Pleyel, Paris, France, 1952; worked w Blind John Davis, Sylvio's, Chicago, 1952; app w Blind John Davis, BIG BILL HILL SHOW, WOPA-radio, Oak Park, IL, 1952; owned/operated tavern, Chicago, 1954; worked Johnson Lounge, Chicago, c1955; Gate of Horn, Chicago, mid-50s; rec Chess label, Chicago, 1955; rec Nixa label, London, Eng, 1955; worked w Pete Seeger, Northwestern Univ, Evanston, IL, 1956 (por rel Verve label); worked Club Montmartre, Copenhagen, Denmark, 1956 (por rel Storyville label); worked local clubs/cabarets, Paris, France, 1956; app in French documentary film LOW LIGHT AND BLUE SMOKE, 1956; rec Columbia label, Paris, 1956; app in Belgian documentary film short BIG BILL BLUES, 1956; rec Philips label, Bearn, Holland, 1956; rec Ricordi label, Milan, Italy, 1956; worked Gate of Horn, Chicago, IL, 1956; rec Folkways label, Chicago, 1956-7; toured w Brother John Sellers working club/TV/radio dates through England, 1957; inactive due to illness and underwent numerous lung operations from 1957; died of cancer in ambulance on way to Billings Hospital; buried Lincoln Cemetery, Worth, IL; heard on ST of film short THIS TRAIN, 1965

Personal: Married Guitrue Embria (1916-); Rosie Syphen (1941-58). Had 5 children. Was half-brother of Robert Brown (Washboard Sam)

Book: Big Bill Blues, Yannick Bruynoghe, Cassell & Company Ltd, 1955

Songs: All by Myself/Baby Don't You Tear My Clothes/Baby I Done Got Wise/Back to Arkansas/Bad Acting Woman/Bad Luck Man/Big Bill Blues/Big Bill's Boogie/Black, Brown and White/Bossy Woman/Bull Cow Blues/By Myself/Cell No 13 Blues/Come Home Early/Come On Back/Country Boy/Diggin' My Potatoes/Do Right Blues/Don't You Be No Fool/Don't You Want to Ride/Down and Lost My Mind/Down the Line Blues/Dreamy Eyed Baby/Five Feet Four/Friendless Blues/Get Away Blues/Get Back/Give Your Mama One Smile/Going to Chicago/Good Jelly/Good Liquor Gonna Carry Me Down/Good Old Cabbage Greens/Good Time Tonight/Goodbye Baby Blues/Green Grass Blues/Hard Hearted Woman/Hey Bud Blues/Hey Hey/Hit the Right Lick/Hollerin' (and Cryin') the Blues/Humble Blues/IC Blues/I Can Fix It/I Don't Know Why/I Feel So Good/I Get the Blues at Bedtime/I Had a Dream/I Know She Will/I Want My Hands on It/I Want You by My Side/I'm Just a Bum/I'm Woke Up Now/It's Your Time Now/Jacqueline/Jivin' Mr Fuller Blues/Just a Dream/Just Got to Hold You/Just Rocking/Keep Your Hands off Her/Key to the Highway/Kind Hearted Blues/Leap Year Blues/Leavin' Day/Let Her Go/Let Me Be Your Winder/Letter to My Baby/Little City Woman/Lonesome/Looking Up at Down/Louise Louise Blues/Lowland Blues/Made a Date with an Angel (Got No Walking Shoes)/Make My Getaway/Martha Blues/Medicine Man Blues/Merry-Go-Round Blues/Messed Up in Love/The Mill Man Blues/Mindin' My Own Business/Mississippi River Blues/Moppers Blues/My Last Goodbye to You/My Little Flower/My Mellow Man/My Old Lizzie/Nappy Head Woman/Night Watchman Blues/Oh, Mama, How I Love You/Oh Yes/Old Man Blues/Pneumonia Blues (I Keep on Aching)/Play Your Hand/Please Believe Me/Plough (Plow) Hand Blues/Ramblin' Bill/Rockin' Chair Blues/Roll Dem Bones/Romance Without Finance/San Antonio Blues/Saturday Evening Blues/She Never/She's Gone with the Wind/Shine On, Shine On/Shoo Blues/Somebody Changed That Lock on My Door/Somebody's Got to Go/Southbound Train/The Southern Blues/Southern Flood Blues/Stomp Blues/Stop and Fix It/Summertime Blues/The Sun Gonna Shine in My Door Someday/Sweet Honey Bee/Tell Me Baby/Texas Tornado/Tomorrow/Trouble and Lying Woman/Trucking Little Woman/Walkin' the Lonesome Road/What Is That She Got?/When I Been Drinking/When Will I Get to be Called a Man?/Who Was That Here a While Ago?/Why Did You Do That to Me?/Why Should I Spend Money?/Willie Mae/You Changed/You Do Me Any Old Way/You Got the Best Go/You Got to Play Your Hand/You Know I Got a Reason/Your Time Now

Awards/Honors: Won *Jazz Podium* magazine (German) Jazz Critics Award as best male traditional vocalist, 1958

Won French Academie du Jazz Record Prix as best traditional blues artist, 1968

Infl by: Jerry Belcher/Blind Blake/John Estes/Papa Charlie Jackson/Blind Lemon Jefferson/Lonnie Johnson/Peetie Wheatstraw

Infl to: John Henry Barbee/George Barnes/James Brewer/John Brim/Robert Brown/Big Boy Crudup/Jack Elliott/Andrew "Smokey" Hogg/Willie B James/Hopson "Hotbox" Johnson/Eddie Kirkland/JB Lenoir/Little Walter/Lazy Bill Lucas/Brownie McGhee/Memphis Slim/Jimmy Rogers/John Sellers/Roebuck Staples/Tarheel Slim/Eddie Vinson/Jimmy Witherspoon/Johnny Young

Quotes: "In the vast field of Negro folk-blues there have been few father figures who have exerted the powerful shaping influences that emanated from Big Bill Broonzy"—Lawrence Cohn, CBS album 52648

"He can safely be ranked as one of the blues immortals"—Bob Groom, *Blues World* magazine (UK), Aug 1970

"A major influence in the growth of the Chicago blues style"—Don Heckman, *BMI, The Many Worlds of Music,* Summer 1969, p 9

References: Big Bill Blues, Yannick Bruynoghe, Cassell & Company Ltd, 1955

CBS album 52648

BROTHER BLUES

(see Dupree, William)

BROTHER GEORGE

(see Fuller, Blind Boy)
(see McGhee, Walter)

BROTHER JOSHUA

(see Joseph, Pleasant)

BROWN, ADA

Born: May 1, 1890, Kansas City (Wyandotte Co), KS
Died: Mar 31, 1950, Kansas City, KS
Inst: Piano

Father was HW Scott, mother was Anna Morris; born Ada Scott; family was musically inclined; interested in music early and frequently sang in local church choir from childhood; worked Bob Mott's Pekin Theater, Chicago, 1910; reportedly worked clubs in Paris, France/Berlin, Germany, during teens; toured with Miller & Lyle's variety show STEP ON IT working theater dates across US, 1922; frequently worked w Bennie Moten Band in local dance halls/clubs in Kansas City, MO, area, early 20s; rec w Bennie Moten Band, OKeh label, St Louis, MO, 1923; frequently worked club dates in Kansas City, MO/St Louis, MO, from mid-20s; rec Vocalion label, Chicago, 1926; app in PLANTATION DAYS Revue, Lafayette Theater, NYC, NY, 1927; worked Perry Theater, Erie, PA, 1927; Riverside Theater, NYC, 1927; Olympia Theater, Lynn, MA, 1928; Music Hall Theater, Lewiston, ME, 1928; Palace Theater, Hartford, CT, 1928; Palace Theater, New Haven, CT, 1928; Rialto Theater, Glens Falls, NY, 1928; Avon Theater, Watertown, NY, 1928; Jefferson Theater, Auburn, NY, 1928; Sheridan Square Theater, Pittsburgh, PA, 1928; Harris Theater, McKeesport, PA, 1928; Davis Theater, Pittsburgh, PA, 1928; Majestic Theater, Butler, PA, 1928; Orpheum Theater, Brooklyn, NY, 1928; Keith Coliseum Theater, NYC, NY, 1928; Madison Theater, Brooklyn, NY, 1928; Proctor's Theater, Mt Vernon, NY, 1928; Proctor's 86th St Theater, NYC, 1928; Proctor's 5th Avenue Theater, NYC, 1928; Royal Theater, NYC, 1928; Tilyou Theater, Brooklyn, NY, 1928; Broadway Theater, NYC, 1928; Jefferson Theater, NYC, 1928; app BANDANNALAND Revue, Lafayette Theater, NYC, 1928; Riviera Theater, Chicago, IL, 1928; Capitol Theater, Flint, MI, 1928; Temple Theater, Saginaw, MI, 1928; Lincoln Theater, Union City, PA, 1928; Cross Keys Theater, Philadelphia, PA, 1928; York Opera House, York, PA, 1928; New State Theater, Harrisburg, PA, 1928; Keith Albee Fordham Theater, NYC, 1928; Colonial Theater, Allentown, PA, 1928; Plantation Cafe, Chicago, c1928; Perry Theater, Erie, PA, 1929; Imperial Theater, Montreal, Can, 1929; Orpheum Theater, Brooklyn, NY, 1929; Capitol Theater, Union Hill, NJ, 1929; Keith-Albee Franklin Theater, NYC, 1929; Scolly Square Theater, Boston, MA, 1929; Avon Theater, Poughkeepsie, NY, 1929; Proctor's 58th St Theater, NYC, 1929; Olympia Theater, New Bedford, MA, 1929; rec OKeh label, NYC, 1929; worked Orpheum Theater, Vancouver, Can, 1929; Orpheum Theater, Seattle, WA, 1929; Orpheum Theater, Denver, CO, 1929; Hill Street Theater, Los Angeles, CA, 1929; Golden Gate Theater, San Francisco, CA, 1929; Orpheum Theater, NYC, 1929; RKO Theater, St Louis, MO, 1929; Main St Theater, Kansas City, MO, 1929; Orpheum Theater, Sioux City, IA, 1929; Hennepin Theater, Minneapolis, MN, 1929; State Lake Theater, Chicago, IL, 1929; Hollywood Theater, Detroit, MI, 1929; Genesee Theater, Waukegan, IL, 1929; Fletcher Theater, Danville, IL, 1929; Iowa

Ada Brown
Courtesy Frank Driggs Collection

Theater, Cedar Rapids, IA, 1929; 105th St Theater, Cleveland, OH, 1929; State Theater, Jersey City, NJ, 1929; app w Fess Williams Band in TAN TOWN TOMALES Revue, Lafayette Theater, NYC, 1930; worked Hippodrome Theater, NYC, 1930; Shea's Hippodrome Theater, Buffalo, NY, 1930; Albee Theater, Providence, RI, 1930; Harris Theater, Pittsburgh, PA, 1930; app w Bill Robinson/Adelaide Hall in musical comedy BROWN BUDDIES, Nixon Theater, Pittsburgh, PA, 1930/Liberty Theater, NYC, 1930/Palace Theater, NYC, 1930-2; app w Bill Robinson in JANGLELAND Revue, Lafayette Theater, NYC, 1931; worked Downtown Theater, Detroit, MI, 1932; Keith Theater, Boston, MA, 1932; Palace Theater, Chicago, IL, 1932; app w Bill Robinson in GOING TO TOWN Revue, Lafayette Theater, NYC, 1932; app on NATIONAL NEGRO FORUM HOUR, WEVD-radio, NYC, 1932; app in SOUTHERN SYNCOPATION REVUE, Harlem Opera House, NYC, 1932; app in revival GOING TO TOWN Revue, Lafayette Theater, NYC, 1934; app in HAWAIIAN MOON Revue, Apollo Theater, NYC, 1934; app in JUNGLE DRUMS Revue, Apollo Theater, NYC, 1934; moved to Chicago, 1936; worked as singer/dancer w Fletcher Henderson Orch, Grand Terrace Cafe, Chicago, IL, 1937-8 (remotes on NBC-radio network); worked The Palladium, London, Eng, 1939; frequently toured club/theater dates across US from 1939 into 40s; app w Fats Waller in film STORMY WEATHER, 1943 (por rel 20th Century Fox/V-Disc labels); worked w Don Redman Orch, Club Zanzibar, NYC, NY, 1943; reportedly app in Ralph Cooper's HARLEM TO HOLLYWOOD Revue, Elks Rendezvous Club, NYC, 1943; app w Bill Robinson in show MEMPHIS BOUND, Broadway Theater, NYC, 1945; moved to Kansas City, KS, and mostly inactive in music from mid-40s; died at home of kidney disease; buried Westlawn Cemetery, Kansas City, KS

Personal: Was cousin of James Scott, noted ragtime

composer/pianist. Sometimes worked as character actress in role of "Aunt Jemima" for stage appearances. Was an original incorporator of The Negro Actors Guild of America, 1936

Billing: Queen of Blues

Quote: "The voice of Ada Brown was full, rich and very mellow . . . one of the forgotten ladies of the blues"—Derrick Stewart-Baxter, *Ma Rainey and the Classic Blues Singers*, Studio Vista Ltd, 1970

BROWN, AMANDA
(see McCoy, Viola)

BROWN, ANDREW
Born: Feb 25, 1937, Jackson (Hinds Co), MS
Died: Dec 11, 1985, Harvey, IL
Inst: Alto Sax/Guitar/Organ

Father was Mose Brown; mother Colma ___; learned guitar as child; often worked in Chicago, IL from 1946; frequently returned to Jackson, MS, to work local shows w Joe Dyson Orch, late 40s; frequently worked local school dances in Chicago, late 40s; worked as sideman at White Rose Club, Phoenix, IL, c1949; Club De Lisa, Chicago, c1949; Grand Ballroom, Chicago, c1949; extensive work as sideman in bands of Little Walter/Muddy Waters/Howlin' Wolf/Jr Wells/Magic Sam/others in local clubs, Chicago area, through 50s; occasionally worked w Eldorados/Moroccos groups in Chicago, late 50s; worked as singer w Andrews Gospel Singers group, Chicago, late 50s; worked/rec as sideman w Freddy King/Shakey Jake/others, Chicago, into early 60s; served briefly in US Army, early 60s; settled in Harvey, IL, 1962; frequently worked in local bands in various club dates, Harvey area, 1962-80s; rec w own band, USA label, c1962; rec 4 Brothers label, mid-60s; rec Brave label, c1973; worked outside music in Harvey area into 80s; toured Europe, 1982; rec Double Trouble label, Holland (rel 1985); died of cancer; buried Washington Memorial Cemetery, Homewood, IL

Songs: Can't Let You Go/First Love/For Liz/Let's Get Together/Something Can Go Wrong/You Better Stop/You Ought to Be Ashamed

Andrew Brown
Photo by Amy O'Neal. Courtesy Living Blues Magazine

Infl by: Wayne Bennett/Albert King/BB King/Aaron "T-Bone" Walker

Quote: "A stalwart of the south [Chicago] suburban blues scene is guitarist and singer Andrew Brown"—Dick Shurman, *Living Blues* magazine, Mar 1976, p 12

Reference: Living Blues magazine, Mar 1976, pp 12-13

BROWN, BESSIE ELIZABETH
(*aka:* Sadie Green/Caroline Lee)

Courtesy Sheldon Harris Collection

Born: Mar 2, 1890, Baltimore (Baltimore Co), MD
Died: Nov 12, 1955, New York, NY

Father was John Brown; mother Laura Clements; frequently worked theater dates in Brooklyn, NY/Chicago, IL, from 1922; app in MOONSHINE Revue, Lafayette Theater, NYC, 1922; app w Doc Straine in THE WHIRL OF JOY musical comedy, Lafayette Theater, NYC, 1922; worked Lafayette Theater, Cleveland, OH, 1925; reportedly app on local radio, Cleveland, mid-20s; rec Pathe/Perfect labels, NYC, 1925; rec Banner/Domino/Oriole labels, NYC, 1926; worked Ritz Cafe Revue, Philadelphia, PA, 1926; worked w Doc Straine (as "Brown & Straine") in local clubs, NYC, from 1926; app in Jimmy Cooper's DARKTOWN FROLICS Revue, Howard Theater, Washington, DC, 1926; frequently worked local club dates, Cleveland, OH, 1927-32; rec Brunswick/Vocalion labels, Chicago, IL, 1928; rec Brunswick/Vocalion labels, Chicago/NYC, 1929; worked Club Madrid, Cleveland, 1932; worked outside music from 1932; suffered fatal heart attack; buried Arlington Memorial Park, Baltimore, MD

Personal: Married William Phillip Brown; three children; not to be confused with Bessie Brown who rec on Columbia label or Vaughn De Leath who used pseudonym Sadie Green
Billing: The Original Bessie Brown

BROWN, BESSIE

George Williams/Bessie Brown. Courtesy Sheldon Harris Collection

Born: c1895, Texas (unconfirmed)
Died: (unknown)

Teamed w George W Williams (as "Williams & Brown") to tour TOBA circuit working theater dates, 1918; Fats Waller joined team to work Putnam Theater, Brooklyn, NY, 1919, and then toured TOBA circuit into 20s; toured w George W Williams (as "Williams & Brown") working vaudeville circuits across US c1922-30; rec duets w George W Williams, Columbia label, NYC, 1923-6; rec (as single) Columbia label, NYC, 1924; headlined w George W Williams, Lafayette Theater, NYC, 1925; worked 81 Theater, Atlanta, GA, 1929; app w George W Williams in S'PRISE ME Revue, Alhambra Theater, NYC, 1930; app in HOT TOWN Revue, Alhambra Theater, NYC, 1930; reportedly retired to live in Cincinnati, OH, from 1932 into 70s

Personal: Married George W Williams. Not to be confused with Bessie Brown who recorded on Pathe and other labels. Possibly used pseudonym "Eliza Brown"

BROWN, BUSTER

Courtesy Sheldon Harris Collection

Born: Aug 15, 1911, Cordele (Crisp Co), GA (unconfirmed)
Died: Jan 31, 1976, Brooklyn, NY
Inst: Harmonica

Mother was Henrietta Davis; one of at least 7 children; raised and worked outside music in Cordele/Albany, GA, area; frequently worked local houseparties in area, 1930s/40s/50s; worked Fort Valley State Col Folk Festival, Fort Valley, GA, 1943 (por rel LC label [unissued]/por rel Flyright-Matchbox label); settled in NYC to work outside music in area from c1956; worked Fed's Chicken & Barbecue Place, NYC (?), 1959; rec Fire label, NYC, 1959-61; reportedly toured South working one-nighters c1960; rec Serock label, NYC, c1962; rec Gwenn label, Chicago, IL, 1962; worked club dates in Chicago, mid-60s; rec Checker label, Chicago, 1965; rec Blue Horizon label, 1968; rec Nocturn label, NYC (?), 1972; died at Brooklyn Hospital, buried local cemetery, Hanover, NJ

Personal: Married/divorced. 2 children. Not to be confused with musician B Daniel Brown (born Jun 18, 1928, Hernando, MS)

Songs: Blues When It Rains/Doctor Brown/Don't Dog Your Woman (When You Ain't Doing Right Yourself)/Fannie Mae/Fannie Mae's Place/Gonna Love My Baby/I'm Going—But I'll Be Back/Lost in a Dream/The Madison Shuffle/Two Women

Infl by: Fats Domino/Sonny Terry

Quote: "Buster's style was firmly set: bawdy, faintly erotic sexual metaphors bawled in his richly unmusical voice interspersed with piercing harmonica breaks—over a raunchy, rolling, sax-filled beat"—Tony Cummings, DJM album 22037

BROWN, CHARLES

Born: Sep 13, 1922, Texas City (Galveston Co), TX
Inst: Organ/Piano

Father Mose Brown; mother Mattie Simpson; studied classical piano in Galveston HS and worked local beach club/church gigs, mid-30s; attended Prairie View A&M Col, Prairie View, TX (earning BS degree) where he frequently worked in school band in late 30s; worked outside music (as teacher), George Washington Carver HS, Baytown, TX, c1942; worked outside music, Pine Bluff, AR, 1943; moved to West Coast to work outside music from 1943; worked International House, Berkeley, CA, 1943; won first prize in amateur show, Lincoln Theater, Los Angeles, CA, 1944; worked in pit band of Bardu Ali, Lincoln Theater, Los Angeles, 1944; worked Ivie's Chicken Shack, Los Angeles, 1944; joined Johnny Moore's Three Blazers working Talk of the Town Club, Beverly Hills, CA, 1944; Swing Club, Hollywood, CA, 1945; Copa Club, Los Angeles, 1945; rec acc to Frankie Laine, Atlas label, Los Angeles, 1945; rec w Johnny Moore's Three Blazers, Aladdin label, Los Angeles, 1945; rec Modern Music label, Los Angeles, 1945; worked Renaissance Casino, NYC, 1945; Apollo Theater, NYC, 1945-6; rec w Three Blazers, Exclusive label, Los Angeles, 1946; toured w Johnny Moore's Three Blazers working theater dates across US, 1946-8; worked The Riviera, St Louis, MO, c1947; rec w own trio, Aladdin label, Los Angeles, 1949; worked Birmingham Theater, Birmingham, AL, 1949; Dreamland Ballroom, Omaha, NE, c1949; rec w own band, Aladdin label, Los Angeles, c1950; toured w own band in R&B package show working theater dates across US through early 50s; toured as single w Johnny Ace package show working concert dates through South, 1954; worked Apache Inn, Day-

Charles Brown *Courtesy* Living Blues *Magazine*

ton, OH, 1954; frequent one-nighters in Los Angeles, CA, area from 1954; Elks Club, Los Angeles, 1954; Club Desire, New Orleans, LA, 1955; rec w Ray Charles Singers, East-West label, Los Angeles (?), 1956; worked The Palladium, San Diego, CA, 1956; toured w Fats Domino on Big Ten R&B package show working theaters through US, 1957; toured w own band working one-nighters through South, 1958; worked Dew Drop Inn, New Orleans, LA, c1959; rec w Amos Milburn, Ace label, New Orleans, 1959; worked w Jimmy Witherspoon at local gambling casinos, Newport, KY, 1959-60; rec King label, Cincinnati, OH (?), 1960; rejoined Johnny Moore to work club dates on West Coast, 1961; worked w own trio in local club dates, Columbus, OH, 1962-4; rec Mainstream label, San Francisco, CA, 1963; rec Mainstream label, NYC, 1964; worked club dates in San Francisco area, 1964-6; w Amos Milburn, Blue Angel Club, Cincinnati, OH, c1966; worked club dates, Anchorage, AK, 1966-7; worked outside music with occasional gigs at The Living Room/Roaring Twenties Club, Cincinnati, OH, 1967; worked outside music on West Coast, 1968-9; worked Ruthie's Inn, Oakland, CA, 1969; rec BluesWay label, Los Angeles, 1969; app on HOMEWOOD SHOW, PBS-TV (syndicated), 1970; worked w Amos Milburn, Viking Lounge, Cincinnati, 1970; Tommy's 250 Club, Richmond, CA, 1971; rec Jewel label, Los Angeles, c1971; worked local club dates, Denver, CO, 1972; rec w T-Bone Walker, Reprise label, Hollywood, CA/NYC, NY, 1973; worked Ruthie's Inn, Berkeley, CA, 1973; Dottie's Stardust Lounge, San Francisco, CA, 1974-6; rec w Johnny Otis, Blues Spectrum label, Los Angeles, c1975; toured Ramada Inn circuit working lounges across US, 1976; worked Club Savoy, San Francisco, 1976; San Francisco Blues Festival, McLaren Park, San Francisco, 1976 (por rel Jefferson label); app on BLUES BY THE BAY, KPFA-FM-radio, Berkeley, CA, 1976; toured club dates through Texas/Louisiana/Mississippi, 1977; worked Lee Magid's Cafe, Tarzana, CA, 1977; Sacramento Blues Festival, William Land Park, Sacramento, CA, 1977

Personal: Married Mabel Scott (1949-53); Eve McGhee (1959-)

Songs: All Is Forgiven/Driftin' Blues/I Want to Go Home/Jilted/Merry Christmas Baby/Please Come Home for Christmas/Tell Me You'll Wait for Me/Trouble Blues

Awards/Honors: The Three Blazers won *Cashbox* magazine and *Billboard* magazine awards as Best R&B trio, 1946

Infl by: Nat Cole/Pha Terrell

Infl to: Johnny Ace/Dave Alexander/Ray Charles/Floyd Dixon/Fats Domino/Johnny Fuller/Candy Green/Bee Houston/BB King/Little Willie Littlefield/Amos Milburn/Johnny Otis/Mel Walker

Quotes: "Charles' vocal style definitely opened the door for a whole school of musicians including Floyd [Dixon]"—Dick Shurman, *Living Blues* magazine, Sept 1975, p 20

"A great contributor to modern blues . . ."—Tom Mazzolini, *Living Blues* magazine, May 1976, p 19

Reference: Living Blues magazine, May 1976, pp 19-27

BROWN, CHOCOLATE
(see Scruggs, Irene)

BROWN, CLARENCE *"Gatemouth"*
Born: Apr 18, 1924, Vinton (Calcasieu Parish), LA
Inst: Bass/Drums/Guitar/Harmonica/Mandolin/Violin

Father was Clarence Brown Sr, a local musician; mother Virginia Frank; one of at least 7 children; moved to Orange, TX, at 3 weeks of age where he was raised; interested in music early and learned guitar from father, 1929, and violin, 1934; frequently worked outside music on father's ranch, Orange, TX, through 30s; joined William Benbow's BROWN SKIN MODELS (as drummer) and toured with group into Midwest, early 40s; served in Engineer Corps of US Army, 1946; worked w Hart Hughes Orch (as drummer) out of San Antonio, TX, 1946; worked Avalon Grill, San Antonio, 1946; The Old Keyhole, San Antonio, 1946; Bronze Peacock, Houston, TX, 1947; rec w Maxwell Davis Orch, Aladdin label, Los Angeles, CA, 1947; frequently rec w Jack McVea's Orch, Peacock label, Houston, 1949-60; worked The Hole, E St Louis, IL, c1949; The Ritz Lounge, Chicago, IL, 1949; extended residency w Jack McVea's Orch, Bronze Peacock, Houston, TX, into 50s/60s; formed own Gates Express group working extended residency at local club, Bogotá, Colombia (SA), c1953; worked Orchid Room, Kansas City, MO, 1954; toured East Coast working club dates, 1954; toured w Big Mama Thornton working concert dates, 1956; app on MACK McCORMICK AND FRIENDS, KUHF-FM-radio, Houston, TX, 1961; worked Longhorn Ranch, Dallas, TX, 1961; frequently worked (as C&W singer) Prentice Alley, Nashville, TN, c1961; frequently worked 400 Club/Playgirl Club (other C&W

Clarence "Gatemouth" Brown *Photo by Norbert Hess. Courtesy* Living Blues *Magazine*

bars/clubs), Denver, CO, early 60s; rec w Paul Bryant, Fantasy label, San Francisco, CA, 1963; rec Cue label, Houston, TX, 1964; settled in Farmington, NM, to work residency at Copper Penny Club from early 60s; rec Hermitage label, Nashville, TN, 1965; app on THE BEAT, WPIX-TV, NYC, NY, 1966; frequently worked Golden Slipper Club, Durango, CO, through 60s into 70s; worked Hurricane Bar, Pittsburgh, PA, 1967; toured w Chicago Blues Festival working concert dates through Europe 1971; app on local TV, Paris, France, 1971; rec Black & Blue label, Paris, 1971; worked Club Jetty, Maui, HI, c1971; 400 Club, Denver, CO, c1973; Montreux Jazz Festival, Montreux, Switzerland, 1973; rec Barclay label, Bogalusa, LA, early 70s; worked Newport Jazz Festival, Philharmonic Hall, NYC, NY, 1973 (por rel Buddah label); Winners Inn, Reno, NV, c1973; Circle Club, Vinton, LA, 1973; Star Casino, Reno, NV, c1973; The Nugget, Carson City, NV, c1974; New Orleans Jazz & Heritage Festival, New Orleans, LA, 1974; rec Blue Star label, Bogalusa, LA, 1974; frequently worked outside music (as Deputy Sheriff of San Juan County, New Mexico) through mid-70s; worked Liberty Hall, Houston, TX, 1976; New Orleans Jazz & Heritage Festival, New Orleans, LA, 1976-7; w Arnett Cobb, Hubers Seafood Restaurant, Houston, 1976; Philadelphia Folk Festival, Schwenksville, PA, 1976; toured for US State Department working concert dates through Africa, 1976; worked Jed's University Inn, New Orleans, LA, 1976; Rosy's Club, New Orleans, 1976; app in local radio commercials for Lone Star Beer Company of Texas, 1976; toured w own group working club dates through Texas, 1976-7; app in AUSTIN CITY LIMITS, PBS-TV (syndicated), 1977-8; worked Miller Theater, Houston, 1977; Mumma's Worry, Beaumont, TX, 1977; Texas Opry House, Houston, TX, 1977; Golden Nugget Saloon, Houston, 1977; worked Newport Jazz Festival Blues Picnic, Waterloo Village, Stanhope, NJ, 1977; North Sea Jazz Festival, Holland, 1977; Nice Jazz Festival, Nice, France, 1977; Monterey Jazz Festival, Monterey, CA, 1977; Coffee Gallery, San Francisco, CA, 1977

Personal: Married Geraldine Paris; Mary Durbin; Yvonne Ramsey. Has 2 children. Half-brother James "Widemouth" Brown was also singer. Name "Gatemouth" given him during childhood and refers to his loud voice. Not to be confused with singer Arnold "Gatemouth" Moore

Songs: A Long Way Home/Ain't That Dandy?/Chicken Shift/Depression Blues/For Now, So Long/Gate Walks to Board/Hot-Club Drive/It's Alright/Just Before Dawn/Just Got Lucky/Leftover Blues/Man and His Environment/Midnight Hour/Please Tell Me Baby/Please Mr Nixon/Swingin' the Gate

Infl by: Louis Jordan/Peetie Wheatstraw/Aaron "T-Bone" Walker

Infl to: Lonnie Brooks/Goree Carter/Albert Collins/Earl Gilliam/Cal Green/Guitar Slim/Bee Houston

Quote: "One of the major figures of the postwar blues scene"—Jim DeKoster, *Living Blues* magazine, Summer 1972, p 36

Reference: Blues Unlimited magazine (UK), Jun 1972, p 8

BROWN, DUSTY

Courtesy Living Blues *Magazine*

Born: Mar 11, 1929, Tralake (Washington Co), MS
Inst: Harmonica

One of 3 children; taught self harmonica at 13 years of age; worked mostly outside music on farm as youth; moved to Chicago, IL, 1946; worked mostly outside music with some sit-in gigs w Muddy Waters/Little Walter/others through 40s into 50s; formed own band to work Lover's Lounge, Chicago, 1953; Casbah Lounge, Chicago, 1953-6; rec Parrot label, Chicago,

1955; worked Charlie's Lounge, Chicago, 1956-60; rec Bandera label, Chicago, 1958; frequently worked small club dates in Chicago, IL/Gary, IN/Michigan City, IN, areas, early 60s; worked mostly outside music from 1964; worked Y'alls Club, Chicago, 1968; Flamingo Club, Chicago, 1970; Tom's Musicians' Lounge, Chicago, 1970; continued outside music work, Chicago, into 70s; toured France working concert dates, 1972

Personal: Married. Has children

Songs: He Don't Love You/Please Don't Go

Infl by: Louis Jordan/Little Walter/Muddy Waters

Quote: "Dusty is a good harp-blower, with the knack of finding simple, catchy and very effective riffs to offset his singing"—Bob Eagle, *Alley Music* magazine (Australia), First Quarter 1971, p 16

Reference: Blues Unlimited magazine (UK), Sept 1971, pp 7-8

BROWN, GABRIEL
Born: c1910, Florida (unconfirmed)
Died: c1972, Florida (unconfirmed)
Inst: Guitar

Believed raised in Florida and worked most of life outside music; rec Library of Congress label, Eatonville, FL, 1935; moved to NYC, NY, to work small cafes in Greenwich Village area from early 40s; rec Joe Davis label, NYC, 1945; rec MGM/Coral labels, NYC, 1949; reported active as street singer in NYC area through 50s; reportedly died in boating accident in Florida

Songs: A Dream of Mine/Bad Love/Black Jack Blues/Cold Love/Don't Worry About It/Down in the Bottom/Going My Way/I Get Evil When My Love Comes Down/I'm Gonna Take It Easy/I've Done Stopped Gambling/I've Got to Stop Drinkin'/It's Getting Soft/Now Now, I'll Tell You When/Stick with Me/You Ain't No Good

Quotes: "An artist of great originality and feeling"—Tony Travers, Policy Wheel album PW 4592

"A superb blues singer and guitarist"—Derrick Stewart-Baxter, *Jazz Journal* magazine (UK), Jun 1975, p 14

BROWN, GATEMOUTH
(see Brown, Clarence)

BROWN, *"Papa"* HENRY
(*aka:* Henry Charles)
Born: July 25, 1908, Troy (Obion Co), TN
Died: Jun 28, 1981, St Louis, MO
Inst: Piano

Father was Will Brown; mother Lemora Steward; to St Louis, MO working rent parties/bars from 1922; worked Blue Flame Club/9-0-5 Club/Jim's Place/Katy Red's (other clubs/bars), St Louis area, through 20s into 30s; rec w Ike Rodgers/Mary Johnson/solo, Brunswick label, Chicago, IL, 1929; rec Paramount label, Richmond, IN, 1929; rec Paramount label, Grafton, WI, 1930; worked mostly outside music in St Louis, MO, from early 30s; rec acc to Mary Johnson and others, Decca label, Chicago, 1934; served in US Army, early 40s; formed own quartet to work occasional local gigs, St Louis, MO, area, from 50s; rec 77 label, St Louis, 1960; continued outside music work, St Louis, through 60s/70s; worked *Becky Thatcher* riverboat, St Louis, 1965 (por rel Storyville/Euphonic labels); rec Adelphi label, St Louis, 1969/74; died of heart disease; buried National Cemetery, Jefferson Barracks, MO

Personal: Not to be confused with guitarist "Hi" Henry Brown

Songs: Blues for Charlie O'Brien/Blues Stomp/Blind Boy Blues/Bottled in Bond/Deep Morgan Blues/Deep Morgan Is Delmar Now/Eastern Chimes Blues/Got It and Cain't Quit It/Handy Man Blues/Henry Brown Blues/Henry's Jive/It Hurts So Good/My Blues Is in the Bottle/O'Fallon Blues/Papa Slick Head/Pickin' 'Em Out Again/Scufflin' Boogie/21st Street Stomp/Websters Blues

Quote: "Brown's extremely economical blues was reflected in the playing of other pianists in St Louis . . ."—Paul Oliver, *The Story of the Blues*, Chilton Book Company, 1969

Reference: 77 album 12-5

BROWN, IDA G *"Baby Blues"*
(*aka:* Baby Blues/Flora Dale/Sadie Jones)
Born: c1900
Died: (unknown)

Active in Lafayette Stock Company, Chicago, IL, late teens; app in musical comedy THIS AND THAT, Avenue Theater, Chicago, 1919; app in musical comedy BABY BLUES, Lafayette Theater, NYC, NY, 1919; app in musical comedy THIS AND THAT, Lafayette Theater, NYC, 1920; app in Irvin Miller's musical comedy BROADWAY RASTUS OF 1920, La-

Courtesy Sheldon Harris Collection

fayette Theater, NYC, 1920; app in musical comedy SULTAN SAM, Lafayette Theater, NYC, 1920; app in ALABAMA BOUND Revue, Lafayette Theater, NYC, 1920; toured w Sheftell's Creole Fashion Revue Company working theaters on Pantages circuit, 1921; frequently app in Joe Sheftell's Revue, Lafayette Theater, NYC, 1922-3; rec Banner label, NYC, 1924; app w Piron Orch, WJZ-radio, NYC, 1924; frequently toured TOBA circuit working theater dates through South, mid-20s; app in THE TROUBADOURS REVUE, New Alhambra Theater, NYC, 1927; app in THE HARLEM ROUNDERS Revue, New Alhambra Theater, NYC, 1927; app in LUCKY NUMBERS Revue, New Alhambra Theater, NYC, 1927; app in PULLMAN DANDIES Revue, New Alhambra Theater, NYC, 1927; app in DIXIE MAGNOLIAS Revue, New Alhambra Theater, NYC, 1927; app in DESIRES OF 1928 Revue, Lincoln Theater, NYC, 1927; app in BROADWAY RASTUS Revue, Lafayette Theater, NYC, 1928; app in HARLEM PASTIMES Revue, Alhambra Theater, NYC, 1928; app in DANCING DANDIES Revue, Alhambra Theater, NYC, 1928; app in GOING UP Revue, Alhambra Theater, NYC, 1928; app in ARE WE HAPPY? Revue, Alhambra Theater, NYC, 1928; app in ON THE AVENUE Revue, Alhambra Theater, NYC, 1928; app in AUTUMN FROLICS Revue, Alhambra Theater, NYC, 1928; app in WINNERS ALL Revue, Alhambra Theater, NYC, 1928; app in QUAKERTOWN SCANDALS Revue, Lincoln Theater, NYC, 1929; app in THE CIRCUS SHOWMAN Revue, Lincoln Theater, NYC, 1929; app in HONEY Revue, Lincoln Theater, NYC, 1929; app in SMALLS PARADISE Revue, Lafayette Theater, NYC, 1929; app in AT THE BARBECUE Revue, Alhambra Theater, NYC, 1930; app in BY MOONLIGHT Revue, Alhambra Theater, NYC, 1930; reportedly app w Bill Robinson in Lew Leslie's BLACKBIRDS OF 1933-4 Revue, 42nd Street Apollo Theater, NYC, 1933-4; reportedly app w Miriam Hopkins in show JEZEBEL, Ethel Barrymore Theater, NYC, 1933; retired from music mid-30s; whereabouts unknown thereafter

BROWN, *"Elder"* **J C**
(see Jefferson, Lemon)

BROWN, JOHN HENRY *"Bubba"*
Born: Dec 5, 1902, Brandon (Rankin Co), MS
Inst: Bass/Guitar/Piano/Violin

Father was musician from whom he learned guitar and violin; frequently worked local parties in area through 20s; moved to Jackson, MS, to work outside music with frequent weekend gigs w Tommy Johnson/Cary Lee Simmons/Johnny Temple/Sam Norwood/Chatmon Brothers/others from 1928 into 30s; moved to Los Angeles, CA, to work mostly outside music from 1963; rec Flyright label, Los Angeles, 1967

Personal: Married. Has 3 children. His son Mel Brown is noted modern jazz guitarist. His son James (Jim) Brown is pianist

Infl to: Boogie Bill Webb

Reference: Blues World magazine (UK), Oct 1968, pp 7-9

BROWN, LILLIAN *"Lillyn"*
(*aka:* Fannie Baker/Elbrown/Mildred Fernandez/Maude Jones)
Born: Apr 24, 1885, Atlanta (Fulton Co), GA
Died: Jun 8, 1969, NYC, NY

Father was Ben Thomas, an Erie Iroquois Indian; mother was Ella Bronks; born Lillian Thomas, an only child; recited poem at Easter Sunday church service at 3 years of age; joined all-girl white string orchestra

John "Bubba" Brown

Photo by Marina Bokelman. Courtesy Dave Evans

Lillian "Lillyn" Brown *Courtesy Sheldon Harris Collection*

(billed as "The Indian Princess") working local theater dates, Atlanta, GA, area, 1894-6; toured w Queen City Minstrels tent show (billed as "The Youngest Interlocutor in the World") working as singing/ dancing male impersonator ("Elbrown"), 1896-7; frequently worked solo act, Baxters Beer Garden, FL, c1897-1908; began singing blues at Little Strand Theater, Chicago, IL, 1908; app in show HARVEST MOON, Dixie Theater, Memphis, TN, c1910; teamed w Billy DeMont (as "Brown & DeMont") to tour vaudeville circuit working theaters through teens; app w DeMont in show THE MISLEADING LADY, Lincoln Theater, NYC, NY, 1916; app w DeMont in show THE COUNTRY BOY, Lincoln Theater, NYC, 1916; replaced Esther Bigeou in Irvin C Miller's BROADWAY RASTUS Revue to tour theater dates, 1918; worked w DeMont, Strand Theater, Halifax, NC, 1918; Music Hall, Lewiston, ME, 1918; The Playhouse, Passaic, NJ, 1918; Proctor's, Elizabeth, NJ, 1918; Halsey Theater, Brooklyn, NY, 1918; Proctor's, Schenectady, NY, 1918; Powers Theater, Camden, NJ, 1919; Standard Theater, Philadelphia, PA, 1919; Keith Theater, Jersey City, NJ, 1919; Harris Theater, Pittsburgh, PA, 1920; Plaza Theater, Bridgeport, CT, 1920; Halsey Theater, Brooklyn, NY, 1920; Proctor's, Elizabeth, NJ, 1920; Howard Theater, Boston, MA, 1920; Standard Theater, Philadelphia, PA, 1921; Strand Theater, Halifax, NC, 1921; rec w own Jazzbo Serenaders, Emerson label, NYC, NY, 1921; worked Lafayette Theater,

NYC, 1921; Lincoln Theater, NYC, 1922; Mountain Park Casino, Holyoke, MA, 1922; app w DeMont in musical comedy BON-BON BUDDY JR, Lafayette Theater, NYC, 1922, then toured; frequently worked Cotton Club/Harlem Opera House/Club Alabam/Calypso Club/others, NYC, into 20s; worked w DeMont, Music Hall, Lewiston, ME, 1923; The Bijou, Bangor, ME, 1923; Empire Theater, Red Bank, NJ, 1923; New Star Casino, NYC, 1923; app in show ROSEANNA, Pitt Theater, Pittsburgh, PA/Riviera Theater, NYC, 1924; app in BANJO LAND Revue, Lafayette Theater, NYC, 1924; app in THE PRICELESS FUNNY REVUE, Lafayette Theater, NYC, 1924; worked Keith's Orpheum Theater, Brooklyn, NY, 1924; app w Florence Mills in DIXIE TO BROADWAY Revue, Broadhurst Theater, NYC, 1924, then toured with show into 1925; worked w DeMont, Lafayette Theater, NYC, 1925; Feeley's Theater, Hazelton, PA, 1925; Capitol Theater, New Britain, CT, 1925; Victory Theater, Holyoke, MA, 1925; Palace Theater, Springfield, MA, 1925; BF Keith Theater, Lowell, MA, 1925; Congress Theater, Saratoga, NY, 1925; Imperial Theater, Montreal, Can, 1926; Keith Theater, Ottawa, Can, 1926; State Theater, New Brunswick, NJ, 1926; Proctor's 25th Street Theater, NYC, NY, 1926; Capitol Theater, Trenton, NJ, 1926; Bellevue Theater, Niagara Falls, NY, 1926; Opera House, Jamestown, NY, 1926; Majestic Theater, Johnstown, PA, 1926; Rialto Theater, Poughkeepsie, NY, 1926; William Penn Theater, Philadelphia, PA, 1926; Orpheum Theater, Germantown, PA, 1926; Strand Theater, E Liverpool, OH, 1926; Ralph Theater, Reading, PA, 1926; State Theater, Harrisburg, PA, 1926; Colonial Theater, Newport, RI, 1926; Mystic Theater, Malden, MA, 1926; app w DeMont in musical comedy ROLL ON, Gibson's Dunbar Theater/Lincoln Theater, NYC, NY/Howard Theater, Washington, DC/Orpheum Theater, Newark, NJ, 1926; worked w DeMont, Gayety Theater, Utica, NY, 1926; Rialto Theater, Glens Falls, NY, 1926; New Boston Theater, Boston, MA, 1926; Federal Theater, Salem, MA, 1926; Palace Theater, Pittsfield, MA, 1926; Capitol Theater, Hartford, CT, 1926; Feeley's Theater, Hazelton, PA, 1927; Kingston Theater, Kingston, NY, 1927; Majestic Theater, Elmira, NY, 1927; Riviera Theater, Brooklyn, NY, 1927; Keith Theater, Portland, ME, 1927; Washington Street Theater, Boston, MA, 1927; Capitol Theater, Hartford, CT, 1927; Orpheum Theater, NYC, NY, 1927; Proctor's Theater, Albany, NY, 1927; Bijou Theater, Woonsocket, RI, 1927; Granada Theater, Waltham, MA, 1927; Brockton Theater, Brockton, MA, 1927; Olympia Theater, Haverhill, MA, 1927; Glove Theater, Gloversville, NY, 1927; St James Theater, Asbury Park, NJ, 1927; Regent Theater, Paterson, NJ, 1927; Proctor's Theater, Newark, NJ, 1928; worked as single from 1928; toured in own company working Palace Theater, Bridgeport, CT, 1928; Loew's State Theater, Montreal, Can, 1928; Capitol Theater, Dunkirk, NY, 1928; Congress Theater, Saratoga, NY, 1928; Palace Theater, Worcester, MA, 1928; Keith Theater, Ottawa, Can, 1928; Scollay Square Theater, Boston, MA, 1928; Proctor's 125th Street Theater, NYC, NY, 1928; Loew's Prospect Theater, Brooklyn, NY, 1928; KA Jefferson Theater, NYC, 1928; Broadway Theater, NYC, 1928; Proctor's Theater, Yonkers, NY, 1928; Proctor's 86th Street Theater, NYC, 1928; Broadway Theater, NYC, 1928; Rivoli Theater, Toledo, OH, 1929; Lyric Theater, Indianapolis, IN, 1929; Pantages Theater, Minneapolis, MN, 1929; Pantages Theater, Edmonton, Can, 1929; Pantages Theater, Tacoma, WA, 1929; Pantages Theater, Portland, OR, 1929; Pantages Theater, San Francisco, CA, 1929; Pantages Theater, Fresno, CA, 1929; Pantages Theater, Los Angeles, CA, 1929; Pantages Theater, San Diego, CA, 1929; Pantages Theater, Long Beach, CA, 1929; Pantages Theater, Ogden, UT, 1929; Pantages Theater, Kansas City, MO, 1929; Earle Theater, Atlantic City, NJ, 1929; Madison Theater, Brooklyn, NY, 1929; Proctor's 58th Street Theater, NYC, NY, 1929; app in musical comedy SAM FROM BAM, Lafayette Theater, NYC, 1929; app in musical comedy HARLEM GIRL, Lafayette Theater, NYC, 1929; app in SAY IT WITH GIRLS Revue, Alhambra Theater, NYC, 1930; app in show QUEEN AT HOME, Times Square Theater, NYC, 1930; app in HOT STUFF Revue, The Embassy, Paris, France, 1930; worked club dates in Spain, 1930; worked Harlem Opera House, NYC, 1931; app in MANHATTAN FROLICS Revue, Harlem Opera House, NYC, 1932; app in HERE 'TIS musical comedy, Lafayette Theater, NYC, 1932; app w Jelly Roll Morton in HEADIN' FOR HARLEM Revue (theater unknown), 1933; worked Lafayette Theater, NYC, 1934; Harlem Opera House, NYC, 1934-5; app in show BABY POMPADOUR, Vanderbilt Theater, NYC, 1934; retired to work outside music in NYC area from mid-30s through 1940s; app in show REGINA, 46th Street Theater, NYC, 1949; app in revival show KISS ME KATE, Broadway Theater, NYC, 1952; app in Equity Library Community Theater Production of revival show MAMBA'S DAUGHTERS, DeWitt Clinton Community Center (and other adult/youth centers), NYC, 1953; owned/operated a downtown acting/sing-ging school and frequently taught at uptown Jarahal School of Music, NYC, through 1950s; active as secretary of Negro Actors Guild, NYC, from 1956; wrote/produced/directed various plays/productions (as PRODIGAL SINGER, Abyssinian Baptist Church, NYC, 1965) in NYC area through 1960s; worked Mamie Smith Benefit Concert, Celebrity Club, NYC, 1964; entered St Rose's Home where she died of cancer; buried Frederick Douglass Memorial Park Cemetery, Staten Island, NY

Personal: Married William "Billy" DeMont (c1915-), an entertainer who later worked as her business manager; married Teddy Wilson (died c1963). Not to be confused with early recording artist Lil Brown

Billings: The Indian Princess/The Kate Smith of Harlem/The Original Gay 90s Gal/The Youngest Interlocutor in the World

Song: Up the Way Bound

Reference: Record Research magazine, Nov 1956, p 12

BROWN, LOTTIE
(see Beaman, Lottie)

BROWN, OLIVE

Born: Aug 30, 1913, St Louis (St Louis Co), MO
Died: May 9, 1982, St Louis, MO
Inst: Drums

Father was Charles Jefferson; mother was Georgia Williams. Born Olive Jefferson; to Detroit, MI at 3 months of age where she was raised, with frequent trips to St Louis, MO; sang at Kennerly Sanctified Temple, St Louis, 1927; left home to work outside music from 1936; worked w Todd Rhoades Orch in BLUES IN THE NIGHT Revue, Club Zombi, Detroit, MI, 1941; Champion Bar, Detroit, 1943; Uncle Tom's Plantation Club, Detroit, 1943; w Earl Bostic Orch/Cecil Scott Orch, Smalls Paradise, NYC, NY, 1943; w Tiny Bradshaw Orch, El Grotto Room, Pershing Hotel, Chicago, IL, 1943; w Teddy Buckner Orch, Club Three Sixes, Detroit, MI, 1944-7; app w

Olive Brown
Photo by Wally Lubzik. Courtesy Jim Taylor

TJ Fowler Band in Paul William's HUCKLE BUCK Revue, Lee's Sensation, Detroit, c1945; w Gene Ammons, Royal Gardens Club, Flint, MI, c1946; rec Our World label, Nashville, TN, c1948; worked w Jackie Wilson, Casbah Club, Detroit, MI, early 50s; Club Moonglow, Buffalo, NY, 1958; Williams Bar, Buffalo, NY, 1958; Key Hole Club, San Antonio, TX, 1958; Sun Valley Motor Motel, Harlingen, TX, 1960; Holiday Inn, Mission, TX, 1960; JP's House of Steaks, Houston, TX, 1960; Tony's Steak House, Houston, 1960; Sho Biz Restaurant, Houston, 1960; Connies on Lenox, NYC, NY, 1960; moved to Toronto, Can, 1963; worked Canadian National Exhibition, Toronto, 1963; Colonial Tavern, Toronto, 1963-7; Westover Hotel, Toronto, 1964; Warwick Hotel, Toronto, 1964; rec w Hallie Ingram, Blues Spectacle label, Toronto, c1964; app on A LA CARTE Show, CBC-TV, Toronto, 1964; app on FESTIVAL PRESENTS THE BLUES, CBC-TV, Toronto, 1964; Waverley Hotel, Toronto, 1964; rec Spivey label, Brooklyn, NY (?), c1965; worked Town Tavern, Toronto, 1965; Ryerson Concert, Toronto, 1965; Golden Nugget, Toronto, 1965-8; Penny Farthing, Toronto, 1965; Club 76, Toronto, 1965; Le Caberett, Toronto, 1965; worked local club dates, Kansas City, MO, 1966; Cab-A-Bob Club, Toronto, 1967-8; w Cy McLean's Trio, Ford Hotel, Toronto, 1967; Town Tavern, Toronto, 1968; w Henry Cuesta Sextet/Toronto Symphony Orch, Massey Hall, Toronto, 1968; Ragtime Society Concert, Toronto, 1968; w Don Ewell, Bakers Keyboard Lounge, Detroit, MI, 1968; worked *Goldenrod/Admiral Streckfuss* riverboats, St Louis, MO, 1970-3; Blues/Jazz Festival, Memphis, TN, 1971; Cotton Festival, Memphis, TN, 1972; Chicago Roadhouse Restaurant, Detroit, 1973; w Gabriel Brothers Band, Detroit Hot Jazz Society Concert, Detroit, 1973; rec w Blues Chasers, JTP label, Detroit 1973; w New McKinney's Cotton Pickers, Hotel Pontchartrain, Detroit, 1973; w Teddy Wilson, Rod's Outdoor Theater, Cool Valley, TX, 1973; w Lee Castle's Dorsey Band, Colliseum, Austin, TX, 1973; w Knocky Parker, Municipal Auditorium, Kerrville, TX, 1973; St Louis Ragtime Festival, St Louis, MO, 1973; Evansville Jazz Festival, Evansville, IN, 1973; w St Louis All-Stars, Big Horn Festival, Mundelein, IL, 1973; Cafe Nostalgique, Detroit, MI, 1974; Highland Park Community Col, Detroit, 1974; Ragtime Festival, Kerrville, TX, 1974; w New McKinney's Cotton Pickers, Carnegie Hall, NYC, NY, 1974; toured college circuit working concerts through Midwest/South from 1975; died of stroke; buried Washington Park Cemetery, Berkeley, MO

Personal: Married 3 times. Has 2 children

Billings: The Princess of the Blues/New Empress of the Blues/Foxy GGM (great-grandmother)

Songs: Monkey on My Back/A Woman's Lament

Infl by: Bessie Smith

Quotes: "Olive Brown sings with expression and feeling and is steeped in the old blues and jazz traditions . . ."—Eric Townley, *Storyville* magazine (UK), Jun 1975, p 197

"I like her as well as any singer I have ever heard, and that includes my idols, Bessie Smith and Ida Cox"—Derrick Stewart-Baxter, *Jazz Journal* magazine (UK) (unknown date)

"The finest blues singer . . . since Bessie Smith"—*Toronto Globe* newspaper (unknown date)

BROWN, RICHARD *"Rabbit"*
Born: c1880, New Orleans (Orleans Parish), LA
Died: 1937, New Orleans, LA
Inst: Guitar

Born and raised in James Alley, a noted gang-fighting area of New Orleans; began singing in streets for tips working through James Alley/Storyville district and other parts of town, New Orleans, into 20s; worked as popular street singer (noted for extemporaneous songs and rhyming names) and frequently worked as singing boatman on Lake Pontchartrain and excursion trains between New Orleans and Baton Rouge, LA, through 20s into 30s; frequently worked Tom Anderson's Saloon/Mama Lou's, New Orleans, through 20s; rec Victor label, New Orleans, 1927; died in poverty

Songs: Downfall of the Lion/Gyp, the Blood

BROWN, ROBERT
(*aka:* Ham Gravy/Shufflin' Sam/Washboard Sam)
Born: Jul 15, 1910, Walnut Ridge (Lawrence Co), AR
Died: Nov 13, 1966, Chicago, IL
Inst: Washboard

Father stated to be Frank Broonzy, a former slave; given grandfather's surname at birth; one of at least 3 children; born/raised on farm; left home to play washboard with local blues groups, Memphis, TN, area, from early 20s; moved to Chicago, IL, working w Hammie Nixon/John Estes on streets for tips from 1932; frequently worked local gigs w Bill Broonzy, Chicago, from 1932; rec Bluebird label, Chicago, 1935-42; rec Vocalion label, Chicago, IL/Aurora, IL, 1935-6; frequently rec acc to Jazz Gillum/Bill Broonzy/Bukka White/others on local labels, Chicago, late 30s into early 40s; rec w State Street Swingers, Vocalion label, Chicago, 1936-7; frequently worked outside

Robert Brown (Washboard Sam)

Courtesy Institute of Jazz Studies

music with local club dates, Chicago, late 30s through 40s; rec Victor label, Chicago, 1947-9; mostly inactive in music, Chicago, from 1949; rec Chess label, Chicago, 1953; worked Fickle Pickle and other clubs/coffeehouses, Chicago, 1963-4; rec Spivey label, Chicago, 1964; brief tour working concerts through Europe, 1964; entered Cook County Hospital where he died of heart disease; buried Washington Memorial Cemetery, Homewood, IL

Personal: Married. 2 children. Was half brother of Bill Broonzy. Not to be confused with Robert Brown (Smoky Babe) or Clarence Todd who used pseudonym Shufflin' Sam or Albert Johnson (from Jeffrey, MS) who used pseudonym Washboard Sam

Songs: Back Door/Block and Tackle/The Blues What Am/Booker T Blues/Bright Eyes/CCC Blues/Chauffeur Blues/Deep Water Blues/Diggin' My Potatoes/Every Tub Stands on Its Own Bottom/Evil Blues/Fast Woman Blues/Fool About That Woman/Get Down Brother/Go Back to the Country/Going Back to Arkansas/Gonna Hit the Highway/Gonna Take My Rap/Good Luck Blues/Good Old Easy Street/Good Time Tonight/Hand Reader Blues/He's a Creepin' Man/Horseshoe over the Door/How Can I Play Fair/I Believe I'll Make a Change/I Laid My Cards on the Table/I Love My Baby/I Won't Be Sober Long/I'm a Lonely Man/I'm a Prowlin' Ground Hog/I'm Gonna Train My Baby/I'm on My Way Blues/I've Been Treated Wrong/It's Too Late Now/Jazz Gillum's Blues/Long Razor Blues/The Longest Train I've Ever Seen/Look What You Are Today/Louise/Lover's Lane Blues/Lowland Blues/Minding My Own Business/My Big Money/Never, Never/99 Blues/Out with the Wrong Woman/Reckless Rider Blues/River Hip Mama/She Fooled Me/She's Just My Size/Shirt Tail/Soap and Water Blues/Stop and Fix It/This Time Is My Time/Warehouse Blues/Wasn't He Bad/Yellow, Black and Brown/You Got to Run Me Down/You Should Give Some Away/You Stole My Love

Infl by: Bill Broonzy

Quotes: "His deep, heavy voice was perfectly suited to the blues he sang, and he had a penchant for better than average lyrics, leavened with a wry sense of humor"—Don Kent, RCA album LPV-577

"One of the most consistently popular Bluebird artists was . . . Robert Brown"—Sam Charters, *The Country Blues*, Rinehart & Company, Inc, 1959

"Washboard Sam is a good blues singer"—(Bill Broonzy) Yannick Bruynoghe, *Big Bill Blues*, Cassell & Company Ltd, 1955

Reference: Big Bill Blues, Yannick Bruynoghe, Cassell & Company Ltd, 1955

BROWN, ROBERT
(*aka:* Smoky Babe)
Born: 1927, Itta Benna (Leflore Co), MS
Died: 1975, Louisiana (unconfirmed)
Inst: Guitar

Born and raised on farm and worked most of life as migrant worker through South; frequently hoboed through South working outside music with frequent houseparties/small dives/bars/tonks/picnics/suppers in Bessemer, AL/New Orleans, LA/Baton Rouge, LA/Scotlandville, LA, through 40s/50s/60s; rec Folk-Lyric label, Scotlandville, 1960-1; rec Folk-Lyric/Storyville labels, Baton Rouge, 1960; rec Bluesville label, Baton Rouge, 1961; continued occasional outside music work with some local parties, Baton Rouge, through 60s; whereabouts unknown thereafter

Personal: Not to be confused with Robert Brown (Washboard Sam)

Songs: Bad Whiskey/Black Ghost/Going Back Home/I'm Broke and I'm Hungry/Mississippi River/My Baby Put Me Down/My Baby She Told Me/Rabbit Blues/Too Many Women/Two Wings

Quote: "Despite his rough and poverty-stricken life, Smoky is full of high exuberance, a joy in life, which he expresses in his dance provoking style"—Harry Oster, Folk-Lyric album 118

Reference: Folk-Lyric album 118

BROWN, ROY JAMES *"Good Rockin"*
(*aka:* Tommy Brown)
Born: Sept 10, 1920, New Orleans (Orleans Par) LA
Died: May 25, 1981, San Fernando, CA
Inst: Piano

Father, Yancy Brown, and mother, Tru-Love Warren (part Algonquin Indian), were musicians/singers who frequently sang in church choirs in area; learned piano from mother at 5 years of age; moved to Eunice, LA, where he was raised and attended elementary school; frequently sang in local church as youth and worked outside music in area into 40s; formed The Rookie Four gospel quartet working local churches in area from 1938; moved to West Coast to work outside music (as professional boxer), Los Angeles, CA, from 1942; won first prize singing pop songs in amateur talent show, Million Dollar Theater, Los Angeles, 1945; frequently worked other amateur talent shows in theaters in Los Angeles area, 1945; extensive residency as MC/pop-blues singer, Billy Riley's Palace Park, Shreveport, LA, 1945; worked w Joe Coleman's group in local club dates, Galveston, TX, 1946; formed The Mellodeers working extended residency at Club Grenada, Galveston, with frequent app on KGBC-radio, Galveston, 1946-7; rec Gold Star label, Galveston, 1947; worked w Clarence Samuels (as "Blues Twins") in residence, Downbeat Club, New Orleans, 1947; rec w Bob Ogden Orch and others, DeLuxe label, New Orleans, LA/Dallas, TX/Cincinnati, OH/Los Angeles, CA, 1947-51; formed own band working Starlight Club, New Orleans, 1947; w Paul Gayten's Band, Club Robin Hood, New Orleans, 1947; toured extensively w own Mighty Men band or as single working one-nighters/clubs/theaters/ballrooms across US from 1947; worked Lincoln Theater, New Orleans, c1947; Rip's Playhouse, New Orleans, c1947; The Hilltop, Pine Bluff, AR, c1948; Ryman Auditorium, Nashville, TN, 1948; The Armory, Flint, MI, 1950; worked Royal Peacock Club, Atlanta, GA/Meadowbrook Club, Savannah, GA/Cavalcade of Jazz, Wrigley Field, Los Angeles, CA/Richmond Auditorium, Los Angeles/5-4 Ballroom (w frequent remotes), Los Angeles/Savoy Ballroom, Los Angeles/Ox Club, Los Angeles/Fox Theater, Brooklyn, NY/Apollo Theater, NYC, NY/Howard Theater, Washington, DC/Royal Theater, Baltimore, MD/others into 1950s; rec King label, New Orleans, LA/Los Angeles, CA/Miami, FL/Cincinnati, OH, 1952-5; frequently toured one-nighters and weekend gigs in clubs/lounges through South, mid-50s; rec w Bill Doggett Band (as "Tommy Brown"), King label, New Orleans, LA, 1956; rec Imperial label, New Orleans, 1956-7; toured as MC on Universal Attractions Rock & Roll package show across US, 1957; frequently worked club dates, Las Vegas, NV, late 50s; rec King label, Cincinnati, OH, 1959; worked Apollo Theater, NYC, NY, 1959; rec Home of the Blues label, Mem-

Roy Brown *Courtesy Sheldon Harris Collection*

phis, TN, 1960-1; settled on West Coast to work mostly outside music, Los Angeles, CA, c1960 to late 60s; rec DRA/Connies/Mobile labels, Los Angeles, 1962; rec Chess label, Chicago, IL, 1963 (unissued); occasional gigs w Johnny Otis Show on West Coast, late 60s into 70s; rec BluesWay label, Hollywood, CA, 1967-8; rec Gert/Summit/Tru-Love labels, Los Angeles, 1968; worked w Johnny Otis Show, Monterey Jazz Festival, Monterey, CA, 1970 (por rel Epic label); formed/rec Friendship label, Los Angeles, 1971; rec Mercury label, Los Angeles, 1971; worked long residency Parisian Room, Los Angeles, 1975; toured Eng/Sweden, 1978; San Francisco Blues Festival, San Francisco, CA, 1979 (por rel Solid Smoke label); toured w Roomful of Blues into 80s; New Orleans Jazz & Heritage Festival, New Orleans, LA, 1981; suffered fatal heart attack; buried Eternal Valley Cemetery, Los Angeles, CA

Songs: Boogie at Midnight/Cryin' with the Blues/Deep Down in My Soul/Driving Me Mad/Fannie Mae/Fore Day in the Morning/Good Rockin' Man/Good Rockin' Tonight/Hard Luck Blues/Hard Times/Higher and Higher/I Want My Fanny Brown/Lollipop Mama/Long About Midnight/Love Don't Love Nobody/Man in Trouble Blues/Miss Fanny Brown/New Orleans Woman/Queen of Diamonds/Soul Lover/Standing on Broadway/Till the End of Never/Travelin' Man/Trouble at Midnight/Woman Trouble Blues/Worried Life Blues/Wrong Woman Blues

Infl by: Wynonie Harris

Infl to: Bobby Bland/Little Milton Campbell/Larry Davis/Little Richard/Little Junior Parker/Tommy Ridgley/Joe Turner/Jackie Wilson

Quote: "Blues shouter extraordinary"—Gary Vontersch, *Blues Unlimited* magazine (UK), Dec 1971, p 25

"He was the first singer of soul"—John Broven, *Walking to New Orleans*, Blues Unlimited, 1974

References: Blues Unlimited magazine (UK), Jan 1977, pp 4-11

Blues Unlimited magazine (UK), Mar 1977, pp 14-21

Walking to New Orleans, John Broven, Blues Unlimited, 1974

BROWN, TOMMY

(see Brown, Roy)

BROWN, WALTER

Courtesy Frank Driggs Collection

Born: Aug c1917, Dallas, TX (unconfirmed)
Died: Jun 1956, Lawton, OK (unconfirmed)

Believed raised in Dallas, TX, area and worked outside music (sometimes in CCC Camps) into 1930s; frequently sang for tips in local bars, Dallas, to late 30s; won first prize in local talent contest, Sunset Crystal Palace, Kansas City, MO, c1937; while singing in local barbecue stand was discovered by Jay McShann in Dallas, 1940; joined Jay McShann Band to work/tour/record, 1940-5; worked w Jay McShann Band in residence, Century Room, Kansas City, MO, 1940; Univ of Missouri, Columbia, MO, 1940; Lincoln Hall, Kansas City, MO, 1940; extensive tour w Jay McShann Band working dances/clubs through Midwest, 1940-1; in residence, Casa Fiesta Club, Kansas City, MO, 1941; Savoy Ballroom, NYC, NY, 1941-2; rec w Jay McShann Band/groups, Decca label, Dallas, TX/Chicago, IL/NYC, NY, 1941-2; rec w Jay McShann Band, Paradise Theater, Detroit, MI, 1942; Michigan Theater, Detroit, 1942; Apollo Theater, NYC, 1942; Royal Theater, Baltimore, MD, 1942; Howard Theater, Washington, DC, 1942; toured extensively w Jay McShann Band working one-nighters in theaters/dances/ballrooms through South/Midwest, 1942-3; worked Kings Ballroom, Lincoln, NE, 1942; app w Jay McShann Band on JUBILEE USA Show, AFRS-radio (Armed Forces Radio Service Broadcast), Chicago, IL, c1943; worked Band Box, Chicago, 1943-4; Congo Club, Detroit,

MI, 1943; Municipal Auditorium, Kansas City, MO, 1944; Two Spot Nite Club, Jacksonville, FL, 1944; Gypsy Tea Room, New Orleans, LA, 1944; in residence at Club Plantation, Los Angeles, CA, 1944; Casa Madrid, Louisville, KY, 1944; Downbeat Club, NYC, NY, 1945; rec w Skip Hall Orch, Queen-King label, NYC, NY, 1945/Cincinnati, OH, 1946; briefly worked some club dates w Earl Hines Orch, c1946; worked small club dates, Newark, NJ, 1947; rec w Tiny Grimes Sextet, Signature label, NYC, 1947; rec w Jay McShann's Quartet, Mercury label, Los Angeles, CA (?), 1948; rec Capitol label, Kansas City, MO, 1949; rec Peacock/Zip labels, c1949; worked local club dates, New Orleans, LA, c1949; reportedly worked in music infrequently working way back to Midwest from c1950; whereabouts unknown thereafter; reportedly died a drug addict

Songs: Confessin' the Blues/Hello and Goodbye/Hootie Blues/Inform Me Baby/Jumping the Blues/Lonely Boy Blues/One Woman's Man/Sloppy Drunk/Supressin' the Blues/WB Blues/What Evil Have I Done?

Infl to: Chuck Berry/Big Miller

Quotes: "Perhaps the most persuasive of carollers of the exploits of wastrels, wanderers and the woes of uncontrolled drunkards and illicit lovers"—(unknown credit) *Metronome* magazine, 1945

"[Jay McShann's] jumping Kansas City Band . . . achieved its greatest success with audiences as a result of the blues singing of Walter Brown and the ballads of Al Hibbler"—Barry Ulanov, *A Handbook of Jazz*, The Viking Press, 1957

BROWN, WILLIE LEE

Born: Aug 6, 1900, Clarksdale (Coahoma Co), MS
Died: Dec 30, 1952, Tunica, MS
Inst: Guitar

Worked outside music on Jim Yeager's Plantation, Drew, MS, from 1911; frequently worked local parties w Charley Patton/Tommy Johnson/others at Webb Jennings Plantation, Drew area, from c1916; frequently worked w Charley Patton on Will Dockery's Plantation, Dockery, MS, early 20s; settled in Robinsonville, MS, c1926; frequently worked local parties/picnics/dances in Robinsonville/Lake Cormorant, MS, areas from c1926; teamed w Son House to work local parties/picnics, Lula, MS, from 1929; frequently worked w Son House at local parties, Banks, MS, area, early 30s; rec Paramount label, Grafton, WI, 1930; frequently worked w Son House/Kid Bailey/others in Cormorant/Farmin, MS, areas through 30s; worked w Robert Johnson in local joints, Walls, MS, c1936; frequently worked w Son House/Robert Johnson/Willie Borum in Memphis, TN, area, late 30s; rec Library of Congress label, Lake Cormorant, MS, 1941; moved to Rochester, NY, to work outside music w Son House from early 40s; moved to Tunica, MS, area to work outside music (as farmer) from c1950; died at home of heart trouble; buried Good Shepherd Cemetery, Prichard, MS

Personal: Married Josie Bush/Rosa ———. Not to be confused with "Little" Willie Brown (harmonica) or bandleader Noble Sissle who used pseudonym "Willie Brown"

Songs: Future Blues/M&O Blues

Infl by: Charley Patton

Infl to: Dick Bankston/Son House/Robert Johnson/Tommy Johnson

Quotes: "Willie Brown was one of Patton's earliest understudies"—David Evans, *Tommy Johnson*, Studio Vista, 1971

"Brown had a rasping, abrasive voice and had developed a dramatic guitar technique . . ."—Paul Oliver, *The Story of the Blues*, Chilton Book Company, 1969

BRYANT, BEULAH

Courtesy Beulah Bryant

Born: Feb 20, 1918, Dayton (Marengo Co), AL
Died: Jan 29, 1988, Roosevelt Is, NY, NY

Father was Austin Walton; mother was Annie Jones; one of 6 children; born Blooma Walton; moved to Birmingham, AL, as infant where she was raised; frequently sang in local church junior choir as child; moved to West Coast, 1936; app in MARINDALE AMATEUR HOUR Show, KFRC-radio (Mutual network), San Francisco, CA, 1937 (winning first prize); formed own trio working extensive club/cocktail lounge dates on West Coast to mid-40s; worked Club Fortune, Reno, NV, 1945; Tower Theater, Kansas City, MO, 1945; settled in NYC, NY, to work/tour as single from 1945; app on ARTHUR GODFREY'S TALENT SCOUTS, CBS-radio (network), c1946; worked The Caverns, Washington, DC/The Riviera Club, St Louis, MO/Club DeLisa, Chicago, IL/ Lucky's Paradise, Montreal, Can/The Cave, Vancouver, Can/others through 40s; app w The Three Flames, NBC-TV, c1948; frequently worked Apollo Theater/Stuyvesant Casino/Central Plaza, NYC, from late 40s; rec Do-Kay-Lo label, NYC, late 40s; rec MGM label, Nashville, TN, late 40s; rec MGM label, NYC, early 50s; continued touring club/theater dates across US into 50s; worked Tom George's Country Club, Juneau, AK, 1951; residency at El Lobby Cafe, Juarez, Mexico, 1952; app on WELCOME TRAVELLERS Show, NBC-radio, early 50s; app on LIVE LIKE A MILLIONAIRE, ABC-TV, c1953; app on ROBERT Q LEWIS SHOW, CBS-TV, c1954; worked Newport Jazz Festival, Newport, RI, 1958 (por shown in film JAZZ ON A SUMMER'S DAY); app on KRAFT TELEVISION THEATER, NBC-TV, c1958; app on ARMSTRONG CIRCLE THEATER, CBS-TV, c1958; toured w Bo Diddley/Little Willie John/others on package rock show working theater dates across US, 1958; toured w Tony Parenti group working dates through New England states, 1960; rec Excello label, Nashville, TN, c1960; app TAMBOURINES TO GLORY, Westport County Theater, Westport, CT, 1961; app on CBS TELEVISION PLAYHOUSE, CBS-TV, c1963; worked Bruce's Log Cabin, Wyandanch, NY, 1965; toured Army/Air Force military bases working concert dates through Germany, 1965-6; worked Club Haven, Westbury, NY, 1966; Sunshine Lounge, Lawrence, NY, 1966; Club Peacock, Atlanta, GA, 1966; Pussy Cat A-Go-Go, Uniontown, AL, 1966; 400 Club, South River, NJ, 1967; worked SS *Independence* cruise ship out of NYC, 1966; Red Carpet Lounge, Cleveland, OH, 1967; Baby Grand, Canton, OH, 1967; Phelps Lounge, Detroit, MI, 1967; The Scene, NYC, 1967; Club Supreme, Elizabeth, NJ, 1967; The Rock Garden, Jamaica, West Indies, 1967; app on ALAN BURKE Show, WNEW-TV, NYC (syndicated), 1967; worked Terrace Lounge, Norwalk, CT, 1967; Lock & Key Club, Astoria, NY, 1967; app on NEW YORKER Show, WNEW-TV, NYC, 1968; worked Paul's Club, Flushing, NY, 1968; The Playpen, Cliffside Park, NJ, 1968; toured w own Beulah Bryant Show working USO concert dates through Korea/Japan/Okinawa/Philippines/Guam, 1968; worked A Giant Step Club, New Rochelle, NY, 1968; app on JOE FRANKLIN Show, WOR-TV, NYC, 1968-9; worked Pine Lounge, Bronx, NY, 1968; Fantasy Lounge, Jackson Heights, NY, 1968; Airways Lounge, NYC, 1968; app on CALLBACK, CBS-TV, 1969; worked Eastwood Country Club, San Antonio, TX, 1969; Cavalier Club, Port Chester, NY, 1969; Al Foxes Den, Astoria, NY, 1969; Fulsome Steak Club, Brooklyn, NY, 1969; King Arthur's Roundtable, Hempstead, NY, 1969; toured w own Beulah Bryant Show working military bases for USO in Vietnam/ Thailand, 1969-70; app on ALMA JOHN Show, WWRL-radio, NYC, 1969; worked Golden Elephant, Bronx, NY, 1969; toured w own Beulah Bryant Show working military bases for USO in Panama/Puerto Rico/Antigua/Cuba/elsewhere, 1970; toured w own Beulah Bryant Show working hospitals for USO through South Korea/Japan, 1970; worked Rainbow Inn, Woodbridge, NJ, 1970; toured w own Beulah Bryant Show working military bases for USO through Greece/Turkey/Spain/N Africa/Germany/elsewhere into 70s; app (as extra) in film THE HOSPITAL, 1971; app (as extra) in film THE TAKING OF PELHAM ONE TWO THREE, 1974; app on BLACK PRIDE, WPIX-TV, NYC, c1975; worked w own Beulah Bryant Show of USO, Diego Garcia Island, Indian Ocean, 1975; Nassau Community Col, Hempstead, NY, 1980; frequent app on local NYC radio talk shows into 80s; BLUES IS A WOMAN concert, Avery Fisher Hall, NYC, 1980; mostly inactive due to illness from 80s; suffered fatal heart attack; buried George Washington Cemetery, Paramus, NJ

Quote: "One of the best R&B people I know"—(Dinah Washington), Dick Edward, *NY News World*, Nov 29, 1979

BUDDY BOY
(see Guy, George)

BUFORD, *"Little"* GEORGE
(*aka:* Mojo/Muddy Waters Jr)
Born: Nov 10, 1929, Hernando (De Soto Co), MS
Inst: Harmonica

Photo by Amy O'Neal. Courtesy Living Blues Magazine

Grandfather was a preacher; father was harmonica player; frequently sang in Church of God & Christ choir as youth; occasionally worked w M&O Gospel Singers in area from 1938; frequently worked outside music with local party work in area to 1944; moved to Memphis, TN, to work mostly outside music, 1944-53; moved to Chicago, IL, 1953; formed The Savage Boys working Walters Show Lounge and other clubs/house parties, Chicago, 1953-5; formed Muddy Waters Jr Band (including Jo Jo Williams) to work Smitty's Corner/Jamboree Club/other bars/clubs/lounges, Chicago, 1956 into 60s; worked w Muddy Waters Band in local club dates, Chicago, 1962; moved to Minneapolis, MN, to work w Jo Jo Williams and others in local clubs/bars from 1963 into 70s; rec Vernon/Folkart labels, Minneapolis, 1963; worked w own trio, Sylvio's, Chicago, IL, 1963; Key Club, Minneapolis, 1963-4; rec Adell/Bangar labels, Minneapolis, 1964; worked Regal Tavern, Minneapolis, 1966-7; Expo 67, Montreal, Can, 1967; Mike's Bar, Minneapolis, 1968; frequently worked outside music at Univ of Chicago, Chicago, IL, through 60s; replaced George Smith in Muddy Waters Band working local clubs, Chicago, 1967-8; worked Cozy Bar, Minneapolis, 1970; rec Garrett/Twin Town labels, Minneapolis, c1971; worked w Muddy Waters Band, Alice's Revisited, Chicago, 1971; toured w Muddy Waters Band working concert dates through US/England/Europe, 1972; worked Montreux Jazz Festival, Montreux, Switzerland, 1972; w Muddy Waters Band, Ann Arbor Blues Festival, Ann Arbor, MI, 1972 (por rel Atlantic label); worked Sweet Queen Bee Lounge, Chicago, IL, 1972-5; Theresa's Tavern, Chicago, 1972-4; Florence's, Chicago, 1974

Personal: Married/divorced. 2 children. Took name "Mojo" from Muddy Waters song "Got My Mojo Working"

Song: Deep Sea Diver

Infl by: BB King/Little Walter/Muddy Waters/Jimmy Reed/Sonny Boy Williamson (Alex Miller)

Reference: Blues Unlimited magazine (UK), Oct/Nov 1970

BULL COW
(see Burnett, Chester)

BUMBLE BEE SLIM
(see Easton, Amos)

BUNN, ALDEN *"Allen"*
(*aka:* Allen Baum/Tarheel Slim)
Born: Sept 24, 1924, Bailey (Nash Co), NC
Died: Aug 21, 1977, Bronx, NY
Inst: Guitar

Father Henry Bunn was guitarist; mother Leonia Owens was church singer; born and raised on farm outside Wilson, NC; interested in music early learning guitar at age of 12; occasionally sang in local churches with frequent outside music work in Wilson/Nash County area, early 40s; worked w The Gospel Four in local churches/schools/auditoriums in area c1945-50; app w The Gospel Four, WPTF-radio, Raleigh, NC, late 40s; app w own Southern Harmoneers on local radio show, Wilson, NC, c1946; frequently toured w Selah Jubilee Singers working local churches in area, 1947-51; app w Selah Jubilee Singers, WPTF-radio, Raleigh, NC, late 40s; rec w Selah Jubilee Singers, Continental/Decca labels, 1947; rec w Southern Harmoneers, Regal label, 1949-50; moved to NYC, NY, to frequently work outside music from 1950; rec w Four Barrons, Regent label, NYC, 1950; app on CHESTERFIELD SUPPER CLUB, NBC-radio, c1950; rec w The Larks (originally Four Barrons), Apollo label, NYC, 1951-2; app w The Larks on ARTHUR GODFREY TALENT SCOUTS, CBS-TV, c1952; app on ZEKE MANNERS Show, local radio, NYC, c1952; app on TED STEELE Show, local radio, NYC, c1952; worked The Palace Theater, NYC, c1952; toured w The Larks on Percy Mayfield package

Alden Bunn (Tarheel Slim) *Photo by Peter B Lowry*

show working theaters through South/Midwest, 1952; frequently worked as single from 1952; rec w Sonny Terry, Apollo label, NYC, 1952; rec Red Robin label, NYC, 1953; worked w The Wheels group in local bars/clubs in NYC area from c1953; rec w The Wheels, Premium label, NYC, 1954; formed duo w "Little" Ann Bunn (as "The Lovers"), rec Lamp label, NYC, c1954; worked w Ann Bunn in local clubs/bars in NYC/NJ area through 50s; rec as "The Lovers," Aladdin label, NYC, 1957; rec as "Tarheel Slim & Little Ann," Fire-Fury label, NYC, 1958-9; frequently worked as session man for Apollo/Jubilee labels, NYC, late 50s/early 60s; frequently worked Cotton Club, Carteret, NJ/Billy's Night Club, Elizabeth, NJ, and other clubs/bars/auditoriums in Newark/Plainfield, NJ, area late 50s to mid-60s; rec Atco label, NYC (?), 1963; worked mostly outside music in NYC area through 60s into 70s; rec Trix label, Montclair, NJ, 1970-1; rec Trix label, Brooklyn, NY, 1972; worked Univ of North Carolina, Chapel Hill, NC, 1973 (por rel Trix/Flyright labels); worked Philadelphia Folk Festival, Schwenksville, PA, 1974; rec w Big Chief Ellis, Trix label, Cottekill, NY, 1974-5; app on Bob Javors SOMETHING INSIDE OF ME, WKCR-FM-radio, NYC, 1975; worked Center for New Music, NYC, 1976; Peace Methodist Church, NYC, 1976; rec Trix label, Hyattsville, MD, 1976; worked The Environ, NYC, 1977; entered Montefiore Hospital where he died of pneumonia; buried Fairlawn Cemetery, Fairlawn, NJ

Personal: Married Carrie Dingle. Married Anna Sandford. 2 children. Name "Tarheel" is reference to North Carolina, the "Tarheel State"

Songs: Baby I'm Going to Throw You Out/Bless You My Darling/Close to You/Dark Shadows/Discouraged/'Fore Day Creep/Forever I'll Be Yours/The Guy with the .45/I Got You Covered/I Submit to You/It's Too Late/Jitterbug Rag/Lock Me in Your Heart (And Throw Away the Key)/Married Woman Blues/Much Too Late/My Baby's Gone/My Kinda Woman/No Time At All/Number Nine Train/180 Days/Open Nose/Screaming and Crying/Security/She'll Be Sorry/So Sweet, So Sweet/Some Cold Rainy Day/Superstitious/Too Much Competition/Walking/Wildcat Tamer/Wine/Wrapped, Tied & Tangled/You're Gonna Reap (Everything You Sow)

Infl by: Bill Broonzy/Blind Boy Fuller/Gary Davis/ Brownie McGhee/Buddy Moss

Quotes: "A sensitive, haunting vocalist and a gentle, melodic guitarist"—Jim O'Neal, *Living Blues* magazine, Spring 1973, p 32

"Slim has a dry acid voice, well suited to the blues"—Derrick Stewart-Baxter, *Jazz Journal* magazine (UK), Mar 1973, p 2

"Tarheel Slim is an artist of great depth, able to go back to the sounds he grew up with with ease, and stretch from there into modern R&B"—Pete Lowry, Trix album 3310

Reference: Trix album 3310

BURNETT, CHESTER ARTHUR
(*aka:* Big Foot/Bull Cow/Howlin' Wolf)
Born: Jun 10, 1910, West Point (Clay Co), MS
Died: Jan 10, 1976, Hines, IL
Inst: Guitar/Harmonica

Father was Dock Burnett; mother was Gertrude ———; one of 6 children; frequently sang in Life Board Baptist Church, Aberdeen, MS, as child; moved to Young & Myers Plantation, Ruleville, MS, to work outside music from 1923; frequently worked local dances/suppers/Saturday-night hops/fish fries/ jukes/streets in area of Drew/Cleveland/Penton/West Point/Ruleville, MS, 1928 into early 30s; moved to Nat Phillips' Plantation, Twist, AR, to work outside music from 1933; frequently worked local joints as Will Weiler's Place/Will Smith's Place/Vandy Cobb's Place as well as frolics/streets in Hughes, AR, area from early 30s; occasionally toured w Robert Johnson/Sonny Boy Williamson (Alex Miller)/Texas Alexander/others, working joints/jukes through Tennessee/Arkansas/Mississippi, from mid-30s; frequently worked w Robert Jr Lockwood/Baby Boy Warren/others, Church's Park (WC Handy Park), Memphis, TN, c1938; worked local juke joints in Robinsonville, MS, 1939-40; worked Dooley Square, Tunica, MS, c1941; served in US Army where he frequently entertained troops, 1941-5; settled in Twist, AR, to work outside music as farmer, 1945; moved to Penton, MS, to continue farm work, 1946-8; formed own band to work jukes, Lake Cummins, MS, 1947; worked jukes, West Memphis, AR, 1948; toured w own group working jukes/barrelhouses/small clubs through South from 1948; app as DJ/singer/producer/advertising salesman, KWEM-radio, West Memphis, AR, 1948-52; rec Sun label (rel Chess label), West Memphis, AR, 1951; rec Chess label, Memphis, TN, 1951-3; rec RPM label, Memphis, 1951; rec RPM label, West Memphis, AR, 1952; app on weekly show, KXJK-radio, Forrest City, AR, 1952; moved to Chicago, IL, to work as single in 708 Club and others from 1952; rec Chess label, Chicago, 1953-66; worked Rock Bottom Club, Chicago, 1953; Club Zanzibar, Chicago, 1953-4; Silkhairs Club, West Memphis, AR, c1954; Hippodrome Ballroom, Memphis, TN, 1954; Sylvio's Lounge, Chicago, 1956; formed own band working 708 Club, Chicago, 1957; Big Squeeze Club, Chicago, 1959; Pepper's, Chicago, 1959; toured w American Blues Festival working concert dates through England/Europe, 1961-4 (por of 1964 Musikhalle concert, Hamburg, Ger, rel Fontana label); worked First International Jazz Festival, Washington, DC, 1962; frequently app on BIG BILL HILL Show, WOPA-radio, Oak Park, IL, during 60s; extensive residency, Sylvio's Lounge, Chicago, IL, 1963-8; Copa Cabana Club, Chicago, 1963-5 (por of a 1963 date rel Chess label); International Jazz Jamboree, Philharmonic Hall, Warsaw, Poland, 1964; app on SHINDIG, ABC-TV, 1965; worked Pepper's, Chicago, 1965; worked Club 47, Cambridge, MA, 1966; Newport Folk Festival, Newport, RI, 1966 (por shown in film FESTIVAL); Big John's, Chicago, 1966; Cafe A-Go-Go, NYC, NY, 1967; Mother Blues, Chicago, 1966-7; Univ of Chicago Folk Festival, Chicago, 1968; app on FOR BLACKS ONLY, local TV, Chicago, c1968; worked Club Key Largo, Chicago, 1968-9; Mariposa Folk Festival, Toronto, Can, 1968; Ash Grove, Los Angeles, CA, 1968; The Scene, NYC, 1968; Cheetah, Chicago, 1968; Ungano's, NYC, 1969; app on local show, WNUR-FM-radio, Evanston, IL, 1969; toured England working club/concert dates, 1969; rec Chess label, London, Eng, 1969; worked Electric Circus, NYC, 1969; toured West Coast working club dates, 1969; worked State Univ of New York, Buffalo, NY, 1969; Ann Arbor Blues Festival, Ann Arbor, MI, 1969-70; Pepper's Lounge, Chicago, IL, 1969-71; Aragon Ballroom, Chicago, 1969; Colonial Tavern, Toronto, Can, 1970-1; Flamingo Lounge, Chicago, 1970-1; The Riviera, Chicago, 1970; Quiet Knight, Chicago, 1970; Sutherland Hotel Lounge, Chicago, 1970; Washington Blues Festival, Howard Univ, Washington, DC, 1970; The Cellar, Chicago, 1970; frequently worked Big Duke's Blue Flame Lounge, Chicago, 1970-3; app in film short WOLF, 1971; worked The Star Dust, Chicago, 1971; Hunter Col, NYC, 1971; Notre Dame Blues Festival, South Bend, IN, 1971; Alice's Revisited, Chicago, 1972 (por rel Chess label); Ann Arbor

Chester Burnett (Howlin' Wolf) *Photo by Doug Fulton. Courtesy* Living Blues *Magazine*

Blues Festival, Ann Arbor, MI, 1972 (por rel Atlantic label); Univ of Waterloo, Waterloo, Can, 1972; Esquire Showbar, Montreal, Can, 1972; Joe's Place, Cambridge, MA, 1973; New Orleans Jazz & Heritage Festival, Municipal Auditorium, New Orleans, LA, 1973; Max's Kansas City, NYC, 1973; Avery Fisher Hall, NYC, 1973; El Mocambo Tavern, Toronto, Can, 1973-5; rec Chess label, Chicago, 1973; worked Grendel's Lair, Philadelphia, PA, 1973; High Chaparral, Chicago, 1974; Pepper's Hideout, Chicago, 1974; Sandy's Concert Club, Boston, MA, 1974; International Blues Festival, Louisville, KY, 1974; Easter Concert, Cocoa Beach, FL, 1974; The Egress, Vancouver, Can, 1974; Urban Blues Festival, Auditorium Theater, Chicago, 1974; rec Chess label, London, Eng, 1974; worked In Concert Club, Montreal, Can, 1974; Richard's Club, Atlanta, GA, 1974; The Stingrey, Chicago, 1974; w BB King, International Amphitheater, Chicago, 1975; Univ of Chicago Circle Campus, Chicago, 1975; New 1815 Club, Chicago, 1975; Eddie Shaw's Place (New 1815 Club), Chicago, 1975; inactive in music through 1975 and entered Veterans Administration Hospital where he was operated on but died of cancer; buried Oakridge Cemetery, Hillside, IL

Personal: Married Willie Brown's sister (during 30s). Second wife was Lillie Handley until his death. 4 children. His half-sister, Mary, married Sonny Boy Williamson (Alex Miller) c1937. Name "Howling Wolf" given him as child for his pranks (or) assumed pseudonym from John (Funny Papa) Smith's hit song of same name during early 1930s

Songs: Ain't Superstitious/CV Wine Blues/California Blues/California Boogie/Call Me the Wolf/Change My Way/Don't Laugh at Me/Forty-Four/Highway 49/How Many More Years?/Howlin' Blues/I Asked for Water/I Better Go Now/I Didn't Know/I Walked from Dallas/I Want to Have a Word with You/I'm the Wolf/I've Been Abused/Just Passing By/The Killing Floor/Look A-Here Baby/Louise/Love Me, Darlin'/ Moanin' at Midnight/Moanin' for My Baby/Moving/ Mr Airplaneman/Mr Highway Man/My Country Sugar Mama/My Friends/My Last Affair/My Mind Is Ramblin'/My Troubles and Me/Natchez Burnin'/Nature/New Crawlin' King Snake/No Place to Go/Oh Red/Ohh Baby Hold Me/Poor Boy/Rocking Daddy/ Saddle My Pony/Smokestack Lightning/So Glad/Stop Using Me/The Sun Is Rising/Tell Me What I've Done/Well That's All Right/When I Laid Down I Was Troubled/Who's Been Talkin'?/Wolf Is at Your Door/Work for Your Money/Worried About My Baby/Worried All the Time

Awards/Honors: Awarded honorary Doctor of Arts degree from Columbia Col, Chicago, IL, 1972

Won Montreux Festival Award for album "Back Door Wolf" (Chess 50045), 1975

Infl by: Blind Lemon Jefferson/Tommy Johnson/Charley Patton/Sonny Boy Williamson (Alex Miller)

Infl to: Woodrow Adams/Butterfield Blues Band/ Cream/John Fogerty/Birmingham Jones/Floyd Jones/Little Wolf/John Littlejohn/Rolling Stones/Sidney Semien/Johnny Shines/The Tail Dragger (James Jones)/Amos Jr Wells/The Yardbirds

Quotes: "One of the major shapers of the electrically amplified modern blues style that has been so dominant an influence on all popular music since his time"—Pete Welding, *Downbeat* magazine, May 6, 1976, p 19

"Howlin' Wolf's voice, dark, brooding, vibrantly rich and immediately recognizable, easily transcended the most banal material"—Amy O'Neal, *Living Blues* magazine, Jan 1976, p 6

"Howlin' Wolf is a true artist in every sense of the word"—(John Broven) Mike Leadbitter, *Nothing But the Blues*, Hanover Books, 1971

References: Blues Unlimited magazine (UK), Mar 1976, pp 4-7

Feel Like Going Home, Peter Guralnick, Outerbridge & Dienstfrey, 1971

Downbeat magazine, May 6, 1976, pp 19-20

BURNS, *"Little"* **EDDIE** *"Guitar"*
(*aka:* Big Ed/Slim Pickens/Swing Brother)
Born: Feb 8, 1928, Belzoni (Humphreys Co), MS
Inst: Guitar/Harmonica

Father was a singing musician who worked medicine/minstrel shows; one of 3 children; raised by grandparents in Webb, MS; taught self harmonica and made first guitar from broom handle as youth; moved to Dublin, MS, to work streets/stores, early 40s; moved to Clarksdale, MS, to work as sideman w Sonny Boy Williamson (Alex Miller)/Pinetop Perkins at local gigs in area, 1943-7; moved to Waterloo, IA, to work outside music with frequent gigs w John T Smith at houseparties/streets/dances at Black Elks Club, 1947; moved to Detroit, MI, to form The Friendly Brothers gospel group working local churches from 1948; rec Holiday label, Detroit, 1948; rec w John Lee Hooker, Sensation label, Detroit, 1949; frequently toured with various blues groups into 50s; sat-in w John Lee Hooker, Monte Carlo Club/Harlem

Photo by Norbert Hess

Inn, Detroit, c1951; formed own band to frequently work Harlem Inn, Detroit, c1951-8; rec DeLuxe label, Detroit, 1952; frequently worked Tavern Lounge, Detroit, c1952-6; frequently worked outside music, Detroit, from c1953; rec Modern/Checker labels, Detroit, 1954; worked Club Plantation, Detroit, c1956; Bank Bar, Detroit, c1956-7; rec JVB label, Detroit, 1957; w Little Sonny Willis working Club Carribe, Detroit, 1958-61; w Louisiana Red, Harlem Inn, Detroit, late 50s; rec Harvey label, Detroit, 1961; worked extensively as sideman in various local bands in Detroit area, 1962 through mid-60s; rec Von label, Detroit, c1965; continued outside music work, Detroit, through 60s; worked Detroit Blues Festival, Detroit, 1970; toured club/concert/radio/TV dates through England/Europe, 1972; rec Big Bear/Action/Transatlantic labels, London, Eng, 1972; worked college circuit across US, 1972; Univ of North Carolina, Chapel Hill, NC, 1973 (por rel Flyright label); Ann Arbor Blues Festival, Ann Arbor, MI, 1973; Highland Park Community College, Detroit, 1974; Triangle Bar, Minneapolis, MN, 1974; worked club/concert dates through England, 1974; toured w American Blues Legends 75 working concert dates through England/Europe, 1975; worked 100 Club, London, Eng, 1975 (por rel Big Bear label); BJ's Buffeteria, Bay City, MI, 1977; Detroit Blues Festival, Detroit, 1977

Personal: Married. Has 6 children

Songs: Biscuit Bakin' Mama/Bull Head, Go Ahead Angie/Bury Me Back in the USA/Detroit Black Bottom/Do It If You Wanna/Every Jug Stands on Its Own Bottom/Hard Hearted Woman/Hello Miss Jessie Lee/I Call It Love/I Wanna Trade with You/I've Got a Lot of Respect/(Don't Be) Messing with My Bread/Mississippi County Farm/Mean and Evil (Baby)/Orange Driver/Pee Pa Pobble/She's in LA/The Thing to Do/Toni Louise/You Say That You're Leaving/Wig Wearing Woman

Infl by: Tommy McClennan/John Lee "Sonny Boy" Williamson/Sonny Boy Williamson (Alex Miller)

Quote: "A man who can cope with everything from straight, country blues to contemporary sounds with practiced ease"—Mike Leadbitter, Action album 100

References: Blues Unlimited magazine (UK), Apr 1972, pp 5-8

Blues World magazine (UK), Spring 1972, p 14

Jazz & Blues magazine (UK), Jan 1972, p 11

BURRIS, JOHNNY CHARLES *'JC'*
Born: Mar 15, 1928, Kings Mountain (Cleveland Co) NC
Died: May 16, 1988, Kings Mountain, NC
Inst.: Bones/Harmonica

Father Clarence Burris Sr; mother Ludava Terrell; entertained by his uncle, Sonny Terry, as child; moved to Bessemer City, NC, after death of mother to work local farms from 1937-48; moved to NYC, NY, to work outside music from 1949; learned harmonica from Sonny Terry and frequently worked streets/coffeehouses/houseparties in NYC area, 1953-60; worked small club dates, Bronx, NY, 1954; rec acc to Sonny Terry, Folkways label, NYC, 1958; rec w Sonny Terry (as "Sonny & Jaycee"), Ember label, NYC, 1958; rec acc to Sticks McGhee, Herald label, NYC, 1960; moved to West Coast to work outside music with occasional street work with local musicians, Los Angeles, CA, 1960-1; frequently worked The Troubador and other folk clubs, Los Angeles, c1961; moved to San Francisco, CA, to frequently work local gigs in North Beach section from 1961; worked Sugar Hill, San Francisco, CA, 1961; Coffee

J C Burris *Photo © Jon Sievert, 1978. Courtesy* Living Blues *Magazine*

& Confusion Coffeehouse, San Francisco, 1964; Spaghetti Factory, San Francisco, c1965; Blue Mirror, San Francisco, c1965; Matrix, San Francisco, c1966; The Cabale, Berkeley, CA, c1966; Mandrakes, Berkeley, c1966; inactive due to illness, 1966-73; frequently worked Coffee Gallery, San Francisco, 1974-5; app on BLUES BY THE BAY, KPOO-FM-radio, San Francisco, 1975; worked Berkeley Blues Festival, Berkeley, CA, 1975; Minnie's Can-Do Club, San Francisco, 1975; frequently sat in with various local blues bands in area, San Francisco, from 1975; worked The Boardinghouse, San Francisco, 1975; Great American Music Hall, San Francisco, 1975-6; McLaren Park Amphitheater, San Francisco, 1975; app on OPEN STUDIO, local TV, San Francisco, 1975; app on A M SAN FRANCISCO, KGED-TV, San Francisco, 1975; worked The Exploratorium, San Francisco, 1975; The Family Light School of Music Blues Festival, Sausalito, CA, 1975; Inn of the Beginning, Cotati, CA, 1975; Univ of California, Santa Cruz, CA, 1975; The Savoy Club, San Francisco, 1975-6; North East Community Center, San Francisco, CA, 1975 (por rel Arhoolie label); West Dakota Club, Berkeley, CA, 1975 (por rel Arhoolie label); City Col, San Francisco, 1976; frequently worked Green Earth Cafe, San Francisco, 1976-7; app in film LEADBELLY, 1976; worked American River Col, Sacramento, CA, 1976; app in film RIVERBOAT 1988, 1976; app in THE SAN FRANCISCO BLUES, PBS-TV, c1976; app on BLUES BY THE BAY, KPFA-FM-radio, Berkeley, CA, 1976-7; worked Keystone, Berkeley, 1977; app on EVENING SHOW, KPIX-TV, San Francisco, 1977; Santa Rosa Folk Festival, Santa Rosa, CA, 1977; Coffee Gallery, San Francisco, 1977; worked clubs/festivals/radio shows/children shows in San Francisco area into 80s; toured Europe w San Francisco Blues Festival, 1980 (por rel Paris Album label); suffered fatal heart attack; buried Adams Chapel Cemetery, Kings Mountain, NC

Songs: Bones Blues/Highway Blues/Hold Me Tight/Inflation Blues/Loneliness/Mr Jack's Dance/One of These Mornings/River of Life/She Can't Be Right Always Doin' Wrong/You Got to Roam/You Keep Doggin' Me

Infl by: Blind Boy Fuller/Sonny Terry

Quote: ". . . he is among the most unique of the country blues performers around today"—Tom Mazzolini, Arhoolie album 1075 (1975)

References: Arhoolie album 1075
Crazy Music magazine (Australia), Jan 1976, pp 4-5

BURSE, CHARLIE *"Uke"*
(*aka:* Ukelele Kid)

Courtesy Sing Out *Magazine*

Born: Aug 25, 1901, Decatur (Morgan Co), AL
Died: Dec 20, 1965, Memphis, TN
Inst: Banjo/Guitar/Mandolin

Father was Robert Burse; mother was Emma Hill; one of about 15 children; frequently played music as child with younger brother Robert on a banjo made from tin can; worked outside music on farm in area through 20s; moved to Memphis, TN, 1928; teamed w Will Shade to work w Memphis Jug Band in local streets/bars/parks (with frequent tours through South), Memphis, from 1928; rec w Memphis Jug Band, Victor label, Memphis, 1928-30; frequently worked outside music in Memphis into 30s; frequently teamed w Will Shade working streets, Memphis, early 30s; rec duo w Will Shade, Champion label, Richmond, IN, 1932; rec w Memphis Jug Band, OKeh label, Chicago, 1934; rec w Robert Burse, OKeh label, Chicago, 1934; rec w own Memphis Mudcats, Vocalion label, Memphis, 1939; worked mostly outside music, Memphis, from c1943 through 60s; often teamed w Will Shade to work local office buildings for tips, Memphis, through 50s; rec w Will Shade, Folkways label, Memphis, 1956; app w Will Shade on tribute to WC Handy, local TV show, Memphis, 1958; mostly inactive into 60s; rec w Will Shade, Rounder label, Memphis, 1963; died at home of heart disease; buried Rose Hill Cemetery, Memphis, TN

Personal: Married Birdie ———. His brother Robert Burse was musician

Songs: Brand New Day Blues/Too Much Beef

BUTLER, GEORGE *"Wild Child"*

Courtesy Living Blues *Magazine*

Born: Oct 1, 1936, Autaugaville (Autauga Co), AL
Inst: Guitar/Harmonica

Mother was Bette Mae ———; family was sharecroppers; one of 12 children; born/raised on farm; interested in music early, first on guitar but changing to harmonica at about 6 years of age; moved to Montgomery, AL, early 40s working local breakdowns/balls in area to mid-40s; moved to Chicago, IL, 1945, then left home to hobo across US working outside music into 50s; returned to Montgomery, AL, to form trio working local juke joints in area from 1956; worked occasional gigs w Sonny Boy Williamson (Alex Miller), Detroit, MI, 1957; frequently worked lounges in Houston, TX, early 60s; rec Sharp label, Montgomery, AL, 1964; rec Jewel label, Shreveport, LA, 1965; worked small clubs/bars in Chicago, IL, area, 1965; app w Jr Wells Band on local TV shows, Chicago, 1966; rec Jewel label, Chicago, 1967; worked local gigs w Lightnin' Hopkins, Houston, TX, area, 1967; app in film THE BLUES ACCORDIN' TO LIGHTNIN' HOPKINS, 1968; rec Mercury label, Chicago, c1968; frequently worked w Sam Lay's Band in local dates, Chicago, late 60s into mid-70s; worked Chicago Blues Festival, Chicago, 1969; Memphis Blues Festival, Memphis, TN, 1969; Court Tavern, New Orleans, LA, 1969; Five Stages, Chicago, 1970; Coq D'or, Toronto, Can, 1971; Toronto Island Festival, Toronto Island, Can, 1974; Theresa's, Chicago, 1974; The Attic, Chicago, 1974; Minstrel's, Chicago, 1974; rec Roots label, Chicago (?), 1976

Personal: Name "Wild Child" given him by mother

Songs: Everybody Got a Mojo/Funky Butt Lover/Gravy Child/Love Like a Butterfly/Love You from Now On/My Baby Got Another Man/My 40 Year Old Woman/None of Nothing/Open Up Baby

Infl by: Lightnin' Hopkins/Sonny Boy Williamson (Alex Miller)

Quote: "A tough, down-home bluesman"—Mike Leadbitter, Carnival album 2941

References: Blues Unlimited magazine (UK), Jun 1973, p 16
Blues Unlimited, Sep 1978, pp 27-30

BUTTERFIELD, PAUL VAUGHN
Born: Dec 17, 1942, Chicago (Cook Co), IL
Died: May 4, 1987, North Hollywood, CA
Inst: Flute/Guitar/Harmonica/Piano

Father was Edwin Butterfield; mother was Elizabeth O'Callahan; sang in church choir as youth while teaching self harmonica; frequently sat-in w Muddy Waters group in local gigs, Chicago, from 1958; attended Univ of Chicago, Chicago, learning classical flute, c1960; worked Blue Flame Club/Pepper's Lounge/1015 Club/others, Chicago, early to mid-60s; worked Big John's Club, Chicago, 1963 (por rel Red Lightning label); formed own Butterfield Blues Band and app local TV shows/clubs/lounges, Chicago, from c1964; worked Sylvio's Lounge, Chicago, 1964; Big John's Club, Chicago, 1964-6; Turks Club, Chicago, 1964; The Village Gate, NYC, 1965; Cafe A-Go-Go, NYC, 1965; Mooncusser, Martha's Vineyard, MA, 1965; Club 47, Cambridge, MA, 1965; The Unicorn, Boston, MA, 1965; Town Hall, NYC, 1965; rec w own band, Elektra label, Chicago, IL, 1965-8; worked w own Butterfield Blues Band, Newport Folk Festival, Newport, RI, 1965 (por shown in film FESTIVAL); Whiskey A-Go-Go, Los Angeles, CA, 1965-6; Chessmate, Detroit, MI, 1966; Rheingold Central Park Music Festival, NYC, NY, 1966-8; Monterey Jazz Festival, Monterey, CA, 1966; International Pop Festival, Monterey, 1967; New Penelope, Montreal, Can, 1967; La Cave, Cleveland, OH, 1967; Cheetah, Chicago, IL, 1968; The Eagles, Seattle, WA, 1968; Civic Auditorium, Santa Monica, CA, 1968; app in film YOU ARE WHAT YOU EAT, 1968; worked

Paul Butterfield
Photo by Julie Snow

Fillmore East, NYC, 1968-70; Carnegie Hall, NYC, 1968; Cafe A-Go-Go, NYC, 1968; Miami Pop Festival, Miami, FL, 1968; Shrine Exposition Hall, Los Angeles, CA, 1968; Kinetic Playground, Chicago, IL, 1969; The Eagles, Seattle, WA, 1969; toured Denmark working concert dates, 1969; worked Fillmore West, San Francisco, CA, 1969; Woodstock Music & Art Fair, Bethel, NY, 1969 (por rel Cotillion label); rec w Muddy Waters, Chess label, Chicago, 1969; worked w Muddy Waters, Super Cosmic Joy-Scout Jamboree, Auditorium Theater, Chicago, 1969 (por rel Chess label); The Pavilion, NYC, NY, 1969; w Janis Joplin, Madison Square Garden, NYC, 1969; Ravinia Park, Chicago, 1969; Civic Center, Baltimore, MD, 1969; Auditorium Theater, Chicago, 1970; Lennie's, Boston, MA, 1970; Washington Univ, St Louis, MO, 1970; Festival for Peace, Shea Stadium, NYC, 1970; Midway Stadium, St Paul, MN, 1971; Sunset Series Concert, Boston, MA, 1972; Tulagi's, Boulder, CO, 1973; Civic Center, Santa Monica, CA, 1973; rec ST for film STEELYARD BLUES, 1973; worked Cowtown Ballroom, Kansas City, MO, 1973; rec Asylum label, Chicago (?), 1973; formed own Better Days group working Capitol Theater, Passaic, NJ, 1973; rec w Better Days group, Warner Brothers-Bearsville label, Chicago, c1974-5; app on BONNIE RAITT & PAUL BUTTERFIELD Show, PBS-TV, 1974; app on MIDNIGHT SPECIAL, NBC-TV, 1974; worked Winterland Auditorium, San Francisco, CA, 1976 (por in film THE LAST WALTZ, 1978/por rel Warner Bros label); Jed's Inn, New Orleans, LA, 1976; app on SATURDAY NIGHT, NBC-TV, 1977; app w Foghat group, The Palladium, NYC, 1977 (por on DON KIRSHNER'S ROCK CONCERT, NBC-TV, 1978); New Orleans Jazz & Heritage Festival, New Orleans, LA, 1979; formed own Danko-Butterfield Band (w bassist Rick Danko) to work clubs/concerts in NYC area through 80s; app ROCK 'N' ROLL TONIGHT, NBC-TV, 1983; died at home of drug/alcohol OD; body cremated

Songs: In My Own Dream/Little Piece of Dying/You Can Run But You Can't Hide

Infl by: Howlin' Wolf/Little Walter/Muddy Waters/ Louis Myers/Jr Wells/Sonny Boy Williamson (Alex Miller)

Quotes: "One of the best of the white American blues performers"—Robert Shelton, *New York Times* newspaper, Mar 11, 1965

"The best harmonica player today, white or black"—Mojo Buford, *Blues Unlimited* magazine (UK), Dec 1970, p 14

"His blues collage is pasted together out of black New York jazz of the early sixties, blue Memphis soul of the late sixties, and moire-screen orientalisms from Frisco '67"—Albert Goldman, *Freakshow*, Atheneum, 1971

Reference: The Illustrated Encyclopedia of Rock, Nick Logan/Bob Woffinden, Hamlyn Publishing Group, 1976

BYRD, ROY *"Bald Head"/"Fess"*
(*aka:* Robert Boyd/Little Loving Henry/Professor Longhair)
Born: Dec 19, 1918, Bogalusa (Washington Parish), LA
Died: Jan 30, 1980, New Orleans, LA
Inst: Drums/Guitar/Piano

Father, James Lucius Byrd, and mother, Ella Mae ———, were musicians; born Henry Roeland Byrd; one of at least 2 children; parents separated and raised in New Orleans, LA, from 2 months of age; learned music basics from mother as child; briefly attended Arthur P Williams elementary school but dropped out early to work outside music through 20s; worked briefly as a kick (stuntman) in CJK Medicine Show, New Orleans, LA, c1926; made own instruments and worked streets as entertainer/singer/dancer for tips, New Orleans, early 30s; formed small group working dancing act at Cotton Club/Porters Inn/The New York Inn/Palace Theater/Lincoln Theater/others, New Orleans, into 30s; worked as guitarist with occasional piano work at local parties from mid-30s; worked w Jack Dupree, Cotton Club, New Orleans, c1937; worked outside music in Civilian Conservation Corps (CCC) travelling through Louisiana, 1937; frequently worked outside music (often as professional gambler), New Orleans, 1937-42; served in US Army, 1942-3; worked mostly outside music, New Orleans, from 1943; frequent gigs at Pepper Pot, Gretna, LA, c1947-9; frequent work w Mid-Drifs group in local club dates, New Orleans, late 40s; formed own Professor Longhair and the Four Hairs combo working Caldonia Inn, New Orleans, 1949; renamed group Professor Longhair and his Shuffling Hungarians and rec Star Talent label, New Orleans, 1949; rec w own Blues Jumpers, Mercury label, New Orleans, 1949; rec Atlantic label, New Orleans, c1949; toured w Dave Bartholomew Band working club dates through Midwest/West Coast, 1949; continued frequent outside music work with occasional club work in New Orleans, LA, area through 50s into 60s; rec Federal label, New Orleans, 1951; rec Wasco label, New Orleans, c1952; rec Atlantic label, New Orleans, 1953; rec Ebb label, New Orleans, 1957; rec Ron label, New Orleans, 1958; rec Rip label, New Orleans, 1962; rec Watch label, New Orleans, 1963-4; frequently worked First Bass Club, New Orleans, 1970; rec demos w Snooks Eaglin, Baton Rouge, LA, 1971; worked w Original Four Hairs Combo, New Orleans Jazz & Heritage Fair, New Orleans, 1971-4; app on DR JOHN Show, PBS-TV, 1971; worked Festival of American Folklife, Washington, DC, 1971; worked local rock/jazz clubs, New Orleans, 1972; Nutcracker Lounge, New Orleans, 1972; Tulane Univ, New Orleans, 1973; Newport Jazz Festival, NYC, 1973; Mason's Lounge, New Orleans, 1973; The Temple Hall, New Orleans, 1973; The Talisman, New Orleans, 1973; toured w Night in New Orleans package show working concert dates through Europe, 1973; worked Montreux Jazz Festival, Montreux, Switzerland, 1973; w own trio at Kenny's Castaways, NYC, 1973; app on DR JOHN'S NEW ORLEANS SWAMP Show, PBS-TV, 1974; worked Liberty Hall, Houston, TX, 1974; rec w Gatemouth Brown, Blue Star label, Bogalusa, LA, 1974; worked Jed's University Inn, New Orleans, 1974-6; app on BLUES PIANO ORGY, WLDC-radio, New Orleans, 1975; worked New Orleans Jazz & Heritage Festival, New Orleans, 1975-9 (por 1976 concert rel Island label); *SS Queen Mary*, Long Beach, CA, 1975 (por rel Harvest label); Philadelphia Folk Festival, Schwenksville, PA, 1975; toured Europe working concert dates, 1975; worked Univ of Chicago, Chiçago, 1976; owned/worked with own Blues Scholars Band, Tipitina Club, New Orleans from 1977; worked Monterey Jazz Festival, Monterey, CA, 1977; Boarding Housé Club, San Francisco, CA, 1977; toured England/Europe working concert dates, 1977-8; rec JSP label, London, Eng, 1978; app in film ALWAYS FOR PLEASURE, 1978; toured club dates/concerts in US/Canada 1979; rec Alligator label, New Orleans, 1979; app in PIANO PLAYERS RARELY EVER PLAY TOGETHER, 1980 (released for PBS-TV, 1984; mostly inactive during 1980s; died in sleep of respiratory disease; buried Mt Olivet Cemetery, New Orleans

Songs: Bald Head/Cry Pretty Baby/Doctor Professor Longhair/Doin' It/Go to the Mardi Gras/Gone So

Roy Byrd (Professor Longhair) *Photo by Norbert Hess. Courtesy* Living Blues *Magazine*

Long/Hadicol Bounce/Hey Now Baby/How Long Has That Train Been Gone?/If I Only Knew/In the Night/Mardi Gras in New Orleans/Mean Ol' World/Meet Me Tomorrow Night/No Buts, No Maybes/Tipitina/Walk Your Blues Away/Who's Been Fooling You?/Willie Mae

Infl by: Robert Bertrand/Kid Stormy Weather/Sullivan Rock/Jimmy Yancey/Jack Dupree

Infl to: James Booker/Ernie K-Doe/Fats Domino/Dr John (Mac Rebennack)/Clarence "Frogman" Henry/Jessie Hill/Earl King/Big Boy Myles/Huey Smith/Allen Toussaint

Quotes: "Professor Longhair was an eccentric original who mixed Louisiana's Latin, blues and jazz elements into an unmistakably personal piano style."—Noah Shapiro, *Sing Out,* Jan-Feb, 1980

"Roy Byrd . . . has long been a staple of the rich and unique New Orleans scene"—Rich Mangelsdorff, *Living Blues* magazine, Summer 1972, p 31

References: Living Blues magazine, Mar 1976, pp 17-29

Downbeat magazine, Mar 28, 1974, pp 18-19

Atlantic album 7225

C

CADILLAC JAKE
(see Harris, James D)

CAGE, JAMES *"Butch"*
Born: Mar 16, 1894, Hamburg (Franklin Co), MS
Died: 1975, Zachary, LA (unconfirmed)
Inst: Fiddle/Fife/Guitar

Mother was songster and dancer; one of 13 children; born/raised on farm outside Hamburg, MS; worked outside music on local farms from childhood; interested in music early learning fife then fiddle from local musicians, 1911; frequently worked local dances/church affairs/picnics/quilting parties in area to 1919; left home to hobo through South working outside music in Meadville, MS/Slaughter, LA/Linsay, LA/Natchez, MS/Fayette, MS/Port Gibson, MS/Cedars, MS, 1919-27; settled in Zachary, LA, to work outside music with occasional local parties/fish fries from 1927; rec w Willie B Thomas, Folk-Lyric label, Zachary, LA, 1959-60; worked Newport Folk Festival, Newport, RI, 1959-61 (por 1959 concert rel Folkways label/por 1960 concert in USIA film short series JAZZ-USA [Nos 20, 22]); rec Decca/Arhoolie labels, Zachary, LA, 1960; app w Willie B Thomas/Victoria Spivey on LYRICS AND LEGENDS (ep: The Blues), WNET-TV, NYC (syndicated), 1963; worked occasional parties in Zachary, LA, area through 60s into 70s; rec ST for UK film BLUES LIKE SHOWERS OF RAIN, 1970; reportedly died at home; clip shown in PEOPLE'S MUSIC—AND ALL THAT JAZZ, BBC-2-TV, London, Eng, 1976

Personal: Married 1913. 2 children. Married Rosie ——— (1919-). Name "Butch" was childhood pet name given him by mother

Infl by: Frank Felters/"Ole Man" Carol Williams

Quote: "A great representative of the now virtually extinct 19th century Negro fiddle tradition"—Dr Harry Oster, Arhoolie album 2018

CAIN, PERRY
(aka: Daddy Deep Throat)
Born: 1929, New Waverly (Walker Co), TX
Inst: Guitar

Moved to Houston, TX, c1945 and took some guitar lessons from Melvyn Martin; worked Casba Bar and other local clubs/bars, Houston, late 40s; rec w own band, Gold Star label, Houston, 1948; frequently worked local clubs w Ben Turner/Buster Pickens, Houston area, late 40s; rec Freedom label, Houston, 1949; frequently worked local clubs as singer/MC, Houston area, into 50s; rec w Henry Hayes, Sittin' In With label, Houston, 1950; worked as DJ (as "Daddy Deep Throat"), KCOH-radio, Houston, through 50s/60s; mostly inactive in music thereafter

Reference: Blues Unlimited magazine (UK), Feb 1968, p 13

CALHOUN, MR
(see Vincent, Monroe)

CALICOTT, JOE
(see Callicott, Joe)

CALLICOTT, *"Mississippi"* **JOE**
(aka: Joe Calicott/Joe Callicutt)
Born: Oct 11, 1900, Nesbit (De Sota Co), MS
Died: 1969, MS (unconfirmed)
Inst: Guitar

Born and raised on farm; began playing guitar at about 15 years of age; worked mostly outside music as youth with frequent work w Garfield Akers at local parties/picnics in area through teens; toured in small medicine shows through Mississippi c1918; frequently worked w Frank Stokes in joints/bars, Memphis, TN, into 20s; returned to Nesbit, MS, to work mostly outside music as farmer with frequent work w Garfield Akers at local country suppers/Saturday-night fish fries/parties, mid-20s into 50s; rec Brunswick label, Memphis, 1930; retired to work outside music from 1959; worked Memphis Folk Blues Festival, Memphis, 1967-8 (por of 1968 concert rel Sire-Blue Horizon label); rec Revival label, Memphis, 1967; worked benefit for Museum of the City of New York, NYC, NY, 1968

Personal: Married

Songs: Great Long Ways from Home/Hoist Your Window and Let Your Curtain Down/Joe's Troubled Blues/On My Last Go Round/Poor Boy Blues

Infl by: Frank Stokes

Quotes: "The simplicity of song, guitar and vocal work gives Joe an identity all his own . . ."—Mike Vernon, Sire album 97003

"... a singer and musician who was quite obviously of no mean quality . . ."—Paul Oliver, *Jazz & Blues* magazine (UK), May 1971, p 18

Reference: Blue Horizon album 7-63227

CALLICUTT, JOE
(see Callicott, Joe)

CAMPBELL, *"Blind"* JAMES
Born: Sept 17, 1906, Nashville (Davidson Co), TN
Inst: Guitar

Began playing guitar at age of 13; worked mostly outside music until he lost eyesight in factory accident, 1936; formed own Nashville Washboard Band working local roadhouses/streets/parties/dances/social functions in Nashville, TN, area, 1936 into 60s; app in film HILLBILLY MUSIC, 1962; rec Arhoolie label, Nashville, 1962-3; worked Vanderbilt Univ, Nashville, early 60s; whereabouts unknown thereafter

Reference: Arhoolie album F-1015

CAMPBELL, MILTON
(aka: Little Milton)
Born: Sept 7, 1934, Inverness (Sunflower Co), MS
Inst: Guitar

Father was Milton Campbell Sr; mother Pearl Tardin; born James Milton Campbell; one of 7 children raised on farm between Greenville/Leland, MS; interested in music early and was singing in local church choir and gospel groups as child; taught self guitar at 12 years of age; worked local parties/picnics in area through 40s; toured w Eddie Kusick Band working jukes through area, 1950-2; app w Willie Nix on KWEM-radio, West Memphis, AR, early 50s; app w Willie Love group, WGVM-radio, Greenville, MS, early 50s; formed own group working local jukes, Memphis, TN, from c1951; rec w Ike Turner and the Playmates of Rhythm, Sun label, Memphis, 1953-4; worked Fireworks Station, E St Louis, IL, 1955; rec Meteor label, Memphis, 1957; worked Regal Theater, Chicago, IL, c1957; rec Bobbin label, E St Louis, IL, 1958, and St Louis, MO, 1958-9; worked frequently in own band in local clubs, E St Louis, IL, through 50s; rec Checker label, Chicago, 1961-9; toured w own band and The Miltonettes working club dates in area through 60s; worked Northside Armory, Indianapolis, IN, 1965; Apollo Theater, NYC, NY, 1966; Regal Theater, Chicago, IL, 1968; Operation Breadbasket Blues Festival, Chicago, 1969; Chicago Blues Festival, Chicago, 1969; app on SOUL, PBS-TV, 1970; worked Burning Spear, Chicago, 1970; formed Camil Productions (a production/booking agency), early 70s; worked w own band at Wattstax 72 Concert, Memorial Coliseum, Los Angeles, CA, 1972 (por shown in film WATTSTAX/por rel Stax label); worked Club Sue-B-Rue, Chicago, 1972; Willy's Inn, Chicago, 1972; Starlight Club, Seffner, FL, 1972-4; Medgar Evers Memorial Festival, Jackson, MS, 1973; Montreux Jazz Festival, Montreux, Switzerland, 1973; Alexandria Lounge, Miami, FL, 1974; High Chaparral, Chicago, 1974-5; Keymen's Club, Chicago, 1974; Continental Showcase, Houston, TX, 1974; Tenampa Ballroom, Chicago, 1974; Club Harlem, Winstonville, MS, 1974; The Coliseum, Jackson, MS, 1974; The International Amphitheater, Chicago, 1975-6; The Stingrey, Chicago, 1975-7; frequently toured club dates through South, 1976; worked Burning Spear, Chicago, 1977

Personal: Briefly married c1948. Not to be confused with "Little" Milton Anderson, musician

Songs: Ain't No Big Deal on You/Beggin' My Baby/Believe in Me/Can't Hold Back the Tears/I Love My Baby/If Crying Would Help Me/If You Love Me/Life Is Like That/Lonesome for My Baby/Rode That Train All Night Long/Runnin' Wild Blues/Somebody Told Me

Infl by: Bobby Bland/Roy Brown/Louis Jordan/BB

Milton Campbell (Little Milton) *Courtesy* Living Blues *Magazine*

King/Willie Love/Joe Turner/Aaron "T-Bone" Walker/Sonny Boy Williamson (Alex Miller)

Infl to: Jimmy Dawkins

Quotes: ". . . talented singer, composer and guitarist . . ."—Peter Shertser, Red Lightnin' album 0011

"An important figure in contemporary black music"—Lynn Summers/Bob Scheir, *Living Blues* magazine, Autumn 1974, p 17

Reference: Living Blues magazine, Autumn 1974, pp 17-24

CANNON, GUS

(aka: Banjo Joe)

Courtesy BMI Archives

Born: Sept 12, 1885, Red Banks (Marshall Co), MS
Died: Oct 15, 1979, Memphis, TN
Inst: Banjo/Fiddle/Guitar/Jug/Kazoo/Piano

Father was John Cannon, a former slave, mother was Ellen ———, both sharecroppers; born on Henderson Newell's Plantation; one of 9 children; worked on farm from childhood; first instrument was a homemade banjo (from a frying pan and racoon skin) and worked local parties in area, 1895-8; ran away from home 1898 to work outside music in Clarksdale, MS, with frequent entertaining at levee camps/plantations/railroad camps/riverboats/sawmills through Delta area, into 1900s; reportedly rec banjo solos, Victor (cylinder) or Columbia (disc) labels, Belzoni, MS, early 1900s; worked outside music on Snooks Dillehunt's Plantation, Ashport, TN, from 1908; formed own jug band trio working parties/suppers/breakdowns in area, 1908-13; teamed w Noah Lewis and frequently worked together in Henning, TN, and elsewhere from c1910; worked small dives/barrelhouses in Memphis, TN, 1910; worked w Jim Jackson in jukes, Hernando, MS, c1912; continued outside music work while frequently working country dances through Arkansas/Illinois/Tennessee c1913-14; toured w Dr Stokey Medicine Show working as a banjo player/juggler/comedian (billed as "Banjo Joe") through Arkansas/Missouri/Illinois, 1914-15; toured w Dr WB Miller Medicine Show working through Midwest, 1916-17; worked outside music as off-season farmer, Ripley, TN, from 1916; frequently worked w Noah Lewis at local parties/streets, Ripley, TN, into 20s; toured w Dr Benson Medicine Show through southeastern US, 1918-27; frequently worked outside music in Memphis, TN, c1918 into 20s; toured w Dr C Hankenson's Medicine Show through North Carolina/Virginia, early 20s; brief tour w Dr Willie Lewis' Medicine Show during 1920s; formed own Jug Stompers to tour (sometimes solo) Arkansas/Mississippi and through South working parties/dances/picnics/suppers/streets, late 20s into 40s; frequently worked solo at Church's Park (WC Handy Park) for tips, Memphis, TN, late 20s into 40s; rec Paramount label, Chicago, IL, 1927; rec Victor label, Memphis, 1928-30; rec w Hosea Woods (as "Cannon and Woods, The Beale Street Boys"), Brunswick label, Chicago, 1929; toured w Dr Streak's Medicine Show working Alabama and Gulf Coast areas, 1929; app in film HALLELUJAH!, 1929; frequently worked outside music in Memphis, TN, through 1930s into 1970s with occasional street singing for tips; worked Cotton Carnival, Peabody Hotel, Memphis, during 1940s; rec Folkways label, Memphis, 1956; app in documentary film THE BLUES, 1963; rec Stax label, Memphis, 1963; worked Old Town North, Chicago, IL, 1963; worked w Furry Lewis/Willie Borum, New York Univ and others, NYC, NY, 1963; Holiday Inn, Memphis, c1965; worked excursion steamer *Memphis Queen* late 60s; rec w Furry Lewis/Bukka White, Adelphi label, Memphis, TN, 1969; mostly inactive in music in Memphis into 70s; app in THE DEVIL'S MUSIC—A HISTORY OF THE BLUES (ep: Work and Mother Wit), BBC-1-TV, Eng, 1976; app on GOOD MORNIN' BLUES, PBS-TV, 1978; died of heart disease; buried Greenview Memorial Cemetery, Nesbitt, MS

Personal: Married at least 3 times

Billing: Banjo Joe

Songs: Lela/Mule Gallop/Walk Right In

Infl by: Bud Jackson/Saul Russell

Quotes: "His beginning parallels the beginnings of the blues itself and his roots dip deeply into this pre-blues body of Negro folk music . . ."—Steve LaVere, Adelphi album AD-1009-S

"The greatest of the Memphis jug bands was led by 'Banjo Joe'—Gus Cannon"—Paul Oliver, *The Story of the Blues*, Chilton Book Company, 1969

Reference: Sweet as the Showers of Rain, Samuel B Charters, Oak Publishers, 1977

CAROLINA SLIM
(see Harris, Edward)

CARR, GUNTER LEE
(see Gant, Cecil)

CARR, LEROY
(*aka:* Blues Johnson)

Courtesy Frank Driggs Collection

Born: Mar 27, 1905, Nashville (Davidson Co), TN
Died: Apr 29, 1935, Indianapolis, IN
Inst: Piano

Father was John Carr; mother was Katie Dozier; moved to Louisville, KY, as child then to Indianapolis, IN, to attend local public schools from 1912; taught self piano and dropped out of school to tour with a travelling circus as teenager; served in US Army c1920; acc many singers in various Midwest dance halls/houseparties/dives, into 20s; frequently worked joints in Covington, KY, area during mid-20s; teamed w Scrapper Blackwell, 1928; frequently toured/rec w Scrapper Blackwell through 20s into 30s; rec Vocalion label, Indianapolis, IN, 1928; rec Vocalion label, Chicago, IL, 1928-31; worked extensively w Scrapper Blackwell in local clubs/theaters, St Louis, MO, area, early 30s; worked Booker T Washington Theater, St Louis, c1931; Jazzland Club, St Louis, c1932; Barrelhouse, Burdette, MS, c1932; rec Vocalion label, NYC, NY, 1932; worked clubs/dives/parties in Indianapolis, IN, early 30s; worked Cotton Club, Indianapolis, c1933; rec Vocalion label, NYC/St Louis, 1934; rec Vocalion label, Chicago, 1935; died of nephritis due to acute alcoholism; buried Floral Park, Indianapolis, IN

Personal: Married (1922-c1930), 1 daughter

Songs: Alki Blues/Baby Come Back to Me/Big Four Blues/Blue 'n' Whistling/Blues Before Sunrise/Bobo Stomp/Carried Water for the Elephant/Corn Likker Blues/E Blues/Florida Bound Blues/How Long Blues/In the Evening When the Sun Goes Down/Leaving You Blues/Love Hides All Faults/Mean Mistreater Mama/Midnight Hour Blues/Naptown Blues/No Good Woman Blues/Prison Bound Blues/Rocks in My Bed/Sally-In-The-Alley Blues/Shady Lane Blues/Six Cold Feet in the Ground/Soft Blues/Take a Walk Around the Corner (Courtroom Blues)/That's All Right for You/The Truth About the Thing/Truthful Blues/Wrong Man Blues/You Got to Reap What You Sow

Infl by: Ollie Akins

Infl to: Little Eddie Boyd/Bumble Bee Slim/Walter Davis/KC Douglas/Jack Dupree/Pete Franklin/Bill Gaither/Cecil Gant/Carol Leigh/Pinetop Perkins/Jimmy Rushing/Otis Spann/Eddie Vinson/Aaron "T-Bone" Walker/Peetie Wheatstraw

Quotes: "It seems that the popularity and importance of Leroy Carr rests on three main points: his talent as a vocalist, the piano-guitar synthesis that he and Scrapper virtually created and the material that he had to work with"—Kip Lornell, Biograph album BLP-C9

"He was exceptionally varied in his choice of songs and poetic in his blues . . ."—Paul Oliver, *Jazz Journal* magazine (UK), Jul 1973, p 33

"In the late 1920s, Leroy Carr almost completely changed the style of popular blues singing. He was a city man, playing the piano, and his singing was much less intense than the singing of the country-blues men"—Samuel B Charters, *The Country Blues*, Rinehart & Company Inc, 1959

References: Columbia album 1799
The Country Blues, Samuel B Charters, Rinehart & Company Inc, 1959

CARRADINE, WILLIAM

(*aka:* Cat-Iron)
Born: c1896, Garden City (Istmary Parish), LA
Died: c1958, Natchez, MS (unconfirmed)
Inst: Guitar

An almost entirely unknown itinerant street singer of both blues and religious music; lived in Buckners Alley, Natchez, MS, through 50s; rec Folkways label, Natchez, 1958; app in SEVEN LIVELY ARTS, CBS-TV, 1958

Personal: Married Fannie ———

Reference: Blues World magazine (UK), Summer 1972, p 9

CARROLL, JEANNE

Courtesy Living Blues *Magazine*

Born: Jan 15, 1931, Ruleville (Sunflower Co), MS
Inst: Guitar

Father was Rubin Simmons; mother Ethel Winters; born Albertha Jeanne Simmons; sang in church at 3; moved to Chicago, IL, where she frequently sang in local church choirs, 1938 into 40s; was member of Metropolitan Opera Guild Choir, Chicago, c1949-51; worked Stage Lounge, Chicago, 1950; Flame Show Bar, Detroit, MI, 1951; worked local club dates, Chicago, IL, through 50s; Stage Lounge, Chicago, 1955; frequently worked w Memphis Slim Band in local clubs, Chicago, late 50s; w Earl Fatha Hines group, Chicago, late 50s; frequently app on CJAY-TV, Winnipeg, Can, 1960; rec Bombay label, Chicago, 1963; app on national TV commercials for Budweiser Beer, mid-60s; toured w Franz Jackson's All-Stars on USO package show working army camps in Pacific Far East, 1967; toured w Franz Jackson Band on USO package show working army camps in Alaska/Aleutian Islands/Bahamas, 1968; frequently w Franz Jackson Band, Red Arrow Club, Stickney, IL, 1968-9; w Franz Jackson Band, Connecticut Jazz Club concert, Meriden, CT, 1968; frequently w Little Brother Montgomery working local club dates, Chicago, IL, 1968-9; toured w Franz Jackson Band on USO package show working army camps in Pacific Far East, 1969; worked Edge Lounge, Chicago, 1969; Chicago Blues Festival, Chicago, 1969; Showboat Sari-S, Chicago, 1969-70; w Salty Dog's Band, Sloppy Joe's, Chicago, 1969; rec w Little Brother Montgomery, Adelphi label, Chicago, 1969; toured w Franz Jackson Band on USO package show working army camps in Vietnam/Thailand, 1970; rec w Little Brother Montgomery, FM label, Chicago, 1969; worked w Franz Jackson in club/concert dates, Edmonton, Can, 1970; w Franz Jackson Band in local jazz club dates, New York/Connecticut, 1971; worked Mr Kelly's, Chicago, 1971; Memorial Concerts, Libertyville, IL, 1971-3; Bourbon Street Banana Factory, Toronto, Can, 1972; Ravina Park Jazz Festival, Chicago, IL, 1972-3; toured w Great Stars of Jazz package show working concert dates across US, 1973; worked Big Horn Jazz Festival, Mundelein, IL, 1973-4; toured w Art Hodes Jazz Four working concert dates across US/Canada, 1974; worked Pheasant Run, St Charles, IL, 1974; w Franz Jackson Band, Donovan's Pub Ltd, Wheeling, IL, 1974; app in BESSIE, BILLIE & BO, musical revue (unknown theater), Chicago, IL, 1975; worked Ratso's, Chicago, 1976 (por on JIMMY MITCHELL Show, WOPA-radio); Club Zodiac, Chicago, 1977; Elsewhere Lounge, Chicago, 1977

Personal: Married 1948. Has children

Song: Penny Pinching Blues

Awards/Honors: Nominated as Blues Singer of the Century by Harriette Choice, *Chicago Tribune* newspaper, 1971

Infl by: Mahalia Jackson/Bessie Smith/Dinah Washington

Quotes: "She has a rich and powerful, full throated voice with a fine acid tang to it . . ."—Derrick Stewart-Baxter, *Jazz Journal* magazine (UK), Jan 1970, p 9

"Miss Carroll's feeling for her music is strong . . ."—Dick Spottswood, Adelphi album 10003

Reference: Jazz Journal magazine (UK), Jan 1970, pp 9-10

CARSON, NELSON
(aka: Nelson Carter)
Born: Sept 18, 1917, New Boston (Bowle Co), TX
Inst: Guitar

Moved to Houston, TX, 1934, where he learned guitar and worked local dances in area to 1942; served in US Army c1942-5; settled in Ashdown, AR, to work local gigs mid-40s; toured w Jay Franks Rockets of Rhythm group to work club dates through South and cruise ships out of Houston, TX, from 1948; toured occasionally w Sonny Boy Williamson (Alex Miller) working club dates, late 40s; rec Sittin' In With label, Houston, 1950; returned to Ashdown, AR, to work locally through 50s/60s/70s; toured w Jay Franks group working club dates through Texarkana, TX, area, 1970

CARTER, BO
(see Chatmon, Armenter)

CARTER, BUNNY
(see Collins, Sam)

CARTER, CHARLIE
(see Jackson, Charlie)

CARTER, JOE
Born: Nov 6, 1927, Midland (Muscogee Co), GA
Inst: Guitar

Was playing home-made instruments as child; learned some guitar from Lee Willis, 1938; began working local houseparties/streets/jukes in Columbus, GA, area, through 40s; moved to Chicago, IL, 1952; formed small group to work local club dates, 1952-5; frequently worked Zanzibar Club/Ricky's Show Lounge/Pepper's/Kersey's Lounge/others, Chicago, 1955-65; worked mostly outside music, Chicago, 1965-70, with occasional club work into 70s; worked

Joe Carter

Photo by Jim O'Neal. Courtesy Living Blues *Magazine*

Louise's South Park Lounge, Chicago, 1974; rec w Chicago Broomdusters, Barrelhouse label, Chicago, 1976

Infl by: Elmore James

Quote: "Coupled with a screaming slide guitar, Joe's intense voice preaches the blues in a manner that few can equal"—George Paulus, Barrelhouse album BH-07

Reference: Barrelhouse album BH-07

CARTER, NELSON
(see Carson, Nelson)

CARY, CLARA
(see Beaman, Lottie)

CASTELL, MICHELE
(aka: Michele)
Born: Nov 27, 1945, Northwood (Middlesex Co), England
Inst: Kazoo

Father was guitarist; mother was singer; one of 2 children; interested in music early and frequently travelled through southern US as child; frequently worked Wembley Jazz Club, London (?), Eng, 1962-4; frequently toured w Steve Lane's Famous Southern Stompers group working jazz clubs/private clubs/festivals/riverboat shuffles through England, 1962-7; occasionally app on RADIO CAROLINE Show, BBC-radio, England, 1963-7; worked Nottingham Blues & Jazz Festival, Nottingham, Eng, 1965; Dunkirk Jazz Festival, Dunkirk, France, c1965; rec w Steve Lane's VJM Washboard Band, Stomp label, London (?), Eng, 1968; w Steve Lane Band, local concerts, London (?), Eng, 1968 (por rel Stomp label); frequently toured w writer Rex Harris working illustrated lectures in universities through England through 1960s into 70s; rec Major-Minor label, London (?), Eng, 1969-70

Personal: Married Robb Castell. 2 children

Infl by: Annette Hanshaw/Bessie Smith

Quote: "I have a great admiration for this singer, in fact I think I would place her as one of our greatest blues singers"—Rex Harris (correspondence)

CASTON, LEONARD *"Baby Doo"*
(aka: Baby Doo/Baby Duke)
Born: Jun 2, 1917, Sumrall (Lamar Co), MS
Died: Aug 22, 1987, Minneapolis, MN
Inst: Guitar/Piano

Father was Eugene Caston; mother Minda King; lived in Bude, MS as child; schooled in Meadville, MS briefly; learned some guitar from cousin Alan Weathersby as youth; worked outside music with occasional gigs at local country suppers/Saturday night parties, Meadville, MS, area from early 30s; moved to Natchez, MS, where he learned piano c1937; moved to Chicago, IL, to work outside music from c1939; worked w Five Breezes group, Martin's Corner/Pink Poodle/Brass Rail/Capitol Lounge/others, Chicago, c1940-2; rec Decca label, Chicago, 1940; rec w Five Breezes, Bluebird label, Chicago, 1940; teamed w Bob Moore to work Briscoli's Grenada Cafe, Peoria, IL, 1942, then formed small group to work residency from 1942; worked many local club dates, Chicago, early 40s; w own group, Swingland Club, Chicago, early 40s; w own Rhythm Rascals Trio working Squires Lounge/Cafe Society/Ship Shore Lounge/others, Chicago, early 40s; toured w Rhythm Rascals on USO R&B package show working army bases through India/China/Burma/Egypt/Africa/Europe, 1945, worked USO command performance for General Eisenhower, Frankfort, Ger, 1945; worked as single at Music Box/Joe's Club/Pink Poodle/others, Chicago, from 1946; together w Willie Dixon/Ollie Crawford formed Big Three Trio working local club dates, Chicago, IL, 1946, then toured Midwest working club dates to 1955; rec w Big Three Trio, Bullet label, Memphis, TN, 1946; rec w Jump Jackson Band, Specialty label, Chicago, 1946; frequently rec acc to Doc Clayton/John Sellers/Big Maceo/Jazz Gillum/Roosevelt Sykes/others, Chicago, 1946-7; rec w Big Three Trio, Columbia label, Chicago, 1947; worked Melody Show Bar, St Louis, MO, c1947; rec w Big Three Trio, Columbia label, Chicago, 1949; rec w Big Three Trio, OKeh label, Chicago, 1951-2; frequently worked as single out of Chicago from 1955; worked Top Hat Club, Chicago, 1961; teamed w Othum "Sonny" Allen working club dates/American Legion Halls through Nebraska, 1962-9; worked clubs/hotels/restaurants/festivals in Minneapolis/St Paul, MN areas from 1969; app in film SURVIVORS, 1985; died of heart failure; buried Crystal Lake Cemetery, Minneapolis

Personal: "Baby Doo" was childhood pet name

Book: From Blues to Pop: The Autobiography of Leonard "Baby Doo" Caston, Jeff Titon, John Edwards Memorial Foundation Inc, 1974

Songs: Blues at Midnight/I'm Gonna Walk Your Log

Infl by: Scrapper Blackwell/Alan Weathersby

Quote: "Baby Doo Caston . . . mixes blues songs, boogie-woogie, light classic pieces and country-western songs in his cocktail bar performances"—Jeff Titon, *Early Downhome Blues*, Univ of Illinois Press, 1977

Reference: From Blues to Pop: The Autobiography of Leonard "Baby Doo" Caston, Jeff Titon, John Edwards Memorial Foundation Inc, 1974

CAT-IRON
(see Carradine, William)

CATJUICE CHARLEY
(see Hicks, Charlie)

CHARITY, PERNELL

Photo by Peter B Lowry

Born: Nov 20, 1920, Waverly (Sussex Co), VA
Died: Apr 12, 1979, Waverly, VA
Inst: Guitar

Interested in music early and made first guitar from cigar box as child; worked mostly outside music in Waverly, VA, area from 30s; occasionally worked w Sam Jones at local dances/parties/picnics/streets, Waverly area, late 30s to 1944; worked mostly outside music, Waverly, from 40s into 70s; rec Trix label, Waverly, 1972; died of cancer

Songs: Blind Man/Pig Meat Mama/War Blues

Infl by: Blind Boy Fuller/Lightnin' Hopkins

Quote: "Pernell Charity is a very fine guitarist and a good singer, as well as being a strong interpreter . . ."—Kip Lornell, Trix album 3309

Reference: Living Blues magazine, Summer 1973, pp 25-7

CHARLES, HENRY
(see Brown, Henry)

CHARLES, RAY
Born: Sept 23, 1930, Albany (Dougherty Co), GA
Inst: Clarinet/Organ/Piano/Saxophone/Trumpet

Father was Bailey Robinson; mother Aretha ———; born Ray Charles Robinson (later dropping last name to avoid confusion with boxing champion of same name); one of 2 children; moved to Greenville, FL, at 2 months of age; interested in music from 3 years of age; frequently sang in local Shiloh Baptist Church from childhood; partially blind at 5 and completely blind at 7 years of age due to possible glaucoma; attended State School for Deaf and Blind Children, St Augustine, FL, where he studied classical piano/clarinet, 1937-45; worked solo or w own school group at tea parties/church socials in area, mid-40s; quit school to work briefly w Henry Washington Band, The Two Spot, Jacksonville, FL, 1946; w Tiny York Combo, Jacksonville, FL, 1947; w Joe Anderson Band, Sunshine Club, Orlando, FL, 1947; w Sammy Glover Combo/AC Price Combo in local club dates, Orlando, FL, 1947; toured w Charlie Brantley Combo out of Tampa, FL, 1947; worked w Manzy Harris Trio, Tampa, FL, 1947; toured w Florida Playboys (a white C&W band) out of Tampa, FL, 1947; worked O'Dells Club, Miami, FL, 1948; moved to Seattle, WA, to form McSon Trio (also spelled Maxim) working Elks Club/Rocking Chair Club/908 Club/Black & Tan Club and others in area, 1948-9; app w McSon Trio on KRSC-radio and own show, local TV, Seattle, WA, 1948; rec w Maxim Trio (others), Swingtime-Downbeat label, Seattle, WA/Los Angeles, CA, 1948-9; toured w Lowell Fulson Band working package R&B shows in theaters through South/Southwest, 1950-2; worked w Lowell Fulson Band, Apollo Theater, NYC, NY, 1950; rec Swingtime-Downbeat label, Los Angeles, CA, 1950-1; rec Atlantic label, NYC, NY/New Orleans, LA (elsewhere), 1952-9; toured as single working club dates across USA, 1952-4; formed own band working back-up for Ruth Brown or as single unit at concerts/dances in Southwest, 1954; rec w Guitar Slim Band, Specialty label, New Orleans,

Ray Charles *Courtesy Sheldon Harris Collection*

1954; toured w own group extensively working one-nighters in clubs/concerts across US, 1955 into 60s; worked Town Hall Ballroom, Philadelphia, PA, 1955; toured on Universal Attractions package Rock & Roll Show working theaters across US, 1957; worked Gleasons, Cleveland, OH, 1957; Howard Theater, Washington, DC, 1957-9; annually at Carnegie Hall, NYC, 1957-9; settled in Los Angeles, CA, 1958; worked Newport Jazz Festival, Newport, RI, 1958 (por rel Atlantic label/por heard CBS-radio); The Showboat, Philadelphia, PA, 1958 (por heard MUSIC USA, VOA-radio); frequently worked Apollo Theater, NYC, 1958-61; Jazz Cruise on SS *Pennsylvania* on Delaware River, 1959; The Auditorium, Oakland, CA, 1959; Cavalcade of Jazz, Academy of Music, Philadelphia, 1959; in concert, Atlanta, GA, 1959 (por rel Atlantic label); rec/produced ABC-Paramount label, NYC/Los Angeles, 1959-68; worked Tivoli Theater, Chicago, 1960; The Auditorium, Oakland, 1960; The Cloister, Los Angeles, 1960; Newport Jazz Festival, Newport, RI, 1960 (por shown in USIA film short series JAZZ-USA [Nos 11, 18, 26]); Longhorn Ranch Club, Dallas, TX, 1961; McCormick Place, Chicago, 1961; Regal Theater, Chicago, 1961; Fox Theater, Detroit, MI, 1961; Hollywood Palladium, Hollywood, CA, 1961; Zebra Lounge, Los Angeles, 1961; toured Europe working concerts/festivals, 1961-2; worked Palais des Sports, Paris, France, 1961; Hollywood Bowl, Hollywood, CA, 1961; worked club dates in Bahama Islands, 1961; Symphony Hall, Boston, MA, 1961; Carnegie Hall, NYC, 1961; w Sarah Vaughan, RKO Palace Theater, NYC, 1961; Smalls Paradise, NYC, 1961; City Auditorium, Memphis, TN, 1961; Convention Hall, Asbury Park, NJ, 1962; app on DINAH SHORE Show, NBC-TV, 1962; app on ED SULLIVAN SHOW, CBS-TV, c1962; worked Tulane Univ, New Orleans, LA, 1962; Southern Methodist Univ, Dallas, TX, 1962; Latin Casino, Philadelphia, PA, 1962; app in film DOUBLE TROUBLE (rel UK as SWINGING ALONG), 1962; heard on ST of film short COSMIC RAY, 1962; formed Ray Charles Enterprises, incorporating Tangerine Records/Tangerine Music/Racer Music Company, 1962-73; worked O'Keefe Center, Toronto, Can, 1963; Arie Crown Theater, Chicago, 1963-6; Music Hall, Cleveland, OH, 1963-7; frequently worked clubs/hotels/casinos, Reno, NV, 1963; Cow Palace, San Francisco, 1963; rec ST for film SCORPIO RISING, 1963; worked The Arena, Long Beach, CA, 1963; toured concert dates through Brazil, 1963; worked Donnelly Theater, Boston, MA, 1963; Kleinhans Music Hall, Buffalo, NY, 1963-6; Miles Col, Birmingham, AL, 1963; Memorial Auditorium, Dallas, TX, 1963; McCormick Place, Chicago, IL, 1963; toured England working concert dates, 1963; toured extensively through Europe/Algeria/Japan/Australia/Hawaii working concert dates, 1964; app in singing/acting role in UK film BALLAD IN BLUE (rel US as BLUES FOR LOVERS), 1964; worked Shrine Auditorium, Los Angeles, CA, 1964 (por rel ABC label); worked Academy of Music, Brooklyn, NY, 1964; Carnegie Hall, NYC, NY, 1965; app on SHINDIG, ABC-TV, 1965; app on IT'S HAPPENING BABY, CBS-TV, 1965; rec ST for film CINCINNATI KID, 1965 (por rel MGM label); app on national radio commercials for Coca Cola, 1966; worked Latin Casino, Philadelphia, PA, 1966; Masonic Auditorium, San Francisco, CA, 1966; The Royal Tahitian, Ontario, CA, 1966; Forest Hills Music Festival, NYC, 1966; app on HOLLYWOOD PALACE, ABC-TV, 1966; app in film THE BIG TNT SHOW, 1966; worked Westbury Music Fair, Westbury, NY, 1966-7; McCormick Place, Chicago, IL, 1966; Memorial Auditorium, Kansas City, MO, 1966; Dinner Key Auditorium, Miami, FL, 1966; Loyola's Auditorium, New Orleans, LA, 1966; rec ST for film IN THE HEAT OF THE NIGHT, 1967 (por rel United Artists label); toured England/Europe working festivals/concerts, 1967; worked Diablo Valley Col, Concord, CA, 1967; Randalls Island Jazz Festival, NYC, NY, 1967-8; app on KRAFT MUSIC HALL, NBC-TV, 1967; app on ANDY WILLIAMS Show, NBC-TV, 1967; toured Australia working concert dates, 1967; worked Harrah's Club, Reno, NV, 1967; Copacabana, NYC, NY, 1967; Center Arena, Seattle, WA, 1967; rec Tangerine label, Los Angeles, CA, 1968-73; app on OPERATION: ENTERTAINMENT, ABC-TV, 1968; worked Circle Star Theater, San Carlos, CA, 1968; Melody Land, Anaheim, CA, 1968; Cocoanut Grove, Los Angeles, CA, 1968; app w Aretha Franklin on national radio commercials for Coca Cola, 1968; app on JOEY BISHOP Show, ABC-TV, 1968-9; worked Apollo Theater, NYC, 1968-9; app on MERV GRIFFIN Show, WNEW-TV, NYC, NY (syndicated), 1968; app on JERRY LEWIS Show, NBC-TV, 1968; worked Central Park Music Festival, NYC, 1968; Newport Jazz Festival, Newport, RI, 1968; toured England/Europe working concert dates, 1968; Antibes Jazz Festival, Antibes, France, 1968; app on OF BLACK AMERICA series, CBS-TV, 1968 (rel as film BODY & SOUL—PART 2); worked Queen Elizabeth Theater, Vancouver, Can, 1968; Minneapolis Auditorium, Minneapolis, MN, 1968; Pittsburgh Jazz Festival, Pittsburgh, PA, 1968; Long Beach Auditorium, Los Angeles, CA, 1968; Shrine Auditorium, Los Angeles, 1968; app on

SMOTHERS BROTHERS COMEDY HOUR, CBS-TV, 1969; app on BOB HOPE SPECIAL, NBC-TV, 1969; toured with own Ray Charles Show package revue working extensive concerts/night clubs/one-nighters across US from 1969 into 70s; worked Elcamino Real, Mexico City, Mexico, 1969; app on DELLA Show, WOR-TV, NYC (syndicated), 1969; worked The Frontier, Las Vegas, NV, 1969; The Soul Bowl, Dallas, TX, 1969; toured England/Europe working club/concert dates, 1969; worked Cocoanut Grove, Los Angeles, CA, 1969; Allentown Fair, Allentown, PA, 1969; Lambertville Music Circus, Lambertville, NJ, 1969; Westbury Music Fair, Westbury, NY, 1969; Pauley Pavilion, Los Angeles, CA, 1969; Univ of California, Los Angeles, 1969; Aces Club, Los Angeles, 1969; Santa Monica Civic Auditorium, Santa Monica, CA, 1970; Now Grove, Los Angeles, 1970; app w Los Angeles Philharmonic, SWITCHED-ON SYMPHONY, NBC-TV, 1970; Palace Theater, Albany, NY, 1970; Sold on Soul concert, Madison Square Garden, NYC, NY, 1970; app on GLEN CAMPBELL GOODTIME HOUR, CBS-TV, 1970; app on JOHNNY CASH SHOW, ABC-TV, 1970; app on ENGELBERT HUMPERDINCK Show, ABC-TV, 1970; app on TOM JONES Show, ABC-TV, 1970; worked Central Park Music Festival, NYC, 1970; Fillmore East, NYC, 1970; app on HEE HAW, CBS-TV, 1970; app on MERV GRIFFIN Show, CBS-TV, 1970; worked Sugar Shack, Boston, MA, 1970; extensive tour working concert dates on college circuit across US, 1970-1; toured Japan working concert dates, 1970-1; worked Jazz Expo 70, London, Eng, 1970; Salle Aleyel, Paris, France, 1970; rec ST for West German film WARNUNG VOR EINER HEILIGEN NUTTE, 1970; served as president of RPM Company (recording/publishing/management), Los Angeles, CA, from early 70s; worked w Aretha Franklin, Fillmore West, San Francisco, CA, 1971 (por rel Atlantic label); worked Symphony Hall, Newark, NJ, 1971; app on FLIP WILSON Show, NBC-TV, 1971; worked as guest soloist w Houston Symphony Orch, Houston, TX, 1971; Auditorium Theater, Chicago, IL, 1971; toured Europe working concert dates, 1971; worked w The Supremes, Circle Star, San Carlos, CA, 1971; app on BILL COSBY Show, NBC-TV, 1971; app on CAROL BURNETT Show, CBS-TV, 1972; co-hosted MIKE DOUGLAS Show, CBS-TV, c1972; app on Johnny Carson's TONIGHT Show, NBC-TV, 1972; app on DICK CAVETT Show, ABC-TV, 1972; worked California State Polytechnic Col, San Luis Obispo, CA, 1972; The Grove, Los Angeles, 1972; Newport Jazz Festival, NYC, 1972 (por heard MUSIC—USA, VOA-radio); Astrodome Jazz Festival, Houston, TX, 1972; Ohio Valley Jazz Festival, Cincinnati, OH, 1972; Summer Festival, Milwaukee, WI, 1972; Meadowbrook Jazz Festival, Detroit, MI, 1972; Mill Run Theater, Niles, IL, 1972; toured England/Europe working concert dates, 1972; worked The Forum, Toronto, Can, 1972; Valley Music Theater, Woodland Hills, CA, 1972; rec ST for film BLACK RODEO, 1972; app on DUKE ELLINGTON SPECIAL, CBS-TV, 1973; worked Philharmonic Hall, NYC, NY, 1973; Ann Arbor Blues Festival, Ann Arbor, MI, 1973; toured England/Europe/Japan working concert dates 1973; app on NBC FOLLIES, NBC-TV, 1973; app on BARBRA STREISAND Show, CBS-TV, 1973; formed own Crossover label to record/produce, 1973-7; worked Empire Room, Waldorf-Astoria Hotel, NYC, 1974; Newport Jazz Festival, NYC, 1974 (por rel Buddah label); worked Caribbean cruise ship SS *Rotterdam*, 1974; app on COTTON CLUB 75, NBC-TV, 1974; app on SMOTHERS BROTHERS Show, NBC-TV, 1975; app on SAMMY AND COMPANY, NBC-TV, 1975; app on DINAH! Show, CBS-TV, 1975; app on EBONY READERS MUSIC POLL AWARD SHOW, PBS-TV, 1975; app on CHER, CBS-TV, 1975; worked Massey Hall, Toronto, Can, 1975; toured Japan/Australia working concert dates, 1975 (por Japan concert rel Crossover label); app in public service radio/TV commercial for Foresters State Service, 1975-6; app Olympia Beer radio commercials, 1975; app in national print ad for Craig Corporation, 1976; app on CELEBRATION: THE AMERICAN SPIRIT, ABC-TV, 1976; app on Johnny Carson's TONIGHT Show, NBC-TV, 1976; app on THE OSCAR PETERSON: VERY SPECIAL, CBC-TV, Toronto, Can, 1976; app on COMEDY IN AMERICA REPORT, NBC-TV, 1976; app on MIDNIGHT SPECIAL, NBC-TV, 1976; worked Carnegie Hall, NYC, 1976; Ambassador Hotel, Los Angeles, 1976; app on MUSIC HALL AMERICA, WPIX-TV, NYC, 1976; worked Great American Music Hall, San Francisco, CA, 1976; rec w Cleo Laine, RCA Victor label, NYC (?), 1976; worked North Sea Jazz Festival 76, Congress Centre, The Hague, Holland, 1976; app on MIKE DOUGLAS Show, CBS-TV, 1977; app on HOLLYWOOD SQUARES game show, ABC-TV, 1977; app on DINAH! Show, CBS-TV, 1977; app in radio/TV commercial for Scotch Brand Recording Tape, 1977; app in public service commercial for United Negro College Fund on national radio/TV, 1977-8; rec Atlantic label, Los Angeles, CA, 1977; worked Back Yard Bandstand, Belmont Racing Park, Elmont, NY, 1977; Eduardo's, Buffalo, NY, 1977; Jones Hall,

Houston, TX, 1977; Hyatt Regency Hotel, Dearborn, MI, 1977; Burning Spear, Chicago, IL, 1977; app on SATURDAY NIGHT, NBC-TV, 1977; app on THE BEATLES FOREVER, NBC-TV, 1977; worked Avery Fisher Hall, NYC, NY, 1977; app on 50 YEARS OF COUNTRY MUSIC, NBC-TV, 1978; app on THE SECOND BARRY MANILOW SPECIAL, ABC-TV, 1978; app on THE CHUCK BARRIS RAH RAH Show, NBC-TV, 1978; app on THANK YOU ROCK 'N' ROLL, WPIX-TV, NYC, NY, 1978; app on JOHNNY CASH: SPRING FEVER, CBS-TV, 1978; hosted SATURDAY NIGHT LIVE, NBC-TV, 1978; app on A SALUTE TO AMERICAN IMAGINATION, CBS-TV, 1978

Personal: Married Eileen ——— (1952-3); Della Beatrice Antwine (1954-75), a gospel singer. 3 children. (Has other children.) Not to be confused with Ray Charles (b Sep 13, 1918), choir director

Billing: The Genius

Books: *Instrumental Folio,* Ray Charles, Progressive Music, 1963

Ray Charles, Sharon Bell Mathis, Crowell, 1973

Brother Ray, Ray Charles' Own Story, Ray Charles/David Ritz, The Dial Press, 1978

Songs: A Fool for You/Ain't That Love/Baby Let Me Hold Your Hand/Blackjack/Confession Blues/Come Back Baby/Don't Tell Me Your Troubles/Don't You Know/Funny But I Still Love You/Get on the Right Track Baby/Hallelujah I Love Her So/I Got A Woman/I Had a Dream/I Want to Know/It's Allright/Jumpin' in the Morning/Leave My Woman Alone/Light Out of Darkness/Mary Ann/Rockhouse/Rockin' Chair Blues/The Snow Is Falling/Sweet Sixteen Bars/Talkin' 'bout You/Tell All the World About You/Tell Me How Do You Feel/Tell the Truth/That's Enough/This Little Girl of Mine/What Kind of Man Are You?/What Would I Do Without You?/What'd I Say?/You Be My Baby

Awards/Honors: Won Grand Prix du Disque Award for Best Jazz Vocal Album, 1958 ("Ray Charles," Atlantic album 8006)

Won *Downbeat* magazine International Critics Poll for Best New Star, Male Singer, 1958

Won *Downbeat* magazine Readers Poll for R&B Personality of the Year, 1958, 1959

Won National Academy of Recording Arts & Sciences Grammy Award for Best Contemporary Rock & Roll Single, 1960 ("Georgia on My Mind")

Won National Academy of Recording Arts & Sciences Grammy Award for Best Male Vocal Performance Single, 1960 ("Georgia on My Mind")

Won National Academy of Recording Arts & Sciences Grammy Award for Best R&B Single, 1960 ("Let the Good Times Roll"); 1961 ("Hit the Road Jack"); 1962 ("I Can't Stop Loving You"); 1963 ("Busted"); 1966 ("Crying Time")

Won National Academy of Recording Arts & Sciences Grammy Award for Best Male Vocal Performance Album, 1960 ("The Genius of Ray Charles," Atlantic album 1312)

Won *Downbeat* magazine International Critics Poll for Best Male Singer, 1961, 1962, 1963, 1964, 1968, 1969, 1973

Won *Downbeat* magazine Readers Poll for Best Male Vocalist, 1963, 1964, 1968, 1969

Won *Swing Journal* magazine (Japan) Best Male Singer Award, 1964, 1965, 1966, 1969, 1970, 1971, 1972

A special commemorative coin for Ray Charles was issued in Paris, France, c1965

A resolution honoring Ray Charles was introduced in the US House of Representatives, 1966

Won Hollywood Radio/TV Society International Broadcasting Award, 1966

Named National Chairman of Sickle Cell Disease Research Foundation, 1967

Awarded honorary degree in Music from Florida A&M Univ, Tallahassee, FL, 1967

A Ray Charles Day was proclaimed by Los Angeles, CA, City Council "for outstanding contributions to the world of entertainment over the past two decades," Jun 8, 1967

Inducted into *Playboy* magazine Jazz & Pop Hall of Fame, 1968

Won The Golden Plate Award of American Academy of Achievement for his outstanding contributions, 1975

Won Man of Distinction Award of National Association for Sickle Cell Disease, 1975

Won Man of the Year Award of B'nai B'rith Lodge, Beverly Hills, CA, 1976

Won National Academy of Recording Arts & Sciences Grammy Award for Best Male Vocal R&B Performance, 1975 ("Living For The City")

Won American Music Conference National Music Award, 1976

Inducted into Songwriters Hall of Fame, NYC, NY, 1976

Won *Playboy* magazine Music Awards Reader Poll as Best Jazz Male Vocalist, 1976

Awarded honorary Doctorate of Humane Letters, Shaw Univ, Raleigh, NC, 1978

Infl by: Alex Bradford/Charles Brown/Nat Cole/Big Boy Crudup/Floyd Dixon/Lloyd Glenn/Mahalia Jackson/Eddie "Guitar Slim" Jones/Louis Jordan/Peggy Lee/Percy Mayfield/Art Tatum/Joe Turner/Muddy Waters

Infl to: Dave Alexander/Eric Burdon/Jerry Burne/Joe Cocker/Bobby Darin/Lee Dorsey/Snooks Eaglin/Sugarcane Harris/Richie Havens/Al Reed/Alvin Robinson/Allen Toussaint/Tommy Tucker

Quotes: "Charles is, let's face it, one of the major performers of our time, a brilliant, compelling singer whose distinctive, emotion-drenched delivery and thrilling dark-hued voice are capable of energizing virtually any type of song"
—Pete Welding, *Downbeat* magazine, May 5, 1977, p 12

"Everyone does—or should—know that Ray is the father of soul, a living legend, the first soul brother, a genius"
—Tony Cummings, *Black Music* magazine (UK), May 1974, p 35

"As far as I'm concerned, Ray Charles is by far the greatest exponent of blues and feeling for what we call soul"
—Joe Williams, *Downbeat* magazine, Oct 5, 1967, p 40

References: Brother Ray, Ray Charles' Own Story, Ray Charles/David Ritz, The Dial Press, 1978

Downbeat magazine, May 5, 1977, pp 12-15

The Great American Popular Singers, Henry Pleasants, Simon & Schuster, 1974

Cadence magazine, Oct 1976, pp 3-4

CHATMAN, BO
(see Chatmon, Armenter)

CHATMAN, PETER
(aka: Leroy/Memphis Slim)
Born: Sept 3, 1915, Memphis (Shelby Co), TN
Died: Feb 24, 1988, Paris, France
Inst: Bass/Celeste/Organ/Piano

Courtesy Sing Out *Magazine*

Father was Peter Chatman Sr, a deacon of local Baptist Church and musician; mother was Ella Kennedy; born John Len Chatman; raised next door to local honky-tonk and was interested in music at early age; taught self piano at about 7 years of age; attended Lester HS where he played bass in school band as youth; worked Midway Cafe, Memphis, TN, 1931; left home to hobo through South working juke joints/dives/dance halls/turpentine camps, 1931-7; settled in Chicago, IL, 1937; worked (as "Memphis Slim") w Bill Broonzy at Ruby's Tavern/Cozy Corner/others, Chicago, 1940-2; rec w own washboard band, OKeh label, Chicago, 1940; rec Bluebird label, Chicago, 1940-1; frequently worked local clubs like 1410 Club/The Beehive/Rap Club and theaters like Regal Theater/8th Street Theater, Chicago, into 40s; frequently worked Plantation Club, Chicago, mid-40s; formed own quintet then enlarged group to "The House Rockers" working local club dates, Chicago, from 1946; rec HyTone label, Chicago, 1946; worked Music at Midnight Concert, Town Hall, NYC, NY, 1947; rec (as "Leroy") United Artist label, NYC, 1947; rec Miracle label, Chicago, 1947-9; worked George Wood's Timber Tap Room, Chicago, 1948; rec Master label, Chicago, 1949; rec King label, Cincinnati, OH, 1949; rec Peacock label, Houston, TX, 1949-52; rec Premium label, Chicago, 1950-2; worked Ralph's Club, Chicago, 1950; rec Mercury label, Chicago, 1951; rec Chess label, Cleveland, OH, 1952; rec United label, Chicago, 1952-4; rec Money label, Los Angeles, CA, 1954; toured Midwest working theater dates in mid-50s; worked Storyville Club, Boston, MA, c1957; The Green Door, Chicago, 1957; rec VJ label, Chicago, 1958-9; rec acc to Willie Dixon,

Bluesville label, Englewood Cliffs, NJ, 1959; rec Folkways label, NYC, 1959-61; worked State Univ of New York, Buffalo, NY, 1959; Carnegie Hall, NYC, 1959 (por rel United Artists label); Town Hall, NYC, 1959; Newport Folk Festival, Newport, RI, 1959; Ash Grove, Los Angeles, 1959; Gate of Horn, Chicago, 1959-61; toured w Willie Dixon working concert dates through England/Europe, 1960; rec Collector/International/Polydor labels, London, Eng, 1960; app in Belgian film MEMPHIS SLIM, 1960; rec Storyville label, Copenhagen, Den, 1960-3; rec Xtra label, Chicago, 1960; rec Prestige-Bluesville/Verve labels, NYC, 1960; worked Village Gate, NYC, 1960 (por rel Folkways label); app on Dave Garroway's TODAY Show, NBC-TV, 1960; worked Basin Street Club, Toronto, Can, 1960; El Macombo Lounge, Chicago, c1960; rec Folkways/Disc labels, Chicago, 1960; rec Candid label, NYC, 1961; rec Strand label, Chicago, 1961; toured concert dates through England/Europe, 1961; rec Fontana label, London, Eng, 1961; rec Agorilla label, Bayonne, France, 1961; rec Odeon label, Paris, France, 1961; app on local show, CBC-radio, Toronto, Can, 1961; worked Blind Pig, Chicago, 1961; toured concert circuit extensively across US, 1961; worked Paris Blues Festival, Paris, France, 1962; rec Vogue/Farandole labels, Paris, France, 1962; app frequently on local TV shows, Paris, France, from 1962; app frequently on local TV shows in Rumania/Yugoslavia/Italy/Belgium / England/Germany / Holland/Poland/Austria/Switzerland through 60s into 70s; worked Blues Festival, Hamburg, Ger, 1962, rec Polydor label, Hamburg, Ger, 1962; worked Les Trois Mailletz Club, Paris, France, 1962 (por rel Polydor label) extended residencies at Mars Club/Les Trois Mailletz, Paris, from 1962 into 70s; toured w Rhythm & Blues USA package show working concert dates through England/Europe, 1962; worked Jamboree Club, Barcelona, Spain, 1963; toured w American Folk Blues Festival working concert dates through England/Europe/Israel 1963 (por shown on I HEAR THE BLUES, Granada-TV, Eng); toured concert dates w Sonny Boy Williamson (Alex Miller) through Poland, 1963; rec acc to Sonny Boy Williamson (Alex Miller), Storyville label, Copenhagen, Den, 1963; rec Fontana label, Bremen, Ger, 1963; worked w Sonny Boy Williamson (Alex Miller), Blues Bar, Paris, France, 1963 (por rel Vogue label); The New Marquee, London, Eng, 1964; National Jazz & Blues Festival, London, 1964; scored ST for French film short VISAGE DES P T T, 1964; toured w Alex Harvey's Band working concert dates through England, 1965; Village Vanguard, NYC, NY, 1965; rec Spivey label, Brooklyn, NY, 1965; worked Newport Jazz Festival, Newport, RI, 1965; Both/And Club, San Francisco, CA, 1966; Ash Grove, Los Angeles, CA, c1966; Monterey Jazz Festival, Monterey, CA, 1966; Palais des Sports, Nanterre, Paris, France, 1967; rec International/Polydor labels, Paris, France, 1967; worked Molde Jazz Festival, Oslo, Norway, 1967; rec Sonet label, NYC, 1967; app in film THE SERGEANT, 1968; worked Jazz on an Island Festival, Yvoir, Belgium, 1968; rec Beacon label, London, Eng, c1968; owned United Black Artists Booking Agency, Paris, France, c1969; extensive tours through England/Europe working concert/club dates, 1969 into 70s; scored ST for French film A NOUS DEUX LA FRANCE, 1970; rec Barclay label, Paris/Herouville, France, 1970; rec Carumet/Jewel labels, France, 1970; rec Warner Bros label, Burbank, CA, 1970; app in film CARRY IT ON (JOAN), 1970; worked Quiet Knight, Chicago, 1971; Queen Elizabeth Hall, London, Eng, 1971; app in French film L'AVENTURE DU JAZZ (UK title: JAZZ ODYSSEY), 1972 (por rel Jazz Odyssey label); rec Trip label, c1972; toured w American Folk Blues Festival working concert dates through Europe, 1972; toured Europe working concert dates, 1973; worked Montreux Jazz Festival, Montreux, Switzerland, 1973; rec w Canned Heat group, Blue Star label, 1973; worked Hot Club of France Concert, Paris, 1975 (por rel Flame label); rec Barclay label, Madison, TN, 1975; worked Ratso's, Chicago, IL, 1975-6; Jazz 200 Festival, Hamburg, Ger, 1976; Haarlem Music Festival, Haarlem, Holland, 1976; North Sea Jazz Festival 76, Congress Centre, The Hague, Holland, 1976; Village Gate, NYC, NY, 1977; clip shown in ROOTS OF COUNTRY MUSIC & BLUES, KGO-TV, San Francisco, 1977; worked Quartier Latin, Berlin, Ger, 1978; Summer Festival, Groningen, Holland, 1978; La Grande Parade Du Jazz, Nice, France, 1978; frequent US club dates into 80s; Centro Cultural de Tarrasa, Tarrasa, Barcelona, Spain, 1982/86; app GOOD TIME GEORGE Show, BBC-2-TV, London, 1983; mostly inactive due to illness during 80s; entered Necker Hospital, Paris, where he died of kidney failure; buried Galilee Memorial Gardens Cemetery, Memphis, TN

Personal: Not to be confused with Cow Cow Davenport who also used pseudonym "Memphis Slim"

Songs: **A Long Time Baby/Ain't Nothing But a Texas Boogie on a Harpsichord/Alberta/All By Myself/Angel Child/The Animal in Me/Baby Doll/Beer Drinking Woman/Bertha May/Between Midnight and Dawn/Big City Girl/Big Time Girl/Black Cat Cross My Trail/Blue and Disgusted/Blue and Lonesome/Blue**

Brew/Blue This Evening/Blues for My Baby/The Blues Is Everywhere/Blues Is Troubles/Bluesingly Yours/Boogie Duo/Born with the Blues/Brenda/ Broadway Boogie/C Rocker/Choo Choo/Christina/ Churnin' Man Blues/Clap Your Hands/The Comeback/Darling I Miss You/Dear Abby and Ann/Don't Doubt Me/Don't Ration My Love/Don't Think You're Smart/Double Crossin' Mamma/Down Home Blues/ Down That Big Road/88 Boogie/European Blues/Everything I Do Is Wrong/Every Day I Have the Blues/Fast and Free/Fat and Forty/Feel Like Screamin' and Cryin'/Feeling the Blues/Forty Years or More/Four O'Clock Boogie/Freedom/French Woman/Gamblers Blues/Gone Again/Good Time Charlie/Got a Little Old Mama/Grinder Man Blues/ Harlem Bound/Havin' Fun/Headed for Nashville/ Help Me Some/Hey Slim/House Cleaning/I Am the Blues/The IC Blues/I Feel Like Ballin' the Jack/I Got the Blues Everywhere/I Guess I'm a Fool/I Wanna Dance/I'm Crying/I'm So All Alone/Jaspers Gal/Jefferson County Blues/Jerusalem/Just Blues/Lend Me Your Love/Let's Get with It/Letter Home/Life Is Like That/Little Lonely Girl/Lonesome Traveler/Lord Have Mercy on Me/Losers Weepers/M&S Boogie/ Marack/Me Myself and I/Mean Mistreatin' Mama/ Memphis on the Mississippi/Memphis Slim USA/ Messing Around/Misery/Mistake in Life/Mister Freddie/Mother Earth/Mr Longfingers/My Baby Left Me/My Dog Is Mean/No/No Strain/Now I Got the Blues/Old Taylor/Only Fools Have Fun/Paris Scene/ People People/Pigalle and Love/Rack 'em Back Jack/ Rainin' in My Heart/Raining the Blues/Ramble This Highway/Really Got the Blues/Reverend Bounce/ Rock Me Woman/Rockin' the Pad/Sail on Blues/Sassy Mae/She's All My Life/Slim's Blues/So Lonely/St Juan Blues/Steady Rolling Blues/Strollin' Thru the Park/ Sunnyland Train/Sweet Root Man/There's a Fool in Town/This Little Woman/Three and One Boogie/ Three Women Blues/Tia Juana/Too Late/Trouble Everywhere I Go/Two of a Kind/Waiting Game/Walkin' the Boogie/Watch Out Baby/What Is the Blues?/When Buddy Come to Town/When I Was Young/When Your Dough Roller Is Gone/Whiskey and Gin Blues/Whiskey Drinking Man/Whizzle Wham/Wish Me Well/Women Blues Boogie/You Called Me at Last/You Don't Know My Mind/You Got to Help Me Some/You're Gonna Need My Help One Day/You're the One/Youth Wants to Know

Awards/Honors: "Memphis Slim and Real Honky Tonk" (Folkways album 3535) won French Academie du Jazz Award as best blues LP of 1965

Infl by: Joshua Altheimer/Bill Broonzy/Pinetop Smith/Roosevelt Sykes

Infl to: Lazy Bill Lucas

Quote: "Slim's blues serves a natural link between earlier blues tradition and the more recent rhythm and blues styles"—LeRoy Jones, Bluesville album 1053

References: Encyclopedia of Pop, Rock & Soul, Irwin Stambler, St Martin's Press, 1974

CHATMAN, SAM
(see Chatmon, Sam)

CHATMON, ARMENTER *"Bo"*
(aka: Bo Carter/Bo Chatman)

Courtesy Record Research Archives

Born: Mar 21, 1893, Bolton (Hinds Co), MS
Died: Sept 21, 1964, Memphis, TN
Inst: Banjo/Bass/Clarinet/Guitar/Violin

Father was Henderson Chatmon, mother was Eliza Jackson, both musicians; born on Dr Dupress' Plantation; one of at least 11 children; worked outside music on local farm, 1912-17; moved to Stovall, MS, to work outside music, 1917-18; formed family string band to work white square dances in area with frequent tours through South from c1917; worked outside music as sharecropper on Kelly Drew's Plantation, Hollandale, MS, with occasional local street/drug store work for tips through 20s; rec Brunswick label, New Orleans, LA, 1928; rec acc Walter Vincent, Brunswick label, Memphis, TN, 1929; rec OKeh/Columbia labels, Atlanta, GA, 1930-1; toured w Mississippi Sheiks group working country dances/picnics/parties/suppers/fish fries throughout Mississippi/Tennessee/Georgia/Louisiana/Illinois/New York, 1930-5; rec w Mississippi Sheiks, OKeh label, Shreveport, LA/San Antonio, TX, 1930; rec w Mississippi Sheiks, OKeh/Columbia labels, Atlanta, GA/NYC, 1930-1; rec w Mississippi Sheiks, Paramount label, Grafton, WI, 1932; rec Bluebird label, San Antonio, TX, 1934 and New Orleans, LA, 1935-6; settled in Glenallen, MS, to work outside music on farm from 1936; suffered blindness and toured with brothers on various minstrel shows working dances/parties/picnics/hotels/streets through Delta area and points south through 30s; rec Bluebird label, San Antonio, TX, 1938; rec Bluebird label, Atlanta, GA, 1940; settled in Memphis, TN, to work mostly outside music from early 40s; suffered cerebral hemorrhage and died Shelby County Hospital; buried Nittayuma Cemetery, Sharkey, MS

Personal: Brother of Sam Chatmon/Lonnie Chatmon/Harry Chatmon/Ty Chatmon. Half-brother of Charley Patton

Songs: Corrine Corrina/New Auto Blues/Policy Blues/Sitting on Top of the World/Sue Cow/Who's Been Here?/You Keep on Spending My Change

Infl to: Sam Chatmon/Johnny Young

Quotes: "One of the giants of country blues"—Dennis Buck, *Living Blues* magazine, Winter 1973, p 31

"One of the bona-fide geniuses of the country blues"—John Miller, Yazoo album L-1034

Reference: Yazoo album L-1034

CHATMON, SAM
(*aka:* Sam Chatman)
Born: Jan 10, 1899, Bolton (Hinds Co), MS
Died: Feb 2, 1983, Hollandale, MS
Inst: Banjo/Bass/Guitar/Harmonica/Mandolin

Father was Henderson Chatmon, a former slave and popular local fiddler; mother was Eliza Jackson, a guitarist; one of at least 11 children (Lonnie/Harry/Bo/Edgar/Willie/Lamar/Larry/Burt/Ty/Charlie); born on John Gettis' plantation and raised/worked outside music there from childhood; interested in music early learning bass at 6 years of age; joined family string band frequently working square dances in Bolton,

Sam Chatmon *Photo by Jim O'Neal. Courtesy* Living Blues *Magazine*

MS, area from c1905 to c1927 with occasional tours through Mississippi/Tennessee/Illinois; worked white dances, Leroy Percy Park, Jackson, MS, 1928; settled in Hollandale, MS, to work streets/drug stores in late 20s; rec acc to Texas Alexander, OKeh label, San Antonio, TX, 1930; rec w Mississippi Sheiks, OKeh label, San Antonio, 1930; toured w Mississippi Sheiks working country dances/picnics/parties through Mississippi/Tennessee/Georgia/Louisiana/Illinois/New York from c1930; rec w Mississippi Sheiks, Bluebird label, San Antonio, 1934; rec w Mississippi Sheiks, Bluebird label, New Orleans, LA, 1935; rec w brother Lonnie Chatmon (as "Chatman Brothers"), Bluebird label, New Orleans, 1936; extensive touring with brothers in local minstrel shows/theater groups working dances/fish fries/ parties/picnics/hotels through South through late 30s; worked outside music (as plantation supervisor), Arcola, MS, late 30s into early 40s; returned to Hollandale, MS, to work mostly outside music, 1942 through 60s; rec Arhoolie label, Hollandale, 1960; worked small folk clubs, Los Angeles, CA/San Diego, CA, areas, 1967 into early 70s; rec Blue Goose label, San Diego, 1971; worked San Diego State Univ Folk Festival, San Diego, 1971-4 (por 1974 concert on KPFK-FM-radio); worked w New Mississippi Sheiks, Univ of Chicago Folk Festival, Chicago, IL, 1972; rec Rounder label, Chicago, 1972; worked Folklore Center, NYC, NY, 1972; River City Blues Festival, Memphis, TN, 1972-3; Smithsonian Festival of American Folklife, Washington, DC, 1972; Community Music Center, San Francisco, CA, 1973; rec Advent label, San Diego, CA, 1973; worked Mariposa Folk Festival, Toronto Island, Can, 1974; app in local country blues show, WMAB-TV (PBS), Jackson, MS, 1974; worked Ritz Theater, Austin, TX, 1974; Winnipeg Folk Festival, Birds Hill Park, Winnipeg, Can, 1975; app on TODAY Show, NBC-TV, 1976; worked Pinewoods Society Concert, NYC, NY, 1976; Washington Square Methodist Church, NYC, 1976; Harbor Col Folk Festival, Wilmington, CA, 1976; New Orleans Jazz & Heritage Festival, New Orleans, LA, 1976; rec Albatross label, 1976; app on THE DEVIL'S MUSIC—A HISTORY OF THE BLUES (ep: Nothing But the Truth/ep: Work and Mother Wit) BBC-1-TV, Eng, 1976; worked Santa Rosa Folk Festival, Santa Rosa, CA, 1977; American Folk Music Festival, Los Angeles Harbor Col, Wilmington, CA, 1977; app GOOD MORNIN' BLUES, PBS-TV, 1978; worked Mississippi Delta Blues Fest, Freedom Village, MS, 1978-82 (por 1980 concert on MISSISSIPPI DELTA BLUES, PBS-TV, 1981); rec Rounder label 1979; app THE LAND WHERE THE BLUES BEGAN, NET-TV, 1980; entered South Washington County Hospital where he died of lung cancer; buried Sanders Garden Cemetery, Hollandale, MS

Personal: Half brother of Charley Patton, singer

Songs: Ash Tray Taxi/B&O Blues/Blues in E/Brown Skin Women Blues/Cool About My Loving/Corrine (Corinne Corinna)/Cross Cut Saw Blues/Don't Sell It, Give It Away/Go Back Old Devil/Old Grey Mule, You Ain't What You Used to Be/Sales Tax/Screwdriver/She's My Baby/Turnup Greens/What's the Name of That Thing?/Winter Time Blues

Infl by: Bo Chatmon/Blind Lemon Jefferson/Lonnie Johnson

Quotes: "He still has the vocal flexibility required to swing between a slow, poignant song with antiphonal mutters and shouts and many different levels of blues expression, so that he becomes, in effect, a living summation of the style"—John S Wilson, *New York Times* newspaper, Jul 21, 1972

References: Blues Unlimited magazine (UK), Jul 1971, pp 9-10

Jazz Journal magazine (UK), Jun 1972, p 18

Sing Out magazine, May-Jun 1977, pp 10-11

CHENIER, CLIFTON

Born: Jun 25, 1925, Opelousas (St Landry Parish), LA
Died: Dec 12, 1987, Lafayette, LA
Inst: Accordion/Harmonica/Organ/Piano

Father Joseph Chenier; mother Olivia ———; born, worked outside music on farm near Opelousas, LA, as child; interested in music early, learning basics from father as youth; worked w brother Cleveland Chenier in Clarence Garlow Band, Lake Charles, LA, 1942; worked outside music, New Iberia, LA, mid-40s; worked outside music with occasional weekend gigs, Port Arthur, TX, 1947-54; formed Hot Sizzling Band working Cajun areas of Port Arthur, TX/Beaumont, TX/Houston, TX/Lake Charles, LA, late 40s into 50s; rec Elko label, Lake Charles, 1954; worked Blue Moon Club, Port Arthur, TX, 1955; toured w own band working dances/parties through South to West Coast, 1955; worked Bon Ton Drive-In, Beaumont, TX, 1955-6; worked 5-4 Ballroom, Los Angeles, CA, 1955; rec Specialty label, Los Angeles, 1955; toured w Bon Ton Garlow working club dates out of Beaumont c1955; frequently toured w R&B acts working theater dates across US, 1955-6; worked Crown Propeller, Chicago, IL, c1955; Doris Miller Auditorium, Aus-

Clifton Chenier

Photo by Michael P Smith. Courtesy C Strachwitz, Arhoolie Records

tin, TX, 1956; rec Argo label, Los Angeles, 1956; rec Checker label, Chicago, 1957; frequently worked local club dates out of Houston, TX, 1958 into early 60s; rec Zynn label, Crowley, LA, 1961; extensive tours as ballad/blues/Zydeco singer working bars/clubs/concerts through east Texas/Louisiana/Florida from early 60s; rec Arhoolie label, Houston, 1964-5; worked Berkeley Blues Festival, Univ of California, Berkeley, CA, 1966 (por rel Arhoolie label); rec Arhoolie/Crazy Cajun labels, Pasadena, CA, 1966; worked Bon Ton Roulet, Lafayette, LA, c1967; Avalon Ballroom, San Francisco, CA, 1967; Ash Grove, Los Angeles, CA, 1967; Newport Folk Festival, Newport, RI, 1969; rec Arhoolie label, Houston, TX, 1969-70; worked Ann Arbor Blues Festival, Ann Arbor, MI, 1969; toured w American Folk Blues Festival working concert dates through England/Europe, 1969; worked Royal Albert Hall, London, Eng, 1967 (por rel CBS label); frequently toured w own group working dances/clubs along Gulf Coast/West Coast/northwest US areas into 70s; toured w Jimmy Reed working concerts through Canada in early 70s; Raven Oyster Bar, Beaumont, TX, 1971; app on own TV show, Lafayette, LA, 1971; worked St Marks Hall, Richmond CA, 1971 (por rel Arhoolie label); worked Ash Grove, Los Angeles, CA, 1971; New Orleans Jazz & Heritage Festival/Fair, New Orleans, LA, 1972-3; app in Les Blank film DRY WOOD AND HOT PEPPER, 1973; Ozark Mountain Folk Fair, AR, 1973 (por in film GETTIN' BACK); worked The Sparkle Paradise Club, Bridge City, TX, 1973-5; rec Arhoolie label, San Francisco, CA, 1973; app in French film WITHIN SOUTHERN LOUISIANA, 1974; worked w own Red Hot Louisiana Band, New Orleans Jazz & Heritage Festival, New Orleans, 1974 into 80s; Blue Morocco, Port Arthur, TX, 1974; Continental Showcase, Houston, TX, 1974; All Hallows Church, San Francisco, CA, 1974; Club Zayante, Felton, CA,

1974; Ruthie's Inn, Berkeley, CA, 1974; Liberty Hall, Houston, 1974; Jed's University Inn, New Orleans, 1975-6; Montreux Rock/Blues Festival, Montreux, Switzerland, 1975 (por rel RCA-Victor label); Embassy Hall, Los Angeles, 1975; The Boarding House, San Francisco, 1975; Contemporary Arts Museum, Houston, 1975; St Francis Church, Houston, 1975; rec Arhoolie label, Bogalusa, LA, 1975; app on AUSTIN CITY LIMITS, PBS-TV, 1976; worked dances/club dates in San Francisco, CA, area, 1976; Mainliner Club, San Francisco, 1976; Antone's, Austin, TX, 1976-8; Rosy's, New Orleans, 1976; St Francis of Assisi Parish Hall, Houston, TX, 1977; Murphy and Me Club, Eugene, OR, 1977; Verbum Dei Auditorium, Los Angeles, 1977; toured Europe working clubs/concerts, 1978; toured US/Canada through 80s; app in Les Blank film J'AI ETE AU BAL, c1990; entered Lafayette General Hospital where he died of chronic kidney disease; buried Loreauville, LA

Billings: The King of the South/King of the Zydeco

Songs: Ain't Gonna Worry Any More/All Day Long/All Night Long/Bad Luck and Trouble/Bayou Drive/Bogalusa Boogie/Blues All the Time/Brown Skin Woman/Calinda/Come Go Along with Me/I Can't Stand/I Woke Up This Morning/I'm a Hog for You/Just a Lonely Boy/Louisiana Blues/My Mama Told Me/One Step at a Time/They Call Me Crazy/Something on My Mind/Worried Life Blues

Awards/Honors: Won *Blues Unlimited* magazine (UK) readers poll as best Cajun artist of 1973

Infl by: Morris Chenier/Bon Ton Garlow

Quotes: "Chenier . . . a blues singer and accordionist extraordinaire, is the foremost practitioner of that black Louisiana-Cajun R&B called Zydeco or, sometimes, Zodico . . ."—Ed Leimbacher, *Rolling Stone* magazine, Dec 23, 1971

"One of the undisputed masters of American French blues"—Pete Welding, *Downbeat* magazine, Oct 10, 1974, p 26

"Chenier is king of Zydeco . . . a cross of Cajun and blues with a grand mélange of other influences"—Roger Misiewicz, *Coda* magazine (Canada), Oct 1973, p 25

Reference: Rolling Stone magazine, Dec 23, 1971

CHICAGO BILL
(see Broonzy, William)

CHICAGO BOB
(see Nelson, Bob)

CHICAGO SUNNY BOY
(see Louis, Joe Hill)

CHOCOLATE BROWN
(see Scruggs, Irene)

CLAYTON, PETER JOE *"Doc"/"Doctor"*
(aka: Peter Cleighton)
Born: Apr 19, 1898, Georgia
Died: Jan 7, 1947, Chicago, IL

Father was Peter Clayton Sr; both parents born in South Africa; raised in St Louis, MO, where he began singing pop ballads in local bars through 20s into 30s; moved to Chicago, IL, in mid-30s where he sang blues in local clubs; reportedly rec Bluebird label, Chicago, 1935; frequently worked Sylvio's, Chicago, late 30s; frequently worked w Robert Jr Lockwood/Sunnyland Slim in local club dates, Chicago, through 30s into 40s; rec OKeh label, Chicago, 1941; rec Bluebird label, Chicago, 1941-2; toured South working club dates, 1942; reportedly worked as itinerant singer in after-hours clubs for tips, Chicago, through 40s; rec Victor label, Chicago, 1946; entered Cook County Hospital where he died of tuberculosis; buried Restvale Cemetery, Worth, IL

Note: Some reports state this singer may have been born in Africa and brought to US at an early age

Personal: Married 1933-7. 4 children. His entire family died in accident, 1937

Billing: Blues Doctor

Songs: Ain't Gonna Drink No More/Ain't No Business We Can Do/Angels in Harlem/Doctor Clayton Blues/Hold That Train Conductor/I Gotta Find My Baby/I Need My Baby/Let Me Play Your Vendor/Moonshine Woman Blues/My Own Blues/Pearl Harbor Blues

Infl to: BB King/Robert Jr Lockwood/Malcolm Willis/Jimmy Witherspoon

Quotes: "Clayton was a meaty, virile singer . . ."—Tony Russell, *Jazz & Blues* magazine (UK), Apr 1971, p 19

"A very distinctive singer and fine songwriter"—Mike Rowe, *Chicago Breakdown*, Eddison Press Ltd, 1973

CLEARWATER, EDDY
(aka: Guitar Eddy)
Born: Jan 10, 1935, Macon (Noxubee Co), MS
Inst: Guitar

Peter "Doc" Clayton

Courtesy Frank Driggs Collection

Father was Ralph Harrington; mother Willie Mae Love; born Eddy Harrington; early influences were Red Foley/Hank Williams; moved to Birmingham, AL, where he taught self guitar and frequently worked with father in local spiritual groups in area c1948-50; moved to Chicago, IL, where he frequently worked local churches from 1950; formed own blues trio working Grand Ballroom, Chicago, c1953; Cadillac Baby, Chicago, c1953; Happy Home Lounge, Chicago, c1953; Skyway Lounge, Chicago, c1955; L&D Lounge, Chicago, c1955; rec Atomic label, Chicago, c1956-9; frequently worked Kirksey's Lounge, Chicago, late 50s; app on Dick Clark's AMERICAN BANDSTAND, ABC-TV, c1959; rec Atomic-H label, Chicago, 1959; rec La Salle/Federal labels, Chicago, 1960; worked Lee's Lounge, Chicago, 1960; rec USA label, Chicago, c1961; frequently worked small clubs, Chicago, through 60s; worked Club Hello, Chicago, 1967; Casa Madrid, Chicago, c1968; El Morocco, Chicago, c1969; Lemon Tree, Chicago, c1969; Starlight Club, Chicago, c1969; Cavalier Show Lounge, Chicago, c1969; The Gold Coast, Chicago, 1970; rec Versa label, Chicago, c1970; was co-owner of Atomic-H label, Chicago, early 70s; frequently worked J&J Lounge, Chicago, 1972; New Party Time Lounge, Chicago, 1972; Tiebiro's Lounge, Chicago, 1972; Sportsman Lounge, Chicago, 1972; Stardust Lounge, Chicago, 1972; Angelo's Speakeasy Lounge, Stone Park, IL, 1972; The Post, Chicago, 1972; This Way Inn, Franklin Park, IL, 1972; Wise Fools Pub, Chicago, 1973-4; app on ATOMIC MAMA'S WANG DANG DOODLE BLUES, WNIB-FM-radio, Chicago, c1973; rec w Bob Riedy Blues Band, Flying Fish label, Chicago, 1974; worked Attic Lounge, Chicago, 1974-5; White Stallion, Chicago, 1974; opened own record store, Chicago, 1974; worked Auditorium Theater, Chicago, 1974; Majestic "M," Chicago, 1975; w Bob Riedy Blues Band, Zoo Bar, Lincoln, NE, 1975; Biddy Mulligan's Bar, Chicago, 1975; Eddie Shaw's Place, Chicago, 1975; Kingston

Eddy Clearwater
Courtesy Living Blues *Magazine*

Mines, Chicago, 1976; Four Locks, Westmont, IL, 1976; Jaspers, Chicago, 1976; Zorba's, Cicero, IL, 1976; Zoo Bar, Lincoln, NE, 1977; The Zodiac, Chicago, 1977

Personal: Married Carol Bellerive (1977-). Named "Clearwater" by booking agent as name-play on singer "Muddy Waters"

Songs: Boogie Woogie Baby/Cool Water

Infl by: Chuck Berry/Magic Sam

Reference: Living Blues magazine, Summer 1972, pp 10-13

CLEIGHTON, PETER
(see Clayton, Peter)

CLEMENS, ALBERT
(see Lofton, Clarence)

CLIFF, DAISY
(see McCoy, Viola)

COBBS, WILLIE
(aka: Willie C)
Born: Jul 15, 1940, Monroe (Monroe Co), AR
Inst: Guitar/Harmonica

One of 11 children; sang with parents in local church choir as child and was leading choir at 8 years of age; toured with local church choir working churches through Arkansas, c1948-9; formed own spiritual quartet with brothers working local churches in area c1950; moved to Chicago, IL, 1951; frequently worked outside music in Chicago from 1951; frequently worked/learned/teamed w Little Walter working Maxwell Street area for tips, Chicago, early 50s; frequently worked w Muddy Waters Band in local club dates, Chicago, c1952; served in US Marines in Japan/Caribbean areas, 1953-7; returned to Chicago, IL, to open own Toast of Town Club, 1957; toured as single working club dates in Memphis, TN/Florida/Texas during late 50s; formed own band to tour club dates through South c1959 into 60s; rec Mojo label, Memphis, 1961; rec C&F label, Memphis, 1962; rec Ruler label, Memphis, 1963; rec JOB label, Chicago, 1963; rec Pure Gold label, 1964; rec Whirl-A-Way label, Memphis, 1965; frequently worked outside music, 1965-8; settled in Stuttgart, AR, to operate local taverns in Dewitt, AR, area from 1969

Songs: While in Korea/You're So Hard to Please

Reference: Blues Unlimited magazine (UK), Jun 1970, p 15

COLEMAN, BURL C *"Jaybird"*
(aka: Rabbit's Foot Williams)
Born: May 20, 1896, Gainesville (Sumter Co), AL
Died: Jun 28, 1950, Tuskegee, AL
Inst: Guitar/Harmonica/Jug

Parents were sharecroppers; one of 4 children; born/raised/worked outside music on farm from childhood; learned harmonica at about 12 years of age; served in US Army at Ft McClellan, Anniston, AL, where he began to sing blues and entertain troops c1917-19; returned to Gainesville, AL, to work outside music from c1920; teamed w Big Joe Williams in Birmingham Jug Band to tour w Rabbit Foot Minstrels working shows through South c1922-4; settled in Bessemer, AL, to work with wife in local church/parties/suppers/picnics in Birmingham/Bessemer, AL, area through 20s; rec Gennett/Silvertone/Black Patti labels, Birmingham, 1927; toured as single working club dates through South, 1929; frequently worked w Birmingham Jug Band in Bessemer/Birmingham/Tuscaloosa, AL, area into 30s; rec w Birmingham Jug Band, OKeh label, Atlanta, GA, 1930; rec Columbia label, Atlanta, GA, 1930; worked mostly outside music with occasional work as single/with other jug bands/or acc sister Lizzie Coleman on streets in Bessemer/Birmingham area through 30s/40s; entered Veterans Administration Hospital where he died of cancer; buried Lincoln Memorial Gardens, Bessemer, AL

Personal: Married Irene ———. Named "Jaybird" while in army service due to his independent manner

Quote: "His technique was close to the field holler with a sung vocal line and then an interpreting response on the harmonica"—Paul Oliver, *The Story of the Blues*, Chilton Book Company, 1969

References: Back Woods Blues, Simon A Napier, Blues Unlimited, 1968
The Bluesmen, Samuel B Charters, Oak Publications, 1967

COLEMAN, NELLY
(see Wilson, Lena)

COLLINS, ALBERT
Born: Oct 3, 1932, Leona (Leon Co), TX
Died: Nov. 24, 1993, Las Vegas, NV
Inst: Guitar

Born and raised on farm; moved to Houston, TX, 1939; attended local high school where he studied piano/guitar, Houston, mid-40s; formed own trio to work local bars/clubs, Houston, from c1948; worked w own The Rhythm Rockers, Manhattan Club, Galveston, TX, c1949-51; frequently worked w Malcolm Moore's Orch in local club dates, Houston, 1951; toured w Piney Brown Orch working club dates through South c1951-4; frequently worked outside music with occasional weekend gigs w Gatemouth Brown, Houston, from 1954; rec Kangaroo label, Houston, 1958; rec Great Scott label, Houston, c1960; rec Hall label, Houston, 1962; formed own small group working club dates in Houston area through 60s; rec 20th Century-Fox label, Houston, 1965; worked w own group at Christian Club, Houston, 1967; Ponderosa Club, Houston, 1968; Chateau Club, Houston, 1968; rec Imperial label, Houston, 1968; worked Ash Grove, Los Angeles, CA, 1968-73; Carousel Club, Oakland, CA, 1968; Santa Monica Civic Auditorium, Santa Monica, CA, 1969; Fillmore West, San Francisco, CA, 1969; Newport 69, Northridge, CA, 1969; Seattle Pop Festival, Duvall, WA, 1969; rec Tumbleweed label, Chicago, IL, 1971; worked Lighthouse, Los Angeles, CA, 1972; Four Muses, San Clemente, CA, 1972; Univ of California, Los Angeles, 1972; Esquire Showbar, Montreal, Can, 1972; Joe's Place, Cambridge, MA, 1972; frequent club dates in Seattle, WA, 1972-5; Fergie's, Goleta, CA, 1973; El Mocambo Tavern, Toronto, Can, 1973; Joint Bar, Minneapolis, MN, 1974; The Rainbow Room, Detroit, MI, 1974; Montreux Jazz Festival, Montreux, Switzerland, 1975; Monkey's Bottom, Portland, OR, 1975; Old Waldorf, San Francisco, CA, 1975; Wilshire Ebell Theater, Los Angeles, CA, 1976; WOW Hall, Eugene, OR, 1976; Murphy & Me Club, Eugene, 1977; frequently worked Green Earth Cafe, San Francisco, 1977; The Lighthouse, Los Angeles, 1977; San Francisco Blues Festival, McLaren Park, San Francisco, 1977

Albert Collins *Courtesy Tom Mazzolini*

Personal: Married (c1968-). Cousin of Lightnin' Hopkins

Songs: Back Yard Back Talk/Collin's Mix/Do What You Want to Do/Don't Lose Your Cool/Dyin' Flu/ Frosty/Got a Good Thing Goin'/Harris County Line-Up/Hot 'n' Cold/Jam It Up/Jawing/Left Overs/ Let's Get It Together/Shiver and Shake/Soul Food/ Talking Slim Blues/Thaw Out/Watcha Say?

Infl by: Clarence "Gatemouth" Brown/BB King/ Aaron "T-Bone" Walker

Quotes: "Albert has taken the post T-Bone Walker/BB King guitar idiom to new exciting levels of creativity and inventiveness"—Pete Welding, BluesTime album BTS-8

"The *best* of the Texas blues guitarists"—Bob Hite, Imperial album LP-12428

References: *Living Blues* magazine, Winter 1973, pp 12-13

Blues Unlimited magazine (UK), May 1969, pp 5-6

COLLINS, LOUIS BO
(*aka:* Mr Bo)

Courtesy Living Blues *Magazine*

Born: Apr 7, 1932, Indianola (Sunflower Co), MS
Inst: Guitar

Raised on farm and learned guitar at 11 years of age; moved to Chicago, IL, to work outside music from 1946; moved to Detroit, MI, 1950 to work outside music; worked w Washboard Willie, Good Time Bar, Detroit, 1956; formed own band to work local club dates in Detroit area, 1958 into 60s; rec w own Blues Boys, Big D/Diamond Jim labels, Detroit, 1966-71; worked w own Blues Boys, The Town House, Dearborn, MI, 1970-3; Detroit Blues Festival, Detroit, 1970; rec own Gold Top label, Detroit, 1972; worked Ann Arbor Blues Festival, Ann Arbor, MI, 1973; frequently worked outside music in Detroit, MI, area through 70s

Personal: Brother of Little Mack Collins, musician

Songs: I Ain't Gonna Suffer/If Trouble Was Money/ Lost Love Affair/Never Love Again

Infl by: BB King

Infl to: Little Joe Blue

Quote: "His clean, polished, BB King-based modern blues sound has kept him in business"—Jim O'Neal, *Living Blues* magazine, Winter 1973, p 10

Reference: *Living Blues* magazine, Winter 1973, p 10

COLLINS, SAMUEL *"Cryin' Sam"*
(*aka:* Bunny Carter/Jim Foster/Salty Dog Sam/Big Boy Woods)
Born: Aug 11, 1887, Louisiana
Died: Oct 20, 1949, Chicago, IL
Inst: Guitar

Father was Samuel Collins Sr; mother was Sophie ———; was raised in McComb, MS, area; reportedly worked w King Solomon Hill at local parties/picnics, McComb area, from 1920; rec Gennett label, Chicago, IL/Richmond, IN, 1927; rec ARC label group, NYC, NY, 1931-2; reportedly worked roadhouses/jukes in northern cities into 30s; reportedly settled in Chicago in late 30s working outside music; died of heart disease at home; buried Burr Oak Cemetery, Worth, IL

Personal: Married Lillie ———

Quote: ". . . there was an intensity to his best work, a brooding sense that fused the awkwardness of his style into a whole expression that was often moving" —Samuel B Charters, *The Bluesmen,* Oak Publications, 1967

COLLINS

Reference: The Bluesmen, Samuel B Charters, Oak Publications, 1967

COLLINS, "*Big*" TOM
(see Dupree, William)
(see McGhee, Walter)

COOK, ANN

Courtesy Institute of Jazz Studies

Born: May 10, 1903, St Francisville (West Feliciana Parish), LA
Died: Sept 29, 1962, New Orleans, LA

Father was Carl Cook; mother was Rose Henderson; one of at least 6 children; raised in New Orleans, LA, area from childhood; reportedly was working in Storyville section of New Orleans as singer from c1915; worked Countess Willie Piazza House, New Orleans, 1918; frequently worked local clubs/bars like Red Onion Cafe/Calliope Street Cafe/others, New Orleans, through teens into 20s; rec w Louis Dumaine Jazzola Eight, Victor label, New Orleans, 1927; frequently worked outside music through 20s/30s; frequently sang in church choir of Greater St Matthew #2 Baptist Church, New Orleans, from 1940s; rec (non-blues) w Wooden Joe Nicholas Band, American Music label, New Orleans, 1949; mostly inactive through 50s; suffered fatal heart attack at home; buried Ellen Cemetery, St Bernard, LA

Note: City of birth listed in some reports as Franzenville or Fazaneville. As there were no such towns in Louisiana at that time, it is likely they are phonetic spellings of above city

Personal: Married Willie Johnson

Song: Mamma Cookie's Blues

Quotes: "She would sing according to the temperament and moods of the customers and could sing endless verses to one song"—Clarence Williams, *Boogie Woogie Blues Folio*, Clarence Williams Publishing Company, 1940

"She was just one of them real outstanding barrelhouse blues singers"—(Earl Humphrey) Karl Gert zur Heide, *Deep South Piano*, Studio Vista Ltd, 1970

COOKER, JOHN LEE
(see Hooker, John Lee)

COOL PAPA
(see Sadler, Haskell)

COOT(S)
(see Grant, Leola B)

CORLEY, DEWEY

Photo by Jim O'Neal. Courtesy Living Blues Magazine

Born: Jun 18, 1898, Halley (Desha Co), AR
Died: Apr 15, 1974, Memphis, TN
Inst: Harmonica/Jug/Kazoo/Piano/Washtub Bass

Father was musician; interested in music early and was playing harmonica as child; ran away from home to hobo across US working outside music into teens; settled in Memphis, TN, 1916 to work outside music with occasional side work as musician into 20s; frequently worked w Memphis Jug Band in Memphis area c1926; frequently w Memphis Jug Band and other bluesmen working WC Handy Park/streets/riverboats, Memphis area, into 30s; frequently worked w Jack Kelly's South Memphis Jug Band at stag parties at Blue Room of Peabody Hotel and other gigs, Memphis, c1933-4; rec w Memphis Jug Band, OKeh label, Chicago, IL, 1934; worked outside music with occasional gigs with local jug bands, Memphis area,

Elizabeth "Libba" Cotten *Photo by Julie Snow*

through 30s/40s/50s; rec Arhoolie label, Tennessee/ Mississippi, mid-60s; rec Rounder label, Memphis, 1967; worked Memphis Blues Festival, Memphis, 1969; rec Adelphi label, Memphis, 1969; worked National Folk Festival, Washington, DC, 1971; River City Blues Festival, Memphis, 1971; rec Albatross label, Memphis, 1972; entered City of Memphis Hospital and died of natural causes; buried local cemetery, Kansas City, MO

Songs: Dewey's Walkin' Blues/Fishing in the Dark

Quote: "He did have a compelling voice and a great ability for impromptu lyrical creation"—Steve LaVere, *Living Blues* magazine, Autumn 1974, p 7

Reference: Living Blues magazine, Autumn 1974, p 7

COTTEN, ELIZABETH *"Libba"*

Born: Jan 5, 1893, Chapel Hill (Orange Co), NC
Died: Jun 29, 1987, Syracuse, NY
Inst: Banjo/Guitar

Father was George Nevilles; mother Louisa Price; born Sis Nevilles; one of 2 children; given first guitar which she taught self and occasionally entertained family/friends from c1904; worked outside music, Chapel Hill, NC, from 1907 into 40s; moved to Washington, DC, to work outside music from 1943; worked outside music (as housekeeper for ethnomusicologist Charles Seeger and family), Chevy Chase, MD, early 50s into 60s; worked Newport Folk Festival, Newport, RI, 1964 (por rel Vanguard label); rec Folkways label, NYC, NY (?), 1967; worked Festival of American Folklife, Washington, DC, 1968-71; Newport Folk Festival, Newport, RI, 1968; Smoky Mountain Folk Festival, Gatlinburg, TN, c1969; Washington Square Church, NYC, 1969; Washington Blues Festival, Howard Univ, Washington, DC, 1970; Mariposa Folk Festival, Toronto, Can, 1970; Philadelphia Folk Festival, Schwenksville, PA, 1972; National Folk Festival, Wolf Trap Farm Park, Vienna, VA, 1973; app in videotape GRASS ROOTS SERIES #1 — OLD TIME MUSIC, 1974; worked McCabe's, Santa Monica, CA, 1974; Binghamton Folk Festival, Binghamton, NY, 1974; Mariposa Folk Festival, Toronto, Can, 1974; Town Crier Cafe, Poughkeepsie, NY, 1975; Reed Col, Portland, OR, 1975; Euphoria Tavern, Portland, OR, 1975; Festival of American Folklife, Washington, DC, 1975; Great American Music Hall, San Francisco, CA, 1976; app on ME AND STELLA, PBS-TV (syndicated), 1977; worked Carnegie Hall, NYC, 1978; app AUSTIN CITY LIMITS, WNET-TV (PBS), 1979; toured US/Europe working clubs/concerts into 80s; worked Smithsonian, Washington, DC, 1983; suffered fatal injuries in a fall; died at Crouse-Irving Hospital; body cremated

Personal: Married Frank Cotten (1907-c1947). 1 child

Songs: Freight Train/I'm Going Away/Washington Blues

Quote: "Her music is rooted in blues, rag, traditional, and religious tunes that were part of her own unique life experience, and the lyrics and musical accompaniments of her songs reflect this individuality and creative outlook on life"—Kristin Baggelaar/Donald Milton, *Folk Music: More Than A Song,* 1976

References: Folk Scene magazine, Apr 1974, pp 14-17
Folk Music: More Than a Song, Baggelaar / Milton, Thomas Y Crowell Company, 1976

COTTON, JAMES *"Jimmy"*

(aka: Joe Denim)
Born: Jul 1, 1935, Tunica (Tunica Co), MS
Inst: Drums/Guitar/Harmonica

Father was a preacher; mother was harmonica player; born/raised/worked on farm as child with some singing in local church choir into 40s; began playing harmonica after hearing Sonny Boy Williamson (Alex Miller) on local radio, 1942; frequently worked streets/local joints/parties for tips, Tunica, MS, from 1944; ran away from home to work w Sonny Boy Williamson (Alex Miller) in Helena, AR, area with occasional app on KING BISCUIT TIME, KFFA-radio, Helena, and frequent tours working jukes through Mississippi/Arkansas, 1945-50; occasionally worked in bands of Howlin' Wolf/Willie Nix/others, West Memphis, AR, area in late 40s; worked w Sonny Boy Williamson (Alex Miller), Be-Bop Hall, West Memphis, 1950; assumed leadership of Sonny Boy Williamson (Alex Miller) Band working local gigs in West Memphis, then toured with band through Tennessee/ Arkansas, 1950-3; frequently worked as single in local jukes/clubs, West Memphis, early 50s; app w Willie Nix on BROADWAY FURNITURE STORE Show, KWEM-radio, West Memphis, c1950; frequently app on HART'S BREAD Show, KWEM-radio, West Memphis, c1952; worked outside music, West Memphis area, c1953-4; rec Sun label, Memphis, TN, 1954; joined Muddy Waters Band in Memphis and toured/worked/recorded off-and-on with band out of Chicago, IL, 1954-66; frequently worked 708 Club/

James "Jimmy" Cotton *Courtesy* Living Blues *Magazine*

Sylvio's/others, Chicago, late 50s into early 60s; w Muddy Waters Band, Carnegie Hall, NYC, NY, 1959 (por rel United Artists label); worked w Muddy Waters Band, Newport Jazz Festival, Newport, RI, 1960 (por rel Chess label/por shown in film THE SUBTERRANEANS); toured w Muddy Waters Band working concert dates through England/Europe, 1961; worked British Beaulieu Jazz Festival, London, Eng, 1961; rec Columbia label, London, 1961; worked w Muddy Waters Band, Carnegie Hall, NYC, 1961; rec w Otis Spann, Vanguard label, Chicago, IL, 1965; rec acc to Johnny Young, Arhoolie label, Chicago, 1965; worked Downbeat Jazz Festival, Chicago, 1965; formed own band to work local club dates, Chicago, from 1966; rec Loma label, Chicago, 1966; worked Mother Blues, Chicago, 1966; The Bowery, Chicago, 1966; Fillmore Auditorium, San Francisco, CA, 1966; Folk Music Festival, Berkeley, CA, 1967 (por shown on syndicated TV); rec Verve label, NYC, NY, 1967; worked Town Hall, NYC, 1967; La Cave, Cleveland, OH, 1967; Living End, Detroit, MI, 1967; Grand Ballroom, Detroit, 1967; Second Fret, Philadelphia, PA, 1967; The Riverboat, Toronto, Can, 1967; Fillmore East, NYC, 1968; The Troubador, Los Angeles, CA, 1968; Loew's King Theater, Brooklyn, NY, 1968; Cafe A-Go-Go, NYC, 1968; Sky River Rock Festival, Sultan, WA, 1968; Fillmore West, San Francisco, CA, 1968; rec Vanguard label, San Francisco, 1968; worked Kaleidoscope, Philadelphia, PA, 1968; Miami Pop Festival, Hallandale, FL, 1968; The Eagles, Seattle, WA, 1969; app on Hugh Hefner's PLAYBOY AFTER DARK, WOR-TV, NYC (syndicated), 1969; worked The Felt Forum, NYC, 1969; worked w Muddy Waters, The Auditorium, Chicago, IL, 1969; International Pop Festival, Lewisville, TX, 1969; Sky River Rock Festival, Tenino, WA, 1969; State Univ of New York, Buffalo, NY, 1969; Colonial Tavern, Toronto, Can, 1969-70; Ann Arbor Blues Festival, Ann Arbor, MI, 1969; The Jazz Workshop, Boston, MA, 1969-71; w Muddy Waters Band, Ungano's, NYC, 1969; app on DIAL M FOR MUSIC, CBS-TV, 1970; worked Pepper's Lounge, Chicago, IL, 1970-1; Blue Flame Lounge, Chicago, 1970-1; Lennie's, Boston, MA, 1970-2; Town Hall, NYC, 1970; rec Capitol label, Los Angeles, CA, early 70s; worked Coq D'or, Toronto, Can, 1971; Kileinhan's Music Hall, Buffalo, NY, 1971; Univ of Detroit, Detroit, MI, 1972; Esquire Showbar, Montreal, Can, 1972; app UK film short PLAYING THE THING, 1972; worked Siena Col Blues Festival, Memphis, TN, 1972; Joe's Place, Cambridge, MA, 1972; Good Rockin' Lounge, Chicago, IL, 1972; Central Park Music Festival, NYC, NY, 1973; w Muddy Waters Band, The Auditorium, Chicago, 1973; Theresa's Lounge, Chicago, 1973-4; Grendel's Lair Coffeehouse, Philadelphia, PA, 1973; Avery Fisher Hall, NYC, 1973; La Bastille, Houston, TX, 1973; Paul's Mall, Boston, MA, 1973; Shaboo Inn, Mansfield, CT, 1973; Sandy's, Beverly, MA, 1973-4; Main Point, Bryn Mawr, PA, 1974-5; Monterey Jazz Festival, Monterey, CA, 1974; Last Chance Saloon, Poughkeepsie, NY, 1974; Checkerboard Lounge, Chicago, IL, 1974; Electric Ballroom, Atlanta, GA, 1974; Univ of Houston, Houston, TX, 1974; Pepper's Hideout, Chicago, 1974; Sweet Queen Bee's, Chicago, 1974; Rainbow Room, Detroit, MI, 1974; rec Buddah label, Quincy, MA, 1974; Easter Concert, Cocoa Beach, FL, 1974; Convention Center, Dallas, TX, 1974; Mondavi Winery Summer Festival, Oakville, CA, 1975; toured w Johnny Winter working concert dates across US, 1975; worked w Johnny Winter, The Spectrum, Philadelphia, PA, 1975; rec Buddah label, New Orleans, LA, 1975; worked The Boston Club, Cambridge, MA, 1975; Aquarius Tavern, Seattle, WA, 1975; Ratso's, Chicago, IL, 1975-6; Peyton Place, Chicago, 1975; Keystone, Berkeley, CA, 1975-6; The Bottom Line, NYC, NY, 1975-6; Sophie's, Palo Alto, CA, 1976; My Father's Place, Roslyn, NY, 1976; Max's Kansas City, NYC, 1976; Outside Inn, Buffalo, NY, 1976; Monterey Jazz Festival, Monterey, CA, 1976; rec w Muddy Waters, Blue Sky label, Westport, CT, 1976; worked The Palladium, NYC, 1977; Elliot's Nest, Rochester, NY, 1977; toured w Muddy Waters/Johnny Winter working concert/college dates across US, 1977; worked Ivanhoe, Chicago, IL, 1977; Liberty Hall, Houston, TX, 1977; Belle Starr, Buffalo, NY, 1977

Personal: Married (1955-). 2 children

Songs: All Walks of Life/Caldonia/Cotton Crop Blues/The Creeper/The Creeper Creeps Again/Down at Your Buryin'/'Fatuation/Feelin' Good/Hold Me in Your Arms/How Long Can a Fool Go Wrong?/I Got a Feelin'/My Baby/One More Mile/Straighten Up Baby

Infl by: Muddy Waters/Sonny Boy Williamson (Alex Miller)

Quote: ". . . one of the better live performers in the blues"—Thomas J Cullen III, *Living Blues* magazine, Winter 1973, p 29

Reference: Blues Unlimited magazine (UK), Jul 1976, pp 4-11

COUNCIL, FLOYD *"Dipper Boy"*
(aka: Devil's Daddy-In-Law)

Photo by Kip Lornell. Courtesy Living Blues *Magazine*

Born: Sept 2, 1911, Chapel Hill (Orange Co), NC
Died: cJun 1976, Sanford, NC (unconfirmed)
Inst: Guitar/Mandolin

Interested in music at early age and learned guitar as child; raised in Chapel Hill, NC, frequently working outside music with occasional entertaining on streets with own small group, late 20s through 30s; frequently worked w Thomas & Leo Strowd in area, late 20s; frequently worked w Blind Boy Fuller on streets for tips, Chapel Hill, through 30s; rec ARC/Vocalion labels, NYC, NY, 1937; frequently worked local country clubs/Elks Homes/local radio, Chapel Hill area, into 40s/50s; mostly inactive due to illness during 60s and settled in Sanford, NC

Billing: Blind Boy Fuller's Buddy

Infl by: Blind Boy Fuller/Peetie Wheatstraw

Quote: "Older musicians around Orange County remembered Floyd as one of the area's best guitarists"—Kip Lornell, *Living Blues* magazine, Mar 1977, p 6

References: Blues Unlimited magazine (UK), Feb 1970, pp 7-8

COUNT ROCKIN' SYDNEY
(see Semien, Sidney)

COUNTRY PAUL
(see Harris, Edward)

COURTNEY, THOMAS *"Tom"/"Tomcat"*

Photo by Virginia Curtiss. Courtesy Living Blues *Magazine*

Born: Jan 23, 1929, Waco (McLennan Co), TX
Inst: Guitar

Father was pianist; ran away from home to work w Bee Kelly's Floor Show (as tap-dancer), Corpus Christi, TX, 1941; toured w Bee Kelly's Floor Show working club dates through area, 1941-2; toured w Dailey Brothers Circus (as dancer) working tent shows through South/Midwest, 1942-6; frequently worked The Greasy Spoon/The Coleman Club (other honky tonks), Lubbock, TX, late 40s into 50s; frequently worked outside music with occasional gigs w Smokey Hogg through Texas during 50s; worked The American Club, Denver, CO, 1960; The Holiday Club, Denver, 1960; frequently toured w Little Johnny Taylor working club dates between Denver, CO, and Los Angeles, CA, 1960-1; moved to Los Angeles to work local gigs, 1961; reportedly worked extensively in Africa, 1962; frequently toured with various blues bands working club dates through California/Texas/Louisiana through 60s; worked w John Hogg's Band in local club dates, Los Angeles, CA, late 60s; settled in San Diego, CA, c1970; formed own Tomcat & The Blues Dusters, working Peoples Club/Folk Arts Store/others, San Diego, into 70s; worked San Diego State Folk Festival, San Diego, 1972; rec Advent label, San Diego, 1973; worked Zebra Club, San Diego, 1975; Peoples Club, Ocean Beach, CA, 1975; Stone Steps Bar, Encinitas, CA, 1975

Personal: Married Smokey Hoggs' niece (1951-)

Songs: Early One Morning/Just Goes to Show You/Somebody's Been Knockin'

Infl by: Aaron "T-Bone" Walker

Reference: Living Blues magazine, Mar 1975, pp 36-7

COUSIN JOE/JOSEPH
(see Joseph, Pleasant)

COVINGTON, *"Bogus"/"Blind"* **BEN**
Born: c1900, Columbus (Lowndes Co), MS
Died: c1935, Homer City, PA (unconfirmed)
Inst: Banjo/Guitar/Harmonica

Reportedly on his own from teens; frequently worked w Big Joe Williams in streets/medicine shows/The Rabbit Foot Minstrels and circuses as musician/singer/human pretzel (side-show attraction) through South into 20s; rec Paramount/Brunswick labels, Chicago, IL, 1928; hoboed extensively through South/North and back into Chicago working odd jobs through 20s into 30s; worked w Big Joe Williams (as fake blind man), Century of Progress World's Fair, Chicago, 1934; whereabouts unknown thereafter

COX, IDA
(*aka:* Velma Bradley/Kate Lewis/Julia Powers/Julius Powers/Jane Smith)
Born: Feb 25, 1896, Toccoa (Stephens Co), GA
Died: Nov 10, 1967, Knoxville, TN

Father was ____ Prather; mother Susie Knox; born Ida Prather; raised in Cedartown, GA learning music early and frequently sang in local African Methodist Church choir as child; ran away from home to tour w White & Clark Black & Tan Minstrels (as a black-face "Topsy") working theater circuits from 1910; toured w Rabbit Foot Minstrels working under canvas through teens; toured w Silas Green from New Orleans Show/Pete Werley's Florida Cotton Blossom Minstrels through late teens; worked briefly outside music (as manager of Douglass Hotel), Macon, GA, c1920; worked w Jelly Roll Morton, 81 Theater, Atlanta, GA, c1920; app on WMC-radio, Memphis, TN, 1923; worked Tom Anderson's Cafe, New Orleans, LA, c1923; rec extensively, Paramount label, Chicago, IL/NYC, NY, 1923-9; frequently toured as feature artist on vaudeville circuit down East Coast through 20s; worked Bijou Theater, Nashville, TN, 1924; Dallas Theater, Dallas, TX, 1926; frequently worked w King Oliver Band, Plantation Club, Chicago, through 20s; worked Grand Theater, Chicago, 1929; toured in own road show revue RAISIN' CAIN working theaters across US, 1929 into early 30s; frequently toured in own DARKTOWN SCANDALS Revue working theaters across US through 30s into 40s; worked w Bessie Smith in FAN WAVES Revue, Apollo Theater, NYC, NY, 1934; w Dede and Billie Pierce working shows through Florida, c1935; app on HOBBY LOBBY, WJZ-radio (Blue Network), 1939; rec w Hot Lips Page/Fletcher Henderson/others, Vocalion/OKeh labels, NYC, 1939-40; worked Cafe Society Downtown, NYC, 1939; From Spirituals to Swing Concert, Carnegie Hall, NYC, 1939-40 (por 1939 concert rel Vanguard label); toured in own show working theater dates in northeast US, 1939; toured w Billie Pierce working theater dates through South, early 40s; app in film WOMAN'S A FOOL, 1947; to Buffalo, NY, where she was inactive in music 1945-9; moved to Knoxville, TN, where she lived from 1949; worked Oshkosh Theater, Oshkosh, WI, c1950; rec w Coleman Hawkins group, Riverside label, NYC, 1961; entered East Tennessee Baptist Hospital where she died of cancer; buried Longview Cemetery, Knoxville, TN

Personal: Married Adler Cox (of Florida Blossoms Minstrel Show) (c1920s); married Jesse Crump, singer/pianist (20s-30s); reportedly married third husband. Had one child. Not to be confused with Sam Fouche, a female impersonator who also used billing "The Sepia Mae West"

Billings: The Sepia Mae West/The Uncrowned Queen of the Blues

Songs: Alphonsia Blues/Bama Bound Blues/Bear-Mash Blues/Blues Ain't Nothin' Else But/Blues for Rampart Street/Cherry Picking Blues/Chicago Bound Blues/Chicago Monkey Man Blues/Come Right In/Crow Jane Woman/Fogyism/Give Me a Break Blues/Graveyard Dream Blues/Hard Oh Lawd/Hard Time Blues/I Love My Man Better Than I Love Myself/I'm Leaving Here Blues/Lawdy Lawdy Blues/

Ida Cox *Photo by J W Miner. Courtesy Frank Driggs Collection*

Lonesome Blues/Lost Man Blues/Lovin' Is the Thing I'm Wild About/Mama Doo Shee Blues/Marble Stone Blues/Mean Papa Turn Your Key/Mercy Blues/Midnight Hour Blues/Misery Blues/Mistreatin' Daddy Blues/Moaning Groaning Blues/Mojo Hand Blues/Pleading Blues/Rambling Blues/Separated Blues/Sobbing Tears Blues/Tree Top Tall Papa/Trouble Trouble Blues/Weary Way Blues/Wild Women Don't Have the Blues/Worn Down Daddy/Worried Any How Blues/You Stole My Man

Infl to: Barbara Dane/Billie Pierce/Irene Scruggs/Aaron "T-Bone" Walker

Quotes: "One of the greatest of all classic blues singers"—Derrick Stewart-Baxter, Fontana album 301

"Ida Cox [combined] the poise and artistry of vaudeville with the passion of the blues and with an armour plated cynicism all her own"—Chris Hillman, *Storyville* magazine (UK), Oct 1976, p 12

Reference: Milestone album MLP-2015

CRAYTON, CONNIE CURTIS *"Pee Wee"*
(aka: Homer the Great)
Born: Dec 18, 1914, Rockdale (Milam Co), TX

Photo by Norbert Hess. Courtesy Living Blues Magazine

Died: Jun 25, 1985, Los Angeles, CA
Inst: Guitar/Trumpet/Ukelele

Father was Samuel Crayton; mother was Louise Smith; raised in Austin, TX from childhood; made first instrument out of cigar box as child; attended Olive C School where he learned trumpet/ukelele and played in school band, Austin, late 20s; moved to Los Angeles, CA, to work outside music in area, 1935 into mid-40s; worked Slim Jenkins Club, Oakland, CA, 1945; formed own trio to work club dates in Oakland/San Francisco/Los Angeles, CA, area through 40s; worked w Ivory Joe Hunter Band in local club dates, Los Angeles area, c1946; rec acc to Ivory Joe Hunter, Pacific label, Los Angeles, 1946; worked Barrelhouse Club, Watts, Los Angeles, CA, late 40s; frequently worked New Orleans Swing Club, San Francisco, CA, 1947 into 50s; rec 4-Star label, Los Angeles, 1947; frequently worked The Colony/The Clef Club/The Elks, Oakland, CA, late 40s into early 50s; rec Modern label, Los Angeles, 1949-51; toured w own band working one-nighters across US, 1949; worked Savoy Ballroom, NYC, NY, 1949; w Joe Turner/Lowell Fulson, Saginaw, MI, 1950; rec w Maxwell Davis Orch, Aladdin label, Los Angeles, 1951; worked Wrigley Field, Los Angeles, 1951; Sam's Barbecue, Richmond, CA, early 50s; rec w Red Callender Sextet, RIH/Hollywood labels, Los Angeles, 1954; worked w Gatemouth Brown, Orchid Room, Kansas City, MO, 1954; toured w Gatemouth Brown working one-nighters on East Coast, 1954; rec Imperial label, New Orleans, LA, 1954-5; worked Apollo Theater, NYC, 1956; worked out of Detroit, MI, frequently touring club dates in South through 50s; rec VJ label, Chicago, IL, 1956-7; frequently worked/toured w Roy Milton/Dinah Washington/Ray Charles/Big Maybelle/others in package shows/theaters/clubs/ballrooms through 50s/60s; rec Fox label, Detroit, 1959-60; rec Jamie/Guyden labels, 1961; rec w RA Blackwell Orch, Smash label, 1962; frequently worked outside music with occasional weekend gigs in Los Angeles, CA, area through 60s into 70s; worked Ash Grove, Los Angeles, 1968; rec Modern label, Hollywood, CA, 1968; worked w Johnny Otis Show, Monterey Jazz Festival, Monterey, CA, 1970 (por rel Epic label); Ann Arbor Blues Festival, Ann Arbor, MI, 1970; toured w Johnny Otis package show working concert dates on West Coast, 1971; rec Vanguard label, Hollywood, 1971; worked Ann Arbor Blues Festival, Ann Arbor, MI, 1973; Fergie's, Goleta, CA, 1973; Topanga Corral, Los Angeles, CA, 1973; Lucille's Place, Los Angeles, 1974-5; rec Blues Spectrum label, Los Angeles, 1974; app on JIMMY

WITHERSPOON Show, KMET-FM-radio, Los Angeles, 1975; worked Parisian Room, Los Angeles, 1975; T-Bone Walker Memorial Show, Musicians Union Hall, Los Angeles, 1975; rec acc to Joe Turner, Pablo label, Los Angeles, 1975; Chantilly's Lace Club, Los Angeles, 1976; Caribbean Lounge, Los Angeles, 1976; Stage Number One Club, Los Angeles, 1976; w own Ultimates of Soul, Roy's Rib Inn, Compton, CA, 1976; Slone's Lounge, Los Angeles, 1977; Santa Barbara Blues Society Concert, Santa Barbara, CA 1977; continued West Coast club/concert gigs into 80s; worked Chicago Blues Festival, Chicago, IL, 1985; suffered fatal heart attack; buried Inglewood Cemetery, Inglewood, CA

Songs: Blues After Hours/Blues for My Baby/Blues in the Ghetto/Don't Forget to Close the Door/In the Evenin'/My Baby's on the Line/Old Fashioned Baby/Pee Wee's Boogie/Phone Call from My Baby/Texas Hop

Infl by: Charlie Christian/John Collins/Aaron "T-Bone" Walker

Quote: "A truly outstanding guitarist in his prime, Crayton bridged the commercial gap between blues and R&B with few reservations"—John Breckow, *Whiskey, Women And . . .* magazine, Feb 1973, p 14

References: Whiskey, Women And . . . magazine, Feb 1973, pp 14-20

Blues Unlimited magazine (UK), Apr 1974, pp 8-9

Living Blues magazine, No. 56-57, 1983

CRIPPEN, "*Little*" KATIE "*Kate*"/"*Kay*"
(*aka:* Ella White)
Born: Nov 17, 1895, Philadelphia (Philadelphia Co), PA
Died: Nov 25, 1929, New York, NY

Father was John Crippen; mother was Catherine Garden; born Catherine Crippen; one of at least 3 children; reportedly settled in NYC, NY, late teens; worked Edmond's Cellar, NYC, c1920; Rafe's Paradise Cafe, Atlantic City, NJ, 1921; rec w Fletcher Henderson Orch, Black Swan label, NYC, 1921; toured in own Liza and Her Shuffling Sextet Revue (including Fats Waller) working theater circuit from c1922-3; toured in own Kate Crippen and Her Kids Revue working vaudeville theater circuit c1923; worked outside music (operating own food concession), Barrons Exclusive Club, NYC, 1924; occasionally worked Bamboo Inn/Nest Club/others, NYC, 1925-9; app in RARIN' TO GO Revue, Lafayette Theater, NYC, 1927; frequently worked Vo-De-Do Club, NYC, 1927-8; toured w Dewey Brown (as "Crippen & Brown") in SHUFFLE ALONG JR musical comedy working Keith-Albee-Orpheum circuit across US/Canada, 1928-9; toured as Crippen & Brown duo act on RKO circuit, 1929; app w Dewey Brown, FIGITY FEET Revue, Lafayette Theater, NYC, 1929; after long illness entered Skin & Cancer Hospital where she died of cancer; buried Marion Cemetery, Philadelphia, PA

Personal: Married Lou Henry, a musician. Not to be confused with Lulu Whidby who also used pseudonym "Ella White"

CRUDUP, ARTHUR WILLIAM *"Big Boy"*
(*aka:* Percy Lee Crudup/Art Crudux/Arthur Crump/Elmer James)
Born: Aug 24, 1905, Forest (Scott Co), MS
Died: Mar 28, 1974, Nassawadox, VA
Inst: Guitar

Mother Minnie Crudup, a musician; interested in music at early age and sang in gospel choirs/quartets at age of 10; moved to Indianapolis, IN, to work outside music, 1916-26; returned to Forest, MS, to work outside music, 1926-c35; moved to Belzoni/Clarksdale, MS, to work outside music in area from c1935; taught self guitar and worked local parties, Clarksdale area, c1939; joined Harmonizing Four gospel quartet and worked churches in Chicago, IL, 1940; frequently worked outside music with street/house party gigs, Chicago, from 1940; rec Bluebird label, Chicago, 1941-2; frequently returned to work outside music in Forest, MS, from c1942; rec US Armed Forces Radio Service transcription (AFRS), early 40s; rec Bluebird label, Chicago, 1944-5; worked Indiana Theater, Chicago, c1945; rec Victor label, Chicago, 1945-51; app on KING BISCUIT TIME, KFFA-radio, Helena, AR, mid-40s; frequently worked outside music with local gigs w Sonny Boy Williamson (Alex Miller), Belzoni, MS, area, 1948; frequently toured w Sonny Boy Williamson (Alex Miller)/Elmore James working small jukes through South, late 40s; rec Victor label, Atlanta, GA, 1952; rec Trumpet/Checker labels, Jackson, MS, 1952; rec Champion label, Jackson, c1952; rec Ace label, Jackson, 1953; rec Groove/Victor labels, Atlanta, 1953-4; worked brief gigs in Florida, c1953; settled in Franktown, VA, to work mostly outside music with occasional gigs w Malibus Family group at local country dances, 1953-69; rec Fire label, Nashville, TN, c1959; worked 50 Grand Club, Detroit, MI, 1965; The Ark, Boston, MA, c1966; The

Arthur "Big Boy" Crudup *Photo by Diana Davies © 1978. Courtesy Sing Out Magazine*

Electric Circus, NYC, c1966; Univ of Chicago R&B Festival, Chicago, 1967; Avant Garde Coffeehouse, Milwaukee, WI, 1967; Central Park Music Festival, NYC, 1967; Philadelphia Folk Festival, Schwenksville, PA, 1967; rec Delmark label, Chicago, 1967; Ann Arbor Blues Festival, Ann Arbor, MI, 1969; Univ of California, Berkeley, CA, 1969; Ash Grove, Los Angeles, CA, 1969; toured England working club/concert/TV dates, 1970-1; app on LATE NIGHT LINE-UP, BBC-2-TV, London, Eng, 1970; rec Liberty label, London, 1970; worked Festival of American Folklife, Washington, DC, 1970; Washington Blues Festival, Howard Univ, Washington, DC, 1970; toured w American Blues Festival working concert dates through Australia, 1972; app in French film OUT OF THE BLACKS INTO THE BLUES (pt 2: A Way to Escape the Ghetto), 1972; worked Univ of Vermont, Burlington, VT, 1972; Siena Col, Memphis, TN, 1972; Newport Jazz Festival, Philharmonic Hall, NYC, 1973 (por rel Buddah label); Mariposa Folk Festival, Toronto, Can, 1973; app on ARTHUR CRUDUP: BORN IN THE BLUES, WETA-TV, Washington, DC, 1973 (also rel as film); toured with Bonnie Raitt working concert dates through Virginia, 1974; worked Hunter Col, NYC, 1974; suffered stroke and died at Northampton-Accomac Memorial Hospital; buried Bethel Baptist Cemetery, Franktown, VA

Personal: Married twice. 4 children. "Big Boy" was childhood nickname

Songs: Black Pony Blues/Coal Black Mare/Death Valley Blues/Ethel May/Greyhound Bus Blues/Hand Me Down My Walking Cane/I Don't Know It/If I Get Lucky/Keep Your Arms Round Me/Keep Your Hands Off That Woman/Look on Yonder(s) Wall/Mean Ole Frisco Blues/My Baby Left Me/Nobody Wants You When You're Old and Grey/Rock Me, Mama/Roe Buck Man/So Glad I'm Livin'/Standing at My Window/That's All Right/Who's Been Fooling You?

Infl by: Bill Broonzy/Papa Floyd

Infl to: Ray Charles/Eddie Kirkland/JB Lenoir/Elvis Presley/Doc Ross/James "Son" Thomas

Quotes: ". . . as a singer he was superb and many of his songs have become classics"—Mike Rowe, *Chicago Breakdown*, Eddison Press Ltd, 1973

"One of the most popular blues singers of the 1940s and one of the finest blues songwriters ever" —Jim O'Neal, *Living Blues* magazine, Spring 1974, p 5

"He bridged the space between, say, Tommy McClennan and Lightnin' Hopkins . . ."—Tony Russell, *Jazz & Blues* magazine (UK), Jul 1972, p 14

References: *Crawdaddy* magazine, Jul 1973, pp 22-3
Downbeat magazine, Nov 11, 1971, p 11

Blues Unlimited magazine (UK), Sept 1970, pp 16-18

CRUDUP, PERCY LEE
(see Crudup, Arthur)

CRUDUX, ART
(see Crudup, Arthur)

CRUMP, ARTHUR
(see Crudup, Arthur)

CRUMP, JESSE *"Tiny"*
Born: 1906, Paris (Lamar Co), TX
Inst: Clarinet/Organ/Piano

Mother was organist; raised in Dallas, TX, area; interested in music early and took piano lessons as child; toured with passing carnivals/girly shows/tent shows working through South as youth; began touring on TOBA circuit from c1919; frequently worked as pianist in local clubs, Helena, AR, area in early 20s; residency at Golden West Cafe, Indianapolis, IN, 1923; rec solo/acc to Nina Reeves/Genevieve Stearns, Gennett label (private issue), Richmond, IN, 1923; rec w Ida Cox, Paramount label, Chicago, IL, 1923; frequently toured as acc to Ida Cox (solo or with own band) on TOBA circuit through South, 1923-36; rec acc to Ida Cox, Paramount label, Chicago, 1925/1928; frequently toured TOBA circuit working as singer/pianist/dancer/comedian through 20s; app w own Jessie Crump & his Cain Raisers on local radio shows, Kansas City, MO, through 20s; rec w Billy McKenzie as "Billy & Jesse," Brunswick label, Chicago, IL, 1929 and as "McKenzie & Crump," Paramount label, Grafton, WI, 1929; toured w Ida Cox in revue RAISIN' CAIN, late 20s into early 30s; settled in Muncie, IN, to frequently work as single at 1100 Club/Main Cafe/Hollywood Bar/The Candlelight Club/others, late 30s to 1951; moved to West Coast working New Orleans Swing Club, San Francisco, CA, 1952; Copa Club, Monterey, CA, 1952; rec acc w Bob Scobey Frisco Band, Good Time Jazz/American Recording Society labels, Oakland, CA, 1956; worked w Marty Marsala's Band, Kewpie Doll, San Francisco, 1960; mostly inactive from early 60s

Personal: Married Ida Cox (20s/30s)

Songs: Alphonsia Blues/Bear-Mash Blues/Black Crepe Blues/Cherry Pickin' Blues/Death Letter Blues/Do Lawd Do/Fare Thee Well Poor Gal/Farewell Sweet Man of Mine/Fogyism/'Fore Day Creep/Gypsy Glass Blues/Hard Oh Lord/Last Mile Blues/Long Distance Blues/Mojo Hand Blues/Someday Blues/That's a Married Man's Weakness/Who's Gonna Do Your Jelly Rollin'?

Infl to: Sammy Price

Quote: "Crump's work was in a vaudeville vein but he could play good blues . . ."—Paul Oliver, *The Story of the Blues*, Chilton Book Company, 1969

Reference: Record Changer magazine, Mar 1952, pp 11, 22

CRYIN' RED
(see Minter, Iverson)

CURTIS, JAMES *"Peck"*

Photo by C Strachwitz, Arhoolie Records

Born: Mar 7, 1912, Benoit (Bolivar Co), MS
Died: Nov 1, 1970, Helena, AR
Inst: Drums/Jug/Washboard

Father was John Curtis; born/raised on farm; moved to Helena, AR, to work outside music from 1929; frequently worked (as washboard/tub player and dancer) in local bands at picnics/parties in area from c1932; frequently toured in various carnivals/minstrel/travelling shows working through South through 30s; frequently worked w South Memphis Jug Band in streets/parks, Memphis, TN, 1933; frequently w Howlin' Wolf at local dances, West Memphis, AR, area, late 30s; frequently toured w Sonny Boy Williamson (Alex Miller)/John Henry Henderson into 40s; frequently app w Sonny Boy Williamson (Alex Miller) on KING BISCUIT TIME, KFFA-radio, Helena, AR, from 1942 into 50s; frequently toured w Sonny Boy Williamson (Alex Miller) working jukes through Little Rock, AR, area, mid-40s; app on KNOE-radio, Monroe, LA, 1945;

teamed off-and-on w Houston Stackhouse to work jukes/cafes/dives through Mississippi Delta area and through South from 1947 into 60s; rec Modern label, 1952; toured w King Biscuit Entertainers Band working picnics/jukes/streets through Arkansas/Missouri, 1952-3; app w King Biscuit Entertainers Band, KLCN-radio, Blytheville, AR, c1953; w Sonny Boy Williamson (Alex Miller) working club dates in Detroit, MI, 1954; settled in Helena, AR, to work occasionally w Houston Stackhouse with some app on local radio shows from early 60s; rec w Houston Stackhouse, Testament label, Dundee, MS, 1967; suffered fatal heart attack at home; buried Magnolia Cemetery, Helena, AR

References: Testament album 2215
Blues Unlimited magazine (UK), Jan/Feb 1970

D

DADDY DEEP THROAT
(see Cain, Perry)

DADDY STOVEPIPE
(see Watson, Johnny)

DALE, FLORA
(see Brown, Ida G)
(see Henderson, Rosa)

DALLAS, LEROY
Born: Dec 12, 1920, Mobile (Mobile Co), AL
Inst: Guitar/Washboard

Born/raised on farm, Mobile, AL; moved to Memphis, TN, to work outside music from c1934; teamed w James McMillan to work jukes/streets through Mississippi/Louisiana/Georgia/Tennessee, late 30s; frequently worked w Frank Edwards in jukes in Mobile, AL (later Georgia Slim added to form trio), with many tours working jukes through South into 40s; app w Frank Edwards in MAJOR BOWES ORIGINAL AMATEUR HOUR, CBS-radio, c1940; worked Apollo Theater, NYC, NY, c1940; settled in Chicago, IL, to work outside music with occasional street singing for tips, 1941-3; settled in Brooklyn, NY, to work outside music from 1943; rec w Brownie McGhee, Sittin' In With label, NYC, 1949; rec Storyville/Milestone labels, NYC, 1962

Songs: Bellevue Blues/Talk to Me Baby

Infl by: Frank Edwards

Quote: "Leroy Dallas was a good rhythm player and a good blues singer . . ."—Brownie McGhee, *Festival of American Folklife* program, 1971

Reference: Nothing But the Blues, Mike Leadbitter, Hanover Books, 1971

DANE, BARBARA

Photo by Carolyn Mugar. Courtesy Barbara Dane

Born: May 12, 1927, Detroit (Wayne Co), MI
Inst: Guitar/Piano

Father was Gilbert Spillman; mother was Dorothy Roleson; born Barbara Jean Spillman; sang in local Sunday school as child; frequently sang in local high school glee club as youth; took piano/voice lessons in early 40s; taught self guitar in early 40s; briefly attended Greenbrier Jr Col, Lewisburg, WV/Wayne State Univ, Detroit, MI, mid-40s; frequently worked outside music, Detroit, from mid-40s; frequently participated/entertained for United Auto Workers labor movement, Detroit, 1945-7; worked w Pete Seeger, Detroit Institute of Art, Detroit, 1946; worked First World Youth Festival, Prague, Czechoslovakia, 1947; moved to San Francisco, CA, working outside music from 1949; app on LIGHT AND MELLOW, KNBC-radio, San Francisco, 1949; app on GOOD OLD DAYS, KNBC-radio, San Francisco, c1949; app on own show series, KPFA-radio, Berkeley, CA, 1949; app on STANDARD SCHOOL BROADCAST, KNBC-radio, San Francisco, CA, 1949; won first prize on MISS US TELEVISION talent contest, KPIX-TV, San Francisco, 1951; app in own series, FOLKSVILLE USA, KGO-TV, San Francisco, 1951; frequently worked w Kid Ory Band/George Lewis Band/others, Tin Angel Club/Fallen Angel Club/others, San Francisco, mid-50s; frequently w Dick Oxtot Bearcats Band in local club dates, San Francisco, 1955; w Turk Murphy Band, Tin Angel Club, San Francisco, 1956; w Dick Oxtot Bearcats, Jack's Waterfront Hangout, San Francisco, 1956-7; rec w George Lewis Band, Score label, San Francisco, 1957; rec Barbary Coast label, San Francisco, 1957; worked The Den, NYC, 1958; worked 400 Club, Hollywood, CA, 1958; Cosmo Alley, Hollywood, 1958; The Limelight, Los Angeles, 1958; International Club, Los Angeles, 1958; w Louis Armstrong, Civic Auditorium, Pasadena, CA, 1958; frequently worked w Jesse Fuller/Gary Davis/Lightnin' Hopkins/Big Joe Williams/Memphis Slim/Little Brother Montgomery/others, Ash Grove, Hollywood, CA, 1958-74 (por 1959 date rel Horizon label); frequently app on Bobby Troup's STARS OF JAZZ, ABC-TV, 1959; app w Louis Armstrong, TIMEX ALL STAR JAZZ Show, CBS-TV, 1959; worked Newport Folk Festival, Newport, RI, 1959 (por rel Vanguard label); rec w Earl Hines group, Dot label, Los Angeles, CA, 1959; toured w Jack Teagarden Sextet working concert dates on East Coast, 1959; worked w Lennie Bruce/others, Gate of Horn, Chicago, IL, 1959-62; Ravinia Folk Festival, Chicago, 1959; The Cloisters, Chicago, 1959; 3525 Club, Dallas, TX, 1959; Jazz Interlude, San Francisco, CA, 1959; Easy Street Club, San Francisco, 1959; Copley Square Hotel, Boston, MA, 1959; American Jazz Festival, Detroit, MI, 1959; rec World Pacific label, Los Angeles (?), 1959; rec Trey label, Los Angeles, 1960; worked w Art Hodes Band, Cafe Continentale, Chicago, 1960; app on PLAYBOY'S PENTHOUSE, syndicated TV, 1960; contributed article to *Downbeat* magazine, 1960; app on own series BARBARA'S BLUES, KPFK-radio, Los Angeles, 1960; worked Civic Auditorium, Santa Monica, CA, 1960; Hungry i, San Francisco, 1960; The Troubadour, Hollywood, CA, 1960; frequently app on PM EAST . . . PM WEST, syndicated TV, 1960; app on CHECKMATE, CBS-TV, c1960; toured w Bob Newhart working concert dates in northwest US/Canada, 1961; owned/operated/performed at Sugar Hill Club, San Francisco, 1961; app 26 weeks on own children's series WAKE UP AND SING, KPIX-TV, San Francisco, c1961; app own series BARBARA'S BLUES, KIBE-radio, Palo Alto, CA/KDFC-FM-radio, San Francisco/KJAZ-radio, San Francisco, 1961; rec w Lightnin' Hopkins, Arhoolie label, Berkeley, CA, 1961; rec Horizon/Capitol labels, Los Angeles, 1961; worked Masonic Hall, San Francisco, 1961; Hollywood Bowl, Hollywood, CA, 1961; app in film THE BLUES, 1962; app on ALFRED HITCHCOCK PRESENTS (ep: Captive Audience), CBS-TV, 1962; app on Johnny Carson's TONIGHT Show, NBC-TV, c1962; app on JACK BRICKHOUSE/EDDIE HUBBARD Show, WGN-radio, Chicago, IL, 1962; app on STEVE ALLEN Show, WABC-TV, NYC, NY (syndicated), 1963; worked Room at the Bottom, NYC, 1963; The Attic, Vancouver, Can, 1963; Cabale Club, Berkeley, CA, 1963; rec w Lu Watters Band, Fantasy label, San Francisco; 1964; UCLA Folk Concert, Los Angeles, 1964; Hootenanny Club, Los Angeles, 1964; rec w Lightinin' Hopkins, Arhoolie label, Berkeley, CA, 1964; walk-on at Newport Folk Festival, Newport, RI, 1964; rec Folkways label, NYC, 1964; worked w Wild Bill Davison Band, Grandview Inn, Columbus, OH, 1964; active in political/social causes and frequently worked concerts/marches/demonstrations/meetings from 1964; active as singing organizer of GI anti-war movement at meetings/concerts/gatherings at army bases/clubs across US/England/Japan/Okinawa/Philippines from mid-60s; worked demonstrations/marches/protest meets/Freedom Schools through Mississippi, 1964; worked The Ark, Vancouver, Can, 1964; Folk Festival, John's Island, SC, 1964; Second Fret, Philadelphia, PA, 1964; app w Bob Dylan, MORE FOLK MUSIC, WOR-TV, NYC, 1964; worked Leadbelly Memorial

Concert, Town Hall, NYC, 1964; contributed articles to *Sing Out* magazine, 1965-76 (member of Advisory Board from 1967); hosted SING OUT series, WBAI-FM-radio, NYC, 1965; toured w Southern Folk Cultural revival group working college concert circuit through South, 1965; worked Gerdes Folk City, NYC, 1965; Cafe A-Go-Go, NYC, 1965; rec w Chambers Brothers, Folkways label, NYC, 1965; initiated/coordinated/entertained at Sing-In for Peace Concert, Carnegie Hall, NYC, 1965; worked Town Hall, NYC, 1965; frequently worked concerts sponsored by Southern Students Organizing Committee and Student Non-Violent Coordinating Committee, 1966; worked concert/local TV dates and interviewed Premier Fidel Castro, Havana, Cuba, 1966; worked Phipps Auditorium, Denver, CO, 1966; worked in concert, Havana, Cuba, 1967; rec Casa de las Americas (private label), Havana, Cuba, 1967; worked Village Theater, NYC, 1967; rec Women Strike for Peace (private label), NYC, 1967; toured w Campaign for Nuclear Disarmament group as peace singer working concerts through West Germany, 1967; worked w Otis Spann, Washington Square Methodist Church, NYC, 1969; rec I Dischi Del Sole label, NYC, 1969; worked Festival of L'Unita, Florence, Italy, then toured Italy with group, 1970; toured for underground worker/student movement group working concerts/meets through Spain, 1970; worked Varadero Pop Song Festival, Havana, Cuba, 1970; worked Vietnamese Tet Celebration, Mutualite, Paris, France, c1971; worked Festival of L'Unita, Turin, Italy, then toured northern Italy with group, 1971; worked Political Song Festival, Berlin, Ger, 1972; formed own Paredon label, NYC, c1972 and rec self/others into 70s; toured w Committee for US-Vietnamese Friendship, Hanoi, Vietnam, 1974-5; worked Women's Music Festival, Univ of Illinois, Urbana, IL, 1974-5; worked Folk City, NYC, 1975; Orphans, Chicago, IL, 1975; Ash Grove, Los Angeles, 1975; All Souls Unitarian Church, Washington, DC, 1975; continued rallies/concert work across US, 1975-8; worked benefits for United Mine Workers, NYC, NY/Massachusetts, 1978; worked Bread & Roses Coffeehouse, Baltimore, MD, 1978; worked solo concert dates in San Francisco, CA, 1978

Personal: Married Rolf Cahn (1946-51). Son is Nick Cahn. Married Byron Menendez (1951-64). 2 children, Paul and Nina

Book: Vietnam Songbook (co-edited w Irwin Silber), 1969

Songs: Just Can't Make It by Myself/Wild Cat Blues/Working Class Woman

Awards/Honors: Won *Playboy* magazine All Star Jazz Poll as One of the Outstanding Jazz Artists of 1960

Infl by: Ida Cox/Leadbelly/Mance Lipscomb/Lizzie Miles/Ma Rainey/Bessie Smith/Mama Yancey

Quotes: "Bessie Smith in stereo!"—Leonard Feather, *Playboy* magazine (issue unknown)

"A woman with a big, bluesy, gutsy voice . . ."—Boris Weintraug, *Washington Star* newspaper, Jun 2, 1975

"Did you get that chick? She's a gasser"—Louis Armstrong, *Time* magazine, Nov 24, 1958

References: Folk Music: More Than a Song, Kristin Baggelaar/Donald Milton, Thomas Y Crowell Company, 1976

Encyclopedia of Folk, Country, and Western Music, Irwin Stambler/Grelun Landon, St Martin's Press, 1969

Sing Out magazine, Apr 1964, p 19

DARBY, *"Big"* IKE

Born: Dec 7, 1929, Philadelphia (Neshoba Co), MS
Died: Sept 6, 1988, Memphis, TN

Father was Victor Vonna Darby; mother was Bertha Brantley; to New Orleans, LA, 1949; in US Army, 1951-3; settled in Mobile, AL, to work outside music, 1953-63; app as DJ on own DAVIS AVENUE BLUES ASSOCIATION Show, WMOO-radio, Mobile, from 1963; frequently worked local club dates, Mobile, 1963 into 70s; frequently worked outside music (in own music store), Mobile, from 1964; frequently app on local shows, WMOO/WGOK-radio, Mobile, late 60s into 70s; worked outside music in own Big Ike's Record Sales music store (2nd store), Mobile, late 60s; rec Mil-Smi/Darby labels, Mobile, 1969 into 70s

Songs: Cryin' the Blues/Your Love Is Like a Checker Game

Reference: Living Blues magazine, Spring 1972, pp 8-10

DARBY, THEODORE *"Blind Blues"/"Teddy"/"Teddy Roosevelt"*

(*aka:* Blind Squire Turner)
Born: Mar 2, 1906, Henderson (Henderson Co), KY
Inst: Guitar/Piano

Mother was guitarist; moved to Indiana as child; moved to St Louis, MO, where he was raised and attended grade school from 1913; served time at Missouri Training School for Boys, Boonville, MO, 1921-2; worked outside music, St Louis, 1922-6; lost eyesight due to glaucoma c1926; served time in local

"Big" Ike Darby *Courtesy* Living Blues *Magazine*

Photo by Diane Allmen. Courtesy Living Blues Magazine

workhouse where he taught self guitar, St Louis, 1927-8; frequently worked for tips at houseparties/sidewalks/clubs/bars, St Louis area, through 20s into 30s; rec Paramount label, Richmond, IN, 1929; moved to East St Louis, IL, to work local club dates with frequent outside music work there and Louisville, KY, area from c1930; rec Victor label, Chicago, IL, 1931; rec Bluebird label, Chicago, 1933; rec Vocalion label, Chicago, 1935; rec Decca label, Chicago, 1937; ordained deacon of King Solomon Holy House of Prayer, East St Louis, IL, 1954; rec (unissued) label, Chicago, 1964

Songs: Bootleggin' Ain't Good No More/Built Right on the Ground/Deceiving Blues/Heart Trouble Blues/Lawdy Lawdy Worried Blues/My Laona Blues/Spike Driver

Infl by: Peetie Wheatstraw

Quote: "His music reflects the traditional country blues he heard as a youth, though modified by the urban blues he heard after moving to the city . . ."—Pete Welding, Origin album OJL-20

References: Living Blues magazine, Autumn 1970, pp 20-21

Blues World magazine (UK), Jun 1970, pp 3-4

DAVENPORT, CHARLES EDWARD *"Charlie"/"Chas"/"Cow Cow"*
(*aka:* Bat the Hummingbird/Georgia Grinder/George Hamilton/Memphis Slim)

Born: Apr 23, 1894, Anniston (Calhoun Co), AL
Died: Dec 3, 1955, Cleveland, OH
Inst: Organ/Piano

Father was Clement Davenport, a preacher; mother was Queen Victoria Jacobs, an organist; one of 8 children; interested in music early and taught self organ in mother's church as child; studied piano briefly at age of 12; attended Alabama Theological Seminary, Selma Univ, Selma, AL, 1910-11 (where he was later expelled for ragging a march at local social function); worked as pianist at local dances/honky tonks/parties/cabarets/backroom joints, Birmingham, AL, from c1912; worked honky tonks/barrelhouses/brothels in Black Bottom district, Atlanta, GA, from c1914; toured w Barkoot's Travelling Carnival troupe working shows under canvas though South, 1917; worked as brothel pianist in Storyville section of New Orleans, LA, c1917; worked w Bessie Smith in local vaudeville show, Augusta, GA, 1917; worked w Haeg's Circus (as black-face singing/dancing minstrel), Macon, GA, and other carnivals/vaudeville shows, late teens, through early 20s; teamed w Dora Carr working as "Davenport & Company," to tour extensively on TOBA and other circuits working theaters through South from 1922; worked Star Theater, Pittsburgh, PA, 1924; Lincoln Theater, NYC, NY, 1924; rec w Dora Carr, Okeh label, NYC, 1924-6; rec w Dora Carr, Gennett label, Richmond, IN, 1925; reportedly toured Europe work-

Courtesy Institute of Jazz Studies

ing shows before royalty, mid-20s; rec Vocal-style label (piano rolls), Cincinnati, OH, 1925-6; worked w Dora Carr, Coliseum Theater, Chicago, 1926; rec w Ivy Smith (or solo), Paramount label, Chicago, 1927; toured w Ivy Smith in Davenport & Smith's CHICAGO STEPPERS Revue working TOBA circuit in late 20s; worked as talent scout/song writer/ recording artist for Vocalion-Brunswick label, Chicago, 1928-9; rec Gennett label, Richmond, IN, 1929-30; frequently worked local houseparties, Chicago, c1929-30; moved to Cleveland, OH, to work outside music (in own music-record shop) c1930-2; toured w own COW COW'S CHICAGO STEPPERS Revue working theater dates through South, c1933-5; returned to Cleveland to work outside music (in own cafe) with occasional local gigs with own band from 1935; rec w Sam Price group, Decca label, NYC, 1938; worked Hot Club of Cleveland, Cleveland, OH, 1939; app on ART HODES Show, WNYC-radio, NYC, c1942; worked outside music (as washroom attendant), Onyx Club, NYC, c1942; worked Musical Bar, Cleveland, c1944; Plantation Club, Nashville, TN, c1945; Starlite Grill, Cleveland, c1945; rec Comet label, Chicago, IL, 1945; worked club date in Bristol, CT, 1945; Blue Note Concert, Town Hall, NYC, 1945; rec w Art Hodes Jazz Record Six, Jazz Record label, NYC, 1946; rec Circle label, Chicago, 1946; worked Mayfair Grill, Cleveland, 1946; Stuyvesant Casino, NYC, 1948; worked mostly outside music, Cleveland, from 1948; worked Carioca Club, Cleveland, late 40s; worked Pin Wheel Club, Cleveland, c1955; died at home of hardening of arteries; buried Evergreen Cemetery, Cleveland, OH

Personal: Married Helen Rivers (1921-2); Iva France (30s?); Carrie Peggy Taylor (40s-50s). "Cow Cow" was childhood pet name and refers to cow catcher on train engine. Not to be confused with Peter Chatman who also uses pseudonym "Memphis Slim"

Songs: Atlanta Rag/Black Gal Gets There Just the Same/Buckwheat Cakes/Chimes Blues/Contribution Box/Cow Cow Blues/Cow Cow Boogie/Do You Call That Religion?/Fifth Street Blues/Goin' Home Blues/Good Women's Blues/He Sho' Don't Mean No Harm/Hobson City Stomp/Hurry and Bring It Home Blues/I Ain't No Ice Man/I'll Be Glad When You're Dead You Rascal You*/I'm Gonna Steal Somebody's Man/Jump Little Jitterbug Jump/Low Down Man Blues/Mama Don't Allow*/Slowdrag/State Street Jive/Stealin' Blues/You Might Pizen Me

(*Claimed to have sold these songs for flat fee and received no composer credit or royalties)

Infl by: Bob Davis

Quotes: "Davenport was a prolific blues composer, pianist and entertainer"—George Hoefer, *Downbeat* magazine, Jan 25, 1956, p 31

"A fine blues pianist and boogie woogie exponent . . . his style was primitive, driving, rough, winning by its honesty and feeling"—Charles Fox/Peter Gammond/Alun Morgan, *Jazz on Record: A Critical Guide*, Hutchinson of London Ltd, 1960

References: *Downbeat* magazine, Jan 25, 1956, p 31
Jazz Journal magazine (UK), May 1959, p 10
The Jazz Record magazine, Dec 1944, p 6

DAVENPORT, JED
Born: Mississippi (unconfirmed)
Died: (unknown)
Inst: Harmonica/Jug/Trumpet

Frequently worked streets of Memphis, TN, from early 20s into 60s; rec Vocalion label, Peabody Hotel, Memphis, 1929; worked w own Beale Street Jug Band, Memphis area, late 20s; rec w own Beale Street Jug Band, Vocalion label, Memphis, 1930; possibly rec w Beale Street Rounders, Vocalion label, Chicago, IL, 1930; rec w Memphis Minnie, Vocalion label, Chicago, 1930; frequently with local jazz bands working clubs/Flamingo Hotel/others, Memphis, c1937; frequently worked w Dub Jenkins/Al Jackson in passing tent shows, Memphis area, through 30s into 40s; whereabouts unknown after 60s

DAVIS, CARL
Born: Mar 5, 1886, Rison (Cleveland Co), AR
Died: (unknown)
Inst: Guitar/Piano

Born/raised on sharecropper farm; taught self guitar at 18 years of age; moved to Louisiana to work as singing guitarist in local clubs, Shreveport, LA, area c1905; frequently teamed with other musicians to work local dances in New Orleans, LA, area into teens; frequently worked w Papa Celestin Band in local club dates, New Orleans, from c1910; frequently toured with travelling carnivals working under canvas through South c1925 into 30s; rec w Dallas Jamboree Jug Band, Vocalion label, Dallas, TX, 1935; frequently worked w Charles Jackson in local bars/clubs, Baltimore, MD, late 30s; toured w Fat Head Williams Band working dances through Illinois into 40s; settled in Toledo, OH, to work small bars/clubs, 1945 through 40s; whereabouts unknown after 60s

Infl by: Lonnie Johnson

DAVIS, *Rev "Blind"* **GARY D**
(*aka:* Blind Gary)

Born: Apr 30, 1896, Laurens (Laurens Co), SC
Died: May 5, 1972, Hammonton, NJ
Inst: Banjo/Guitar/Harmonica/Piano

Father was John Davis; mother was Evelina———; born on farm between Clinton and Laurens, SC; one of 8 children; suffered ulcerated eyes and was partially blinded at 2 months of age; interested in music at early age and taught self harmonica at 5 years of age, banjo at 6, guitar at 7; raised and worked outside music on farm with occasional local parties/picnics in area and frequent singing at Center Raven Baptist Church, Gray Court, SC, from childhood; frequently worked in local string band, Greenville, SC, 1910 into 20s; attended Cedar Springs School for Blind People, Spartanburg, SC, c1914-15; was totally blind by 1926; moved to Durham, NC, to work outside music c1927; worked as street singer, Asheville, NC, area through late 20s; ordained minister of Free Baptist Connection Church, Washington, NC, 1933; toured as singing gospel preacher working camp meetings/revival meets/country churches/streets through Carolinas in early 30s; settled in Durham, NC, working streets/parties/dances/chittlin' struts/churches from c1935; rec blues/religious songs, ARC label group, NYC,

"Blind" Gary Davis
Photo by Julie Snow. Courtesy Sing Out Magazine.

1935; moved to NYC becoming ordained minister of Missionary Baptist Connection Church, 1940; frequently worked as singing preacher on local streets/folk concerts/local radio, NYC, into 40s; rec Asch label, NYC, c1945; worked as teacher at Brownie McGhee's Home of the Blues Music School, NYC, c1948; rec Lenox label, NYC, 1949; continued working as singing street preacher in NYC area through 40s/50s; worked Leadbelly Memorial concert, Town Hall, NYC, 1950; rec Stinson label, NYC, 1954; rec Riverside label, NYC, 1956; rec Folk-Lyric label, NYC, 1957; worked Folk Concert, Boston, MA, 1958; Carnegie Hall, NYC, 1958; Newport Folk Festival, Newport, RI, 1959; Mariposa Folk Festival, Toronto, Can, 1959 (por rel Kicking Mule label); Town Hall, NYC, 1960; rec Bluesville-Prestige label, NYC, 1960-1; worked Mother Blues, Chicago, IL, c1961; First Step, Tucson, AZ, c1961; Retort Club, Detroit, MI, c1961; Second Fret, Philadelphia, PA, c1961; Philadelphia Folk Festival, Paoli, PA, 1961-3 (por 1963 concert rel Prestige-International label); Golden Vanity, Boston, MA, 1961; Purple Onion, Toronto, Can, 1962; Pot Pourri, Montreal, Can, 1962; Swarthmore Col, Swarthmore, PA, 1962 (por rel Transatlantic label); worked as assistant pastor of True Heart Baptist Church, Bronx, NY, 1963; worked Here Coffeehouse, Minneapolis, MN, 1963; Gerdes Folk City, NYC, 1963; Le Hibou Club, Ottawa, Can, 1963; Fifth Dimension, Montreal, Can, 1963; Cafe Yana, Boston, MA, 1963; Cabale Club, Berkeley, CA, 1964; Hunter College, NYC, 1964; Village Corner, Toronto, Can, 1964; app in film short BLIND GARY DAVIS IN NEW YORK, 1964; rec Folkways label, NYC, 1964; worked Univ of California Folk Concert, Los Angeles, CA, 1964; Mariposa Folk Festival, Toronto, Can, 1964; Bohemian Embassy Coffee House, Toronto, 1964; toured w Blues Caravan working concert dates through England, 1964; worked The Ark, Vancouver, Can, 1965; Newport Folk Festival, Newport, RI, 1965; toured England working club/concert dates, 1965; worked Imbroglio, Boston, MA, 1965; Gaslight Cafe, NYC, 1965-6; Club 47, Cambridge, MA, 1965; Carnegie Hall, NYC, 1965; Jordan Hall, Boston, 1965; Philadelphia Folk Festival, Spring Mount, PA, 1965; Univ of Chicago Folklore Society Festival, Chicago, IL, 1966; Ash Grove, Los Angeles, CA, 1966; Rheingold Music Festival, NYC, 1966; rec Folkways label, NYC, 1966; app w Pete Seeger, RAINBOW QUEST, WNDT-TV, NYC, 1967; worked Mariposa Folk Festival, Toronto, Can, 1967; app in film short REVEREND GARY DAVIS, 1967; worked North Carolina Baptist Convention, 1968; Michigan State Univ, East Lansing, MI, 1968 (por rel Kicking Mule label); Newport Folk Festival, Newport, RI, 1968 (por rel Vanguard label); Harvard Univ, Cambridge, MA, c1968 (por rel Fontana label); Electric Circus, NYC, 1969; Philadelphia Folk Festival, Schwenksville, Pa, 1969; rec Adelphi label, Silver Spring, MD, 1969; toured England working club/concert dates, 1969; worked Ash Grove, Los Angeles, CA, 1969; The Onion, Toronto, Can, 1969; Quiet Knight, Chicago, IL, 1969; Back Door Coffee House, Montreal, Can, 1970; Temple Univ, Philadelphia, PA, 1970; Berkeley Blues Festival, Berkeley, CA, 1970; app on LIKE IT IS, ABC-TV, 1970; app in film documentary BLACK ROOTS, 1970; worked Univ of Pittsburgh Blues Festival, Pittsburgh, PA, 1971; Cambridge Folk Festival and others, Cambridge, Eng, 1971; rec Biograph label, NYC, 1971; worked w Sister Davis, Little Mt Moriah Baptist Church, NYC, 1971-2; Festival of American Folklife, Washington, DC, 1971; frequently worked local concert/college dates in New York/New Jersey area, 1971-2; app in French film bio BLIND GARY DAVIS, 1972; while en route to a Newtonville, NJ, concert date suffered heart attack; died William Kessler Memorial Hospital; buried Rockville Cemetery, Lynbrook, NY

Books: The Holy Blues (a collection of spirituals), Robbins Music Corporation, 1970

Rev Gary Davis/Blues Guitar, Stefan Grossman, Oak Publications, 1974

'Oh, What A Beautiful City', Robert Tilling, Paul Mill Press (UK), 1992

Songs: All My Friends Are Gone/Baby Let Me Lay It on You/Candyman/Cincinnati Flow Rag/Cocaine Blues/Cross and Evil Woman Blues/Death Don't Have No Mercy/Delia/Dun Goin' Down/I Am the Light of This World/I Heard the Angels Singing/I Will Do My Last Singing in This Land Somewhere/I'm Throwing Up My Hand/It's a Mean World Till You Die/Let Us Get Together Right Down Here/Lo, I'll Be with You Always/(Lord) Search My Heart/O, Glory How Happy I Am/Out on the Ocean/Pure Religion/Right Now/Sailing/Sally, Where'd You Get the Liquor From?/Samson & Delilah/Say No to the Devil/Soon My Work Will All Be Done/There Was a Time When I Went Blind/Whistlin' Blues/You Got to Go Down/You've Got to Move

Infl by: Blind Blake/Craig Fowler

Infl to: Roy Bookbinder/Bull City Red/Andy Cohen/Ry Cooder/Donovan/Bob Dylan/Blind Boy Fuller/George Gritzbach/Stefan Grossman/Hot Tuna/Larry Johnson/Nick Katzman/Dave Lieberson/Brownie

McGhee/Ralph McTell/Taj Mahal/Woody Mann/Al Mattes/Alec Seward/Tarheel Slim/John Townley/Dave Van Ronk/John Weiss

Quotes: "Behind . . . the gospel songs and holy blues of the Reverend Gary Davis lies a long tradition of Negro folksong"—Kenneth S Goldstein, Riverside album RLP-148

"His voice, though strained through years of street-singing, has a fierce kind of beauty, imbued with a special kind of loneliness that surely only a blind person can feel"—Gillian Cook, Xtra album 1009

"One of the finest gospel, blues, ragtime guitarists and singers"—Robert Tilling, *Jazz Journal* magazine (UK), Jul 1972, p 19

References: Blues World magazine (UK), Spring/ Summer 1972

Blues magazine (Canada), Apr/Jun, 1976

Sing Out magazine, Mar/Apr 1974, pp 2-5

'Oh, What A Beautiful City', Robert Tilling, Paul Mill Press (UK), 1992

DAVIS, *"Maxwell Street"* **JIMMY**
(see Thomas, Charles)

DAVIS, *"Blind"* **JOHN HENRY**
Born: Dec 7, 1913, Hattiesburg (Forrest Co), MS
Died: Oct 12, 1985, Chicago, IL
Inst: Piano

Photo by Amy O'Neal. Courtesy Sheldon Harris Collection

Father John Wesley Davis; mother Lillie Iverson; one of 4 children; to Chicago where he was raised lost eye-sight due to tetanus infection, 1923; taught self piano and worked as entertainer in local speakeasies, Chicago, from 1926 into 30s; formed own Johnny Davis' Original Music Masters to work local club dates, Chicago, from 1938 through 40s; rec Vocalion label, Chicago, 1938; frequently worked as house pianist for Bluebird label and rec acc to Doc Clayton/John Lee "Sonny Boy" Williamson/Lonnie Johnson/Bill Broonzy/others, Chicago, late 30s into 40s; rec w own trio, MGM label, Chicago, 1949-51; worked w Kansas City Red Band in local club dates, Chicago, early 50s; toured w Bill Broonzy working concert dates through Europe, 1952 (frequently thereafter); rec acc to Bill Broonzy/or with own trio/or solo, Vogue label, Paris, France, 1952; worked w Bill Broonzy, Sylvio's, Chicago, 1952; app w Bill Broonzy on BIG BILL HILL SHOW, WOPA-radio, Oak Park, IL, 1952; worked local road houses/clubs/taverns through Illinois through 50s; worked Easy Street Club, Chicago, 1956-7; Tony's Cellar, Chicago, 1959; Tony's Upstairs, Chicago, 1959; Ravinia Folk Festival, Chicago, 1959; rec w Al Wynn Band, Riverside label, Chicago, 1961; worked Fickle Pickle, Chicago, 1963; w Bob Scobey Band, Bourbon Street, Chicago, 1963; Newport Folk Festival, Newport, RI, 1964; Showboat Sari-S, Chicago, 1965; frequently worked w Judge Riley (drums) as Johnny Davis Duo working local club dates, Chicago, 1966-73; toured England/ Europe working concert dates, 1973-4; rec Happy Bird label, Hamburg, Ger, 1973; rec Chrischaa label, Bonn, Ger, 1973; rec Oldie Blues label, Veenendaal, Holland, 1974; frequently worked Maxwell Street area for tips, Chicago, 1974; Mariposa Folk Festival, Toronto, Can, 1975; Ratso's, Chicago, 1975; Univ of Chicago, Chicago, 1975; Milwaukee Jazz Festival, Milwaukee, WI, 1975; Chicago Blues Festival, Jane Addams Theater, Chicago, 1975; Midwest Blues Festival, Univ of Notre Dame, South Bend, IN, 1975; Shiers Coffee House, Toronto, Can, 1976; The Riverboat, Toronto, 1976; Fiddler's Green, Toronto, 1976; Winnipeg Folk Festival, Winnipeg, Can, 1976; John Henry Folk Festival, Camp Virgil Tate, Princeton, WV, 1976; rec Sirens label, Chicago, 1976; worked Orphans, Chicago, 1976; toured Europe working concert dates, 1977; worked Northern Illinois Univ, DeKalb, IL, 1977; Univ of Chicago Folk Festival,

Chicago, 1977; Miller Theater, Dallas, TX, 1977; Elsewhere Club, Chicago, 1977; app on MADE IN CHICAGO, WTTW-TV, Chicago, 1977; worked The Rising Sun, Montreal, Can, 1978; toured Europe/Mexico working concerts, 1979; worked club/concerts in Chicago/NYC, NY area into 80s; app in film MAXWELL STREET BLUES, 1980; suffered fatal heart attack; buried Burr Oak Cemetery, Worth, IL

Personal: Married (1938-55). Not to be confused with John "Johnny" Davis (harmonica)/or John Henry Davis Jr (guitarist/bassist)/or John Davis, formerly with the Georgia Sea Island Singers, all unrelated

Songs: A Little Every Day/Davis Boogie/Everybody's Boogie/If I Had a Listen/My Own Boogie/Rockin' Chair Boogie/Run Away Boogie

Quote: "John was the greatest and most prolific pre-war piano-accompanist"—Martin Van Olderen, Oldie Blues Album 2803

Reference: Blues Unlimited magazine (UK), Nov 1969, p 14

DAVIS, LARRY *"Totsy"*

Courtesy Sheldon Harris Collection

Born: Dec 4, 1936, Kansas City (Jackson Co), MO
Inst: Bass/Drums/Guitar/Piano/Tenor Saxophone

Mother Mattie——— was singer; raised in Little Rock/England/Pine Bluff, AR, area from childhood; began playing drums at about 9 years of age; sat-in w BB King Band, Club Morocco, Little Rock, AR, c1951; frequently toured w Bill Fort Band/Hugh Holloway Band through Arkansas in mid-50s; toured w Billy Gayles group working clubs from St Louis, MO, to Los Angeles, CA, 1957-8; rec w Fention Robinson, Duke label, Houston, TX, 1958-9; formed own group to work club dates in Little Rock, AR, area in 1958; frequently toured w own group working clubs from Little Rock to St Louis through late 50s into 60s; worked w Albert King Band, mid-60s; frequently worked clubs in St Louis area in late 60s; rec Virgo label, St Louis, 1968; toured Texas/Arizona/New Mexico working one-nighters in late 60s; rec Kent label, Los Angeles, 1969; worked Steve Paul's Scene, NYC, 1969; learned guitar and worked Gingerbread House/Persian Room/Cavalier Club/others, Little Rock, AR, area, 1970 into 70s; rec Hub City label, Memphis, TN, early 70s; worked Convention Center Auditorium, Pine Bluff, AR, 1976

Songs: Tears of Sorrow/Texas Flood

Infl by: Roy Brown/Little Willie John/BB King

Quote: "At the relatively young age of 40, Larry Davis has established himself as one of the most polished and distinctive blues stylists now working in Arkansas. He is also one of the most cosmopolitan"—Louis Guida, *Living Blues* magazine, May 1977, p 29

References: Blues Unlimited, Jun 1973, pp 12-14
Blues Unlimited, Mar/Jun, 1979, pp. 4-7

DAVIS, WALTER
(*aka:* Hooker Joe)

Courtesy Frank Driggs Collection

Born: Mar 1, 1912, Grenada (Grenada Co), MS
Died: Oct 22, 1963, St Louis, MO (unconfirmed)
Inst: Piano

Born/raised/worked on farm; ran away from home to hobo to St Louis, MO, c1925; unconfirmed report he rec Paramount label (under unknown pseudonym), late 20s; worked JC Nightclub, East St Louis, IL, late 20s; frequently toured w Henry Townsend/Brother Fox/others working club dates through Texas/Missouri/Tennessee/Mississippi/South Carolina, late 20s through 30s; rec Victor label, Cincinnati, OH, 1930; rec Victor label, Louisville, KY/Chicago, IL, 1931; rec Victor label, Dallas, TX, 1932; rec Victor/Bluebird labels, Chicago, 1933; rec Bluebird label, Chicago, 1935-6; rec Bluebird label, Aurora, IL, 1937-8; rec Bluebird label, Chicago, 1939-41; worked Nat Love's Club, East St Louis, IL, c1940; rec Victor label, Chicago, 1946-7; rec Bullet label, Chicago, 1949-50; rec Victor label, Chicago, 1952; suffered illnesses and was inactive in music from c1953; settled in St Louis to work outside music with frequent work as preacher from c1953; worked outside music (as night clerk/switchboard operator) at Calumet Hotel/Albany Hotel, St Louis, into 60s

Note: Unconfirmed reports exist regarding this singers' death date and place, as well as other possible birth places

Personal: Not to be confused with Walter Davis Jr, a contemporary jazz pianist who is not related

Songs: Ashes in My Whiskey/Biddle Street Blues/Blue Blues/Blue Ghost Blues/Broke and Hungry/Corrine/Cuttin' Off My Days/Dentist Blues/Doctor Blues/Don't You Want to Go?/Down and Out/Early This Morning/Everything Is OK/Falling Rain/Frisco Blues/Goodbye/Got to See Her Every Night/Hello Baby/Hijack Blues/Homesick/Howling Wind Blues/I Can Tell by the Way You Smell/I Feel All Right/I Like the Way You Spread Your Wings/I Would Hate to Hate You (Like I Love You)/If It Hadn't Been for You/If You Treat Me Right/If You'll Only Understand/It's Been So Long/Just One More Time/L&N Blues/Let Me in Your Saddle/M&O Blues/Mercy Blues/Minute Man Blues/Mojo Blues/Moonlight Is My Spread/Move Back to the Woods/My Friends Don't Know Me/New B&O Blues/New Orleans/Oh Me Oh My Blues/One Sweet Letter from You/The Only Woman/Please Remember Me/Root Man Blues/Sad and Lonesome Blues/Santa Claus Blues/Sweet Sixteen/Teasin' Brown Skin/That Stuff You Sell Ain't No Good/Things Ain't Like They Use to Be/Think You Need a Shot/Travellin' This Lonesome Road/The Way I Love You/What Have I Done Wrong?/When You Need My Help/Wonder What I'm Doing Wrong/You've Got to Reap What You Sow/Your Time Is Coming

Infl by: Leroy Carr/Henry Townsend

Infl to: Gus Jenkins/St Louis Jimmy

Quotes: "Probably the most original of them all with his deeply moving singing and lyrical piano style"—Mike Rowe, *Chicago Breakdown*, Eddison Press Ltd, 1973

"We must consider Walter Davis to be an important voice from the blues world of the thirties"—Neil Slaven, RCA-International album 1085

DAWKINS, JAMES HENRY *"Fast Fingers"/"Jimmy"*

Born: Oct 24, 1936, Tchula (Holmes Co), MS
Inst: Guitar

Was an only child; moved to Pascagoula, MS, where he was raised from early 40s; taught self guitar in 1953; left home to work outside music, Chicago, IL, 1955-7; teamed w Lester Hinton to work streets for tips, Chicago, 1957-60; formed own band to work Pink Poodle Club/Big Squeeze Club/others, Chicago, 1957 into 60s; frequently w Jimmy Rogers Band in local club dates, Chicago, c1958; frequently w Magic Sam group in local club dates, Chicago, into 60s; toured w own band working local club dates in Chicago area, early 60s; frequently rec as sideman w Sonny Thompson/Wild Child Butler/Johnny Young/others, Chicago, through 60s; worked w JT Brown Band in local supper clubs, Grand Rapids, MI, 1963; w own band at Copa Cabana Club, Chicago, 1964 (with frequent radio remotes); rec Bea & Baby label, Chicago, 1966; rec acc to Johnny Young, Arhoolie label, Chicago, 1967; w Johnny Young Orch, Blues Festival, Madison, WI, 1968; rec Delmark label, Chicago, 1968; app in documentary bio film (unknown title), 1969; worked Ann Arbor Blues Festival, Ann Arbor, MI, 1969-70; rec acc to Luther Allison, Delmark label, Chicago, 1969; worked Univ of Minnesota, Minneapolis, MN, 1970-1; J&P Lounge, Chicago, 1970; Texas Lady, Chicago, 1970; Five Stages, Chicago, 1970; Beloit Col, Beloit, WI, 1970; toured w John Lee Hooker/Carey Bell/Eddie Taylor working concert dates through Europe, 1970; worked Alice's Revisited, Chicago, 1970-1; app w Carey Bell on local shows, WFXM/WNUS-radio, Chicago, 1970; worked Notre Dame Blues Festival, South Bend, IN, 1970; Union Theater, Chicago, 1971; Lovia's Lounge,

James "Jimmy" Dawkins

Photo by Jim Falconer. Courtesy Sheldon Harris Collection

Chicago, 1971; Kent State Univ, Kent, OH, 1971; toured w Chicago Blues Festival working concert dates through Europe, 1971-2; app on local TV show, Paris, France, 1971; rec Vogue/Black & Blue labels, Paris, 1971; worked Psychedelic Shack, Chicago, 1971; Big T Lounge, Chicago, 1971; rec Delmark label, Chicago, 1971-3; worked w Otis Rush Band, Ann Arbor Blues Festival, Ann Arbor, MI, 1972 (por rel Atlantic label); Univ of Miami Blues Festival, Silver Springs, FL, 1972; toured w American Folk Blues Festival working concert dates through England/Europe, 1972; rec Excello label, London, Eng, 1972; worked Montreux Jazz Festival, Montreux, Switzerland, 1972 (por rel Excello label); Ma Bea's Lounge, Chicago, 1972-5 (por 1975 date rel MCM label); Ratso's, Chicago, 1973; app on ATOMIC MAMA'S WANG DANG DOODLE BLUES, WNIB-FM-radio, Chicago, 1973; worked Teddy's Club, Milwaukee, WI, 1973; Univ of Vermont, Burlington, VT, 1973; Univ of Wisconsin, Madison, WI, 1973; Festival of American Folklife, Washington, DC, 1973 (por shown in videotape BORN IN THE BLUES); Club H, Bowling Green, OH, 1974; Kings Club Waveland, Chicago, 1974; Joe's Place, Boston, MA, 1974; Wise Fools Pub, Chicago, 1974-6; Uprising Tavern, DeKalb, IL, 1974; Biddy Mulligan's, Chicago, 1974; Minstrel's, Chicago, 1974; Peanut Barrel, Chicago, 1974; Ann Arbor Blues & Jazz Festival, Windsor, Can, 1974; toured w Chicago Blues Festival working concert dates through Europe, 1974 (por Paris, France, concert rel Black & Blue label); worked Soap Creek Saloon, Austin, TX, 1974; Ritz Theater, Austin, 1974; app in film SINCERELY THE BLUES, 1975; worked Cafe Campus, Montreal, Can, 1975; Eddie's Place, Chicago, 1975; app on TODAY Show, NBC-TV, 1975; worked The Zoo Bar, Lincoln, NE, 1975-6; Biddy Mulligan's, Chicago, 1976; Green Earth Cafe, San Francisco, CA, 1976; Winterland

Auditorium, San Francisco, 1976; Jazz Showcase, Chicago, 1976; rec Delmark label, Chicago, 1976; worked The Bayou, Washington, DC, 1976; Theater 1839, San Francisco, 1977; app on BLUES BY THE BAY, KPFA-FM-radio, Berkeley, CA, 1977; Intersection Tavern, Grand Rapids, MI, 1977; clip shown in ROOTS OF COUNTRY MUSIC & BLUES, KGO-TV, San Francisco, 1977

Personal: Married. 5 children

Songs: Ain't Never Had Nothing/All for Business/Blues in the Ghetto/Born in Poverty/Casino Trick Stick/Chicago on My Mind/Close Down Boogie/Cold Sweat Blues/I Want to Know/It Serves You Right to Suffer/Let Me Have My Way/Lick for Licks/Life Is a Mean Mistreater/Marcelle Jacques et Luc/Mean Atlantic Ocean/Mississippi Bound/No More Trouble/Off Business/1011 Woodland/Out of Business/Stoned Dead/Tribute to Orang/The Way She Walks/Welfare Line/You've Got to Keep On Trying

Awards/Honors: Won Grand Prix du Disque de Jazz of Hot Club of France for best jazz/blues guitar album of 1971 ("Fast Fingers," Delmark album 623)

Won *Downbeat* magazine International Critics Poll as best rock/pop/blues group deserving wider recognition, 1974

Infl by: Smiley Lewis/Little Milton/Guitar Watson

Quotes: "Known among his peers as a consummate guitarist"—Hamilton Bims, *Ebony* magazine, Mar 1972, p 86

". . . artists like Jimmy Dawkins prove that blues can evolve creatively yet be perpetuated in a relevant manner"—Doug Langille, *Coda* magazine (Canada), Dec 1976, p 9

Reference: Living Blues magazine, Spring 1972, pp 18-21

DE FORREST, MAUDE

Born: c1900, Philadelphia (Philadelphia Co), PA (unconfirmed)
Died: (unknown)

Was working theaters w Gus Smith Trio from early teens; worked w Gus & Virginia Smith in singing/dancing act at Lyric Theater, New Orleans, LA, 1922; worked Academy of Music, Wilmington, NC, 1922; Douglass Theater, Baltimore, MD, 1922; Standard Theater, Philadelphia, PA, 1922; toured w Ethel Waters/Fletcher Henderson Jazz Masters in Black Swan Troubadours troupe working theater circuit through Midwest/South in 1922; rec w Fletcher Henderson, Black Swan label, NYC, NY, 1923; rec w Leroy Tibbs, Paramount label, NYC, 1923; app in PLANTATION DAYS Revue, Lafayette Theater, NYC, 1923; app in musical comedy NORTH AIN'T SOUTH, Lafayette Theater, NYC, 1923, then toured with show; app in 7-11 Revue, Cleveland, OH, 1924; teamed w George McClennon (clarinetist) to tour in own act on burlesque circuit, 1925; replaced Josephine Baker in show REVUE NEGRE, Champs-Elysees Theater, Paris, France, 1925-6 then toured Europe with show into late 20s; app in CABIN CLUB FOLLIES, Cabin Club, NYC, 1929; frequently worked local club dates, NYC, NY/Philadelphia, PA, 1929 into 30s; app in MANHATTAN FROLICS Revue, Harlem Opera House, NYC, 1932; reportedly inactive in music from mid-30s and whereabouts unknown thereafter

DEE, MERCY

(see Walton, Mercy Dee)

DELANEY, THOMAS HENRY *"Tom"*

Courtesy Merrill M Hammond

Born: Sept 14, 1889, Charleston (Charleston Co), SC
Died: Dec 16, 1963, Baltimore, MD
Inst: Piano

Father was Abral Delaney; mother was Roxanna Gasson; raised in Jenkins Orphanage, Charleston, SC, from childhood; formed The Springfield Minstrels while at Jenkins Orphanage to write/perform with group from 1901; teamed w Henderson Mitchell (as "Mitchell & Delaney") to tour as singing/dancing act on vaudeville circuit/theaters/dance halls/amusement parks/cabarets on East Coast c1910-17; worked as single on vaudeville circuit from c1917 to 1921; teamed w Pearl Mason working as singing/dancing/monologist act at Regent Theater, Baltimore, MD, 1921, then touring as team on vaudeville circuit to 1923; toured as acc/manager to Ethel Waters working theater dates through 20s; rec Columbia label, NYC, NY, 1925; extensive residency w John J Quigley, Glass Pavilion, Steeplechase Park, Brooklyn, NY, late 20s into 30s; app w Bertha Idaho on local talk show, WCBM-radio, Baltimore, MD, c1932; occasional theater work in NYC area to 1935; settled in Baltimore to work mostly outside music with occasional entertaining w Marjorie Wilson in local clubs/jazz organizations/others, 1935 through 50s; worked Washington Jazz Club concert, Charles Hotel, Washington, DC, c1956; entered Provident Hospital where he died of hardening of arteries; buried Mt Auburn Cemetery, Baltimore, MD

Personal: Married Pearl Mason (c1918-died 1928), 1 son; married Marjorie Wilson (c1929-1963)

Songs: Absent Minded Blues/At the (New) Jump Steady Ball/Bow-Legged Mamma/Buttin' in Other Folks Buzzness/Cootie for Your Tootie/Death House Blues/Down Home Blues/Down on Pennsylvania Avenue/Everybody Wants to Go to Heaven But Nobody Wants to Die/Everybody's Blues/Follow the Deal On Down/Georgia Stockade Blues/Give Me That Old Slow Drag/Good Times Up in Harlem/Graveyard Love/Hard Boiled Papa/Honey Where You Been So Long?/I Don't Care Where You Take It/I Love You Daddy But You Don't Mean Me No Good/If I Lose Let Me Lose/I'm a Back-Bitin' Mama/I'm a Good Hearted Mama/I'm Leavin' Just to Ease My Worried Mind/I've Cried My Last Time over You/Jazz Me Blues/Let the Good Times Roll/Log Cabin Blues/Low Down Mama Blues/Meet Me Up in Harlem/Miss Lizzie Can't Strut No More/Mournful Blues/Move It On Out of Here/Mr Leader Man Swing That Band/Never Drive a Beggar from Your Door/New York Glide/Nobody Knows the Way I Feel This Mornin'/Parson Jones/Police Blues/Poon Tang/Slow and Steady/Somethin' Goin' On Wrong/South Bound Blues/Strollin' Down Pennsylvania Ave/Thing Called Love's Done Made a Fool Out of Me/Troublesome Blues/Walk That Broad/Way Down in Bam/When I Get Blues/When I Leave This Time Baby/Working Man Blues/You May Go But You'll Come Back Some Day

DELTA JOE
(see Luandrew, Albert)

DELTA JOHN
(see Hooker, John Lee)

DENIM, JOE
(see Cotton, James)

DETROIT JR
(see Williams Jr, Emery)

DETROIT RED
(see Perryman, Rufus)

DEVIL'S DADDY-IN-LAW
(see Council, Floyd)

DEVIL'S SON-IN-LAW
(see Wheatstraw, Peetie)

DIAMOND, WILLIAM *"Do Boy"*
Born: c1913, Canton (Madison Co), MS
Inst: Guitar

Born/raised/worked farm from childhood; one of 13 children; taught self guitar and frequently worked local dances/jukes/cafes in Canton, MS, area from c1938 into 50s; continued outside music work, Canton, into 70s; rec Revival label, Canton, 1967; inactive in music from 60s

Personal: Married twice. 3 children

References: Blow My Blues Away, George Mitchell, Louisiana State Univ Press, 1971

DIDDLEY, BO
(see McDaniel, Ellas)

DIRTY RED
(see Wilborn, Nelson)

DIXON, FLOYD *"Skeet"*
Born: Feb 8, 1929, Marshall (Harrison Co), TX
Inst: Piano

Taught self piano in early 40s; moved to Los Angeles, CA, where he was raised from c1942; won first prize in

Photo by Norbert Hess

amateur show, Million Dollar Theater, Los Angeles, c1948; won talent contest, Barrelhouse Club, Los Angeles, c1949; rec Modern label, Los Angeles, 1949-52; rec w Eddie Williams and the Brown Buddies, Supreme label, Los Angeles, c1949; rec w Johnny Moore's Three Blazers, Aladdin label, Los Angeles, 1950-1; toured extensively w Frank Bull/Gene Norman's Blues Jubilee/other package shows working Riviera Club, St Louis, MO/Flame Show Bar, Detroit, MI/Howard Theater, Washington, DC/Royal Theater, Baltimore, MD/Regal Theater, Chicago, IL/Primalon, San Francisco, CA, and other theaters/clubs/one-nighters across US from early 50s; rec Aladdin label, Los Angeles, 1952; rec Speciality label, Los Angeles, 1953; rec w own band, Cat label, California, 1954; app on GENE NORMAN SHOW, KLAC-radio, Los Angeles, mid-50s; rec Cash label, Los Angeles, 1957; rec Ebb label, Los Angeles, c1957; rec Kent label, Los Angeles, 1958; rec Checker label, Chicago, 1958; rec Swingin' label, 1960; rec Dodge label, Houston, TX, 1961; rec Chatta-Hoo-Chie label, 1962; toured Midwest working one-nighters in early 60s; worked mostly outside music, Los Angeles, 1963 into 70s; worked occasional gigs, Mr Jones Pub, Venice, CA, c1971; Sweet Pea, Santa Monica, CA, c1971; rec w Charles Brown, Jewel label, Los Angeles, c1971; worked w ZZ Hill in local club dates, Beaumont, TX, 1971; worked mostly outside music, San Francisco, early 70s; app on BLUES BY THE BAY, KPOO-FM-radio, San Francisco, 1974; worked Minnie's Can-Do Club, San Francisco, 1975; Cat's Cradle, San Francisco, 1975; San Francisco Blues Festival, McLaren Park Amphitheater, San Francisco, 1975; Scandinavian Blues Association Concert, Orebro, Sweden, 1975 (por rel Great Dame label); app on PERSPECTIVE Show, KGO-TV, San Francisco, 1975; worked Ruthie's, Berkeley, CA, 1975-6; The Exploratorium, San Francisco, 1975; Sierra Club, Stockton, CA, 1976; Festival of Arts Concert, Univ of Chicago, Chicago, 1976; R&B Festival, Groningen, Netherlands, 1978

Personal: Not to be confused with at least two other Floyd Dixons who worked Texas/Florida clubs during the 1950s/60s

Songs: Dallas Blues/Floyd's Blues/For You/Homesick Blues/Operator 210/Two Piano Blues/When I Get Lucky

Inf by: Charles Brown/Louis Jordan/Amos Milburn

Infl to: Dave Alexander/Ray Charles

Quotes: "Floyd shows more vibrancy and exuberance than Charles [Brown], excelling at jump tunes and rocking piano boogies. He also begs comparison to Louis Jordan and Ray Charles . . ."—Dick Shurman, *Living Blues* magazine, Sept 1975, p 20

"The role Floyd Dixon has played in the evolution of the West Coast blues scene has long been overlooked"—Tom Mazzolini, *Living Blues* magazine, Sept 1975, p 14

Reference: *Living Blues*, Sept 1975, pp 14-21

DIXON, *"Big"* WILLIE JAMES

Born: Jul 1, 1915, Vicksburg (Warren Co), MS
Died: Jan 29, 1992, Burbank, CA
Inst: Bass/Guitar

Father was Charlie Dixon; mother was Daisy McKenzie; one of 14 children; raised/worked on farm from childhood; moved to Chicago, IL, to work outside music, 1926-9; returned to Vicksburg, MS, to work in Union Jubilee Singers group w frequent Saturday parties, 1929-32; returned to Chicago, IL, to work outside music from c1932; won Golden Gloves amateur heavyweight boxing title (as James Dixon), Chicago, 1936; then turned professional in 1937; learned string bass and worked w Five Breezes group and others at Cafe Society/Martin's Corner/Pink Poodle/Brass Rail/Capitol Lounge/others, Chicago, c1940-42; rec w Five Breezes, Bluebird label, Chicago, 1940; formed Jumps of Jive group work-

The Big Three Trio ([t] Willie Dixon/[m] Leonard Caston [b] Ollie Crawford) *Courtesy Frank Driggs Collection*

ing local club dates, 1945-6; rec w Four Jumps of Jive, Mercury label, Chicago, 1945; formed Big Three Trio working local club dates, Chicago, from 1946 with frequent tours working clubs through Midwest to 1952; rec w Big Three Trio, Bullet label, Memphis, TN, 1946; rec w Big Three Trio, Columbia label, Chicago, 1947; rec w Memphis Slim & His House Rockers, Miracle label, Chicago, 1947; worked Melody Show Bar, St Louis, MO, c1947; rec w Big Three Trio, Columbia label, Chicago, 1949; frequently rec acc to various bluesmen, Aristocrat label, Chicago, 1949-52; rec w Big Three Trio, OKeh label, Chicago, 1951-2; worked as A&R/producer/composer/musician/talent scout/arranger for Chess Record Company, Chicago, 1952-6; worked w Elmore James Broomdusters, Sylvio's and others, Chicago, 1955; rec w The All Stars, Checker label, Chicago, 1955; worked as A&R for Cobra/Abco labels/others, Chicago, 1956-60; toured w Otis Rush group working one-nighters through Florida/Texas/Mississippi, 1956-7; formed own Ghana Music Publishing Company, Chicago, 1957 (later sold to ARC Music Corp); worked Charisse Lounge, Chicago, 1957; w Memphis Slim, Gate of Horn, Chicago, 1959-61; rec w Memphis Slim, Bluesville label, Englewood Cliffs, NJ, 1959; worked Storyville Club, Boston, MA, c1959; toured w Memphis Slim working concert dates through England/Europe, 1960; worked The Village Gate, NYC, NY, 1960 (por rel Folkways label); app w Memphis Slim, Dave Garroway's TODAY Show, NBC-TV, 1960; rec w Memphis Slim, Verve/Folkways labels, NYC, 1960; worked Ash Grove, Los Angeles, CA, 1960; continued to work as singer/A&R/producer for Chess Record Company, Chicago, 1960 into early 70s; toured w Rhythm & Blues USA package show working concert dates through England/Europe, 1962 (por rel Atlantic label); worked w Memphis Slim at Blues Concert, Hamburg, Ger, 1962 (por rel German Brunswick label); w Memphis Slim, Trois Mailletz Club, Paris, France, 1962 (por rel Polydor label); worked New Alex Club, Chicago, 1963; toured w Folk Blues Festival working concert dates through England/Europe, 1963-4 (por 1963 concert shown I HEAR THE BLUES, Granada-TV, London, Eng/por 1964 Musikhalle Concert, Hamburg, Ger, rel Fontana label); rec Fontana label, Bremen, Ger, 1963; rec Amiga label, Berlin, Ger, 1964; rec Spivey label, Chicago, IL, 1964; worked Newport Jazz Festival, Newport, RI, 1965; Village Vanguard, NYC, 1965; app on FESTIVAL PRESENTS THE BLUES, CBC-TV, Toronto, Can, 1966; worked The Kibitzeria, Toronto, 1968; formed The Chicago All-Stars group to tour US/Europe working jazz/folk clubs/concerts, 1968 into 70s; worked Hunter Col, NYC, 1969; Electric Circus, NYC, 1969; Half Note, NYC, 1969; rec Spivey label, Chicago, 1969; rec w Chicago All-Stars, MPS label, Cologne, Ger, 1969; worked Chicago Blues Festival, Chicago, 1969; rec

Blue Horizon label, Chicago, 1969; worked Ash Grove, Los Angeles, CA, 1969; Five Stages, Chicago, 1970; rec Columbia label, NYC, 1970; toured w American Folk Blues Festival working concert dates through England/Europe, 1970 (por Frankfort, Ger, concert rel Scout label); worked Jazz Expo 70, London, Eng, 1970; Berlin Jazz Days Festival, Berlin, Ger, 1970; app in UK film CHICAGO BLUES, 1970 (shown on OMNIBUS, BBC-1-TV, London, Eng); formed own Blues Factory/Soul Productions (a talent/recording/production agency), Chicago, IL, c1970-4; formed/rec Yambo/Spoonful labels, Chicago, c1970; worked Blues Festival, Liberty Hall, Dallas, TX, 1971; Alice's Revisited, Chicago, 1972; Ann Arbor Blues Festival, Ann Arbor, MI, 1972; Univ of California, Irvine, CA, 1972; Earth Breeze, Vancouver, Can, 1972; toured w Chicago All-Stars working concert dates on college circuit through Canada, 1972-3; worked Montreux Jazz Festival 72, Montreux, Switzerland, 1972; rec Ovation label, Chicago, 1973; worked Medgar Evers Memorial Festival, Jackson, MS, 1973; El Mocambo, Toronto, Can, 1973; app in film OUT OF THE BLACKS INTO THE BLUES (pt 2: A Way to Escape the Ghetto), 1972; worked Grendel's Lair, Philadelphia, PA, 1973-5; Kenny's Castaways, NYC, 1973-4; rec Spivey label, Brooklyn, NY, c1974; app on SOUNDSTAGE, PBS-TV, 1974; worked Lincoln Center, NYC, 1974; Joe's Place, Boston, MA, 1974; toured w Chicago Blues All-Stars working concert dates through Australia/New Zealand, 1974; worked Teddy's Club, Milwaukee, WI, 1974; Toronto Blues Festival, Olympic Island, Toronto, Can, 1974; The Cabooze, Minneapolis, MN, 1974; Keystone Korner, Berkeley, CA, 1974; In Concert Club, Montreal, Can, 1975; Embassy Hall, Los Angeles, CA, 1975; Foundation Tavern, Tacoma, WA, 1975; Univ of Oregon, Eugene, OR, 1975; w Chicago All-Stars, My Father's Place, Roslyn, NY, 1976; Bottom Line, NYC, 1976; Wise Fools Pub, Chicago, IL, 1976; New England Blues Festival, Providence, RI, 1976; Toad's Place, New Haven, CT, 1976; Howard Street Tavern, Omaha, NE, 1976; Rising Sun, Montreal, Can, 1977; w Chicago Blues All-Stars, The Music Hall, Atlanta, GA, 1977; hosted New Generation of Chicago Blues package group, Berlin Jazztage Festival, Berlin, Ger, 1977 (por shown in film WILLIE DIXON AND THE NEW GENERATION OF CHICAGO BLUES, Ger/UK TV); Quasimodo Club, Berlin, 1977; Joe's Bierhaus, Berlin, 1977; extensive touring working clubs/concerts/festivals in US/Mexico through 80s; worked Delta Blues Fest, Freedom Village, MS, 1980 (por shown MISSISSIPPI DELTA BLUES, PBS-TV, 1981); semi-retired to Glendale, CA, 1984; app in film SURVIVORS, 1985; died of heart failure; buried Burr Oak Cemetery, Worth, IL

Book: I Am The Blues: The Willie Dixon Story, Willie Dixon/Don Snowden, Da Capo. 1989

Songs: After Five Long Years/Alone/Axe and the Wind/Back Door Man/Big Boat/Big Boss Man/Big Momma, Little Momma/Bills Bills and More Bills/ Blues You Can't Lose/Born to Love Me/Born Too Late/Bring It On Home/Broken Hearted Blues/Built for Comfort/Business Man/Bye Bye Bird/Close to You/Country Style/Crazy for My Baby/Crazy Love/ Crazy Mixed Up World/Do Me Right/Do Something Baby/Do the Do/Do What You Want to Do, Be What You Want to Be/Don't Go No Further/Don't Let That Music Die/Don't Mess with the Messer/Down in the Bottom/Earthquake and Hurricane/East Baby/ Every Girl I See/Evil Is Going On/Fire/Get to My Baby/God's Gift/Goin' Home/The Gravedigger Cried/Groaning the Blues/Hidden Charms/Hold Me Baby/Home to Mamma/Hoo Doo Blues/Howlin' for My Baby/The Hunt/I Ain't Superstitious/I Am the Blues/I Can't Quit You Baby/I Don't Care Who Knows/I Don't Want Maybe/I Got a Strange Feeling/ I (Just) Want to Make Love to You/I Need More and More/I'd Give My Life for You/If You Were Mine/I'm Ready/I'm Shorty/I'm Worried/I'm Your Hoochie Coochie Man/Insane Asylum/It's in the News/Jelly Jam/Jump Sister Bessie/Just Like I Treat You/Just Make Love to Me/Keep On Running/Let Everybody Boogie/Let Me Love You, Baby/Little Baby/Little Red Rooster/Love Me to Death/My Babe/My Baby/ My Baby's Sweeter/My Hoodoo Doctor/My John the Conquer Root/My Love Will Never Die/Need More Baby/Nervous/One Day You're Going to Get Lucky/ One More Time/One Way Out/Peace?/Put It All in There/Rub My Root/The Same Thing/The Seventh Son/Sex Appeal/Shake for Me/Shaky/Sittin' and Cryin' the Blues/Slave to Love/Somebody Please Play the Blues/Southern Women/Spoonful/Stop Ducking Me Baby/Sure Is Fun/Tail Dragger/That's All I Want/300 Pounds of Joy/Tiger in Your Tank/Tollin' Bells/Too Late/Too Many Ways/29 Ways/Un Huh My Baby/ Violent Love/Walking Blues/Wang Dang Doodle/ What Ever I Am You Made Me/What in the World You Goin' to Do?/When I Make Love/When My Left Eye Jumps/When the Eagle Flies/The Wiggling Worm/Yes, It's Good for You/You Can't Judge a Book by Its Cover/You Know My Love/You Shook Me/ You'll Be Mine/Young Fashioned Ways

Awards/Honors: Won *Blues Unlimited* magazine (UK) Readers Poll as best blues bassist, 1973

Infl by: Little Brother Montgomery

Quotes: "In any definitive review of the postwar Chicago [and urban] blues, Willie Dixon's diverse contributions as composer, arranger, performer and organizer stand out as a major and energizing force that helped shape the blues of his era . . ."—Tom Fiofori, *Downbeat* magazine, Aug 6, 1970, p 18

References: *Downbeat* magazine, Aug 6, 1970, p 18
Blues Unlimited magazine (UK), Oct 1964, p 3
I Am The Blues: The Willie Dixon Story, Willie Dixon/Don Snowden, Da Capo, 1989

DOCTOR CLAYTON'S BUDDY
(see Luandrew, Albert)

DOMINO, ANTOINE *"Fats"*

Courtesy Sheldon Harris Collection

Born: Feb 26, 1928, New Orleans (Orleans Parish), LA
Inst: Piano

Father was violinist; one of 9 children; mostly self-taught on piano from about 10 years of age; worked local honky tonks/bars/clubs for tips, New Orleans, LA, from 1938; dropped out of school to work outside music with frequent small club dates, New Orleans, into 40s; worked Al's Starlight Inn, New Orleans, late 40s; Crystal Gazers Club, New Orleans, late 40s; w Billy Diamond Combo, The Hideaway Club, New Orleans, c1948-9; Blue Monday Club, New Orleans, c1949; rec w Dave Bartholomew Band, Imperial label, New Orleans, 1949; toured w Dave Bartholomew Band working club dates to West Coast, 1949; worked w Roy Brown Band in local club dates, Kansas City, MO, 1949; rec extensively, Imperial label, New Orleans, LA (occasionally Los Angeles, CA), 1950-63; formed own group to tour extensively working clubs/concerts/theaters across US from c1950; worked Five-Four Ballroom, Los Angeles, 1954; Laurel Garden, NYC, NY, 1954; The Showboat, Philadelphia, PA, 1955; Palms Club, Hallandale, FL, 1955; Paramount Theater, Brooklyn, NY, 1956; app in film SHAKE RATTLE AND ROCK, 1956; app in film THE GIRL CAN'T HELP IT, 1956; toured extensively w own band on Big Ten R&B package shows working theater/concert dates across US/Canada from 1956; worked Palomar Gardens, San Jose, CA, 1956; The Blue Note, Chicago, IL, 1956; app in film JAMBOREE, 1957; app in film THE BIG BEAT, 1957; app on DICK CLARK'S SATURDAY NIGHT BEECHNUT Show, ABC-TV, c1958; app on Dick Clark's AMERICAN BANDSTAND, ABC-TV, 1958; frequently worked West Coast club dates from c1958 into 60s; worked Fabian's Fox Theater, Brooklyn, NY, 1959; Apollo Theater, NYC, NY, 1960; frequently worked club/hotel dates on Las Vegas, NV, hotel circuit from 1961; worked Antibes Jazz Festival, Antibes, France, 1962; rec ABC-Paramount label, Nashville, TN, 1963-5; worked Flamingo Hotel, Las Vegas, 1963-5 (por 1965 date rel Mercury label); Showboat Club, Philadelphia, PA, 1963; Small's Paradise, NYC, NY, 1963; Sands Club, New Orleans, LA, 1965; Village Gate, NYC, 1966; Al Hirt's Club, New Orleans, 1966-70; Scotch Mist, Chicago, IL, 1967-8; toured England working club dates, 1967; worked Saville Theater, London, Eng, 1967; owned/rec Broadmoor label, New Orleans, 1967; worked Central Park Music Festival, NYC, 1968; rec Reprise label, New Orleans, 1968-70; app on MONKEES SPECIAL, NBC-TV, 1969; worked Fillmore East, NYC, 1969-70; Hollywood Bowl, Los Angeles, CA, 1969; Harrah's, Lake Tahoe, NV, 1969; Plugged Nickel, Chicago, IL, 1969; owned/managed chain of drive-in restaurants, 1969-70; app on MIKE DOUGLAS Show, CBS-TV, 1970;

worked Carnegie Hall, NYC, 1971; Sho-Bar, New Orleans, 1971; Rock & Roll Revival Show, Madison Square Garden, NYC, 1972; Summer Festival, Milwaukee, WI, 1972; toured Europe working concert dates, 1973; worked Montreux Jazz Festival, Montreux, Switzerland, 1973 (por rel Atlantic label); Flamingo Hotel, Las Vegas, NV, 1973-4 (por 1973 date shown in film LET THE GOOD TIMES ROLL); rec ST for film AMERICAN GRAFFITI, 1973; worked La Bastille, Houston, TX, 1973; El Mocambo, Toronto, Can, 1973-4; Fontainebleau Hotel, New Orleans, LA, 1973; toured Japan working concert dates c1974; toured France working concert dates, 1974; worked Hilton Lounge, Las Vegas, NV, 1975; app on MERV GRIFFIN Show, WNEW-TV (syndicated), NYC, 1975-6; app on AMERICAN BANDSTAND's 23rd BIRTHDAY SPECIAL, ABC-TV, 1975; rec ST for film RETURN TO MACON COUNTY, 1975; worked Academy of Music, NYC, 1975; New Orleans Jazz & Heritage Festival, New Orleans, LA, 1975; toured England/Australia working concert dates in 1975; worked New Victoria Theater, London, Eng, 1976; Rock & Roll Spectacular, Madison Square Garden, NYC, 1976-7; Newport Jazz Festival, NYC, 1976; rec ST for Miller Beer national TV commercial, 1976; worked Five Star Playhouse, New Orleans, LA, 1976; Fairmont Hotel, New Orleans, 1977; Stardust Inn, Waldorf, MD, 1977; toured Europe working concert dates, 1977; worked Mill Run Theater, Chicago, IL, 1977; Ivanhoe, Chicago, 1977; New Orleans Jazz & Heritage Festival, New Orleans, 1977; app on THE CAPTAIN & TENNILLE IN NEW ORLEANS, ABC-TV, 1978

Personal: Married Rosemary——— (1945-). 8 children

Songs: Ain't That a Shame?/All by Myself/Be My Guest/The Big Beat/Cheatin'/Detroit City Blues/Don't Come Knockin'/Don't Lie to Me/Every Night About This Time/The Fat Man/Fats Frenzy/Goin' Home/Going to the River/Hey Fat Man/Hide Away Blues/I Wanna Walk You Home/I Want You to Know/If You Need Me/I'll Be Gone/I'm Gonna Be a Wheel Someday/I'm in Love Again/I'm Walking/It's You I Love/La La/Let the Four Winds Blow/Please Don't Leave Me/Poor Poor Me/Rooster Song/Rose Mary/She's My Baby/Valley of Tears/Walkin' to New Orleans/Whole Lotta Lovin'/Yes My Darling/You Can Pack Your Suitcase/You Said You Love Me

Awards/Honors: Won *Billboard* magazine Triple Crown Award (four times) during 1950s

Won *Downbeat* magazine Readers Poll as best R&B personality of year, 1956, 1957

Infl by: Charles Brown/Roy Byrd/Jack Dupree/Leon Gross/Louis Jordan/Willie Littlefield/Amos Milburn/Roosevelt Sykes/Harrison Verrett

Infl to: Chuck Berry/Boogie Jake/Lonnie Brooks/Buster Brown/Chubby Checker/Lee Dorsey/Jessie Hill/Wilbert Harrison/Clarence Henry/Ernie K-Doe/Jerry Lee Lewis/Little Richard/Allen Toussaint

Quotes: "One of the first to penetrate the white record market was a chubby, shy man who combined blues feeling with an almost childlike sound"—Arnold Shaw, *The World of Soul*, Cowles Book Company, Inc, 1970

"Fats Domino has enjoyed greater popularity than most singers working in the blues idiom in the post-war years"—(Paul Oliver) McCarthy/Morgan/Oliver/Harrison, *Jazz on Record*, Hanover Books, 1968

References: United Artists album UPS-9958

Encyclopedia of Pop, Rock & Soul, Irwin Stambler, St Martin's Press, 1974

Walking to New Orleans, John Broven, Blues Unlimited, 1974

DOOLEY, *"Blind"* SIMMIE
Born: Jul 3, 1881, Hartwell (Hart Co), GA
Died: Jan 17, 1961, Spartanburg, SC
Inst: Guitar

Was a blind itinerant singer who worked streets for tips in Spartanburg, SC, area from c1900; worked w Pink Anderson at local country picnics/parties in Spartanburg area from 1916; frequently worked w Pink Anderson in Doc WR Kerr's Indian Remedy Company Medicine Show into 20s; continued working streets/store fronts/fish fries/picnics through Spartanburg area into 30s; rec w Pink Anderson, Columbia label, Atlanta, GA, 1928; believed mostly inactive in music from 30s; entered General Hospital where he died of heart disease; buried City Cemetery, East Spartanburg, SC

Infl to: Pink Anderson

DORSEY, THOMAS ANDREW *"Tom"*
(*aka:* Barrelhouse Tommy/Georgia Tom/Memphis Jim/Memphis Mose/Railroad Bill/George Ramsey (?)/Smokehouse Charley/Texas Tommy)
Born: Jul 1, 1899, Villa Rica (Carroll Co), GA
Died: Jan 23, 1993, Chicago, IL
Inst: Guitar/Piano

Courtesy Living Blues *Magazine*

Father was Thomas Madison Dorsey, a revival running Baptist minister; mother was Etta Plant, an organist; born/raised on farm; moved to Atlanta, GA, where he sang in local church choir from c1904; worked outside music (as water boy) in local circus and then as soft drink peddler at 81 Theater, Atlanta, from c1910; learned to read music from local theater pianists and worked local dance halls/private parties/gin palaces (as "Barrelhouse Tommy"), Atlanta, c1910-16; briefly attended Morehouse Col, Atlanta, c1916; moved north to work outside music, Chicago, IL/Gary, IN, areas while working w own five piece group in local clubs, Chicago, from 1916; attended Col of Composition and Arranging, Chicago, c1919-21; worked w Will Walker's Whispering Syncopators in local clubs, Chicago, 1922-3; acc Ma Rainey, Grand Theater, Chicago, 1924; toured w own Wildcats Jazz Band in Ma Rainey show working TOBA theater circuit through Midwest/South, 1924-8; frequently worked as music demonstrator in local music stores, Chicago, from c1928; worked as music arranger for Chicago Music Publishing Company/Vocalion Record Company, Chicago, from c1928; rec (as "Georgia Tom") Vocalion label, Chicago, 1928-9; teamed w Tampa Red working house rent parties/theaters/dance halls/juke joints/excursion boats in Chicago area with frequent tours (as team) on TOBA theater circuit through South, 1928-9; rec w Tampa Red, Vocalion label, Chicago, 1928-31; rec w Hokum Jug Band, Vocalion label, Chicago, 1928-30; rec w Hokum Boys, Paramount label, Chicago, 1928-9; frequently rec acc to Ma Rainey and others on local labels, Chicago, 1928 into early 30s; rec (under own name) Vocalion label, Chicago, 1928-9; rec Gennett label, Richmond, IN, 1928-30; worked as talent scout/music arranger/recording advisor for Brunswick Record Company, Chicago, from 1929; rec Brunswick label, Chicago, 1929; rec w Black Hill Billies, Vocalion label, Chicago, 1929; rec w Famous Hokum Boys/Hannah May, ARC label group, NYC, 1930; rec (as "Georgia Tom") on ARC label group, NYC, 1930; rec Champion label, Richmond, IN, 1930; rec Paramount label, Grafton, WI, 1930; formed Thomas A Dorsey Gospel Songs Music Publishing Company and active as composer of gospel music, Chicago, from 1930; rec Melotone label, Chicago, 1932; rec w Tampa Red/Memphis Minnie, Vocalion label, NYC, 1932; left blues field to work as choral director of Pilgrim Baptist Church, Chicago, from 1932; rec (gospel songs) Vocalion label, NYC, 1932; app w own University Gospel Singers, WLFL-radio (others), Chicago, 1932-7; frequently worked w Sallie Martin in local church concerts, Chicago, 1932; toured extensively with Gospel Choral Union in An Evening with Dorsey gospel program working churches/concerts/recitals across US/Europe/Mexico/North Africa, 1932-44; founded The National Convention of Gospel Choirs and Choruses Inc, Chicago, 1933 (serving with group into 70s); rec (gospel songs) Vocalion label, Chicago, 1934; served as Dean of Evangelistic Musical Research and Ministry of Church Music (for the Gospel Choral Union of Chicago), Chicago, from 1940; continued extensive gospel work/song writing through 40s/50s; served as assistant pastor of Pilgrim Baptist Church, Chicago, through 60s/70s; frequently toured as after dinner speaker/lecturer for schools/clubs/church affairs/others across US through 60s into 80s; app on THE DEVIL'S MUSIC - A HISTORY OF THE BLUES (ep: Crazy Blues/ep: The Movements of Providence), BBC-1-TV, Eng, 1976; app in film SAY AMEN, SOMEBODY, 1982; died of alzheimer's disease; buried Oakwood Cemetery, Chicago

Personal: Credited with terming the name "Gospel Song" during the 1920s. Not to be confused with big-band leader Thomas (Tommy) Dorsey (1905-1956)

Books: Inspirational Thoughts, Thomas A Dorsey, 1934

The Life and Works of Thomas Andrew Dorsey, Ruth A Smith, 1935
My Ups and Downs, Thomas A Dorsey, 1938
Dorsey's Book of Poems, Tom Dorsey, 1941
Rise of Gospel Blues, Michael Harris, 1992

Songs: A Little Talk with Jesus/At the Golden Jubilee/Beedle Um Bum/Been Mistreated Blues/Bessemer Bound Blues/Better Cut That Out/Black Cat Hoot Owl Blues/Blame It on the Blues/Broke Man Blues/Caught Him Doing It/Chain Gang Blues/Come On In/Count the Days I'm Gone/The Day Is Past and Gone/Don't Shake It No More/Double Trouble Blues/Down Home Blues/Eagle Rock Me Papa/Explainin' the Blues/Fix It/Freight Train Blues/Gee But It's Hard/Georgia Stockade Blues/Glory for Me/Grieving Blues/He Knows How Much You Can Bear/Hide Me in Thy Bosom/Hip Shakin' Strut/How About You?/I Don't Know Why/I Had to Give Up Gym/I Just Want a Daddy I Can Call My Own/I Surely Know There's Been a Change in Me/I Thank God for My Song/I Will Trust in the Lord/If You See My Saviour/If You Sing a Gospel Song/I'll Never Turn Back/I'll Tell It Wherever I Go/I'm Gonna Live the Life I Sing About in My Song/I'm Leavin' Just to Ease My Worried Mind/It's My Desire/It's Tight Like That/Just One Step/Keep Praying All the Time/Last Minute Blues/Leave My Man Alone/Levee Bound Blues/Log Camp Blues/The Lord Has Laid His Hands on Me/Maybe It's the Blues/Memphis Bound Blues/Miss Anna Brown/Miss Baker's Blues/Muddy Water Blues/Night Time Blues/Old Ship of Zion/Pat-A-Foot Blues/Peace in the Valley/Pig Meat Blues/Precious Lord Take My Hand/Riverside Blues/Rock Me/Search Me Lord/Second Hand Woman Blues/Selling That Stuff/Singing in My Soul/Slave to the Blues/Someday Somewhere/Stormy Sea Blues/Sweet Bye and Bye/Tell Jesus Everything/Terrible Operation Blues/That's Good News/Thy Kingdom Come/Today/Traveling On/29th and Dearborn/Victim of the Blues/Watching and Waiting/What Could I Do?/When I've Done the Best I Can/When the Gates Swing Open/When the Last Mile Is Finished/Where Did You Stay Last Night?/Wings over Jordan/You May Go But You'll Come Back Some Day

Awards/Honors: Awarded honorary degree of Doctor of Gospel Music by The Simmons Institute of South Carolina, 1946

Won American Music Conference National Music Award, 1976

Infl by: CH Tindley

Quotes: "[Dorsey] raised blues music to new levels of inventiveness, and brought a degree of wit and sophistication that had never previously been known to blues lyrics"—Stephen Calt, Yazoo album L-1041

"His great ability to compose and perform in almost any blues field from country to hokum jazz to gospel must make him one of black music's great men"—John Stiff, *Jazz Journal* magazine (UK), Jul 1974, p 76

"Everything contemporary music aims for, Dorsey accomplished, welding gospel, blues, jazz and country music into a distinctive musical style"—Tony Heilbut, *The Gospel Sound,* Simon & Schuster, 1971

References: Living Blues magazine, Mar 1975, pp 17-34

The Rise of Gospel Blues: The Music of Thomas Andrew Dorsey In The Urban Church, Michael W. Harris, Oxford Press, 1992

DOUGLAS, K C

Photo by Tom Mazzolini. Courtesy Living Blues *Magazine*

Born: Nov 21, 1913, Sharon (Madison Co), MS
Died: Oct 18, 1975, Berkeley, CA
Inst: Guitar

Father was John Douglas; born/raised on family farm outside Sharon, MS; interested in music from 10 years of age; left home to work outside music in Sharon area, 1934-6; briefly worked outside music, Grenada, MS, 1936; worked outside music, Carthage, MS, 1936-40; frequently worked w Tommy Johnson in local streets/parties, Jackson, MS, area, 1940-5; moved to Vallejo, CA, to work outside music, 1945 into 50s; formed own Lumberjacks group working small clubs, Richmond, CA, area from 1947 into 50s; rec Downtown label, Oakland, CA, 1948; rec Rhythm label, Oakland, 1954; app on local show, KPFA-radio, Berkeley, CA, 1955; frequently worked dances/parties/small clubs/bars in Oakland area, 1955-60; rec Cook label, Oakland, 1955; worked w Jessie Fuller, Ash Grove, Los Angeles, CA, 1960; rec Bluesville label, Oakland, 1960; worked Sugar Hill, San Francisco, CA, 1961; Cabale Club, Berkeley, CA, 1963; rec Arhoolie label, Berkeley, 1963; frequently worked outside music (for city Public Works Dept), Berkeley, from c1963 into mid-70s; rec Fantasy label, Oakland, c1967; briefly worked joints/roadhouses/jukes in Jackson/Canton, MS, area in 1968; worked Berkeley Blues Festival, Berkeley, CA, 1970; formed own quartet working coffee houses/clubs/bars in East Bay/Modesto/Stockton, CA, area into 70s; rec Arhoolie label, Berkeley, 1973-4; worked Univ of California Extension Center, San Francisco, CA, 1973; The Continental Club, Oakland, CA, 1973; San Francisco Bay Blues Festival, San Francisco, 1973-4; Community Music Center, San Francisco, 1973; The Refectory, Dublin, CA, 1973-4; app on BLUES BY THE BAY, KPOO-FM-radio, San Francisco, 1973; worked w own Mississippi Blues Band, Spaghettery, Redwood City, CA, 1974; Village Rest, Modesto, CA, 1974; app on local show, KGED-TV, San Francisco, 1974; worked Berkeley Blues Festival, Berkeley, CA, 1975; The Square Rigger, Napa, CA, 1975; Jack's, Modesto, CA, 1975; app on local news show, KGO-TV, San Francisco, 1975; worked Western Bicentennial Folk Festival, Berkeley, CA, 1975; suffered fatal heart attack at home; buried Pleasant Green Cemetery, Sharon, MS

Personal: Married 4 times. Given names are initials only

Songs: Born in the Country/Broken Heart/Catfish Blues/Country Girl/Fanny Lou/Good Looking Women/Hear Me Howlin'/Hen House Blues/High Water Rising/KC's Doctor Blues/Love Me All Night Long/Mercury Boogie/No More Cryin'/Wake Up Workin' Woman/Watch Dog Blues/Woke Up This Morning

Infl by: Leroy Carr/Blind Lemon Jefferson/Lonnie Johnson/Tommy Johnson

Quotes: "KC Douglas was one of the last great rural stylists of the San Francisco/Oakland area"—Tom Mazzolini, *Living Blues* magazine, Nov 1975, p 5

"He is first and foremost, a down to earth blues singer . . ."—Larry Cohn, Prestige album 1023

References: *Living Blues* magazine, Winter 1973, pp 15-19

Blues Unlimited magazine (UK), Apr 1971, pp 11-13

DOUGLAS, LIZZIE *"Minnie"/"Kid"*
(*aka:* Gospel Minnie/Minnie McCoy/Memphis Minnie/Texas Tessie)
Born: Jun 3, 1897, Algiers (Orleans Parish), LA
Died: Aug 6, 1973, Memphis, TN
Inst: Guitar/Banjo

Father was Abe Douglas, mother was Gertrude Wells; one of 13 children; born/raised on farm; moved to Walls, MS, at 7 years of age; learned banjo at 10 years of age, guitar at 11 and frequently worked local parties in area from c1908; ran away from home to work (as "Kid Douglas") in streets and Church's Park (WC Handy Park), Memphis, TN, from c1910; toured w Ringling Brothers Circus working tent shows through South, 1916-20; settled in Memphis to work saloons/bars/streets along Beale Street through 20s; frequently worked w Joe McCoy in Jed Davenport's Beale Street Jug Band in streets/parks, Memphis, late 20s; rec w Joe McCoy, Columbia label, NYC, 1929; rec w Memphis Jug Band, Victor label, Memphis, 1930; worked North Memphis Cafe, Memphis, c1930; rec Vocalion label, Memphis, TN/Chicago, IL, 1930-2; together w Joe McCoy moved to Chicago to form own blues group to work Music Box Club/Mike DeLisa Club/Martin's Corner/Ruby Lee Gatewood's Tavern (where she frequently held her "Blue Monday" parties) and other bars/clubs in area, 1930 into early 40s; rec OKeh label, NYC, NY, 1933; won first prize (over Bill Broonzy) in local blues contest, Chicago, 1933; toured w Bill Broonzy working club dates during 30s; rec Vocalion label, Chicago, 1934-9; rec Decca label, Chicago, 1934-5; rec Bluebird label, Chicago, 1935; rec w Bumble Bee Slim, Vocalion label, Chicago, 1936; worked w Black Bob, Tramor Hotel, Chicago, 1936; worked w "Fiddlin' " Joe Martin in local jukes, Jackson, MS, c1939; rec OKeh label, Chicago, 1940-1; worked White Elephant Club, Chicago, 1941; Don's Den, Chicago, 1942; 230 Club, Chicago, 1942; 708 Club, Chicago, c1943; rec OKeh/Columbia labels, Chicago, 1944; worked Indiana Theater, Chicago, mid-40s; together w St Louis Jimmy owned/operated a blues club in Indianapolis, IN, during 40s; worked/lived (for 3 years) in Detroit, MI, during 40s; rec Columbia label, Chicago, 1946-7; formed own vaudeville troupe working theater dates through South in late 40s; rec Columbia label, Chicago, 1949; rec w Sunnyland Slim, Regal/Biograph

Lizzie Douglas (Memphis Minnie)

Courtesy Sing Out Magazine

labels, Chicago, 1949; worked w Little Son Joe, 708 Club, Chicago, 1949; continued working local club dates, Chicago area, early 50s; rec Checker label, Chicago, 1952; rec JOB label, Chicago, 1954; returned to Memphis, TN, and inactive in music from mid-50s; rec (unissued) label, Memphis, 1959; suffered illnesses from late 50s and lived later part of life in various local nursing homes; suffered fatal stroke at home of sister Daisy Johnson; buried New Hope Cemetery, Walls, MS

Personal: Married singers/musicians Casey Bill Weldon (during 20s); Kansas Joe McCoy (1929-35); "Little Son Joe" Ernest Lawlars (1939-61)

Book: Woman With Guitar: Memphis Minnie's Blues, Paul and Beth Garon, Da Capo, 1992

Songs: Bumble Bee/I Want to Do Something for You/Meningitis Blues/Nothing in Rambling/Queen Bee

Infl to: John Lee Granderson/Jo-Ann Kelly/Mance Lipscomb/Big Mama Thornton/Mama Yancey

Quotes: "Acknowledged by her contemporaries among blues singers as the greatest of the women singers outside the 'classic' vein"—(Paul Oliver) Albert McCarthy/Alun Morgan/Paul Oliver/Max Harrison, *Jazz on Record,* Hanover Books Ltd, 1968

"In my opinion, Memphis Minnie was without doubt the greatest of all female blues singers ever to record"—Chris Strachwitz, Blues Classics album 13

"The most popular female country blues singer of all time"—Steve LaVere, *Living Blues* magazine, Autumn 1973, p 5

References: Living Blues magazine, Autumn 1973, p 5

Blues Unlimited magazine (UK), Dec 1970, pp 8-9

Sweet as the Showers of Rain, Samuel B Charters, Oak Publications, 1977

DRIFTIN' SLIM/SMITH
(see Mickle, Elmon)

DUKES, *"Little"* LAURA
(aka: Little Laura)
Born: Jun 10, 1907, Memphis (Shelby Co), TN
Inst: Banjo/Uke

Father was a drummer with the WC Handy Band; one of 4 children; worked w Laura Smith as child singer in local theater dates, Memphis, TN, c1913; worked (as dancer) in local clubs along Beale Street, Memphis, early 20s; frequently toured as singer/dancer in passing carnivals out of Memphis working amusement parks/tent shows through Arkansas/Texas/Illinois, 1928 into 30s; learned guitar from Robert Nighthawk, 1933; teamed w Robert Nighthawk to work local joints, East St Louis, IL, mid-30s; worked (as dancer/musician) w Will Batts South Memphis Jug Band at local dances/parties/clubs, Memphis, from c1938 with frequent tours through Mississippi/Arkansas/Indiana, to c1956; rec w Will Batts Novelty Band, Flyright label, Cleveland, OH (?), 1954; occasionally worked w Son Smith's Band, Memphis, TN, through 60s; occasionally worked local dates/riverboats out of Memphis through 60s into 70s; rec Albatross label, Memphis, 1972; worked w Charlie Banks and his Beale Street Originals, River City Blues Festival, Memphis, 1973; worked A Salute to WC Handy, Henderson, KY, 1974; Hotel Pontchartrain, Detroit, MI, 1974; app on THE DEVIL'S MUSIC—A HISTORY OF THE BLUES (ep: Crazy Blues), BBC-1-TV, Eng, 1976; worked w Charlie Banks Band, Memphis Riverfront Festival, Tom Lee Park, Memphis, 1976

Personal: Has 1 child

Infl by: Robert Nighthawk

Reference: Blues Unlimited magazine (UK), Jul/Aug 1977, pp 19-21

DUNBAR, SCOTT
Born: 1904, Deer Park Plantation (Wilkinson Co), MS
Died: (unknown)
Inst: Guitar

Photo by Bill Ferris, Center for Southern Folklore

Father was born a slave and worked on Deer Park Plantation between Mississippi River and Old River Lake (Lake Mary); born/raised on plantation, unschooled, working as field hand on local farms from childhood; taught self guitar on home-made instrument and frequently worked local parties/picnics/dances/suppers in area for tips from 8 years of age; continued outside music work with frequent work as single or w Lee Baker String Band at local picnics/square dances/parties on Deer Park Plantation, MS, into 50s; rec Folkways label, Lake Mary (area), MS, 1954; app on local TV show, Baton Rouge, LA, 1954; worked outside music (as guide and professional fisherman) on Lake Mary with frequent work at lodge parties/juke joints/fishing camps/dances/wedding receptions, Deer Park Plantation, from 50s into 70s; film clip shown on ANATOMY OF POP: THE MUSIC EXPLOSION, ABC-TV, 1966 (rel as film AMERICAN MUSIC—FROM FOLK TO JAZZ AND POP); rec Matchbox label, Lake Mary, MS, 1968; rec Ahura Mazda label, Lake Mary, 1970; app in film short THINKING OUT LOUD, 1972

Personal: Married 3 times. 6 children

Song: Jaybird

Quote: "Resident blues singer of Woodville and rural Wilkinson County, Mississippi"—Karl Michael Wolfe, Ahura Mazda album 505-1

References: Blues World magazine (UK), Summer 1971, pp 3-7
Been Here and Gone, Frederic Ramsey Jr, Rutgers Univ Press, 1960

DUNN, ROY SIDNEY

Photo by Tom Hill. Courtesy Peter B Lowry

Born: Apr 13, 1922, Eatonton (Putnam Co), GA
Died: Mar 2, 1988, Atlanta, GA
Inst: Guitar/Harmonica

Father was Willie Dunn; mother was Estella Griggs; one of 12 children; moved to Kelly, GA, where he took interest in guitar from c1931; moved to Covington, GA, learning some guitar from Curley Weaver and frequently worked in The Dunn Brothers family gospel group in local churches in area c1935-8; left home to tour extensively w All National Independents/Victory Bond Spiritual Singers/Rainbow Gospel Four/Golden Gospel Singers/other gospel groups through South/West of US c1938 into 40s; frequently worked w Blind Willie McTell/Curley Weaver/Buddy Moss/others in local gigs, Atlanta, GA, area, through 40s; settled in Atlanta to work mostly outside music, early 50s; served sentence for manslaughter c1956-60; returned to Atlanta to continue outside music work with occasional weekend gigs c1960-8; mostly inactive due to accident from 1968; rec Trix label, Covington, GA 1971-2; rec Trix label, Conyers, GA, 1972-3; worked Univ of North Carolina, Chapel Hill, NC, 1973 (por rel Flyright label); rec Trix label, Atlanta, 1974-5; often worked Blind Willie's, Atlanta during 80s; died of liver failure; buried Resthaven Garden of Memories, Decatur, GA

Songs: Everything I Get Ahold To/She Cook Corn Bread for Her Husband/Tired of Living a Bachelor/You're Worrying Me

Quote: "Roy Dunn is an eclectic artist, a writer of a couple of good songs, a nice player of the guitar, and a marvelous singer"—Pete Lowry, Trix album 3312

Reference: Trix album 3312

DUPREE, WILLIAM THOMAS *"Champion Jack"* (*aka:* Brother Blues/Big Tom Collins/Blind Boy Johnson/Meathead Johnson/Willie Jordan/Lightnin' Jr)
Born: Jul 4, 1910, New Orleans (Orleans Parish), LA
Died: Jan 21, 1992, Hanover, Ger
Inst: Drums/Guitar/Piano

Father was George Dupree of French heritage; mother Georgana ——— was Cherokee; after parents died in fire was placed in Colored Waifs' Home for Boys, New Orleans, LA, c1911-24 where he learned piano; left home to work outside music with frequent entertaining w pianist Drive 'em Down (Willie Hall) in local barrelhouses and solo street work for tips in French Quarter, New Orleans, from 1924; frequently worked w Papa Celestin Band/Chris Kelly Band/Kid Rena Band from back of wagons, New Orleans, through 20s; worked as singing pianist at local parties/Delpee's Club and other clubs/dives, New Orleans, late 20s; hoboed extensively working outside music across US, late 20s into 30s; frequently worked house parties, Chicago, IL, from c1930; worked outside music as professional boxer (107 bouts), 1932-40; worked Astoria Club, Indianapolis, IN, c1939; worked as singer/dancer/pianist/MC (frequently w Ophelia Hoy) at Cotton Club, Indianapolis, c1939-40; rec OKeh label, Chicago, 1940-1; worked outside music in NYC, NY, area with some club work through Midwest, 1940-1; worked Lincoln Theater, New Orleans, 1941; served in US Navy (as cook) in Pacific Theater of Operations, 1941-5; rec Folkways label, NYC, 1942; rec Solo label, NYC, 1943; rec Asch label, NYC, 1944; rec Continental/Lenox labels, NYC, 1945; returned to NYC to work outside music (as cook) from c1945; worked Ringside Ball/The Spotlight Club/Mayfair Club/Italian Franks/others, NYC, from mid-40s; rec Joe Davis/Alert/Celebrity labels, NYC, 1946; rec w Brownie McGhee, Savoy label, NYC, 1947; rec Apollo label, NYC, 1949-50; worked local restaurant in Coney Island, Brooklyn, NY, late 40s; Central Plaza, NYC, 1949; rec Gotham/Apex labels, NYC, 1950; rec w Brownie McGhee, King label, NYC, 1951; worked Harlem Club, NYC, 1952; rec Harlem label, NYC, 1952; rec Red Robbin label, NYC, 1953;

William "Champion Jack" Dupree *Photo by Guy Schoukroun. Courtesy Living Blues Magazine*

rec King label, Cincinnati, OH/NYC, NY, 1953/1955; worked Apollo Theater, NYC, c1955; toured in own revue for Universal Attractions working concerts/clubs through Southwest, 1955; rec Groove label, NYC, 1956; rec Vik label, NYC, 1957; rec Atlantic label, NYC, 1958; toured w Nappy Brown Revue working shows across US, 1958; extensive residency at Celebrity Club, Freeport, NY, 1958-9; toured England/Europe working concert/club dates, 1959; rec Atlantic label, London, Eng, 1959; rec Sonet/Storyville labels, Copenhagen, Den, 1959-63; worked Concert Hall, Stockholm, Sweden, 1960; settled in Zurich, Switzerland, 1960; toured extensive club/concert dates through England/Europe from 1960; rec Impulse label, Koblenz, Ger, 1963; worked Trois Mailletz Club, Paris, France, 1963; Africana Club, Zurich, Switzerland, 1964; worked w Chris Barber Band, New Marquee Club, London, 1964 (por shown JAZZ 625, BBC-2-TV, London, Eng); rec w Keith Smith's Climax Jazz Band, Decca label, London, 1964; worked Northampton Jazz Festival, Northampton, Eng, 1964; toured w Keith Smith's Climax Jazz Band working club dates through England, 1965; settled in Copenhagen, Den, to work local club/concert dates with frequent tours through England/Norway from 1965; rec Ace of Clubs label, London, 1966; rec w John Mayall, London label, London, 1966; worked college circuit through England, 1967-8; rec Sire label, London, 1967; toured Switzerland working club dates, 1967; toured Poland working club dates, 1968; worked Conway Hall, London, Eng, 1968; rec Blue Horizon label, London, 1968-9; rec w Mickey Baker, Vogue label, Paris, France, 1968; toured w Blues Scene 69 working concert dates through England, 1969; toured Norway working clubs/radio/TV, 1969; worked Jazz Expo, London, Eng, 1969-70; toured w American Folk Blues Festival working concerts through England/Scotland, 1969; toured w American Folk Blues Festival working concerts through England/Europe, 1970 (por Frankfurt, Ger, concert rel Scout label); worked Ronnie Scott Club, London, Eng, 1970 (por shown JAZZ SCENE

AT RONNIE SCOTT'S, BBC-2-TV); worked Hot Jazz Concert, Hamburg, Ger, 1970; Montreux Jazz Festival, Montreux, Switzerland, 1970 (por shown PBS-TV, US-Canada, 1972/por rel Atlantic label); rec w Sonny Terry, Scout label, Frankfurt, Ger, 1970; settled in Halifax, Eng, with frequent tours working club\concert dates through England from 1971; app 24 HOURS, BBC-2-TV, London, 1971; app in film BLACK, WHITE & BLUES, 1971; rec w Mickey Baker, Crescendo label, Paris, France, 1971; worked Umea Jazz Festival, Stockholm, Sweden, 1971; extensive tours working clubs/concerts through England/Europe, 1971-5; rec Sonet label, London, Eng, 1972; toured clubs/concerts through Denmark, 1972; worked Quartier Latin, Berlin, Ger, 1973; app in film IF YOU GOT THE FEELIN', 1973; settled in Bollerup, Sweden, c1974; frequently toured concert dates through Germany/Switzerland, 1974; worked Jazz 200, Hamburg, Ger, 1976; Blues-Jazz Festival, Tibble Theater, Stockholm, Sweden, 1976; formed/rec Friendship label, Hamburg (?), Ger, 1974; worked Quartier Latin, Berlin, 1977-9/82-3; North Sea Jazz Festival, Holland, 1977; moved to Hanover, Ger, c1977; Cafe De Beyerd, Breda, Holland, 1978; American Folk & Blues Fest, Milan, Italy, 1979; Bern Jazz Fest, Bern, Switzerland, 1979; rec Free Bird label, Paris, 1979; Montreux Jazz Festival, Montreux, Switzerland, 1979; app in Swedish/Eng film FRIENDSHIP, c 1979; toured w American Blues Stars, Ger, 1980; worked Tramps, NYC, NY, 1981; often worked European club/concert/festival circuit through 80s; worked New Orleans Jazz & Heritage Festival, New Orleans, LA, 1990-1; Lone Star, NYC, 1991; rec Bullseye-Rounder label, New Orleans/Boston, MA, 1991; Chicago Blues Festival, Chicago, IL, 1991; toured US working club dates, 1991; died at home of cancer; body cremated

Songs: A Good Woman Is Hard to Find/A Racehorse Called Mae/Ain't That a Shame/Bad Blood/Bad Life/Black Wolf Blues/The Blues Got Me Rockin'/Broken Hearted Blues/Cabbage Greens/Camille/Chicken Shack/Come Back Baby/Cryin' Woman Blues/The Death of Big Bill Broonzy/The Death of Louis/The Death of Luther King/Dupree's Special/Everybody's Blues/Everything's Gonna Be Alright/Evil Woman/FDR Blues/Fisherman's Blues/Free and Equal/Get with It/Goin' to Paris/Going (Back) to Louisiana/Grandma/Hard Feelings Blues/Hare Lip Blues/House Rent Party/I Had a Dream/I Love You So/I'll Try/I'm Happy to Be Free/I'm Having Fun/It's a Hard Pill to Swallow/I've Been Mistreated/Jail House Junker's Blues/Me and My Mule/Mercy on Me/Met My Mule/Miss Ada Blues/Mother-In-Law Blues/Mr Dupree Blues/My Black and White Dog/My Heart Beats for You/My Home's in Hell/Oh Lawdy/Old and Grey/Old Women Blues/One Scotch, One Bourbon, One Beer/Poor Boy Blues/President Kennedy Blues/Rampart Street Special/Right Now/School Day/Shirley Mae/Slow Drag/Snaps Drinking Woman/Sneaky Pete/Speakeasy Days/Sporting Life Blues/Street Wailing Woman/Strollin' TB Blues/Take Me Back Baby/Talk to Me Baby/Talkin' Out of My Head/Tell Me When/Tongue Tied Blues/Too Evil to Cry/The Tricks/Trouble Trouble/24 Hours/Ugly Woman/Wailing the Blues/Walkin' Upside Your Head/Walking the Blues/When a Young Girl Is 18/Whiskey Head Woman/Young Girl Blues

Infl by: Leroy Carr/John Davis/"Drive 'Em Down"/Brownie McGhee/Peetie Wheatstraw

Infl to: Roy Byrd/Fats Domino

Quotes: ". . . simple, uninhibited, unsophisticated and aggressive"—Dean Tudor, *Coda* magazine (Canada), Jun 1972, p 21

"His blues lyrics are a happy blend of the country and urban style, quite in keeping with his life's experiences"—Duncan P Schiedt, OKeh album 12103

References: *Living Blues* magazine, May 1977, pp 10-14

The Legacy of the Blues, Sam B Charters, Calder & Boyars Ltd, 1975

Mississippi Rag magazine, Jul 1993, pp 21-6

DURHAM, EDWARD LEE *"Mr Buddy"*
Born: 1915, Ashburn (Turner Co), GA
Inst: Guitar

Father was local musician; one of 6 children; born/raised on farm from childhood; began playing guitar c1936; left home to hobo through Georgia as singing guitarist through 30s into 40s; served in US Army in 1942-5; settled in Tifton, GA, to work outside music with frequent gigs at local picnics/frolics in area c1945 into 50s; moved to Albany, NY, to work mostly outside music from 1955; worked Empire State Col, Albany, NY, 1973; rec Flyright label, Albany, NY, 1973

Personal: Nephew of Lightnin' Hopkins. Not to be confused with jazz musician Eddie Durham

Reference: *Living Blues* magazine, Winter 1973, pp 22-3

E

EAGER, JIMMY
(see Whittaker, Hudson)

EAGLIN, FIRD *"Blind Snooks"/"Snooks"/"Ford"*

Photo by Norbert Hess

Born: Jan 21, 1936, New Orleans (Orleans Parish), LA
Inst: Guitar/Tom Toms

Father was Fird Eaglin Sr; mother was Myrtle Riley; suffered blindness after operation for glaucoma and brain tumor at 19 months of age; taught self to play guitar at 6 years of age; frequently sang in local Baptist churches in New Orleans, LA, area through 40s; won first prize in local talent show, WNOE-radio, New Orleans, 1947; frequently worked w Flamingoes R&B group/or as single on streets for tips, New Orleans, from 1952; rec Folkways label, New Orleans, 1958; rec Folk-Lyric label, New Orleans, 1960; rec Imperial label, New Orleans, 1960-1; rec Prestige-Bluesville/Storyville/Heritage labels, New Orleans, 1961; frequent residency at Playboy Club, New Orleans, 1963 through 60s; worked New Orleans Jazz & Heritage Festival, New Orleans, 1969-74; worked occasional gigs w Prof Longhair in New Orleans area, early 70s; rec Sonet label, New Orleans, 1971; rec w Prof Longhair (unissued demos), Baton Rouge, LA, 1971; rec Arhoolie label, New Orleans, c1971; worked Tulane Univ, New Orleans, 1973; w Prof Longhair, The Temple Hall, New Orleans, 1973; w Prof Longhair at private parties, London, Eng, 1973; worked 501 Club, New Orleans, 1975

Personal: Married Doretha ——— (1960-). Named "Snooks" as a child after the popular mischievous radio character "Baby Snooks"

Songs: Don't Leave No News/That Same Old Train

Infl by: Ray Charles

Quotes: "His assets include a wide range of guitar styles and an incredible bluesy voice"—Simon Napier, *Blues Unlimited* magazine (UK), Oct 1971, p 26

"He's a brilliant guitarist and a sensitive singer, with a warm, strong voice . . ."—Sam Charters, Sonet album 625

Reference: The Legacy of the Blues, Sam B Charters, Calder & Boyars Ltd, 1975

EASTON, AMOS
(*aka:* Amos/Shelley Armstrong/Bumble Bee Slim)
Born: May 7, 1905, Brunswick (Glynn Co), GA
Died: c May, 1968 (unconfirmed)
Inst: Guitar/Piano

One of 6 children; interested in music early; worked outside music (as barber) from childhood; left home to tour with passing circus c1920; hoboed extensively as singing guitarist working streets/parks/jukes across US through 20s; worked jukes in Indianapolis, IN, from 1928; settled in Chicago, IL, c1930; worked bars/halls/dives/parties in Chicago area with frequent tours to Grand Rapids, MI/Los Angeles, CA, and elsewhere through 30s; rec Paramount label, Grafton, WI, 1931; rec Vocalion label, NYC/Chicago, 1932; rec Vocalion label, Chicago, 1934-7; rec Bluebird label, Chicago, 1934-5; rec Decca label, Chicago, 1934-6; lived in Atlanta, GA, area in mid-30s; worked 81 Theater, Atlanta, 1935; rec Decca label, NYC, 1936; settled in Los Angeles working mostly outside music from early 40s; rec Fidelity label, Los Angeles, 1951; rec Marigold/Specialty labels, Los Angeles, c1952; rec Pacific Jazz label, Los Angeles, 1962; worked outside music in Chicago in late 60s

Personal: Married

Songs: Chain Gang Bound/Cry On! Cry On!/Direct

Amos Easton (Bumble Bee Slim)

Georgia White

Courtesy Frank Driggs Collection

South/Funny Feelin'/He Caught That B&O/I'll Meet You in the Bottom/I'm the One/Keep On Sailing/Let Your Money Talk/Lonesome Old Feeling/Lonesome Trail Blues/Meet Me in the Bottom/New B&O Blues/No Woman No Nickel/Puppy Love/Sad and Lonesome/Sail On Little Girl/Strange Angel/There You Stand/Wake Up in the Mornin'

Infl by: Leroy Carr

Quotes: "His ubiquity in the recording studios and his prolific abilities as a song writer were responsible for the development of the so-called 'Chicago Blues' school of the 1930s . . ."—Pete Welding, World Pacific album ST 20150

"He was one of the most popular and one of the most prolific of blues singers of the thirties"—Paul Oliver, International Polydor album 423-243

Reference: Pacific Jazz album 910

EDWARDS, CHARLES
(*aka:* Good Rockin' Charles)
Born: Mar 4, 1933, Pratts (Barbour Co), AL (unconfirmed)
Inst: Harmonica

Moved to Chicago, IL, to work w Willie "Long Time" Smith at Brown Derby, 1949; worked local clubs w Lee Jackson/James Richardson, Chicago, c1950; learned harmonica and teamed w Johnny Young to work Maxwell Street area, Chicago, from c1950; frequently worked w Big Boy Spires/Otis Smothers/Otis Rush/others in local clubs/bars, Chicago, early 50s; worked local clubs w Louis Myers Band, Chicago, 1954; frequently worked local club dates w Jimmy Rogers, Chicago, 1955; frequently worked Cotton Club, Chicago, late 50s; frequently worked w Johnny Young in local houseparties, Champaign, IL, area in late 50s; worked mostly outside music in Chicago from c1960 into 70s; worked Detroit Blues Festival, Detroit, MI, 1970; occasionally worked w Lee Jackson/Jimmy Rogers/others in local clubs, Chicago, into 70s; rec Mr Blues label, Chicago, 1975; worked Elsewhere Lounge, Chicago, 1977; Rob Michael's Club, Chicago, 1977; Fat Chance Saloon, Chicago, 1977

Songs: Five Years in Prison/Green Country Gal/Rockin' at Midnight

Quote: "He blends pure blues feeling, an infectious and unique approach, and mastery of his tradition" —Dick Shurman, Mr Blues album 7001

Reference: Mr Blues album 7001

Charles Edwards (Good Rockin' Charles)
Photo by Steve Tomashefsky. Courtesy Delmark Records

EDWARDS, DAVID *"Honeyboy"*
(aka: Honey Eddie/Mr Honey)
Born: Jun 28, 1915, Shaw (Sunflower Co), MS
Inst: Guitar/Harmonica

Father was Henry Edwards, a local musician; mother was Pearl Phillips; born on farm outside Shaw, MS, in Sunflower County; one of 6 children; began playing guitar at 14 years of age; moved to Greenwood, MS, area to work outside music from 1931; teamed w Big Joe Williams to work parties/dances through Mississippi/Louisiana and into Gulf Coast area, 1932-3; frequently worked w Tommy McClennan on streets/country dances/parties, Greenwood, MS, area, 1933-4; toured briefly w Charley Patton working parties/country stores on/about Will Dockery's Plantation, Ruleville, MS, 1934; worked w Memphis Jug Band in local streets/Church's Park (WC Handy Park), Memphis, TN, 1935-6; teamed w Big Walter Horton working streets/jukes/parties, Memphis, 1936; worked w JD Short at local joints/parties, St Louis, MO, 1937-8; worked w Robert Johnson at local jukes/parties, McComb, MS, area, 1938; frequently worked local bars/jukes between Greenwood, MS/Memphis, TN, 1938-9; worked local parties and Maxwell Street area for tips, Chicago, with frequent tours through South, 1939 into 40s; rec Library of Congress label, Clarksdale, MS, 1942; worked briefly outside music, Portland, OR, 1945; worked w Little Walter Jacobs in local clubs, St Louis, MO/East St Louis, IL, 1945; frequently worked w Little Walter in Maxwell Street area, Chicago, IL, from 1945; continued extensive one-nighters/odd gigs in and out of Chicago working through South to 1954; rec ARC label group, Houston, TX, 1951; rec Chess label (as "Honey Eddie"), Chicago, 1951/3; settled in Chicago, 1954; worked Anglish Lounge, Chicago, 1954; 708 Club, Chicago, 1954; Cozy Inn, Chicago, 1954-7; Cadillac Baby's, Chicago, 1957; worked mostly outside music, Chicago, late 50s through 60s and occasionally thereafter; rec w John Lee Henley, Milestone label, Chicago, 1964; worked Saxes Lounge, Chicago, c1965; rec Adelphi/Blue Horizon labels, Chicago, 1969; worked w Magic Slim, Elite Arabian Sands, Chicago, 1970; 1125 Club, Chicago, 1970; Alice's Revisited, Chicago, 1970; Florence's Lounge, Chicago, 1972; Univ of Chicago Folk Festival, Chicago, 1973; 1125 Club, Chicago, 1975; toured Europe working concert dates, 1975-6; rec Roots label, Vienna, Austria, 1975; worked World Surrealist Exhibition, Chicago, 1976; Washington Square Methodist Church, NYC, NY, 1976; Alternative Center for International Arts, NYC, 1976-7; Village Gate, NYC, 1977; Elsewhere Club, Chicago, 1977; w Foghat group, The Palladium, NYC, 1977 (por shown DON KIRSHNER'S ROCK CONCERT, NBC-TV, 1978); app on GOOD MORNIN' BLUES, PBS-TV, 1978

Personal: Married Bessie Mae ——— (1947-72). 3 children. Cousin of JD Short. Not to be confused with Frank Patt who also used pseudonym "Honeyboy"

Songs: Blues, Blues/Build Myself a Cage/Hot Springs Blues/Howling Wind/I Love You Baby/Take Me in Your Arms/When You Get Lonesome

Infl by: Charley Patton/Big Joe Williams

Quote: "He [sings] in a strong, keening voice and accompanies himself with dazzling guitar runs and a buoyant, steady rhythm"—Robert Palmer, *New York Times* newspaper, Oct 12, 1976

References: ***Living Blues*** magazine, Winter 1970, pp 19-24

Blues Unlimited magazine (UK), Jun 1968, pp 3-12

David "Honeyboy" Edwards *Photo by Jim O'Neal. Courtesy* Living Blues *Magazine*

EDWARDS, FRANK
Born: Mar 20, 1909, Washington (Wilkes Co), GA
Inst: Guitar/Harmonica/Jug/Washboard

Moved to St Petersburg, FL, area as child where he learned guitar; left home to work local gigs in area from c1923; worked briefly w Tampa Red in St Augustine, FL, 1926; hoboed widely working as single or in string/jug bands through South through 20s into 30s; added harmonica rack, 1934; frequently worked jukes/carnivals/theater contests/stage shows/medicine shows across US through 30s into 50s; app w Leroy Dallas, MAJOR BOWES ORIGINAL AMATEUR HOUR, CBS-radio, c1940; worked Apollo Theater, NYC, NY, c1940; rec OKeh label, Chicago, IL, 1941; worked w local bluesmen in local club dates, Chicago, early 40s; rec Savoy label, Atlanta, GA, 1949; frequently worked local gigs, Atlanta area, through 50s into 60s; worked outside music with frequent church work, Atlanta, from c1965 into 70s; rec Trix label, Conyers, GA, 1972; worked Univ of North Carolina, Chapel Hill, NC, 1973 (por rel Flyright label); Atlanta Blues Festival, Atlanta, 1976; Georgia Grassroots Music Festival, Atlanta, 1976

Songs: Alcatraz Blues/Chicken Raid/Love My Baby/

Frank Edwards

Photo by George Mitchell. Courtesy Peter B Lowry

Mini Dress Wearer/Put Your Arms Around Me/ Throw Your Time Away

Infl by: Tampa Red/John Lee "Sonny Boy" Williamson

Infl to: Leroy Dallas/Robert Fulton

Quote: "As a blues artist, Frank is uniquely identifiable — his guitar, harmonica and voice sound like nobody else . . ."—Pete Lowry, *Blues Unlimited* magazine (UK), Feb 1973, p 10

References: Blues Unlimited magazine (UK), Feb 1973, pp 10-11
Trix album 3303

EDWARDS, SUSIE

(aka: Susie)
Born: 1896, Pensacola (Escambia Co), FL
Died: Dec 5, 1963, Chicago, IL

Father was George Hawthorn; mother was Marguerite Wellington; born Susie Hawthorn; left home to tour w Tolliver's Circus and Musical Extravaganza Show working (as cakewalk dancer) under canvas across US c1910-16; worked Charlie Douglas Theater, Macon, GA, c1915; teamed w Jody Edwards (billed as "Edwards and Hawthorn," then "Edwards and Edwards" and later "Butterbeans and Susie") working exclusively as singing/dancing comedic team mostly on TOBA circuit through South from c1916; while Jody Edwards was in military service frequently worked w Butler "Stringbeans" May touring theaters on TOBA circuit c1917-18; worked w Trixie Smith in local vaudeville shows, Pittsburgh, PA, 1920; worked Koppin Theater, Detroit, MI, 1921; w Ethel Waters, Booker T Washington Theater, St Louis, MO, 1922; worked Lincoln Theater, NYC, NY, 1922; Star Theater, Shreveport, LA, 1923; 81 Theater, Atlanta, GA, c1924; Lincoln Theater, NYC, 1924; rec w Jody "Butterbeans" Edwards (or solo), OKeh label, NYC, NY/

Butterbeans & Susie (Jody Edwards/Susie Edwards) *Courtesy Frank Driggs Collection*

Atlanta, GA/Chicago, IL, 1924-30; frequently toured w Butterbeans in Rabbit Foot Minstrels working shows in South through 20s; app w Butterbeans in a Vaudeville Comedy Club Presentation, Lafayette Theater, NYC, 1925; worked Grand Theater, Chicago, 1925; Coliseum Theater, Chicago, 1926; app w Butterbeans in Jimmie Cooper's BLACK & WHITE REVUE, Columbia Theater, NYC/Empire Theater, Brooklyn, NY/Hurtig & Seamon New Theater, NYC/Miner's Theater, Bronx, NY/Casino Theater, Brooklyn, NY, 1926/Lafayette Theater, NYC, 1927, then toured with show working theaters through South in 1927; app w JIMMIE COOPER'S REVUE, Gayety Theater, Toronto, Can, 1927; app w Jimmie Cooper's OKEH REVUE, Lafayette Theater, NYC, 1927; app w Jimmie Cooper's 1928 REVUE, Lafayette Theater, NYC, 1927; app in own BUTTERBEANS & SUSIE REVUE, Grand Central Theater, Chicago, 1927/Howard Theater, Washington, DC, 1927; toured in various Butterbeans & Susie Revues working theaters/music halls/clubs/cabarets across US, 1927-36; app in Jimmie Cooper's HIGH JINKS Revue, Lafayette Theater, NYC, 1928; app w Ethel Waters, Oriole Terrace Club, Detroit, MI, 1928; app w Butterbeans in LAUGHING LIGHTNING Revue, Lafayette Theater, NYC, 1929; app w Butterbeans in RADIO FOLLIES Revue, Lincoln Theater, NYC, 1929; worked Elmore Theater, Pittsburgh, PA, 1929; Orpheum Theater, Newark, NJ, 1930; app w Butterbeans, BUTTERBEANS & SUSIE 1930 REVUE, Lafayette Theater, NYC, 1930; app w Butterbeans in FROLICS OF 1930 Revue, Lafayette Theater, NYC, 1930; app w Butterbeans/Fess Williams Band in musical comedy EASE ON DOWN, Lafayette Theater, NYC, 1930; toured w Butterbeans working theater dates in Midwest and West, 1931; app w Butterbeans, NOTORIETIES Revue, Lafayette Theater, NYC, 1931; app w Butterbeans, HARLEM BOUND Revue, Lafayette Theater, NYC, 1932; app w Butterbeans in musical comedy HERE 'TIS, Lafayette Theater, NYC, 1932; worked w Nicholas Brothers, Cotton Club, NYC, early 30s; app w Bessie Smith in HOT STUFF OF 1933 Revue, Lincoln Theater, Philadelphia, PA, 1932; worked w Butterbeans, Harlem Opera House, NYC, 1933; frequently w Butterbeans at Lafayette Theater, NYC, 1933-4; toured w Ethel Waters troupe working vaudeville circuit across US, 1935-7; worked w Ethel Waters, Apollo Theater, NYC, 1938; app w Ethel Waters in show CABIN IN THE SKY, Martin Beck Theater, NYC, 1940-1; toured vaudeville circuit into 40s; worked w Butterbeans, Rialto Theater, Chicago, IL, 1943; w Butterbeans, Apollo Theater, NYC, 1944; mostly inactive in music, settling in Chicago, c1945-50; frequently worked Apollo Theater, NYC, from 1950; worked Sugar Hill Club, NYC, 1952; toured with a white vaudeville troupe working theater dates through Midwest into late 50s; app in THE RIVERBOAT FOLLIES OF 1959, Big Mama Showboat Theater, Pittsburgh, PA, 1959; rec w Butterbeans, Festival label, NYC, 1960; worked Tivoli Theater, Chicago, 1963; suffered heart attack at home; DOA at Michael Reese Hospital; buried Mount Glenwood Cemetery, Bloom, IL

Personal: Married Jody "Butterbeans" Edwards (1916-1963), singer/comedian/dancer (born Jul 19, 1895-died Oct 28, 1967)

Billings: Butterbeans & Susie/Queen of the Blues

Songs: I Got Your Bath Water On/When My Man Shimmies

Quotes: "Susie Edwards [had] always been one of the most underrated singers in the field. Her sensitive and warmly expressive voice [was] complemented by the driving vehemence of her husband's declarations" —Yannick Bruynoghe, Festival album 7000

"[Butterbeans & Susie] very occasionally sang blues or blues exchanges but their singing was rich in blues inflection and timing"—Paul Oliver, *The Story of the Blues*, Chilton Book Company, 1968

EGGE, RAY
(see Agee, Raymond)

ELBROWN
(see Brown, Lillian)

ELLIOTT, *"Ramblin' "* JACK
Born: Aug 1, 1931, Brooklyn (Kings Co), NY
Inst: Guitar/Harmonica

Father was a doctor; born Elliott Charles Adnopoz; ran away from home to work outside music (as groom) w Colonel Jim Eshew's JE Ranch Rodeo, Washington, DC, and elsewhere, 1945; hitched to West Coast in late 40s; returned to Brooklyn, NY, to attend Erasmus Hall HS, then Adelphi Col, Garden City, NY/Univ of Connecticut, Storrs, CT, late 40s; frequently entertained in Washington Square Park, NYC, late 40s into 50s; teamed w Woody Guthrie (on and off) to tour at rallies/folk meets/worker groups for union/socio-political/conservational causes across US, 1951-4; worked outside music in California, 1955; rec Elektra label, California (?), 1955; toured England/Europe working clubs/concerts/radio/TV shows, 1955-8;

Photo by Diana Davies © 1978. Courtesy Sing Out Magazine

worked Blue Angel Club, London, Eng, c1957; Brussels World Fair, Brussels, Belgium, c1958; frequently app on local TV shows, Scandinavian countries, c1958; continued travelling across US from 1958; worked Manny Greenhill's, Boston, MA, 1959; w Cisco Houston, Club Renaissance, Los Angeles, CA, 1959; toured w Jesse Fuller/The Weavers/others working concerts through England/Europe, 1959-61; rec Prestige-International label, NYC, 1960-1; worked Gerde's Folk City, NYC, 1961; Bassins, Washington, DC, 1961; Ash Grove, Los Angeles, 1961; Philadelphia Folk Festival, Paoli, PA, 1962; frequent concert tours through Europe during 1960s; worked Newport Folk Festival, Newport, RI, 1963 (por rel Vanguard label); Boston Arts Festival, Boston, MA, 1964; Odyssey Coffeehouse, Boston, 1965; Town Hall, NYC, 1965; Folk Song 65 Concert, Carnegie Hall, NYC, 1965; Ash Grove, Los Angeles, 1965; Goliard Club, Forest Hills, NY, 1965; app w Pete Seeger, RAINBOW QUEST, WNJU-TV, Newark, NJ, c1965; worked Newport Folk Festival, Newport, RI, 1966-9; Gaslight Cafe, NYC, 1967-9; Ash Grove, Los Angeles, 1968; Woody Guthrie Memorial Concert, Carnegie Hall, NYC, 1968 (por rel Columbia label); Matrix, San Francisco, CA, 1969; Berkeley Blues Festival, Berkeley, CA, 1970; Mariposa Folk Festival, Toronto, Can, 1970; Woody Guthrie Memorial Concert, Hollywood Bowl, Hollywood, CA, 1970 (por rel Warner Brothers label); app on JOHNNY CASH Show, ABC-TV, 1970; app in film short RAMBLIN', 1970; worked Quiet Knight, Chicago, IL, 1970; app on BOBOQUIVARI, PBS-TV, 1971; continued club/concert work across US into 70s; worked Golden State Country Bluegrass Special, Sausalito, CA, 1974; Mariposa Folk Festival, Toronto, Can, 1975; worked w Bob Dylan's ROLLING THUNDER Revue, Astrodome, Houston, TX, 1976; Felt Forum, NYC, 1976; Bottom Line, NYC, 1977; Winnipeg Folk Festival, Winnipeg, Can, 1977; McCabe's, Los Angeles, CA, 1977

Personal: Married June Hammerstein (1955-); Martha ——— (c1964-), 1 child. Not to be confused with John "Jack" Elliott, composer/arranger

Song: Just Stopped by to Get a Cup of Coffee

Infl by: Gene Autry/Bill Broonzy/Woody Guthrie/ Brownie McGhee

Infl to: Bob Dylan/London Wainwright III

Quotes: ". . . a major link between the legendary personalities of a bygone age and the contemporary folk scene"—Kristin Baggelaar/Donald Milton, *Folk Music: More Than a Song*, Thomas Y Crowell Company, 1976

"He is original . . . an interpreter of the highest artistry, in a great American folk tradition"—Bob Atkinson, *Sing Out* magazine, Mar 1970, p 9

References: Sing Out magazine, Nov 1965, pp 25-8/ Mar 1970, pp 2-10

Folk Music: More Than a Song, Kristin Baggelaar/Donald Milton, Thomas Y Crowell Company, 1976

ELLIS, WILBERT THIRKIELD *"Big Boy"/"Big Chief"*
(aka: Big Chief)
Born: Nov 10, 1914, Birmingham (Jefferson Co), AL
Died: Dec 20, 1977, Birmingham, AL
Inst: Piano

Father was Lem Ellis; mother was Climmie Reddlery, a Black Creek Indian; raised in Mason City, a suburb of Birmingham, AL, then moved to Eylton, AL, then Titiville, AL, c1923; taught self piano as youth and worked local parties/dances through 20s; left home to travel widely working outside music from early 30s; worked outside music in NYC, NY, from 1936; served in US Army, 1939-42; settled in NYC to

Photo by Cletha Francis. Courtesy Living Blues *Magazine*

work outside music (as bartender), Manhattan Bar & Grill and others, from 1942; rec Lenox label, NYC, 1945; frequently rec acc to many bluesmen in NYC area from 1945; worked occasional house rent parties/clubs/bars in NYC area through 40s into 50s; rec Sittin' In With label, NYC, 1949; rec acc to Sonny Terry/Brownie McGhee, Capitol label, NYC, 1950; inactive in music from 1955; moved to Washington, DC, area to work mostly outside music from 1972; rec Trix label, Cottekill, NY, 1974-5; worked National Folk Festival, Washington, DC, 1974; Philadelphia Folk Festival, Schwenksville, PA, 1974; National Folk Festival, Wolf Trap Farm Park, Vienna, VA, 1975; formed own Barrelhouse Rockers to frequently work local club dates, Washington, DC, area, 1975-7; rec Trix label, Hyattsville, MD, 1976; worked National Folk Festival, Wolf Trap Farm Park, Vienna, VA, 1977; John Henry Folk Festival, Camp Virgil Tate, Princeton, WV, 1977; died in University Hospital of cardiac failure; buried Shadow Lawn Cemetery, Birmingham, AL

Personal: Married Mattie Lee Pennington (1936-77). 4 children. "Chief" was childhood nickname

Songs: All Down Blues/Blues for Moot/Chief's E-Flat Blues/Dices Oh Dices/Prison Bound

Infl by: Prince Linnear

Quote: "He is a sensitive and critical man . . ." — Richard K Spottswood, Trix album 3316

Reference: Cadence magazine, Mar 1978, pp 3-4, 6, 18

EMERSON, WILLIAM ROBERT *"Billy the Kid"*
Born: Dec 21, 1929, Tarpon Springs (Pinellas Co), FL
Inst: Organ/Piano

Father was NT Emerson who frequently sang blues; learned piano as youth and frequently entertained family and friends into 40s; frequently worked w Billy Battle Band in Tarpon Springs, FL, area, 1946; frequently worked w Charley Bantley Combo/Manzy Harris Combo/Alonzo Broom group/others in Tarpon Springs area, 1946-52; served in US Air Force, 1952-4; worked w Ike Turner Band in local club dates, Memphis, TN, area, 1954-5; rec Sun label, Memphis, 1954-5; settled in Chicago, IL, 1955; rec VJ label, Chicago, 1955-7; rec Chess label, Chicago, 1958-9; rec Mad label, Chicago, 1960; rec M-Pac label, Chicago, c1963; rec USA label, Chicago, 1963; formed/rec Tarpon label, Chicago, from mid-60s; worked The Clock Lounge, Chicago, 1970; Kingston Mines, Chicago, 1976; Earl's Shangri-La Lounge, Chicago, 1977

ERBY, JOHN J
(aka: George Seymour/Guy Smith/J Guy Suddoth)
Born: Sept 20, 1902, Fort Worth (Tarrant Co), TX
Inst: Clarinet/Guitar/Piano/Sax/Trombone/Trumpet/Violin

Interested in music at young age and was playing piano/composing/arranging at 9 years of age; attended Wilberforce Univ, Wilberforce, OH, 1920-4 (earning BA degree); worked outside music (as school teacher), 1924; worked as composer for Chicago Music Company, Chicago, IL, mid-20s; rec Columbia label, Chicago, 1926; worked w Margurite Johnson in local club dates, St Louis, MO, 1926; reportedly rec QRS label (piano rolls) in late 20s; worked as talent scout for OKeh Record Company through 20s into early 30s; rec acc to Victoria Spivey, OKeh label, NYC/St Louis, 1926-7; rec acc to Lonnie Johnson, OKeh label, St Louis, 1927; toured w Martin & Walker Show, 1927; toured w Victoria Spivey on various road shows, late 20s; worked w WC Handy Presentations, St Louis, late 20s; rec Paramount label, Chicago, 1929; settled

Courtesy Bob Eagle/Record Research Archives

in Milwaukee, WI, early 30s; frequently worked La Fiesta Cafe, Manitowoc, WI (and other night clubs/ cafes in Milwaukee, WI, area), early 30s; moved to Los Angeles, CA, 1936; frequently worked as song writer/personal appearance pianist for Hattie McDaniel/Helen Humes/others, Los Angeles, late 30s into 50s; formed/directed/rec on A Natural Hit label, Los Angeles, late 40s; inactive in music in Los Angeles from early 60s

Personal: Married singer Monette Moore (c1925-c1927). One child. Married Learless Grady (c1927-early 30s). Name mislabeled as "Jack Erby" on some early recordings

Billing: The Singing Pianist

Songs: Black Spatch Blues/Graveyard Bound Blues/ Guess I'd Better Knock on Wood/He May Be Yours But He Ain't Yours All Alone/I Couldn't Take It/I Offer You/Lot's of Luck to You/Love Sick/Moanin' Groanin' Blues/Play My Baby's Blues/Praying Blues/ Show Girl Blues/Skeleton Key Blues/Somebody All My Own/That's My Specialty/This Christmas I Give Love/Toad Frog Blues

Reference: Record Research magazine, Mar 1973, pp 1-5

ESTES, *"Sleepy"* JOHN ADAMS
Born: Jan 25, 1899, Ripley (Lauderdale Co), TN
Died: Jun 5, 1977, Brownsville, TN
Inst: Guitar

Father Daniel Estes was guitarist; mother was Millie Thornton; one of at least 10 children; moved to Jones, TN, to work mostly outside music from childhood; blinded in right eye due to baseball accident at 6 years of age; moved to Brownsville, TN, to work outside music (as farmer), 1915-19; interested in music early and learned guitar on home-made cigar box instrument to work local houseparties, Brownsville, from 1916; teamed w Yank Rachell to work local streets/ country suppers/picnics/houseparties/radio shows, Brownsville area, 1919-27; teamed w Hammie Nixon to work picnics/dances in Brownsville area with frequent hoboing through Arkansas/Missouri, 1924-7; frequently worked w Hammie Nixon (and occasionally w Yank Rachell/Jab Jones as Three J's Jug Band) in streets/hotels/houseparties and Blue Heaven Club, Memphis, TN, 1927-30; rec Victor label, Memphis, 1929-30; worked mostly outside music (as farmer), Brownsville, 1930-1; moved to Chicago, IL, to work local house rent parties/street corners, 1931-7; served as judge in local blues contest, Chicago, 1933; rec Champion label, Chicago, 1935; rec Decca label, NYC, 1937-8; teamed w Hammie Nixon to hobo across US working fish fries/parties/dances/hobo camps/streets, 1937-41; toured w Hammie Nixon working Rabbit Foot Minstrel Show and Dr Grim(m)'s Medicine Show c1939; rec Decca label, Chicago, 1940; rec Bluebird label, Chicago, 1941; returned to Brownsville to work outside music, 1941-62; was completely blind by 1950; rec w Hammie Nixon, Ora Nelle label, Chicago, c1950; rec w Hammie Nixon, Sun label, Memphis, c1950; app in documentary film CITIZEN SOUTH—CITIZEN NORTH, 1962; worked Univ of Illinois, Urbana, IL, 1962; Harvard Univ, Cambridge, MA, 1962; Purdue Univ, Lafayette, IN, 1962; Westminster Col, Fulton, MO, 1962; rec Delmark label, Saukville, WI, 1962; worked The Limelight Theater, Chicago, 1962; Le Gallerie Flambeau, Baltimore, MD, 1962; app in Sam Charters film THE BLUES, 1963; worked Fickle Pickle, Chicago, 1963; Queens Col, Queens, NY, 1963; Gerdes Folk City, NYC, NY, 1963; rec Delmark label, Chicago, 1963-4; worked First Floor Club, Toronto, Can, 1964; Club 68, Hamilton, Can, 1964; app on ASSIGNMENT Show, local radio, Toronto, Can, 1964; app on THE OBSERVER Show, CBC-TV, Toronto, Can, 1964; worked Newport Folk Festival, Newport, RI, 1964 (por rel Vanguard label); toured w American Folk Blues Festival working TV/radio/con-

"Sleepy" John Estes

Photo by Julie Snow

cert dates through England/Europe, 1964 (por of Musikhalle concert, Hamburg, Ger, rel Fontana label); rec Storyville label, Copenhagen, Den/London, Eng, 1964; worked New Gate of Cleve, Toronto, Can, 1965; Second Fret, Philadelphia, PA, 1965, toured w American Folk Blues Festival working concert dates through England/Europe, 1966 (por Berlin, Ger, concert rel Fontana label); rec Delmark label, Chicago, 1966; worked Avant Garde, Milwaukee, WI, 1966; Ash Grove, Los Angeles, 1967; frequently worked local coffeehouses, Memphis, TN, 1968; Rockford Col, Rockford, IL, 1968; The Quiet Knight, Chicago, 1969; Newport Folk Festival, Newport, RI, 1969; Chicago Blues Festival, Chicago, 1969; Memphis Blues Festival, Memphis, TN, 1969; rec Blue Thumb label, Memphis, 1969; worked Ann Arbor Blues Festival, Ann Arbor, MI, 1969; Festival of American Folklife, Washington, DC, 1970; rec Delmark label, Chicago, 1970; rec Adelphi label, Memphis, c1970; worked Washington Blues Festival, Howard Univ, Washington, DC, 1970; River City Blues Festival, Memphis, 1971; Univ of Arkansas, Fayetteville, AR, 1972; app in film short THINKING OUT LOUD, 1972; worked Festival of American Folklife, Washington, DC, 1973 (por shown in videotape BORN IN THE BLUES); rec Albatross label, Memphis, 1972; toured w Memphis Blues Caravan working concert/college dates through Midwest, 1973-4; worked Newport Jazz Festival, NYC, 1974; toured Europe working concert dates, 1974; toured w Blues Festival working concert dates through Japan, 1974; worked Yubin Chokin Hall, Tokyo, Japan, 1974 (por rel Trio-Delmark label); worked Jubilee Jazz Hall, Memphis, TN, 1975; Xanadu Ballroom, Memphis, 1975 (por remote WLYX-FM-radio); John Henry Folk Festival, Camp Virgil Tate, Princeton, WV, 1976; Old Town School of Folk Music, Chicago, IL, 1976; toured Japan working concert dates, 1976; suffered stroke and died at Haywood Park General Hospital; buried family plot, Durhamville Baptist

Church Cemetery, Durhamville, TN

Personal: Married Olie ——— (1948-). 6 children. Married second wife. His daughter Virginia Estes married blues singer Hammie Nixon. Was cousin of blues musician Charlie Pickett. Named "Sleepy" as youth due to a chronic blood pressure problem or his continual exhaustion from outside music work causing him frequently to nap. Some unconfirmed sources give birth years between 1899-1904

Songs: Airplane Blues/Beale Street Sugar/Black Mattie/Broke and Hungry/Broken Hearted, Ragged and Dirty Too/Brownsville Blues/Death Valley Blues/Diving Duck Blues/Down South Blues/Drop Down Mama/80 Highway/Electric Chair/Fire Department/Freedom Loan/The Girl I Love/I Stayed Away Too Long/(I Will Never Forget That) Floating Bridge/I'd Been Well Warned/I'm a Tearing Little Daddy/I'm Going Home/Jailhouse Blues/Lawyer Clark/Married Woman Blues/Milk Cow Blues/Need More Blues/Olie Blues/Rats in My Kitchen/Shelby County Work House Blues/Someday Baby/Special Agent/Stop That Thing/Vernita/Working Man Blues/You Got to Go/You Oughtn't Do That

Infl by: David Campbell/Hambone Willie Newbern

Infl to: Big Bill Broonzy/Arthur Crudup/John Lee Williamson/Johnny Young

Quotes: "The emotional impact of his singing is overwhelming and when he really gets wound up in his music he sings with great power"—John Norris, *Jazz Beat* magazine, Apr 1964, p 17

"An extraordinarily affecting folk poet"—Pete Welding, *Downbeat Music: 1968,* p 59

"One of the greatest pure country blues singers"—Derrick Stewart-Baxter, *Jazz Journal* magazine (UK), Oct 1970, p 10

References: Living Blues magazine, Jul 1977, pp 11-14

Downbeat magazine, Nov 11, 1971, pp 10, 29

Sweet as the Showers of Rain, Samuel B Charters, Oak Publications, 1977

EVANS, MARGIE

Born: Jul 17, 1940, Shreveport (Caddo Parish), LA

Father was preacher; mother played piano; born Marjorie Ann Johnson; raised in Algiers, LA, where she sang in local churches as child; attended Grambling College, Grambling, LA, late 50s; moved to Los Angeles, CA, to work with local pick-up groups and Billy Ward Sextet in local club dates, 1958-64; rec

Courtesy Living Blues *Magazine*

Dore label, Hollywood, CA, c1963 (unreleased); toured w Ron Marshall Orch working colleges/clubs/hotels/concerts on US West Coast/Canada, 1964-9; worked Tiki's, Monterey Park, LA, 1967; rec w Johnny Otis Band, Epic label, Los Angeles, 1969; toured extensively w Johnny Otis Show working concert dates across US/Far East, 1969-72; worked w Johnny Otis Show, Monterey Jazz Festival, Monterey, CA, 1970 (por shown in film MONTEREY JAZZ/por rel Epic label); Ash Grove, Los Angeles, CA, 1970-3; app on Wally Thompson HOT SAUCE JAZZ Show, KTYM-radio, Inglewood, CA, c1970; app on HOMEWOOD Show, PBS-TV (syndicated), 1970; app w Johnny Otis on BLUE MONDAY Show, KPPC-radio, Pasadena, CA, 1971; toured w Johnny Otis Show working concert dates through Japan/Guam/China/Philippines/Thailand/Okinawa (with app on local radio/TV shows in Hong Kong, China), 1971; rec Yambo label, Chicago, IL, 1972; toured w Willie Dixon's Chicago All Stars working college circuit through Canada, 1972-3; worked Topanga Corral, Los Angeles, 1973; Fergies, Goleta, CA, 1973; rec United Artists label, Los Angeles, 1973; opened Kolbeh Club, Berlin, Ger, 1974; rec Buddah label, Los Angeles, c1974; toured w Rhythm & Blues: Roots of

Rock Show working concert dates through Europe, 1975; worked Parisian Room, Los Angeles, c1975; Chantilly's Lace Club, Los Angeles, 1976; Monterey Jazz Festival, Monterey, CA, 1976; app in show SHOWBOAT, Civic Light Opera Theater, Glendale, CA, 1976; toured through Germany/Italy working concert dates, 1977

Personal: Married James Evans (1958). One child. No relation to Delmar Evans, musician

Song: Louisiana Woman

Awards/Honors: Received an appreciation award from Senator Dymally of California

Infl by: Billie Holiday/Bessie Smith

EVERSON, LOTTIE
(see Beaman, Lottie)

FEELGOOD, DOCTOR
(see Perryman, William)

FENTION
(see Robinson, Fention)

FERNANDEZ, MILDRED
(see Brown, Lillian)

FLOWERS, ***"Evangelist"*** **MARY**
(see Miles, Josephine)

FLOYD, FRANK ***"Rambling King"***
(aka: Harmonica Frank/The Silly Kid)

Photo by Steve LaVere

Born: Oct 11, 1908, Toccopola (Pontotoc Co), MS
Died: Aug 7, 1984, Blanchester, OH
Inst: Footdrum/Guitar/Harmonica/Kazoo

Father Bruce Floyd and mother Stella Miles were musicians; born without given name (gave self name as teenager); one of 3 children; raised/worked on farm from childhood; taught self harmonica at 10 years of age; left home to work outside music with frequent work as comedian/singing harmonicist in carnivals/amateur shows/streets/tonks/parks through South/West c1922 through 20s; taught self guitar, mid-20s; worked w Cole Brothers Carnival through South in late 20s; toured w WE West's Motorized Show through South, 1928-9; toured as one man band w Happy Phillipson's Medicine Show, 1932; worked gigs in Juarez, Mexico, 1932; app w Buster Steele's Log Cabin Wranglers, KELW-radio, Burbank, CA, 1932; toured w Dr Hood's Medicine Show through South, 1933-4; app on own show, KLCN-radio, Blytheville, AR, during 30s; app on KTHS-radio, Hot Springs, AR, during 30s; app on WOBT-radio, Union City, TN, early 40s; frequently worked outside music (as farmer), mid-40s; frequently toured w Eddie Hill's Troupe and app with troupe on WMC-radio, Memphis, TN, late 40s into 50s; app on local radio, Valdosta, GA, 1949; worked Rainbow Lake Club, Memphis, early 50s; rec Chess label, Memphis, 1951; rec Sun label, Memphis, 1954; app on own show, local radio, Dyersburg, TN, early 50s; frequently worked outside music in Memphis area through 50s; formed/rec on own The F&L label, Memphis, 1958; worked outside music in Dallas, TX, early 60s; worked Sports Arena, Dallas, early 60s; worked mostly outside music, Memphis, through 60s; worked outside music, Millington, TN, into 70s; worked Mid-South Jamboree, Linden Circle Theater, Memphis, 1971; Hot Mama's Coffeehouse, Memphis, 1972; Univ of Chicago, Chicago, IL, 1972; Univ of Illinois, Urbana, IL, 1972; River City Blues Festival, Memphis, 1972; First Church Congregational, Cambridge, MA, 1972; rec Adelphi label, Silver Spring, MD, 1972-4; toured w Memphis Blues Caravan working concert dates through Midwest, 1973; worked Univ of California, Santa Barbara, CA, 1974; San Diego State Univ, San Diego, CA, 1974 (por remote KPFK-FM-radio); rec Barrelhouse label, Chicago, 1975; worked coffeehouses/blues festivals\university concerts through 70s; entered Continental Hospital where he died of pneumonia; buried Clover Cemetery, Bethel, OH

Songs: From Memphis to New Orleans/The Great Medical Menagerist/Married Man's Blues/Ring Tailed Tom/Rockin' Chair Daddy/Train Whistle Boogie

Infl by: DeFord Bailey/Blind Lemon Jefferson/ Palmer McAbee/Jimmie Rodgers

Quotes: "Floyd's music belongs to the American disenfranchised of the 1920s, 1930s and 1940s. He is a self-proclaimed spokesman for the rounders, backwoods rebels, poor farmers, sharecroppers, labourers, drifters, hobos and alley people of that hardtime period"—Doug Langille, *Coda* magazine (Canada), Feb 1977, p 28

Reference: Blues Unlimited magazine (UK), Apr 1973, pp 37-40

FOREST *"Forrest"* CITY JOE
(see Pugh, Joe)

FORTESCUE, JOHN HENRY
(aka: Guitar Shorty)

Photo by Peter B Lowry

Born: Jan 24, 1923, Belhaven (Beaufort Co), NC
Died: May 26, 1976, Rocky Mount, NC
Inst: Guitar

Father was Bud E Fortescue; mother was Agnes Lewis; born/worked outside music on farm from childhood; learned guitar from uncle as teenager; left home to hobo through North Carolina working outside music with frequent street singing for tips from 40s into 60s; continued working odd jobs outside music in Elm City/Sharpsburg, NC, with occasional parties/gatherings/street work from c1967 into 70s; rec Flyright label, Elm City, NC, 1970/Wilson, NC, 1971; rec Trix label, Elm City, NC, 1972-3; worked Univ of North Carolina, Chapel Hill, NC, 1973 (por rel Flyright label); frequently worked local coffeehouses, Chapel Hill, NC, from 1973; continued outside music work to 1976; entered Nash General Hospital where he died of cirrhosis of the liver; buried North Eastern Cemetery, Rocky Mount, NC

Personal: Not to be confused with David William Kearney who also used pseudonym "Guitar Shorty" and rec on Cobra and Pull labels

Songs: Drinkin' Wine/FBI Blues/Goin' Down in Georgia/Hold On Baby/Hoogle-De-Doo/I'm Goin' Home/My Mind Never Changed/Scat Boogie

Quotes: "His music is always highly rhythmic, he sings in a variety of styles and is, in fact, a free form player even within the looseness of the blues tradition"—Valerie Wilmer, *Melody Maker* magazine (UK), Sept 2, 1972

"He is a total musical animal, often spontaneously creating material on the spot"—William Bentley, Trix album 3706

Reference: Blues Unlimited magazine (UK), Jul 1976, pp 20-21

FOSTER, JIM
(see Collins, Sam)

FOSTER, LEROY
(aka: Baby Face/Baby Face Leroy)
Born: Feb 1, 1923, Algoma (Pontotoc Co), MS
Died: May 26, 1958, Chicago, IL
Inst: Drums/Guitar

Father was Tony Foster; mother was Mandie Miller (unconfirmed); raised/worked outside music in Coffeeville, MS, area; left home for Chicago, IL, working Maxwell Street area for tips from c1944; frequently worked w Sunnyland Slim/Lee Brown/John Lee "Sonny Boy" Williamson in local clubs/house rent

Courtesy Betty Foster/Mike Rowe/Living Blues Magazine

parties, Chicago, from 1946; worked 21 Club/Tuxedo Lounge/Kenny Lester's Sporting House, Chicago, late 40s; worked w Muddy Waters Band, Du Drop Inn/Club Zanzibar/Boogie Woogie Inn/708 Club/others, Chicago, 1948; rec acc to Floyd Jones, Tempo-Tone label, Chicago, 1948; rec Aristocrat label, Chicago, 1949; rec w Muddy Waters/Little Walter, Parkway label, Chicago, 1950; rec w own Baby Face Trio, Savoy label, Chicago, 1950; frequently worked as single in local clubs/lounges, Chicago, into 50s; rec JOB label, Chicago, 1950-2; rec Chess label, Chicago, 1952; worked w Johnny Temple, The Spot, Chicago, c1952; frequently worked w Homesick James/Snooky Pryor/Lazy Bill, Club Jamboree, Chicago, mid-50s; mostly inactive in music thereafter; reportedly suffered heart attack and DOA at AM Billings Hospital; buried Fern Oak Cemetery, Griffith, IN

Personal: Married Betty Arnold (1947-58). First cousin of musicians Johnnie Jones and Little Willie Foster

Song: The Devil Is Going to Get You

Infl by: Robert Johnson

Quote: "He was a fine singer with a warm insinuating voice which, like the late Sonny Boy's, 'got to the people' "—Mike Rowe, *Chicago Breakdown,* Eddison Press Ltd, 1973

Reference: Chicago Breakdown, Mike Rowe, Eddison Press Ltd, 1973

FOSTER, *"Little"* WILLY /WILLIE
Born: Apr 5, 1922, Clarksdale (Coahoma Co), MS
Inst: Harmonica/Piano

Father was Will Foster, a sharecropper who played piano; born/raised/worked on farm from childhood; learned piano from father as youth; moved to Chicago, IL, to work outside music from 1941; learned harmonica from Walter Horton and frequently worked Maxwell Street area for tips through 40s; frequently worked w Floyd Jones group, Club Jamboree/520 Club, Chicago, late 40s; frequently worked as sideman w Baby Face Leroy/Snooky Pryor/Lazy Bill Lucas/others in local clubs, Chicago, into 50s; w Floyd Jones group, Vi's Lounge, Chicago, early to mid-50s; rec Parrot/Blue Lake labels, Chicago, 1954; rec Cobra label, Chicago, 1956; inactive in music due to illness, Chicago, 1956 into 70s; sat-in w Willie Johnson Band, Washburne Lounge, Chicago, c1971; w Hayes Ware group in local clubs, St Louis, MO, 1972; reportedly served time for fatal shooting from 1974

Personal: Married Marie ———. Cousin of musicians Robert Earl Foster/Leroy Foster

Infl by: Walter Horton

Reference: Blues Unlimited magazine (UK), Dec 1973, p 23

FRANK, JOHNNY
(see Sellers, John)

FRANKLIN, EDWARD LAMONTE *"Pete"*
(aka: Guitar Pete)
Born: Jan 16, 1928, Indianapolis (Marion Co), IN
Died: Jul 31, 1975, Indianapolis, IN
Inst: Guitar/Piano

Father was Julius Franklin; mother Flossie Woods was musician; interested in music early and taught self piano as child; taught self guitar at about 11 years of age; dropped out of Crispus Attucks HS to work local club dates, Indianapolis, IN, c1945; served in US Army Special Services Unit working as entertainer, 1945-7; worked in San Francisco, CA, 1947; rec Victor label, Chicago, IL, 1947; returned to Indianapolis to work outside music with frequent local club/party work from late 40s into 70s; rec w John Brim, JOB label, Chicago, 1954; rec Bluesville label, Indianapolis, 1961; worked Eleventh Hour Coffee

Edward "Pete" Franklin

Courtesy Living Blues *Magazine*

House, Indianapolis, 1965; National Folk Festival, Wolf Trap Farm Park, Vienna, VA, 1971; rec Blue Goose label, Indianapolis (?), c1972; died at home of heart disease; buried Crown Hill Cemetery, Indianapolis

Personal: His mother Flossie Woods Franklin wrote many songs for Leroy Carr

Song: Guitar Pete's Blues

Infl by: Leroy Carr/Jesse Eldridge

Quote: "He is a powerful and original singer"—Art Rosenbaum, Bluesville album BV-1068

References: Living Blues magazine, Summer 1972, pp 18-21

Bluesville album BV-1068

FRAZIER, CALVIN H

Born: Feb 16, 1915, Osceola (Mississippi Co), AR
Died: Sept 23, 1972, Detroit, MI
Inst: Guitar

Father was Dan Frazier; mother was Belle ———; one of 3 children; most of family were musicians and became interested in music early; learned guitar as youth and frequently worked w Robert Johnson in local street group in Osceola, AR, area c1930 through 30s; frequently app on KLCN-radio, Blytheville, AR, mid-30s; moved to Detroit, MI, late 30s to work outside music; rec w Sampson Pittman, Library of Congress label, Detroit, 1938; frequently worked as sideman in local blues bands in local clubs, Detroit, from early 40s through 50s; toured in JUNGLE JIVE REVUE working 161 Club, Buffalo, NY/St Michele Club, Montreal, Can/others, 1946; rec w TJ Fowlers Band, Savoy label, Detroit, 1951; worked Palmer House, Detroit, 1956 (por rel JVB label); rec JVB label, Detroit, c1958; frequently worked outside music, Detroit, through 50s/60s; formed own band working local club dates, Detroit, c1970; rec acc to Washboard Willie, Barrelhouse label, Chicago, IL, 1972; entered Zieger Osteopathic Hospital where he died of cancer; buried United Memorial Gardens Cemetery, Plymouth, MI

Calvin Frazier

Courtesy Barrelhouse Records/Living Blues *Magazine*

Personal: Married Frances M Dunlap. Cousin of Johnny Shines, singer/musician

Infl by: Robert Johnson

Infl to: Bobo Jenkins

FROST, FRANK OTIS
Born: Apr 15, 1936, Augusta (Woodruff Co), AR
Inst: Guitar/Harmonica/Organ/Piano

Father was Theodore Roosevelt Frost; mother Darthula Winston; learned piano in church; to St Louis, MO, to work outside music with occasional local club gigs from 1951; learned harmonica from Sonny Boy Williamson (Alex Miller), mid-50s; frequently worked w Sonny Boy Williamson (Alex Miller) in local club dates, St Louis, 1956-9; moved to Lula, MS, to work outside music from 1960; frequently worked w Sam Carr in local jukes/clubs/dances in Lula/Clarksdale, MS, area, 1960 into 70s; frequently app w Sonny Boy Williamson (Alex Miller) on KING BISCUIT TIME, KFFA-radio, Helena, AR, early 60s; worked w Sonny Boy Williamson (Alex Miller) in local club dates, Marvell, AR, 1962; rec Phillips International label, Memphis, TN, 1963; frequently toured w Albert King/BB King/Little Milton/others out of Clarksdale, MS, as well as white country groups like Carl Perkins/Conway Twitty through 60s; toured w Robert Nighthawk's Nighthawks Trio in early 60s; rec Jewel label, Nashville/Memphis, TN, 1966; frequently worked w own group, City Auditorium, Clarksdale, MS, late 60s; worked The Barn, Tunica, MS, late 60s; Ann Arbor Blues Recital, Ann Arbor, MI, 1971; White Swan Club, Helena, AR, 1974; The Black Fox, Clarksdale, 1975; frequently w Sam Carr in local clubs, Lula, MS/Helena, AR, areas, 1977; worked Top & Lanes, Helena, 1977

Billing: The Rhythm & Blues King

Songs: Harp and Soul/Lucky to Be Living/My Back Scratcher/Pocket Full of Money/Pocket Full of Shells/Ride with Your Daddy Tonight/So Tired of Living By Myself/Things You Do/You're So Kind

Infl by: Robert Nighthawk/Jimmy Reed/Sonny Boy Williamson (Alex Miller)

Quote: "Mississippi singer-multi-instrumentalist Frank Frost and his band were responsible for some of the finest southern blues records of the 1960's"—Jim O'Neal, *Living Blues* magazine, Nov/Dec 1977, p 24

Reference: Living Blues magazine, Winter 1971, pp 26-8

Frank Frost *Photo by Jim O'Neal. Courtesy Living Blues Magazine*

FULLER, BLIND BOY
(aka: Brother George)
Born: 1908, Wadesboro (Anson Co), NC
Died: Feb 13, 1941, Durham, NC
Inst: Guitar

Father was Calvin Allen; mother was Mary Jane Walker; born Fulton Allen; one of 10 children; moved to Rockingham, NC, where he learned guitar and frequently worked streets/country suppers/houseparties in area through mid-20s; was partially blinded (reportedly due to ulcerated eyes) in 1926 and completely blind c1928; left home to work as itinerant musician from 1928; worked for tips in tobacco warehouses, Winston-Salem, NC, 1928; briefly worked streets of Danville, VA, c1928; settled in Durham, NC, to work as street singer c1929-34; teamed w Sonny Terry to work streets/fish fries/houseparties (occasionally w Bull City Red and Gary Davis) in Wadesboro/Watha/Durham, NC, 1934-8; frequently worked Lincoln Cafe, Durham, mid-30s; rec extensively for ARC label group, NYC, 1935-8; travelled widely working tobacco plants/farms/fairs/streets of Burlington/Raleigh/Greensboro/Chapel Hill, NC, and Memphis, TN, areas in late 30s; rec Decca label, NYC, NY, 1937; rec Vocalion label, Columbia, SC, 1938; rec Vocalion label, Memphis, 1939; mostly inactive in music, Durham, NC, 1939-40; rec Vocalion label, NYC, 1940; rec OKeh label, NYC/Chicago, 1940; underwent kidney operation, 1940, but later suffered resultant blood poisoning and died at home; buried Grove Hill Cemetery, Durham, NC

Personal: Married first wife during 20s. Second wife was Cora Mae Martin (1927-). One adopted child

Songs: Piccolo Man/Red River Blues/Working Man Blues/You've Got Something There

Infl by: Blind Blake/Blind Gary Davis

Infl to: JC Burris/Carolina Slim/Pernell Charity/Floyd Council/Arthur Gunter/Alvin Hankerson/Sonny

Courtesy Sheldon Harris Collection

Jones/Brownie McGhee/Doug Quattlebaum/Peg Richardson/Tarheel Slim/Baby Tate/Rich Trice/Welly Trice/Curley Weaver/Ralph Willis

Quotes: "[Fuller was] a fine eclectic artist, a synthesizer who was capable of assimilation and able to transform into his own individual style on the broad base of the Piedmont blues . . ."—Bruce Bastin, *Crying for the Carolines*, Studio Vista Ltd, 1971

"The language of Fuller's music has become a part of the mainstream of the folk blues tradition"—John Norris, *Coda* magazine (Canada), Jan 1968

"Carolina style? . . . Blind Boy Fuller style, rather"—Paul Oliver, Blues Classics album 11

References: Crying for the Carolines, Bruce Bastin, Studio Vista Ltd, 1971

Blues Unlimited magazine (UK), Dec 1969, p 6

FULLER #2, BLIND BOY
(see McGhee, Walter)

FULLER, JESSE *"Lone Cat"*
Born: Mar 12, 1896, Jonesboro (Clayton Co), GA
Died: Jan 29, 1976, Oakland, CA
Inst: Drums/Fotdella/Guitar/Harmonica/Kazoo/Washboard

One of 3 children; born/worked on farm from childhood; dropped out of school at third grade to continue outside music work in area; first instrument was homemade stringed mouth bow, 1901; raised with Wilson family in Macedonia, GA, 1902-6; ran away from home to work outside music through area, 1906 into 20s; learned guitar from Big Stella and frequently worked dances/suppers/picnics in Atlanta, GA, area through teens; worked outside music in Cincinnati, OH, c1918; travelled w Hagenbeck Wallace Circus (as tent-stretcher) through US/Canada from 1920; hoboed across US working streets for tips c1921-2; settled in California to work outside music, 1922; frequently worked as hot-dog stand attendant, Santa Monica, CA, and sold own cloth-covered wooden snakes on streets of Los Angeles, CA, into 20s; app (as extra) in Douglas Fairbanks film THE THIEF OF BAGDAD, 1924; app (as extra) in Pola Negri film EAST OF SUEZ, 1924; worked outside music in Bakersfield, CA, 1928; app (as extra) in film HEARTS IN DIXIE, 1929; app (as extra) in film END OF THE WORLD, 1929; settled in Oakland, CA, to work outside music (for Southern Pacific Railroad), 1929 into 40s; worked outside music (in local shipyard), San Francisco, CA, from early 40s; occasionally worked local parties/clubs as songster and tap dancer, San Francisco area, from 1943; worked occasionally w Leadbelly in local clubs, Hollywood, CA, mid-40s; continued working outside music through 40s into 60s; worked as one-man band with own fotdella (washboard/kazoo/harmonica/foot operated bass/cymbals) and app on local TV amateur shows, San Francisco, from 1951; app on DON SHERWOOD Show, local TV, San Francisco, early 50s; app on YOU'RE NEVER TOO OLD, local TV, Los Angeles, early 50s; rec World Folk Song label, San Francisco, 1954; rec Cavalier label, San Francisco, 1955-6; worked Cabo-Verdi Cafe, San Francisco, 1956; w Marty Marsala group in local jazz concert, Carmel, CA, 1957; rec Good Time Jazz label, Los Angeles, 1958; worked Sail'n Club, San Francisco, 1958; frequently worked Haight Street Barbeque Club, San Francisco, late 50s; app on Bobby Troup's STARS OF JAZZ, ABC-TV, 1959; worked Univ of California, Berkeley, CA, 1959; Monterey Jazz Festival, Monterey, CA, 1959-60; The Troubadour, Hollywood, CA, 1960; Sugar Hill Club, San Francisco, 1960-1; Blind Lemon Jefferson Club, San Pablo, CA, 1960; Univ of San Francisco, San Francisco, 1960; Ash Grove, Hollywood, CA, 1960-1; rec Good Time Jazz label, Los Angeles, 1960-1; toured w Chris Barber's Band working clubs/concerts through England/Ireland/Europe, 1960-1; app in film THE BLUES, 1962; worked Univ of Chicago, Chicago, 1962; Univ of Michigan, Ann Arbor, MI, 1962; rec Folk Lyric label, San Francisco, 1962; worked Gerde's Folk City, NYC, NY, 1962; rec Good Time Jazz label, Los Angeles, 1963; rec Bluesville label, San Francisco, 1963; worked Cabale Club, Berkeley, CA, 1963; Folk Festival, Sun Valley, ID, 1963; Brandeis Univ, Waltham, MA, 1963-4; Newport Folk Festival, Newport, RI, 1964; rec Prestige label, San Francisco, 1964;

Jesse "Lone Cat" Fuller *Photo by Julie Snow*

worked Swarthmore Folk Festival, Swarthmore, PA, 1964; Village Corner, Toronto, Can, 1964-5; Odyssey Coffeehouse, Boston, MA, 1965; app on LES CRANE Show, ABC-TV, 1965; toured England working clubs/concerts/TV shows, 1965; rec Fontana label, London, Eng, 1965; worked Indiana Univ, Bloomington, IN, 1965; Books, Strings & Things Coffeehouse, Blacksburg, VA, 1965; app on FESTIVAL PRESENTS THE BLUES, CBC-TV, Toronto, Can, 1966; worked Chessmate, Detroit, MI, 1966; St Peter's, NYC, NY, 1967; Klay Folk Festival, NYC, 1967; toured England working club/concert dates, 1967; worked Rheingold Music Festival, Central Park, NYC, 1967; Philadelphia Folk Festival, Schwenksville, PA, 1967; Berkeley Folk Festival, Berkeley, CA, 1968 (por shown on PBS-TV), app in film short JESSIE "LONE CAT" FULLER, 1968; worked Electric Circus, NYC, 1969; Newport Folk Festival, Newport, RI, 1969; Festival of American Folklife, Washington, DC, 1969; State Univ of New York at Buffalo, Buffalo, NY, 1969; Mariposa Folk Festival, Toronto, Can, 1969; rec ST for film THE GREAT WHITE HOPE, 1970; worked Berkeley Blues Festival, Berkeley, CA, 1970; Oakland Museum, Oakland, CA, 1971; Festival of American Folklife, Washington, DC, 1971; app in film ROOTS OF AMERICAN MUSIC: COUNTRY & URBAN MUSIC (pts 1&2), 1971; mostly inactive in music due to illnesses from 1971; worked Fresno State Univ, Fresno, CA, 1973; San Francisco Blues Festival, Golden Gate Park, San Francisco, 1974; entered Dowling Convalescent Hospital where he died of heart disease; buried Evergreen Cemetery, Oakland, CA

Personal: Married Curley Mae ——— (1916-28); Gertrude Johnson (1935-). 3 children

Songs: Beat It On Down the Line/Brownskin Gal I Got My Eyes on You/Buck and Wing/Cincinnati Blues/Crazy 'bout a Woman/Down Home Waltz/Drop Out Song/Fables Aren't Nothing But Doggone Lies/Hey Hey/Hump in Your Back/I Got a Mind to Ramble/Leavin' Memphis/Let Me Hold You in My Arms Tonight/Little Black Train/Memphis Boogie/Midnight Cold/The Monkey and the Engineer/Morning Blues/Move On Down the Line/New Corrine/99 Years and One Dark Day/Railroad Blues/San Francisco Bay Blues/Take It Slow an' Easy/The Way You Treat Me/You Can't Keep a Good Man Down/You're No Good

Infl to: John Koerner

Quotes: "He is the last of the great race of Negro minstrels"—Robert Tilling, *Jazz Journal* magazine (UK), Aug 1972

"A genuine folk-jazz musician of great originality and power"—Pete Clayton, Fontana album 5313

References: Blues World magazine (UK), Oct 1969/Jan 1970

Jazz Journal magazine (UK), Aug 1972, pp 25-6

FULLER, JOHNNY

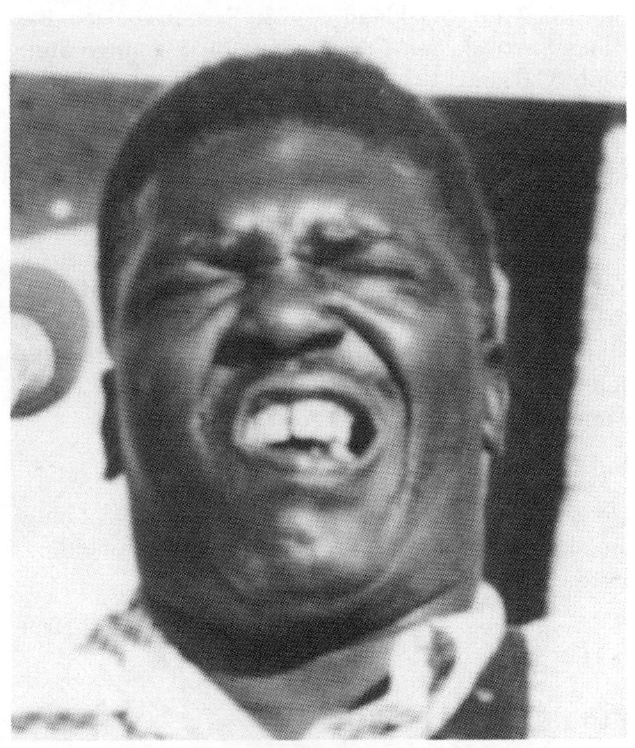

Photo by Jerry Haussler. Courtesy Tom Mazzolini

Born: Apr 20, 1929, Edwards (Hinds Co), MS
Died: May 20, 1985, Oakland, CA
Inst: Guitar/Organ/Piano

Father was Major Fuller, local musician; mother Beatrice Cox; to Vallejo, CA 1935 to teach self guitar at 7 years of age; frequently sang in local churches, Vallejo area, from 1944; formed own Teenage Gospel Singers (later changed to Golden West Gospel Singers) working locally from 1946; rec gospel songs, Jackson label, CA, c1948; app on KWBR-radio, Oakland, CA, late 40s; app on KRE-radio, Berkeley, CA, early 50s; rec Heritage label, Oakland, c1950; taught self organ/piano and began singing blues in early 50s; frequently toured as sideman in various package rock shows working theaters across US through 50s; rec w own band, Rhythm label, Oakland, 1954-5; rec Aladdin label, Hollywood, CA, 1955; toured w Paul Anka package show working concert dates in Hawaii, late 50s; toured w Frankie Avalon package show working concerts through Europe, 1959; frequently toured w Jimmy McCracklin/Eddie Boyd working concert dates, 1962; frequently worked outside music, Oakland, CA, area through 60s; worked Tommy's 250 Club, Richmond, CA, 1969; Lloyd's Club, Hayward, CA, 1970; continued outside music work, Oakland area, into 70s; rec Bluesmaker label, Hollywood, CA, 1973; worked Univ of California Extension Center, San Francisco, CA, 1973; Continental Club, Oakland, 1973; San Francisco Bay Blues Festival, San Francisco, 1973; Flamingo Steer Club, Oakland, 1974; Esther's Orbit Room, Oakland, 1974-5; Minnie's Can-Do Club, San Francisco, 1975; w own band, Crab Tree Brothers Club, Richmond, CA, 1975; Ruthie's, Berkeley, CA, 1976; worked West Coast clubs into 80s; died of vascular disease; buried Evergreen Cemetery, Oakland, CA

Songs: A Good Letting Alone/Back Home/Bad Luck Overtook Me/Buddy/Crying Won't Make Me Stay/Hard Times/The Haunted House/It's Your Life/Johnny Ace's Last Letter/Johnny's Lowdown Blues/Mercy Mercy/1009 Blues/Prowling Blues

Infl by: Johnny Ace/Charles Brown

Quote: "One of the mainstays of the West Coast blues for almost a quarter of a century"—Pete Welding, Bluesmaker album 3801

Reference: Blues Unlimited magazine (UK), Dec 1969, p 11

FULLER, LITTLE BOY
(see Trice, Richard)

FULLER, PLAYBOY
(see Minter, Iverson)

FULLER, RICHARD LEE
(see Minter, Iverson)

FULLER, ROCKY
(see Minter, Iverson)

FULSOM, LOWELL
(see Fulson, Lowell)

FULSON, LOWELL
(aka: Lowell Fulsom/Tulsa Red)
Born: Mar 31, 1921, Tulsa (Tulsa Co), OK
Inst: Guitar

Grandfather was hoedown violinist who spelled name "Fulsom"; three uncles were ministers; father was Martin Fulson, a Cherokee Indian; mother Mammie Wilson was a singing guitarist; moved to Atoka, OK, to work outside music as field hand from c1927; occasionally sang at local church affairs and tap danced at local events into early 30s; attended high school in Coalgate, OK, mid-30s; taught self guitar to frequently work churches/picnics/country dances while working outside music through 30s; worked w Dan Wright's String Band at local dances, Ada, OK, 1938-9; frequently worked as single (as C&W musician) at country suppers/gambling houses/beer joints/houseparties through area, 1939; teamed w Texas Alexander working jukes/joints through western Oklahoma/Texas, 1939-40; continued working outside music in Ada, OK/Gainesville, TX, areas, 1941-3; served in US Navy, 1943-5, and frequently entertained at USO shows in Guam, 1945; returned to Duncan, OK, briefly in 1945, then moved to West Coast to work outside music with occasional small club work in Richmond/Oakland, CA, area from 1945; formed small group w brother Martin Fulson and rec Big Town/Swingtime labels, Oakland, CA, 1946-52; rec Downtown/Trilon labels, Oakland, CA, 1946-8; extensive residency at Savoy Club, Richmond, CA, late 40s; frequently worked The Showboat, Vallejo, CA, late 40s; rec Aladdin label, Oakland, CA, 1949; worked frequently w Ivory Joe Hunter in local clubs/ballrooms in Oakland/San Francisco, CA, area, early 50s; worked w Bullmoose Jackson, Avalon Ballroom, San Francisco, CA, early 50s; worked w Joe Turner/Pee Wee Crayton in local club dates, Saginaw, MI, 1950; toured w own band working package R&B shows in theaters across US, 1950-3; worked Apollo Theater, NYC, NY, 1950; rec Aladdin label, New Orleans, LA, 1953; toured spot work fronting bands or working w Hot Lips Page/Choker Campbells Band/others, 1953-4; worked Crown Lounge, Chicago, IL, 1954; Cadillac Club, Chicago, 1954; toured w Clifton Chenier working club dates through South, mid-50s; rec Checker label, Dallas, TX, 1954; rec Checker label, Los Angeles, CA, 1955-62; worked Five-Four Ballroom, Los Angeles, 1955; toured one-nighters down West Coast, 1956; frequently worked Savoy Club, Richmond, CA, late 50s into early 60s; app in film THE BLUES, 1962; rec Kent label, Los Angeles, CA, 1963-7; worked Rhumboogie Club, Oakland, CA, early 60s; rec Movin' label, Los Angeles, 1964; worked Continental Club, Oakland, CA, 1964; Apollo Theater, Brooklyn, NY, c1965; Shelly's Manne-Hole, Los Angeles, CA, mid-60s; Pepper's, Chicago, IL, 1966; Sylvio's, Chicago, 1966; Blue Gardenia, Birmingham, AL, 1967; Grand Terrace, Birmingham, AL, 1967; Ash

Lowell Fulson *Courtesy* Living Blues *Magazine*

Grove, Hollywood, CA, 1968; rec Jewel label, Dallas, TX/Muscle Shoals, AL, 1968-9; worked The Auditorium, Santa Monica, CA, 1968; Electric Circus, NYC, NY, 1969; toured England/France working club/concert dates, 1969; toured one-nighters through Texas c1969; Old Dixie Ballroom, Los Angeles, CA, 1969; app on HOMEWOOD Show, PBS-TV (syndicated), 1970; worked Ann Arbor Blues Festival, Ann Arbor, MI, 1970; High Chaparral, Chicago, IL, 1970; Club Long Island, San Francisco, CA, 1970; S&R Room, Oakland, CA, 1970; Liberty Hall, Houston, TX, 1971; Alice's Revisited, Chicago, IL, 1971; Continental Club, Oakland, CA, 1973 (por shown on ALL TOGETHER NOW, KPIX-TV, San Francisco, CA); Joe's Place, Cambridge, MA, 1973; Topanga Corral, Los Angeles, CA, 1973-4; Fergie's, Goleta, CA, 1973; Joe's Melody Club, Vallejo, CA, 1974; Amvets, Oakland, CA, 1974; rec Warner Brothers label, Memphis, TN, 1974; worked Ruthie's, Berkeley, CA, 1975; Univ of Chicago Folk Festival, Chicago, IL, 1975; Montreux Rock/Blues Festival, Montreux, Switzerland, 1975 (por rel Utopia label); T-Bone Walker Memorial Concert, Musicians Union Hall, Los Angeles, CA, 1975; Dottie's Stardust Club, San Francisco, CA, 1975; Cat's Cradle, San Francisco, 1975; Upper Haight Street Club, San Francisco, 1976; rec Granite label, Memphis, TN/Hollywood, CA, 1976; Wilshire Ebell Theater, Los Angeles, CA, 1976; McCabe's Club, Santa Monica, CA, 1977; El Ray, Los Angeles, 1977; Club La Veek, Houston, TX, 1977; The Starwood, Hollywood, 1977; Coffee Gallery, San Francisco, 1977; Sacramento Blues Festival, William Land Park, Sacramento, CA, 1977

Personal: Married Adena ——— (1939-c1949); married/divorced Minnie Lou ——— (early 50s) who owned/operated Minnie Lou's Club in Richmond, CA. Managed brother Martin Fulson (musician, died 1959)

Songs: Blue Soul/Check Yourself/Cloudy Day/Comin' Home Someday/Country Boy Blues/Crying Won't Help/Do You Love Me?/Don't Be So Evil/Don't Destroy Me/Every Second a Fool Is Born/Fed Up/I Still Love You Baby/Have You Changed Your Mind?/I Want to Know/It's a Long Time/It's Your Own Fault/Just a Kiss/KC Bound/Lady in the Raw/Lonely Hours/Love Grow Cold/Love 'n' Things/Lovin' You/Low Society/Man on the Run/Market Street Blues/Miss Lillie Brown/Name of the Game/Pay Day Blues/Poor Boy Blues/Reconsider Baby/Rock 'em Dead/Rock This Morning/Rollin' Blues/Shed No Tears/Sinner's Prayer/Sleeper/So Long So Long/So Many Tears/Something's Wrong/Step at a Time/Stoned to the Bone/Swingin' Party/Teach Me/Three O'Clock Blues/Took a Long Time/Tramp/Trouble Everywhere/Trouble Trouble/Trouble with the Blues/Walk On/Why Don't You Write Me?/Worry Worry

Infl by: Texas Alexander/Blind Lemon Jefferson/Lonnie Johnson/Jimmy Rushing/Joe Turner/Aaron "T-Bone" Walker

Infl to: Bobby Bland/Ray Charles/Lloyd Glenn/BB King/Magic Sam/Al K Smith

Quotes: "Lowell's heritage may be Indian but he rides to the rhythm of a guitar . . . and he comes into his own when he sings the blues"—Paul Oliver, International-Polydor album 423250

"In 26 years of recording, Lowell Fulson has successfully coped with all the changing trends in blues adapting his very personal style to suit each successive generation"—Mike Leadbitter, Polydor album 2384038

References: *Living Blues* magazine, Summer 1971, pp 19-25

Living Blues magazine, Autumn 1971, pp 11-20

Honkers and Shouters, Arnold Shaw, Collier Books, 1978

G

GANT, CECIL
(aka: Gunter Lee Carr)
Born: Apr 4, 1913, Nashville (Davidson Co), TN
Died: Feb 4, 1951, Nashville, TN
Inst: Piano

Born/raised in Nashville, TN; worked local clubs and app on local radio broadcasts from mid-30s; formed own band to tour South working club dates, late 30s; served in US Army on West Coast, 1944; rec Gilt Edge label, Los Angeles, CA (billed as "The GI Sing-Sation"), 1944-5; served as US saving bond promoter with frequent gigs in local clubs, Los Angeles area, 1944-7; worked Lincoln Theater, Los Angeles, 1944; toured as single working one-nighters across US from mid-40s; worked Paradise Theater, Detroit, MI, c1945; Club Zanzibar, Nashville, TN, c1945; rec 4 Star label, Los Angeles, CA, c1947; rec King label, Cincinnati, OH, 1947; worked Dew Drop Inn, New Orleans, LA, 1947; rec Bullet label, Nashville, TN, 1948-9; worked Manhattan Club, Newport, KY, 1948; rec Downbeat/Swingtime labels, Los Angeles, CA, 1949; rec Imperial label, New Orleans, LA, 1950; rec Decca label, NYC, NY, 1950-1; entered Hubbard Hospital where he died of pneumonia; buried in Cleveland, OH

Personal: Married Alma———

Billing: The GI Sing-Sation

Songs: Boogie Woogie Baby/Cecil Boogie/Cecil's Jam Session/Deal Yourself Another Hand/I Ain't Gonna/I Wonder/If It's True/Jump Jack/Loose as a Goose/Nashville Jump/Nobody Love You/Playin' Myself the Blues/Screwy Boogie/Sloppy Joe's/Special Delivery/Train Time Blues/Wake Up Cecil Wake Up/Way Down/What's on Your Worried Mind?

Infl by: Leroy Carr

Quotes: "Cecil Gant [had a] highly individual talent for blues singing, boogie piano-playing and general good feeling"—Tony Russell, Flyright album 3710

"Not only a remarkable piano player, Cecil Gant was also a fascinating singer with a ringing voice who knew, through mocking comments, how to give a lot of life and humor to his songs"—Virgile Degand, Riverboat album 900.260

Reference: Honkers and Shouters, Arnold Shaw, Collier Books, 1978

GARLOW, CLARENCE JOSEPH *"Bon Ton"*
(aka: Parran)

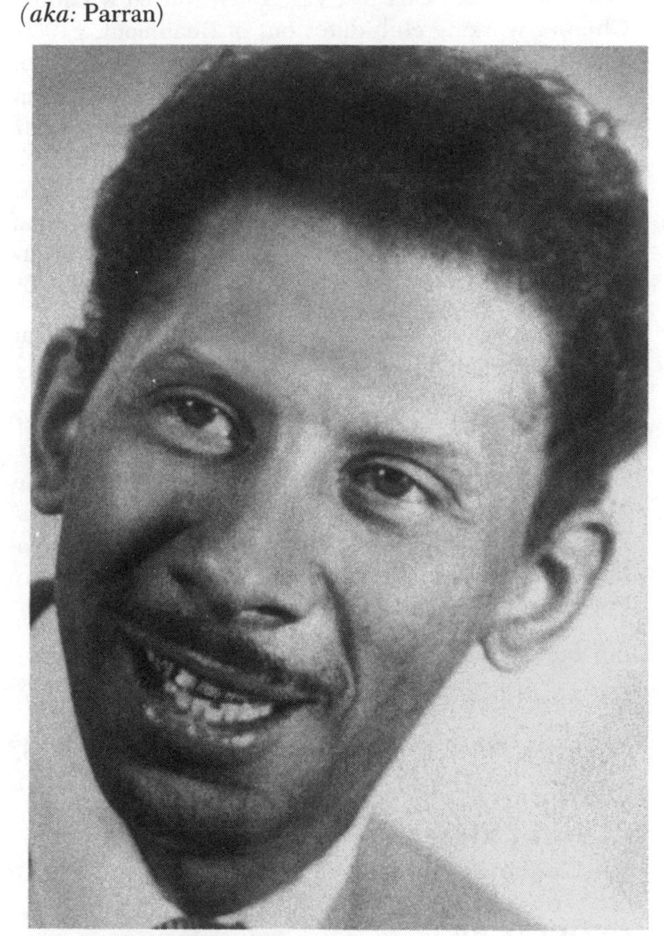

Courtesy W D Shook III, MD

Born: Feb 27, 1911, Welsh (Jefferson Davis Parish), LA
Died: Jul 24, 1986, Beaumont, TX
Inst: Accordion/Fiddle/Guitar/Violin

Father was Compton Garlow, a singer/musician and leader of local string band; mother was Ophelia Broussard; moved to Beaumont, TX, at 5 months of age; interested in music early, learning fiddle at 8 years of age and later guitar/violin/accordion; occasionally worked in father's string band as youth; worked mostly outside music, Beaumont, from early 30s; rec Macy's label, Houston, TX, 1949; formed own Bon Ton Boys working local clubs, Beaumont, from 1949 then touring clubs through Texas/Louisiana into 50s; rec Feature label, Crowley, LA, 1951; rec Lyric label, Lake Charles, LA, 1951; rec w Henry Mesner Band, Aladdin label, New Orleans, LA, 1952; owned/operated The Bon Ton Drive In, Beaumont,

TX, 1952-6; moved to West Coast working club dates in Malibu/Ocean City/Ocean Park/San Bernadino, CA, areas, 1953-4; rec Flair label, Culver City, CA, 1954; rec Feature label, Crowley, LA, 1954; rec Folk Star label, Lake Charles, LA, 1954; toured w Clifton Chenier working club dates out of Beaumont, c1955; app (as DJ) on own BON-TON Show, KJET-radio, Beaumont, 1955-61, and occasionally thereafter on KJET-radio, Beaumont/KLVI-radio, Beaumont/KZEY-radio, Tyler, TX/KOGT-radio, Orange, TX, into 60s; rec Goldband label, Lake Charles, LA, 1956-7; rec acc to T Baby Green on own Bon-Ran label, Beaumont, 1962; worked outside music, Beaumont from mid-60s; some club/concert dates 1984-6

Personal: Name "Bon Ton" from his song "Bon Ton Roula" (French colloquial for "Good Times Roll")

Songs: Bon Ton Roula/Bound To Lose My Mind/Crawfishin'/Dreaming/I Called You Up Daddy/I Feel Like Calling You/If I Keep On Worrying/In a Boogie Mood/Jumpin' for Joy/Let Me Be Your Santa/Louisiana Blues/New Bon Ton Roula/No No Baby/Please Accept My Love/Route 90/She's So Fine/Sound the Bell/Train Fare Home

Infl by: Aaron "T-Bone" Walker

Infl to: Clifton Chenier/Johnny Winter

Reference: Blues Unlimited magazine (UK), Jan 1968, p 7

GAYNO, CREOLE
(see Guesnon, George)

GEORGIA BILL
(see McTell, Willie)

GEORGIA GRINDER
(see Davenport, Charles)

GEORGIA PINE
(see Harris, Edward)

GEORGIA PINE BOY
(see McCoy, Joe)

GEORGIA SLIM
(see Seward, Alexander)

GEORGIA TOM
(see Dorsey, Thomas A)

GIBBONS, IRENE
(see Taylor, Eva)

GIBSON, CLIFFORD *"Grandpappy"*
(aka: Sluefoot Joe)
Born: Apr 17, 1901, Louisville (Jefferson Co), KY
Died: Dec 21, 1963, St Louis, MO
Inst: Guitar

Father was William Gibson, mother Letha ———; reportedly moved to St Louis, MO, late 20s; frequently worked local club dates, St Louis, late 20s into early 30s; rec QRS label, Long Island City, NY, 1929; rec Victor label, NYC, 1929; rec acc to Jimmie Rodgers/RT Hanen (or as single), Victor label, Louisville, KY, 1931; worked almost exclusively as itinerant street musician (with a trained dog) for tips, St Louis area, through 30s/40s/50s; rec Bobbin label, St Louis, 1960; worked Gaslight Square, St Louis, 1963; died of pulmonary edema; body donated to local medical center

Personal: Married Johnnie Mae ———

Songs: Bad Luck Dice/Hard Headed Blues/Ice and Snow Blues/Tired of Being Mistreated

Infl by: Lonnie Johnson

Quote: "One of the most inspired of all country blues guitarists"—Stephen Calt, Yazoo album 1027

GILLUM, WILLIAM McKINLEY *"Bill"/"Jazz"*
(aka: Bill McKinley)

Courtesy Frank Driggs Collection

Born: Sept 11, 1904, Indianola (Sunflower Co), MS
Died: Mar 29, 1966, Chicago, IL
Inst: Harmonica/Harmonium

Father was Irving Gillum, mother was Celia Buchanan; one of a few children; after parents died was raised by uncle Ed Buchanan (local church deacon) from infancy; interested in music early and taught self harmonium and frequently played for local church functions/parties as child; taught self harmonica c1910; ran away from home to live with relatives in Charleston, MS, 1911-15; worked outside music (as field hand), Minter City, MS, 1915-18; worked outside music with frequent street work for tips, Greenwood, MS, 1918-23; moved to Chicago, IL, to work mostly outside music from 1923; occasionally worked w Bill Broonzy in local club dates through 20s; frequently acc local bluesmen in local record dates, Chicago, into 30s; rec Bluebird label, Chicago, 1934; rec Bluebird/ARC label group, Chicago, 1936; rec Bluebird label, Aurora, IL, 1937-8; rec Bluebird label, Chicago, 1939-42; rec Vocalion label, Chicago, 1940; served in US Army c1942-5; continued to work outside music, Chicago, from c1945 through 50s; rec Bluebird label, Chicago, 1945; rec Bluebird/Victor labels, Chicago, 1946-7; rec Victor label, Chicago, 1949; rec w Memphis Slim, Folkways/Candid labels, NYC, NY, 1961; worked mostly outside music in Hammond, IN, from c1961; worked Fickle Pickle, Chicago, 1963; suffered gunshot head wound during an argument, DOA at Garfield Park Hospital; buried Restvale Cemetery, Worth, IL

Personal: Married. Had children. Name "Jazz" was given him during childhood.

Songs: Got to Reap What You Sow/I Got Somebody Else/I'll Get Along Somehow/It Looks Too Bad for You/It's All Over Now/Me and My Buddy/One Letter Home/Riley Springs/She Won't Treat Me Kind/Woke Up Cold in Hand/You Drink Too Much Whiskey/You're Laughing Now

Quotes: "Gillum's music [was] highly individual and there was a distinctive character and charm to his records that kept him a popular name in the Bluebird catalogue until its demise"—Neil Slaven, RCA-International album 1177

"Gillum has emerged as an important figure in the growth of the southern blues tradition"—Iola/Ray Flerlage, Folkways album FT3826

References: RCA-International album 1177
Folkways album FT3826

GILMORE, BOYD
Born: Jun 12, 1910, Belzoni (Humphreys Co), MS
Died: Dec 23, 1976, Fresno, CA
Inst: Guitar

Father Sam Gilmore; mother Luella Bryant; raised at Paines-Deadman Plantation, Honey Is, MS; was working jukes in Helena, AR, area c1942; worked Bloomfield's Gambling Joint, Vance, MS, c1943; reportedly served in US Army, early 40s; lived/worked on RL Shurden Plantation, Drew, MS, from 1946; worked w Ike Turner group in local clubs, Clarksdale, MS, 1951; frequently worked local jukes in Greenville, MS, area in 1952; rec w Ike Turner, Modern label, Greenville, 1952; formed own Boogie Ramblers group working local jukes/clubs in Drew, MS, area in early 50s; worked w own group, Fireworks Station, East St Louis, IL, c1955; Little Rabbit Night Club, Pine Bluff, AR, late 50s; frequently worked w own group in local clubs/bars in Pine Bluff, AR, 1962-4; worked Oakland, CA area from mid-60s into 70s; suffered fatal heart attack at home; buried Odd Fellows Cemetery, Fresno, CA

Personal: Reportedly cousin of Elmore James

Reference: Blues Unlimited magazine (UK), Dec 1974, p5

GITFIDDLE JIM
(see Arnold, James)

GLAZE, RED HOT WILLIE
(see McTell, Willie)

GOOD ROCKIN' CHARLES
(see Edwards, Charles)

GOOD ROCKING SAM
(see Maghett, Samuel)

GORDON, ODETTA FELIOUS
(*aka:* Odetta)
Born: Dec 31, 1930, Birmingham (Jefferson Co), AL
Inst: Guitar

Father was Reuben Holmes; mother was Flora Sanders; born Odetta Holmes, an only child; after death of father assumed surname of stepfather Zadock Felious; moved to Los Angeles, CA, where she was raised from 1937; interested in music early and sang in junior high school glee club with some vocal training as teenager; worked as amateur at Turnabout Theater, Hollywood, CA, 1945; graduated Belmont HS, Los Angeles, 1947; worked outside music with some clas-

Odetta Gordon (Odetta)

Photo by Julie Snow

sical music studies at City College, Los Angeles, through 40s; app in chorus of show FINIAN'S RAINBOW, Greek Theater, Los Angeles, 1949, then toured West Coast with show; taught self guitar and worked as folk singer at local parties in Los Angeles/ San Francisco, CA, areas from c1949; impromptu singing at Hungry i club, San Francisco, c1952; worked residency at Tin Angel, San Francisco, 1953; Yugoslav Hall, NYC, NY, 1953; Blue Angel, NYC, 1953; Turnabout Theater, Hollywood, CA, c1954-5; app in film THE LAST TIME I SAW PARIS, 1954; app in film CINERAMA HOLIDAY, 1955; in residence at Gate of Horn, Chicago, IL, 1956-7 (por 1957 date rel Tradition label); Wilshire Ebell Theater, Los Angeles, 1956; rec Tradition label, San Francisco, 1956; worked Bill Broonzy Benefit concert, KAM Temple, Chicago, 1957; Academy of Music, Brooklyn, NY, 1957; extensive tours working clubs/coffeehouses/concerts across US/Canada, 1958; worked Town Hall, NYC, 1959; w Count Basie Orch, Hunter Col, NYC, 1959; Newport Jazz/Folk Festivals, Newport, RI, 1959-60 (por 1959 folk concert rel Vanguard label); Ash Grove, Los Angeles, 1959; app w Langston Hughes on LAMP UNTO MY FEET, CBS-TV, 1959; app on TONIGHT WITH BELAFONTE, CBS-TV, 1959; worked Village Gate, NYC, 1960; Eaton Auditorium, Toronto, Can, 1960-1; Jordan Hall, Boston, MA, 1960; Storyville, Boston, 1960; w Pete Seeger, Yale Univ, New Haven, CT, 1960; Carnegie Hall, NYC, 1960 (por rel Vanguard label); app w William Warfield on PARABLE IN THE PARK, NBC-TV, 1960; worked Berkshire Music Barn, Lenox, MA, 1960; Apollo Theater, NYC, 1960; Blue Angel, NYC, 1960; Monterey Jazz Festival, Monterey, CA, 1960-1; app in film SANCTUARY, 1960, Gate of Horn, Chicago, IL, 1961-2; frequent club/concert dates in San Francisco, CA, area, 1961; worked Orchestra Hall, Chicago, 1961; w Fred Kaz Trio, One Sheridan Square, NYC, 1961; Town Hall, NYC, 1961; app (in non-singing role) in HAVE GUN WILL TRAVEL (ep: The Hanging of Aaron Gibbs), CBS-TV, 1961; worked Ravinia Park, Chicago, 1961; The Renaissance, Los Angeles, 1961; rec w Sonny Terry, Victor label, NYC, 1962; rec w Buck Clayton group, Victor label, NYC, 1962; rec Riverside label, NYC, 1962; worked Hungry i club, San Francisco, 1962; toured

Europe working concert dates, 1962-3; worked American Society of African Culture Center Concert, Lagos, Nigeria, 1962; Southern Methodist Univ, Dallas, TX, 1962; app on HARRY BELAFONTE SPECIAL, CBS-TV, 1962; worked Sheraton Park Hotel, Washington, DC, 1963 (por shown on DINNER WITH THE PRESIDENT, CBS-TV); app w Bob Dylan on SONGS OF FREEDOM, NBC-TV, 1963; frequently worked Village Gate, NYC, 1963-8; Berkshire Music Barn, Lenox, MA, 1964; Newport Folk Festival, Newport, RI, 1964-5 (por shown in film FESTIVAL); Carnegie Hall, NYC, 1964; app on LLOYD THAXTON Show, WPIX-TV, NYC (syndicated), 1964; worked Shadows Club, Washington, DC, 1964; toured concert dates through Australia/Japan, 1965; app on KALEIDOSCOPE 4, NBC-TV, 1965; app on EASTER SPECIAL, CBS-TV, 1965; app on NIGHTLIFE, ABC-TV, 1965; worked Mother Blues, Chicago, IL, 1965; Town Hall, NYC, NY, 1965; New Gate of Cleve, Toronto, Can, 1965; La Cave, Cleveland, OH, 1965; Gaslight, South Miami, FL, 1965; Birtian Club, Chicago, 1966; Orchestra Hall, Chicago, 1966; Moondial, Boston, MA, 1966; toured England working concert dates, 1966; worked Lewisohn Stadium, NYC, 1966; The Troubadour, Los Angeles, 1966; Central Park Music Festival, NYC, 1966-7; The Riverboat, Toronto, Can, 1966; Apollo Theater, NYC, 1966-7; app on THE WORLD OF MUSIC, CBC-TV, Toronto, Can, 1966; toured Australia/New Zealand working concert/TV dates, 1966-7; worked Olin Hotel, Denver, CO, 1967; app on FROM THE BITTER END, WOR-TV, NYC, 1967; app on JOEY BISHOP Show, ABC-TV, 1967; app on TWANG, ABC-TV, 1967; worked Carnegie Hall, NYC, 1968; app in INAUGURAL EVENING AT FORD'S THEATER, Ford's Theater, Washington, DC, 1968 (por shown CBS-TV); worked Chateau Restaurant, Denver, CO, 1968; Woody Guthrie Memorial Concert, Carnegie Hall, NYC, 1968 (por rel Columbia label); app on WITH PIERRE SALINGER, WNEW-TV, NYC, 1968; toured Israel working concert dates, 1968; worked Main Point, Bryn Mawr, PA, 1968; app on MERV GRIFFIN Show, CBS-TV, 1968; worked Kaleidoscope, Philadelphia, PA, 1968; Philadelphia Folk Festival, Schwenksville, PA, 1968-9; worked college circuit concert dates across US, 1968-9; Pavilion Folk Festival, NYC, 1969; toured Japan working concert dates, 1969; app on JOEY BISHOP Show, ABC-TV, 1969; worked Jazz by the Bay concert, San Diego, CA, 1969; app on DELLA Show, WOR-TV, NYC (syndicated), 1969; app on MIKE DOUGLAS Show, CBS-TV, 1970; app on DAVID FROST Show, WNEW-TV, NYC (syndicated), 1970; worked Woody Guthrie Memorial Concert, Hollywood Bowl, Hollywood, CA, 1970 (por rel Warner Brothers label); The Centaur, Montreal, Can, 1970; The Bitter End, NYC, 1970; Playhouse in the Park, Boston, MA, 1970; app in film short RAMBLIN', 1970; app on VIRGINIA GRAHAM Show, WOR-TV, NYC (syndicated), 1971; app on LIKE IT IS, ABC-TV, 1971; worked Metropolitan Museum, NYC, 1971; Fillmore East, NYC, 1971; app on BOBOQUIVARI, PBS-TV, 1971; worked w Rochester Philharmonic Orch, Carnegie Hall, NYC, 1972; app on THE GREAT AMERICAN DREAM MACHINE, PBS-TV, 1972; toured Israel working concert dates, 1972; worked Tangiers 72 Jazz Festival, Tangier, Morocco, 1972; Club des Rhythms Africans, Tangier, Morocco, 1972; Berlin Jazz Festival, Berlin, Ger, 1973; Max's Kansas City, NYC, 1973; Academy of Music, Brooklyn, NY, 1974; Music Festival, Martinique, West Indies, 1974; Playhouse in the Park, Boston, MA, 1974; app in THE AUTOBIOGRAPHY OF MISS JANE PITTMAN, CBS-TV, 1974 (rel as film of same title); worked Reno Sweeney, NYC, 1975; Amazingrace, Evanston, IL, 1976; app on BLACK CONVERSATIONS, WPIX-TV, NYC, 1976; app on JOE FRANKLIN Show, WOR-TV, NYC, 1976; worked Carnegie Hall, NYC, 1976; John Henry Folk Festival, Camp Virgil Tate, Princeton, WV, 1976; Montreux Music Festival, Montreux, Switzerland, 1976 (por shown on MUSIC FROM MONTREUX, BBC-2-TV, London, Eng); worked Best of Harlem Club, Stockholm, Sweden, c1976 (por rel Four Leaf Clover label); New Orleans Jazz Festival, New Orleans, 1977; toured Japan working concert dates, 1977; toured w Sammy Price working concert dates through Europe, 1977; worked Cascais Jazz Festival, Cascais, Portugal, 1977 (por shown on RTP-TV, Portugal); Newport Jazz Festival Blues Picnic, Waterloo Village, Stanhope, NJ, 1977; Town Hall, NYC, 1977; The Cookery, NYC, 1977; Philadelphia Folk Festival, Schwenksville, PA, 1977

Personal: Married Dan Gordon (1959 to mid-60s); Gary Shead (late 60s); Iverson Minter (Louisiana Red) (c1977-)

Song: Hit or Miss

Awards/Honors: Won Sylvania Award for excellence for TONIGHT WITH BELAFONTE, CBS-TV, 1959

Presented with Key to City by Birmingham, AL, 1965

Infl by: Bessie Smith

Infl to: Janis Joplin

Quotes: "One of the more exciting singers to emerge during the current [1960] renaissance of interest in American folk music is Odetta, who belongs to the great tradition of Leadbelly, Bessie Smith and Mahalia Jackson"—(unknown credit) *Current Biography*, HW Wilson Company, 1960

"Odetta's voice remains a remarkably flexible instrument, capable both of soft-spun timbres and one with a powerful cutting edge, equally convincing in resonant, low tones and scat-like passages way up high"—Robert Sherman, *New York Times* newspaper (unknown issue), 1971

". . . one of the great figures in American folk music"—Adam Barnes, Victor album LPM 2573

References: Current Biography, HW Wilson Company, 1960

Folk Music: More Than a Song, Kristin Baggelaar/Donald Milton, Thomas Y Crowell Company, 1976

Encyclopedia of Folk, Country & Western Music, Stambler/Landon, St Martin's Press, 1969

GORDON, SLIM

(see Weaver, Curley)

GORGEOUS WEED

(see Phelps, Arthur)

GOSPEL MINNIE

(see Douglas, Lizzie)

GRANDERSON, JOHN LEE

Born: Apr 11, 1913, Ellendale (Shelby Co), TN
Died: Aug 22, 1979, Chicago, IL
Inst: Guitar/Kazoo

Father was Louis Granderson; mother Bertha Brooks; was playing guitar by age of 9; often worked with John Estes/Hammie Nixon/others in area through 20s; left home to hobo North c1927; settled in Chicago, IL, to work outside music from 1928; worked w John Lee "Sonny Boy" Williamson, Chicago, mid-30s; frequently worked parties/clubs/lakeboats/streets for tips, Chicago area, through 30s/40s/50s; suffered injury and worked full time in music from 1964; worked

John Lee Granderson *Photo by Ray Flerlage (Kinnara Collection). Courtesy Sing Out Magazine*

w Robert Nighthawk, Diz's Club, Chicago, 1964; frequently worked w John Wrencher and others on Maxwell Street, Chicago, through 60s/70s; rec Testament label, Chicago, 1964-6; formed own The Streetmonders trio working locally (and with local gospel group), Chicago, through 60s; rec w Chicago String Band, Testament label, Chicago, 1966; rec Adelphi label, Chicago, 1969; worked Alice's Revisited, Chicago, 1970; inactive in music through 70s; died of cancer at Cook County Hospital; buried locally, Brunswick, TN

Songs: A Man for the Nation/Girl at the Bottom/Going 'round the World/I Can't Do Nothing But Boogie/ John Lee's Dirty Dozen

Infl by: Blind Lemon Jefferson/Memphis Minnie

Quote: "An excellent singer with a low, introspective voice"—Clas Ahlstrand, *Blues Unlimited* magazine (UK), Feb 1968, p 10

Reference: Blues Unlimited (UK), Feb 1968, pp 10-11

GRANT, LEOLA B *"Coot"*
(aka: Coot(s)/Patsy Hunter/Leola B Pettigrew/Leola B Wilson)

Courtesy Sheldon Harris Collection

Born: Jun 17, 1893, Birmingham (Jefferson Co), AL
Died: c1960 (unconfirmed)

Father was owner of local honky-tonk; mother was of Indian heritage; born Leola B Pettigrew, one of 15 children; interested in music early and learned cakewalk dances from father as child; frequently danced at local parades, Birmingham, AL, c1898; frequently worked local amateur vaudeville shows, Atlanta, GA, c1900; toured w Mayme Remington's Pickaninnies (as pick and dancer) working theaters across US/ Europe/South Africa, 1901-9; worked w Wesley Wilson in local vaudeville shows, Jacksonville, FL, from 1905; teamed w Wesley Wilson (as "Coot Grant & Socks Wilson") to tour vaudeville circuit extensively through Midwest/West/South c1912 into 30s; rec w Wesley Wilson, Paramount label, NYC, NY/Chicago, IL, 1925; rec w Fletcher Henderson Orch, Paramount label, NYC, 1925; rec w Blind Blake, Paramount label, Chicago, 1926; rec extensively w Wesley Wilson, Columbia/ QRS/ OKeh labels/others, NYC, 1928-33; toured w Wesley Wilson (as "Grant & Wilson") in musical comedy THE CHOCOLATE SCANDALS working theaters, 1928, then Lafayette Theater, NYC, 1928; app w Wesley Wilson in BACK HOME AGAIN Revue, Lincoln Theater, NYC, 1928; app w Wesley Wilson in PITTER PATTER Revue, Alhambra Theater, NYC, 1929; app w Wesley Wilson in LOUISIANA Revue, Lafayette Theater, NYC, 1929; app w Wesley Wilson in film EMPEROR JONES, 1933; app w Wesley Wilson in HOLIDAY IN HARLEM Revue, Apollo Theater, NYC, 1934; rec Decca label, NYC, 1938; frequently worked outside music in NYC area from 1939; worked occasional local concert dates in NYC area into 40s; rec w Mezzrow-Bechet Quintet, King Jazz label, NYC, 1946; app w Mezz Mezzrow, Really the Blues Concert, Town Hall, NYC, 1947; app on THIS IS JAZZ, WOR-radio (Mutual network), NYC, 1947; formed own HOLIDAY IN BLUES Revue working local theater dates, Newark, NJ, 1948; worked Bessie Smith Memorial Concert, Town Hall, NYC, 1948; Stuyvesant Casino, NYC, 1949; worked outside music, Los Angeles, CA, 1951-5; moved to Whitesboro, NJ, and inactive in music from 1955; whereabouts unknown thereafter

Personal: Married Wesley Wilson (c1912-died 1958). One son. "Coot" was childhood pet name for "Cutie"

Songs: Blue Monday Up on Sugar Hill/Boodle Boo/ Come On, Coot, Do That Thing/Crying Won't Make Him Stay/Deceiving Man Blues/Dish Rag Blues/Do You Call That a Buddy?/Down in the Country/Down in the Dumps/Get Off with Me/Gimme a Pigfoot/He's a Good Meat Cutter/I Ain't Going to Sell You None/ Rollin' Mill Blues/Scoop It/Skrontch/Stevedore Man/Take Me for a Buggy Ride/When Your Man Is Going to Put You Down/Wilson Dam/Your Kitchen Floor Is Plenty Good for Me

GRAY, *"Blind"* **ARVELLA**
Born: Jan 28, 1906, Somerville (Burleson Co), TX
Died: Sept 7, 1980, Chicago, IL
Inst: Guitar

Courtesy Living Blues *Magazine*

Father was Tom Allen, mother was Dora Dickerson; reportedly born Walter Dixon; one of 8 children; worked outside music (as farm hand) from age of 4; unschooled and ran away from home after death of mother, 1919; hoboed extensively working outside music (as plantation worker/levee camp worker/factory worker/construction worker/gandy-dancer on B&O railroad/others) through Texas into 20s; toured w Ringling Brothers Circus working outside music (as roustabout) across US through 20s; lost eyesight and two fingers of left hand due to shotgun accident in Peoria, IL, 1930, and was institutionalized; ran away to Chicago, IL, to learn guitar and work for tips on Maxwell Street/buses/trains/streetcars from early 30s; continued to travel widely working as street singer for tips at Kentucky Derby, Louisville, KY, and other points across US from 30s into 60s; worked Univ of Chicago Folkfest, Chicago, IL, early 60s; rec Heritage/Decca labels, Chicago, 1960; frequently app on local radio/TV programs, Chicago, from early 60s; worked Limelight Theater, Chicago, 1962; app in film short AND THIS IS FREE, 1963; formed/rec on own Gray label, Chicago, c1965; narrated UK film documentary BLUES LIKE SHOWERS OF RAIN, 1970; worked Alice's Revisited, Chicago, 1970; continued working streets/shopping centers/buses/bus stops frequently w sister Clara Alma Allen ("Granny") Littricebey/Moody Jones/others, Chicago, through 70s; rec Birch label, Harvey, IL, 1972; worked college circuit concert dates in early 70s; Univ of Wisconsin, Madison, WI, 1973; app in film SAVE THE CHILDREN, 1973; frequently worked streets of San Francisco, CA, 1974; worked Juicy John Pink's Coffeehouse, DeKalb, IL, 1974; Two Fools Club, DeKalb, 1975; app in film MAXWELL STREET BLUES, 1980; died of cancer; buried Restvale Cemetery, Worth, IL

Personal: Reportedly changed name after leaving Institution for the Blind in early 30s

Quote: "Arvella's a folk singer with a head full of stories"—Cary Baker, Birch album 60091

Reference: Living Blues, Winter 1972, pp 32-3

GRAY, HENRY
(*aka:* Little Henry)

Photo by Norbert Hess

Born: Jan 19, 1925, Kenner (Jefferson Parish), LA
Inst: Organ/Piano

Raised on farm near Alsen, LA, from infancy; interested in music early and taught self piano at 8 years of age; frequently played in local churches in area through 30s; served in US Army in early 40s; settled in Chicago, IL, to work w Little Hudson's Red Devil Trio in local club dates in area, 1946-9; frequently worked w Little Walter group in local gigs, Chicago, 1950; w Jimmy Rogers group in local clubs, Chicago, 1951; worked Upstairs Lounge, Chicago, 1951; teamed w Morris Pejoe working local gigs, Chicago, 1952-6; rec as sideman w Junior Wells Eagle Rockers,

States label, Chicago, 1953; rec w Morris Pejoe, Checker label, Chicago, 1954; rec w Dusty Brown, Parrot label, Chicago, 1955; extensive touring w Howlin' Wolf Band as sideman working clubs/recording dates out of Chicago, 1956-68; worked extensively as session man for many bluesmen including Jimmy Reed/Billy Boy Arnold/others, Chicago, through 60s; returned to Alsen, LA, to work outside music with occasional dates in local bars/lounges from 1969; rec Arhoolie/Excello labels, Baton Rouge, LA, 1970; worked w Henry Gray Cats, New Orleans Jazz & Heritage Festival, New Orleans, LA, 1974/6-7; toured Germany/Belgium/Holland working concert dates, 1977; rec Bluebeat label, Ger, 1977; worked R&B Festival, Groningen, Netherlands, 1978

Songs: The Blues Won't Let Me Take My Rest/Can't Last Too Long/Cold Chills/Gray's Bounce/Lucky Lucky Man/Showers of Rain/You're My Midnight Dream

Infl by: Big Maceo Merriweather/Roosevelt Sykes

Quote: "Henry successfully amalgamate[s] his wild, tough Chicago blues background with the voluptuous indolence of Louisiana blues to create a fascinating explosive sound of his own"—Robert Sacre, *Living Blues* magazine, May/Jun 1977, p 32

Reference: Blues Unlimited magazine (UK), Jul 1970, pp 6-9

GREEN, CLARENCE *"Candy"/"Galveston"*

Born: Mar 15, 1929, Galveston Is (Galveston Co) TX
Died: Apr 3, 1988, Galveston, TX
Inst: Piano

Mother was Viola Bell, a pianist; taught self piano as child; frequently worked local honky-tonks for tips, Galveston, TX, early 40s; served in Merchant Marine travelling to Europe/Asia, 1945-8; worked local club dates with own band, Galveston, 1947; returned to Galveston to app on local DJ show, KGBC-radio, Galveston, 1948; rec Eddie's label, Houston, TX, 1948; toured as single working bars/gambling joints through Texas/Louisiana, late 40s; rec Peacock label, Houston, 1950; served in US Army, 1951-3; rec Essex/Monarch labels, Houston, 1952; worked w Paul Love Band in local club dates, Mexico City, Mexico, 1954; owned/managed/performed at Echo Club, Mexico City, 1954-8; rec Chess label, Houston, 1959; toured as single in Copenhagen, Denmark/Oslo, Norway/Helsinki, Finland/elsewhere to 1964; worked w Leo Wright's Band in local clubs, Berlin, Ger, 1964-5; rec Supraphon label, Berlin, Ger (?), c1965; continued touring as single through Europe with occasional return trips to Galveston, 1966-72; frequently worked outside music during 60s; operated bar in Palma de Mallorca, Spain, 1969; worked Laurita's Club, London, Eng, 1973; toured as single through Scandinavian countries, 1973; settled in Galveston, TX, c1974; worked clubs/concerts in Houston, TX, from 1975; worked Galveston Col, Galveston, 1976; Hyatt Regency Hotel, Houston, 1976; sat-in w Caroline Jones, Astrodome Holiday Inn, Houston, 1976; Harrigan's, Houston, 1976; Danny Boy's, Houston, 1976; residency at Warners, Galveston, 1977; toured concerts/clubs in Europe, 1978; extended residence at the Wentletrap Restaurant, Galveston, TX, 1979; died of diabetic coma; buried locally

Photo by Norbert Hess

Personal: No relation to guitarists Clarence Green/Cal Green. Name "Candy" refers to his reputation as a ladies' man

Songs: Galveston/Green's Bounce/Thunder and Lightning

Infl by: Charles Brown

Quote: "Candy is a pianist with real class, playing and

singing with relaxed assurance a mixed bag of Texas blues and boogies . . ."—Mike Leadbitter, *Blues Unlimited* magazine (UK), Oct 1973, p 37

Reference: Jazz Journal magazine (UK), Jul 1973, pp 22-3

GREEN, CORNELIUS
(aka: Lonesome Sundown)

Photo by Frank Scott

Born: Dec 12, 1928, Donaldsonville (Rice Parish), LA
Inst: Guitar/Piano

One of 12 children; taught self piano while still in school, mid-40s; moved to New Orleans, LA, to work outside music from 1948; took some guitar lessons, 1950; moved to Jeanerette, LA, to work outside music, 1952; went to Port Arthur, TX, to work outside music with occasional local gigs from 1953; worked w Clifton Chenier Band, Blue Moon Club, Port Arthur, 1955; toured w Clifton Chenier Band working dances/parties through South to West Coast, 1955; worked w Clifton Chenier Band, 5-4 Ballroom, Los Angeles, CA, 1955; rec w Clifton Chenier Band, Specialty label, Los Angeles, 1955; settled in Opelousas, LA, to work w Lloyd Reynaud Trio in local club dates, 1955; frequently worked Domino's Lounge, Eunice, LA, mid-50s; frequently rec Excello label, Crowley, LA, 1956-65; formed own 5-piece combo working local club dates in Opelousas, LA, area through 50s; frequently worked outside music with occasional local club dates, Opelousas, early 60s; worked Twist City Club, Chicago, IL, c1964; joined Apostolic Church and continued outside music work, Opelousas, from 1965; rec Joliet label, Los Angeles, 1977; worked The Bluebird, Santa Barbara, CA, 1977

Personal: Married (1955—separated). 7 children

Songs: Do What You Did/Gonna Stick to You Baby/Hoodoo Woman Blues/I Had a Dream Last Night/I Woke Up Cryin'/I'm a Mojo Man/I'm Glad She's Mine/If You See My Baby/Learn to Treat Me Better/Leave My Money Alone/Lonesome Lonely Blues/Lost Without Love/Love Me Now/Please Be on That 519/When I Had I Didn't Need

Infl to: Phillip Walker

Quote: "As a blues singer Lonesome Sundown has few equals. He has a rich, strong voice—not frantic but intense"—Bruce Bromberg, Excello album 8012

Reference: Blues Unlimited magazine (UK), Feb 1971, pp 5-6

GREEN, LILLIAN *"Lil"*
Born: Dec 22, 1919, Mississippi
Died: Apr 14, 1954, Chicago, IL

Father was Elias Johnson; mother was Ida Crocket; one of 10 children; after death of parents left home to work outside music from c1929; settled in Chicago, IL, to attend school with frequent work at local school concerts from c1934; dropped out of school to work as singing waitress in local clubs, Chicago, late 30s; worked All Star Club, Chicago, late 30s; Manchester Grill, Chicago, c1940; rec w Bill Broonzy, Bluebird label, Chicago, 1940-5; worked 308 Club, Chicago, 1941; toured w Bill Broonzy/Tiny Bradshaw Orch working dance dates in Detroit, MI/Chicago, IL, and through South, 1941-2; frequently worked w Tiny Bradshaw Orch, Apollo Theater, NYC, NY, 1941-6; worked Savoy Ballroom, NYC, 1942; Cafe Society, NYC, c1942; w Tiny Bradshaw Orch, Plantation Club, St Louis, MO, c1943; Lido Ballroom, NYC, 1943; w Tiny Bradshaw Orch, Elks Ball, The Gardens, Pittsburgh, PA, 1943; Tic Toc Club, Boston, MA, 1943; Royal Theater, Baltimore, MD, 1944; toured w Luis Russell Orch on 3-Star package revue working one-nighters/clubs/theaters in Cleveland, OH/Youngstown, OH/Chattanooga, TN/elsewhere, 1944; worked Regal Theater, Chicago, 1944; rec w Howard Callender Orch, Victor label, Chicago, 1946-7; worked Club De Lisa/Chez Paree, Chicago, late 40s; rec Aladdin label, Chicago, 1949; rec Atlantic label, Chicago, 1951; inactive due to illness in early 50s; died at home of bronchial pneumonia; buried Oak Hill Cemetery, Gary, IN

Songs: Knockin' Myself Out/Now What Do You Think?/Romance in the Dark

Quotes: ". . . a beautiful jazz and blues singer . . . she had a superb sense of timing"—Derrick Stewart-Baxter, *Jazz Journal* magazine (UK), Feb 1972, p 25

"A wonderful entertainer"—Little Brother

Lillian "Lil" Green
Courtesy Frank Driggs Collection

Montgomery, *Jazz Journal* magazine (UK), Feb 1972, pp 25

References: Jazz Journal magazine (UK), Feb 1972, pp 25, 39

Encyclopedia of Pop, Rock & Soul, Irwin Stambler, St Martin's Press, 1974

GREEN, NORMAN G *"Slim"*
(aka: Guitar Slim)
Born: Jul 25, 1907, Bryan (Brazos Co), TX
Died: Sept 28, 1975, Los Angeles, CA
Inst: Guitar

Father was Eli Green; moved to Christie, OK, as youth where he worked outside music; learned guitar and frequently worked local parties/suppers in area from c1935; moved to Las Vegas, NV, where he worked outside music from early 40s; moved to West Coast working outside music with occasional local parties, Los Angeles, CA, from 1947; rec J&M Fulbright label, Los Angeles, 1948; rec Murray label, Los Angeles, 1948; moved to Fresno, CA, to work outside music through 50s; moved to Los Angeles to work outside music from 1957; rec Dig label, Los Angeles, 1957; rec Canton label, Los Angeles, c1957; worked McDaniel's Lounge, Houston, TX, 1965; Nola's, Houston, 1968; rec Geenote label, Los Angeles (?), 1968; worked small clubs in Los Angeles area, late 60s; rec w Johnny Otis group, Kent label, Los Angeles, 1970; frequently worked local bars, Las Vegas, NV, into 70s; entered Martin Luther King Jr General Hospital where he died of cancer; buried Angeles Abbey Cemetery, Los Angeles, CA

Personal: Not to be confused with Eddie Jones/Alexander Seward who have also used pseudonym "Guitar Slim"

Songs: Big Fine Thing/Bumble Bee Blues/Fifth Street Alley Blues/Make Love All Night/My Little Angel Child/Old Folks Boogie/Play On Little Girl/Shake 'em Up/You Make Me Feel So Good

Photo by Frank Scott

Infl by: Aaron "T-Bone" Walker

Reference: Blues Unlimited magazine (UK), Jun 1969, p 11

GREEN, ROSA
(see Henderson, Rosa)

GREEN, SADIE
(see Brown, Bessie)

GREEN, VIOLET
(see Smith, Clara)

GRIFFITH, SHIRLEY
Born: Apr 26, 1908, Brandon (Rankin Co), MS
Died: Jun 18, 1974, Indianapolis, IN
Inst: Guitar

Father was Willie Griffith; mother was Maggie McDonald; moved to Fannin, MS, to work outside music from childhood while briefly attending school; interested in music early and learned guitar from an aunt and uncle at age of 10; moved to Jackson, MS, to work outside music c1925; learned some guitar from Tommy Johnson c1926; moved to Indianapolis, IN, to work outside music with occasional gigs w Scrapper Blackwell at local parties/clubs/taverns, 1928 into 70s; rec Bluesville label, Indianapolis, 1961; toured w Yank Rachell working club dates on East Coast, 1968; worked Ann Arbor Blues Festival, Ann Arbor, MI, 1969; Notre Dame Blues Festival, South Bend, IN, 1971; Univ of Iowa, Iowa City, IA, 1973; rec Blue Goose label, NYC, NY (?), 1973; died of heart disease; buried Crown Hill Cemetery, Indianapolis, IN

Note: This is a male singer

Songs: "A" Jump/Bad Luck Blues/Bright Street Jump/Cool Kind Papa from New Orleans/Delta Haze Blues/Flying Eagle Blues/Going Away Blues/Indiana Avenue Blues/King of Spades/River Line Blues/Shaggy Hound Blues/Walkin' Blues

Infl by: Scrapper Blackwell/Ishmon Bracey/Tommy Johnson

Quote: "Shirley's controlled and expressive voice and his consummate mastery of the guitar enable him to perform well many kinds of blues"—Arthur Rosenbaum, Bluesville album 1087

GROSS, LEON T
(*aka:* Archibald/Archie Boy)
Born: Sept 14, 1912, New Orleans (Orleans Parish), LA
Died: Jan 1973, New Orleans, LA
Inst: Piano

Interested in music at early age and learned piano as child; worked outside music with frequent entertaining at local parties/fraternity houses, New Orleans, LA, through 20s/30s; served in US Army in Bombay, India, early 40s; returned to New Orleans to work local clubs/bars in French Quarter from c1945; rec Imperial/Colony labels, New Orleans, 1950; rec Imperial label, New Orleans, 1952; extended residency at Poodle Patio Club, New Orleans, through 60s; worked Nero's Club, Chicago, IL, 1968; frequently worked w Smilin' Joe at Court of Two Sisters, New Orleans, late 60s; died of heart attack

Songs: Balling with Archie/Little Miss Muffet/Scattered Everywhere/Shake Baby Shake/Stack-o-Lee

Infl by: Burnell Santiago/Isidoe "Tuts" Washington

Infl to: James Booker/Fats Domino/Dr John/Huey Smith/Alan Toussaint

Quote: "Archibald was one of the last in the long line of traditional New Orleans pianist entertainers"—John Broven, *Walking to New Orleans*, Blues Unlimited, 1974

Reference: Blues Unlimited magazine (UK), Oct 1970, pp 9-10

GUESNON, *"Creole"* **GEORGE** *"Curly"*
(aka: Creole Gayno)

Courtesy The Al Rose Collection, Tulane University Library

Born: May 25, 1907, New Orleans (Orleans Parish), LA
Died: May 5, 1968, New Orleans, LA
Inst: Banjo/Guitar/Trumpet/Ukulele

Father was George Guesnon Sr; mother was Marie Blache; raised in New Orleans, LA, working outside music as boy; first instrument was toy ukulele which he taught self to play c1918; worked outside music (as father's apprentice), New Orleans, 1923-7; worked w Kid Clayton's Happy Pals, Hummingbird Cabaret, New Orleans, 1927-8; learned banjo while working in Kid Clayton's Band with some later lessons from John Marrero; frequently sat-in w Kid Rena/Buddy Petit/Chris Kelly/other bands, in local clubs, New Orleans, 1927-8; worked w Papa Celestin's Tuxedo Orch at local dances, New Orleans area, 1928; w Willie Pajeaud Band, Alamo Ballroom, New Orleans, 1929; w Sam Morgan's Jazz Band at local dances with frequent tours through South, 1930-5; w Lou Johnson's Californians working clubs out of Monroe, LA, 1935; toured w Little Brother Montgomery's Southland Troubadors Orch out of Jackson, MS, 1935-6; rec w Little Brother Montgomery, Bluebird label, New Orleans, 1936; toured w FS Wolcott's Rabbit Foot Minstrels (as banjo soloist) working shows through Delta area, 1936-8; settled in New Orleans to work in local bands, 1938-40; rec Decca label, NYC, NY, 1940; rec (as "Creole Gayno") Lissen label, NYC, c1940; worked outside music in New Orleans, 1941-2; served in US Merchant Marine, 1942-6; returned to New Orleans to work mostly as sideman in local bands from 1946; rec w Kid Thomas Algiers Stompers, American Music label, New Orleans, 1951; rec w Emile Barnes Storyville Ramblers (unissued label), New Orleans, 1951; rec w Kid Clayton's Band, Folkways label, New Orleans, 1952; worked w Percy Humphrey's Band, Mardi Gras Lounge, New Orleans, 1953; w Kid Howard group, Childs Restaurant, NYC, c1954; toured w George Lewis Band working concert dates across US, 1955-6; rec w George Lewis New Orleans Band, Blue Note label, Hackensack, NJ, 1955; app on ART FORD'S JAZZ PARTY, WNTA-TV, NYC, NY, 1958; rec solo and w New Orleans Stompers, Icon label, New Orleans, 1959; rec w Kid Thomas Creole Jazz Band, 77/Arhoolie labels, New Orleans, 1959; rec New Orleans Jazz Society label, New Orleans, 1959; worked w Kid Thomas Algiers Stompers at local dances, New Orleans, 1960; rec w Kid Thomas Creole Jazz Band, Icon label, New Orleans, 1960; rec (solo) on Jazz Crusade label, New Orleans, 1960; rec Arhoolie label, New Orleans, 1960; rec w Jim Robinson's New Orleans Band, Riverside label, New Orleans, 1961; frequently worked w Kid Clayton's Happy Pals Band in local club dates, New Orleans area, from early 60s; worked frequently as music teacher in New Orleans from early 60s; app on DAVID BRINKLEY'S JOURNAL, NBC-TV, 1961; frequently worked w own band (or as sideman), Preservation Hall, New Orleans, c1961-5 (por rel Atlantic label); rec Icon label, New Orleans, 1961-2; rec w Kid Howard Band, Music of New Orleans label, New Orleans, 1962; rec 77/Music of New Orleans/San Jacinto labels, New Orleans, 1963; app on NEW ORLEANS JAZZ, PBS-TV, 1964 (por rel New Orleans Rarities label); rec w Kid Howard New Orleans Jazz Band, Nobility label, New Orleans, 1964; rec w Jim Robinson New Orleans Band, GHB/Pearl labels, New Orleans, 1964; worked w George Lewis/Keith Smith group, San Jacinto Hall, New Orleans, 1965 (por rel 77 label); rec w Percy Humphrey Crescent City Joymakers, Pearl label, New Orleans, 1965; rec GHB/Jazz Crusade labels, New Orleans, 1965; mostly inactive in music in New Orleans from 1965; app w Kid Sheik Cola Band in US Information film (unknown title), 1967 (shown on local TV show, Japan/por rel [unissued] label); died of natural causes; buried St Louis No 2 Cemetery, New Orleans, LA

Personal: Married. 1 daughter. Frequently sang in Gombo French dialect

Billing: Banjo King of the Southland

Songs: Goodbye Good Luck to You/Iberville and Franklin/King Zulu/Last Go-Round Blues/Sunflower Country Blues

Quote: "When Creole George sings the blues, his guitar playing is corollary in the tradition of the country blues singer"—Grayson Mills, Icon album LP-1

Reference: Storyville magazine (UK), Aug 1968, pp 17-22

GUITAR EDDY
(see Clearwater, Eddy)

GUITAR JR
(see Brooks, Lonnie)

GUITAR NUBBITT
(see Hankerson, Alvin)

GUITAR PETE
(see Franklin, Pete)

GUITAR RED
(see Minter, Iverson)

GUITAR SHORTY
(see Fortescue, John Henry)

GUITAR SLIM
(see Green, Norman)
(see Jones, Eddie)
(see Seward, Alexander)

GUNTER, ARTHUR NEAL
Born: May 23, 1926, Nashville (Davidson Co), TN
Died: Mar 16, 1976, Port Huron, MI
Inst: Guitar

Father William Gunter was preacher; mother was Fannie Morrison; one of at least 3 children; raised in Nashville, TN, and formed family gospel group The Gunter Brothers to work local churches as youth; learned guitar from older brother Larry Gunter as youth; rec w The Leapfrogs (as sideman), Excello label, Nashville, 1954; moved to Port Huron, MI, c1955; frequently rec w Kid King Combo, Excello label, Nashville, 1955-61; frequently toured w Kid

Photo by Norbert Hess

King Combo, working club dates through South, late 50s into 60s; worked The Hilltop, Little Rock, AR, late 50s; worked mostly outside music in Port Huron, MI, area, 1966 into 70s; worked local rock festival, Port Huron, 1973; Ann Arbor Blues Festival, Ann Arbor, MI, 1973; won Michigan State lottery and inactive in music thereafter, 1973-6; died at home of pneumonia; buried Caswell Cemetery, Kimball, MI

Personal: Frequently worked gigs with brother "Little" Al Gunter, musician

Songs: Baby Can't You See/Baby Let's Play House/Blues After Hours/I Want Her Back/Ludella/No Naggin' No Draggin'/She's Mine All Mine/Working for My Baby

Infl by: Larry Gunter/Blind Boy Fuller/BB King/Jimmy Reed

Quote: "Arthur had a pleasant, forthright nature, a smoky, appealing voice, and a pure, simple country blues guitar style, as well as a talent for song writing" —Jim O'Neal, *Living Blues* magazine, May 1976, p 9

References: Blues Unlimited magazine (UK), Feb 1971, p 12
Living Blues magazine, May 1976, p 9

GUTHRIE, WOODROW WILSON *"Woody"*
Born: Jul 14, 1912, Okemah (Okfuskee Co), OK
Died: Oct 3, 1967, Queens, NY
Inst: Fiddle/Guitar/Harmonica/Mandolin

Woodrow "Woody" Guthrie *Courtesy Frank Driggs Collection*

Father was Charles Edward Guthrie, a singing guitarist/banjoist; mother was Nora Belle Tanner; one of 5 children; sang/danced for pennies on streets as child, Okemah, OK; frequently worked outside music in Okemah area, 1922-8; left home to hobo to Galveston/Houston, TX, area to work outside music with frequent work in local saloons/barber shops/shine stands/pool halls/streets for tips from 1929; settled w uncle Jeff Guthrie, Pampa, TX, c1929; taught self guitar to tour w Jeff Guthrie/Jack Guthrie (cousin) in travelling magic show working rodeos/fairs/carnivals/parades/ranch parties/dances in Pampa, TX, area, 1931-2; worked outside music (with frequent hobo trips to West), Pampa area, through 30s; hoboed to Los Angeles, CA, to work outside music, 1937; teamed w Jack Guthrie to work Radio Stars Jamboree, Shrine Auditorium, Los Angeles, 1937; Grand Theater, Long Beach, CA, 1937; app w Jack Guthrie on own shows, KFVD-radio, Los Angeles, 1937; teamed w Lefty Lou Crissman (female singer) to app on own WOODY AND LEFTY LOU Show, KFVD-radio, Los Angeles, 1937-8; app briefly w Lefty Lou, XELO-radio, Tijuana, Mexico, c1938; app w Lefty Lou (and solo), KFVD-radio, Los Angeles, 1938-9; frequently entertained at migrant labor camps on West Coast, 1938; wrote daily "Woody Sez" column (with own sketches) for *People's Daily World* newspaper, 1939-41; toured w actor Will Geer/singer Cisco Houston to entertain migratory workers/farm pickers/strikers at benefits/union forums/rallies/picnics/picket lines and others through California from 1939; hoboed east to work solo in local taverns/bars/flophouses/IWO lodges/folk-social gatherings, NYC, NY, from 1940; contributed articles to *The Daily Worker* newspaper, NYC, c1940; worked benefit, Mecca Temple, NYC, 1940; app on PURSUIT OF HAPPINESS, CBS-radio, 1940; app on SCHOOL OF THE AIR, CBS-radio, 1940; app on ADVENTURES IN MUSIC, WNYC-radio, NYC, 1940; app w Leadbelly on FOLK SONGS OF AMERICA, WNYC-radio, NYC, 1940; app on CAVALCADE OF AMERICA, NBC-radio, 1940; app on WE THE PEOPLE, CBS-radio, 1940; app on PIPE SMOKING TIME, CBS-radio, 1940; app on AMERICAN MUSIC FESTI-

VALS, WNYC-radio, NYC, 1940; app on BACK WHERE I COME FROM, CBS-radio, 1940; rec w Leadbelly, Biograph label, NYC, 1940; rec extensively for Library of Congress label, Washington, DC, 1940; teamed w Pete Seeger to tour migrant camps/union meetings through South/Midwest, 1940; rec Victor label, NYC, c1941; hoboed as itinerant musician with frequent outside music work through South/West c1941; worked as song writer for Bonneville Power Administration, 1941 (some songs used in film THE COLUMBIA, 1948); rec w Almanac Singers, General Records label, NYC, 1941; toured w Almanac Singers/Pete Seeger working union halls/meetings/picnics/farm-factory worker groups/parties across US, 1941-2; toured w Pete Seeger working West Coast into Mexico, 1941; frequently worked w Headline Singers (including Leadbelly/Sonny Terry/Brownie McGhee/others) at local houseparties/hootenannies/lofts in NYC area, 1942-3; app w Pete Seeger on Office of War Information (OWI) radio broadcasts c1942; contributed article to *New York Times* newspaper, NYC, 1943; served frequently w Cisco Houston in Merchant Marine in Africa/Sicily/United Kingdom, 1943-5; worked w Almanac Singers in NYC area c1944-5; rec w Sonny Terry, Asch label, NYC, 1944; served in US Army where he frequently entertained at military camps in US, 1945; rec Asch label, NYC, 1946; formed Woody Guthrie Singers (including Sonny Terry/Brownie McGhee) working lofts/hoots/parties in NYC area c1946; served on executive committee of People's Songs (a songwriters' cooperative), NYC, c1946-9; worked w Josh White, Town Hall, NYC, 1946; settled in Brooklyn, NY, c1946; app in Alan Lomax OWI film short TO HEAR YOUR BANJO PLAY, 1947; worked Central Plaza, NYC, 1949; briefly attended Brooklyn Col, Brooklyn, NY, 1950; worked Leadbelly Memorial Concert, Town Hall, NYC, 1950; continued to work/tour at rallies/folk meets/worker groups for sociopolitical/union/conservational causes across US c1951-4; rec w Sonny Terry, Stinson/Archive of Folk Music labels, NYC, 1952; frequently worked Washington Square Park, NYC, mid-50s; mostly inactive in music due to illness from c1955; app on Oscar Brand's FOLKSONG FESTIVAL, WNYC-radio, NYC, late 50s; frequently hospitalized through 50s into 60s; entered Creedmore State Hospital where he died of Huntington's chorea, a hereditary nervous disease; buried Greenwood Cemetery, Brooklyn, NY; memorial concerts were held in Carnegie Hall, NYC, 1968, and Hollywood Bowl, Hollywood, CA, 1970; film biography BOUND FOR GLORY was released in 1976

Personal: Married Mary Esta Jennings (1933-41), 3 children; married Marjorie Mazie Greenblatt (1945-c53), 4 children; married Anneka Louise Van Kirk (c1954-). His son Arlo Davy Guthrie (born 1947) and daughter Noralee Guthrie (born 1950) are singers/musicians

Books: *Bound for Glory* (autobiography), Woody Guthrie, EP Dutton & Company, 1943

American Folksong: Woody Guthrie, Disc Company of America, 1947

California to the New York Island (song collection), Guthrie Children's Trust Fund, 1958-60

Ballads of Sacco and Vanzetti, Woody Guthrie, Oak Publications, 1960

Woody Guthrie Folk Songs: A Collection of Songs by America's Foremost Balladeer, Pete Seeger, Ludlow Music, 1963

Born to Win (collection prose/poems), Robert Shelton (ed), Macmillan Company, 1965

A Woody Guthrie Bibliography 1912-1967, Richard Reuss (ed), Woody Guthrie Publications, 1968

A Mighty Hard Road, Henrietta Yurchenco, McGraw-Hill Company, 1970

A Tribute to Woody Guthrie, Guthrie/Lampell/Wood, Ludlow Music, 1972

Woody Sez (Articles from "People's World," 1939-40), Grosset & Dunlap, 1975

Seeds of Man, William Doerflinger (ed), EP Dutton & Company, 1976

The Woody Guthrie Songbook, Harold Leventhal/Marjorie Guthrie (eds), Grosset & Dunlap, 1976

Songs: Ain't a Gonna Do/At My Window/Ballad of Harriet Tubman/Ballad of Harry Bridges/Been in Jail/The Biggest Thing That Man Has Ever Done/Blowing Down This Old Dusty Road/Boomtown Bill/Dead from the Dust/Deportee/The Do-Re-Mi/Dust Bowl Refugee/Dust Pneumonia Blues/The Dying Miner/The Ferguson Brother's Killing/Go and Leave Me/Good Night Little Arlo/Good Old Union Feeling/Gotta Get to Boston/Grand Coulee Dam/The Great Dust Storm/The Great Historical Bum/Hang Knot/Hard Travelling/Hooversville/I Ain't Got No Home in This World Anymore/Jesus Christ/The Ludlow Massacre/The Mound of Your Grave/The 1913 Massacre/Oklahoma Hills/Old Army Mule/On My Way/Pastures of Plenty/Philadelphia Lawyer/Plane Wreck at Los Gatos/Pretty Boy Floyd/Reuben James/Roll On Columbia/Round Round Hitler's Grave/Share Cropper Song/So Long It's Been Good to Know You/Talking Columbia (Blues)/Talking Dust Bowl Blues/Talking Miner/Talking Subway Blues/This

Land Is Your Land/Tom Joad/Union Maid/Waiting at the Gate/What Shall It Profit a Man?

Awards/Honors: Awarded Conservation Service Award by US Department of Interior, 1966

Won American Music Conference National Music Award, 1976

Infl by: Jeff Guthrie/Leadbelly

Infl to: Eric Anderson/Joan Baez/Len Chandler/Judy Collins/Bob Dylan/Jack Elliott/Arlo Guthrie/Phil Ochs/Tom Paxton/Mark Spolestra

Quotes: "He was a master of the subtleties of creating and performing talking blues in the best folk tradition"—Jerry Silverman, *Folk Blues*, The Macmillan Company, 1958

"The best folk-ballad composer whose identity has ever been known"—(Alan Lomax) John Greenway, *American Folksongs of Protest*, Univ of Pennsylvania Press, 1953

"He was an authentic American genius, a common man with uncommon gifts. In his songs and writings he combined country wit, pioneer traditions, and colorful and unhackneyed country language with a skilled writer's art. He represents, better than anyone else, the human unity of rural and urban America"—Henrietta Yurchenco, *A Mighty Hard Road*, McGraw-Hill Company, 1970

References: *A Mighty Hard Road*, Henrietta Yurchenco, McGraw-Hill Company, 1970

Woody Guthrie and Me, Ed Robbin, 1979

Woody Guthrie: A Life, Joe Klein, c1980

Pastures of Plenty: A Self Portrait, Dave Marsh/Harold Leventhal, 1990

GUY, GEORGE *"Buddy"*
(aka: Buddy Boy)
Born: Jul 30, 1936, Lettsworth (Pointe Coupee Parish), LA
Inst: Guitar

Father Sam Guy; mother Isabell Toliver; made own guitar at 13 years of age; taught self guitar and worked

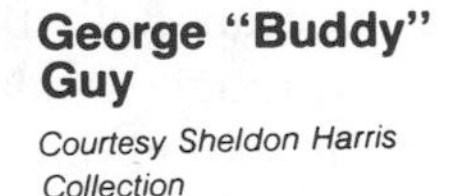

George "Buddy" Guy

Courtesy Sheldon Harris Collection

occasional weekend gigs in area with some outside music work from c1953; worked as sideman in Big Poppa John Tilley Band, Baton Rouge, LA, area, c1953; frequently gigged/sat-in w Lightnin' Slim/Lazy Lester/Slim Harpo/others in local clubs, Baton Rouge area, through 50s; moved to Chicago, IL, to work outside music with frequent local gigs from 1957; sat-in w Otis Rush, 708 Club, Chicago, 1957; w own trio, 708 Club, Chicago, 1957; w Rufus Foreman Band, Squeeze Club, Chicago, 1957-8; frequently worked Theresa's Lounge, Chicago, 1958-70; w BB King, Trianon Ballroom, Chicago, 1958; won "Battle of Blues" over Magic Sam/Otis Rush/Junior Wells at Blue Flame Club, Chicago, 1958; rec w Magic Sam, Cobra label, Chicago, 1958; rec w own band, Artistic label, Chicago, 1958; frequently worked local club dates, Gary, IN, area, late 50s to early 60s; rec w Willie Dixon, Chess label, Chicago, 1960-7; worked Club Tay May, Chicago, 1960; frequently worked as house guitarist for Chess label, Chicago, from 1960; rec Argo label, Chicago, 1963; worked w Guitar Jr Band, Curley's Bar, Chicago, 1964; Big John's, Chicago, 1965; toured w American Folk Blues Festival working concert dates through England/Europe, 1965-7 (por 1965 Hamburg, Ger, concert rel Fontana label); rec acc to Big Mama Thornton, Arhoolie label, London, Eng, 1965; rec w Jr Wells, Vanguard label, Chicago, 1965; frequently worked as team w Jr Wells from c1966; worked w Jr Wells, Pepper's Lounge, Chicago, 1966-8 (por rel Vanguard label); worked Club Alex, Chicago, 1966; Univ of Chicago, Chicago, 1966; The Riverboat, Toronto, Can, 1967-9; The Avalon, San Francisco, CA, 1967; Mariposa Folk Festival, Toronto, 1967; rec w Jr Wells, Atlantic label, Chicago, c1968; rec w Otis Spann, Vanguard label, Chicago, 1968; worked Univ of Chicago R&B Festival, Chicago, 1968; app on CAMERA THREE (ep: Really the Country Blues), CBS-TV, 1968; worked The Generation, NYC, NY, 1968; Philadelphia Folk Festival, Schwenksville, PA, 1968; Newport Folk Festival, Newport, RI, 1968; Central Park Music Festival, NYC, 1968; Canadian National Exhibition, Toronto, Can, 1968; Club 47, Cambridge, MA, 1968; The Scene, NYC, NY, 1968; The Fillmore West, San Francisco, 1968-70; New Orleans House, Berkeley, CA, 1968 (por rel Vanguard label); Village Gate, NYC, 1969; rec Vanguard label, NYC, 1969; app on local TV programs, London, Eng, 1969; worked Main Point, Bryn Mawr, PA, 1969; toured for US State Department working concert dates through central/east Africa, 1969; worked Ann Arbor Blues Festival, Ann Arbor, MI, 1969-70; app on local program, WXPN-FM radio, Philadelphia, PA, 1969; worked Kinetic Playground, Chicago, IL, 1969; The Pavilion, NYC, 1969; State Univ of New York, Buffalo, NY, 1969; Laurel Pop Festival, Laurel, MD, 1969; Sky River Rock Festival, Tenino, WA, 1969; Lennie's, Boston, MA, 1969; Monterey Jazz Festival, Monterey, CA, 1969; The New Thing, Washington, DC, 1969; Auditorium Theater, Chicago, 1969; toured w Canadian Festival Express Show working concert dates through Canada, 1970; worked w Lonnie Johnson, Massey Hall, Toronto, Can, 1970; rec Atco label, Miami, FL, 1970; rec w Jr Wells, Delmark label, Chicago, c1970; app in film THE BLUES IS ALIVE AND WELL IN CHICAGO, 1970; worked Pepper's Lounge, Chicago, 1970; The Berkey, Boston, MA, 1970; toured w The Rolling Stones working concert dates through Europe, 1970; rec w Memphis Slim, Barclay label, Herouville, France, 1970; worked Palais Des Sports, Paris, France, 1970; Fillmore East, NYC, 1970; Washington Blues Festival, Howard Univ, Washington, DC, 1970; Five Stages, Chicago, 1970; app in UK film SUPERSHOW, 1970; app in UK film CHICAGO BLUES, 1970 (shown on OMNIBUS, BBC-1-TV, London, Eng, 1971); worked Notre Dame Blues Festival, South Bend, IN, 1971; owned/worked Checkerboard Lounge, Chicago, 1972-9; owned/worked Buddie's Club, Chicago, 1972; clip shown in French film BLUES UNDER THE SKIN, 1972; app in French film OUT OF THE BLACKS INTO THE BLUES (pt 2: A Way to Escape the Ghetto), 1972; worked Univ of Vermont, Burlington, VT, 1972; rec Atco label, Boston, MA, 1972; toured w American Blues Festival, working concert dates through Australia, 1972; worked Keystone Korner, Berkeley, CA, c1972-4; Minnie's Can-Do, San Francisco, CA, c1973; Sandy's Club, Beverly, MA, 1973-4; Felt Forum, NYC, NY, 1973; El Mocambo Tavern, Toronto, Can, 1973; Sports Arena, Toledo, OH, 1974; Hunter Col, NYC, 1974; Vibes Lounge, Chicago, IL, 1974; Toronto Blues Festival, Olympic Island, Toronto, Can, 1974; Joint Bar, Minneapolis, MN, 1974; Montreux Blues Festival, Montreux, Switzerland, 1974; Newport Jazz Festival, NYC, 1974; app on SOUNDSTAGE, PBS-TV (syndicated), 1975; worked Univ of Miami Blues Festival, Coral Gables, FL, 1975; Univ of North Florida, Jacksonville, FL, 1975; toured w blues package working concert dates through Japan/Europe, 1975; worked Yubin Chokin Hall, Tokyo, Japan, 1975 (por rel Bourbon label); worked Civic Auditorium, Portland, OR, 1975; Univ of Vermont, Burlington, VT, 1975; In Concert Club, Montreal, Can, 1975; Great American Music Hall, San Francisco,

CA, 1976; El Mocambo, Toronto, Can, 1976; Belle Star, Colden, NY, 1976-7; New England Blues Festival, Providence, RI, 1976; Jazz Life Festival, Dortmund, Ger, 1976; The Bottom Line, NYC, 1976; Opry Club, Burlington, VT, 1977; Sandy's Jazz Revival, Beverly, MA, 1977; The Lighthouse, Los Angeles, CA, 1977; Nancy Jazz Festival, Nancy, France, 1977; Cafe Campus, Montreal, Can, 1978; Bottom Line, NYC, 1978

Personal: Married (1959-). 3 children. Brother Philip (Phil) Guy is musician

Songs: A Man and the Blues/A Man of Many Words/Come See About Me/Hold That Plane/I Can't Quit the Blues/I Found a True Love/I Got My Eyes on You/I Had a Dream Last Night/I'm Not the Best/In the Wee Wee Hours/Jam on a Monday Morning/Just Playing My Axe/Leave My Girl Alone/No Lie/Shake It Baby/She Suits Me to a Tee/Slow Slow/Stomach Ache/Stone Crazy/Ten Years Ago/This Old Fool/Watch Yourself/We're Ready/You Were Wrong

Infl by: John Lee Hooker/Lightnin' Hopkins/BB King/Lightnin' Slim/Aaron "T-Bone" Walker

Infl to: Chicago Bob Nelson/Fenton Robinson

Quotes: "A performer who is possibly one of the finest guitarists (of any kind), a magnetic singer, and a consummate showman"—Dick Flohil, *Coda* magazine (Canada), Sept 1967, p 38

"Brilliant guitarist, incredible showman"—*New York Times* newspaper (credit/issue unknown)

References: Living Blues, Summer 1970, pp 3-9

Damn Right I've Got The Blues: Buddy Guy & The Blues Roots of Rock-and-Roll, Donald E. Wilcock/Buddy Guy, Woodford Press, 1993

HALL, VERA
(*aka:* Nora Reed/Vera Hall Ward)

Courtesy Sing Out *Magazine*

Born: c1906, Livingston (Sumter Co), AL
Died: Jan 29, 1964, Tuscaloosa, AL

Born on farm and lived/worked outside music in or about Livingston, AL, almost all of life; rec Library of Congress label, Livingston, 1937/1939-40; rec Folkways label, Livingston, c1948-50; worked Folk Song concert, Columbia Univ, NYC, c1949; rec Atlantic/Prestige labels, Livingston, 1959; active in local Baptist Church in Tuscaloosa-Livingston, AL, area, through 40s/50s/60s; inactive due to illness with loss of eyesight in early 60s; reportedly died Druid City Hospital; buried Livingston Negro Cemetery, Livingston, AL

Personal: Was cousin of Doc Reed. Recorded both secular and religious songs

Infl by: Richard Amerson/Blind Jesse Harris

Quote: "Her singing is like a deep-voiced shepherd's flute, mellow and pure in tone . . ."—Alan Lomax, *The Rainbow Sign,* Duell, Sloan and Pearce, 1959

Reference: The Rainbow Sign, Alan Lomax, Duell, Sloan and Pearce, 1959 (under pseudonym "Nora Reed")

HALLELUJAH JOE
(see McCoy, Joe)

HAM GRAVY
(see Brown, Robert)

HAMFOOT HAM
(see McCoy, Joe)

HAMILTON, GEORGE
(see Davenport, Charles)

HAMMIE
(see Nixon, Hammie)

HAMMOND, JOHN PAUL
Born: Nov 13, 1942, New York (New York Co), NY
Inst: Guitar/Harmonica

Father was John Henry Hammond Jr, noted talent scout/executive/producer/entrepreneur; raised in

Photo by Julie Snow

NYC, NY, where he studied art and sculpture as youth; interested in blues as teenager; learned guitar and harmonica while attending Antioch Col, Yellow Springs, OH, early 60s; worked local coffeehouses, Los Angeles, CA, 1962; rec Vanguard label, NYC (?), 1963-5; worked Club Yana, Boston, MA, 1963; Newport Folk Festival, Newport, RI, 1963-4 (por 1963 concert rel Vanguard label); worked Village Vanguard, NYC, 1964; Gaslight Club, NYC, 1964; Ash Grove, Los Angeles, c1964; Fat Black Pussycat, Lansing, MI, 1965; toured England/Europe working club dates, 1965; app on CLAY COLE R&B Show, local TV, Eng (?), 1965; worked Odyssey Club, Boston, MA, 1965; Village Gate, NYC, 1964-5; Cafe A-Go-Go, NYC, 1965; rec Spivey label, Brooklyn, NY, 1965; worked Massey Hall, Toronto, Can, 1965; Folk Song 65, Carnegie Hall, NYC, 1965; Mooncusser, Martha's Vineyard, MA, 1965; Club 47, Cambridge, MA, 1965; Mariposa Folk Festival, Toronto, Can, 1965; Foghorn, Baltimore, MD, 1966; Gaslight Cafe, NYC, 1967-9; rec Atlantic label, 1967; worked Main Point, Bryn Mawr, PA, 1968; app on PETER MARTIN Show, WPIX-TV, NYC, 1968; worked The Scene, NYC, 1968; Ash Grove, Los Angeles, CA, 1968; Fillmore East, NYC, 1969-70; app on Johnny Carson's TONIGHT Show, NBC-TV, 1969; worked The Riverboat, Toronto, Can, 1969; Guelph Folk Festival, Toronto, Can, 1969; The Matrix, San Francisco, 1969; Second Fret, Philadelphia, PA, 1969; rec ST for film LITTLE BIG MAN, 1970; worked Olympic Auditorium, Los Angeles, 1970; Summerthing Concert, Boston, MA, 1970; directed film short LARRY JOHNSON, 1970; rec w Larry Johnson, Biograph label, NYC, 1971; worked Ash Grove, Los Angeles, 1971; Liberty Hall, Dallas, TX, 1971; rec CBS label, NYC, 1971; worked Gaslight Cafe, NYC, 1971; rec w Mike Bloomfield/Dr John, Columbia label, NYC, 1973; worked Lion's Share, San Anselmo, CA, 1973; Mariposa Folk Festival, Toronto, Can, 1973-4; Capitol Theater, Montreal, Can, 1973; app on SOUNDSTAGE, PBS-TV, 1975; worked Winnipeg Folk Festival, Birds Hill Park, Winnipeg, Can, 1975; Bottom Line, NYC, 1976; Le Coq D'or, Toronto, Can, 1976; Mariposa Folk Festival, Toronto Island, Toronto, 1977; Winnipeg Folk Festival, Winnipeg, 1977; New Yorker Theater, Toronto, 1977; Basin Street Club, Toronto, 1977; McCabe's, Santa Monica, CA, 1977; Theater 1839, San Francisco, CA, 1977; Bottom Line, NYC, 1978

Personal: Married. Has 1 child. Not to be confused with Johnny Hammond, jazz organist

Song: Baby, Won't You Tell Me?

Infl by: John Lee Hooker/Lightnin' Hopkins/Blind Lemon Jefferson/Robert Johnson/Muddy Waters/Big Joe Williams

Quotes: "By the mid-60s, John Hammond was regarded as one of the foremost white urban interpreters of the Mississippi Delta blues sound"—Kristin Baggelaar/Donald Milton, *Folk Music: More Than a Song*, Thomas Y Crowell Company, 1976

"Hammond has developed into a first rate master of the blues tradition in all its subtlety and stylistic idiosyncrasies"—Barry Kittleson, Vanguard album 9178

References: Folk Music: More Than a Song, Kristin Baggelaar/Donald Milton, Thomas Y Crowell Company, 1976

Blues Magazine (Canada), Aug 1977, pp 11-22

HANKERSON, ALVIN
(*aka:* Guitar Nubbitt)
Born: 1923, Fort Lauderdale (Broward Co), FL
Inst: Guitar

Moved to Gaynesboro, GA, to work outside music (on farm) from 1932; moved to Savannah, GA, to work outside music from 1939; continued outside music work in Valdosta/Atlanta, GA, into 40s; worked outside music, Boston, MA, from 1945; taught self guitar,

1948, and occasionally worked with local bands in club dates, Boston, into 50s; rec Bluestown label, Boston, 1962-4; continued outside music work with occasional work at Club 47/private parties, Boston, through 60s

Personal: Lost tip of right thumb as child which earned him name "Nub" or "Nubbitt"

Infl by: Blind Boy Fuller

References: Blues Unlimited magazine (UK), Nov 1964, p 5

Whiskey, Women, And . . . magazine, Feb 1973, p 11

HARMONICA FRANK
(see Floyd, Frank)

HARMONICA HARRY
(see Mickle, Elmon)

HARMONICA KING
(see Smith, George)

HARMONICA SLIM
(see Blaylock, Travis)
(see Moore, James)

HARPO, SLIM
(see Moore, James)

HARRIS, DON *"Sugarcane"*

Photo by Norbert Hess. Courtesy Living Blues Magazine

Born: Jun 18, 1938, Pasadena (Los Angeles Co), CA
Inst: Guitar/Harmonica/Piano/Violin

Parents were entertainers who worked in West Coast carnival during 1930s; interested in music early playing on home-made comb-brush instrument at 6 years of age; studied classical violin with LC Robinson, 1944-54; attended Manual Arts HS, Los Angeles, CA, mid-50s; formed The Squires band working locally in 1956; teamed with Dewey Terry (as "Don & Dewey") to tour w Johnny Otis Show working West Coast gigs in late 50s; rec (as "Don & Dewey") Specialty label, Los Angeles, late 50s; rec Eldo label, Los Angeles, c1961; toured w Little Richard show working shows/concerts across US/Europe, early 60s; rec w Little Richard, VJ label, Los Angeles, 1964; rec w Frank Zappa, Bizarre label, Los Angeles, late 60s; rec w Johnny Otis Band, Epic label, Los Angeles, 1969; worked w Johnny Otis Show, Basin Street West, San Francisco, CA, 1970; toured w John Mayall working concerts, 1970-1; rec w John Mayall, Polydor label, NYC, 1970; w Johnny Otis package show at Monterey Jazz Festival, Monterey, CA, 1970 (por shown in film MONTEREY JAZZ); rec under own name, Epic label, Los Angeles, 1970; worked Old Cellar, Vancouver, Can, 1970; Ash Grove, Los Angeles, 1970; worked w John Mayall, Whiskey A-Go-Go, Los Angeles, 1971; The Auditorium, Long Beach, CA, 1971; Berlin Jazz Days 71 Festival, Berlin, Ger, 1971 (por rel MPS label); worked w rock group Pure Food & Drug Act, Alice's Revisited, Chicago, IL, 1972; Ash Grove, Los Angeles, 1972; Gassy Jack's Place, Vancouver, Can, 1972; Lion's Share, San Anselmo, CA, 1973; rec w Dewey Terry (as "Don & Dewey"), MPS label, Los Angeles, 1973; toured w Dewey Terry (as "Don & Dewey") w Rhythm & Sounds Concert 73 Show working concert dates across Europe in 1973; toured Europe working concert dates, 1974; residency at Parisian Room, Los Angeles, CA, 1974

Personal: Name "Sugarcane" given him by musician Johnny Otis and refers to his reputation as a ladies' man

Songs: A Little Soul Food/Elim Stole My Baby/Funk and Wagner/Leavin' It All Up to You/Take It All Off/Yours Eternally

Awards/Honors: Won *Jazz & Pop* magazine International Critics Award as best pop violinist of 1970

Infl by: Bobby Bland/Ray Charles/Miles Davis/BB King/Little Walter/LC Robinson

Infl to: Jerry Goodman

Reference: Downbeat magazine, May 8, 1974, p 13

HARRIS, EDWARD P *"Ed"/"Eddie"*
(*aka:* Carolina Slim/Country Paul/Georgia Pine/Jammin' Jim/Lazy Slim Jim)
Born: Aug 22, 1923, Leasburg (Caswell Co), NC
Died: Oct 22, 1953, Newark, NJ
Inst: Guitar

Father was local songster; interested in music early and learned guitar from father as youth; spent most of life as itinerant singer working joints through backwoods and hamlets of the South/Southwest for tips; reportedly settled in Newark, NJ, early 50s; rec Sharp/Acorn/King/Savoy labels, Newark, NJ (?)/Cincinnati, OH (?), early 50s; entered St James Hospital for back surgery and suffered fatal heart attack during operation; burial details unknown

Songs: Ain't It Sad?/Black Cat Trail/Blues Knock at My Door/I'll Never Walk in Your Door/One More Time/Rag Mama/Shake Boogie/Sidewalk Boogie/Since I Seen Your Smiling Face/Slow Freight Blues/Su Garee/Winehead Baby/Your Picture Done Faded

Infl by: Blind Boy Fuller/Lightnin' Hopkins

Quotes: "Carolina Slim sang homespun, down home, absolutely informal compulsively rhythmic blues . . ."—Wilson Winslow, Sharp album 2002

HARRIS, HI TIDE
Born: Mar 26, 1946, San Francisco (San Francisco Co), CA
Inst: Guitar

True name reportedly Willie Boyd or Willie Gitry; raised in Richmond, CA, from childhood; sang in small "doo wop" school groups in area, early 60s; learned some guitar from Herbert Owens c1963; frequently toured w Johnny Taylor/Ella Thomas & The Dollettes/Lowell Fulson and other groups/bands from c1964; toured w Jimmy McCracklin Band working club/concert dates through South, 1965; w Jimmy

Hi Tide Harris
Photo by Dave Patrick. Courtesy Living Blues Magazine

McCracklin Band, Continental Club, West Oakland, CA, c1965; worked w Roger Collins Band, 1966; toured w Big Mama Thornton working college concert circuit on West Coast, 1967; w Big Mama Thornton, Univ of California, Berkeley, CA, 1967; toured w Bob Geddins Jr group working concert dates through Japan/Philippines, 1968; frequently worked w Shakey Jake's group in local gigs, Los Angeles, CA, area, 1969-71; formed own band to work local blues shows in Los Angeles area, 1971-2; worked Rick's Bar, Los Angeles, CA, c1972; The Gackscraggle Coffeehouse, San Francisco, c1972; worked w Charlie Musselwhite, Tenth Street Inn, Berkeley, CA, 1973; toured w Charlie Musselwhite group working club/college gigs across US, 1973; toured one-nighter club dates down West Coast, 1974; toured/recorded w John Mayall Band working concert dates across US/Europe/Australia/Japan, 1974; worked w own blues band, Minnie's Can-Do Club, San Francisco, 1975; San Francisco Blues Festival, McLaren Park, San Francisco, 1975-6 (por 1976 concert rel Jefferson label); Moonlight Club, San Francisco, 1975; Blues Room, Los Angeles, 1975; The Savoy Club, San Francisco, 1975; wrote theme song for film MANDINGO, 1975; app on BLUES BY THE BAY, KPOO-FM-radio, San Francisco, 1975; rec ST as lead singer in film LEADBELLY, 1976; worked w Sonny Rhodes, Shalimar Club, Oakland, CA, 1976; Green Earth Cafe, San Francisco, 1976-7; rec Messaround label, San Francisco, 1976; worked New Old Waldorf, San Francisco, 1977; La Pena, Berkeley, CA, 1977; Sacramento Blues Festival, William Land Park, Sacramento, CA, 1977

Songs: Born in This Time/Never Will Forget Your Love

Infl by: Elmore James/Little Willie John

Quote: "A singer in his own right, and an excellent guitarist in both the slide and regular finger-styles" —Alan Stewart, *Blues Unlimited* magazine (UK), Jun 1974, p 11

Reference: Crazy Music magazine (Australia), Sept 1975, pp 4-7

HARRIS, HOMER
Born: May 6, 1916, Drew (Sunflower Co), MS

Moved to Chicago, IL, to work outside music from 1943; worked occasionally as singer in local club dates from mid-40s; rec Testament label, Chicago, 1946; frequently worked w Memphis Jimmy and others in Flame Club/Sylvio's/Caldonia Lounge/Club 34/others, Chicago, through 40s-early 50s; frequently worked w Johnnie Jones in local club dates, Chicago, 1952-6; worked mostly outside music in Chicago from mid-50s

Reference: Living Blues magazine, Spring 1973, p 37

HARRIS, JAMES D *"Jimmie"/"Jimmy"*
(*aka:* Cadillac Jake/Shakey Jake)
Born: Apr 12, 1921, Earle (Crittenden Co), AR
Died: Mar 2, 1990, Forrest City, AR
Inst: Harmonica

Father was James Harris Sr; mother Lizzie Ashford; moved to Chicago, IL working odd jobs from 1928; taught self harmonica as child; frequently returned to Earle, AR, to work outside music during 30s; dropped out of Wendell Phillips HS, Chicago, to serve in US Army in early 40s; returned to Chicago to work outside music with frequent local club dates as sideman from 1946; frequently sat-in bands of Muddy Waters/Little Walter/others in local clubs, Chicago, late 40s into 50s; formed own band working local club dates, Chicago, from 1952; worked Hob Nob Club, Chicago, 1955; Bee Hive Club, Chicago, c1955; Wagon Wheel, Chicago, 1956; Pepper's Lounge, Chicago, 1956; Mel's Hideaway, Chicago, c1957; rec Artistic label, Chicago, 1958; worked frequently w Magic Sam Band in local club dates, Chicago, late 50s; rec Prestige-Bluesville label, NYC, NY, 1959-60; frequently worked w own quartet in local clubs, Chicago area, into 60s; toured w Rhythm & Blues USA package show working concerts/festivals through England/Europe, 1962; rec Polydor label, Hamburg, Ger, 1962; worked New Alex Club, Chicago, 1963; Sylvio's, Chicago, 1966; w Magic Sam at Copacabana Club, Chicago, 1966; moved to Los Angeles, CA, to work local club dates in area, 1968 into 70s; rec World Pacific label, Los Angeles, 1968; worked Playa Del Ray, Los Angeles, 1969; toured college circuit working concert dates c1969-70; rec Polydor label, Los Angeles, 1971; app in film short CONVERSATIONS WITH SHAKEY JAKE, 1972; worked Chantilly's/Ash Grove, Los Angeles during 70s; rec Grenade label, Los Angeles c1976; owned/rec Good Time label, Los Angeles, 1977-82; owned/worked Safara Lounge, Los Angeles, 1977-8; inactive in music during 80s; died of pneumonia; buried Stanley Grove Cemetery, Pine Tree, AR

Personal: Married twice. Uncle of Magic Sam. Named "Shakey Jake" due to his proficiency at dice

Songs: A Hard Road to Travel/Bad Luck Time/Call Me When You Need Me/Easy Baby/Family Blues/

James Harris (Shakey Jake) *Courtesy Institute of Jazz Studies*

Foolish Heart/Gimme a Smile/Good Times/Hold That Bus, Conductor/Huffin' and Puffin'/I Will Always Love You/It Won't Happen Again/Jake's Blues/Jake's Cha Cha/Just Shakey/Keep A-Loving Me Baby/Let Me Be Your Loverman/Love My Baby/Mouth Harp Blues/My Blues Advice/My Broken Heart/Ragged and Dirty/Remembering/Respect Me Baby/Roll Your Money Maker/Save Your Money Baby/Still Your Fool/Strollin' on the Strip/Sunset Blues/Tear Drops/Things Is Alright/Three Times Seven/Too Hot to Hold/Worried Blues/You Spoiled Your Baby

Infl by: Little Walter/John Lee "Sonny Boy" Williamson

Quote: "One of the most colorful figures associated with the modern Chicago blues scene is James D Harris"—Pete Welding, *Living Blues* magazine, Autumn 1972, p 10

Reference: Living Blues magazine, Autumn 1972, pp 10-16

HARRIS, MAE
(see Henderson, Rosa)

HARRIS, MAMIE
(see Henderson, Rosa)

HARRIS, PEARL
(see Miles, Josephine)

HARRIS, PEPPERMINT
Born: c1925, Texas (unconfirmed)
Inst: Guitar

Born Harrison Nelson; reportedly born/raised in Texas working mostly outside music from 1940s; rec Gold Star label, Houston, TX, 1947; rec Sittin' In With/Modern/Time labels, Houston and elsewhere, 1950-1; reportedly worked outside music on West Coast from early 50s; rec Aladdin label, Los Angeles, CA, 1951-3; rec Money label, Los Angeles, 1954; rec

Peppermint Harris
Courtesy Institute of Jazz Studies

X label, Los Angeles, 1955; rec Dart label, Lake Charles, LA, c1960; rec Duke label, Houston, TX; 1960; app on MACK McCORMICK AND FRIENDS, KUHF-FM-radio, Houston, 1961; rec Jewel label, Tyler, TX, 1965-6; reportedly worked outside music in Houston, 1966/Chicago, IL, c1967/New Orleans, LA, c1968/Texarkana, TX, 1970

Quote: "He represents the generation after Smokey Hogg, Lightnin' Hopkins, Brownie McGhee and Big Bill Broonzy"—Bob Shad, Time album 5

HARRIS, SUGARCANE
(see Harris, Don)

HARRIS, WYNONIE *"Mr Blues"*
Born: Aug 24, 1915, Omaha (Douglas Co), NE
Died: Jun 14, 1969, Los Angeles, CA
Inst: Drums

Father was Luther Harris; mother was Mallie Hood; was only child; attended Technical HS and Central HS, Omaha, NE, late 20s into 30s; attended Creighton Univ, Omaha, early 30s; dropped out to work as comedian/dancer at Jim Bell's Harlem Club/McGill's Blue Room/Apex Bar/others, Omaha, through 30s; taught self drums and formed own small combo to work local clubs/bars, Omaha area, into 40s; moved to West Coast to work as MC/singer, Club Alabam, Los Angeles, CA, early 40s; app (as dancer) in film HIT PARADE OF 1943, 1943; frequently produced stage shows, Lincoln Theater, Los Angeles, 1944; worked Chez Paree Club, Kansas City, MO, 1944; Club Rhumboogie, Chicago, IL, 1944; w Lucky Millinder Orch, Savoy Ballroom, Los Angeles, 1944; rec w Lucky Millinder Orch, Decca label, NYC, NY, 1944; w Lucky Millinder Orch, Tic Toc Club, Boston, MA, 1944; Loew's State Theater, NYC, 1944; Apollo Theater, NYC, 1944; rec w Johnny Otis All Stars,

Courtesy Frank Driggs Collection

Aladdin label, Los Angeles, 1945; rec w Illinois Jacquet Orch/Jack McVea All Stars/Oscar Pettiford All Stars/others, Apollo label, Los Angeles, 1945; toured w Illinois Jacquet Orch working gigs in mid-40s; rec w Hamp-Tone All Stars, Hamp-Tone label, Los Angeles, 1945; rec Bullet label, Nashville, TN, 1946; rec Aladdin label, NYC, 1946-7; worked Club 845, Bronx, NY, 1946; w Ernie Fields Band, Apollo Theater, NYC, 1946; rec extensively King label, NYC, 1947-57; worked Foster's Rainbow Room, New Orleans, LA, 1947; toured w Lionel Hampton Orch working club dates, late 40s; app on local radio show, Geneva, NY, 1948; toured w Big Joe Turner working club dates through South, 1949; toured w Dud Bascomb's Combo working one-nighters c1949; rec w Lucky Millinder Orch, King label, NYC, 1950; toured w Larry Darnell working theater dates, 1951; worked Regal Theater, Chicago, IL, 1951; toured on package shows working theaters/clubs and many one-nighters across US, early 50s; settled in St Albans, NY, to work outside music from c1953; owned/operated a cafe in Brooklyn, NY, late 50s to 1963; rec Atco label, NYC (?), c1960; rec Roulette label, NYC (?), c1960; owned/operated a cafe in Los Angeles, CA, from 1963; rec Cadet label, Chicago, 1963; worked Shrine Auditorium, Los Angeles, 1963; worked mostly outside music, Los Angeles, through 60s; worked Apollo Theater, NYC, 1967; entered USC Medical Center where he died of cancer; buried Woodlawn Cemetery, Los Angeles, CA

Personal: First marriage, 1934-46; son Wesley Devereaux is singer/guitarist; second marriage to Gertrude ———

Billings: The Mississippi Mockingbird/Peppermint Cane

Songs: All She Wants to Do Is Rock/Big City Blues/Bite Again, Bite Again/Blowin' to California/Drinkin' by Myself/Good Morning Corrine/Grandma Plays the Numbers/Here Come the Blues/My Playful Baby's Gone/Quiet Whiskey/That's the Stuff You Gotta Watch/Wynonie's Boogie

Infl by: Louis Jordan/Jimmy Rushing

Infl to: Roy Brown/Screaming Jay Hawkins

Quotes: ". . . Harris could sing either [blues or ballads] though the blues was really where he shone"—Ralph Gleason, *New York Post* newspaper, Sept 2, 1969

"Everything about Wynonie was strong . . . a set of vocal chords seemingly made of steel"—Jack Schiffman, *Uptown*, Cowles Book Company, Inc, 1971

HARRISON, VERNON

(*aka:* Boogie Woogie Red)
Born: Oct 18, 1925, Rayville (Richland Parish), LA
Died: Jul 2, 1992, Detroit, MI
Inst: Piano

Father was George Harrison; mother Minnie Swift; moved to Detroit, MI, 1927; interested in blues music early and taught self piano at 8 years of age; frequently worked local school functions, Detroit, late 30s; dropped out of school to work outside music, 1940-5; weekend residency at King Solomon Bar, Detroit, 1945; frequently worked w Sonny Boy Williamson (Alex Miller) in local clubs/bars, Detroit, 1945-8; worked Tempo Tap Club, Chicago, IL, c1948; residency at Nat Ivory's Playground Club, Chicago, 1948; George Wood's Timber Tap Club, Chicago, 1948; teamed w Baby Boy Warren to work local bars, Detroit, MI, from c1948; frequently worked Bronx Bar, Detroit, c1949; rec acc to Baby Boy Warren, Staff label, Detroit, 1950; worked w Washboard Willie, Golden Bell, Detroit, early 50s; rec w Baby Boy Warren group, JVB/Drummond/Excello/Blue Lake/

Sampson labels, Detroit, c1953-4; frequently worked w John Lee Hooker Band, Henry's Swing Club/The Harlem Inn/Club Carribe, Detroit, with frequent US/Canadian tours and recordings, early 50s into early 60s; rec under own name, Decca label, Detroit, 1960; worked mostly outside music in Detroit through 60s; worked w Baby Boy Warren in local clubs/ festivals, Saginaw, MI, 1971; Ann Arbor Blues Festival, Ann Arbor, MI, 1972-3 (por 1972 concert rel Atlantic label); toured w Baby Boy Warren working concert dates through England/Europe, 1972; rec Trix label, Detroit, MI, 1972; frequently worked Blind Pig, Ann Arbor, MI, 1973-5 (por rel Blind Pig label); Univ of North Carolina, Chapel Hill, NC, 1973 (por rel Flyright label); toured w American Blues Legends 73 working concert/TV/radio dates through England/Europe, 1973; rec Big Bear-Polydor label, London, Eng, 1973; worked Highland Park Community Col, Detroit, MI, 1974; Blues & Jazz Festival, Grand Valley State Col, Allendale, MI, 1974-5; frequent club dates in Grand Rapids, MI, 1974; worked Ann Arbor Blues & Jazz Festival, Windsor, Can, 1974; Inner-Section, Grand Rapids, MI, 1975; Rudolf's Roaring 20s Club, Saginaw, MI, 1975; Elsewhere, Chicago, IL, 1976; Jazzlife Festival, Dortmund, Ger, 1976; BJ's Buffeteria, Bay City, MI, 1977; rec Blind Pig label, Farmington, MI, 1977; worked Blind Pig club, Ann Arbor, MI into 80s; worked infrequently in area due to illness through 80s; died of kidney failure; buried Lincoln Memorial Park, Mt Clemens, MI

Courtesy Cadence Magazine

Songs: After Hours/Beer Drinkin' Woman/Carnegie Boogie/Easy Listening/Mess Up/Old Time Shuffle/ Red's "A" Train/Red's Boogie/Red's Rhumba/ Relaxin'/Sisterly Love/Spider in the Web/Strollin' Down State Street/Take Five/Viper Song/When I Was Young

Infl by: Big Maceo

Quote: "[An] immensely talented Detroit blues pianist and showman"—Doug Langille, *Coda* magazine (Canada), Sept 1975, p 20

References: Trix album 3311

HATCH, PROVINE, JR
Born: Oct 25, 1921, Sledge (Quitman Co), MS
Inst: Harmonica

Moved to Tunica, MS, to work outside music from age of 12; served in US Navy, 1943-6; settled in Kansas City, MO, to work outside music from 1946; formed own band to work local club dates, Kansas City, MO, from 1962; rec w own Little Hatchet Band, M&M label, Kansas City, 1970

HAVENS, RICHARD PIERCE *"Richie"*
Born: Jan 21, 1941, Brooklyn (Kings Co), NY
Inst: Guitar/Koto/Sitar

Father Richard P. Havens Sr was pianist; mother Mildred Gay; raised in Bedford-Stuyvesant area where he frequently worked streets for tips as youth; formed McCrea Gospel Singers working locally, Brooklyn, 1955; dropped out of Franklin K Lane HS to work outside music from 1958; frequently worked as portrait artist in Greenwich Village area, NYC, from 1959; taught self guitar and frequently sat-in/worked Cafe Wha?/Cafe Bizarre/Why Not?/Fat Black Pussy Cat and other cafes/coffeehouses, NYC, 1962-6; rec Douglas International-Transatlantic label, NYC, c1963; toured w Nina Simone in Ford Motor Company Show working dates, 1963; rec Verve-Folkways label, NYC, 1966; worked Newport Folk Festival, Newport, RI, 1966; Monterey Jazz Festival, Monterey, CA, 1967 (por shown MONTEREY JAZZ

Richard "Richie" Havens

Photo by Julie Snow

FESTIVAL, PBS-TV (syndicated)/por shown in film MONTEREY JAZZ); Fillmore Auditorium, San Francisco, CA, 1967; rec w Jeremy Steig group, Verve-Forecast label, NYC, 1967; worked Expo 67 Fair, Montreal, Can, 1967; Second Fret, Philadelphia, PA, 1967; Cafe A-Go-Go, NYC, 1967-8; Canterbury House, Ann Arbor, MI, 1967; toured college circuit working concert dates across US, 1967; worked Club 47, Cambridge, MA, 1968; app on PETER MARTIN Show, WPIX-TV, NYC, 1968-70; app on TODAY Show, NBC-TV, 1968; worked Woody Guthrie Memorial Concert, Carnegie Hall, NYC, 1968 (por rel Columbia label); app on Johnny Carson's TONIGHT Show, NBC-TV, 1968; worked Academy of Music, Brooklyn, NY, 1968; Brooklyn Col, Brooklyn, 1968; The Troubador, Los Angeles, CA, 1968; app on NEW YORKER Show, WNEW-TV, NYC, 1968; app on STEVE ALLEN Show, WOR-TV, NYC (syndicated), 1968; worked Central Park Music Festival, NYC, 1968; Civic Auditorium, Santa Monica, CA, 1968; Philharmonic Hall, NYC, 1968; Fillmore East, NYC, 1968-9; toured college circuit working concerts on West Coast, 1968-9; worked Univ of Buffalo Music Festival, Buffalo, NY, 1968; Miami Pop Festival, Hallandale, FL, 1968; formed own Stormy Forest Production Company (a film/TV/theater production house), 1969; app in show PETER AND THE WOLF, New York City Center, NYC, 1969; worked Westbury Music Fair, Westbury, NY, 1969; app on ED SULLIVAN Show, CBS-TV, 1969; app on COUSIN BRUCIE Show, WOR-TV, NYC, 1969; app on MIKE DOUGLAS Show, CBS-TV, 1969; worked solo concert, The Pavilion, NYC, 1969; app on MUSIC SCENE, ABC-TV, 1969; toured Denmark working concert/radio/TV dates, 1969; worked Isle of Wight Festival, Isle of Wight, Eng, 1969; Woodstock Music & Art Fair, Bethel, NY, 1969 (por shown in film WOODSTOCK/por rel Cotillion label); app on DAVID FROST Show, WNEW-TV, NYC (syndicated), 1969-70; frequently produced/recorded, Stormy Forest label, NYC, 1970-3; worked Washington Blues Festival, Howard Univ, Washington, DC, 1970; Woody Guthrie Memorial Concert, Hollywood Bowl, Hollywood, CA, 1970 (por rel Warner Brothers label); worked Sold on Soul concert, Madison Square Garden, NYC, 1970; Festival for Peace concert, Shea Stadium, NYC, 1970; Carnegie Hall, NYC, 1970; Aragon Ballroom, Chicago, IL, 1970-2; Village Gate, NYC, 1971; Fillmore East, NYC, 1971; Civic Auditorium, Santa Monica, CA, 1971; The Spectrum, Philadelphia, PA, 1971; Univ of Vermont, Burlington, VT, 1971; Painters Mill Theater, Baltimore, MD, 1971-2; app on Johnny Carson's TONIGHT Show, NBC-TV 1972; app on PERPETUAL PEOPLE PUZZLE, ABC-TV, 1972; app in show TOMMY (unknown theater), NYC, 1972; app/scored film CATCH MY SOUL, 1973; app on ROCK CONCERT, WNEW-TV, NYC, 1973; worked as American representative to International Festival of Song, Rio de Janeiro, Brazil, 1974; app in film ALI THE MAN, 1975; worked The Astrodome, Houston, TX, 1976; app on WONDERAMA, WNEW-TV, NYC, 1976; app on BROOKLYN COLLEGE, PBS-TV, 1976; app on Johnny Carson's TONIGHT Show, NBC-TV, 1976; worked The Ivanhoe Theater, Chicago, IL, 1976-7; app in film GREASED LIGHTNING, 1977; worked Colonial Tavern, Toronto, Can, 1977; Dr Pepper's Central Park Music Festival, NYC, 1977; Carnegie Hall, NYC, 1978; app on MIKE DOUGLAS Show, CBS-TV, 1978

Personal: Married Nancy ——— ; 2 children

Book: Richie Havens Anthology, The Big Three Music Corporation, 1972

Songs: Adam/Babe I'm Leavin'/Bright Lights in the City/Chain Gang/Daddy Roll 'em/Do You Feel Good?/Don't Listen to Me/For Haven's Sake/Handsome Johnny/I'm Gonna Make You Glad/I'm on My Way/Indian Rope Man/Inside of Him/It Hurts Me/Just Above My Hobby Horse's Head/Nora's Dove/The Parable of Ramon/Putting Out the Vibrations and Hoping It Comes Home/Run, Shaker Life/Somethin' Else Again/Stop Pulling and Pushing Me/Three Day Eternity/What More Can I Say John?

Infl by: Ray Charles/Nina Simone/Bukka White

Quotes: ". . . [his] style is a mournful mixture of Ray Charles, Bob Dylan and Mississippi John Hurt . . ." —Donald Bogle, *Ebony* magazine, May 1969

"Whether he is performing material by the Beatles, Bob Dylan, Jesse Fuller, Gordon Lightfoot or songs penned by his own hand, Richie Havens consistently produces a result which is uniquely his own"—Kristin Baggelaar/Donald Milton, *Folk Music: More Than a Song*, Thomas Y Crowell Company, 1976

References: Folk Music: More Than a Song, Kristin Baggelaar/Donald Milton, Thomas Y Crowell Company, 1976

Encyclopedia of Pop, Rock & Soul, Irwin Stambler, St Martin's Press, 1974

HAWKINS, JALACY J *"Screamin' Jay"/"Jay"*
Born: Jul 18, 1929, Cleveland (Cuyahoga Co), OH
Inst: Piano/Sax

Father was Gleason (?) Ward; mother Marie Kathy Hawkins; placed in orphanage, adopted at 18 months; was interested in music early taking some piano lessons as youth; occasionally worked local bars for tips, Cleveland, into 40s; won Golden Gloves as amateur boxer c1943; dropped out of high school to work in Special Services Division of US Army/US Air Force entertaining at service clubs through US/Germany/Japan/Korea, 1945-52; worked as boxer through 40s winning middleweight championship of Alaska, 1949; rec w Tiny Grimes Band, Gotham label, Philadelphia, PA, 1952; toured w Tiny Grimes Band (as chauffeur/musician) working club dates up East Coast US into Canada, 1953-4; worked Royal Theater, Baltimore, MD, 1953; rec w Tiny Grimes Band, Atlantic/Timely/Apollo labels, NYC, NY, 1953; rec w Leroy Kirkland Band, Mercury/Wing labels, NYC, 1954; rec Grand label, Philadelphia, PA, 1954; toured w Fats Domino group working club dates/dances across US, 1954; frequently worked resort area of Atlantic City, NJ, with some road work c1954-5; rec OKeh/Epic labels, NYC, 1956-7; worked Baby Grand, NYC, c1956; toured w Alan Freed Summer Festival package show working theaters, 1957; extensive touring as single on theater circuit working concerts/rock shows across US, late 50s; worked Regal Theater, Chicago, IL, c1957; app in film MISTER ROCK AND ROLL, 1957 (cut in release); worked Apollo Theater, NYC, 1957; rec Red Top label, c1958; settled in Honolulu, HI, frequently working as MC/entertainer at Forbidden City Club and other clubs/hotels, 1960-4 (por 1963 date rel Sounds of Hawaii label); rec w

Jalacy "Screamin' Jay" Hawkins
Courtesy Frank Driggs Collection

Chicken Hawks, Enrica label, NYC, 1962; rec w Pat Newborn, Chancellor label, Philadelphia, PA, 1962; rec Roulette label, NYC, 1963; rec Planet label, London, Eng, 1964; toured England working concert dates, 1965; rec Providence label, NYC, 1965; frequently worked local theater/club dates in NYC area, 1965-6; Apollo Theater, NYC, 1966; rec Decca label, NYC, 1967; app on BRUCE MORROW Show, ABC-TV, 1967; returned to Honolulu, HI, to work local clubs/hotels, 1967-70; rec Philips label, Hollywood, CA/Houston, TX, 1969-70; settled in NYC to work local clubs/bars/theaters in area from 1970; frequently worked Apollo Theater, NYC, 1970-2; Academy of Music, NYC, 1971; rec Hot Line label, Nashville, TN, 1973; app on JOE FRANKLIN Show, WOR-TV, NYC, 1974; rec RCA-Victor label, NYC, 1974; toured South/East Coast working concert dates, 1975-6; toured w Rhythm & Blues: Roots of Rock Show working concert dates through Europe, 1975; worked Virginia Theater, Alexandria, VA, 1976; app in film AMERICAN HOT WAX, 1978

Personal: Married Virginia "Ginny" ——— (in Hawaii)

Songs: Baptize Me in Wine/Feast of the Mau Mau/Frenzy/I Found My Way to Wine/I Hear Voices/I Put a Spell on You/She Put the Whammee on Me/Talk About Me/There's Something Wrong with You/There's Too Many Teardrops/Well I Tried

Infl by: Wynonie Harris/Louis Jordan/Jimmy Rushing/Devonia Williams

Infl to: David Bowie/Arthur Brown/Alice Cooper/Little Richard/Dr John/Screamin' Lord Sutch

Quote: "Jalacy J Hawkins is known as a weird, wild blues singer, rhythm & blues shouter and rock 'n' roll star"—Norbert Hess, *Blues Unlimited* magazine (UK), Sept 1976, p 4

Reference: Blues Unlimited magazine (UK), Sept 1976, pp 4-14

HEGAMIN, LUCILLE

(*aka:* Fanny Baker)
Born: Nov 29, 1894, Macon (Bibb Co), GA
Died: Mar 1, 1970, New York, NY

Father was John Nelson, mother was Minnie Wallace; born Lucille Nelson; one of 5 children; interested in music early and frequently sang in local church choirs/theater affairs, Macon, GA, as child; toured w Leonard Harper Minstrel Stock Company working as singing entertainer in theaters/tent shows through

Courtesy Record Research Archives

South from c1909; settled in Chicago, IL, 1914; worked (frequently as "Georgia Peach") w Bill Hegamin at Bill Lewis' Mineral Cafe/Charlie Letts Cafe/ Sherman Blackwell Club/Elite No 2 Club (acc by Tony Jackson)/DeLuxe Cafe (acc by Jelly Roll Morton)/Panama Cafe/Bud Sneeze's Forest Inn Cafe/others, Chicago, 1914-18; worked w Bill Hegamin at Hite's Cabaret/Bill Brown's Club/Los Angeles Broadway Theater, Los Angeles, CA, 1918; Harris' Cabaret, Seattle, WA, 1918; moved to NYC, NY, 1919; worked Dolphin Cafe, NYC, 1919; Connors Club, NYC, 1919; Libya Cafe, NYC, 1919-20; w Happy Rhone's All Star Show, Manhattan Casino, NYC, 1920-1; rec w Fletcher Henderson, Victor label, NYC (unissued), 1920; rec w Harris' Blues & Jazz Seven, Arto label, NYC, 1920; formed Blue Flame Syncopators Band (w Bill Hegamin) and toured vaudeville circuit through Pennsylvania/West Virginia/Ohio, 1921; rec w Blue Flame Syncopators, Arto label, NYC, 1921-2; opened Shuffle Inn, NYC, 1921; w Noble Sissle Orch, Manhattan Casino, NYC, 1922; w Happy Rhone Orch, New Star Casino, NYC, 1922; app in musical comedy SHUFFLE ALONG (company #2) touring one-nighters through New England area, 1922; app in HURRY ON Revue, Lafayette Theater, NYC, 1922; app in BLACK BEAUX BELLES Revue (unknown theater), NYC, early 20s; toured w Johnny Dunn Band in own JAZZ JUBILEE Revue working Warwick Theater, Brooklyn, NY/Metropolitan Theater, Brooklyn, NY/Lincoln Square Theater, NYC/State Theater, NYC/Boulevard Theater, NYC/Gates Avenue Theater, Brooklyn, NY/Howard Theater, Boston, MA, and other Loew's theaters across US in 1922; rec w Blue Flame Syncopators/Sam Wooding's Society Entertainers, Paramount label, NYC, 1922; rec Cameo label, NYC, 1922-6; app in CREOLE FOLLIES Revue, Lafayette Theater, NYC, 1923; worked Lincoln Theater, NYC, 1923; Loew's Greely Square Theater, NYC, 1923; Avenue Theater, Chicago, IL, 1923; toured extensively as solo act on Keith vaudeville circuit across US, 1923-4; worked w Andy Preer's Cotton Club Syncopators, Cotton Club, NYC, 1925; frequently app on WHN-radio, NYC, from 1925; worked Artist & Movie Ball, Renaissance Ballroom, NYC, 1926; app in CLARENCE WILLIAMS REVUE, Lincoln Theater, NYC, 1926; frequently worked w own Sunnyland Cotton Pickers Band, Lincoln Theater, NYC, 1926 with tours to Baltimore, MD/New Haven, CT/elsewhere, 1926-7; rec w Clarence Williams Band, Columbia label, NYC, 1926; co-starred w Adelaide Hall in LINCOLN FROLICS Revue, Lincoln Theater, NYC/Broadway Theater, Washington, DC, 1926; worked Club Alabam, Philadelphia, PA, 1927; app in SHUFFLIN' FEET Revue, Lincoln Theater, NYC, 1927; app in musical comedy THE MIDNIGHT STEPPERS, Lafayette Theater, NYC, 1928; frequently toured w George "Doc" Hyder's Southernaires working halls/theaters, late 20s; app on NEGRO ACHIEVEMENT HOUR, WABC-radio, NYC, 1929; app w Claude Hopkins' Savoy Bohemians in NEW YEAR'S REVELS Revue, Lafayette Theater, NYC, 1930-1; rec OKeh label, NYC, 1932; worked Paradise Cafe, Atlantic City, NJ, 1933-4; app in Frank Montgomery's PARADISE CLUB REVUE, Lafayette Theater, NYC, 1933; worked mostly outside music (as registered nurse) in NYC, 1934 through 50s; rec w Willie The Lion and His Cubs, Prestige-Bluesville label, Englewood Cliffs, NJ, 1961; rec Spivey label, NYC, 1962; worked Mamie Smith Benefit concert, Celebrity Club, NYC, 1964; mostly inactive due to illness; entered Harlem Hospital Center where she died of natural causes; buried Cemetery of the Evergreens, Brooklyn, NY

Personal: Married Bill Hegamin, pianist (c1914-23); married ——— Allen

Billings: The Blues Singer Supreme/The Cameo Girl/Chicago Cyclone/Georgia Peach/Harlem's Favorite

Songs: Lonesome Monday Mornin' Blues/Mississippi Blues

Infl by: Ruth Etting/Annette Hanshaw

Quotes: "[She typified] the Negro vaudeville performer of the 20s, with a strong tendency towards refinement and a 'torch-blues' style reminiscent of Ethel Waters and Ruth Etting . . ."—Chris Albertson, Prestige-Bluesville album 1052

"She was an extremely good singer of jazz based blues . . ."—Derrick Stewart-Baxter, *Ma Rainey and the Classic Blues Singers*, Studio Vista Ltd, 1970

"She displayed a vigorous powerful voice, deep and resonant, youthful and exuberant. If anything, the passing years added conviction to her blues presentation"—Len Kunstadt, *Record Research* magazine, Nov 1961, p 3

References: Record Research magazine, Nov 1961/Jan 1962/Feb 1962/May 1962

Jazz Journal magazine (UK), Jul 1967/Aug 1967

HENDERSON, CATHERINE
(see Taylor, Eva)

HENDERSON, KATHERINE
Born: Jun 23, 1909, St Louis (St Louis Co), MO

Father was Griffin Henderson; mother was Kitty Gibbons; toured w Josephine Gassman and her Pickaninnies (working as pick) from 1912; toured w Josephine Gassman Phina & Company Show working theaters in Australia/Tasmania/New Zealand, 1915-17; continued tours w Josephine Gassman troupe (as singer/dancer/impersonator) on Albee & Keith circuits across US, 1917-21; settled in NYC, NY, to attend local schools from 1921; brief tours on vaudeville circuit as single (or w Eva Taylor) in theater dates in NYC, NY/Youngstown, OH/elsewhere, mid-20s; occasionally substituted for Eva Taylor on local radio shows, NYC, through 20s; brief app in (unknown) revue, New Douglas Theater, NYC, 1926; rec w Clarence Williams' Blue Five, Brunswick label, NYC, 1927; app w Eva Taylor in show BOTTOMLAND, Savoy Theater, Atlantic City, NJ, 1927/Princess Theater, NYC, 1927; worked for Clarence Williams' Music Publishing Company, NYC (as clerk and song demonstrator), through 20s; worked Kathleen Kirkwood Underground Theater, Greenwich Village, NYC, 1928; rec QRS/Paramount labels, Long Island City, NY, 1928; app in musical show KEEP SHUFFLIN', Pearl Theater, Philadelphia, PA, 1929; app w Eva Taylor in non-singing role, CARELESS LOVE Show, WEAF-radio, NYC (NBC-Network), 1931; mostly inactive in music from early 1930s; app w Eva Taylor in FOLKS FROM DIXIE, NBC-Network-radio, 1933; worked w Sylvester Wolfson Orch in long residency at Joe & Rose Beer Garden, Queens, NY, early 40s; moved to St Louis, MO, 1944; inactive in music thereafter

Courtesy Spencer Williams

Personal: Married John Jackson (1928-c1948). 3 children. No relation to singer Rosa Henderson or musician Fletcher Henderson. Not to be confused w Eva Taylor (her aunt) who used pseudonym "Catherine Henderson"

Billing: Only Me

Infl by: Eva Taylor

HENDERSON, ROSA *"Rose"*
(*aka:* Flora Dale/Rosa Green/Mae Harris/Mamie Harris/Sara Johnson/Sally Ritz/Josephine Thomas/Gladys White/Bessie Williams)
Born: Nov 24, 1896, Henderson (Henderson Co), KY
Died: Apr 6, 1968, New York, NY

Born Rosa Deschamps; left home to join uncle's carnival show and frequently toured various tent/plantation shows through South from 1913; teamed w

Slim Henderson to work as duo on southern vaudeville circuit from c1918; toured w Slim Henderson and John Mason in Mason-Henderson troupe working vaudeville circuit across US into 20s; worked w Slim Henderson Company, Lincoln Theater, NYC, NY, 1922; app in GO GET IT Revue (unknown theater), NYC, c1923; rec Victor/Paramount/Vocalion/Columbia/Ajax/Pathe-Actuelle labels, NYC, 1923; app w Fletcher Henderson, WDT-radio, NYC, 1923; rec Brunswick/Emerson/Banner/Edison/Vocalion labels, NYC, 1924; app in THE PRICELESS FUNNY REVUE, Lafayette Theater, NYC, 1924; rec Ajax label, NYC, 1924-5; worked w Slim Henderson, Lincoln Theater, NYC, 1925; rec Vocalion label, NYC, 1925-6; rec Columbia label, NYC, 1926; app in QUINTARD MILLER'S REVUE, Lincoln Theater, NYC, 1926; rec Pathe-Actuelle label, NYC, 1926-7; app in SEVENTH AVENUE AFFAIRS Revue, Lincoln Theater, NYC, 1927; app in THE HARLEM ROUNDERS Revue, New Alhambra Theater, NYC, 1927; app in BRUNETTES PREFERRED Revue, New Alhambra Theater, NYC, 1927; app in SITTING PRETTY Revue, New Alhambra Theater, NYC, 1927; app in SEVENTH AVENUE STROLLERS Revue, New Alhambra Theater, NYC, 1927; app in RAMBLIN' AROUND Revue, New Alhambra Theater, NYC, 1927; app in FLAMING FOLLIES Revue, New Alhambra Theater, NYC, 1927; app in RODEO GIRLS REVUE, New Alhambra Theater, NYC, 1927; app in AND HOW Revue, Lincoln Theater, NYC, 1928; app in GOING STRONG Revue, Lincoln Theater, NYC, 1928; app in SITTING PRETTY Revue, Lincoln Theater, NYC, 1928; app in BE YOURSELF Revue, Lincoln Theater, NYC, 1928; app in BLACKOUTS OF 1929 Revue, Lafayette Theater, NYC, 1929; app in CHOCOLATE MUSIC BOX musical comedy, Lincoln Theater, NYC, 1929; app in local shows/revues, Atlantic City, NJ, into 30s; app in BLACKBERRIES Revue, Lafayette Theater, NYC, NY, 1930; rec w James P Johnson, Columbia label, NYC, 1931; app in YEAH-MAN Revue, Park Lane Theater, NYC, 1932; worked mostly outside music in NYC from c1932; entered Bird S Coler Hospital, Welfare Island, NY, and after long illness died of natural causes; buried Frederick Douglass Memorial Park Cemetery, Staten Island, NY

Courtesy Record Research Archives

Personal: Married comedian Douglas "Slim" Henderson (c1918-died 1928). 2 children. No relation to Fletcher/Katherine/Edmonia Henderson. Had used sister's name "Sally Ritz" on some recordings. Not to be confused with Viola McCoy who also used pseudonym "Bessie Williams"

Quotes: ". . . Rosa Henderson had a fine throaty booming blues voice (with) swinging rhythmic qualities . . ."—Len Kunstadt, *Record Research* magazine, Apr 1966, p 3

"Rosa Henderson was one of the most outstanding of the many early women vaudeville-blues singers to record for the race record companies in the early twenties"—Bill Daynes-Wood, *Jazz Journal* magazine (UK), Jul 1968, p 16

References: *Record Research* magazine, Apr 1966, p 3
Jazz Journal magazine (UK), Jul 1968, p 16

HENDRIX, JAMES MARSHALL *"Jimi"/"Jimmi"*
(*aka:* Jimmy James)
Born: Nov 27, 1942, Seattle (King Co), WA
Died: Sept 18, 1970, London, England
Inst: Bass/Drums/Guitar/Organ/Piano

Father was James Allen Hendrix; mother was a Cherokee Indian; one of 2 children; learned guitar at 11 years of age; worked in local bands, Seattle, WA, from 1956; dropped out of Garfield HS to work outside music, 1958-60; served in 101st Airborne Division of US Army, 1960-1; toured w The Flames group working club dates through South, 1961; frequently toured as sideman w BB King/Chuck Jackson/Sam Cooke/Little Richard/Ike & Tina Turner/King Curtis/others

Courtesy BMI Archives

in theater dates/R&B shows/auditoriums across US, 1961-4; worked w Curtis Knight & the Squires at Purple Onion/The Lighthouse/Club Cheetah/Ondines Club, NYC, NY/George's Club-20, Hackensack, NJ, and other clubs in NYC area, 1964-6; rec w Isley Brothers, Buddah label, NYC, c1965; rec w Curtis Knight, Capitol label, NYC, 1965/7; worked w The Blue Flames, Cafe Wha?, NYC, 1966; worked Blaise's Club, London, Eng, 1966; formed own The Jimi Hendrix Experience to work The Olympia Theater, Paris, France/The Tivoli, Stockholm, Sweden/Sports Arena, Copenhagen, Den/Bag O'Nails Club, London, Eng, 1966; rec Polydor-Reprise label, London, 1966-7; app on READY STEADY GO Show, BBC-TV, London, 1966; worked Saville Theater, London, 1967 (por shown on THE JIMI HENDRIX EXPERIENCE AT THE SAVILLE THEATER, 1967, syndicated on local TV, Europe); toured England/Europe working club/concert dates, 1967; worked Odeon Theater, Ipswich, Eng, 1967 (por shown on French TV); rec w Paul McCartney, Parlophone label, London, 1967; worked International Pop Festival, Monterey, CA, 1967 (por shown in film MONTEREY POP/por rel Reprise-Atlantic label); Central Park Festival, NYC, 1967; toured briefly w The Monkees group working concert dates across US, 1967; worked Hollywood Bowl, Hollywood, CA, 1967; Fillmore West, San Francisco, CA, 1967; worked concert dates in England/Europe, 1967-8; worked Convention Hall, Anaheim, CA, 1968; Olympia Theater, Paris, France, 1968; Underground Pop Festival, Miami, FL, 1968; rec w Timothy Leary, Douglas label, CA (?), c1968; worked The Scene, NYC, 1968; Fillmore East, NYC, 1968; Singer Bowl, NYC, 1968; Cafe A-Go-Go, NYC, 1968; Philharmonic Hall, NYC, 1968; toured England working concert dates/TV shows, 1969; app on THROUGH THE EYES OF TOMORROW, CBC-TV, Toronto, Can, c1969 (produced England); app w The Experience, Albert Hall, London, Eng, 1969 (por rel Ariola-Ember label/por shown in film short EXPERIENCE); rec ST for film EASY RIDER, 1969; worked Municipal Auditorium, Kansas City, MO, 1969; app on DICK CAVETT Show, ABC-TV, 1969; app on Johnny Carson's TONIGHT Show, NBC-TV, 1969; worked Salvation Club, NYC, 1969; Civic Center, Baltimore, MD, 1969-70; Boston Garden, Boston, MA, 1969; Toronto Pop Festival, Toronto, Can, 1969 (por shown in film SWEET TORONTO and short film version KEEP ON ROCKIN'); Maple Leaf Gardens, Toronto, 1969; Denver Festival, Denver, CO, 1969; disbanded The Experience to work Newport 69 Festival, Northridge, CA, 1969; Woodstock Music & Art Fair, Bethel, NY, 1969 (por shown in film WOODSTOCK/por rel Cotillion label); formed The Band of Gypsies group to work Fillmore East, NYC, 1969 (por rel Capitol-Track label); Madison Square Garden, NYC, 1970; disbanded Band of Gypsies group in early 1970; worked Cincinnati Gardens, Cincinnati, OH, 1970; Community Theater, Berkeley, CA, 1970 (por rel Polydor/Reprise labels); app in film JIMI PLAYS BERKELEY, 1970; toured Hawaii working concert dates, 1970; app in film RAINBOW BRIDGE, 1970 (por rel Reprise label); owned/operated Electric Lady Studios, NYC, 1970; worked The Coliseum, Seattle, WA, 1970; Isle of Wight Festival, Isle of Wight, Eng, 1970 (por rel Polydor label); toured Europe working concert dates, 1970; sat-in w Eric Burdon & War group, Ronnie Scott's Club, London, Eng, 1970; suffered consequence of barbiturate intoxication at Samarkand Hotel and DOA at St Mary Abbot's Hospital; buried Greenwood Cemetery, Renton, WA; posthumous film releases: DYNAMITE CHICKEN (1971), JIMI HENDRIX (1973) (por rel Reprise label)

Books: Hendrix, Chris Welch, 1972
Jimi, Curtis Knight, Praeger Publishing Company, 1974

Songs: Angel/Are You Experienced?/Can You Hear Me?/Castles Are Made of Sand/Crosstown Traffic/Electric Church/51st Anniversary/First Look Around the Corner/Foxy Lady/I Don't Live Today/Let Me Stand Next to Your Fire/Love and Confusion/Manic Depression/May This Be Love/Purple Haze/Red

House/Remember/Third Stone from the Sun/Voodoo Child

Awards/Honors: Won *Disc* magazine (UK) Musician of Year Award, 1967/1968

Won *Melody Maker* magazine (UK) Pop Musician of Year Award, 1967

Won *Billboard* magazine Artist of Year Award, 1968

Won *Rolling Stone* magazine Performer of Year Award, 1968

Won *Rolling Stone* magazine American/British Rock 'n' Roll Album of Year Award, 1968 ("Electric Ladyland," Reprise 6307)

Presented with key to city by Mayor of Seattle, Washington, 1968

Won Academie Charles Cros Award (French) as Best Pop Singer of Year Award, 1969

Won *Playboy* magazine Artist of the Year Award, 1969

Won *Jazz & Pop* magazine International Critics Poll as Best Pop Guitarist of Year Award, 1970

Won *Downbeat* magazine Readers Poll Hall of Fame Award, 1970

Infl by: Chuck Berry/Earl Hooker/Elmore James/Robert Johnson/Albert King/BB King/Aaron "T-Bone" Walker/Muddy Waters/Johnny "Guitar" Watson

Infl to: Eddie Jones (Guitar Slim)

Quotes: "Hendrix' absolute command of the many facets of Afro-American music—beginning with primitive blues, extending through soul, R&B and improvisatory jazz/energy music—made him a total player"—Charles Mitchell, *Downbeat* magazine, Jun 19, 1975, p 24

"The very best of his lyrics fall someplace between outerspace imagery and the directness of the blues"—John Burks, *Rolling Stone* magazine, Oct 15, 1970, p 8

"He was a genius black musician, a guitarist, singer and a composer of brilliantly dramatic power" —Michael Lydon, *Rock Folk,* Dial Press, 1971

References: Hendrix, Chris Welch, 1972

Jimi, Curtis Knight, Praeger Publishing Company, 1974

Jimi Hendrix: A Visual Documentary -- His Life, Loves and Music, Tony Brown, Omnibus, London, Eng, 1992

HENLEY, JOHN LEE

(*aka:* John Lee)
Born: Feb 13, 1919, Canton (Madison Co), MS
Inst: Harmonica

Grandfather was a preacher; father was a cotton farmer; born/raised on farm; taught self harmonica as youth; frequently worked w Buddy Cobbs and others at local suppers/frolics/parties/dances/country functions, Canton, MS, area through 30s into 40s; moved to Chicago, IL, to work outside music from 1943; sat-in w Muddy Waters group, Purple Cat, Chicago, c1945; frequently worked w Big Boy Spires Rocket Four in local club dates, Chicago, early 50s; rec w Big Boy Spires, Chance label, Chicago, 1953; frequently worked sit-in with many blues groups in local clubs, Chicago, through 50s; rec JOB label, Chicago, 1958; rec Testament label, Chicago, 1963; worked outside music, Chicago, through 60s; worked w Big Joe Williams, Fickle Pickle, Chicago, 1964

Infl by: John Lee "Sonny Boy" Williamson/Sonny Boy Williamson (Alex Miller)

Reference: Nothing But the Blues, Mike Leadbitter, Hanover Books, 1971

HENSLEY, WILLIAM PADEN

(*aka:* Washboard Willie)
Born: Jul 24, 1909, Ft Mitchell (Russell Co), AL
Died: Aug 24, 1991, Detroit, MI
Inst: Drums/Washboard

Father was Clabe Hensley; mother Annie Ezekiel; raised in Columbus, GA; played drums by age of 6; moved to Detroit, MI, 1945; together w Eddie Burns formed own group working locally in late 40s; formed own Washboard Willie and His Super Suds of Rhythm working Golden Bell and other clubs in Detroit area from c1950; rec w Washboard Willie and His Suds of Rhythm, JVB label, Detroit, 1956; worked Good Time Bar, Detroit, 1956; Calumet Show Club, Detroit, 1960; Monterey Jazz Festival, Monterey, CA, 1964; rec Von label, Detroit, c1964; worked Univ of Detroit, Detroit, 1965; rec Herculon label, Detroit, 1966; frequently worked bars/lounges in Detroit/Ann Arbor, MI, areas, 1966-7; worked Epworth Bar, Detroit, 1970; Detroit Blues Festival, Detroit, 1970; w own Super Suds of Rhythm, Mackinac Jack's, Ann Arbor, 1972; rec Barrelhouse label, Chicago, IL, c1972; toured w American Blues Legends 73 working TV/radio/concert dates through England/Europe, 1973; rec Big Bear-Polydor label,

William Hensley (Washboard Willie)

Photo by Amy O'Neal. Courtesy Living Blues Magazine.

London, Eng, 1973; worked Ann Arbor Blues Festival, Ann Arbor, 1973; Highland Park Community College, Detroit, 1974; worked clubs/festivals in Detroit area to mid-80s; mostly inactive thereafter; died of heart attack; buried Detroit Memorial Park; Warren, MI

Song: I Feel So Fine

Quote: "A major figure on the Detroit blues scene."—*Living Blues* magazine, Jan/Feb, 1992, p 39

HI-HAT HATTIE
(see McDaniel, Hattie)

HICKS, CHARLIE *"Charley"*
(*aka:* Catjuice Charley/Charley-Charlie Lincoln/ Laughing Charley)
Born: Mar 11, 1900, Lithonia (DeKalb Co), GA
Died: Sept 28, 1963, Cairo, GA
Inst: Guitar

Father was Charlie Hicks Sr; mother was Mary Harris; born/raised on farm; worked outside music (on farm) from childhood; interested in music early and learned guitar as teenager from Savannah Weaver (mother of Curley Weaver); frequently worked local suppers/frolics/picnics in Lithonia, GA, area to 1920; moved to Atlanta, GA, to work mostly outside music with occasional gigs with brother Robert Hicks from c1920 into 50s; rec w/Robert Hicks, Columbia label, Atlanta, 1927-30; served time for murder in local prison, Cairo, GA, 1955-63; died of cerebral hemorrhage; buried Lincoln Cemetery, Atlanta, GA

Personal: Married first wife in early 20s; second wife was Annie Thomas. Was older brother of Robert Hicks, musician/singer

Infl to: Curley Weaver

Quote: "When it comes to country blues and the first popular recording artists of Atlanta, one must look at Peg Leg Howell and, especially, Robert 'Barbecue Bob' Hicks and his brother Charlie 'Lincoln' Hicks"—Pete Lowry, *Blues Unlimited* magazine (UK), Aug 1973, p 15

References: Blues Unlimited magazine (UK), Aug 1973, p 15
Sweet as the Showers of Rain, Samuel B Charters, Oak Publications, 1977

HICKS, EDNA
(*aka:* Mae Alix/Lila Vivian)
Born: Oct 14, 1895, New Orleans (Orleans Parish), LA
Died: Aug 16, 1925, Chicago, IL
Inst: Piano

Father was Victor Landreaux; mother was Rena ———; born Edna Landreaux; reportedly came north in mid-teens; app in show FOLLOW ME, Casino Theater, NYC, NY, 1916; app in Billy King's musical comedy OVER THE TOP, Lafayette Theater, NYC, 1919; toured TOBA circuit working theater dates out of Chicago, IL, from c1919; app in THE NEW AMERICAN musical comedy, Lafayette Theater, NYC, NY, 1921; app in musical comedy A TRIP AROUND THE WORLD, Lafayette Theater, NYC, 1921; app in musical comedy DERBY DAY IN DIXIE, Lafayette Theater, NYC, 1921; worked Lyceum Theater, Cincinnati, OH, 1921; worked New Star Casino, NYC, 1923; rec Victor/Brunswick/Gennett/Vocalion/Ajax/Columbia labels, NYC, 1923; rec Paramount label, NYC, 1923-4; suffered gasoline accident at home; entered Provident Hospital where she died of burns; buried Holy Sepulchre Cemetery, Worth, IL

Personal: Married Will Benbow (pre-20s); married John Hicks (c1923-5). Sister of Herb Morand of Harlem Hamfats group. Half sister of Lizzie Miles

Songs: Hard Luck Blues/Poor Me Blues

HICKS, OTIS V
(*aka:* Lightnin' Slim)
Born: Mar 13, 1913, St Louis (St Louis Co), MO
Died: Jul 27, 1974, Detroit, MI
Inst: Guitar

Born/raised on farm outside of St Louis, MO; one of 4 children; interested in music early and learned guitar from father as child; moved to St Francisville, LA, to work outside music from 1926; dropped out of school to continue outside music work through 30s; learned some guitar from brother Layfield Hicks and frequently sat-in with local bands at country suppers/picnics, St Francisville, late 30s into 40s; moved to Baton Rouge, LA, to work outside music with frequent work in small combos in back street ghetto joints from 1946; worked w Big Poppa's Band, Johnny's Cafe, Baton Rouge, c1948; frequently worked w Schoolboy Cleve in local clubs/radio shows, Baton Rouge, into 50s; rec Feature label, Crowley, LA, 1954; rec Ace label, Jackson, MS, 1954; frequently worked w Slim Harpo/Jeffrey Tyson in local club dates, Baton Rouge area, mid-50s; rec Excello label, Crowley, LA, 1955-66; formed own band to work

Otis Hicks (Lightnin' Slim)
Photo by Doug Fulton. Courtesy Living Blues *Magazine*

dance halls/parties/country suppers in Crowley area from mid-50s into 60s; worked w Whispering Smith in Baton Rouge area, 1960-2; moved to Detroit, MI, to work outside music with occasional house parties in area from c1965; worked w Slim Harpo in local club dates, Chicago, IL, c1967; w Slim Harpo, The Scene, NYC, NY, 1968; Grand Ballroom, Detroit, 1970; Univ of Chicago Folk Festival, Chicago, 1971; rec Excello label, Sheffield, AL, 1971; worked Ann Arbor Blues Festival, Ann Arbor, MI, 1972; toured w American Folk-Blues Festival working concert dates through England/Europe, 1972; rec Blue Horizon label, London, Eng, 1972; worked Marquee Club, London, 1972; worked solo at Concord Club, Southampton, Eng, 1972; Montreux Jazz Festival, Montreux, Switzerland, 1972 (por rel Excello label); toured w American Blues Legends working concert/TV/radio dates through England/Europe 1973 (por shown in film BLUES LEGENDS 73); rec Big Bear-Polydor label, London, 1973; worked local concert, Windsor, Can, 1973; entered Henry Ford Hospital where he died of cancer; buried Oak Hill Cemetery, Pontiac, MI

Personal: Married Slim Harpo's sister. Had children

Songs: Bad Luck Blues/GI Slim/Goin' Home/Help Me Spend My Gold/I Got a Little Woman/Just Made Twenty-One/Lonesome Cabin Blues/Love Bug/Miss Sarah's a Good Girl/My Starter Won't Work/Nobody Loves Me But My Mother/Voodoo Blues

Infl by: Lightnin' Hopkins/Muddy Waters/John Lee "Sonny Boy" Williamson/Sonny Boy Williamson (Alex Miller)

Infl to: Buddy Guy/Slim Harpo/Silas Hogan/Boogie Jake

Quotes: "He was, in his own way, one of the truly great, 'unspoiled' bluesmen of the post-war era"—Mike Leadbitter, *Crowley Louisiana Blues*, Blues Unlimited, 1968

"Lightnin' Slim was the king of the blues in Louisiana, he influenced everybody"—Matthew "Boogie Jake" Jacobs, *Living Blues* magazine, Mar 1977, p 26

References: Blues Unlimited magazine (UK), May 1972, pp 15-17

Crowley Louisiana Blues, Mike Leadbitter, Blues Unlimited, 1968

HICKS, ROBERT *"Bob"*
(*aka*: Barbecue Bob)

Courtesy Frank Driggs Collection

Born: Sept 11, 1902, Walnut Grove (Walton Co), GA
Died: Oct 21, 1931, Lithonia, GA
Inst: Guitar

Father was Charlie Hicks Sr; mother was Mary Harris; one of at least 3 children; worked outside music on various farms from childhood; interested in music early and learned guitar from brother Charlie Hicks as youth; moved to Atlanta, GA, to work outside music from c1920; frequently worked Tidwell's Barbecue Place/parties/suppers/picnics in Atlanta area from c1924 into 30s; rec Columbia label, Atlanta, 1927-30; rec Columbia label, NYC, NY, 1927; occasionally toured with travelling medicine shows out of Atlanta, late 20s; rec w Curley Weaver/Buddy Moss (as Georgia Cotton Pickers), Columbia label, Atlanta, 1931; died of pneumonia; buried local cemetery, Walnut Grove, GA

Personal: Married (c1925-30). Younger brother of musician/singer Charlie Hicks. Named "Barbecue Bob" due to frequent entertaining at Tidwell's Barbecue Place, Atlanta, GA

Songs: Mississippi Heavy Water Blues/Waycross Georgia Blues

Infl to: John Jackson/Curley Weaver

Quotes: "When it comes to country blues and the first popular recording artists of Atlanta, one must look at Peg Leg Howell and, especially, Robert 'Barbecue Bob' Hicks and his brother Charlie 'Lincoln' Hicks"—Pete Lowry, *Blues Unlimited* magazine (UK), Aug 1973, p 15

"For sheer musical verve and punch, Hicks easily rivals Charley Patton . . ."—Stephen Calt, Mamlish album S-3808

References: Blues Unlimited magazine (UK), Aug 1973, p 15

Sweet as the Showers of Rain, Samuel B Charters, Oak Publications, 1977

HILL, BERTHA *"Chippie"*

Courtesy Frank Driggs Collection

Born: Mar 15, 1905, Charleston (Charleston Co), SC
Died: May 7, 1950, New York, NY

Father was John Hill; mother was Ida Jones; one of 16 children; interested in music early and was singing in local churches at 9 years of age; left home at early age working as dancer on bill w Ethel Waters, LeRoy's, NYC, NY, 1919; worked William Banks Cafe, NYC, c1919; toured w Rabbit Foot Minstrels working shows as singer/dancer into 20s; toured as single on TOBA circuit working theaters in South through 20s; worked w Ethel Waters, Edmond's Cellar, NYC, c1922; rec w Louis Armstrong, OKeh label, Chicago, IL, 1925-6; frequently worked Plantation Cabaret/Dreamland Cafe, Chicago, mid-20s; worked residency w King Oliver Band, Palladium Dance Hall, Chicago, c1926; worked Coliseum Theater, Chicago, 1926; rec w Richard M Jones Jazz Wizards, OKeh label, Chicago, 1926-7; rec w Georgia Tom/Tampa Red, Vocalion label, Chicago, 1928-9; worked Elite #2 Club, Chicago, 1929; toured w Lovie Austin, 1929; settled in Chicago to work mostly outside music, 1930-4; frequently worked Annex Buffet, Chicago, 1934-7; w Jimmie Noone Orch, Cabin Inn, Chicago, 1937; worked Club De Lisa, Chicago, 1939-40; mostly inactive in music, Chicago, 1940-6; rec w Lovie Austin Blues Serenaders/Montana Taylor, Circle label, Chicago, 1946; worked Club De Lisa, Chicago, 1946-7; app on THIS IS JAZZ, WOR-radio (Mutual Network), 1947 (rebroadcast to Europe by US Department of State/por rel Circle label); worked w James P Johnson, Spanish War Relief Concert, Ziegfeld Theater, NYC, NY, 1947; Village Vanguard, NYC, 1947-8; Jimmy Ryan's, NYC, 1947-8; w Kid Ory Band, Carnegie Hall, NYC, 1948; Town Hall, NYC, 1948; Semaine du Jazz Concert, Paris, France, 1948; Central Plaza, NYC, 1949; Riviera Club, NYC, 1949-50; residency w Art Hodes Quintet, The Blue Note, Chicago, IL, 1950; Stuyvesant Casino, NYC, 1950; suffered multiple injuries in hit and run auto accident and died at Harlem Hospital; buried Lincoln Cemetery, Chicago, IL

Personal: Married John Offett (1929-). 7 children. Named "Chippie" by owner of LeRoy's in 1919 due to her young age

Songs: Atomic Blues/Blackmarket Blues/Pratt City Blues

Quotes: "One of the best accompanied, biggest toned, most swinging blues singer of the twenties . . ."—Barry Ulanov, *A Handbook of Jazz,* Viking Press, 1955

"She was a rough country contralto singer, but could fill a noisy club with her big voice"—Walter C Allen, Biograph album BLP-C6

". . . expressive, deep and beautiful voice, full of haunting inflections"—Rudi Blesh, *Shining Trumpets,* Alfred A Knopf, 1946

Reference: Playback magazine, Feb 1950, pp 3-4

HILL, BEVERLY JEAN *"Bev"*
(*aka:* Big Mama Bev)
Born: Jan 6, 1938, Birmingham (Oakland Co), MI
Died: Nov 26, 1978, Detroit, MI

Father was Charles Cecil Hill; mother Mae Bowling; both of French/Indian heritage; worked Ramoda Inn, San Jacinto, CA, 1959; worked local piano bars in Detroit, MI, with frequent work outside music into 60s; worked Ralph's Lounge, Hazel Park, MI, 1961; began singing blues at Peanut Cellar, Union Lake, MI, 1968; Rogers Roost, Warren, MI, 1968-75; worked w Tailgate Ramblers/Father Joseph Dustin's

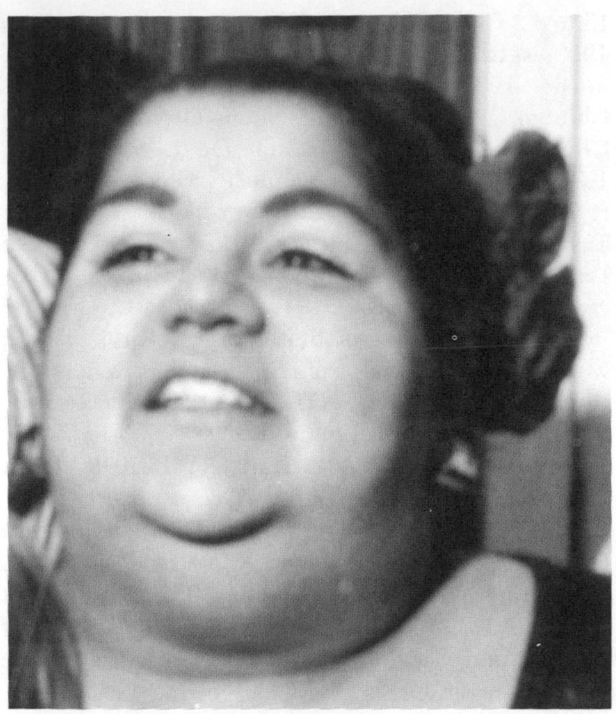
Courtesy Beverly Hill

Band/other traditional jazz groups in local clubs, Detroit area, 1968 into 70s; w Tailgate Ramblers, Troy Hilton/Sheraton Cadillac/Red Garter Club/others, Detroit area, 1971-2; w Al Hirt, Al Hirt's Club, New Orleans, LA, 1971; Coach Stop, Detroit, 1971-4; w Red Garter Banjo Band, Red Garter Club, Detroit, 1971-4; Tin Lizzie Club, Lansing, MI, 1972; w Mother's Boys jazz group, St Louis Ragtime Festival, St Louis, MO, c1972; w own DRC Dixielanders, DRC Racetrack, Detroit, 1972; w Flat Rock Society Orch, Hotel Pontchartrain, Detroit, 1972; w Bob Snyder All Stars, Flying Dutchman Club, Harbor Springs, MI, 1973; app w Red Garter Band, WKBD-TV, Detroit, 1973; app on TV commercials for local products, Detroit, early 70s; rec w Tailgate Ramblers, Jazzology label, Detroit, 1972; worked Dick Saunders' Memorial Concerts, Royal Oak, MI, 1973-5; frequently entertained for Lyons Club/Times-Picayune Newspaper Guild/other local organizations, Detroit area, early 70s; worked Detroit-Windsor Jazz/Ragtime Festival, Detroit, 1974; frequently worked w Flat Rock Society Orch at private parties in Detroit area from 1974; w Cellar Dwellers, Rogers Roost, Warren, MI, 1974; w The Nickelodeon Band, Rogers Roost, Warren, 1976; inactive from 1976; died as consequence of obesity; body cremated

Personal: Married twice; one child

Infl by: Lizzie Miles/Bessie Smith

HILL, KING SOLOMON
(see Holmes, Joe)

HILL, ROSA LEE *"Rosalie"*
Born: Sept 25, 1910, Como (Panola Co), MS
Died: Oct 22, 1968, Senatobia, MS
Inst: Guitar

Father was Sidney Hemphill, a local musician who toured in Rabbit Foot Minstrels Show and other minstrel/circus shows; mother was Zoolenia Harris, also a musician; born Rosa Lee Hemphill; one of 3 children; interested in music early and learned guitar from father as child; worked in Sidney Hemphill Band at parties/dances in Como, MS, area c1917; moved to Crenshaw, MS, to attend school, 1920-2; dropped out of school to work outside music with occasional gigs in father's cafe, Sardis, MS, 1922-4; continued outside music work with frequent gigs in father's band, Crenshaw, 1924 through 30s; worked mostly outside music with only occasional gigs in father's band into 50s; rec Atlantic label, Senatobia, MS, 1959; after death of father worked outside music in Coldwater/Senatobia/Como, MS, areas from 1961; rec Arhoolie label, Como (?), MS, 1968; died of heart failure; buried New Salem Baptist Church Cemetery, Senatobia, MS

Personal: Married Ruffan Hill (1941-68)

Reference: Blow My Blues Away, George Mitchell, Louisiana State Univ Press, 1971

HILLERY, MABLE
Born: Jul 22, 1929, La Grange (Troupe Co), GA
Died: Apr 26, 1976, New York, NY

Father was Clarence Henderson; mother was Mamie Zachery; raised in Coweta County, GA, working outside music as youth; interested in music at early age; moved to Brunswick, GA, to work outside music c1960; app on ALAN LOMAX FOLK SPECIAL, CBS-TV, 1961; toured w Georgia Sea Island Singers (as religious/folk singer) working college campuses/festivals/coffeehouses on college circuit, 1961-5; worked w Georgia Sea Island Singers, Ash Grove, Los Angeles, CA, 1965; Cafe A-Go-Go, NYC, NY, 1965; Berkeley Folk Festival, Berkeley, CA, c1965; Philadelphia Folk Festival, Spring Mt, PA (?), c1965; Smithsonian Folk Festival, Washington, DC, c1965; frequently toured as blues singer w Southern Folk Festival working college circuit/prisons through South c1966-75; app on FESTIVAL PRESENTS THE BLUES, CBC-TV, Toronto, Can, 1966; app on

Photo by Julie Snow

WBAI-FM-radio, NYC, c1966; frequently worked folk festivals on Johns Island, SC, late 60s; toured England working concert/TV dates, 1968; rec Xtra label, London, Eng, 1968; settled in NYC to work w Interdependent Learning Model's Follow-Thru Program (City Univ of New York) developing material for teachers on black culture that was used in schools/seminars, 1968-76; worked Folklore Center concert, NYC, 1968; Manhattan Community College, NYC, 1969; worked w Barbara Dane at Festival L'Unita, Turin, Italy, 1971; worked as teacher at Bank Street Col of Education, NYC, early 70s; worked Puerto Rican Solidarity Day, Madison Square Garden, NYC, 1974; Univ of Miami Blues Festival, Coral Gables, FL, 1975; Civic Center, Atlanta, GA, 1975; toured Louisiana working prisons/reform schools/old folks homes, 1975; entered St Luke's Hospital where she died of heart attack; buried Strangers Cemetery, St Simons Island, GA

Personal: Married Will Adams (1950s). 6 children. Was member of Board of Directors of Southern Folk Cultural Revival Project (SFCRP). Was consultant to New York City Head Start Program.

Songs: He Was More Than a Friend of Mine/Who Am I and Who Are You?

Quote: "Mable Hillery is a fine singer of traditional Afro-American folk music: blues, ballads and children's songs"—Pete Seeger (source/date unknown)

Reference: Sing Out magazine, May/Jun 1976, p 38

HITE, MATTIE/MATIE
(*aka:* Nellie Hite?)
Born: c1890, New York (New York Co), NY (unconfirmed)
Died: c1935, New York, NY (unconfirmed)

Reportedly born/raised in New York, NY; moved to Chicago, IL, c1915; frequently worked w Alberta Hunter/Florence Mills/others, Panama Club, Chicago, c1917-19; returned to NYC, 1919; worked Barron Wilkin's Cafe, NYC, 1919-20; Edmond's Cellar, NYC, 1920; LeRoy's, NYC, c1920; rec w Julian Motley, Victor label, NYC, 1921 (unissued); worked Rafe's Paradise Theater, Atlantic City, NJ, 1921; rec w Fletcher Henderson, Pathe label, NYC, 1923; app in HOT FEET Revue, Lafayette Theater, NYC, 1928; app in TIP-TOP REVUE, Lincoln Theater, NYC, 1928; Pod's & Jerry's Club, NYC, c1928; The Nest Club, NYC, c1929; app in CHOCOLATE BLONDES Revue, Lafayette Theater, NYC, 1929; app in THE TEMPLE OF JAZZ Revue, Lafayette Theater, NYC, 1929; app in DESIRES OF 1930 Revue, Lafayette Theater, NYC, 1930; rec w Cliff Jackson, Columbia label, NYC, 1930; app w Ralph Cooper's Band, THAT GETS IT Revue, Lafayette Theater, NYC, 1932; whereabouts unknown thereafter

Personal: Reportedly niece of Les Hite, musician and band leader. Bell recordings released as by Nellie Hite may be this singer or her sister

Quote: "One of the greatest cabaret singers of all time"—James P Johnson, *Jazz Review* magazine, Mar/Apr 1960, p 13

HITE, NELLIE
(see Hite, Mattie)

HOGAN, SILAS
Born: Sept 15, 1911, Westover (West Baton Rouge Parish), LA
Inst: Guitar/Harmonica

Moved to Irene, LA, where he was raised from 1913; worked outside music as youth; learned some guitar from uncles in late 20s; frequently worked local house parties/country jukes/picnics in Irene area into 30s; frequently worked jukes w Henry Gaines/Willie B. Thomas/Butch Cage in Irene area through 30s; moved

Photo by Terry Pattison. Courtesy Living Blues Magazine

to Scotlandville, LA, working mostly outside music, 1939 into late 50s; formed own band working joints/cafes/jukes in Baton Rouge, LA, area, 1958-65; rec Excello label, Crowley, LA, 1962-6; formed trio (w Guitar Kelley/Gene Douzier) to work clubs/bars/dances in Baton Rouge, 1966 into 70s; rec Reynaud-Flyright label, Opelousas, LA, late 60s; rec w Guitar Kelley, Arhoolie/Excello labels, Baton Rouge, 1970; worked New Orleans Jazz & Heritage Fair, New Orleans, LA, 1972; Aretha King's Club, Baton Rouge, 1974-5

Personal: Married. His son Samuel Hogan is musician

Songs: Airport Blues/Baby Please Come Back to Me/Born in Texas/Dark Clouds Rolling/Dry Chemical Blues/Everybody Needs Somebody/Honey Bee Blues/I Didn't Tell Her to Leave/I'm Gonna Quit You Baby/Just Give Me a Chance/Let Me Be Your Hatchet/Lonesome La La/So Long Blues/Trouble at Home Blues/You're Too Late, Baby

Infl by: Lightnin' Slim/Jimmy Reed

Reference: Blues Unlimited magazine (UK), Apr 1970, p 15

HOGG, ANDREW *"Smokey"/"Smoky"*
Born: Jan 27, 1914, Westconnie (Nacogdoches Co), TX
Died: May 1, 1960, McKinney, TX
Inst: Guitar/Piano

Father was Frank Hogg; mother was Money Royal; born on farm between Cushing and Westconnie, TX; one of 7 children; interested in music early and learned guitar from father as youth; frequently worked w Black Ace at local dances/parties, Greenville, TX, early 30s; frequently worked outside music with occasional work for tips on streets/picnics/country dances/jukes/taverns in Cushing, TX, area through 30s into 40s; rec Decca label, Chicago, IL, 1937; served in US Army, early 40s; frequently worked local streets/jukes/parties in Greenville/Dallas, TX, area from mid-40s into 50s; frequently worked local club dates between Houston, TX/Los Angeles, CA, late 40s; rec Exclusive label, Los Angeles, 1947; rec Bullet/Modern label, Dallas, TX, 1948; worked w Frankie Lee Sims, Empire Room, Dallas, c1948; rec acc to Frankie Lee Sims, Blue Bonnet label, Dallas, 1948; rec Modern label, Los Angeles, 1948-50; rec Specialty label, Dallas (?), 1949; rec Macy's label, Houston, 1949; rec Independent/Imperial labels, Houston (?), 1949; rec Mercury/SIW labels, Houston, 1950; rec Fidelity label, Los Angeles, 1952; rec Rays Record label, San Diego, CA, 1952; frequently worked local clubs/lounges on West Coast through 50s; rec Federal/Imperial labels, Los Angeles, 1953; rec Crown/Show Time labels, Los Angeles, 1954; frequently worked streets of Houston, late 50s; rec Ebb label, Los Angeles, 1958; entered Veterans Adminstration Hospital for cancer treatment; died of ulcer hemorrhage; buried in family cemetery, Westconnie, TX

Courtesy Sheldon Harris Collection

Personal: Married twice. 2 children. First cousin of John Hogg. Cousin of Lightnin' Hopkins. Not to be confused with Willie Anderson Hogg or Will Hodges who have also called themselves "Smokey Hogg." Generally considered to be the original "Smokey Hogg"

Billing: Little Peetie Wheatstraw

Songs: Coming Back to You Again/Look in Your Eyes, Pretty Mama

Infl by: Bill Broonzy/Peetie Wheatstraw

Quote: "His familiar guitar playing, his burred voice and his combination of new blues themes with the elements of the older traditions earned him the acclaim of both the younger Negroes and their parents"—Paul Oliver, International Polydor album 423-243

References: Blues Unlimited magazine (UK), Sept 1968, pp 9-10
Blues Unlimited magazine (UK), Jul 1968, pp 3-5
Blues World magazine (UK), Mar 1970, pp 13-14

HOGG, JOHN

Photo by Frank Scott

Born: 1912, Westconnie (Nacogdoches Co), TX
Inst: Guitar

One of 9 children; raised in Greenville, TX, and worked mostly outside music through 30s; worked outside music (as rodeo performer) on rodeo circuit through Oklahoma, late 30s; worked outside music, Dallas, TX, 1939, then Denver, CO, c1941, then Los Angeles, CA, 1942; learned some guitar from Pee Wee Crayton, early 40s; worked outside music with occasional gigs in Los Angeles area from 1942; occasionally worked with other singers/musicians in area, late 40s; rec Mercury/Octive labels, Los Angeles, 1951; continued outside music work with frequent weekend club dates, Los Angeles area, through 50s/60s; worked w own band in local clubs, Los Angeles area, late 60s; continued outside music work, Los Angeles, into 70s; worked San Diego Folk Festival, San Diego, CA, 1974; rec Advent label, Los Angeles (?), 1974

Personal: Cousin of Andrew "Smokey" Hogg. Reportedly cousin of Willie Anderson "Smokey" Hogg

Infl by: Texas Alexander/Black Ace/Blind Blake/Elmore James/Blind Lemon Jefferson

Reference: Eureka magazine, May 1960

HOGG, WILLIE ANDERSON *"Smokey"*

Born: Nov 19, 1908, Centerville (Leon Co), TX
Inst: Guitar

Grandfather Anderson Hogg was banjo player; father Isaac Andrew Hogg was guitar/piano player; learned guitar from father as child; ran away from home to tour w JC O'Brien's Georgia Minstrels working tent shows across US, 1921-8; reportedly rec for Black Swan label, Brooklyn, NY, late 20s; rec Victor label, Chicago, IL, 1931; rec extensively as acc to other bluesmen through 30s; frequently worked as acc to other bluesmen and solo in after-hour clubs through 30s/40s/50s; worked local club dates on West Coast, late 50s; settled in Brooklyn, NY, to work outside music from c1960; rec Spivey label, Brooklyn, NY, 1970

Personal: Married Laura ———. 1 child. Reportedly half-brother of Leroy Carr and cousin of John Hogg. Claimed to have used father's name on early recordings. Named "Smokey" by JC O'Brien due to his preference for smoked hamhocks. Not to be confused with singer Andrew "Smokey" Hogg

Quote: "He's an extemporaneous free-verse blues

troubadour in the Walt Whitman tradition"—Len Kunstadt, Spivey album LP-1011

Reference: Spivey album LP-1011

HOLDER, *"Ram"* JOHN WESLEY

Courtesy Sheldon Harris Collection

Born: c1939, Georgetown, British Guiana
Inst: Guitar

Father was Methodist preacher who played guitar; mother played piano/organ; one of 10 children; interested in music at early age and learned guitar at 6 years of age; frequently entertained at Saturday night outdoor meetings and church affairs from late 40s; was preaching sermons at 7 years of age; frequently sang in calypso group in area as teenager; moved to US to attend Free Methodist God's Bible School, Cincinnati, OH, 1954; attended Ohio State Univ, Columbus, OH, c1957; occasionally worked w Isley Brothers group in local church dates, Columbus, late 50s; frequently worked in local gospel groups with occasional preaching in area, Cincinnati, OH, late 50s; rec Guyanese folksongs on Afquest label (USA) c1958; formed own calypso group touring college circuit c1959-60; moved to East Coast to work as folk-blues singer in local coffeehouses, NYC, NY, 1960-3; worked New York Summer Festival, NYC, 1960; owned/performed Cafe Rafio, NYC, 1961-2; to England to tour folk club circuit, 1963; long residency at Witches Cauldron, Hampstead, Eng, c1964-5; rec local labels, London, Eng, from 1964; worked residency, Marquee Club, London, Eng, late 60s; worked local bars/clubs, London, Eng, 1968; scored RAINBOW CITY series, BBC-TV, England, late 60s; app in/scored UK films TWO GENTLEMEN SHARING/LEO THE LAST, late 60s; app in Royal Shakespeare Company Show, GOD BLESS AMERICA, Aldwych Theater, London, Eng, 1968; rec Beacon-Philips label, London, Eng, c1968; scored UK film TAKE A GIRL LIKE YOU, 1970; rec Melodisc label, London, Eng, c1970; app in show NIGHT GUITAR, Sussex Univ, Brighton, Eng, 1970; extensive England/Europe tours into 70s; rec Beacon label, London, Eng, 1971; app in non-singing role in ROBINSON CRUSOE, NBC-TV, 1974

Personal: Married (c1962-4)

Songs: Bed Sitter Girl/Black London Blues/Blues in Moscow/Blues over Europe/Brixton Blues/Definition Blues/Freedom I'm Ready/Hampstead Blues/Hampstead to Lose the Blues/Ladbroke Grove Blues/London Paris Rome Blues Express/Low Down in Paris/Notting Hill Eviction Blues/Picadilly Circus Blues/Pub Crawling Blues/Saturday's Child/Sleeping Alone Tonight Blues/Too Much Blues/Way Up High/Wimpy Bar Blues

Quotes: ". . . a true artist"—Derrick Stewart-Baxter, *Jazz Journal* magazine (UK), Aug 1969

Reference: Jazz Journal magazine (UK), Aug/Sept 1969

HOLLINS, TONY

Born: c1900-15, Clarksdale (Coahoma Co), MS (unconfirmed)
Died: c1959, Clarksdale, MS (unconfirmed)
Inst: Guitar

Raised on Lucky's Plantation, near Clarksdale, MS, working mostly outside music into 30s; learned guitar and frequently worked jukes in Dublin, MS, area through 30s; frequently worked w Brother Johnny in Clarksdale, MS, area through 30s into 40s; rec OKeh label, Chicago, IL, 1941; served in US Army c1943-5; returned to Clarksdale area to work local jukes c1945-50; moved to Chicago to work local clubs from c1950; rec w Sunnyland Slim, Decca label, Chicago, 1952; reportedly worked outside music, Chicago, from early 50s

Songs: Crawlin' King Snake/Married Women Blues/Wine-O-Woman

HOLMES, JOE

(*aka:* King Solomon Hill)
Born: 1897, McComb (Pike Co), MS
Died: 1949, Sibley, LA
Inst: Guitar/Harmonica

Learned guitar as child; moved to Sibley, LA, to work local jukes from 1915; frequently worked parties/dances in McComb, MS, area into 20s; reportedly worked w Sam Collins, McComb area, from 1920; worked w Blind Lemon Jefferson, Wichita Falls, TX, c1928; frequently worked w Ramblin' Thomas, Shreveport, LA, area, late 20s; returned to Sibley, LA, to work jukes/barrelhouses in area into 30s; rec Paramount label, Grafton, WI, 1932; hoboed through Louisiana/Texas/Arkansas through 30s into 40s; worked mostly outside music in Sibley area through 40s; died of hemorrhage

Personal: Married Roberta Allums (1918-   ). 1 child

Billing: Blind Lemon's Buddy

Songs: Down on My Bended Knee/My Buddy Blind Papa Lemon/Whoopee Blues

Reference: 78 Quarterly magazine, Autumn 1967, pp 6-9

HOLMES, WRIGHT

Born: Jul 4, 1905, Hightower, TX (unconfirmed)
Inst: Guitar

Raised/worked outside music as youth; moved to Houston, TX, to work local speakeasys/jukes in area from 1930; worked outside music in Detroit, MI/Chicago, IL, areas, early 40s; returned to Houston to work Club DeLisa/Whispering Pine/Ebony Club from c1946; frequently app on KTRH-radio, Houston, c1947; rec Gold Star/Miltone/Gotham labels, Houston, 1947; mostly inactive in music working frequently at local church services/evangelistic meets, Houston, from 1950

Personal: Married Elzadie ———

Reference: Blues Unlimited magazine (UK), Aug 1967, pp 13-16

HOLT, MORRIS

(*aka*: Magic Slim)
Born: Aug 7, 1937, Grenada (Grenada Co), MS
Inst: Guitar

Interested in music early and made own first instrument as child; attended school with Magic Sam, late

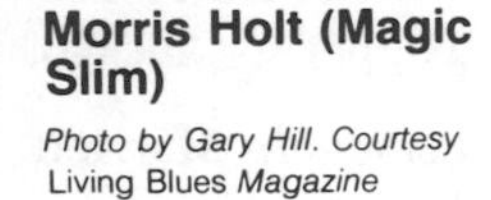

Morris Holt (Magic Slim)

Photo by Gary Hill. Courtesy Living Blues *Magazine*

40s; moved to Chicago, IL, to work outside music with occasional sit-in gigs w Magic Sam group at Ray's Lounge, Chicago, from 1955; frequently sat-in w Shakey Jake Band in local clubs, Chicago, late 50s; returned to Grenada, MS, to work outside music c1959-62; returned to Chicago to work outside music with frequent gigs at Cedar Club and others in Chicago area from c1962; frequently worked w Little Hite group, Chicago, c1966; rec w Little Hite, Ja-Wes label, Chicago, c1966; worked w Magic Sam at Club 99, Joliet, IL, c1967; formed own The Ter-Drops group, 1967; worked The Bat Man Club, Chicago, 1967; frequent residency at 1125 Club, Chicago, 1967-75; Flamingo Lounge, Chicago, 1972; frequently worked Florence's Lounge, Chicago, 1972-7; frequently worked dances/parties in Grenada/ Indianola, MS, area, early 70s; frequently worked schools/colleges in Chicago area, early 70s; frequently worked Josephine's, Chicago, 1974-7; The Peanut Barrel, Chicago, 1974; Arabian Sands, Chicago, 1974; Wise Fools, Chicago, 1974-5; rec Mean Mistreater label, Chicago, c1975; app w own Ter-Drops on TILMON TEMPO Show, WMAQ-TV, Chicago, 1975; worked Zoo Bar, Lincoln, NE, 1976-7; Biddy Mulligan's, Chicago, 1976; Midwest Blues Festival, Univ of Notre Dame, South Bend, IN, 1976; worked Pepper's, Chicago, 1977

Personal: Married. 6 children. His brothers Nick/ Douglas Holt are musicians. Lost little finger of right hand in accident during youth. Named "Magic Slim" by singer Magic Sam

Quote: "Slim has remained true to the rough, down home clientele that has long been the source and main audience for the blues"—Dick Shurman, *Crazy Music* magazine (Australia), Jun 1976, p 4

References: Blues Unlimited magazine (UK), Oct 1972, p 13

Crazy Music magazine (Australia), Jun 1976, pp 4-9

HOLTS, ROOSEVELT

Born: Jan 15, 1905, Tylertown (Walthall Co), MS
Inst: Guitar

Born/raised on farm; interested in music from 1924; moved to Pike County to learn guitar from Harrison Smith/Tommy Johnson during 30s; teamed w Tommy Johnson to work dances/parties in Jackson, MS, area, 1937; returned to Tylertown, MS, to work w Babe Stovall and others in area from 1938; frequently worked jukes/clubs in Tylertown area through 40s; spent time in Parchman Farm Prison Camp for shoot-

Photo by David Evans

ing incident early 50s; settled in Bogalusa, LA, to work mostly outside music through 50s; moved to Franklinton, LA, to work outside music early 60s; rec w Babe Stovall, Blue Horizon label, New Orleans, LA/ Bogalusa, LA/Franklinton, LA, 1966; rec Decca-Rounder label, Bogalusa, LA, 1966; worked briefly outside music in Folsom, LA, c1966; frequently worked w brother in local party work, Bogalusa area, from c1967; worked with local blues group, Pasadena, CA, 1968; rec Arhoolie label, Bogalusa/Clifton/New Orleans, LA, 1969-70; rec Bluesman label, Bogalusa, c1969/71; was jailed briefly for peddling own records on streets of Bogalusa, early 70s

Songs: Another Mule Kickin' in My Stall/Barrelhouse Blues/I'll Catch the Train and Ride/Leaving This Town, Won't Be Back to Fall/Packing Up Her Trunk to Leave/She Put Me Outdoors

Infl by: Tommy Johnson

Quote: "A man who [is] steeped in the country blues tradition [and] has refused to let his music remain static"—David Evans, Arhoolie album 1057

Reference: Blues Unlimited magazine (UK), Nov 1975, pp 9-11

HOMER THE GREAT

(see Crayton, Connie)

HOMESICK JAMES
(see Williamson, John A)

HONEY EDDIE
(see Edwards, David)

HONEYBOY
(see Patt, Frank)

HONEYDRIPPER, THE
(see Sykes, Roosevelt)

HOOKER, EARL ZEBEDEE
Born: Jan 15, 1930, Clarksdale (Coahoma Co), MS
Died: Apr 21, 1970, Chicago, IL
Inst: Banjo / Drums / Guitar / Harmonica / Mandolin / Organ / Piano

Father was Earl Hooker Sr who played harmonica/ guitar; mother was Mary Blare, a singer w Rabbit Foot Minstrels; one of 3 children; interested in music early and taught self guitar at 10 years of age; moved to Chicago, IL, where he attended Lyon & Healy Music School from 1941; occasionally worked streets w Bo Diddley and others for tips, Chicago, early 40s; learned some guitar technique from Robert Nighthawk and worked small gigs, Chicago, 1945; app w Robert Nighthawk group, KFFA-radio, Helena, AR, c1947; toured w Ike Turner group working jukes/ clubs thorugh Tennessee/Mississippi/Florida, 1949 into 50s; frequently app w Sonny Boy Williamson (Alex Miller) on KING BISCUIT TIME, KFFA-radio, Helena, AR, 1949 into mid-50s; frequently worked Wades Club, Cairo, IL, early 50s; rec Rockin' label, Memphis, TN, 1952; rec King label, Memphis, 1953; toured w own group working clubs across US, mid-50s; often worked w Otis Rush Band in local club dates, Chicago, IL/Gary, IN, 1956; toured Indiana/ Ohio working club dates, late 50s; rec Bea & Baby label, Chicago, 1959; frequently worked w Lillian Offitt at Robert's Show Lounge, Chicago, into 60s; rec acc w Lillian Offitt, Chief label, Chicago, c1960; rec w own Roadmasters and others, CJ label, Chicago, 1960-1; rec acc w Ricky Allen, Age label, Chicago, 1962; rec Checker/Age labels, Chicago, 1962-3; mostly inactive due to illness from 1963; frequently worked local hospital benefits, Chicago, mid-60s; frequently worked w Jr Parker's Band in local clubs,

Earl Hooker
Photo by Norbert Hess

Chicago, mid-60s; rec Mil-Lon label, Chicago, 1965; frequently worked Tri-State Inn, Gary, IN, through 60s; worked Rock's Tavern, Rockford, IL, mid-60s; frequently worked Pepper's Lounge/Blue Flame Club, Chicago, IL, through 60s; formed The Invaders to work on Joe Hinton Show at concert dates in Paris, France, 1965; app w The Beatles on READY STEADY GO Show, BBC-TV, London, Eng, 1965; rec CJ label, Chicago, IL, 1966; rec Cuca/BluesWay/Red Lightnin' labels, Sauk City, WI, 1967; worked White Horse Inn, Chicago, IL, 1968; rec Arhoolie label, Chicago, 1968; w Jr Wells Band, Kinetic Playground, Chicago, 1969; Alex Club, Chicago, 1969; Chicago Blues Festival, Chicago, 1969; rec Arhoolie label, Berkeley, CA, 1969; rec Blue Thumb label, CA (?), 1969; rec BluesWay label, Los Angeles, CA, 1969; toured w American Folk-Blues Festival working concert dates through England/Europe, 1969; worked Royal Albert Hall, London, Eng, 1969 (por rel CBS label); worked w own Electric Dust Band, Theresa's Lounge, Chicago, 1969; entered Municipal Tuberculosis Sanitarium where he died of pulmonary tuberculosis; buried Restvale Cemetery, Worth, IL

Personal: Married Bertha Nixon. Was cousin of musicians John Lee Hooker/Joe Hinton and nephew of Kansas City Red

Songs: Bertha/Blue Guitar/Blue Shadows Fall/Conversion Blues/Country & Western/Don't Have to Worry/Earl Hooker Blues/End of the Blues/Going Up and Down/Guitar Rag/Hold On, I'm Comin'/Hooker 'n' Steve/Hooker Special/Hookin'/Hot & Heavy/The Leading Brand/Moon Is Rising/Off the Hook/Something You Ate/Two Bugs and a Roach/Universal Rock/You Don't Want Me/You Got to Lose/Wah Wah Blues

Infl by: Leo & Kinky Blevins/Robert Nighthawk/Aaron "T-Bone" Walker

Infl to: Elvin Bishop/Jimi Hendrix/Ike Turner

Quotes: "Earl Hooker had the greatness which enabled him to successfully bring new techniques to an old tradition"—Peter Hatch, *Coda* magazine (Canada), Jun 1970, p 14

"... Earl Hooker, one of the finest, though underappreciated, guitarists in modern blues and long considered by his Chicago peers the man to beat"—Pete Welding, *Downbeat* magazine (issue unknown)

Reference: Blues Unlimited magazine (UK), Jan 1969, pp 7-9

HOOKER JOE

(see Davis, Walter)

HOOKER, JOHN LEE

(*aka:* Birmingham Sam/John Lee Booker/Boogie Man/John Lee Cooker/Delta John/Johnny Lee/Texas Slim/Johnny Williams)
Born: Aug 22, 1917, Clarksdale (Coahoma Co), MS
Inst: Guitar

Father was William Hooker; mother Minnie Ramsey; raised/worked outside music on stepfather William Moore's farm from childhood; frequently sang spirituals in local church, Clarksdale, MS, late 20s; first instrument was inner-tube on barn door, later learning some guitar from William Moore as youth; frequently worked w William Moore at local country suppers/fish-fries/dances in area c1929-31; ran away from home to work outside music in Memphis, TN, from 1931; worked w Robert Nighthawk/Eddie Love/Joe Willard/others in local clubs/tonks/joints, Memphis, 1931-3; moved to Cincinnati, OH, to work outside music, 1933 into 40s; frequently worked with gospel groups such as The Big Six (1938), The Delta Big Four (1940), The Fairfield Four (1942) in Cincinnati area through 30s into 40s; moved to Detroit, MI, to work outside music from 1943; formed own group working Monte Carlo Club/New Olympia Club/Henry's Swing Club/Apex Club/Forest Inn/JB Bar/Club Basin/Vogue Lounge/Huddy Color Bar/Sensation Club/others in Detroit area from late 40s; rec Modern label, Detroit, 1948-54; rec King label, Detroit, 1948-50; rec Regent/Savoy labels, Detroit, c1948; rec Staff/Sensation labels, Detroit, c1949-50; frequently worked jazz concerts/local TV shows, Detroit area, 1949; rec Regal label, Detroit, 1950; rec Gone label, Detroit, 1951; worked Music Inn, Lenox, MA, 1951; rec Acorn/Chance labels, Detroit, c1951; worked Harlem Inn, Detroit, 1951; frequent road tours out of Detroit, 1951; worked Club Carribe, Detroit, 1951; rec Chess label, Detroit, 1951-4; rec DeLuxe label, Detroit, MI/Cincinnati, OH, 1952-3; rec Gotham label, Philadelphia, PA, 1952; worked briefly as DJ on local radio show, Detroit, 1952; toured w Muddy Waters Band working clubs through South, 1952; toured extensively as single working clubs/bars/concerts/coffeehouses in major cities of US through 50s; worked Circle Club, Flint, MI, early 50s; rec JVB label, Detroit, 1953; rec Savoy label, Newark, NJ, c1954; rec Specialty label, Detroit, 1954; rec VJ label, Chicago, IL, 1955-62; rec Fortune label, Detroit, 1956; frequently worked Harlem Inn, Detroit,

John Lee Hooker

Courtesy Sheldon Harris Collection

through 50s; rec Fortune label, Detroit, 1959-60; worked Newport Folk Festival, Newport, RI, 1959; Gerde's Folk City, NYC, NY, 1959; rec Lauren/Galaxy labels, Culver City, CA, 1959; rec Riverside label, Detroit, 1959-60; rec Prestige label, Chicago, IL, c1959; worked Newport Folk/Jazz Festival, Newport, RI, 1960 (por shown in USIA film short series JAZZ USA [Nos 19, 22]/por rel VJ/Vanguard labels); worked Village Gate, NYC, 1960; rec Decca label, NYC, 1960; worked Golden Vanity, Boston, MA, 1960-1; Counterpoint, Chicago, IL, 1960; extensively toured coffeehouses/college circuit, 1960-1; worked Second Fret, Philadelphia, PA, 1961; rec Atco label, Miami, FL, 1961; worked Fifth Peg, Toronto, Can, 1961; Ascot Club, Toronto, 1961; Town Hall, NYC, 1961; Sugar Hill Club, San Francisco, 1961-2 (por 1962 date rel Galaxy/Fantasy labels); Gerde's Folk City, NYC, 1962; toured w Rhythm & Blues USA package show working concerts/festivals through England/Europe, 1962; rec Polydor label, Hamburg, Ger, 1962; worked Raven Gallery, Detroit, MI, 1963; Newport Folk Festival, Newport, RI, 1963 (por rel Vanguard label); The Establishment, Toronto, Can, 1963; app on LYRICS AND LEGENDS (ep: Singing Styles), WNET-TV, NYC (syndicated), 1963; worked Copa Cabana, Chicago, IL, 1964; Western Hall, Chicago, 1964-6; Newport Jazz Festival, Newport, RI, 1964 (por rel VJ label); rec ST for Democratic National Committee TV commercial, 1964; toured England/Europe w own John Lee's Ground Hogs group working concert dates, 1964; worked w John Mayall's Bluesbreakers, Flamingo Club, London, Eng, 1964; toured w/American Folk Blues Festival working concert dates through England/Europe, 1965 (por Hamburg, Ger, concert rel Fontana label); rec Verve-Folkways label, London, Eng, 1965; worked Gerde's Folk City, NYC, NY, 1965; Blues Unlimited Club, Detroit, MI, 1965; Apollo Theater, NYC, 1965-6; New Gate of Cleve, Toronto, Can, 1965; Cafe A-Go-Go, NYC, 1965-6 (por rel Verve/BluesWay labels); app on KALEIDOSCOPE 4, NBC-TV, 1965; rec Impulse label, NYC, 1965; app on SOME OF THE PEOPLE, KUHF-FM-radio, Houston, TX, 1965; worked Motor Inn, Fairfield, CT, 1966; Sylvio's, Chicago, IL, 1966; rec Chess label, Chicago, 1966; toured England working concert dates, 1966-7; worked Rheingold Central Park Music Festival, NYC, 1966-7; Club 47, Cambridge, MA, 1966; Community Theater, Berkeley, CA, 1967; rec BluesWay label, NYC, 1967; worked Basin Street West, San Francisco, CA, 1967; American Festival of Music, Boston, MA, 1967; Golden Bear, Huntington Beach, CA, 1968; toured w American Folk Blues Festival working concerts through England/Europe, 1968; app in UK film AMERICAN FOLK BLUES FESTIVAL, 1968 (shown on BBC-TV, London, Eng); worked Ash Grove, Los Angeles, CA, 1968; Rapa House, Detroit, MI, 1968; toured w Eddie Vinson working concert dates through England/Europe, 1969; worked Antibes Jazz Festival, Paris, France, 1969; Blues Scene 69, London, Eng, 1969; Electric Circus, NYC, 1969; app on DICK CAVETT Show, ABC-TV, 1969; worked Central Park Music Festival, NYC, 1969; Ungano's, NYC, 1969-70; Loeb Student Center, NYC, 1969; Ann Arbor Blues Festival, Ann Arbor, MI, 1969-70; Jazz Workshop, Boston, MA, 1969; Main Point, Bryn Mawr, PA, 1969; rec w Earl Hooker, BluesWay label, Los Angeles, 1969; worked Temple Music Festival, Temple University, Ambler, PA, 1970; Auditorium Theater, Chicago, IL, 1970; rec Stax label, Memphis, TN, c1970; toured w Carey Bell working concert dates through Europe, 1970; rec ABC label, San Francisco, CA, 1970-1; rec w Canned Heat group, Liberty label, Los Angeles, CA, 1970; toured w Canned Heat group working concert dates across US, 1970-1; worked Keystone Korner, Berkeley, CA, 1971; Kabuki Theater, San Francisco, 1971 (por rel ABC-BluesWay label); Carnegie Hall, NYC, NY, 1971; Boston Univ, Boston, MA, 1971; Liberty Hall, Houston, TX, 1971; Ash Grove, Los Angeles, 1971-3; Hunter Col, NYC, 1971; app in film ROOTS OF AMERICAN MUSIC: COUNTRY & URBAN MUSIC (Pt 1), 1971; toured England working concert/club dates, 1971; worked local club dates, Vancouver, Can, 1972; Funky Quarters, San Diego, CA, 1972; The Lighthouse, Los Angeles, 1972; in concert at Correctional Training Facility, Soledad, CA, 1972 (por rel ABC label); app in French film L'AVENTURE DU JAZZ (UK title, JAZZ ODYSSEY), 1972 (por rel Jazz Odyssey label); rec ST for film MISTER BROWN, 1972; worked Esquire Showbar, Montreal, Can, 1972-3; Nutcracker Lounge, New Orleans, LA, 1972; Siena Col Blues Festival, Memphis, TN, 1972; Joe's Place, Cambridge, MA, 1972; The Unicorn, Boston, MA, 1972; Shaboo Inn, Mansfield, CT, 1973; Capitol Theater, Montreal, Can, 1973; Lincoln Center, NYC, 1973; Ozark Mountain Folk Fair, Arkansas, 1973 (por shown in film GETTIN' BACK); worked Ann Arbor Blues Festival, Ann Arbor, MI, 1973; Topanga Corral, Los Angeles, 1974; Hunter Col, NYC, 1974; My Father's Place, Roslyn, NY, 1974-5; Academy of Music, Brooklyn, NY, 1974-5; Nixon Theater, Pittsburgh, PA, 1974; worked w Coast to Coast Blues Band, Sand Dunes, San Francisco, 1974; Rainbow Room, Detroit, MI, 1974; Ann Arbor Blues/Jazz Festival, Windsor, Can, 1974; Toronto Blues Festival, Olympic Island, Toronto, Can, 1974; app on MIDNIGHT SPECIAL, NBC-TV, 1974; worked Keystone Korner, Berkeley, CA, 1974; Sandy's Concert Club, Boston, MA, 1974; Balcony Hall, Scottsdale, AZ, 1975; Tote's Place, New Haven, CT, 1975; Liberty Hall, Houston, TX, 1975; Blackbeard's, Santa Barbara, CA, 1975; In Concert Club, Montreal, Can, 1975; El Mocambo, Toronto, Can, 1975; w Coast to Coast Blues Band, The Savoy Club, San Francisco, CA, 1976; Hunter Col, NYC, NY, 1976; toured Europe working club/concert dates, 1976; worked North Sea Jazz Festival 76, Congress Centre, The Hague, Holland, 1976; Antone's, Austin, TX, 1976; Wise Fools Pub, Chicago, IL, 1976-7; New Orleans Jazz & Heritage Festival, New Orleans, LA, 1976; Murphy & Me Tavern, Eugene, OR, 1977; Miller Theater, Houston, TX, 1977; Main Point, Bryn Mawr, PA, 1977; Rainbow Tavern, Seattle, WA, 1977; The Rising Sun, Montreal, Can, 1977; The Keystone, Palo Alto, CA, 1977 (por rel Tomato label); The Red Creek, Rochester, NY, 1977; Belle Starr, Buffalo, NY, 1977; app w Foghat group, The Palladium, NYC, 1977 (por on DON KIRSHNER'S ROCK CONCERT, NBC-TV, 1978)

Personal: Married Martella ——— (1943-). 4 children. His sons Robert and John Jr are musicians and have worked/recorded with him. Cousin of musician Earl Hooker. Not to be confused with Johnny Williams, guitarist, or Robert Warren who also used pseudonym Johnny Williams

Songs: A Sheep Out on the Foam/Alimonia Blues/Apologize/Baby Be Strong/Baby I Love You/Ballad to Abraham Lincoln/Bang Bang Bang Bang/Behind the Plow/Birmingham Blues/Blacksnake/Bluebird/Blue Monday/Blues For My Baby/Boogie Chillen/Boogie Everywhere I Go/Boogie with the Hook/Boom Boom Boom Boom/Bumblebee Bumblebee/Burning Hell/Bus Station Blues/Church Bell Tone/Cold Chills/Country Boy/Crawling King Snake/Cruel Little Baby/Deep Down in My Heart/Democrat Man/Devils Jump/Dimples/Do You Remember Me?/Doin' the Shout/Don't Be Messin' with My Bread/Don't Go Baby/Don't Look Back/Don't Turn Me Away from Your Door/Down at the Landing/Dreamin' Blues/Dusty Road/Endless Boogie/Feel So Bad/The Feelin' Is Gone/Get Back Home to the USA/Goin' South/Goin' to Louisiana/Graveyard Blues/Grinder Man/Guitar Lovin' Man/Half a Stranger/Hard Headed Woman/Have Mercy on My Soul/High Priced Woman/Hit the Floor/Hit The Road/Hobo Blues/Hold It/House Rent Boogie/I Don't Need No Steam Heat/I Don't Wanna Go to Vietnam/I Don't Want Your Money/I Just Can't Hold On Much Longer/I

Just Don't Know/I Like to See You Walk/I Need Some Money/I Need You/I Want to Shout/I Was Standing by the Wayside/I Wonder Why/If You Got a Dollar/I'll Know Tonight/I'm Bad Like Jesse James/I'm Going Upstairs/I'm in the Mood/I'm Just a Drifter/I'm Leaving/I'm Prison Bound/It's a Crazy Mixed Up World/It's My Own Fault/It's You I Love Baby/Jackson Tennessee/The Journey/Kick Hit 4 Hit Kix U/Late Last Night/Leave My Wife Alone/Left My Wife and My Baby/Let's Make It/Letter to My Baby/Little Wheel/Look at the Rain/Lost My Job/Love Is a Burning Thing/Love My Baby/Mad with You Baby/Mean Mean Woman/Messin' with the Hook/Might as Well Say We're Through/Mini Skirts/Misbelieving Baby/Moaning Blues/My Baby Don't Love Me/My Baby Put Me Down/My Best Friend/My First Wife Left Me/Never Get Out of These Blues Alive/Night Mare Blues/No Shoes/Nothin' But Trouble/One Way Ticket/Peace Lovin' Man/Poor Me/Pots On, Gas on High/Pouring Down Rain/Queen Bee/Ramblin' by Myself/Run On Babe/Send Me Your Pillow/She's Long She's Tall (Weeping Willow)/Serve Me Right to Suffer/Seven Days and Seven Nights/Sittin' Here Thinking/Sittin' in My Dark Room/Sometimes You Made Me Feel So Bad/Stella Mae/Stuttering Blues/Sugar Mama/TB Is Killing Me/TB Sheets/Take Me As I Am/Talk About Your Baby/Teachin' the Blues/Thinking Blues/This World/Travelin' Day and Night/Tupelo/Walkin' the Boogie/Wednesday Evening Blues/What's the Matter Baby/Whiskey and Wimmen/Wobblin' Baby/Women and Money/You Been Dealin' with the Devil/You Gonna Miss Me/You Lost a Good Man/Your Love/You're Looking Good Tonight

Awards/Honors: Won French Academie du Jazz Record Prix for Best Urban Blues Artist of 1968

Won *Jazz & Pop* magazine International Critics Poll for Best Blues Album, 1968 ("Urban Blues," BluesWay BL-6012)

Won *Jazz & Pop* magazine International Critics Poll for Best Blues Album, 1969 ("Simply the Truth," BluesWay BL-6023)

Won *Ebony* magazine Black Music Poll Blues Hall of Fame, 1975

Infl by: Coot Harris/William Moore/James Smith

Infl to: Canned Heat/Buddy Guy/John Hammond/Pat Hare/Eddie Kirkland/Robert Lowery/Maxwell Street Jimmy/John Mayall/Junior Parker/Sidney Semien/Johnny Winter

Quotes: "One of the most gripping and powerful singers the blues has yet produced and a guitarist whose playing all but overwhelms one with its ferocity and rhythmic tension"—Pete Welding, Buddah album 7506

"His chanting voice, inventive guitar, and insistent foot-tapping make for a one man orchestra which is hard to beat"—Alan Wilson, Specialty album 2125

"A prolific creater of songs in the blues vein, reflecting a depth of involvement in the entire spectrum of black music . . ."—Don Heckman, *BMI: The Many Worlds of Music,* Summer issue, 1969

References: Nothing But the Blues, Mike Leadbitter, Hanover Books, 1971

Downbeat magazine, Oct 3, 1968, pp 15-17

Living Blues magazine, Autumn 1979 (No. 44), pp 14-22

HOPKINS, JOEL *"Squatty"*
Born: Jan 3, 1904, Centerville (Leon Co), TX
Died: Feb 15, 1975, Galveston, TX
Inst: Guitar

Father was Abe Hopkins; mother was Janie Washington; one of 6 children; born/raised on farm; ran away from home to hobo across US working outside music from 1913; taught self guitar c1914; frequently toured with medicine caravans/tent shows working as buck dancer into 20s; frequently worked/toured w/Blind Lemon Jefferson through Texas, 1922-7; continued outside music work while hoboing through South working as singing guitarist in jukes/dives into 30s; occasionally served time in county farm work gangs during 30s; rec w Lightnin' Hopkins, Gold Star label, Houston, TX, 1947; worked outside music (as caretaker) in Darlington, TX, through 50s; rec Candid label, Dickinson, TX, 1959; app on MACK McCORMICK AND FRIENDS, KUHF-FM-radio, Houston, TX, 1960; frequently worked outside music in Houston area through 60s into 70s; rec w Lightnin' Hopkins, Arhoolie label, Waxahachie, TX, 1964; rec w Lightnin' Hopkins, Arhoolie label, Houston, TX, 1965; app w Lightnin' Hopkins in film THE BLUES ACCORDING TO LIGHTNIN' HOPKINS, 1968; mostly inactive in music from late 60s; entered Univ of Texas Medical Branch Hospital where he died of cardiovascular disease; buried Centerville Cemetery, Centerville, TX

Personal: Older half-brother of musician/singer Sam "Lightnin' " Hopkins

Infl to: Lightnin' Hopkins

HOPKINS, JOHN HENRY
Born: Feb 3, 1901, Centerville (Leon Co), TX
Died: (unknown)
Inst: Guitar

Father was Abe Hopkins; mother was Frances Sims; one of 6 children; ran away from home at early age to hobo across US working outside music; spent many years in various work farms/prisons; settled in Waxahachie, TX, during 50s; rec w Lightnin' Hopkins, Arhoolie label, Waxahachie, 1964; worked mostly outside music thereafter

Personal: Brother of Sam "Lightnin'" Hopkins

HOPKINS, SAM *"Lightnin' "*
Born: Mar 15, 1912, Centerville (Leon Co), TX
Died: Jan 30, 1982, Houston, TX
Inst: Guitar/Organ/Piano

Father Abe Hopkins was musician; mother was Frances Sims; one of 6 children; after death of father moved to Leona, TX, where he was raised from c1915; frequently worked outside music (on local farms) with occasional local church choir singing from childhood; first instrument was homemade cigar box at 8 years of age; learned some guitar from brother Joel Hopkins as child; dropped out of school to hobo through Texas from c1920; worked dances/picnics/

Sam "Lightnin' " Hopkins
Photo by Chris Strachwitz. Courtesy Arhoolie Records

streets in Buffalo, TX, area early 20s; travelled widely through Texas working for tips in bars/joints/clubs/taverns through 20s; worked w Texas Alexander, Rainbow Theater, Houston, TX, c1927; teamed w Texas Alexander to work streets/dives, Houston, late 20s, with frequent tours as team through East Texas to mid-30s; served time in Houston County Prison Farm, late 30s; returned to Houston to work outside music with occasional tours working parties/frolics through South from late 30s into 40s; worked The Beer Garden, Yazoo City, MS, 1939; frequently worked w Texas Alexander on streets/buses, Houston, 1945 into 50s; rec w Thunder Smith, Aladdin label, Los Angeles, CA, 1946-7; worked local dance halls, Los Angeles, 1946-7; rec w Joel Hopkins, Gold Star label, Houston, 1947-9; rec extensively on many independent labels, various locations in Texas, late 40s into early 50s; rec Mainstream label, NYC, 1950; rec Mercury label, Houston, TX, 1952; frequently worked Pop's Place/Silver Dollar #2 and other clubs/jukes/bars, Houston, through 50s into 60s; rec Decca label, NYC, 1953; rec Herald label, Houston, 1954; rec Folkways label, Houston, 1959; rec Tradition/77 labels, Los Angeles, CA/Houston, TX, 1959-60; app on FOLKSAY, KUHF-FM-radio, Houston, 1959; worked Hootenanny-in-the-Round, Alley Theater, Houston, 1959; Univ of California Folk Festival, Berkeley, CA, 1960; rec World Pacific label, Los Angeles, 1960; toured college circuit on West Coast, 1960; worked The Troubador, Los Angeles, 1960; app on (unknown) show, CBC-TV, Toronto, Can, 1960; rec Decca label, Houston, 1960; worked Carnegie Hall, NYC, 1960; frequently worked Ash Grove, Los Angeles, 1960-70 (por 1960 dates rel VJ label); Irene's, Houston, 1960; Sputnik Bar, Houston, 1960; app on MACK McCORMICK AND FRIENDS, KUHF-FM-radio, Houston, 1960-1; rec Prestige-Bluesville label, Houston, TX, and elsewhere, 1960-3; rec Fire/Candid labels, NYC, 1960; app on A PATTERN OF WORDS AND MUSIC, CBS-TV, 1960; worked Sugar Hill Club, San Francisco, CA, 1961; toured w Clifton Chenier's Band working dances/clubs through Texas, 1961; worked Rainbow Room, Dallas, 1961; Shriners Auditorium, Dallas, 1961; rec Arhoolie label, Berkeley, CA, 1961; app in film THE BLUES, 1962; worked Village Gate, NYC, 1962-3; rec Arhoolie label, Houston, 1962; rec Prestige label, NYC, 1963-5; worked Retort Club, Detroit, 1963; Second Fret, Philadelphia, PA, 1963 (por rel Prestige label); worked Cabale Coffeehouse, Berkeley, CA and other clubs/coffeehouses/concerts in Berkeley/Oakland, CA, areas, 1963; toured w American Folk Blues Festival working concert dates through England/Europe, 1964 (por Musikhalle Concert, Hamburg, Ger, rel Fontana label); rec Arhoolie label, Waxahachie, TX, 1964; worked Continental Club, Los Angeles, 1964; Cabale Club, Berkeley, CA, 1964 (por rel Arhoolie label); Carnegie Hall, NYC, 1964; Bird Lounge, Houston, 1964 (por rel Guest Star label); rec Home Cooking label, Houston (?), mid-60s; rec Arhoolie label, Houston, 1965; worked Western Hall, Chicago, IL, 1965-6; Pepper's Lounge, Chicago, 1965; rec Jewel label, Houston, 1965; frequently worked local bars/clubs/joints, Houston, late 60s into 70s; worked Gaslight Club, NYC, 1965; The Good Buddy, San Francisco, 1965; Newport Folk Festival, Newport, RI, 1965; The Matrix, San Francisco, 1965; rec Verve label, Los Angeles, 1965; worked Longhorn Jazz Festival, Austin, TX, 1966; Berkeley Blues Festival, Univ of California, Berkeley, CA, 1966 (por rel Arhoolie label); Sylvio's, Chicago, IL, 1966; Lou's Rickshaw Room, Houston, 1966; app on SOME OF THE PEOPLE, KUHF-FM-radio, Houston, 1966; app in Les Blank film short THE SUN'S GONNA SHINE, 1967; worked The Showboat, Houston, 1967; rec Arhoolie label, Houston, TX, 1967; worked Pacific Jazz Festival, Costa Mesa, CA, 1967; app in Les Blank film short THE BLUES ACCORDIN' TO LIGHTNIN' HOPKINS, 1968; worked Festival of American Folklife, Washington, DC, 1968; Civic Auditorium, Santa Monica, CA, 1969; rec International Artists label, Houston, 1968; worked Blossom Music Center, Cleveland, OH, 1969; Ann Arbor Blues Festival, Ann Arbor, MI, 1969; King Hall, Berkeley, CA, 1969; Mandrake's, Berkeley, 1969; rec Liberty label, Hollywood, CA, 1969; worked Fillmore West, San Francisco, CA, 1969; Notre Dame Blues Festival, South Bend, IN, 1970; rec Avco label, Houston (?), c1970; rec ST for UK film BLUES LIKE SHOWERS OF RAIN, 1970; worked The Boarding House, San Francisco, c1971; La Bastille, Houston, c1971; Raven Oyster Bar, Beaumont, TX, 1971; app on ARTISTS IN AMERICA, PBS-TV, 1971 (rel as film short SAM LIGHTNIN' HOPKINS); app on BOBOQUIVARI, PBS-TV, 1971; app in Univ of Washington film short A PROGRAM OF SONGS BY LIGHTNIN' SAM HOPKINS, 1971; rec ST for film SOUNDER, 1972; worked Carnegie Hall, NYC, 1973; Quiet Knight, Chicago, IL, 1973; Univ of Vermont, Burlington, VT, 1973; The Temple Hall, New Orleans, LA, 1973; Lincoln Center, NYC, 1974; New Orleans Jazz & Heritage Festival, New Orleans, 1974-7 (por 1976 concert rel Island label); Effie's Go-Go, Beaumont, TX, 1974; Mother Blues, Dallas, 1974; rec Sonet label, Houston, 1974; worked Great Southeast Music Hall, Atlanta, GA, 1974; Castle Creek, Austin, TX, 1974; Keystone Korner, Berkeley, CA, 1975-6; Liberty Hall, Houston, 1975; Simon Fraser Univ, Burnaby, Can, 1975; Univ of Saskatchewan, Saskatoon, Can, 1975; Atlanta Blues Festival, Great Southeast Music Hall, Atlanta, GA, 1976; Sophie's, Palo Alto, CA, 1976; Jed's University Inn, New Orleans, LA, 1976; New Yorker Theater, Toronto, Can, 1977; The Lighthouse, Los Angeles, 1977; Miller Theater, Houston, 1977; Liberty Hall, Houston, 1977; Granada Theater, Dallas, 1977; toured Europe working concert dates, 1977; worked Rotterdam Jazz Festival '3-3', Rotterdam, Netherlands, 1977; Dortmund Jazz Life Festival, Dortmund, Ger, 1977; The Rising Sun, Montreal, Can, 1978; toured US/Canada working clubs/concerts from 1978; app AUSTIN CITY LIMITS, NET-TV (PBS), 1979; New Orleans Jazz & Heritage Fest, New Orleans, 1979; Tramps, NYC, 1980-1; died of cancer; buried Forest Park Cemetery, Houston

Personal: Took name "Lightnin'" from his early association w pianist Wilson "Thunder" Smith

Songs: A Man Like Me Is Hard to Find/Abilene/Ain't It Crazy?/Airplane Blues/All I Got Is Gone/At Home Blues/Baby You're Not Going to Make a Fool Out of Me/Bald Headed Woman/Ball of Twine/Beans Beans Beans/Big Car Blues/Black and Evil/Black Cat Bone/Black Ghost Blues/Blues for Queen Elizabeth/Blues Is a Feeling/Born in the Bottoms/Bud Russell Blues/Burnin' in LA/Business You're Doin'/California Showers/Can't Be Successful/Can't Get That Woman off My Mind/Change Your Way/Christmas Time Is Coming/Coffee Blues/Come Back Baby/Crying for Bread/Cut Me Out Baby/Dark and Cloudy/Death Bells/December 7, 1941/Don't Embarrass Me Baby/Don't Treat That Man the Way You Treat Me/Down Baby/Fast Life Woman/Feel Like Balling the Jack/Feel So Bad/Footrace Is On/Get Off My Toe/Give Me Time to Think/Go Ahead/Goin' Away/Goin' to Dallas/Good Times Here/Got to Move You Baby/Grandma Told Grandpa/Grosebeck Blues/Happy Blues for John Glenn/Hard to Love a Woman/Have You Ever Loved a Woman?/Hello Central/Honey Babe/How Have You Been?/I Asked the Bossman/I Don't Need You Woman/I Got Tired/I Heard My Children Crying/I Went to Louisiana/I Wish I Was a Baby/I Wonder Where She Can Be Tonight/Ice Storm Blues/Ida Mae/I'm Goin' to Build a Heaven of My Own/I'm Gonna Meet My Baby Somewhere/I'm Taking a Devil of a Chance/I've Had My Fun/The Jet/Katie Mae/Last Night Blues/Leave Jike Mary Alone/Lightnin' Don't Feel Well/Lightnin's Love/Little and Low/Little Antoinette/Little Mama Blues/Little Sisters Boogie/Lonesome Graveyard/Long Gone/Mama's Baby Child/Meet You at the Chicken Shack/Miss Loretta/Mister Charlie/Mistreated Blues/Mojo Hand/Morning Blues/Movin' Out/My Grandpa Is Old Too/Old Man/Old Woman Blues/Once Was a Gambler/Open Up Your Door/Rollin' and Rollin'/Rollin' Woman Blues/Sad News from Korea/Santa Fe Blues/Send My Child Home to Me/75 Highway/Shinin' Moon/Short Haired Woman/Shotgun/Sinner's Prayer/Slavery/So Long Baby/Somebody's Got to Go/Stool Pigeon Blues/Stranger Here/Take a Walk/Take It If You Want It/Tim Moore's Farm (Blues)/T-Model Blues/Too Many Drivers/Trouble Blues/Up on Telegraph Avenue/Wake Up Old Lady/Walkin' Blues/Walking This Road/The War Is Over/War News Blues/The World's in a Tangle/You Better Stop Her/You One Black Rat/You Treat Po' Lightnin' Wrong

Awards/Honors: Won *Downbeat* magazine International Jazz Critics Poll as New Star, Male Singer, 1962

Film THE BLUES ACCORDIN' TO LIGHTNIN' HOPKINS won Gold Hugo Award of Chicago Film Festival as best documentary of 1970

Infl by: Texas Alexander/Joel Hopkins/Blind Lemon Jefferson/Lonnie Johnson

Infl to: Wild Child Butler/Carolina Slim/Pernell Charity/Buddy Guy/John Paul Hammond/Larry Johnson/Guitar Kelley/Eddie Kirkland/JB Lenoir/Lightnin' Slim/Louisiana Red/Robert Lowery/Luke Miles/LC Robinson/Arthur Spires/Hound Dog Taylor/Eddie Vinson/LC Williams/Robert Pete Williams

Quotes: "He is—in the finest sense of the word—a minstrel: a street-singing, improvising song maker born to the vast tradition of the blues. His only understanding of music is that it be as personal as a hushed conversation"—Mack McCormick, Tradition album TLP-1035

"His blues are poetic, personal recollections and observations, and he delivers them with a sense of humor and sincerity"—Chris Albertson, Barnaby album 30247

"The most creative folk poet of our time who is without a doubt the King of the Blues"—Chris Strachwitz, Arhoolie album 200

Reference: The Country Blues, Samuel B Charters, Rinehart & Company Inc, 1959

HORTON, JOANNE BARBARA *"Pug"*

Courtesy Joanne Horton

Born: May 30, 1932, Sheffield (York Co), England

Father was Herbert Kitcheman; mother was Florence Amelia Draper; born Joanne Barbara Kitcheman; raised/schooled in Sheffield, Eng; interested in music early and sang w Colin Whitehead Dance Band at about 7 years of age; occasionally worked in various bands in local Working Men's clubs, Sheffield, 1947-50; worked Milestone Inn, Derbyshire, Eng, 1949; worked as entertainment organizer for Butlin Holiday Camps in England, 1950-2; worked as dancer w Carroll Gibbons Company, Savoy Hotel, London, 1952-3; frequently worked outside music as fashion model and in promotional activities in England, 1953-4; moved to Ontario, Can, to work outside music in public relations business with appearances on CBC-TV and radio shows, 1954-6; moved to Florida to continue outside music work with some appearances in local TV commercials and in documentary film THE SPANISH MONASTERY, Miami/Palm Beach, FL, 1956-9; toured South America as ambassador of good will for the US government and the Miami, FL, Chamber of Commerce, 1957-8; app as extra in film HOLE IN THE HEAD, 1959; returned to England to work outside music with some app on local TV shows, 1959-60; returned to US to continue fashion work/local TV appearances while active in many volunteer/charity affairs, Albany, NY, from 1960; returned to musical work to gigs w Skip Parson's Riverboat Band at local county fairs/clubs/hotels in Albany, NY, area, 1961-8; app on EARLE PUDNEY Show, WRGB-TV, Schenectady, NY, 1962-3; frequently worked w Wild Bill Davison/Jack Stewart Band, Stockbridge Inn, Stockbridge, MA, 1964-5; worked w Frank Laidlaw All Stars, Egremont Inn, South Egremont, MA, 1964-5; frequently worked/toured in local theater groups out of Albany, NY, from 1965; app on LET'S CHAT weekly show, WAMC-radio, Albany, 1967-8; worked w Jazz Cellar Six, Manassas Jazz Festival, Manassas, VA, 1970 (por rel Fat Cat label); frequently worked clubs/restaurants w Riverboat Jazz Band/Pug Horton's All-Stars, early 70s; attended Empire State Col, Albany, obtaining BA degree, 1973; formed own Joanne B Horton Fashion Enterprises Inc to work outside music, Albany, from 1973; worked w Climax Jazz Band, DJ's Tavern, Toronto, Can, 1975-6; w Climax Jazz Band, Hayloft Dinner Theater, Manassas, VA, 1975 (por rel Fat Cat label); w Bob Wilber, Carnegie Hall, Newport Jazz Festival, NYC, NY, 1976; attended St Rose Graduate School, Albany, obtaining MA degree, 1976; active as producer/writer/editor of TV documentaries, 1976; hosted weekly ARTS ACTION Show, local educational-TV station, Albany, 1976-7; toured as singer/dancer w Bob Wilber and Newport All-Stars working college circuit through Midwest, 1977; worked Pizza Express, London, Eng, 1977; Uncle Po's Club, Hamburg, Ger, 1977; The Wequasset Inn, East Harwich, MA, 1977; Manassas Jazz Festival, Manassas, VA, 1977; toured Europe, 1978; worked Nice Jazz Festival, Nice, France, 1978

Personal: Married John Horton, 3 children; married Bob Wilber, musician (1978-). Served on Board of Directors of Albany Symphony Orch, Albany, 1967-75; elected to Zonta Organization for Business & Professional Women, 1969

Awards/Honors: Named as "one of the outstanding women of our community," American Association of University Women, 1976

Infl by: Lizzie Miles/Bessie Smith

Quotes: ". . . a very interesting vocal personality in her own right"—John S Wilson, *New York Times* newspaper, Jul 1976

"Pug Horton's blues interpretations are clearly influenced by Bessie Smith but, unlike many contemporary followers of Bessie, there is no sign of direct imitation in her style. Her voice is deeper than Bessie's and her style has great elegance and sophistication . . ."—Bob Wilber (correspondence)

HORTON, WALTER *"Shakey"*
(*aka:* Big Walter/Mumbles/Shakey Walter/Tangle Eye/Walter)

Photo by Chris Strachwitz. Courtesy Arhoolie Records

Born: Apr 6, 1918, Horn Lake (DeSoto Co), MS
Died: Dec 8, 1981, Chicago, IL
Inst: Harmonica

Father was Albert Horton Sr; mother Emma McNaire; taught self harmonica at 5 years of age; to Mound City, AR, then Memphis, TN, working outside music with frequent street work for tips from early 20s; rec w Memphis Jug Band, Victor label, Chicago, IL, 1927; worked w Memphis Jug Band, Grand Central Theater, Chicago, 1927; w Memphis Jug Band on Ma Rainey Show, Gary, IN, 1927; frequently worked as sideman in various blues bands that toured South through 20s into 30s; worked for tips in Church's Park (WC Handy Park), Memphis, 1935; worked w Honey Boy Edwards on streets/jukes/parties, Memphis, 1936; teamed w Little Buddy Doyle/Homesick James/others working streets in Memphis area, late 30s; rec w Buddy Doyle Trio, OKeh/Vocalion labels, Memphis, 1939; settled in Chicago, IL, to frequently work Maxwell Street area for tips from c1940; worked outside music in Chicago/Memphis through 40s; worked w Eddie Taylor Band, Club Jamboree, Chicago, 1949; rec Modern/RPM labels, Memphis, 1951; rec Chess label, Memphis, 1952; rec Sun label, Memphis, 1953; frequently worked w Muddy Waters Band in local clubs, Chicago, 1953; w Johnny Shines, Frosty Corner, Chicago, c1953; rec w Johnny Shines, JOB label, Chicago, 1953; worked w Johnny Shines, Purple Cat Club, Chicago, 1953; formed own combo to rec States label, Chicago, 1954; worked Cosy Inn, Chicago, 1954-5; frequently worked Turner's Lounge, Chicago, from 1955; Hollywood Rendezvous, Chicago, 1955; rec w Jimmy Rogers Band, Chess label, Chicago, 1956; rec w Otis Rush, Cobra label, Chicago, 1956; frequently worked w Jimmy Rogers group and others or with own group in local clubs/bars, Chicago, through 50s into 60s; worked Drummers Lounge, Chicago, early 60s; Fickle Pickle Club, Chicago, 1963; Grinnell Folk Festival, Grinnell, IA, 1963; frequently worked w Sonny Boy Williamson (Alex Miller)/Howlin' Wolf/others in local club dates, Chicago, 1963-4; rec Decca/Argo labels, Chicago, 1964; worked w Johnny Young Band, Kelly's Blue Lounge, Chicago, 1965; toured w American Folk Blues Festival working concerts through England/Europe, 1965 (por Hamburg, Ger, concert rel Fontana label); rec acc to Big Mama Thornton, Arhoolie label, London, Eng, 1965; rec Vanguard/Testament labels, Chicago, 1965; worked Turner's Lounge, Chicago, 1966; Monterey Jazz Festival, Monterey, CA, 1966; rec w Johnny Shines, Testament label, Chicago, 1966; worked Mariposa Folk Festival, Toronto, Can, 1966; Knox Col, Galesburg, IL, 1966; rec w Johnny Young, Arhoolie label, Chicago, 1967; worked w Johnny Shines, Univ of Chicago R&B Festival, Chicago, IL, 1968; toured w American Folk Blues Festival working club/concert dates through England, 1968; app in UK film AMERICAN FOLK BLUES FESTIVAL, 1968 (shown on BBC-TV, London, Eng); rec Sire label, London, 1968; worked w Johnny Shines, Ash Grove, Los Angeles, CA, 1968-9; rec w Johnny Shines, Blue Horizon label, Chicago, 1968; worked Hunter Col, NYC, NY, 1969; Half Note, NYC, 1969; toured w Chicago Blues All Stars working US/European jazz/folk clubs/concert dates, 1969; rec w Chicago Blues All Stars, MPS label, Cologne, Ger, 1969; worked Chicago Blues Festival, Chicago, 1969; rec Adelphi/Blue Horizon labels, Chicago, 1969; worked Electric Circus, NYC, 1969; rec w Johnny Winter, Columbia label, Nashville, TN, 1969; rec w Johnny Shines, Testament label, Los Angeles, 1969; worked Rose & Kelly's, Chicago, 1970; toured w American Folk Blues Festival working concert dates through England/Europe, 1970 (por Frankfort, Ger, concert rel Scout label); worked Jazz Expo 70, London, Eng, 1970; Berlin Jazz Days Festival, Berlin, Ger, 1970; Wise Fools, Chicago, 1970; Turner's Blue Lounge, Chicago, 1970; rec w Floyd Jones, Delta label, Chicago, 1970; rec w Willie Dixon, Yambo label, Chicago, c1970; toured w Chicago Blues All Stars working concerts through Europe, 1971; worked Festival of American Folklife, St Helen's Island, Montreal, Can, 1971; rec Xtra label, Edmonton, Can, 1972; rec w Hot Cottage group, Transatlantic label, Edmonton, 1972; worked Alice's Revisited, Chicago, 1972; rec w Carey Bell, Alligator label, Chicago, 1972; rec Red Lightnin' label, Chicago, 1972; worked Florence's Lounge, Chicago, 1972; Ann Arbor Blues Festival, Ann Arbor, MI, 1973; El Mocambo, Toronto, Can, 1973; Joe's Place, Boston, MA, 1973; Univ of Miami, Miami, FL, 1974; Richard's, Atlanta, GA, 1974; Kings Club Waveland, Chicago, 1974; occasionally worked Maxwell Street area for tips, Chicago, 1974; Urban Blues Festival, Auditorium Theater, Chicago, 1974; Smithsonian Festival of American Folklife, Washington, DC, 1975; Keystone Korner, Berkeley, CA, 1975; Monterey Jazz Festival, Monterey, CA, 1975 (por on KEST-radio, San Francisco, CA); Univ of Chicago Folk Festival, Chicago, 1975; Reed College, Portland, OR, 1975; Euphoria Tavern, Portland, OR, 1975; 1125 Club, Chicago, 1975; rec w Floyd Jones, Magnolia label, Chicago, 1975; Univ of Nebraska, Lincoln, NE, 1975; Midwest Blues Festival, Univ of Notre Dame, South Bend, IN, 1975; Vegetable Buddies Club, South Bend, 1976; The Fugue, NYC, NY, 1976; Red Creek Bar, Rochester, NY, 1977; Belle Star, Colden, NY, 1977; Knickerbocker Cafe, Westerly, RI, 1977; The Speakeasy Club, Cambridge, MA, 1977; Lupo's, Providence, RI, 1977; Keystone Korner, Berkeley, CA, 1977; rec w Muddy Waters, Blue Sky label, Westport, CT, 1977; worked club dates w Jimmy Rogers Band 1977; app on GOOD MORNIN' BLUES, NET-TV (PBS), 1978; worked clubs/concerts on East Coast/Mexico through 70s; Carnegie Hall, NYC, 1979; app in film BLUES BROTHERS, 1980; toured concerts in Europe, 1981; died as consequence of alcoholism; buried Restvale Cemetery, Worth, IL

Songs: Big Walter's Boogie/Black Gal/Blues in the Morning/Christine/Cotton Patch Hot Foots/Easy/Hard Hearted Woman/I Got the Blues/I Need Your Love/Joe Chicago/Jumpin' Blues/Little Boy Blues/Lovin' My Baby/Need My Baby/So Long Woman/South Indiana/Tell Me Baby/That Ain't It/They Call Me Big Walter/Train Time/Walter's Blues

Infl by: John Lee "Sonny Boy" Williamson

Info to: Carey Bell/Julio Finn/Forest City Joe/Willie Foster/Little Walter Jacobs/Jerry Portnoy

Quotes: "In the first rank of Chicago's harp players"—Mike Rowe, *Chicago Breakdown*, Eddison Press Ltd, 1973

"Horton's understated, warm, raspy vocals are secondary to his absolutely superb harp playing"—Robert Rusch, *Downbeat* magazine, Jan 18, 1973, p 26

References: *Blues Unlimited* (UK), Mar 1965, p 8
Living Blues, Spring 1982 (No. 52), pp 52-3

HOT SHOT WILLIE
(see McTell, Willie)

HOUSE, EDDIE JAMES, JR *"Son"*

Born: Mar 21, 1902, Riverton (Coahoma Co), MS
Died: Oct 19, 1988, Detroit, MI
Inst: Guitar

Father was Eddie House Sr; mother was Maggie ________ ; born on plantation between Clarksdale and Lyon, MS; one of at least 3 children; family moved often through Mississippi/Louisiana when child; was preaching sermons in local churches at 15 years of age; frequently worked outside music through Louisiana/Tennessee into 20s; served as pastor of local Baptist church in Lyon, MS, area in early 20s with some preaching later in Colored Methodist Episcopal Church; worked outside music in St Louis, MO/East St Louis, IL, areas c1922-3; worked outside music, Lyon area, from c1923; taught self guitar and worked with local bluesmen at house parties/dances/picnics, Robinsonville/Lyon, MS, areas from 1927; worked briefly in Dr McFadden's Medicine Show, Ruleville, MS, c1928; served time in Parchman State Farm, Parchman, MS, c1928-9; worked w Charley Patton, Jeffrey's Plantation, Lula, MS, 1929; frequently worked solo at country dances/bars/levee camps, Clarksdale, MS, area, late 20s into 30s; rec Paramount label, Grafton, WI, 1930; frequently worked outside music while working w Willie Brown at picnics/parties/dances/juke joints/plantations, Lake Cormorant/Robinsonville/Banks/Tunica, MS, areas/Memphis, TN, area, 1930-42; rec Library of Congress label, Lake Cormorant, MS, 1941/Robinsonville, MS, 1942; moved to Rochester, NY, to work outside music with occasional local gigs from 1943; inactive in music, 1948-64; rec Blue Goose label, Washington, DC, c1964; worked Ontario Place, Washington, DC, 1964; Univ of Chicago, Chicago, IL, 1964-5; Philadelphia Folk Festival, Paoli, PA, 1964; Newport Folk Festival, Newport, RI, 1964-6 (por 1966 concert shown in film FESTIVAL/por 1965 concert rel Vanguard label); Indiana Univ, Bloomington, IN, 1964; rec Columbia label, NYC, 1965; worked Wayne State Univ, Detroit, MI, 1965; Univ of California Folk Festival, Los Angeles, CA,

Eddie "Son" House *Photo by Jeff Todd Titon. Courtesy* Living Blues *Magazine*

1965; Swarthmore Folk Festival, Swarthmore, PA, 1965; Folksong 65, Carnegie Hall, NYC, 1965; Mariposa Folk Festival, Toronto, Can, 1965; Club 47, Cambridge, MA, 1965-6; New Gate of Cleve, Toronto, Can, 1965; Fool's Mate, Westport, CT, 1965; Knox College, Galesburg, IL, 1965; Lake Forest Col, Lake Forest, IL, 1965; Folklore Center, NYC, 1965; Gaslight Cafe, NYC, 1965; Cafe A-Go-Go, NYC, 1965-6 (por 1966 date rel Verve label); La Faim Foetale, Montreal, Can, 1965; Orleans, Boston, MA, 1965; Grinnell College, Grinnell, IA, 1965; Oberlin College, Oberlin, OH, 1965; app on SOME OF THE PEOPLE, KUHF-FM-radio, Houston, TX, 1965; Boston Folk Festival, Boston, 1966; Univ of Cincinnati, Cincinnati, OH, 1966; Rheingold Central Park Music Festival, NYC, 1967; toured w American Folk Blues Festival working concert dates through England/Europe, 1967; worked Philadelphia Folk Festival, Schwenksville, PA, 1967-8; The Avalon Ballroom, San Francisco, CA, 1968; app on CAMERA THREE (ep: Really the Country Blues), CBS-TV, 1968; app in film short SON HOUSE, 1969; worked Electric Circus, NYC, 1969; Newport Folk Festival, Newport, RI, 1969 (por rel Vanguard label); Ann Arbor Blues Festival, Ann Arbor, MI, 1969-70; King Hall, Berkeley, CA, 1969; Notre Dame Univ, South Bend, IN, 1969; rec Roots label, Rochester, NY, 1969; worked Wisconsin Blues Festival, Beloit, WI, 1970; Stanford Univ, Stanford, CA, 1970, Montreux Jazz Festival, Montreux, Switzerland, 1970; toured England working college/club dates, 1970; worked 100 Club, London, Eng, 1970 (por rel Liberty label); rec w Stefan Grossman, Transatlantic label, London, 1970; app on LATE NIGHT LINE-UP, BBC-2-TV, London, 1970; worked Univ of Minnesota, Minneapolis, MN, 1971; app in film ROOTS OF AMERICAN MUSIC: COUNTRY & URBAN MUSIC (pt 1), 1971; mostly inactive in music due to poor health, Buffalo, NY, 1971-6; worked Univ of Vermont, Burlington, VT, 1972; Toronto Island Blues Festival, Toronto Island, Can, 1974; moved to Detroit, MI, and mostly inactive in music from 1976; clip shown in ROOTS OF COUNTRY MUSIC & BLUES, KGO-TV, San Francisco, 1977; entered Harper Hospital where he died of cancer of the larynx; buried Mt Hazel Cemetery, Detroit, MI

Personal: Married Carrie Martin (c1928-); Evie McGown (c1934-88)

Songs: A Down the Staff/DT Moan/Death Letter Blues/Dry Spell Blues/Empire State Express/Grinnin' in Your Face/Hobo/Lake Cormorant Blues/Levee Camp Moan/Louise McGhee/Mississippi County Farm Blues/My Black Mama/Pearline/Pony Blues/Preachin' the Blues/Rochester Blues/Son's Blues/Soon in the Morning/Sundown/This War Will Last You for Years/Trouble Blues

Infl by: Willie Brown/Rubin Lacy/James "Jim" McCoy/Charley Patton/Willie Wilson

Infl to: Robert Johnson/Bonnie Raitt/Muddy Waters

Quotes: "The integration in tone and rhythm between the two voices, the guitar's and his own, was perhaps the most sensitive that any blues singer has ever achieved"—Samuel B Charters, *The Bluesmen*, Oak Publications, 1967

"One of the greatest performers of the taut, anguished Mississippi blues"—Pete Welding, *Downbeat Music: 1968*, p 86

"Son House is the greatest blues singer alive today"—Julius Lester, *Sing Out* magazine, Jul 1965, p 38

References: Living Blues magazine, Mar/Apr 1977, pp 14-22

The Bluesmen, Samuel B Charters, Oak Publications, 1967

Sounds & Fury magazine, Dec, 1965, pp 18-21

HOUSTON, EDWARD WILSON *"Bee"*
Born: Apr 19, 1938, San Antonio (Bexar Co), TX
Died: Mar 19, 1991, Inglewood, CA
Inst: Guitar

Father was Wilson Edward Houston; mother was Mellone Edwards; played in HS drum & bugle corps as youth; taught self guitar and formed small group to work local dances, San Antonio, TX, area, late 50s; frequently toured as back-up band for Little Willie John/Jr Parker/Bobby Bland/others working shows through Texas/New Mexico into 60s; served in US Army c1960-1; moved to West Coast to work outside music in Los Angeles, CA, from 1961; frequently rec acc to local bluesmen on West Coast through 60s into 70s; toured/rec extensively w Big Mama Thornton on West Coast, mid to late 60s; worked w Big Mama Thornton, Monterey Jazz Festival, Monterey, CA, 1968; rec Arhoolie label, Los Angeles, CA, 1968; frequently worked local club dates, Los Angeles area, into 70s; rec Arhoolie label, Hollywood, CA, 1970; worked Roaring '20s Cafe, Los Angeles, early 70s; Topanga Corral, Los Angeles, 1974; Berkeley Blues Festival, Berkeley, CA, 1975; mostly inactive through 70s/80s; died of complications of gastric ulcer; body cremated

Edward "Bee" Houston

Courtesy Living Blues Magazine

Infl by: Bobby Blue Band/Charles Brown/Gatemouth Brown/BB King/Aaron "T-Bone" Walker

Quote: "His earthy voice makes for a fine compliment to his strong guitar work . . ."—Chris Strachwitz, Arhoolie album 1050

HOVINGTON, FRANKLIN *"Frank"*

Born: Jan 9, 1919, Reading (Berks Co), PA
Died: Jun 21, 1982, Felton, DE
Inst: Banjo/Guitar/Ukulele

One of at least 3 children; moved to Frederica, DE, as child where he was raised; was playing ukulele at 5 years of age and banjo at 11 years of age; worked mostly outside music in Frederica, late 30s into 40s; teamed w William Walker working local parties/dances, Frederica, c1937; teamed w Gene Young to work parties/dances, Frederica area, c1938-48; moved to Washington, DC, to work outside music with occasional work in Stewart Dixon's Golden Stars gospel group/Ernest Ewins Jubilee Four/The Four H's gospel group/others, 1948 through 60s; occasionally worked w Smilin' Billy Stewart's Band and others at local dances, Washington, DC, area to 1967; moved to Felton, DE, to work outside music with occasional party work from 1967 into 80s; worked Smithsonian Folk Festival, Washington, 1971; rec Flyright label, Felton, 1975; died of heart failure

Infl by: Adam Greenfield/William Walker

Quote: "One of the finest rural songsters to be found in the United States"—Bruce Bastin, Flyright album 522

Reference: Flyright album 522

HOWARD, ROSETTA

Born: c1914, Chicago (Cook Co), IL

Raised in Chicago, IL; worked as dancer at The Bungalow, Chicago, early 30s; began singing to juke-box songs, The Bungalow, Chicago, into 30s; frequently worked locally w Herb Morand & Odell Rand, Chicago, mid-30s; rec w The Harlem Hamfats,

Courtesy Frank Driggs Collection

Decca label, NYC/Chicago, 1937-8; worked w Jimmie Noone Orch, Savoy Club, Chicago, 1938; worked w Eddie Smith's Band in local clubs, Chicago, 1938-9; rec w Blues Serenaders, Decca label, NYC, 1939; worked w Lillian Allen, 333 Club, Chicago, c1940; w Sonny Thompson's Band, Apex Grill, Robbins, IL, 1941; worked as single in local clubs, Chicago, into 40s; rec w The Big Three and others, Columbia label, Chicago, 1947; app on Studs Terkel I COME FOR TO SING, local TV, Chicago, late 40s; retired to work outside music with frequent work w Thomas A Dorsey at Pilgrim Baptist Church, Chicago, from early 50s

Billing: The Viper Girl

Infl by: Billie Holiday

HOWELL, JOSHUA BARNES *"Peg Leg"*
Born: Mar 5, 1888, Eatonton (Putnam Co), GA
Died: Aug 11, 1966, Atlanta, GA
Inst: Guitar

Father was Thomas Howell, a farmer; mother was Ruthie Myrick; born/raised on farm; taught self guitar c1909; dropped out of school early to work outside music (as farmer) in Eatonton, GA, area to 1916; suffered loss of leg due to gunshot wound, 1916; worked outside music in Eatonton area into 20s; moved to Atlanta, GA, c1923; formed own Peg Leg Howell and His Gang (usually w Henry Williams/Eddie Anthony) to work streets/parks for tips, Atlanta, 1923-34; served time for bootlegging, River Camp Prison, Atlanta, 1925; rec w own group (or as single), Columbia label, Atlanta, 1926-9; rec duet w Jim Hill, Columbia label, Atlanta, 1929; worked outside music with occasional street work for tips, Atlanta, 1934 into 50s; lost second leg due to diabetes, 1952; mostly inactive into 60s; rec Testament label, Atlanta, 1963; entered Grady Memorial Hospital where he died of chronic nervous disease; buried Chestnut Hill Cemetery, Atlanta, GA

Personal: Married Aldora Benford

Songs: Ball and Chain Blues/Coal Man Blues/Fo' Day Blues/Hobo Blues/Moanin' Groanin'/Peg Leg/Please Ma'am/Rocks and Gravel/Skin Game Blues/Too Tight

Quotes: "One of the earliest and most important country blues artists to record was Joshua Barnes Howell . . ."—Pete Welding, Testament album 2204

"Peg Leg Howell was one of the first Atlanta musicians to be recorded, and his music reflected a patchwork of old work songs, traditional verses and

Courtesy Frank Driggs Collection

his own material"—Giles Oakley, *The Devil's Music —A History of the Blues*, British Broadcasting Corp, 1976

References: Nothing But the Blues, Mike Leadbitter, Hanover Books, 1971
Sweet as the Showers of Rain, Samuel B Charters, Oak Publications, 1977

HOWLIN' WOLF

(see Burnett, Chester)
(see Smith, John T)

HUFF, LUTHER HENRY

Photo by Darryl Stolper. Courtesy Living Blues Magazine

Born: Dec 5, 1910, Fannin (Rankin Co), MS
Died: Nov 18, 1973, Detroit, MI
Inst: Guitar/Mandolin/Organ

Father was John Huff; mother was Lizzie Taylor; interested in guitar from age of 6; taught self organ at about 7 years of age; teamed w brother Percy Huff to work local country picnics in Fannin, MS, area from c1925; left home w brother Percy Huff to hobo through Delta area working as itinerant musicians from c1927; frequently worked w brother Percy Huff at parties/breakdowns at Big John's Plantation, Belzoni, MS, 1928 into 30s; continued working parties/picnics/dances in Belzoni area through 30s; taught self mandolin, 1936; served in US Army in England/Europe theater of operations, 1942-6; returned to Detroit, MI, to work mostly outside music, 1947 through 50s; rec w brother Percy Huff, Trumpet label, Jackson, MS, 1951; mostly inactive due to disability from 1957; rec Adelphi label, Detroit, 1968; entered St Joseph Hospital where he died of hardening of arteries; buried Lincoln Memorial Park, Macomb County, MI

Personal: Married Ledella Ford. 12 children. Brothers Willie/Percy Huff were musicians

Infl by: Charlie McCoy

Reference: Living Blues magazine, Jul 1975, pp 33-4

HUMES, HELEN ELIZABETH

Born: Jun 23, 1913, Louisville (Jefferson Co), KY
Died: Sep 13, 1981, Santa Monica, CA
Inst: Harmonium/Organ/Piano

Father John Henry Humes was a lawyer; mother Emma Johnson was school teacher of Cherokee Indian heritage; learned piano early and frequently sang in North Street Baptist Church choir, Louisville, KY, as child; frequently sang w Dickie Wells/Jonah Jones in Miss Bessie Allen's Booker T Washington Community Center Junior Band at country fairs/outings/dances in area through 20s; worked w Miss Bessie Allen's Junior Band, Palace Theater, Louisville, 1927; rec OKeh label, St Louis, MO/NYC, NY, 1927; graduated local high school to work outside music with some dance/theater work, Louisville, c1929 into 30s; worked w Al Sears Band, Spider Web Club, Buffalo, NY, 1936; Vendome Hotel, Buffalo, 1936; app in local radio shows, Schenectady, NY, 1936; worked outside music (as restaurant operator), Albany, NY, 1936; worked w Al Sears Band at local dances, Cincinnati, OH, 1937; w Doc Wheeler's Sunset Royal Band, Cotton Club, Cincinnati, 1937; w Vernon Andrades Orch, Renaissance Ballroom, NYC, 1937; rec w Harry James Orch, Brunswick label, NYC, 1937-8; worked amateur show, Apollo Theater, NYC, 1937; rec w Count Basie Quintet, Vanguard label, NYC, 1938; replaced Billie Holiday in Count Basie Orch, 1938; worked w Count Basie Orch, Famous Door, NYC, 1938, then toured extensively w Count Basie Orch working one-nighters across US, 1938-42; rec w Count Basie Orch, Decca label, NYC, 1938-9; worked w Count Basie group, From Spirituals to Swing Concert, Carnegie Hall, NYC, 1938; rec w Count Basie Orch, Vocalion label, NYC, NY/Chicago, IL, 1939; rec w Count Basie Orch, Columbia label, NYC, 1939-40; worked w Count Basie Orch, Southland Cafe, Boston, MA, 1940; rec w Count Basie Orch, OKeh label, NYC/Chicago, 1940-1; worked as single at Cafe Society Downtown, NYC, 1941-3; Famous Door, NYC, 1942; rec w Pete Brown Band, Decca label, NYC, 1942; worked Three Deuces, NYC, 1942; w Eddie Heywood, Village Vanguard, NYC, 1942; toured w Ernie Fields Band working dances through

Helen Humes
Courtesy Living Blues *Magazine*

Midwest, 1942; w Don Byas group, Minton's, NYC, c1942 (por rel Onyx label); toured w Clarence Love Orch working one-nighters, 1943-4; worked w Norman Granz's Jazz at the Philharmonic group, Carnegie Hall, NYC, 1944, with frequent tours across US working concert dates into 50s; rec w Leonard Feather's Hiptet, Savoy label, NYC, 1944; frequently worked Small's Paradise, NYC, 1944-5; moved to West Coast to work concert/club dates/TV shows, 1944-55; worked Streets of Paris Club, Hollywood, CA, 1944; rec w Bill Doggett Octet, Philo/Aladdin labels, Los Angeles, CA, 1945; rec w own All Stars group, Aladdin label, Los Angeles, 1945; rec w Buck Clayton All Stars, B&W/Mercury labels, Los Angeles, 1946-7; worked w JATP, Symphony Hall, Boston, MA, 1946; app in NEW REVUE OF STARS Revue, Small's Paradise, NYC, 1946; worked w JATP Academy of Music, Brooklyn, NY, 1946; app w Dizzy Gillespie Orch in film JIVIN' IN BEBOP, 1947 (por adapted and shown in film shorts EE-BABA-LEE-BA/TAN AND TERRIFIC); worked Baby Grand, NYC, 1947; rec with the Marshall Royal Orch, Discovery label, Los Angeles, 1950, worked w Roy Milton Band, Blues Jubilee Concert, Shrine Auditorium, Los Angeles, 1950 (por rel Gene Norman/Modern/Discovery labels); rec w Dexter Gordon Orch, Discovery label, Los Angeles, 1950; rec ST for film PANIC IN THE STREETS, 1950; rec ST for film MY BLUE HEAVEN, 1950; app w Count Basie in telescription films IF I COULD BE WITH YOU/I CRIED FOR YOU, c1950; app w Count Basic Orch in film short COUNT BASIE AND HIS ORCHESTRA, 1951; rec w Count Basie Orch, Camay label, Los Angeles (?), 1951; toured w JATP group working concert dates in Hawaii, 1951; rec w Gerald Wiggins Orch, Los Angeles, 1952; worked w Gerald Wiggins Orch in local club dates, Los Angeles, 1952; worked Just Jazz/Blues Jubilee Concert, Pasadena Auditorium, Los Angeles, 1952 (por rel Decca label); toured Hawaii working concert dates, 1952; app w Count Basie Orch, HARLEM VARIETY REVUE, Apollo Theater, NYC, early 50s (por shown on SHOWTIME AT THE APOLLO, syndicated TV, 1955/por shown in films HARLEM JAZZ FESTIVAL, 1955/BASIN STREET REVUE, 1956); app in singing/acting role in show SIMPLY HEAVENLY (unknown theater), Los Angeles, 1955; toured w Red Norvo group working through Australia, 1956; worked w Red Norvo group in local club dates, Hollywood, CA, c1956; app in singing/acting role in show IT'S GREAT TO BE ALIVE (unknown theater), Los Angeles, 1957; rec w Red Norvo Orch, Victor label,

Los Angeles, 1958; worked Newport Jazz Festival, Newport, RI, 1959; French Lick Jazz Festival, French Lick, IN, 1959; Westover Hotel, Toronto, Can, 1959; rec Contemporary label, Los Angeles, 1959-61; worked Monterey Jazz Festival, Monterey, CA, 1960; The Renaissance, Los Angeles, 1960; residency at Shelly's Manne Hole, Los Angeles, 1961; Beach Walk Ebbtide Hotel, Honolulu, HI, 1961-2; toured Australia working concert dates, 1962; worked Monterey Jazz Festival, Monterey, CA, 1962; toured w Rhythm & Blues USA package revue working festivals/concerts through England/Europe, 1962-3; worked Playboy Club, Chicago, IL, 1964; toured Australia extensively working concert/club dates, 1964; worked Shelly's Manne Hole, Los Angeles, CA, 1967; Redd Foxx Club, Los Angeles, 1967; retired to work outside music, Louisville, KY, 1967-73; worked Newport Jazz Festival, NYC, NY, 1973-5 (por 1973/1975 concerts on MUSIC-USA, VOA-radio); Louis Armstrong Memorial Concert, Shea Stadium, NYC, 1973; toured France working concert dates, 1973-4; rec Black & Blue label, France, 1973; worked Jazz Festival Baden 73, Baden, Switzerland, 1973; Montreux Blues Festival, Montreux, Switzerland, 1974 (por rel Black Lion label); toured England working club/concert dates, 1974; rec w Connie Berry & Her Jazz Hounds, Jazzology label, Atlanta, GA, 1974; worked Blues Alley, Washington, DC, 1974; Half Note, NYC, 1974; rec w Milt Larkins Orch, Columbia label, NYC, 1974; extended solo residencies at The Cookery, NYC, 1974-7; app on JOE FRANKLIN Show, WOR-TV, NYC, 1975; worked New York Jazz Museum concert, NYC, 1975; app on TODAY Show, NBC-TV, 1975; worked Overseas Press Club concert, NYC, 1975; worked Nice Jazz Festival, Nice, France, 1975; Sandy's Jazz Revival, Boston, MA, 1975; app on SOUNDSTAGE (ep: The World of John Hammond), PBS-TV, 1975; worked The Rainbow Grill, NYC, 1975; The Lighthouse, Los Angeles, CA, 1975; Broadmoor Hotel, Colorado Springs, CO, 1975; Monterey Jazz Festival, Monterey, CA, 1975-6 (por on KEST-radio, San Francisco); El Matador, San Francisco, 1975; Ratso's, Chicago, IL, 1975; New York Univ Loeb Student Center, NYC, 1976-7; Channel Gardens, Rockefeller Center, NYC, 1976; Milwaukee Lakefront Festival, Milwaukee, WI, 1976; Concert by the Sea, Redondo Beach, CA, 1976; Statler Hilton Downtown Room, Buffalo, NY, 1976 (por remote WBFO-radio); Sandy's Jazz Revival, Beverly, MA, 1977; Showboat Lounge, Silver Spring, MD, 1977; Holiday Inn, Chicago, 1977; Storyville Club, NYC, 1977; Gulliver's, West Paterson, NJ, 1977; worked w Alberta Hunter, The Cookery, NYC, 1977 (por remote JAZZ ALIVE, WNYC-FM-National Public radio); Sibi Club, NYC, 1978; app on BIG BAND BASH, PBS-TV, 1978; opened Norman's, NYC, 1978; worked concerts in Eng/France/Germany, 1978; then clubs/festivals across US, 1978-9; residency at The Cookery, NYC, 1980; entered Beverly Manor Convalescent Hospital where she died of cancer; buried Inglewood Cemetery, Inglewood, CA

Awards/Honors: Won Hot Club of France Award for Best Album of 1973 (Black & Blue album 33050)

Quote: "The 30s produced three quintessential swing vocalists: Mildred Bailey, Ella Fitzgerald and Helen Humes. Of these three, only Miss Humes has established any kind of reputation as a blues singer . . ."—John McDonough, *Downbeat* magazine, Aug 14, 1975, p 26

References: *Storyville,* Apr 1976, pp. 126-30
Mississippi Rag, May 1979, pp 1-2
Downbeat, May 20, 1976, pp. 17-18

HUNTER, ALBERTA

(*aka:* May Alix/Josephine Beatty/Helen Roberts)
Born: Apr 1, 1895, Memphis (Shelby Co), TN
Died: Oct 17, 1984, Roosevelt Is, NY, NY

Father was Charles Hunter; mother was Laura Peterson; one of 4 children; frequently sang at local school concerts as child; moved to Chicago, IL, where she was raised and frequently worked outside music from 1907; worked Dago Frank's Cafe, Chicago, 1912-13; Hugh Hoskins Club, Chicago, 1914-16; worked Panama Cafe/De Luxe Cafe/Paradise Gardens/Elite #2 (w Tony Jackson)/Pekin Theater Cabaret/Phoenix Club/Sunset Cafe/others, Chicago, 1917 into 20s; worked Lyceum Theater, Chicago, 1918; worked w King Oliver and others, Dreamland Cabaret, Chicago, c1920-3; Lorraine Gardens #2, Chicago, 1921; rec w Fletcher Henderson Orch, Black Swan label, NYC, NY, 1921; rec Paramount label, NYC/Chicago, 1922-4; worked Lafayette Theater, NYC, 1922; replaced Bessie Smith in musical comedy HOW COME, 42nd Street Apollo Theater, NYC/Lafayette Theater, NYC/Shubert Theater, Newark, NJ, 1923, then toured with road company working theaters across US, 1923; worked Century Theater, NYC, 1923; w Edith Wilson, 44th Street Theater, NYC, 1924; worked Sam Langford testimonial, Lafayette Theater, NYC, 1924; Happy Rhones Orchestra Club, NYC, 1924; rec w Louis Armstrong's Red Onion Jazz Babies, Gennett label, NYC, 1924; worked Halsey

Alberta Hunter *Courtesy Frank Driggs Collection*

Theater, Brooklyn, NY, 1925; Proctor's Theater, Albany, NY, 1925; Lincoln Theater, NYC, 1925; Columbia Theater, Sharon, PA, 1925; worked w own trio, Keeney's Bay Ridge Theater, Brooklyn, NY, 1925; Lafayette Theater, NYC, 1925; rec OKeh label, NYC, 1925-6; worked The Coliseum, Chicago, 1926; rec Victor label, NYC, NY/Camden, NJ, 1927; worked Lincoln Theater, Philadelphia, PA, c1927; Michaelson's, Cincinnati, OH, 1927; Green Park Hotel, London, Eng, 1927; Palace Hotel, Nice, France, 1927; Knickerbocker Hotel, Monte Carlo, Monaco, 1928; The Palladium, London, Eng, 1928; Florida Club, London, 1928; Argyle, London, 1928; Royal Palace Hotel, London, 1928; app w Paul Robeson/Edith Day in show SHOWBOAT, Drury Lane Theater, London, 1928-9; worked Grande Carte, Paris, France, 1929; The Cotton Club, Paris, 1929; Chez Florence Jones Cabaret, Paris, 1929; rec Columbia label, NYC, 1929; worked Keith's State Theater, Jersey City, NJ, 1929; RKO Bushwick Theater, Brooklyn, NY, 1929; Keith Theater, Yonkers, NY, 1929; app in show CHANGE YOUR LUCK, George M Cohan Theater, NYC, 1930; app on NEGRO ACHIEVEMENT HOUR, WABC-radio, NYC, 1930; worked Connie's Inn, NYC, 1930; app in CHERRY LANE FOLLIES Revue, Cherry Lane Theater, NYC, 1930; app in THANKSGIVING REVELS Revue, Alhambra Theater, NYC, 1930; The Nest Club, NYC, 1931; The Hotfeet Club, NYC, 1931; w Earl Hines, Grand Terrace Ballroom, Chicago, IL, c1932; Harlem Opera House, NYC, 1932; app in FOUR STAR REVUE, Lafayette Theater, NYC, 1932; app in show STRUTTIN' TIME, George M Cohan Theater, NYC, 1933, then toured with show; worked The Clam House, NYC, 1933; Kings Hall, Bournemouth, Eng, 1933; La Gaite Cabaret, Amsterdam, Holland, 1933; The National Scala, Copenhagen, Den, 1934; The Little Club, Paris, France, 1934; Boues Sur Tois Club, Paris, 1934; replaced Josephine Baker at Casino de Paris, Paris, 1934-5; app w Henry Hall BBC Dance Orch, BBC-radio, London, 1934; w Lou Preager's Orch, Club Ramonaga, London, 1934 (remotes on BBC-radio); w Jack Jackson Orch, Dorchester Hotel, London, 1934-5; rec w Jack Jackson Orch, HMV label, London, 1934; worked Theater Royal, Edinburgh, Scotland, 1934; Tivol Theater, Aberdeen, Scotland, 1934; The Pavilion, London, 1934; Shakespeare Theater, Liverpool, Eng, 1934; app in UK film RADIO PARADE OF 1935 (RADIO FOLLIES), 1934; w Louis Armstrong, Connie's Inn, NYC, c1936; extensive tour working clubs/concerts/hotels like The Old Laurie, Copenhagen, Den/La Femina Club, Athens, Greece/Excelsior Club, Alexandria, Egypt/The Continental, Cairo, UAR/Shepheard's Hotel, Cairo/Jardins des Petite Champs, Istanbul, Turkey/elsewhere, 1936-8; app w Teddy Hill Band in COTTON CLUB REVUE, The Palladium, London, 1937; The Baltabaris Club, The Hague, Netherlands, 1938; frequently app w Henry Levine Orch on ALBERTA HUNTER Show, WJZ/WEAF/WOR-radio, NYC, 1938-40; app w Ethel Waters in non-singing role in show MAMBA'S DAUGHTERS, Empire Theater, NYC, 1939, then toured with show into 1940 with a return to Broadway Theater, NYC, 1940; rec w Charlie Shavers Quartet, Decca label, NYC, 1939; rec w Eddie Heywood Jr, Bluebird label, NYC, 1940; extended residency at Downbeat Room, Garrick Lounge, Chicago, 1943-4; worked Paris Qui Chante Supper Club, NYC, 1944; toured extensively on many USO package shows working China/Burma/India/Korea/Egypt/Africa/European Theater of Operations and military bases throughout the world, 1944-53; worked USO command performance for General Eisenhower, Frankfurt, Ger, 1945; worked w Eddie Heywood Band, Apollo Theater, NYC, 1946; 845 Club, Bronx, NY, 1946; Mayfair Club, Boston, MA, 1946; rec Juke Box/Regal labels, NYC, 1950; worked Club La Commedia, NYC, 1951; frequently worked Latin Quarter, Montreal, Can, and other clubs in Montreal/Toronto area, 1953; app as understudy to Eartha Kitt is show MRS PATTERSON, National Theater, NYC, 1954-5; worked Bon Soir Club, NYC, 1955; app in show DEBUT, Holiday Theater, NYC, 1956; worked outside music (as nurse in local hospitals), NYC, 1957-77; rec w Buster Bailey's Blues Busters, Prestige-Bluesville label, NYC, 1961; rec w Lovie Austin Blues Serenaders, Riverside label, Chicago, IL, 1961; rec w Jimmy Archey Group, Folkways label, NYC, 1962; app in FACES IN JAZZ (taped in NYC), Scandinavian TV-Network, 1971-2; worked solo residencies at The Cookery, NYC, 1977-84; app TODAY Show, NBC-TV, 1977-8; app on ARLENE FRANCIS Show, WOR-radio, NYC, 1977; app on MIKE DOUGLAS Show, CBS-TV, 1977-8; rec Columbia label, NYC, 1977; worked St Peter's Lutheran Church, NYC, 1977; worked w Helen Humes, The Cookery, NYC, 1977 (por remote JAZZ ALIVE, WNYC-FM-National Public radio); app on CAMERA THREE (ep: One Hundred Years from Today), CBS-TV, 1978; app on TO TELL THE TRUTH, WPIX-TV, NYC (syndicated), 1978; app on JACK O'BRIEN Show, WOR-radio, NYC, 1978; app in national TV commercial for Clairol Hair products,

1978; worked Newport Jazz Festival, NYC, 1978; app on DICK CAVETT SHOW, PBS-TV, 1978; app on 60 MINUTES, CBS-TV, 1978; wrote/rec ST for film REMEMBER MY NAME, 1978; app concerts/clubs across US into 80s; Smithsonian Institute, Washington, DC, 1982 (por rel JAZZ AT THE SMITHSONIAN, Sony Video label); app BLUES AT THE COOKERY, (1981), NET-TV, 1983; toured concerts in Europe, 1982 and US/Brazil, 1984; died natural causes; body cremated

Billings: America's Foremost Brown Blues Singer/ Marian Anderson of the Blues

Songs: Chirping the Blues/Downhearted Blues/Down South Blues/Experience Blues/I Got a Mind to Ramble/I Got Myself a Working Man/I Want a Two-Fisted, Double-Jointed, Rough-and-Ready Man/I Want to Thank You Lord for My Blessings/Kind Treatment/The Love I Have for You/Mistreated Blues/My Castle's Rocking/Now I'm Satisfied/ Remember My Name/Streets Paved with Gold/ What's The Matter Baby?/Will the Day Ever Come When I Can Rest?/You Better Change Your Way of Livin'/You Got to Reap Just What You Sow

Awards/Honors: Awarded meritorious service medal for USO work during 1940s

Infl by: Sophie Tucker

Quotes: ". . . American blues singer Alberta Hunter . . . gave the raw material of the folk-song of her people an artistic veneer that helped popularize it with the world at large"—Brian Rust, *The Dance Bands*, Arlington House, 1974

"Perhaps the most influential of all American blues singers in Europe . . ."—Barry Ulanov, *A Handbook of Jazz*, Viking Press, 1957

References: *Storyville* magazine (UK), Aug 1975, pp 223-4

Who's Who of Jazz, John Chilton, Bloombury Book Shop, 1970

HUNTER, PATSY
(see Grant, Leola B)

HUNTER, SLIM
(see Broonzy, William)

HURT, *"Mississippi"* JOHN SMITH
Born: Jul 3, 1893, Teoc (Carroll Co), MS
Died: Nov 2, 1966, Grenada, MS
Inst: Guitar/Harmonica

Father was Isom Hurt; mother was Mary Jan McCain; one of 3 children; moved to Avalon, MS, at age of 2 where he was raised and frequently sang in local church as child; dropped out of school to work outside music from 1902; interested in music early and taught self 3 finger style guitar, 1903; frequently worked local dances/parties in Carroll County area from c1904; frequently worked local parties/picnics in Jackson, MS, area c1912; worked mostly outside music (as farmer & odd jobs) with occasional work at local parties/picnics/country dances/school and church functions in Avalon, MS, area to 1963; rec OKeh label, Memphis, TN/NYC, NY, 1928; worked Ontario Place, Washington, DC, 1963 (por rel Piedmont label); The Showboat, Washington, DC, 1963; The Brickseller, Washington, DC, 1963; Newport Folk Festival, Newport, RI, 1963-5 (por of 1963-4 concert rel Vanguard label/por shown in film FESTIVAL, 1967); Philadelphia Folk Festival, Paoli, PA, 1963; Second Fret, Philadelphia, PA, c1963; app on Johnny Carson's TONIGHT Show, NBC-TV, c1963; rec Library of Congress label, Washington, DC, 1964; worked Cafe Yana, Boston, MA, 1964; Columbia Univ, NYC, c1964; Gaslight Cafe, NYC, 1964-5; Hunter Col, NYC, 1964; Retort Club, Detroit, MI, c1964; Ash Grove, Los Angeles, CA, 1964; Carnegie Hall, NYC, 1964; rec Piedmont label, Falls Church, VA, 1964; worked Mariposa Folk Festival, Toronto, Can, 1964; New Gate of Cleve, Toronto, 1965; app on THIS HOUR HAS SEVEN DAYS, CBC-TV, Toronto, 1965; rec Rebel label, Ontario, Can, c1965; worked Town Hall, NYC, 1965; New York Folk Festival, Carnegie Hall, NYC, 1965; Massey Hall, Toronto, 1965; Philadelphia Folk Festival, Spring Mount, PA, 1965; Univ of Chicago, Chicago, IL, 1965; Cafe A-Go-Go, NYC, 1965; Oberlin Col, Oberlin, OH, 1965 (por rel Vanguard label); app on SOME OF THE PEOPLE, KUHF-FM-radio, Houston, TX, 1965; app w Pete Seeger on RAINBOW QUEST Show, WNDT-TV, NYC, c1966; worked Univ of Cincinnati, Cincinnati, OH, 1966; Overton Park, Memphis, TN, 1966; rec Vanguard label, NYC, 1966; suffered heart attack and died at Grenada County Hospital; buried St James Cemetery, Avalon, MS

Personal: Married Jessie ———. 14 children

Songs: Avalon Blues/Big Leg Blues/Candy Man Blues/Coffee Blues/Cow Hooking/Got the Blues, Can't Be Satisfied/I Been Cryin' Since You Been Gone/Lazy Blues/Let the Mermaids Flirt with Me/ Louis Collins/Monday Morning Blues/Nobody Cares for Me/Nobody's Dirty Business/Payday/Pera Lee/

"Mississippi" John Hurt *Photo by Julie Snow*

Richland Women Blues/Salty Dog/Sliding Delta/Spanish Fandango/Spike Driver Blues/Talkin' Casey/Trouble I've Had It All My Days/Weeping and Wailing

Infl by: Jimmie Rodgers

Infl to: John Jackson

Quotes: "He was, and is, one of the greatest bluesmen of all time"—(Dick Spottswood) Mike Leadbitter, *Nothing But the Blues*, Hanover Books, 1971

"He is a brilliant guitarist and a singer with a fine sense of phrasing and emotional communication" —Sam B Charters, *The Country Blues*, Rinehart & Company, Inc, 1959

"The colors of the blues are pervasive in all his work, but they are of many different hues . . ." —Nat Hentoff, Vanguard album 79220

References: Piedmont album 13157

Jazz Journal magazine (UK), Feb 1964, pp 24-6

HUTTO, JOSEPH BENJAMIN *"JB"*
(aka: JB)
Born: Apr 29, 1926, Elko (Barnwell Co), SC
Died: Jun 12, 1983, Harvey, IL
Inst: Drums/Guitar/Piano

Father was Calvin Hutto, a deacon; mother Susie Johnson; to Augusta, GA 1929; frequently sang in family group, The Golden Crowns Gospel Singers, working local churches in Augusta area, late 30s into 40s; moved to Chicago, IL, to work outside music while learning guitar, mid-40s; worked occasional gigs w Johnny Ferguson and His Twisters group at local clubs/taverns, Chicago, from c1946; formed own JB and the Hawks group working parties/basement jumps as well as 1015 Club/Club Playtime/Happy Home Club/Globetrotter Lounge/Sylvio's and other bars/clubs/lounges, Chicago, late 40s into 50s; worked w Hawks, Red's Upstairs Lounge, Chicago, 1954; rec w Hawks, Chance label, Chicago, 1954; worked mostly outside music, Chicago, c1955-65; rec Vanguard label, Chicago, 1965; worked frequently w

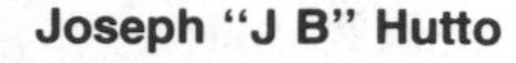

Joseph "J B" Hutto

Photo by Ray Flerlage (Kinnara Collection). Courtesy Living Blues *Magazine*

Hawks at Turner's Blue Lounge, Chicago, 1966 into 70s; Univ of Chicago, Chicago, 1966; Ash Grove, Los Angeles, CA, 1966; rec Testament label, Chicago, 1966; rec Delmark label, Chicago, 1966; Univ of Chicago R&B Festival, Chicago, 1968; Univ of Wisconsin Blues Festival, Madison, WI, 1968; rec w Sunnyland Slim, Delmark label, Chicago, 1968; Jazz Institute of Chicago Concert, Chicago, 1969; Univ of Notre Dame, South Bend, IN, 1969-70; Ash Grove, Los Angeles, 1969; The Sweet Pea, Chicago, 1969; Jet Star Club, Chicago, 1969; Ann Arbor Blues Festival, Ann Arbor, MI, 1969; Second Fret, Philadelphia, PA, 1969; Electric Circus, NYC, 1969; Rose & Kelly's, Chicago, 1970; Alice's Revisited, Chicago, 1970; Wisconsin Blues Festival, Beloit, WI, 1970; Mariposa Folk Festival, Toronto, Can, 1970; Washington Blues Festival, Howard Univ, Washington, DC, 1970; app on MADE IN CHICAGO, WTTW-TV, Chicago, c1970; app in UK film CHICAGO BLUES, 1970 (shown on OMNIBUS Show, BBC-1-TV, London, Eng, 1971); worked Mr Henry's, Washington, DC, 1970-1; Washington Square Church, NYC, 1971; Boston Blues Society Concert, Harvard Univ, Cambridge, MA, 1971; toured England working 100 Club/Marquee Club and other club/college dates, 1972 (por rel Flyright label); Florence's Lounge, Chicago, 1972-4; Joe's Place, Cambridge, MA, 1972; rec Delmark label, Chicago, 1972; worked Univ of North Carolina, Chapel Hill, NC, 1973 (por rel Flyright label); Wise Fools Pub, Chicago, 1973-4; The Kove, Kent, OH, 1973; El Mocambo, Toronto, Can, 1973; app on ATOMIC MAMA'S WANG DANG DOODLE BLUES Show, WNIB-FM-radio, Chicago, c1973; worked Peanut Barrel, Chicago, 1974; Sports Arena, Toledo, OH, 1974; Minstrel's, Chicago, 1974; Biddy Mulligan's, Chicago, 1974-6; Cafe Campus, Montreal, Can, 1975; toured Europe working concert/TV dates, 1976-7; rec Amigo label, Stockholm, Sweden, 1976; worked The Bayou, Washington, DC, 1976; Sweet Lips Club, Chicago, IL, 1976; International People's Appeal Blues Concert, Chicago, 1976; NAIRD Convention, O'Hare Motor Inn, Chicago, 1977; Bona Vista, Buffalo, NY, 1977; Coffee Gallery, San Francisco, CA, 1977; Ken's Afterglow, Portland, OR, 1977; Portland State Col, Portland, OR, 1977; toured concerts in Austria, 1977 (por rel Wolf label); Sandy's Jazz Revival, Beverly, MA, 1978 (por rel Baron label); worked clubs/cabarets on West Coast/Can, 1978; frequent East Coast club/college dates, 1979-82; toured Eng/Europe working concert dates, 1979; toured US working club/concert dates into 80s; toured Europe working concerts/one-nighters, 1981-2 (por 1982 Montreux Jazz Festival rel Montreux label, Montreux, Switzerland); worked Gulf Coast club dates, 1982; rec Black & Blue label, Carlisle, MA, 1982; entered Ingalls Hospital where he died of cancer; buried Restvale Cemetery, Worth, IL

Songs: Blues Do Me a Favor/Blues for Fonessa/Blues Stay Away from Me/Boogie Right-On/Chicago Boogie/Diabetic Blues/Feeling Is Gone/Girl I Love/Going Ahead/Goodnight Boogie/Hawk Squat/Hip-Shakin'/If You Change Your Mind/Letter from My Baby/Lulu Belle's Here/Married Woman Blues/My Kind of Woman/Notoriety Woman/Pet Cream Man/Please Help/Precious Stone/Same Mistake Twice/She's So Sweet/Shy Voice/Slide Winder/Sloppy Drunk/Speak My Mind/Stranger Blues/That's the Truth/Things Are So Slow/Too Late/Too Much Alcohol/Too Much Pride/20% Alcohol/Young Hawks Crawl

Awards/Honors: Won *Downbeat* magazine International Critics Award for Rock-Pop-Blues group deserving of wider recognition, 1969

Infl by: Elmore James/Muddy Waters/Aaron "T-Bone" Walker

Infl to: Edward Williams

Quotes: "Hutto is unequivocally the most exciting bluesman today working in the modern style"—Pete Welding, *Blues Unlimited* magazine (UK), Feb 1967, p 10

"JB's music has always been so strong . . . almost violently strong . . . that just about everything he's ever done is worth listening to"—Bob Koester, *Living Blues* magazine, Nov 1976, p 23

Reference: Living Blues magazine, Nov 1976, pp 14-24

I

IVORY LEE
(see Semien, Lee)

J

JB
(see Hutto, Joseph)
(see Lenoir, JB)

JACKSON, ARTHUR *"Sam"*
(*aka:* Peg-Leg Sam/Peg Pete)

Photo by Norbert Hess. Courtesy Living Blues Magazine

Born: Dec 18, 1911, Jonesville (Union Co), SC
Died: Oct 27, 1977, Jonesville, SC
Inst: Harmonica

Mother was a church organist; born/raised on farm; taught self harmonica at 9 years of age; ran away from home to hobo across US/Cuba/Haiti/Jamaica/Bahamas to work outside music with frequent work as itinerant musician in streets/fairs/picnics/ships from c1921; frequently toured w Doc Thompson Carnival/Emmet Smith Medicine Show/Doc WR Kerr's Indian Remedy Company Medicine Show (w Pink Anderson) and other carnivals/medicine shows from 1933 through 50s; frequently app on FENNER'S WAREHOUSE Show, WEED-radio, Rocky Mount, NC, 1936-51; frequently toured w Chief Thundercloud Medicine Show working streets/lots/picnics/fairs through South from 1950s to 1972; frequently worked w Rufe Johnson at local parties, Spartanburg, SC, area, through 60s; rec in performance w Chief Thundercloud Medicine Show, Flyright label, Pittsboro, NC, 1972; rec Trix label, Jonesville, SC, 1972; rec acc to Ruff Johnson, Trix label, Jonesville/Union, SC, 1972; worked w Ruff Johnson at blues festivals/bars, Chapel Hill, NC, 1972; Univ of North Carolina, Chapel Hill, 1973 (por rel Flyright label); Duke Univ, Durham, NC, 1973; Philadelphia Folk Festival, Schwenksville, PA, 1974 (por shown on PHILADELPHIA FOLK FESTIVAL, PBS-TV, 1975); Univ of Chicago Folk Festival, Chicago, IL, 1975; Folk City, NYC, NY, 1975; rec w Louisiana Red, Blue Labor label, White Plains, NY, 1975; worked Academy of Music, Brooklyn, NY, 1975; National Folk Festival, Wolf Trap Farm Park, Vienna, VA, 1975; John Henry Memorial Concert, Clifftop, WV, 1975; w Louisiana Red at The Riverboat, Toronto, Can, 1976; Atlanta Blues Festival, Great Southeast Music Hall, Atlanta, GA, 1976; New Orleans Jazz & Heritage Festival, New Orleans, LA, 1976; inactive since 1976 due to illness; worked Mariposa Folk Festival, Toronto Island, Toronto, Can, 1977; died of natural causes

Personal: Lost lower part of right leg due to train accident and thus called "Peg-Leg." Not to be confused with "One-Leg" Sam Norwood

Infl by: Pink Anderson/Elmon "Shorty" Bell

Quotes: ". . . an amazing story-teller, toast-giver, reciter of poetry, dancer, singer, and a master of the French harp"—Pete Lowry, Trix album 3302

References: Trix album 3302
Living Blues, Nov/Dec 1977, p. 39

JACKSON, BENJAMIN JOSEPH *"Bull Moose"*
Born: Apr 22, 1919, Cleveland (Cuyahoga Co), OH
Died: Jul 31, 1989, Cleveland, OH
Inst: Saxophone/Violin

Father was Benjamin Jackson Sr; mother Margaret Washington; with Avery Church Choir at 3; received violin/vocal instruction from 4 years of age; was featured violinist in local grade school orchestra at 6 years of age; attended Central HS working in school band through 30s; after graduating toured w Freddie Webster Harlem Hotshots Band working dances through northern Ohio, 1939 into early 40s; worked w local dance bands, Moon Glo Club/Little Harlem Club and other cafes/ballrooms, Buffalo, NY, c1942; worked in house band of Cedar Gardens Club, Cleve-

Benjamin "Bull Moose" Jackson *Courtesy Frank Driggs Collection*

land, OH, 1943; extensive touring w Lucky Millinder Band working dances/clubs/theaters across US, 1943-7; app in soundie film BIG FAT MAMAS c1943; app w Lena Horne on JUBILEE USA, AFRS-radio, Hollywood, CA (syndicated), 1944; rec w own band, King label, 1945; rec w Lucky Millinder Orch (as sideman or vocalist), Decca label, NYC, NY, 1945-7; w Lucky Millinder Band, Club Riviera, St Louis, MO, 1946; Apollo Theater, NYC, 1946; rec Superdisc label, NYC, 1947; rec w own Buffalo Bearcats, King label, NYC, 1947-52; toured w own Buffalo Bearcats working theaters/clubs/ballrooms across US c1947 into 50s; app w Lucky Millinder Orch in film BOARDING HOUSE BLUES, 1948; w own band, Apollo Theater, NYC, 1948; Avalon Ballroom, San Francisco, CA, c1950; rec w Tiny Bradshaw Band, King label, Cincinnati, OH, 1952; app in SMART AFFAIRS Revue, Regal Theater, Chicago, IL, 1954; worked Latin Quarter, Montreal, Can, 1954; Club Miami, Hamilton, Can, 1955; Weekes Club, Atlantic City, NJ, 1955; Pep's Musical Bar, Philadelphia, PA, 1955; Zanzibar Club, Buffalo, NY, 1956; Carr's Beach Club, Annapolis, MD, 1956; 4400 Club, Brentwood, MD, 1956; toured South working club dates, 1957; worked outside music through 50s/60s; app in film SINCERELY THE BLUES, 1975; toured Europe/Africa, 1977; worked occasional one-nighters into 80s; worked w The Flashcat's from 1983; toured Europe, 1985; rec Bogus label, Pittsburgh, PA, 1985; died of cancer; buried Lincoln Cemetery, Suitland, OH

Quote: "One of the founding fathers of R&B."—David Nelson, *Living Blues* Dec 1989, p 36

JACKSON, BESSIE
(see Bogan, Lucille)

JACKSON, BILL
Born: Feb 22, 1906, Granite (Baltimore Co), MD
Inst: Guitar

One of 5 children; born/raised/worked outside music on farm from youth; learned guitar from Jim Fuller and frequently worked local house parties/community work parties/country suppers/dances in Granite, MD, area from c1921-8; moved to Philadelphia, PA, to work mostly outside music work from c1928 into 70s; rec Testament/Storyville labels, Philadelphia, 1962-3

Personal: Married. 1 child

Song: 22nd Day of November

Quote: "Bill Jackson . . . in whose wistful, ingenuous singing and nimble fingers are carried the Negro folksong traditions of his native Maryland"—Pete Welding, Testament album 201

Reference: Testament album 201

JACKSON, *"Papa"* CHARLIE
(*aka:* Charlie Carter)

Courtesy Sheldon Harris Collection

Born: New Orleans (Orleans Parish), LA (unconfirmed)
Died: Spring 1938, Chicago, IL
Inst: Banjo/Guitar/Ukulele

Reportedly worked as singer/performer on various touring minstrel/medicine shows across US during teens; frequently worked for tips on Maxwell Street, Chicago, IL, through 20s and 30s; frequently worked west side club dates, Chicago, from c1924; rec Paramount label, Chicago, 1924-9; rec w Ida Cox, Paramount label, Chicago, 1925; rec w Freddie Keppard's Jazz Cardinals, Paramount label, Chicago, 1926; rec acc to Lucille Bogan and others, Paramount label, Chicago, 1927; worked Kentucky State Fair, Lexington, KY, 1928; rec Paramount label, Grafton, WI, 1929-30; continued working club dates in Chicago into 30s; rec OKeh label, Chicago, 1934; rec w Big Bill Broonzy, ARC label group, Chicago, 1935; was living on west side of Chicago at time of death

Personal: Not to be confused with guitarist Charlie Jackson who had worked with Tiny Parham Band

Songs: Airy Man Blues/Baby Don't You Be So Mean/Baby Please Loan Me Your Heart/Blue Monday Morning Blues/Bright Eyes/Coalman Blues/Coffee Pot Blues/Corn Liquor Blues/Don't Break Down on Me/Drop That Sack/The Faking Blues/Fat Mouth Blues/Gay Cattin'/Hot Papa Blues/I Got What It Takes but It Breaks My Heart to Give It Away/I'll Be Gone Babe/I'm Alabama Bound/Jackson's Blues/Look Out Papa Don't Tear Your Pants/Maxwell Street Blues/Mister Man/Mumsy Mumsy Blues/Papa Do Do Do Blues/Papa's Lawdy Lawdy Blues/Salty Dog (Blues)/Self Experience/Shake That Thing/She Belongs to Me Blues/Sheik of Desplaines Street/Skoodle Um Skoo/Take Me Back Blues/Texas Blues/We Can't Buy It No More/You Got That Wrong/Your Baby Ain't Sweet Like Mine

Infl to: Bill Broonzy

Quotes: "Medicine show singer 'Papa' Charlie Jackson was the first Negro folk singer to record"—Paul Oliver, *The Story of the Blues*, Chilton Book Company, 1969

"He was a sophisticated all-round entertainer, with comic songs, vaudeville and minstrel-sounding material as well as blues . . ."—Giles Oakley, *The Devil's Music—A History of the Blues*, British Broadcasting Corp, 1976

Reference: Yazoo album 1029

JACKSON, JIM

Courtesy Sheldon Harris Collection

Born: c1890, Hernando (De Soto Co), MS
Died: 1937, Hernando, MS (unconfirmed)
Inst: Guitar

Interested in music early and learned guitar from father as youth; frequently worked as singer/musician/dancer in local medicine shows in area from c1905; frequently worked w Robert Wilkins/Gus Cannon in local dances/parties/picnics/fish fries/jukes in Hernando, MS, area c1912; frequently toured w Silas Green Minstrel Show/Abbey Sutton Show/Rabbit Foot Minstrels Show/others working out of Memphis, TN, through southern states from c1915; formed group w Furry Lewis/Will Shade/Gus Cannon to work streets and clubs like Pee Wee's/Big Grundy's/Cham Fields'/BB Anderson's/others, Memphis, TN, c1916 into 20s; toured w Dr WB Miller Medicine Show working through Midwest, 1916-17; frequently toured w Dr Benson Medicine Show working through Southeast, 1918-27; worked Peabody Hotel, Memphis, TN, c1919; toured w Dr C Hankenson's Medicine Show working through Tennessee/North Carolina/Virginia, early 20s; toured w Birmingham Jug Band on Doctor Willie Lewis Medicine Show working through South into 20s; toured w Rabbit Foot Minstrels tent show through South c1923; continued to work solo (or w Gus Cannon) on local streets/gambling joints/parties/suppers in Memphis through 20s; rec Vocalion label, Chicago, IL, 1927-30; rec Victor label, Memphis, 1928; toured w Speckled Red in Red Rose Minstrel/Medicine Show working through Mississippi/Arkansas/Alabama, 1928-31; frequently worked w Speckled Red in local bars/joints, Memphis, 1929; rec w Tampa Red/Tom Dorsey/Speckled Red, Vocalion label, Memphis, 1929; toured w Doctor Streaks Medicine Show working through Alabama/Gulf Coast areas, 1929; app in film HALLELUJAH!, 1929; continued working out of Memphis, TN, in various travelling shows/local jukes/bars/streets through 30s

Song: Kansas City Blues

Infl by: Frank Stokes

Infl to: JB Lenoir

Quotes: "One of the great Memphis-based entertainers and a medicine show favorite"—Pete Welding, Fantasy album 24703

"Jim Jackson was a successful blues singer and his recording of 'Kansas City Blues' was one of the most popular in the idiom"—Paul Oliver, *The Story of the Blues*, Chilton Book Company, 1969

Reference: Memphis Blues, Bengt Olsson, Studio Vista, 1970

JACKSON, *"Mississippi"* JOHN H

Born: Feb 25, 1924, Woodville (Rappahannock Co), VA
Inst: Banjo/Guitar/Piano

"Mississippi" John Jackson *Courtesy* Living Blues *Magazine*

Parents were farmers who also worked local parties as singing musicians; born/raised on farm in FT Valley, between Woodville and Sperryville, VA; one of 14 children; interested in music early and learned guitar at 4 years of age; dropped out of school early to work outside music on farm with frequent work in family band at local parties/dances/picnics in valley area through 30s/40s; moved to Fairfax, VA, to work mostly outside music with occasional dance gigs at local hunt club from 1949 into 60s; worked Ontario Place, Washington, DC, 1964; Newport Folk Festival, Newport, RI, 1965; rec Arhoolie label, Fairfax, VA, 1965; worked Georgia Festival of Folkmusic, Atlanta, GA, 1966-7 (por 1967 concert shown local TV); Washington Folk Festival, Washington, DC, 1966; Smithsonian Folklife Conference, Washington, DC, 1967; Philadelphia Folk Festival, Schwenksville, PA, 1967-70; Festival of American Folklife, Washington, DC, 1967-70; rec Arhoolie label, Fairfax Station, VA, 1967; worked Univ of Chicago Folk Festival, Chicago, IL, 1968; toured w American Folk Blues Festival working concert dates through England/Europe,

1969-70; worked Royal Albert Hall, London, Eng, 1969 (por rel CBS label); rec Arhoolie label, Stuttgart, Ger, 1969; worked Berkeley Blues Festival, Univ of California, Berkeley, CA, 1970; Ann Arbor Blues Festival, Ann Arbor, MI, 1970; Washington Blues Festival, Howard Univ, Washington, DC, 1970; app on local show, WTTG-TV, Washington, DC, 1970; worked Festival of American Folklife, Montreal, Can, 1971; Mariposa Folk Festival, Toronto Islands, Can, 1971; National Folk Festival, Wolf Trap Farm Park, Vienna, VA, 1971; Mariposa Folk Festival, Toronto Islands, Can, 1973; toured concert dates through Latin America, 1973; toured England/Europe working concert dates, 1973; Five College Folk Festival, Amherst, MA, 1974; worked Festival of American Folklife, Washington, DC, 1975; Mariposa Folk Festival, Toronto Islands, Can, 1976; toured concert dates through Europe, 1976; Winnipeg Folk Festival, Winnipeg, Can, 1977; National Folk Festival, Wolf Trap Farm Park, Vienna, VA, 1977; Philadelphia Folk Festival, Schwenksville, PA, 1977; George Washington Univ, Washington, DC, 1977

Personal: Married Cora Lee ———. 7 children

Songs: John Jackson Breakdown/Poor Boy

Infl by: Barbecue Bob (Robert Hicks)/Blind Blake/Jim Clark/"Happy"/John Hurt/Blind Lemon Jefferson

Quotes: "Jackson's music combines the traditions of Carolina blues, old-time white hillbilly music, medicine show entertainment tunes, and ragtime"—Bruce Iglauer, *Downbeat* magazine, Nov 12, 1970, p 29

"He is by classification a songster and not a bluesman, although he will play and sing more blues on a good night's parlor concert than some Delta bluesmen may have known in a lifetime"—Bruce Cook, *Listen to the Blues*, Charles Scribner's Sons, 1973

References: *Blues* magazine (Canada), Aug 1976, pp 19-31

Arhoolie album 1025

JACKSON, LEE

(*aka:* Warren Lee)
Born: Aug 18, 1921, Gill, AR (unconfirmed)
Died: Jul 1, 1979, Chicago, IL
Inst: Guitar

Father George Hardin Lee; mother Ada Hartmon; born Warren George Hardin Lee; interested in music early; often at Alf Bonner's place, Gill, AR, where he learned guitar on homemade instrument during teens; later worked local house parties/roadhouses in Marianna, AR, area; left home to hobo through Mississippi/Alabama/Georgia/Oklahoma/Florida/elsewhere working outside music with frequent work at parties/picnics/fish fries/suppers from c1932 through 1940s; rec (unissued) tests, Memphis, TN, c1932; app w own Warren Lee & The Drops of Joy, KXJK-radio, Forrest City, AR, 1949; settled in Chicago, IL, to frequently work outside music from c1950; frequently sat-in/rec as sideman with local blues groups with frequent work on Maxwell Street for tips, Chicago, through 50s; worked Tuxedo Lounge, Chicago, c1952; w Johnny Shines, Frosty Corner, Chicago, c1953; rec Chess label (unissued), Chicago, early 50s; rec VJ label (unissued), Chicago, 1955; worked w Elmore James Band, Ft Worth, TX, mid-50s; frequently worked w Big Walter Horton, Turner's Lounge, Chicago, late 50s; rec Cobra label, Chicago, 1956-7; continued working as sideman in local clubs, Chicago, into 60s; rec Keyhole label, Chicago, 1961; rec w JB Hutto Hawks, Testament label, Chicago, 1966; rec w Cadillac Baby Specials group, Bea and Baby label, Chicago, 1967; rec w JB Hutto Band, Delmark label, Chicago, 1968; worked Turner's Blue Lounge, Chicago, 1968-70; Electric Circus, NYC, NY, 1969; continued outside music work, Chicago, into 70s; toured w Chicago Blues All Stars on American Blues Festival tour working concert dates through England/Europe, 1970 (por Frankfort, Ger, concert rel Scout label); worked Jazz Expo, London, Eng, 1970; Wisconsin Blues Festival, Beloit, WI, 1970; toured w Chicago Blues All Stars working concert dates through Europe, 1971; rec Bea & Baby label (unissued), Chicago, 1971; worked Big Duke's Blue Flame Lounge, Chicago, 1972; Florence's Lounge, Chicago, 1972; The Post, Chicago, 1972; w JB Hutto Band, Univ of North Carolina, Chapel Hill, NC, 1973; rec BluesWay label, Chicago, 1973; w JB Hutto, Delmark label, Chicago, c1973; rec CJ label, Chicago, 1974; worked Michigan Cafe Society, Chicago, 1975; Alibi Inn, Chicago, 1975; Kingston Mines, Chicago, 1976; Elsewhere Club, Chicago, 1977-8; B.L.U.E.S, Chicago, 1978-9; killed in family argument; buried Mt Glenwood, Glenwood, IL

Songs: All Around Man/Came Home This Morning/Country Girl/I Had a Dream Last Night/Juanita/Lonely Girl/Lonely Without Love/Neck Bones/Old Aunt Jane/The Sky Above/When I First Came to Chicago

Quote: "[His method] is one of innovation: a synthesis of new and old material, of standard blues forms and more unusual changes"—Justin O'Brien, *Living Blues* magazine, Sept/Oct 1977, p 16

Lee Jackson
Courtesy Living Blues *Magazine*

Reference: Living Blues magazine, Jul-Aug/Sept-Oct 1977

JACKSON, MELVIN *"Lil Son"*
Born: Aug 16, 1915, Barry (Navarro Co), TX
Died: May 30, 1976, Dallas, TX
Inst: Guitar

Father was Johnny Jackson, a singer and musician; mother was Ivora Allen; born/raised on grandfather's farm where he later worked outside music as sharecropper; frequently sang in choir at Holiness Church, Tyler, TX, as youth; interested in music and learned guitar from father as teenager; ran away from home to work outside music in Dallas, TX, from early 30s; frequently worked w Blue Eagle Four Spiritual group in local churches, Dallas, through 30s; served in Quartermaster Corps of US Army in Wales/France/Germany, 1944-6; returned to Dallas to work outside music from 1946; rec Gold Star label, Houston, TX, 1948-9; formed own band to tour dances/clubs through Texas/Oklahoma, late 40s into 50s; rec Imperial label, 1950-4; worked mostly outside music with frequent local church work, Dallas, from 1954; rec Arhoolie/Decca labels, Dallas, 1960; rec (unknown) label, Houston, 1963; mostly inactive due to illness from early 70s; entered Veterans Administration Hospital where he died of cancer; buried Lincoln Memorial Park Cemetery, Dallas, TX

Songs: Charlie Cherry/Everybody's Blues/Mr Blues/Restless Blues/Rockin' and Rollin'/Rocky Road/Thrill Me Baby/Time Changes Things/Travelin' Woman/Two Timin' Women/Young Woman Blues

Infl by: Texas Alexander/Lonnie Johnson

Infl to: Robert Lowery

Quote: "[Jackson is] possessed of a distinctive, almost laconic vocal style and a guitar approach that is both full and rhythmically relaxed . . ."—Pete Welding, Imperial album LM-94000

Reference: Nothing But the Blues, Mike Leadbitter, Hanover Books, 1971

Melvin "Lil Son" Jackson *Courtesy C Strachwitz, Arhoolie Records*

JACOBS, MARION WALTER
(aka: Little Walter/Little Walter J)
Born: May 1, 1930, Marksville (Avoyelles Parish), LA
Died: Feb 15, 1968, Chicago, IL
Inst: Guitar/Harmonica

Father was Adams Jacobs; mother was Beatrice Leviege; born and raised on farm; interested in music early and taught self harmonica at age of 8; ran away from home to form own group and work streets/small clubs, New Orleans, LA, 1942; worked Liberty Inn Club, Monroe, LA, 1943; app on KING BISCUIT TIME, KFFA-radio, Helena, AR, c1944; worked w Houston Stackhouse in local club dates, Helena area, from c1944; app w Dudlow Taylor on MOTHER'S BEST FLOUR HOUR, KFFA-radio, Helena, 1945-6; worked small clubs, East St Louis, IL/St Louis, MO, 1945; settled in Chicago, c1946; frequently worked Maxwell Street area for tips from c1946; frequently worked w Tampa Red/Bill Broonzy/Memphis Slim/others in local clubs, Chicago, IL, from c1946; rec Ora Nelle label, Chicago, 1947; worked Purple Cat, Chicago, 1947; worked w Muddy Waters Band in Du Drop Inn/Club Zanzibar/Boogie Woogie Inn/Romeo's Place/708 Club/others, Chicago, 1948-9; rec Tempo-Tone label, Chicago, 1948; toured extensively w Muddy Waters Band working clubs through South, 1949-50; app w Muddy Waters Band, KATZ CLOTHING STORE Show, KFFA-radio, Helena, AR, 1949; rec Parkway/Regal labels, Chicago, 1950; rec as sideman on many local sessions, Chicago, through 50s; toured w Muddy Waters Band working clubs through South, 1952; w Muddy Waters Band, Club Zanzibar, Chicago, 1952; Apollo Theater, NYC, NY, 1952; w Louis Myers' Four Aces, Hollywood Rendezvous, Chicago, 1952; toured w All-Girl Band on package show, 1952; rec frequently Checker-Chess label, Chicago, IL, 1952-66; toured w Louis Myers' Aces (as "The Night Cats," later renamed "The Jukes") working auditoriums/dance halls/road houses/night clubs across US, 1952-3; worked Club Zanzibar, Chicago, IL, 1953; Ricky's Show Lounge, Chicago, 1953; Apollo Theater, NYC, NY, 1953; app

Courtesy Institute of Jazz Studies

at Alan Freed's Holiday Ball, The Armory, Akron, OH, 1953; toured w The Jukes and other groups working one-nighters in Grand Rapids/Pontiac/Battle Creek, MI, area, 1954; Club Hollywood, Chicago, 1954; The Royal Peacock, Atlanta, GA, 1954; toured Texas working club one-nighters, 1954; worked Hippodrome Ballroom, Memphis, TN, 1954; worked Jam With Sam package show, Madison Rink, Chicago, 1954; 708 Club, Chicago, 1954; toured w Jukes working concerts/clubs across US, 1954; worked Alan Freed's Diddley Daddy package show, Loew's State, Boston, MA, 1955; Barrelhouse Lounge, Chicago, 1955; Club Zanzibar, Chicago, 1956-8; Ricky's Show Lounge, Chicago, 1957; Regal Theater, Chicago, c1957; rec acc Otis Rush, Cobra label, Chicago, 1957; worked Temple Room, Baton Rouge, LA, 1958; frequently inactive due to illnesses from 1958; toured as single working one-nighters in major cities of US, 1959 into early 60s; worked Hernando's Hideaway, Chicago, c1962; toured in Rhythm & Blues USA package show working concerts/festivals through England/Europe, 1962; worked Pride & Joy Club, Chicago, 1964; Mandel Hall, Chicago, 1964-6; toured w Rolling Stones group (and as single) in clubs/concerts through England, 1964; rec w Muddy Waters, Checker label, Chicago, 1967; toured w American Folk Blues Festival working concert dates through England/Europe, 1967; worked w Sam Lay Band, L&H Club, Chicago, 1968; Theresa's, Chicago, 1968; suffered injuries in street fight that later resulted in blood clot at home (coronary thrombosis); DOA Provident Hospital; buried St Mary's Cemetery, Evergreen, IL

Personal: Married Pearl Lee ——— (c1945). Was second cousin of Boogie Jake (Matthew Jacobs). Pseudonym "Little Walter J" also used by Walter J Westbrook, singer. Not to be confused with musician/singer Walter Jacobs Vinson

Songs: Ah'w Baby/Back Track/Blue Lights/Blues with a Feeling/Break It Up/Can't Hold Out Much Longer/Crazy Legs/Everything Gonna Be Alright/Flying Saucer/I Got to Find My Baby/I Got to Go/I Just Keep Loving Her/It Ain't Right/Juke/Just a Feeling/Just Your Fool/Last Night/Leaving in the Morning/Lights Out/Mean Old World/Moonshine Blues/Muskadine/Off the Wall/Oh Baby/One More Chance with You/Quarter to Twelve/Rock Bottom/Rocker/Sad Hours/Shake Dancer/Take Me Back/Teenage Beat/Tell Me Mama/Thunderbird/The Toddle/Up the Line/You Better Watch Yourself/You're So Fine

Awards/Honors: Won *Blues Unlimited* magazine (UK) Readers Poll for best blues harmonica player, 1973

Infl by: Big Maceo/Bill Broonzy/Big Walter Horton/Moody Jones/Tampa Red/Aaron "T-Bone" Walker/John Lee "Sonny Boy" Williamson/Sonny Boy Williamson (Alex Miller)

Infl to: Billy Boy Arnold/Carey Bell/Billy Branch/Dusty Brown/George Buford/Paul Butterfield/Eric Clapton/Cyril Davies/Shakey Jake Harris/Sugarcane Harris/Lazy Lester/Little Mack/Jerry McCain/Magic Sam/Johnny Mars/Charlie Musselwhite/Louis Myers/Raful Neal/Jerry Portnoy/George Smith/Henry Strong/Little Sonny Willis

Quotes: "He almost single-handedly fashioned the stylistic approach for harmonica which has since become standard for the genre and has been emulated by virtually every blues harmonica player"—*Downbeat* magazine, Apr 4, 1968, p 10

"My favorite singer"—(John Lee Hooker) Mike Leadbitter, *Nothing But the Blues*, Hanover Books, 1971

"Walter Jacobs was one of the very greatest, most exciting and original interpreters the blues has ever seen"—Pete Welding, Chess album 416

Reference: Living Blues, Winter 1971, pp 17-25

JACOBS, MATTHEW
(aka: Boogie Jake)

Photo by Stan Smith. Courtesy Living Blues Magazine

Born: c1929, Marksville (Avoyelles Parish), LA
Inst: Guitar/Piano

Interested in music early and played piano in local church as child; learned guitar as youth; frequently worked outside music with occasional local party work, Marksville, LA, area into 50s; worked w Little Walter Jacobs, Golden Lantern, Marksville, mid-50s; moved to Baton Rouge, LA, late 50s; frequently worked w Joe Hudson (drummer) as duo at Apex Club/Rhythm Club/others, Baton Rouge, late 50s; rec acc to Slim Harpo, Excello label, Crowley, LA, 1957; rec under own name, Excello-Flyright label, Crowley, 1957; rec Minit label, Baton Rouge, 1959; formed own 5-piece band to tour club dates through South, 1959-61; settled in Berkeley, CA, 1961; worked outside music with occasional house parties/Mason halls/others in San Francisco, CA, area, 1961-74; worked San Francisco Blues Festival, Golden Gate Park, San Francisco, 1974; The Sand Dunes, San Francisco, 1974; app on BLUES BY THE BAY Show, KPOO-FM-radio, San Francisco, 1974; worked Minnie's Can-Do Club, San Francisco, 1975; James Lick Jr HS, San Francisco, 1976; Green Earth Cafe, San Francisco, 1976-7; Playboy Club, Richmond, CA, 1976; Goldie's Saloon, Burlingame, CA, 1976; Spider's Web, Oakland, CA, 1977; rec Blues Connoisseur label, San Francisco, CA, 1977; worked San Francisco Blues Festival, McLaren Park Amphitheater, San Francisco, 1977; Eugene Blues Festival, Eugene, OR, 1977; app on BLUES BY THE BAY Show, KPFA-FM-radio, Berkeley, CA, 1977

Personal: Married Jessie ———. Second cousin of Little Walter Jacobs

Infl by: Nappy Brown/Fats Domino/Lightnin' Slim

Reference: Living Blues magazine, Mar/Apr 1977, pp 24-6

JACOBS, WALTER
(see Jacobs, Marion Walter)
(see Vinson, Walter Jacobs)

JAMES, BILLY
(see Phelps, Arthur)

JAMES, ELMER
(see Crudup, Arthur)

JAMES, ELMORE *"Elmo"/"Joe Willie"*

Courtesy Mike Rowe /Jim Gregory /Living Blues Magazine

Born: Jan 27, 1918, Richland (Holmes Co), MS
Died: May 24, 1963, Chicago, IL
Inst: Guitar

Mother was Learo Brooks; given surname of stepfather Joe Willie James; raised on various farms in Durant/Pickens/Goodman/Lexington, MS, area; interested in music early and learned on home-made lard can instrument as child; frequently worked dances/barrelhouses (as "Cleanhead" or Joe Willie James) through Delta area from 1932; frequently worked outside music with party/picnic work at Daybreak/Kincaid/Turner Brothers Plantations, Belzoni, MS, area, 1937-40; frequently worked w Robert Johnson/Sonny Boy Williamson (Alex Miller) or single, Harlem Tavern and others, Belzoni, MS, 1937-8; formed own combo working jukes/theaters/dances, Belzoni area, 1939; frequently toured w Sonny Boy Williamson (Alex Miller) working jukes through South, late 30s to 1942; worked w Sonny Boy Williamson (Alex Miller), New York Inn, New Orleans, LA, early 40s; served in US Navy in Guam, 1943-5; worked as single in local jukes, Belzoni, MS, area, 1945-6; worked w Homesick James/Eddie Taylor in local jukes, Memphis, TN, 1946; worked outside music in Jackson, MS, 1946; worked outside music on Silver Creek Plantation, Belzoni, 1947-8; frequently worked Webber's Inn, Belzoni, 1947-8; app w Sonny Boy Williamson (Alex Miller), KING BISCUIT TIME, KFFA-radio, Helena, AR, 1947; app w Sonny Boy Williamson (Alex Miller), TALAHO SYRUP Show, WAZF-radio, Yazoo City, MS, 1947-8 (also heard on WJPR-radio, Greenville, MS/WROX-radio, Clarksdale, MS); frequently worked w Sonny Boy Williamson (Alex Miller)/Big Boy Crudup in local gigs, Belzoni area, 1948; app w Willie Love Three Aces, WGVM-radio, Greenville, 1949; app w Sonny Boy Williamson (Alex Miller)/Willie Nix on HADACOL Show, KWEM-radio, West Memphis, AR, 1949; frequently worked local clubs/jukes, West Memphis, 1949-50; worked w Sonny Boy Williamson (Alex Miller) in local clubs, Jackson, MS, 1951; rec w Sonny Boy Williamson (Alex Miller)/Willie Love, Trumpet label, Jackson, MS, 1951-2; worked w Kansas City Red, Chuck's Club, Chicago, IL, 1951; Club Bizarre, Canton, MS, 1951-3; Tuxedo Lounge, Chicago, c1952; 708 Club, Chicago, 1952; rec w Johnnie Jones Group, Meteor label, Chicago, 1952; rec w own Broodusters, Checker label, Chicago 1953-6; rec Flair label, Chicago, 1953-5; frequently worked conventions/country clubs/sawmills/jukes in Canton, MS, area, 1953-4; rec acc to Joe Turner, Atlantic label, Chicago, 1953-5; worked Tuxedo Lounge/Square Deal Club, Chicago, c1955; Key Largo, Chicago, 1955; Club Alex, Chicago, 1955; worked w Johnnie Jones group, Sylvio's Club, Chicago, 1955-7; toured w Willie Nix group through South/Midwest, 1955-6; rec Chief label, Chicago, 1957-60; frequently worked Thelma's Lounge/Charlie's Lounge/Smitty's Corner, Chicago, 1957-60; frequently app on club remotes on BIG BILL HILL Show, WOPA-radio, Oak Park, IL, late 50s into 60s; worked as DJ on WOKJ/WRBC-radio, Jackson, MS, 1958; worked club dates in Chicago, IL/Gary, IN/Detroit, MI/St Louis, MO, 1958; rec Fire label, NYC, NY, 1959-61; toured extensively with own band working one-nighters through Atlanta, GA/Mississippi/Arizona/Texas/Mexico, late 50s into 60s; worked Grand Terrace Ballroom, Chicago, 1959; Tay May Club, Chicago, 1959; rec Chess label, Chicago, 1960; w own Broomdusters, Globetrotter Lounge/West Roosevelt Club/Cadillac Baby Lounge, Chicago, early 60s; Mr. P's Club, Jackson, MS, 1962; Copacabana Club, Chicago, 1963; suffered fatal heart attack; buried in unmarked grave, New Port Cemetery, Ebenezer, MS; grave marker placed/dedicated 1992

Personal: Married Josephine Harris (1937-); Georgianna Crump (1947-); Janice ——— (c1954-). Had 3 children. His son, Elmore James Jr is musician. Was cousin of musicians Homesick James/Boyd Gilmore

Songs: Baby Please Set a Date/Bobby's Rock/Can't Stop Loving My Baby/Canton Mississippi Breakdown/Coming Home/Country Boogie/Done Somebody Wrong/1839 Blues/Elmo's Shuffle/Elmore Jumps One/Fine Little Mama/Hand in Hand/Hawaiian Boogie/I Believe/I Gotta Go Now/I Have a Right to Love My Baby/I Held My Baby Last Night/I Need You/I See My Baby/I'm Worried/It Hurts Me Too/Knocking on Your Door/Late Hours at Midnight/Long Tall Woman/Madison Blues/Make My Dreams Come True/Manhattan Slide/Mean Mistreatin' Mama/My Best Friend/My Bleeding Heart/Please Find My Baby/Quarter Past Nine/Rock My Baby Tonight/Shake Your Money Maker/Sho Nuff I Do/Sinful Woman/The Sky Is Crying/So Mean to Me/Something Inside of Me/Standing at the Crossroads/Strange Kinda Feeling/The Sun Is Shining/Sunnyland/Take Me Where You Go/Talk to Me Baby/Tool Bag Boogie/Where Can My Baby Be?/Whose Muddy Shoes?/Wild About You Baby/Worried About My Baby

Infl by: Kokomo Arnold/Robert Johnson/Robert Nighthawk

Infl to: Joe Carter/Hi Tide Harris/Jimi Hendrix/John Hogg/Homesick James/JB Hutto/BB King/Freddy King/John Littlejohn/Jimmy Reed/Hound Dog Taylor/James "Son" Thomas/Johnny Winter

Quotes: "Elmore followed through the logical development [of Mississippi blues] and modernized them for all time"—Mike Rowe, *Chicago Breakdown*, Eddison Press Ltd, 1973

". . . one of the most prominent and influential bluesmen of his, or any time"—Michael Bromberg, Kent album 9010

"Elmore James' career was of consistent brilliance"—Simon Napier, Sue album 927

Reference: Blues Unlimited magazine (UK), May 1972, pp 5-10

JAMES, ELMORE, JR
(see Minter, Iverson)

JAMES, HOMESICK
(see Williamson, John A)

JAMES, JIMMY
(see Hendrix, James)

JAMES, NEHEMIAH *"Skip"*

Photo by Julie Snow

Born: Jun 9, 1902, Bentonia (Yazoo Co), MS
Died: Oct 3, 1969, Philadelphia, PA
Inst: Guitar/Kazoo/Organ/Piano

Father was Rev Eddie James, a Baptist minister and musician; mother was Phyllis Jones; born/raised on Woodbine Plantation outside Bentonia, MS; interested in music early and learned guitar at 8 years of age; attended Yazoo City HS where he learned piano basics and later played piano/organ in local church as youth, Bentonia; dropped out of school to hobo through Mississippi/Arkansas working outside music from c1917; worked w Henry Stuckey in local barrelhouses, Bentonia area, from c1918; frequently worked country frolics/parties/picnics/road houses/dance halls in various towns through South/Midwest into 20s; frequently worked local barrelhouses/dives/jukes in Memphis, TN, early 20s; attended a local divinity school, Yazoo City, MS, from mid-20s; settled in Jackson, MS, becoming active in ministry work with some side music instruction and local party work (w Johnnie Temple) c1929-31; rec Paramount label, Grafton, WI, 1931; moved to Dallas, TX, 1931; formed The Dallas Texas Jubilee Singers to work local churches (with some preaching) and frequent tours through Texas/Oklahoma/Arkansas/Mississippi/Kansas working churches/concerts, 1931-5; was ordained Baptist minister at father's Missionary Baptist Church, Birmingham, AL, 1932; frequently worked outside music with local preaching in churches in area, Birmingham, into 40s; was ordained a Methodist minister, Meridian, MS, 1946; moved to Hattiesburg, MS, to work outside music (as preacher) in area through 40s; worked outside music in Tunica/Dundee, MS, areas from 1951; returned to blues to work Bitter Lemon Coffeehouse, Memphis, TN, 1964; Newport Folk Festival, Newport, RI, 1964 (por rel Vanguard label); Mariposa Festival, Toronto, Can, 1964; Ontario Place, Washington, DC, 1964; Montgomery Junior Col, Takoma Park, MD, 1964; The Unicorn, Boston, MA, 1964; The Gaslight, NYC, NY, 1964; Second Fret, Philadelphia, PA, 1964-5; toured w John Hurt working concert dates on East Coast, 1964; rec Melodeon label, Falls Church, VA, 1964; rec Herwin label, Boston, 1964; rec Vanguard label, NYC, 1965; worked Folksong 65, Carnegie Hall, NYC, 1965; Cafe A-Go-Go, NYC, 1965-6 (por 1966 gig rel Verve label); Club 47, Cambridge, MA, 1965; Philadelphia Folk Festival, Spring Mount, PA, 1965; Fool's Mate, Westport, CT, 1965; Orleans Club, Boston, 1965; Ash Grove, Los Angeles, CA, 1966; Sign of the Sun, San Diego, CA, 1966; Jabberwock, Berkeley, CA, 1966; Newport Folk Festival, Newport, RI, 1966; Chicago Folk Festival, Chicago, IL, 1967; toured w American Folk Blues Festival working concert dates through England/Europe, 1967; worked Univ of Chicago, Chicago, 1968; Hampton Institute Jazz Festival, Hampton, VA, 1968; Fillmore East, NYC, 1968; Festival of American Folklife, Washington, DC, 1968; mostly inactive due to illness from 1968; entered Univ of Pennsylvania Hospital where he died of cancer; buried Mercon Cemetery, Bala-Cynwyd, PA

Personal: Married Lorenzo M ——— (mid-20s); married Mabel ——— (c1947). Named "Skip" (short for "Skippy") as child

Songs: All Night Long/Be Ready When He Comes/ Cherry Ball Blues/Crow Jane/Cypress Grove Blues/ Devil Got My Woman/Drunken Spree/4 O'Clock Blues/Hard-Luck Child/Hard Time Killin' Floor Blues/How Long Buck?/I Don't Want a Woman to Stay Out All Night Long/I'm So Glad/If You Haven't Any Hay Get on Down the Road/Illinois Blues/Little Cow and Calf Is Gonna Die Blues/Look Down the Road/ My Gal/Sick Bed Blues/Special Rider Blues/22-20 Blues/Washington DC Hospital Center Blues

Infl by: Will Crabtree/Rich Griffith/Little Brother Montgomery/Henry Stuckey

Infl to: Robert Johnson/Johnnie Temple

Quotes: "Skip James is the greatest artist that ever came from the Mississippi Delta . . ."—Ed Morris, Melodeon album 7321

"The one characteristic of Skip James' music that strikes one most . . . is the perfect blend of voice, accompaniment and lyrics"—Bruce Jackson, Vanguard album 79219

"His style was one of the most distinctive to come out of the Delta, and it was dominated by an intense lyricism that shaped every element of the music"—Samuel B Charters, *The Bluesmen*, Oak Publications, 1967

References: Feel Like Going Home, Peter Guralnick, Outerbridge & Dienstfrey, 1971

The Bluesmen, Samuel B Charters, Oak Publications, 1967

Sing Out magazine, Jan 1966, pp 26-31

JAMMIN' JIM
(see Harris, Edward)

JAXON, FRANKIE *"Half-Pint"*
(*aka:* Cotton Thomas)
Born: Feb 3, 1895, Montgomery (Montgomery Co), AL
Died: c1940, CA(unconfirmed)
Inst: Piano/Sax

One of 3 children; parents died when he was young and worked outside music (as house boy) at 10 years of age; moved to Kansas City, MO, to attend Attuck Grammar School, 1906-9; frequently worked outside music with occasional work in local amateur shows/ theaters/bars for tips, Kansas City, 1910-15; toured w (Henry) McDaniel Company show working character parts through Oklahoma/Texas from 1910; teamed w Gallie DeGaston to tour as singing/dancing act work-

Frankie "Half-Pint" Jaxon *Courtesy Sheldon Harris Collection*

ing vaudeville circuit through South, 1912-14; worked Bailey's Theater, Atlanta, GA, 1912; teamed briefly w Buzzin' Burton to work vaudeville theaters, c1915; worked Whitley Brothers Show, Gibson Theater, Philadelphia, PA, 1916; frequently worked as singer/producer, New World Cafe, Atlantic City, NJ, 1916-19; frequently worked Rafe's Paradise Theater, Atlantic City, 1916-21; frequently worked w King Oliver/Freddie Keppard/others, Sunset Cafe/Plantation Club/others, Chicago, 1917-22; frequently produced shows/revues at Apollo Theater, NYC, NY, c1919; worked New Cabaret, Atlantic City, 1919; teamed w Helen Lee to work vaudeville theaters (as blackface comedian or female impersonator) c1920; frequently produced revues w Ethel Waters/Bessie Smith/others, Rafe's Paradise Theater, Atlantic City, 1922-6; teamed w Mae Dix working (as comedian) in local theaters, Detroit, MI/St Louis, MO/elsewhere, 1926; produced shows/revues, Miller's Grand Theater and others, Chicago, IL, 1927-9; rec Gennett/Black Patti labels, Chicago, 1927; rec Vocalion label, Chicago, 1928-30; rec w Tampa Red/Georgia Tom (as "The Black Hillbillies"), Vocalion label, Chicago, 1929; rec w Cotton Top Mountain Sanctified Singers/Bill Johnson's Jug Band/Banjo Ikey Robinson, Brunswick label, Chicago, 1929; worked w Bennie Moten Band in local club dates, Kansas City, MO, 1930; formed own Quarts of Joy group working/producing shows in local clubs, Chicago, 1930-1; frequently app on MUSCLE-TONE Show and others, WJJD/WBBM/WMAQ/WCFL-radio, Chicago, IL/Aurora, IL, 1931-41; app on own show from Century of Progress World's Fair, Chicago, 1933; rec w own Hot Shots, Vocalion label, Chicago, 1933; worked Harlem Opera House, NYC, NY, 1934; toured w own band working local radio shows in Midwest, 1936; toured w own band working hotel dates in Midwest, 1937-41; rec w Harlem Hamfats, Decca label, Chicago, 1937; rec Decca label, NYC, 1938-40; app in James P Johnson show POLICY KINGS, Nora Bayes Theater, NYC, 1938-9; settled in Washington, DC, to work outside music, c1940; moved to Los Angeles, CA to work mostly outside music, c1940; unconfirmed report of death in California Veterans Hospital

Personal: Named "Half-Pint" due to his short stature. Some sources spell this singer's surname "Jaxson"

Songs: Callin' Corrine/Fan It/Fifteen Cents

Quote: "[He] moved from jazz band to show business to hokum Chicago folk band with considerable ease" —Paul Oliver, *The Story of the Blues*, Chilton Book Company, 1969

JEFFERSON, BONNIE

Born: Jun 28, 1919, Shoal Creek (Logan Co), AR
Inst: Guitar

Father was Clark A Lewis; mother was Clara E ———; born Bonnie Lewis; one of 7 children; interested in music early and frequently sang in local Baptist church choir at 6 years of age; frequently toured w family choir to work churches across Arkansas c1929 into 30s; learned guitar from mother as teenager; attended vocational school on music scholarship c1936 and frequently worked outside music through 30s; worked outside music in Ft Smith, AR/Omaha, NE, area, from 1943; moved to San Diego, CA, to work outside music, 1951 into 70s; app at San Diego Folk Festival, San Diego, c1971; rec Advent label, San Diego, 1973; rec Blue Goose label, San Diego (?), c1973; worked occasional concert dates on college circuit on West Coast, early 70s

Personal: Married Calvin Jefferson (1947-)

Songs: Got the Blues So Bad/Take Me Back

Infl by: Mamie Scott

Quote: "An excellent guitarist, a good singer and . . . an audience pleaser and a good performer, too"—Lou Curtiss, *Living Blues* magazine, Summer 1974, p 8

Reference: Living Blues magazine, Summer 1974, p 8

JEFFERSON, *"Blind"* LEMON

(aka: Deacon LJ Bates/Elder JC Brown)
Born: Jul 11, 1897, Couchman (Freestone Co), TX
Died: Dec 1929, Chicago, IL (unconfirmed)
Inst: Guitar

Father Alec Jefferson was farmer; mother was Classie Banks; one of 7 children; born blind on farm outside Wortham, TX; worked as itinerant singing beggar at farm parties/picnics/streets in Wortham, TX, area from c1912; frequently worked streets/brothels/parties in East Dallas/Silver City/Galveston, TX, c1914; frequently worked Taborian Park for tips, Waco, TX, 1914; frequently worked streets/barrelhouses/brothels/saloons of Upper Elm Street area, Dallas, TX, from c1915; worked briefly outside music (as wrestler), Dallas, 1917; worked Alf Bonner's Place, Gill, AR, c1917; hoboed extensively working as itinerant singer (solo or with others) on streets through Louisiana/Mississippi/Alabama/Virginia/elsewhere into 20s; frequently worked picnics/suppers/parties in Wichita Falls/Leona/Buffalo/Galveston, TX, areas, early 20s; frequently worked house rent parties, Chicago, IL, from mid-20s; rec (religious songs)

"Blind" Lemon Jefferson *Courtesy Frank Driggs Collection*

Paramount label, Chicago, c1926; rec Paramount label, Chicago, 1926-9; worked Booker T Washington Theater, St Louis, MO, mid-20s; rec OKeh label, Atlanta, GA, 1927; continued working as street singer through Ft Worth/Waco/McHale/Dallas, TX, areas through 20s; worked briefly in local medicine show, Crystal Springs, MS, c1928; worked w Rubin Lacy in Greenwood/Moorhead, MS, c1929; rec Paramount label, Richmond, IN, 1929; reportedly suffered heart attack and died on street of exposure; buried Wortham Negro Cemetery, Wortham, TX; grave marker placed and dedicated Oct 15, 1967

Personal: Married Roberta ——— (c1922-). His son Miles Jefferson and sister Mabel Jefferson were musicians

Book: Blind Lemon Jefferson, Bob Groom, Blues World, 1970

Songs: Bad Luck Blues/Bakershop Blues/Bed Springs Blues/Beggin' Back/Big Night Blues/Black Horse Blues/Blind Lemon's Penitentiary Blues/Booger Rooger Blues/Booster Blues/Broke and Hungry/Chinch Bug Blues/Chock House Blues/Competition Bed Blues/Corinna Blues/Deceitful Brownskin Blues/Dry Southern Blues/Dynamite Blues/Eagle Eyed Mama/Gone Dead on You Blues/Got the Blues/Hang Man's Blues/Jack O Diamond Blues/Lemon's Cannon Ball Moan/Lemon's Worried Blues/Long Distance Moan/Long Lonesome Blues/Matchbox Blues/Mosquito Moan/Old Rounders Blues/One Dime Blues/Peach Orchard Mama/Piney Woods Money Mama/Pneumonia Blues/Prison Cell Blues/Rabbit Foot Blues/Sad News Blues/Saturday Night Spender Blues/See That My Grave Is Kept Clean/Shuckin' Sugar Blues/Southern Woman Blues/Stocking Feet Blues/That Black Snake Moan/That Crawlin' Baby Blues/Tin Cup Blues/Wartime Blues/Yo Yo Blues

Awards/Honors: A Blind Lemon Jefferson Club was opened in San Pablo, CA, 1960

A Blind Lemon Jefferson Club was opened in NYC, NY, 1962

A Jefferson Airplane rock group was popular during the 1960s

Infl by: Hobart Smith

Infl to: JT Adams/Louis Armstrong/Bill Broonzy/Sam Chatmon/KC Douglas/Frank Floyd/Lowell Fulson/John Lee Granderson/John Paul Hammond/John Hogg/Lightnin' Hopkins/Howlin' Wolf/John Jackson/Bunk Johnson/Curtis Jones/Moody Jones/Albert King/BB King/Leadbelly/John Arthur Lee/JB Lenoir/Mance Lipscomb/Brownie McGhee/Jelly Roll Morton/Buddy Moss/Muddy Waters/Jimmie Rodgers/LC Robinson/Alec Seward/Tom Shaw/Johnny Shines/Bessie Smith/Hobart Smith/Aaron "T-Bone" Walker/Josh White/Big Joe Williams/Robert Pete Williams/Hop Wilson

Quotes: "Blind Lemon Jefferson, the greatest of the early country blues singers, perhaps the first to codify blues in the form that is familiar to us today"—Charles Fox, Polydor album 545-019

"An exceptional poet, an outstanding guitar player, and a dark, haunting vocalist, he was one of the best selling artists of his time [c1925-30] and some of his efforts rank as all-time greats in the field of blues recordings"—Larry Cohn, Biograph album 12000

"One of America's outstanding original musicians"—Blind Lemon Jefferson's grave marker

References: The Country Blues, Samuel B Charters, Rinehart & Company, Inc, 1959

The Bluesmen, Samuel B Charters, Oak Publications, 1967

Blues World magazine (UK), Jan/Jul/Oct 1968; Apr/Jul/Oct 1969; Feb/Mar/Apr/May/Oct/Nov 1970; Autumn 1971

JEFFERY, ROBERT ERNEST LEE *"Bob"*
Born: Jan 14, 1915, Tulsa (Tulsa Co), OK
Died: Jul 20, 1976, San Diego, CA
Inst: Guitar/Piano

Father George Jeffery was musician; mother was Sarah Franklin; learned piano from uncle as child and entertained at local parties through 20s; left home to tour w JJ Collins Medicine Show working through Midwest into 30s; returned to Midwest to work outside music with occasional party work w Aaron "T-Bone" Walker, Kingfisher, OK, 1936; moved to Bakersfield, CA, to work outside music (in own auto repair shop) from mid-30s; moved to San Diego, CA, c1939; frequently worked w Tom Shaw, Little Harlem Chicken Shack, San Diego, CA, and other clubs/parties/Saturday night dates in area into 60s; continued outside music work, San Diego, to early 70s; toured college circuit working concert dates on West Coast, 1972; worked San Diego Univ Folk Festival, San Diego, 1972; rec Advent label, San Diego, 1973; worked Sweets Mill Folk Festival, San Diego, c1973; w Phillip Walker Blues Band, San Diego State Univ Folk Festival, San Diego, 1974 (por remote KPFK-FM-radio); w Bob Riedy Blues Band, Biddy Mulligan's Bar, Chicago, IL, 1975; worked Festival of American Folklife, Washington, DC, 1975; suffered

Robert "Bob" Jeffery

Photo by Virginia Curtiss /Folk Arts, San Diego /Living Blues Magazine

heart attack at home and died at Community Hospital of San Diego; buried Cypress View Cemetery, San Diego, CA

Personal: Married Ruby Lee Brunner. First cousin of Aaron "T-Bone" Walker

Songs: Gasoline Rationing Blues/73 Hop/Watergate Blues/Watergate Boogie Woogie

Reference: Living Blues magazine, Winter 1973, p 11

JENKINS
(see Wilson, Wesley)

JENKINS, AUGUSTUS *"Gus"*
(aka: Gus Jinkins/Little Temple/The Young Wolf)
Born: Mar 24, 1931, Birmingham (Jefferson Co), AL
Died: Dec 22, 1985, Inglewood, CA
Inst: Piano

Father Andrew Jenkins; mother Minnie Kate Forbes; taught self piano at 6 years of age; frequently entertained at local parties, Birmingham, AL, from childhood; won talent contest at Frolic Theater, Birmingham, as youth; dropped out of school to work local club dates, Birmingham, late 40s; toured w Willie Mae Thornton in Sammy Green's Hot Harlem Revue working shows through South c1948; toured w Percy Mayfield on package shows on West Coast, late 40s; worked Regal Theater, Chicago, IL, 1949; Joe's Deluxe Club, Chicago, 1949; frequently worked as studio musician for Chess Record Company, Chicago, 1950-2; worked with many local blues groups in club dates, Chicago, from early 50s; rec Chess label (unissued), Chicago, 1951-2; toured w Little Walter Jacobs group working clubs/dances across US, c1952; attended Frank Wiggins Trade School, Los Angeles, CA, 1952; frequently worked outside music with occasional night gigs, Los Angeles, 1952-4; rec Combo label, Los Angeles, 1952; rec Specialty label, Los Angeles, 1954; rec Cash label, Los Angeles, c1955; toured w Gene & Eunice in package show working theaters across US, 1955-6; rec Flash label, Los Angeles, 1956-8; frequently rec own Pioneer label (later renamed International Commander), Los Angeles, 1959-62; frequently toured w Johnny Otis

Courtesy Sheldon Harris Collection

Revue working concerts/TV shows on West Coast, early 60s; rec Catalina label, Los Angeles, 1963; frequently worked outside music (in own picture frame business), Los Angeles, early 60s into 70s; rec General Artist label, Los Angeles, c1965; frequently toured in package shows w Ray Charles/Amos Milburn/Little Richard/others through 60s; toured concert dates through Europe, late 60s; worked Univ of CA, Santa Barbara, CA, 1974; worked mostly outside music into 80s; died of hardening of arteries; buried Rose Hills Cemetery, Whittier, CA

Songs: Bloodstains on the Wall/I Ate the Wrong Part/Release Me/Tricky/You Told Me

Infl by: Walter Davis

References: Blues Unlimited magazine (UK), Apr 1971, pp 6-7

Whiskey, Women, And Jun 1973, pp 4-7

JENKINS, JOHN PICKENS *"Bobo"*
Born: Jan 7, 1916, Forkland (Greene Co), AL
Died: Aug 15, 1984, Detroit, MI
Inst: Guitar/Harmonica

Father was sharecropper; mother Mary Taylor; frequently sang in family church choirs at 5 years of age; formed own gospel quartet working local churches/funerals/friendship schools in Forkland, AL, area from c1925; ran away from home to work outside music in Memphis, TN, c1928; hoboed extensively through Mississippi/Arkansas working outside music through 30s; worked outside music, Tuscaloosa, AL, 1938-42; app on KING BISCUIT TIME, KFFA-radio, Helena, AR, c1941; served in US Army c1942-4; settled in Detroit, MI, working outside music from 1944; taught self guitar, 1954; worked Big George's Club Carribe, Detroit, c1954; formed own band frequently working club dates, Detroit, MI/St Louis, MO, areas from 1954; continued outside music work, Detroit, 1950s through 80s; rec Chess label, Detroit, 1954; rec Boxer label, Chicago, IL, 1955; rec Fortune label, Detroit, 1956; rec Big Star label, Detroit, c1964; worked Hurricane Lounge, Detroit, 1969; Idle Hour Lounge, Detroit, 1970; Detroit Blues Festival, Detroit, 1970; worked outside music (owned Fort Boulevard Recreation Bowling Alley/Bar), Detroit, 1970; formed/rec Big Star Recording Studio, Detroit, 1972-3; app BLUES AFTER HOURS Disc-jockey Show, WDET-FM-radio, Detroit early 70s; worked St Lawrence Centre, Toronto, Can, 1972; Ann Arbor Blues Festival, Ann Arbor, MI, 1973; Windsor

Courtesy Living Blues Magazine

Concert, Windsor, Can, 1973; Sports Arena, Toledo, OH, 1974; Highland Park Community Col, Detroit, 1974; Eddie Shaw's Place, Chicago, IL, 1975; Ethel's Lounge, Detroit, 1975; Golden 20s Club, Detroit, 1975; formed (served as president) Detroit Blues Club, Detroit, 1975; worked Detroit Blues Club Festival, Detroit, 1976-8; worked occasional local festivals into 80s; worked European Blues Festival, 1982; died of high blood pressure and diabetes; buried Detroit Memorial Park, Warren, MI

Songs: Bad Luck and Trouble/Cold Hearted Blues/Democrat Blues/Have You Heard the News?/Here I Am a Fool in Love Again/I Love That Woman/Monkey Not for Sale/Playboy Blues/Reeling and

Rocking/Shake 'em On Down/Sharecropper's Blues/ Solid Gold/Somebody Been Talkin'/Tell Me Who/24 Years/Watergate Blues/When I First Left Home/You Will Never Understand

Infl by: Calvin Frazier/Albert Witherspoon

Quote: "In addition to being a creative blues poet and warm personality, he can lay down some solid down-home blues"—Doug Langille, *Living Blues* magazine, Mar 1976, p 32

Reference: Living Blues magazine, Autumn 1970, pp 9-12; Winter 1970, pp 27-8

JICK (AND HIS TRIO)
(see Williamson, John A)

JINKINS, GUS
(see Jenkins, Gus)

JOHNSON, ALONZO *"Lonnie"*
(aka: Jimmy Jordan/Tom Jordan)

Courtesy Sing Out *Magazine*

Born: Feb 8, 1889, New Orleans (Orleans Parish), LA
Died: Jun 16, 1970, Toronto, Canada
Inst: Guitar/Harmonium/Kazoo/Piano/Violin

Father was musician; one of about 12 children; interested in music early and studied guitar and violin as child; dropped out of school to work outside music, New Orleans, LA, c1902; frequently worked w Punch Miller in Raceland, LA, area, as youth; frequently worked solo in redlight district of Storyville, New Orleans, 1910-17; worked frequently as violinist in father's family band at local banquets/weddings/street corners, New Orleans, 1914-17; worked w brother James "Steady Roll" Johnson, Iroquois Theater, New Orleans, c1917; Frank Pineri's Place, New Orleans, c1917; app in stock company in (unknown) musical revue, London, Eng, 1917-19; worked w Charlie Creath Jazz-O-Maniacs Band on Mississippi riverboat SS *St Paul* out of St Louis, MO, 1920-2; w Fate Marable Band on Mississippi riverboat SS *Capitol*, 1920-2; toured as single or w Clenn & Jenkins (comedic dancers) working TOBA/RKO theater circuits through South, 1922-4; frequently worked outside music in New Orleans, LA/Galesburg, IL/St Louis, MO, 1924-5; worked w brother James "Steady Roll" Johnson at Katy Red's Club, E St Louis, IL, 1925; won first prize in eight-week blues contest, Booker T Washington Theater, St Louis, 1925; rec w Charlie Creath Jazz-O-Maniacs, OKeh label, St Louis, 1925; frequently worked as staff musician, OKeh label, St Louis, MO/NYC, NY/Chicago, IL, 1925-32; frequently worked house parties, Chicago, from c1925; worked The Coliseum Theater, Chicago, 1926; rec w Louis Armstrong Hot Five, OKeh label, Chicago, 1927; worked local club dates, NYC, 1927; rec w Duke Ellington Orch/Chocolate Dandies, OKeh label, NYC, 1928; won second prize (to Lillian Glinn) in blues contest, Ella B Moore Theater, Dallas, TX, 1928; rec w Louis Armstrong Savoy Ballroom Five, OKeh label, NYC, 1929; frequently led pit band, Stanton Theater, Philadelphia, PA, 1929; toured w Bessie Smith in MIDNIGHT STEPPERS Revue working theaters through South, 1929; frequently app on own LONNIE JOHNSON, RECORDING GUITARIST Show, WPAP/WOV-radio, NYC, 1929-30; rec Columbia label, NYC, 1931-2; rec acc to Martha Raye, Victor label (unissued), NYC, 1932; settled in Cleveland, OH, to work outside music with app w Putney Dandridge on local shows on WTAM/WJAY/WHK-radio and local club dates from early 30s; frequently worked w Baby Dodds, Club Three Deuces, Chicago, IL, 1937-40; rec Decca label, Chicago/NYC, 1937-8; formed own trio to work Boulevard Lounge/Squyres Club/Flame Club/Plantation Club/The Gate/others, Chicago, c1938 to early 40s; rec Bluebird label, Chicago, 1939-44; toured one-nighters in Kansas City, MO/St Louis, MO/ Detroit, MI, and then to West Coast, 1940-4; worked Hughes DeLuxe Club, Chicago, 1943; rec Disc label, NYC, 1946; worked Martin's Corner, Chicago, c1946; Sportree Musical Bar, Detroit, 1946; rec Aladdin label, Chicago, 1947; worked w John Lee "Sonny Boy" Williamson, Club Georgia, Chicago, 1947; rec King label, Cincinnati, OH, 1947-52; worked Three Sixes Club, Detroit, MI, 1948; Apollo Theater, NYC, NY, 1948; Baby Grand, NYC, 1948; w Kid Ory Band, Carnegie Hall, NYC, 1948; frequently worked outside music in Cincinnati, late 40s to early 50s; worked Fairfield Lounge, Chicago, 1950; worked club/

concert dates in England, 1952; rec Parade/Paradise/Rama labels, Cincinnati, mid-50s; worked outside music (at Ben Franklin Hotel), Philadelphia, PA, late 50s; rec Prestige-Bluesville label, Englewood Cliffs, NJ, 1960-1; worked The Center, Philadelphia, 1960; Playboy Club, Chicago, 1960; Town Hall, NYC, 1960-1; Cafe Galerie, Detroit, MI, 1961; app on local shows, WDET/WJR-radio, Detroit, 1961; worked w Victoria Spivey, Gerdes Folk City, NYC, 1961; Sugar Hill Club, San Francisco, CA, 1962; toured w American Folk Blues Festival working club/concert dates through England/Europe, 1963 (por shown on I HEAR THE BLUES, Granada-TV, Eng); rec w Otis Spann, Storyville label, Copenhagen, Den, 1963; rec Fontana label, Bremen, Ger, 1963; worked The Cellar, Philadelphia, 1963; Philadelphia Folk Festival, Paoli, PA, 1963; rec Spivey label, Brooklyn, NY, 1963-5; worked Downstairs Club, Hamilton, Can, 1963; The Gaslight, NYC, NY, 1965; The Owl, NYC, 1965; Gerdes Folk City, NYC, 1965; settled in Toronto, Can, to work New Gate of Cleve, 1965-6; Penny Farthing, Toronto, 1965; Steele's Tavern, Toronto, 1965; Castle George, Toronto, 1966; owned/worked Home of the Blues Club, Toronto, 1966; George's Kibitzeria, Toronto, 1967-8; Club Alley Cat, Toronto, 1967; The Gaslight, Toronto, 1968-9; The Golden Nugget, Toronto, 1968; mostly inactive due to illness, Toronto, from 1969; rec ST of UK film BLUES LIKE SHOWERS OF RAIN, 1970; worked w Buddy Guy, Massey Hall, Toronto, 1970; suffered fatal stroke at home; buried local cemetery, Philadelphia, PA

Personal: Married blues singer Mary Smith (1925-32). 6 children. His son Clarence Johnson is recorded singer/musician. Brother of James "Steady Roll" Johnson. Reportedly related to Tommy Johnson's father, Idell Johnson

Billing: The World's Greatest Blues Singer

Songs: Another Night to Cry/Be Careful/Blue Ghost Blues/Blues 'Round My Door/Clementine Blues/Crowing Rooster Blues/Death Valley Is Just Half-Way to My Home/Devil's Got the Blues/Don't Drive Me from Your Door/Don't Ever Love/End It All/Evil Woman/Feelings from the Fingers/Fine Booze and Heavy Dues/Flood Water Blues/Fly Right Baby/Four Walls and Me/Friendless and Blue/Get Yourself Together/Good Luck Darling/Goodbye Kitten/Got the Blues for the West End/Hard Times Ain't Gone Nowhere/Hell Is a Name for All Sinners/Home Wrecker's Blues/I Ain't Gonna Be Your Fool/I Don't Hurt Anymore/I Got News for You Baby/I'm Nuts over You/I've Got to Get Rid of You/Jelly Jelly/Jelly Roll Baker/Last Call/Leave Me or Love Me/Lines in My Face/Lonnie's Traveling Light/Love Cry Shadows Calling Me Home/Make Love to Me Baby/Man Killing Broad/Men Get Wise to Yourself/Moaning Blues/Mr Johnson Swing/My Little Kitten Susie/My Love Don't Belong to You/My Love Is Down/New Orleans Blues/New Years Blues/No Love for Sale/No More Cryin'/Nuts About That Gal/Oh Yes Baby/Please Baby/Please Help Me/Pleasing You/Raining on the Cold Cold Ground/Roamin' Rambler/She Devil/She Don't Know Who She Wants/She's Drunk Again/Slow and Easy/Some Day Baby/Something Fishy/Southbound Backwater/Swing Out Rhythm/Swinging with Lonnie/Too Late to Cry/Unselfish Love/Working Man Blues/You Are My Life/You Don't Move Me/You Have No Love in Your Heart/You Will Need Me/You Won't Let Me Go

Infl to: Bill Broonzy/Sam Chatmon/Charlie Christian/Carl Davis/KC Douglas/Lowell Fulson/Clifford Gibson/Sam "Lightnin' " Hopkins/Little Son Jackson/Robert Johnson/Albert King/BB King/Freddy King/Little Hudson/Willie McTell/Willie Reed/Walter Roland/Alec Seward/Johnny Shines/Sluefoot Joe/Cal Smith/Tallahassee Tight/Rambling Thomas/Henry Townsend/Aaron "T-Bone" Walker

Quotes: "The late Lonnie Johnson was without doubt a musical giant of the 20th century: An exceptionally gifted instrumentalist, a sensitive, moving vocalist and a composer of thoughtful, often highly original blues . . ."—Bob Groom, *Blues World* magazine (UK), Oct 1970, p 3

". . . a major figure throughout virtually the entire history of the blues . . ."—Don Heckman, *BMI, The Many Worlds of Music,* Summer 1969, p 9

"He has been more notable as a moulder of the city blues than as an exponent of the primitive forms of the music"—Paul Oliver, Storyville album 616-010

References: Blues World magazine (UK), Oct 1970, pp 3-10

Storyville album 616-010
Mamlish album S-3807

JOHNSON, BIG BILL
(see Broonzy, William)

JOHNSON, BLIND BOY
(see Dupree, William)

JOHNSON, BLUES
(see Carr, Leroy)

JOHNSON, DINK
(see Johnson, Oliver)

JOHNSON, EASY PAPA
(see Sykes, Roosevelt)

JOHNSON, EDITH NORTH
(*aka:* Maybelle Allen/Hattie North)
Born: Jan 2, 1903, St Louis (St Louis Co), MO
Died: Feb 28, 1988, St Louis, MO
Inst: Piano

Father was King North; mother Hattie———; born Edith North; worked outside music (as salesperson in Jessie Johnson's DeLuxe Music Shop), St Louis, through 20s/30s; frequently toured South working as talent scout, late 20s; rec QRS label, Long Island City, NY, 1928; rec Paramount label, Richmond, IN/Grafton, WI, 1929; rec OKeh label, Chicago, IL, 1929; rec Vocalion label, Kansas City, MO, 1929; reportedly worked mostly outside music with occasional local private party work, St Louis, from c1930 into 50s; owned/operated DeLuxe Restaurant, St Louis from late 50s; suffered heart failure; buried National Cemetery, Jefferson Barracks, MO

Personal: Married Jessie Johnson (during 20s). Sister-in-law of James "Stump" Johnson

Songs: Beat You Doing It/Can't Make Another Day/Cornet Pleading Blues/Eight Hour Woman/Good Chib Blues/Honey Dripper Blues/Nickel's Worth of Liver Blues/That's My Man/Whispering to My Man

Infl by: Victoria Spivey

JOHNSON, ELLA
Born: Jun 22, 1923, Darlington (Darlington Co), SC

Father Reese Johnson; mother Rosanna Rouse; to NYC 1937; worked w Buddy Johnson's Combo, Barney Gallant's Club, NYC, 1939; rec w Buddy Johnson's Band/Orch, Decca label, NYC, 1940-2; worked w Buddy Johnson group, Paradise Theater, Detroit, MI, 1943; frequently worked Apollo Theater, NYC, 1943-6; toured w Buddy Johnson group working dances through Midwest/South, 1943; worked Gypsy Tea Room, New Orleans, LA, 1944; rec Decca label, NYC, 1944-5; rec Gotham label, NYC, c1945; toured exclusively w Buddy Johnson's Orch working theaters/dances/shows across US from mid-40s to 1959; worked w Buddy Johnson Orch, Riviera Club, St Louis, MO, 1946; Regal Theater, Chicago, IL, 1946; Paradise Theater, Detroit, 1946; Adams Theater, Newark, NJ, 1946; The Armory, NYC, 1946; rec w

Courtesy Frank Driggs Collection

Buddy Johnson Orch, Decca label, NYC, 1947/1949/1950-2; frequently worked w Buddy Johnson Orch, Savoy Ballroom, NYC, early 50s; rec w Buddy Johnson Orch, Mercury label, NYC, 1953-6; worked w Buddy Johnson Orch, Alan Freed's R&B Package Show, Loew's State, Boston, MA, 1955, then toured with show; toured w Buddy Johnson on Jocko & His Rocketship Rock 'N' Roll Stars package show working theaters c1957; rec w Buddy Johnson Orch, Roulette label, NYC, 1958; mostly inactive in music in NYC from early 60s; active at Salem Methodist Church, NYC, from 60s

Personal: Married Odell Day (c1940-). 1 child. Her brother Woodrow Wilson "Buddy" Johnson was pianist/band leader

Quote: ". . . one of the great individualists of modern blues singing"—Leonard Feather, *The New Encyclopedia of Jazz,* Horizon Press, 1960

JOHNSON, FANNIE
(see McCoy, Viola)

JOHNSON, GLADYS
(see McCoy, Viola)

JOHNSON, HENRY
(see McGhee, Walter Brown)

JOHNSON, HENRY *"Rufe"*

Photo by Amy O'Neal. Courtesy Living Blues Magazine

Born: Dec 8, 1908, Union (Union Co), SC
Died: Feb 1974, Union, SC (unconfirmed)
Inst: Guitar/Harmonica/Piano

Born on farm between Union/Jonesville, SC; learned guitar from older brother Roosevelt Johnson as youth; worked outside music (on farm) and frequently sang in local church, Union, SC, from 15 years of age; taught self piano and frequently worked local churches, Union area, from c1933; app w West Spring Friendly Four, WSPA-radio, Spartanburg, SC, during 30s; app w Silver Star Quartet, WBSU-radio, Union, SC, during 30s; worked outside music in Union from mid-30s into 70s; occasionally worked local parties, Union, from 1952; app w Peg Leg Sam on WBSU-radio, Union, early 70s; rec w Peg Leg Sam, Trix label, Jonesville, SC/Union, SC, 1972; worked w Peg Leg Sam at local blues concert and bars, Chapel Hill, NC, 1972; Univ of North Carolina, Chapel Hill, 1973 (por rel Flyright label); Duke Univ, Durham, NC, 1973; reportedly died of kidney failure; buried local cemetery

Personal: Name "Rufe" given him as child and is corruption of pet name "Rooster"

Songs: Had a Little Woman/Join the Army/Me and My Dog/My Baby's House/Sittin' Down Thinkin'/Union County Slide

Infl by: Blind Blake/JT Briggs/Roosevelt Johnson/Thelmon Johnson

Quotes: "Johnson is a fine guitarist and sings in a grainy, blues tinged voice"—Derrick Stewart-Baxter, *Jazz Journal* magazine (UK), Mar 1974, p 20

References: *Living Blues* magazine, Winter 1972, p 29
Trix album 3304

JOHNSON, JAMES *"Steady Roll"*

Born: c1888, New Orleans (Orleans Parish), LA (unconfirmed)
Died: Early 1960s, E St Louis, IL, area (unconfirmed)
Inst: Banjo/Celeste/Guitar/Piano/Violin

One of about 12 children; family musically inclined; interested in music early and learned multiple instruments as teenager; worked w father's family band at local banquets/weddings/street corners, New Orleans, LA, from c1914; worked w Lonnie Johnson, Iroquois Theater/Frank Pineri's Place/elsewhere, New Orleans, c1917; worked w Lonnie Johnson in Charlie Creath's Jazz-O-Maniacs on Mississippi riverboat SS *St Paul* out of St Louis, MO, 1920-2; settled in St Louis to work local club dates from early 20s; worked w Lonnie Johnson, Katy Red's Club, E St Louis, IL, 1925; frequently toured (as first violinist) in Ethel Waters' Company working theater dates through 20s; rec acc to Lonnie Johnson (or under own name), OKeh label, NYC, NY, 1926-7/9; worked as studio musician acc many blues singers, Gennett label, Richmond, IN, 1927; frequent residency at Waterfront Club, Newport, IL, from c1931 to 1960; frequently worked Harlem Club, Brooklyn, NY, during 1950s; whereabouts unknown thereafter

Personal: Brother of singer/musician Alonzo "Lonnie" Johnson. Not to be confused with musician James "Stump" Johnson

Infl to: Henry Townsend

JOHNSON, JAMES *"Stump"*

(aka: Little Man/Snitcher Roberts/Shorty George)
Born: c1905, St Louis, MO (unconfirmed)
Died: c1972, St Louis, MO (unconfirmed)
Inst: Piano

Taught self piano to work local sporting houses, St Louis, MO, as youth; rec QRS label, Long Island City, NY, 1929; rec Brunswick label, Chicago, IL, 1929; rec Paramount label, Richmond, IN, 1929; rec OKeh label, Chicago, 1929; rec Paramount label, Grafton, WI, 1930; worked occasional club dates in St Louis into 30s; rec Victor label, Dallas, TX, 1932; rec Bluebird label, Chicago, 1933; reportedly frequently worked outside music, St Louis, from mid-30s into

50s; together w Edith North Johnson operated DeLuxe Restaurant, St Louis, from late 50s; continued outside music work, St Louis, into 60s; mostly inactive due to illness in late 60s; rec Euphonic label, St Louis, c1970; rec ST for UK film BLUES LIKE SHOWERS OF RAIN, 1970

Personal: Brother of Jessie Johnson (A&R man) who married singer Edith North. Named "Stump" from fact he was short and stocky. Not to be confused with musician James "Steady Roll" Johnson

Songs: Baby B Blues/Duck's Yas Yas/The Snitcher's Blues/Soaking Wet Blues/Transom Blues/You Buzzard You

Infl by: Son Long

JOHNSON, JOE
Born: Jan 19, 1942, Independence (Tangipahoa Parish), LA
Inst: Guitar/Harmonica

Raised in Greensboro, LA; taught self harmonica as youth; frequently worked with high school gospel group in late 50s; frequently worked w Guitar Grady's Strings of Rhythm group in local clubs (later changed to Blue Flames), Greensboro, from 1959 through 60s; rec w Guitar Grady's Strings of Rhythm, A-Bet label, Crowley, LA, c1966; rec Kry label, Crowley, LA, 1967; formed own group to tour clubs in east Texas area, 1971-2; worked Candle Lit Club, Dallas, TX, 1972; Landmark, Dallas, 1972

Personal: Not to be confused with drummer Joe "Smokey" Johnson

Songs: Alimony Blues/Dirty Woman Blues

Reference: Blues Unlimited magazine (UK), Apr 1972, p 18

JOHNSON, LARRY
Born: May 15, 1938, Atlanta (Fulton Co), GA
Inst: Banjo/Guitar/Harmonica

Father Rev Leo Johnson; mother Thelma Prichett; to Wrightsville, GA, where he was raised from c1940; learned harmonica and frequently toured with father on southern gospel circuit as youth; returned to Atlanta, GA, to work local house parties, 1954-5; served in US Navy in Okinawa, 1955-9; returned to Atlanta, then NYC, NY, 1959; worked outside music while studying guitar with Gary Davis and working an occasional Greenwich Village coffeehouse into 60s; rec w Bobby Robinson, Blues Soul label, NYC, 1962; rec acc to Big Joe Williams, Bluesville label, NYC, 1962; frequently worked w Henry Adkins (as "Larry & Hank") in local clubs, NYC, through 60s; rec w Henry "Hank" Adkins, Prestige label, NYC, 1965; rec w Alec Seward, Prestige-Bluesville label, NYC, 1965; rec Blues Soul/Blue Horizon labels, NYC, 1966; rec acc to Gary Davis, Adelphi label, Silver Spring, MD, 1969; worked Electric Circus, NYC, 1969; rec w Charles Walker, Fury label, NYC, c1970; worked Judson Memorial Church, NYC, 1970; Washington Square Church, NYC, 1970; Gaslight Cafe, NYC, 1970; app on BOB FASS Show, WBAI-FM-radio, NYC, 1970; app in film short LARRY JOHNSON, 1970; worked Pine Woods Folk Festival, (unknown location) 1970; toured England/Europe working club/concert dates 1970; worked Sports Guild, Manchester, Eng, 1970; 100 Club, London, Eng, 1970; rec Blue Horizon label, London, 1970; rec Blue Goose label, NYC, 1970; app on SAY BROTHER, unknown TV, Boston, MA, c1970; app w Gary Davis in documentary film BLACK ROOTS, 1970; worked Univ of Pittsburgh Blues Festival, Pittsburgh, PA, 1971; rec w John Paul Hammond, Biograph label, NYC, 1971; worked Hunter Col, NYC, 1971; Mariposa Folk Festival, Toronto, Can, 1971; app w Gary Davis in French film BLIND GARY DAVIS, 1972; worked Mariposa Folk Festival, Toronto, 1973-5; formed own trio working local club dates, NYC, 1973; worked National Folk Festival, Wolf Trap Farm Park, Vienna, VA, 1973; rec acc to Charles Walker, Oblivion label, NYC, 1973; worked w Doc Watson, Yale Univ, New Haven, CT, 1973; Max's Kansas City, NYC, 1973; Kenny's Castaways, NYC, 1973; toured England working club dates c1973; app on Tom Pomposello's SOMETHING INSIDE OF ME Show, WKCR-FM-radio, NYC, 1973; worked Philadelphia Folk Festival, Schwenksville, PA, 1973 (por shown PHILADELPHIA FOLK FESTIVAL, PBS-TV); Seaport Museum Concert, NYC, 1974; rec Spivey label, Brooklyn, NY, c1974; Huntington Folk Society Concert, Huntington, NY, 1975; app on TOUGHING IT OUT, PBS-TV, 1976

Personal: Married. Has children

Songs: Beat from Rampart Street/Charlie Stone/Death Call/Lucille Blues/My Game Blues/Red River Dam Blues

Infl by: Gary Davis/Lightnin' Hopkins/Muddy Waters

Quote: "Johnson is not just a proficient guitarist, he's quite superb"—Tony Russell, *Jazz & Blues* magazine (UK), Jun 1971, p 15

References: Living Blues magazine, Spring 1974, pp 16-22
Sing Out magazine, Jul/Aug 1974, pp 1-3

Larry Johnson *Courtesy Sing Out Magazine*

JOHNSON, LEMUEL CHARLES *"Deacon"/"Lem"*
Born: Aug 6, 1909, Oklahoma City (Oklahoma Co), OK
Inst: Clarinet/Saxophone

Attended Douglass HS, Oklahoma City, OK, as youth; frequently worked outside music (as carpenter) with part time gigs in Oklahoma City from mid-20s; worked w The Jolly Harmony Boys in local dances, Oklahoma City, c1928; worked w Walter Page Blue Devils, Shawnee, OK, 1928; frequently worked as team w Sammy Price (as "Samuel B and Lemuel C") on local radio shows, Oklahoma City, 1928; toured w Gene Coy 101 Ranch Show working Wild West shows through Midwest, 1930; frequently worked as sideman w Gene Coy's Black Aces/Hobart Banks Band/ Grant Moore Band/Eli Rice Band/others in Minneapolis, MN, areas into 30s; toured w Earl Hines Band working dance dates, 1937; settled in NYC, NY, to work locally from 1937; worked w Fess Williams Band, NYC area, 1937; rec w Louis Jordan Band, Decca label, NYC, 1938-9, with frequent local

Lem Johnson *Courtesy Jack Bradley Collection*

gigs; worked w Luis Russell Band, NYC, c1939; frequently worked as sideman (with some recordings) w Buster Harding Band/Eddie Durham/Edgar Hayes/ Sidney Bechet/Claude Hopkins/Lucky Millinder/ Skeets Tolbert's Gentlemen of Swing/others, NYC area, c1939-41; rec w Sammy Price, Decca label, NYC, 1940-2; worked w own sextet at Onyx Club, NYC, c1941; The Place, NYC, c1942; Zorita's 606 Club, NYC, early 40s; frequently worked outside music with occasional USO tours to Europe/Near East from c1943-6; formed own trio to work residency, Kelly's Stable, NYC, 1944; Cameo Club, Rochester, NY, 1944; app on TOLERANCE THROUGH MUSIC Show, local radio, NYC, 1944; rec Queen label, NYC, 1946; worked mostly outside music with occasional band work in NYC area from mid-40s; rec w own band, MGM label, NYC, c1953; occasionally worked with calypso bands in local club dates, NYC, through 60s

Reference: Jazz Journal magazine (UK), Dec 1967, pp 16, 44

JOHNSON, LESLIE
(aka: Lazy Lester/Henry Thomas)
Born: Jun 20, 1933, Torras (Pointe Coupee Parish), LA
Inst: Harmonica

Father was Robert Johnson; mother Maggie Hartford; to Scotlandville, LA to work outside music in area

Leslie Johnson *Courtesy Sheldon Harris Collection*

from 40s; taught self harmonica and formed The Rhythm Rockers working local dances, Scotlandville area, from c1952; frequently worked w Lightnin' Slim Band at dances/parties/suppers in Crowley, LA, area from mid-50s; rec Excello label, Crowley, 1956-64; rec (as Henry Thomas) Bluesville label, early 60s; continued working outside music in Scotlandville through 60s; worked w Buddy Guy/Jr Wells/Jimmy Reed, Pepper's Lounge, Chicago, IL, 1970; Univ of Chicago Folk Festival, Chicago, 1971

Infl by: Jimmy Reed/Little Walter

Quote: "There are few artists of his calibre around, who can provide us with the real blues in the best alley traditions, today"—Mike Leadbitter, Blue Horizon album 2431-007

Reference: Blues Unlimited magazine (UK), Sept 1970, pp 4-6

JOHNSON, LONNIE
(see Johnson, Alonzo)

JOHNSON, LUTHER *"Georgia Boy"/"Snake"*
(aka: Little Luther/Luther King)
Born: Aug 30, 1934, Davisboro (Washington Co), GA
Died: Mar 18, 1976, Boston, MA
Inst: Bass/Drums/Guitar

Father Willis Johnson was guitarist; mother was Lillian Lee; born Lucius Brinson Johnson; one of at least 10

Photo by Guy Schoukroun

children; raised/worked outside music on farm into 40s; learned guitar at 7 years of age; ran away from home and was placed in reform school where he was active in music, Milwaukee, WI, c1947-50; served in US Army where he frequently entertained at service clubs c1950-3; frequently worked w Milwaukee Supreme Angels Gospel group at local churches, Milwaukee, from mid-50s; formed own blues trio working club dates, Milwaukee, late 50s into early 60s; moved to Chicago, IL, to frequently sit-in with various blues groups from early 60s; worked w Elmo James, Cadillac Baby Lounge, Chicago, early 60s; rec (as "Little Luther") Checker label, Chicago, 1964; formed own trio to work Trocadero Lounge, Chicago, c1965; w Muddy Waters Band, Univ of Chicago Folklore Society Festival, Chicago, 1966; w Otis Spann, Cafe A-Go-Go, NYC, NY, 1966; rec w Otis Spann, Spivey/BluesWay labels, NYC, 1966; rec w Muddy Waters Blues Band, Spivey label, Chicago (?), 1966; toured extensively w Muddy Waters Blues Band working clubs/concerts/festivals across US, 1966-7; rec w Muddy Waters Band, Douglas label, Chicago (?), 1967; worked w Bill Dicey's Atlantic Blues Band, Electric Circus, NYC, 1969; Loeb Student Center, New York Univ, NYC, 1969; moved to Boston, MA, 1970; formed own band to work local club dates, Boston, from 1970; worked The Village Gate, NYC, 1971; Sandy's, Beverly, MA, 1972; toured w Chicago Blues Festival working concert dates through Europe, 1972; rec Black & Blue label, Bordeaux, France, 1972; worked The Sting, Burlington, VT, 1974; Univ of Vermont, Burlington, 1975; The Boston Club, Cambridge, MA, 1975; toured w Chicago Blues Festival working concert dates through Europe, 1975; entered St Elizabeth's Hospital where he died of cancer; buried Mt Hope Cemetery, Mattapan, MA

Personal: Married (late 50s). His brother Arthur Johnson is guitarist. Not to be confused with Luther Johnson Jr, blues singer/musician

Songs: Aces Blues/Born in Georgia/Excuse Me Baby/Impressions from France/Looking for My Baby/My Daddy Told Me/Natural Wig/On the Road Again/Sad Day Uptown/She Moves Me/Snake/Somebody Loan Me a Dime/Sting It/Take Enough of Him/Top of the Boogaloo/Why Don't You Leave Me Alone?/Woman Don't Lie/You Know You Don't Love Me Baby/You Move Me/You Told Me You Love Me

Infl by: Muddy Waters

Quotes: "Luther is indeed one of the great vocal finds . . . rural, powerful, packed with emotion in the Muddy Waters mold"—Len Kunstadt, *Record Research* magazine, Jan 1968, p 5

"Of all the Muddy Waters emulators, 'Georgia Boy' perhaps best conveyed the raw, powerful sound and feeling of the Chicago blues master"—Jim O'Neal, *Living Blues* magazine, Mar 1976, p 8

Reference: Cadence magazine, May 1976, pp 3-6

JOHNSON, LUTHER, JR *"Guitar Jr"*
(aka: Black Jr/Little Jr)
Born: Apr 11, 1939, Itta Benna (Leflore Co), MS
Inst: Guitar

Father is Luther Johnson Sr; mother Lucille Robinson; to Greenwood, MS area and attended school in Phillip, MS, as youth; frequently sang in New Hope Baptist Church choir, Minter City, MS, as youth; taught self guitar c1954; formed own The Spirit of Minter City gospel group working local churches, Minter City/Greenwood areas, c1955; frequently worked as blues singer at local picnics/parties in Greenwood area c1955; moved to Chicago, IL, to work w Ray Scott Band in residence at Scotty's Rock 'n' Roll Inn, 1955-7; worked w Little Jr Robinson Blues Band in local club dates, St Louis, MO, area, 1957; rejoined Ray Scott Band working local club dates, Chicago area, c1957-62; worked w Magic Sam

Band in local club dates, Chicago, c1962-4; w Bobby Rush Band in local gigs, Chicago, c1964; rec acc w Bobby Rush, unknown label, Chicago, 1964; worked mostly outside music with occasional weekend dates with own group at Globetrotter Lounge, Chicago, from 1964 into 70s; app on BIG BILL HILL Show, WOPA-radio, Oak Park, IL, 1971; app w Muddy Waters in film DYNAMITE CHICKEN, 1971; rec Big Beat label (as L Johnson Jr), Chicago, 1972; toured w Soulful Mary's Band working club dates through South, 1972; worked w Muddy Waters Band, White Stable Club, East Lansing, MI, 1973; frequently toured/rec w Muddy Waters Band into 70s; worked Sweet Queen Bee's, Chicago, 1974; toured w Muddy Waters Band working concert dates through Australia/New Zealand, 1974; worked Ma Bea's, Chicago, 1975 (por rel MGM label); toured w Muddy Waters Band working concerts through England/Europe, 1976; worked Miller Theater, Houston, TX, 1976; w Muddy Waters Band, Newport Jazz Festival Blues Picnic, Waterloo Village, Stanhope, NJ, 1977; Nice Jazz Festival, Nice, France, 1977

Personal: Married/separated. Not to be confused with singers Guitar Jr (Lonnie Brooks) or Luther "Snake" Johnson

Song: You Got to Have Soul

Infl by: Albert Collins/Albert King/Muddy Waters

Photo by Martin Feldman /Michael Alexander. Courtesy Living Blues *Magazine*

References: Cadence magazine, Aug 1976, pp 8-11
Crazy Music magazine (Australia), Dec 1974, pp 16-18

JOHNSON, MARGARET
(see Martin, Sara)

JOHNSON, MARTHA
(see Beaman, Lottie)

JOHNSON, *"Signifyin'"* MARY

Courtesy Frank Driggs Collection

Born: c1900, Eden Station (Yazoo Co), MS
Died: c1970, St Louis, MO (unconfirmed)

Mother was Emma Williams; born Mary Smith, an only child; moved to St Louis, MO, to work outside music from 1915; frequently worked Jazzland/Chauffeurs Club/other clubs/bars, St Louis, c1925-7; frequently worked with Lonnie Johnson in local clubs, St Louis/NYC, late 20s; won blues contest, Booker T Washington Theater, St Louis, 1929; rec Brunswick label, Chicago, IL, 1929-30; rec Paramount label, Grafton, WI, 1930; worked Jazzland Club, St Louis, 1932; rec Champion label, Richmond, IN, 1932; worked mostly outside music with occasional local club dates, St Louis, from c1932 into 40s; rec Decca label, Chicago, 1934-6; active in church work in St Louis area through 40s/50s/60s; worked outside music (as hospital worker), St Louis, to c1959 when she retired

Personal: Married blues singer Alonzo "Lonnie" Johnson (1925-32). 6 children

Songs: Baby Please Don't Go*/Barrelhouse Flat Blues/Black Gal Blues/Black Men Blues/Dream Daddy Blues/Key to the Mountain Blues/Mary Johnson Blues/Mean Black Man Blues/Prison Cell Blues/Rattlesnake Blues/Tornado Blues
*("Baby Please Don't Go" is usually credited to Big Joe Williams who has stated that this singer is author)

Infl by: Victoria Spivey

Quote: "She had a determined delivery with no frills . . ."—Paul Oliver, Riverside album 8819

Reference: Conversation with the Blues, Paul Oliver, Horizon Press, 1965
Agram album AB 2014

JOHNSON, MEATHEAD
(see Dupree, William)

JOHNSON, OLIVER *"Ollie"/"Dink"*
Born: Oct 28, 1892, Biloxi (Harrison Co), MS
Died: Nov 29, 1954, Portland, OR
Inst: Clarinet/Drums/Piano

Father was Jeff Johnson; mother was Hattie ———; learned piano/drums as youth; toured w Freddie Keppard Band out of New Orleans, LA, working to West Coast, 1912; renamed band The Original Creole Orch to tour theaters on Orpheum Circuit c1913; formed own Louisiana Six working South from c1915; worked w Kid Ory Band c1920; formed Five Hounds of Jazz working Paradise Garden, Los Angeles, CA, 1921; rec as sideman w Kid Ory Sunshine Orch, Nordskog label, Los Angeles, 1922; renamed band Los Angeles Six to work local clubs, Chicago, IL, 1924; worked as solo pianist in local club dates, Los Angeles, late 20s; worked outside music, Los Angeles, from early 30s; worked outside music (as restaurant owner), Los Angeles, early 40s; worked outside music, Portland, OR, from 1944; rec American Music label, Los Angeles, 1946-7; rec Euphonic label, Los Angeles, 1948; rec New Orleans Louisiana label, Los Angeles, 1950; entered Multnomah Hospital where he died of hemorrhage; buried Greenwood Cemetery, Portland, OR

Personal: His brother Bill Johnson was musician with King Oliver Band and sister Anita Gonzales was married to pianist Jelly Roll Morton

Song: Dink's (Final) Blues

Reference: Who's Who of Jazz, John Chilton, Bloomsbury Book Shop, 1970

JOHNSON, ROBERT L
Born: May 8, 1911, Hazlehurst (Copiah Co), MS
Died: Aug 16, 1938; Greenwood, MS
Inst: Guitar/Harmonica

Father was Noah Johnson; mother Julia Major; moved with mother to Leatherman Plantation, Commerce, MS, where he was raised by stepfather Robert "Dusty" Willis from childhood; worked outside music on farm from childhood and received little education; learned harmonica as youth; ran away from home to learn some guitar from Son House in area c1930; frequently worked w Son House in juke joints/Saturday night balls, Banks, MS, early 30s; frequently worked w Son House/Willie Brown/Willie Borum in Church's Park (WC Handy Park) for tips, Memphis, TN, early 30s; frequently hoboed from town to town working solo in small clubs/bars/barrelhouses/jukes/streets in Helena/Marvell/Elaine/Greenville, AR, through 30s; teamed w Johnny Shines to work bars/dances/fish fries/house parties/streets/cafes/levee camps/coal yards/taverns/speakeasies/lumber camps through Arkansas/Tennessee/Missouri/Illinois/Texas/Kentucky/New York/New Jersey and west to Dakotas c1934-7; worked w Henry Townsend, Ernest Walker's house party, St Louis, MO, area, 1935; rec Vocalion/ARC label group, San Antonio/Dallas, TX, 1936-7; app w Johnny Shines, THE ELDER MOTEN HOUR, local radio, Detroit, MI, 1937; frequently worked w Sonny Boy Williamson (Alex Miller)/Howlin' Wolf/Elmore James in jukes in Moorhead/Greenwood, MS, area, 1937-8; worked w Honey Boy Edwards at jukes/parties in Macomb, MS area, 1938; was poisoned while working at Three Forks Roadhouse, Greenwood, MS; died at home; buried Zion Churchyard, Greenwood; gravestone erected 1991

Personal: Married Estella Coleman, mother of blues singer/guitarist Robert Jr Lockwood

Books: Robert Johnson, Bob Groom, Blues World, 1969

Robert Johnson, Samuel B Charters, Oak Publishers, 1973

Searching For Robert Johnson, Peter Guralnick, EP Dutton, 1989

Songs: Come On in My Kitchen/Crossroads Blues/Dead Shrimp Blues/Drunken-Hearted Man/From Four Till Late/Hell Hound on My Trail/Honeymoon Blues/I Believe I'll Dust My Broom/I'm a Steady Rollin' Man/Kind Hearted Woman/Last Fair Deal Gone Down/Little Queen of Spades/Love in Vain/Malted Milk/Me and the Devil Blues/Milkcow's Calf Blues/Phonograph Blues/Preachin' Blues/Ramblin' on My Mind/Stones in My Passway/Stop Breakin' Down Blues/Sweet Home Chicago/Take a Little Walk with Me/Terraplane Blues/32-20 Blues/Traveling Riverside Blues/Walkin' Blues/When You Got a Good Friend

Awards/Honors: Won American Music Conference National Music Award, 1976

Won *The Blues* magazine (Japan) Readers Poll as The Greatest Bluesman, 1976

Infl by: Kokomo Arnold/Willie Brown/Son House/Skip James/Lonnie Johnson/Charley Patton

Infl to: Leroy Foster/Calvin Frazier/John Paul Hammond/Jimi Hendrix/Graham Hine/Roger Hubbard/Elmore James/Floyd Jones/Robert Jr Lockwood/Clayton Love/Robert Lowery/Taj Mahal/Muddy Waters/Robert Nighthawk/Bonnie Raitt/Johnny Shines/Eddie Taylor/Baby Boy Warren/Johnny Winter/Keith Richards/Eric Clapton

Quotes: "Robert Johnson is acknowledged as perhaps the most accomplished and certainly the most influential of all bluesmen"—Peter Guralnick, *Feel Like Going Home*, Outerbridge & Dienstfrey, 1971

"His music [has] become the root source for a whole generation of blues and rock and roll musicians"—Samuel B Charters, *Robert Johnson*, Oak Publishers, 1973

"Robert Johnson is a chilling confrontation with aspects of the American consciousness. He is a visionary artist with a terrible kind of information about his time and place and personal experience"—Mack McCormick, *Biography of a Phantom* (unpublished manuscript)

References: Robert Johnson, Samuel B Charters, Oak Publishers, 1973

Blues Unlimited, Nov 1971, pp 12-14

Searching For Robert Johnson, Peter Guralnick, EP Dutton, 1989

JOHNSON, SARA
(see Henderson, Rosa)

JOHNSON, STUMP
(see Johnson, James)

JOHNSON, SYL
Born: 1937, Centerville (Hickman Co), TN
Inst: Guitar/Harmonica

Father was Sam Thompson, a harmonica/guitar player; born Sylvester Thompson; one of 3 children; interested in music early and learned guitar from father as child; moved to Chicago, IL, to attend local school, 1946-51; dropped out of school to work w Eddie Boyd Band in local club dates, early 50s; frequently worked as sideman w Jr Wells/Elmore James/Jimmy Reed/Billy Boy Arnold/Howlin' Wolf/Shakey Jake/others in local club dates, Chicago, through 50s; worked w Magic Sam Band, 708 Club, Chicago, 1955; worked Pepper's Lounge, Chicago, c1955; assumed leadership of Magic Sam's Band (while Magic Sam was in service) to work Just Me Lounge, Chicago, 1959-60; formed own band to work local club dates, Chicago, 1960; worked Dirty Girty Club, Chicago, 1960; frequently worked clubs/lounges/bars in Gary, IN/Chicago, IL, areas through 60s; rec Tmp-Ting/Zachron labels, Chicago, mid-60s; rec Twilight-Twinight label, Chicago, 1967-71; worked L&A Lounge, Chicago, 1969; Peacock Alley, Minneapolis, MN, 1969; Apollo Theater, NYC, c1969; frequently toured one-nighters, 1969 into 70s; rec Hi label, Memphis, TN, from 1971; worked Keymen's Club, Chicago, 1972; Stingrey, Chicago, 1975

Personal: His brothers Mack Thompson and Jimmy Johnson (born Nov 25, 1928) are musicians

Song: Come On, Sock It to Me

Infl to: Magic Sam

Quote: ". . . one of black music's most persuasively

seductive voices, a high, bluesily-flexible voice, a voice which brilliantly combines flourishes of grit and anguish with a unique melismatic wail"—Tony Cummings, *Black Music* magazine (UK), Jun 1974, p 47

JOHNSON, TOMMY

Courtesy Sheldon Harris Collection

Born: c1896, Terry (Hinds Co), MS
Died: Nov 1, 1956, Crystal Springs, MS
Inst: Guitar/Kazoo

Father was Idell Johnson; mother was Mary Ella Wilson; born on George Miller Plantation, outside Terry, MS; one of 13 children; moved to Crystal Springs, MS, c1910 where he took interest in guitar, learning some from brother LeDell Johnson; ran away from home to work as itinerant musician in Boyle/Rolling Fork, MS, area c1912-14; frequently worked local country parties/dances in Crystal Springs area, 1914-16; worked outside music on Tom Sander Plantation, Drew, MS, from 1916; frequently worked w Willie Brown/Dick Bankston/Charley Patton on Webb Jennings Plantation, Drew, MS, through teens; hoboed extensively through Arkansas/Louisiana/Mississippi working jukes/streets c1917-20; frequently worked jukes/parties/frolics in Crystal Springs area from c1920; occasionally worked w Charley Patton in local jukes, Greenwood/Moorhead, MS, early 20s; frequently worked outside music (as farmer) in Delta area into 20s; worked outside music on Bernard Graff Plantation, Rolling Fork, MS, with frequent wanderings through Delta area working for tips, 1924-7; frequently worked w Rubin Lacy/Son Spand/Charley McCoy/John Byrd/Walter Vincent/Ishmon Bracey/others at local dances/parties/streets with some outside music work, Jackson, MS, through 20s; rec Victor label, Memphis, TN, 1928; rec Paramount label, Grafton, WI, 1930; owned/worked in small cafe, Jackson, into 30s; continued street/party/picnic/supper work through Mississippi/New Orleans, LA, into early 30s; frequently toured w Ishmon Bracey working in Doctor Simpson's Medicine Show and others as well as jukes/parties/dances through Delta area, early to mid-30s; worked local parties, Tylertown, MS, c1935; worked house parties in Angie, LA/Tylertown, MS/Jackson, MS, c1936; worked w Roosevelt Holts/KC Douglas/others at local parties/streets of Jackson from 1937 into 50s; suffered fatal heart attack after working local house party; buried Warm Springs Methodist Church Cemetery, Crystal Springs, MS

Personal: Married Maggie Bidwell (c1914-17); Ella Hill (early 20s); Rosa Youngblood (c1935-9); Emma Downes (during 40s). His father was reportedly related to Alonzo "Lonnie" Johnson, blues singer. His brothers Clarence/LeDell/Mager Johnson were musicians

Songs: Big Fat Mama Blues/Big Road Blues/Black Mare Blues/Bye Bye Blues/Canned Heat Blues/Cool Water Blues/I Wonder to Myself/Lonesome Home Blues/Louisiana Blues/Maggie Campbell Blues/Slidin' Delta

Infl by: Dick Bankston/Willie Brown/Ben Maree/Charley Patton

Infl to: James Brewer/KC Douglas/Shirley Griffith/Roosevelt Holts/Howlin' Wolf/Clarence Johnson/LeDell Johnson/Mager Johnson/Floyd Jones/Otis Spann/Houston Stackhouse/Babe Stovall/Johnny Temple/Boogie Bill Webb

Quotes: "For about 30 years Tommy Johnson was perhaps the most important and influential blues singer in the state of Mississippi"—Dave Evans, *Tommy Johnson*, Studio Vista, 1971

"One of the major figures of the Mississippi blues"—Pete Welding, Testament album 2215

"It is true to say that here was one of the finest of all the Mississippi singers, and probably the most imitated or admired"—Simon A Napier, *Blues Unlimited* magazine (UK), Feb 1966, p 14

Reference: Tommy Johnson, Dave Evans, Studio Vista, 1971

JOHNSON, WILLIE LEE
Born: Mar 4, 1923, Senatobia (Tate Co), MS
Inst: Guitar

One of 6 children; first instrument was homemade guitar and frequently worked local parties in area from late 30s; worked w Howlin' Wolf, Dooley Square, Tunica, MS, c1941; moved to Memphis, TN, to work in local groups from mid-40s; frequently worked w Matt Murphy/Calvin Newborn in local clubs, Memphis, 1947-9; worked w Willie Love in local club dates, Memphis, 1949; frequently w Howlin' Wolf Band in local club dates, Memphis, from c1950; rec w Howlin' Wolf Band, RPM label, Memphis, 1951; frequently worked w Willie Nix Band in local club dates, Memphis, 1951-2; rec w Willie Nix Band, RPM label, Memphis, 1951; rec w Willie Nix Band, Checker label, Memphis, 1952; rec w Howlin' Wolf Band, Chess label, Memphis, 1952; formed own band to work club dates through Tennessee/Mississippi, 1952; frequently toured as sideman w Little Jr Parker/Roscoe Gordon/Bobby Bland/Elmore James/Sonny Boy Williamson (Alex Miller)/others, early 50s; rec under own name, Sun label, Memphis, 1955; moved to Chicago, IL, 1955; frequently worked Maxwell Street area for tips, Chicago, from 1955; frequently toured w Howlin' Wolf Band working club dates out of Chicago, c1956-61; rec w Howlin' Wolf Band, Chess label, Chicago, 1956; formed own band to work frequently at Blanche's Lounge, Chicago, 1961-3; frequently toured as sideman w JT Brown and others working club dates through 60s; worked Washburne Lounge, Chicago, 1970-1; frequently worked outside music into 70s

Reference: Blues Unlimited magazine (UK), Jul 1972, pp 4-7

JONES, AUGUSTA
(see Miles, Josephine)

JONES, B B
(see Nichols, Alvin)

JONES, BIRMINGHAM
Born: Jan 9, 1937, Saginaw (Saginaw Co), MI
Inst: Guitar/Harmonica/Saxophone

Born Wright Birmingham; one of 7 children; moved to Chicago, IL, c1950; learned sax and worked as sideman w JB Lenoir group and others in local club dates, Chicago, early 50s; learned guitar and worked w Elmore James group/JB Lenoir group/others, Chicago, through 50s; learned harmonica and formed own Birmingham Jones and His Lover Boys group

Courtesy Record Research Archives

working local club dates, Chicago, from mid-50s; rec Ebony label, Chicago, c1956; rec VJ label, Chicago, c1963; rec Vivid label, Chicago, 1965; toured w Muddy Waters group working clubs/concerts across US, 1968; worked w Little Addison's Band, Eddie Shaw's, Chicago, 1969; w Johnny Young Band, Wisconsin Blues Festival, Beloit, WI, 1970; frequently worked w Eddy Clearwater Band in local club dates, Chicago, 1970-1; worked New Party Time Lounge, Chicago, 1972; mostly inactive into 70s; worked club dates in Chicago, 1977

Personal: Married. 2 children

Infl by: Howlin' Wolf/Lester Young

Reference: Record Research magazine, May 1968, p 8

JONES, CURTIS
Born: Aug 18, 1906, Naples (Morris Co), TX
Died: Sept 11, 1971, Munich, Germany
Inst: Guitar/Organ/Piano

Father Willie Jones was farmer; mother was Agnes Logan; one of 7 children; raised/worked on father's farm from 8 years of age; learned guitar at 10 years of age, later learned piano; formed own group working local vau-

Courtesy Sheldon Harris Collection

deville shows, Naples, TX, c1922; ran away from home to work outside music (and served short sentence for bootlegging) with frequent gigs as singing pianist in local bars/joints/resorts, Dallas, TX, 1922-9; rec w Papa Chittlins (Alex Moore) on (unissued) label, Dallas, c1925; frequently hoboed through western US working clubs/gambling houses/barrelhouses, mid-20s into early 30s; worked outside music with occasional club dates, Wichita, KS, 1929; worked Nate's Club, Kansas City, MO, c1931; The Panama Club, Kansas City, c1931; worked w The Georgia Colored Strollers (a vaude-minstrel troupe) in local theater, Cheyenne, WY, then toured theaters through Midwest, 1932; frequently toured as single working joints/houses/bars through Midwest/Southwest c1933; frequently worked w Lee Collins' Band and others, Astoria Hotel and other hotels/clubs, New Orleans, LA, c1933-5; worked Anchorage Club, West Baton Rouge, LA, c1935; settled in Chicago, IL, to work outside music from 1936; formed own group to work rent parties/south side joints/bars, Chicago, 1936 into 40s; rec Vocalion label, Chicago, 1937-9; rec Bluebird label, Aurora, IL/Chicago, IL, 1937/1940; rec OKeh label, Chicago, 1940-1; worked w Johnny Shines, Don's Den, Chicago, 1942; worked mostly outside music, Chicago, into 50s; rec Parrot label, Chicago, 1952; worked local club dates, Toledo, OH, 1953; w Lee Collins, Olympic Hotel/Victory Club, Chicago, c1953; formed own group to work Blind Pig, Chicago, 1960-1; rec Prestige-Bluesville label, NYC, NY, 1960; worked Univ of Illinois, Urbana, IL, 1961; The Birdhouse, Chicago, 1961; Hoolies Club, Chicago, 1961; Univ of Chicago, Chicago, 1961; rec Delmark label, Chicago, 1962; worked Gate of Horn, Chicago, 1962; worked club dates in Zurich, Switzerland, area, 1962; worked The Birdhouse, Chicago, 1962; settled in France to work Trois Mailletz, Paris, 1962; worked concert dates/film scoring, Lille, France, 1962; app on local TV show, Belgium, 1963; app on local radio show, London, Eng, 1963; toured club/concert dates through Germany, 1963; rec Impulse label, Koblenz, Ger, 1963; rec Decca-Ace of Clubs label, London, 1963; frequently worked w Chris Barber Band in local club dates, London, 1963; toured solo working club dates through England, 1964-5; frequently worked Basin Street Bar, Casablanca, Morocco, with frequent tours working bars/casinos/clubs/TV shows through North Africa, 1965-6; toured Spain/Greece/southern France working concert dates, 1966; frequently worked Trois Mailletz, Paris, 1966-7; toured w American Folk Blues Festival working concert dates through England/Europe, 1968; app in UK film AMERICAN FOLK BLUES FESTIVAL, 1968 (shown on BBC-TV, England); worked Conway Hall, London, 1968; rec Blue Horizon label, London, 1968; frequently toured Europe working concert/club dates into 70s; suffered heart failure and died Schwabinger Krankenhaus Hospital; buried Friedhof am Perlacher Forst Cemetery, Munich, Ger

Personal: Married Lula ("Lulu") Stiggars (early 30s-1937); married Bertha ——— (late 30s)

Songs: Alley Bound Blues/Curtis Jones Boogie/Decoration Day Blues/Dryburgh Drive/Gee Pretty Baby/Good Time Special/Good Woman Blues/Highway 51 Blues/I Got a Whole Lot of Talk for You/I'm Feeling Low Down/Let Your Hair Down/Lonesome Bedroom Blues/Love Season Blues/Low Down Dirty Shame/Low Down Worried Blues/Morocco Blues/Please Believe Me/Shake It Baby/Skid Row/Soul Brother Blues/Suicide Blues/Syl-vous Play Blues/Tin Pan Alley Blues/Weekend Blues/Young Generation Boogie

Infl by: Blind Lemon Jefferson

Quotes: "Every chord, every note in his economical style lends full support to his unusual vocal style, sometimes in unison, at other times in accompaniment"—Robert G Koester, Delmark album 605

"He is the bluesman's blues singer"—Paul Oliver, Decca album 3587

References: Blue Horizon album 7703

Rhythm & Blues magazine, Apr 1964, p 20

JONES, EDDIE
(aka: Guitar Slim)

Courtesy Institute of Jazz Studies

Born: Dec 10, 1926, Greenwood (Leflore Co), MS
Died: Feb 7, 1959, New York, NY
Inst: Guitar

Raised in Hollandale, MS, from early age; interested in music and frequently sang in local church choir as youth; formed trio w pianist Huey Smith working club dates in New Orleans, LA, area, late 40s; worked as single, Dew Drop Inn/Moonlight Inn/Club Tijuana, New Orleans, 1949-51; rec Imperial label, New Orleans, 1951; rec JB label, Nashville, TN, 1952; reportedly served in US Army in Korea c1952; rec Specialty label, New Orleans, LA/Chicago, IL/Los Angeles, CA, 1953-6; toured w Lloyd Lambert Band working dances/concerts mainly through South and Southwest, 1953-9; worked Apollo Theater, NYC, NY, 1954; Gleason's, Cleveland, OH, 1954; Club Walahuje, Atlanta, GA, 1954; Ebony Club, Cleveland, OH, 1955; (unknown) club, Pahokee, FL, 1955; rec Atco label, NYC, 1956-8; worked w Lloyd Lambert Band, The Palms Club, Hallandale, FL, 1957; died of pneumonia; buried local cemetery, Thibodeaux, LA

Personal: Married (?). 2 children. One son works as singer/guitarist in New Orleans, LA, as "Guitar Slim Jr." Not to be confused with Norman Green or Alexander Seward who also used pseudonym "Guitar Slim"

Songs: Along About Midnight/Bad Luck Blues/Guitar Slim/I Got Sumpin' for You/Our Only Child/Something to Remember You By/The Story of My Life/Sufferin' Mind/The Things That I Used to Do/Trouble Don't Last/Well, I Done Got Over It

Infl by: Gatemouth Brown/Aaron "T-Bone" Walker

Infl to: Ray Charles/Jimi Hendrix

Quotes: "Guitar Slim was not only a great blues performer, but one of the most original and impassioned lyricists ever to work in the blues form"—Barret Hansen, Specialty album 2120

"One of the greatest bluesmen of the fifties"—Ronald Weinstock, *Alley Music* magazine (Australia), May 1970, p 9

JONES, FLOYD

Photo by Peter B Lowry

Born: Jul 21, 1917, Marianna (Lee Co), AR
Died: Dec 19, 1989, Chicago, IL
Inst: Guitar

Father was Robert Jones; mother Minnie ____; moved to Delta area of Mississippi during childhood; learned guitar in early 30s; ran away from home to hobo through Mississippi/Arkansas working jukes/fish fries/picnics from 1933 into 40s; settled in Chicago, IL, c1945; frequently worked w Baby Face Leroy/Moody Jones/others in Maxwell Street area for tips, Chicago, from c1945; frequently toured w Snooky Pryor/Moody Jones/Homesick James at Club Jamboree, Chicago, through late 40s; rec w Snooky Pryor, Marvel label, Chicago, 1947; rec w Sunnyland Slim, Tempo Tone label, Chicago, 1948; formed own band working frequently at Vi's Lounge, Chicago, early 50s through 1957; rec JOB label, Chicago, 1952; rec Chess label, Chicago, 1952-3; rec VJ label, Chicago, 1954-5; frequently worked outside music, Chicago, from c1957; worked w Sunnyland Slim, Univ of Wisconsin, Milwaukee, WI, 1962; Fickle Pickle, Chicago, 1963; Theresa's Bar, Chicago, 1963; Kansas City Red's Shangri-la Lounge, Chicago, 1966; rec Testament label, Chicago, 1966; app in UK film CHICAGO BLUES, 1970 (shown on OMNIBUS Show, BBC-1-TV, England); rec w Walter Horton, Delta label, Chicago, 1970; continued working outside music, Chicago, into 70s; worked Univ of Chicago Folk Festival, Chicago, 1973; King's Club Waveland, Chicago, 1974; rec w Walter Horton, Magnolia label, Chicago, 1975; worked Chicago Blues Festival, Jane Addams Theater, Chicago, 1975; Kingston Mines, Chicago, 1975; frequently worked Elsewhere Club, Chicago, 1976-8; Univ of Notre Dame, South Bend, IN, 1976; worked B.L.U.E.S, club, Chicago, 1979; app in film MAXWELL STREET BLUES 1980; inactive from mid-80s; died of heart attack; buried Mt Glenwood, Willow Springs, IL

Songs: Big World/Cryin' the Blues/Dark Road/Falling Rain Blues/Hard Times/M&O Blues/On the Road Again/Rising Wind/School Days/Stockyard Blues

Infl by: Howlin' Wolf/Tommy Johnson/Robert Johnson/Charley Patton/Johnny Shines

Quote: "Floyd Jones is one of the handful of excellent composers of blues to have emerged in the postwar blues idiom"—Pete Welding, Testament album 2214

Reference: Testament album 2214

JONES, JOHN *"Johnnie"/"Little Johnny"*
(aka: Little Johnny)
Born: Nov 1, 1924, Jackson (Hinds Co), MS
Died: Nov 19, 1964, Chicago, IL
Inst: Harmonica/Piano

John Jones/Syl Johnson *Courtesy Letha Jones/*Living Blues *Mag*

Father was George Jones; mother was Mary Crusoe; both musicians; one of 3 children; interested in music early and was playing harmonica and piano as youth; moved to Chicago, IL, c1945; frequently worked w Tampa Red Band in local club dates, Chicago, 1947-52; worked w Tampa Red, C&T Lounge, Chicago, 1948; rec acc to Tampa Red, Victor label, Chicago, 1949-53; rec w Muddy Waters, Aristocrat label, Chicago, 1950; worked w Elmore James, 708 Club and others, Chicago, c1952-4; frequently toured w Little Walter working club dates, 1953-5; extensive studio work rec acc to Joe Turner/Albert King/JB Hutto/Magic Sam/Howlin' Wolf/Elmore James/others, Chicago, 1952-64; rec w own Chicago Hound Dogs, Flair label, Chicago, 1953; rec Atlantic label, Chicago, 1954; worked w Elmore James Broomdusters in local club dates, Chicago, 1955; frequently toured w Elmore James out of Chicago working club dates through Georgia/Mississippi/Arizona/Texas/Mexico through 50s; worked 34 Club, Chicago, c1955; worked local club dates, Atlanta, GA, 1955-61; Sylvio's Lounge, Chicago, c1956; frequently worked w Magic Sam in local club dates, Chicago, c1959-64; worked Scotty's, Chicago, 1963; rec w Eddie Taylor's Band, Vivid label, Chicago, 1964; entered Cook County Hospital where he died of bronchopneumonia; buried Restvale Cemetery, Worth, IL

Personal: Married Letha ——— (1952-). Was first cousin of pianist Otis Spann. Not to be confused with Johnny Jones (guitarist) who worked in Bobby Blue Bland Band during mid-70s

Songs: Big Town Playboy/Chicago Blues/Hoy Hoy/Shelby County Blues/Up the Line/Wait Baby

Infl by: Big Maceo Merriweather/Otis Spann

Quotes: "He had a relaxed but bluesy vocal style which enhanced the brilliance of his playing"—Bob Eagle, *Living Blues* magazine, Spring 1973, p 29

"Little Johnny Jones was one of the best pianists to appear on the blues scene after the second world war"—Pete Lowry, Atlantic album 7227

Reference: Living Blues magazine, Spring 1973, pp 28-9

JONES, MAGGIE
(aka: Fae/Faye Barnes)

Courtesy Record Research Archives

Born: c1900, Hillsboro (Hill Co), TX (unconfirmed)
Died: (unknown)
Inst: Piano

Born Fae Barnes; reportedly moved to NYC, NY, to work local club dates from c1922; worked Princess Theater, Harrisburg, PA, 1922, then frequently toured TOBA circuit working theaters to c1926; rec Black Swan/Victor/Pathe labels, NYC, 1923; rec Paramount label, NYC, 1924; frequently rec w Louis Armstrong/Fletcher Henderson/Clarence Williams/others, Columbia label, NYC, 1924-6; frequently worked w Clarence Muse Vaudeville Company in local theater dates, NYC, 1927; worked w Hall Johnson Singers, Roxy Theater, NYC, 1927; frequently worked outside music (owned/operated dress store), NYC, from 1927; worked local blues contest, Ella B Moore Theater, Dallas, TX, 1928; app w Bill Robinson in Lew Leslie's BLACKBIRDS OF 1928 Revue, Eltinge Theater/Liberty Theater, NYC, 1928-9, then toured with show across US/Canada; worked in own revue in theaters in Dallas/Ft Worth, TX, areas, early 30s; worked All American Cabaret, Ft Worth, 1934; reportedly mostly inactive in music thereafter and whereabouts unknown

Billing: The Texas Nightingale

Songs: Northbound Blues/Screamin' the Blues/Single Woman's Blues/Undertaker's Blues

Quote: "Maggie Jones was a real blues artist and together with such singers as Clara and Bessie Smith, Sippie Wallace, Ma Rainey and Victoria Spivey formed the bedrock of the classic blues singers"—Derrick Stewart-Baxter, VJM album VLP25

JONES, MAMIE
(see Waters, Ethel)

JONES, MAUDE
(see Brown, Lillian)

JONES, SADIE
(see Brown, Ida G)

JOPLIN, JANIS LYN

Photo by Julie Snow

Born: Jan 19, 1943, Port Arthur (Jefferson Co), TX
Died: Oct 4, 1970, Hollywood, CA
Inst: Autoharp

Father was Seth Ward Joplin; mother was Dorothy Bonita East; one of 3 children; sang in local church choir/glee club as child; graduated Thomas Jefferson HS, 1960; briefly attended Lamar State Col of Technology, Beaumont, TX/Univ of Texas, Austin, TX/Port Arthur Col, Port Arthur, TX, with frequent outside music work c1960-1; left home to work with The Waller Creek Boys (bluegrass band) at local parties/coffeehouses/The Ghetto Club/Threadgills Bar, Austin, 1961; hitched to West Coast to work Coffee Gallery, San Francisco, CA, 1961-2; frequently worked folk/blues bars/hootenannies with frequent outside music work, San Francisco, CA/Venice, CA, area to 1965; returned to Port Arthur briefly to attend Lamar State Col, Beaumont, 1965; dropped out to return to West Coast joining Big Brother & the Holding Company (rock group), 1966-9; worked Avalon Ballroom/Fillmore Auditorium (por rel Columbia label)/Winterland/Panhandle Park/Golden Gate Park, San Francisco, CA, 1966; rec w Big Brother group, Mainstream label, Chicago, IL, 1967; worked Mother Blues, Chicago, 1967; International Pop Festival, Monterey, CA, 1967 (por shown in film MONTEREY POP); Monterey Jazz Festival, Monterey, CA, 1967; The Eagles, Seattle, WA, 1967; Straight Theater, San Francisco, CA, 1967; Golden Bear Club, Huntington Beach, CA, 1967; Psychedelic Super Market, Boston, MA, c1967; Anderson Theater, NYC, NY, 1968; New Generation Club, NYC, 1968; Fillmore East, NYC, 1968; app on HOLLYWOOD PALACE, ABC-TV, 1968; worked Univ of Buffalo Music Festival, Buffalo, NY, 1968; Newport Folk Festival, Newport, RI, 1968-9; Avalon Ballroom, San Francisco, 1968; Fillmore West, San Francisco, 1968-70; Electric Theater, Chicago, 1968; Kinetic Playground, Chicago, 1968; Whiskey-A-Go-Go, Los Angeles, CA, 1968; rec w Big Brother group, Columbia label, NYC, 1968; worked Electric Factory, Philadelphia, PA, 1968; Singer Bowl, NYC, 1968; Tyrone Guthrie Theater, Minneapolis, MN, 1968; Winterland, San Francisco, 1968-9; left Big Brother group to form Janis Revue and Main Squeeze (later renamed Kozmic Blues) to work Memphis Mid-South Coliseum, Memphis, TN, 1968; Fillmore East, NYC, 1969; Music Hall, Boston, MA, 1969; rec w Main Squeeze group, Columbia label, NYC, 1969; app on ED SULLIVAN SHOW, CBS-TV, 1969; worked Newport 69, Northridge, CA, 1969; Woodstock Music & Art Fair, Bethel, NY, 1969; app on 60 MINUTES, CBS-TV, 1969; app on MUSIC SCENE, ABC-TV, 1969; worked Toronto Pop Festival, Toronto, Can, 1969 (por rel in film SWEET TORONTO/short film version rel as KEEP ON ROCKIN'); Pop Festival, Atlantic City, NJ, 1969; Texas International Pop Festival, Lewisville, TX, 1969; New Orleans Pop Festival, Baton Rouge, LA, 1969; toured England/Europe working concert/radio/TV dates, 1969; app on TOM JONES Show, ABC-TV, 1969; worked Madison Square Garden, NYC, NY, 1969; Quaker City Rock Festival, Philadelphia, PA, 1969; Civic Center, Baltimore, MD, 1969; Rock Festival, West Palm Beach, FL, 1969; Curtis Hixon Hall, Tampa, FL, 1969; formed own Full Tilt Boogie group working Freedom Hall, Louisville, KY, 1970; extensive touring working concert dates on college circuit across US, 1970; worked Harvard Stadium, Cambridge, MA, 1970; app on DICK CAVETT Show, ABC-TV, 1970; toured w Canadian Festival Express Show working concerts in Calgary/Toronto and across Canada, 1970; worked Ravinia, Los Angeles, 1970; Festival for Peace, Shea Stadium, NYC, 1970; rec w Full Tilt group, Columbia label, Hollywood, CA, 1970; died of drug OD at Hollywood Landmark Motor Hotel; body cremated and ashes scattered over the Pacific Ocean; a full-length film documentary, JANIS, was produced 1974 (por rel Columbia label)

Books: ***Janis,*** David Dalton, Simon and Schuster, 1971 (revised as *Piece of My Heart,* 1985)
Buried Alive, Myra Friedman, William Morrow & Company, 1973
Going Down with Janis, Peggy Caserta, Lyle Stuart Inc, 1973
Love, Janis, Laura Joplin, Villard Books, 1992
Pearl, Ellis Amburn, Warner Books, 1992

Songs: Comin' Home/Down on Me/I Need a Man to Love/Kozmic Blues/Move Over/One Good Man/Turtle Blues

Awards/Honors: Won *Jazz & Pop* magazine International Critics Poll for Best Female Vocal Album of 1968 ("Cheap Thrills," Columbia album KCS 9700)
Won *Jazz & Pop* magazine International Critics Poll for Best Female Pop Singer of the Year, 1968, 1969
Won *Jazz & Pop* magazine Readers Poll for Best Female Pop Singer of the Year, 1968

Infl by: Leadbelly/Mance Lipscomb/Odetta/Otis Redding/Bessie Smith/Big Mama Thornton

Quotes: "A mixture of Leadbelly, a steam engine, Calamity Jane, Bessie Smith, an oil derrick, and rotgut bourbon funneled into the 20th century somewhere between El Paso and San Francisco"—(credit unknown) *Cashbox* magazine, 1966

"Janis was a blues singer of right now"—**Ralph Gleason, *Rolling Stone* magazine, Oct 29, 1970, p 16**

References: Janis, David Dalton, Simon and Schuster, 1971

Buried Alive, Myra Friedman, William Morrow & Company, 1973

Going Down with Janis, Peggy Caserta, Lyle Stuart Inc, 1973

JORDAN, CHARLES *"Charley"/"Charlie"*
(aka: Charley Jordon/Uncle Skipper [?])

Courtesy Paul Garon /Living Blues Magazine

Born: c1890, Mabelvale (Pulaski Co), AR
Died: Nov 15, 1954, St Louis, MO
Inst: Guitar

Reportedly raised in Mabelvale, AR, through teens; served in US Army c1918-19; hoboed as itinerant musician working through Delta area/Kansas City, MO/Memphis, TN/elsewhere in early 20s; settled in St Louis, MO, 1925; worked/assisted Roosevelt Sykes/Memphis Minnie/Casey Bill/others, St Louis, from 1925 into 50s; suffered permanent spine injury due to bootlegging shooting incident, 1928; rec Vocalion label, Chicago, 1930-1; rec Vocalion label, NYC, NY, 1932; rec Vocalion label, Chicago, 1934; frequently served as talent scout for Vocalion/Decca Record Companies through 30s; frequently toured/rec w Peetie Wheatstraw out of St Louis through 30s; rec Decca label, Chicago, 1935; rec w Charlie Manson (as "The Two Charlies"), ARC label group, NYC, 1936; frequently worked w Big Joe Williams in St Louis Club, St Louis, late 30s through 40s; mostly inactive in music from late 40s; entered Homer Phillips Hospital where he died of pneumonia; buried Oakdale Cemetery, St Louis, MO

Song: Honeysucker Blues

Quote: "Jordan was one of the major figures in St Louis, personally and musically . . ."—Don Kent, Yazoo album L-1003

Reference: 78 *Quarterly* magazine, Autumn 1967, pp 39-41

JORDAN, JIMMY
(see Johnson, Alonzo)

JORDAN, LOUIS THOMAS

Courtesy Sheldon Harris Collection

Born: Jul 8, 1908, Brinkley (Monroe Co), AR
Died: Feb 4, 1975, Los Angeles, CA
Inst: Clarinet/Saxophone

Father was Jim Jordan, a musician and teacher; mother was Adelle ———; studied clarinet with father from age of 7; attended Arkansas Baptist Col, Little Rock, AR, while working outside music (as ball player), late 20s; occasionally toured w Rabbit Foot Minstrels working as band member/dancer in shows through South during school vacations, late 20s into 30s; briefly toured w Ma Rainey Show working TOBA circuit through Mississippi, late 20s; worked w Ruby "Tuna Boy" Williams Belvedere Orch, Green Gables Club, Hot Springs, AR, late 20s; worked local dates w Jimmy Pryor's Imperial Serenaders, Little Rock, AR, 1929; rec w Jungle Band, Brunswick label, NYC, NY, 1929; reportedly app w Chick Webb Band in vitaphone film short AFTER SEBEN, 1929; rec w Louis Armstrong Orch, Victor label, Camden, NJ, 1932; worked w Charlie Gaines Orch, Standard Theater (others), Philadelphia, PA, 1932-5; briefly worked local dates w Jim Winters Band, Philadelphia, 1932; rec w Clarence Williams Orch, Vocalion label, NYC, NY, 1934; worked Apollo Theater, NYC, c1935; w Kaiser Marshall Band, Ubangi Club/Harlem Opera House/Elks Rendezvous, NYC, 1935; toured w Kaiser Marshall Band working dance dates through New York/New Jersey/Massachusetts/Connecticut, 1935; toured w Leroy Smith Orch working dance dates from New York to Cleveland, OH, 1935; worked w Chick Webb Band, Savoy Ballroom, NYC, 1936; toured (as singer/sideman/announcer) w Chick Webb Savoy Ballroom Band working ballrooms/dances across US, 1936-8; rec w Chick Webb Orch, Decca label, NYC, 1936-8; rec w Ella Fitzgerald Savoy Eight, Decca label, NYC, 1937-8; formed own 9-piece band working long residency, Elks Rendezvous, NYC, 1938 into 40s; rec w own Elks Rendezvous Band, Decca label, NYC, 1938; app in film SWINGIN' THE DREAM, 1939; renamed band Tympany Five (usually 7-8 pieces) to rec extensively Decca label, NYC, 1939-47; extensive residency w Tympany Five, Capitol Lounge, Chicago, IL, 1941; rec w Tympany Five, Decca label, Chicago, 1941; toured extensively w Tympany Five working The Fox Head Tavern, Cedar Rapids, IA/The Tic Toc Club, Boston, MA/Lakota's Lounge, Milwaukee, WI/The Garrick, Chicago, IL/The Top Hat, Toronto, Can/Adams Theater, Newark, NJ/Oriental Theater, Chicago, IL/State Theater, Hartford, CT/Riverside Theater, Milwaukee, WI/Royal Theater, Baltimore, MD/The Beachcomber, Omaha, NE, and other one-nighters/clubs/theaters/bars/concerts across US into 40s; app in soundie film shorts DOWN DOWN DOWN (1942)/FUZZY WUZZY (1942)/THE OUTSKIRTS OF TOWN (1942)/FIVE GUYS NAMED MOE (1942)/OLD MAN MOSE (1942)/GI JIVE (1943)/HEY TOJO COUNT YO' MEN (c1943)/HONEY CHILE (c1943)/IF YOU CAN'T SMILE AND SAY YES (c1943); rec V-Disc label, Los Angeles, CA, 1943-4; worked Swing Club, Hollywood, CA, 1943; Orpheum Theater, Hollywood, 1943-4; Paradise Theater, Detroit, MI, 1943; frequently worked Apollo Theater, NYC, 1944-6; worked Club Bali, Washington, DC, 1944; Howard Theater, Washington, DC, 1944; Hollywood Canteen, Hollywood, CA, 1944; Silver Slipper, San Diego, CA, 1944; The Coliseum, New Orleans, LA, 1944; residency at Trocadero Club, Hollywood, CA, 1944; app on Al Jarvis' DOWNBEAT DERBY, Mutual-radio network, 1944; app on JUBILEE USA, AFRS-radio (syndicated), 1944-5 (por 1945 shows rel Rarities label); app on COMMAND PERFORMANCE Show, AFRS-radio (syndicated), 1944; app in film FOLLOW THE BOYS, 1944; app in film MEET MISS BOBBY SOCKS, 1944; app in RADIO HALL OF FAME Show, ABC-Blue Network radio, 1944; app in soundie film shorts JUMPIN' AT THE JUBILEE (1944)/RATION BLUES (1944)/DON'T CRY AND SAY NO (1944)/JORDAN JIVE (1944)/LOUIS JORDAN MEDLEY NOS 1 & 2 (c1945)/BUZZ ME (1945)/CALDONIA (1945)/TILLIE (1945); worked Paramount Theater, NYC, NY, 1945-6; app in all-Negro musical comedy film short CALDONIA, 1945; app in film SWING PARADE OF 1946, 1946; app in film BEWARE, 1946; app in film LOOK OUT SISTER, 1948; worked Billy Berg's Swing Club, Hollywood, CA, 1946; Esquire Jazz Concert, City Center Casino, NYC, 1946; 400 Club, NYC, 1946; Regal Theater, Chicago, IL, 1946; app in film short REET, PETITE AND GONE, 1947; worked Club Troubadour, NYC 1947; rec Decca label, Los Angeles, CA, 1947; rec Decca label, NYC/Los Angeles, 1949; app on Ed Sullivan's TOAST OF THE TOWN, Show, CBS-TV, 1949; worked Bop City, NYC, 1950; rec w Tympany Five, Decca label, NYC, 1950-5; rec w own band, Decca label, NYC, 1951; extensive touring w own band/Tympany Five/or single working dances/clubs/hotels across US from 1951; frequently worked Celebrity Club, Providence, RI, 1951-4; Golden Club, Reno, NV, 1953; State Line, Lake Tahoe, NV, 1953; rec w Nelson Riddle Orch, Decca label, Los Angeles, CA, 1953; worked Pep's Musical Show Bar, Philadelphia, PA, 1954-6; rec Aladdin label, NYC, 1954; worked Apollo Theater, NYC, 1954; frequently worked Howard Theater, Washington, DC, 1954-7; Tiffany Club, Los Angeles, 1954; The Royal, Baltimore, MD, 1954; El Rancho, Chester, PA, 1954; toured Texas/Midwest working club dates, 1955; worked The Sands, Las Vegas, NV,

1955; Harrah's, Lake Tahoe, NV, 1955-6; Club Calvert, Miami, FL, 1955-6; Flame Show Bar, Detroit, 1956; rec Mercury label, NYC/Los Angeles, 1956; worked The Riviera, St Louis, MO, 1956; Orchid Club, Kansas City, MO, 1956; Zardi's Jazzland, Hollywood, CA, 1956; Ko Ko Club, Phoenix, AZ, 1956; toured South/Midwest working club dates, 1957; worked Apollo Theater, NYC, 1957; Robert's Show Lounge, Chicago, IL, 1957; Slim Jenkins' Club, Oakland, CA, 1957; Easy Street, San Francisco, CA, 1958; Club 53, San Francisco, 1958; app on SINGING, SWINGING YEARS, (unknown network) TV, 1960; worked The Metropole, NYC, 1960; Apollo Theater, NYC, 1960; Basin Street East, NYC, 1961; worked as single w Dobby Hayes Show, Java Lanes, Long Beach, CA (w tours to other clubs/lounges/bowling alleys in area), 1961; toured w Chris Barber Band working concert dates through England, 1962; rec w Chris Barber Band, Black Lion label, London, Eng, 1962; reformed Tympany Five group to tour night clubs/Nevada show lounges/service clubs/festivals mostly on West Coast from 1963; rec Tangerine label, Los Angeles, CA (?), 1964; toured Asia working concert dates, 1967-8; rec w Teddy Edwards Orch, Pzazz label, Los Angeles, 1968; worked Apollo Theater, NYC, NY, 1973; rec Blues Spectrum label, Los Angeles, 1973; worked Newport Jazz Festival, Radio City Music Hall, NYC, 1973 (por heard MUSIC-USA, VOA-radio); toured Europe working concerts/festivals, 1973; rec Black & Blue label, France, 1973; worked Marriott Hotel, New Orleans, LA, 1974; inactive due to illness, 1974; suffered fatal heart attack at home; buried Mt Olive Cemetery, St Louis, MO

Personal: Married Ida ——— (-died 1943); Fleecie Ernestine Moore (1943-); Martha Weaver

Billing: King of the Jukeboxes

Songs: Boogie Woogie Blue Plate/But I'll Be Back/Doug the Jitterbug/Early in the Mornin'/'Fore Day Blues/Honey in the Bee Ball/I Know What You're Puttin' Down/I Like 'em Fat Like That/Ice Man/Is You Is Or Is You Ain't My Baby?/Look Out/Push Ka Pee Shee Pie/Ration Blues/Reet Petite and Gone/Run Joe/Saturday Night Fish Fry/You Ain't Nowhere/You Will Always Have a Friend

(*Note:* While song "Caldonia" is copyrighted by wife Fleecie Moore, Louis Jordan has claimed authorship)

Infl to: Chuck Berry/Little Joe Blue/Clarence "Gatemouth" Brown/Dusty Brown/Ray Charles/Bo Diddley/Floyd Dixon/Fats Domino/Wynonie Harris/Jay Hawkins/Freddy King/Little Milton

Quotes: "In the years immediately following World War II, no black singer-instrumentalist was more successful in bodying forth the tough and pleasurable excitement of R&B—it was not yet known as that—than Louis Jordan & his Tympany Five"—Arnold Shaw, *The World of Soul*, Cowles Book Company Inc, 1970

"Jordan was an admirable showman, full of vitality, and with the intelligence to create an individual and very popular style for his small group. Jordan himself had a smooth voice and a strong blues feeling"—(Yannick Bruynoghe) Stanley Dance (ed), *Jazz Era: The 'Forties*, MacGibbon & Kee, 1961

"Jordan, perhaps, did the most to revolutionize (post-war) black music with an emphasis on humorous lyrics and a wailing, tight, small-combo blues sound . . ."—Mike Leadbitter, Polydor album 2343048

References: Let The Good Times Roll: The Story of Louis Jordan and His Music, John Chilton, Quartet, 1992

Blues Unlimited magazine, Feb/Mar 1974, p 12

Honkers and Shouters, Arnold Shaw, Collier Books, 1978

JORDAN, TOM

(see Johnson, Alonzo)

JORDAN, WILLIE

(see Dupree, William)

JORDON, CHARLEY

(see Jordan, Charles)

JOSEPH, PLEASANT

(*aka:* Brother Joshua/Cousin Joe/Cousin Joseph/Cousin Joe Pleasant/Pleasant Joe/Smiling Joe)
Born: Dec 20, 1907, Wallace (St John the Baptist Parish), LA
Died: Oct 2, 1989, New Orleans, LA
Inst: Guitar/Piano/Ukulele

Father was Stewart Joseph; mother Elizabeth Clark; to New Orleans, LA c1910; sang in church choir, New Orleans, c1914-25; interested in music early, playing uke at local high school football games into 20s; frequently worked outside music in New Orelans area c1919 through 20s; frequently worked gambling houses and riverboats for tips in New Orleans area from c1923; formed own band working Black Gold Club, New Orleans, 1930; Grand Terrace, New Orleans, c1932; Gypsy Tea Room, New Orleans, 1934; worked w Billie and Dede

Photo by Norbert Hess. Courtesy Living Blues *Magazine*

Pierce, Kingfish Club, New Orleans, 1935; taught self piano, mid-30s; worked w AJ Piron, Silver Slipper Club, New Orleans, late 30s (por remote WWL-radio); worked w own band, Battle Club, New Orleans, late 30s; frequently worked w own Jazz Jesters, Famous Door Lounge, New Orleans, late 30s into 40s; w Harold DeJean's Band, The Steamship SS *Dixie* out of New Orleans, 1938; toured w Joe Robichaux working club dates through Florida c1938; w Joe Robichaux Band, National Theater, Havana, Cuba, 1938; toured w Jazz Jesters working club dates through Midwest-Southwest US, 1939-40; worked Cotton Club, Indianapolis, IN, c1940; formed own Smiling Joe's Blues Trio working club dates in New Orleans, 1941-2; worked Onyx Club/Small's Paradise/Spotlight Club/others, NYC, NY, 1943-7; rec w Leonard Feather's Hiptet, Philo label, NYC, 1945; worked w Sidney Bechet group, Savoy Club, Boston, MA, 1945; frequently worked concert dates w Sidney Bechet, Washington, DC, c1945; rec w Sam Price/Mezzrow-Bechet Septet, King Jazz label, NYC, 1945; rec w Pete Brown's Brooklyn Blowers, Savoy label, NYC, 1945; worked w Tiny Grimes Band, Downbeat Club, NYC, 1945; rec w Earl Bostic Sextet, Gotham label, NYC, 1946; rec Savoy/Signature/Decca labels, NYC, 1947; worked 21 Club, Chicago, IL, 1948; rec w Paul Gayten, DeLuxe label, New Orleans, 1948; worked extensive residency, Absinthe House, New Orleans, 1948 through late 60s; rec Imperial label, New Orleans, 1951; worked w Freddie Kohlman Band, Artesan Hall, New Orleans, 1952; rec w Freddie Kohlman Band, Decca label, New Orleans, 1952; worked w Lizzie Miles/New Orleans Sextet, Orleans Mardi Gras Lounge, New Orleans, 1952, frequently worked Balloy Club/Preservation Hall/others, New Orleans, through 50s; rec Imperial label, New Orleans, 1954; worked Village Gate, NYC, 1963; Folk City, NYC, 1963; Jimmy Ryan's, NYC, 1963; Take Three Coffee House, NYC, 1963-5; app on local TV show, Beaumont, TX, 1963; Hunter Col, NYC, 1964; toured w American Blues Caravan working concerts through England (por shown on BLUES & GOSPEL TRAIN Show, Granada-TV), then toured France working concert dates, 1964; worked International Jazz Festival, New Orleans, 1965; extensive residency, Court of Two Sisters, New Orleans, 1964-71; Dillard Univ, New Orleans, 1966; Top of the Gate, NYC, 1968-9; Club 77, New Orleans, 1968; New Orleans Jazz Festival, New Orleans, 1969-70; toured w Chicago Blues Festival working concert dates through Europe, 1971; app on local TV shows, Paris, France, 1971; rec Black & Blue label, Paris, France, 1971; rec BluesWay label, New Orleans, c1973; worked Folk Life Festival, Washington, DC, 1973; La Strada Club, New Orleans, 1974; toured w American Blues Legends through Eng/Europe, 1974 (por rel Big Bear label); app on OLD GREY WHISTLE TEST Show, BBC-2-TV, London, 1974; worked Easy Eddie's, New Orleans, 1974-5; toured Eng/Europe, 1975-7; Jazz Fest, Montreux, Switzerland, 1975 (por rel Big Bear label); Jazz & Heritage Fest, New Orleans 1976 into 80s; worked clubs/concerts in US through 80s; rec Great Southern Records label, New Orleans, 1985; died in sleep of heart disease; buried in Mt Olivet Mausoleum, New Orleans

Book: Cousin Joe: Blues From New Orleans, Pleasant Joseph/Harriet Ottenheimer, Univ of Chicago, 1987

Songs: ABC's/Baby You Don't Know/Bachelor's Blues/Bad Luck Blues/Barefoot Boy/Begging Woman/Box Car Shorty/Chicken a la Blues/Death House Blues/Evolution Blues/Fly Hen Blues/I Can't Lose with the Stuff I Use/I Had to Stop to Conquer You Baby/It's Dangerous to Be a Husband/Lightnin' Struck the Poorhouse/Little Eva/Lonesome Man Blues/My Tight Woman/Phoney Women Blues/Postwar Future Blues/Too Tight to Walk Loose/Touch Me/Wedding Day Blues/You Ain't (So) Such-A-Much

Infl by: Battleaxe/Edgar Blanchard

Quotes: "Cousin Joe is certainly one of the most unique of all bluesmen . . . unique in that he sings in a very sophisticated blues ballad fashion, yet accompanies himself with a rough, barrelhouse blues piano style . . ."—Hammond Scott, *Living Blues* magazine, Jan 1975, p 20

"His deep growling voice, huge infectious laugh and a sly sense of humour are aided by a knocked-out piano style which harks back to a previous age"—John Broven, *Walking to New Orleans*, Blues Unlimited, 1974

"A unique entertainer who'll wow an audience with rolling boogie and deft blues piano and haunting, whiskey-soaked vocals"—Tony Cummings, *Black Music* magazine (UK), Sept 1974, p 58

Reference: Cousin Joe: Blues From New Orleans, Pleasant Joseph/Harriet Ottenheimer, Univ of Chicago, 1987

K

KANSAS JOE
(see McCoy, Joe)

KELLEY, ARTHUR *"Guitar"*

Photo by Terry Pattison. Courtesy Living Blues Magazine

Born: Nov 14, 1924, Clinton (East Feliciana Parish), LA
Inst: Guitar

Born/raised/worked outside music (on farm), Clinton, LA, to 1947; was playing guitar by 14 years of age; moved to Baker, LA, to work outside music with occasional local parties/suppers in area, 1947 into 50s; frequently worked w Lightnin' Slim at local parties, Baker, LA, area through 50s into 60s; frequently worked w Silas Hogan at clubs/bars/dances in Baton Rouge, LA, 1966 into 70s; rec Arhoolie/Excello labels, Baton Rouge, 1970; worked New Orleans Jazz & Heritage Fair, New Orleans, LA, 1972; Aretha King's Club, Baton Rouge, 1974-5

Songs: Count the Days I'm Gone/How Can I Stay When All I Have Is Gone?/Hurry Down Sunshine/I Got a Funny Feeling/If I Ever Get Back Home/Kelly's Killer/Number Ten at the Station and Number Twelve Is on the Road/Somebody Stole My Baby and Gone/Talk to Me Baby

Infl by: Lightnin' Hopkins

Quote: "He is truly representative of traditional Louisiana blues . . ."—Terry Pattison, *Blues Unlimited* magazine (UK), Sept 1970, p 7

Reference: Blues Unlimited magazine (UK), Sept 1970, pp 7-8

KELLY, JO-ANN

Photo by Norbert Hess

Born: Jan 5, 1944, London, England
Died: Oct 21, 1990, London, Eng (unconfirmed)
Inst: Guitar

Learned some guitar from brother Dave Kelly, early 60s; worked London Blues Society Convention, Conway Hall, London, Eng, 1968; rec Immediate label, London, 1968; rec Sunset label, London (?), c1968; app on local show, Radio-1, London, 1968; toured w Blues Scene 69 working concert dates through England, 1969; worked blues concert, Oslo, Norway, 1969; Arts Festival, Town Hall, London, 1969; rec Epic label, NYC, NY (?), 1969; worked Memphis Blues Festival, Memphis, TN, 1969; 100 Club, London, 1969; Gaslight Cafe, NYC, 1970; rec w John Fahey, Blue Goose label, NYC (?), c1972; formed own Spare Rib group touring pubs/clubs through England, 1972-3; toured as single working clubs/concert dates across US, 1973; worked Boogie Woogie Festival, Cologne, Ger, 1974; rec w Pete Emery, Red Rag label, London (?), 1976; worked Quartier Latin, Berlin, Ger, 1977; worked Axel Melhardt's Jazzland Club, Vienna, Austria, 1977 (por rel Columbia label); club-concert work into 80s; Cambridge Folk Fest, Cambridge, Eng, 1990; died of tumor

Songs: Jinx Blues/Man I'm Lovin'/Sit Down on My Knee/Yellow Bee Blues

Infl by: Memphis Minnie

Quotes: "Her voice is hard and rough, her words and phrases come in clumps, stubby and aggressive . . . a fine blues singer"—Mike John, *New York Times* newspaper, May 8, 1970

KELLY, WILLIE
(see Sykes, Roosevelt)

KID THOMAS
(see Watts, Louis)

KIDD, KENNETH
(*aka*: Prez Kenneth)
Born: c1935, Newton (Newton Co), MS
Inst: Bass/Guitar

Father was Claude Kidd; mother was Mattie ———; one of 2 children; born/raised in Newton, MS, and frequently sang in local church choir as child; dropped out of school, left home to work outside music in Yazoo, MS/New Orleans, LA, areas, early 50s; settled in Chicago, IL, to work outside music from 1956; interested in music and learned guitar to work as sideman in local club dates from early 60s; frequently worked w Sheppards group in local clubs, Chicago, mid-60s; rec Biscayne label, Chicago, 1965-6; worked w OC Perkins (as bassist) in local clubs, Chicago area, late 60s; formed/rec Kenneth label, Chicago, c1969; continued outside music work in Chicago into 70s

Personal: Married (c1953). 2 children

Reference: Blues Unlimited magazine (UK), Feb 1973, pp 14-15

KIMBROUGH, LENA
(see Beaman, Lottie)

KIMBROUGH, LOTTIE
(see Beaman, Lottie)

KING, AL
(*aka:* Al K Smith)

Photo by Denis Lewis. Courtesy Living Blues Magazine

Born: Aug 8, 1926, Monroe (Ouachita Parish), LA

Born Alvin K Smith; frequently sang in local churches, Monroe, LA, from 1936; moved to Los Angeles, CA, to work outside music from 1947; frequently worked local talent shows, Los Angeles area, through 40s; worked w Johnny Otis Revue in Los Angeles area into 50s; rec w The Savoys, Combo label, Los Angeles, 1953; frequently worked w The Savoys group in local club dates, Los Angeles, c1953; rec Music City label, Oakland, CA, 1953; reportedly worked outside music, Los Angeles area, into 60s; rec Shirley label, Los Angeles, 1964; formed and rec Flag label, Los Angeles, 1965; rec Sahara label, NYC, NY, 1966; frequently toured w Jimmy McCracklin group working concerts/clubs through South, late 60s; rec

Modern label, Los Angeles, 1968; worked Continental Club, Oakland, CA, 1970; continued outside music work with occasional local weekend club work, San Francisco, CA, area into 70s; worked San Francisco Blues Festival, McLaren Park, San Francisco, 1977; Sacramento Blues Festival, William Land Park, Sacramento, CA, 1977

Personal: Name legally changed to Al King (1964). Not to be confused with Albert King, singer/guitarist

Songs: Better to Be by Yourself/I'll Rock You Baby/ I'm Your Part Time Love/My Last Letter/On My Way/This Thing Called Love

Infl by: Lowell Fulson/Jimmy McCracklin

Reference: Blues Unlimited magazine (UK), Jul 1970, p 15

KING, ALBERT
Born: Apr 25, 1923, Indianola (Sunflower Co), MS
Died: Dec 21, 1992, Memphis, TN
Inst: Drums/Guitar

Father was Albert Nelson; mother Mary Gilmore; born Albert Nelson; raised/worked on local plantation and frequently sang in local church, Arcola, MS; lived/worked outside music in Forrest City/Osceola, AR, area, 1931 into 40s; learned guitar on homemade instrument, late 30s; frequently worked road houses in Osceola area from 1939; frequently worked w Harmony Kings Gospel Quartet in local churches, South Bend, IN, 1949-51; worked briefly in St Louis, MO, late 40s; frequently worked w In the Groove Boys group at George York Cafe/T-99 Club/others, Osceola, from late 40s; occasionally app w In the Groove

Albert King *Courtesy BMI Archives*

Boys on KOSE-radio, Osceola, c1948-51; moved north to work outside of music w frequent gigs w Jimmy Reed, Pulaski Hall and others, Gary, IN, 1952-3; worked w Homesick James in local club dates, South Bend, 1953; frequently worked local club dates in Chicago, IL, 1953-4; rec Parrot label, Chicago, 1953; returned south to work outside music with frequent gigs w In the Groove Boys, Osceola, 1954-6; moved to St Louis, MO, 1956; formed own trio (later enlarged) to work local club dates, St Louis area, 1956-64; rec Bobbin label, St Louis, 1959-62; rec King label, St Louis, 1962; rec Coun-Tree label, E St Louis, IL, 1964; worked The Manhattan Club and other one-armed gambling joints, E St Louis area, 1964-5; worked Fillmore Auditorium, San Francisco, CA, 1966-7; Winterland, San Francisco, 1966; rec Stax label, Memphis, TN, 1966-9; worked The Club, Chicago, 1966; frequently worked club dates, Birmingham, AL, 1967; Cafe A-Go-Go, NYC, 1968; Fillmore West, San Francisco, 1968-71 (por of 1968 date rel Stax label); Ash Grove, Los Angeles, 1968; Whiskey A-Go-Go, Hollywood, CA, 1968; The Auditorium, Santa Monica, CA, 1968; The Shrine, Los Angeles, 1968; Winterland, San Francisco, 1968; app on Dick Clark's AMERICAN BANDSTAND, ABC-TV, 1968; worked Club Paradise, Memphis, TN, 1968; Mid-South Coliseum, Memphis, 1968; Fillmore East, NYC, 1968-71; Regal Theater, Chicago, 1968; Father Blues, Chicago, 1968; toured w own band working club dates through England, 1968; app on UPBEAT, WPIX-TV, NYC (syndicated), 1968; worked The Scene, NYC, 1968; Carnegie Hall, NYC, 1968; The Village Gate, NYC, 1969; rec Atlantic label, Memphis, TN, 1969; worked The Kinetic Playground, Chicago, 1969; app on MERV GRIFFIN Show, WNEW-TV, NYC (syndicated), 1969; worked Univ of California, Berkeley, CA, 1969; Rock Pile, Toronto, Can, 1969; Hunter Col, NYC, 1969; The Pavilion, NYC, 1969; Barnaby's, Chicago, 1969; The Licking Stick, Chicago, 1969; Colonial Tavern, Toronto, Can, 1969; toured w American Folk Blues Festival working club/concert dates through England, 1969; worked Ronnie Scott's, London, Eng, 1969 (por shown JAZZ SCENE AT RONNIE SCOTT'S, BBC-2-TV, 1970); worked Jazz Expo 69, London, 1969; Lennie's, Boston, MA, 1969; St Louis Univ, St Louis, MO, 1969; in concert w St Louis Symphony Orch, Powell Symphony Hall, St Louis, 1969; The Creation, Encino, CA, 1970; Five Stages, Chicago, 1970; Olympic Auditorium, Los Angeles, 1970; Ann Arbor Blues Festival, Ann Arbor, MI, 1970; Newport Jazz Festival, Newport, RI, 1970; Madison Square Garden, NYC, 1970; app on national television commercial for Miller Beer, 1970; worked The Burning Spear, Chicago, 1970-1; app on FAREWELL TO FILLMORE EAST, PBS-TV, 1971; owned/operated Harlem Club, Osceola, AR, early 70s; worked Ash Grove, Los Angeles, 1971-2; Funky Quarters, San Diego, CA, 1972; Wattstax '72 concert, Memorial Coliseum, Los Angeles, 1972 (por shown in film WATTSTAX); worked The Beach House, Venice, CA, 1972; rec Stax label, Memphis, TN, 1972-4; worked New Orleans Jazz & Heritage Festival, Municipal Auditorium, New Orleans, LA, 1973; Carnegie Hall, NYC, 1973; Montreux Jazz Festival, Montreux, Switzerland, 1973; Keystone Korner, Berkeley, CA, c1973; The Burning Spear, Chicago, IL, 1974; High Chaparral, Chicago, 1974-5; International Blues Festival, Louisville, KY, 1974; Golden Checkmate, Chicago, 1974; The Stingrey, Chicago, 1974-5; Stouffer's Riverfront Inn, St Louis, MO, 1974; Richard's Club, Atlanta, GA, 1974; rec Stax label, Hollywood, CA/Muscle Shoals, AL, c1974; worked Utopia Club, West Oakland, CA, 1975; Robert Motel, Chicago, 1975; Academy of Music, Brooklyn, NY, 1975; Balmoral Racetrack, Chicago, 1975; Blue Moon Ballroom, Elgin, IL, 1975; Ratso's, Chicago, 1975-6; Community Theater, Berkeley, CA, 1975; Montreux Rock/Blues Festival, Montreux, Switzerland, 1975 (por rel Utopia label); International Amphitheater, Chicago, 1975-6; rec Utopia label, Hollywood/NYC, 1975; worked Midwest Blues Festival, Univ of Notre Dame, South Bend, IN, 1975-6; Silver Shadow Show Lounge, Chicago, 1975; toured college circuit working concert dates across US, 1976; worked Bottom Line, NYC, 1976; My Father's Place, Roslyn, NY, 1976; Great American Music Hall, San Francisco, 1976; Ethel's, Detroit, MI, 1976; Antone's, Austin, TX, 1976; The Cellar Door, Washington, DC, 1976; New Orleans Jazz & Heritage Festival, New Orleans, LA, 1976; Liberty Hall, Houston, TX, 1977; New Old Waldorf, San Francisco, 1977; Keystone Korner, Berkeley, CA, 1977; Burning Spear, Chicago, 1977; Continental Showcase, Houston, TX, 1977; Belle Starr, Buffalo, NY, 1977; Radio City Music Hall, NYC, 1977; app SOUNDSTAGE, PBS-TV, 1978; toured w BB King, 1978; toured Eng/Belgium/France, 1978; toured Sweden, 1979; toured extensive concerts/clubs in US/Canada through 80s; suffered fatal heart attack; buried, Edmondson, AR

Songs: Blues at Sunrise/Blues Power/California/Cold Feet/Cross Cut Saw/Don't Throw Your Love on Me/Down Don't Bother Me/Dyna Flow/Funk-Shun/I Get Evil/I Walked All Night Long/I've Made Nights by Myself/Laundromat Blues/Let's Have a Natural

Ball/Look Out/Merry Way/Murder/Ooh-ee Baby/ Overall Junction/This Morning/Travelin' Man/ Travelin' to California/What Can I Do to Change Your Mind?/Wild Woman/Won't Be Hanging Around/ Wrapped Up in Love Again/You Threw Your Love on Me Too Strong/You're Gonna Need Me

Infl by: Dorphy Bailey/Blind Lemon Jefferson/Lonnie Johnson/BB King/Aaron "T-Bone" Walker/Mercy Dee Walton

Infl to: Luther Allison/Andrew Brown/Eric Clapton/ Jimi Hendrix/Luther Johnson Jr/Al Kooper/Taj Mahal/William Norris/Jimmy Page/Robbie Robertson/Otis Rush/Son Seals/Johnny Winter

Quotes: "His husky and smoky baritone conveys the worldly credibility necessary for the gamut of human emotions covered in his songs"—Chuck Berk, *Downbeat* magazine, Nov 4, 1976, p 18

"Albert is a punchier, more deliberate and direct singer [than BB King], more in the manner of Midwesterners like Kansas City's Big Joe Turner"—Robert Palmer, Utopia album CYL2-2205

". . . one of a handful of preeminent blues singers in the world"—Edmund Newton, *New York Post* newspaper, Oct 28, 1976

References: Encyclopedia of Pop, Rock & Soul, Irwin Stambler, St Martin's Press, 1974

Guitar Player magazine, Sep 1977, pp 38-9, 66,68,70,72,76

KING, B B
(see King, Riley)

KING, FREDDIE *"Freddy"*
Born: Sept 3, 1934, Gilmer (Upshur Co), TX
Died: Dec 28, 1976, Dallas, TX
Inst: Guitar

Father was JT Christian; mother was Ella Mae King; both mother and uncle Leon King were guitarists; interested in music early and learned guitar from mother at 6 years of age; moved to Chicago, IL, to work outside music, 1950-8; frequently sat-in with local bluesmen in local clubs, Chicago, from 1951; worked Red's Playmore Lounge, Chicago, 1951; Kitty Cat Club, Chicago, 1952; formed own Every Hour Blues Boys (w Jimmy Lee Robinson) to work Cadillac Baby's Club and others, Chicago, 1952-3; frequently worked w Little Sonny Cooper Band in local club dates, Chicago, 1953; rec w Sonny Cooper Band, Parrot label, Chicago, 1953; frequently worked w Earlee Payton's Blues Cats in local club dates, Chicago, 1954-8; rec w Earlee Payton's Blues Cats, Parrot label, Chicago, 1954; worked w own band at Ricky's Show Lounge/Club Zanzibar/Sylvio's/Casbah/Mel's Hideaway Lounge/Walton's Corner/Squeeze Club/ others, Chicago, 1955-60; rec El-Bee label, Chicago, 1956; rec Cobra label (unissued), Chicago, late 50s; worked Cotton Club, Argo, IL, 1958; rec Federal/ King labels, Cincinnati, OH, 1960-6; toured w own band working club dates across US, 1960-3; frequently worked extensively as local rec session man, Chicago, into 60s; worked package blues show, Fillmore Auditorium, San Francisco, CA, 1961; Cadillac Baby's Club, Chicago, c1962; Civic Auditorium, Chicago, c1962; settled in Dallas, TX, to work local gigs from 1963; w BB King, Ashland Auditorium, Chicago, 1964; app w Clarence "Gatemouth" Brown, THE BEAT, WPIX-TV, NYC, 1966; toured England working club/pub dates, 1967-9; worked Ash Grove, Los Angeles, CA, 1968-70; Hunter Col, NYC, 1969; Texas International Pop Festival, Lewisville, TX, 1969; Ann Arbor Blues Festival, Ann Arbor, MI, 1969; rec Cotillion label, NYC, 1969-70; worked Electric Circus, NYC, 1969; Univ of Chicago Folk Festival, Chicago, 1969; Walton's Corner, Chicago, 1969; app on BOBOQUIVARI, PBS-TV, 1971; rec Shelter label, Chicago, 1971; toured England working club/concert dates, 1971 (por rel Black Bear Series private label); worked Fillmore West, San Francisco, 1971; New Ruthie's Inn, Oakland, CA, 1971; Keystone Korner, Berkeley, CA, 1971; Liberty Hall, Houston, TX, 1971; Fillmore East, NYC, 1971; Tom's Musicians Club, Chicago, 1971; Whiskey A-Go-Go, Los Angeles, CA, 1971; Ann Arbor Blues Festival, Ann Arbor, MI, 1972-3 (por 1972 concert rel Atlantic label); Gaslight A-Go-Go, NYC, 1972; Univ of Waterloo, Waterloo, Can, 1972; rec Shelter label, Memphis, TN/Hollywood, CA, 1972; worked Mother Blues, Dallas, TX, 1972; rec Shelter label, Tia Juana, OK, 1973; worked Montreux Jazz Festival, Montreux, Switzerland, 1973; Univ of Minnesota, Minneapolis, MN, 1973; Philharmonic Hall, NYC, NY, 1973; Joe's Place, Cambridge, MA, 1973; Capitol Theater, Montreal, Can, 1973; The Metro, NYC, 1974; toured England/Europe/Australia working concert dates, 1974; worked Antibes Jazz Festival, Antibes, France, 1974; rec RSO label, Miami, FL/Oxfordshire, Eng, 1974; worked Topanga Corral, Los Angeles, CA, 1974; Aragon Ballroom, Dallas, TX, 1974; The Winterland, San Francisco, CA, 1974; Pepper's Hideout, Chicago, IL, 1974; Minneapolis State Fair, Minneapolis, MN, 1974; Liberty Hall, Houston, TX, 1974; Electric Ballroom, Atlanta,

Freddie "Freddy" King *Photo by Doug Fulton. Courtesy* Living Blues *Magazine*

GA, 1974; Tomorrow Club, Youngstown, OH, 1974; Agora Club, Cleveland, OH, 1974; The Bottom Line, NYC, 1975; Armadillo World Headquarters, Austin, TX, 1975; rec RSO label, Hollywood/NYC/Austin, TX/London, Eng, 1975; toured Australia/New Zealand working concert dates, 1975; worked In Concert Club, Montreal, Can, 1975; Starwood, Los Angeles, CA, 1975; Civic Auditorium, Jacksonville, FL, 1975; Great American Music Hall, San Francisco, CA, 1976; Blues Festival, Lenox, MA, 1976; Ratso's, Chicago, IL, 1976; New England Blues Festival, Providence, RI, 1976; Jed's Inn, New Orleans, LA, 1976; Rosy's Club, New Orleans, 1976; entered Presbyterian Hospital where he died of hepatitis and other complications; buried Hillcrest Memorial Park Cemetery, Dallas, TX

Personal: Married Jessie ———; His brothers Benny/Bobby Turner are musicians. Reportedly half-brother of Albert King (per Albert King which Freddie King denied). No relation to BB King. Not to be confused with guitarist "Little" Freddie King

Songs: Cloud Sailin'/Double Eyed Whammy/Driving Sideways/Freeway 75/Funky/Funny Bone/Hide Away/High Rise/It's Too Bad Things Are Going So Tough/Just Pickin'/King-A-Ling/Manhole/My Feeling for the Blues/Play It Cool/Pulp Wood/Sen-Sa-Shun/She Put the Whammy on Me/She's the King/Side Tracked/Someday After a While/Stumble/Texas Flyer/Texas Oil/Tore Down/Use What You Got/Walk Down That Aisle/Wash Out/Wide Open/You Got to Love Her with a Feeling/You Know That You Love Me/You Was Wrong

Infl by: Elmore James/Lonnie Johnson/Louis Jordan/BB King/Muddy Waters/Jimmy Rogers/Eddie Taylor/Aaron "T-Bone" Walker

Infl to: Luther Allison/Eric Clapton/Peter Green/Paul Kossoff/Magic Sam/Mick Taylor/Stan Webb

Quotes: "Freddie King . . . was essentially a tough, driving and powerful urban blues exponent, a modern bluesman with Texas roots and R&B leanings . . ."—Max Jones, *Melody Maker* magazine (UK), Jan 15, 1977

"His vocals were distinctive, restrained and smokey with none of the overt emotionalism of other fleet-fingered guitarists"—Bez Turner, *Blues Unlimited* magazine (UK), Jan 1977, p 26

Reference: Living Blues magazine, Mar 1977, pp 7-11

KING IVORY LEE
(see Semien, Lee)

KING, LUTHER
(see Johnson, Luther)

KING, RILEY B *"BB"*

Courtesy Bill Greensmith /Living Blues *Magazine*

Born: Sept 16, 1925, Indianola (Sunflower Co), MS
Inst: Clarinet/Guitar

Grandfather was bottleneck guitarist; father Albert King and mother Nora Ella Pully were singers; born on plantation between Itta Bena/Indianola, MS (birth registered in Indianola); one of 5 children; sang in local churches from 4 years of age; parents separated and he moved with mother to Kilmichael, MS, area to attend one-room school house w frequent singing in school spiritual quartet, 1929-34; after death of mother quit school to work outside music (as farmhand) on local plantation, 1934-9; returned to Indianola to live with father and work outside music with occasional church choir singing, 1939-43; taught self guitar forming Elkhorn Singers (gospel) quartet to work local churches c1940-3; served briefly in US Army and sang blues for troops at Camp Shelby, Hattiesburg, MS/Ft Benning, GA, 1943; returned to Indianola, MS, to work outside music with occasional church/street singing in area, 1943-6; app w St John Gospel Singers on WJPM-radio, Greenwood, MS/WJPR-radio, Greenville, MS, 1945-6; hitched to

Memphis, TN, 1946; worked amateur shows at WC Handy Theater/Palace Theater, Memphis, 1947-8; occasionally sang in local streets/parks for tips, Memphis, 1947-8; frequently worked w Bobby Bland/ Johnny Ace/Earl Forrest (later called "The Beale Streeters") in local bars/clubs in Memphis area, 1948-9; worked Square Deal Cafe, West Memphis, AR, 1948-9; app w Sonny Boy Williamson (Alex Miller) on HADACOL Show, KWEM-radio, West Memphis, 1949; worked 16th Street Grill, Memphis, 1949; app on own PEPTICON BOY Show, WDIA-radio, Memphis (with frequent local club work), 1949-50; rec w Tuff Green Band, Bullet label, Memphis, 1949; app as DJ (billed as "Riley King, The Blues Boy from Beale Street," later shortened to "Beale Street Blues Boy," then to "Blues Boy," then to "BB"), WDIA-radio, Memphis, 1950-3; rec RPM label, Memphis, 1950-2; w Floyd Dixon, Club Morocco, Little Rock, AR, 1951; worked small clubs/bars in Chicago, IL/NYC, NY, 1952; rec w Sonny Boy Williamson (Alex Miller), Trumpet label, Jackson, MS, 1953; formed own group, touring club dates through southern US, 1953; rec RPM label, Houston, 1953-5; worked City Auditorium, Houston, 1954; w Bill Harvey Band working club dates on West Coast, 1954; worked Apollo Theater, NYC, 1954; Graystone Ballroom, Detroit, MI, 1955; toured extensively with own group working one-nighters in clubs/theaters/concerts/package shows across US, 1955-61; worked Robert's Show Lounge, Chicago, 1956; rec RPM label, Los Angeles, CA, 1956-7; operated Blues Boys Kingdom label c1957; worked w Buddy Guy, Trianon Ballroom, Chicago, 1958; rec Kent/Crown labels, Los Angeles, 1958-62; Longhorn Ranch Club, Dallas, TX, 1960-2; worked Apollo Theater, NYC, 1961; Mardi Gras, Kansas City, MO, 1962; rec ABC label, Los Angeles, 1962-3; California Hotel, Oakland, CA, 1963; toured w Jackie Wilson Revue working theaters/concerts across US, 1964; worked Corner Tavern, Cleveland, OH, 1964; Regal Theater, Chicago, IL, 1964 (por rel ABC-Paramount label); Ashland Auditorium, Chicago, 1964; rec ABC-Paramount label, Chicago, 1964-6; worked Sweet's Ballroom, Los Angeles, 1964; The Show Boat, Los Angeles, 1964; Apollo Theater, NYC, 1964-7; Leo's Casino, Cleveland, OH, 1965; The Showcase, Oakland, CA, 1965-7; Fillmore Auditorium, San Francisco, 1966-7; The Club, Chicago, 1966-7; Club DeLisa, Chicago, 1966 (por rel ABC-BluesWay label); worked Circle Ballroom, Cleveland, 1966; toured one-nighters through Texas, 1966; worked 20 Grand Club, Detroit, MI, 1967; Jazzville, San Diego, CA, 1967; Gazzarri's, Los Angeles, CA, 1967; rec ABC-BluesWay label, NYC, NY, 1967-9; worked Cafe A-Go-Go, NYC, 1967-8; toured w Rhythm & Blues Show working theaters across US, 1967; worked Monterey Jazz Festival, Monterey, CA, 1967 (por shown on MONTEREY JAZZ FESTIVAL, PBS-TV [syndicated]/por shown in film MONTEREY JAZZ); worked The Eagles, Seattle, WA, 1967; app on TWANG, ABC-TV, 1967; toured Europe working concert dates, 1967-8; app on NET JAZZ, PBS-TV (syndicated), 1968; rec ST for film FOR THE LOVE OF IVY, 1968 (por rel ABC label); worked Regal Theater, Chicago, IL, 1968; Burning Spear, Chicago, 1968-9; Club Jamaica, Columbus, OH, 1968; Ken Hawkins Club, Cleveland, OH, 1968; toured one-nighters through South, 1968; worked Club Paradise, Memphis, TN, 1968; Club Streamline, Port Allen, LA, 1968; Elks Club, Montgomery, AL, 1968; New Generation Club, NYC, NY, 1968; Stardust Inn, Chester, PA, 1968; Central Park Music Festival, NYC, 1968-9; app on STEVE ALLEN Show, WOR-TV, NYC (syndicated), 1968; worked Anderson Theater, NYC, 1968; Randalls Island Festival, NYC, 1968-9; The Scene, NYC, 1968; Wonder Garden, Atlantic City, NJ, 1968; Newport Folk Festival, Newport, RI, 1968-9; Quaker City Rock Festival, Philadelphia, PA, 1968; Village Gate, NYC, 1968; Fillmore West, San Francisco, 1968-70; app on DIAL M FOR MUSIC, CBS-TV, 1969; app on MERV GRIFFIN Show, WNEW-TV, NYC (syndicated), 1969; app on SOUL, PBS-TV, 1969-70; worked Fillmore East, NYC, 1969-71; Grand Ballroom, Detroit, MI, 1969; toured Mexico working concert dates, 1969; app in national radio commercials for Axion Soap/Pepsi Cola/ American Telephone & Telegraph, 1969; app on UP-BEAT, WNEW-TV, NYC (syndicated), 1969; app on Johnny Carson's TONIGHT Show, NBC-TV, 1969-70; worked Village Gate, NYC, 1969 (por rel ABC-BluesWay label); Kinetic Playground, Chicago, IL, 1969; Boston Globe Jazz Festival, Boston, MA, 1969-70; toured England/Europe working concert/ radio/TV dates, 1969; worked Electric Factory, Philadelphia, PA, 1969; Civic Center, Baltimore, MD, 1969; Plugged Nickel, Chicago, 1969; MC Lounge, Gary, IN, 1969; The Living Room, Cincinnati, OH, 1969; Rutgers Univ Jazz Festival, New Brunswick, NJ, 1969; app on DICK CAVETT Show, ABC-TV, 1969; Massey Hall, Toronto, Can, 1969; Tyrone Guthrie Theater, Minneapolis, MN, 1969; Texas International Pop Festival, Lewisville, TX, 1969; Harlem Cultural Festival, Mt Morris Park, NYC, NY, 1969; Blossom Music Center, Cleveland, OH, 1969; Longhorn Jazz Festival, Houston, TX, 1969; Berkshire Music Festival, Lenox, MA, 1969-70; Ravinia Park Festival, Chicago, IL, 1969; Ann Arbor

Blues Festival, Ann Arbor, MI, 1969-70; app on MUSIC SCENE, ABC-TV, 1969; worked w Ike & Tina Turner/Rolling Stones Rock Show, The Forum, Los Angeles, CA, then toured with show working concerts across US, 1969; Hollywood Bowl, Los Angeles, 1969; 5-4 Ballroom, Los Angeles, c1969; Carousel Theater, Framingham, MA, 1969; Jazz Concert, Tanglewood, MA, 1969; Ohio Valley Jazz Festival, Cincinnati, OH, 1969-71; Ungano's, NYC, NY, 1969; Lennie's, Boston, MA, 1969; Pep's, Philadelphia, PA, 1969; app on BARBARA McNAIR Show, WNEW-TV, NYC (syndicated), 1969; worked Caesar's Palace, Las Vegas, NV, 1970-1; app on DAVID FROST Show, WNEW-TV, NYC (syndicated), 1970; worked Whiskey A-Go-Go, Los Angeles, CA, 1970; app on FLIP WILSON Show, NBC-TV, 1970-2; worked Djon Ballroom, Los Angeles, 1970; Lampertville Concert, Philadelphia, PA, 1970; King's Castle, Lake Tahoe, NV, 1970; Basin Street West, San Francisco, CA, 1970; app on ED SULLIVAN Show, CBS-TV, 1970; worked Ruggles, Chicago, IL, 1970; Washington Blues Festival, Howard Univ, Washington, DC, 1970; extensively toured college circuit entertaining/lecturing on blues into 70s; worked Univ of California, Berkeley, 1970; Carnegie Hall, NYC, 1970; Apollo Theater, NYC, 1970; Royal Box, Hotel Americana, NYC, 1970; Shrine Auditorium, Los Angeles, CA, 1970; Mr Kelly's, Chicago, IL, 1970; frequently worked Cook County Jail concerts, Chicago, from 1970 (por 1970 date rel ABC-Dunhill label/por 1973 date shown on BB KING REVISITS COOK COUNTY JAIL, PBS-TV) with other prison benefit concerts across US into 70s; app in film BLACK MUSIC IN AMERICA—FROM THEN TIL NOW, 1970; worked Man and His World Concert, Montreal, Can, 1970; Newport Resort Motel, Miami Beach, FL, 1970; app on VIRGINIA GRAHAM Show, WOR-TV, NYC (syndicated), 1971; worked Pepper's Lounge, Chicago, IL, 1971; Burning Spear, Chicago, 1971; toured England/Europe working club/concert dates, 1971; rec ABC label, London, Eng, 1971; rec ABC label, Los Angeles, CA, 1971-2; rec Probe label, Los Angeles, 1971; worked Place des Arts, Montreal, Can, 1971; The Loser's Club, Dallas, TX, 1971-3; Oakland Univ, Rochester, MI, 1971; Hunter Col, NYC, 1971; app in film MEDICINE BALL CARAVAN (UK title: WE HAVE COME FOR YOUR DAUGHTERS), 1971; app on national TV commercials for Tijuana Smalls (Consolidated Cigar Corp), 1971; app on PEARL BAILEY Show, ABC-TV, 1971; app on MIKE DOUGLAS Show, CBS-TV, 1971; app on FANFARE, PBS-TV, 1971; app on ONE NIGHT STAND, NBC-TV, 1971; toured w Sonny Freeman & the Unusuals working concert dates through Japan, 1971-2; worked Memorial Auditorium, New Orleans, LA, 1971; Univ of California, Santa Barbara, CA, 1971; rec ST for film THE SEVEN MINUTES, 1971; worked The Flamingo, Las Vegas, NV, 1971; rec ST for film cartoon FRITZ THE CAT, 1971; rec ST for film BLACK RODEO, 1972; app on DICK CAVETT SHOW, ABC-TV, 1972; app on SOUL TRAIN, WNEW-TV NYC (syndicated), 1972-3; app on KUP'S SHOW, WOR-TV, NYC, 1972; co-founded Foundation for the Advancement of Inmate Rehabilitation and Recreation (FAIRR), 1972; worked Queen Elizabeth Theater, Vancouver, Can, 1972; New Orleans Jazz & Heritage Festival, New Orleans, LA, 1972-3; Puerto Rico Music Festival, San Juan, PR, 1972; Univ of Detroit, Detroit, MI, 1972; Civic Center, Baltimore, MD, 1972; Newport Jazz Festival, NYC, 1972 (por rel Cobblestone label/por on MUSIC—USA, VOA-radio); Summer Festival, Milwaukee, WI, 1972; Sunset Series Concert, Boston, MA, 1972; toured extensively working concert dates in Europe/Africa and other countries around the world, 1972-3; app in French film BLUES UNDER THE SKIN, 1972; app in French film OUT OF THE BLACKS INTO THE BLUES (pt 2: A Way to Escape the Ghetto), 1972; worked Astrodome Jazzfest, Houston, TX, 1972; Civic Arena, Pittsburgh, PA, 1972; Ohio Valley Festival, Cincinnati, OH, 1972; Public Hall, Cleveland, OH, 1972; Blossom Music Center, Cleveland, 1972; Mill Run Theater, Niles, IL, 1972-4; Valley Music Theater, Woodland Hills, CA, 1972; Capitol Theater, Passaic, NJ, 1972; Sing Sing Prison, Ossining, NY, 1972 (por shown in film SING-SING THANKSGIVING, 1974); app on WHAT'S MY LINE?, NBC-TV, c1972; toured England/Europe working concert dates, 1973; app on IN CONCERT, ABC-TV, 1973; app on HELEN REDDY Show, NBC-TV, 1973; app on GEORGE CARLIN MONSANTO CHEMICAL SPECIAL, ABC-TV, 1973; app on MIDNIGHT SPECIAL, NBC-TV, 1973-4; hosted Medgar Evers Memorial Festival, Jackson/Fayette, MS, 1973-5; worked Central Park Music Festival, NYC, NY, 1973; Newport Jazz Festival, NYC, 1973 (por rel Buddah label); app on DICK CLARK PRESENTS THE ROCK & ROLL YEARS, ABC-TV, 1973; app on public service national radio commercial for Council of Foods and Nutrition, 1973; app on ALL TOGETHER NOW, KPIX-TV, San Francisco, CA, 1973; app on POSITIVELY BLACK, NBC-TV (syndicated), 1973; app on IN SESSION, ABC-TV (syndicated), 1973; worked Mississippi Homecoming Festival, Fayette, MS, 1973-4; Massey Hall, Toronto, Can, 1973;

Flamingo Hotel, Las Vegas, NV, 1973-4; Hilton Hotel, Las Vegas, 1973-5; rec ST for film LET THE CHURCH SAY AMEN, 1973; worked Caribe Hilton Hotel, San Juan, PR, 1973; Academy of Music, NYC, NY, 1973; Capitol Theater, Montreal, Can, 1973; contributed articles to *Sounds* magazine, Canada, 1974; worked The Warehouse, Denver, CO, 1974; International Blues Festival, Louisville, KY, 1974; London House, Chicago, IL, 1974; rec ABC label, Las Vegas, NV, 1974; rec w Bobby Bland, ABC-Dunhill label, Los Angeles, CA, 1974; worked Ann Arbor Blues/Jazz Festival, Windsor, Can, 1974; O'Keefe Center, Toronto, Can, 1974; Philharmonic Hall, Hamilton, Can, 1974; Apollo Theater, NYC, 1974; Newport Jazz Festival, NYC, 1974-5 (por 1975 concert on MUSIC—USA, VOA-radio); app on RHYTHM & BLUES, NBC-TV, 1974; app on FEELING GOOD, PBS-TV, 1974; worked The Winterland, San Francisco, CA, 1974-5; Hollywood Bowl, Los Angeles, CA, 1974; High Chaparral, Chicago, IL, 1974-5; toured Australia/New Zealand working concert/TV/radio dates, 1974; worked Richard's Club, Atlanta, GA, 1974; Continental Showcase, Houston, TX, 1974; app w Bobby Bland, SOUL TRAIN, WNEW-TV, NYC (syndicated), c1975; worked Hook & Ladder, Toronto, Can, 1975; app on MERV GRIFFIN Show, WNEW-TV, NYC (syndicated), 1975-7; rec ABC label, Los Angeles, CA, 1975; worked Memorial Auditorium, Burlington, VA, 1975; New Orleans Jazz & Heritage Festival, New Orleans, LA, 1975-6; Convention Hall, Miami, FL, 1975; Civic Center, San Gabriel, CA, 1975; Heritage House Nightclub, Seattle, WA, 1975; Sportsman's Park, Chicago, IL, 1975; Municipal Auditorium, New Orleans, LA, 1975; International Amphitheater, Chicago, 1975-6; The Stingrey, Chicago, 1975-6; Constitution Hall, Washington, DC, 1975; toured Japan working concert dates, 1975; app in film GIVE MY POOR HEART EASE: MISSISSIPPI DELTA BLUESMEN, 1975; app in MIDNIGHT SPECIAL, NBC-TV, 1976; worked w Bobby Bland, Beacon Theater, NYC, 1976; Marco Polo Hotel, Miami, FL, 1976; w Bobby Bland, Concerts at the Grove, Los Angeles, 1976 (por rel ABC-Impulse label); Electric Ballroom, Atlanta, GA, 1976; app on SAMMY AND COMPANY, NBC-TV, 1976; worked Capitol Theater, Chicago, 1976; Ambassador Hotel, Los Angeles, 1976; Great American Music Hall, San Francisco, 1976; Kool Jazz Festival, The Astrodome, Houston, TX, 1976; app on GET DOWN, WPIX-TV, NYC, 1976; worked New England Blues Festival, Providence, RI, 1976; Antone's, Austin, TX, 1976; Civic Auditorium Music Hall, Omaha, NE, 1976; New Burning Spear, Chicago, 1976-7; Terrace Ballroom, Salt Lake City, UT, 1976; Louisville Gardens, Louisville, KY, 1976; toured Australia/New Zealand working concert dates, 1976; app on SANFORD AND SON, NBC-TV, 1977; app w/Bobby Bland, SOUNDSTAGE (ep: Together in the Blues), PBS-TV, 1977; worked Swinger's Lounge, Marco Polo Hotel, Miami, FL, 1977; app in national print ad for Gibson guitars, 1977; worked Tropicana Hotel, Las Vegas, NV, 1977; Shea's Buffalo Theater, Buffalo, NY, 1977; My Father's Place, Roslyn, NY, 1977; Lucifer's, Boston, MA, 1977; Beale Street Blues Festival, Memphis, TN, 1977; Hammersmith Odeon, London, Eng, 1977; The Congresge Bouw, The Hague, Holland, 1977; Nancy Jazz Festival, Nancy, France, 1977; Colonial Tavern, Toronto, Can, 1977; clip shown in ROOTS OF COUNTRY MUSIC & BLUES, KGO-TV, San Francisco, 1977; worked Melody Fair, Buffalo, NY, 1977; Radio City Music Hall, NYC, 1977; app on DONAHUE! Show, WGN-radio, Chicago, 1977; narrated GOOD MORNIN' BLUES, PBS-TV, 1978

Personal: No relation to Albert King/Freddie King. "BB" is short for "Blues Boy"

Billings: Beale Street Blues Boy/Blues Boy/The Blues Boy from Beale Street/The King of the Blues/The Bossman of the Blues

Books: *BB King Songbook*, Gibson Inc, 1971
BB King, Harvey Vinson (Ed), Amsco Music, 70
BB King: The World's Greatest Living Blues Artist, John Haag (Ed), West Coast Pub, 1971
Blues Guitar: A Method By BB King, Jerry Snyder (Ed), Indianola Productions, 1973
Arrival of BB King, C Sawyer, Doubleday, 1980

Songs: A Fool Too Long/Ain't Gonna Worry My Life Anymore/All over Again/Ask Me No Questions/BB's Gibson Guitar Blues/Bad Luck/Beautician Blues/Blind Love/Boogie Rock/Can't You Hear Me Talking to You?/Chains and Things/Come by Here/Country Girl/Cryin' Won't Help You Now/Dance with Me/Darlin' You Know I Love You/Did You Ever Love a Woman?/Don't Have to Cry/Everybody Lies a Little/Fine Looking Woman/Friends/Gambler's Blues/Get Off My Back Woman/Get Out of Here/Ghetto Woman/Go Underground/Gonna Keep On Lovin' You/Good Livin' Good Lovin' Blues/Gotta Find My Baby/Having My Say/Heartbreaker/Highway Bound/Hold That Train/I Can't Explain/I Done Got Wise/I Got Some Help I Don't Need/I Know the Price/I Want You So Bad/I'm Cracking Up over You/I'm Gonna Do What They Do to Me/I'm Gonna Quit My Baby/I'm Not Wanted Any More/I'm with You/I've Been Blue Too Long/Just a Little Love/Keep Movin' On/King's Special/Let Me Love You/Let's Do the Boogie/Let's Get Down to Business/Losing Faith in You/Love Speaks Louder Than Words/Lucille/Lucille's Granny/Lucille Talks Back/Lying Signifying/Many Hard Years/Meet My Happiness/Midnight/My Baby's Comin' Home/My Mood/My Own Fault/My Own Life to Live/My Silent Prayer/Neighborhood Affair/Nobody Loves Me But My Mother/No Good/Now That You've Lost Me/Outside Help/Paying the Cost to Be the Boss/Please Accept My Love/Please Help Me/Please Love Me/Praying to the Lord/Rainin' All the Time/Raining in My Heart/Rock Me Baby/Shot Gun Blues/Shouldn't Have Left Me/Skinny Minnie/Sneakin' Around/So Excited/Stop Putting the Hurt on Me/Sweet Little Angel/Sweet Sixteen/Sweet Thing/Talkin' the Blues/Ten Long Years/That Evil Child/That's Wrong Little Mama/Think It Over/Three O'Clock Blues/Tomorrow Is Another Day/Troubles Don't Last/Troubles Troubles Troubles/Until I Found You/Until I'm Dead and Cold/Waitin' on You/Walkin' Dr Bill/We Can't Make It/What Happened?/When I'm Wrong/When My Heart Beats Like a Hammer/Whole Lot of Lovin'/Why I Sing the Blues/Woke Up This Morning/Worried Dream/Worst Thing in My Life/You Didn't Want Me/You Don't Know/You Know I Love You/You Move Me So/You Upset Me Baby/You're Gonna Miss Me/You're Losing Me/You're Mean/You're Still My Woman/Young Dreamers

Awards/Honors: Won *Jazz & Pop* magazine Readers Poll for Best Male Jazz Singer of Year, 1968

Won NATRA Golden Mike Award for Best Blues Singer of the Year, 1969, 1974

Won French Academie du Jazz Award for Best Blues Album of Year, 1969 ("Lucille," ABC-BluesWay BLS-6016)

Won National Academy of Recording Arts & Sciences Grammy Award for Best R&B Vocal performance by a male, 1970 ("The Thrill Is Gone," ABC-BluesWay BLS-6037)

Won *Downbeat* magazine International Critics Poll for Best Rock-Pop-Blues Group, 1970, 1971, 1972, 1973, 1974, 1975

Won *Guitar Player* magazine Readers Poll for World's Most Popular Guitarist (Top Blues Guitarist of Year), 1970, 1971, 1972, 1973, 1974

Honored with a Day of Blues by city of Memphis, TN (Aug 27, 1971)

Awarded Key to the City by Mayor Carl B Stokes, Cleveland, OH, 1971

A BB King watch marketed, 1971

Honored with a BB King Day by Gov Bill Waller of the state of Mississippi, 1972

Awarded Honorary Doctorate of Humanities from Tougaloo College, Tougaloo, MS, 1973

Awarded Humanitarian Award by B'nai B'rith Music & Performance Lodge of New York, 1973

Won *Blues Unlimited* magazine (UK) Readers Poll for Best Blues Guitarist, 1973

Won *Melody Maker* (World Section) magazine (UK) Jazz Poll for Best Blues Artist of Year, 1973

Won *Ebony* magazine Black Music Poll for Blues Hall of Fame, 1974

Won *Ebony* magazine Black Music Poll for Best Blues Album, 1974 ("Live at the Regal," ABC-724)

Won *Ebony* magazine Black Music Poll for Best Blues Album, 1975 ("To Know You Is to Love You," ABC-794)

Won *Ebony* magazine Black Music Poll for Best Blues Instumentalist, 1974, 1975

Won *Ebony* magazine Black Music Poll for Best Male Blues Singer, 1974, 1975

Won NAACP Image Award, 1975

Honored with BB King Day by city of Berkeley, CA (Jun 12, 1976)

Awarded Honorary Doctor of Music, Yale University, New Haven, CT, 1977

Infl by: Charles Brown/Doc Clayton/Archie Fair/Lowell Fulson/Al Hibbler/Elmore James/Blind Lemon Jefferson/Lonnie Johnson/Sam McQuery/Jimmy Rushing/Joe Turner/Aaron "T-Bone" Walker/Bukka White

Infl to: Luther Allison/Mickey Baker/Elvin Bishop/Bobby Bland/Mike Bloomfield/Lonnie Brooks/Andrew Brown/George Buford/Eric Clapton/Albert Collins/Louis Bo Collins/Larry Davis/Arthur Gunter/Buddy Guy/Sugarcane Harris/Jimi Hendrix/Bee Houston/Luther Johnson Jr/Albert King/Freddie King/Carol Leigh/Little Joe Blue/Little Mack/Little Milton/John Littlejohn/Magic Sam/Johnny Mars/Chicago Bob Nelson/Alvin Nichols/William Norris/Andrew Odom/Fenton Robinson/Otis Rush/Son Seals/Lucille Spann/Ted Taylor/Johnny Twist/Phillip Walker/Albert Washington/Joe Leon Williams/Johnny Winter/Mighty Joe Young

Quotes: "BB is the first and greatest bluesman of the modern age of electronic communications"—Barret Hansen, Kent album 9011

"A superb showman, King is one of the world's greatest guitar soloists, and is certainly the best known and most influential bluesman of them all . . ."—Nick Logan/Bob Woffinden, *The Illustrated Encyclopedia of Rock*, Hamlyn Pub Group, 1976

"BB King has earned his title ('King of the Blues') because he is simply the best blues singer of his generation"—Ralph Gleason, ABC-BluesWay album 6037

References: Great American Popular Singers, Henry Pleasants, Simon & Schuster, 1974

Downbeat magazine, Oct 5, 1978/Oct 19, 1978

Rolling Stone magazine, Oct 20, 1970, pp 37-8

The Arrival of BB King, Charles Sawyer, Doubleday, 1980

KIRK, EDDIE
(see Kirkland, Eddie)

KIRKLAND, *"Little"* EDDIE
(*aka*: Eddie Kirk)

Photo by Peter B Lowry

Born: Aug 16, 1928, Jamaica, British West Indies
Inst: Guitar/Harmonica/Organ

Father was Major Kirkland; mother Dixie Rainey; raised in Dothan, AL; learned harmonica and frequently worked streets for tips as child; learned guitar from Blind Murphy, Dothan, c1936; frequently sang in local Sanctified Church choir as youth; ran away from home to tour w Sugar Girls Medicine Show working through North, 1940-2; settled in New Orleans, LA, to work outside music as amateur boxer c1942; frequently worked w Louisiana Six in local club dates, New Orleans, c1942; moved to Dunkirk, IN, to complete high school from c1943; settled in Detroit, MI, to work outside music with occasional local gigs w Percy Webb's Band from c1948; worked extensively w John Lee Hooker (as singer/musician/song writer), Detroit area (with frequent tours), 1949-54; rec w John Lee Hooker, RPM label, Detroit, 1952; rec King label, Detroit, 1953-4; worked local clubs, Detroit, from 1954; worked w Percy Webb's Band in local clubs, Detroit, 1956-8; formed own band working local club dates, Detroit, from 1958; rec Fortune label, Detroit, 1959; worked w own band, Apex Club, Detroit, 1960; Swann's Paradise Bar, Grand Rapids, MI, 1960; occasional club dates in NYC, NY, 1961; rec w King Curtis Band, Prestige-Tru Sound label, Bergenfield, NJ, 1961; worked as DJ on (unknown) radio, Moultrie, GA, c1961; settled in Macon, GA, 1962; formed own band/own club to work frequently, Macon, from 1962; worked outside music, Macon, from early 60s; toured briefly w Otis Redding package show through South, 1964; rec King label, 1964; rec Volt label, 1965; rec w John Lee Hooker, BluesWay label, Detroit, 1968; rec Trix label, Macon, GA, 1970-1; frequently worked w Soul-Blue group in local clubs, Macon, early 70s; rec Trix label, Lake Hill, NY, 1972; worked Univ of North Carolina, Chapel Hill, NC, 1973 (por rel Flyright label); Ann Arbor Blues Festival, Ann Arbor, MI, 1973; app on Bob Javors' SOMETHING INSIDE OF ME Show, WKCR-FM-radio, NYC, 1976; worked Joe's East West, New Paltz, NY, 1977; app w Foghat group, The Palladium, NYC, 1977 (por on DON KIRSHNER'S ROCK CONCERT, NBC-TV, 1978)

Personal: Married. 12 children

Billing: The Blues Man

Songs: Baby You Know It's True/Burnin' Love/Daddy Please Don't Cry/The Devil/Done Somebody Wrong/Don't Take My Heart/Down on My Knees/Eddie's Boogie Chillen/Georgia Woman/Goin' Back to Mississippi/Got to Love My Baby/Hard to Raise a Family Today/Have Mercy on Me/Have You Seen That Lonesome Train?/I Need a Lover Not Just a Friend/I Tried/I Tried to Be a Friend/I'm Goin' to

Keep Lovin' You/I'm Going to Wait for You/I'm Gonna Forget You/I've Got an Evil Woman/I Walked Twelve Miles/Jerdine/Lonesome Talkin' Blues/Man of Stone/Mink Hollow Slide/Mother-In-Law/Nora/Pity on Me/Rollin' Stone Man/Saturday Night Stomp/ Something's Gone Wrong in My Life/Spank the Butterfly/Tell Me Baby/Train Done Gone/When I First Started Hoboing

Infl by: Junior Daddy Bailey/Blind Murphy/Big Bill Broonzy/Big Boy Crudup/John Lee Hooker/Lightnin' Hopkins

Quotes: "An original guitar stylist . . . as well as an impassioned singer"—Pete Lowry, Trix album 3301

"... a leaping, somersaulting, soul-blues shouter"—James O'Neal, *Downbeat* magazine, Apr 24, 1975, p 20

References: Trix album 3301

Blues Unlimited magazine (UK), Feb 1971, pp 9-10

KITTRELL, JEAN

Courtesy Jean Kittrell

Born: Jun 27, 1927, Birmingham (Jefferson Co), AL
Inst: Piano

Father was David McCarty, mother was Dorothy Ethel Clark, both singers; born Ethel Jean McCarty; interested in music early and studied piano at 5 years of age; frequently played piano and sang in choir of Southern Baptist Church, Birmingham, AL, as child; attended Blue Mountain Col, Blue Mountain, MS (receiving BA degree), 1947; attended Univ of Chicago, Chicago, IL (receiving MA degree), 1951; frequently worked outside music with occasional social/party work through 50s; worked w Chesapeake Bay Jazz Band, Norfolk, VA, area, 1957-9; worked Boat Club, Norfolk, 1958-9; Norfolk Yacht Club, Norfolk, 1958-9; Officers' Club, Cherry Point, NC, 1959; toured w Chicago Stompers working Storyville Club, Frankfort, Ger/New Orleans Bier Bar, Dusseldorf, Ger, and other clubs/concerts through Europe, 1959; worked w Chicago Stompers, Red Arrow Club, Chicago, 1959-60; worked mostly outside music through 60s; worked Texas State Fair, Dallas, TX, 1967; frequently worked St Louis Ragtime & Jazz Festival, St Louis, MO, 1967-75; app on ST LOUIS JAZZ, CBS-TV, 1967; worked Levee House, St Louis, 1967-9; rec w Tony Parenti's Blues Blowers, Jazzology label, Columbia, SC, 1967; worked Hemisfair, San Antonio, TX, 1968; app on NEGRO MUSIC IN AMERICA, National/Midwestern educational radio, 1968; frequently app on local radio/TV programs out of Southern Illinois Univ, Carbondale, IL, 1968-72; worked w Boll Weevil Jazz Band, Goldenrod Showboat, St Louis, MO, 1969; frequently worked St Louis Country Club, St Louis, 1969-75; frequently app on various shows, Midwestern educational TV, 1970-1; worked Memphis Cotton Carnival, Memphis, TN, 1970; Big Horn Jazz Festival, Mundelein, IL, 1971-3; w Dan Havens Boll Weevil Jazz Band, Lakefront Jazz Festival, Milwaukee, WI, 1971; Manassas Jazz Festival, Manassas, VA, 1971; Univ of Tennessee, Knoxville, 1971; attended Southern Illinois Univ, Carbondale (receiving PhD degree), 1973; toured Japan working club/concert/lecture/college dates, 1973; worked Bethel College, McKenzie, TN, 1973; Memphis Cotton Carnival, Memphis, 1973; Paris-Henry County Arts Council Concert, Paris, TN, 1973; St Bridget's of Erin Church, St Louis, MO, 1974; worked w Jazz Cats, 7-11 Club, Chilton Inn, St Louis, 1974; Hayloft Dinner Theater, Manassas, VA, 1975; St Louis Ragfest, Goldenrod Showboat, St Louis, 1975-7; worked outside music (in English Dept of Southern Illinois Univ), Carbondale, IL, mid-70s; frequently toured w Mississippi Mudcats working concert/club dates, mid-70s; worked Jazz Festival, Mattoon, IL, 1975; Ramada Inn and Jazz Emporium, Rochester, MN, 1975; Broomcorn Festival, Arcola, IL, 1975; frequently worked local parties/concerts/ lectures at private clubs/jazz clubs/churches/ universities/schools/civic organizations through

Illinois/Missouri, 1976-7; worked w Dan Havens Mississippi Mudcats, Cotton Bowl, Edwardsville, IL, 1976-7; w Muggsy Sprecher's Jazz Band, Airport Hilton Inn, St Louis, MO, 1976; w Old Guys Jazz Band, Bradley Univ, Alton, IL, 1976; w Dan Havens-Jean Kittrell Mound City All-Stars, Central Illinois Jazz Festival, Decatur, IL, 1977 (por rel Jim Taylor Presents label); worked Blackburn Col, Carlinville, IL, 1977; Herman Park, St Louis, MO, 1977; rec w Old Guys Jazz Band, Meridian 8 label, Glen Carbon, IL, 1977; worked The Hermitage, St Louis, 1977; w Muggsy Sprecher's Jazz Band, Ramada Inn, Springfield, IL, 1977; residency Lt Robert E Lee Riverboat, St Louis, 1978

Personal: Married Edward Kittrell (1949-62). 2 children

Billing: Jazzie Jeanie

Songs: I'm a One Man Woman But I Never Found My Man/I'm Goin' to Quit Saying Goodbye/Mr Shoe Man Blues

Infl by: Mahalia Jackson/Ma Rainey/Bessie Smith

Quote: "In national jazz circles, Jean Kittrell is well received as a blues vocalist who can tame a piano and belt out a tune with the best of them"—Ron Freeberg, *Post-Bulletin* newspaper, Mar 8, 1975

KOERNER, JOHN *"Spider"*
Born: Aug 31, 1938, Rochester, (Monroe Co), NY
Inst: Guitar/Harmonica

Raised in Rochester, NY, area through 50s; attended Univ of Minnesota, Minneapolis, MN, late 50s; settled on West Coast to work as folk singer in local coffeehouses, San Francisco, CA, area, from c1960; worked Bitter End, NYC, NY, 1963; Newport Folk Festival, Newport, RI, 1964-5 (por 1964 concert rel Vanguard label/por shown in film FESTIVAL); The

Photo by Julie Snow

Loft, Boston, MA, 1965; Club 47, Cambridge, MA, 1965; Mooncusser, Martha's Vineyard, MA, 1965; Ash Grove, Los Angeles, CA, 1966; Club 47, Cambridge, MA, 1968; toured England working club dates, 1968; rec Elektra label, c1968; worked Triangle Bar, Minneapolis, MN, 1969; Newport Folk Festival, Newport, RI, 1969

Personal: Married/divorced

Infl by: Jesse Fuller/Leadbelly

L

LACY, Rev **RUBIN (RUBEN)** *"Rube"*
Born: Jan 2, 1902, Pelahatchie (Rankin Co), MS
Died: Nov 14, 1969, Corcoran, CA
Inst: Guitar/Mandolin

Father Perry Lacy; mother Missouri Frazier; one of 13 children; raised by grandfather who was a preacher with an African Methodist church in area; dropped out of school to work outside music as youth; learned guitar in late teens; left home to team w Son Spand to work local jukes, Jackson, MS, area from 1921; hoboed extensively working outside music in Mississippi/Iowa/Illinois/elsewhere, 1923-5; returned frequently to work w Son Spand/Charlie McCoy/Tommy Jackson/Tommy Johnson/Ishmon Bracey/others in local jukes/streets/dances/parties, Jackson, MS, area from 1925; formed own group to work streets out of Yazoo City, MS, from 1927; frequently worked outside music on Roy Flowers Plantation, Mattson, MS, from 1927; rec Columbia label, Memphis, TN, 1927; rec Paramount label, Chicago, IL, 1928; reportedly acc to many bluesmen on local recordings in Mississippi, c1929-32; ordained minister of Missionary Baptist Church and worked as preacher in churches through Mississippi/Arkansas/Missouri/California from 1932 through 50s; settled in Los Angeles, CA, late 50s; frequently preached in local churches in northern towns of California, late 50s into 60s; served as pastor of Union Baptist Church, Ridgecrest, CA, through 60s; rec (religious songs) Advent label, Ridgecrest, CA, c1966; moved to Bakersfield, CA, to preach in local churches from 1966; suffered fatal heart attack after sermon; buried unmarked grave, Union Cemetery, Bakersfield; gravestone erected/dedicated, 1992

Personal: Married twice. 6 children

Infl by: George "Crow Jane" Hendrix

Infl to: Ishmon Bracey/Son House/Tommy McClennan/Charlie McCoy

Quote: ". . . [He] made a major contribution to the study of blues history, preaching, and religious folksong and his career had been an important one in the fields of both blues and religious work"—David Evans, *Blues Unlimited* magazine (UK), Jul 1975, p 23

Rev Rubin Lacy and wife *Photo by David Evans*

References: Nothing But the Blues, Mike Leadbitter, Hanover Books, 1971
Blues Unlimited magazine (UK), Jul 1975, p 23

LAMB, NATALIE

Courtesy Natalie Lamb

Born: Nov 10, c1940, New York (New York Co), NY
Inst: Guitar

Father was Norman Elston, a professional musician; mother was Genevieve Hart; born Natalie Elston; studied classical voice as youth; attended Hunter Col, NYC, NY, late 50s (receiving BA degree); interested in music and frequently worked as folk/pop singer at local parties/clubs/social events, NYC area, late 50s; worked outside music (as teacher) in NYC area through 60s into 70s; debut at Town Hall, NYC, 1965; rec w Sammy Price, Columbia label (unissued test), NYC, 1965; worked One Fifth Avenue Club, NYC, 1966; app on JOE FRANKLIN Show, WOR-TV, NYC, 1966; worked Paddock Club, Yonkers, NY, 1966; San Roc Club, Hastings-on-Hudson, NY, 1966; Sheraton-Tenny Club, Queens, NY, 1966; worked w Red Onion Jazz Band, Town Hall, NYC, 1969 (por rel Biograph label); frequently worked w Red Onion Jazz Band at local parties/private jazz clubs/associations/concerts in New York/New Jersey/Connecticut areas from 1969; worked St Louis Ragtime Festival, St Louis, MO, 1969; Pee Wee Russell Memorial Stomp, Martinsville Inn, Martinsville, NJ, 1969-72; Park 100 Restaurant, NYC, 1970; Roosevelt Grill, NYC, 1970; app on NEWARK ARTS FESTIVAL Show, WNJU-TV, Newark, NJ, c1972; worked Princeton Univ, Princeton, NJ, c1972; Three Sisters, West Paterson, NJ, c1973; Manassas Jazz Festival, Manassas, VA, 1973-5 (por 1973 concert rel Fat Cat label); International Center, NYC, 1973; attended Hunter Col, NYC, c1973 (receiving MA degree); worked Connecticut Traditional Jazz Club concert, Meriden, CT, 1974 (por rel Fat Cat label); Big Horn, Mundelein, IL, 1974; New Orleans Jazz Club of North California, San Francisco, CA, 1974; Mariott Hotel, New Orleans, LA, 1974; International Center, NYC, 1974; long residency w Red Onion Jazz Band, O'Connor's Ale House, Watchung, NJ, 1974-6; worked World Champions of Jazz Jam Session, Indianapolis, IN, 1974; Stouffer's Inn, Indianapolis, 1975; Pee Wee Russell Memorial Stomp, Martinsville Inn, Martinsville, NJ, 1976; Breda Jazz Festival, Breda, Holland, 1976, then toured club dates through Denmark/France/Austria; worked Newport Jazz Festival, Waterloo Village, Stanhope, NJ, 1976; Meadowbrook Ballroom, Cedar Grove, NJ, 1976; Cassell's Lounge, Long Island City, NY, 1977; Long Island Traditional Jazz Club, Babylon, NY, 1977; Manassas Jazz Festival, Manassas, VA, 1977; Essex Hunt Club, Peapack, NJ, 1977; w Lee's Imperial Jazz Band, Detroit Hot Jazz Society, Detroit, MI, 1978

Personal: Married Bob Thompson, leader of Red Onion Jazz Band (1972-)

Infl by: Ma Rainey

Quote: "Miss Lamb has successfully captured the spirit and tone of her predecessors . . ."—Chris Albertson, *Downbeat* magazine, Jun 26, 1969, p 32

LAUGHING CHARLEY
(see Hicks, Charlie)

LAWLARS, ERNEST
(aka: Little Son Joe/Son Joe)
Born: May 18, 1900, Hughes (St Francis Co), AR
Died: Nov 14, 1961, Memphis, TN
Inst: Guitar/Washboard

Raised in Hughes, AR, where he frequently worked outside music through 20s; teamed w Robert Wilkins to work local jukes/streets, Memphis, TN, c1931-6; rec w Robert Wilkins, Vocalion label, Jackson, MS, 1935; frequently worked w local jug bands at house parties/dances/streets/elsewhere, Memphis area, c1936-8; rec w Memphis Minnie, Vocalion label, Chicago, IL, 1938-9; rec w Memphis Minnie, OKeh label, Chicago, 1940-1; frequently worked w Memphis Minnie (or as single) in local clubs, Chicago, from early 40s; rec w Memphis Minnie, OKeh/Columbia labels, Chicago, 1944; worked w Memphis Minnie, Indiana Theater, Chicago, mid-40s; rec OKeh/Columbia labels, Chicago, 1946-7/9; toured w Willie Love's Three Aces working clubs through Delta area of Mississippi, late 40s; worked w Memphis Minnie, 708 Club, Chicago, 1949; worked occasional local club dates, Chicago area, early 50s; rec acc to Memphis Minnie, Regal label, Chicago, 1950; rec Checker label, Memphis, TN, 1952; rec JOB label, Chicago, 1954; frequently worked outside music, Chicago area, through 50s; mostly inactive due to illness from 1957; retired to Memphis, TN, c1960; entered John Gaston Hospital where he died of heart disease; buried New Hope Cemetery, Walls, MS

Personal: Married musician/singer Lizzie Douglas (Memphis Minnie) (1939-61)

Songs: Afraid to Trust Them/Every Time My Heart Beats/Flying Crow Blues/I'm Not the Lad/Levee Camp (Blues)/Life Is Just a Book/My Feet Jumped Salty/She Belongs to the Devil

LAZY LESTER
(see Johnson, Leslie)

LAZY SLIM JIM
(see Harris, Edward)

LEADBELLY/LEAD BELLY
(see Ledbetter, Huddie)

LEDBETTER, HUDDIE WILLIAM
(aka: Leadbelly/Lead Belly)
Born: Jan 20, 1889, Mooringsport (Caddo Parish), LA
Died: Dec 6, 1949, New York, NY
Inst: Accordion/Bass/Guitar/Harmonica/Mandolin/Piano/Windjammer

Father was Wesley "Wes" Ledbetter, a farmer and musician; mother was Sallie Pugh, part Cherokee Indian; born on Jeter Plantation outside Mooringsport, LA; was only child; moved to Leigh, TX, where he was raised from 5 years of age; learned Cajun accordion (windjammer) from uncle Terril Ledbetter as youth; later learned guitar/harmonica and frequently worked backwood dances/breakdowns/sooky jumps in Leigh, TX, area to c1906; left home to hobo to Dallas/Fort Worth, TX, areas working outside music c1906; hoboed to Shreveport, LA, to work outside music, 1906-8; worked outside music in New Orleans, LA, 1909; frequently hoboed through Southwest working outside music with some street singing, 1910-16; served as leadman for Blind Lemon Jefferson on streets of West Dallas, TX, c1912; worked w Blind Lemon Jefferson, Big Four Club, Dallas, c1912; worked outside music, New Boston, TX, c1914; served term for assault in Harrison County Prison, TX, c1916 (later escaping); served term for murder in Shaw State Prison Farm, Huntsville, TX (alias Walter Boyd), 1918-25; hoboed to Mooringsport, LA, to work outside music, 1926-30; served term for attempted homicide, Louisiana State Penitentiary, Angola, LA, 1930-4; rec Library of Congress label, Angola, LA, 1933; worked as chauffeur/assistant/folksinger for folklorist John A Lomax, Sr touring universities/colleges/prisons/plantations through East, 1934-5; rec extensively on Library of Congress label at various locations across US, 1934-5/1937-8; toured college circuit working concerts through New York/Connecticut, 1935; worked Lafayette Theater, NYC, NY, 1935; rec ARC group/Folkways/Biograph labels, NYC, 1935; app w John Lomax in documentary newsfilm MARCH OF TIME, 1935; worked outside music, Shreveport, LA, 1935-7; moved to NYC to work local parties/lofts/political rallies/clubs from 1937; worked Columbia Univ, NYC, 1939; rec Musicraft label, NYC, 1939; served term for assault, New York State prison, Rikers Island, NYC, 1939; frequently worked outside music, NYC, 1940-4; rec w Golden Gate Quartet, Victor label, NYC, 1940; rec Bluebird/Biograph labels, NYC, 1940; worked Riverside Stadium, Washington, DC, 1940; frequently worked w Josh White, Village Vanguard, NYC, 1940; app on own weekly series FOLK SONGS OF AMERICA, WNYC-radio, NYC, 1940; app on BACK WHERE I COME FROM, CBS-radio Network, 1940; rec Asch label, NYC, 1941-3; app on Office of War Information radio shows (frequently heard on BBC-radio, London, Eng), early 40s; frequently worked w Sonny Terry/Brownie McGhee/Woody Guthrie (as "Headline Singers") at hootenannies/house parties in NYC area, 1942-3; rec Stinson label, NYC, 1944; rec Capitol label, Hollywood, CA, 1944; worked local folk clubs/concert dates/private parties, Hollywood, CA, area, 1944-6; app on own show, KRE-radio, Los Angeles, CA, 1945; app in film short THREE SONGS BY LEADBELLY, 1945; University of Utah, Salt

Huddie Ledbetter (Leadbelly)
Courtesy BMI Archives

Lake City, UT, 1946; toured w People's Songs Inc group working folk festivals/colleges across US c1946; w Sonny Terry, Town Hall, NYC, 1946; frequently worked solo at school concerts/church affairs/private club parties, NYC area, from c1947; worked Times Hall, NYC, 1948; app on WNYC JAZZ FESTIVAL series, WNYC-FM-radio, NYC, 1948 (por rel Xtra label); rec Folkways label, NYC, 1948; worked Central Plaza, NYC, 1949; app on THE CHAMBER MUSIC SOCIETY OF LOWER BASIN STREET, NBC-radio (Blue Network), 1949; worked Fondation des Etats-Unis Concert, Paris Jazz Fair, Paris, France, 1949; rec w Bill Dillard on (unissued) label, Paris, 1949; worked Univ of Texas, Austin, 1949 (por rel Playboy label); entered Bellevue Hospital where he died of lateral sclerosis; buried Shiloh Baptist Church Cemetery, between Mooringsport/Blanchard, LA; a Leadbelly Memorial concert was held at Town Hall, NYC, 1950/1964; heard on ST of Dutch film HET COMPROMIS, 1968; heard on ST of film BLACK MUSIC IN AMERICA: FROM THEN TIL NOW, 1970; film bio LEADBELLY released 1976; gravestone erected/dedicated c1972; second gravestone erected/dedicated, 1993

Personal: Had 2 children by Margaret Coleman c1905; married Aletha Henderson (c1908-); married Martha Promise (1935-49). The name "Leadbelly" was given him as 1) corruption of name Ledbetter or 2) reference to his strength or 3) reference to buckshot wound in his stomach

Billing: The King of the 12 String Guitar Players of the World

Books: Negro Folk Songs as Sung by Lead Belly, John A Lomax/Alan Lomax, The Macmillan Company, 1936

A Tribute to Huddie Ledbetter, Max Jones/ Albert McCarthy, Jazz Music Books, 1946

The Leadbelly Songbook, Asch-Lomax, Oak Publications, 1962

The 12 String Guitar as Played by Leadbelly, Pete Seeger/Julius Lester, Oak Publications, 1965

The Midnight Special, Richard M Garvin/ Edmond Addeo, Bernard Geis Associates, 1971

Leadbelly, Judy Bell (ed), Trio Folkways Music, 1976

The Life and Legend of Leadbelly, Charles Wolfe/Kip Lornell, Harper-Collins Pub, 1992

Songs: Ain't Goin' Let You Worry My Life No More/ Alberta/Back Slider Fare You Well/Becky Deem/ Black Girl/Blind Lemon/The Boll Weevil/The Bourgeois Blues/Bring Me a Little Water, Silvy/Bull Cow/Corn Bread Rough/Cotton Fields (Old Cotton Fields at Home/The Cotton Song)/DeKalb Blues/ Death Letter Blues/Don't Lie Buddy/Don't You Love Your Daddy No More?/Ella Speed/Fort Worth and Dallas Blues/Four Day Worry Blues/The Gallis Pole/Go Down Ol' Hannah/Good Mornin' Blues/ Goodnight Irene/Governor OK Allen/Governor Pat Neff/Green Corn/The Grey Goose/Gwine Dig a Hole/Ha, Ha Thisaway/Henry Ford Blues/Hindenburg Disaster/Kansas City Papa/Keep Your Hands off Her/Laura/Leavin' Blues/Little Children's Blues/The Medicine Man/The Midnight Special/Mr Tom Hughes Town (Fannin' Street)/Old Riley (Here Rattler Here)/Packin' Trunk Blues/Pick a Bale O' Cotton/Po' Howard/Polly Wee/Pretty Papa/Red Cross Store/Red River/Redbird/Roberta/Rock Island Line/ Roosevelt Song/Scottsboro Blues/Silver City Bound/ Take a Whiff on Me/Take Me Back/Turn Your Radio On/We Shall Be Free/When I Was a Cowboy/Whoa, Back, Buck/Yellow Gal/You Cain' Lose-A Me Cholly

Infl by: Blind Lemon Jefferson/Terril Ledbetter

Infl to: Barbara Dane/Paul Geremia/Woody Guthrie/ Janis Joplin/John Koerner/Brownie McGhee/Pete Seeger/Sonny Terry/Eric Von Schmidt/The Weavers

Quotes: "Leadbelly was a man of many facets: minstrel, blues artist, musically adept at several instruments, singer extraordinaire, raconteur, people's songbook, etc"—Lawrence Cohn, Elektra album 301

"Leadbelly was the most versatile of all singers in the Afro-American tradition and was deeprooted in its folkways"—Ross Russell, *Downbeat* magazine, Aug 6, 1970, p 12

"His singing represented the ideal stage in the development of Negro folksong, an intermediate point between the primitive performance of a Blind Lemon and the sophisticated production of a Josh White"—John Lucas, *Basic Jazz on Long Play*, Carleton Jazz Club, 1954

References: Negro Folk Songs as Sung by Lead Belly, John A Lomax/Alan Lomax, The Macmillan Company, 1936

Elektra album 301

Downbeat magazine, Aug 6, 1970, pp 12-14, 33

LEE, BESSIE
(see Smith, Trixie)

LEE, CAROLINE
(see Brown, Bessie)

LEE, JIMMY
(see Robinson, Jimmy Lee)

LEE, JOHN
(see Henley, John Lee)

LEE, JOHN ARTHUR

Photo by Peter B Lowry

Born: May 24, 1915, Mt Willing (Lowndes Co), AL
Inst: Guitar/Kazoo/Piano

Father Climon Lee and mother Vallie ——— were musicians; born on Judge Wood's Plantation; one of 9 children; interested in music early and taught self guitar at 6 years of age; moved to Milton Moore's farm, Evergreen, AL, where he was raised/worked outside music from 1922; frequently worked fish fries/ house and school parties/jukes/dances, Evergreen, AL, area to 1933; left home to hobo across US working outside music, 1933-7; worked outside music, Cantonment, FL, c1938-9; settled in Montgomery, AL, 1945; worked outside music with frequent gigs at local clubs/private parties/dances/night spots, Montgomery, AL, 1945 to mid-50s; frequently app on WMGY-radio, Montgomery, late 40s to 1951; rec Federal label, Montgomery, 1951; worked mostly outside music, Montgomery, c1955 into 70s; worked Travel Lodge, Montgomery, 1973 (por rel Rounder label); National Folk Festival, Wolftrap Farm, Vienna, VA, 1974; Toronto Blues Festival, Olympic Island, Toronto, Can, 1974; Down East Festival, Cambridge, MA, 1974; The Physical World, Cambridge, 1974 (por rel Rounder label)

Personal: Married Nellie ——— (1938-)

Songs: Alabama Boogie/Baby Blues/Circle Around the Sun/Depot Blues/Somebody's Been Fooling You/ Where My Money Goes

Infl by: Blind Lemon Jefferson/Levi Kelley/Ellie Lee

Quote: "John Lee's repertoire is one of the most varied of any blues performer"—Robert Gear, Rounder album 2010

References: *Blues Unlimited* magazine (UK), May 1975, pp 12-13

Living Blues magazine, Autumn 1974, pp 13-14

LEE, JOHNNY

(see Hooker, John Lee)

LEE, JULIA

Born: Oct 13, 1903, Boonville (Cooper Co), MO
Died: Dec 8, 1958, Kansas City, MO
Inst: Piano

Father George Lee Sr was violinist; mother was Katie Redmond; interested in music early and began singing with father's string trio at 4 years of age; moved to Kansas City, MO, as child; studied piano w Scrap

Julia Lee
Courtesy Frank Driggs Collection

Harris and Charles Williams from 1912; frequently worked house parties/high school events/skating rinks/socials/amateur shows, Kansas City, MO, 1916-20; attended local university where she studied advanced piano from c1918; worked as pianist, Novelty Club, Kansas City, MO, c1920; worked w brother George E Lee, Lyric Hall, Kansas City, 1920; joined brother George E Lee's Band to work local clubs with extensive tours through Southwest working clubs/dances/ballrooms, 1920-33; rec OKeh label (unissued test), Chicago, IL, 1923; rec w George E Lee and His Novelty Singing Orch, Meritt label, Kansas City, MO, 1927; worked w George E Lee's Novelty Singing Orch, Reno Club, Kansas City, MO, c1928; rec w George E Lee Orch, Brunswick label, Kansas City, 1929; worked w Bunk Johnson, Yellow Front Cafe, Kansas City, 1931; w George E Lee Orch, Cherry Blossom Club, Kansas City, 1933; extensive residency (as single) at Milton's Taproom, Kansas City, 1933-48; w Baby Dodds, Three Deuces, Chicago, 1939; Off Beat Club, Chicago, 1939; The Beachcomber, Omaha, NE, 1943; Silver Frolics, Chicago, 1943; Downbeat Room, Chicago, 1943; rec w Jay McShann's Kansas City Stompers, Capitol label, Kansas City, MO, 1944; rec w Tommy Douglas Orch, Premium label, Kansas City, 1945; rec w Baby Lovett Boy Friends, Capitol label, Los Angeles, CA, 1946-7; worked command performance for President Harry Truman at the White House, Washington, DC, 1948; frequently worked club/theater dates on West Coast, 1948-9; worked Ciro's, Los Angeles, 1949; Tiffany, Los Angeles, 1949; rec w Boy Friends, Capitol label, Kansas City, MO, 1949-52; worked Rossonian Club, Denver, CO, 1950; Theater Lounge, Denver, 1950; frequently worked The Cuban Room, Kansas City, early 50s; rec Foremost label, Kansas City, 1956-7; app w Bill Nolan Trio in film THE DELINQUENTS, 1957; frequently worked Hi-Ball Bar, Kansas City, late 50s; suffered fatal heart attack at home; buried Highland Cemetery, Kansas City, MO

Personal: Married Johnny Thomas (1920s)

Songs: Come On Over to My House/Dream Lucky Blues/Gotta Gimme Whatcha Got/Julee Boogie/Julia's Blues/That's What I Like

Infl by: Etta Moten

Quotes: "Julia Lee was probably one of the finest blues artists on record"—Sally Ann Worsfold, *Jazz Journal* magazine (UK), Mar 1971, p 23

"One of the finest jazz singers from the Kansas City era of jazz"—Monette Moore, *Jazz Journal* magazine (UK), Apr 1963, p 8

References: *Jazz Journal* magazine (UK), Mar 1972, pp 23-4

Downbeat magazine, Jan 15, 1947, p 12

LEE, KING IVORY
(see Semien, Lee)

LEE, LONESOME
(see Robinson, Jimmy Lee)

LEE, WARREN
(see Jackson, Lee)

LEIGH, CAROL ANN

Courtesy Carol Leigh

Born: Dec 25, c1937, San Francisco, CA (unconfirmed)
Inst: Piano

Grandfather was violinist; born Carol Ann Karney; raised in San Francisco, CA; interested in music at early age and was singing at local amateur shows/lodge meetings from 5 years of age; attended San Jose State Col, San Jose, CA, 1956-7; worked outside music, San Francisco area, from c1957; worked w Alan Hall's Jazz Band, The Swinging Door Club, San Mateo, CA, c1960; The Hotsy-Totsy Club, San Francisco, 1961-2; La Hora del Pueblo, Cuernavaca, Mexico, 1962; app on AL COLLINS Show, KPIX-TV, San Francisco, 1963; rec Epitaph label, Redondo Beach, CA, 1963; frequently worked club dates in San Francisco area, 1963-8; worked w Slim Gaillard, Casuals on the Square, Oakland, CA, mid-60s; app w Bill Cosby/Slim Gaillard, KDIA-radio, Oakland, CA, c1965; worked Sabella's, San Francisco, 1968; in residence w Bill Napier, Pier 23 Cafe, San Francisco, 1968-71; worked Pu'o'Oro Plage Club, Papeete, Tahiti, 1970; w Osaka Rascals, Earthquake McGoon's, San Francisco, late 60s into 70s; toured w Big Tiny Little working concert dates, 1971; app w Tiny Little on BOB BRAUN Show, WLWD-TV, Dayton, OH/WLWT-TV, Cincinnati, OH, 1971; formed own trio to tour Holiday Inn circuit across US, 1972; worked w Dave Frishberg at Southern California Hot Jazz Society Concert, Los Angeles, CA, 1972; app as extra in film YOUR THREE MINUTES ARE UP, 1972; moved to and frequently worked local club dates, Chicago, IL, from 1973; worked Big Horn Jazz Festival, Mundelein, IL, 1974; Gaslight Club, Chicago, 1974; The Inkwell, Chicago, 1974; w Original Salty Dogs, St Louis Ragfest, Goldenrod Showboat, St Louis, MO, 1974-7; frequently worked w Truck Parham Trio in local club dates, Chicago, 1974-5; worked Kingston Mines, Chicago, 1975; rec w Original Salty Dogs, GHB-Jazzology label, Chicago, 1975; worked w Original Salty Dogs, New Black Eagle Hall, Hopkinton, MA, 1975; w Johnny Faren Jazz Band, Indianhead Lounge, Lemont, IL, 1976; Buffalo Nickel, Buffalo Grove, IL, 1976; w Climax Jazz Band, DJ's Bar, Toronto, Can, 1976-7; Bogart's, Cincinnati, OH, 1976; toured w Original Salty Dogs working club dates through Delaware/Massachusetts, 1976; worked w Hall Brothers Jazz Band, Emporium of Jazz, Mendota, MN, 1976-7; Central Illinois Jazz Festival, Decatur, IL, 1977; settled in Syracuse, NY, 1977; worked w Jack Maheu's Salt City Six in residency at Carriage House, Rochester, NY, 1977; Big Horn Jazz Festival, Ramada Inn, Mundelein, IL, 1977; residencies at Dinkler Motor Inn, Syracuse, NY, 1977-8; toured w Original Salty Dogs working club/concert dates through New England states, 1977; worked Sandy's Jazz Revival, Beverly, MA, 1977-8; app on PETER APPLEYARD PRESENTS THE CLIMAX JAZZ BAND WITH CAROL LEIGH, CHCH-TV, Hamilton, Can, 1978; worked Maryland Inn, Annapolis, MD, 1978

Personal: Married James Leigh, trombonist (divorced); married Russ Whitman (1977-)

Infl by: Leroy Carr/BB King/Ma Rainey/Bessie Smith

Quote: "She is a dynamic performer, filled with the enthusiasm of living, and her in-person appearances are always a thrill . . ."—George H Buck Jr, GHB-Jazzology album GHB-88

LENOIR, J B

(*aka:* JB/JB Lenore)
Born: Mar 5, 1929, Monticello (Lawrence Co), MS
Died: Apr 29, 1967, Urbana, IL
Inst: Guitar/Harmonica

Father was Dewitt Lenoir, mother was Roberta Ratliff, both guitarists; raised/worked on father's farm from childhood; learned guitar from father, 1937; left home to work outside music through South from early 40s; worked w Sonny Boy Williamson (Alex Miller)/Elmore James, New York Inn, New Orleans, LA, early 40s; settled in Chicago, IL, 1949; worked outside music with frequent night gigs w Memphis Minnie/Big Maceo/Muddy Waters in local club dates, Chicago, 1949 into 50s; worked w Bill Broonzy, Sylvio's, Chicago, 1949; formed own JB and His Bayou Boys working club dates, Chicago, from 1950; rec Chess label, Chicago, 1951; rec JOB label, Chicago, 1952-4; rec Parrot label, Chicago, 1954-5; frequently w own band at White Rose Tavern/Sylvio's/Happy Home Club/Pepper's/Gate of Horn/others, Chicago, through 50s into 60s; rec Checker label, Chicago, 1955-8; owned/operated Club Lolease, Chicago, late 50s; worked Bill Broonzy Benefit Concert, KAM Temple, Chicago, 1957; rec Shad label, NYC, 1958; worked State Univ of New York, Buffalo, NY, 1959; Tay May Club, Chicago, c1960; rec VJ/Decca/Blue Horizon labels, Chicago, 1960; rec USA label, Chicago, 1963; worked Fickle Pickle, Chicago, 1963; rec CBS label, Chicago, 1965; worked Western Hall, Chicago, 1965; toured w American Folk Blues Festival working concert dates through England/Europe, 1965 (por of Hamburg, Ger, concert rel Fontana label); worked Sylvio's, Chicago, 1966; rec Polydor label, Champaign, IL, c1966; toured Europe working concerts, 1966; suffered injuries in auto accident, consequently suffering heart attack; DOA Mercy Hospital; buried Salem Church Cemetery, Monticello, MS; heard on ST of UK film BLUES LIKE SHOWERS OF RAIN, 1970

Personal: Married Ella Louise. 3 children. Given names were initials only

Songs: Born Dead/Carrie Lee/Don't Dog Your Woman/Don't Touch My Head/Eisenhower Blues/Feeling Good/I'm in Korea/Korea Blues/Natural Man/Need Somebody's Help/Round and Round/Slow Down/Vietnam Blues/What Have I Done?

J B Lenoir *Photo by Sylvia Pitcher. Courtesy* Living Blues *Magazine*

Infl by: Bill Broonzy/Big Boy Crudup/Lightnin' Hopkins/Jim Jackson/Blind Lemon Jefferson

Quote: "JB Lenoir was consistently good, and at times brilliant. His vocals were high pitched, relaxed, smooth, full of enthusiasm, his guitar simple and effective"—John Holt, *Blues World* magazine (UK), Jul 1967, p 6

References: Chicago Breakdown, Mike Rowe, Eddison Press Ltd, 1973
Blues Unlimited magazine (UK), Sept 1964, pp 5, 6

LENORE, J B
(see Lenoir, J B)

LEROY
(see Chatman, Peter)

LEROY, BABY FACE
(see Foster, Leroy)

LEVEE JOE
(see Weldon, Will)

LEWIS, FURRY
(see Lewis, Walter)

LEWIS, JOHNIE *"Johnnie"*
Born: c1910, Eufaula (Barbour Co), AL
Inst: Guitar

Born/raised on farm; left home to hobo through Mississippi/Georgia working outside music from 14 years of age; taught self guitar in late 20s; continued working outside music with frequent party work through South through 30s; settled in Chicago, IL, late 30s; worked outside music with some club work, Chicago, late 30s into 70s; app in UK film CHICAGO BLUES, 1970 (shown on OMNIBUS, BBC-1-TV, London, Eng); rec Arhoolie label, Chicago, 1970-1; worked Univ of Chicago Folk Festival, Chicago, 1972

Personal: Married (1933-)

Johnie Lewis *Photo by C Strachwitz/Arhoolie Records*

Songs: Baby Listen to Me Howl/Can't Hardly Get Along/Hobo Blues/I'm Gonna Quit My Baby/Mistake in My Life/My Little Gal/My Mother Often Told Me/North Carolina Blues/Uncle Sam

Infl by: Aaron "T-Bone" Walker

Quote: "Johnnie Lewis is a real find, a singer of calibre and a fine slide guitarist"—Paul Oliver, *Jazz Journal* magazine (UK), Oct 1971, p 31

LEWIS, JOHNNY
(see Louis, Joe Hill)

LEWIS, KATE
(see Cox, Ida)

LEWIS, NOAH
Born: Sept 3, 1895, Henning (Lauderdale Co), TN
Died: Feb 7, 1961, Ripley, TN
Inst: Harmonica

Father was Daniel Lewis, a farmer; born on Glimpse farm outside Henning, TN; taught self harmonica as child; frequently worked outside music on local farms from childhood; moved to Ripley, TN, where he worked parties/streets for tips from c1912; frequently w Gus Cannon working streets/dances in Ripley area, 1916-20; frequently worked outside music in area with some house parties/picnics w Sleepy John Estes, Brownsville, TN, through teens; frequently worked as single or with local musicians/bands at country dances/frolics/picnics/parties/crap games/suppers/coalyards between Ripley/Henning, TN, areas through 20s; frequently worked as single or with Memphis Jug Band on streets/parks for tips, Memphis, TN, c1926-30; rec w Gus Cannon's Jug Stompers, Victor label, Memphis, 1928; rec under own name, Victor label, Memphis, 1929-30; rec w own jug band, Victor/Bluebird label, Memphis, 1930; returned to Ripley, TN, to work outside music with occasional club/juke/dance/party work in area, c1930 through 40s; mostly inactive due to illness, Ripley, from 50s; suffered frost

Cannon's Jug Stompers (Gus Cannon/Ashley Thompson/Noah Lewis) *Courtesy Sheldon Harris Collection*

bite and entered Lauderdale Hospital where both feet were amputated but died of blood poisoning; buried Morrow Cemetery, Henning, TN

Personal: Married. 1 child

Song: Minglewood Blues

Quotes: "One of the greatest pre-World War II harmonica players"—Bob Eagle, *Alley Music* magazine (Australia), May 1970, p 13

"His playing had a very beautiful, controlled quality, emotionally expressive and intensely personal"—Bengt Olsson, *Memphis Blues*, Studio Vista, 1970

Reference: Memphis Blues, Bengt Olsson, Studio Vista, 1970

LEWIS, SMILEY *"Smiling"*

Courtesy Institute of Jazz Studies

Born: Jul 5, 1920, Union (St James Parish), LA
Died: Oct 7, 1966, New Orleans, LA
Inst: Piano

Father was Amos Lemons; mother was Lilly Johnson; born Overton Amos Lemons; interested in music early; moved to New Orleans, LA, to work frequently in Thomas Jefferson Band in area from 1931; frequently worked local clubs like Beck's Restaurant/Dalio's/The Court of Two Sisters/other clubs/bars/tea rooms/terminals in New Orleans area, late 30s through 40s; rec DeLuxe label, New Orleans, 1947; worked Dew Drop Inn/The Hideaway/others, New Orleans, LA, late 40s; worked El Morocco Club, New Orleans, 1949; frequently rec Imperial label, New Orleans, 1950-60; frequently worked as single in local clubs/lounges in New Orleans and often toured through Tennessee/Ohio/Gulf Coast areas working clubs through 50s; rec ST for film BABY DOLL, 1956; rec OKeh/Dot labels, New Orleans (?), mid-60s; rec Loma label, New Orleans, 1965; died of cancer; buried St James AMH Cemetery, Convent, LA

Personal: Married Dorothy Estes

Songs: The Bells Are Ringing/Blue Monday/Down the Road/Down Yonder We Go Ballin'/Hook, Line and Sinker/I Hear You Knocking/One Night of Sin/Real Gone Lover/Some Day/Tee-Nah-Nah/Too Many Drivers

Infl by: Roosevelt Sykes/Isidoe "Tuts" Washington

Infl to: Jimmy Dawkins

Quotes: "One of the greatest blues shouters of the 1950s"—Mike Leadbitter, *Blues Unlimited* magazine (UK), Dec 1971, p 29

"Smiley Lewis was a particularly important artist in the cosmic scheme of New Orleans R&B . . ." —John Broven, *Blues Unlimited* magazine (UK), Mar 1975, p 12

"Smiley Lewis . . . was among the very most enjoyable of the artists who recorded in the New Orleans R&B heyday of the 1950s . . ."—Jim DeKoster, *Living Blues* magazine, Mar 1977, p 32

Reference: Blues Unlimited, Mar/Apr 1975, p 12

LEWIS, TOMMY
(see Watts, Louis)

LEWIS, WALTER *"Furry"*
Born: Mar 6, 1893, Greenwood (Leflore Co), MS
Died: Sep 14, 1981, Memphis, TN
Inst: Guitar/Harmonica

Father Walter Lewis Sr; mother Victoria Jackson; learned music on homemade guitar at about 6 years of age; moved to Memphis, TN, to work streets for tips from c1900; ran away from home to follow Jim Jackson in passing medicine shows c1906-8; returned to Memphis to work w WC Handy Orch (or single) in local taverns/speakeasies/dance halls/house parties/streets/suppers/picnics/frolics/fish fries/dances or occasional passing tent/medicine shows through area, c1908-16; frequently hoboed through South working as itinerant singer/guitarist and suffered loss of leg in train accident, 1916; returned to Memphis to form group w Jim Jackson/Will Shade/Gus Cannon working Pee Wee's/Big Grundy's/Cham Fields/BB Ander-

Photo by Steve LaVere

son's/other clubs and occasional street work c1916 into 20s; toured w Doctor Willie Lewis Medicine Show working through Arkansas/Mississippi c1920; frequently worked w Memphis Minnie/Blind Lemon Jefferson/Texas Alexander/others in riverboats/jukes/dives through South into 20s; worked mostly outside music with occasional house parties in Memphis area, 1923-66; occasionally worked w Will Shade's Memphis Jug Band in Church's Park (WC Handy Park)/streets/clubs/dances/parties in Memphis with some touring late 20s; rec Vocalion label, NYC, NY, 1927; rec Victor label, Memphis, 1928; rec Vocalion label, Memphis, 1929; rec Folkways label, Memphis, 1959; rec Prestige-Bluesville label, Memphis, 1961; app in documentary film THE BLUES, 1963; worked Bitter Lemon Coffeehouse, Memphis, c1963; worked w Willie Borum/Gus Cannon, New York Univ and other concert dates, NYC, 1963; Chicago Folk Festival, Chicago, IL, 1964; rec Rounder label, Memphis, 1963; worked Memphis Blues Festival, Memphis, 1966-9 (por 1968 concert rel Sire-Blue Horizon label); toured w Memphis Blues Society Show working concert dates across US, 1966; rec Rounder label, Memphis, 1967-8; toured w Alabama State Troupers rock road show working concert dates, late 60s; worked Preservation Hall, New Orleans, LA, 1968; rec Biograph/Matchbox labels, Memphis, 1968; rec w Bukka White, Asp label, Memphis, 1968; worked Electric Circus, NYC, 1969; rec w Bukka White and others, Adelphi label, Memphis, 1969; worked Cafe A-Go-Go, NYC, c1970; Berkeley Blues Festival, Univ of California, Berkeley, CA, 1970; Beloit Col, Beloit, WI, 1970; app on HOMEWOOD SHOW, PBS-TV, 1970; worked Washington Blues Festival, Howard Univ, Washington, DC, 1970; app in film ROOTS OF AMERICAN MUSIC: COUNTRY & URBAN MUSIC (pt 1), 1971; worked Gaslight Club, NYC, 1971 (por rel Ampex label); River City Blues Festival, Ellis Auditorium, Memphis, TN, 1971-3 (por 1973 concert heard VOA-radio); worked Long Beach Civic Auditorium, Long Beach, CA, 1971 (por rel Elektra label); Pasadena Civic Auditorium, Pasadena, CA, 1971 (por rel Elektra label); Univ of Chicago, Chicago, IL, 1972; Delta Blues Festival, Univ of Arkansas, Fayetteville, AR, 1972; app in French film BLUES UNDER THE SKIN, 1972; app in French film OUT OF THE BLACKS INTO THE BLUES (pt 1: Along the Old Man River), 1972; app in film short THINKING OUT LOUD, 1972; toured w Memphis Blues Caravan working college circuit across US, 1972-6; rec w Don Nix, Stax label, Memphis, c1974; app on Johnny Carson's TONIGHT Show, NBC-TV, 1974; worked A Salute to WC Handy Show, Henderson, KY, 1974; Hotel Pontchartrain, Detroit, MI, 1974; Peanut's Pub, Memphis, TN, 1974; app in film WW & THE DIXIE DANCEKINGS, 1975; worked Jubilee Jazz Hall, Memphis, 1975; film clips shown on OMNIBUS Show (ep: The Friendly Invasion), BBC-TV, London, Eng, 1975; worked Cornell Folk Festival, Ithaca, NY, 1975; w Memphis Blues Caravan, Performing Arts Center, Milwaukee, WI, 1976; app on MAC DAVIS Show, NBC-TV, 1977; app on GOOD MORNIN' BLUES, PBS-TV, 1978; worked occasional festivals into 80s; app in film, THIS IS ELVIS, 1981; died of lung cancer; buried Hollywood Cemetery, Memphis

Personal: "Furry" was childhood pet name

Songs: A Chicken Ain't Nothin' But a Bird/Brownsville/East St Louis/Furry's (Worried) Blues/Grand Central Station/I Will Turn Your Money Green/I'm Black/I've Got a Bird to Whistle/Judge Boyshoy Blues/Let's Shake Hand in Hand/My Dog Got the Measles/Oh Babe/Paer Lee/Skinny Woman/Take Your Time Rag/Why Don't You Come Home Blues?

Award/Honor: Made Honorary Colonel of the State of Tennessee, 1973

Infl by: Blind Joe

Infl to: Dave Van Ronk

Quotes: "Furry's expressiveness and subtlety have an almost intimate feeling. He is in many ways one of the most personal blues singers"—Sam B Charters, Folkways album FA-3823

"His individuality lies in his unconventional use of the guitar as a percussive instrument and as a supplementary vocal line"—Pete Welding, Fantasy album 24703

"His style is highly anecdotal and emotionally charged, brimming with tales of hard times"—Martha Gilmore, *Downbeat* magazine, Feb 4, 1971, p 28

References; Playboy magazine, Apr 1970, pp 100-4, 114, 193-4

Memphis Blues, Bengt Olsson, Studio Vista Ltd, 1970

Sweet as the Showers of Rain, Samuel B Charters, Oak Publications, 1977

LIGHTFOOT, ALEXANDER *"George"/"Papa"*
(aka: Little Papa Walter/Papa George)
Born: Mar 2, 1924, Natchez (Adams Co), MS
Died: Nov 28, 1971, Natchez, MS
Inst: Harmonica/Washboard

Father was Andrew Lightfoot; mother was Marie Donaldson; taught self harmonica as youth; frequently worked outside music, Natchez, MS, into 40s; worked Project Bar and other clubs/bars in Natchez, MS/New Orleans, LA, late 40s into 50s; rec w The Gondoliers, Peacock label, Houston, TX, 1949; rec Sulton label, Natchez, 1950; rec Aladdin label, New Orleans, 1952; toured w Jack Dupree working club dates through

Alexander "George" Lightfoot
Photo by Steve La Vere. Courtesy Living Blues *Magazine*

South, 1953; rec w Jack Dupree, King label, Cincinnati, OH, 1953; toured extensively as sideman in various package shows including Fats Domino/Dinah Washington/Sonny Boy Williamson (Alex Miller)/others through 50s; rec Imperial/Aladdin labels, New Orleans, 1954; rec Savoy label, Atlanta, GA, 1954; won Horace Heidt talent contest and then toured extensively w Horace Heidt Orch working theater circuit, 1954-8; toured w Smiley Lewis working club dates through Tennessee/Ohio through 50s; app in film short SPOOKY LOOT, c1956; worked as DJ/entertainer on local radio show, Natchez, MS, late 50s; worked mostly outside music, Natchez, from late 50s; rec Vault label, Jackson, MS, 1969; worked Ann Arbor Blues Festival, Ann Arbor, MI, 1970; entered Natchez Charity Hospital where he died of respiratory/cardiac arrest; buried Natchez Colored Cemetery, Natchez, MS

Songs: Ah Come On Honey/I Heard Somebody Cryin'/Love My Baby/My Woman Is Tired of Me Lyin'/New Mean Old Train/Night Time/Take It Witcha/Wine, Women, Whiskey

Quote: "One of the most original and imaginative harmonica players in Rhythm & Blues"—Steve LaVere, *Living Blues* magazine, Summer 1973, p 6

References: Blues Unlimited magazine (UK), Dec 1969, p 12
Living Blues magazine, Summer 1973, p 6

LIGHTNIN' JR
(see Dupree, William)
(see Williams, L C)

LIGHTNIN' SLIM
(see Hicks, Otis)

LINCOLN, CHARLEY/CHARLIE
(see Hicks, Charlie)

LIPSCOMB, MANCE
Born: Apr 9, 1895, Navasota (Brazos Co), TX
Died: Jan 30, 1976, Navasota, TX
Inst: Fiddle/Guitar

Mance Lipscomb *Photo by Jim Marshall. Courtesy C Strachwitz/Arhoolie Records*

Father was Charlie Lipscomb, a former slave who became professional fiddler after emancipation; mother was Janie Pratt; born on farm near Navasota, TX; one of 11 children; raised/worked on farm from childhood; learned fiddle from father (later taught self guitar) and frequently acc father at local picnics/dances/breakdowns/suppers/parties, Navasota area, c1909-11; worked mostly outside music (as sharecropper farmer) in Brazos bottom area with frequent work at suppers/dances/schools/beer joints/church meetings, 1911-56; moved to Houston, TX, to work outside music, 1956-7; returned to Navasota to work outside music, 1958 into 60s; rec 77/Arhoolie/Decca labels, Navasota, 1960; worked Texas Heritage Festival, Houston, 1960-1; app on MACK McCORMICK AND FRIENDS, KUHF-FM-radio, Houston, 1960-1; worked Univ of California Folk Music Festival, San Francisco, CA, 1961; Berkeley Folk Festival, Univ of California, Berkeley, CA, 1961-3; worked small clubs/coffeehouses on West Coast, early 60s; rec Reprise label, Houston, TX, 1961; worked Sugar Hill, San Francisco, 1961; app in film THE BLUES, 1962; worked Ash Grove, Los Angeles, CA, 1963; Univ of California, Los Angeles, 1963; Monterey Folk Festival, Monterey, CA, 1963; Cabale Club, Berkeley, CA, 1963-4 (por 1964 concert rel Arhoolie label); rec Arhoolie label, Berkeley, 1964; worked Town Hall, NYC, NY, 1965; Univ of Chicago Folklore Society, Chicago, IL, 1965; Newport Folk Festival, Newport, RI, 1965; Brandeis Univ, Waltham, MA, 1965; Berkeley Blues Festival, Univ of California, Berkeley, 1966 (por rel Arhoolie label); Univ of California, Santa Barbara, CA, 1966 (por rel Arhoolie label); app on SOME OF THE PEOPLE, KUHF-FM-radio, Houston, TX, 1966; app in film THE BLUES ACCORDIN' TO LIGHTNIN' HOPKINS, 1968; worked Festival of American Folklife, Washington, DC, 1968; Univ of Texas, Houston, TX, 1968; rec Arhoolie label, Navasota, TX, 1968; worked King Hall, Berkeley, CA, 1969; rec Arhoolie label, Berkeley, 1969; worked Wisconsin Blues Festival, Beloit, WI, 1970; Ann Arbor Blues Festival, Ann Arbor, MI, 1970; rec ST for UK film BLUES LIKE SHOWERS OF RAIN, 1970; worked Festival of American Folklife, Washington, DC, 1970; Washington Blues Festival, Howard Univ, Washington, DC, 1970; app in film ROOTS OF AMERICAN MUSIC: COUNTRY & URBAN MUSIC (pt 1), 1971; app in Les Blank film bio A WELL SPENT LIFE, 1971; worked Texas Rose Cafe, Houston, TX, 1971; Liberty Hall, Dallas, TX, 1971; Notre Dame Blues Festival, South Bend, IN, 1971; Univ of Pittsburgh Blues Festival, Pittsburgh, PA, 1971; Boston Univ, Boston, MA, 1971; Ash Grove, Los Angeles, CA, 1971-3; Mother Blues, Dallas, TX, 1972; The Basement Coffee House, College Station, TX, 1972; clip shown in French film BLUES UNDER THE SKIN, 1972; app in French film OUT OF THE BLACKS INTO THE BLUES (pt 2: A Way to Escape the Ghetto), 1972; worked Philadelphia Folk Festival, Schwenksville, PA, 1972; Sonoma State Col, Rohnert Park, CA, 1972; Univ of Utah, Salt Lake City, UT, 1972; rec Arhoolie label, Berkeley, CA, 1973; worked Folk Festival, San Antonio, TX, 1973; Monterey Jazz Festival, Monterey, CA, 1973; Univ of Vermont, Burlington, VT, 1973; mostly inactive in music from 1974 due to illness; entered Grimes Memorial Hospital where he died of heart trouble; buried Rest Haven Cemetery, Navasota, TX

Songs: Ain't You Sorry?/Black Gal/Blues in G/Blues in the Bottle/'Bout a Spoonful/Captain, Captain/I'm Looking for My Jesus/Knocking Down Windows/Long Tall Girl Got Stuck on Me/Mama Don't Dog Me/Mance's Blues/Mother Had a Sick Child/Mr Tom/Rag in G/Run Sinner Run/Shake Shake Mama/So Different Blues/Sugar Babe It's All Over Now/Take Me Back Babe/Texas Blues/What You Gonna Do When Death Comes Creepin' at Your Room?/Whiskey Blues/Willie Poor Boy/You Gonna Quit Me Baby?

Infl by: Blind Lemon Jefferson/Memphis Minnie/Robert Timm/Hamp Walker

Infl to: Bob Baxter/Chambers Brothers/Dave Cohen/Barbara Dane/Bob Dylan/The Grateful Dead/Janis Joplin/Luke Miles/Bernard Pearl/Mark Spolestra/Kurt Van Sickle

Quotes: "Mance Lipscomb is *not* properly a blues singer. He is more—being of that generation when the blues were but one, unseparate stream in the vast flow of Negro traditions. From such a man you will hear ballads, breakdowns, reels, shouts, drags, jubilees *and blues.* You will hear the firm, brisk rhythm meant for dancers, the clear ring of expressive song, and the energetic melding of tradition and personal creation. And if you describe the artist with accuracy, it will be with his own apt word: songster"
—Mack McCormick, Arhoolie album F1001

"Although he never recorded until he was 65, he came to be regarded as one of the finest country blues singer-guitarists active in the 1960s and 70s"
—Jim O'Neal, *Living Blues* magazine, Jan 1976, p 8

References: I Say Me For A Parable: The Oral Autobiography of Mance Lipscomb, Texas Bluesman, Glen Alyn, WW North & Co, 1993

Guitar Player magazine, Mar 1974, pp 12, 26

LISTON, VIRGINIA

Courtesy Sheldon Harris Collection

Born: c1890 (unconfirmed)
Died: Jun 1932, St Louis, MO (unconfirmed)

Reportedly sang blues at Segal Theater, Philadelphia, PA, c1912; settled in Washington, DC, where she was known for her open-house hospitality to musicians/singers into early 20s; teamed w Sam H Gray to tour (as "Liston & Liston") TOBA circuit working vaudeville theaters through South, 1920-3; worked Lyric Theater, New Orleans, LA, 1921; Monogram Theater, Philadelphia, PA, 1921; Rafe's Paradise Theater, Atlantic City, NJ, 1921; settled in NYC to frequently work Harlem theaters from c1923; rec w Clarence Williams/Louis Armstrong/others, OKeh label, NYC, 1923-5; rec w Sam Gray, OKeh label, NYC, 1924; worked Elmore Theater, Pittsburgh, PA, 1924; worked theater dates in Detroit, MI, 1924-6; toured theaters on East Coast, 1924; toured in ELIZA SCANDALS Revue working theaters through Georgia/North Carolina/Florida, 1925; rec Vocalion label, NYC, 1926; worked theater dates, Indianapolis, IN, 1927; rec w Clarence Williams Washboard Band, OKeh label, NYC, 1929; reportedly retired to St Louis, MO, to become active in church work from c1929

Personal: Married Sam H Gray, actor/musician (c1920-5); married Charles Harry Lee Smith (1929-32)

Songs: Bed Time Blues/Bill Draw/Don't Agitate Me Blues/Don't Irritate Me Blues/Happy Shout/Jealous Hearted Blues/Night Latch Key Blues/Oh What a Time/Put Your Mind on No One Man/Sally Long Blues/You Don't Know My Mind Blues/You Thought I Was Blind But Now I Can See

Quote: "One of the earliest recorded Negro singers was Virginia Liston"—Paul Oliver, Blue Horizon album 763227

LITTLE BOY BLUE
(see Williamson, Sonny Boy)

LITTLE BROTHER
(see Montgomery, Eurreal)

LITTLE ESTHER
(see Phillips, Esther)

LITTLE HENRY
(see Gray, Henry)

LITTLE HUDSON
(see Shower, Hudson)

LITTLE JOE
(see Louis, Joe Hill)

LITTLE JOHNNY
(see Jones, John)

LITTLE JUNIOR/JR
(see Johnson, Luther)
(see Parker, Herman)

LITTLE LAURA
(see Dukes, Laura)

LITTLE LOVIN' HENRY
(see Byrd, Roy)

LITTLE LUTHER
(see Johnson, Luther)

LITTLE MACK
(see Simmons, Mack)

LITTLE MAN
(see Johnson, James)

LITTLE MILTON
(see Campbell, Milton)

LITTLE OTIS
(see Rush, Otis)

LITTLE PAPA JOE
(see Williams, Joseph Leon)

LITTLE PAPA WALTER
(see Lightfoot, Alexander)

LITTLE RAY
(see Agee, Raymond)

LITTLE RICHARD
(see Penniman, Richard)

LITTLE SAM
(see Broonzy, William)

LITTLE SISTER
(see Scruggs, Irene)

LITTLE SON
(see Broonzy, William)

LITTLE SON JOE
(see Lawlars, Ernest)

LITTLE SONNY
(see Willis, Aaron)

LITTLE T-BONE
(see Rankin, R S)

LITTLE TEMPLE
(see Jenkins, Gus)

LITTLE WALTER
(see Jacobs, Marion Walter)

LITTLE WALTER J
(see Jacobs, Marion Walter)

LITTLE WALTER JR
(see Smith, George)

LITTLE WOLF
(see Shines, John)

LITTLEFIELD, *"Little"* WILLIE
Born: Sept 16, 1931, Houston (Harris Co), TX
Inst: Guitar/Piano

Interested in music at early age and sang/played guitar in local Baptist church at about 6 years of age; took some piano lessons at about 7 years of age; worked El Dorado Ballroom, Houston, TX, c1945; rec Eddie's label, Houston, 1946; settled in Los Angeles, CA, working locally from 1949; rec Modern label, Los Angeles, 1949-51; rec Federal label, Los Angeles, 1952-3; formed own band and toured clubs across US from early 50s; rec Federal label, Cincinnati, OH, 1953; rec Argyle label, 1956; rec Rhythm label, 1958; worked mostly clubs/bars in San Francisco, CA, area c1962-8; worked club dates, Sunnydale, CA, 1967; Red Stag Club, San Jose, CA, 1968-70; Univ of California Extension Center, San Francisco, 1973; San Francisco Bay Blues Festival, San Francisco, 1973; Red Carpet Club, San Jose, 1973; Delta Bell, Bethel Island, CA, 1974; Minnie's Can Do Club, San Francisco, 1975; Mac's Old House, Antioch, CA, 1975-6; Red Stag Club, San Jose, 1976-7; worked club dates in Santa Cruz, CA, 1976; Green Earth Cafe, San Francisco, 1977; Angeleo's Steak House, San Jose, 1977; San Francisco Blues Festival, McLaren Park, San Francisco, 1977

Songs: Kansas City/Little Willie's Boogie/Ruby, Ruby

Infl by: Charles Brown

Infl to: Fats Domino

Reference: Blues Unlimited magazine (UK), Mar 1969, pp 12, 14

LITTLEJOHN, JOHN *"Johnny"*
Born: Apr 16, 1931, Lake (Scott Co), MS
Inst: Guitar

Born John Funchess; born/raised/worked on farm from childhood; moved to Jackson, MS, c1937; taught self guitar at about 9 years of age; left home to work outside music with frequent work at fish fries/house parties through Delta area into 40s; formed own band to work local dances/picnics/parties while continuing outside music work, Drew, MS, late 40s; app on WOKJ-radio, Jackson, MS, late 40s; left home to continue working outside music through Arkansas/New York/Indiana/Illinois into 50s; formed own group to work club dates, Ann Arbor, MI/Detroit, MI, area, early 50s; occasionally worked w John Brim Band, early 50s; worked Club 99, Joliet, IL, 1951-5; Twist City, Chicago, IL, c1952; w Jimmy Reed, Pulaski

"Little" Willie Littlefield

Photo by E Andrew McKinney. Courtesy Living Blues Magazine

John Littlejohn *Photo by Chris Strachwitz, Arhoolie Records*

Hall, Gary, IN, 1952-4; rec Ace label, New Orleans, LA, early 50s; settled in Chicago, IL, to work outside music c1953 into 70s; worked Pete's Tavern, Chicago, 1953; Club Zanzibar, Chicago, 1954; rec acc to many bluesmen, Chicago, into 60s; rec Margaret/Weis/TDS/Arhoolie labels, Chicago, 1968; toured w Howlin' Wolf Band working clubs/concerts/festivals out of Chicago into Toronto, Can, 1968; worked Sportsman's Club, Chicago, 1968; Chicago Blues Festival, Chicago, 1969; Bill Street Club, Chicago, 1969; Walton's Corner, Chicago, 1969; George's Log Cabin, San Francisco, CA, 1969; Sylvio's, Chicago, 1970; Flamingo Club, Chicago, 1970; Riviera Lounge, Chicago, 1970-2; Alice's Revisited, Chicago, 1970; Five Stages, Chicago, 1970; Florence's Lounge, Chicago, 1970; app on MADE IN CHICAGO, WTTW-TV, Chicago, c1970; toured w Jimmy Rogers group working club dates on East Coast, 1970; frequently w Jimmy Rogers at Big Duke's Club, Chicago, 1971; worked Ma Bea's Lounge, Chicago, 1971-5; toured Finland working concert dates, 1971; worked Notre Dame Blues Festival, South Bend, IN, 1971; Colonial Tavern, Toronto, Can, 1971; Wise Fools, Chicago, 1972; Diamond's Den, Chicago, 1972; Golddigger Lounge, Chicago, 1972; Avenue Lounge, Chicago, 1972; The Post, Chicago, 1972; The Dump, Detroit, MI, 1972; rec w Bob Riedy Band, Rounder label, Chicago, 1973; rec BluesWay label, Chicago (?), 1973; worked The Attic, Chicago, 1974; Urban Blues Festival, Auditorium Theater, Chicago, 1974; Shamrock Lounge, DeKalb, IL, 1975; Wise Fools, Chicago, 1975; Pori Jazz Festival, Pori, Finland, 1975; Eddie Shaw's Place, Chicago, 1975; Biddy Mulligan's Bar, Chicago, 1975; Zoo Bar, Lincoln, NE, 1976; Zorba's, Cicero, IL, 1976; Riviera Lounge, Chicago, 1976; Kingston Mines, Chicago, 1977

Personal: Married. Has children. Surname also "Little John" in early references

Songs: Been Around the World/Dream/Johnny's Jive/Reelin' and Rockin'/Slidin' Home/Treat Me Wrong/Worried Head

Infl by: Howlin' Wolf/Elmore James/BB King/Henry Martin/Muddy Waters

Quote: "One of Chicago's finest guitarist-singers" —Jeff Carlson, *Whiskey, Women And . . .* magazine, Jun 1973, p 12

References: Blues Unlimited magazine (UK), Jun 1972, pp 12-14

Whiskey, Women And . . . magazine, Jun 1973, pp 12-13

LOCKWOOD, ROBERT *"Junior"/"Jr"*
(aka: Robert Jr)
Born: Mar 27, 1915, Marvell (Phillips Co), AR
Inst: Guitar/Harmonica

Father was Robert Lockwood, mother Estella Coleman; one of 2 children; mother later married Robert Johnson, noted bluesman; moved to Helena, AR, as child; moved briefly to St Louis, MO, at 7 years of age; returned to Helena but dropped out of school to work outside music, late 20s; first interest in music was piano but switched to guitar, early 30s, with some lessons from Robert Johnson; frequently worked local house parties, Helena area, from early 30s; left home to hobo widely as itinerant musician working parties/picnics/streets through Delta area of Mississippi through 30s; worked w Sonny Boy Williamson (Alex Miller) in Clarksdale, MS, area, 1938-9; frequently worked w Howlin' Wolf/Baby Boy Warren/others or solo, Church's Park (WC Handy Park), Memphis, TN, c1938; frequently worked St Louis, MO, area, 1939-40; frequently rec acc to various bluesmen in Chicago, IL, 1940; rec Bluebird label, Chicago, 1941; frequently worked w Sonny Boy Williamson (Alex Miller) on local streets for tips, Helena, AR, 1941 to mid-40s; app w Sonny Boy Williamson (Alex Miller) on KING BISCUIT TIME, KFFA-radio, Helena, 1941-3; toured w King Biscuit Time Boys working theaters/clubs/jukes out of Helena, 1941-3; app w Starkey Brothers on MOTHER'S BEST FLOUR HOUR Show, KFFA-radio, Helena, 1943-4; continued working jukes/parties in W Memphis, AR/St Louis, MO/Chicago, IL, c1944-9; app on KXLR-radio, Little Rock, AR, 1947; frequently worked w BB King Beale Streeters in local clubs/bars, Memphis, TN, 1948; settled in Chicago, IL, 1950; rec Mercury label, Chicago, 1951; worked as sideman w Eddie Boyd/Roosevelt Sykes/Muddy Waters/others in local club dates, Chicago, through 50s; rec JOB label, Chicago, 1953; rec acc w Little Walter, Checker label, Chicago, 1953-7; rec w Otis Spann, Candid label, NYC, NY, 1960; worked w Sunnyland Slim, Buckingham Club, Chicago, 1960; rec w Sunnyland Slim, Decca label, Chicago, 1960; frequently worked/rec w Willie Mabon Band, Mad label, Chicago, 1960; moved to Cleveland, OH, to work outside music, 1961 into 70s; formed own band to frequently work Wonder Bar Club and others, Cleveland, through 60s; worked Chicago Blues Festival, Chicago, 1969; rec ST for UK film BLUES LIKE SHOWERS OF RAIN, 1970; worked Ann Arbor Blues Festival, Ann Arbor, MI, 1970; Smithsonian Festival, Washington, DC, 1971; Festival of American Folklife, Montreal, Can, 1971; w Dave Griggs Band at local club/concert dates,

Robert Jr Lockwood *Photo by Doug Fulton. Courtesy* Living Blues *Magazine*

Cleveland, 1971; rec Big Star label, Detroit, MI (?), c1972; worked Ann Arbor Blues Festival, Ann Arbor, MI, 1972; rec w The Aces, Delmark label, Chicago, 1972; worked Univ of Miami Blues Festival, Coral Gables, FL, 1972-5; St Lawrence Centre, Toronto, Can, 1972; toured college circuit working concerts/festivals across US, 1972; worked Joe's Place, Cambridge, MA, 1973; The Kove, Kent, OH, 1973; rec acc to Roosevelt Sykes, Delmark label, Chicago, 1973; rec Trix label, Hiram, OH/Cleveland, OH, 1973; worked Richard's, Atlanta, GA, 1974; Ann Arbor Blues/Jazz Festival, Windsor, Can, 1974; toured w Blues Festival working concert dates through Japan, 1974; worked Yubin Chokin Hall, Tokyo, Japan, 1974 (por rel Trio/Advent labels); worked w Willie Mabon, Berlin Jazz Festival, Berlin, Ger, 1974; Smiling Dog Saloon, Cleveland, OH, 1974; The Grapes of Wrath, Cleveland, 1974; Keystone Korner, Berkeley, CA, 1975; Monterey Jazz Festival, Monterey, CA, 1975 (por heard KEST-radio, San Francisco); Nassau Community Col, Garden City, NY, 1975; Univ of Vermont, Burlington, VT, 1975; rec Trix label, Parma, OH, 1975; worked The Flipside, Cleveland, OH, 1975-6; Faragher's Back Room, Cleveland, 1976; Midwest Blues Festival, Univ of Notre Dame, South Bend, IN, 1976; rec Trix label, Cleveland, 1976; worked State Univ of New York, Buffalo, NY, 1977; John Henry Folk Festival, Camp Virgil Tate, Princeton, WV, 1977; Elsewhere Lounge, Chicago, IL, 1977; Coach House, Cleveland, 1977

Note: Although this singer is commonly known as Robert Jr Lockwood, ostensibly after stepfather (Robert Johnson), name is actually Robert Lockwood Jr, after true father

Personal: Married Annie ———. 2 children

Songs: Little Boy Blue/My Daily Wish/That's All Right

Infl by: Charlie Christian/Doc Clayton/Robert Johnson

Infl to: Luther Tucker/Jimmy Rogers/Joe Willie

Quotes: "Lockwood has real class . . . he is a consummate guitarist and vocalist"—Steve Tomashefsky, *Living Blues* magazine, Autumn 1974, p 11

"He is the most innovative and creative guitar style in current blues"—Pete Crawford, *Living Blues* magazine, May 1975, p 44

References: Living Blues magazine, Spring 1973, pp 18-19

Blues Unlimited magazine (UK), Jun 1973, pp 20, 30

LOFTON, *"Cripple"* CLARENCE
(aka: Albert Clemens?)

Courtesy Sheldon Harris Collection

Born: Mar 28, 1887, Kingsport (Sullivan Co), TN
Died: Jan 9, 1957, Chicago, IL
Inst: Piano

Father was Walter Lofton; mother was Annie Washington; reportedly disabled from birth and raised in Kingsport, TN, area; moved to Chicago, IL, 1917; frequently worked local bars/rent parties/cutting contests, Chicago, IL, 1917 through 40s; reportedly rec w Sammy Brown, Gennett label, Chicago, 1927; reportedly rec acc to many bluesmen in Chicago into early 30s; rec Vocalion/ARC label group, Chicago, 1935; owned/operated/performed at The Big Apple Tavern, Chicago, through late 30s; rec Yazoo label, Chicago, c1937; rec SoloArt/Riverside labels, Chicago, c1939; suffered accident and worked mostly outside music, Chicago, from c1940; rec Pax/Session labels, Chicago, 1943; worked occasional concert dates, Chicago, early 40s; worked local boogie woogie concert, Chicago, 1951; worked mostly outside music, Chicago, through 50s; entered Cook County Hospital where he died of blood clot in the brain; buried Mount Glenwood Cemetery, Bloom, IL

Personal: Married Estelle ———

Songs: Brown Skin Gals/I Don't Know/Mercy

Blues/Mistaken Blues/Pitchin' Boogie/Streamline Train/Travelling Blues/You've Done Tore Your Playhouse Down

Infl by: Jimmy Yancey

Infl to: Erwin Helfer/Meade Lux Lewis/John Mayall

Quotes: "Clarence Lofton was the archetypal rent party entertainer, singing, whistling, drumming and tap dancing as an adjunct to his piano playing"—Don Heckman, *BMI: The Many Worlds of Music*, Summer 1969

"Clarence Lofton was probably one of the finest and most popular pianists (especially amongst jazz fans) there has ever been"—Bob Hall/Richard Noblett, *Blues Unlimited* magazine (UK), May, 1975, p 14

Reference: Blues Unlimited magazine (UK), May 1975, pp 14-16

LONESOME LEE
(see Robinson, Jimmy Lee)

LONESOME SUNDOWN
(see Green, Cornelius)

LOUIS, JOE HILL
(aka: Chicago Sunny Boy/Johnny Lewis/Little Joe)

Courtesy Frank Driggs Collection

Born: Sept 23, 1921, Raines (Shelby Co), TN
Died: Aug 5, 1957, Memphis, TN
Inst: Drums/Guitar/Harmonica/Jew's Harp

Father was Robert Hill; mother was Mary Wilson; born Lester Hill; learned some harmonica/guitar from Will Shade as youth in early 30s; ran away from home to work outside music with frequent work in streets/dives in Robinsonville, MS, area from c1935; worked outside music at Peabody Hotel, Memphis, TN, in late 30s; frequently worked w Eddie Taylor/Willie Borum/Will Shade/Lockhart Hill/others in gambling houses/streets, Memphis, TN/West Memphis, AR, areas, early 40s; frequently worked as one man band in streets/road houses, Memphis area, through 40s; frequently hoboed through Tennessee/Arkansas/Mississippi working dances/suppers/ballgame intermissions, late 40s into 50s; rec Columbia label, NYC, NY, 1949; took over PEPTICON BOY Show (from BB King) working as "Joe Hill Louis, The Be-Bop Boy and His One Man Band," WDIA-radio, Memphis, TN, 1950; rec Modern label, Memphis, 1950-3; worked Blue Light Club, Memphis, early 50s; Brown Jug, West Memphis, AR, early 50s; Tennessee House, West Memphis, early 50s; rec Rockin' label, Memphis, 1952; rec w Walter Horton, Checker label, Chicago, IL, 1952; rec w Billy Love, Sun label, Memphis, 1953; rec Meteor label, Chicago, 1953; rec Bigtown label, Memphis, 1954; rec Ace label, West Memphis, c1954; rec House of Sound label, Memphis, 1957; entered John Gaston Hospital where he died of tetanus infection; buried Ford Chapel Cemetery, West Junction, TN

Personal: Married twice (Polly/Dorothy Mae). His brother Lockhart Hill was musician. Took name "Joe Louis" in honor of boxing champion

Songs: Blue in the Morning/Gotta Go Baby/Highway 99/I Love My Baby/Mistreat Me Woman/Nappy Head Woman/Western Union Man

Quote: "From the late 'forties until 1956, Joe Hill Louis was among the most popular figures in Memphis and the rural areas of Tennessee, Arkansas and Mississippi"—Bengt Olsson, *Memphis Blues*, Studio Vista, 1970

References: Polydor album 2383214
Memphis Blues, Bengt Olsson, Studio Vista, 1970

LOUIS, TOMMY
(see Watts, Louis)

LOUISIANA RED
(see Minter, Iverson)

LOVE, CLAYTON
Born: Nov 15, 1927, Mattson (Coahoma Co), MS
Inst: Piano

Born/raised on farm; one of 6 children; moved to Clarksdale, MS, c1939; frequently sang in local churches/schools as youth; served in US Navy where he learned piano during mid-40s; returned to Mississippi to attend Alcorn A&M Col, Lorman, MS, late 40s; worked outside music (as high school coach), Clarksdale, MS, from early 50s; occasionally worked local gigs, Clarksdale, into 50s; rec as Clayton Love & His Shufflers, Trumpet label, Jackson, MS, 1951; rec w Ray Hill Orch, Aladdin label, Chicago, IL, 1952; rec Modern/Groove labels (possibly others) through 50s; rec w Kings of Rhythm, Federal label, late 50s; moved to St Louis, MO, late 50s; worked w Ike Turner and others in local gigs through 60s; rec Bobbin label, St Louis (?), during 60s; formed own group to work hotels/lounges/clubs, St Louis, into 70s; worked Mid-Town North, St Louis, 1976; Carousel Motor Hotel, St Louis, 1976 (por rel Flash Back label); Talk of the Town, St Louis, 1976; Voyager Lounge, St Louis, 1976; w own St Louis Combo, Robert's Motel 500 Room, Chicago, IL, 1976

Songs: The Big Question/It's You/Limited Love

Infl by: Robert Johnson/Willie Love

Reference: Flash Back album MK 57-411

LOVE, WILLIE

Born: Nov 4, 1906, Duncan (Bolivar Co), MS
Died: Aug 19, 1953, Jackson, MS
Inst: Piano

Father was Willie Love Sr; mother was Ann Sheardeforee; one of at least 3 children; born/raised/worked on farm from childhood; interested in music as youth; left home to hobo through Clarksdale/Drew/Tunica/Belzoni, MS, areas working joints/barrelhouses from mid-30s; toured w Barber Parker Silver Kings Band working jukes through Mississippi, 1938-40; worked w Pinetop Perkins in jukes/clubs, Indianola, MS, late 30s; worked w Doc Ross (or as single) in gambling joints/clubs, Indianola/Greenville, MS, areas, 1940 to early 50s; frequently app on KING BISCUIT TIME, KFFA-radio, Helena, AR, from 1942; frequently toured w King Biscuit Time Boys working jukes/streets out of Helena through 40s; formed own The Three Aces group working jukes in Tunica, MS/Memphis, TN, with frequent tours through Delta area, mid-40s into 50s; worked Casa Blanca Club, Greenville, MS, 1946; app w Elmore James on WGVM-radio, Greenville, 1948-9; frequently toured w Sonny Boy Williamson (Alex Miller)/Willie Nix/Joe Willie Wilkins (as Four Aces) working jukes through Arkansas/Tennessee/Mississippi, 1949-50; app w Sonny Boy Williamson (Alex Miller), HADACOL Show, KWEM-radio, West Memphis, AR, 1949; app on own BROADWAY FURNITURE STORE Show, KWEM-radio, West Memphis, 1949-50; frequently worked outside music in Jackson, MS, from c1949 into 50s; worked Silver Dollar Cafe, Greenville, MS, 1950; rec w Sonny Boy Williamson (Alex Miller), Trumpet label, Jackson, 1951; frequently rec (under own name or w Three Aces) Trumpet label, Jackson, 1951-3; worked w Baby Boy Warren, Harlem Inn, Detroit, MI, 1952; toured w Sonny Boy Williamson (Alex Miller) working jukes through Louisiana/Texas, 1952-3; entered Baptist Hospital where he died of bronchopneumonia; buried Elmwood Cemetery, Jackson, MS

Personal: His brothers Jasper/Eddie Love were musicians. Not to be confused with pianist "Red" Billy Love

Song: Nelson Street Blues

Infl to: Little Milton/Clayton Love

Quote: "A proficient blues pianist"—Mike Leadbitter, *Blues Unlimited* magazine (UK), Oct 1973, p 13

References: Blues Unlimited magazine (UK), Oct 1973, p 13

Nothing But the Blues, Mike Leadbitter, Hanover Books, 1971

LOWERY, ROBERT *"Bob"*

Photo by Paul Kohl. Courtesy Tom Mazzolini

Born: 1932, Shuler (Union Co), AR
Inst: Guitar

Reportedly raised/worked outside music in Shuler/El Dorado, AR, areas through 40s/50s; taught self guitar by age of 17; moved to West Coast to work outside music in Oakland, CA, 1956-7, then Santa Cruz, CA, from 1958; frequently worked clubs/parties/streets in Santa Cruz/San Francisco/Capitola, CA, from 1958; sat-in w Big Mama Thornton group, Beachcomber/Gate Way Clubs, Santa Cruz, CA, early 60s; worked mostly outside music in Santa Cruz area through 60s; worked Spaulding's Club, Santa Cruz, 1973; United Bar, Santa Cruz, c1974; San Francisco Blues Festival, Golden Gate Park, San Francisco, CA, 1974; rec Blues Connoisseur label, San Francisco (?), c1974; worked Univ of California, Santa Cruz, 1975; Sophie's, Palo Alto, CA, 1975-6; Bodega, Campbell, CA, 1975; w Canned Heat group, The Savoy Club, San Francisco, 1976; Univ of Chicago Folk Festival, Chicago, IL, 1976; Santa Rosa Folk Festival, Santa Rosa, CA, 1976; app on TRADITIONAL MUSIC COLLECTIVE CONCERT, KPFA-FM-radio, Berkeley, CA, 1976; app on BLUES BY THE BAY, KPFA-FM-radio, Berkeley, 1976; worked Club Zayante, Felton, CA, 1976; rec Messaround label, San Francisco, 1976; worked American River Col, Sacramento, CA, 1976; San Francisco Blues Festival, McLaren Park, San Francisco, 1976 (por rel Jefferson label); WOW Hall, Eugene, OR, 1976

Infl by: John Lee Hooker/Lightnin' Hopkins/Lil Son Jackson/Robert Johnson/Muddy Waters

Quote: "His vocal and guitar intonations are remarkably close to [Robert] Johnson's and if one should happen to shut one's eyes, the feeling could be that Robert Johnson is performing"—Tom Mazzolini, *Living Blues* magazine, May 1976, p 33

Reference: Living Blues magazine, May 1976, p 33

LUANDREW, ALBERT
(aka: Delta Joe/Doctor Clayton's Buddy/Sunnyland [Sunny Land] Slim)
Born: Sept 5, 1907, Vance (Quitman Co), MS
Inst: Organ/Piano

Father was Rev TW Luandrew, a preacher; mother was Martha ———; born/raised/worked on farm from childhood; interested in music early and taught self piano/organ as child; frequently ran away from home to work outside music with some country dances/house parties/juke joints/roadside taverns out of Vance, MS, from c1918 into early 20s; worked Hot Shot's Club, Vance, MS, 1922; frequently hoboed through South working jukes/parties c1923-5; worked as moving picture theater pianist, Lambert, MS, 1924; settled in Memphis, TN, c1925; frequently worked w Walter Sykes and others or as single at Panama Club/Harlem Night Club/Goshorn Quarters/Pee Wee's/Hole in the Wall/others, Memphis, from c1925 through 30s; frequently toured through South working barrelhouses/honky-tonks/parties through 20s/30s; reportedly app briefly in Ma Rainey's ARKANSAS SWIFT FOOT REVUE, Pollocksville, NC, 1931; worked w Sonny Boy Williamson (Alex Miller) in local clubs, Caruthersville, MO, early 30s; settled in Chicago, IL, to work outside music from 1942; worked Flame Club, Chicago, 1943; w Tampa Red at local clubs, Gary, IN, mid-40s; w Baby Face Leroy/Doc Clayton, 21 Club, Chicago, 1946; Martin's Corner, Chicago, c1946; rec w Jump Jackson Band, Specialty label, Chicago, 1946-7; frequently worked w Little Walter/Muddy Waters/others in local clubs, Chicago, through 40s; rec Victor label, Chicago, 1947; rec w Muddy Waters, Aristocrat

Albert Luandrew (Sunnyland Slim)
Courtesy Living Blues *Magazine*

label, Chicago, 1947-8; rec Tempo Tone label, Chicago, 1948; worked w Tampa Red, 21 Club, Chicago, 1948; rec Hy-Tone/Mercury labels, Chicago, 1949; rec Apollo label, Chicago, 1950; rec JOB label, Chicago, 1950-4; rec Regal/Mercury labels, Chicago, 1951; rec Opera/Chance/Constellation labels, Chicago, 1953; rec Blue Lake/VJ labels, Chicago, 1954; rec Club label, Chicago, 1955; rec Cobra label, Chicago, 1956; worked Smitty's Corner, Chicago, 1957; Bill Broonzy Benefit Concert, KAM Temple, Chicago, 1957; Cadillac Baby's Lounge, Chicago, 1958 (por rel Bea & Baby label); Buckingham Club, Chicago, 1960; rec w Little Brother Montgomery, 77 label, Chicago, 1960; rec Prestige-Bluesville label, Newark, NJ, 1960; worked Blind Pig, Chicago, 1961; rec Miss label, Chicago, 1961; worked Univ of Wisconsin, Milwaukee, WI, 1962; Univ of Chicago, Chicago, 1963; rec Delmark label, Chicago, 1963; worked Fickle Pickle Club, Chicago, 1963; Theresa's Bar, Chicago, 1963; Grinnell Folk Festival, Grinnell, IA, 1963; toured Europe working concert dates, 1963; worked Antibes Festival, Antibes, France, 1963; toured w Otis Rush working club/concert dates through Midwest, 1963; toured w American Blues Festival working concert dates through England/Europe/Soviet Union, 1964 (por of Soviet Union concert rel Airway label/por Musikhalle Concert, Hamburg, Ger, rel Fontana label); rec Storyville label, Copenhagen, Den, 1964; rec Amiga label, East Berlin, Ger, 1964; owned/operated/performed at Rock's Tavern, Rockford, IL, 1964; rec Spivey label, Chicago, 1964; worked w JB Lenore Band, Western Hall, Chicago, 1965; Mariposa Folk Festival, Toronto, Can, 1966; app on FESTIVAL PRESENTS THE BLUES, CBC-TV, Toronto, 1966; worked Shangri-la Lounge, Chicago, 1966; app on BLUES INTERNATIONAL SHOW, WXFM-radio, Elmwood Park, IL, c1968; worked The Kibitzeria, Toronto, 1968; rec w JB Hutto, Delmark label, Chicago, 1968; rec w Walter Horton/Johnny Shines, Blue Horizon label, Chicago, 1968; rec Liberty label, Los Angeles, CA, 1968; worked Hunter Col, NYC, NY, 1969; Electric Circus, NYC, 1969; Half Note, NYC, 1969; The Sweet Pea, Chicago, 1969; Chicago Blues Festival, Chicago, 1969; rec Adelphi label, Chicago, 1969; toured w Chicago All Stars working jazz/folk clubs/concerts through US/Europe, 1969; worked Antibes Jazz Festival, Paris, France, 1969; rec w Chicago

All Stars, MPS label, Cologne, Ger, 1969; rec ST for UK film BLUES LIKE SHOWERS OF RAIN, 1970; worked William's Lounge, Chicago, IL, 1970; Wisconsin Blues Festival, Beloit Col, Beloit, WI, 1970; Sylvio's, Chicago, 1970; J&P Lounge, Chicago, 1970; Washburne Lounge, Chicago, 1970; Alice's Revisited, Chicago, 1970-2; Ann Arbor Blues Festival, Ann Arbor, MI, 1970; Flamingo Lounge, Chicago, 1970-1; app w Howlin' Wolf in film short WOLF, 1971; worked w Howlin' Wolf, Big Duke's Blue Flame Lounge, Chicago, 1971; Festival of American Folklife, Montreal, Can, 1971; Hunter Col, NYC, NY, 1971; Colonial Tavern, Toronto, Can, 1971-4; Univ of Notre Dame Blues Festival, South Bend, IN, 1971; rec Jewel label, Chicago, 1971; worked Univ of Waterloo, Waterloo, Can, 1972; Smithsonian Blues Festival, Washington, DC, 1972; Jazz Workshop, Boston, MA, 1972; toured England/Europe working concert dates, 1973; rec Sonet label, Stockholm, Sweden, 1973; rec BluesWay label, Chicago, 1973; app on ATOMIC MAMA'S WANG DANG DOODLE BLUES SHOW, WNIB-FM-radio, Chicago, c1973; formed own Airway record company, Chicago, 1973; rec Airway label, Chicago, 1974; worked Bethune Col, Toronto, Can, 1974; Toronto Blues Festival, Olympic Island, Toronto, 1974; Ann Arbor Blues & Jazz Festival, Windsor, Can, 1974; Monterey Jazz Festival, Monterey, CA, 1974-5 (por 1975 concert heard KEST-radio, San Francisco); formed own trio to tour US working one-nighters/college dates, 1974; worked Great American Music Hall, San Francisco, 1974; Berlin Jazz Festival, Berlin, Ger, 1974, then toured w Jimmy Dawkins Band working concert dates through Europe, 1974; worked Sand Dunes, San Francisco, 1974; Mondavi Winery Summer Festival, Oakville, CA, 1975; Keystone Korner, Berkeley, CA, 1975; long weekly residency at Elsewhere Lounge, Chicago, 1975-8; occasionally worked outside music, Chicago, from 1975; worked Chicago Blues Festival, Jane Addams Theater, Chicago, 1975; Egerton's, Toronto, Can, 1975; Univ of Chicago Folk Festival, Chicago, 1976; Midwest Blues Festival, Univ of Notre Dame, South Bend, IN, 1976; rec Sirens label, Chicago, 1976; worked Wilshire Ebell Theater, Los Angeles, CA, 1976; Pepper's, Chicago, 1977; Club Zodiac, Chicago, 1977; frequently worked Louise's Palace, Chicago, 1977; Colonial Tavern, Toronto, Can, 1977; The Rising Sun, Montreal, Can, 1978

Personal: Married Freddie Lee (died 1959); Bonnie Mae ———, a singer. Named "Sunnyland Slim" due to his frequent singing of song "Sunnyland Train" as youth

Songs: Across the Hall Blues/Anna Lou Blues/Bassology/Be My Baby/Bob Martin Blues/Broke & Hungry/Brown Skin Woman/Canadian Walk/Couldn't Find a Mule/Cuttin' Out Blues/Depression Blues/Devil Is a Busy Man/Drinking/Every Time I Gets to Drinking/Get Hip to Yourself/Going Back to Memphis/Gonna Be My Baby/Got a Bad Break/(She's) Got a Thing Going On/Got to Get to My Baby/Gotta See My Lawyer/Harlem Can't Be Heaven/Heartache/I Done You Wrong/I Got the Blues About My Baby/I Had It Hard/Illinois Central/It's You Baby/Johnson Machine Gun/La Salle Street Boogie/Layin' in My Cell Sleepin'/Little Girl Blues/Lowland Blues/Midnight Jump/Miss Bessie Mae/Mr Cool/My Past Life/No Special Rider/No Whiskey Blues/Rice, Salmon and Black-Eyed Peas/Sad and Lonesome Blues/She Used to Love Me/She's So Mellow/Slim's Shout/Smile on My Face/Stella Mae/Stepmother/Substitute Woman/Sunnyland Special/Sweet Lucy Blues/That's All Right/Tin Pan Alley/Trembling Blues/Unlucky One/When Your Mama Quit Your Papa/Woman I Ain't Gonna Drink No More Whiskey/Won't Do That No More/You Used to Love Me/Your Fine Brown Frame

Infl by: PR Gibson/Little Brother Montgomery/Jeff Morris/Peetie Wheatstraw

Infl to: Lazy Bill Lucas/Willie Mabon

Quotes: "To the blues of others and to his own compositions Sunnyland Slim brings his own brand of music—loud, declamatory, filling the room with his immense voice, he whoops and yells, sings falsettos with ear-splitting volume in person"—Paul Oliver, Storyville album 616-012

"Sunnyland is, was and always will be a strict bluesman—a good, solid and honest craftsman . . ." —Mike Rowe, Blue Horizon album 763213

"It was during the 50s that Sunnyland established himself as one of the leading blues pianists of the postwar Chicago school . . ."—Harold Brenner, Airway album 3220

References: Airway album 3220

The Legacy of the Blues, Samuel B Charters, Calder & Boyars Ltd, 1975

LUCAS, JANE
(see Spivey, Victoria)

LUCAS, WILLIAM *"Bill"/"Lazy Bill"*

Photo by Jeff Todd Titon. Courtesy University of Illinois Press

Born: May 29, 1918, Wynne (Cross Co), AR
Died: Dec 12, 1982, Minneapolis, MN
Inst: Guitar/Organ/Piano

Father was Eddie Lucas; mother Lula Hunt; born nearly blind due to nervous condition; to Advance, MO, to work outside music on farm from 1924; taught self guitar and frequently worked streets for tips, Advance area, from c1930; taught self piano c1932; left home to work as hillbilly guitarist, Cape Girardeau, MO, 1936-7; worked streets, Commerce, MO, 1937-9; worked w Big Joe Williams (or solo) on streets, St Louis, MO, 1940; moved to Chicago, IL, 1941; frequently worked w John Lee "Sonny Boy" Williamson in Maxwell Street area for tips, Chicago, from 1941; toured w John Lee "Sonny Boy" Williamson working club dates in South Bend, IN/Battle Creek, MI/elsewhere, through 40s; worked w Earl Dranes/Willie Mabon, Tuxedo Lounge, Chicago, 1946; worked w Little Walter in Maxwell Street area, Chicago, c1946; w Little Walter, Purple Cat, Chicago, 1947; w Homesick James/Snooky Pryor (or single) at Club Jamboree/1015 Club/others, Chicago, c1948-early 50s; app w own trio on BIG BILL HILL SHOW, WOPA-radio, Oak Park, IL, early 50s; worked w Little Hudson and Red Devil Trio, Plantation Club and others, Chicago, from 1951; rec w Homesick James, Chance label, Chicago, 1952-3; worked Sylvio's, Chicago, 1952; rec w Snooky Pryor, Parrot label, Chicago, 1953; rec w Little Willie Foster, Blue Lake/Cobra labels, Chicago, 1953; rec w own Lazy Bill and His Blue Rhythms, Chance label, Chicago, 1954; worked w Homesick James, Cotton Club, Chicago, 1954; w JoJo Williams Band in local club dates, Argo, IL, c1954; rec w Blues Rockers, Excello label, Nashville, TN, 1955; continued working as sideman/solo in clubs/coffeehouses, Chicago, late 50s-1964; worked Fickle Pickle, Chicago, early 60s; w Little Hudson, Regent Ballroom, Chicago, 1964; w Mojo Buford Band, Key Club, Minneapolis, MN, 1964; The Lighthouse, Lake Minnetonka, MN, 1964; moved to Minneapolis, MN, c1964; frequently worked Triangle Bar/Scholar Coffeehouse/Broken Drum/Mike's Bar/Cozy Bar and other clubs/bars/church concerts, Minneapolis, through 60s; rec Wild label, Minneapolis, 1969; worked Wisconsin Blues Festival, Beloit, WI, 1970; Ann Arbor Blues Festival, Ann Arbor, MI, 1970; rec w own Lazy Bill and His Friends, Lazy label, Minneapolis, 1970; rec Philo label, Minneapolis, 1971; frequently worked Silver Dollar Cafe, Minneapolis, 1971; Univ of Minnesota, Minneapolis, 1973; toured college circuit through northeast US, early 70s; rec Philo label, N Ferrisburg, VT, 1973; worked Kingston Mines, Chicago, IL, 1976; Midwest Blues Festival, Univ of Notre Dame, South Bend, IN, 1976; worked folk/blues clubs such as Artist's Quarter/Sebastian's/Homestead Pickin' Parlor/Extempore Coffee House/others in Minneapolis-St Paul area into 80s; died in sleep; buried Burr Oak Cemetery, Worth, IL

Songs: I Had a Dream/I Lost My Appetite/Johnny Mae/My Best Friend's Blues/Sara Jane/She Got Me Walkin'

Infl by: Big Bill Broonzy/Memphis Slim/Sunnyland Slim

Quote: "Lucas sings and plays in an authentic tempered barrelhouse, chordal boogie style"—Paul Siber, *Cadence* magazine, Jun 1976, p 41

References: Philo album 1007
Blues Unlimited magazine (UK), Mar/Apr/May/Jun 1969

M

MABON, WILLIE

(*aka:* Big Willie)

Courtesy Living Blues *Magazine*

Born: Oct 24, 1925, Hollywood (Shelby Co), TN
Died: Apr 19, 1985, Paris, France
Inst: Harmonica/Piano

Mother was church choir singer; born in suburb of Memphis, TN; taught self piano at 16 years of age; moved to Chicago, IL, 1942 attending DuSable HS; took formal piano lessons, taught self harmonica and worked outside music, 1942-4; served in US Marine Corps, 1944-6; returned to Chicago to work w Lazy Bill Lucas/Earl Dranes, Tuxedo Lounge, Chicago, 1946; formed own Blues Rockers working Tempo Tap/Harmony Lounge/other clubs, Chicago, 1947 into 50s; rec Apollo label, Chicago, 1949; rec Aristocrat/Chess labels, Chicago, 1950; rec Chess label, Chicago, 1952-6; frequently toured with many R&B package shows out of NYC, NY, 1953 through 50s; often worked Flame Club, Chicago, 1954; Ralph's Club, Chicago, 1954; 708 Club, Chicago, 1954; toured one-nighters through South, 1956; worked Palms Club, Hallandale, FL, 1956; rec Federal label, Chicago, 1957; mostly inactive due to illness late 50s/early 60s; rec Mad label, Chicago, 1960; rec Formal label, Chicago, 1962; worked Club Arden, Chicago, 1962; Theresa's Bar, Chicago, 1963; Mr Lee's Lounge, Chicago, 1963; rec USA label, Chicago, 1963-5; worked Western Hall, Chicago, 1965; worked mostly outside music in Chicago, 1965-9; worked Rock and Roll Show of 1967 in local theaters, Chicago area, 1967; worked w Howlin' Wolf's Band, Sylvio's, Chicago, 1967; Toast of the Town Club, Chicago, 1969; The Clock Lounge, Chicago, 1970; North Park Hotel, Chicago, 1971; Betty Lou's Package Goods, Chicago, 1972; rec Antilles label, Chicago, c1972; toured England/Europe working concert dates; 1972-3; rec Black & Blue label, Bordeaux, France, 1972; worked Montreux Jazz Festival, Montreux, Switzerland, 1973; Trois Mailletz Club, Paris, France, 1973-4; rec America label, France, 1973; rec w Mickey Baker, Big Bear label, London, Eng, 1973; rec Black & Blue label, Toulouse, France, 1973; worked w Robert Jr Lockwood, Berlin Jazz Festival, Berlin, Ger, 1974; toured w Jimmy Dawkins Band working concert dates through Europe, 1974 (por Paris, France, concert rel Black & Blue label); rec Esceha label, Frankfurt, West Ger, 1974; worked Jazz Festival, Groningen, Holland, 1975; toured w Chicago Blues Festival working concert dates through Europe, 1975; worked Ratso's, Chicago, 1975-6; rec Sirens label, Chicago, 1976; worked Elsewhere Lounge, Chicago, 1976-7; Festival of Arts Concert, Univ of Chicago, Chicago, 1976; toured Europe working concerts/festivals/clubs in Switzerland/Spain/Italy/Holland/Germany into 80s; death details unknown

Personal: Married. 2 children

Songs: Baby Why Don't You Write Me?/Blue Piano in Bordeaux/Blues for Chantal/Cold Chilly Woman/Come On Baby/Discotheque Special/Evening Shadows/Fooling Around/Going to Get You/Got to Have Some/Guilty Blues/Hang Loose Baby/Harmonica Special/Hey Girl/I Don't Know/I Enjoy Myself in Pau/I Still Don't Know/I Wonder/I'll Keep On Hurtin'/I'm Going to Get You/I'm Hungry/I'm Mad/Keep My Lover with Me/Klickety Klock/Lover Girl/Lonely Blues/Lucinda/Mabon's Boogie/Michelle/My Baby Won't Write to Me/Poison Ivy/Riverboat/Round for You/Ruby's Monkey/Shakin' the Boogie/Somebody Got to Pay/Thinking About You/Trouble Blues/Why Did It Happen to Me?/World of Trouble/Worry Blues

Infl by: Big Maceo Merriweather/Muddy Waters/Sunnyland Slim/Roosevelt Sykes

MABON

Infl to: Mose Allison

Quotes: ". . . his singing . . . can register a wide range of emotions, from the sly, almost wicked insinuation of his signature tune 'I Don't Know' all the way through to the touching emotional directness of the blues at their most basic, and make each equally, fully convincing"—Pete Welding, Antilles album 7013

"Sharp, slick, smooth, sophisticated"—John J Broven, *Blues Unlimited* magazine (UK), Feb 1973, p 17

References: Blues Unlimited magazine (UK), May 1973, p 17

Nothing But the Blues, Mike Leadbitter, Hanover Books, 1971

MACON, JOHN WESLEY
(*aka:* Mr Shortstuff)

Photo by Len Kunstadt. Courtesy Record Research Archives

Born: 1923, Crawford (Lowndes Co), MS
Died: Dec 28, 1973, Macon, MS
Inst: Guitar

Father was Albert Macon; mother was Louvenia Hall; taught self guitar at 9 years of age; raised/worked outside music with occasional local party work, Crawford, MS, area into 60s; worked w Big Joe Williams in local club dates on West Coast c1964; w Big Joe Williams at Bard Col, Annandale-on-Hudson, NY, 1964; rec w Big Joe Williams, Spivey/Folkways labels, NYC, NY, 1964; worked w Big Joe Williams, Gaslight Cafe, NYC, 1965; returned south to work outside music in Crawford/Starkville, MS, area into 70s; entered Noxubee County Hospital where he died of heart trouble; buried Cross Road Cemetery, Starkville, MS

Personal: Was cousin of Big Joe Williams

Quote: "His hollered, modal vocals indicated the persistence of the oldest blues forms"—Paul Oliver, *The Story of the Blues,* Chilton Book Company, 1969

MAGHETT, SAMUEL *"Sam"*
(*aka:* Good Rocking Sam/Magic Sam/Magic Singing Sam)

Photo by Ray Flerlage. Courtesy Living Blues Magazine

Born: Feb 14, 1937, Grenada (Grenada Co), MS
Died: Dec 1, 1969, Chicago, IL
Inst: Guitar

Father was Jessie Maghett; mother was Hetha Anna Henderson; born/raised on farm outside of Grenada, MS; taught self on home-made guitar at 10 years of age; attended local school w Magic Slim (Morris Holt), Grenada, MS, late 40s; frequently worked outside music, Grenada, through 40s; moved to Chicago, IL, 1950 attending Drake HS; worked w Morning View Special gospel group in local churches, Chicago, from early 50s; worked w Homesick James Band, Cotton Club, Chicago, c1954; formed own band to work 708 Club, Chicago, 1955; Ray's Lounge, Chicago, c1955; w Shakey Jake Band, Wagon Wheel, Chicago, 1955; worked Kirksey's Lounge, Chicago, 1957; rec Cobra label, Chicago, 1957-8; worked Blue Flame Club, Chicago, late 50s; rec w Shakey Jake, Artistic label, Chicago, 1958; worked 1815 Club, Chicago, 1959; Eddie Shaw's Place, Chicago, 1959; Pepper's Lounge, Chicago, 1959; Just Me Lounge, Chicago, 1959; served in US Army in 1959 but deserted in 1960; rec Chief label, Chicago, 1960-1; frequently worked Club Tay May, Chicago, 1960-4; New Alex Club, Chicago, 1963; Tambo Lounge, Chicago, 1963; rec CBS label, Chicago, 1964; worked Copa Cabana Club, Chicago, c1964-8 (frequently remote on BIG BILL HILL SHOW, WOPA-radio); worked Big John's, Chicago, 1965; Eldridge Club, Chicago, 1965; Sylvio's, Chicago, 1966-8; Pershing Lounge, Chicago, 1966; Cal's Corner, Chicago, 1966; rec Delmark/Crash labels, Chicago, 1966; worked Univ of Chicago, Chicago, 1967; Club 99, Joliet, IL, c1967; Mother Blues, Chicago, 1968; Father Blues, Chicago, 1968; Sitzmark, Chicago, 1968; worked w Otis Rush Band in local club dates, Chicago, 1968; worked Univ of Wisconsin, Madison, WI, 1968; Avalon Ballroom, San Francisco, CA, 1968; Fillmore West, San Francisco, 1968; rec Delmark label, Chicago, 1968-9; worked The Log Cabin, San Francisco, c1968; Winterland, San Francisco, 1969; Aragon Ballroom, Chicago, 1969; app on MARTY FAYE Show, local TV, Chicago, 1969; worked L&A Lounge, Chicago, 1969; Ann Arbor Blues Festival, Ann Arbor, MI, 1969; Shrine Auditorium, Los Angeles, CA, c1969; The Catacombs, Boston, MA, c1969; Guild Theater, Louisville, KY, c1969; Black Dome, Cincinnati, OH, c1969; toured w American Folk Blues Festival working concert dates through England/Europe, 1969; worked Royal Albert Hall, London, Eng, 1969 (por rel CBS label); Main Point, Bryn Mawr, PA, 1969; Univ of Chicago, Chicago, 1969; Ash Grove, Los Angeles, 1969; suffered heart attack at home and DOA St Anthony Hospital; buried Restvale Cemetery, Worth, IL

Personal: Married Leola ———; married Georgia Flangan. Had 4 children. "Shakey" Jake Harris was uncle and sometime manager. Had used pseudonym "Good Rocking Sam" early in career but later changed to "Magic Sam" (an adaptation of his name) due to prior use of the former pseudonym

Songs: All My Whole Life/All Night Long/All Your Love/Easy Baby/Everything Gonna Be All Right/Look Whatcha Done/Looking Good/Love Me This Way/Love Me with a Feeling/Magic Rocker/21 Days in Jail

Infl by: Lowell Fulson/Homesick James/Syl Johnson/BB King/Freddie King/Little Walter/Muddy Waters/Jimmy Rogers

Infl to: Luther Allison/Eddy Clearwater

Quotes: "Sam's sound was unique, his guitar playing amazingly lyrical and his high-pitched voice unforgettable"—Gary Von Tersch, *Blues World* magazine (UK), Dec 1970, p 20

"Part of what might be called the second wave of blues artists to move north and east from Mississippi, Magic Sam was an important link in the blues tradition of such first-wave stars as Muddy Waters and Howlin' Wolf"—Irwin Stambler, *Encyclopedia of Pop, Rock & Soul*, St Martin's Press, 1974

". . . a distinct and superior bluesman"—Robert Cappuccio, *Living Blues* magazine, Summer 1973, p 13

References: Blues Unlimited magazine (UK), Feb 1970, pp 16-17

Jazz Journal magazine (UK); Nov 1969, pp 5-6

MAGIC SAM
(see Maghett, Samuel)

MAGIC SINGING SAM
(see Maghett, Samuel)

MAGIC SLIM
(see Holt, Morris)

MAHAL, TAJ
Born: May 17, 1942, New York (New York Co), NY
Inst: Banjo/Bass/Cello/Dulcimer/Fife/Guitar/Harmonica/Kalimba/Mandolin/Piano/Vibes

Father was Henry Fredericks Sr, a West Indian; mother Mildred Constance Shields; born Henry Saint Claire Fredericks, one of 9 children; interested in music early and was singing by 6 years of age; lived in Brooklyn, NY, then raised in Springfield, MA, where he learned guitar at 15 years of age; attended Univ of Massachusetts, Amherst, MA (receiving BA in Animal Husbandry), c1964; worked local coffeehouses, Boston, MA, area, c1964; moved to Los Angeles, CA, 1965; frequently worked w Ry Cooder in Rising Sons group in local folk clubs, Hollywood, CA, 1965-6; w Canned Heat Electric Band, Ash Grove, Los Angeles, CA, 1967; frequently worked as single, Ash Grove, Los Angeles, 1967-70; won banjo contest, Topanga Canyon Fiddlers Convention, Topanga, CA, c1967; frequently rec Columbia label, Los Angeles (?),

Taj Mahal

Courtesy Sheldon Harris Collection

1967-76; worked Newport Folk Festival, Newport, RI, 1968; Fillmore East, NYC, NY, 1969-70; Fillmore West, San Francisco, CA, 1969; Newport '69, Northridge, CA, 1969; Boston Tea Party, Boston, MA, 1969; Salvation Club, NYC, 1969; Mariposa Folk Festival, Toronto, Can, 1969; app on UPBEAT, WPIX-TV, NYC (syndicated), 1969; app on NET PLAYHOUSE (ep: Thoughts of the Artist on Leaving the Sixties), PBS-TV, 1970; app on THE SHOW, PBS-TV, 1970; worked Ludlow Garage, Cincinnati, OH, 1970; Ungano's, NYC, 1970; toured as itinerant musician working streets/cafes through Spain, 1970, then worked coffeehouses/clubs through Europe to 1971; worked The Royal Albert Hall, London, Eng, 1971 (por shown in film SOUNDS OF THE SEVENTIES); worked Fillmore East, NYC, 1971; Swing Auditorium, San Bernardino, CA, 1971; Folk Festival, Big Sur, CA, 1971; Folk Concert, Washington, DC, 1971; rec w BB King, Probe label, Los Angeles, CA, 1971; rec ST for film CLAY PIGEON, 1971; app on FREE TIME, PBS-TV, 1971; app on MARK OF JAZZ, PBS-TV, c1971; worked Palladium, Hollywood, CA, 1971; rec w BB King, ABC-Dunhill label, Los Angeles, 1971; worked Civic Center, Baltimore, MD, 1971; State Penitentiary Concert, Walla Walla, WA, 1971; Ebonee Ballroom, Seattle, WA, 1971; National Folk Festival, Wolf Trap Farm Park, Vienna, VA, 1971; The Auditorium, Long Beach, CA, 1972; Four Muses, San Clemente, CA, 1972; Philharmonic Hall, NYC, 1972; Winterland, San Francisco, c1972; The Soundtrack, Denver, CO, 1972; scored/app in film SOUNDER, 1972 (por rel Columbia label); app on SOUL, PBS-TV, 1972; worked Lincoln Center, NYC, 1972-3; The Bitter End, NYC, 1972; Boarding House, San Francisco, 1972 (por shown BOARDING HOUSE, PBS-TV); Mariposa Folk Festival, Toronto Islands, Can, 1972; app on TILMON TEMPO Show, WMAQ-TV, Chicago, IL, 1972; app on FLIP WILSON Show, NBC-TV, 1973; worked New Orleans Jazz & Heritage Festival, Municipal Auditorium, New Orleans, LA, 1973; Manhattan Center, NYC, 1973; Ahmanson Theater, Los Angeles, CA, 1973; rec acc to Bonnie Raitt, Warner Brothers label (?), Los Angeles (?), 1973; worked Ebbet's Field, Denver, CO, 1973; Great Southeast Music Hall, Atlanta, GA, 1973; Topanga Corral, Los Angeles, 1973; Tufts Univ, Medford, MA, 1973; Avery Fisher Hall, NYC, 1973; John Henry Memorial Concert, Clifftop, WV, 1974; rec ST for film FIGHTING FOR OUR LIVES, 1974; worked Liberty Hall, Houston, TX, 1974; Pilgrimage Theater, Hollywood, CA, 1974; Boarding House, San Francisco, 1974 (por shown KQED-TV); app on PLAY IT AGAIN SAM, PBS-TV, 1975; worked Shakespeare Theater, Stratford, CT, 1975; Balcony Hall, Scottsdale, AZ, 1975; Music Festival, Civic Center, San Francisco, 1975; Berkeley Jazz Festival, Berkeley, CA, 1975; Roxy Theater, Hollywood, CA, c1975; Bijou Cafe, Philadelphia, PA, 1975; Family Light School of Music Blues Festival, Sausalito, CA, 1975; Academy of Music, Philadelphia, 1975; app on APOLLO, WNEW-TV, NYC, 1976; worked Unicorn Club, Rochester, NY, 1976 (por shown AT THE TOP, PBS-TV); app on DINAH! Show, CBS-TV, 1976; worked Mariposa Folk Festival, Toronto Islands, Can, 1976-7; app in film SCOTT JOPLIN, 1976; app in film PART II SOUNDER, 1976; worked New Yorker Theater, Toronto, Can, 1976; Georgetown Univ, Washington, DC, 1976; rec Columbia label, San Francisco (?), c1976; worked Dooley's, Phoenix, AZ, 1977; rec ST for film BROTHERS, 1977; app on SATURDAY NIGHT, NBC-TV, 1977; app on ME AND STELLA, PBS-TV (syndicated), 1977; app on MIKE DOUGLAS Show, CBS-TV, 1978

Personal: Married Inshirah ———. Also known as an accomplished painter/sculptor

Songs: The Big Blues/Done Changed My Way of Living/Eighteen Hammers/Going Up to the Country/Paint My Mailbox Blues/Good Morning Miss Brown/Oh Susannah/Queen Bee/Riverside/Southbound with the Hammer Down/Sweet Mama Janisse

Infl by: Gary Davis/Robert Johnson/Albert King/Hammie Nixon/Sonny Terry

Quotes: ". . . a man whose music is rooted in the country blues, sunk deep down into the mud of the Mississippi Delta . . ."—Patrick William Salvo, *Black Music* magazine (UK), Feb 1975, p 31

"Taj is a clever musician and a charismatic performer"—Peter Keepnews, *Downbeat* magazine, Apr 26, 1973

"One of the best of today's young blues singers"—Jack Bradley, *Coda* magazine (Canada), Jun 1969, p 38

References: *Downbeat* magazine, Feb 12, 1976, pp 18-19

Encyclopedia of Pop, Rock & Soul, Irwin Stambler, St Martin's Press, 1974

MAIDEN, SIDNEY

Born: 1923, Mansfield (De Soto Parish), LA
Inst: Harmonica

Interested in music early, playing harmonica as child; raised in Louisiana, then left home to drift to West Coast in early 40s; frequently worked outside music in Richmond, CA, from early 40s; teamed w KC Douglas working local club dates in Richmond area, 1947 into 50s; rec w KC Douglas, Downtown label, Oakland, CA, 1948; settled in Fresno, CA, working mostly outside music from late 40s; rec Imperial label, San Francisco, CA, 1952; rec Dig/Flash labels, Los Angeles, CA, 1957; rec w Mercy Dee, Arhoolie label, Stockton, CA, 1961; rec Prestige-Bluesville label, Berkeley, CA, 1961; formed own group working local dances in Fresno, CA, area through 60s; whereabouts unknown thereafter

Songs: Blues and Trouble/Buy Me an Airplane/Hand Me Down Baby/San Quentin Blues/Sidney's Worried Life Blues

Quote: "Sidney Maiden is worthy of being mentioned along with the select few greats of the mouth-harp . . ."—Larry Cohn, Prestige-Bluesville album 1035

Reference: Prestige-Bluesville album 1035

MAMA CAN CAN

(see Rainey, Gertrude)

MARS, JOHN *"Johnny"*

Photo by Bill Greensmith. Courtesy Living Blues Magazine

Born: Dec 7, 1942, Laurens (Laurens Co), SC
Inst: Guitar/Harmonica

Father was itinerant farmer; one of 2 children; frequently moved through Florida and southeast coastal states following family from 3 years of age; frequently worked outside music from childhood; taught self harmonica at 13 years of age; continued outside music work through 50s; moved to New Paltz, NY, 1957;

formed Johnny Mars and the Cotton Brothers rock group working school dances/hops/parties, New Paltz, from 1957; continued outside music work, New Paltz, into 60s; frequently worked w The Train Riders Band at local dances, New Paltz area, from 1961; worked w The Burning Bush Band, Spinelli's Club, New Paltz, c1965; rec Mercury label, New Paltz (?), 1967; moved to San Francisco, CA, 1967; worked w The Last Mile Band at local clubs, San Francisco, 1967; formed Johnny Mars Blues Band working local clubs, San Francisco area, c1967; toured w Magic Sam Band working clubs/ballrooms, San Francisco area, c1968; returned east to form own The Blue Flames group working club dates through upstate NY, 1968-71; toured Europe working club dates, 1971; worked First Birmingham Boogie Convention, Birmingham, Eng, 1972; rec Polydor label, London, Eng, 1972; toured England/Europe working concert/club dates, 1973-4; worked concert dates in Gothenburg, Sweden, 1974; toured West Coast working club dates, 1975; app on BLUES BY THE BAY, KPOO-FM-radio, San Francisco, 1975; worked concert dates in Holland/England, 1976; rec Big Bear label, London, Eng, 1976

Songs: Bring It On Home/Cruisin'/Deep in the Wilderness/Honey Bee/I've Been Down So Long/If I Had a Woman/Love Is a Wonderful Thing/My Dream

Infl by: BB King/Little Walter/Jimmy Reed/Sonny Terry/Junior Wells/Sonny Boy Williamson (Alex Miller)

Quote: ". . . his wailing harmonica and tough, gruff vocals are unlikely candidates in the commercialise-blues-and-sell-it-as-rock stakes"—Tony Cummings, *Black Music* magazine (UK), Jul 1974, p 35

Reference: Blues Unlimited magazine (UK), Oct 1973, pp 5, 16

MARS, SYLVIA

Born: c1933, Abbeville (Abbeville Co), SC

Grandfather Willie Henry was local songster/musician; father Jules Mars and mother Thelma Henry were singers/musicians; born/raised on farm; moved to Boston, MA, late 40s; attended Boston Univ, Boston, early 50s; frequently worked outside music, Boston, through 50s; active in Boston Folksong Society, Boston, through 50s; worked w Lionel Hampton Band, Storyville Club, Boston, early 60s; app w Pete Seeger on local TV show, Boston, early 60s; frequently toured folk clubs/night clubs/coffeehouses through New England area of US and into Canada, early 60s; rec Folk-Lyric label, Boston (?), c1962; whereabouts unknown thereafter

MARTIN, CARL

Photo by Mike Joyce

Born: Apr 1, 1906, Big Stone Gap (Wise Co), VA
Died: May 10, 1979, Pontiac, MI
Inst: Bass/Guitar/Mandolin/Violin

Father was Frank "Fiddlin" Martin, a musician and former slave; mother Mary McMahon; took to music early and frequently sang in church choir as child; learned guitar at about 10 years of age; moved to Knoxville, TN, 1920; frequently worked w Roland Martin's Band in streets/medicine shows/country breakdowns in Knoxville from 1920; frequently toured w Roland Martin's Band working dances through Kentucky/Virginia/West Virginia into early 20s; teamed w Howard Armstrong to form Tennessee Chocolate Drops (later renamed "Wandering Troubadors") working dances/parties/radio shows (WROL-radio), Knoxville, through 20s; frequently toured with group working streets/barber shops/restaurants/parties/jail houses through Virginia/West Virginia through 20s; teamed w Ted Bogan to rename group The Four Keys String Band working dances/picnics/weddings/taverns, Knoxville area (with occasional tours into West Virginia), from 1930; frequently app on WROL-radio, Knoxville, TN/WOPI-radio, Bristol, TN, 1930-2; rec w The Four Keys (as "The Tennessee Chocolate Drops"), Vocalion label, Knoxville, 1930; toured w Ted Bogan working clubs in Kalamazoo, MI/South Bend, IN, 1932; worked w Leroy Carr in local dives, Indianapolis, IN, c1933; moved to Chicago, IL, to work frequently w Ted Bogan in streets/stockyards/theaters/parties, 1933-7; frequently rec acc to Bumble Bee Slim/Big Bill Broonzy/Tampa Red/others, Chicago, during 30s; rec Bluebird label, Chicago, 1934-5; rec OKeh/Vocalion/Decca labels, Chicago, 1935; rec Champion label, Chicago, 1936;

worked mostly outside music with occasional club dates w Ted Bogan, Chicago, from 1937-41; learned mandolin, 1941; served in US Army in Hawaii/Philippines, 1941-5; returned to Chicago to work mostly outside music with occasional club dates, 1945 through 60s; rec Testament label, Chicago, 1966; worked w Ted Bogan, Festival of American Folklife, Washington, DC, 1970; Philadelphia Folk Festival, Schwenksville, PA, 1971; Univ of Chicago Folk Festival, Chicago, 1972; frequently w Ted Bogan in own group working local club dates, Chicago, 1972-4; rec w Ted Bogan, Rounder label, Chicago, 1972; worked Smithsonian Blues Festival, Washington, DC, 1972; Mariposa Folk Festival, Toronto, Can, 1972; Earl of Old Town, Chicago, 1973-4; formed Martin, Bogan and The Armstrongs quartet to tour college concert dates in Chicago area, 1973-4; rec w Ted Bogan, Flying Fish label, Chicago, 1973; worked Binghamton Folk Festival, Binghamton, NY, 1974; National Folk Festival, Washington, DC, 1974; Mendota Jazz Festival, Minneapolis, MN, 1974; toured w Martin, Bogan and The Armstrongs quartet on Music of the People—USA tour working concert dates through Central & South America under auspices of US State Department, 1975; worked Portland State Col, Portland, OR, 1975; Univ of Oregon, Eugene, OR, 1975; Oregon State Univ, Corvallis, OR, 1975; Philadelphia Folk Festival, Schwenksville, PA, 1975-6; Mariposa Folk Festival, Toronto, Can, 1975; San Diego Univ Folk Festival, San Diego, CA, 1975; Artpark Theater, Lewiston, NY, 1975; Univ of Notre Dame, South Bend, IN, 1975; Juicy John Pink's Club, DeKalb, IL, 1975; Vegetable Buddies Club, South Bend, IN, 1976; Bobby McGhee's, Cleveland, OH, 1976; Kent State Folk Festival, Kent, OH, 1976; Winnipeg Folk Festival, Winnipeg, Can, 1976; Northwestern Univ, Evanston, IL, 1976; Sylvester's, Chicago, IL, 1976; NAIRD Convention, O'Hare Motor Inn, Chicago, 1977; John Henry Folk Festival, Camp Virgil Tate, Princeton, WV, 1977; Charlotte's Web, Rockford, IL, 1977; Northern Illinois Univ Folk Festival, DeKalb, IL, 1977; Univ of Notre Dame, South Bend, IN, 1978; Blues Festival, Utrecht, Holland, 1979; solo tour of US concert dates, 1979; died of bronchopneumonia; buried Restvale Cemetery, Worth, IL

Songs: Barnyard Dance/Joe Louis Blues/New Deal Blues/1937 Flood

Quote: "Carl Martin is a musician, a songster and entertainer, a bluesman who, quite simply, has been making music all of his life"—Bo Basiuk, *Blues* magazine (Canada), Aug 1975, p 26

References: *Cadence* magazine, Aug 1977, pp 17-20
Blues (Canada), Aug 1975, pp 26-33
Living Blues (No. 43), 1979, pp. 28-9

MARTIN, *"Blind"* GEORGE
(see Phelps, Arthur)

MARTIN, *"Fiddlin'"* JOE

Photo by Marina Bokelman. Courtesy Dave Evans

Born: Jan 8, 1900, Edwards (Hinds Co), MS
Died: Nov 21, 1975, Walls, MS
Inst: Bass/Drums/Guitar/Mandolin/Trombone/Washboard

Father was Carter Martin; mother was Elnora Graham; interested in music early and learned guitar as boy; moved to Mound Bayou, MS, c1914; frequently played trombone in local school marching band as youth; moved to Hollandale, MS, to work outside music with occasional local juke work c1917; frequently worked w Charley Patton/Willie Newbern/Johnnie Temple/Bubba Brown/Little Milton/others in juke joints through Mississippi Delta area, 1918-35; settled in Robinsonville, MS, to work w Son House/Willie Brown in local jukes from 1935; worked w Memphis Minnie in local jukes, Jackson, MS, c1939; rec w Son House/Willie Brown on Library of Congress label, Lake Cormorant, MS, 1941; worked w Memphis Minnie/Tampa Red/others in local bars/churches, Chicago, IL, early 40s; worked w Son House in local clubs, Rochester, NY, c1945; worked briefly in Ringling Brothers Circus, mid-40s; worked w Howlin' Wolf Band, Lake Cummins, MS, area, 1947-52; worked w Daddy Stovepipe in Maxwell Street area, Chicago, late 40s; app w Woodrow Adams on WDIA-radio, Memphis, TN, early 50s; rec acc to Woodrow

Adams, Checker label, Memphis, 1952; settled in Memphis, TN, to work local club dates through 50s; rec acc to Woodrow Adams, Meteor label, Memphis, 1955; rec Home of the Blues label, Memphis, 1961; moved to Robinsonville, MS, to work occasionally w Woodrow Adams Trio in local jukes through 60s; rec Flyright label, Robinsonville, 1967; died of natural causes; buried Mullins Cemetery, Clock, MS

Personal: Was cousin of Chatmon Brothers and Jake Martin, musicians

Infl by: Jake Martin/Frank Nash

Reference: Living Blues magazine, Mar 1976, p 10

MARTIN, SARA *"Sarah"*
(*aka:* Margaret Johnson/Sally Roberts)
Born: Jun 18, 1884, Louisville (Jefferson Co), KY
Died: May 24, 1955, Louisville, KY

Father was William Dunn; mother was Katie Pope; born Sara Dunn; raised in Louisville, KY; moved north to form own singing act working vaudeville circuit out of Chicago, IL, from c1915; frequently worked local clubs/cabarets, NYC, NY, 1922; rec w Clarence Williams, OKeh label, NYC, 1922-8; rec w Fats Waller, OKeh label, NYC, 1922; rec w own Brown Skin Syncopators, Columbia label, NYC, 1922; app in JUMP STEADY Revue, Lafayette Theater, NYC, 1922; toured in show UP AND DOWN working theaters on East Coast, 1922; toured w Fats Waller on TOBA circuit, 1922-3; worked Princess Theater, Harrisburg, PA, 1922; Bijou Theater, Nashville, TN, 1923; Lyric Theater, New Orleans, 1923; Regent Theater, Baltimore, MD, 1923; New Star Casino, NYC, NY, 1923; Monogram Theater, Chicago, IL, 1923; Paradise Cabaret, Atlantic City, NJ, 1923; toured w WC Handy Band working theater dates on TOBA circuit through South, 1923; worked Star Theater, Shreveport, LA, 1923; rec w Eva Taylor/Shelton Brooks/Clarence Williams, OKeh label, NYC, NY, 1923; worked Lafayette Theater, NYC, 1923; toured extensively working club dates through South/Midwest/Texas, 1923-4; app on WFAA-radio, Dallas, TX, 1924; worked club dates, Topeka, KS, 1924; toured extensively working theater dates through Alabama/Tennessee/Illinois and across US, 1924-5; worked Dunbar Theater, Columbus, OH, 1925; Howard Theater, Washington, DC, 1925; Grand Theater, Chicago, IL, 1925; The Coliseum Theater, Chicago, 1926; rec (religious music) w Arizona Dranes, Okeh label, Chicago, 1926; app w Clarence Williams Trio, WHN-radio, NYC, c1927; rec (religious music) w Sylvester Weaver, OKeh label, NYC, 1927; worked w

Courtesy Spencer Williams

Doc Straine Company, Lincoln Theater, NYC, 1927; app w Eva Taylor in musical comedy BOTTOMLAND, Savoy Theater, Atlantic City, NJ, 1927/Princess Theater, NYC, 1927; worked Roosevelt Theater, NYC, 1927; app in film HELLO BILL, c1927; toured in William Benbow's GET HAPPY FOLLIES Revue working theaters in Cuba/Jamaica/San Juan, PR/elsewhere, 1928; rec w Clarence Williams Orch, QRS label, Long Island City, NY, 1928; app w Mamie Smith in musical comedy SUN-TAN FROLICS, Lincoln Theater, NYC, 1929; toured East Coast working theater dates, 1930; worked club dates, Cleveland, OH, 1931; worked mostly w Thomas A Dorsey in local church/gospel activities, Chicago, IL, from 1932; worked outside music in NYC, into 40s; owned/operated private nursing home, Louisville, KY, through 40s; entered Louisville General Hospital where she died of a stroke; buried Louisville Cemetery, Louisville, KY

Personal: Married Hayes Withers (1929-). Not to be confused with Margaret Johnson, a singing pianist from Kansas City, MO

Billings: The Blues Sensation from the West/Queen of the Blues

Songs: Cage of Apes/Can't Find Nobody to Do Like My Old Daddy Do/Daddy Ease This Pain of Mine/Death Sting Me Blues/Don't You Quit Me Daddy/Down at the Razor Ball/Every Woman Needs a Man/Gonna Be a Lovin' Old Soul/Good Bye Blues/Got to Leave My Home Blues/Green Gal Can't Catch On/Guitar Blues/Guitar Rag/I Can Always Tell When (My/A) Man Is Treatin' Me Cool/I Won't Be Back If I Don't Find My Brown at All/I'll Forget You Blues/I'm Gonna Hoodoo You/I'm Sorry Blues/I've Got to (Go and) Leave My Daddy Behind/It's Too Late Now to Get Your Baby Back/Longing for Daddy Blues/Mama's Got the Blues/Mistreating Man Blues/Papa Papa Blues/Roamin' Blues/Sad and Sorrow Blues/Squabbling Blues/Strange Lovin' Blues/Sweet Man's the Cause of It All/Troubled Blues/Uncle Sam Blues/What More Can a Monkey Woman Do?/You Don't Want Me Honey/Your Going Ain't Giving Me the Blues

Infl to: Victoria Spivey

Quotes: "Remembered for her dramatic stage presence and uninhibited delivery in performance"—(Paul Oliver) McCarthy/Morgan/Oliver/Harrison, *Jazz on Record*, Hanover Books Ltd, 1968

"One of the more dramatic blues artists"—Brian Rust, Swaggie album S-1240

MASKED MARVEL, THE
(see Patton, Charley)

MAXWELL STREET JIMMY
(see Thomas, Charles)

MAYALL, JOHN

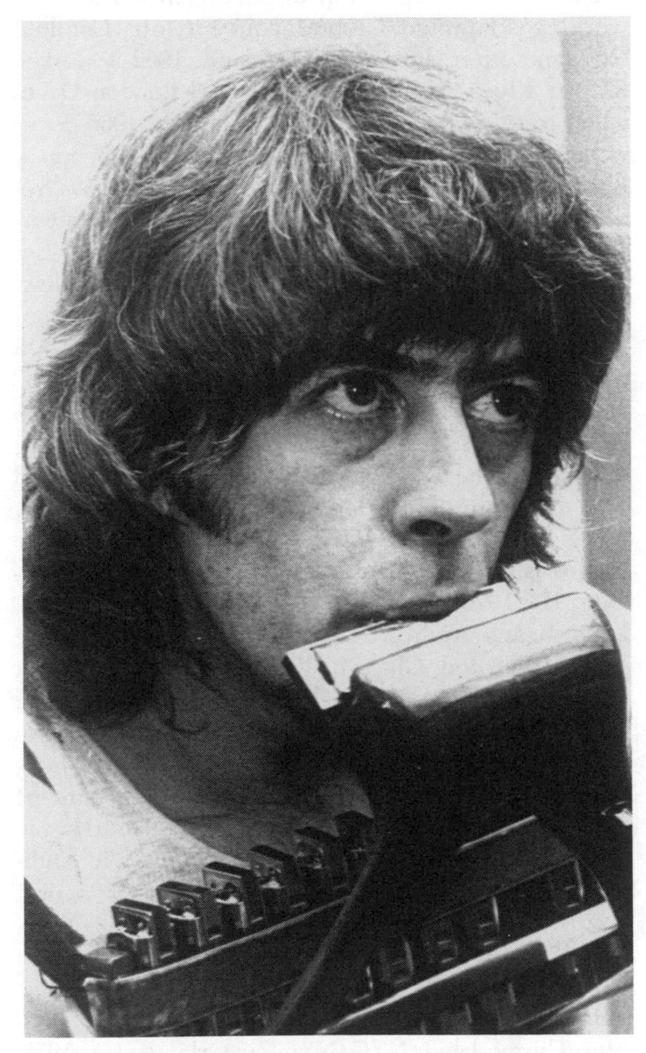

Courtesy Living Blues *Magazine*

Born: Nov 29, 1933, Macclesfield (Cheshire Co), England
Inst: Guitar/Harmonica/Harmonium/Harpsichord/Organ/Piano/Tambourine\Ukulele

Father was jazz guitarist; interested in music early and was playing guitar/uke at 12 years of age; attended Manchester Junior School of Art, Manchester, Eng, 1947-9; frequently worked outside music with occasional blues/boogie piano gigs, late 40s; served in British Army in Korea, 1951-5; attended Col of Art, Manchester, Eng, 1955-9; frequently worked in student band while in college, late 50s; formed own Powerhouse Four working local dances, Manchester, from 1956; worked outside music (as advertising artist), late 50s into 60s; frequently worked w Blues Syndicate Band at local gigs, Manchester, late 50s into 60s; formed Bluesbreakers, 1962; frequently w Bluesbreakers as backup group to American blues artists working Flamingo Club/Marquee Club, London, Eng, and other clubs across England, 1962-8; worked Klook's Kleek, London, 1964 (por rel London-Decca label); rec London-Decca label, London, 1966-8; rec w Jack Dupree, London label, London, 1966; app w Bob Dylan in film DON'T LOOK BACK, 1967; frequently toured England/Europe working concert dates, 1968 into 70s; worked Whisky A-Go-Go, Los Angeles, CA, 1968-71; Newport Jazz Festival, Newport, RI, 1969; Fillmore East, NYC, NY, 1969-71 (por 1969 date rel Polydor label); frequently toured US working concert dates from 1969; app on MUSIC SCENE, ABC-TV, 1969; worked Fillmore West, San Francisco, CA, 1969-70; Foxboro Raceway, Boston, MA, 1969; rec Polydor label, NYC, 1970-5; worked The Spectrum, Philadelphia, PA, 1970; Ungano's, NYC, 1970; The Loser's Club, Dallas, TX, 1970; State Fair Music Hall, Dallas, 1970; Aragon Ballroom, Chicago, IL, 1970; Painters Mill, Baltimore, MD, 1971; Long Beach Auditorium, Los Angeles, CA, 1972; Alice's Revisited, Chicago, 1972; toured w own sextet working concert dates through Australia, 1972; worked Arie Crown Theater, Chicago, 1972; Aragon Ballroom, Chicago, 1972; Carnegie Hall, NYC, 1972-3; toured England/Europe working concert dates, 1973; toured Australia/New Zealand/Hawaii working concert dates, 1973-4; worked Civic Auditorium, Santa Monica, CA, 1973; worked w own Jazz/Blues Fusion group, Philharmonic Hall, NYC, NY, 1973; Academy of Music, NYC, 1973; Newport Jazz Festival, NYC, 1973; toured USA/Europe/Australia/Japan working concert dates, 1974; rec ABC-Blue Thumb label, NYC, NY/New Orleans, LA, 1975; toured US working concert dates, 1975; worked Old Waldorf, San Francisco, CA, 1977; Bottom Line, NYC, 1977; Ivanhoe Theater, Chicago, 1977; My Father's Place, Roslyn, NY, 1977; Aladdin, Las Vegas, NV, 1977

Billing: The Father of British Blues

Songs: Blues City Shake Down/I'm Gonna Fight for You JB/Jenny/The Laws Must Change/Mr James/Room to Move/Sitting in the Rain/So Hard to Share

Awards/Honors: Won *Jazz & Pop* magazine Readers Poll as best pop harmonica player, 1969

Won *Melody Maker* magazine Jazz Poll (British Section) as best blues artist of 1973

Infl by: John Lee Hooker/Clarence Lofton/Sonny Boy Williamson (Alex Miller)

Quotes: "Mayall is the big daddy of the British blues scene in that his successive bands have virtually acted as a finishing school for many of Britain's leading instrumentalists"—Nick Logan/Bob Woffinden, *The Illustrated Encyclopedia of Rock*, Hamlyn Publishing Group, 1976

"John Mayall, [a] master musician and bluesman . . ."—Fred Kirby, *Billboard* magazine, May 1, 1971

"His music is personal, very true to the blues and always somehow new"—Mike Bourne, *Downbeat* magazine, Nov 9, 1972, p 23

References: The Illustrated Encyclopedia of Rock, Nick Logan/Bob Woffinden, Hamlyn Publishing Group, 1976

Encyclopedia of Pop, Rock & Soul, Irwin Stambler, St Martin's Press, 1974

Goldmine magazine, Sept 3, 1993

MAYES, ETHEL
(see Moore, Monette)

MAYFIELD, PERCY

Photo by Norbert Hess

Born: Aug 12, 1920, Minden (Webster Parish), LA
Died: Aug 11, 1984, Los Angeles, CA
Inst: Piano

Father was Penn Mayfield; mother was Addis Carter; left home to hobo through Midwest working outside music from 1935; settled in Houston, TX, working outside music from c1938; moved to West Coast to frequently work outside music from mid-40s; rec Supreme label, Los Angeles, CA, 1947; toured package shows on West Coast, late 40s; rec Specialty label, early 50s; severe auto accident causing disfigurement, 1952; rec Chess label, Chicago, IL, 1955; Imperial label, 1959; rec Cash label, c1960; worked as song writer for Ray Charles, 1962-3; worked McKie's Club, Chicago, 1963; Sportsman Club, Oakland, CA, 1964; Playboy Club, Chicago, 1966; Fillmore Auditorium, San Francisco, CA, late 60s; West Coast concerts, 70s into 80s; app in film POET LAUREATE OF THE BLUES, 1981; toured Europe, 1982; died of heart attack; buried Inglewood Cem, Inglewood, CA

Songs: A Lying Woman/But on the Other Hand, Baby/The Country/Danger Zone/Hide nor Hair/The Highway Is Like a Woman/Hit the Road, Jack/Life Is Suicide/Live Today Like the Day Before/Lost Love/My Error/My Friend/Painful Party/Please Send Me Someone to Love/Strange Things Are Happening/This Time You Suffer Too/To Claim It's Love/To Live the Past/Two Years of Torture/Yes, You'll Play/You Wear Your Hair Too Long

Infl to: Mose Allison/Ray Charles

Quote: "Probably the most consistently good blues writer today"—Pete Lowry, *Blues Unlimited* magazine (UK), Sept 1971, p 23

MAYS, CURLEY
Born: Nov 26, 1938, Maxie (Acadia Parish), LA
Inst: Guitar

Father was guitarist; one of 3 children; moved to Beaumont, TX, where he was raised from childhood; taught self guitar at about 14 years of age; frequently worked street dances, Beaumont, from c1953; frequently worked Chaney's Club, Beaumont, mid-50s; frequently worked with local groups in clubs, Dallas, TX, late 50s; toured w Etta James Revue working theaters/ballrooms/supperclubs across US, 1959-63; worked Cinder Club, Houston, TX, 1964-5; frequently toured as sideman w The Five Royales/James Brown Show/Tina Turner Show/Julius Jones and the Rivieras and other shows/revues working concerts through Oklahoma/Texas through 60s; frequently worked as sideman in hotels, Las Vegas, NV, 1965; formed own band to work King Arthur's Court, San Antonio, TX, 1966; worked Eastwood Country Club, San Antonio, TX, 1966-7; Cinder Club, Houston, TX, 1968-9; Eastwood Country Club, San Antonio, 1970-2; continued working clubs/bars in San Antonio area into 70s

Personal: Married. 1 child. Nephew of "Gatemouth" Brown and cousin of Phillip Walker, musicians/singers

Quote: "With his showmanship and ability on the guitar he should please any blues audience . . ."—Bob Eagle, *Living Blues* magazine, Winter 1973, p 28

Reference: *Living Blues* magazine, Winter 1973, pp 27-8

McCAIN, JERRY *"Boogie"*

Courtesy Living Blues *Magazine*

Born: Jun 19, 1930, Gadsden (Etowah Co), AL
Inst: Drums/Guitar/Harmonica/Jew's Harp/Trumpet

Mother was guitarist; one of 5 children; interested in music early and learned harmonica at 5 years of age; frequently worked streets/cafes/radio shows for tips, Gadsden, AL, through 40s into 50s; formed own The Upstarts group to work local joints/jukes, Gadsden, early 50s; rec Trumpet label, Jackson, MS, 1953-4; rec Excello label, Nashville, TN, 1956-9; rec Rex label, Birmingham, AL, 1958-9; worked mostly outside music, Gadsden, AL, through 60s; rec OKeh label, Nashville, TN, 1962; inactive in music, 1962-5; rec RIC label, Nashville, 1965; rec Continental label, Birmingham, AL, 1965; rec Jewel label, Shreveport, LA, 1965-6; rec Royal American label, Nashville, c1970; worked outside music (as private investigator), Gadsden, AL, into 70s; rec Romulus label, Nashville, c1972; rec Jewel label, Shreveport, LA (or Nashville, TN), 1972; worked National Folk Festival, Wolf Trap Farm Park, Vienna, VA, 1977

Personal: Married

Songs: East of the Sun/Funky Down Easy/Here's Where You Get It/Homogenized Love/Hop Stroll/I'm in Trouble/Jet Stream/Juicy Lucy/Love Ain't Nothin' to Play With/Love Me Right/Pokey/Popcorn/Put It Where I Can Get It/Ruff Stuff/Run Uncle John Run/728 Texas/She's Crazy 'Bout Entertainers/She's Tough/Somebody's Been Talking/Soul Spasm/Steady/Sugar Baby/Things Ain't Right/Ting-Tang-Tigalu/Turn the Lights on Popeye/Twist '62'/What About You?/Wine-O-Wine

Infl by: Little Walter

Reference: Blues Unlimited magazine (UK), Jan 1971, pp 14-15

McCLENNAN, TOMMY
Born: Apr 8, 1908, Yazoo City (Yazoo Co), MS
Died: c1958-62, Chicago, IL (unconfirmed)
Inst: Guitar

Born on JF Sligh farm outside Yazoo City, MS, where he was raised and worked from childhood in area; learned guitar as youth and frequently worked streets for tips in Yazoo City area through 20s; worked outside music in Itta Bena/Greenwood, MS, area, early 30s; frequently worked w Honeyboy Edwards on streets/country dances/parties, Greenwood, MS, area, 1933-4; frequently worked w Robert Petway at local house parties, Itta Bena, MS, area, late 30s; moved to Chicago, IL, c1939; rec Bluebird label, Chicago, 1939-42; frequently worked outside music with occasional local club dates, Chicago, through 40s into 50s; mostly inactive, Chicago, through 50s; reportedly died destitute

Songs: Bottle (Shake) It Up and Go/I Love My Baby

Infl by: Rubin Lacy

Infl to: Eddie Burns/Robert Petway

Courtesy Sheldon Harris Collection

Quotes: "In spite of his small stature, Tommy McClennan has a fierce voice and powerful delivery which made him one of the most striking of blues singers on record"—(Paul Oliver) McCarthy/Morgan/Oliver/Harrison, *Jazz on Record*, Hanover Books Ltd, 1968

"His singing was often a toneless shout, a harsh, almost formless vocal line with sudden moments of excitement or laughter"—Samuel B Charters, *The Bluesmen*, Oak Publications, 1967

Reference: The Bluesmen, Samuel B Charters, Oak Publications, 1967

McCOY, CHARLES *"Charlie"/"Papa"*
(*aka:* Mississippi Mudder/Papa Charlie)
Born: May 26, 1909, Jackson (Hinds Co), MS
Died: Jul 26, 1950, Chicago, IL
Inst: Guitar/Mandolin

Father was Patrick McCoy; one of at least 3 children; interested in music early and taught self guitar as youth; frequently worked w Rubin Lacy/Son Spand/Walter Vinson/Tommy Johnson/Ishmon Bracey/others at local dances/parties/streets, Jackson, MS, area through 20s; worked w Johnny Temple at local house parties, Chicago, IL, late 20s; rec acc to Ishmon Bracey, Victor label, Memphis, TN, 1928; rec acc to Alec Johnson, Columbia label, Atlanta, GA, 1928; rec w Bo Chatmon, Brunswick label, New Orleans, LA, 1928; rec w Chatmon's Mississippi Hot Footers, Brunswick label, Memphis, 1929; rec w Mississippi Hot Footers and others, OKeh label, Atlanta, 1929-30; frequently rec acc to other bluesmen, Brunswick label, Memphis, 1930; rec w Bo Chatmon, OKeh label, Atlanta, 1930; rec w Mississippi Black Snakes, Brunswick label, Chicago, 1931; rec Vocalion label, NYC, NY, 1932; rec Decca label, Chicago, 1934-5; frequently rec acc to Red Nelson/Casey Bill/Johnny Temple/others, Chicago, from 1935; rec acc to Bill Broonzy, ARC label group, Chicago, 1936; rec w own Papa Charlie's Boys, Bluebird label, Chicago, 1936; formed/rec w Harlem Hamfats, Decca label, Chicago/NYC, 1936-9; rec acc to Rosetta Howard/Frankie Jaxon/others, Decca label, NYC, 1937; rec acc to Memphis Minnie, Vocalion label, Chicago, 1938; rec acc to John Lee "Sonny Boy" Williamson, Bluebird label, Chicago, 1941; rec w Big Joe (McCoy) and His Rhythm, Bluebird label, Chicago, 1941-2/44; worked w Joe McCoy, Martins Corner, Chicago, c1946; mostly inactive in Chicago through 40s; entered Psychopathic Hospital where he died of paralytic brain disease; buried Restvale Cemetery, Worth, IL

Personal: Brother of Joe McCoy, blues musician/singer. Not to be confused with musicians Charlie Davis or Charlie Jackson who also used pseudonym "Papa Charlie," or Charlie McCoy (harmonica), a later Nashville musician

Infl by: Rubin Lacy

Infl to: Luther Huff/Johnny Young

Quote: ". . . one of the most prolific accompanists in blues history"—Tony Russell, *Jazz & Blues* magazine (UK), May 1971, p 29

McCOY, JOE

(*aka:* Big Joe/Georgia Pine Boy/Hallelujah Joe/Hamfoot Ham/Kansas Joe/Mississippi Mudder/Mud Dauber Joe/Bill Wilber)
Born: May 11, 1905, Raymond (Hinds Co), MS
Died: Jan 28, 1950, Chicago, IL
Inst: Guitar/Mandolin

Courtesy Sheldon Harris Collection

Father was Patrick McCoy; one of at least 3 children; interested in music early and taught self guitar as youth; frequently worked local dances/parties/streets, Jackson, MS, area, through 20s; rec acc to Alec Johnson, Columbia label, Atlanta, GA, 1928; teamed w Memphis Minnie to work clubs/taverns, Memphis, TN, 1929 through mid-30s; frequently worked w Memphis Minnie in Jed Davenport's Beale Street Jug Band, local streets/parks, Memphis, c1929; rec w Memphis Minnie, Columbia label, NYC, NY, 1929; rec w Memphis Minnie, Vocalion label, Memphis, TN/Chicago, IL, 1930; worked North Memphis Cafe, Memphis, c1930; frequently worked w Memphis Minnie at Music Box Club/Mike DeLisa Club/Gatewood's Tavern/other clubs/bars/taverns, Chicago, 1930-5; rec w Memphis Minnie, Vocalion label, Chicago, 1931; rec w Memphis Minnie (and solo), Vocalion label, NYC, 1932; rec Decca label, Chicago, 1934; frequently rec acc to local bluesmen, Champion/Bluebird labels, Chicago, 1935; formed Harlem Hamfats and rec Decca label, Chicago/NYC, 1936-9; rec w Palooka Washboard Band, Decca label, Chicago, 1937; reportedly worked as preacher, Chicago, from c1937; rec as Big Joe and His Rhythm, Bluebird label, Chicago, 1941-2/44; worked mostly outside music, Chicago, through 40s; worked w Charlie McCoy, Martin's Corner, Chicago, c1946; mostly inactive in late 40s; died at home of heart disease; buried Restvale Cemetery, Worth, IL

Note: Some unconfirmed reports claim this singer's given name to be "Wilber"

Personal: Married Lizzie Douglas (Memphis Minnie) (1929-35); Virginia ——— (late 30s). 2 children. Was brother of blues musician/singer Charlie McCoy. Not to be confused with blues singer Joe Lee Williams who uses pseudonym "Big Joe"

Songs: I Got Somebody Else/I'm a Fool/I'm Going to St Louis/If I Didn't Love You/It Looks Bad for You/ Just Rockin'/Let Me Dig It/Love Me/Oh Baby/Oh Joe/Oh Red/Southern Blues/We Gonna Pitch a Boogie Woogie/What You Gonna Do?/Why Don't You Do Right?/Yes, I Got Your Woman

Quote: "His blues recordings under a number of colourful pseudonyms . . . often popularized country themes, but McCoy's musicianship was not in doubt"—Paul Oliver, *The Story of the Blues*, Chilton Book Company, 1969

McCOY, MINNIE
(see Douglas, Lizzie)

McCOY, ROBERT EDWARD *"Bob"/"Cyclone"*
Born: Mar 31, 1910, Aliceville (Pickens Co), AL
Died: Feb 12, 1978, Birmingham, AL
Inst: Piano

Father was Joseph McCoy; mother Janie Bonner; born Robert Jesse McCoy, later changing middle name; moved to North Birmingham, AL, where he was raised from 2 months of age; heard Cow Cow Davenport/Pinetop Smith who frequently played at his home during 20s; taught self piano and frequently worked local dances/rent parties/clubs, Birmingham, AL, from 1927; worked Paradise Inn, Montgomery, AL, 1929; frequently worked as accompanist to local singers in clubs, Birmingham area, through 20s/30s; worked w Charlie Campbell's Red Peppers in Birmingham area from mid-30s; reportedly rec w Charlie Campbell's Red Peppers, Vocalion label, Birmingham, 1937; rec acc to Peanut the Kidnapper/Guitar Slim, ARC label group, Birmingham, 1937; reportedly worked w Bogan's Birmingham Busters in local clubs, Birmingham area, c1938; served in US Army, early 40s; worked mostly outside music with only occasional local party work, Birmingham, through 40s/ 50s/into 60s; rec Vulcan label, Birmingham, 1963; formed own band to tour club dates through South, 1964; worked Royal Peacock Club, Atlanta, GA, 1964; 27-28 Club, Birmingham, 1964; Famous Club, Birmingham, 1964; rec Soul-O label, Birmingham, 1964; Grand Terrace Ballroom, Birmingham, 1965; Woodland Club, Birmingham, 1967; worked mostly as deacon of local church, Birmingham, into 70s; died of cancer; buried Grace Hill Cem, Birmingham

Personal: Not to be confused with guitarist Robert Nighthawk who used pseudonym "Robert Lee McCoy"

Song: McCoy Boogie

Infl by: Leroy Carr/Cow Cow Davenport/Pinetop Smith

Reference: Oldie Blues album OL-2814

McCOY, ROBERT LEE
(see Nighthawk, Robert)

McCOY, VIOLA
(*aka:* Amanda Brown/Daisy Cliff/Fannie Johnson/ Gladys Johnson/Violet McCoy/Clara White/Bessie Williams/Susan Williams)

Courtesy Frank Driggs Collection

Born: c1900, Memphis (Shelby Co), TN
Died: c1956, Albany, NY (unconfirmed)
Inst: Kazoo

True name may be Amanda Brown; reportedly settled in New York, NY, to work local cabarets from early 20s; app in MOONSHINE Revue, Lafayette Theater, NYC, 1922; frequently worked Lincoln Theater, NYC, 1922-3; app in FROLICERS Revue, Lafayette Theater, NYC, 1923; rec Gennett/Columbia/Ajax labels, NYC, 1923; rec Vocalion label, NYC, 1923-6; rec Pathe/Banner labels, NYC, 1924; rec w Fletcher Henderson's Jazz Five, Brunswick label, NYC, 1924; rec w Choo Choo Jazzers, Ajax label, NYC, 1924; rec w Kansas City Five, Edison label, NYC, 1924; worked Lafayette Theater, NYC, 1924; app in WHO STOLE THE MONEY? musical comedy, Lafayette Theater, NYC, 1924; app in HIDDEN TREASURE musical comedy, Lafayette Theater, NYC, 1924; rec Cameo label, NYC, 1926-7; worked Club Alabam, Philadelphia, PA, 1926; frequently toured TOBA/RKO theater circuits working vaudeville shows through 20s; briefly owned/operated/performed at Jack's Cabaret, NYC, 1927; app in RARIN' TO GO Revue, Park Theater, Bridgeport, CT, 1927/Lafayette Theater, NYC, 1927; app in SETTING THE PACE Revue, Lafayette Theater, NYC, 1927; app in NEW YORK REVUE, Lincoln Theater, NYC, 1928; app in FLYING HIGH Revue, Alhambra Theater, NYC, 1928; app in JOYLAND Revue, Alhambra Theater, NYC, 1928; app in HAPPINESS Revue, Alhambra Theater, NYC, 1928; app in BROWNSKIN BREVITIES Revue, Alhambra Theater, NYC, 1928; app in LAUGHING THROUGH Revue, Alhambra Theater, NYC, 1928; app in SOUTHBOUND Revue, Alhambra Theater, NYC, 1928; rec Columbia label, NYC, 1929; app in THE SURPRISE PARTY Revue, Alhambra Theater, NYC, 1929; app in READY MONEY Revue, Alhambra Theater, NYC, 1929; app in EGG NOG Revue, Alhambra Theater, NYC, 1929; app in HOP OFF Revue, Alhambra Theater, NYC, 1929; app in SWEETHEARTS ON PARADE Revue, Alhambra Theater, NYC, 1929; app in PEARLS OF INDIA Revue, Alhambra Theater, NYC, 1929; app in THE CONJURE MAN Revue, Alhambra Theater, NYC, 1929; app in musical comedy THE CRAZY HOTEL, Alhambra Theater, NYC, 1929; app in AT THE BARBECUE Revue, Alhambra Theater, NYC, 1930; app in BY MOONLIGHT Revue, Alhambra Theater, NYC, 1930; app in SNAKE HIPS REVUE, Alhambra Theater, NYC, 1930; app in FASHION PLATE FROLICS Revue, Alhambra Theater, NYC, 1930; app in IN THE SWIM Revue, Alhambra Theater, NYC, 1930; owned/operated an (unknown) nightclub, Saratoga, NY, 1930; app in SCRAMBLIN' ROUN' Revue, Lafayette Theater, NYC, 1930; app in EDITH WILSON REVUE, Alhambra Theater, NYC, 1930; app w Troy "Bear" Brown, BABY'S BIRTHDAY Revue, Alhambra Theater, NYC, 1930; worked Standard Theater, Philadelphia, PA, 1931; app in SWEET PAPA GARBAGE Revue, Lafayette Theater, NYC, 1931; app in PLENTY OF IT Revue, Lafayette Theater, NYC, 1932; app w Fletcher Henderson Orch, HARLEM HIGH STEPPERS Revue, Public Theater, NYC, 1932; worked Harlem Opera House, NYC, 1933; app w Gladys Bentley's UBANGI CLUB REVUE, Lafayette Theater, NYC, 1934; app w Tiny Bradshaw Orch, WALKING ON AIR Revue, Apollo Theater, NYC, 1934; w Leroy Smith Band, Harlem Opera House, NYC, 1935; frequently worked club/theater dates, Philadelphia, PA, 1935-6; settled in Albany, NY, and mostly inactive in music from c1938

Personal: Not to be confused with Rosa Henderson who also used pseudonym "Bessie Williams"

Quote: "She belongs to the great vaudeville tradition, but in all she does there is a strong jazz strain"—Derrick Stewart-Baxter, *Ma Rainey and the Classic Blues Singers*, Studio Vista Ltd, 1970

McCOY, VIOLET

(see McCoy, Viola)

McCRACKLIN, JIMMY

Born: Aug 13, 1921, St Louis (St Louis Co), MO
Inst: Harmonica/Piano

Born/raised in St Louis, MO; served in US Navy, early 40s; settled in Watts area, Los Angeles, CA, working as professional boxer (23 bouts) from mid-40s; learned some piano from JD Nicholson c1945; rec w JD Nicholson group, Globe label, Los Angeles, 1945; worked outside music in Santa Barbara, CA, area, c1945-6; rec Excelsior label, Los Angeles, 1945; worked outside music with frequent local club dates, Los Angeles area, through 40s; rec Cavatone label, Oakland, CA, 1947; rec J&M Fulbright label, Oakland, CA, 1948; rec w own Blues Blasters, Downtown label, Oakland, 1949-50; rec Trilon label, Oakland, 1949; rec RPM/Modern labels, Oakland, 1950; rec Swingtime label, Los Angeles, 1951; rec Peacock label, Houston, TX, 1952-3; rec Peacock label, Oakland, 1953-4; rec Modern-Crown label, Oakland, 1954-5; rec Hollywood label, Oakland, 1955; rec Irma label, Oakland (?), 1956; worked Savoy Club, Richmond, CA, c1956; reportedly app w Frankie Lee Sims, Dick Clark's AMERICAN BANDSTAND, ABC-TV, c1957; rec Checker label, Chicago, IL, 1957; rec Mercury label, Chicago, 1957-9; formed own Art-Tone label, Oakland, c1962; toured w Eddie Boyd working concert dates, 1962; formed own band to tour South working club/concert dates from 1965; owned/managed/performed, Continental Club, Oakland, CA, c1965-73 (por 1973 date shown on ALL TOGETHER NOW, KPIX-TV, San Francisco, CA); rec Stax label, California, c1971; worked Univ of

Jimmy McCracklin *Photo by Dave Patrick. Courtesy* Living Blues *Magazine*

California Extension Center, San Francisco, 1973; Joe's Melody Club, Vallejo, CA, 1974; La Jolla Club, San Francisco, 1974; San Francisco Blues Festival, McLaren Park Amphitheater, San Francisco, 1975; rec Vanguard label, NYC, 1975; worked Cassidy Hotel, Richmond, CA, 1975; West Dakota Club, Berkeley, CA, 1975; Singleton's, Houston, TX, 1975; Eli's Mile High Club, San Francisco, 1976; Green Earth Cafe, San Francisco, 1976; app on BLUES BY THE BAY, KPFA-FM-radio, Berkeley, 1976; worked WOW Hall, Eugene, OR, 1977; Slats, San Francisco, 1977

Personal: Married Minnie ———

Songs: By Myself/Every Night and Every Day/How About That?/I Had to Get With It/I Just Got to Know/Shame Shame Shame/Take a Chance/Tramp/What's Going On?/You Ain't Nothing But a Devil/You Know Who to Turn To/You're in My Book First/You've Got Me Licked

Infl to: Al K Smith

McDANIEL, ELLAS
(*aka:* Bo Diddley)

Courtesy BMI Archives

Born: Dec 30, 1928, McComb (Pike Co), MS
Inst: Guitar/Harmonica/Trombone/Violin

Father was —— Bates, mother Ethel Wilson; born Ellas Bates on farm between McComb and Magnolia, MS; adopted by the McDaniel family; moved to Chicago, IL, 1934; studied violin w Prof OW Frederick, musical director of Ebenezer Baptist Church (later working in that church orchestra), Chicago, 1934-46; attended Foster Vocational HS and taught self guitar, Chicago, early 40s; formed school band (w Earl Hooker/others) called The Langley Avenue Jive Cats to work local streets for tips, Chicago, from 1941; worked as trombonist in Baptist Congress Band, Chicago, early 40s; formed own washboard trio to work amateur shows/house parties/streets, 1946-51; frequently worked outside music (sometimes as semi-pro boxer), Chicago, late 40s into 50s; worked 708 Club, Chicago, 1951; Sawdust Trail, Chicago, 1954; Castle Rock, Chicago, 1954; rec extensively Checker-Chess label, Chicago, 1955-74; app on Ed Sullivan's TOAST OF THE TOWN Show, CBS-TV, 1955; worked Alan Freed's Diddley Daddy R&B package show, Loew's State, Boston, MA, 1955; worked Carnegie Hall, NYC, 1955; Figueroa Ballroom, Los Angeles, CA, 1955; frequently worked Dr Jive's R&B Revue, Apollo Theater, NYC, 1955-60; Howard Theater, Washington, DC, c1955; Gleason's Lounge, Cleveland, OH, 1956; toured w Red Prysock Rock 'N' Roll Orch in Biggest Rock 'N' Roll Show of 1956 package show working dances/concerts/theaters across US/Australia, 1956; toured w Alan Freed Presents The Big Beat package show working theaters across US, 1956; toured w Alan Freed's Easter Jubilee package show, 1957 (and other package shows through 1950s); extensively toured US/Canada working club/vaudeville circuit, late 50s; formed own ARC Music Publishers Company, Chicago, c1960; frequently worked/rec as session musician/director on various labels, Chicago, into 60s; toured one-nighters working clubs through South and western US, early 60s; toured England working concert dates, 1963; worked Esquire Showbar, Montreal, Can, 1964; extensive tours on college circuit working concert dates across US, 1964; app on SHINDIG, ABC-TV, 1965; worked Basin Street East, NYC, NY, 1965; toured England/Europe working club/concert dates, 1965; worked Apollo Theater, NYC, 1965-7; Le Coq D'or, Toronto, Can, 1966; app in film THE LEGEND OF BO DIDDLEY, 1966; app in film THE BIG TNT SHOW, 1966; worked Opera House, Seattle, WA, 1967; Fillmore Auditorium, San Francisco, CA, 1967; rec w Muddy Waters, Checker label, Chicago, IL, 1967; worked Barnaby's, Chicago, 1968; Winterland, San Francisco, 1969; Ice Palace, Las Vegas, NV, 1969; Chicago Blues Festival, Chicago, 1969; Seattle Pop Festival, Duvall, WA, 1969; Toronto Pop Festival, Toronto, Can, 1969 (por shown in film SWEET TORONTO and abridged film version KEEP ON ROCKIN'); worked Rock & Roll Revival Show, Madison Square Garden, NYC (with frequent US tours), 1969-74; settled in New Mexico c1970; worked Man and His World Exhibit, Montreal, Can, 1970; app in MUSIC SCENE, ABC-TV, 1970; worked Auditorium Theater, Chicago, 1970; Civic Opera House, Chicago, 1970; app on MIKE DOUGLAS Show, CBS-TV, 1971; toured w Creedence Clearwater rock group working concert dates across US, 1971; worked The Forum, Los Angeles, CA, 1971; The Lighthouse, Los Angeles, 1971; Long Beach Arena, Los Angeles, 1971; rec ST for cartoon film FRITZ THE CAT, 1971; worked Gassy Jack's Place, Vancouver, Can, 1972; International Art of Jazz Festival, NYC, 1972; Esquire Showbar, Montreal, Can, 1972; Montreux Jazz Festival, Montreux, Switzerland, 1972; Villageast, NYC, 1972; app in film LET THE GOOD TIMES ROLL, 1973; app in DICK CLARK PRESENTS THE ROCK & ROLL YEARS, ABC-TV, 1973; toured Australia working annual concert dates, 1973-5; worked Monterey Jazz Festival, Monterey, CA, 1973-4; Philharmonic Hall, NYC, 1974; El Mocambo, Toronto, 1974; The Boarding House, San Francisco, 1974; Great American Music Hall, San Francisco, 1974; The Attic, Chicago, 1974; In Concert Club, Montreal, 1974; Ritz Theater, Austin, TX, 1974; served as deputy sheriff of New Mexico police force, 1974-5; app on MIDNIGHT SPECIAL, NBC-TV, 1975; worked Radio City Music Hall, NYC, 1975; rec RCA-Victor label, Seattle, WA/Los Angeles, CA/NYC, NY/Miami, FL, c1975; worked Greenwood Inn, Portland, OR, 1975; toured w Rhythm & Blues: Roots of Rock Show working concert dates through Europe, 1975; app on DONNY & MARIE Show, ABC-TV, 1976; app on DICK CLARK'S GOOD OLD DAYS Show, NBC-TV, 1977; app on DICK CLARK'S LIVE WEDNESDAY, NBC-TV, 1978

Personal: Married Ethel Mae Smith (1946-divorced); 2 children. Married Kay ———; 2 children. "Bo Diddley" was childhood name and refers to a mischievous or "bully" boy

Billings: The Black Gladiator/500% More Man

Songs: Bo Diddley/Bo Diddley Is Loose/Bo Diddley's a Gun Slinger/Bo's a Lumberjack/Bo's Blues/Bring It to Jerome/Crackin' Up/Dearest Darling/Diddley Daddy/Down Home Special/Hey Bo Diddley/Hush Your Mouth/I'm a Man (Manish Boy)/I'm Bad/I'm Looking for a Woman/Mona/Mr Khrushchev/Ooh Baby/Oh Yea/Pretty Thing/Road Runner/Say Man/Who Do You Love?/You Don't Love Me

Infl by: Louis Jordan/Muddy Waters

Infl to: The Animals/Elvis Presley/The Rolling Stones/The Yardbirds

Quotes: "A major figure in the R&B scene since 1955"—(Paul Oliver) McCarthy/Morgan/Oliver/Harrison, *Jazz on Record*, Hanover Books, 1968

"When he laid aside his patented jive line and got stuck into some serious blues [singing], he proved himself to be almost in the same league as fellow Chess artists like Muddy Waters and Howlin' Wolf"—Charles Sharr Murray, *New Musical Express* (UK), Feb 8, 1975

"More than anything else, Bo Diddley brought a mesmeric rhythm to rock music in the mid-fifties"—Chris May, *Rock 'n' Roll*, Socion Books, 1973

References: Blues Unlimited magazine (UK), Apr 1970, pp 4-6; May 1970, pp 11-12

Chess album 60005

Encyclopedia of Pop, Rock & Soul, Irwin Stambler, St Martin's Press, 1974

McDANIEL, HATTIE

(*aka:* Hi-Hat Hattie)
Born: Jun 10, 1895, Wichita (Sedgwick Co), KS
Died: Oct 26, 1952, Hollywood, CA
Inst: Drums

Father was Henry McDaniel, a Baptist minister who operated own McDaniel Company touring show from c1910; mother was Susan Holbert, a singer; one of 13 children; moved to Denver, CO, as child where she was raised; interested in music early and learned many songs from mother as child; attended East Denver HS, Denver, from c1910; frequently toured w Spikes Brothers Comedy Stars troupe working theaters on West Coast during vacations c1910-13; worked amateur theater shows in area, Denver, through teens; occasionally toured w brother Otis McDaniel Company working tent shows through Midwest from c1917; app on local amateur talent radio shows, Denver, early 20s; frequently worked (as singer/musician) w George Morrison's Orch in Maple Leaf Club and other social/private parties/dances, Denver area, 1922-5; toured w George Morrison's Orch working Shrine & Elks Indoor Circuses, Denver, CO/Salt Lake City, UT/El Paso, TX/elsewhere c1922; worked w George Morrison's Orch, Latino Americano, Juarez, Mexico, c1922; toured (as singer/recitalist) w George Morrison's Orch on Pantages vaudeville circuit working auditoriums/theaters through Minnesota/western Canada/Washington/Oregon/California/Arizona/Missouri, 1924-5; rec Meritt label, Kansas City, MO, 1926; rec w Lovie Austin's Serenaders/Richard M Jones Jazz Wizards and others, OKeh label, Chicago, IL, 1926-7; worked outside music with occasional dates in local vaudeville theaters, Kansas City, MO, through 20s; rec Paramount label, Chicago, 1929; frequently headlined floor show, Sam Pick's Suburban Inn, Milwaukee, WI, 1929-31; app in road-company unit of show SHOW BOAT touring major theaters across US, 1929-30; app frequently (as "Hi-Hat Hattie") on weekly OPTIMISTIC DONUT'S variety show, KNX-radio, Los Angeles, CA, 1931; settled in Hollywood, CA, to work outside music, 1931; app in non-singing role in film BLONDE VENUS, 1932; app in film GOLDEN WEST, 1932; app in film HYPNOTIZED, 1932; app in film WASHINGTON MASQUERADE, 1932; app in SHOW BOAT, NBC-radio Network musical series, 1932-3; app thereafter as non-singing film actress (usually in maid/mammy roles) w Bill Robinson/Shirley Temple/Mae West/Clark Gable/Al Jolson/others; app in film THE STORY OF TEMPLE DRAKE, 1933; app in film I'M NO ANGEL, 1933; app in film JUDGE PRIEST,

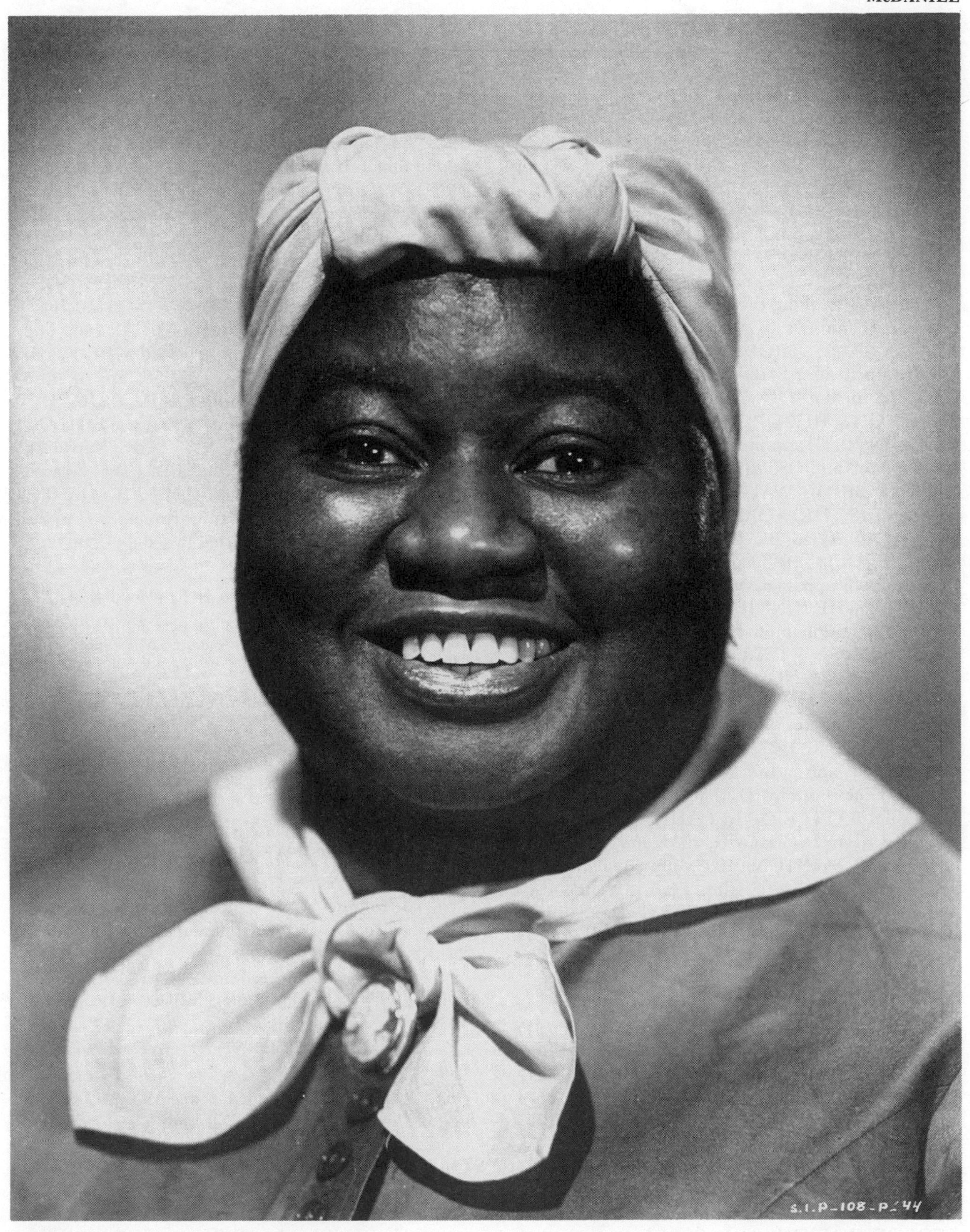

Hattie McDaniel *Courtesy Sheldon Harris Collection*

1934; app in film OPERATOR THIRTEEN, 1934; app in film LOST IN THE STRATOSPHERE, 1934; app in film BABBITT, 1934; app in film IMITATION OF LIFE, 1934; app in film LITTLE MEN, 1934; app in Charley Chase film shorts, FATE'S FATHEAD (1934)/CHASES OF PIMPLE STREET (1934)/OKAY TOOTS! (1935)/FOUR-STAR BOARDER (1935); app in film MUSIC IS MAGIC, 1935; app in film ANOTHER FACE, 1935; app in film ALICE ADAMS, 1935; app in film CHINA SEAS, 1935; app in film TRAVELING SALESLADY, 1935; app in film THE LITTLE COLONEL, 1935; frequently toured w John Erby working theater concert dates on West Coast from mid-30s; app in Our Gang film shorts, ANNIVERSARY TROUBLE (1935)/ARBOR DAY (1936); app in film SHOW BOAT (in musical role), 1936; app in film THE FIRST BABY, 1936; app in film HEARTS DIVIDED, 1936; app in film HIGH TENSION, 1936; app in film STAR FOR A NIGHT, 1936; app in film POSTAL INSPECTOR, 1936; app in film THE BRIDE WALKS OUT, 1936; app in film VALIANT IS THE WORD FOR CARRIE, 1936; app in film CAN THIS BE DIXIE?, 1936; app in film GENTLE JULIA, 1936; app in film NEXT TIME WE LOVE, 1936; app in film LIBELED LADY, 1936; app in film THE SINGING KID, 1936; app in film REUNION, 1936; app in film RACING LADY, 1937; app in film DON'T TELL THE WIFE, 1937; app in film THE CRIME NOBODY SAW, 1937; app in film TRUE CONFESSION, 1937; app in film OVER THE GOAL, 1937; app in film 45 FATHERS, 1937; app in film SARATOGA, 1937; app in film NOTHING SACRED, 1937; app in film MERRY-GO-ROUND OF 1938, 1937; app in film THE WILD CATTER, 1937; app in film BATTLE OF BROADWAY, 1938; app in film THE SHINING HOUR, 1938; app in film THE MAD MISS MANTON, 1938; app in film CAREFREE, 1938; app in film THE SHOPWORN ANGEL, 1938; app in film EVERYBODY'S BABY, 1939; app in film ZENOBIA, 1939; app in film GONE WITH THE WIND, 1939; app in film MARYLAND, 1940; worked w Harry James Orch, Paramount Theater, NYC, NY, 1940; app in film AFFECTIONATELY YOURS, 1941; app in film THE GREAT LIE, 1941; app in film THEY DIED WITH THEIR BOOTS ON, 1941; app in film YOU'RE IN THE ARMY NOW, 1941; app on RUDY VALLEE Show, NBC-radio Network, c1941; app on Eddie Cantor's TIME TO SMILE Show, NBC-radio Network, c1941; worked w Count Basie Orch, Strand Theater, NYC, NY, 1941; app in film THE MALE ANIMAL, 1942; app in film IN THIS OUR LIFE, 1942; app in film GEORGE WASHINGTON SLEPT HERE, 1942; toured w Ethel Waters and others working military bases/veterans' hospitals through California from 1942; app on BLUEBERRY HILL, CBS-radio, 1943; app in film THANK YOUR LUCKY STARS (in musical role), 1943; app in film JOHNNY COME LATELY, 1943; app in film SINCE YOU WENT AWAY, 1944; app in film THREE IS A FAMILY, 1944; app in film JANIE, 1944; app in film HI BEAUTIFUL, 1944; app frequently on BILLIE BURKE Show, CBS-radio Network, c1945; app frequently on AMOS 'N' ANDY Show, NBC-radio Network, 1945-7; app in film MARGIE, 1946; app in film NEVER SAY GOODBYE, 1946; app in film JANIE GETS MARRIED, 1946; app in film SONG OF THE SOUTH, 1946; app in film THE FLAME, 1947; app in lead in BEULAH, CBS-radio Network series, 1947-50; app in film MICKEY, 1948; app in film FAMILY HONEYMOON, 1948; app on Bing Crosby's PHILCO RADIO TIME, WJZ-radio, NYC (ABC Network), 1949; app in film THE BIG WHEEL, 1949; replaced Ethel Waters as lead in series BEULAH, ABC-TV, 1951-2; entered Motion Picture Home & Hospital where she died of cancer; buried Rosedale Cemetery, Los Angeles, CA

Personal: Married James Lloyd Crawford (1941-); Larry C Williams (1949-50); plus had an earlier marriage. Her brother Sam "Deacon" McDaniel (died 1962) was film actor

Billings: The Colored Sophie Tucker/The Female Bert Williams

Book: Hattie: The Life Of Hattie McDaniel, Carlton Jackson, Madison Books, 1989

Songs: Any Kind of a Man Would Be Better Than You/Boo Hoo Blues/I Wish I Had Somebody/That New Love Maker of Mine

Awards/Honors: Won White Women's Christian Temperance Association Dramatic Art Medal, Wichita, KS, 1916

Won Academy Award for Best Supporting Actress in film GONE WITH THE WIND, 1939

Was first Negro to receive an Academy Award (1939)

Quotes: "Hattie McDaniel . . . was the possessor of one of the biggest voices of all, and her deep tragic expressiveness was second only to Ma Rainey's"—Chris Hillman, *Storyville* magazine (UK), Oct 1976, p 13

"Hattie McDaniel was one of the screen's greatest presences, a pre-Felliniesque figure of the absurd and a marvel of energetic verve and enthusiasm"—Donald Bogle, *Toms, Coons, Mulattoes, Mammies and Bucks*, Viking Press, 1973

Reference: Current Biography, HW Wilson Company, 1940

McDOWELL, *"Mississippi"* FRED

Photo by Julie Snow

Born: Jan 12, 1904, Rossville (Feyette Co), TN
Died: Jul 3, 1972, Memphis, TN
Inst: Guitar

Father was Jimmy McDowell and mother was Ida Cureay, both farmers; one of 2 children; parents died when he was youth; worked outside music (on farm) to 1926; taught self guitar and frequently worked local dances, Rossville, TN, area, 1918-26; left home to work outside music, Memphis, TN, 1926; frequently hoboed as itinerant musician working suppers/picnics/house parties/fish fries/dances in Red Banks/Cleveland/Lamar/Holly Springs, MS (and elsewhere through Delta area), through 20s/30s; settled in Como, MS, to work outside music (as farmer) with occasional Saturday night dances/house parties/picnics in area from 1940; rec Atlantic/Prestige labels, Como, MS, 1959; frequently worked Stuckey's candy store for tips, Como, early 60s; continued working outside music with frequent work at local parties/dances/church affairs in Como area through 60s; worked Univ of Chicago Folk Festival, Chicago, IL, 1963; rec w Annie Mae McDowell, Testament label, Como, MS, 1963-4; rec Arhoolie label, Como, MS, 1964; worked Ash Grove, Los Angeles, CA, 1964; Newport Folk Festival, Newport, RI, 1964 (por rel Vanguard label/por shown in film FESTIVAL); New School for Social Research, NYC, NY, 1965; toured West Coast working club/coffeehouse dates, 1965; frequently app on WSAO-radio, Como, MS, 1965; rec Arhoolie label, Berkeley, CA/Como, MS, 1965; toured w American Folk Blues Festival working concert dates through England/Europe, 1965 (por Hamburg, Ger, concert rel Fontana label); rec acc to Big Mama Thornton, Arhoolie label, London, Eng, 1965; app on local TV programs, Holland, 1965; worked Berkeley Folk Festival, Berkeley, CA, 1965-6 (por 1965 concert rel Arhoolie label); rec International-Polydor/Black Lion labels, Como, MS, 1965; rec Arhoolie label, Como, 1966; rec Testament label, Chicago, IL, 1966; worked Univ of Chicago Folklore Society Festival, Chicago, 1966; toured w Memphis Blues Society package show working concert dates across US, 1966; worked Univ of California, Los Angeles, CA, 1966 (por rel Milestone label); Avant Garde Coffeehouse, Milwaukee, WI, 1967; rec w Johnny Woods, Revival label, Como, MS, 1967; worked Newport Folk Festival, Newport, RI, 1968; Arts Society concert, Phoenix, AZ, 1968; app in documentary film short THE BLUES MAKER, 1968; toured w Blues Scene 69 working concert dates through England/Europe, 1969 (por of London concert rel Sire label); rec Transatlantic label, London, Eng, 1969; rec Capitol/Just Sunshine/Antilles labels, Jackson, MS, 1969; rec Biograph label, Como, MS, 1969; app in film short FRED McDOWELL, 1969; worked Sky River Rock Festival, Tenino, WA, 1969; Memphis Blues Festival, Memphis, TN, 1969-70; rec Arhoolie label, Memphis, TN/Berkeley, CA, 1969; worked Ann Arbor Blues Festival, Ann Arbor, MI, 1969-70; Wisconsin Delta Blues Festival, Beloit College, Beloit, WI, 1970; Mariposa Folk Festival, Toronto, Can, 1970; Village Gaslight, NYC, NY, 1970-1 (por of 1971 date rel Oblivion label); Washington Blues Festival, Howard Univ, Washington, DC, 1970; Philadelphia Folk Festival, Schwenksville, PA, 1970-1 (por of 1971 concert shown on PHILADELPHIA FOLK FESTIVAL, PBS-TV); Notre Dame Blues Festival, South Bend, IN, 1970-1; toured concert dates through East/Midwest, 1971; app in film ROOTS OF AMERICAN MUSIC: COUNTRY & URBAN MUSIC (pt 3), 1971; worked River City Blues Festival, Memphis, TN, 1971; Boston Blues Society concert, Boston, MA, 1971; Univ of Pittsburgh Blues Festival, Pittsburgh, PA, 1971; Ash Grove, Los Angeles, CA, 1971; Texas Blues Festival, Liberty Hall, Houston, TX, 1971; The Alley, Ann Arbor, MI, 1971; mostly inactive due to illness, 1972; entered Baptist Hospital where he died of cancer; buried Hammond Hill Church Cemetery, Como, MS

Personal: Married Annie Mae Collins (1940-72), a singer. 1 child

Songs: Annie Mae Blues/Baby Let Me Lay Down/Black Minnie/Do My Baby Ever Think of Me/Eyes Like an Eagle/Fred's Worried Life Blues/Frisco Line/Goin' Down to the River/Gravel Road Blues/I Ain't Gonna Be Bad No More/I Don't Need No Heater/I Heard Somebody Call/I Looked at the Sun/I Walked All the Way from E St Louis/I'm Crazy About You Baby/Kokomo Blues/The Lovin' Blues/Mercy/Mortgage on My Soul/My Second Mind/My Trouble Blues/Over the Hill/Rap/Somebody Keeps Calling Me/Someday/Take Your Picture Darling/The Train I Ride/White Lightnin'/Write Me a Few Lines/You Gonna Be Sorry/You (You've) Got to Move

Infl by: Eli Green/Sid Hemphill/Vandy McKenna/Charley Patton/Raymond Payne

Infl to: Bonnie Raitt

Quote: "Fred McDowell is a blues singer-guitarist of such extraordinary power, emotional intensity and strong individuality that he must be counted among the most significant blues discoveries of recent years [1964]"—Pete Welding, Polydor album 236570

References: Arhoolie album F-1027
Lightnin' Express magazine #3 (1975-6), pp 32-3
Blues Unlimited magazine (UK), Jul 1965, p 4

McGHEE, GRANVILLE H *"Stick(s)"/"Globetrotter"*
Born: Mar 23, 1918, Knoxville (Knox Co), TN
Died: Aug 15, 1961, New York, NY
Inst: Guitar

Father was George Duffield McGhee, a singer/musician; mother was Zella Henely; one of 5 children; moved to farm near Vonore, TN, 1928; raised in Kingsport, TN, where he learned guitar as a pastime c1933; dropped out of school to work outside music in Kingsport area, late 30s; briefly worked outside music, Portsmouth, VA, c1940-1; served in US Army in Pacific Theater of Operations, c1942-6; settled in New York, NY, to work outside music from c1946; rec w Brownie McGhee/Dan Burley, Circle label, NYC, 1946; rec w Brownie McGhee, Harlem label, NYC, 1947; rec w own Sticks McGhee and His Buddies, Decca label, NYC, 1947; frequently worked w Dan Burley in local clubs, NYC, c1948; rec Atlantic label, NYC, 1949-51; rec London label, NYC, 1951; worked local club dates, Cleveland, OH, 1951; rec Essex label, NYC, 1952; rec King label, NYC, 1953; rec w Sonny Terry, Red Robin label, NYC, c1953; rec w own Sticks McGhee and the Ramblers, Savoy label, NYC, 1954-5; rec King label, NYC, 1955; rec w Sonny Terry, Groove label, NYC, 1955; rec w Sonny Terry, Folkways label, NYC, 1958; rec w Sonny Terry, Prestige-Bluesville/Herald labels, NYC, 1960; entered Francis Delafield Hospital where he died of cancer; buried Long Island National Cemetery, Pinelawn (Long Island), NY

Courtesy Big Chief Ellis/Peter B Lowry

Personal: Married Lillie Francis ———; brother of Brownie McGhee, blues singer/musician. Named "Stick" due to his frequent pushing of invalid brother Brownie in a cart with a stick as youth

Songs: Bones Blues/Dealin' from the Bottom/Drink of

Wine, Mop Mop/Drinkin' Wine, Spo-Dee-O-Dee/ Get Your Mind Out of the Gutter/Jailhouse Blues/ Jungle Juice/My Baby Gone Home/So Bad Glad/ Whiskey, Women and Loaded Dice

Reference: Nothing But the Blues, Mike Leadbitter, Hanover Books, 1971

McGHEE, WALTER BROWN *"Brownie"*
(*aka:* Brother George/Big Tom Collins/Blind Boy Fuller #2/Henry Johnson/Spider Sam/Tennessee Gabriel/Blind Boy Williams)

Courtesy Sheldon Harris Collection

Born: Nov 30, 1915, Knoxville (Knox Co), TN
Inst: Banjo/Guitar/Jazz-horn/Kazoo/Piano

Father was George Duffield McGhee, a singer/musician; mother was Zella Henely; one of 5 children; moved to Kingsport, TN, at 4 years of age where he contracted poliomyelitis that resulted in a short right leg; first instrument was a home-made guitar at about 6 years of age; learned guitar from father c1922; moved to Lenoir City, TN, where he worked as guitarist/pianist/organist (with some singing) in local Baptist church choir from early 20s; attended high school in Maryville, TN, c1927-8; dropped out of school to hobo as itinerant musician working summer resort areas/carnivals/medicine shows/minstrel shows/picnics/dances/dives/buses/trains through Tennessee, late 20s; briefly worked w Mighty Hagg Carnival/ Rabbit Foot Minstrels, early 30s; returned to Maryville, TN, to work with father in Golden Voices Gospel Quartet, 1934-6; formed own washboard band (including Robert Young/Leroy Dallas) to work streets/picnics/dances/parties in Maryville area, mid-30s; moved to Kingsport, TN, to work outside music while completing high school with occasional street work, 1936; left home to hobo through South working streets/highways/road houses/bars/dens/jukes/ churches from c1936; worked w Leslie Riddle, Gym Theater, Kingsport, c1939; met Sonny Terry while passing through Burlington, NC, 1939 and worked as team almost continuously thereafter; worked w Sonny Terry/Paul Robeson, Riverside Stadium, Washington, DC, 1940; worked w Sonny Terry on streets of Durham, NC, for tips, 1940; settled in New York, NY, to work w Sonny Terry/Leadbelly/Bill Broonzy/Pete Seeger/Josh White/others at parties/streets from 1940; rec OKeh label, Chicago, IL, 1940-1; rec w Sonny Terry, OKeh label, NYC, 1941; toured (as "Blind Boy Fuller #2") working bars/jukes through Carolinas, 1941; frequently worked w Leadbelly/Sonny Terry/Woody Guthrie/others as Headline Singers on streets/at house parties/hootenannies/lofts, NYC, 1942; rec w Sonny Terry/Leadbelly, Library of Congress label, Washington, DC, 1942; rec w Jack Dupree, Folkways label, NYC, 1942; owned/operated Home of the Blues Music School (later renamed BM Studio), NYC, 1942-50; worked w Sonny Terry, Stuyvesant Casino/ Central Plaza, NYC, early 40s; rec w Sonny Terry, Savoy label, NYC, 1944; rec w Sonny Terry, Solo label, NYC, 1945; app on Office of War Information radio shows (frequently on BBC-radio, London, Eng), mid-40s; worked w Woody Guthrie/Sonny Terry as Woody Guthrie Singers at local hoots/concerts in NYC area c1946; rec (as "Tennessee Gabriel") Circle label, NYC, 1946; rec Alert/Jazz Record labels, NYC, 1946; worked w Sonny Terry, Blues at Midnight Concert, Town Hall, NYC, 1946; rec Capitol/Disc labels, NYC, 1947; app w Sonny Terry/Woody Guthrie in Alan Lomax OWI film short TO HEAR YOUR BANJO PLAY, 1947; frequently rec acc to many folk/blues singers in NYC through 40s into 50s; rec Savoy label, NYC, 1947-8; rec ST for documentary film THE ROOSEVELT STORY, 1947; occasionally worked outside music (selling voodoo charms on street), NYC, 1947; rec w Stick McGhee, Decca/Harlem labels, NYC, 1947; formed own The Three B's group to work local Harlem clubs, NYC, 1947-8; formed own The Mighty House Rockers group to work club dates, Elizabeth, NJ, from c1948 into early 50s; rec Sittin' In With label, NYC, 1948; rec Atlantic label, NYC, 1949-50; worked w Sonny Terry, Leadbelly Memorial Concert, Town Hall, NYC, 1950; worked w Sonny Terry at local clubs/rent parties/lofts/barbecues, NYC, 1950-5; rec Capitol label, NYC, 1950; rec Gramercy label, NYC, 1950-1; rec w Sugarmen/Jook Block Busters/Juke House Rockers/others on various small labels, NYC, early 50s; rec w Sonny Terry, Gotham label, NYC, 1951-2; rec w Ralph Willis Country Boys, Prestige label, NYC, 1952; rec w Jack Dupree, Red Robin label, NYC, 1953; rec w Ralph Willis, King label, NYC, 1953; rec acc to Big Maybelle, OKeh label, NYC, 1953; rec w Sonny Terry, Savoy/Groove labels, NYC, 1954-5; rec Folkways label, NYC, 1955; worked Berkshire Music Barn, Lenox, MA, 1955; app w Sonny Terry in show CAT ON A HOT TIN ROOF, Morosco Theater, NYC, 1955-7, then toured with show; app in Langston Hughes' show SIMPLY HEAVENLY, 85th Street Playhouse, NYC, 1957 (por rel Columbia label); rec ST for film A FACE IN THE CROWD, 1957; rec Fantasy label, San Francisco, CA, 1957; rec w Sonny Terry/Bill Broonzy, Folkways/Xtra labels, Chicago, IL, 1957; rec w Sonny Terry, Folkways label, NYC, 1957-8; worked Gate of Horn, Chicago, 1958; Ash Grove, Los Angeles, CA, 1958-62; toured w Sonny Terry working concert dates through England/Europe, 1958; rec Nixa label, London, Eng, 1958; formed The Folkmasters to work local folk clubs/coffeehouses, NYC, late 50s; rec Savoy/Folkways labels, NYC, 1958; worked Oakdale Musical Theater, Wallingford, CT, 1958 (por rel Metro Jazz label); rec Old Town/Choice labels, NYC, 1959; toured w Sonny Terry working concert dates through England, 1959; rec Columbia label, London, Eng, 1959; rec World Pacific label, Los Angeles, 1959-60; rec Fantasy label, San Francisco, 1959; app on TONIGHT WITH BELAFONTE Show, CBS-TV, 1959; worked Newport Folk Festival, Newport, RI, 1959 (por rel Vanguard/Folkways labels); toured w Sonny Terry for US State Department working concert dates through India, 1959-60; worked Gerdes Folk City, NYC, 1960; Town Hall, NYC, 1960; One Sheridan Square, NYC, 1960; Fifth Peg, Toronto, Can, 1960-1; rec Prestige-Bluesville label, NYC, 1960; rec VJ/Verve/Archive of Folk Music labels, Los Angeles, CA, 1960; toured w Sonny Terry working concert dates through Europe, 1960; toured w Sonny Terry working concert dates through England, 1961; rec Folkways/Choice labels, NYC, 1961; worked Golden Vanity, Boston, MA, 1961; Berkshire Music Barn, Lenox, MA, 1961; rec w Luke Miles, Smash label, Los Angeles, 1961; worked Sugar Hill Club, San Francisco, 1961 (por rel Fantasy label); toured college circuit working concert dates across US, 1962; worked L'Hibou Coffeehouse, Ottawa, Can, 1962; app w Sonny Terry on local show, CBC-TV, Toronto, Can, 1962; worked Finjan Club, Montreal, Can, 1962; rec Prestige-Bluesville label, NYC, 1962; worked Second Fret, Philadelphia, PA, 1962 (por rel Prestige label); toured w Rhythm & Blues USA package group working concert dates through England/Europe, 1962; rec Polydor label, Hamburg, Ger, 1962; worked Raven Gallery, Detroit, MI, c1962; frequently toured w Harry Belafonte Show working theaters/concerts across US, 1962-5; worked Village Gate, NYC, 1963; Newport Folk Festival, Newport, RI, 1963 (por rel Vanguard label/por shown in film FESTIVAL); app on national TV commercial for Alka Seltzer c1963; worked Hunter Col, NYC, 1964; app on A LA CARTE Show, CBC-TV, Toronto, Can, 1964; toured w American Blues Caravan working concert dates through England, 1964 (por shown on BLUES & GOSPEL TRAIN Show, Granada-TV, Eng); app w Pete Seeger on ROOMFUL OF MUSIC, WNDT-TV, NYC, 1965; worked Fisher Theater, Detroit, MI, 1965; Apollo Theater, NYC, 1965-7; toured Australia working concert dates, 1965; worked Jordan Hall, Boston, MA, 1965; frequently worked Riverboat Coffeehouse, Toronto, Can, 1965-73; Jazz Workshop, San Francisco, CA, 1966-7; Univ of Illinois, Urbana, IL, 1966; app on STROLLIN' 20s, CBS-TV, 1966; app on FESTIVAL PRESENTS THE BLUES, CBC-TV, Toronto, Can, 1966; worked Rheingold Central Park Music Festival, NYC, NY, 1966; rec acc to Alec Seward, Blue Labor label, NYC, 1966; worked The Troubador, Los Angeles, CA, 1966; app on THE WORLD OF MUSIC, CBC-TV, Toronto, 1966; worked Mariposa Folk Festival, Toronto, 1966; Ash Grove, Los Angeles, 1967-73; New Penelope, Montreal, Can, 1967-8; toured w American Folk Blues Festival working concert dates through England/Europe, 1967; worked The Bitter End, NYC, 1967; Arts Festival, Cleveland, OH, 1967; rec Fontana label, Chicago, IL, c1967; worked Woody Guthrie Memorial Concert, Carnegie Hall, NYC, 1968; app w Pete Seeger, RAINBOW QUEST, WNDT-TV, NYC, 1968; worked Riverqueen Coffeehouse, Vancouver, Can, 1968-9; Mandrake's, Berkeley, CA, 1969; El Matador, San Francisco, CA, 1969; rec BluesWay label, Los Angeles, CA, 1969; toured w Sonny Terry/BB King working concert dates through England/Europe, 1969; worked Newport Folk Festival, Newport, RI, 1969; Folk City, NYC, NY, 1969; Berkeley Blues Festival, Univ of California, Berkeley, CA, 1969-70; Quiet Knight, Chicago, IL, 1970-1; toured w American Folk Blues Festival working concert dates through England/Europe, 1970 (por Frankfurt, Ger, concert rel Scout label); worked Jazz Expo '70, London, Eng, 1970; app on THE HART & LORNE TERRIFIC HOUR, CBC-TV, Canada, 1970; worked The Gaslight, NYC, 1971; Four Muses, San Clemente, CA, 1971; Univ of British Columbia Student Union, Vancouver, Can, 1971; New Paltz Col, New Paltz, NY, 1971-2; app on VIRGINIA GRAHAM Show, WOR-TV, NYC (syndicated), 1971; app in film ROOTS OF AMERICAN MUSIC: COUNTRY & URBAN MUSIC (pt 2), 1971; worked Back Door Coffeehouse, Montreal, 1971; toured Denmark working schools/clubs, 1971; rec Storyville label, Copenhagen, Den, 1971; worked His Father's Mustache, Montreal, 1971; Funky Quarters, San Diego, CA, 1972; Esquire Showbar, Montreal, 1972; Univ of Waterloo, Waterloo, Can, 1972; app in French film BLUES UNDER THE SKIN, 1972; app in French film OUT OF THE BLACKS INTO THE BLUES (pt 1: Along the Old Man River/pt 2: A Way to Escape the Ghetto), 1972; rec ST for film BUCK AND THE PREACHER, 1972; rec ST for film BOOK OF NUMBERS, 1972; rec A&M/Impress labels, Hollywood, CA, 1972; worked Max's Kansas City, NYC, 1972-3; The Boarding House, San Francisco, CA, 1973; Mandrake's, Berkeley, CA, 1973; Lion's Share, San Anselmo, CA, 1973; Inn of the Beginning, Cotati, CA, 1973; app on ONE OF A KIND, PBS-TV, 1973; worked Joe's Place, Cambridge, MA, 1973; toured England/Europe working club/concert/college dates, 1973-4; worked Montreux Jazz Festival, Montreux, Switzerland, 1973; app in film BLUES FOR A BLACK FILM, 1973; worked Philadelphia Folk Festival, Schwenksville, PA, 1973; Great Southeast Music Hall, Atlanta, GA, 1973-4; Avery Fisher Hall, NYC, NY, 1973; Michigan State Univ, E Lansing, MI, 1973; Liberty Hall, Houston, TX, 1973; frequently toured New Zealand/Australia working concert dates, 1973-6; Hunter Col, NYC, 1974; Academy of Music, Brooklyn, NY, 1974; Bottom Line, NYC, 1974; rec Blue Labor label, NYC, 1974; rec w Big Chief Ellis, Trix label, Cottekill, NY, 1974-5; worked Univ of Louisville, Louisville, KY, 1974; McCabe's, Santa Monica, CA, 1974; Univ of North Carolina, Raleigh, NC, 1974; Frog & Nightgown Club, Raleigh, 1974; Shaboo Inn, Mansfield, CT, 1974; Convocation Hall, Toronto, Can, 1975; Berkeley Blues Festival, Berkeley, CA, 1975; app in film SINCERELY THE BLUES, 1975; worked Juicy John Pink's Folk Center, DeKalb, IL, 1975; Good Karma Coffeehouse, Madison, WI, 1975; Milwaukee Summer Festival, Milwaukee, WI, 1975; Euphoria Tavern, Portland, OR, 1975; app on AM SAN FRANCISCO, KGED-TV, San Francisco, CA, 1975; worked Sophie's, Palo Alto, CA, 1975; The Bodega, Campbell, CA, 1975; My Father's Place, Roslyn, NY, 1975; Egyptian Theater, DeKalb, IL, 1975; rec Trix label, Hyattsville, MD, 1976; worked The Lighthouse, Los Angeles, 1976; The Riverboat, Toronto, Can, 1976; rec ST for film LEADBELLY, 1976; app on national TV commercial for Blues Filter Cigarettes, Australia, 1976; worked Quiet Knight, Chicago, 1976-7; The Raven Gallery, Detroit, 1976-7; toured Europe working concert dates, 1977; worked Ivanhoe, Chicago, 1977; Charlotte's Web, Rockford, IL, 1977; Back Door, San Diego, CA, 1977; The Lighthouse, Los Angeles, 1977; University of Toronto, Toronto, Can, 1977; The Rising Sun, Montreal, Can, 1978; The Crystal Saloon, Juneau, AK, 1978; app in film THE JERK, 1979

Personal: Granville McGhee, singer, was brother

Songs: A Cheater Can't Win/Back to New Orleans/BM Special/Baby How Long?/Barking Bull Dog/Beggin' and Cryin'/Big Question/Black Cat Bone/Blowin' the Fuses/Blue Feeling/Blues for the Lowlands/The Blues Had a Baby/Blues of Happiness/Born to Live the Blues/Brownie's (New) Blues/The CC and O Blues/Corn Bread, Peas and Black Molasses/C'mon If You're Comin'/The Death of Blind Boy Fuller/The Devil's Gonna Get You/Diamond Ring/Dissatisfied Blues/Don't Mistreat Me/Don't Pity Me/Don't Wait for Me/Don't You Lie to Me/Door to Success/East Coast Blues/Everything I Had Is Gone/Evil Hearted Me/Freight Train/Gone Baby Gone/Gone But Not Forgotten/Gone Gal/Hand in Hand/Hold Me in Your Arms/Hole in the Wall/House Lady/Howdy Blues/I Ain't Gonna Scold You/I Can't Sleep at Night/I Couldn't Believe My Eyes/I Don't Know the Reason/I Feel Alright Now/I Gotta Look Under Your Hood/I Know Better/I Woke Up One Morning and I Could Hardly See/I'd Love to Love You/I'll Be Anything/I'm Prison Bound/Jealous Man/Jump Little Children/Keep On Walkin'/Let Me Be Your Big Dog/Life Is a Gamble/Little Black Engine/Lonesome Day/Love, Truth and Confidence/Love's a Disease/Me and My Dog/Me and Sonny/Memories of My Trip/My Fault/My Last Suit/My Plan/Night and Day/On the Road Again/One Thing for Sure/Packin' Up, Gettin' Ready/Parcel Post Blues/Pawn Show/Please Don't Dog Your Woman/Rainy Rainy Day/Ride and Roll/Seaboard and Southern/Sittin' Pretty/So Much Trouble/Sonny's Squall/Southern Train/Sporting Life Blues/Stranger Blues/Stranger Here/Sweet Lovin' Kind/Tell Me Why/That's How I Feel/Too Nicey Mama/Treated Wrong/Tryin' to Win/Trying to Deceive Me/Understand Me/Up, Sometimes Down/Walk On/Walkin' My Blues Away/The Way I Feel/We Have No Friends/When It's Love Time/

Wholesale Dealin' Papa/Worried Life Blues/Worry Worry Worry/Wrong Track/You Don't Know/You Just Using Me for a Convenience/You'd Better Mind

Infl by: Big Bill Broonzy/Gary Davis/Blind Boy Fuller/Blind Lemon Jefferson/Leadbelly/Tampa Red

Infl to: Jack Dupree/Jack Elliott/Alec Seward/Tarheel Slim

Quotes: "Few singers evoke as forcefully as Brownie the many-sideness of heritage. The narrative gift of the ballad, echoes of hymns, spirituals, work songs and minstrels . . . and the worried and lonely blues"—Charles Edward Smith, Folkways album 2422

"[His voice is] astonishingly rich in texture, although he can give it a cutting edge when the material demands it"—Ron Brown, Storyville album SLP 217

References: *Living Blues* magazine, Summer 1973, pp 18-23

The Country Blues, Samuel B Charters, Rinehart & Company, Inc, 1959

McHOUSTON, ED
(see Baker, McHouston)

McKINLEY, BILL
(see Gillum, William)

McMAHON, ANDREW *"Blueblood"*
Born: Apr 12, 1926, Delhi (Richland Parish), LA
Died: Feb 17, 1984, Monroe, LA
Inst: Bass/Guitar

Born/raised on farm; interested in music early and took some guitar lessons at 7 years of age; ran away from home to hobo as itinerant musician working streets/jukes/bars through South from 1937 through 40s; settled in Chicago, IL, late 40s; formed own band to work local club dates, Chicago, through 50s; worked Cadillac Baby's Lounge, Chicago, 1958 (por rel Bea & Baby label); toured extensively w Howlin' Wolf Band working clubs/concerts across US, 1960-73; frequently rec as acc to many bluesmen, Chicago, through 60s; frequently worked as sideman w Muddy Waters Band in local clubs, Chicago, early 70s; worked w Howlin' Wolf Band, Ann Arbor Blues Festival, Ann Arbor, MI, 1972 (por rel Atlantic label); app

Andrew "Blueblood" McMahon *Courtesy* Living Blues *Magazine*

on ATOMIC MAMA'S WANG DANG DOODLE BLUES SHOW, WNIB-FM-radio, Chicago, c1973; rec (under own name) Dharma label, Chicago, 1973; formed Blossom Blues Band working clubs in Chicago/Northern Illinois/Southern Wisconsin areas, 1974-7; moved to Monroe, LA working mostly outside music, c1977; died of cancer

Songs: Baby Child/Fast As My Legs Can Go/Gold Teeth/Guitar King/I Can't Stay Here/Orphan Home Blues/The Sky's the Limit

McTELL, WILLIE SAMUEL *"Blind Willie"*
(*aka:* Barrelhouse Sammy/Blind Doogie/Blind Sammy (Sammie)/Blind Willie/Georgia Bill/Red Hot Willie Glaze/Hot Shot Willie/Pig 'n' Whistle Red/Red Hot Willie)

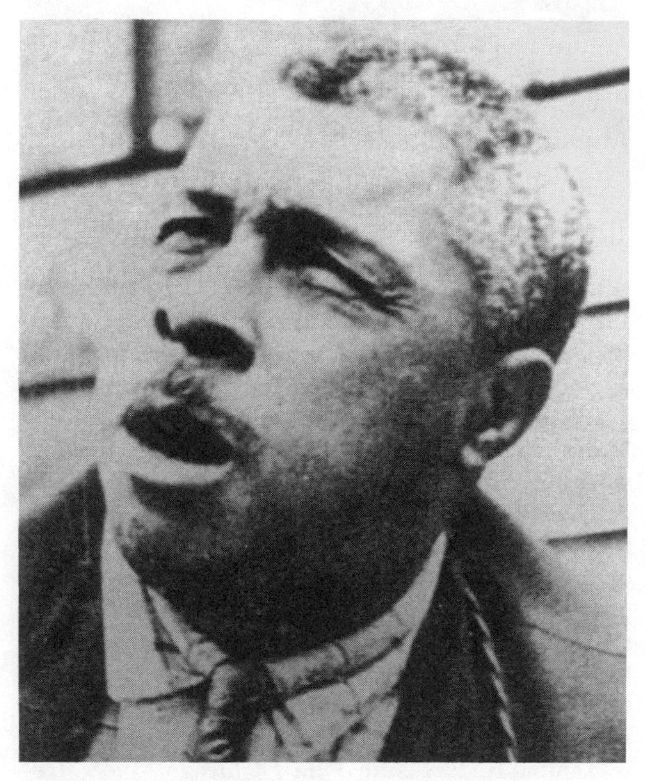

Courtesy Living Blues *Magazine*

Born: May 5, 1901, Thomson (McDuffie Co), GA
Died: Aug 19, 1959, Milledgeville, GA
Inst: Accordion/Guitar/Harmonica/Kazoo/Violin

Father Ed McTier and mother Minnie Watkins were guitarists; born Willie McTier; one of 2 children; born almost totally blind; moved to Statesboro, GA, where he was raised by mother from c1910; learned guitar from mother at about 13 years of age; ran away from home to follow various touring carnivals/minstrel/medicine shows in early teens; toured w John Roberts Plantation Show working through South, 1916-17; worked outside music, southern Georgia, into 20s; attended State School for the Blind, Macon, GA, 1922-5; attended School for the Blind, NYC, NY, 1925-6; hoboed extensively working streets/parks/picnics/resort areas on East Coast through 20s/30s; rec Victor label, Atlanta, GA, 1927-9; rec Columbia label, Atlanta, 1929-31; rec OKeh label, Atlanta, 1931; rec Victor label, Atlanta, 1932; rec Vocalion label, NYC, 1933; frequently worked w Blind Willie Johnson on street corners/highways/stores/parks through South, early 30s; worked outside music, Atlanta, 1935; frequently worked w Buddy Moss/Curley Weaver (or solo) at private parties/dances/parking lots/drug stores/open air drive-ins (like The Pig 'n' Whistle)/streets in Atlanta area through 30s into 50s; worked 81 Theater, Atlanta, 1935; rec Decca label, Chicago, IL, 1935; toured in passing medicine shows through Georgia/Kentucky c1935-6; rec w Piano Red, Vocalion label (unissued), Augusta, GA, 1936; frequently toured w Curley Weaver/Buddy Moss/others working clubs/tobacco markets through Tennessee/Alabama/North Carolina through 30s; rec Library of Congress label, Atlanta, 1940; reportedly app on local radio shows, Augusta, GA, early 40s; worked (as singing car-hop), Blue Lantern Drive-In Restaurant, Atlanta, late 40s; rec Atlantic label, Atlanta, 1949-50; rec Regal/Biograph labels, Atlanta, c1949-50; rec Prestige-Bluesville label, Atlanta, 1956; active as preacher at Mt Zion Baptist Church, Atlanta, from c1957; suffered strokes in Atlanta/Thomson, GA, 1959; entered Milledgeville State Hospital where he died of cerebral hemorrhage; buried Jones Grove Church cemetery, Thomson, GA

Note: Death records and gravestone mistakenly listed him as "Eddie McTier"

Personal: Married Ruth Kate Williams (1933-41), a singer/dancer; married Helen Edwards (1950s)

Songs: Atlanta Strut/Blues Around Midnight/Broke Down Engine Blues/Cigarette Blues/Come On Around to My House Mama/Death-Cell Blues/Dying Crapshooter's Blues/Kill It Kid/Last Dime Blues/Lay Some Flowers on My Grave/Little Delia/Married Life's a Pain/On the Cooling Board/The Razor Ball/Southern Can Is Mine/Statesboro Blues/Ticket Agent Blues

Infl by: Lonnie Johnson/Blind Willie Johnson

Quotes: "Blind Willie McTell is a bridge between the gentle sound of the Piedmont guitarist and the more powerful styles of Atlanta, playing 12 string guitar with both dexterity and sensitivity"—Bruce Bastin, *Crying for the Carolines*, Studio Vista Ltd, 1971

"He has the compelling dramatic voice of the best bluesmen coupled with the wit and imagery of the greatest folk-poet"—Simon A Napier, Atlantic album 7224

"One of [the] great figures of the 20s was the blind Georgia singer Willie McTell, whose poetic, deeply personal performances were among the most appealing of the entire period"—Samuel B Charters, Prestige-Bluesville album BV-1040

References: Blues Unlimited magazine (UK), Jul/Aug, Sept/Oct, Nov/Dec 1977

Blues Access magazine, Fall 1992 (No. 11), pp 30-35

Sweet as the Showers of Rain, Samuel B Charters, Oak Publishing Company, 1977

MEMPHIS BLUES BOY
(see Nix, Willie)

MEMPHIS JIM
(see Dorsey, Thomas A)

MEMPHIS MINNIE
(see Douglas, Lizzie)

MEMPHIS MOSE
(see Dorsey, Thomas A)

MEMPHIS SLIM
(see Chatman, Peter)
(see Davenport, Charles)

MEMPHIS WILLIE B
(see Borum, William)

MERCY DEE
(see Walton, Mercy Dee)

MEYERS, LOUIE
(see Myers, Louis)

MERRIWEATHER, MAJOR *"Maceo"*
(*aka:* Big Maceo)
Born: Mar 31, 1905, Atlanta (Fulton Co), GA
Died: Feb 26, 1953, Chicago, IL
Inst: Piano

Father was Christopher "Kit" Merriweather; mother was Ora ———; one of 11 children; raised on farm between Newman/Atlanta, GA, where he worked

Courtesy Sheldon Harris Collection

outside music until 1920; moved to College Park, GA, 1920; taught self piano and worked parties in College Park/Atlanta area, 1920-4; moved to Detroit, MI, to work outside music with frequent house parties/club dates like The Post Club/Brown's Bar/Crystal Bar/El Vido's/others, 1924-41; moved to Chicago, IL, to work outside music with occasional gigs w Bill Broonzy Quartet in local clubs/parties/theaters from 1941; rec w Tampa Red, Bluebird label, Chicago, 1941-2; frequently worked H&T Club/Gatewoods Club/others, Chicago, into 40s; toured clubs through Tennessee/Georgia, 1944-5; rec w Tampa Red, Bluebird/Victor labels, Chicago, 1945-6; rec w Bill Broonzy, Columbia label, Chicago, 1945; rec w John Lee "Sonny Boy" Williamson, Victor label, Chicago, 1945; worked w Tampa Red, Flame Club, Chicago, 1945; frequently worked Sylvio's, Chicago, c1945-6; w Bill Broonzy, Harmonia Hotel, Chicago, 1946; partially paralyzed by stroke but continued to play piano right-handed from 1946; rec w Eddie Boyd, Victor label, Chicago, 1947; rec w Tampa Red, Specialty label, Chicago, 1948; app on Studs Terkel's I COME FOR TO SING, (unknown) TV, Chicago, late 40s; toured Kentucky/Tennessee/Louisiana working club dates, 1950; worked w John Brim in local club dates, Detroit, MI, c1950; rec w John Brim, Fortune label, Detroit, 1952; suffered fatal heart attack at home; buried local cemetery, Detroit, MI

Personal: Married Rossell Hattie Bell Spruel (c1924-53). 1 child. His brother Rozier "Bob" Merriweather ("Little Maceo") is musician and nephew Roy Meriwether (sic) is rock/jazz/blues pianist

Songs: Anytime for You/Big City Blues/Broke and Hungry Blues/Chicago Breakdown/Country Jail Blues/Do You Remember?/Maceo's 32-20/Poor Kelly Blues/Since You Been Gone/Texas Blues/Texas Stomp/Worried Life Blues

Infl to: Boogie Woogie Red/Little Eddie Boyd/Maceo Charles/Henry Gray/Little Johnny Jones/Little Walter/Willie Mabon/Otis Spann

Quotes: "The directness and energy of his piano playing, with little light or shade, contrasted perfectly with his singing, his smoky brown voice investing the songs with a depth unequaled by most of his contemporaries"—Mike Rowe, *Chicago Breakdown*, Eddison Press Ltd, 1973

"His voice thrillingly dark and gritty, his phrasing as forthright, rhythmically insinuating and emotionally persuasive as his direct, rolling piano"—Pete Welding, *Downbeat* magazine, Oct 9, 1975, p 30

References: Blues Unlimited magazine (UK), Feb/Mar 1974, pp 5-8

The Art of Jazz, Martin T Williams, Oxford Univ Press, 1959

MICHELE
(see Castell, Michele)

MICKEY
(see Baker, McHouston)

MICKLE, ELMON
(*aka:* Driftin' Slim/Drifting Smith/Harmonica Harry/Model T Slim)
Born: Feb 24, 1919, Keo (Lonoke Co), AR
Died: Sept 15, 1977, Los Angeles, CA
Inst: Drums/Guitar/Harmonica

Father was William Mickle; mother was Eva Todd; learned some harmonica from John Lee "Sonny Boy" Williamson as youth; frequently worked w Sonny Boy Williamson (Alex Miller)/Peck Curtis in local jukes/clubs, Little Rock, AR, area, mid-40s; frequently app on KDRK/KGHI-radio, Little Rock, through mid-40s; frequently worked outside music, Little Rock area, into 50s; formed own band w Baby Face Turner/Junior Brooks/Bill Russell to rec Modern label, North Little Rock, AR, 1951; frequently worked w own band

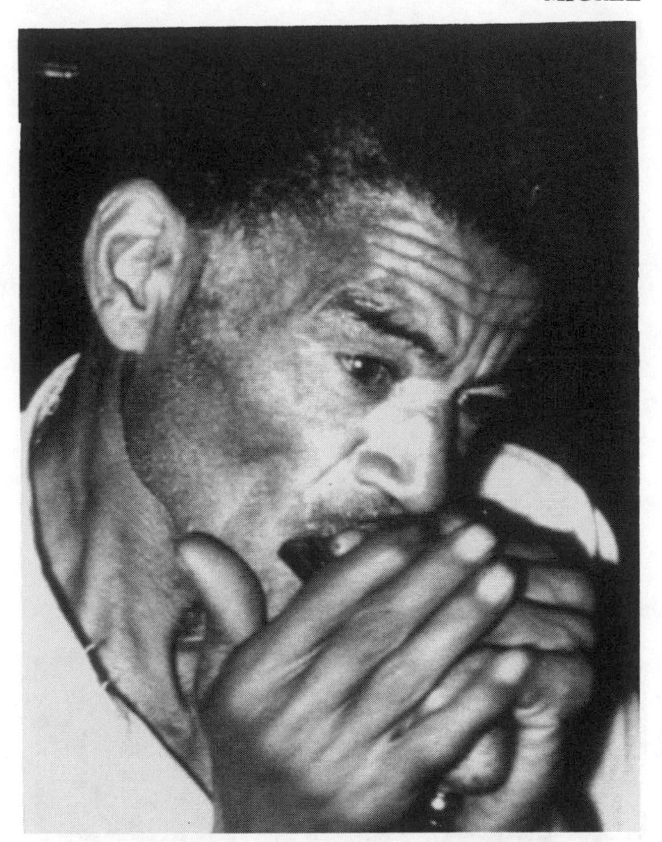

Photo by Frank Scott. Courtesy Living Blues Magazine

at local dances/clubs in Little Rock into 50s; rec RPM label, North Little Rock; learned guitar/drums, late 50s; moved to Los Angeles, CA, 1957; worked as one man band at local parties/suppers with frequent outside music work, Los Angeles area, from 1957; rec own Elko/EM labels, Los Angeles, 1959; rec J Gems label, Los Angeles, early 60s; rec Wonder/Magnum labels, Los Angeles, 1966; rec Blue Horizon/Milestone labels, Los Angeles, 1966; worked Ash Grove, Los Angeles, 1967; Univ of Southern California, Los Angeles, 1967; Folk Music Festival, San Diego, CA, 1971; mostly inactive due to poor health into 70s; died at home of lung cancer; buried Paradise Cemetery, Los Angeles, CA

Personal: Married Mary Lee Green. Had children

Infl by: John Lee "Sonny Boy" Williamson

Quote: "Slim, in addition to being a good bluesman, is an excellent storyteller . . ."—Bruce Bromberg, Kent album KST-9007

Reference: Blues Unlimited magazine (UK), Jan 1967, pp 5-8

MILBURN, AMOS

Courtesy Sheldon Harris Collection

Born: Apr 1, 1927, Houston (Harris Co), TX
Died: Jan 3, 1980, Houston, TX
Inst: Piano

Father was Amos Milburn Sr; mother Amelia Henry; learned piano at about 5 years of age; dropped out of school to serve in US Navy in Pacific Theater of Operations where he entertained at local camp shows, 1942-5; returned to Houston, TX, to form own sextet working small clubs in area from 1946; worked Key Hole Club, San Antonio, TX, 1946; rec Aladdin label, Los Angeles, CA, 1946-8; worked Savoy Club, Los Angeles, 1946-7; toured as single working clubs/bars in Texas/Louisiana, 1947-9; worked Million Dollar Theater, Los Angeles, 1949; rec w own Aladdin Chicken Shackers, Aladdin label, Los Angeles, 1949-52; worked w own band, Gleason's Club, Cleveland, OH, 1952; worked Circle Club, Flint, MI, early 50s; rec w own band, Aladdin label, NYC/Los Angeles, 1953-6; app in HARLEM VARIETY REVUE, Apollo Theater, NYC, early 50s (por shown SHOWTIME AT THE APOLLO, syndicated TV, 1955/por shown in films HARLEM JAZZ FESTIVAL [1955], RHYTHM & BLUES REVUE [1955], BASIN STREET REVUE [1956]); worked extensively as single in local clubs/bars/lounges in Washington, DC/Chicago, IL/NYC, NY, 1954 into 60s; Manor Plaza Hotel, San Francisco, CA, 1954; w Johnny Otis group, Barrelhouse, Los Angeles, CA, mid-50s; Farmdell Club, Dayton, OH, 1955; toured one-nighters on West Coast, 1956; toured w Charles Brown Band working one-nighters through South, 1958; rec w Johnny Mandel Band, Aladdin label, Los Angeles, 1958; rec w Charles Brown, Ace label, New Orleans, LA, 1959; rec King label, Cincinnati, OH (?), 1961; worked Tia Juana Club, Cleveland, OH, 1963; Midway Club, Cleveland, 1964; Blue Angel Club, Cincinnati, c1964-6; worked w own trio, Elite Club, Dallas, TX, 1966; frequently worked outside music in Cincinnati, late 60s; rec Motown label, Detroit, late 60s; worked Satan's Den, Cincinnati, 1970-1; w Charles Brown, Viking Lounge, Cincinnati, 1970; suffered strokes and inactive in music, Cleveland from 1970; retired to Houston, early 70s; rec Blues Spectrum, Los Angeles, 1973; died of heart attack; buried National Cemetery, Houston

Songs: All Is Well/Chicken Shack Boogie/Good Good Whiskey/Hold Me Baby/House Party/I'm Still a Fool for You/Let's Have a Party/My Happiness Depends on You/My Luck Is Bound to Change/Number 12 Is at the Station/That's What I've Been Thru

Infl by: Charles Brown

Infl to: Floyd Dixon/Fats Domino

Quote: "His warm, lancinating voice, his robust piano in melodious boogie-woogies and fascinating slow blues won him a prodigious success"—Virgile Degand, Riverboat album 900.266

Reference: *Blues Unlimited* magazine (UK), Jul/Sept, 1971

MILES, ELIZABETH *"Lizzie"*

(*aka:* Mandy Smith)
Born: Mar 31, 1895, New Orleans (Orleans Parish), LA
Died: Mar 17, 1963, New Orleans, LA

Father was Victor Landreaux; mother Ramise Fazand; born Elizabeth Mary Landreaux; interested in music and was singing hymns in local Sunday school at 5 years of age; dropped out of school to sing at local house parties/lawn dances/Saturday-night fish fries/neighborhood charity events/churches in New Orleans, LA, as teenager; frequently worked w King Oliver/Kid Ory/Bunk Johnson/AJ Piron and others at Dixie Park/Lincoln Park/moving picture houses/riv-

Courtesy David Griffiths

erboats/clubs/cabarets/local halls (as Frances Amis Hall/Equite Hall/Artesan Hall/Hopes Hall/others), New Orleans, 1909-11; toured w Will and Edna Benbow in Benbow Stock Company working theaters through South from 1911; toured w Jones Brothers & Wilson Circus working (as "Queen Elleezee") in tent shows through Florida/Alabama, 1914-15; toured w Cole Brothers Circus working as featured singer/performer/animal act elephant rider in tent shows c1916; frequently worked as song plugger for Clarence Williams in New Orleans, LA/Chicago, IL, from c1916; briefly worked under canvas w Alabama Minstrels/Rabbit Foot Minstrels c1917; worked w Manuel Manetta Band, Martin's Cabaret, Bucktown District, New Orleans, 1917; w George Thomas Orch, Pythian Temple Roof Garden, New Orleans, 1919; frequently worked club dates in French Quarter of New Orleans into 20s; worked w King Oliver/Louis Armstrong, Dreamland Cafe, Chicago, IL, c1921; w Freddie Keppard Band, The Entertainers Club, Chicago, c1921; w Glover Compton, De Luxe Cafe, Chicago, c1921; w boxer Jack Johnson, Club DeLuxe, NYC, NY, c1921; rec OKeh label, NYC, 1922-3; rec w Creole Jazz Hounds/Clarence Williams, Emerson label, NYC, 1923; rec Columbia/Victor labels, NYC, 1923; worked New Star Casino, NYC, 1923; w Armand Piron Band, Cotton Club, NYC, c1923; Capitol Palace Cabaret, NYC, 1924; w Sam Wooding's Orch, Nest Club, NYC, 1924; Herman's Inn, NYC, 1924; w Alexander Shargenski Troupe, Chez Mitchell Club, Paris, France, 1924; toured Europe working concert/club dates 1924-5; worked w New Orleans Creole Jazz Band in local clubs, New Orleans, 1925; frequently worked Capitol Palace Cafe/Nest Club/Cotton Club/Club Bamville/Herman's Inn/others, NYC, 1926 into 30s; worked Ebony Club, NYC, 1927; rec OKeh label, NYC, 1927; rec Banner/Conqueror labels, NYC, 1927-8; rec Columbia label, NYC, 1928; rec w Jasper Davis Orch, Harmony label, NYC, 1929; rec w Jelly Roll Morton, Victor label, NYC, 1929; rec Victor label, NYC, 1930; mostly inactive in music due to illness from 1931; app in films THE STARDUST RING/TICK TACK TOE, early 30s (?); worked w Paul Barbarin Band, Strollers Club, NYC, 1935; w Fats Waller, Capitol Palace Cafe, NYC, 1938; worked local club dates, Chicago, 1938; mostly inactive in New Orleans, 1938-9; rec w Melrose Stompers, Vocalion label, Chicago, IL, 1939; worked local club dates, Chicago, 1939-42; worked outside music, New Orleans, 1942-50; app on POPPA STOPPA Show, WJMR-radio, New Orleans, c1950; worked The Paddock Lounge, New Orleans, c1950; frequently w Freddy Kohlman's Band in residence, Mardi Gras Lounge, New Orleans, c1951-8; rec w New Orleans Boys, Circle label, New Orleans, 1952; rec w Sharkey's Kings of Dixieland, Capitol label, New Orleans, 1952; frequently in residence, Parisian Room, New Orleans, from early 50s; w George Lewis Ragtime Band in residence, Hangover Club, San Francisco, CA, 1953-4 (por frequently on remote radio/por rel Dawn Club label); worked Blue Note, Chicago, IL, 1954; rec w Red Camp/Tony Almerico's Parisian Room Band/others, Cook label, New Orleans, 1954-6; worked w Bob Scobey Band, Show Boat, Oakland, CA, 1955-7; w Wally Rose, Tin Angel, San Francisco, CA, 1955; rec w Bob Scobey Band, Verve label, Los Angeles, CA, 1956; worked w Bob Scobey Band, The Flamingo Hotel and others, Las Vegas, NV, 1956-7; app on DU PONT SHOW OF THE MONTH (ep: Crescendo), CBS-TV, 1957; app on MUSIC USA, Voice of America-radio, 1957; worked w Bob Scobey's Band, Zardi's Jazzland, Hollywood, CA, 1957; w Joe Darensbourg Band, Easy Street Club, San Francisco, 1958; Civic Auditorium, Pasadena, CA, 1958; 400 Club, Los Angeles, 1958; Monterey Jazz Festival, Monterey, CA, 1958-9; worked w Paul Barbarin's Band on SS *President* steamer out of New Orleans, 1958 (por shown on Dave Garroway's WIDE WIDE

WORLD, NBC-TV); worked New Orleans Jazz Club Concert, New Orleans, 1959; toured West Coast working clubs/concerts, 1959; retired to devote time to Sisters of Holy Family Chapel and Jesuit Church, New Orleans, 1959-63; died of heart attack at Lafon's Catholic nursing home; buried St Louis Cemetery, New Orleans, LA

Personal: Married JC Miles (d 1918); August Pajaud (cousin of Willie Pajeaud [sic], musician. Half sister of Edna Hicks

Billings: The Creole Songbird/Queen Elleezee/La Rose Noire de Paris (The Black Rose of Paris)

Infl by: Tillie Johnson/Sophie Tucker

Infl to: Big Mama Bev/Barbara Dane/Pug Horton

Quotes: ". . . Lizzie Miles, a large woman with an equally large voice. Her repertoire was fantastically wide, including everything from vaudeville ballads, Creole songs (sung in Creole French) to the more earthy blues"—Derrick Stewart-Baxter, *Ma Rainey and the Classic Blues Singers*, Studio Vista Ltd, 1970

"She was magnetic Lizzie Miles, acclaimed one of the most powerful voices in the history of jazz"—Laurraine Goreau, *Jazz Journal* magazine (UK), Jan 1964, p 8

References: *Jazz Journal* magazine (UK), Jan 1964, pp 8-10

Who's Who of Jazz, John Chilton, Bloombury Book Shop, 1970

MILES, JOSEPHINE *"Josie"*
(*aka:* Evangelist Mary Flowers/Pearl Harris/Augusta Jones)
Born: c1900, Summerville (Dorchester Co), SC
Died: c1953-65, Kansas City, MO

Reportedly moved to NYC, NY, early 20s; app briefly in touring company of musical comedy SHUFFLE ALONG, c1922; rec Black Swan label, NYC, 1922-3; toured w Black Swan Troubadours group working theater circuit, 1923; worked theater dates in Columbus, OH, 1923; app in RUNNIN' WILD Revue, Colonial Theater, NYC, 1923; app on WDT-radio, NYC, 1923; rec Gennett label, NYC, 1923-4; rec Ajax label, NYC, 1924-5; rec Edison label, NYC, 1924; rec w Jazz Casper, Banner label, NYC, 1924; rec Banner label, NYC, 1925; reportedly rec (religious songs) Gennett label, Richmond, IN, 1928; reportedly settled in Kansas City, MO, where she was mostly active in church activities from early 30s; reportedly died in automobile accident

Courtesy Frank Driggs Collection

MILES, LUKE *"Long Gone"*
Born: May 8, 1925, Lachute (Caddo Parish), LA
Died: Nov 22, 1987, Los Angeles, CA

Father was Jim Miles; mother Silvester Brown; worked on farm, Lachute area to 1952; to Houston, TX to work w Lightnin' Hopkins from 1952; rec w Lightnin' Hopkins, Tradition label, Houston, 1959; moved to Los Angeles, CA, 1961; worked frequently at Insomniac Club, Hermosa Beach, CA, 1961; w Lightnin' Hopkins, Sugar Hill, San Francisco, CA, 1961; frequently worked Ash Grove, Los Angeles, through 60s; rec w Sonny Terry/Brownie McGhee, Smash label, Los Angeles, 1961; rec World Pacific label, Los Angeles, 1964; rec Two Kings label, Los Angeles, 1965; intermittent music work into 80s due to illness; died of lung cancer; body cremated

Songs: Bad Luck/I Feel All Right/Long Gone/Miss Hazel Mae/No Money No Honey

Infl by: Lightnin' Hopkins/Mance Lipscomb/John Lee "Sonny Boy" Williamson

MILLER, CLARENCE HORATIO *"Big"*
Born: Dec 18, 1922, Sioux City (Woodbury Co), IA
Died: Jun 9, 1992, Edmonton, Can
Inst: Bass/Drums/Harmonica/Trombone

Father was Henry Miller, a Sioux Indian and preacher; mother was Nora Epperson; was an only child; to Kansas City, KS to study piano as child; studied bass and trombone at St John's Catholic School for Boys, Leavenworth, KS, as youth; formed own school band working local dances, late 30s; moved to Wichita, KS, late 30s, then hoboed through South into early 40s; served in US Army where he later formed own band to entertain/produce/write shows, Hawaii/Iwo Jima, 1943-6; returned to Wichita, KS, to form own quintet to work Greentree Inn, 1946; frequently toured with group through Kansas/Oklahoma/Texas and South to 1949; worked Snow Flakes Club, New Orleans, LA, c1946; Eldorado Room, Houston, TX, 1947; The Flamingo, Kansas City, MO, 1948; toured w Lionel Hampton Orch working dances, 1949; toured w Jay McShann Orch working clubs/dances, 1949-54; toured w Duke Ellington Orch working concert dates c1955; worked (as MC/producer/entertainer) The Loop Inc/The Crown Propeller/Club DeLisa/Cotton Club, Chicago, IL/Birdland, NYC, NY, 1956-8; worked Village Vanguard, NYC, 1956; toured w Al Grey Band working club dates out of Cincinnati, OH, late 50s; worked Flame Showbar, Detroit, MI, c1957; Pep's, Philadelphia, PA, 1957; settled in New York, NY, to work outside music from 1957; rec w own Five Pennies, Savoy label, NYC, 1957; worked Baby Grand, NYC, 1958; w Rex Stewart All-Stars, Great South Bay Jazz Festival, Great River, NY, 1958 (por rel United Artists label); rec w Bob Brookmeyer Kansas City Seven, United Artists label, NYC, 1958; worked Boston Jazz Festival, Boston, MA, 1958; Storyville Club, Boston, c1958; worked (as maitre d'/producer/entertainer) Copa City, Jamaica, NY, 1958; app on ART FORD'S JAZZ PARTY, WNTA-TV, NYC, 1958; rec w Budd Johnson Orch, United Artists label, NYC, 1959; worked w Nat Pierce Band, Birdland, NYC, 1959; Monterey Jazz Festival, Monterey, CA, 1960-1; The Lamp Post, Syosset, NY, 1960; Carnegie Hall, NYC, 1960; Shelly's Manne-Hole, Hollywood, CA, 1960; rec Columbia label, Los Angeles, CA, 1960; toured w Nat Pierce group working college circuit through New Jersey, 1960; worked The Cloister Club, Chicago, IL, 1960; Newport Jazz Festival, Newport, RI, 1961; toured w Shelly Manne & His Men working college dates through Midwest, 1961; worked Jazz Workshop, San Francisco, CA, 1961; Kismet Club, Los Angeles, CA, 1961; The Summit, Hollywood, CA, 1961; app on BARBARA'S BLUES, KDFC-FM-radio, San Francisco, 1961; app on Groucho Marx's YOU BET YOUR LIFE, NBC-TV, 1961; worked The Encore, Los Angeles, 1961; formed own trio working The Lighthouse, Los Angeles, 1962; w Count Basie Orch, Birdland, NYC, 1962; w Inzy Matthews Band, Virginia Club, Los Angeles, 1962; app on ART LINKLETTER Show (HOUSE PARTY), CBS-TV, 1962; worked w Don Thompson Band, Blues Ball, Toronto, Can, 1962; app on STEVE ALLEN Show, WABC-TV, NYC (syndicated), 1963; app on SUE LEE Show, local TV, Honolulu, HI, 1962; app on DON HO Show, local TV, Hawaii, 1962; app on TOMMY BANKS Show, CBC-TV, Canada, 1963; extensive tours through Australia/Japan/Europe working concert dates, 1963-6; app in film IT'S A MAD MAD MAD MAD WORLD, 1963; app on own show, CFRN-radio, Edmonton, Can, 1964; worked (as manager/entertainer) Club Copacabana, Honolulu, HI, 1964-5; worked Forbidden City/Mongin Club/The Clouds Club/others, Honolulu, 1964-5; Club Morocco, Winnipeg, Can, 1964-5; frequently worked The Embers/The Sheraton Caravan Penthouse/Saxony Motor Inn/others, Edmonton, Can, 1964-5; The Sheraton Motor Cavalier, Saskatoon, Can, 1964; Univ of British Columbia, Vancouver, Can, 1966; Shaleey's Pizza Parlour, Vancouver, 1966; Town Tavern, Toronto, Can, 1967; The New Penthouse, Vancouver, 1967-8; The Cave Supper Club, Vancouver, 1968; Isy's Club, Vancouver, 1968; The New Westminster Hotel, Vancouver,

Clarence "Big" Miller *Photo by Lyseng Studios. Courtesy Clarence Miller*

1968-9; The Georgia Hotel, Vancouver, 1968; Vancouver Hotel, Vancouver, 1969; Bayshore Inn, Vancouver, 1969; Oil Can Harry's, Vancouver, 1969; Villa Motor Hotel, Vancouver, 1969; owned/operated Milro Productions Ltd booking agency, Edmonton, Can, from 1969; app in THE OCCULT series, CBC-TV, Canada, 1969; app on SPEAKING OF BLUES, Access-radio, Canada, 1970; app in Canadian film THE BEGINNING (Evil Doing), 1970; app in Canadian (?) film CROWFOOT, early 70s; frequently app on own show, CKUA-radio, Edmonton, Can, early 70s; app in THE HISTORY OF JAZZ series, Access-TV, Canada, 1973; rec GRT label, Edmonton, 1973; worked Mayfair Park, Edmonton, 1974; app on THE CHILDER HOUR, CBC-TV, Canada, 1975; served on panel of Jazz Workshop, Banff Centre School of Fine Arts, Banff, Can, 1976-80s; worked The Hovel, Edmonton, 1977; w Tommy Bank's Band, JAZZ RADIO—CANADA, CBC-radio, Canada, 1977; toured w own band working school/college concerts across western Canada, 1977; toured w Phil Nimmons Band working concerts/workshops across eastern Canada, 1977; app on 90 MINUTES LIVE, CBC-TV, Canada, 1977-8; worked Caravan Hotel, Edmonton, 1977; Jazz Fest, Montreux, Switzerland, 1978 (por rel CBC label); toured clubs/festivals in Switzerland/Japan/Canada, 1979; often app on Canadian radio/TV shows/lectures through 80's/90's; app in bio film BIG AND THE BLUES, 1981; toured concerts in Canada, 1991; suffered fatal heart attack; body cremated

Songs: Hello Little Girl/Lament to Love/Monterey Story

Infl by: Walter Brown/Joe Turner/Jimmy Rushing/Aaron "T-Bone" Walker/Jimmy Witherspoon

Quotes: "Big's style is unique among blues singers. Among other attributes he has the surprising ability to shift unpredictably from an earthy folk blues style to a sudden fusillade of notes straight out of bop"—Leonard Feather, *Downbeat* magazine, Jul 6, 1961, p 17

Reference: Downbeat magazine, Jul 6, 1961, pp 16-17

MILLER, JIM
(see Moss, Eugene)

MILTON, ROY *"Bunny"*
Born: Jul 31, 1907, Wynnewood (Garvin Co), OK
Died: Sept 18, 1983, Canoga Park, CA
Inst: Drums

Father Jeff Milton, a gospel singer; mother Janie Eastman; sang in church choir as child, Tulsa, OK;

Courtesy Living Blues *Magazine*

worked in local high school brass band, Tulsa, mid-20s; formed own combos working social functions in Tulsa area, 1929; attended Univ of Texas (on football scholarship), Austin, TX, c1929-31; worked w Ernie Fields Band at local dances, Tulsa, 1931-3; moved to West Coast to work beer joints/clubs, San Pedro, CA, 1935-8; formed own Roy Milton & His Solid Senders frequently working Louis' Cafe, Los Angeles, CA, 1938-42; app in soundie film 47th STREET JIVE, 1942; app in soundie film HEY LAWDY MAMA, c1942; app in soundie film RIDE ON RIDE ON, 1944; owned/operated Roy's Night Spot, working there as well as Cobra Room/Cherryland/Royal Room/others, Los Angeles, mid-40s; formed own Roy Milton label to rec w Solid Senders, Los Angeles, 1945; rec w own sextet, Hamp-Tone label, Los Angeles, 1945; worked w Solid Senders, Suzie-Q Club, Hollywood, CA, 1946; Paradise Theater, Detroit, MI,

1946; Apollo Theater, NYC, 1946; rec extensively on Specialty label, Los Angeles, 1947-54; toured w own band working one-nighters across US, c1947-c1953; worked w own band, Blues Jubilee Concert, Shrine Auditorium, Los Angeles, 1950 (por rel Gene Norman/Modern/Discovery labels); rec Dootone label, Los Angeles, 1955; worked Ma Cumba, San Francisco, 1956; Ebony Club, Cleveland, OH, 1956; Apache Club, Dayton, OH, 1956; rec King label, Cincinnati, OH/Los Angeles, 1956-7; worked Crown Propeller Club, Chicago, late 50s; rec Warwick label, NYC, 1960; worked mostly outside music in Los Angeles area from early 60s; worked Ash Grove, Los Angeles, 1970; rec w Johnny Otis group, Kent label, Los Angeles, 1970; worked w Johnny Otis Show, Monterey Jazz Festival, Monterey, CA, 1970 (por rel Epic label); worked Topanga Corral, Los Angeles, 1973; w Johnny Otis Show, New Orleans Club, Los Angeles, 1976; Hollywood Palladium, Hollywood, CA, 1976; rec Black & Blue label, Toulouse, France, 1977; died of blood clot; body cremated

Songs: Best Wishes/Bye Bye Baby Blues/Christmas Time Blues/Cold Blooded Woman/Information Blues/It's Later Than You Think/It's Too Late/Little Boy Blue/Make Me Know It/Milton's Boogie/The Number's Blues/RM Blues/So Tired/True Blues

Infl to: Little Joe Blue/Bill Gaither

Quote: "Milton was one of the real rhythm and blues pioneers . . ."—Mike Leadbitter, *Blues Unlimited* magazine (UK), Jul 1975, p 6

References: Blues Unlimited magazine (UK), Jun/Jul 1974, pp 5-6
Blues Unlimited magazine (UK), Aug/Sept 1974, p 19

MINTER, IVERSON *"Red"*
(*aka:* Iverson Bey/Cryin' Red/Playboy Fuller/Richard Lee Fuller/Rocky Fuller/Guitar Red/Elmore James Jr/Louisiana Red/Rockin' Red/Walkin' Slim)
Born: Mar 23, 1936, Vicksburg (Warren Co), MS
Inst: Guitar/Harmonica

Grandparents were musicians; mother died when he was one week old; father lynched by KKK in 1941; raised by grandmother in New Orleans, LA, then lived in orphanage where he taught self harmonica, early 40s; lived briefly in Waco, TX, early 40s; settled in Pittsburgh, PA, mid-40s; learned guitar, 1947, and often worked streets for pennies, Pittsburgh, late 40s; frequently app on local DJ radio blues shows, Pittsburgh, late 40s; sat-in w Muddy Waters Band, Skyline Club, Pittsburgh, c1949; moved to Chicago, IL, 1949;

Photo by Kevin R Doherty. Courtesy Living Blues Magazine

rec Checker label, Chicago, 1949; served year in reformatory, c1950; worked w John Lee Hooker, Club Karen, Detroit, MI, 1951; served in US Army Air Force in England/Korea, 1951-8; rec (as "Rocky Fuller") Chess label, Philadelphia, PA, 1953; frequently worked w John Lee Hooker, Harlem Inn, Detroit, 1958-9; worked club dates through South, late 50s; frequently worked w James Wayne Nighthawks, Elizabeth, NJ, late 50s-early 60s; rec Atlas label, NYC, 1960; frequently worked outside music into early 60s; rec Roulette label, NYC, 1962; worked w Jimmy Reed, Brevoort Theater, Brooklyn, NY, early 60s; w Jimmy Reed, Shug's Cozy Spot, Newark, NJ, early 60s; active in Black Muslims and The Rev Ike movement with frequent outside music work, Lincolnton, GA, 1966-72; app w Searles Gospel Singers on local show, WJBF-TV, Augusta, GA, late 60s; worked outside music in Okefenokee swamp area, Florida, into 70s; formed own The Bluesettes, working club dates in Atlanta/Augusta, GA, area, c1971; rec Atco label, NYC, 1971; worked Joe's Place, Cambridge, MA, 1972; Buffalo Folk Festival, Buffalo, NY, 1973; Philadelphia Folk Festival, Schwenksville, PA, 1973; rec Blue Labor label, White Plains, NY, 1975; worked Academy of Music, Brooklyn, NY, 1975; Old Reliable Bar, NYC, 1975; Folk City, NYC, 1975; Little Joe's Bar, Newark, NJ, 1975; Montreux Rock/Blues Festival, Montreux, Switzerland, 1975 (por rel Utopia label); Bottom Line, NYC, 1975; El Mocambo, Toronto, Can, 1975; Mike Porco's Folk City, NYC, 1976; Riverboat, Toronto, 1976; Atlanta Blues Festival, Great Southeast Music Hall, Atlanta, GA, 1976; Dr Generosity, NYC, 1976; Gerde's Folk City, NYC, 1976; app on Bob Javors SOMETHING INSIDE ME Show, WKCR-FM-radio, NYC, 1976; toured concert dates through France/Germany, 1976; rec Black & Blue label, France, 1976; worked The Casino, Bern, Switzerland, 1976; John Henry Folk Festival, Camp Virgil Tate, Princeton, WV, 1976; The Raven Gallery, Detroit, MI, 1976; toured concerts in Germany/Japan, 1977; Newport Jazz Festival Blues Picnic, Waterloo Village, Stanhope, NJ, 1977; Club Zircon, Cambridge, MA, 1977; Philadelphia Folk Festival, Schwenksville, PA, 1977; frequently toured clubs/concerts in England/Europe, 1977; rec Chrischaa label, Hanover, W Ger, 1977; worked Nancy Jazz Festival, Nancy, France, 1977; app on OLD GREY WHISTLE TEST Show, BBC-2-TV, London, Eng, 1977

Personal: Married Ealase ——— (1963-died 1973). 3 children. Married blues singer Odetta Gordon (c1977-). Not to be confused with guitarists Paul Johnson/Vincent Duling who have also used pseudonym "Guitar Red"

Songs: Back on the Road Again/Bad Case of the Blues/Caught My Man and Gone/Cold Feeling/Cold White Sheet/Country Playboy/Dead Stray Dog/Death of Ealase/Don't Cry/First Degree/Freight Train to Ride/Going Home/Had a Date with Barbara Last Night/Held Up in One Town/I Was Out Walking/I Wonder Who/I'm a Roaming Stranger/I'm Going Back to Georgia/I'm Lousiana Red/Keep Your Hands off My Woman/My Baby's Coming Home/New Jersey Women/Red's Dream/Sad News/Some Day/Sugar Hips/Sweet Alesse/Sweetblood Call/Thirty Dirty Women/Too Poor to Die/Two Fifty Three/Where Is My Friend?/Who Been Fooling You?/The Whole World/Working Man Blues

Infl by: Lightnin' Hopkins/Jimmy Reed

Quote: ". . . he has the ability to make a guitar talk and a harmonica cry in the manner of the great bluesmen of the past"—Herb Abramson, *Living Blues* magazine, Jan 1972, p 8

References: Blues Unlimited magazine (UK), Oct 1972, pp 8-9
Living Blues magazine, Winter 1973-4, pp 6-7

MISS RHAPSODY
(see Wells, Viola)

MISSISSIPPI MATILDA
(see Witherspoon, Matilda)

MISSISSIPPI MUDDER
(see McCoy, Charles)
(see McCoy, Joe)

MODEL T SLIM
(see Mickle, Elmon)

MOJO
(see Buford, George)

MONROE, VINCE
(see Vincent, Monroe)

MONTGOMERY, E
(see Montgomery, Eurreal)

MONTGOMERY, EURREAL WILFORD *"Little Brother"*
(*aka:* Little Brother)
Born: Apr 18, 1906, Kentwood (Tangipahoa Parish), LA
Died: Sep 6, 1985, Chicago,IL
Inst: Piano

Father was Harper Montgomery, a musician who operated local barrelhouse; mother was Dicy Burten; born Euel Wilford Montgomery; taught self piano at 5 years of age; frequently sang in local Baptist church as child; dropped out of school to leave home and work jukes in Holden, LA, 1917-19; worked Tom Kirby Club, Plaquemine, LA, early 20s; Henderson's Royal Garden, Ferriday, LA, c1922; hoboed extensively working Benny Star's Club, Tallulah, LA/Zack Lewis Club, Vicksburg, MS/Bell's Cafe, Vicksburg, MS/Steamboat Exchange, Vicksburg, MS/The Titanic, Picayune, MS/Will Thomas' Place, Giles Corner, MS/Princess Theater, Vicksburg/Ware's Tonk, Vicksburg/Red Bob's Place, New Orleans, LA/DoDo's Club, New Orleans/The Entertainers, New Orleans, 1922-3; w Leonard Parker's Band, Slidell, LA, c1924; formed own band working dances at Curtis Coleman Club, Gulfport, MS, 1924; worked w Buddy Petit Rhythm Aces, Bogalusa, LA, c1925; frequently sat-in w Sam Morgan Band/Eugene Watt's Serenaders in local club dates, New Orleans, through 20s; frequently toured w Big Joe Williams working brothel circuit/lumber camps/logging camps through Mississippi/Louisiana during 20s; worked King Tut's Tomb,

Eurreal "Little Brother" Montgomery

Photo by Jean-Claude Lejeune. Courtesy Living Blues *Magazine*

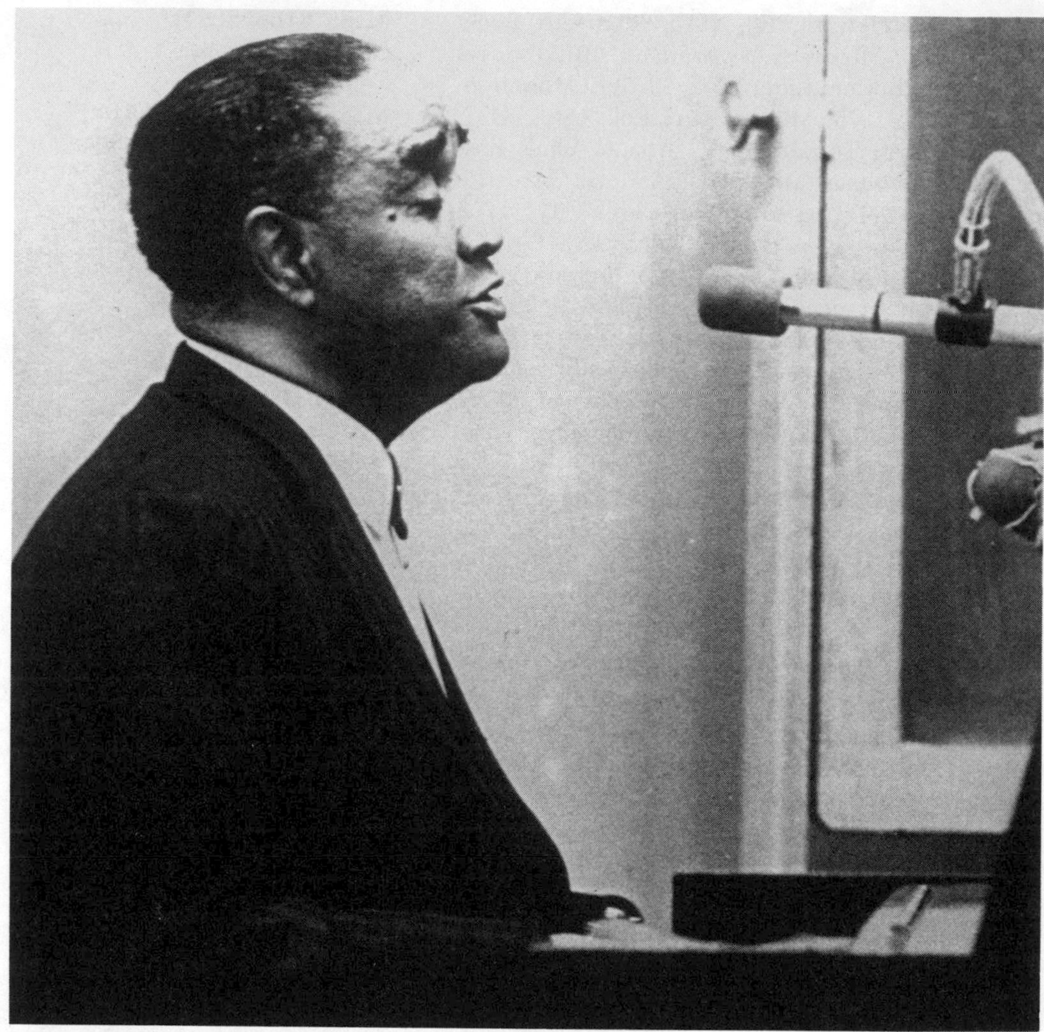

Chicago, IL, 1926; frequently worked local house parties, Chicago, 1926; toured w Danny Barker working juke dances through Mississippi, 1927; toured w Clarence Desdunes Joyland Revellers working dances through South/Midwest to Omaha, NE, 1928; settled in Chicago, IL, 1928, to frequently work house rent parties/joints/gin mills/club dates/hotels, from 1928 into 30s; worked The Hollywood Show Lounge, Chicago, late 20s; The Brass Rail, Chicago, late 20s; Preview Lounge, Chicago, c1930; Olympic Hotel, Chicago, c1930; rec solo (and as acc to other blues singers) Paramount/Broadway labels, Grafton, WI, 1930; toured as acc to Irene Scruggs working TOBA theater circuit, 1931; rec acc to Minnie Hicks, Melotone label, Chicago, 1931; returned to Jackson, MS, to form own Southland Troubadors (renamed Collegiate Ramblers for college dates) frequently working one-nighters/concerts/radio shows out of Jackson, MS, touring Louisiana/Midwest, 1931-9; rec Bluebird label, New Orleans, LA, 1935-6; worked as single in local jukes/barrelhouses, Hattiesburg, MS/Beaumont, TX, areas, 1940-1; returned to Chicago, IL, 1942; frequently worked outside music with work as single (or with own group) at house parties/clubs/dance halls/lounges like Hollywood Show Lounge/Casablanca Club/Moulin Rouge/Moose Hall/Diamond Lounge/Lord Liquor Club/Tin Pan Alley Club/Victory Club/others, Chicago, 1942 into 50s; rec Century label, Chicago, 1946; rec Disc-Delmark label, Chicago, 1947; toured w Kid Ory Band working clubs/concerts across US, 1948; w Kid Ory Band, Carnegie Hall, NYC, 1949; worked w Franz Jackson Band/Al Wynn Band (or as single) in local clubs, Chicago area, through 50s; rec Windin' Ball label, Chicago, 1954; rec Ebony label, Chicago, 1956-60; toured w Otis Rush group working one-nighters through Texas/Mississippi/Alabama/Georgia, 1956; worked Bill Broonzy Benefit concert, KAM Temple, Chicago, 1957; rec acc to Otis Rush, Cobra label, Chicago, 1958; worked Ravinia Folk Festival, Chicago, 1959; Bambu Club, Chicago, 1959; frequently worked club dates in Joliet, IL, 1959; rec w Franz Jackson All-Stars, Phillips label, Chicago, 1959; rec Folkways/Decca/77/Polydor labels, Chicago, 1960; rec Prestige-Bluesville label, NYC, 1960; toured club/concert dates through England, 1960; rec Columbia label, London, 1960; worked w Gold Coast Jazz Band, Gate of Horn, Chicago, 1960; Hey Rube Club, Chicago, 1961; rec Riverside label, Chicago, 1961; worked Camelot Club, Chicago, 1961-2; Plugged Nickel Club, Chicago, 1962-3; Loyola Univ, Chicago, 1963; w Franz Jackson Band, Red Arrow Club, Chicago, 1963; Touch of Olde Club, Chicago, 1964-5; Club Hello Dolly, Chicago, 1964; Gerdes Folk City, NYC, 1965; rec Spivey label, NYC (?), 1965; worked Newport Jazz Festival, Newport, RI, 1965; Mother Blues, Chicago, 1965; McPartlan's Lounge, Chicago, 1966-8; toured w American Folk Blues Festival working concert dates through England/Europe, 1966 (por of Berlin, Ger concert rel Fontana/Amiga labels); formed/rec FM label, Chicago, 1966/9; frequently worked w Franz Jackson Band in local club dates, Chicago, 1968; worked Univ of Wisconsin, Milwaukee, WI, 1969; Edge Lounge, Chicago, 1969; Chicago Blues Festival, Chicago, 1969; Sam Ferrera's Lounge, Chicago, 1969; Sloppy Joe's, Chicago, 1969; rec Blackbird/Adelphi labels, Chicago, 1970; worked Shrimp Walk, Chicago, 1970; Ann Arbor Blues Festival, Ann Arbor, MI, 1970; heard on ST of UK film BLUES LIKE SHOWERS OF RAIN, 1970; worked w Franz Jackson Band in jazz club/concert dates in New York/Connecticut, 1971; worked Festival of American Folklife, Montreal, Can, 1971; Notre Dame Blues Festival, South Bend, IN, 1971; Alice's Revisited, Chicago, 1971; Mr Kelly's, Chicago, 1971; Univ of Chicago Folk Festival, Chicago, 1972-4; toured concert/club dates through England/Europe, 1972; worked Bajes Club, Amsterdam, Holland, 1972 (por rel Blues Beacon label); rec Matchbox label, Chicago, 1972; contributed articles to *Jazz Journal* magazine (UK), 1972; worked Kenny's Castaways, NYC, 1973; McPartlan's Lounge, Chicago, 1973-4; rec Delmark label, Chicago, 1973-6; worked Northeastern Illinois Univ, Chicago, 1973; w Samuel Dent Memorial Jazz Band, Donovan's Pub, Wheeling, IL, 1974; Pheasant Run, St Charles, IL, 1974; w Banjo Ikey Robinson, Berlin Jazz Festival, Berlin, Ger, 1974; worked Jazz at Noon, Marina City Towers, Chicago, 1974; National Folk Festival, Washington, DC, 1974; Philadelphia Folk Festival, Schwenksville, PA, 1974; Lake Meadows Park, Chicago, 1975; Nassau Community Col, Garden City, NY, 1975; worked concert dates in Holland, 1975; Festival of Arts Concert, Univ of Chicago, Chicago, 1976; w Edith Wilson, Goodtime Jazz Club Concert, The Cabriolet, Libertyville, IL, 1976; Wilshire Ebell Theater, Los Angeles, CA, 1976; app on THE DEVIL'S MUSIC—A HISTORY OF THE BLUES (ep: Nothing But the Truth/ep: Crazy Blues/ep: Work and Mother Wit/ep: The Movements of Providence), BBC-1-TV, England, 1976; worked New Orleans Jazz & Heritage Festival, New Orleans, LA, 1976; Avery Fisher Hall, NYC, 1977; app w Edith Wilson on MADE IN CHICAGO, WTTW-TV, Chicago, 1977; toured Australia, 1979; app TV production JAZZ: AMERICAN CLASSIC (ep: Chicago, Jazz Age), 1979; worked clubs/concerts into 80s; died of heart failure; buried Oak Woods Cemetery, Chicago

Personal: Named "Little Brother" during childhood

Book: Deep South Piano, Karl Gert zur Heide, Studio Vista Ltd, 1970

Songs: A&V Railroad Blues/Bass Key Boogie/Brothers Boogie/Chinese Man Blues/Cooney Vaughn's Tremblin' Blues/Dangerous Blues/Deep Fried/Dud Low Joe/Farish Street Jive/The First Time I Met You/Frisco Hi-Ball Blues/How Long Brother?/I Was So in Love with You/Jim Jam Blues/Lakeshore Blues/Leaving Town Blues/London Shout/Lonesome Mama Blues/Louisiana Blues/Mama You Don't Mean Me No Good/Miles Davis Blues/Misled Blues/Mistreatin' Woman Blues/My Electrical Invention Blues/Never Go Wrong Blues/No Special Boogie/No Special Rider Blues/Out West Blues/Pleading Blues/Santa Fe Blues/(New) Satellite Blues/Shreveport Farewell/Something Keeps A-Worryin' Me/Sorrowfull Blues/Sweet Momma/Talkin' Boogie/Tantalizing Blues/Tasty Blues/That's Why I Keep Drinkin'/Tremblin' Blues/Vanado Anderson Blues/Vicksburg Blues/West Texas Blues/Willie Anderson's Blues/The Woman I Love Blues

Infl by: Bob Alexander/Cooney Vaughn

Infl to: Willie Dixon/Skip James/Otis Spann/Sunnyland Slim

Quotes: "It is his blues singing and piano . . . that mark him as an exceptional and creative musician"—Eric Kriss, *Six Blues-Roots Pianists*, Oak Publications, 1973

"A fair performer of hymns and pop tunes, an excellent traditional jazz man, a fascinating singer, Brother stands out as one of the greatest blues soloists and accompanists"—Karl Gert zur Heide, *Deep South Piano*, Studio Vista Ltd, 1970

"Little Brother Montgomery, barrelhouse pianist, blues singer and entertainer extraordinary"—Derrick Stewart-Baxter, Saydisc album 213

References: Deep South Piano, Karl Gert zur Heide, Studio Vista Ltd, 1970

Mississippi Rag magazine, Apr 1974/ Jan 1975

MOORE, ALEXANDER HERMAN *"Whistling Alex"*
(*aka:* Papa Chittlins)

Photo by Chris Strachwitz, Arhoolie Records. Courtesy Living Blues Magazine

Born: Nov 22, 1899, Dallas (Dallas Co), TX
Died: Jan 20, 1989, Dallas, TX
Inst: Harmonica/Piano

After death of father, quit school to work outside music, Dallas, TX, from 1911; learned harmonica and occasionally app on WRR-radio, Dallas, 1915; learned piano, 1916; served in US Army, 1916; worked mostly outside music, Dallas, through 20s; frequently worked house parties/bars, Dallas area, 1923 into 30s; worked White's Road House, Dallas 1928; rec Columbia label, Dallas, 1929; frequently worked Misty Lounge/Hungry Eye Club/The Gay Nineties/The Green Parrot/The Brown Derby/The Three B's/This Is It Club/Pam's Striptease Bar & Dance Lounge/Silver Slipper/400 Club/others, Dallas, TX, through 30s/ 40s/50s; rec Decca label, Chicago, IL, 1937; worked Southern Steak House, Dallas, 1947-50; rec Highway label, Dallas, 1947; rec RPM/Kent labels, Dallas, 1951; worked mostly outside music, Dallas, from c1960 into 70s; rec Arhoolie/Decca labels, Dallas, 1960; app on MACK McCORMICK AND FRIENDS, KUHF-FM-radio, Houston, TX, 1961; app in film THE BLUES, 1962; toured w American Folk Blues Festival working concerts through England/Europe, 1969; worked Royal Albert Hall, London, Eng, 1969 (por rel CBS label); rec Arhoolie label, Stuttgart, Ger, 1969; frequently worked local parties, Dallas area, from 1969 into 70s; worked Mother Blues, Dallas, 1972; worked clubs in Dallas-Austin areas into 80s; West Coast Festivals/clubs mid-80s; rec Rounder label, Dallas (?), 1988; died of heart attack

Songs: Across the Atlantic Ocean/Alex Thinking/Black Eyed Peas and Hog Jowls/Boogie in the Barrel/Come and Get Me/Flossie Mae/Frisky Gal/From North Dallas to the East Side/Having Fun Here and There/July Boogie/Just a Blues/Miss No Good Weed/Neglected Woman/Pretty Woman with a Sack Dress On/Rock and Roll Bed Blues/Rolling Around Dallas/Rubber Tyred Hack/Southern House Blues/West Texas Woman/Whistling Alex Moore's Blues/You Say I'm a Bad Feller

Quote: "He is a true original, a folk blues singer of the city who can sit at the piano and improvise endlessly piano themes and blues verses that are sometimes startling, sometimes comic, sometimes grim and very often are pure poetry"—Paul Oliver, Arhoolie album 1008

References: Blues Unlimited magazine (UK), Aug/ Sept 1974, p 14

Blues World magazine (UK), Jan 1966, pp 3-5

Living Blues magazine, Nov/Dec 1977, pp 8-10

MOORE, *Rev* **ARNOLD DWIGHT** *"Gatemouth"*
Born: Nov 8, 1913, Topeka (Shawnee Co), KS

Mother was Georgia ———; moved to Memphis, TN, where he was raised from childhood; frequently sang in local church choirs as child; briefly worked w Bennie Moten Band, Cherry Blossom Club, Kansas City, MO, c1929; left home to tour w Ida Cox's DARKTOWN SCANDALS Revue/Rabbit Foot Minstrels/ Silas Green from New Orleans/Pork Chop Chapman's Show/Sammy Green's Down in Dixie Minstrels/Sam Dale's Circus/Beckman & Garrity Carnival/Winter Erlich & Hearst Carnival/others working shows across

US/Canada from c1930 through 30s; worked 81 Theater, Atlanta, GA, 1934; worked local club dates, Chicago, IL, c1935; toured briefly w Nat Cole group, mid-30s; worked w King Kolax Band, late 30s; w Erskine Tate Band, Savoy Ballroom, Chicago, late 30s; toured w Walter Barnes Band working ballrooms through South, 1939-40; worked club dates in Memphis, TN, 1940; frequently w Carolina Cotton Pickers, Gilmore's Chez Paree, Kansas City, MO, 1941-5 (por rel Gilmore's Chez Paree label); toured extensively w Carolina Cotton Pickers working clubs/theaters across US, early 40s; w Carolina Cotton Pickers, Town Hall, Philadelphia, PA, 1943; worked Stardust Inn, Washington, DC, 1943; frequently worked Apollo Theater, NYC, 1943-5; rec Damen/National labels, Kansas City, MO, 1945; worked Rhumboogie Club, Chicago, 1945; rec w Al Budd Johnson Orch/Tiny Grimes Swingtet, National label, NYC, 1946; worked (as MC/singer) 845 Club, Bronx, NY, 1946; Civic Opera House, Chicago, 1946; Brown Derby, Chatanooga, TN, c1946; Club De Lisa, Chicago, 1946-7; rec King label, Cincinnati, OH/Chicago, IL, 1947; left blues field to become ordained minister of Church of God in Christ Church, Memphis, 1948, and served into 60s; app as (religious) DJ, WDIA-radio, Memphis, through 50s; toured as singing preacher working revivals/churches through South through 50s into 70s; app on WEDR-radio, Birmingham, AL, mid-50s; app on WOPA-radio, Chicago, 1957; rec religious music into 60s; app on own show, WCIU-TV, Chicago, c1960; app on WBEE-radio, Chicago, into 60s; served as pastor of Wesley Chapel Community Church, Chicago, from c1962; rec religious music, BluesWay label, Chicago, c1973; worked (as blues singer) Cadillac Bob's Toast of the Town Club, Chicago, 1974

Personal: Married. 4 children. Not to be confused with blues musician/singer Clarence "Gatemouth" Brown

Billing: Mr Blues

Song: Did You Ever Love a Woman?

Infl to: Alex Bradford/Rufus Thomas

Reference: Blues Unlimited magazine (UK), Aug/Sept 1974, p 13

MOORE, JAMES
(*aka:* Harmonica Slim/Slim Harpo)
Born: Jan 11, 1924, Lobdell (West Baton Rouge Parish), LA
Died: Jan 31, 1970, Baton Rouge, LA
Inst: Harmonica

Courtesy Sheldon Harris Collection

One of at least 4 children; raised in Port Allen, LA; after parents died he dropped out of school to work outside music in Baton Rouge/New Orleans, LA, areas from mid-30s; taught self harmonica and worked local bars/clubs in Baton Rouge, early 40s; hoboed extensively (as "Harmonica Slim") working jukes/clubs/streets/parties/picnics in Crowley/Lafayette/Opelousas/St Martinville/New Iberia, LA/elsewhere, c1945 into 50s; rec acc to Lightnin' Slim, Excello label, Crowley, LA, 1955-6; rec (as "Slim Harpo") Excello label, Crowley, LA, and elsewhere, 1957-69; toured South working one-nighters, early 60s; rec Imperial label, New Orleans, LA, 1962; worked w James Brown, Madison Square Garden, NYC, NY, 1966; worked outside music (in own trucking business) with occasional work in local clubs, Baton Rouge, LA, from c1966; worked w Lightnin' Slim in local clubs, Chicago, IL, c1967; worked Whiskey A-Go-Go, Los Angeles, CA, 1968; The Scene, NYC, 1968; Apollo Theater, NYC, c1968; Fillmore East, NYC, 1969; Hunter Col, NYC, 1969; Electric Circus, NYC, 1969; rec Excello label, Los Angeles, c1969; entered General Hospital where he died of heart attack; buried local cemetery, Port Allen, LA

Personal: Married Lovell ——— (1948-). 2 children. Wife was co-author of many of his songs. Sister married Otis Hicks (Lightnin' Slim)

Songs: A Man Is Crying/Baby Scratch My Back/Bobby Sox Baby/Buzz Me Baby/Buzzin'/Don't Start Crying Now/Got Love If You Want It/Harpo's Blues/Hey Little Lee/I Just Can't Leave You/I'm a King Bee/I'm Gonna Keep What I've Got/I'm So Sorry/I'm Your Bread Maker Baby/I've Been a Good Thing for You/I've Got to Be with You Tonight/I Love the Life I'm Living/Just for You/Late Last Night/Mailbox Blues/Moody Blues/My Baby She's Got It/Please Don't Turn Me Down/Rainin' in My Heart/Shake Your Hips/Sittin' Here Wondering/Snoopin' Around/Something Inside Me/Strange Love/Te-Ni-Nee-Ni-Nu/That's Why I Love You/Tip On In/What's Goin' On Baby?/Wondering and Worryin'

Infl by: Lightnin' Slim/Muddy Waters/Jimmy Reed

Quotes: "Slim Harpo, the man with the guitar and harmonica, has molded his art into a pure classical style and has become a legend in his own time"—Robert Holmes, Excello album 8008

"One of the best proponents of [the] rural American blues form is Slim Harpo"—Dick Allen, Excello album 8003

References: Crowley Louisiana Blues, Mike Leadbitter, Blues Unlimited, 1968

Blues Unlimited magazine (UK), May/Jun 1966, pp 8-9

MOORE, JOHNNY BELLE

Born: Jan 24, 1950, Clarksdale (Coahoma Co), MS
Inst: Drums/Guitar

Father was Floyd Moore; mother was Ruth Mae Pernell; interested in music early, learning guitar from about age of 13; worked w Spiritual Harmonism Gospel group in local churches, Clarksdale, MS, early 60s; worked w Soul Revival Gospel group in local churches in Clarksdale, mid-60s; moved to Chicago, IL, to work outside music with frequent church work w Gospel Keys group, c1964 into 70s; frequently worked w Charles Spiers group in local club dates, Chicago, c1969; frequently sat-in with various bands in local clubs, Chicago, late 60s into 70s; worked w LC Roby & The Presidents, Majestic "M" Club, Chicago, 1975; formed own trio working local club dates, Chicago, from 1975

Personal: Not to be confused with musician Johnny Moore of the Three Blazers group

Reference: Living Blues magazine, Sept 1975, pp 11-12

Johnny Moore
Photo by Erik Lindahl. Courtesy Living Blues *Magazine*

MOORE, MONETTE
(*aka:* Ethel Mayes/Nettie Potter/Susie Smith/Grace White)

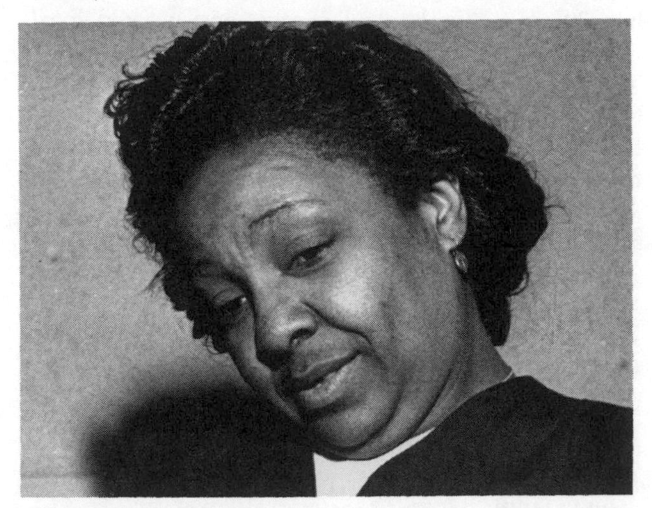

Courtesy Frank Driggs Collection

Born: May 19, 1902, Gainesville (Cooke Co), TX
Died: Oct 21, 1962, Garden Grove, CA
Inst: Piano

Father was Karl Moore; liked music early and sang in local school chorus as child; taught self piano c1915; moved to Kansas City, MO, to work outside music with frequent dates as theater pianist in local movie houses, early 20s; rec Paramount label, NYC, NY, 1923-4; rec w Clarence Jones/Paramount Trio, Paramount label, Chicago, IL, 1923-4; rec Vocalion label, NYC, 1924; worked Clara Smith's Theatrical Club, NYC, 1924; Blue Butterfly Inn, NYC, 1924; rec w Choo Choo Jazzers/Texas Trio, Ajax label, NYC, 1924-5; rec Columbia label, NYC, 1925; worked w Sunshine Sammy Troupe, Koppin Theater, Detroit, MI, c1925; app in musical comedy LUCKY SAMBO, Colonial Theater, NYC, 1925; rec Victor label, NYC, 1926-7; long residency, Sheid's Plaza, Lindenhurst, NY, 1926-7; frequently worked Connie's Inn, NYC, 1927-32; w Charlie Johnson's Paradise Band, Small's Paradise, NYC, c1927; rec w Charlie Johnson's Original Paradise Ten, Victor label, Camden, NJ, 1927-8; worked w Walter Page Blue Devils, Kansas City, MO/Oklahoma City, OK, late 20s; app on A NIGHT IN HARLEM, WMSG-radio, NYC, 1929; app in MESSIN' AROUND Revue, Hudson Theater, NYC, 1929; app in LUCKY STARS Revue, Alhambra Theater, NYC, 1929; app in CRAZY QUILT REVUE, Lafayette Theater, NYC, 1929; app in HIGH SPOTS Revue, Alhambra Theater, NYC, 1929; app in BROWN PEPPER REVUE, Lafayette Theater, NYC, 1930; app w Ada Brown/Bill Robinson in all-Negro show BROWN BUDDIES, RKO-Palace Theater, NYC, 1930; app in musical comedy COOL RHYTHM, Alhambra Theater, NYC, 1931; app w Lucky Millinder Band, HAPPY-GO-LUCKY Revue, Lafayette Theater, NYC, 1931; app in SARATOGA FROLICS REVUE, Saratoga Club, NYC, 1931; worked w Mae Barnes, Covan's Club Morocco, NYC, 1932; app in musical comedy FLYING COLORS, Imperial Theater, NYC, 1932; worked Tyler's Theatrical Grill, NYC, 1932; worked w Fess Williams Band, Lafayette Theater, NYC, 1933; Savoy Ballroom, NYC, 1933; owned/operated/performed at Monette's Place, NYC, 1933; app in THE LAST ROUND-UP Revue, Lafayette Theater, NYC, 1933; frequently worked Harlem Opera House, NYC, 1933-5; worked residency, Sunset Beer Garden, NYC, 1933-4; residency at Brittwood Grill, NYC, 1934; toured (as understudy to Ethel Waters) in musical revue AS THOUSANDS CHEER, 1934; worked Poosepahtuck Club, NYC, 1934-5; rec w Swing Shop Boys, Decca label, NYC, 1936; toured (as understudy to Ethel Waters) in AT HOME ABROAD Revue, 1936; worked w Zinky Cohn group, The Annex, Chicago, IL, 1937; Uptown House Cafe, NYC, 1938; frequently worked outside music in NYC, NY, late 30s into 40s; worked residency w Ernie Henry's Band, 721 Club, NYC, 1941; Sunset Club, NYC, 1941; The Frogs, Detroit, MI, 1942; moved to West Coast to work residency at Casablanca Club, Los Angeles, CA, 1942-5; Club Alabam, Los Angeles, 1942-5; rec w Teddy Bunn, Gilt Edge label, Los Angeles, 1946; worked Streets of Paris Club, Hollywood, CA, 1946-7; rec w Sammy Price Trio, NYC, 1947; frequently worked outside music, Los Angeles, CA, late 40s into 50s; rec w Harmony Girls, A Natural Hit label, Los Angeles, c1949; app w James P Johnson in show SUGAR HILL, Las Palmas Theater, Los Angeles, 1949 (por rel Columbia label); worked Central Plaza, NYC, 1949; app in film YES SIR MR BONES, 1951; app on THE AMOS 'N' ANDY Show, CBS-TV, 1951-3; rec w George Lewis Ragtime Band, Jazzman label, Los Angeles, 1953; app in film A STAR IS BORN, 1954; frequently worked w Nappy Lamare Band on West Coast dates through 50s; worked Beverly Caverns, Los Angeles, c1959; w South Bay Jazz Band, Green Bull, Hermosa Beach, CA, 1960; frequently worked w Young Men from New Orleans Band, Mark Twain Riverboat at Disneyland Park, Anaheim, CA, 1961-2; app w Louis Armstrong on WONDERFUL WORLD OF COLOR (ep: Disneyland After Dark), NBC-TV, 1962 (rel as film DISNEYLAND AFTER DARK); app in film THE OUT-

SIDER, 1962; while working Disneyland Park gig suffered emphysema attack; DOA at Palm Harbor General Hospital; buried Holy Cross Cemetery, Los Angeles, CA

Personal: Married John Erby (mid 20s-late 20s). 1 child. Not to be confused with Ethel Mayes who worked Georgia Smart Set Minstrels troupe during 1920s

Billing: The Girl of Smiles

Songs: Show Girl Blues/Treated Wrong Blues

Infl by: Mamie Smith

Quote: "Blues singer and long time performer in the field of entertainment"—Douglas Hague, *Jazz Journal* magazine (UK), Apr 1963, p 7

References: Jazz Journal magazine (UK), Apr 1963, pp 7-10

Who's Who of Jazz, John Chilton, Bloomsbury Book Shop, 1970

MOORE, WILLIE C
(*aka:* Boll Weenie Bill/Boll Weevil Bill)

Photo by John Rodgers. Courtesy *Living Blues Magazine*

Born: Apr 22, 1913, Kinston (Lenoir Co), NC
Died: May 2, 1971, Albany, NY
Inst: Guitar

Father was Rod Rouse; mother was Mary Dawson; learned some guitar from father at 13 years of age; worked mostly outside music, Kinston, NC, area from late 20s; won local talent contest and worked local house parties/suppers in Kinston area through 30s; rec (as "Boll Weenie Bill"), ARC label group (unissued), NYC, 1934; rec w Blind Boy Fuller/Sonny Terry/Gary Davis, Bluebird label, NYC, 1937; continued outside music work, Kinston area, through 30s; served in US Army, 1940-4; continued outside music work, Kinston, c1944-8; moved to Albany, NY, to work outside music from 1948 into 60s; frequently worked w Bill Broonzy in Chicago, IL, area, mid-50s; worked occasional local bar dates, Albany, NY, through 60s; entered St Peter's Hospital where he died of bronchopneumonia; buried Elmwood Hills Cemetery, Troy, NY

Personal: Was married. Not to be confused with "Wild" Willie Moore, musician

Reference: Living Blues magazine, Summer 1971, pp 15-16

MOOSE JOHN
(see Walker, John)

MORAN, MAE
(see Beaman, Lottie)

MORGANFIELD, McKINLEY
(*aka:* Muddy Waters)
Born: Apr 4, 1915, Rolling Fork (Sharkey Co), MS
Died: Apr 30, 1983, Westmont, IL
Inst: Guitar/Harmonica

Father was Ollie Morganfield, a farmer and musician; mother was Bertha Jones; one of 10 children; born on Kroger Plantation; after death of mother moved to live with grandmother in Stovall-Clarksdale, MS, area, 1918; received some schooling and worked mostly outside music (as farmer) in area through 20s into 30s; frequently sang in local church choirs as youth; taught self harmonica at about 9 years of age and frequently worked local parties, Clarksdale, MS, area, through 20s; taught self guitar c1932; frequently worked w own string group or w Scott Bohanna in juke joints/suppers/picnics/parties/Sunday get-togethers in Clarksdale area through 30s; worked briefly in St Louis, MO, 1940; worked mostly outside music with occasional local dances/jukes/fish fries, Stovall-Clarksdale, MS, area, 1940-3; briefly toured w Silas Green from New Orleans Minstrel/Carnival Show, 1941; rec Library of Congress label, Stovall, MS, 1941-2; moved to Chicago, IL, 1943; worked mostly

McKinley Morganfield (Muddy Waters) *Courtesy Sheldon Harris Collection*

outside music with frequent work on Maxwell Street for tips with occasional parties/south side taverns, Chicago, from 1943; frequently sat-in w Eddie Boyd in west side club dates, Chicago, c1943; worked w John Lee "Sonny Boy" Williamson, Plantation Club, Chicago, 1943; The Spot, Gary, IN, 1943; w Jimmy Rogers, David & Mason's Club, Chicago, 1945; The Flame Club, Chicago, 1945; Cotton Club, Chicago, 1945; Chicken Shack, Chicago, 1945-6; frequently w Tampa Red/Doc Clayton/others at Sylvio's, Chicago, from mid-40s; worked Purple Cat, Chicago, c1945; Tom's Tavern, Chicago, c1946; rec Columbia-Testament label, Chicago, 1946; rec Aristocrat label, Chicago, 1947-50; formed own trio (w Jimmy Rogers/Little Walter), then enlarged to include Sunnyland Slim/Leroy Foster/Johnny Jones/Otis Spann/others from 1948; worked Boogie Woogie Inn, Chicago, 1948; Romeo's Place, Chicago, c1948; Du Drop Inn, Chicago, 1948-9; 708 Club, Chicago, 1948; Club Zanzibar, Chicago, 1948-54; Club 99, Joliet, IL, 1948; Skyline Club, Pittsburgh, PA, 1948; toured w own band working jukes/dances/clubs through South, 1949-50; app on KATZ CLOTHING STORE Show, KFFA-radio, Helena, AR, 1949; worked Owl Cafe, Helena, AR, 1949; Ebony Lounge, Chicago, 1950; rec w Baby Face Trio, Parkway label, Chicago, 1950; rec extensively on Chess label, Chicago, 1951-66; toured w John Lee Hooker working club dates through South, 1952; worked 708 Club, Chicago, 1953; toured w own band working one-nighters through South, 1953-4; worked Hippodrome Ballroom, Memphis, TN, 1954; Alan Freed's Moondog Coronation Ball, Newark, NJ, 1954; worked club dates in Birmingham, AL, 1954; toured w own band working concert dates across US, 1954; worked Graystone Ballroom, Detroit, MI, 1954; Five-Four Ballroom, Los Angeles, CA, 1954; Apollo Theater, NYC, c1955; frequently worked Smitty's Corner, Chicago, 1955-61; frequently app as DJ on WOPA-radio, Chicago, 1956; worked Regal Theater, Chicago, c1957; F&J Lounge, Gary, IN, 1958-60; toured w Chris Barber Band working club/concert dates through England, 1958; worked Carnegie Hall, NYC, 1959-61 (por 1959 concert rel United Artists label); Newport Jazz Festival, Newport, RI, 1960 (por rel Chess label/por shown in USIA film short series JAZZ-USA [Nos 19, 20, 22]/por shown in film THE SUBTERRANEANS); worked Club Tay May, Chicago, 1960; app on BIG BILL HILL Show, WOPA-radio, Oak Park, IL, 1960; worked Pepper's Lounge, Chicago, 1961-5; Orchard Lounge, Chicago, 1961; Playmate Club, Chicago, 1961; McKie's Club, Chicago, 1962-5; Alex Club, Chicago, 1962-3; Copa Cabana Club, Chicago, 1963 (por rel Argo label); Civic Opera House, Chicago, 1963; The Bear, Chicago, 1963; Tally Ho Club, Highwood, IL, 1963; app on INTERNATIONAL HOUR, CBS-TV, 1963; toured w American Folk-Blues Festival working concert dates through England/Europe, 1963 (por shown on I HEAR THE BLUES, Granada-TV, England); rec Fontana label, Bremen, Ger, 1963; worked Hunter Col, NYC, 1964; First Floor Club, Toronto, Can, 1964; Jazz Workshop, Boston, MA, 1964-5; Cafe A-Go-Go, NYC, 1964-6; Newport Folk Festival, Newport, RI, 1964; Bon-Ton Cavern, Buffalo, NY, 1964; toured w Blues Caravan working concert dates through England, 1964 (por shown on BLUES AND GOSPEL TRAIN Show, Granada-TV, England); worked Showboat Club, Philadelphia, PA, 1965; Blues Unlimited Club, Detroit, MI, 1965; Apollo Theater, NYC, 1965-7; Jazz Festival, Pittsburgh, PA, 1965; Museum of Modern Art, NYC, 1965; Newport Jazz Festival, Newport, RI, 1965; New York Folk Festival, Carnegie Hall, NYC, 1965; Downbeat Jazz Festival, Chicago, IL, 1965; Big John's, Chicago, 1965; Jazz Workshop, San Francisco, CA, 1965; Chateau de Count et Eve Club, Indianapolis, IN, 1965; Massey Hall, Toronto, Can, 1965; Illinois Governor's Ball, Oak Brook, IL, 1965; Bohemian Caverns Club, Washington, DC, 1965; Univ of Chicago Folklore Society Festival, Chicago, 1966; app on FESTIVAL PRESENTS THE BLUES, CBC-TV, Toronto, 1966; worked Boston Folk Festival, Boston, MA, 1966; Club 47, Cambridge, MA, 1966; The Troubador, Los Angeles, CA, 1966; Berkeley Blues Festival, Univ of California, Berkeley, CA, 1966; Queen Elizabeth Theater, Vancouver, Can, 1966; rec Spivey label, Chicago (?), 1966; worked Central Park Music Festival, NYC, 1966; Monterey Jazz Festival, Monterey, CA, 1966; app on DATELINE BOSTON, WHDH-TV, Boston, MA, 1966; worked Pacific Jazz Festival, Costa Mesa, CA, 1966; Big John's, Chicago, 1966; rec w Little Walter, Checker label, Chicago, 1967; rec Douglas label, Chicago (?), 1967; worked Carnegie Recital Hall, NYC, 1967; Apollo Theater, NYC, 1967; Expo '67 Fair, Montreal, Can, 1967; Boston-American Festival of Music, Boston, MA, 1967; State Univ of New York, Albany, NY, 1967; The Living End, Detroit, MI, 1967; Newport Folk Festival, Newport, RI, 1967; Electric Circus, NYC, 1967-9; The Jazz Workshop, San Francisco, 1967; New Penelope, Montreal, Can, 1967; app on LIKE YOUNG Show, local TV, Montreal, Can, 1967; worked Village Vanguard, NYC, 1968; Hampton Institute Jazz Festival, Hampton, VA, 1968; Central Park Music Festival, NYC, 1968; Monterey Jazz Festival, Monterey, CA, 1968; Jazz Expo

'68, London, Eng, 1968; toured England/Europe working concert dates, 1968; app on JAZZ AT THE MALTINGS, BBC-2-TV, London, Eng, 1968; worked Retinal Circus, Vancouver, Can, 1968; Tyrone Guthrie Theater, Minneapolis, MN, 1968-9; Cozy Bar, Minneapolis, c1968; Festival of American Folklife, Washington, DC, 1968; Mother Blues, Chicago, 1968; Sylvio's, Chicago, 1968; Shelly's Manne-Hole, Los Angeles, 1968; Family Circle, Dallas, TX, 1968; Disciples of Christ Church, Chicago, 1968; app on FOR BLACKS ONLY, local TV, Chicago, c1968; worked Electric Factory, Philadelphia, PA, 1968; Eagles, Seattle, WA, 1969; Winterland, San Francisco, 1969; Museum of Modern Art, NYC, 1969; Ungano's, NYC, 1969-70; app on BLACK-BOOK Show, WPVI-TV, Philadelphia, 1969; worked Rock Pile, Toronto, Can, 1969; The Pavilion, NYC, 1969; Colonial Tavern, Toronto, 1969; Kinetic Playground, Chicago, 1969; rec Chess label, Chicago, 1969; worked Super Cosmic Joy-Scout Jamboree, Auditorium Theater, Chicago, 1969 (por rel Chess label); Chicago Blues Festival, Chicago, 1969; Newport Folk Festival, Newport, RI, 1969; State Univ of New York, Buffalo, NY, 1969; Ann Arbor Blues Festival, Ann Arbor, MI, 1969; The Plugged Nickel, Chicago, 1969; Jazz Workshop, Boston, MA, 1969-71; Main Point, Bryn Mawr, PA, 1969; Washington Blues Festival, Howard Univ, Washington, DC, 1970; White Rose Club, Chicago, 1970; app on local talk show, WMAQ-TV, Chicago, 1970; worked Alice's Revisited, Chicago, 1970-1; Wise Fools, Chicago, 1970; Bad Sign, Chicago, 1970; Quiet Knight, Chicago, 1970; Theresa's, Chicago, 1970; Five Stages, Chicago, 1970; Sutherland Hotel Lounge, Chicago, 1970; app in film THE BLUES IS ALIVE AND WELL IN CHICAGO, 1970; app in UK film CHICAGO BLUES, 1970 (shown on OMNIBUS, BBC-1-TV, England); worked Lennie's, Boston, MA, 1970; Temple Univ, Philadelphia, PA, 1970; Arlington Street Church, Boston, 1970; Ungano's, NYC, 1970; toured Denmark/Finland working concert dates, 1970; worked White Stable Club, East Lansing, MI, c1971; Burning Spear, Chicago, 1971; app on DAVID FROST Show, WNEW-TV, NYC (syndicated), 1971; worked Village Gaslight, NYC, 1971 (por rel Chess label); Esquire Showbar, Montreal, 1971; Mr Kelly's, Chicago, 1971-2 (por rel Chess label); app on CROMIE CIRCLE talk show, WGN-TV, Chicago, 1971; app in film BLACK, WHITE & BLUES, 1971; Body Politic, Chicago, 1971; Ash Grove, Los Angeles, CA, 1971; app in film DYNAMITE CHICKEN, 1971; worked Pepper's, Chicago, 1971; Colonial Tavern, Toronto, Can, 1971-4; Notre Dame Blues Festival, South Bend, IN, 1971; John F Kennedy Center for the Performing Arts Festival, Washington, DC, 1971; Ann Arbor Blues Festival, Ann Arbor, MI, 1972 (por rel Atlantic label); La Bastille, Houston, TX, c1972; Silver Dollar Club, Minneapolis, MN, 1972; Univ of Detroit, Detroit, MI, 1972; Jazz Workshop, Boston, MA, 1972; Landmark Hotel, Kansas City, MO, 1972; Siena Col Blues Festival, Memphis, TN, 1972; Fresh Air Tavern, Seattle, WA, 1972; toured w Chicago Blues Band working concert dates through England/Europe, 1972; rec Chess label, London, 1972; worked Bajes Cooper Station, Amsterdam, Holland, 1972 (por rel Blues Beacon label); Montreux Jazz Festival '72, Montreux, Switzerland, 1972 (por rel Chess label); The Maisonette, NYC, 1972; Cook County Jail Concert, Chicago, IL, 1972; rec Chess label, Chicago, c1973-4; worked Lincoln Center, NYC, 1973; Tulagi's, Boulder, CO, 1973; Carnegie Hall, NYC, 1973; toured Australia/New Zealand working concert dates, 1973-4; worked Winterland, San Francisco, CA, 1973; Max's Kansas City, NYC, 1973; Central Park Music Festival, NYC, 1973; Newport Jazz Festival, Philharmonic Hall, NYC, 1973 (por rel Buddah label); Richard's Club, Atlanta, GA, 1973; The Auditorium, Chicago, 1973; Avery Fisher Hall, NYC, 1973; Mandrake's, Berkeley, CA, c1973; Paul's Mall, Boston, 1973; formed own Muddy Waters Productions/Watertoons Music, Chicago, 1974; worked Quiet Knight, Chicago, 1974-5; Sports Arena, Toledo, OH, 1974; Sandy's, Beverly, MA, 1974; Crystal Lake Ballroom, Ellington, CT, 1974; Jazz Festival, Antibes, France, 1974; Richard's Club, Atlanta, 1974; app on SOUNDSTAGE, PBS-TV, 1974; rec ST for film STREET GIRLS, 1974; worked Montreux Blues Festival, Montreux, Switzerland, 1974; rec Chess label, London, Eng, 1974; worked The Egress, Vancouver, Can, 1974; rec ST for film MANDINGO, 1975; app on ATOMIC MAMA'S WANG DANG DOODLE BLUES SHOW, WXFM-FM-radio, Elmwood Park, IL, 1975; worked The Bottom Line, NYC, 1975; The Boston Club, Cambridge, MA, 1975; In Concert Club, Montreal, Can, 1975; Aquarius Tavern, Seattle, WA, 1975; Keystone Korner, Berkeley, CA, 1975; Southern Illinois Univ, Edwardsville, IL, 1975; Main Point, Bryn Mawr, PA, 1975-6; Atlanta Blues Festival, Great Southeast Music Hall, Atlanta, GA, 1976; Uncle Sam's Club, Macon, GA, 1976; Northern Illinois Univ, DeKalb, IL, 1976; Holmes Center Ballroom, DeKalb, IL, 1976; New Orleans Jazz & Heritage Festival, New Orleans, 1976; Newport Jazz Festival, NYC, 1976; El Mocambo, Toronto, Can, 1976; Blues Festival, Lenox, MA, 1976; Belle Starr, Buffalo, NY, 1976; New England Blues Festival, Providence, RI, 1976; Antone's, Austin, TX, 1976; rec Blue Sky label, Westport, CT, 1976-7; Winterland Auditorium, San Francisco, 1976 (por shown in film THE LAST WALTZ, 1978/por rel Warner Bros label); worked Jazz Jamboree '76, Warsaw, Poland, 1976 (por rel Poljazz label); Jazz Life Festival, Dortmund, Ger, 1976; Palazetto Dello Sport, Turin, Italy, 1976; app on MIKE DOUGLAS Show, CBS-TV, 1977; app w Foghat group, The Palladium, NYC, 1977 (por shown DON KIRSHNER'S ROCK CONCERT, NBC-TV, 1978); Elliot's Nest, Rochester, NY, 1977; toured w Jimmy Cotton/Johnny Winter working concert/college dates across US, 1977; worked Miller Theater, Dallas, TX, 1977; Newport Jazz Festival Blues Picnic, Waterloo Village, Stanhope, NJ, 1977; Univ of Oregon, Eugene, OR, 1977; Theater 1839, San Francisco, 1977; New Victoria, London, Eng, 1977; app on national radio commercial for Schlitz Beer, 1977; worked North Sea Jazz Festival, Holland, 1977; Nice Jazz Festival, Nice, France, 1977; Mill Run Theater, Niles, IL, 1977; The Roxy, Hollywood, CA, 1977; Granada Theater, Dallas, TX, 1977; Colonial Tavern, Toronto, Can, 1977; clip shown in ROOTS OF COUNTRY MUSIC & BLUES, KGO-TV, San Francisco, 1977; worked Belle Starr, Buffalo, NY, 1977; toured Eng/Europe, 1978-9; worked Newport Jazz Festival, Saratoga Springs, NY, 1979; (por shown SUMMERFEST '79, WNET-TV (PBS), NYC); worked US bars/clubs/concerts into 80s; app in film ERIC CLAPTON & HIS ROLLING HOTEL, 1980; app FROM JUMP STREET (ep: City-Country Blues), WNET-TV (PBS), NYC; suffered heart attack; buried Restvale Cemetery, Worth, IL

Personal: Named "Muddy Waters" as child because he often played in the waters of local Deer Creek

Books: *Music for Groups*, Muddy Waters, ARC Music, 1970

Bossmen: Bill Monroe & Muddy Waters, James Rooney, Dial Press, 1971

Songs: All Aboard/Appealing Blues/Blind Man/Blow Wind Blow/The Blues Had a Baby and They Named It Rock and Roll/Bus Driver/CC Woman/Canary Bird/Can't Get No Grindin'/Country Boy/County Jail/Crosseyed Cat/Deep Down in Florida/Down South Blues/Drive My Blues Away/Early Morning Blues/Evil/Find Yourself Another Fool/Forty Days and Forty Nights/Funky Butt/Gonna Need My Help/Got My Mojo Working/Green Flowers/Gypsy Woman/Hard Days/Honey Bee/I Can't Be Satisfied/I Done Got Wise/I Got My Brand on You/I Want to Be Loved/I Want You to Love Me/It's All Over/Jealous Hearted Man/Katie/Kind Hearted Woman/Kinfolk's Blues/Little Geneva/Lonesome Road Blues/Little Girl/Long Distance Call/Louisiana Blues/Love Weapon/Lovin' Man/Making Friends/Mean Disposition/Mean Mistreater/Mojo Hand/Mother's Bad Luck Child/Mud in Your Ear/Muddy Waters Shuffle/Mule Kicking in My Stall/My Home Is in the Delta/My Life Is Ruined/Remember Me/Rock Me Baby/Rollin' and Tumblin'/Rollin' Stone/Sad Letter/Sad Sad Day/Screamin' and Cryin'/She Moves Me/She's All Right/She's Nineteen Years Old/She's So Pretty/Someday I'm Gonna Ketch You/Standin' 'Round Crying/Still a Fool/Strange Woman/Sugar Sweet/They Call Me Muddy Waters/Too Young to Know/Train Fare Blues/Trouble No More/Two Steps Forward/Walking Thru the Park/What Is That She Got?/Where's My Woman Been?/Whiskey Ain't No Good/Whiskey Blues/Who's Gonna Be Your Sweet Man When I'm Gone?/You Can't Lose What You Ain't Never Had/You Gonna Need My Help

Awards/Honors: Won *Downbeat* magazine Critics Poll as Male Singer Deserving Wider Recognition, 1964

Won *Downbeat* magazine International Critics Award for Best Rock-Pop-Blues group, 1968, 1969

Won National Academy of Recording Arts & Sciences Grammy Award for Best Ethnic/Traditional recording, 1971 ("They Call Me Muddy Waters," Chess 1553)

Won *Billboard* magazine Trendsetter Award, 1971

Won National Academy of Recording Arts & Sciences Grammy Award for Best Ethnic/Traditional recording, 1972 ("The London Muddy Waters Sessions," Chess 50012)

Won *Blues Unlimited* magazine (UK) Readers Poll as Best Male Blues Singer, 1973

Won *Blues Unlimited* magazine (UK) Readers Poll as Best Blues Band, 1973

Won *Ebony* magazine Readers Poll Black Music Hall of Fame Award, 1973

Won National Academy of Recording Arts & Sciences Grammy Award for Best Ethnic/Traditional recording, 1975 ("Muddy Waters Woodstock," Chess 60035)

Infl by: Son House/Blind Lemon Jefferson/Robert Johnson/Robert Nighthawk/Charley Patton

Infl to: Mose Allison/The Beatles/Mike Bloomfield/Bo Diddley/Dusty Brown/George Buford/Paul Butterfield/Ray Charles/Jimmy Cotton/John Paul Hammond/Jimi Hendrix/JB Hutto/Larry Johnson/Luther "Georgia Boy" Johnson/Luther "Guitar Jr" Johnson/Lightnin' Slim/John Littlejohn/Freddie King/Robert Lowery/Willie Mabon/Magic Sam/Jimmy Reed/The Rolling Stones/Doc Ross/Otis Rush/Slim Harpo/Eddie Taylor/Sidney Semien/Jr Wells

Quotes: "Virtually alone, Muddy Waters developed the ensemble style of play which has come to characterize . . . Chicago Blues"—Peter Guralnick, *Feel Like Going Home*, Outerbridge & Dienstfrey, 1971

"From its earliest days, the hectic, vital postwar Chicago blues scene was dominated by one towering figure: Muddy Waters. It was he who led the way—in style, sound, repertoire, instrumentation, in every way . . ."—Pete Welding, *Downbeat* magazine, Feb 27, 1975, p 17

"Muddy Waters I think is one of the greatest of greats . . ."—(BB King) Lawrence N Redd, *Rock Is Rhythm and Blues*, Michigan State Univ Press, 1974

References: Bossmen: Bill Monroe & Muddy Waters, James Rooney, The Dial Press, 1971

Feel Like Going Home, Peter Guralnick, Outerbridge & Dienstfrey, 1971

Downbeat magazine, Feb 27, 1975, pp 17-18, 34, 36

MOSS, EUGENE *"Buddy"*
(*aka:* Jim Miller)
Born: Jan 26, 1906, Jewel (Warren Co), GA
Died: Oct 19, 1984, Atlanta, GA
Inst: Guitar/Harmonica

Father was sharecropper; mother Ida Moss; one of 12 children; moved to Augusta, GA, where he frequently played harmonica at local parties from c1918; moved to Atlanta, GA, 1928; taught self guitar and frequently worked w Barbecue Bob in local gigs, Atlanta, into 30s; reportedly rec w Georgia Cotton Pickers, Harmony (?) label, Atlanta, 1930; worked w Blind Willie McTell and others at local barbecue stands/parties/dives, Atlanta, through 30s; rec extensively on ARC label group, NYC, 1933-5; served time for killing wife, Greensboro, GA, during 30s; occasionally toured w Willie McTell working clubs through Tennessee/Alabama/North Carolina, late 30s; worked outside music, Burlington, NC, late 30s; rec OKeh/Columbia labels, NYC, 1941; worked outside music in Richmond, VA/Durham, NC, through 40s; worked outside music with occasional gigs w Curley Weaver and others, Atlanta, 1951 into 70s; worked Atlanta Jazz Festival, Atlanta, 1965; rec Columbia label, Nashville, TN, 1966; worked Folklore Society of Greater Washington concert, Washington, DC,

Photo by Julie Snow

1966; Gaslight Auditorium, Washington, DC, 1966 (por rel Biograph label); Electric Circus, NYC, 1969; Newport Folk Festival, Newport, RI, 1969; John Henry Memorial Concert, Beckley, WV, 1973; John Henry Memorial Concert, Clifftop, WV, 1974; frequently worked local parks for tips, Atlanta, through 70s; worked annual Georgia Grassroots Festival, Atlanta into 80s; suffered fatal heart attack; body cremated

Personal: Married Dorothy Beadles

Songs: V-8 Ford/When I'm Dead and Gone

Infl by: Blind Blake/Blind Lemon Jefferson

Infl to: Tarheel Slim

Quotes: "Probably the finest of the North Carolina school of Piedmont blues artists was the young harmonica player, Eugene 'Buddy' Moss . . ."—Bruce Bastin, *Crying for the Carolines*, Studio Vista Ltd, 1971

"Moss, today, is . . . still a brilliant guitarist and musician . . ."—Samuel B Charters, *Sweet as the Showers of Rain*, Oak Publications, 1977

References: Blues Unlimited magazine (UK), Jan 1976, pp 18-21
Biograph album 12019
Sweet as the Showers of Rain, Samuel B Charters, Oak Publications, 1977

MR BO
(see Collins, Louis)

MR HONEY
(see Edwards, David)

MR SHORTSTUFF
(see Macon, John)

MUD DAUBER JOE
(see McCoy, Joe)

MUDDY WATERS
(see Morganfield, McKinley)

MUDDY WATERS JR
(see Buford, George)

MUMBLES
(see Horton, Walter)

MUSE, LEWIS ANDERSON *"Rabbit"*

Courtesy Cadence Magazine

Born: May 11, 1908, Rocky Mount (Franklin Co), VA
Inst: Flute/Guitar/Kazoo/Ukulele

Parents were musicians; was only child; learned music at early age; frequently worked in family band at local picnics/fairs/parties from 12 years of age; frequently worked as dancer/comedian/singer in passing minstrel shows/bands/hillbilly groups in area through 20s; frequently worked outside music in Rocky Mount/Roanoke, VA, area through 20s/30s; formed own band to tour (also frequently as single) local dances/fairs/hospitals/radio shows through Virginia/South Carolina during 30s; continued outside music work and work as single in area from 1940s; app w The Tide Family, CLUB 88 SHOW, WSLS-TV, Roanoke, VA, c1950; rec Outlet label, Rocky Mount, VA, 1975

Personal: Married c1945. 4 children. Named "Rabbit" as youth while active as baseball player

Song: Cincinnati Shout

Infl by: Cab Calloway/Bessie Smith

Quote: "While Rabbit is not the skilled technician [Jesse] Fuller and [John] Hurt were, he does have an immediate infectious joy in his playing . . ."—Bob Rusch, *Cadence* magazine, Jan 1978, p 60

Reference: Cadence magazine, Aug 1977, pp 3-5, 12

MUSSELWHITE, CHARLES DOUGLAS *"Charlie"*

Photo by Dave Patrick. Courtesy Living Blues Magazine

Born: Jan 31, 1944, Kosciusko (Attala Co), MS
Inst: Guitar/Harmonica

Father was Charles Musselwhite II, a mandolin maker and musician; mother was Maxine ———, of Choctaw Indian heritage; moved to Memphis, TN, where he was raised from 1947; frequently worked in family shows as child; learned harmonica at 13 years of age; worked outside music, Memphis, late 50s to 1962; moved to Chicago, IL, 1962; worked outside music while occasionally sitting-in w Robert Nighthawk/Homesick James/others at Hideaway Club/C&J Lounge/Turner's Blue Lounge, Chicago, from 1962; worked w Johnny Young in Maxwell Street area for tips, Chicago, 1964; worked w Johnny Young, Pasa Tiempo, Chicago, c1965; Kelly's Blue Lounge, Chicago, 1965; I Spy Club, Chicago, 1965; J&L Lounge, Chicago, 1965; worked w JB Hutto Band in local clubs, Chicago, mid-60s; frequently worked w John Lee Granderson in Maxwell Street area for tips, Chicago, mid-60s; app w Mike Bloomfield-Barry Goldberg Blues Band, WBBM-TV, Chicago, 1966; rec Vanguard label, Los Angeles, CA, 1966-8; app w own band on local TV show, Detroit, MI, c1968; rec Vanguard label, Chicago, 1969; worked Folk Festival, St Cloud, MN, c1969; rec w Chicago Blues Stars, Blue Thumb label, Hollywood, CA, 1969; worked Ann Arbor Blues Festival, Ann Arbor, MI, 1960; rec acc to Big Joe Williams, Arhoolie label, Berkeley, CA, 1969; worked w own band, Keystone Korner, San Francisco, CA, 1970; Whiskey A-Go-Go, Los Angeles, 1970; rec Paramount label, Memphis, TN, c1970; rec Cherry Red label, Los Angeles, c1970; toured w own band working college/club circuit on West Coast, 1970-1; worked Ash Grove, Los Angeles, 1971; rec w John Lee Hooker, ABC-Dunhill label, San Francisco, 1971; rec Arhoolie label, Berkeley, 1971; rec acc to Johnie Lewis, Arhoolie label, Chicago, 1971; worked w own band at Gassy Jack's Place, Vancouver, Can, 1972; San Francisco Bay Blues Festival, San Francisco, 1973; toured East Coast/Midwest working club/concert dates, 1973; worked Joe's Place, Cambridge, MA, 1973; Shelter Saloon, San Jose, CA, 1973; Tenth Street Inn, Berkeley, CA, 1973; Ritz Barbeque Club, Richmond, CA, 1973; Stanford Univ, Stanford, CA, 1974; rec Arhoolie label, San Francisco, 1974; rec Capitol label, Los Angeles, 1975; worked Minnie's Can-Do Club, San Francisco, 1975; Slat's, San Francisco, 1975-6; Anchorage Jazz Festival, Anchorage, AK, 1975; West Dakota Club, Berkeley, CA, 1975; Family Light School of Music, Sausalito, CA, 1975; San Francisco Blues Festival, McLaren Park, San Francisco, 1975; The Savoy Club, San Francisco, 1975; mostly inactive in music due to ill health from mid-70s; worked WOW Hall, Eugene, OR, 1976; sat-in w JB Hutto, Coffee Gallery, San Francisco, 1977

Personal: Married twice

Songs: Arkansas Boogie/Baby Will You Please Help Me?/Blue Feeling Today/Candy Kitchen/Finger Lickin' Good/Highway Blues/Long As I Have You/Skinny Woman/Strange Land/Stranger/Takin' My Time/Taylor's Arkansas/39th and Indiana/Up and Down the Avenue

Infl by: Carey Bell/Little Walter/Louis Myers/Will Shade/Jr Wells

Infl to: Felix Cabrera

Quote: "He is one of the finest blues harmonica players in the country, and many people, unless they prefer Paul Butterfield, say he is the best white musician playing a blues harmonica"—Don Branning, *San Francisco Examiner* newspaper, Mar 15, 1973

Reference: San Francisco Examiner newspaper, Mar 15, 1973

MYERS, LOUIS
(*aka:* Louie Meyers)
Born: Sept 18, 1929, Byhalia (Marshall Co), MS
Inst: Guitar/Harmonica

Parents were farmers/musicians who had worked w Washboard Sam/Blind Boy Fuller/Charley Patton/others; born/raised on farm; taught self guitar at about 8 years of age; moved to Chicago, IL, 1941; frequently worked after-school house parties, Chicago, from early 40s; formed The Little Boys group (w Jr Wells/Dave Myers) working C&T Lounge, Chicago, 1948; renamed group The Three Deuces to work local clubs, Chicago, 1948-9; renamed group The Three Aces working local club dates, Chicago, c1949; renamed group The Four Aces (w Fred Below) working Brookmont Hotel/Club Jamboree/others, Chicago, 1948-52; worked w Muddy Waters, Ebony Lounge, Chicago, c1949; w Bill Broonzy, Miss King's, Chicago, c1951; w Four Aces (with Little Walter replacing Jr Wells) at Hollywood Rendezvous, Chicago, 1952; Four Aces toured w Little Walter (as Little Walter & His Night Cats, later renamed The Jukes) working auditoriums/dance halls/road houses/night clubs across US, 1952-3; rec acc w Little Walter & His Night Cats/Jukes, Checker label, Chicago, 1952-4; worked w Four Aces, 708 Club, Chicago, 1952; Apollo Theater, NYC, 1953; rec

Louis Myers

Photo by Doug Fulton. Courtesy Living Blues Magazine

acc w Jr Wells Eagle Rockers, States label, Chicago, 1953; formed new band w Otis Spann and others, working local club dates, Chicago, 1953; formed new band w Good Rocking Charles/Luther Tucker/others working local club dates, Chicago, 1954; rec acc to Lazy Bill and His Blue Rhythms, Chance label, Chicago, 1954; w Otis Rush Band working Jazzville/New Castle Rock/others, Chicago, then toured south working club dates, 1955-6; rec under own name, Abco label, Chicago, 1955; frequently worked club dates in Chicago, IL/Gary, IN, areas, 1956; rec acc w Otis Rush group, Cobra label, Chicago, 1958; w Otis Rush Trio, 708 Club, Chicago, 1958; New Jazz Castle Rock Club, Chicago, 1958; formed own rock band working 1049 Club and others, Chicago, 1958-62; rec extensively as session man for many bluesmen with frequent local club work, Chicago, through 50s/60s; rec Delmark label, Chicago, 1968; toured France/Spain working concert dates, 1970; rec Black & Blue label, Bordeaux, France, 1970; rec acc to Jr Wells/Buddy Guy, Delmark label, Chicago, c1970; toured w Jr Wells group working one-nighters/club dates across US, 1971; reformed The Aces to work/tour continuously, 1971-6; rec Vogue label, Chicago, 1971; frequently worked Theresa's Lounge, Chicago, 1971-4; Florence's Lounge, Chicago, 1972-4; rec w Jimmy Rogers, Shelter label, Los Angeles, CA, 1972; worked w The Aces, Montreux Jazz Festival, Montreux, Switzerland, 1972 (por rel Big Bear/Polydor/Excello labels); w Muddy Waters Band, Ann Arbor Blues Festival, Ann Arbor, MI, 1972 (por rel Atlantic label); toured w Chicago Blues Festival working concert dates through Europe, 1973; rec Black & Blue label, Toulouse, France, 1973; worked South Park Lounge, Chicago, 1974; toured w Sunnyland Slim Trio working one-nighters/college dates across US, 1974; toured w Blues Festival working concert dates in Japan, 1974; worked Yubin Chokin Hall, Tokyo, Japan, 1974 (por rel Advent label); worked Louise's South Park Lounge, Chicago, 1975-6; Ma Bea's, Chicago, 1975 (por rel MCM label); app on MUSIC IN AMERICA, PBS-TV, 1976; w The Aces, New 1815 Club, Chicago, 1976 (por shown on THE DEVIL'S MUSIC—A HISTORY OF THE BLUES [ep: Sticking with the Blues] BBC-1-TV, England); disbanded The Aces to work as single/pickup man from 1976; rec acc to Andrew Odom, WASP label, Chicago, 1976; worked Pepper's, Chicago, 1977; Kingston Mines, Chicago, 1977; Wise Fools, Chicago, 1977; toured Europe/Japan working concert dates, 1977; worked Elsewhere Lounge, Chicago, 1977; Rob Michael's Club, Chicago, 1977; Fat Chance Saloon, Chicago, 1977

Personal: His brothers Dave/Bob Myers are also musicians

Songs: Ace's Shuffle/Blues for Marcelle/Just Whaling/LM Blues/Off the Wall

Infl by: Willie B Sesserly/Little Walter

Infl to: Paul Butterfield/Charlie Musselwhite/Arthur Spires

Quote: "His warm and rich voice is ideal for the blues"—Willie Leiser, Vogue album 30174

Reference: Blues Unlimited magazine (UK), Nov 1976, pp 4-14

MYERS, SAMMY *"Sam"*
Born: Feb 19, 1936, Laurel (Jones Co), MS
Inst: Drums/Harmonica

Photo by Jim O'Neal. Courtesy Living Blues Magazine

Worked mostly outside music in Jackson, MS, area, from 1956; worked w Elmore James Broomdusters in local club dates, Chicago, IL, mid-50s; rec w King Mose Royal Rockers, Ace label, Jackson, MS, 1957; worked w King Mose Royal Rockers, 1957-63; rec Fury label, New Orleans, LA, 1960; occasionally w Elmore James, Mr P's Club, Jackson, MS, 1962; formed own band to tour clubs through South, 1968-74; worked Sunset Inn, Jackson, MS, 1969-70; Richard's Playhouse, Jackson, MS, 1970; Push & Pull Club, Lula, MS, 1972; Fosters Club, Jackson, MS, 1974; w Robert Miller and his Downbeats, 1974-5; worked Club Sunset, Jackson, MS, 1975; Richard's Playhouse, Jackson, MS, 1975; frequently worked w Sound Corporation group, Camelot Club/Subway Lounge, Jackson, MS, from 1975; Palms Garden, Jackson, MS, 1977; sat-in Elsewhere Lounge, Chicago, IL, 1977

Personal: Is partially blind

Reference: Living Blues magazine, Autumn 1970, pp 19, 21

N

NASH, LEMOINE *"Lemon"*

(*aka:* Banjo Boy)
Born: Apr 22, 1898, Lakeland (Pointe Coupee Parish), LA
Died: Dec 27, 1969, New Orleans, LA
Inst: Banjo/Guitar/Mandolin/Ukulele

Father was musician; mother was Rose Nero; moved to New Orleans, LA, where he was raised from 2 months of age; learned guitar at about 13 years of age, later learning mandolin and ukulele; frequently worked in small groups in local clubs, New Orleans, late teens into 20s; left home to hobo through South working outside music with some party/dance work, late teens; frequently worked local railroad stations for tips, New Orleans area, c1918; frequently worked w Peter Williams Band/Noon Johnson Trio/others at local parties/dances/clubs, New Orleans, early 20s; worked Tumble Inn, New Orleans, 1922; frequently toured w John Robinson Circus/Taylor & Mack troupe/Downey Brothers/Sells-Eloto/Big Chief Indian & Western Cowboy Medicine Show working (as bally-man/entertainer) through South through 20s; worked Eagle Theater, Asheville, NC, late 20s; app on WSM-radio, Nashville, TN, late 20s; worked outside music (as teacher) at Morris Music Co, New Orleans, into 30s; occasional solo gigs in local clubs, New Orleans, during 30s; worked Absinthe House, New Orleans, c1941; Pat O'Brien's, New Orleans, c1941; served in US Merchant Marine, early 40s; formed own quartet touring club dates up East Coast to New York from mid-40s; worked outside music with some club work, New Orleans, into 50s; rec Storyville label, Baton Rouge, LA, 1958; frequently worked parties/streets for tips, New Orleans through 60s; worked Red Garter, New Orleans, 1968; French Market Coffee Shop, New Orleans, 1968; reportedly died of natural causes; buried Mt Olivet Cemetery, New Orleans, LA

Personal: Married (1925-)

Billing: The Banjo Boy

Song: She Was Born in New Orleans

Quote: ". . . he was, for the most part, a musician, a singer, a serenader"—Bruce Cook, *Listen to the Blues*, Charles Scribner's Sons, 1973

NATCHEZ

(see Broonzy, William)

NEAL, RAFUL

Born: 1936, Baton Rouge (East Baton Rouge Parish), LA
Inst: Harmonica

Born/raised in Baton Rouge, LA, where he was taught harmonica by Ike Brown, 1958; frequently worked outside music with occasional work in local clubs, Baton Rouge, through 50s into 60s; toured w Little Eddie Lang working club dates through South, early 60s; formed trio to tour Texas/Louisiana/Mississippi working club/college circuit through 60s; continued outside music work, Baton Rouge, through 60s into 70s; rec Peacock label, Baton Rouge (?), 1968; rec La Louisianne label, Baton Rouge (?), 1969; rec Whit label, Baton Rouge (?), 1970; worked Six O'Clock Club, Scotlandville, LA, 1970; Dream Club, Scotlandville, LA, early 70s; Spooners Club, Irwinville, LA, early 70s; Ernie's Club, Irwinville, LA, early 70s

Infl by: Little Walter

Quote: "Raful is a fine singer and very nice harmonica player much in the Slim Harpo manner"—Frank Scott, *Blues Unlimited* magazine (UK), Dec 1971, p 16

Reference: Blues Unlimited magazine (UK), Dec 1971, pp 16-17

NELSON, *"Chicago"* BOB

(*aka:* Chicago Bob)
Born: Jul 4, 1944, Bogalusa (Washington Parish), LA
Inst: Harmonica

Father Versie Nelson was harmonica player; frequently sang in local churches as child; worked local bars/joints/taverns, New Orleans, LA, 1956-9; moved to Gary, IN, 1959; toured w Earl Hooker working club dates through Indiana/Ohio, late 50s; frequently worked as sideman w JB Hutto/Howlin' Wolf/Muddy Waters/other groups in local clubs, Chicago, early 60s; formed Chicago Bob Blues Band working local dates, Chicago, mid-60s; moved to Boston, MA, late 60s; worked mostly outside music, Boston, late 60s into 70s; formed own band working Louie's Lounge/The Unicorn/others, Boston, early 70s; toured w John Lee Hooker/Johnny Shines working concert dates, early 70s; worked w John Lee Hooker in local clubs, Oakland, CA, 1972

Personal: His brother "Louisiana" Earl Nelson has worked as musician in this singer's band

Infl by: Buddy Guy/BB King/Jr Wells

Quote: "Chicago Bob is one of the most exciting young blues performers around today, bar none . . ." —Joe McEwen, *Blues Unlimited* magazine (UK), Jul 1972, p 9

Reference: Blues Unlimited magazine (UK), Jul 1972, p 9

NELSON, IROMEIO *"Romeo"*

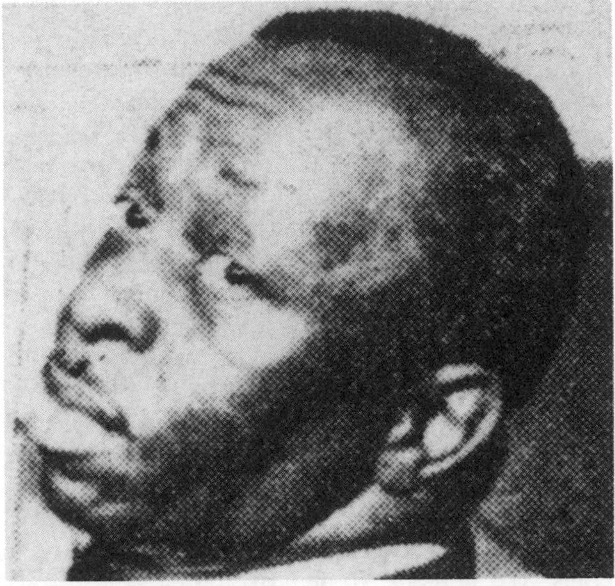

Courtesy Living Blues *Magazine*

Born: Mar 12, 1902, Springfield (Robertson Co), TN
Died: May 17, 1974, Chicago, IL
Inst: Piano

One of at least 2 children; moved to Chicago, IL, where he was raised from age of 6; moved to E St Louis, IL, where he learned some piano, 1915-19; returned to Chicago to work mostly house rent parties c1919 into 40s; rec Vocalion label, Chicago, 1929; frequently worked The Subway/Tip Top Club/Swan Club/others, Chicago, into 30s; worked mostly outside music in Chicago from early 40s; entered Mount Sinai Hospital Medical Center where he died of kidney failure; buried Restvale Cemetery, Worth, IL

Personal: Married

Songs: Dying Rider/Getting Dirty Just Shaking That Thing/Head Rag Hop (Hop Head Rag)

Infl by: Pinetop Smith/Clarence Williams

Quote: ". . . a pianist of complex, dynamic energy and a singer of markedly personal style"—Rudi Blesh, *Shining Trumpets*, Alfred A Knopf, 1946

Reference: Origin album OJL-15

NELSON, RED
(see Wilborn, Nelson)

NICHOLS, ALVIN *"Youngblood"*
(*aka:* BB Jones)

Courtesy Living Blues *Magazine*

Born: Feb 10, 1947, Camden (Madison Co), MS
Inst: Bass/Guitar

Born/raised/worked outside music in Camden, MS, to 1964; moved to Chicago, IL, to work outside music from 1964; worked w Heavenly Kings Gospel Quartet, New Mount Pilgrim Church, Chicago, from mid-60s; worked w Johnny Littlejohn group, Sportsman's Lounge, Chicago, 1968; rec w Johnny Littlejohn group, Arhoolie label, Chicago, 1968; toured w Howlin' Wolf Band working club dates, 1968; worked Ash Grove, Los Angeles, CA, 1968; frequently worked as sideman in various blues bands out of Chicago into 70s; formed own band to work Sportsman's Lounge, Chicago, c1971; worked Pepper's Lounge, Chicago, c1971; rec Magic Touch label, Chicago, 1972; worked Track II Lounge, Grand Rapids, MI, 1976

Infl by: BB King

Quote: "Not only does he sing, play, and talk like BB—he looks like him, too"—Jim O'Neal, *Living Blues* magazine, Sept/Oct 1975, p 10

Reference: Living Blues magazine, Sept/Oct 1975, pp 10-11

NICHOLS, JIMMY
(see Nicholson, James)

NICHOLSON, JAMES DAVID *"JD"*
(*aka:* Jimmy Nichols)
Born: Apr 11, 1917, Monroe (Ouachita Parish), LA
Died: Jul 27, 1991, Los Angeles, CA
Inst: Guitar/Piano/Saxophone/Trombone

Father was Nathaniel Nicholson; mother Mattie Moore; was playing piano at age 7; moved to Los Angeles, CA, where he was raised, 1926-34; left home to hobo across US working outside music, 1934-40; settled in Los Angeles working outside music from 1941; worked occasional club dates, Los Angeles, through 40s; rec w Jimmy McCracklin, Globe label, Los Angeles, 1945; worked Lincoln Gardens, Los Angeles, c1948; rec Courtney label, Los Angeles, 1948; together w Jimmy McCracklin formed own band to work local club dates, Los Angeles, early 50s; frequently worked outside music in Santa Barbara, CA, area, early 50s; formed own The Jiving Five working local club dates, Los Angeles area, from early 50s; renamed group The All Stars to tour Texas/Oklahoma/Arkansas/Arizona working one-nighters through mid-50s; reportedly rec w Smokey Hogg, Modern/Hollywood labels, Los Angeles, during 50s; rec w Harmonica Slim, Aladdin label, Los Angeles, 1956; frequently worked Lake View Inn/Cotton Club/Brown Derby/Holiday Inn/Whiskey A-Go-Go/Golden Bear/others in Los Angeles/Bakersfield, CA, area, 1958-63; owned/operated/performed at The Go-Go Club, Bakersfield, CA, from 1963; frequently worked w George Smith's Bacon Fat group in Los Angeles, CA, clubs, 1968-70; frequently worked outside music into 80s; toured Japan w own group The Soulbenders, mid-70s; often worked clubs in Los Angeles/Las Vegas, NV areas through 80s; died of accidental burns; buried Inglewood Cemetery, Inglewood, CA

Reference: Living Blues, Jan 1991, pp 36-40

NICKERSON, HAMMIE
(see Nixon, Hammie)

NIGHTHAWK, ROBERT
(*aka:* Robert Lee McCoy/Pettie's Boy/Ramblin' Bob)
Born: Nov 30, 1909, Helena (Phillips Co), AR
Died: Nov 5, 1967, Helena, AR
Inst: Guitar/Harmonica

Father was ——— McCollum; mother was ——— McCoy; born Robert Lee McCollum; born/raised/worked on farm from childhood; left home to hobo widely working outside music with frequent juke work through South from mid-20s; worked w Will Shade in Memphis Jug Band in local parks/dances/streets, Memphis, TN, from mid-20s; worked w William Warren at Black Cat Drug Store, Hollandale, MS, late 20s; worked w Houston Stackhouse at local jukes/parties, Hollandale area, late 20s into early 30s; worked w brother Percy McCollum/Houston Stackhouse at local parties/dances/picnics, Crystal Springs, MS, area, 1932; app w Houston Stackhouse, WJDX-radio, Jackson, MS, early 30s; frequently worked jukes in Vicksburg, MS, area, early 30s; worked w John Lee Hooker in local jukes/tonks, Memphis, early 30s; frequently worked w Mississippi Sheiks/Henry Townsend/Joe Williams/others in Friar's Point, MS/St Louis, MO/Chicago, IL/elsewhere into 30s; worked w Jimmie Rodgers, Jackson, MS, 1931; worked w Laura Dukes in local joints, E St Louis, IL, mid-30s; frequently toured in carnivals during 30s; frequently rec as house musician, Bluebird label, Chicago, 1937-40; rec w Speckled Red Trio, Bluebird label, Aurora, IL, 1938; rec Decca label, Chicago, 1940; frequently worked bars/joints/clubs/parties in Helena, AR, area, through 40s/50s; app on BRIGHT STAR FLOUR Show/MOTHER'S BEST FLOUR HOUR Show, KFFA-radio, Helena, 1943-7, with frequent local tours; frequently app on WROX-radio, Clarksdale, MS/WDIA-radio, Memphis, TN, during 40s/50s; rec Chess/Aristocrat labels, Chicago, IL, 1948-50; worked club dates in Cairo, IL, 1949-50; formed Nighthawks Trio touring club dates through South c1949 into 50s; rec United/States labels, Chicago, 1951-4; worked Ned Love's Moonlight Inn, St Louis, MO, early 50s; continued local jukes/clubs/parties/picnics/fish fries in Helena, AR, area through 50s into early 60s; worked Maxwell Street area for tips, Chicago, 1963; app in film short AND THIS IS FREE, 1963; formed own Flames of Rhythm working local clubs/taverns, Chicago, 1964; rec Decca/Testament labels, Chicago, 1964; worked w Little Walter, Mandel Hall, Univ of Chicago, Chicago, 1964; First Floor Club, Toronto, Can, 1964; Diz's Club, Chicago, 1964; worked clubs in Jackson,

Robert Nighthawk
Courtesy Sheldon Harris Collection

MS, 1965; worked outside music (as migrant worker) through Florida 1965; app on KING BISCUIT TIME, KFFA-radio, Helena, AR, 1965; worked outside music with occasional club work in Helena, AR/Lula, MS, areas, 1965-7; rec acc to Houston Stackhouse, Testament label, Dundee, MS, 1967; entered Helena Hospital where he died of heart failure; buried Magnolia Cemetery, Helena, AR

Personal: Was married. His son Sam Carr worked in Nighthawks group. His brother Percy McCollum was musician. Sister was Joe Willie Wilkins' first wife. Reportedly cousin of Houston Stackhouse/Joe & Charlie McCoy. Frequently used mother's maiden name of McCoy during the 1930s. Assumed name "Nighthawk" from his recording of "Prowling Nighthawk" in 1937. Not to be confused with pianist Robert "Cyclone" McCoy

Songs: Annie Lee/Bricks in My Pillow/Feel So Bad/ Kansas City/Maggie Campbell/The Moon Is Rising/ Nighthawk Boogie/Seventy-Four/Sweet Black Angel/Take It Easy, Baby/US Boogie/You Missed a Good Man

Infl by: Robert Johnson/Houston Stackhouse/Tampa Red/Peetie Wheatstraw

Infl to: Frank Frost/Earl Hooker/Elmore James/ Muddy Waters/Frank Seals

Quotes: "One of the most imaginative and distinctive interpreters of the blues"—Pete Welding, Testament album T-2215

"Nighthawk's doom laden, brooding blues merged the slide, which seemed to make his guitar literally weep, with deep, solemn vocals"—Jim O'Neal, Pearl album PL-11

". . . a brooding voice and chilly guitar"—Mike Leadbitter, *Blues Unlimited* magazine (UK), Nov 1971, p 7

Reference: Blues Unlimited magazine (UK), Nov 1971, pp 4-7

NIX, WILLIE
(*aka:* Memphis Blues Boy)
Born: Aug 6, 1918, Memphis (Shelby Co), TN
Died: Jul 8, 1991, Leland, MS
Inst: Drums/Guitar

Born Willie Nicks; toured w Rabbit Foot Minstrels (as dancing comedian) working shows through South late 30s; toured w Royal American Show, early 40s; frequently worked parks/streets in Memphis, TN, area through mid-40s; app w Robert Jr Lockwood on KXLR-radio, Little Rock, AR, 1947; toured w Sonny Boy Williamson (Alex Miller)/Willie Love/Joe Willie Wilkins (as "The Four Aces") working jukes through

Courtesy Steve La Vere /Patty Nix /Living Blues Magazine

Arkansas/Tennessee/Mississippi, 1949-50; app w BB King/Joe Hill Louis on THE PEPTICON BOY Show, WDIA-radio, Memphis (with frequent local club work), 1949-50; frequently worked w Beale Streeters in local bars/clubs, Memphis, 1949; app w Willie Love's Three Aces on BROADWAY FURNITURE STORE Show, KWEM-radio, West Memphis, AR, 1949-50, then taking over show in 1950; app w Beale Streeters, WDIA-radio, Memphis, early 50s; worked Palace Theater, Memphis, c1951; worked w own group at local dances/parties, West Memphis, early 50s; rec RPM label, Memphis, 1951; w Joe Willie Wilkins, Hippodrome Theater, Memphis, early 50s; rec Checker label, Memphis, 1952; app w Jimmy Cotton's group, HART'S BREAD Show, KWEM-radio, West Memphis, c1952; rec (as "Memphis Blues Boy") Sun label, Memphis, 1953; moved to Chicago, IL, 1953; frequently worked w Elmore James/Sonny Boy Williamson (Alex Miller)/Sunnyland Slim/others in local clubs, Chicago, 1953-8; w Johnny Shines, Frosty Corner, Chicago, c1953; rec w own combo, Chance/Sabre labels, Chicago, 1953; toured w Elmore James working clubs through South/Midwest, 1955-6; worked Smitty's Corner, Chicago, 1957; returned to Memphis to serve time in prison, 1958-9; continued to hobo widely working outside music (as migrant worker) with frequent work in jukes/parties, 1959 into 60s; frequently worked local jukes/clubs, West Memphis, AR, area through 60s; worked w Big Amos Patton, West Memphis, late 60s; worked w Willie Cobbs Band in clubs through Mississippi, 1967; rec w Willie Cobbs Band, Riceland label, Memphis, TN, 1968; continued outside work with frequent entertaining for migrant workers through South into 70s; settled in Leland, MS, to work occasional clubs from mid-70s; suffered fatal heart attack; buried Bogue Memorial Gardens, Leland

Songs: Baker Shop Boogie/Seems Like a Million Years/Try Me One More Time

Infl by: Aaron "T-Bone" Walker

Quote: "His abilities as a drummer and vocalist are superb and his few existing recordings are all superior examples of post-war blues"—Steve La Vere, Polydor album 2383-214

References: *Living Blues,* Winter 1972, pp 17-19
Living Blues, Summer 1979, pp 9-13
Living Blues, Jan/Feb, 1992, pp 35-36

NIXON, ELMORE *"Elmo"*
Born: Nov 17, 1933, Crowley (Acadia Parish), LA
Died: c1975, Houston, TX (unconfirmed)
Inst: Drums/Organ/Piano

Moved to Houston, TX, where he was raised from 1939; frequently sang in local elementary school glee club, Houston, as youth; encouraged to learn music by Henry Hayes and learned drums, then piano, mid-40s; reportedly rec Sunset label, New Jersey, c1946; frequently worked local club dates, Houston, late 40s into 50s; rec acc to various gospel singers, Houston, through 50s; rec Lucky Seven label, Houston, 1949; rec w Henry Hayes Four Kings, Peacock label, Houston, 1950-1; rec w Henry Hayes Hadacol Boys, Sittin' In With label, Houston, 1950-1; rec w Henry Hayes Rhythm Kings, Mercury label, Houston, 1951; rec Savoy label, Houston, 1952; rec Post/Imperial labels, Houston, 1955; frequently toured with own band working club dates out of Houston to West Coast and into Mexico into 70s; whereabouts unknown thereafter

Reference: Blues Unlimited magazine (UK), Jul 1966, pp 4-5

NIXON, HAMMIE
(aka: Hammie/Hammie Nickerson)

Photo by Steve LaVere

Born: Jan 22, 1908, Brownsville (Haywood Co), TN
Died: Aug 17, 1984, Jackson, TN
Inst: Guitar/Harmonica/Jew's Harp/Jug/Kazoo/Tub Bass/Washboard

Father was Green Nixon; mother Martha Davis; born Hammie Davis; raised with a white family until 10 years of age; interested in music early and worked local parties as youth; teamed w John Estes working country dances/picnics in Brownsville, TN, area with frequent hoboing through Arkansas/Missouri, 1924-7; worked w John Estes in streets/hotels/house parties and Blue Heaven Club, Memphis, TN, 1927-30; worked mostly outside music (as farmer), Brownsville, 1930-1; moved to Chicago, IL, to work local house rent parties/street corners for tips, 1931-7; worked w Son Bonds on streets, Chicago, 1934; rec w Son Bonds, Decca label, Chicago, 1934; rec w John Estes, Champion label, Chicago, 1935; rec w John Estes, Decca label, Chicago, 1937; teamed w John Estes to hobo across US working fish fries/parties/dances/hobo camps/streets, 1937-41; toured w John Estes working Rabbit Foot Minstrels Show and Dr Grim(m)'s Medicine Show c1939; returned to Brownsville to work outside music, 1941-62; rec w John Estes, Ora Nelle label, Chicago, c1950; rec w John Estes, Sun label, Memphis, c1950; rec w John Estes, Delmark label, Saukville, WI, 1962; rejoined John Estes working as team almost continuously thereafter from 1963; worked w John Estes (and as single), Fickle Pickle Club, Chicago, 1963; rec acc to John Estes/Yank Rachell, Delmark label, Chicago, 1963-4; Queens College, Queens, NY, 1963; Gerde's Folk City, NYC, NY, 1963; rec Bea & Baby label, Chicago, c1963; worked w John Estes/Yank Rachell, First Floor Club, Toronto, Can, 1964; Club 68, Hamilton, Can, 1964; app on ASSIGNMENT Show, local radio, Toronto, 1964; app on THE OBSERVER Show, CBC-TV, Toronto, 1964; worked Newport Folk Festival, Newport, RI, 1964 (por rel Vanguard label); toured w American Folk Blues Festival working TV/radio/concert dates through England/Europe, 1964 (por Musikhalle concert, Hamburg, Ger, rel Fontana label); rec Storyville label, Copenhagen, Den/London, Eng, 1964; continued working clubs/concerts w John Estes through 60s; toured w American Folk Blues Festival working concert dates through England/Europe, 1966 (por Berlin, Ger, concert rel Fontana label); worked w Jimmy Collins in local clubs, Gary, IN, 1966; worked Festival of American Folklife, Washington, DC, 1970; Washington Blues Festival, Howard Univ, Washington, DC, 1970; River City Blues Festival, Memphis, TN, 1971; Univ of Arkansas, Fayetteville, AR, 1972; rec Albatross label, Memphis, 1972; worked Festival of American Folklife, Washington, DC, 1973 (por shown in videotape BORN IN THE BLUES); toured w Memphis Blues Caravan working concert/college dates through Midwest, 1973-4; worked Newport Jazz Festival, NYC, 1974; toured Europe working concert dates, 1974; toured w Blues Festival working concert dates through Japan, 1974; worked Yubin Chokin Hall, Tokyo, Japan, 1974 (por rel Trio-Delmark label); worked Xanadu Ballroom, Memphis, TN, 1975 (por on WLYX-FM-radio); John Henry Folk Festival, Camp Virgil Tate, Princeton, WV, 1976-7; Old Town School of Folk Music, Chicago, 1976; toured Japan working concerts, 1976; rec Albatross label, 1976; worked festivals/concerts w Beale Street Jug Band in Memphis/MS/elsewhere into 80s; suffered fatal cerebral hemorrhage; buried Rosenwald Cemetery, Brownsville, TN

Songs: Airplane Blues/Down South Blues/Floating Bridge/Government Money/I Ain't Gonna Be Worried No More/I Want To Tear It All the Time/Jack and Jill Blues/Minnie's Blues/Need More Blues/Poor Man's Friend/Someday Baby Blues/Stop That Thing/Vernita Blues/Who's Been Telling You Buddy Brown Eyes?

Infl to: Taj Mahal/John Lee "Sonny Boy" Williamson

Quotes: "He can make his harmonica cry and moan like John [Estes'] voice, and both create a blues atmosphere which is almost unbearable"—George Adins, *Jazz Journal* magazine (UK), Aug 1963, p 11

"Nixon is a fascinating example of the religious and secular influences residing in one body"—John Jeremy, *Jazz Journal* magazine (UK), Dec 1974, p 32

References: Living Blues magazine, Jan 1975, pp 13-19

Cadence magazine, May 1978, pp 3, 5, 7

NOLAN, DIXIE
(see Scruggs, Irene)

NORRIS, WILLIAM JAMES *"Dead Eye"*

Photo by Erik Lindahl. Courtesy Living Blues Magazine

Born: Oct 12, 1951, Jackson (Hinds Co), MS
Inst: Bass/Drums/Guitar/Organ/Piano/Sax/Trumpet

Father was Roosevelt Norris, a harmonica player; mother was Juanita Williams; moved to Chicago, IL, where he was raised from c1955; frequently sang in local church choirs, Chicago, c1963-6; taught music by Leo Wilson from c1965; frequently worked in local high school band, Chicago, mid-60s; served time in Cook County Jail where he frequently worked in prison band, Chicago, 1968-71; worked Nonie's Lounge, Chicago, 1972; toured w Arelean Brown working clubs through South c1972-3; frequently worked w Little Mack Simmons in local clubs, Chicago, early 70s; frequently sat-in with many local bluesmen in club dates, Chicago, early 70s; worked w Wild Fire Band at Smitty & Sadie's Club/Minnie's Club/others, Chicago, 1974-5

Infl by: Sam Cooke/Al Green/Albert King/BB King

Reference: Living Blues magazine, Sept 1975, pp 13, 44

NORTH, HATTIE
(see Johnson, Edith)

NORWOOD, SAM *"One Leg"/"Peg Leg"/"RD"*
Born: c1900, Crystal Springs (Copiah Co), MS
Died: c1967, Chicago, IL (unconfirmed)
Inst: Guitar/Mandolin

Reportedly worked in Jackson, MS, from c1920 into 30s; rec w Jaybird Coleman, Gennett label, Birmingham, AL, 1927; rec w Slim Duckett (religious songs as "Pig Norwood"), OKeh label, Atlanta, GA, 1930; frequently worked between Chicago, IL/Jackson, MS, from c1932; worked in Canton, MS, area c1935; settled in Chicago to frequently work Maxwell Street area for tips from c1948 into 60s; whereabouts unknown thereafter

O

OAK CLIFF T-BONE
(see Walker, Aaron)

ODEN, JAMES BURKE *"Jimmie"/"Jimmy"/"Old Man"*
(aka: Big Bloke/Poor Boy/St Louis Jimmy)

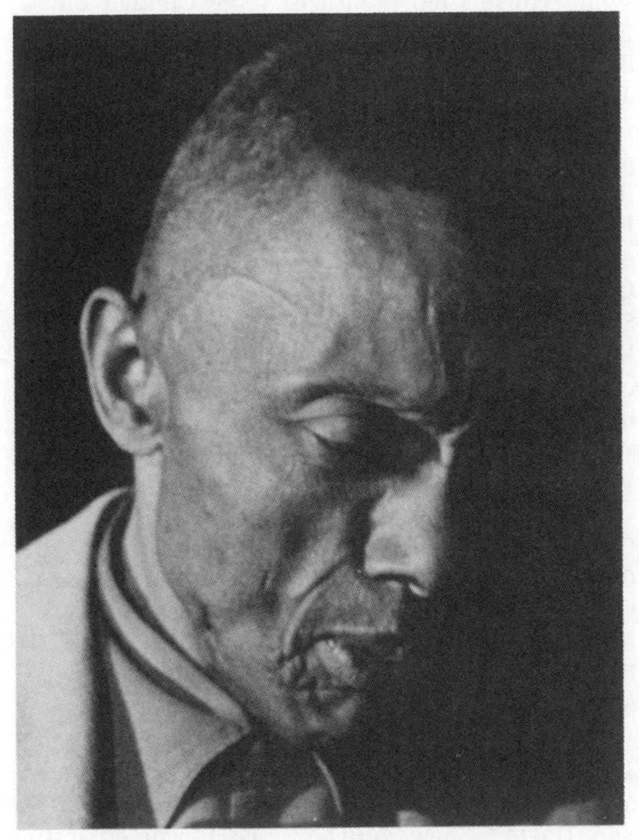

Photo by Ray Flerlage (Kinnara Collection). Courtesy Sing Out Magazine

Born: Jun 26, 1903, Nashville (Davidson Co), TN
Died: Dec 30, 1977, Chicago, IL
Inst: Piano

Father Henry Oden was dancer; mother was Leana West; one of 4 children; parents died early; raised as orphan, Nashville, TN; moved to St Louis, MO, to work outside music from c1917; frequently hoboed through area working outside music into 20s; taught self piano, mid-20s; frequently worked w Big Joe Williams at local house parties, St Louis, MO, c1929; frequently worked w Roosevelt Sykes in local bars/clubs, St Louis, into 30s; rec w Roosevelt Sykes, Champion label, Richmond, IN, 1932; moved to Chicago, IL, 1933; frequently worked local parties/bars, Chicago, through 30s; rec Bluebird label, Chicago, 1933; rec Decca label, Chicago, 1934-7; rec w Roosevelt Sykes, Decca label, Chicago, 1937; toured w Roosevelt Sykes working clubs/theaters/one-nighters across US, late 30s; rec w Roosevelt Sykes, Bluebird label, Chicago, 1941; rec w Bill Broonzy, Bluebird label, Chicago, 1942; together w Memphis Minnie owned/operated a blues club, Indianapolis, IN, during 40s; rec w Roosevelt Sykes, Bluebird/Victor labels, Chicago, 1944; rec w Roosevelt Sykes, B&W label, Chicago, 1945; rec w Jump Jackson Band, Columbia label, Chicago, 1945; rec Bullet label, Chicago, 1947; rec Miracle label, Chicago, 1948; rec w Muddy Waters Blues Combo, Aristocrat label, Chicago, 1948; rec Mercury label, Chicago, 1949; co-founded JOB Record Company, Chicago, 1949; rec JOB/Apollo labels, Chicago, 1949; rec Savoy label, Chicago, 1951; rec Duke label, Houston, TX, 1952; rec Herald/Opera labels, Chicago, 1953; frequently worked as manager of Eddie Boyd Band, Chicago, through 50s; after serious accident worked mostly as song writer, Chicago, from 1957; was living with Muddy Waters family, Chicago, late 50s into 60s; rec Bluesville/Barnaby-Candid labels, NYC, 1960; rec Delmark label, Chicago, 1963; rec Spivey label, Chicago, 1964; mostly inactive in music, Chicago, through 60s; worked Ann Arbor Blues Festival, Ann Arbor, MI, 1969; rec ST for UK film BLUES LIKE SHOWERS OF RAIN, 1970; mostly inactive due to illness, Chicago, into 70s; entered Rush Presbyterian—St Luke's Medical Center Hospital where he died of bronchopneumonia; buried Restvale Cemetery, Worth, IL

Personal: Was married/divorced

Songs: Bad Condition/Come Day, Go Day/Coming Up Fast/Dog House Blues/Evil Ways/Goin' Down Slow/Goody Goody Goody/Half Ain't Been Told/I Have Made Up My Mind/I'm St Louis Bound/Monkey Faced Woman/Mothers Day/My Heart Is Loaded with Trouble/Nothing But the Blues/Poor Boy Blues/Sitting Down Thinking Blues/Some Sweet Day/Soon Forgotten/Speak Now Woman/Sweet as She Can Be/What a Woman

Infl by: Walter Davis

Quote: "His lean, economical style of half-sung, half spoken verses mark[ed] him out as an individual artist"—Paul Oliver, Riverside album 8819

"One of the premier song writers of the blues"—Jim O'Neal, *Living Blues* magazine, Jan/Feb 1978, p 30

References: Prestige album 1028
Living Blues magazine, Jan/Feb 1978, p 30

ODETTA
(see Gordon, Odetta)

ODOM, *"Little"* ANDREW *"Voice"*
(aka: BB Jr/Big Voice/Blues Boy)

Courtesy Living Blues *Magazine*

Born: Dec 15, 1936, Denham Springs (Livingston Parish), LA
Died: Dec 23, 1991, Chicago, IL

Father was Guy Odom; mother was Lula ———; one of 7 children; sang in local church choir as child; moved to E St Louis, IL, 1955, then to St Louis, MO; frequently worked w Albert King's Band/Johnny Twist Band/Johnny O'Neal's Hound Dog Band in local clubs, St Louis, from 1956-60; reportedly rec (as "King Odom") Perspective label, St Louis, 1959; moved to Chicago, IL, 1960; worked/toured w Earl Hooker Band out of Chicago through 60s; rec Nation label, Chicago, 1967; frequently worked outside music, Chicago, through 60s into 70s; rec w Earl Hooker Band, Arhoolie label, Chicago, 1968; worked White Horse Club, Chicago, 1968; Chicago Blues Festival, Chicago, 1969; rec w Earl Hooker Band, BluesWay label, Los Angeles, CA, 1969; rec under own name, BluesWay label, Los Angeles, 1969; worked Theresa's Lounge, Chicago, 1969-70; Pepper's Lounge, Chicago, 1970; rec w Jimmy Dawkins Band, Delmark label, Chicago, 1971; worked w Jimmy Dawkins, Big T Lounge, Chicago, 1971; Alice's Revisited, Chicago, 1971; Florence's Lounge, Chicago, 1972; Univ of Miami Blues Concert, Silver Springs, FL, 1972; toured w American Folk Blues Festival working concert dates through England/Europe, 1972; worked Mr M's, Chicago, 1972; Checkerboard Lounge, Chicago, 1973-4; rec w Jimmy Dawkins, Delmark label, Chicago, 1973; worked Univ of Wisconsin, Madison, WI, 1973; Brown's Lounge, Chicago, 1974; Club Aquarius, Chicago, 1974; Sweet Queen Bee's, Chicago, 1974; Theresa's Lounge, Chicago, 1974; Show & Tell, Chicago, 1974; Brown's, Chicago, 1974; toured w Jimmy Dawkins Band working concert dates through Europe, 1974; rec Black & Blue label, Paris, France, 1974; worked Sackedelic Shack, Chicago, 1974; Eddie Shaw's Place, Chicago, 1975; w Jimmy Dawkins Band, Ma Bea's, Chicago, 1975 (por rel MCM label); rec w The Earbenders, WASP label, Chicago, 1976; toured Europe 1977-8; app TODAY Show, NBC-TV, 1981; worked festivals/clubs in Chicago area through 80s; died in auto accident; buried Washington Cemetery, Homewood, IL

Songs: Come to Me/Don't Ever Leave Me All Alone/Feel So Good/I Got the Feelin'/Long About Sunrise/No More Troubles/Sweet Laura/Tell Me Woman

Infl by: Bobby Bland/BB King

Quote: "He has perfect [control] of his powerful, ringing voice that is yet always slightly muffled by the intense emotion that comes from his singing"—Marcelle Morgantini, Black & Blue album 33.510

Reference: *Blues Unlimited,* Jan 1972, pp 14-15

OFFITT, LILLIAN
Born: Nov 4, 1938, Nashville (Davidson Co), TN

Born/raised in Nashville, TN; attended Tennessee Agricultural & Industrial State Univ, Nashville, late 50s; rec Excello label, Nashville, 1957-8; moved to Chicago, IL, to work Regal Club, 1958; rec Chief label, Chicago, c1959-60; worked residency w Earl Hooker Band, Robert's Show Lounge, Chicago, into 60s; worked Shangri-la Lounge, Chicago, 1966; frequently worked outside music, Chicago, through 60s into 70s; app in Streakers Rated-X Revue, Shadowland Ballroom, St Joseph, MI, 1974

OLIVER, KINE
(see Alexander, Alger)

ONE-ARMED JOHN
(see Wrencher, John)

P

PAGE, ORAN THADDEUS *"Hot Lips"/"Lips"*
(*aka:* Papa Snow White)

Courtesy Frank Driggs Collection

Born: Jan 27, 1908, Dallas (Dallas Co), TX
Died: Nov 5, 1954, New York, NY
Inst: Mellophone/Trumpet

Father was Greene Page; mother was Maggie Beal, a school teacher and musician who taught him music basics; learned trumpet at age of 12 and worked w Lux Alexander Youth Band at local weddings/picnics/parades in Dallas, TX, area into early 20s; frequently worked outside music with occasional gigs in passing carnival/minstrel shows, Dallas, from early 20s; worked in pit band of Ma Rainey show, then toured TOBA circuit working summer theater dates (including Lincoln Theater, NYC, NY/81 Theater, Atlanta, GA/others), 1924; worked in house band at Novelty Club, Kansas City, MO, mid-20s; frequently worked in high school band, Corsicana, TX, mid-20s; attended Texas Col, Tyler, TX, c1926-7; worked w Troy Floyd Band in local clubs, San Antonio, TX, c1927; toured w Sugar Lou & His Sugar Foot Stompers working dances in Dallas/Tyler/Austin, TX areas, 1927; w Frenchy's Orch in local clubs, New Orleans, LA, 1927; toured w Walter Page Blue Devils working dances through Oklahoma/Texas/Missouri/Kansas, 1927-9; rec w Walter Page Blue Devils, Vocalion label, Kansas City, MO, 1929; worked Cinderella Dance Palace, Little Rock, AR, 1929; toured w Bennie Moten Kansas City Orch working dance/club dates across US, 1930-5; rec w Bennie Moten Kansas City Orch, Victor label, Kansas City, MO, 1930; rec w Bennie Moten Kansas City Orch, Victor label, NYC/Camden, NJ, 1931-2; worked w Bennie Moten Kansas City Orch, Pearl Theater, Philadelphia, PA, 1931; Savoy Ballroom, NYC, NY, 1932; Champion Theater, Birmingham, AL, 1933; worked w Count Basie Quintet, Sunset Club and others, Kansas City, MO, 1935; w Count Basie Orch (as MC/musician/singer), Reno Club, Kansas City, 1935-6 (por remote, W9XBY-radio/WHB-radio); toured w Andy Kirk Orch working dances through Midwest, 1936; worked w Louis Metcalf Orch, Renaissance Casino, NYC, 1936; settled in New York, NY, working locally from 1937; worked Bedford Ballroom, Brooklyn, NY, 1937; Onyx Club, NYC, 1937-8; formed own band to work in residence, Small's Paradise, NYC, 1937-8; rec w Chu Berry Stompy Stevedores, Variety label, NYC, 1937; worked in residence, Plantation Club, NYC, 1938; frequently worked Savoy Ballroom/Hotel American/Cafe Society Downtown/others, NYC, 1938 into 40s; worked w All Star Band, St Regis Hotel, NYC, 1938; rec w own band, Decca/Bluebird labels, NYC, 1938; worked w Count Basie Orch, From Spirituals to

PAGE

Swing Concert, Carnegie Hall, NYC, 1938 (por rel Vanguard label); Brick Club, NYC, 1938; The Friday Club, Park Lane Hotel, NYC, 1938; app on ESQUIRE SWING SHOW, local radio, NYC, 1938-9; worked Golden Gate Ballroom, NYC, 1939; w Max Kaminsky Orch working dances in Boston, MA, area, 1939; rec w Billie Holiday/Ida Cox/Pete Johnson/others, Vocalion label, NYC, 1939; worked Kelly's Stable, NYC, 1939-41; rec w own band, Decca label, NYC, 1940; rec w own trio, Bluebird label, NYC, 1940; toured w Bud Freeman/Joe Marsala Orchs working one-nighters, 1940; worked private parties, NYC, 1940 (por rel Onyx label); worked Hickory House, NYC, 1940; West End Theater Club, NYC, 1940-1; frequently worked Minton's/Jimmy Ryan's, NYC, from 1941 (por Minton's gig rel Onyx/Esoteric labels); worked Monroe's, NYC, c1941; rec w Chu Berry Jazz Ensemble, Commodore label, NYC, 1941; toured w Artie Shaw Orch working one-nighters through New England, 1941; rec w Artie Shaw Orch, Victor label, NYC, NY/Chicago, IL, 1941-2; worked The Beachcomber, Providence, RI, 1941; w Fats Waller, Carnegie Hall, NYC, 1942; Village Vanguard, NYC, 1942; Eddie Condon's, NYC, 1942; Eddie Condon Presents, Town Hall, NYC, 1942; toured w own band working concert/club dates down East Coast, 1942-4; rec w Ben Webster Quintet, World Transcription label, NYC, 1943; worked Famous Door, NYC, 1943; w Count Basie Orch, Apollo Theater, NYC, 1943; Garrick Bar, Chicago, IL, 1943; rec w Albert Ammons Rhythm Kings (and own band), Commodore label, NYC, 1944; rec Savoy/Continental/V-Disc labels, NYC, 1944; worked w Eddie Condon Band, Town Hall, NYC, 1944 (por remote EDDIE CONDON'S JAZZ CONCERT Show, NBC-radio Network/por rel Armed Forces Radio Service and V-Disc labels); worked w Louis Jordan, Apollo Theater, NYC, 1944; worked Salute to Fats Waller Concert, Carnegie Hall, NYC, 1944; Onyx Club, NYC, 1944-5; w Don Redman Orch, Apollo Theater, NYC, 1945; rec w Mezzrow-Bechet Septet, King Jazz label, NYC, 1945; rec w own band, Melotone/Continental labels, NYC, 1945; app on ART FORD'S NEW SUNDAY SWING SESSION, local radio, NYC, 1945; rec w Pete Johnson All Stars, National label, NYC, 1946; rec Swan/Hub/Apollo labels, NYC, 1946; worked Fans Theater, Philadelphia, PA, 1945; Savoy Club, Boston, MA, mid-40s; Hotel Sherman, Chicago, IL, mid-40s; The Spotlight Club, NYC, 1946; worked Really The Blues Concert, Town Hall, NYC, 1947; rec w own band, Columbia/Harmony labels, NYC, 1947; rec acc to Wynonie Harris/Marion Abernathy, Federal/King labels, Cincinnati, OH, 1947; frequently sat-in w Bertha Chippie Hill, Jimmy Ryan's, NYC, 1947-8; frequently worked Eddie Condon's Club, NYC, late 40s into early 50s; worked Stuyvesant Casino, NYC, 1947; app on THREE FLAMES SHOW, NBC-TV, 1948; app on ADVENTURES IN JAZZ, CBS-TV, 1949; rec w own band, Columbia/Harmony labels, NYC, 1949; rec duet w Pearl Bailey, Harmony label, NYC, 1949; worked Salle Pleyel Jazz Festival, Paris, France, 1949; Jimmy Ryan's, NYC, 1949; Birdland, NYC, 1949; app on Eddie Condon's FLOOR SHOW, NBC-TV, 1949; worked w Bertha Chippie Hill, Riviera Club, NYC, 1949-50; Leadbelly Memorial Concert, Town Hall, NYC, 1950; rec Columbia label, NYC/Chicago, 1950; worked Brass Rail, Chicago, 1950; Central Plaza, NYC, 1950-1; Lou Terrassi's, NYC, 1950; rec Circle label, NYC, 1951; app w Pearl Bailey on Ed Sullivan's TOAST OF THE TOWN, CBS-TV, 1951; extensive tours working jazz concerts through Europe, 1951-2; rec w Andre Reweliotty's Orch, King label, Paris, France, 1952; rec King label, NYC, 1952-3; toured in various jazz package shows working theaters across US, 1952; worked Cafe Society, NYC, 1953; w Marion McPartland Trio, Fort Monmouth Concert, Fort Monmouth, NJ, 1953 (por rel Brunswick label); mostly inactive due to illness through 1954; entered Harlem Hospital where he died of pneumonia; buried Dallas Cemetery, Dallas, TX

Personal: Married Myrtle ___; 1 child. Married Mary Elizabeth Lawson (1949-54)

Songs: Ashes on My Pillow/Big "D" Blues/Dance of the Tambourine/Florida Blues/I Keep Rollin' On/I Won't Be Here Long/It Ain't Like That/Rumba Negro/7-8-9-10 Blues/They Raided the Joint (Raidin' the Joint)/Uncle Sam Blues/Walkin' in a Daze

Infl by: Louis Armstrong/Beno Kennedy/Harry Smith

Quotes: "Lips was a master of the blues: vocal or instrumental, happy or sad, fast, medium or slow"—Dan Morgenstern, *Jazz Journal* magazine (UK), Jul 1962, p 6

"He was one of the greatest players of blues on any instrument . . . he was blues all the way through"—Hank Jones, *Downbeat* magazine, Oct 30, 1958, p 22

Reference: Jazz Journal magazine (UK), Jul/Aug, 1962
Mississippi Rag, Feb 1992

PAPA CHARLIE
(see McCoy, Charles)

PAPA CHITTLINS
(see Moore, Alexander)

PAPA GEORGE
(see Lightfoot, Alexander)

PAPA SNOW WHITE
(see Page, Oran)

PARKER, HERMAN *"Little Junior"*
(*aka:* Little Junior)

Courtesy Living Blues *Magazine*

Born: Mar 27, 1932, Clarksdale (?), MS
Died: Nov 18, 1971, Blue Island, IL
Inst: Harmonica

Father was Herman Parker, Sr; mother was Jeannetta Henry; frequently sang with local gospel quartets as child; frequently worked local streets for tips as child; worked outside music in Clarksdale, MS, as youth; worked w Sonny Boy Williamson (Alex Miller)/Howlin' Wolf/others in local clubs, West Memphis, AR, area, 1949; toured w Howlin' Wolf Band (eventually assuming leadership) working clubs through Arkansas/Alabama/Mississippi/Missouri into early 50s; worked w BB King's Beale Streeters group in Memphis, TN, area, early 50s; formed own Blue Flames group working clubs in Memphis area, c1951-2; rec w Blue Flames, Modern label, Memphis, 1952; rec Sun label, Memphis, 1953; worked in Johnny Ace Revue in Memphis, 1953-4; teamed w Bobby Bland and assumed leadership of Johnny Ace Revue to tour w Blues Consolidated Package show working theaters/club dates across US, 1954-61; rec Duke label, Houston, TX, 1954-8; worked 5-4 Ballroom, Los Angeles, CA, 1960; Civic Auditorium, Chicago, IL, c1960; Ashland Auditorium, Chicago, 1964; Apollo Theater, NYC, 1964-6; Cozy Bar, Minneapolis, MN, c1968; Regal Theater, Chicago, 1968; rec Minit label, Los Angeles, CA (?), 1969; rec Mercury-Blue Rock label, Chicago (?), c1969; worked Burning Spear, Chicago, 1970-1; Ann Arbor Blues Festival, Ann Arbor, MI, 1970; High Chaparral, Chicago, 1970; rec Groove Merchant label, NYC (?), 1971; rec United Artists label, Chicago, c1971; rec w Jimmy McGriff, Capitol label, 1971; worked w Jimmy McGriff, Golden Slipper, Newark, NJ, c1971 (por rel United Artists label); entered St Francis Hospital where he was operated on and died of brain tumor; buried West Memphis, TN

Personal: Married Geraldine "Jerri" Cox

Songs: Bare Foot Rock/Blue Shadows Falling/How Long Can This Go On?/I'll Forget About You/Love My Baby/Man or Mouse/No One Knows/Pretty Baby/Stand by Me

Infl by: Roy Brown/John Lee Hooker/Jr Wells/Sonny Boy Williamson (Alex Miller)

Infl to: Bobby Bland/Little Frankie Lee/Little Mack/Big Mama Thornton/Jr Wells

Quotes: "He was one of the greatest blues singers of them all"—Purvis Spann, *Living Blues* magazine, Winter 1971, p 6

"Junior's music is warm, earthy and it swings . . ."—Jim Delehant, Mercury album 21101

PARRAN
(see Garlow, Clarence)

PATT, FRANK
(*aka:* Honeyboy)
Born: Sept 1, 1928, Fostoria (Lowndes Co), AL
Inst: Bass/Guitar

One of 7 children; was singing in local church choir as child; moved to Birmingham, AL, to work mostly outside music c1941 into 50s; moved to Los Angeles, CA, to work outside music from 1952; taught self guitar, early 50s; rec Specialty label, Los Angeles, 1954; reportedly rec w Gus Jenkins, Combo label, Los Angeles, 1954/Flash label, Los Angeles, 1956; rec Flash label, Los Angeles, 1956-7; frequently worked w Gus Jenkins/Chuck Higgins/Pee Wee Crayton/George Smith/others in local club dates, Los Angeles

Photo by Norbert Hess

area, through 50s into 60s; worked mostly outside music in Los Angeles, 1960/70s; app on Johnny Otis BLUE MONDAY Show, KPPC-radio, Pasadena, CA, 1970; worked w Jay Hodges Band in local club dates, Los Angeles, 1970; frequently worked as session man in Los Angeles into 70s

Personal: Not to be confused with singer David "Honeyboy" Edwards

Reference: Blues Unlimited magazine (UK), Feb 1971, p 11

PATTERSON, LILA
(see Rainey, Gertrude)

PATTERSON, OTTILIE
Born: Jan 31, 1932, Comber (County Down), Northern Ireland
Inst: Piano/Tambourine

Born Anna-Ottilie Patterson of Irish/Latvian parentage; interested in blues as hobby and frequently sang locally in late 40s into 50s; toured w Chris Barber's Band working concert dates through England from 1950; w Chris Barber's Band, Royal Festival Hall, London, Eng, 1955 (por rel Decca [Eng] label); app w Chris Barber's Band in UK film MOMMA DON'T ALLOW, 1955; rec frequently w Chris Barber's Band, Nixa label, London, 1955-8; worked w Chris Barber's Band, Royal Festival Hall, London, 1956 (por rel Nixa label); toured w Chris Barber's Band working concert dates through England, 1956; app w Chris Barber's Band in UK film CHRIS BARBER'S JAZZ BAND, 1956; rec ST in UK film short HOLIDAY, 1957; worked Town Hall, Birmingham, Eng, 1958 (por rel Nixa label); rec w Chris Barber's Band, Columbia (Eng) label, London, 1959-64; toured w Chris Barber's Band working concerts across US, 1959; worked Town Hall, NYC, NY, 1959; Monterey Jazz Festival, Monterey, CA, 1959; New Orleans Jazz Club concerts, New Orleans, LA, 1959-60; toured w Chris Barber's Band working halls/clubs/concerts/colleges across US/Canada, 1960; worked The Dixieland Jubilee, Hollywood Bowl, Hollywood, CA, 1960; Central Plaza, NYC, NY, 1960; Municipal Auditorium, New Orleans, LA, 1960; Concert Hall, Stockholm, Sweden, 1960; International Jazz Festival, Washington, DC, 1962; worked w Chris Barber's Band, Richmond Jazz Festival, Richmond, Eng, 1962 (por shown in UK film CHRIS BARBER BANDSTAND); app in UK film IT'S TRAD, DAD, 1962; toured w Chris Barber's Band working concert dates through Miskolc/Pecs, Hungary, 1962; rec Qualiton label, Budapest, Hungary, 1962; rec Supraphon label, Prague, Czechoslovakia, 1963; worked

Ottilie Patterson/Chris Barber Courtesy Chris Barber

Bath Jazz Festival, Bath, Eng, 1963; toured w Chris Barber's Band working concert/TV dates through England, 1964; worked New Marquee Club, London, 1964; toured w Chris Barber's Band working concert dates through Switzerland, 1964; worked National Jazz & Blues Festival, London, Eng, 1964; rec ST for UK film WHERE HAS POOR MICKEY GONE?, 1964; mostly inactive in music devoting time to song writing and poetry in London area from mid-60s

Personal: Married Chris Barber (1959-)

Song: Where Has Poor Mickey Gone?

Awards/Honors: Won *Melody Maker* magazine Jazz Poll as Best Female Singer in England, 1958

Quotes: "Influenced by folk-blues singers, she was the first European artist to sing in this [blues] style with conviction and authenticity"—Leonard Feather, *The New Encyclopedia of Jazz,* Horizon Press, 1960

"One of the few British singers who can sound convincing on the blues"—Doug Murray, *Storyville* magazine (UK), Jun 1975, p 195

PATTON, CHARLEY/CHARLIE
(*aka:* The Masked Marvel/Charley Peters)

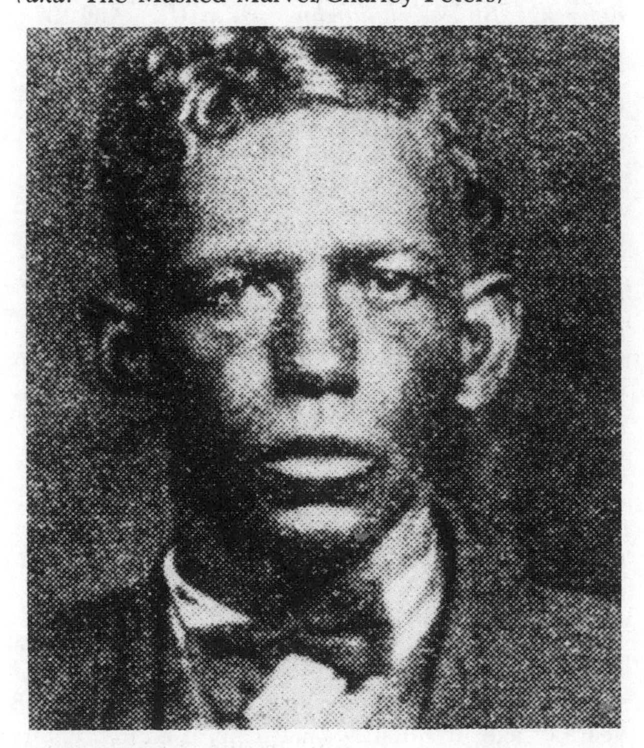

Courtesy Sheldon Harris Collection

Born: Apr, 1891, Edwards (Hinds Co), MS
Died: Apr 28, 1934, Holly Ridge, MS
Inst: Guitar

Father was Bill Patton, a preacher; mother was Amy ———; born on farm between Edwards/Bolton, MS; one of 12 children; worked on farm from childhood; moved to Will Dockery's Plantation to work outside music with frequent work at local meetings/socials/suppers/dances in Ruleville, MS, area, 1897-1929; frequently worked w Tommy Johnson/Willie Brown/Dick Bankston/others at local parties on Webb Jennings Plantation, Drew, MS, area from c1916; frequently worked w Tommy Johnson at local jukes in Greenwood/Moorhead, MS, areas c1923; frequently hoboed through Mississippi working logging camps/parties/streets during mid-20s; rec Paramount label, Richmond, IN, 1929; rec Paramount label, Grafton, WI, 1929-30; frequently worked Jeffrey's Plantation, Lula, MS, 1929-30; settled in Holly Ridge, MS, to work country dances/juke joints/weekend picnics/fish fries/cabins/road houses/back yards/sandlot ball games/barbecues in Boyle/Cleveland/Stringtown/Leland, MS, areas, 1930-4; rec Vocalion label, NYC, 1934; worked w Honeyboy Edwards at parties/country stores, near Dockery's Plantation, Ruleville, 1934; died of heart disease; buried New Jerusalem Churchyard, Holly Ridge; gravestone erected 1991

Personal: Was half-brother of the Chatmon brothers

Books: *Charley Patton,* John Fahey, Studio Vista Ltd, 1970

King of the Delta Blues: The Life & Music of Charlie Patton, Stephen Calt/Gayle Dean Wardlow, Rock Chapel Press, 1988

Songs: Banty Rooster Blues/Bird Nest Bound/Black Cow Blues/Circle Round the Moon/Devil Sent the Rain Blues/Down the Dirt Road Blues/Dry Well Blues/Elder Greene Blues/Going to Move to Alabama/Green River Blues/Hammer Blues/Heart Like Railroad Steel/High Sheriff Blues/High Water Everywhere/I'm Goin' Home/It Won't Be Long/Jersey Bull Blues/Jim Lee Blues/Lord I'm Discouraged/Love Is My Stuff/Magnolia Blues/Mean Black Cat Blues/Mean Black Moan/Moon Going Down/Pea Vine Blues/Pony Blues/Poor Me/Rattle Snake Blues/Revenue Man Blues/Runnin' Wild Blues/Screamin' and Hollerin' the Blues/Shake It and Break It But Don't Let It Fall Mama/Some Happy Day/Some of These Days I'll Be Gone/Some Summer Day/Spoonful Blues/Tom Rushen Blues/When Your Way Gets Dark/You're Gonna Need Somebody When You Die

Infl by: Henry Sloan

Infl to: Kid Bailey/Dick Bankston/Willie Brown/Honeyboy Edwards/Son House/Howlin' Wolf/Tommy

Johnson/Robert Johnson/Floyd Jones/Bertha Lee/ Fred McDowell/Johnny Shines/Henry Sims/Roebuck Staples/Eddie Taylor/Muddy Waters/Bukka White

Quotes: "Charley Patton is without question one of the most impressive and important of bluesmen on record . . ."—(Paul Oliver) McCarthy/Morgan/ Oliver/Harrison, *Jazz on Record*, Hanover Books, 1968

"Patton takes his place with the finest of the country blues singers of the late 1920s"—Samuel B Charters, *The Country Blues*, Rinehart & Company Inc, 1959

"One of the progenitors of the Mississippi Delta blues style"—Pete Welding, *Downbeat Music: 1968*, p 91

References: 78 Quarterly magazine, Autumn 1967, pp 10-17

Blues World magazine (UK), Aug 1970, pp 11-15

The Bluesmen, Samuel B Charters, Oak Publishing Company, 1967

PAYTON, EARLEE

Photo by Jim O'Neal. Courtesy Living Blues *Magazine*

Born: Nov 24, 1923, Pine Bluff (Jefferson Co), AR
Inst: Harmonica

Born/raised in Pine Bluff, AR, and worked outside music while learning to play harmonica to 1942; moved to Chicago, IL, to work outside music from 1942; frequently sat-in w Muddy Waters group, Du Drop Inn, Chicago, 1948; frequently worked as side-man in many local blues groups at clubs/dances in Chicago area through 40s/50s; rec w own Blues Cats, Parrot label, Chicago, 1954; worked w Blues Cats in local clubs, Chicago, 1954 into 60s; worked w Otis Rush, Club Alibi, Chicago, 1955; rec w Freddy King, El-Bee label, Chicago, 1956; worked w Blues Cats, Ricky's Show Lounge, Chicago, 1957; Zanzibar Club, Chicago, c1958; Cotton Club, Chicago, c1958; Indiana Theater, Chicago, c1959; occasionally worked with local blues groups in club dates, Chicago area, c1959; worked mostly outside music in Chicago from c1959 into 70s; worked Kingston Mines, Chicago, 1977; w Tail Dragger Band, Golden Slipper, Chicago, 1977

Personal: Given name also listed as "Earl" in some references

Reference: Blues Unlimited magazine (UK), Aug 1974, p 15

PEETIE WHEATSTRAW'S BUDDY
(see Ray, Harmon)

PEETIE'S BOY
(see Nighthawk, Robert)

PEG-LEG SAM
(see Jackson, Arthur)

PEG PETE
(see Jackson, Arthur)

PENNIMAN, RICHARD WAYNE

(*aka:* Little Richard)
Born: Dec 25, 1935, Macon (Bibb Co), GA
Inst: Piano

Father Charles Penniman; mother Leva Mae ___; was singing/dancing on streets of Macon, GA, for tips at 7 years of age; won talent show in Atlanta, GA, at 8 years of age; frequently sang in local church choirs where he learned to play piano as youth; worked Tick Tock Club, Macon, c1948; toured w Dr Hudson's Medicine Show/Sugar Foot Sam from Alabam/other medicine shows working as singer/dancer/pianist (while selling herb tonic) through South c1949 into

Courtesy Frank Driggs Collection

50s; won talent contest, 81 Theater, Atlanta, GA, 1951; rec Victor label, Atlanta, 1951-2; formed own band to work one-nighters at local schools/dances/clubs, Atlanta, c1952; worked w Tempo Toppers, Club Tijuana, New Orleans, LA, 1953-4; rec w Tempo Toppers, Peacock label, Houston, TX, 1953; frequently worked outside music, Macon, GA, c1954-5; rec w own band, Specialty label, New Orleans, 1955-8; app in film THE GIRL CAN'T HELP IT, 1956; app in film DON'T KNOCK THE ROCK, 1957; app in film SHE'S GOT IT, c1957; app in film MISTER ROCK AND ROLL, 1957; toured in Big 10 Package Shows working concert dates across US/Australia, 1957-8; left field to enter Oakwood College Seminary, Huntsville, AL (receiving BA degree in theology), 1958-61; was ordained minister of Seventh Day Adventist Church, c1961; rec (religious music) Mercury/20th Century-Fox/Atlantic labels and frequently toured churches through South as preacher and hymn singer, early 60s; rec w The Upsetters (Tempo Toppers), Little Star label, Alabama (?), c1961; returned to work w The Beatles/The Rolling Stones groups in concert dates, London, Eng, 1962; toured Europe/Orient/Australia working concert dates from 1962; app on own special, Granada-TV, London, Eng, c1963; worked City Opera House, Chicago, IL, c1963; rec Specialty label, Los Angeles, CA, 1964; rec VJ/Modern labels, Los Angeles, 1964-5; rec OKeh label, Los Angeles (?), c1965; worked Paramount Theater, NYC, 1965; toured England/Europe working concert dates, 1966; worked Brevoort Theater, Brooklyn, NY, 1966; app on JERRY BLAVAT Show, WOR-TV, NYC, 1967; worked Eden Rock, Las Vegas, NV, 1967; Concord's Coliseum, San Francisco, CA, 1967; Basin Street West, San Francisco, 1967; rec Brunswick label, Los Angeles (?), 1968-9; app Johnny Carson's TONIGHT Show, NBC-TV, 1968-71; worked Central Park Music Festival, NYC, 1968-9; Ish's, Vancouver, Can, 1968; Caesar's Roman Theater, Aladdin Hotel, Las Vegas, NV, 1969; app on MONKEES SPECIAL, NBC-TV, 1969; worked Toronto Pop Festival, Toronto, Can, 1969 (por in film SWEET TORONTO and short version KEEP ON ROCKIN'); Pop Festival, Atlantic City, NJ, 1969; Whiskey A-Go-Go, Los Angeles, 1969-70; Cocoanut Grove, Los Angeles, 1970; Berkeley Community Center, Berkeley, CA, 1970; app in film JIMI PLAYS BERKELEY, 1970; toured concert dates through South, 1970; rec Reprise label, Muscle Shoals, AL, 1970; app on MIKE DOUGLAS Show, CBS-TV, 1970-1; app on SMOTHERS BROTHERS Show, ABC-TV, 1970; worked Apollo Theater, NYC, 1970; Fillmore East, NYC, 1970; Rock & Roll Revival Show, The Felt Forum, Madison Square Garden, NYC, 1970; Olympic Auditorium, Los Angeles, 1970; Electric Circus, NYC, 1970-1; app w Dick Clark on AMERICAN BANDSTAND, ABC-TV, 1971-2; app on MERV GRIFFIN Show, WNEW-TV, NYC (syndicated), 1971-2; app on GLEN CAMPBELL GOOD TIME HOUR, CBS-TV, 1971; worked The Forum, Los Angeles, 1971; The Palladium, Hollywood, CA, 1971; rec ST for film $ (DOLLARS), 1971; worked Oriental Theater, Chicago, 1971; Wembley Stadium, London, Eng, 1972; app on TOM JONES Show, WNEW-TV, NYC (syndicated), 1972; rec ST for film BLACK RODEO, 1972; app in film LET THE GOOD TIMES ROLL, 1973; app in film JIMI HENDRIX, 1973; toured Australia working concert dates, 1974; worked Rock 'n' Roll Revival Spectacular, Madison Square Garden, NYC, 1974; app in ROCK & ROLL REVIVAL, ABC-TV, 1974; app in MIDNIGHT SPECIAL, NBC-TV, 1974; worked Radio City Music Hall, NYC, 1975; app on DINAH!, CBS-TV, 1976; app on MIDNIGHT SPECIAL, NBC-TV, 1976-7; app on DONNY & MARIE SHOW, ABC-TV, 1976; left field to serve mostly as singing minister from mid-70s

Book: The Life & Times of Little Richard: The Quasar of Rock, Charles White, Harmony, 1984

Songs: Directly from My Heart to You/Early One Morning/Every Hour/Freedom Blues/Jenny Jenny/Keep A-Knockin'/Long Tall Sally/Lucille/Oh My Soul/She Knows How to Rock/She's Got It/Slippin' 'n' Slidin'/Thinkin' 'Bout My Mother/Tutti Frutti

Infl by: Alex Bradford/Roy Brown/Fats Domino/Jay Hawkins

Infl to: The Beatles/Lonnie Brooks/James Brown/Jerry Lee Lewis/Billy Preston/Elvis Presley/Otis Redding/Rolling Stones

Quote: "[A] pioneer of the rock revolution . . . Little Richard gained fame from songs, usually of his own composition, with nonsense lyrics and a wild, driving rhythm"—Irwin Stambler, *Encyclopedia of Pop, Rock & Soul*, St Martin's Press, 1974

Reference: Encyclopedia of Pop, Rock & Soul, Irwin Stambler, St Martin's Press, 1974

PERKINS, JOE WILLIE *"Pinetop"*

Photo by Doug Fulton. Courtesy Living Blues Magazine

Born: Jul 7, 1913, Belzoni (Humphreys Co), MS
Inst: Guitar/Piano

Parents were farmers; born on farm outside Belzoni, MS; was one of many children; moved to Paines-Deadman Plantation, Honey Island, MS, where he was raised; taught self guitar working local parties/dances in area from c1923; learned piano and frequently worked The Old Barrelhouse Honkeytonk, Honey Island, MS, from c1926; frequently worked outside music in Indianola, MS, area through 20s; continued outside music work with frequent gigs in local dives/bars in Indianola area into early 30s; frequently worked jukes in Tutwiler, MS, mid-30s; teamed w Willie Love to work local jukes, Indianola, late 30s; worked w Big Joe Williams, St Louis, MO, c1941; worked outside music on Harold Hopkins Plantation, Clarksdale, MS, with occasional weekend juke work, 1941-3; worked w Boyd Gilmore in local gambling houses, Vance, MS, 1943; teamed w Robert Nighthawk working club dates in Helena, AR, area, 1943; app w Robert Nighthawk on MOTHER'S BEST FLOUR HOUR/BRIGHT STAR FLOUR Shows, KFFA-radio, Helena, AR, 1943 into mid 40s with frequent local tours; frequently app w Sonny Boy Williamson (Alex Miller) on KING BISCUIT TIME, KFFA-radio, Helena, with frequent local tours, 1943-8; worked w Houston Stackhouse, Green Spot, Clarksdale, MS, 1947; worked outside music, Greenwood, MS, c1948; worked w Robert Nighthawk in local clubs, Cairo, IL, 1949-50; rec acc to Robert Nighthawk, Aristocrat label, Chicago, IL, 1950; frequently worked outside music with some club work, Cairo, IL, 1950-3; toured w Earl Hooker Band working club dates in Sarasota/Bradenton, FL, 1953, with many clubs through Midwest into mid-50s; rec w Earl Hooker, King label, Memphis, 1953; worked w Johnny O'Neal's Hound Dogs, Moonlight Bar, East St Louis, IL, mid-50s; frequently worked w Little Milton/Albert King/others in East St Louis area through 50s; settled in Chicago, IL, to work mostly outside music from early 60s; rec w Earl Hooker, Arhoolie label, Chicago, 1968; replaced Otis Spann in Muddy Waters Band, 1969, with frequent tours/concerts/clubs with band into 70s; worked Ann Arbor Blues Festival, Ann Arbor, MI, 1969; Electric Circus, NYC, 1969; rec w Carey Bell, Delmark label, Chicago, 1970; worked Notre Dame Blues Festival, South Bend, IN, 1971; Alice's Revisited, Chicago, 1971; rec acc to Willie Wilkins, Supreme Blues label, Chicago, 1971; toured w Muddy Waters Chicago Blues Band working concert dates through England/Europe, 1972; worked Ann Arbor Blues Festival, Ann Arbor, MI, 1972 (por rel Atlantic label); Newport Jazz Festival, NYC, 1973; Shaboo Inn, Mansfield, CT, 1973; w Hound Dog Taylor, Avery Fisher Hall, NYC, 1974; Sweet Queen Bee's, Chicago, 1974; Montreux Blues Festival, Montreux, Switzerland, 1974; rec acc w Muddy Waters Band, Chess label, Chicago, 1974; frequently worked outside music, Chicago, through 70s; worked w Muddy Waters Band, Belle Starr Club, Buffalo, NY, 1976; toured w Muddy Waters Band working concert dates through England/Europe, 1976; rec acc w Muddy Waters, Blue Sky label, Westport, CT, 1976-7; extensive touring w Muddy Waters Band working concerts/college dates across US, 1977; worked Miller Theater, Houston, TX, 1977; Newport Jazz Festival Blues Picnic, Waterloo Village, Stanhope, NJ, 1977; Nice Jazz Festival, Nice, France, 1977; app SOUNDSTAGE PBS-TV, 1978

Personal: Cousin of Elmore James

Song: Pinetop's Boogie Woogie (claimed to have given this uncopyrighted song to Pinetop Smith)

Infl by: Percy "Fast Black" Brown/Leroy Carr/Ernest "44" Johnson/Pinetop Smith/Roosevelt Sykes

References: *Cadence* magazine, Jan 1976, pp 8-10
Blues Unlimited magazine (UK), Aug 1973, pp 7-8

PERRYMAN, RUFUS G
(*aka:* Detroit Red/Speckled Red)
Born: Oct 23, 1892, Monroe (Ouachita Parish), LA
Died: Jan 2, 1973, St Louis, MO
Inst: Organ/Piano

Father was Henry Perryman, a blacksmith; mother was Ada Westmorland; one of 16 children; moved to Hampton, GA, as infant; moved with mother to Detroit, MI, where he was raised with frequent returns

Rufus Perryman (Speckled Red) *Photo by Greg Roberts. Courtesy Delmark Records*

to Hampton; worked outside music with frequent organ work in local churches, Hampton, 1912-17; moved to Atlanta, GA, c1920-4; returned to Detroit to work outside music with occasional house rent parties/brothels in area c1924-8; worked w Wolverine Nighthawks in local clubs, Detroit, 1927; teamed w Jim Jackson to tour w Red Rose Minstrel/Medicine Show working through Mississippi/Arkansas/Alabama, 1928-31; frequently worked w Jim Jackson/Tampa Red in local bars/joints, Memphis, TN, 1929; rec w Jim Jackson, Vocalion label, Memphis, 1929; rec Brunswick label, Memphis, 1929-30; frequently worked excursion trains into New Orleans, LA, c1931; frequently worked Saturday Night jumpups in Truman, AR, early 30s; hoboed extensively working taverns/jukes/bars/parties through South/Midwest, 1931-41; rec w own trio, Bluebird label, Aurora, IL, 1938; frequently worked w Jim Jackson in local bars/clubs, Memphis, late 30s; settled in St Louis, MO, 1941; frequently worked outside music with occasional work in local bars/taverns from 1941; frequently worked w Dixie Stompers group as intermission pianist in local clubs, St Louis, into 50s; worked World's Fair Bar, St Louis, 1953-5; Club Jakovac, St Louis, 1955; St Louis Jazz Club Concert, St Louis, 1955; worked w Gene Mayl's Dixieland Rhythm Kings as intermission pianist in local clubs, Dayton, OH, 1955; worked McMillan's Bar, St Louis, 1956; rec Tone/Delmark labels, St Louis, 1956-7; worked Westminster Col, Fulton, MO, 1957; toured southern California working traditional club concert dates c1958; worked Bourbon Street Club, Hollywood, CA, c1958; toured England/Europe working concert dates, 1959-60; worked Roundhouse Club, London, Eng, 1960 (por rel VJM label); rec Folkways/Storyville labels, Copenhagen, Den, 1960; app w Piano Red on WAOK-radio, Atlanta, GA, 1960; worked St Louis Jazz Club concert, St Louis, 1961; Captain's Table, St Louis, 1962; Univ of Chicago Folk Festival, Chicago, IL, 1962; Gate of Horn, Chicago, 1962; mostly inactive in music in St Louis through 60s; worked Levee House, Minneapolis, MN, 1968; rec ST for UK film BLUES LIKE SHOWERS OF RAIN, 1970; entered Homer G Phillips Hospital where he died of cancer; buried Oakdale Cemetery, St Louis Co, MO

Personal: Had been married. Was an albino Negro and named "Speckled Red" due to his pink and speckled skin pigmentation. Older brother of Willie "Piano Red" Perryman. No relation to Gus Perryman, pianist

Songs: After Dinner Blues/Ain't Gonna Cry No More/All on Account of You/Blues on My Brain/Cryin' in My Sleep/Early Morning Blues/I Had My Fun/If You Ever Been Down/Little Girl/Oh Red!/Red's Boogie Woogie/Red's Own Blues/The Right String But the Wrong Yo Yo/St Louis Stomp/Wilkin's Street Stomp

Infl by: Paul Seminole

Quotes: "His harsh yet humourous voice and his clipped, percussive and powerful piano playing stamped him as one who could take his place among the elite of the barrelhouse and boogie pianists"—Tony Standish, Storyville album SLP-117

"His playing blends folk traditions and an adapted ragtime style into an original piano music representative of those early barrelhouse musicians . . ."—Eric Kriss, *Six Blues-Roots Pianists*, Oak Publications, 1973

References: *Jazz Journal* magazine (UK), Jun 1960, pp 3-6

Living Blues magazine, Winter 1972, p 4

PERRYMAN, WILLIAM LEE *"Willie"*
(aka: Doctor Feelgood/Piano Red)

Photo by Cheryl Evans. Courtesy David Evans

Born: Oct 19, 1911, Hampton (Henry Co), GA
Died: Jul 25, 1985, Decatur, GA
Inst: Piano

Father was Henry Perryman, a blacksmith; mother was Ada Westmorland; one of 16 children; to Atlanta, GA, where he was raised from 1920; learned some piano from father at 12 years of age; won talent contest on WAOK-radio, Atlanta, c1934; frequently worked outside music with occasional weekend club/party work, Atlanta, through 30s; worked The Chitter-Chatter Club, Atlanta, 1934; Moose Club, Atlanta, 1934; frequently hoboed w Jack Hemphill/Tom Fletcher working parties/jukes/dances/halls/summer resorts through South through 30s; reportedly rec w Willie McTell, Vocalion label, Atlanta, 1936; frequently worked Hole in the Wall Club, Atlanta, from 1936 into 40s; app on local radio show, Decatur, GA, 1950; rec Victor label, Atlanta, 1950-2; rec Victor label, NYC, 1952-3; app as DJ/singer/musician on WAOK-radio, Atlanta, 1953-67; rec Groove label, NYC, 1954-6; worked Univ of Georgia, Athens, GA, c1954; rec Groove label, Nashville, TN, 1955-6; rec Jax label, 1958; rec OKeh label, Atlanta, 1961; rec Epic label, 1961; rec OKeh label, Nashville, 1962-3; worked w own Interns, Magnolia Ballroom, Atlanta, 1962; frequently toured w own Dr Feelgood and the Interns working college circuit across US, 1962-7; worked Harvard Univ, Cambridge, MA, c1965; Apollo Theater, NYC, c1965; app w Aretha Franklin, (unknown) show, local TV, Nashville, c1966; extensive residency at Muhlenbrink's Saloon (Underground Atlanta), Atlanta, GA, 1969-79 (por rel Warped label); rec King label, Atlanta(?), c1970; rec Arhoolie label, Macon, GA, 1972; app in film THE CATCHER, 1972; worked Last Chance Saloon, Poughkeepsie, NY, 1974; Montreux Blues Festival, Montreux, Switzerland, 1974-5 (por 1974 concert rel Black Lion label); toured England/Europe working concert/radio dates, 1977; app on BLUES AM DIENSTAG Show, NDR-radio, Hamburg, Ger, 1977; toured Europe, 1978; worked clubs/festivals mostly in Atlanta area into 80s; died of cancer; buried Dawn Memorial Garden, Decatur

Personal: Was an albino Negro. Brother of Rufus Perryman. Not to be confused w John Williams/Vernon Harrison/Vance Patterson who have used the name "Piano Red" or similar variances

Billing: Mr Boogie 'n' Blues

Songs: Atlanta Bounce/Blues Blues Blues/Count the Days I'm Gone/Diggin' the Boogie/Do She Love Me?/Let's Get It On/My Baby Left Me/Pushing That Thing/Red's Boogie/Rockin' with Red/Ten Cent Shot/Well Well Baby/Wild Fire/You Ain't Got a Chance

Infl by: Fats Waller

Infl to: Dr John

Quote: "When it comes to the blues and the question of sincerity then [his blues] mark him as an expert in the field"—Alun Morgan, Black Lion album 30162

References: Blues Unlimited magazine (UK), Sept/Oct 1977, pp 18-22

Blues Unlimited magazine (UK), Apr 1970, pp 7-8

PETERS, CHARLEY
(see Patton, Charley)

PETTIGREW, LEOLA B
(see Grant, Leola)

PHELPS, ARTHUR

(*aka:* Blind Arthur/Blind Blake/Gorgeous Weed/Billy James/Blind George Martin)
Born: c1890-5, Jacksonville (Duval Co), FL (unconfirmed)
Died: c1933, Florida (unconfirmed)
Inst: Guitar

Reportedly moved to Georgia as youth; frequently worked as blind street musician in towns through Georgia and points south, late teens into 20s; worked w Bill Williams singing for road gangs near Bristol, TN, 1921; hoboed extensively working as itinerant musician through Florida/Georgia and north to Ohio on streets/at picnics/parties/suppers/fish fries into 20s; settled in Chicago, IL, mid-20s; rec acc to Ma Rainey/Charlie Jackson/others, Paramount label, Chicago, through 20s; rec Paramount label, Chicago, 1926-9; rec Paramount label, Richmond, IN, 1929; rec Paramount label, Grafton, WI, 1929-32; toured in show HAPPY GO LUCKY c1930-1; whereabouts unknown thereafter; possibly returned to Jacksonville, FL, area, early 30s

Note: There have been numerous unconfirmed and conflicting reports regarding this singer's birth/death facts as well as his true name

Personal: Reportedly had son. Not to be confused with Blake Higgs, a Bahamian calypso singer who uses pseudonym "Blind Blake"

Songs: Baby Lou Blues/Bad Feeling Blues/Black Dog Blues/Blake's Worried Blues/Bootleg Whiskey/Buck-Town Blues/Chump Man Blues/Cold Hearted Mama Blues/Cold Love Blues/Come On Boys Let's Do that Messin' Around/Detroit Bound/Diddie Wa Diddie/Doing a Stretch/Early Morning Blues/Fightin' the Jug/Georgia Bound/Goodby Mama Moan/Hard Pushing Papa/Hard Road Blues/Ice Man Blues/New Style of Loving/No Dough Blues/Notoriety Woman Blues/One Time Blues/Panther Squall Blues/Poker Woman Blues/Police Dog Blues/Ramblin' Mama Blues/Rope Stretching Blues/Sea Board Stomp/

Arthur Phelps (Blind Blake) *Courtesy Sing Out Magazine*

Search Warrant Blues/Skeedle Loo Doo Blues/ Southern Rag/Sweet Papa Low Down/Tampa Bound/That Will Never Happen No More/Too Tight Blues/Walkin' Across the Country/West Coast Blues

Infl to: Bill Broonzy/Gary Davis/Blind Boy Fuller/ John Hogg/Homesick James/Roger Hubbard/John Jackson/Rufe Johnson/William Moore/Buddy Moss/ Josh White/Bill Williams

Quotes: "Blind Blake's music did much to shape the style of the younger singers who were to become prominent in the thirties"—Dr Hans Rookmaaker, Biograph album 12003

". . . his voice was quiet, slightly wistful, giving his blues the feeling of self-depreciating irony"—Giles Oakley, *The Devil's Music—A History of the Blues,* British Broadcasting Corporation, 1976

"Blind Blake, a very good guitar player, about the best for my money"—Josh White, *Blues Unlimited* magazine (UK), Jul 1968, p 17

Reference: Sweet as the Showers of Rain, Samuel B Charters, Oak Publications, 1977

PHILLIPS, ESTHER

(aka: Little Esther)

Photo by Norbert Hess. Courtesy Living Blues Magazine

Born: Dec 23, 1935, Galveston (Galveston Co), TX
Died: Aug 7, 1984, Torrance, CA
Inst: Drums/Organ/Piano/Trumpet

Father was Arthur Jones; mother was Lucille Washington; born Esther Mae Jones; moved to Houston, TX, at 3 months of age; moved with mother to Watts area of Los Angeles, CA (with frequent return trips to Houston), where she was raised from 1940; frequently sang in local sanctified church and local amateur shows in Los Angeles area, 1940-9; won first prize in amateur show, Largo Theater, Los Angeles, 1949; won first prize in amateur show, The Barrelhouse, Los Angeles, 1949; rec w Johnny Otis Orch, Savoy label, Los Angeles, 1949-50; rec w Johnny Otis Orch, Modern label, Los Angeles, 1950; dropped out of school to tour w Mel Walker in Johnny Otis's Rhythm & Blues Caravan package revue working one nighter club/theater dates/dance halls/auditoriums/tobacco warehouses from West Coast across US, 1950-1; worked Civic Auditorium, Atlanta, GA, 1950; frequently worked Apollo Theater/Village Gate/Baby Grand, NYC, NY, from 1950; rec w Nic Nacs group, RPM label, Los Angeles, 1950; rec Modern label, Los Angeles, 1950; rec Federal label, Cincinnati, OH/NYC, NY, 1951; worked Howard Theater, Washington, DC, 1951; The Paradise, Detroit, MI, 1951; rec w Little Willie Littlefield and others, Federal label, Los Angeles, 1952; toured w Johnny Otis Barrelhouse Revue package show working dance halls across US, 1952-3; rec Federal label, Los Angeles, 1953; rec Decca label, NYC, 1954; worked w Rhythm & Blues Jubilee package show in local theaters, Los Angeles area, 1954; toured briefly w Slide Hampton (and family band) working club dates through California, 1954; worked club dates in Los Angeles area, 1954; settled in Houston, TX, and mostly inactive in music, 1954-62; rec Savoy label, NYC, 1956/9; rec Warwick label, NYC, 1960; worked Paul's Sidewalk Cafe, Houston 1962; rec Lenox label, Nashville, TN, 1962; rec Atlantic label, NYC, 1963-6; app w The Beatles, READY, STEADY, GO, BBC-TV, London, Eng, 1965; rec Atlantic label, Hollywood, CA/Los Angeles, CA, 1966; worked Newport Jazz Festival, Newport, RI, 1966; entered Synanon Drug Treatment Center, Santa Monica, CA (and other California centers), where she was mostly inactive in music, 1966-9; rec Roulette label, NYC, 1969; rec Epic label, Santa Monica, CA (?), 1969; worked Ash Grove, Los Angeles, 1969-70; Monterey Jazz Festival, Monterey, CA, 1969-70 (por 1970 concert shown in film MONTEREY JAZZ/por rel Epic label); app on Johnny Carson's TONIGHT Show, NBC-TV, 1969; app w Johnny Otis Revue on HOMEWOOD Show, PBS-TV, 1970; worked Quaker City Jazz Festival, Philadelphia, PA, 1970; toured US working colleges/state fairs, 1970; worked The Apartment, Chicago, IL, 1970; rec w Dixie Flyers, Atlantic label, Miami, FL, 1970; worked Freddie Jett's Pied Piper Club, Los Angeles, 1970 (por rel Atlantic label); frequently worked Memory Lane Club, Los Angeles, 1970-3; app on SOUL, PBS-TV, 1971; worked Mr Henry's, Washington, DC, 1971; New Ruthie's Inn, Oakland, CA, 1971; rec Kudu label, NYC, 1971-5; worked w Freddie Hubbard group, Civic Opera House, Chicago, 1972; Felt Forum, Madison Square Garden, NYC, 1972; toured w Freddie Hubbard group working concert dates through Holland/Germany, 1972; worked Philharmonic Hall, Lincoln Center, NYC, 1972; Berkeley Community Center, Berkeley, CA, 1972; The Lighthouse, Los Angeles, 1972; York Club, Los Angeles, 1972; Hollywood Bowl, Los Angeles, 1972 (por rel CTI label); app on Johnny Carson's TONIGHT Show, NBC-TV, 1972; worked Ronnie Scott's Club, London, Eng, 1973; The Palladium, Hollywood, CA, 1973;

Keystone Korner, Berkeley, CA, 1973; Memory Lane Supper Lounge, West Santa Barbara, CA, 1973; The Boarding House, San Francisco, 1974-5 (por of 1974 date shown on BOARDING HOUSE, PBS-TV); In Concert Club, Montreal, Can, 1974; Stardust Lounge, San Francisco, 1974; Paul's Mall, Boston, MA, 1974; Just Jazz, Philadelphia, PA, 1974; The Orphanage, San Francisco, 1974; The Viking Lounge, Cincinnati, OH, 1974; Robert's 300 Room, Chicago, IL, 1974; app on AFRICAN VIBRATIONS, WIIN-radio, Atlanta, GA, 1975; app on SATURDAY NIGHT, NBC-TV, 1975; app on AM AMERICA, ABC-TV, 1975; worked Felt Forum, Madison Square Garden, NYC, 1975; Buddy's Place, NYC, 1975; Apollo Theater, NYC, 1975; Ratso's, Chicago, 1975; Roxy, Los Angeles, CA, 1975; Concerts at the Grove, Los Angeles, 1975; app on DON KIRSHNER'S ROCK CONCERT, WNEW-TV, NYC (syndicated), 1976; app on DINAH! Show, CBS-TV, 1976; worked The Bottom Line, NYC, 1976; Village Gate, NYC, 1976; Ratso's, Chicago, 1977; Colonial Tavern, Toronto, 1977; Concert by the Sea, Los Angeles, 1977; worked festivals/TV shows in Europe, 1978 (por Switzerland concert shown RAY CHARLES AT MONTREUX, PBS-TV); worked clubs across US into 80s; app on BUFFALO BILL SHOW (ep: Hit The Road Jack), NBC-TV, 1983; died of cirrhosis of liver; buried Lincoln Cemetery, Compton, CA

Awards/Honors: Won *Rolling Stone* magazine Best R&B Singer Award, 1974

Won *Ebony* magazine Black Music Poll for Best Female Blues Singer, 1974, 1975

Won NAACP Image Award, 1975

Won French Academie du Jazz Award, 1975

Infl by: Billie Holiday/Sarah Vaughan/Dinah Washington

Quotes: "More subtle than Tina Turner, less sophisticated than Dinah Washington, she is in her way a great blues singer"—Steve Voce, *Jazz Journal* magazine (UK), Aug 1972, p 36

"Esther Phillips sings blues with as much hurt as any singer around"—Herb Nolan, *Downbeat* magazine, Mar 28, 1974, p 27

References: *Living Blues,* Summer 1974, pp 13-17
Black Music, May 1976, pp 6-7

PIANO RED
(see Perryman, William)

PICHON, WALTER G *"Fats"*

Courtesy Frank Driggs Collection

Born: Apr 3, 1906, New Orleans (Orleans Parish), LA
Died: Feb 26, 1967, Chicago, IL
Inst: Piano

Father was Walter Pichon Sr; mother was Cecelia Parrell; interested in music early and learned piano as child; moved to New York, NY, c1922; formed own quartet to work Atlantic Hotel, Belmar, NJ, c1923; attended New England Conservatory of Music, Boston, MA, to mid-20s; toured w Eleven Aces group working dances through Mexico c1925; returned to New Orleans, LA, 1926; frequently worked w Sidney Desvigne Orch in local clubs, New Orleans, 1926; frequently worked (as arranger) for Sam Morgan Band, New Orleans, late 20s; worked w Sidney Desvigne Orch on *SS Inland Queen* Riverboat on excursions between New Orleans/Cincinnati, OH, 1927, with frequent tours through South; worked w own band at Pelican Cafe, New Orleans, 1927; frequently worked w Elmer Snowden Orch in NYC, 1927-30; w Amos Riley Band, Danger Bar, New Orleans, 1928; rec w QRS Boys, QRS label, Long Island City, NY, 1929; rec under own name, Victor label, NYC, 1929; rec w Luis Russell Burning Eight, OKeh label, NYC, 1929; rec w King Oliver Orch, Victor label, NYC, 1929; toured w Dusky Stevedores band working dances through Texas, 1929; rec w Fess Williams Band, Victor label, NYC, 1930; worked w Otto Hardwick Band, NYC, 1930; frequently worked w Fess Williams Orch/Lucky Millinder Band/others, NYC, c1931-2; frequently worked (as arranger) for Chick Webb Band, NYC, early 30s; returned to New Orleans, 1931; frequently worked w Sidney Desvigne Band/Armand Piron Band on riverboats/clubs/dances in New Orleans area into 30s; toured in pit-band of Mamie Smith's YELPING HOUNDS Revue, 1932-4; formed own band to work dances in Memphis from 1935; worked solo in residence at Absinthe House, New Orleans, 1941 into 50s; worked Cafe Society, NYC, 1944; rec Raynac label, New Orleans, 1945; rec DeLuxe label, New Orleans, 1947; worked Cafe Society, NYC, 1948; toured as soloist working hotels through Caribbean area, 1952; rec Decca label, New Orleans, 1956; moved to Chicago, IL, c1962; frequently worked solo in local clubs/radio/TV in Chicago, IL/Milwaukee, WI, areas (with occasional New Orleans gigs) through 60s; entered Jackson Park Hospital where he died of heart disease; buried St Louis #2 Cemetery, New Orleans, LA

References: Who's Who of Jazz, John Chilton, Bloomsbury Book Shop, 1970

Jazz: New Orleans (1885-1957), Samuel B Charters, Jazz Monographs #2, 1958

PICKENS, EDWIN GOODWIN *"Buster"*
Born: Jun 3, 1916, Hempstead (Waller Co), TX
Died: Nov 24, 1964, Houston, TX
Inst: Piano

Father was Eli Pickens; mother was Bessie Gage; ran away from home to hobo through Louisiana/Mississippi/Arkansas/Tennessee through 20s; frequently worked w guitarist Otis Cook as itinerant musician entertaining migrant cotton pickers and working dives/barrelhouses/saw mill camps/fast houses/cabarets/bars through Texas/Louisiana/elsewhere through 30s; frequently worked club dates through Mexico, 1938; served in US armed forces in England/France, early 1940s; returned to Houston, TX, to work clubs/dives through area from mid-40s into 50s; rec w Benton's Busy Bees, Freedom label, Houston, TX, 1950; toured w Doc Sugar's Medicine Show through Texas c1960; occasionally worked w Lightnin' Hopkins in local clubs, Houston, into 60s; rec Decca/Heritage labels, Houston, 1960-1; app on MACK McCORMICK AND FRIENDS, KUHF-FM-radio, Houston, 1960; rec w Lightnin' Hopkins, Prestige-Bluesville label, Houston, 1962; app in film THE BLUES, 1962; was fatally shot during an argument in local bar; buried Brenham Cemetery, Hempstead, TX; heard on ST of UK film BLUES LIKE SHOWERS OF RAIN, 1970

Personal: Married Ethel ———

Quote: "Pickens was one of the finest [early blues pianists] of them all"—Derrick Stewart-Baxter, *Jazz Journal* magazine (UK), Oct 1966, p 10

PICKENS, SLIM
(see Burns, Eddie)

PIERCE, BILLIE

Photo by Andrew Wittenborn

Born: Jun 8, 1907, Marianna (Jackson Co), FL
Died: Sept 29, 1974, New Orleans, LA
Inst: Organ/Piano

Father Madison H Goodson and mother Sarah Jenkins were musicians; born Wilhelmina ("Willie") Madison Goodson; one of 7 children; moved to Pensacola, FL, where she was raised from infancy; taught self piano at about 7 years of age; frequently worked (as dancer) in local theaters, Pensacola, early 20s; worked in chorus line of Bessie Smith's touring show, Belmont Theater, Pensacola, 1922; replaced Clarence Williams as Bessie Smith's accompanist to tour with show working theaters, through Florida, 1922; frequently worked as accompanist for Ma Rainey/Ida Cox/Mary Mack/others, Belmont Theater, Pensacola, early 20s; worked in pit band of Joe Jesse's Orch, Belmont Theater, Pensacola, early 20s; toured w sister Edna Goodson in Mighty Wiggle Carnival working Gulf Coast night spots as singer/dancer/pianist c1922-7; toured in own revue working theater dates through South from 1925; frequently worked w Slim Hunter Orch in local clubs, Mobile, AL, late 20s; app w Slim Hunter on WODX-radio, Mobile, AL, c1928; frequently worked w The Nighthawks Orch in local clubs, Selma/Bessemer/Birmingham, AL, 1929; worked w Buddy Petit Orch on steamer SS *Madison* out of New Orleans, LA, 1929; w Lawrence Martin Band at local dances, Covington, LA, 1929; toured w Mack's Merrymakers working dances through Florida/Louisiana/Alabama, early 30s; toured w Joe Peoples Band working dances in Orlando, FL, area, early 30s; frequently worked Cat and the Fiddle Club/Popeye's/Charlie Palooka's/Steil's Wiggling Wagon/New Cocoanut Club/Harmony Inn/River Bell and other honkytonks/waterfront taverns, New Orleans, LA, from early 30s into 40s; frequently worked w Armand Piron/Alphonse Picou Orch/George Lewis Orch at Absinthe House, New Orleans, from early 30s; frequently w Alphonse Picou Orch at Rialto Nightclub, New Orleans, early 30s; worked Kingfish Club, New Orleans, 1935; w George Lewis Band, Blue Jay Club, New Orleans, 1935; brief tour w Ida Cox working shows through Florida, c1935; teamed w Dede Pierce to work together almost exclusively from 1935; frequently worked extended residencies, Luthjen's Dance Hall, New Orleans, c1935-59 (por rel Center label, 1953); worked Club Playtime, Bunkie, LA, early 40s; Maker's Nightclub, Pensacola, FL, early 40s; Kings Motor Court, Panama City, FL, 1944; toured w Ida Cox working theaters through South, early 40s; worked w Alphonse Picou at Club Pig Pen, New Orleans, late 40s; worked w Paul Barnes, Harmony Inn, New Orleans, 1947; rec w Emile Barnes New Orleans Band, American Music/Folkways labels, New Orleans, 1951; rec Folkways label, New Orleans, 1954; rec solo on Tone label, New Orleans, 1956; mostly inactive in music due to illness, New Orleans, c1956-9; rec Folk-Lyric label, New Orleans, 1959; rec Icon/Arhoolie labels, New Orleans, 1960; worked Tulane Univ, New Orleans, 1960; app on DAVID BRINKLEY'S JOURNAL, NBC-TV, 1961; worked Lee Roy's Club, New Orleans, 1961; rec Riverside label, New Orleans, 1961; frequently worked Press Club, New Orleans, c1961; formed Preservation Hall Jazz Band working extensive residencies at Preservation Hall, New Orleans, 1961 into 70s; worked Club 76, Toronto, Can, 1962; rec Atlantic label, New Orleans, 1962; rec Jazzology/77/Music of New Orleans labels, New Orleans, 1963; worked Borenstein's Art Gallery, New Orleans, 1963; Contemporary Art Festival, Houston, TX, 1963; The Royal Orleans, New Orleans, 1964; app on NEW ORLEANS JAZZ, PBS-TV, 1964; worked w Preservation Hall Jazz Band, Cotton Carnival, Memphis, TN, 1965; Music Hall, Memphis, 1966-7; app in film clip in ANATOMY OF POP: THE MUSIC EXPLOSION, ABC-TV, 1966 (rel as film AMERICAN MUSIC—FROM FOLK TO JAZZ AND POP); worked Newport Folk Festival, Newport, RI, 1966; Jazz Concert, Afton, MN, 1966; worked steamer SS *President* out of New Orleans, 1966; rec Preservation Hall label, New Orleans, 1966; toured w own band working college circuit through Midwest to West Coast, 1967; worked Stanford Univ, Stanford, CA, 1967-9; toured w Preservation Hall Jazz Band working concerts/radio/TV broadcasts through Europe, 1967; app w Herb Alpert and the Tijuana Brass, THE BEAT OF THE BRASS, national TV, 1968; toured w Preservation Hall Jazz Band working concert dates through Midwest into Mexico, 1968; worked w Preservation Hall Jazz Band at annual concerts, Philharmonic Hall, NYC, 1968-73; Guilford Col, Greensboro, NC, 1968; w Dixieland Jazz Quintet, Community Playhouse, Atlanta, GA, 1968; Theater Atlanta, Atlanta, 1968; Duke Univ, Durham, NC, 1968; Univ of North Carolina, Greensboro, NC, 1968-9; toured w Preservation Hall Jazz Band working concert dates through Midwest to New England, 1969; worked Fillmore East, NYC, 1969; Fillmore West, San Francisco, 1969; Univ of California, Los Angeles, 1969; Temple Univ, Philadelphia, PA, 1969; Newport Jazz Festival, Newport, RI, 1970; Lisner Auditorium, Washington, DC, 1970; rec ST for UK film BLUES LIKE SHOWERS OF RAIN, 1970; app w Preservation Hall Jazz Band on national TV commercial for Rainier Brewing Company, 1971; worked Univ of California, Berkeley, CA, 1971; New Orleans Jazz & Heritage Festival, New Orleans, LA, 1972-3; Onondaga Community Col, Syracuse, NY, 1972; Stanford Univ, Stanford, CA, 1972; Colgate Univ, Hamilton, NY, 1972; Blossom Music Center, Cleveland, OH, 1972; York Univ, Toronto, Can, 1973; Stern Grove Concert, San Francisco, CA, 1973; inactive after death of husband, from 1973; entered Sara

Mayo Hospital where she died of natural causes; buried St Louis #2 Cemetery, New Orleans, LA

Personal: Married musician Joseph "Dede" Pierce (1935-died 1973). Her sister Sadie Foster is pianist

Songs: Billie's Gumbo Blues/Freight Train Moanin' Blues/Going Back to Florida/Good Tonk Blues/In the Racket

Infl by: Ida Cox/Bessie Smith

Quotes: "A rough, vigorous pianist and a moving singer, she was one of the last remaining performers in the classic blues style as well as an excellent band pianist"—Paige Van Vorst, *Downbeat* magazine, Nov 21, 1974, p 10

"The Bessie Smith influence on Billie's vocal style . . . is still evident"—Larry Borenstein/Bill Russell, *Preservation Hall Portraits*, Louisiana State Univ Press, 1968

Reference: Preservation Hall Portraits, Borenstein/Russell, Louisiana State Univ Press, 1968

PIG 'n' WHISTLE RED
(see McTell, Willie)

PIGMEAT PETE
(see Wilson, Wesley)

PINEWOOD TOM
(see White, Joshua)

PITTS, Rev **ALFRED**
(see Watson, Johnny)

PLEASANT, COUSIN JOE
(see Joseph, Pleasant)

PLEASANT JOE
(see Joseph, Pleasant)

POLKA DOT SLIM
(see Vincent, Monroe)

POOR BOB
(see Woodfork, Robert)

POOR BOY
(see Oden, James)

POOR CHARLIE
(see West, Charles)

POOR JIM
(see Rachell, James)

POPPA/POPPY HOP
(see Wilson, Harding)

POTTER, NETTIE
(see Moore, Monette)

POWELL, VANCE *"Tiny"*
Born: May 17, 1922, Warren (Bradley Co), AR
Died: Feb 5, 1984, Oakland, CA

Father was Rev George Powell; mother was Kattie Watts; moved to St Louis, MO, mid-30s to work as singer in local churches and arranger for The Evening Melody Boys of St Louis gospel group, St Louis, from c1939; frequently worked w The Friendly Brothers of Dallas/The Flying Clouds of Detroit/The Pilgrim Travelers/The Blind Boys of Jackson, Mississippi, and other gospel groups in St Louis area into 40s; served in US Army c1945-6; returned to settle in Oakland, CA, c1946; frequently worked w The Paramount Singers of Oakland gospel group c1946-60; rec (blues) Wax label, Oakland, 1964; rec Ocampo label, Oakland, 1965; rec Early Bird label, Oakland (?), 1968; frequently worked w Johnny Talbot Band in local club dates in San Francisco, CA, area through 60s; frequently toured w Jimmy McCracklin Band into 70s; worked blues festivals in San Francisco/Sacramento, CA, 1977-8; worked outside music into 80s; died of cirrhosis of liver; buried Rolling Hills Memorial Park, El Sobrante, CA

Infl by: Sam Cooke/Claude Jeter/James Walker

Reference: Blues Unlimited (UK), Oct 1969, p 14

POWERS, JULIA/JULIUS
(see Cox, Ida)

PRICE, KERRY
Born: Mar 6, 1939, Louisville (Jefferson Co), KY
Inst: Piano

Father, William Albert Price, and mother, Anna Blye Blakey, were musicians; interested in music early and took piano lessons at 5 years of age; attended Indiana Univ, Bloomington, IN, late 50s (received BA in music education); worked as public school music teacher, Detroit, MI, area, 1960-71; frequently worked Bimbo's, Ann Arbor, MI, 1965-7; app w The Gaslighters, WXYZ-TV, Detroit, 1965-6; attended Univ of Michigan, Ann Arbor, mid-60s (received MA in music); worked Lulu's Storyville Saloon, Ann Arbor, 1967-8 (por 1967 date rel GHB label); frequently

Vance "Tiny" Powell *Photo by David Patrick. Courtesy* Living Blues *Magazine*

Photo by Walt Gower © 1978. Courtesy Kerry Price

worked w Mother's Boys Jazz Band at local clubs/colleges/dances in Detroit/Midwest/Toronto, Can, from 1967; worked St Louis Ragtime Festival, St Louis, MO, 1968-70; rec w Mother's Boys, Audiophile label, Ann Arbor, 1968; worked International Ragtime Festival, Minneapolis, MN, 1968; Jazz Concert, Waukesha, WI, 1969; frequently worked w Original Salty Dogs, Sloppy Joe's, Chicago, IL, 1969; Baker's Keyboard Lounge, Detroit, MI, 1969; Ragtime Bash of Toronto Ragtime Society, Toronto, Can, 1969-77; Manassas Jazz Festival, Manassas, VA, 1969 (por rel Fat Cat's Jazz label); sat-in at Red Arrow Club, Osaka, Japan, 1970; rec w Mother's Boys, Audiophile label, Plymouth, MI, 1970; worked w Mother's Boys, Georgian Inn, Roseville, MI, 1971; Hotel Pontchartrain, Detroit, MI, 1973; Bix Beiderbecke Memorial Jazz Festival, Davenport, IA, 1974-5 (por 1974 concert rel Bix Beiderbecke Memorial Society label); w Mother's Boys, Detroit-Windsor Jazz-Ragtime Festival, Detroit, 1974; w Mother's Boys, Dick Saunders' Memorial Concert, Royal Oak, MI, 1974; Dakota Inn, Detroit, 1974; Klip Joint, Cadillac Hotel, Detroit, 1974; Bimbo's, Ann Arbor, 1975; New Orleans Jazz Festival 75, New Orleans, LA, 1975; frequent one-woman musical programs working civic/social/church groups in Detroit area from 1976; worked w Mother's Boys, Detroit Hot Jazz Society Concert, Presidential Inn, South Gate, MI, 1976; w Mother's Boys, Schuss Mountain Jazz Symposium, Mancelona, MI, 1976; w Red Garter Band, Greenbriar Country/Golf Club, WV, 1976-8; w Mother's Boys, Henry Ford Museum, Detroit, 1977; Detroit Athletic Club, Detroit, 1977; Michigan Inn, Detroit, 1977; Clamdiggers Piano Bar, Detroit, 1977; served as director of Royal Oak Musicale Chorus, Royal Oak, MI, from 1977; served as director of music at Pilgrim Congregational Church, Birmingham, MI, from c1978; worked New Orleans Jazz Club Concert, New Orleans, LA, 1978

Personal: Married Walter Gower, musician (1971-)

Infl by: Claire Austin/Ma Rainey/Bessie Smith

Quote: "Ms Price is a blues shouter with a little girl quality"—Robert Morris, *Mississippi Rag* magazine, Nov 1975, p 13

PRICE, WALTER TRAVIS
(*aka:* Big Walter)

Courtesy Norbert Hess

Born: Aug 2, 1917, Gonzales (Gonzales Co), TX
Inst: Organ/Piano

Born, raised and worked farm from childhood; moved to San Antonio, TX, 1928; frequently worked w Northern Wonders gospel group in local churches with frequent outside music work, San Antonio area, through 30s; dropped out of school to work outside music in San Antonio area from early 40s; formed The Thunderbirds group to rec TNT label, San Antonio,

1955; rec w Little Richard, Peacock label, Houston, TX, 1956; rec Goldband label, Lake Charles, LA, 1956-7; frequently app on local TV/radio shows in San Antonio/Dallas, TX, through 50s into 60s; rec Myrl label, Houston, 1962; worked outside music (as owner of record/candy store/cafe), Houston, 1964; worked local concert, Houston, 1965 (por rel Flyright label); owned Sunshine Record Company, Houston, 1966; worked The Red Barn, Houston, 1967; worked w own Thunderbirds, Paladium Ballroom, Houston, 1969; worked outside music with frequent work as intermission musician/singer at local strip joints, Houston, from 1969; sat-in w John Lee Hooker, Miller Theater, Houston, 1977

Personal: Not to be confused with Walter Horton who has also used pseudonym "Big Walter"

Billing: Big Walter, The Thunderbird from Coast to Coast

Songs: Nothing But the Blues/Shirley Jean/Torn to Pieces

Infl by: Willie Pickett

Quote: "He is a great blues pianist and singer . . ."—Mike Leadbitter, Flyright album LP4700

Reference: Blues Unlimited magazine (UK), Feb 1965, pp 8-9

PROFESSOR LONGHAIR
(see Byrd, Roy)

PRYOR, JAMES EDWARD *"Snooky"/"Bubba"*
(aka: Snooky)
Born: Sept 15, 1921, Lambert (Quitman Co), MS
Inst: Drums/Harmonica

Father was James Edward Pryor, Sr, a minister; mother was Willie Terry; taught self harmonica and drums at 14 years of age; frequently worked w James Scott at local house parties, Lambert, MS, area 1935-7; moved to Helena, AR, 1937; left home to hobo through Arkansas/Missouri/Illinois working as itinerant musician, 1937-41; settled in Chicago, IL, 1940-c42; served in US Army in Pacific Theater of Operations frequently entertaining troups on USO shows c1942-5; returned to Chicago to work w Floyd Jones/Johnny Young on Maxwell Street and local house parties from 1945; worked w John Lee "Sonny Boy" Williamson/Homesick James, Purple Cat, Chicago, c1945; worked One Way Inn, Chicago, mid-40s; formed own band working The 24 Club and others, Chicago, 1946-7; frequently worked w Bill Broonzy/Memphis Minnie/Son Joe in Chicago, late 40s; rec Planet label, Chicago, 1948; frequently rec as sideman w Floyd Jones/John Brim/others, Chicago, into 50s; rec JOB label, Chicago, 1950-3; rec Parrot label, Chicago, 1953; rec VJ label, Chicago, 1954; rec w Sunnyland Slim, Blue Lake label, Chicago, 1954; rec w Floyd Jones, VJ label, Chicago, 1954; frequently worked w Baby Face Leroy/Homesick James, Club Jamboree/708 Club, Chicago, mid-50s; rec under own name, VJ label, Chicago, 1956; frequently toured w own band working club dates through Tennessee/Mississippi/Arkansas/Ohio through 50s into 60s; rec JOB label, Chicago, 1963; worked mostly outside music in Chicago area, 1963 into 70s; worked North Park Hotel, Chicago, 1971; Brown Shoe, Chicago, 1972; rec Today label, Chicago, 1972; app on ATOMIC MAMA'S WANG DANG DOODLE BLUES Show, WNIB-FM-radio, Chicago, 1972-3; toured w Homesick James and American Blues Legends '73 working concerts/TV/radio dates through England/Europe, 1973; rec w Homesick James, Big Bear-Polydor label, London, Eng, 1973; rec Blues-Way label, New Orleans, LA, 1973; worked Otto's, Chicago, 1975

Personal: "Snooky" is pet name given him by Floyd Jones

Courtesy Living Blues *Magazine*

Songs: After You There Won't Be Nobody Else/Break It On Down/Call the Doctor/Can Be Your Friend/Can I Be Your Man a Little While?/Cross Town/Dangerous Woman/Dirty News/Do It If You Want To/I Feel Alright/I Want to Go Fishin'/Keep Your Fat Mouth Out of My Business/Miss Matie Mae/Mr Charlie Mule/Nothing But Trouble/The One I Crave/Somebody Been Ramblin' in My Drawers/She Knows How to Love Me/Sloppy Drunk/Stop Teasing Me/Sweet as an Apple in a Tree/Take It Kind of Easy/Time Waits on No One/Trying to Sell My Monkey/Wrapped in Sin/You Wait Too Long

Infl by: John Lee "Sonny Boy" Williamson/Sonny Boy Williamson (Alex Miller)

Quote: ". . . the sides he recorded between 1947 and 1962, singing and playing harmonica, rank as classics in the Chicago postwar blues style"—Amy O'Neal, *Living Blues* magazine, Autumn 1971, p 4

Reference: Living Blues magazine, Autumn 1971, pp 4-6

PRYOR, MARTHA
(see Waters, Ethel)

PUGH, JOE BENNIE
(*aka:* Forest "Forrest" City Joe)
Born: Jul 10, 1926, Hughes (Crittenden Co), AR
Died: Apr 3, 1960, Horseshoe Lake, AR
Inst: Guitar/Harmonica/Piano

Father was Moses Pugh; mother was Mary Walker; raised on various farms in Hughes/West Memphis, AR, areas from childhood; frequently worked local juke joints in Hughes area as youth; left home to hobo through Arkansas working jukes/clubs/dives through 40s; worked w Big Joe Williams in St Louis, MO, late 40s; worked frequently in Chicago, IL, from 1947; rec Aristocrat label, Chicago, 1949; returned to Hughes, AR, 1949; app w Howlin' Wolf/Sonny Boy Williamson (Alex Miller) on HADACOL Show, KWEM-radio, West Memphis, AR, 1949; app w Willie Love's Three Aces on BROADWAY FURNITURE STORE Show, KWEM-radio, West Memphis, 1949; returned to Chicago, IL, 1949; worked w Otis Spann Combo, Tick Tock Lounge and other local clubs, Chicago, 1949-54; returned to Hughes, AR, to work outside music with occasional weekend gigs w Willie Cobbs in pool rooms/streets/jukes from 1955; rec Atlantic label, Hughes, 1959; while returning home from a dance suffered fatal injuries in truck accident; buried National Cemetery, Memphis, TN

Personal: Was married

Infl by: Walter Horton/John Lee "Sonny Boy" Williamson

Quotes: ". . . the fact remains [that] anybody who heard Forrest City Joe knows he's the baddest harp player that ever lived"—Louis Myers, *Blues Unlimited* magazine (UK), Nov 1976, p 8

"One of the best"—Otis Spann, *Blues Unlimited* magazine (UK), Mar 1975, p 9

Reference: Blues Unlimited magazine (UK), Mar 1975, p 9

Q

QUATTLEBAUM, DOUGLAS ELIJAH *"Doug"*
Born: Jan 22, 1927, Florence (Florence Co), SC
Inst: Guitar

Was an only child; first instrument was homemade from screen wire and stick as child; frequently sang in family quartet at 7 years of age; moved with mother to Philadelphia, PA, c1941; taught self guitar in early 40s; dropped out of school to work outside music, Philadelphia, c1943; frequently worked w Haze Quartet of Lake City, South Carolina gospel group, in local churches, Philadelphia area, into 40s; occasionally worked as a local preacher, Philadelphia, through 40s; toured w Charity Gospel Singers working churches/radio shows through Tennessee/Louisiana/Florida into 50s; toured w Bells of Joy gospel singers working

Courtesy Sheldon Harris Collection

churches through South, 1950-3; rec w Bells of Joy, Peacock label, Texas, c1952; toured w The Harlem Gospel Singers working churches through South Carolina into 50s; rec Gotham label, Philadelphia, 1953; frequently worked outside music with occasional gospel/blues work, Philadelphia, through 50s/60s; frequently toured w The Ward Singers gospel group, 1960-2; worked Purple Onion, Toronto, Can, 1961; rec Storyville/Bluesville labels, Philadelphia, PA, 1961; worked Gerde's Folk City, NYC, NY, 1962; worked w The Musicalaires gospel group, Philadelphia, 1962; worked Playboy Club, Chicago, IL, 1963; continued outside music work, Philadelphia, through 60s into 70s; reportedly entered ministry, Philadelphia, early 70s

Personal: Arthur Crudup was brother of his stepfather

Infl by: Blind Boy Fuller

Quote: "In his earnest, exultant singing several main currents of Afro-American folksong come together, for his forceful, individual style is an effective amalgam of urban and rural blues approaches and is further energized by his extensive gleanings from . . . Gospel music"—Pete Welding, Prestige-Bluesville album 1065

Reference: Prestige-Bluesville album 1065

R

RACHELL, JAMES *"Yank"*
(*aka*: Poor Jim)

Photo by Julie Snow

Born: Mar 16, 1910, Brownsville (Haywood Co), TN
Inst: Guitar/Harmonica/Mandolin/Violin

Father was George Rachell; mother was Lula Taylor; one of 3 children; born/raised/worked on farm from childhood; encouraged to learn music by uncle Daniel Taylor as child; first instrument was mandolin at 8 years of age; occasionally worked w Hambone Willie Newbern at local country dances/fish fries/suppers in Brownsville, TN, area c1919; teamed w John Estes to work streets/picnics/house parties/suppers/radio shows, Brownsville area, 1919-27; worked mostly outside music (on L&N railroad), c1928-9; formed Three J's Jug Band (w John Estes/Jab Jones) to work (occasionally w John Estes as team) local streets/parties in Paducah, KY/Memphis, TN, areas, 1929; rec w John Estes, Victor label, Memphis, 1929; worked mostly outside music (as farmer) in Brownsville, TN, area through 30s; worked w John Lee "Sonny Boy" Williamson, Blue Flame Club, Jackson, TN, 1933; rec w Dan Smith, ARC label group, NYC, 1934; rec w John Lee "Sonny Boy" Williamson, Bluebird label, Aurora, IL, 1938; frequently rec acc to other bluesmen through 30s; frequently worked between Brownsville, TN/St Louis, MO, late 30s; continued outside music work in Brownsville, 1938-58; worked w Peetie Wheatstraw, St Louis, 1940; rec Bluebird label, Chicago, IL, 1941; moved to Indianapolis, IN, to work outside music, 1958 into 60s; rejoined John Estes to tour college circuit, 1962-3; rec w John Estes, Delmark label, Chicago, 1963-4; worked Zapot Coffee House, Louisville, KY, 1963; Fickle Pickle, Chicago, 1963; Univ of Chicago,

Chicago, c1963; Oberlin Col, Oberlin, OH, c1963; Cornell Univ, Ithaca, NY, c1963; Queens College, Queens, NY, 1963; Gerde's Folk City, NYC, NY, 1963; Le Gallerie Flambeau, Baltimore, MD, c1964; First Floor Club, Toronto, Can, 1964; Club 68, Hamilton, Can, 1964; app on ASSIGNMENT, local radio, Toronto, Can, 1964; app on THE OBSERVER Show, CBC-TV, Toronto, 1964; worked w John Estes, Newport Folk Festival, Newport, RI, 1964 (por rel Vanguard label); worked New Gate of Cleve, Toronto, 1965; toured w American Folk Blues Festival working concert dates through England/Europe, 1966 (por Berlin, Ger, concert rel Fontana label); worked Avant Garde, Milwaukee, WI, 1966; Ash Grove, Los Angeles, CA, 1967; toured w Shirley Griffith working concert dates on East Coast, 1968; worked Newport Folk Festival, Newport, RI, 1969; Chicago Blues Festival, Chicago, IL, 1969; Quiet Knight, Chicago, 1969; Memphis Blues Festival, Memphis, TN, 1969; Ann Arbor Blues Festival, Ann Arbor, MI, 1969; Festival of American Folklife, Washington, DC, 1970; Washington Blues Festival, Howard Univ, Washington, DC, 1970; continued outside music work, Indianapolis, IN, into 70s; rec Blue Goose label, Indianapolis, 1973; worked National Folk Festival, Wolf Trap Farm Park, Vienna, VA, 1973; Univ of Iowa, Iowa City, IA, 1973; worked w own Indianapolis Blues Band, Crazy Al's, Indianapolis, 1975; Elsewhere Lounge, Chicago, 1976-7; John Henry Folk Festival, Camp Virgil Tate, Princeton, WV, 1977

Personal: Married Ella Mae Johnson (1937-61). 4 children. His son JC Rachell is gospel singer. Named "Yank" by grandmother as child.

Songs: Gravel Road Woman/Hobo Blues/Insurance Man Blues/Pack My Clothes/Peach Tree Blues/Rainy Day Blues/Shot Gun Blues/Skinny Woman Blues/Stack O' Dollars Blues/Sugar Farm Blues/Tappin' That Thing/Texas Tony/34 Blues/Wadie Green

Infl by: John Lee "Sonny Boy" Williamson

Infl to: Blue Smitty

Quotes: ". . . a terrific showman"—(Paul Garon) Mike Leadbitter, *Nothing But the Blues*, Hanover Books, 1971

"Yank Rachell has always been an animated performer, enthusiastically shouting and clowning with his audiences"—C Chris Sautter, *Living Blues* magazine, May-Jun 1975, p 45

References: Nothing But The Blues, Mike Leadbitter, Hanover Books, 1971

Cadence magazine, Aug 1977, pp 8, 10, 20

RAILROAD BILL
(see Dorsey, Thomas A)

RAINEY, GERTRUDE *"Ma"/"Madame"*
(*aka*: Mama Can Can/Lila Patterson/Anne Smith)

Courtesy Sheldon Harris Collection

Born: Apr 26, 1886, Columbus (Muscogee Co), GA
Died: Dec 22, 1939, Columbus, GA

Father was Thomas Pridgett Sr, mother was Ella Allen, both minstrel troupers; born Gertrude Pridgett; one of 5 children; baptized in First African Baptist Church, Columbus, GA; worked as singer/dancer in talent show A BUNCH OF BLACKBERRIES, Springer Opera House, Columbus, 1900; reportedly was singing blues by 1902; teamed w William "Pa" Rainey to tour as song and dance team working tent shows/levee camps/cabarets through South from 1904; frequently toured circuits working theater dates through South/Midwest from teens into 20s; worked w Pa Rainey/Bessie Smith in Moses Stokes Show, Ivory Theater, Chattanooga, TN, 1912; toured w Bessie Smith in Fat Chappelle's Rabbit Foot Minstrels tent show through South c1915; frequently toured w Florida Cotton Blossoms Show/Donald MacGregor's Carnival Show/The Smart Set Show/CW Parks

Minstrels/Tolliver's Circus and Musical Extravaganza Show from mid-teens into 20s; worked w Silas Green from New Orleans minstrel show, Ella B Moore Theater, Dallas, TX, c1917; toured w own Madam Gertrude Rainey and Her Georgia Smart Sets working theater dates through South, 1917; retired to Mexico briefly in early 20s; rec w Lovie Austin Blues Serenaders, Paramount label, Chicago, IL, 1923-4; rec w own Georgia Band, Paramount label, NYC, NY/Chicago, IL, 1924-7; toured w own Georgia (Wild Cats) Jazz Band working theater dates on TOBA vaudeville circuit through Midwest/South, 1924-35; worked Grand Theater, Chicago, 1924; Lincoln Theater, NYC, 1924; Temple Theater, Cleveland, OH, 1924; Bijou Theater, Nashville, TN, 1924; Lincoln Theater, Pittsburgh, PA, 1924; Frolic Theater, Birmingham, AL, 1925; Lincoln Theater, NYC, 1926; toured w own LOUISIANA BLACKBIRDS Revue working theater dates through South, 1927; rec w Tub Jug Washboard Band/Tom Dorsey/Papa Charlie Jackson/others, Paramount label, Chicago, IL, 1928; toured w Boisy De Legge and His Bandanna Girls in BANDANNA BABIES Revue working theaters through Arkansas, 1930; toured in own ARKANSAS SWIFT FOOT Revue working theaters through South from 1930; toured w Al Gaines Carnival Show working under canvas through Southwest, 1933-5; retired from music to live with brother Thomas Pridgett Jr, a deacon, Columbus, GA, from 1935; active in Friendship Baptist Church activities and owned/operated The Lyric/Airdrome Theaters in Rome/Columbus, GA, through 30s; suffered heart attack and died in City Hospital; buried in family grave, Porterdale Cemetery, Columbus, GA

Personal: Married William "Pa" Rainey (Feb 2, 1904). Her sister Malissa Nix was singer. Not to be confused w singer Lilian Glover (Memphis Ma Rainey)

Billings: Black Nightingale/The Golden Necklace of the Blues/Mother of the Blues/The Paramount Wildcat/Rainey and Rainey, Assassinators of the Blues/Songbird of the South

Book: ***Mother of the Blues: A Study of Ma Rainey,*** **Sandra Lieb, Univ of Massachusetts Press, 1981**

Songs: Army Camp Harmony Blues/Big Boy Blues/Blues Oh Blues/Bo Weavil Blues/Broken Hearted Blues/Cell Bound Blues/Countin' the Blues/Damper Down Blues/Dead Drunk Blues/Don't Fish in My Sea/Dream Blues/Farewell Daddy Blues/Four Day Honory Scat/Gone Daddy Blues/Goodbye Daddy Blues/Hear Me Talking to You/Hustlin' Blues/Jelly Bean Blues/Lawd Send Me a Man Blues/Leaving This Morning/Log Camp Blues/Lost Wandering Blues/Louisiana Hoo Doo Blues/Misery Blues/Moonshire Blues/Morning Hour Blues/Oh My Babe Blues/Oh Papa Blues/Prove It On Me Blues/Rough and Tumble Blues/Run Away Blues/Screech Owl Blues/See See Rider Blues/Shave 'em Dry Blues/Sissy Blues/Sleep Talking Blues/Slow Driving Moan/Soon This Morning/Southern Blues/Stormy Sea Blues/Those Dogs of Mine (Famous Cornfield Blues)/Titanic Man Blues/Tough Luck Blues/Victim of the Blues/Walking Blues/Weepin' Woman Blues/Yonder Come the Blues

Infl to: Barbara Dane/Jean Kittrell/Natalie Lamb/Carol Leigh/Kerry Price/Bessie Smith/Tampa Red/Big Mama Thornton/Dinah Washington/Pat Yankee

Quotes: "Ma Rainey differed from most, if not all, of the great women blues singers in that her style was directly influenced by rural Afro-American folk music, even while the content tended more and more to be that of urban blues—love misery, with its deep pathos and wry humor"—Charles Edward Smith, Milestone album 2008

"Ma Rainey was not strictly a blues singer, although she was an excellent one, nor was she a total jazz singer . . . she was a performer, a dancer, singer of vaudeville songs and of bawdy, double-entendre offerings . . . a consummate singer-artist whose skills and talents were considerable"—Lawrence Cohn, Biograph album 12001

"Well maybe I'm partial, but far as I'm concerned, Ma was the greatest of the blues singers . . ."—Georgia Tom Dorsey, *Living Blues* magazine, Mar 1975, p 28

References: Storyville magazine (UK), Jun 1971, pp 173-5

Milestone album 2008

Notable American Woman (1607-1950), Radcliffe College, Cambridge, MA (nd)

RAITT, BONNIE LYNN

Born: Nov 8, 1949, Burbank (Los Angeles Co), CA
Inst: Guitar

Father John Raitt is noted stage and film singer/actor; mother is Marjorie ———; one of 3 children; moved to New York, NY, where she was raised from infancy; returned to Los Angeles, CA, 1957; took some piano lessons as child; learned guitar at 9 years of age; attended University HS, Hollywood, CA, early 60s; worked Hoot Night, The Troubadour, Los Angeles,

Bonnie Raitt *Courtesy Sheldon Harris Collection*

1964; attended a Quaker secondary school, Poughkeepsie, NY, mid-60s; attended Radcliffe College, Cambridge, MA, 1967; frequently worked outside music with some work at local hootenannies, Cambridge area, from 1967; worked w Sweet Stavin' Chain Band, Second Fret, Philadelphia, PA, c1968; worked w John Hammond Jr at local clubs, Cambridge, late 60s; frequently toured w Son House/Fred McDowell/Robert Pete Williams/others working concert dates into 70s; worked outside music for American Friends Service Committee, Philadelphia, c1970; worked local clubs in Boston, MA/Philadelphia, PA, areas c1970; worked Gaslight Club, NYC, NY, 1970; Main Point; Bryn Mawr, PA, 1970; Philadelphia Folk Festival, Schwenksville, PA, 1970; frequently toured East Coast working college concerts, early 70s; rec Warner Brothers label, Lake Minnetonka, MN/NYC, NY/ Los Angeles, CA, from 1971; worked Univ of Vermont, Burlington, VT, 1972; Ann Arbor Blues Festival, Ann Arbor, MI, 1972 (por rel Atlantic label); Quiet Knight, Chicago, IL, 1972; Philadelphia Folk Festival, Schwenksville, PA, 1972; Carnegie Hall, NYC, 1973; toured w Big Boy Crudup working concert dates through Virginia, 1974; worked Bottom Line, NYC, 1974; Checkerboard Lounge, Chicago, 1974; app on BONNIE RAITT & PAUL BUTTERFIELD Show, PBS-TV, 1974; app on SOUNDSTAGE, PBS-TV, 1975; worked Civic Auditorium, Portland, OR, 1975; Wolf Trap Farm Park, Vienna, VA, 1975 (por shown IN PERFORMANCE AT WOLF TRAP, PBS-TV); Ambassador Hotel, Los Angeles, CA, 1976; Great American Music Hall, San Francisco, CA, 1976; toured England working concert dates, 1976; app on MIDNIGHT SPECIAL, NBC-TV, 1977; worked Univ of Oregon, Eugene, OR, 1977; Avery Fisher Hall, NYC, NY, 1977; New Orleans Jazz & Heritage Festival, New Orleans, LA, 1977 (por heard on national public radio); app on SATURDAY NIGHT LIVE, NBC-TV, 1978

Song: Give It Up

Infl by: Son House/Robert Johnson/Fred McDowell/ Sippie Wallace

Quotes: "Bonnie Raitt is an impressive writer and interpreter of blues and modern material and an entertainer with a sincere and irrepressible nature"—Kristin Baggelaar/Donald Milton, *Folk Music: More Than a Song*, Thomas Y Crowell Company, 1976

Reference: Folk Music: More Than a Song, Kristin Baggelaar/Donald Milton, Thomas Y Crowell Company, 1976
Guitar Player magazine, May 1977

RAMBLIN' BOB
(see Nighthawk, Robert)

RAMSEY, GEORGE
(see Dorsey, Thomas A)

RANKIN, R S
(*aka*: Little T-Bone/T-Bone Walker Jr)

Photo by Norbert Hess. Courtesy Living Blues Magazine

Born: Feb 22, 1933, Royse City (Rockwell Co), TX
Inst: Guitar

One of 9 children; raised and worked on farm as child; received some guitar lessons from T-Bone Walker, 1946; rec Miltone label, Houston, TX, 1947; briefly toured w T-Bone Walker (as valet) from 1949, eventually working in his band into 50s; rec as sideman w T-Bone Walker Band, Imperial label, Hollywood, CA, 1952-3; worked w T-Bone Walker, Apollo Theater, NYC, NY, early 50s; Flame Showbar, Detroit, MI, 1954-5; Blue Mirror Club, San Francisco, CA, c1956; formed band to work 5-4 Ballroom, Los Angeles, CA, 1956; then toured West Coast through 50s; rec as sideman w T-Bone Walker Band, Atlantic label, Los Angeles, 1959; app on SOUPY SALES Show, ABC-TV, c1960; rec w Curtis Tillman Band, Midnight label, Los Angeles, 1962; worked mostly outside music in Los Angeles area from c1964 into 70s; worked Moon Man Club, Los Angeles, 1974; T-Bone Walker Memorial concert, Musicians Union Hall, Los Angeles, 1975

Personal: Aaron "T-Bone" Walker was his uncle. Not to be confused with Roy Gaines who also used pseudonym "Little T-Bone." Given names are initials only

Song: Midnight Bells

Infl by: Aaron "T-Bone" Walker

Reference: Blues Unlimited magazine (UK), Sept 1975, p 19

RAWLS, LOUIS ALLEN *"Lou"*

Courtesy Sheldon Harris Collection

Born: Dec 1, 1935, Chicago (Cook Co), IL

Father was Baptist minister; sang in junior church choir from 7 years of age; graduated Dunbar HS, Chicago, IL, c1953; attended Art Institute (commercial art course), Chicago, c1954; worked outside music with occasional singing with local gospel groups, Chicago, mid-50s; moved to Los Angeles, CA, c1955;

toured w Pilgrim Travelers gospel group working churches/gospel programs across US, mid-50s; worked Apollo Theater, NYC, NY, c1955; served in 82nd Airborne Division of US Army, Ford Bragg, NC, 1956-7; returned to West Coast to rejoin Pilgrim Travelers group (w Sam Cooke) with frequent tours, 1958-9; worked as single in small clubs/cafes/beer joints in West/Midwest, 1959; app in non-singing role, BOURBON STREET BEAT, ABC-TV, 1959; app in non-singing role, 77 SUNSET STRIP, ABC-TV, 1959; worked w Dick Clark Show, Hollywood Bowl, Los Angeles, CA, 1959; Pandora's Box, Hollywood, CA, 1961; rec w Les McCann Trio, Capitol label, Los Angeles, 1961; app on NEW STEVE ALLEN Show, ABC-TV, 1961; app on FRANKLY JAZZ, KTLA-TV, Los Angeles, 1962; toured club dates in major cities of US c1962; rec under own name, Capitol label, Los Angeles, 1963-70; app on Johnny Carson's TONIGHT Show, NBC-TV, 1963; app on MIKE DOUGLAS Show, local TV, Cleveland, OH, 1963; app on JACK BARRY Show, KABC-TV, Hollywood, CA, 1963; worked w Louis Bellson Orch in club/hotel dates, Las Vegas, NV, 1963; Leo's Casino, Cleveland, OH, 1963-5; Purple Onion, Hollywood, 1963; Small's Paradise West, Los Angeles, 1963; Adams West, Los Angeles, 1963; Twenty Grand, Detroit, MI, 1963; The Palladium, Hollywood, 1963; app on JAZZ SCENE USA, WGBH-TV, Boston, MA, 1963; worked Sportsman Club, Oakland, CA, 1964; Showcase, Oakland, 1964; Ohio Valley Jazz Festival, Cincinnati, OH, 1964; Monterey Jazz Festival, Monterey, CA, 1964; Bohemian Caverns, Washington, DC, 1964; Louann's Club, Dallas, TX, 1964; The Lighthouse, Los Angeles, 1965; Jazz Workshop, San Francisco, 1965; app w Stan Kenton Band, JAMBOREE, KCOP-TV, Los Angeles, 1965; worked Grand Lounge, Detroit, 1965; Baker's Keyboard, Detroit, 1965; Ward's Jazzville, San Diego, CA, 1965; Parisian Room, Los Angeles, 1965; app on COLOR ME JAZZ (syndicated TV), 1965; app on JACK BENNY PROGRAM, NBC-TV, 1965; worked Riviera Civic Center, St Louis, MO, 1965; Back Bay Theater, Boston, 1965; Eden Roc Hotel, Miami Beach, FL, 1965; Pep's, Philadelphia, PA, 1966; Grand Bar, Detroit, 1966; Apollo Theater, NYC, 1966-9; Freemont Hotel, Las Vegas, NV, 1966; Living Room, Los Angeles, 1966; Village Gate, NYC, 1966; Masonic Temple, Detroit, 1966; New York Jazz Festival, Randalls Island, NYC, 1966-9; app on JOHN GARY Show, CBS-TV, 1966; Carnegie Hall, NYC, 1966-7; Arie Crown, Chicago, IL, 1966; Royal Tahitian, Ontario, CA, 1966; Carter Barron Amphitheater, Washington, DC, 1966; Lyric Auditorium, Baltimore, MD, 1966; Academy of Music, Philadelphia, PA, 1966; Admiral Steamship, St Louis, MO, 1966; app on ED SULLIVAN Show, CBS-TV, 1966-8; app on THE BEAT, WPIX-TV, NYC, 1966; worked The Music Hall, Cincinnati, OH, 1966; The Arena, Seattle, WA, 1966; Kleinhan's Music Hall, Buffalo, NY, 1966; app on MIKE DOUGLAS Show, CBS-TV, 1967; worked Pied Piper, Los Angeles, CA, 1967; Convention Center, Louisville, KY, 1967; Kansas City Jazz Festival, Kansas City, MO, 1967; Dinner Key Auditorium, Miami, FL, 1967; Cocoanut Grove, Los Angeles, 1967-8; Municipal Auditorium, New Orleans, LA, 1967; State Fair Music Hall, Dallas, TX, 1967; Penthouse Supper Club, Cleveland, OH, 1967; app on UPBEAT (syndicated TV), 1967; rec w Pilgrim Travelers, Capitol label, Los Angeles, c1967; toured w Pigmeat Markham working theater dates through Midwest, 1967; worked Central Park Music Festival, NYC, 1967-8; Town Hall, Philadelphia, PA, 1967; app on STEVE ALLEN COMEDY HOUR, CBS-TV, 1967; worked International Pop Festival, Monterey, CA, 1967; Hollywood Bowl, Los Angeles, 1967; Fairmont Hotel, San Francisco, 1967; worked A Program of Blues and Ballads, Carnegie Hall, NYC, 1967; Symphony Hall, Newark, NJ, 1967; app on DATELINE: HOLLYWOOD, ABC-TV, 1967; worked Carousel Theater, Los Angeles, 1967; Cobo Hall, Detroit, MI, 1967-70; Civic Center, Baltimore, MD, 1967; Memorial Auditorium, Dallas, TX, 1968; app on JOEY BISHOP Show, ABC-TV, 1968-9; app on RED SKELTON Show, CBS-TV, 1968-9; worked Redd Foxx's Club, Los Angeles, 1968; Royal Box, Hotel Americana, NYC, 1968; toured concert dates on college circuit through California, 1968; app on THE NOW GENERATION, ABC-TV, 1968; app on SOUL, NBC-TV, 1968; worked Constitution Hall, Washington, DC, 1968; app on BOB HOPE Show, NBC-TV, 1968; toured concert/TV dates through England/Europe, 1968; worked Bill of Fare, Los Angeles, 1968; app on DONALD O'CONNOR Show, WNEW-TV, NYC (syndicated), 1968; app on HOLLYWOOD PALACE, ABC-TV, 1968; app on BEAUTIFUL PHYLLIS DILLER Show, NBC-TV, 1968; app in film RIOT, 1968; worked Ravinia Theater, Chicago, IL, 1968; Marco Polo Club, Vancouver, Can, 1968; Leo's Casino, Cleveland, OH, 1968; app in New York State Public Service TV commercial, 1969; worked at President Richard Nixon/Duke Ellington Award Presentation, The White House, Washington, DC, 1969; app in THE BIG VALLEY, ABC-TV, 1969; app on DEAN MARTIN Show, NBC-TV, 1969-70; worked Imperial Hotel, Honolulu, HI, 1969; The Coliseum, Oakland, CA, 1969; app on

THE GOING THING, ABC-TV, 1969; worked Melody Land Theater, Los Angeles, 1969; Academy of Music, Philadelphia, PA, 1969; hosted JOEY BISHOP Show, ABC-TV, 1969; worked Century Plaza Hotel, Los Angeles, 1969-72; Ice Palace, Las Vegas, NV, 1969; app on PLAYBOY AFTER DARK (Hugh Hefner Show), WOR-TV, NYC (syndicated), 1969; app on MUSIC SCENE, ABC-TV, 1969; app on DELLA Show, WOR-TV, NYC (syndicated), 1969-70; app on Johnny Carson's TONIGHT Show, NBC-TV, 1969-71; app in film THE CULT OF THE DAMNED (Angel Angel Down We Go), 1969; worked Fairmont Hotel, Dallas, TX, 1969-71; Univ of Kansas, Lawrence, KS, 1969; hosted (10 weeks) DEAN MARTIN Show ("Lou Rawls & the Gold Diggers"), NBC-TV, 1969; app on BARBARA McNAIR Show, WNEW-TV, NYC (syndicated), 1969; formed Dead End Productions to assist disadvantaged youngsters in recording industry, 1969; formed Crossroads (TV) Productions Company c1969; app on MERV GRIFFIN Show, CBS-TV, 1969-71; app on ENGELBERT HUMPERDINCK Show, ABC-TV, 1970; frequently sang national anthem at sporting events across US into 70s; app on MIKE DOUGLAS Show, CBS-TV (syndicated), 1970; app on SESAME STREET, PBS-TV (syndicated), 1970; app on TOM JONES Show, ABC-TV, 1970; app on ACADEMY AWARDS PRESENTATION, ABC-TV, 1970; app on THE HOLLYWOOD SQUARES game show, NBC-TV, 1970; app on KRAFT MUSIC HALL, NBC-TV, 1970; app on CONTACT, WPIX-TV, NYC, 1970; worked Constitution Hall, Washington, DC, 1970; app on local TV shows, London, Eng, 1970; toured clubs/concerts/military bases through Europe, 1970; worked concert dates through Australia/Japan/Far East, 1970; app in film BELIEVE IN ME, 1971; worked Ohio Valley Jazz Festival, Cincinnati, OH, 1971; rec MGM label, Los Angeles, CA (?), 1971-2; app on LOU RAWLS Show, CBS-TV, 1971; app on VIRGINIA GRAHAM Show, WOR-TV, NYC (syndicated), 1971; worked Disneyland Park, Anaheim, CA, 1972; 270 Garden Restaurant, St Louis, MO, 1972; Newport Jazz Festival, NYC, 1972, then toured with festival working concerts in major cities of US, 1972; worked Newport Hotel, Miami Beach, FL, 1972; Sunset Series Concert, Boston, MA, 1972; Astrodome Jazz Festival, Houston, TX, 1972; Lookout House, Cincinnati, OH, 1972; Palmer House, Chicago, 1972; Terrace Room, Jacksonville, FL, 1972; Pirates Den, Jacksonville, 1972; The Thunder Bird, Jacksonville, 1972; The Maisonette, NYC, 1972; app on MIKE DOUGLAS Show, CBS-TV (syndicated), 1972; app on DAVID FROST Show, WNEW-TV, NYC (syndicated), 1972; worked The Warehouse, Denver, CO, 1973; Mr Kelly's, Chicago, IL, 1973; MGM Grand Hotel, Las Vegas, NV, 1974; app w BB King, RHYTHM & BLUES, NBC-TV, 1974; app on SOUL TRAIN, WNEW-TV, NYC (syndicated), 1975; worked Buddy's Place, NYC, 1975; app on MIDDAY LIVE, WNEW-TV, NYC, 1975; app on POSITIVELY BLACK, NBC-TV (syndicated), 1975; app on MERV GRIFFIN Show, WNEW-TV, NYC (syndicated), 1975-7; app on Johnny Carson's TONIGHT Show, NBC-TV, 1975-6; app on SAMMY AND COMPANY, NBC-TV, 1975; app on DINAH! Show, CBS-TV, 1976-7; app on MIDNIGHT SPECIAL, NBC-TV, 1976-7; app on BICENTENNIAL MINUTE, CBS-TV, 1976; app on AUSTIN CITY LIMITS, PBS-TV, 1976; rec CBS label, Philadelphia, PA, 1976; app on MIKE DOUGLAS Show, CBS-TV (syndicated), 1976-8; app on DON KIRSHNER'S ROCK CONCERT, WNEW-TV, NYC (syndicated), 1976-7; app in radio commercial for Eastern Airlines, 1976-7; app on AMERICAN MUSIC AWARDS, ABC-TV, 1977-8; app on CAPTAIN & TENNILLE Show, ABC-TV, 1977; app in national print/TV commercials for Budweiser Beer, 1977-8; app TV CRITICS CIRCLE AWARDS, CBS-TV, 1977; app on LOU RAWLS—SPECIAL, ABC-TV, 1977; app on DISCO '77, WOR-TV, NYC (syndicated), 1977; app on MUPPET SHOW, CBS-TV, 1977; app on MIDDAY LIVE, WNEW-TV, NYC, 1977; app on DINAH! Show, WPIX-TV, NYC, 1977; app on LOU RAWLS ON ICE, WNEW-TV, NYC, 1978; app on GRAMMY AWARDS, CBS-TV, 1978; app on NATIONAL COLLEGIATE CHEERLEADING CHAMPIONSHIPS, CBS-TV, 1978; worked Latin Casino, Philadelphia, PA, 1978; Westbury Music Fair, Westbury, NY, 1978; app on AMERICA 2-NIGHT, WOR-TV, NYC (syndicated), 1978; app DICK CLARK AND A CAST OF THOUSANDS, NBC-TV, 1978; worked solo concert, Mark Hellinger Theater, NYC, 1978 (por rel Philadelphia International label)

Personal: Married Lana Jean ——— (1962-72). 2 children

Songs: Breaking My Back/Mean Black Snake

Awards/Honors: Won *Downbeat* magazine International Critics Poll for Male Singer deserving wider recognition, 1966

Won *Downbeat* magazine Readers Poll for Best Male Vocalist, 1967

Won National Academy of Recording Arts & Sciences Grammy Award for Best Male

R&B vocal performance, 1967 ("Dead End Street")

Presented award and a Lou Rawls Day proclaimed by city of Los Angeles in honor of his contribution to music and to the children of Los Angeles, CA, 1968

Won NATRA Award as Best Male Jazz Vocalist, 1969

Cited in Congressional Record for his efforts to encourage children to remain in school, 1969

Won National Academy of Recording Arts & Sciences Grammy Award for Best Male R&B Performer, 1971, 1977

Infl by: Sam Cooke/Al Hibbler/Joe Williams

Quotes: "Lou Rawls is a mixture of Blues/Soul/Jazz"—Frank Lieberman, *Los Angeles Herald Examiner* newspaper (date unknown)

". . . an established music industry great"—Irwin Stambler, *Encyclopedia of Pop, Rock & Soul,* St Martin's Press, 1974

References: Encyclopedia of Pop, Rock & Soul, Irwin Stambler, St Martin's Press, 1974.

Los Angeles Times newspaper, Apr 20, 1969

RAY, HARMON *"Herman"*
(*aka*: Peetie Wheatstraw's Buddy)

Photo by Tony Russell. Courtesy Living Blues Magazine

Born: 1914, Indianapolis (Marion Co), IN

Moved to St Louis, MO, as youth; was working local club dates, St Louis, early 30s; worked Cabin Inn, St Louis, 1935; worked w Peetie Wheatstraw in local club with frequent tours working clubs through South through 30s; rec w Joe McCoy's Big Joe & His Rhythm, Bluebird label, Chicago, IL, 1942; served in US Navy in France/Aleutian Islands, 1942-6; worked Martin's Corner and other clubs, Chicago, c1946 through 50s; rec (unissued) label, Chicago, 1947; reportedly rec Hy Tone label, Chicago, 1947; rec Decca label, NYC, NY, 1949; mostly inactive in music due to poor health, Chicago, early 60s

Songs: Brown Skin Woman/Check Up on My Baby/Come Over and See Me/Hearseman Blues/Please Baby Come Home to Me/President's Blues

Infl by: Peetie Wheatstraw

Quote: ". . . a thoughtful songwriter and quite an interesting bluesman of his period"—Tony Russell, *Living Blues* magazine, Mar 1976, p 14

Reference: Living Blues magazine, Mar 1976, pp 14-15

RAY, ISOM
(see Agee, Raymond)

RED DEVIL
(see Milborn, Nelson)

RED HOT WILLIE
(see McTell, Willie)

RED NELSON
(see Wilborn, Nelson)

REED, MATHIS JAMES *"Jimmy"*
Born: Sept 6, 1925, Dunleith (Washington Co), MS
Died: Aug 29, 1976, Oakland, CA
Inst: Guitar/Harmonica

Father Joseph Reed and mother Virginia Ross were sharecroppers on Mr Johnny Collier's Plantation outside Dunleith, MS; one of 10 children; often sang in local church choirs as child; raised w Eddie Taylor from 7 years of age and later learned guitar from him as youth; dropped out of school to work outside music (as farmer), Duncan, MS, c1939; moved to Meltonia, MS, to work outside music with some local church choir singing at Pilgrim Rest Baptist Church, 1940-3;

Mathis James "Jimmy" Reed *Photo by Jim O'Neal. Courtesy* Living Blues *Magazine*

moved to Chicago, IL, to work outside music, 1943-4; served in US Navy, 1944-5; returned to Dunleith, MS, to work outside music, 1945-8; moved to Gary, IN, to work outside music from 1948; frequently worked w John Brim's Gary Kings at Club Jamboree, Chicago, IL/Pulaski Lounge, Gary, IN, and other clubs, 1948 into early 50s; frequently worked w Willie Joe "Jody" Duncan on streets for tips, Chicago Heights, IL, c1949; worked w Eddie Taylor almost continually from 1949 through 60s; worked Velma's Tavern, Chicago, 1952; frequently w Albert King, Pulaski Hall, Gary, 1952-3; residency w Kansas City Red Band, Black & Tan Club, Chicago Heights, IL, c1953; rec w Eddie Taylor, Chance label, Chicago, 1953; rec w John Brim, Parrot label, Chicago, 1953; rec extensively on VJ label, Chicago, 1953-65; worked on Roy Hamilton R&B package show, Trianon Club, Chicago, c1954 with tours through Illinois/Indiana/Wisconsin/Michigan; rec w John Lee Hooker, VJ label, Chicago, 1955; worked w John Lee Hooker, Apex Club, Detroit, c1955; toured extensively across US/Mexico working colleges/concerts/auditoriums and clubs like The Peacock, Atlanta, GA/The Harlem Square Club, Miami, FL/Castle Farm, Cincinnati, OH/Stemp Hall, St Paul, MN/Civic Auditorium, Albuquerque, NM/others from 1955 into 60s; worked Doris Miller Auditorium, Austin, TX, 1956; frequent club dates in San Francisco, CA, area, 1959; worked Club DeLisa, Chicago, IL, 1960; Brevoort Theater, Brooklyn, NY, early 60s; rec w John Lee Hooker, VJ label, Chicago, 1961; worked Univ of Florida, Gainesville, FL, 1961; Empire Room, Dallas, TX, 1961; Carnegie Hall, NYC, 1961-3; w John Brim Band, Club 99, Joliet, IL, 1962; Rockland Palace, NYC, 1963; Prince Hall, Detroit, 1963; toured England working concert dates, 1963-4; app on READY,

STEADY, GO, BBC-TV, London, Eng, 1964; rec w Eddie Taylor, Vivid label, Chicago, 1964; worked Blues Unlimited Club, Detroit, 1965; Apollo Theater, NYC, 1965-6; The Coliseum, Washington, DC, 1966; rec Exodus label, Chicago, 1966; rec ABC-BluesWay label, Chicago, 1966-8; toured West Coast working club dates, 1966; worked Playboy Club, Chicago, 1966; Pussy Cat-A-Go-Go, Birmingham, AL, 1966; Community Theater, Berkeley, CA, 1967; Basin Street West, San Francisco, CA, 1967; The Golden Bear, Huntington Beach, CA, 1968; toured w American Folk Blues Festival working concert dates through England/Europe, 1968 (por shown in UK film AMERICAN FOLK BLUES FESTIVAL which was shown on BBC-TV, London); mostly inactive in music due to illness, Chicago, through 60s; worked w BB King, Shrine Auditorium, Los Angeles, 1970; rec Roker label, Chicago, 1970; toured w Clifton Chenier working concert dates through Canada, early 70s; rec Blues on Blues label, Chicago, 1971; worked Big Duke's, Chicago, 1971; Pepper's Lounge, Chicago, 1971; North Park Hotel, Chicago, 1971; Mother Blues, Dallas, TX, 1972; Nutcracker Lounge, New Orleans, LA, 1972; rec Magic label, Chicago, 1972; worked Ethel's, Detroit, MI, c1972; High Chaparral, Chicago, 1973; Ann Arbor Blues Festival, Ann Arbor, MI, 1973; Le Coq D'or Tavern, Toronto, Can, 1973; La Bastille, Houston, TX, 1973; rec ABC-BluesWay label, Chicago, IL, c1973; app on ATOMIC MAMA'S WANG DANG DOODLE BLUES, WNIB-FM-radio, Chicago, c1973; mostly inactive in music due to illness, 1974; worked Theresa's Lounge, Chicago, 1974; Antone's, Austin, TX, 1975; Golden Checkmate, Chicago, 1975; Wise Fools Pub, Chicago, 1975; The Stingrey, Chicago, 1975; The New 1815 Club, Chicago, 1975; Kingston Mines, Chicago, 1975; Liberty Hall, Houston, 1975; Atlanta Blues Festival, Great Southeast Music Hall, Atlanta, GA, 1976; West Dakota Club, Berkeley, CA, 1976; Savoy Club, San Francisco, 1976; app on BLUES BY THE BAY, KPFA-FM-radio, Berkeley, 1976; suffered epilepsy attack and died in sleep of respiratory failure; buried Lincoln Cemetery, Blue Island, IL

Personal: Married Mary Lee "Mama" Davis (1945-c1974) who wrote many of his songs. Had 9 children. His son Jimmy Reed Jr is a guitarist, daughter Malinda Reed is singer. AC (Aaron Corthen) Reed (unrelated) is musician/singer. Nephew Jesse Reed is guitarist. Had suffered from epilepsy since 1957

Songs: A New Leaf/Ain't No Big Deal/Ain't No Time for Fussin'/Ain't That Lovin' You Baby?/Aw Shucks Hush Your Mouth/Baby What You Want Me to Do?/Baby's So Sweet/Blue Carnegie/Boogie in the Dark/Bright Lights, Big City/Caress Me Baby/Close Together/Crazy About Oklahoma/Down the Road/Ends and Odds/Fifteen Years/Found Love/Found My Baby Gone/Go on to School/Going by the River/Going Fishing/Going to New York/Good Lover/Got Nowhere to Go/Got to Be a Reason/Heartaches and Trouble/Help Yourself/High and Lonesome/Honest I Do/Hush Hush/I Ain't from Chicago/I Ain't Got You/I Got to Keep Rolling/I Know It's a Sin/I Love You Baby/I Wanna Be Loved/I Was So Wrong/I'm Leaving/I'm Mr Luck/I'm Nervous/I'm Trying to Please You/Just a Poor Country Boy/Kansas City Baby/Keep the Faith/Kind of Lonesome/Knocking on Your Door/Laughing at the Blues/Left Handed Woman/Mary Mary/Meet Me/The Moon Is Rising/My Baby Told Me/My Bitter Seed/New Chicago Blues/Oh John/Peepin' and Hidin'/Shame Shame Shame/Take It Slow/Take Out Some Insurance/Tell Me What You Want Me to Do/Tell The World I Do/Tribute to a Friend/Turn Me On Like a TV/Up Side the Wall/Up Tight/Wake Me Up in the Morning/Wake Up at Daybreak/Wear Something Green/When I Woke Up This Morning/Where Can You Be?/Yes Yes Yes/You Don't Have to Go/You Got Me Crying/You Got Me Dizzy/You Got Me Running/You Know You're Looking Good/You're My Baby/You're Something Else

Infl by: Elmore James/Muddy Waters/Eddie Taylor/Sonny Boy Williamson (Alex Miller)

Infl to: Lonnie Brooks/Juke Boy Bonner/George Buford/Frank Frost/Arthur Gunter/Blind Joe Hill/Silas Hogan/Lazy Lester/Little Mack/Louisiana Red/Johnny Mars/Brewer Phillips/Jimmy Reeves Jr/Slim Harpo/Jo Jo Williams

Quotes: "Mathis James Reed sang, played and composed an enormously influential style of blues based on simplicity and a warm, relaxed sort of charm"—Jim O'Neal, *Living Blues* magazine, Sept 1976, p 5

"Jimmy Reed is a stunningly individual blues performer"—Pete Welding, VJ album 1035

"Jimmy was easily the last and the most successful of the 50s Chicago bluesmen"—Mike Rowe, *Blues Unlimited* magazine (UK), Sept 1976, p 16

References: *Living Blues* magazine, May 1975, pp 16-41

Blues Unlimited magazine (UK), Aug 1974, pp 5-8

Guitar Player magazine, Dec 1976

REED, NORA
(see Hall, Vera)

RICHARDSON, CLARENCE CLIFFORD *"CC"/ "Peg"*

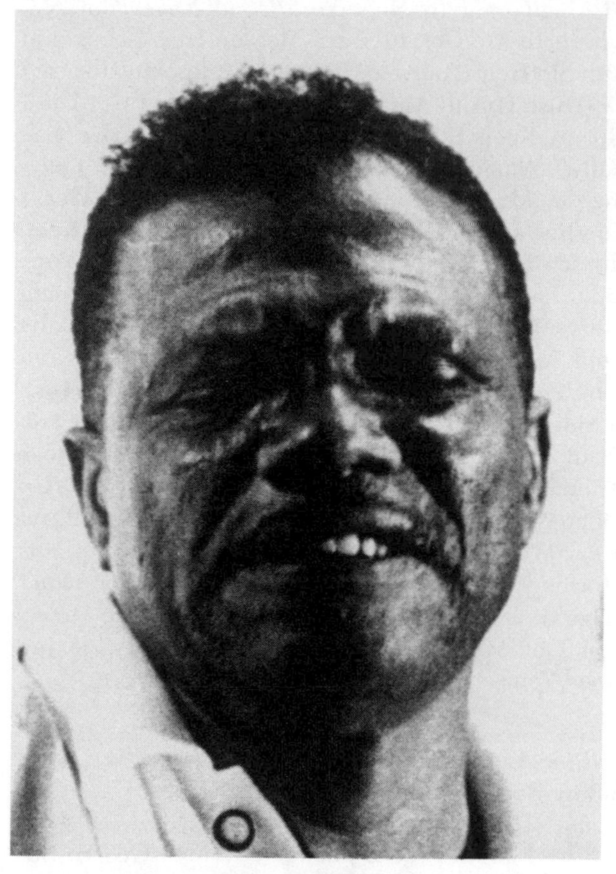

Photo by Amy O'Neal. Courtesy Living Blues Magazine

Born: Dec 18, 1918, Sumter (Sumter Co), SC
Died: Jan 30, 1984, Charleston, WV
Inst: Guitar

Mother was Essa Richardson; lost part of foot in train accident as child; sang in gospel quartet in Brown Chapel Church, Sumter, SC, as youth; left home to tour w Silas Green from New Orleans minstrel tent show working as singer/dancer through South through 30s; toured w Blake's Carnival through South, early 40s; frequently toured w Benny Carter Band/Jay McShann Band/Nat Cole group working clubs/dances across US through 40s into 50s; worked Al Hammer Club, Charleston, WV, 1949-51; settled in Charleston, WV, to work mostly outside music, 1962 into 70s; rec Duo label, Nashville, TN, c1969; rec on own Richardson label, Charleston (?), c1971; worked John Henry Memorial Concert, Beckley, WV, 1973; app on TALENT HUNCH Show, WOWK-TV, Huntington, WV, 1973; rec Bluejay label, Huntington, 1973; worked John Henry Memorial Concert, Cliff Top, WV, 1974; John Henry Folk Festival, Camp Virgil Tate, Princeton, WV, 1976-7; worked mostly outside music into 80s; died of heart disease; buried Spring Hill Cemetery, Charleston

Infl by: Blind Boy Fuller

Reference: Whiskey, Women, And . . . magazine, Feb 1973, pp 4-6

RIDGLEY, TOMMY

Courtesy Living Blues Magazine

Born: Oct 30, 1925, New Orleans (Orleans Par), LA
Inst: Piano

Father was Emanuel Ridgley; mother Rebecca Wilson; was playing piano w local Dixieland groups, New Orleans, LA, late 40s; worked w Earl Anderson's Band, Starlight Club, New Orleans, 1949; rec Imperial label, New Orleans, 1949; rec Decca label, NYC, NY, 1951; rec Atlantic label, New Orleans, 1953-4; frequently worked residency w own The Untouchables, The Municipal Auditorium, New Orleans, 1957-65; rec Herald label, New Orleans, 1957; toured college circuit working concerts through Mississippi/ Louisiana, late 50s; worked Pimloco Club, New Orleans, 1959; rec Ric label, New Orleans, 1960-1; frequently worked w own The Untouchables in local club dates, New Orleans area, early 70s; worked w Irma Thomas, Marriott Hotel, New Orleans, 1973;

New Orleans Jazz & Heritage Festival, New Orleans, 1973-7; St Bernard Civic Auditorium, New Orleans, 1973; active in record production in New Orleans from 1973; worked 38 Colt Club, New Orleans, 1976; worked The Steamboat *Natchez* out of New Orleans, 1976; residency at Aristocrat Club, New Orleans, 1977

Personal: Married. 2 children

Songs: Baby Do Liddle/Double Eye Whammy/The Girl Across the Street/The Girl from Kooka Monga/In the Same Old Way/Let's Try and Talk It Over/Shewsberry Blues/Tra La La/When I Meet My Girl

Infl by: Roy Brown

Infl to: Willie Tee

RITZ, SALLY
(see Henderson, Rosa)

ROBERT JR
(see Lockwood, Robert Jr)

ROBERTS, HELEN
(see Hunter, Alberta)

ROBERTS, SALLY
(see Martin, Sara)

ROBERTS, SNITCHER
(see Johnson, James "Stump")

ROBINSON, FENTION/FENTON
(*aka*: Fention)
Born: Sept 23, 1935, Greenwood (Leflore Co), MS
Inst: Guitar

Born/raised/worked on cotton/corn plantation from childhood; moved to Memphis, TN, 1953; learned guitar and frequently worked w Bobby Bland/Roscoe Gordon in local jukes in area from 1956; rec w Dukes, Meteor label, Memphis, 1957; worked w Billy Gayles group in local clubs, St Louis, MO/Los Angeles, CA, 1957; rec Duke label, Houston, TX, 1958-9; worked w Larry Davis in local clubs, Little Rock, AR, area c1959; formed own group to work local club dates, Little Rock area, into 60s; moved to Chicago, IL, 1961; frequently worked w Jr Wells/Otis Rush/Prince James Jazz Combo/Sonny Boy Williamson (Alex Miller)/others in local club dates into 60s; worked Theresa's Lounge, Chicago, 1964; worked w own band at Pepper's Lounge, Chicago, 1964-71; rec Giant label,

Photo by Mike Joyce

Chicago, 1965; rec USA label, Chicago, 1966; rec Palos/Giant labels, Chicago, 1967; rec Giant label, Chicago, 1969; rec Sound Stage label, Chicago, c1970; worked Tom's Lounge, Chicago, 1970; Sportsman's Lounge, Chicago, 1970, Full Note, Chicago, 1970; rec 77 label, Nashville, TN/Memphis, TN, 1971; worked Alice's Revisited, Chicago, 1971; toured w Charlie Musselwhite Band working club dates in San Francisco, CA, area, 1971; worked w Charlie Musselwhite Band, Gassy Jack's Place, Vancouver, Can, 1972; Checkerboard Lounge, Chicago, 1972; Silver Moon, Chicago, 1972; frequently worked club dates in Memphis, 1973; app on ATOMIC MAMA'S WANG DANG DOODLE BLUES, WNIB-FM-radio, Chicago, c1973; rec Alligator label, Chicago, 1974; worked Ma Bea's Lounge, Chicago, 1974; 1815 Club, Chicago, 1974; Florence's, Chicago, 1974; Hill's Fox Hole, Chicago, 1975; served sentence for involuntary manslaughter (in 1969 auto accident), Joliet Penitentiary, Joliet, IL, 1975; worked Midwest Blues Festival, Univ of Notre Dame, South Bend, IN, 1975-6; Wise Fools Pub, Chicago, 1975; Big Duke's Blue Flame Lounge, Chicago, 1976; New 1815 Club, Chicago, 1976 (por shown in THE DEVIL'S MUSIC—A HISTORY OF THE BLUES [ep: Sticking with the Blues], BBC-1-TV, England); Pepper's Lounge, Chicago, 1976; The Bayou, Washington, DC, 1976; Northern Illinois Univ, DeKalb, IL, 1977; Iowa State Univ, Ames, IA, 1977; Grand Valley State Col, Allendale, MI, 1977; Intersection Club, Grand Rapids, MI, 1977; Golden Slipper, Chicago, 1977; rec Alligator label, Chicago, 1977

Songs: Checking on My Woman/The Getaway/Give You Some Air/Gotta Wake Up/I Hear Some Blues Downstairs/I've Changed/Little Turch/Somebody Loan Me a Dime/Texas Flood/You Know What Love Is

Infl by: Buddy Guy/BB King/Charles McGowan/Jr Wells/Aaron "T-Bone" Walker

Quote: "One of the finest, most creative artists in modern blues . . . an unusually gifted and introspective man whose progressive musical ideas and continual reshapings of the blues form set him apart from his contemporaries"—Jim O'Neal, Alligator album 4705

Reference: Crazy Music magazine (Australia), Sept 1974, pp 9-14

ROBINSON, JAMES *"Bat"*
(aka: Bat the Humming-Bird)
Born: Dec 25, 1903, Algiers (Orleans Parish), LA
Died: Mar 2, 1957, St Louis, MO
Inst: Drums/Piano

Father was John Richard, a pianist; mother was Bessie Robinson; moved to Memphis, TN, where he was raised from childhood; learned piano and drums from father as youth; moved to Chicago, IL, c1922; frequently worked w Bertha "Chippie" Hill/Eppie Moan/Elzadie Robinson/others in local club dates, Chicago, from c1922; worked w Louis Armstrong, Sunset Cafe, Chicago, c1927; moved to St Louis, MO, c1930; frequently worked outside music, St Louis, with occasional touring with various medicine shows, early 30s into 50s; rec Champion label, Richmond, IN, 1931; occasionally worked w Jimmy Crutchfield in local club dates, St Louis, 1955; frequently worked (as drummer) in Dollar Bill group in local club dates, St Louis, c1957; rec Tone label, St Louis, 1957; entered St Louis City Hospital where he died of tuberculosis; buried Oakdale Cemetery, Lemay, MO

Personal: "Bat the Humming-Bird" refers to his style of singing. Not to be confused with Cow Cow Davenport who also used pseudonym "Bat the Hummingbird"

Quote: "He had a little trick of singing that set him apart, a falsetto 'throat whistle' which his friends called 'humming' "—Paul Oliver, Riverside album 8809

ROBINSON, JIMMY LEE
(aka: Jimmy Lee/Lonesome Lee)
Born: Apr 30, 1931, Chicago (Cook Co), IL
Inst: Bass/Drums/Guitar

Courtesy Bandera Records /Living Blues *Magazine*

Born/raised in Chicago, IL; learned some guitar basics from Blind Percy and frequently worked as team on Maxwell Street/churches, Chicago, 1944-9; frequently worked outside music, Chicago, through 40s; worked Vi's Lounge, Chicago, c1949; w Eddie Taylor, Jake's Tavern, Chicago, 1949; Club Alibi, Chicago, 1949; frequently worked w Eddie Taylor on Maxwell Street for tips, Chicago, 1949-50; briefly attended Chicago School of Music, Chicago, c1949-50; served sentence in Cook County Jail, Chicago, 1950-2; formed Every Hour Blues Boys (w Freddie King) working Cadillac Baby's Club and others, Chicago, 1952-3; worked w Sonny Cooper Band in local club dates, Chicago, 1953; rec w Sonny Cooper Band, Parrot label, Chicago, 1953; frequently worked w Elmore James group in local clubs, Chicago, mid-50s; toured frequently w Little Walter's Band working clubs across US, 1955-8; rec Bandera label, Chicago, 1959-60; frequently worked w Magic Sam/Jimmy Reed/Willie Mabon/others in local clubs, Chicago, from 1959 into early 60s; rec as sideman w Shakey Jake, Bluesville label, NYC, NY, 1960; rec w St Louis Jimmy, Bluesville label, NYC, 1960; worked w Detroit Jr Band in local clubs, Chicago, c1961; rec Bandera label, Chicago, 1962; rec as sideman w Willie Mabon, Formal label, Chicago, 1962; worked w Willie

Mabon, Mr Lee's Lounge, Chicago, 1963; w Sunnyland Slim, Rock's Tavern, Rockford, IL, 1964; toured w American Folk Blues Festival working concert dates through England/Europe, 1965 (por Hamburg, Ger, concert rel Fontana label); worked mostly outside music, Chicago, from c1965 into 70s; worked Rat Trap Inn, Chicago, 1974; toured w American Blues Legends '75 working concert dates through England/Europe, 1975; worked 100 Club, London, Eng, 1975 (por rel Big Bear label); toured w Rhythm & Blues: Roots of Rock Show working concert dates through Europe, 1975

Personal: Reportedly changed to Muslim name Latif Aliomar (c1966)

Infl to: Eddie Taylor

Reference: Blues Unlimited magazine (UK), Oct 1965, pp 11-13

ROBINSON, LOUIS CHARLES *"L C"/"Good Rockin"*

Courtesy Living Blues *Magazine*

Born: May 15, 1915, Brenham (Washington Co), TX
Died: Sept 26, 1976, Berkeley, CA
Inst: Guitar/Harmonica/Violin

Father was AC Robinson, a harmonica player; mother was Mary Jane Washington; born/raised on farm and began playing guitar at 9 years; teamed w brother AC Robinson to work local dances/parties in Brenham, TX, area, late 20s into 30s; toured w West Coast Carnival and Seven Black Aces working shows/dances through Texas from 1934; app w Three Hot Brown Boys, KTEM-radio, Temple, TX, c1934-7; frequently worked for tips at local dances/streets, Temple, TX, area, late 30s; worked outside music in Abilene, TX, c1939; together w brother AC Robinson moved to West Coast to work outside music with frequent gigs in San Francisco, CA, area from 1940; formed Three Hot Brown Boys (later changing name to Combo Boys) working local Army/Navy bases, San Francisco area, early 40s; worked w Johnny Otis Band, The Barrelhouse, Los Angeles, CA, 1944; rec w AC Robinson (as "The Robinson Brothers"), B&W label, Los Angeles, 1945; frequently worked Moonlight Club/The Boat House/The House of Joy/Fillmore Auditorium/Louisiana Club, San Francisco area, late 40s; worked Crystal Grill, Oakland, CA/The Savoy Club, Richmond, CA/126 Club, Vallejo, CA, and other clubs/auditoriums/theaters on West Coast, late 40s into 50s; settled in Oakland, CA, to work mostly outside music, early 50s into 70s; rec w AC Robinson, Rhythm label, Oakland, 1954; worked Slim Jenkins' Club, Oakland, 1956; frequently worked w own California Blues Band (or as single), Savoy Club, North Richmond, CA, late 50s into 60s; rec acc to Mercy Dee, Arhoolie label, Stockton, CA, 1961; frequently worked Ruthie's Inn, Berkeley, CA, 1966-9; rec Liberty label, San Francisco, 1968; rec World Pacific label, Berkeley, 1968; worked Berkeley Blues Festival, Berkeley, CA, 1970; Ruthie's Inn, Oakland, CA, 1970-1 (por 1970 date shown on PBS-TV); Dumbarton Club, East Palo Alto, CA, 1970; Keystone Korner, Berkeley, CA, 1971; rec w Muddy Waters Blues Band, Arhoolie label, San Francisco, 1971; worked w John Lee Hooker, Kabuki Theater, San Francisco, 1971 (por rel BluesWay label); Ruthie's Inn, Richmond, CA, 1971; Community Theater, Aquatic Park, Berkeley, CA, 1972; Bluebird Cafe, Santa Barbara, CA, 1973-4; Univ of California Extension Center, San Francisco, 1973; Continental Club, Oakland, CA, 1973; San Francisco Bay Blues Festival, San Francisco, 1973-4; Community Music Center, San Francisco, 1973; Stardust Lounge, San Francisco, 1974; rec BluesWay label, San Francisco, 1974; worked Ruthie's Inn, Berkeley, CA, 1974; app on (unknown) show, KGED-TV, San Francisco, 1974; worked Club La Jolla, San Francisco, 1974; Club Shalimar, Berkeley, CA, 1974-5; Berkeley Blues Festival, Berkeley, CA, 1975; Minnie's Can-Do Club, San Francisco, 1975; Brentwood Lounge, San Francisco, 1975; My Club, Oakland, CA, 1975; St Francis Parish Hall, East Palo Alto, CA, 1975; Butch's Club, La Honda, CA, 1975; Scandinavian Blues Association Concert, Orebro, Sweden, 1975; Cat's Cradle, San

Francisco, 1975; West Dakota Club, Berkeley, CA, 1975; rec Mr Blues label, San Francisco (?), 1975; worked The Savoy Club, San Francisco, 1975-6; The Bunk House, San Francisco, 1976; app w brother Deacon AC Robinson on TRADITIONAL MUSIC COLLECTIVE CONCERT, KPFA-FM-radio, Berkeley, CA, 1976; app on BLUES BY THE BAY, KPFA-FM-radio, Berkeley, CA, 1976; worked Green Earth Cafe, San Francisco, 1976; Eli's Mile High Club, San Francisco, CA, 1976; Festival of American Folklife, Washington, DC, 1976; American River College, Sacramento, CA, 1976; Slat's, San Francisco, 1976; suffered heart attack at home, DOA at Herrick Memorial Hospital; buried Cypress Lawn Memorial Park, Colma, CA

Personal: Married Peggy ——— (divorced). 1 child. His brother Arthur C "AC" Robinson was also musician. Reportedly was brother-in-law of Blind Willie Johnson, religious street singer

Songs: Across the Bay Blues/Hobo's Meditation/House Cleanin' Blues/I've Got to Go/Mojo in My Hand/Rockin' with Peggy/Separation Blues/She Got It from the Start/Southern Bound/Standin' in Line/Stop and Jump/Stop Now/Summerville Blues/Texas Blues/Trailing My Baby/Train Time/Ups and Downs

Infl by: Lightnin' Hopkins/Blind Lemon Jefferson/Blind Willie Johnson/Leon McAuliffe/Henry Rattler/Bob Wills

Infl to: Sugarcane Harris

Quote: "LC 'Good Rockin' Robinson is one of the most dynamic artists to have emerged from the San Francisco/Oakland blues scene"—Tom Mazzolini, *Living Blues* magazine, Jul 1975, p 17

Reference: Living Blues magazine, Jul 1975, pp 16-21

ROCKIN' RED
(see Minter, Iverson)

ROCKIN' SYDNEY
(see Semien, Sidney)

RODGERS, JAMES CHARLES *"Jimmie"*
Born: Sept 8, 1897, Pine Springs (Lauderdale Co), MS
Died: May 26, 1933, New York, NY
Inst: Banjo/Guitar

Courtesy Frank Driggs Collection

Father was Aaron Rodgers, a railroad foreman; mother was Eliza Bozeman; one of 3 children; moved to Scooba, MS, then Meridian, MS, as child; raised in and around railroad yards learning songs/instruments from workers as youth; won amateur contest in local theater, Meridian, 1911, then toured briefly with a passing medicine show; worked outside music (as section hand on Mobile & Ohio Railroad), 1911-12; continued working outside music (on various railroad jobs) through Mississippi/Louisiana/Texas, 1913-23; toured briefly w Billy Terrell's Comedians, 1923; frequently entertained for friends/social groups/gatherings in Meridian through 20s; continued outside music work, 1924-7; retired from railroad work (due to illness) and settled in Asheville, NC, to work outside music with frequent work at local parties/dances in area from 1927; app on WWNC-radio, Asheville, 1927; formed Jimmie Rodgers Entertainers working Kiwanis Carnival, Johnson City, TN, 1927; rec Victor label, Bristol, TN/Camden, NJ, 1927; worked occasional theater/club dates, Washington, DC, 1927-8; app on MONDAY NIGHT FEATURE, WTFF-radio, Washington, DC, 1928; toured Loew's vaudeville circuit working theaters through South/Southeast, 1928; rec Victor label, Camden, NJ/Atlanta, GA, 1928; toured w Paul English Players working theater dates, 1929; rec Victor label, NYC, NY/New Orleans, LA/Dallas, TX/Atlanta, GA, 1929; app in film short THE SINGING BRAKEMAN, 1929; worked Majestic Theater, San Antonio, TX, 1929; toured Keith-Orpheum-Interstate circuit working theater dates through South, 1929; settled in Kerrville, TX, 1929; toured w Swain's Hollywood Follies working theaters through South, 1930; rec Victor label, Hollywood, CA, 1930; settled in San Antonio, TX, 1930; toured w Will Rogers working charity shows through Texas/Oklahoma, 1931; worked Leslie E Kell Shows, Houston/San Antonio, TX, 1931; rec Victor label, San Antonio, TX/Dallas, TX/ Louisville, KY, 1931-2; worked w Robert Nighthawk in Jackson, MS, 1931; app on own show, KMAC-radio, San Antonio, 1932; brief tour w J Doug Morgan Show, 1932; rec Victor label, NYC, 1933; died of pulmonary TB; buried Oak Grove Cemetery, Meridian, MS

Personal: Married Stella Kelly (1917-19); 1 child. Carrie Cecil Williamson (1920-33). 2 children

Billings: America's Blue Yodeler/The Singing Brakeman

Books: My Husband, Jimmie Rodgers, Mrs Jimmie Rodgers, San Antonio Southern Literary Institute, 1935

Blue Yodel, Peer International, 1943

Supreme Edition, Peer-Southern, 1943

Jimmie the Kid, Mike Paris/Chris Comber, Eddison Music Books, 1977

The Recordings of Jimmie Rodgers, Johnny Bond, The John Edwards Memorial Foundation, Inc, Univ of California, Los Angeles, CA, 1978

Jimmie Rodgers: The Life & Times of America's Blue Yodeler, Nolan Porterfield, U of IL, 1979

Songs: Anniversary Blue Yodel/Any Old Time/Blue Yodel (12 versions)/Brakeman's Blues/Daddy and Home/Desert Blues/Home Call/I'm Lonesome Too/In the Jailhouse Now/Lullaby Yodel/Mississippi Moon/My Old Pal/Never No Mo' Blues/T for Texas/The TB Blues/Waiting for a Train/Way Out on the Mountain/Why Should I Be Lonely?/Yodeling Cowboy/You and My Old Guitar

Awards/Honors: A statue was erected in Meridian, MS, 1953

Elected one of first members of Country Music Hall of Fame, Nashville, TN, Nov 3, 1961

Won American Music Conference National Music Award, 1976

A US commemorative postage stamp was issued in his honor, 1978

Infl by: Blind Lemon Jefferson

Infl to: John Arnold/Frank Floyd/Merle Haggard/John Hurt/Kenneth Threadgill/Ernest Tubb

Quotes: "Although generally neglected by historians of the blues, his adherence to the twelve-bar, three-phrase form helped promote and sustain this as the most common blues vehicle and made country music say, 'Blues, How Do You Do?' "—(John P Morgan) Melvin Shestack, *Country Music Encyclopedia*, Thomas Y Crowell Company, 1974

"The accuracy and authenticity of his blues singing stand as an instructive early memorial—on records—to the interaction of white and black that has so profoundly enriched western music in the cities and the heartlands of America"—Henry Pleasants, *The Great American Popular Singers*, Simon & Schuster, 1974

"Rodgers' efforts crystalized the white blues form and insured its future in country music"—Tony Russell, *Blacks, Whites and Blues*, Studio Vista Ltd, 1970

References: My Husband Jimmie Rodgers, Mrs Jimmie Rodgers, San Antonio Southern Literary Institute, 1935

The Great American Popular Singers, Henry Pleasants, Simon & Schuster, 1974

Jimmie the Kid, Mike Paris/Chris Comber, Eddison Music Books, 1977

ROGERS, JAMES *"Jimmy"*

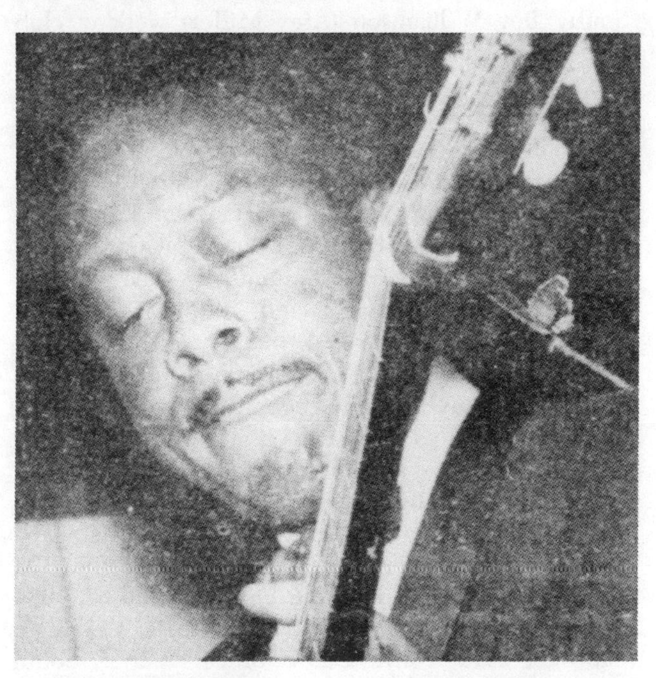

Courtesy Living Blues *Magazine*

Born: Jun 3, 1924, Ruleville (Sunflower Co), MS
Inst: Guitar/Harmonica/Piano

Father was Roscoe Lane; mother Grozie Jackson; born James A Lane, assuming stepfather's surname Rogers as child; raised in Atlanta, GA 1926-34; taught self harmonica at 8 years of age; attended school w Snooky Pryor, Vance, MS, mid-30s; frequently moved to West Memphis, AR/Memphis, TN/elsewhere from 1934; taught self guitar on home-made instrument c1935; worked w Little Arthur Johnson in local house parties, Minter City, MS, area, late 30s into 40s; frequently worked Nat Love's Club, East St Louis, IL, c1938-41; frequently worked streets, Chicago, IL, from 1939; moved to Chicago to frequently work outside music with occasional work on Maxwell Street for tips from 1941; frequently worked Tom's Tavern/Purple Cat and other clubs/bars/parties, Chicago, through 1940s; worked w Claude "Blue Smitty" Smith Band in local clubs, Chicago, mid-40s; w Sunnyland Slim, 21 Club, Chicago, 1946; w Daddy Stovepipe, 708 Club, Chicago, c1946; worked as sideman w Muddy Waters Band, Boogie Woogie Inn/708 Club/Ebony Lounge/Club Zanzibar/Du Drop Inn/Romeo's Place/others, Chicago, from 1948 with frequent tours/club/concert work to 1955; rec extensively as session man on local record dates, Chicago, late 40s into 50s; rec under own name, Ora-Nelle label, Chicago, c1947; app w Muddy Waters, KATZ CLOTHING STORE Show, KFFA-radio, Helena, AR, 1949; rec Regal label, Chicago, 1949; rec w own Rocking Four, Chess label, Chicago, 1950-9; toured w Sonny Boy Williamson (Alex Miller) working club dates through South, early 50s; worked w Howlin' Wolf in West Memphis, AR, early 50s; worked w Sunnyland Slim in St Louis, MO, early 50s; formed own band to work local club dates, Chicago, from 1955; worked 708 Club, Chicago, 1958; toured w own Headhunters group working club dates on East Coast, late 50s; worked w Mighty Joe Young at Castle Rock Lounge, Chicago, 1959; frequently worked w Howlin' Wolf Band, Sylvio's and other local clubs, Chicago, 1959-61; worked mostly outside music, Chicago, 1959-69; worked w Sonny Boy Williamson (Alex Miller), Sylvio's, Chicago, 1963; w John Littlejohn/Bob Riedy, Florence's Lounge, Chicago, 1970; frequently worked Alice's Revisited, Chicago, 1970-3; toured w John Littlejohn working club dates in Philadelphia, PA/Cleveland, OH/Memphis, TN/elsewhere, 1970; worked Liberty Hall, Houston, TX, 1971; w John Littlejohn, Big Duke's Club, Chicago, 1971; w Bob Riedy's Blues Band, Ma Bea's Lounge, Chicago, 1971; Notre Dame Blues Festival, South Bend, IN, 1971; Ash Grove, Los Angeles, CA, 1971; rec Shelter label, Los Angeles, 1972; toured w American Folk Blues Festival working concert dates through England/Europe, 1972; worked w Bob Riedy's Blues Band, 1815 Club, Chicago, 1972; The Post, Chicago, 1972; Wise Fools, Chicago, 1972; rec w Bob Riedy's Blues Band, Rounder label, Chicago, 1973; toured w Chicago Blues Festival working concert dates through Europe, 1973; rec Black & Blue label, Toulouse, France, 1973; worked Topanga Corral, Los Angeles, CA, 1974; Milwaukee Summerfest, Milwaukee, WI, 1975; worked mostly outside music (as manager of apartment buildings), Chicago, from 1975; worked club dates, Austin, TX, and northeast US through 1977; worked The Speakeasy Club, Cambridge, MA, 1977; rec w Muddy Waters, Blue Sky label, Westport, CT, 1977

Personal: Married. Has children

Songs: Act Like You Love Me/Back Door Friend/Blues Leave Me Alone/Broken Hearted Blues/Brown Skinned Woman/Chicago Bound/Goin' Away Baby/Gold Tailed Bird/House Rocker/I Lost the Good Woman/I Used to Have a Woman/Last Time/Live at Ma Bea's/Lonesome Blues/Ludella/Money Marbles and Chalk/Out on the Road/Shelby County/Sloppy Drunk/That's All Right/Tricky Woman/Walking by Myself/You Are So Sweet/You're the One

Infl by: Bill Broonzy/Robert Jr Lockwood/Houston Stackhouse

Infl to: Freddy King/Magic Sam

Quotes: "Jimmy Rogers, the superb guitarist and singer . . . brightened all Muddy Waters' great early sessions"—Alex Cramer, *Coda* magazine (Canada), Jul 1974, p 6

"His superb voice is friendly and warm, possessing a very personally revealing quality . . ."—Keith Tillman, Python album PLP-KM6

References: *Coda* magazine (Canada), Jul 1974, pp 6-8
Living Blues, Autumn 1973, pp 11-20

ROSS, CHARLES ISAIAH *"Doc"*

Born: Oct 21, 1925, Tunica (Tunica Co), MS
Died: May 28, 1993, Flint, MI
Inst: Drums/Guitar/Harmonica/Kazoo

Grandparents were Indians; father was Jake Ross, a farmer who played harmonica; born/raised on farm; one of 11 children; interested in music early and learned harmonica at 6 years of age; occasionally

Photo by Bill Greensmith. Courtesy Living Blues Magazine

worked local churches/parties in Tunica, MS, area, from 1934; worked w George P Jackson at local roadhouses/jukes, Tunica, 1936; teamed w Willie Love to tour w Barber Parker Silver Kings Band working dances through Mississippi, late 30s; worked w Wiley Galatin (or solo) at local house parties, Tunica area, 1942-3; served in US Army in Philippines/Pacific Theater of Operations frequently entertaining troops, 1943-7; returned to Tunica to work outside music (on farm) from 1947; app on WROX-radio, Clarksdale, MS, 1947; frequently worked local dances/parties/picnics in Tunica area through 40s; app w own Doc Ross & His Jump and Jive Boys on KATZ CLOTHING STORE Show, KFFA-radio, Helena, AR, 1949; worked Owl Cafe, Helena, 1949; Hole-In-The-Wall, Helena, 1950; Isidore's Bar, Helena, 1950; Roger's Club, Helena, 1950; app w Sonny Boy Williamson (Alex Miller) on KING BISCUIT TIME, KFFA-radio, Helena, 1950; app w own Doc Ross & His Jump and Jive Boys, WDIA-radio, Memphis, TN, 1950; served again in US Army, 1950-1; rec w Doc Ross & His Jump and Jive Boys, Chess label, Memphis, 1951; rec Sun label, Memphis, 1951-4; toured w King Biscuit Boys working jukes through Arkansas/Missouri, early 50s; app on KLCN-radio, Blytheville, AR, 1953; worked outside music, Champaign, IL, 1953; app on DOC ROSS Show, WDIA-radio, Memphis, 1953-4; formed Dr Ross and the Interns group working local club dates, Memphis, 1953-4; moved to Flint, MI, to work outside music, 1954 into 90s; often worked as one-man band in Flint, MI/Detroit, MI/Chicago, IL, from 1954 into 70s; rec own DIR label, Flint, 1958; rec Fortune label, Detroit, 1959; rec Hi-Q label, Detroit, 1961-3; rec Testament label, Flint, 1965; worked Univ of Illinois, Urbana, IL, 1965; toured w American Folk Blues Festival working concert dates through England/Europe, 1965 (por Hamburg, Ger, concert rel Fontana label); rec Blue Horizon/Xtra labels, London, Eng; 1965; worked Univ of Detroit, Detroit, 1965; rec Xtra label, Flint, 1966; worked Ann Arbor Blues Festival, Ann Arbor, MI, 1970; Holiday Inn Bar, Saginaw, MI, 1971; Mariposa Folk Festival, Toronto, Can, 1971; rec w The Disciples, Fortune label, Detroit, 1971; toured England/Europe working concert dates/radio/TV shows, 1972; rec Big Bear-Munich label, London, Eng, 1972; rec Esceha label, Koblenz, W Ger, 1972; worked Montreux Jazz Festival, Montreux, Switzerland, 1972 (por rel Big Bear-Polydor/Excello labels); Ann Arbor Blues Festival, Ann Arbor, 1973; toured w American Blues Legends working concert dates through England/Europe, 1974 (por rel Big Bear label); app on IN CONCERT Show, Radio-4, London, Eng, 1974; worked BJ's Buffeteria, Bay City, MI, 1977; toured Europe working concert dates, 1977

Personal: Married (1952-3); married (1954-). 2 children. Name "Doc" is reference to some medical knowledge he obtained while in service

Billing: Flying Eagle (due to his on-stage stance and gestures)

Songs: Bad Whiskey Bad Women/Boogie Disease/Chicago Breakdown/Come Back Baby/Country Clown/Do the Boogie Woogie/Doctor Ross Rockin'/Don't Worry 'bout the Bear/Dr Ross Breakdown/Freight Train/General Motors Blues/Going Away Baby/Going Back South/Going to the River/Good Thing Blues/Good Things Come to My Mind/Harmonica Boogie/How Much More Long/I Am Not Dead/I Got Something to Tell You/I Want All My Friends to Know/I'd Rather Be an Old Woman's Baby Than a Young Woman's Slave/Industrial Blues/It Seem Like a Dream/Juke Box Boogie/Let's Boogie All Night Long/Little Soldier Boy/Memphis Boogie/Miss Elvira/Miss Ledora Blues/Mississippi Blues (Cat Squirrel)/Mother Before This Time Another Year/My Airplane Chick/My Be Bop Gal/On My Way to

School/Rockin' After Midnight/San Francisco Breakdown/Shake-A My Hand/Stop Crying/Sugar Gal/Sweet Black Angel/Train Fare Home/Turkey Leg Woman

Infl by: DeFord Bailey/Arthur Crudup/Lonnie Glossen/George Jackson/Muddy Waters/John Lee "Sonny Boy" Williamson

Quotes: "There can be little doubt that Dr Ross is one of the most individual and expressive blues singers and players around today [1965]"—Peter J Welding, Testament album 2206

"[Ross] has the artistic ability and lifetime experience to create significant blues"—Doug Langille, *Coda* magazine (Canada), Aug 1975, p 22

Reference: Blues Unlimited magazine (UK), Dec 1972, pp 4-6

RUSH, OTIS
(*aka*: Little Otis)

Courtesy Sheldon Harris Collection

Born: Apr 29, 1934, Philadelphia (Neshoba Co), MS
Inst: Drums/Guitar/Harmonica/Jew's Harp

Father was OC Rush, mother was Julia Boyd, both farmers; one of 7 children; born/raised/worked farm from childhood; taught self guitar at 8 years of age; occasionally sang in local church choirs as youth; moved to Chicago, IL, 1948; worked outside music with occasional gigs in local clubs, Chicago, 1948 to mid-50s; worked (solo) Club Alibi, Chicago, 1953; formed own group (as "Little Otis") working local club dates, Chicago, 1955-60; worked Club Alibi, Chicago, 1955; frequently worked Jazzville Club, Chicago, from 1955; worked 708 Club, Chicago, 1956-8; rec Cobra/Blue Horizon labels, Chicago, 1956-8; toured Texas/Mississippi/Georgia/Florida working one-nighters, 1956-7; frequently app on BIG BILL HILL Show, WOPA-radio, Oak Park, IL, 1956-8; frequently worked as session man in local rec dates, Chicago, late 50s; worked Pepper's Lounge, Chicago, 1957-9; Blue Flame Club, Chicago, 1958; frequently worked Harmonium Lounge/Castle Rock Lounge/Alex Club/Mr Lee's/others, Chicago, late 50s into early 60s; rec Chess label, Chicago, 1960; worked F&J Lounge, Gary, IN, 1960; toured w Jimmy Reed group working one-nighters through South, early 60s; worked w Aaron "T-Bone" Walker, Regal Theater, Chicago, c1962; rec Duke label, Chicago, 1962; worked w Little Richard, City Opera House, Chicago, c1963; Twist City, Chicago, 1963; 633 Club, Chicago, 1964; Pepper's Lounge, Chicago, 1964; rec Vanguard label, Chicago, 1965; Club Alibi, Chicago, c1965; worked Big John's, Chicago, 1966; Curley's Bar, Chicago, 1966; toured w American Folk Blues Festival working concert dates through England/Europe, 1966 (por Berlin, Ger, concert rel Fontana/Amiga labels); worked Smoot's, Chicago, 1966; Mother Blues, Chicago, 1966-7; Club 47, Cambridge, MA, 1967; rec Cotillion label, Muscle Shoals, AL, 1968; worked The L&A Lounge, Chicago, 1968; Univ of Wisconsin Blues Festival, Madison, WI, 1969; The I Spy Club, Chicago, 1969; Don's Cedar Club, Chicago, 1969-70; Ann Arbor Blues Festival, Ann Arbor, MI, 1969-70; 1815 Club, Chicago, 1970; Apollo Theater, NYC, c1970; Alex Club, Chicago, 1970; Tom's Musicians Lounge, Chicago, 1970; Texas Lady, Chicago, 1970; Alice's Revisited, Chicago, 1970-2; Notre Dame Blues Festival, South Bend, IN, 1970-1; frequently worked Wise Fools Pub, Chicago, 1971-6; toured one-nighter club dates through Iowa, 1971; worked Fillmore West, San Francisco, CA, c1971; rec Capitol-Bullfrog label, San Francisco, 1971; rec acc to Jimmy Dawkins, Delmark label,

Chicago, 1971; worked Ann Arbor Blues Festival, Ann Arbor, MI, 1972-3 (por 1972 concert rel Atlantic label); Harvard Univ, Cambridge, MA, 1972; Amazingrace, Evanston, IL, 1972; Philadelphia Folk Festival, Schwenksville, Pa, 1972; Joe's Place, Cambridge, MA, 1972-3; Joint Bar, Minneapolis, MN, 1974; Majestic M, Chicago, 1974-5; White Stallion, Chicago, 1974; Minstrel's, Chicago, 1974; Peanut Barrel, Chicago, 1974; Wise Fools, Chicago, 1974; toured w Jimmy Dawkins working concert dates through Europe, 1974 (some French concerts rel Black & Blue label); toured w Blues Festival working concert dates through Japan, 1974-5 (por of 1974-5 Tokyo concerts rel Trio label); worked Avenue Lounge, Chicago, 1975; rec Delmark label, Chicago, 1975; worked Washington Univ, St Louis, MO, 1975; Midwest Blues Festival, Univ of Notre Dame, South Bend, IN, 1975; Biddy Mulligan's, Chicago, 1976; Eddie Shaw's New 1815 Club, Chicago, 1976; Wise Fools Pub, Chicago, 1976-7; The Bayou, Washington, DC, 1976; Univ of Oregon, Eugene, OR, 1977; Coffee Gallery, San Francisco, 1977; app on BLUES BY THE BAY, KPFA-FM-radio, Berkeley, CA, 1977; toured West Coast working club dates, 1977; The Lighthouse, Hermosa Beach, CA, 1977; toured Europe working concert dates, 1977 (por Sweden concert rel Sonet label); worked Nancy Jazz Festival, Nancy, France, 1977; Village Gate, NYC, NY, 1978; app on JAZZ ALTERNATIVES, WKCR-FM-radio, NYC, 1978

Personal: Married second wife Kathy Guyton; 4 children. Blues musician Bobby Rush (Emmett Nelson) is not related

Songs: All Your Love/Double Trouble/Easy Go/It Takes Time/Keep On Loving Me Baby/My Love Will Never Die/Right Place Wrong Time/So Close/Take a Look Behind/Three Times a Fool

Awards/Honors: Won *Downbeat* magazine International Critics Awards for Rock-Pop-Blues group deserving wider recognition, 1975

Won *Downbeat* magazine International Critics Award for Soul-R&B artist deserving wider recognition, 1978

Infl by: Kenny Burrell/Albert King/BB King/Muddy Waters/Jimmy Smith/Aaron "T-Bone" Walker

Infl to: Luther Allison/Tyrone Davis/Jimmy Johnson

Quotes: "Otis Rush . . . has displayed profound vocal delivery [he adopts the trembling, flailing falsetto], fine lyrical composition, good melodic and rhythmic sense, and above all great musicianship"—Graham L Jackson, *Jazz Journal* magazine (UK), May 1974, p 8

"His singing is full of dramatic, pain-filled intensity which invites comparison with the work of the finest vocalists in blues history"—Pete Welding, Chess album LP-1538

Reference: Living Blues magazine, Jul 1976, pp 10-28

RUSHING, JAMES ANDREW *"Jimmy"*

Born: Aug 26, 1902, Oklahoma City (Oklahoma Co), OK

Died: Jun 8, 1972, New York, NY

Inst: Piano/Violin

Father Andrew Rushing and mother Cora Freeman were musicians; interested in music early and learned violin as child; studied musical theory at Douglass HS, Oklahoma City, OK, as youth; encouraged to play piano by uncle Wesley Manning, a sporting house singing pianist; frequently sang in local church choirs/school pageants/glee clubs/opera houses in Oklahoma City area as teenager; frequently left home to hobo through Midwest/Texas and up to Chicago, IL, during teens; attended Wilberforce Univ, Wilberforce, OH, early 20s; dropped out of school to move to West Coast working outside music, Los Angeles, CA, 1924-6; occasionally worked w Jelly Roll Morton at local private parties, Los Angeles, c1924-5; worked as singing pianist, Jump Steady Club, Los Angeles, c1924; Quality Night Club, Los Angeles, 1924-5; toured briefly w Walter Page in Billy King Road Show Revue, 1925; returned to Oklahoma City to work outside music (in father's cafe), 1926-7; toured w Walter Page's Blue Devils working dances through South/Southwest, 1928-9; worked w Walter Page's Blue Devils, Cinderella Dance Palace, Little Rock, AR, 1929; rec w Walter Page's Blue Devils, Vocalion label, Kansas City, MO, 1929; toured w Bennie Moten's Kansas City Orch working dances/club dates extensively across US, 1929-35; rec w Bennie Moten Kansas City Orch, Victor label, Chicago, 1930-1; worked w Bennie Moten's Kansas City Orch, Pearl Theater, Philadelphia, PA, 1931; app w Bennie Moten's Band, MUSIC AND LAUGHTER Revue, Lafayette Theater, NYC, 1931; app w Bennie Moten's Band, WHITMAN SISTERS Revue, Lafayette Theater, NYC, 1931; worked Champion Theater, Birmingham, AL, 1933; toured w Count Basie Orch/groups working dances/clubs/hotels/concerts extensively across US, 1935-50; worked w/Count Basie Orch, Reno Club, Kansas City, MO, 1935-6 (frequent remotes W9XBY-radio/WHB-radio); Grand Terrace Ballroom, Chicago, 1936; rec w Jones-Smith Inc (Count Basie

RUSHING

James "Jimmy" Rushing
Courtesy Frank Driggs Collection

Quintet), Vocalion label, Chicago, 1936; worked Roseland Ballroom, NYC, NY, 1936; rec w Benny Goodman Orch, Victor label, NYC, 1936; worked Chatterbox Room, William Penn Hotel, Pittsburgh, PA, 1936-7 (with frequent radio remotes); Ritz Carlton Hotel, Boston, MA, c1937; rec w Count Basie Orch, Decca label, NYC, 1937-9; worked Apollo Theater, NYC, 1937; Savoy Ballroom, NYC, 1937-8 (with frequent radio remotes); The Meadowbrook, Cedar Grove, NJ, 1937; The Famous Door, NYC, 1937-9; frequently w Count Basie Orch, Paramount Theater, NYC, from 1938 into 40s; w Count Basie Orch, Martin Block Carnival of Swing Show, Randalls Island, NYC, 1938; w Count Basie Orch, From Spirituals to Swing Concert, Carnegie Hall, NYC, 1938; Cafe Society, NYC, 1939; rec Columbia label, NYC/Chicago, 1939-42; rec Vocalion label, NYC/Chicago, 1939; rec OKeh label, NYC, 1940-2; worked Hotel Sherman, Chicago, 1940; Golden Gate Theater, San Francisco, CA, 1941; app w Count Basie Orch in film short BIG NAME BANDS NO 1, 1941; app w Count Basie Orch in soundie film AIR MAIL SPECIAL, 1941; app w Count Basie Orch in soundie film TAKE ME BACK BABY, 1941; app w Count Basie, PABST BLUE RIBBON SHOW, local radio, NYC, 1942; app w Count Basie Orch in film CRAZY HOUSE (Funzapoppin'), 1943; app in film TOP MAN, 1943; app w Count Basie Orch in film short CHOO CHOO SWING, 1943; app on COMMAND PERFORMANCE Show/JUBILEE USA Show, Armed Forces Radio Service (AFRS) (syndicated), 1943; rec w Count Basie Orch, V-Disc label, Hollywood, CA, 1943; worked w Count Basie Orch, Apollo Theater, NYC, 1943-4; worked residency w Count Basie Orch, Blue Room, Lincoln Hotel, NYC, 1943-4 (with frequent remotes, WGN-radio); Roxy Theater, NYC, 1944; Salute to Fats Waller Concert, Carnegie Hall, NYC, 1944; Orpheum Theater, Los Angeles, 1944; Club Plantation, Los Angeles, 1944; rec V-Disc label, NYC, 1944-5; rec Columbia label, NYC, 1944-6; worked Avodon Ballroom, Los Angeles, 1946-7; Golden Gate Theater, San Francisco, 1946; Lincoln Theater, Los Angeles, 1946; Million Dollar Theater, Los Angeles, 1946; rec w Johnny Otis Orch, Excelsior label, Los Angeles, 1946; worked one-nighter club dates w Jimmy Mundy Orch, Los Angeles, 1946; w Count Basie Orch, Exhibition Hall, Columbus, GA, 1946; Palace Theater, Columbus, OH, 1946; rec w Count Basie Orch, Victor label, NYC/Los Angeles/ Chicago, 1947; toured w Count Basie group working one-nighters, late 40s; rec w Count Basie Orch, Victor label, NYC, 1949; formed own septet to work long residency, Savoy Ballroom, NYC, 1950-2; rec King label, NYC, 1951-2; frequently toured as single working club dates in major cities of US from 1952; rec Gotham label, Philadelphia, PA, c1952; app on OMNIBUS Show, CBS-TV, 1953; worked Stuyvesant Casino, NYC, 1953; rec w Frank Culley's Combo, Parrot label, Chicago, 1953; worked w Count Basie Orch, Birdland, NYC, 1954 (por remote on Steve Allen's TONIGHT Show, NBC-TV); rec Vanguard label, NYC, 1954-7; worked Newport Jazz Festival, Newport, RI, 1955-6 (por on MUSIC USA, VOA-radio); Berkshire Music Barn, Lenox, MA, 1955; Stratford Festival, Stratford, Can, 1956; app on Steve Allen's TONIGHT Show, NBC-TV, 1956; rec Columbia label, NYC, 1956-60; app on THE SEVEN LIVELY ARTS (ep: The Sound of Jazz), CBS-TV, 1957 (rel as film THE SOUND OF JAZZ); rec OKeh label, NYC, 1957; worked w Count Basie Orch, Newport Jazz Festival, Newport, RI, 1957 (por rel Verve label/por on MUSIC USA, VOA-radio); Great South Bay Festival, Great River, NY, 1957 (por on MUSIC USA, VOA-radio); Downbeat Club, San Fransisco, 1957; Jazz Night, Hollywood Bowl, Hollywood, CA, 1957; toured as single working club/concert dates through England/Europe, 1957-8; worked w Benny Goodman Orch, Newport Jazz Festival, Newport, RI, 1958 (por remote CBS-radio); worked w Benny Goodman Orch, Brussels World's Fair, Brussels, Belgium, 1958 (por shown on Eurovision TV-Network/por shown NBC-TV/por heard Westinghouse radio network/por rel Columbia label); app on SUBJECT IS JAZZ, WNDT-TV, NYC, 1958; app on JOHN GUNTHER'S HIGH ROAD, ABC-TV (syndicated), 1959; worked Westover Hotel, Toronto, Can, 1959; app on JACK KANE Show, CBC-TV, Toronto, Can, 1959; worked Toronto Jazz Festival, Toronto, 1959; worked w Buck Clayton, Newport Jazz Festival, Newport, RI, 1959 (por rel Atlantic label); worked French Lick Jazz Festival, French Lick, IN, 1959; Playboy Jazz Festival, Chicago Stadium, Chicago, IL, 1959; Blue Note, Chicago, 1959; toured w Buck Clayton group working concert dates through England/Europe, 1959; worked Mosque Theater, Newark, NJ, 1960; Tally Ho Club, Philadelphia, PA, 1960; Northeastern Univ, Boston, MA, 1960; Mike White Club, Toronto, Can, 1960; Newport Jazz Festival, Newport, RI, 1960 (por shown in film THE SUBTERRANEANS); rec w Dave Brubeck Quartet, Columbia label, NYC, 1960; worked w Joe Newman Sextet and others, Museum of Modern Art, NYC, 1960-2; The Roundtable, NYC, 1960; Jazz Festival, Saugatuck, MI, 1960; Monterey Jazz Festival, Monterey, CA, 1960-1; Hangover Club, San Francisco, CA, 1960; w Dave Brubeck Quartet, Basin Street East, NYC, 1960; Colonial Park, NYC, 1961; toured briefly w Harry James Orch/Benny Goodman Orch, early 60s; frequently worked Colonial Tavern, Toronto, Can, 1961-8; Indiana Jazz Festival, Evansville, IN, 1961; Jazz Festival, Virginia Beach, VA, 1961; Sugar Hill Club, San Francisco, CA, 1961-2; Playboy Club, Chicago, IL, 1962; w Count Basie Orch, Newport Jazz Festival, Newport, RI, 1962 (por rel in film NEWPORT JAZZ FESTIVAL, 1962); Sound Track Night Club, New Haven, CT, 1962; Monterey Jazz Festival, Monterey, CA, 1962; worked club dates in Miami, FL, 1962; toured w Thelonious Monk working concert dates through Japan, 1963; w Benny Goodman, Yale Univ, New Haven, CT, 1963; frequently worked Lennie's, Boston, MA, 1963-9; w Count Basie Orch, Salle Pleyel, Paris, France, 1963; worked Jazz Festival, Landskrona, Sweden, 1963; Webster Hall, NYC, NY, 1963 (por rel Columbia-Pix label); Apollo Theater, NYC, 1963; Town Hall, NYC, 1963; app on JAZZ CASUAL, PBS-TV, 1964; worked w Count Basie Orch, Singer Bowl, NYC, 1964; toured w Eddie Condon All Stars working concert dates through Australia/New Zealand/Japan, 1964; worked Front Room, Newark, NJ, 1964; Boston Arts Festival, Boston, MA, 1964; toured w Count Basie Orch working concert dates through Europe, 1964; worked Jazz Workshop, San Francisco, CA, 1965-6; frequently worked Half Note, NYC, 1965-72; app on KALEIDOSCOPE 4, NBC-TV, 1965; worked w Buddy Tate Band, Museum of Modern Art, NYC, 1965; Jazz Workshop, Boston, MA, 1965; Blues Alley, Washington, DC, 1965; The Lighthouse, Los Angeles, CA, 1966; w Count Basie Orch, Newport Jazz Festival, Newport, RI, 1966 (por heard MUSIC USA, VOA-radio); Molde Jazz Festival, Oslo, Norway, 1966; app on MIKE DOUGLAS Show, WOR-TV, NYC, 1967; rec w Earl Hines/All Stars, MJR label, NYC, 1967; rec ABC-BluesWay label, NYC, 1967-8; worked Jazz Workshop, San Francisco, CA, 1967; Byrd's Nest, Washington, DC, 1968; Pep's Musical Bar, Philadelphia, PA, 1968; Fordham Univ, Bronx, NY, 1968; app (in singing/acting role) in film THE LEARNING TREE, 1969; worked Monterey Jazz Festival, Monterey, CA, 1969-70 (por 1970 concert shown in film MONTEREY JAZZ); Downbeat Club, NYC, 1969; Town Tavern, Toronto, Can, 1969-71; Blues Alley, Washington, DC, 1969; Town Hall, NYC, c1970; Ash Grove, Los Angeles, CA, 1970; Kansas City Jazz Festival, Kansas City, MO, 1971; rec RCA-Victor label, NYC, 1971; app on OUR AMERICAN MUSICAL HERITAGE, CBS-TV, 1971; mostly inactive in music due to illness from 1971; worked Half Note, NYC, 1972; entered Flower & Fifth Avenue Hospital where he died of leukemia; buried Maple Grove Cemetery, Kew Gardens, Queens, NY

Personal: Married Connie Ingram

Billing: Mr Five By Five

Songs: Baby Don't Tell on Me/Blues in the Dark/Bran' New Wagon/Bye Bye Baby/Did You Ever?/Don't You Miss Your Baby?/Don't You Want a Man Like Me?/Evil Blues/Go Get Some More You Fool/Goin' to Chicago/Good Morning Blues/How Do You Want Your Lovin' Done?/I Left My Baby/If This Ain't the Blues/In the Moonlight/Jimmy's Blues/Jimmy's Round the Clock Blues/Leave Me/MJR Blues/My Baby Business/Nobody Knows/Please Come Back/Rock and Roll/Sent for You Yesterday/She's Mine She's Yours/Somebody's Spoiling These Women/Sometimes I Think I Do/Take Me Back Baby/Thursday Blues/Undecided Blues/The Way I Feel/You Can't Run Around

Awards/Honors: Won *Melody Maker* magazine (UK) Critics Poll as Best Male Singer, 1957, 1958, 1959, 1960

Won *Jazz Podium* magazine (German) Jazz Critics Award as Best Male Jazz Vocalist, 1958

Won *Downbeat* magazine International Critics Poll as Best Male Singer, 1958, 1959, 1960, 1972

Won *Jazz & Pop* magazine Critics JAY Award as Best Blues Singer, 1967

Won Kansas City Jazz Festival Jazz Hall of Fame Award, 1971

Won *Downbeat* magazine International Critics Poll Record of the Year Award, 1972 ("The You and Me That Used to Be," RCA-Victor 4566)

Won *Swing Journal* magazine (Japanese) Award as Best Vocalist, 1972 ("The You and Me That Used to Be," RCA-Victor 4566)

Infl by: Leroy Carr/Wesley Manning/Bessie Smith/Mamie Smith/Gerry Stone/George "Fat Head" Thomas

Infl to: Lowell Fulson/Wynonie Harris/Jay Hawkins/Al Hibbler/BB King/Big Miller/Joe Turner/Aaron "T-Bone" Walker/Jimmy Witherspoon

Quotes: "Of all the vocalists whose careers have been linked to the blues, Jimmy Rushing's is the one which has reached the furthest and has spread the appeal of the blues on a wider area than anyone had thought of before"—Frank Driggs, *Evergreen Review* magazine, Apr 1966, p 64

"He is first of all a jazz singer who can handle anything from ballads to rhythm tunes and then also a man who sings the blues extremely well"—Dan Morgenstern, *Downbeat* magazine, Oct 14, 1971, p 30

"One of the significant aspects of his art is the imposition of a romantic lyricism upon the blues tradition . . ."—Ralph Ellison, *New York Times* newspaper, Jun 9, 1972

References: *Count Basis and His Orchestra*, Raymond Horricks, Citadel Press, 1957

Downbeat magazine, Nov 13, 1969, pp 17, 38

Who's Who of Jazz, John Chilton, Bloomsbury Book Shop, 1970

S

SADLER, HASKELL ROBERT

(aka: Cool Papa)

Born: Apr 6, 1935, Denver (Denver Co), CO
Inst: Guitar

Interested in country & western music from about 14 years of age; taught self guitar and frequently played in local high school Mellow Tones Blues Band, Denver, CO, into 50s; worked local club dates, Denver, from 1951; moved to West Coast to work w BB Brown/Sidney Maiden Band in local club dates, Los Angeles, CA, from 1954; rec Flash label, Los Angeles, 1957; worked w Roy Brown in local clubs, Las Vegas, NV, late 50s; frequently toured as sideman w Earl King/Aaron "T-Bone" Walker/Lowell Fulson/BB King/others working club dates through South/Southwest into 60s; toured w Fast Twice Together group working concert dates through Northwest during 60s; worked San Francisco Blues Festival, Golden Gate Park, San Francisco, CA, 1974; Joe's Melody

Courtesy Living Blues *Magazine*

Club, Vallejo, CA, 1974; Amvets, Oakland, CA, 1974; The Rainbow Sign, Los Angeles, 1975; Laws of London, San Francisco, 1975; Klassic Kitten, El Sobrante, CA, 1975; House of Joy, Oakland, CA, 1975; Playboy Club, Richmond, CA, 1975; Moonlight Club, San Francisco, 1975-6; Berkeley Music Festival, Provo Park, Berkeley, CA, 1975; Playboy Club, San Francisco, 1976

Personal: Married Jane ——— (c1961-). 1 child

Songs: I Should Have Known/That Was Yesterday

Reference: Blues Unlimited magazine (UK), Nov 1970, pp 15-16

SALTY DOG SAM
(see Collins, Sam)

SAMPSON, SAMMY
(see Broonzy, William)

SAYLES, CHARLES *"Charlie"*
Born: Jan 4, 1948, Woburn (Middlesex Co), MA
Inst: Cymbal/Harmonica

One of a few children; moved to West Medford, MA, at 2 weeks of age; raised with grandparents in Andover, MA, from 1950-9; lived in Boys Home, Salem, MA, 1959 into 60s; served in US Army in Vietnam, 1967-70, then Germany, 1971; worked outside music in Roxbury, MA, 1971; taught self harmonica then hoboed across US working outside music with frequent street work for tips from 1972; worked local bars, Nashville, TN, 1973; frequently worked clubs/streets in Atlanta, GA, 1973-5; worked streets for tips, NYC, NY, 1975-6; worked Bottom Line, NYC, 1975; American Folklife Festival, Washington, DC, 1975-6; app on Bob Javors' SOMETHING INSIDE OF ME Show, WKCR-FM-radio, NYC, 1975; worked National Folk Festival, Wolf Trap Farm Park, Vienna, VA, 1975-6; John Henry Memorial Concert, Clifftop, WV, 1975; toured Louisiana working concerts in prisons/reform schools/old age homes, 1975; worked streets for tips, Los Angeles, CA, 1975; El Cafe, NYC, 1976; Folk City, NYC, 1976; The New School for Social Research, NYC, 1976; Whitey's Tavern, NYC, 1976; app on OMNIBUS, BBC-1-TV, London, Eng (filmed in NYC), 1976; rec Dusty Road label, Brooklyn, NY/Rockaway, NY, 1976; worked Philadelphia Folk Festival, Schwenksville, PA, 1977

Photo by Kevin R Doherty. Courtesy Living Blues *Magazine*

Songs: Almost Gone/Atlanta Boogie/Baby You Done Wrecked My Life/Banjo/Goin' Up, Goin' Down/Here Comes the Train/I'm Mad with You/Makin' Love to Music/New York—St Louis/Vietnam

Infl by: Sonny Boy Williamson (Alex Miller)

Quote: "He is a superb and talented harmonica player with stunningly individual songs of his own creation performed in a fine vocal style"—Dave Sax, *Blues Unlimited* magazine (UK), Jul 1976, p 22

Reference: Blues Unlimited magazine (UK), Jul 1976, p 22-3

SCHOOLBOY CLEVE

(see White, Cleve)

SCOTT, GENEVIA

(see Sylvester, Hannah)

SCRUGGS, IRENE

(*aka:* Chocolate Brown/Little Sister/Dixie Nolan)
Born: Dec 7, 1901, Mississippi
Died: (unknown)

Reportedly raised in St Louis, MO; won first prize in local amateur contest, Booker T Washington Theater, St Louis, 1924; rec w Clarence Williams, OKeh label, NYC, 1924; toured TOBA circuit working theater dates out of St Louis through 20s; rec w King Oliver Band, Vocalion label, Chicago, 1926; rec w Lonnie Johnson, OKeh label, St Louis, 1927; formed own band working local club dates, St Louis, late 20s; worked w Erskine Tate Vendome Orch, Vendome Theater, Chicago, IL, c1928; worked w Dave Peyton Band in local clubs, Chicago, late 20s; worked Lincoln Theater, NYC, c1928; rec (as "Dixie Nolan") w Johnny Hardge (as "Johnny Hodges"), Victor label, Memphis, TN, 1929; rec (as "Chocolate Brown"), Paramount label, Grafton, WI, 1930; rec Gennett/Champion labels, Richmond, IN, 1930; frequently worked Town Club, Cicero, IL, c1930; toured w Little Brother Montgomery working theater dates on TOBA circuit, 1931; worked 81 Theater, Atlanta, GA, 1931; Grand Theater, Chicago, c1932; worked w daughter Baby Scruggs (a dancer), Kelly's Stable, Chicago, 1934; retired to St Louis and inactive in music from c1935; frequently travelled as companion to daughter Baby Scruggs to England/Europe during 50s; worked NFJO Jazz Band Ball, London, Eng, 1953; app on BALLADS AND BLUES, BBC-radio, London, Eng, 1953; app on BLUES FOR MONDAY, AFN-radio, London, 1953; reportedly settled in Paris, France, mid-50s, then Germany into 70s; whereabouts unknown thereafter

Personal: Married (c1920). Her daughter Leazar "Baby" Scruggs is dancer (born 1921). Reportedly married a Frenchman (mid-50s?)

Songs: Back to the Wall/Borrowed Love/Cherry Hill Blues/Cruel Papa But a Good Man to Have Around/Everybody's Blues/Home Town Blues/My Daddy's Calling Me/Sorrow Valley Blues/You Got What I Want

Infl by: Ida Cox/Bessie Smith

SEALS, FRANK JUNIOR *"Son"*

Born: Aug 13, 1942, Osceola (Mississippi Co), AR
Inst: Drums/Guitar

Father was Jim "Son" Seals, a musician with FS Wolcott's Rabbit Foot Minstrels and owner of Dipsy Doodle Club, Osceola, AR; mother Eula Mae Dilworth; one of 13 children; father bought him first set of drums and taught him music basics c1953; frequently worked w Sonny Boy Williamson (Alex Miller) Band/Robert Nighthawk Band/others, Dipsy Doodle Club, Osceola, from c1955; worked w Earl Hooker Band in Little Rock, AR, area c1956; learned guitar to form own band working Chez Paris Club, Little Rock, c1959-63; frequently sat-in with various bands in local club dates, Little Rock area, into 60s; frequently worked/toured w Earl Hooker's Roadmasters out of Chicago, IL, 1963-5; rec w own band, (unknown) label, Chicago (?), 1963; toured w Albert King working club dates, 1966-8; worked w Albert King Band, Fillmore West, San Francisco, CA, 1968 (por rel Stax label); frequently worked in various blues bands in Blue Goose Club/Harlem Club/others, Osceola, AR, 1968-71; settled in Chicago, IL, to work outside music from 1971; worked w Hound Dog Taylor, Psychedelic Shack, Chicago, 1971; formed own group to work Expressway Lounge, Chicago, 1972; Flamingo Club, Chicago, 1972; rec Alligator label, Chicago, 1973; worked Ratso's, Chicago, 1973; Kove, Kent, OH, 1973; Florence's, Chicago, 1974; Wise Fools, Chicago, 1974; Minstrel's, Chicago, 1974; toured Sweden/Finland working concert dates, 1974; worked Univ of Miami Blues Festival, Coral Gables, FL, 1975; Univ of Vermont, Burlington, VT, 1975; Midwest Blues Festival, Univ of Notre Dame, South Bend, IN, 1975; Northern Illinois Univ, DeKalb, IL, 1976; Holmes Center Ballroom, DeKalb, IL, 1976; frequent residencies at Sweet Queen Bee's Lounge, Chicago, 1976-7; Grand Valley State Col Festival, Allendale, MI, 1976; rec Alligator label, Chicago, 1976; Louise's, Chicago, 1976; The Bottom Line, NYC, 1977-8; The Belle Star, Colden, NY, 1977; Joe's East West, New Paltz, NY, 1977; The Childe Harold, Washington, DC, 1977; Intersection Tavern, Grand Rapids, MI, 1977; Lupo's, Providence, RI, 1977; Zoo Bar, Lincoln, NE, 1977; toured Europe working concerts, 1977; worked Nancy Jazz Festival, Nancy, France, 1977; w BB King, Hammersmith Odeon, London, Eng, 1977; Wise Fools Pub, Chicago, 1977-8; Lawrence Opera House, Lawrence, KS, 1977; The Rising Sun, Montreal, Can, 1978

Personal: Married. 8 children

Songs: Cotton Picking Blues/Don't Bother Me/Don't

Frank "Son" Seals

Photo by Marc Pokempner. Courtesy Sheldon Harris Collection

Fool with My Baby/Four Full Seasons of Love/Going Back Home/Hot Sauce/How Could She Leave Me?/ Look Now Baby/No No Baby/Now That I'm Down/On My Knees/Sitting at My Window/Strung Out Woman/Your Love Is Like a Cancer

Awards/Honors: Won *Chicago Reader* magazine Music Writers Award as Best Chicago Blues Artist of the Year, 1974

Won *Downbeat* magazine International Critics Award for soul-R&B artist deserving wider recognition, 1977

Infl by: Albert King/BB King/Robert Nighthawk

Quotes: "One of the most exciting and hard driving blues guitarists on the scene today"—Roy Greenberg, *Living Blues* magazine, May 1977, p 32

"For 16 years, Son's been playing and singing his fierce, unrelenting style of blues, night after night"—Richard McLeese, Alligator album 4708

References: Alligator album 4703

Blues Unlimited magazine (UK), Sept 1972, p 18

Downbeat magazine, Apr 6, 1978, pp 14-15

Brother John Sellers

Courtesy Brother John Sellers

SELLERS, BROTHER JOHN
(aka: Johnny Frank)
Born: May 27, 1924, Clarksdale (Coahoma Co), MS
Inst: Guitar/Tambourine

Father was Charles Sellers; mother Lettie Buchanan; to Burdett, MS c1927; Leland MS c1931-2; raised in Greenville, MS where he lived in sporting house that catered to travelling shows as child; attended local elementary school briefly while working frequently outside music, Greenville, into 30s; frequently worked as singer/dancer in local minstrel show talent contests, Greenville, early 30s; moved to Chicago, IL, where he attended local high school from 1933; frequently worked outside music with occasional work at local churches/revival meetings/religious concerts, Chicago area, through 30s; frequently toured w Mahalia Jackson/Emma Jackson and other gospel singers/groups or as single through South into 40s; extensive tours as single working club/theater dates through US/Canada, 1941 into 50s; rec religious songs, Cincinnati/King/Decca/Southern labels, NYC, 1945; worked w Dizzy Gillespie, Apollo Theater, NYC, 1946; toured w Don Archer's Band working clubs through South, 1947; rec Victor/Miracle/Gotham labels, Chicago, 1947; replaced Bill Broonzy, Blue Note Club, Chicago, 1950; rec w Annisteen Allen, King label, 1951; rec Chance label, Chicago, 1952; worked w Sonny Terry, Tanglewood Festival, Lenox, MA, 1954; rec Vanguard label, NYC, 1954; rec (as "Johnny Frank") Herald label, NYC, 1955; toured w Bill Broonzy working club dates/radio/TV shows, 1951; rec Decca-London label, London, Eng, 1957; rec Columbia (French)/Pathe-Marconi labels,

Paris, France, 1957; app in European film ETHNIC FOLK SONGS OF THE SOUTHLAND, 1957; extensive tours working festivals/churches/concerts across US from 1958; worked Gate of Horn, Chicago, 1959; Ravinia Folk Festival, Chicago, 1959; rec Monitor label, NYC, 1959; worked Town Hall Folk Festival, NYC, 1959; Fifth Peg, NYC, 1960; worked as MC/performer, Gerde's Folk City, NYC, 1960-1; rec Decca label, Chicago, 1960; Jazz & Folk Music Festival, Castle Frank, Toronto, Can, 1961; app on CAMERA THREE, CBS-TV, 1962; worked Montreal Jazz Festival, Montreal, Can, 1962; Traditional Jazz Club Concert, Montreal, 1962; toured w Alvin Ailey American Dance Company for US State Department Cultural Exchange Program working shows through Japan / Australia / Philippines / India / Korea / Europe, 1962; worked East Harlem Plaza, NYC, 1962; app in Langston Hughes show TAMBOURINES TO GLORY, Little Theater, NYC, 1963; worked Trois Mailletz Club, Paris, France, 1964; toured Australia working concert dates, 1965; worked Carnegie Hall, NYC, 1965; served as minister of music, Spencer Memorial Church, NYC, 1967; worked Gerde's Folk City, NYC, c1967; toured w Alvin Ailey American Dance Company working shows through England, 1970; worked w Alvin Ailey American Dance Company, New York City Center, NYC, 1971-2; toured as Brother John and His Soul Sisters working night club circuit across US, 1972; worked Folk City, NYC, 1973; weekend residency, The Cookery, NYC, 1973; continued frequent tours w Alvin Ailey group working shows across US into 70s

Note: "Brother" is true given name

Songs: Chicago Hop/I Have the Blues Every Day/I Want a True Lover/Love Is a Story/Lucy Mae Blues/Oh Little Girl/Oh What Kind of Woman/They Call Me a Blind Man/You've Been Gone Too Long

Infl by: Big Bill Broonzy/Mahalia Jackson

References: Jazz Journal (UK), Feb 1957, p 1
Record Research magazine, Nov 1961, p 8

SEMIEN, *"Ivory"* LEE
(aka: Ivory Lee/King Ivory Lee)
Born: Sept 13, 1931, Washington (St Landry Parish), LA
Inst: Drums

Father taught him guitar/sax/drums as youth; moved to Houston, TX, 1949; frequently worked w Raymond Trimbel in local clubs, Houston, 1949 into 50s; frequently toured w Hop Wilson working club dates through Texas/Louisiana, 1956-60; rec Goldband label, Lake Charles, LA, 1958; rec Goldband label, Houston, 1959; formed/rec Alameda label, Houston, c1959; formed/rec Ivory label, Houston, 1960-2; worked mostly outside music (in own TV repair shop), Houston, through 60s; continued recording local artists on own Ivory label, Houston, into 70s; worked C&P Lounge, Houston, 1970; formed own band to work Irene's, Houston, early 70s; Hollywood Lounge, Houston, 1970

Song: Woke Up This Morning

Reference: Nothing But the Blues, Mike Leadbitter, Hanover Books, 1971

SEMIEN, SIDNEY
(aka: Count Rockin' Sydney/Rockin' Sydney)
Born: Apr 9, 1938, Lebeau (St Landry Parish), LA
Inst: Guitar/Harmonica

Grandfather was accordionist who worked in local Zydeco band; interested in music early and learned guitar at about 13 years of age; frequently worked in uncle's band working dances in Lebeau, LA, area from 1953 (eventually assuming leadership); rec Fame label, Lake Charles, LA, 1959; rec w All Stars, Jin label, Ville Platte, LA, 1959/1963-4; frequently worked local club dates in Lake Charles, early 60s; rec w Dukes, Goldband label, Lake Charles, 1965; worked Casa Blanca Club, New Iberia, LA, 1966; rec Goldband label, New Iberia, 1966; toured w Dukes working club dates through Louisiana, late 60s; rec Flyright label, Lake Charles, 1969; frequently worked clubs/bars in Lake Charles area into 70s

Songs: Boogie in the Mud/If I Could I Would/I'm Walking Out/It Really Is a Hurtin' Thing/Keep On Pushing/No Good Woman/Past Bedtime/They Call Me Rockin'/You Ain't Nothin' but Fine

Infl by: John Lee Hooker/Howlin' Wolf/Muddy Waters

Reference: Blues Unlimited magazine (UK), Nov-Dec 1976, p 3

SEWARD, ALEXANDER T *"Alec"/"Slim"*
(aka: Blues Boy/Blues King/Georgia Slim/Guitar Slim)
Born: Mar 16, 1902, Charles City (Charles City Co), VA
Died: May 11, 1972, New York, NY
Inst: Guitar

Father was Isaac Seward; mother was Martha Johnson; one of 14 children; moved to Newport News,

Photo by Peter B Lowry

VA, where he was raised; taught self guitar at about 18 years of age and frequently worked local parties/country dances in Newport News, 1920-3; moved to New York, NY, 1923; worked outside music with frequent party work in NYC, 1923 through 30s/40s; frequently worked w Sonny Terry/Brownie McGhee at local house parties/lofts/hoots in NYC area, early 40s; rec w Louis Hayes as The Blues Boys, Superdisc/Tru Blue labels, NYC, c1947; rec w Louis Hayes as The Backporch Boys, Apollo label, NYC, 1947; rec w Louis Hayes (as "The Blues King"), Solo label, NYC, c1947; rec w Louis Hayes, MGM label, NYC, c1947; worked w Leadbelly at local parties, NYC area, late 40s; attended Brownie McGhee's Home of the Blues Music School, NYC, c1949; rec w Sonny Terry, Archive of Folk Music label, NYC, 1952; rec w Sonny Terry, Elektra label, NYC, 1953; worked mostly outside music, NYC, from 1957; rec w Larry Johnson, Prestige-Bluesville label, NYC, 1965; rec w Sonny Terry/Brownie McGhee, Blue Labor label, NYC, 1966; entered Flower & Fifth Avenue Hospital where he died of natural causes; buried Hackensack Cemetery, Hackensack, NJ

Personal: Married Juanita ———. Not to be confused with Norman Green or Eddie Jones who also used pseudonym "Guitar Slim"

Songs: Big Hip Mama/Creepin' Blues/Evil Woman Blues/Late One Saturday Evening/Let a Good Thing Do/Some People Say/Sweet Woman

Infl by: Gary Davis/Blind Lemon Jefferson/Lonnie Johnson/Brownie McGhee/Sonny Terry

Quote: "There wasn't none better'n him at singing"—Sonny Terry, Blue Labor album 103

SEYMOUR, GEORGE
(see Erby, John)

SHADE, WILL
(*aka:* Son Brimmer)
Born: Feb 5, 1898, Memphis (Shelby Co), TN
Died: Sept 18, 1966, Memphis, TN
Inst: Guitar/Harmonica/Jug/"Streamline" Bass

Father was Will Shade Sr; mother was Mary Brimmer; raised by grandmother Annie Brimmer from childhood; interested in music early and learned some music from mother and "Hucklebones" as teenager; frequently followed street singer "Tee Wee" Blackman through Memphis, TN, c1915-17; frequently worked w Furry Lewis Jug Band at Pee Wee's/Red Onion/Vintage and other tonks/jukes, Memphis, from c1917; frequently worked outside music in Memphis area into 20s; frequently toured with passing medicine shows out of Memphis, early 20s; frequently worked w Jennie Mae Clayton in local bars/clubs, Memphis, early 20s; formed Memphis Jug Band (which at various times included Ben Ramey/Will Weldon/Roundhouse/Charlie Burse/Furry Lewis/Vol Stevens/Jab Jones/Ham Lewis/Charlie Pierce and others) to work Church's Park (WC Handy Park)/Chickawaw Country Club/Peabody Hotel/streets/dances/clubs/parties with some tours out of Memphis, mid-20s to mid-30s; frequently worked Mardi Gras in New Orleans, LA, late 20s; rec w Memphis Jug Band, Victor label, Memphis, TN/Chicago, IL/Atlanta, GA, 1927; worked w Memphis Jug Band, Grand Central Theater, Chicago, 1927; w Memphis Jug Band in Ma Rainey Show, Gary, IN, 1927; rec under own name, Victor label, Memphis, 1928; frequently rec as acc on Victor label, Memphis and elsewhere, 1928-30; frequently teamed w Charley Burse to work streets for tips, Memphis, early 30s; rec w Picaninny Band, Champion label, Richmond, IN, 1932; rec OKeh label, Chicago, 1934; frequently worked outside music, Memphis, through 30s/40s/50s; frequently worked w Willie Borum/Joe Hill Louis in jukes/gambling houses/streets of Memphis, TN/West Memphis, AR, areas, early 40s; occasionally worked w Charlie Burse in local office buildings/streets for tips, Memphis, through 40s/50s; rec w Charlie Burse, Folkways label, Memphis, 1956; app w Charlie Burse on tribute to WC Handy, local TV, Memphis, 1958; rec Decca label, Memphis, 1960; mostly inactive due to illness into 60s; rec Rounder label, Memphis, 1963; entered

John Gaston Hospital where he died of pneumonia; buried Shelby County Cemetery, Memphis, TN

Personal: Married Jennie "Jenny" Mae Clayton who frequently worked/recorded with this singer. Named "Son Brimmer" during childhood while living with grandmother, Annie Brimmer

Songs: Boodie Bum Bum/Going Back to Memphis/ Hurry Down Sunshine (See What Tomorrow Bring)/It Won't Act Right/Jug Band Waltz/Kansas City Blues/ Memphis Jug Blues/Newport News Blues/State of Tennessee Blues/Sun Brimmer's Blues

Infl by: Tee Wee Blackman

Infl to: Charlie Musselwhite

Quotes: "The heart of the Memphis Jug Band was the musicianship and the enthusiasm of Son and Charlie Burse"—Samuel B Charters, *The Country Blues*, Rinehart & Company, Inc, 1959

"A perfectionist"—Bengt Olsson, *Memphis Blues*, Studio Vista Ltd, 1970

References: The Country Blues, Samuel B Charters, Rinehart & Company, 1959

Memphis Blues, Bengt Olsson, Studio Vista Ltd, 1970

Sweet as the Showers of Rain, Samuel B Charters, Oak Publications, 1977

SHAKEY JAKE
(see Harris, James)

SHAKEY WALTER
(see Horton, Walter)

SHAW, ROBERT WILLIAM *"Fud"*
Born: Aug 9, 1908, Stafford (Fort Bend Co), TX
Died: **May 16, 1985, Austin, TX**
Inst: Piano

Father Jesse Shaw; mother Hettie Brown, a musician; born/raised on fathers' cattle ranch; taught self piano as youth working local parties from mid-20s; left home to work as itinerant pianist in juke joints/ bordellos/barrelhouses/tonks in Sugarland/Richmond/Houston/Galveston/Kingsville/Kilgore, TX, and up to Kansas City, MO, through late 20s into 30s; worked Black Orange Cafe, Kansas City, MO, 1932; app on own show, KFXR-radio, Oklahoma City, OK, 1933; worked local cabaretts/parties/dances, Oklahoma City, 1933-5; worked Jim Hotel Dance Hall, Ft Worth, TX, c1933; briefly worked club dates in Kansas City, MO, c1935; settled in Austin, TX, to work outside music (in own Shaw's Food Market) with occasional private party work from mid-30s into 70s;

Photo by C Strachwitz, Arhoolie Records

app on MACK McCORMICK AND FRIENDS, KUHF-FM-radio, Houston, TX, 1960; rec Almanac label, Austin, TX, 1963; app on SOME OF THE PEOPLE, KUHF-FM-radio, Houston, 1966; worked Festival of American Folklife, Washington, DC, 1968; Festival of American Folklife, Montreal, Can, 1971; Berlin Jazz Festival, Berlin, Ger, 1974; Montreux Jazz Festival, Montreux, Switzerland, 1975; Festival on the Strand, Galveston, TX, 1976; app on VISIONS (ep: Charlie Smith and the Fritter Tree), PBS-TV (syndicated), 1978; app AUSTIN CITY LIMITS, PBS-TV, 1979; worked club dates, Austin area into 80s; suffered fatal heart attack; buried Memorial Hill Park Cemetery, Austin

Songs: Black Gal/Hattie Green/The Ma Grinder

Infl by: All Night Jack/Black Boy Shine (Harold Holiday)/Rob Cooper/Bernice Edwards

Quote: "He is . . . a gruff, easeful blues singer, telling stories that came out of his audience's lives"—Nat Hentoff, *HiFi/Stereo Review* magazine, Dec 1966

References: Almanac album 10

Blues Unlimited magazine (UK), Mar/Apr 1978, pp 13-21

SHAW, THOMAS EDGAR *"Tom"*

Photo by Frank Scott

Born: Mar 4, 1908, Brenham (Washington Co), TX
Died: Feb 24, 1977, San Diego, CA
Inst: Guitar/Harmonica

Father was Louis Shaw; mother was Emma Benton; one of 5 children; interested in music early and taught harmonica by father and guitar by cousin Willie Shaw Jr at 9 years of age; worked outside music with occasional work on streets for tips, Brenham, TX, late teens; worked outside music, Moody, TX, c1920; worked outside music, Brenham, TX, early 20s; left home to hobo through Texas working outside music with occasional party work w Blind Lemon Jefferson and others through 20s; worked local jukes/parties/marathon dances, Wichita Falls/Odell, TX, 1929; worked w JT Smith in Frederick, OK, area, 1930-1; worked local dances, Moody, TX, area, 1932; toured w Rambling Thomas working parties in West Texas area c1933; settled in San Diego, CA, working outside music, 1934 into 70s; frequently toured club dates through southern California through 30s; app on own show XEMO-radio, Tijuana, Mexico, 1935; frequently worked w Bob Jeffery at own club, Little Harlem Chicken Shack (and local parties/Saturday night dates), San Diego, CA, early 40s through 60s; served mostly as a reverend at Noah's Temple of the Apostolic Faith, San Diego, late 60s into 70s; rec Blue Goose/Advent labels, San Diego, c1969; worked San Diego State Col Folk-Blues Festival, San Diego, 1970-2; California State Polytechnic Col Folk Festival, San Luis Obispo, CA, 1971; toured England/Europe working club/concert dates, 1972; rec Blues Beacon label, Baambrugge, Holland, 1972; worked Community Music Center, San Francisco, 1973; Blues Society Concert, Santa Barbara, CA, 1973; rec Advent label, San Diego, 1973; mostly inactive in music due to illness with occasional West Coast gigs through mid-70s; entered Donald Sharp Memorial Hospital where he died during open heart surgery of cardiac failure; buried Mt Hope Cemetery, San Diego, CA

Personal: Married (c1930); married Catherine Henderson (1934-   ). Had children

Songs: Baby Be a Boy Child Named After Me/Hey Mr Nixon/Martin Luther King/Mean Little Woman/Prowling Ground Hog/Rock/Stop in the Valley/WPA Blues

Infl by: Blind Lemon Jefferson/JT Smith

Quote: "The greatest Texas blues discovery since Mance Lipscomb"—(*Billboard* magazine) *Living Blues* magazine, Jul 1977, p 5

Reference: Living Blues magazine, Summer 1972, pp 24-7

SHELBY, JAMES *"Son"*

Born: 1927, Jasper (Jasper Co), TX
Inst: Guitar/Harmonica

Father was local musician; was born blind; learned harmonica from father and frequently worked local dances, Jasper, TX, early 40s; learned guitar from Charlie Hafford; moved to Beaumont, TX, to work as street musician for tips, 1948 through 60s; worked South Texas State Fair, Beaumont, TX, 1970-2; frequently worked streets/shopping centers for tips, Beaumont, into 70s; rec Swoon label, Neches, TX, 1972; worked Univ of Texas, Austin, TX, 1972

Infl by: Charlie Hafford

Reference: Living Blues magazine, Winter 1972, p 12

SHINES, JOHN NED *"Johnny"*
(aka: Little Wolf/Shoe Shine Johnny)
Born: Apr 25, 1915, Frayser (Shelby Co), TN
Died: Apr 20, 1992, Tuscaloosa, AL
Inst: Guitar

Father was John Shines Sr; mother was Vernether Frazier, a guitarist; moved to Memphis, TN, 1921; briefly attended Manassa Street Grade School, Memphis, c1924; worked outside music in Memphis through 20s; moved frequently through area into 30s; frequently worked in small children's group on local streets for tips, Memphis, early 30s; moved to Hughes, AR, to work outside music (as sharecropper) from 1932; learned guitar and occasionally worked get-backs (open houses)/plantations/roadhouses, Hughes area, 1932-4; worked Church's Park (WC Handy Park)/Saturday night parties for tips, Memphis, 1934; worked local jukes/backwoods farmhouses, Helena, AR, area, 1934-5; teamed w Robert Johnson to hobo (off and on) working bars/dances/fish fries/house parties/streets/roadside cafes/speakeasies/taverns/levee camps/sawmills/coal yards through South, then north into Canada, 1935-7; app w Robert Johnson on THE ELDER MOTEN HOUR, local radio, Detroit, MI, 1937; settled in Memphis to work outside music with occasional tours w Baby Boy Warren and others into Tennessee/Arkansas/Missouri, 1937-41; moved to Chicago, IL, to frequently work outside music with occasional gigs for tips on Maxwell Street from 1941; formed own trio working Big Jerry Johnson's Cozy Corner Club/Frosty Corner/Tom's Tavern/Club DeLisa, Chicago, 1941; worked Don's Den, Chicago, 1942; Ma's Place, Chicago, 1942; formed own Dukes of Swing working Apex Chateau, Robbins, IL, 1943-5; rec Columbia-Testament label, Chicago, 1946; continued mostly outside music work, Chicago, into 50s; rec Chess label, Chicago, 1950; rec JOB label, Chicago, 1952-3; worked Frosty Corner, Chicago, c1953; frequently rec acc to many bluesmen with frequent gigs in local groups, Chicago, through 50s; worked w Sonny Boy Williamson (Alex Miller) Band, Chicago, 1956-7; worked outside music, Chicago area, 1957-64; rec Vanguard label, Chicago, 1965; rec Testament label, Chicago, 1966; rec Blue Horizon label, Chicago, 1968; worked Univ of Chicago R&B Festival, Chicago, 1968; frequently worked Ash Grove, Los Angeles, CA, 1968-72; New Orleans House, Los Angeles, 1968; Hunter Col, NYC, NY, 1969; Half Note, NYC, 1969; Electric Circus, NYC, 1969; toured w Chicago All Stars working jazz/folk clubs through US/Europe, 1969; rec w Chicago All Stars, MPS label, Cologne, Ger, 1969; rec Testament label, Los Angeles, 1969; worked Chicago Blues Festival, Chicago, 1969; rec Adelphi label, Chicago, 1969; moved to Holt, AL, to work outside music from 1969; worked Vieux Carre Club/61 Club/Down Under Coffeehouse/others, Holt, AL, from 1970; toured England working club/concert dates, 1970; worked Berlin Jazz Days Festival, Berlin, Ger, 1970; Wisconsin Blues Festival, Beloit, WI, 1970; Ann Arbor Blues Festival, Ann Arbor, MI, 1970; Old Cellar, Vancouver, Can, 1970; rec Testament label, Altadena, CA, 1970; worked Memphis Blues Festival, Memphis, TN, 1970; app in film THE VELVET VAMPIRE, 1971; toured East Coast working club dates, 1971; worked Boston Blues Society Concert, Harvard Univ, Cambridge, MA, 1971; Washington Blues Festival, Washington, DC, 1971; Festival of American Folklife, Washington, DC, 1971; app in film ROOTS OF AMERICAN MUSIC: COUNTRY & URBAN MUSIC (pt 2), 1971; Mariposa Folk Festival, Toronto, Can, 1971; toured w own Stars of Alabama working club dates through Alabama/Mississippi, early 70s; app on local show, WCFT-TV, Tuscaloosa, AL, c1972; worked Ann Arbor Blues Festival, Ann Arbor, MI, 1972 (por rel Atlantic label); Univ of Miami Blues Festival, Silver Springs, FL, 1972; Harpur Col, Binghamton, NY, 1972; rec Advent label, Los Angeles, CA, c1972; rec Biograph label, NYC, 1972; toured w Chicago Blues Festival working concert dates through Europe, 1972 (por Bordeaux, France, concert rel Black & Blue label); worked John Henry Memorial Concert, Beckley, WV, 1973; National Folk Festival, Wolf Trap Farm Park, Vienna, VA, 1973; app in videotape JOHNNY SHINES: BLACK AND BLUES, 1973; worked The Boarding House, San Francisco, CA, 1974; app on NATCH'L BLUES, CKUA-radio, Edmonton, Can, 1974; rec Xtra label, Edmonton, Can, 1974; rec Biograph label, NYC, 1974; worked New Orleans Jazz & Heritage Festival, New Orleans, LA, 1974; toured w Southern Folk Festival working college circuit, 1974; worked Newport Jazz Festival, NYC, 1974; John Henry Memorial Concert, Clifftop, WV, 1974-5; Univ of Miami Blues Festival, Coral Gables, FL, 1975; Univ of North Florida, Jacksonville, FL, 1975; toured w blues package show working concerts through Japan, 1975; worked Yubin Chokin Hall, Tokyo, Japan, 1975 (por rel Bourbon label); worked American Folklife Festival, Washington, DC, 1975; Mariposa Folk Festival, Toronto, Can, 1975; Our Lady of Peace RC Church, NYC, 1975; rec w Louisiana Red, Blue Labor label, White Plains, NY, 1975; app on BOB FASS Show, WBAI-FM-radio, NYC, 1975; worked Civic Center, Atlanta, GA, 1975;

John "Johnny" Shines *Photo by Doug Fulton. Courtesy* Living Blues *Magazine*

Schubert Theater, Los Angeles, CA, 1975; Cornell Folk Festival, Ithaca, NY, 1975; McCabe's, Santa Monica, CA, 1976; Winnipeg Folk Festival, Winnipeg, Can, 1976; John Henry Folk Festival, Camp Virgil Tate, Princeton, WV, 1976-7; Midwest Blues Festival, Univ of Notre Dame, South Bend, IN, 1976; Monterey Jazz Festival, Monterey, CA, 1976; New Orleans Jazz & Heritage Festival, New Orleans, LA, 1976; Red Creek Bar, Rochester, NY, 1977; toured w Portable Folk Festival working concert dates through South, 1977; app on local show, WACT-radio, Tuscaloosa, AL, 1977; worked Belle Star, Colden, NY, 1977; Knickerbocker Cafe, Westerly, RI, 1977; The Speakeasy Club, Cambridge, MA, 1977; app on GOOD MORNIN' BLUES, PBS-TV, 1978; toured concerts/festivals w Robert Jr Lockwood in US/Europe/Eng/Can/Australia from 1978; worked Mississippi Delta Blues Fest, Greenville, MS, 1979-80 (por 1980 concert shown MISSISSIPPI DELTA BLUES, PBS-TV); suffered stroke 1980 but continued US touring through 80s; app THE SEARCH FOR ROBERT JOHNSON, CH 4-TV (UK), c1991; left leg amputated, 1992; died of lung disease; buried Cedar Oak Memorial Park, Tuscaloosa

Songs: Abide My Wish/Arguing and Boodling/As Long as the World Stands/Back to the Steel Mill/Blood Ran Like Wine/The Blue Horizon/Can't Get Along with You/Chief Tuscaloosa/Deep Freeze/Delta Pine/Devil's Daughter/Down in Spirit/Evening Sun/Evil Hearted Women Blues/Fat Mama/For the Love of Mike/Freight Train/CB Blues/Give My Heart a Break/Gladrags/Goodbye/I Believe I Make a Change/I Cry I Cry/I Know the Winds Are Blowing/I Want to Warn You Baby/I'm Getting Old/Jim String/Just a Little Tenderness/Just Call Me/Little Wolf/Lost Love Letter Blues/Mean Black Gobbler/Moaning and Groaning/Mother's Place/Mr Cover Shaker/My Best Friend/My Love Can't Hide/Nobody's Fault But Mine/Pet Rabbit/Poor Man's Tonic/Ramblin'/Shotgun Whupin'/Skull and Crossbone Blues/Slavery Time Breakdown/So Cold in Vietnam/Stand by Me/Stop Cryin'/This Morning/Till I Made My Tonsils Sore/Tom Green's Farm/Too Lazy/Too Long Freight Trains/Vallie Lee/Worried Blues Ain't Bad/You Don't Have to Go/You're the One I Love

Infl by: Scrapper Blackwell/Howlin' Wolf/Blind Lemon Jefferson/Lonnie Johnson/Robert Johnson/Charley Patton/Willie Reed/Peetie Wheatstraw
Infl to: Floyd Jones/Johnny Winter

Quotes: "[He rates] among the most important and individualistic blues stylists of the post-war years"—Pete Welding, Testament album 2212

"A forceful explosive singer whose strong, vibrato laden voice possesses a range and sensitivity which is rivaled by few other bluesmen"—Peter Guralnick, *Feel Like Going Home*, Outerbridge & Dienstfrey, 1971

References: Living Blues magazine, Jul 1975, pp 23-32
Feel Like Going Home, Peter Guralnick, Outerbridge & Dienstfrey, 1971
Blues World magazine (UK), Winter 1973, pp 3-13

SHOE SHINE JOHNNY

(see Shines, John)

SHORT, JD *"Jaydee"/"Jelly Jaw"*

Courtesy Sing Out *Magazine*

Born: Dec 26, 1902, Port Gibson (Claiborne Co), MS
Died: Oct 21, 1962, St Louis, MO
Inst: Clarinet/Cymbals/Drums/Guitar/Harmonica/Piano/Saxophone

Father was Preston Short, a guitarist; parents were migrant farmers and he frequently moved through Hollandale/Shoals, MS, area from childhood; raised/worked outside music on farm, Clarksdale, MS, area c1912-23; learned guitar/piano and frequently worked local parties/suppers in Delta area of Mississippi, 1919-23; moved to St Louis, MO, to work outside music with occasional weekend gigs/street work w Neckbones/Henry Spaulding/others, 1923 into 30s; rec Paramount label, Grafton, WI, 1930; rec Vocalion label, NYC, 1932; frequently worked w Douglas Williams Band (as sideman) in local club dates, East St Louis, IL, from mid-30s; worked w Honeyboy Edwards at local joints/parties, St Louis, MO, 1937-8; served in US Army (receiving medical discharge), 1942-3; returned to St Louis, MO, to work as one-man band through area with frequent outside music work through 40s/50s; frequently worked w Big Joe Williams (or as single) in local hillbilly taverns, St Louis, late 50s; rec Delmark label, St Louis, 1958; rec Folkways/Sonet labels, St Louis, 1962; suffered heart attack at home and DOA Homer G Phillips Hospital, buried Jefferson Barracks Cemetery, St Louis, MO; app in documentary film THE BLUES, rel 1963

Personal: Married Pearl ———; married Lola Belle ———. Cousin of Big Joe Williams and Honeyboy Edwards. Unconfirmed report to have rec as Joe C Stone (Stoat). Incorrectly reported in early references to have been JT "Funny Papa (Paper)" Smith, singer/musician. Named "Jelly Jaw" due to his noticeable mouth vibrato during performances. Given names are initials only

Songs: By the Spoonful/Drafted Mama/East St Louis/Help Me Some/I'm Just Wastin' My Time/Lonesome Swamp Rattlesnake/Make Me Down a Pallet/My Rare Dog/The Red River Run/Sliding Delta/So Much Wine/Starry Crown Blues/Telephone Arguin' Blues/Train Bring My Baby Back/Wake Up Bright Eye Mama/You're Tempting Me

Infl by: Son Harris/Willie Johnson/JT Smith

Quote: "[His] singing is pure Delta, but with the unique vibrato he had that made his music so individual"—Samuel B Charters, Sonet album 648

Reference: Delmark album 609

SHORTY GEORGE
(see Johnson, James "Stump")

SHOWER, HUDSON
(aka: Little Hudson)
Born: Sept 6, 1919, Anguilla (Sharkey Co), MS
Inst: Guitar

Father was Elijah Shower, a guitarist; mother was Ida Belle, a pianist/guitarist; moved to Louise, MS, where he was raised from 1928; learned guitar from uncle at about 12 years of age; moved to Chicago, IL, to work outside music from 1939; frequently worked w Willie Mabon/Lazy Bill/others in local club dates, Chicago, 1946 into 50s; formed own Red Devil Trio working Plantation Club/Club Alibi/Du Drop Inn/Cotton Club/Club Platmond/Evergreen Club/Zanzibar Club/Upstairs Lounge/others, Chicago, from 1951; rec JOB label, Chicago, 1953; worked The Shed Club, Robbins, IL, late 50s; Apex Club, La Grange, IL, late 50s (remote on WTAQ-radio); long residence at Hard Knob Club, Chicago, late 50s into 60s; worked Fickle Pickle, Chicago, 1963; Regent Ballroom, Chicago, 1964; frequently worked mostly outside music, Chicago, from 1964

Note: Some references incorrectly give surname as "Showers"

Song: Rough Treatment

Infl by: Lonnie Johnson

Quote: "A painstaking craftsman with decided views on the music"—Mike Rowe, *Blues Unlimited* magazine (UK), Dec 1974, p 16

Reference: Blues Unlimited magazine (UK), Dec 1974, p 16

SHUFFLIN' SAM
(see Brown, Robert)

SIB
(see Williamson, Sonny Boy)

SILLY KID, THE
(see Floyd, Frank)

SIMMONS, *"Little"* MACK *"Mac"*
(aka: Little Mack/Mac Sims/St Louis Mac)
Born: Jan 25, 1934, Twist (Cross Co), AR
Inst: Harmonica

Born/raised/worked farm from childhood; interested in music early and taught self harmonica as youth; frequently worked outside music with some local party work, Twist, AR, area, late 40s; moved to St Louis, MO, 1952; worked outside music with occasional work w Robert Nighthawk, St Louis, 1952-4; moved to Chicago, IL, 1954; formed own group to work Pete's Place, Chicago, 1954; Cadillac Baby Lounge, Chicago, 1954-8 (por 1958 date rel Bea & Baby label); Pepper's Lounge, Chicago, 1956-9; Sylvio's, Chicago, 1959; rec CJ label, Chicago, 1959; rec Bea & Baby label, Chicago, 1960; rec Checker/Pacer

Courtesy Sheldon Harris Collection

labels, Chicago, 1961; worked Walton's Corner, Chicago, c1961; w own group, Mr Lee's Lounge, Chicago, 1963; frequently worked as rec session musician with some local club work, Chicago, through 60s; rec Miss label, Chicago, 1969; worked w own Royal Aces, Pepper's Lounge, Chicago, 1969-72; Ash Grove, Los Angeles, CA, 1969; Chicago Blues Festival, Chicago, 1969; Sportsman's Club, Chicago, 1970; Tom's Musicians Lounge, Chicago, 1970; Blue Flame, Chicago, 1970-1; Don's Cedar Club, Chicago, 1970; worked club dates in Seattle, WA, 1970; Salt & Pepper Ballroom, Chicago, 1971 (remote on WOPA-radio); Banner Show Lounge, Chicago, 1972 (remote on WOPA-radio); app on BIG BILL HILL Show, WOPA-radio, Oak Park, IL, 1972; worked Chicago Auditorium, Chicago, 1973; rec Blue Light label, Chicago (?), c1973; worked Pepper's Hideout, Chicago, 1974-6; Fox Hole, Chicago, 1974; Green Bunny Lounge, Chicago, 1975; toured w Chicago Blues Festival working concert dates through Europe, 1975; worked The Amphitheater, Chicago, 1975; New Burning Spear, Chicago, 1976; rec PM label, Chicago, c1976; owned/operated/worked Club Zodiac, Chicago, 1976-7

Personal: Not to be confused with Little Mack Collins, bassist

Song: Come Back to Me Baby

Infl by: BB King/Jr Parker/Jimmy Reed/Little Walter

Reference: Blues Unlimited magazine (UK), Jun 1972, pp 15-16

SIMS, FRANKIE LEE
Born: Apr 30, 1917, New Orleans (Orleans Parish), LA
Died: May 10, 1970, Dallas, TX
Inst: Guitar

Father Henry Sims and mother Virginia Summuel were guitarists; one of 13 children; moved to Marshall, TX, c1927-9; taught self guitar late 20s; ran away from home to work local country dances/school closings/country parties, Crockett/Centerville, TX, area c1929 into 30s; attended Wiley Col, Marshall, TX, mid-30s; worked outside music (as elementary school teacher), Palestine, TX, late 30s; served in US Marines, c1942-5; settled in Dallas, TX, to work frequently w Aaron "T-Bone" Walker and others in local clubs, 1945 into 50s; worked w Smokey Hogg, Empire Room, Dallas, c1948; rec w Smokey Hogg, Blue Bonnet label, Dallas, 1948; worked The Longhorn, Dallas, 1948; rec Specialty label, Dallas, 1953; toured w Memphis Slim working theater dates through Midwest, mid-50s; rec Specialty/Ace labels, Jackson, MS/Dallas, TX, 1957; briefly worked local gigs in Chicago, IL, from c1957; worked Regal Theater, Chicago, c1957; reportedly app w Jimmy McCracklin on Dick Clark's AMERICAN BANDSTAND, ABC-TV, c1957; settled in Dallas, TX, to work local gigs from late 50s through 60s; worked Cabale Club, Berkeley, CA, c1963; entered Woodlawn Hospital where he died of pneumonia; buried Lincoln Memorial Cemetery, Dallas, TX

Personal: Married. His son Little Frankie Lee is recording artist. Was cousin of Lightnin' Hopkins. Reportedly nephew of Texas Alexander

Songs: Boogie Cross the Country/Cryin' Won't Help You/Don't Take It Out on Me/Frankie's Blues/I Done Talked and I Done Talked/Jelly Roll Baker/Lucy Mae Blues/Married Woman/Raggedy and Dirty

References: Blues Unlimited magazine (UK), Nov 1976, pp 20-2
Specialty album 2124

Frankie Lee Sims
Courtesy C Strachwitz, Arhoolie Records

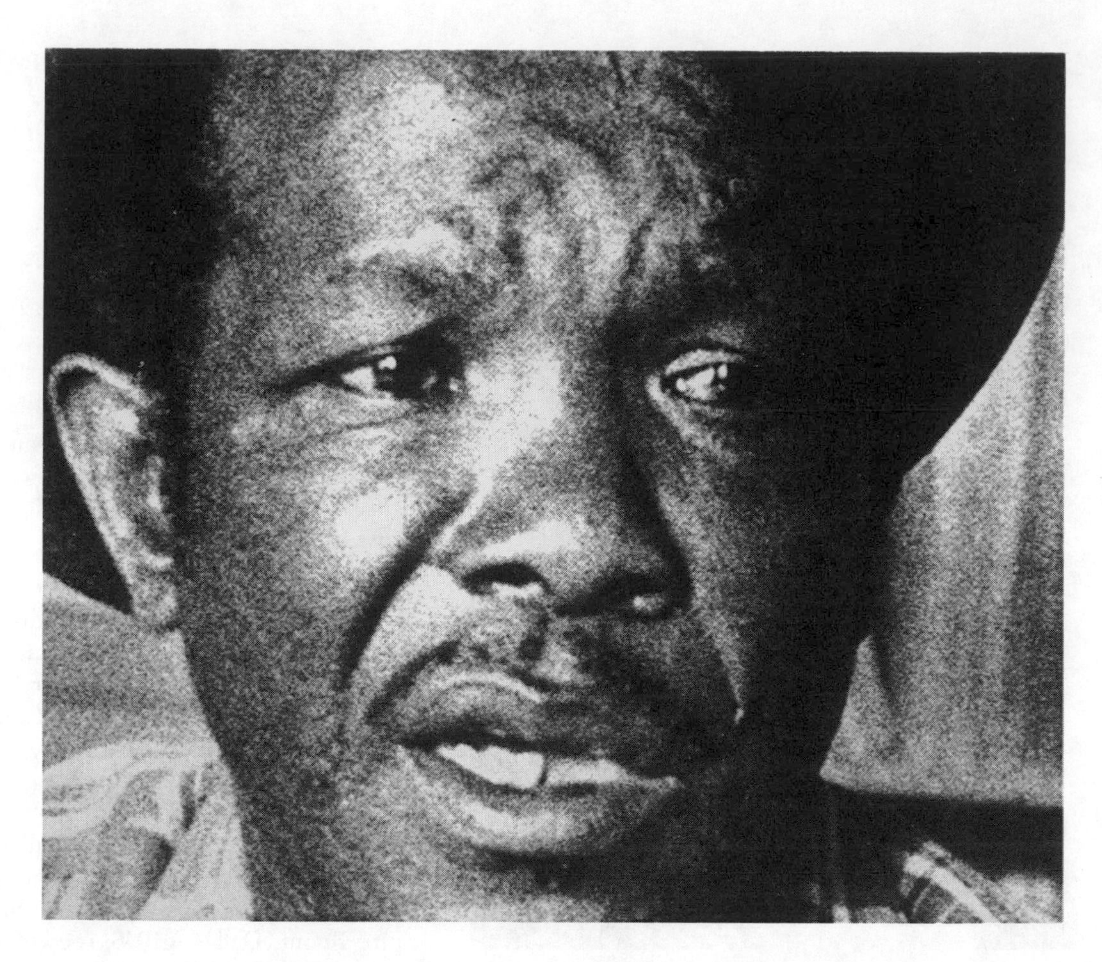

SIMS, MAC
(see Simmons, Mack)

SINGING CHRISTIAN, THE
(see White, Joshua)

SLIM HARPO
(see Moore, James)

SLIM PICKENS
(see Burns, Eddie)

SLUEFOOT JOE
(see Gibson, Clifford)

SMILING JOE
(see Joseph, Pleasant)

SMITH, AL K
(see King, Al)

SMITH, ANNE
(see Rainey, Gertrude)

SMITH, BESSIE

Born: Apr 15, 1894, Chattanooga (Hamilton Co), TN
Died: Sept 26, 1937, Clarksdale, MS

Father was William Smith, a part-time Baptist preacher; mother was Laura ———; one of 7 children; parents died before she was 8 years of age; frequently sang on streets for pennies, Chattanooga, TN, from c1903; worked w Ma Rainey, Moses Stokes Show, Ivory Theater, Chattanooga, 1912; toured (as chorus girl) in Irvin C Miller's tent show working under canvas through South c1912; worked 81 Theater, Atlanta, GA, 1913; teamed w Buzzin' Burton (as "Smith & Burton") working as singer/dancer in PARK'S BIG REVUE, Dixie Theater, Atlanta, 1914; toured w Ma Rainey in Fat Chappelle's Rabbit Foot Minstrels tent show through South c1915; toured w Pete Werley Florida Cotton Blossoms Minstrel Show/Silas Green Minstrel Show/others through South from mid-teens; worked Paradise Cafe, Atlantic City, NJ, 1917; teamed w Hazel Green working Douglas Gilmore Theater, Baltimore, MD, 1918; app (as singer/dancer/male impersonator) in own LIB-

Bessie Smith

Courtesy Frank Driggs Collection

ERTY BELLES Revue, 91 Theater, Atlanta, 1918-19; frequently worked w Charley Taylor Band in local club dates, Atlantic City, NJ, early 20s; worked w Charles Johnson Band, Paradise Gardens, Atlantic City, 1920-2; worked Horan's Madhouse Club, Philadelphia, PA, 1920-3; possibly rec test for Black Swan/Emerson labels, NYC, NY, 1921; frequently toured Milton Starr's Negro vaudeville circuit working theaters into 20s; frequently worked w own band, Standard Theater, Philadelphia, from 1921; app w Sidney Bechet in musical comedy HOW COME, Dunbar Theater, Philadelphia, 1923; app in musical revue TUNES AND TOPICS, Dunbar Theater, Philadelphia, 1923; possibly rec test for OKeh label, NYC, NY, 1923; rec extensively Columbia label, NYC, 1923-31; worked New Star Casino, NYC, 1923; 81 Theater, Atlanta, GA, 1923-5 (por 1923 date remote WSB-radio); Frolic Theater, Birmingham, AL, 1923-5; Lyric Theater, New Orleans, 1923; Bijou Theater, Nashville, TN, 1923-5; Beale Street Palace Theater, Memphis, TN, 1923-4 (por remote WMC-radio); Koppin Theater, Detroit, MI, 1923-9; Globe Theater, Cleveland, OH, 1923-9; Douglass Theater, Baltimore, MD, 1923; Orpheum Theater, Nashville, TN, 1924; Avenue Theater, Chicago, IL, 1924; Franklin Theater, Birmingham, AL, 1924; Roosevelt Theater, Cincinnati, OH, 1924-9; Lincoln Theater, Pittsburgh, PA, 1924; Star Theater, Philadelphia, 1924; app on WCAE-radio, Pittsburgh, 1924; worked The Nest Club, NYC, 1924; frequently worked as headliner, Lafayette Theater, NYC, 1924-7; Grand Theater, Chicago, 1924-7; Howard Theater, Washington, DC, 1924; Liberty Theater, Chattanooga, TN, 1925; frequently toured w own HARLEM FROLICS show working through South, 1925-9; worked Orpheum Theater, Newark, NJ, 1925-7; Paradise Gardens, Chicago, IL, 1925; Frolic Theater, Bessemer, AL, 1925-6; Booker T Washington Theater, St Louis, MO, 1927; Pythian Theater, Columbus, OH, 1927; frequently app in own YELLOW GIRL REVUE, Lincoln Theater, NYC, 1927-9; Lincoln Theater, Kansas City, MO, 1927; Alhambra Theater, NYC, 1927; app in musical comedy MISSISSIPPI DAYS, Lafayette Theater, NYC, then toured on TOBA circuit on East Coast, 1928; worked Belmont Theater, NYC, 1928; toured w own STEAMBOAT DAYS

Revue working theaters through South, 1928-9, then Lincoln Theater, NYC, 1929; worked Wallace Theater, Indianapolis, IN, 1929; app in HARLEM FROLICS Revue, Lincoln Theater, NYC, 1929; app in show PANSY, Belmont Theater, NYC, 1929; app in RCA Phototone 2-reel film short ST LOUIS BLUES, 1929 (por rel Circle label); app in musical comedy LATE HOUR DANCERS, Lafayette Theater/Lincoln Theater, NYC, 1929; app in musical comedy THE JAZZ REGIMENT, Lafayette Theater, NYC, 1929; toured w Lonnie Johnson in MIDNIGHT STEPPERS Revue working theaters through South, 1929; toured in MOANIN' LOW Revue working theaters on TOBA circuit, 1930; worked Pearl Theater, Philadelphia, PA, 1930; frequently worked Apollo Theater, NYC, 1930-6; app in own BESSIE SMITH REVUE, Alhambra Theater, NYC, 1930; app in own HAPPY TIMES Revue, Standard Theater, Philadelphia, 1930; worked Lincoln Theater, New Orleans, LA, 1930; Central Theater, Dallas, TX, 1930; Kit Kat Club, NYC, 1930; toured in BROADWAY REVUE working theaters, 1931; app in GOSSIPING LIZA Revue, Standard Theater, Philadelphia, 1931; worked Forrest Theater, Philadelphia, 1931; app in HOT STUFF OF 1933 Revue, Lincoln Theater, Philadelphia, 1932; worked Grand Theater, Chicago, 1932; Roosevelt Theater, Pittsburgh, PA, 1933; rec w Benny Goodman and others, OKeh label, NYC, NY, 1933; worked Lafayette Theater, NYC, 1933; app in CHRISTMAS REVELS Revue, Harlem Opera House, NYC, 1933-4; app w Miff Mole in (unknown) jazz series, NBC-radio Network, c1933; app w Ida Cox in FAN WAVES Revue, Apollo Theater, NYC, 1934; toured in HOT FROM HARLEM Revue working theaters through South, 1934; app w Don Redman Orch, Harlem Opera House, NYC, 1934; Apollo Theater, NYC, 1934; Lincoln Theater, Philadelphia, PA, 1935; app in BLACKBIRDS Revue, Cotton Club, NYC, 1935; app in STARS OVER BROADWAY Revue, Connie's Inn, NYC, 1936; worked Famous Door, NYC, 1936; Savoy Ballroom, NYC, 1936; app in LEAGUE OF RHYTHM Revue, Apollo Theater, NYC, 1936; worked Art's Cafe, Philadelphia, PA, 1936; Wander Inn, Philadelphia, 1937; toured w BROADWAY RASTUS Revue working theaters through South, 1937; while touring with that show suffered major injuries and shock in auto accident at Coahoma, MS; entered Afro-American Hospital where her arm was amputated but died of her injuries; buried Mount Lawn Cemetery, Sharon Hill, PA; a Bessie Smith Memorial Concert was held in Town Hall, NYC, 1948; an Edward Albee show DEATH OF BESSIE SMITH was produced, 1959, opened West Berlin, Ger, 1960, and NYC, 1961; a film short BESSIE SMITH was rel, 1968; a gravestone was erected and dedicated, 1970; a musical revue ME AND BESSIE played Ambassador Theater, NYC 1975-6, with tours into 1977

Note: Other reports on the circumstances of this singer's death have proven incorrect.

Personal: Married Earl Love (c1920-deceased); Jack Gee (1923-9). Adopted Jack Gee Jr, 1926. No relation to singers Clara Smith/Mamie Smith/Trixie Smith. Not to be confused with Bessie Mae Smith, OKeh recording artist

Billing: Empress of the Blues

Books: *Bessie Smith,* Paul Oliver, Cassel Ltd, 1959
Somebody's Angel Child, Carman Moore, Thomas Y Crowell Company, 1969
Bessie, Chris Albertson, Stein & Day, 1972
Bessie Smith, Empress of the Blues, Chris Albertson, Walter Kane & Son, Inc, 1975
Bessie Smith, Elaine Feinstein, 1985

Songs: Baby Doll/Backwater Blues/Blue Blues/Death Valley Moan/Dirty No-Gooder's Blues/Dixie Flyer Blues/Don't Fish in My Sea/Foolish Man Blues/Golden Rule Blues/Hard Time Blues/He's Gone Blues/Hot Springs Blues/In the House Blues/It Makes My Love Come Down/Jailhouse Blues/Jot 'em Down Blues/Lonesome Desert Blues/Long Old Road/Lost Your Head Blues/My Man Blues/Pickpocket Blues/Pinch Backs, Take 'em Away/Please Help Me Get Him off My Mind/Poor Man's Blues/Reckless Blues/Rocking Chair Blues/Safety Mama/Shipwreck Blues/Soft Pedal Blues/Sorrowful Blues/Spider Man Blues/Standin' in the Rain Blues/Sweet Potato Blues/Telephone Blues/Thinking Blues/Wasted Life Blues/Young Woman's Blues

Awards/Honors: Won *Record Changer* magazine All-Time All-Star Poll, 1951
Won *Downbeat* magazine International Jazz Critics Hall of Fame Award, 1967
A Bessie Smith commemorative medal was issued by American Negro Commemorative Society, 1971
The Columbia record album series "The World's Greatest Blues Singer" won Grand Prix du Disque, Montreux Jazz Festival, Montreux, Switzerland, 1971
Won American Music Conference National Music Award, 1976

Infl by: Cora Fisher/Blind Lemon Jefferson/Ma Rainey

Infl to: Louis Armstrong/Mildred Bailey/Connie Boswell/Olive Brown/Big Mama Bev/Barbara Dane/Margie Evans/Lillian Glinn/Billie Holiday/Pug Horton/Mahalia Jackson/Janis Joplin/Jean Kittrell/Carol Leigh/Odetta/Billie Pierce/Kerry Price/Jimmy Rushing/Irene Scruggs/Carrie Smith/Lucille Spann/Victoria Spivey/Jack Teagarden/Joe Turner/Tampa Red/Blanche Thomas/Big Mama Thornton/Dinah Washington/Mama Yancey/Pat Yankee

Quotes: "Bessie Smith's magnificent voice, majestic phrasing, clear and unaffected diction, and incomparable rhythmic sureness have had a far-reaching influence on the development of jazz singing"—Dan Morgenstern, *Downbeat* magazine, Aug 24, 1967, p 22

". . . Bessie Smith was destined to be the greatest Negro recording artist of her day and one of the most outstanding figures in the whole history of American music"—Paul Oliver, *Bessie Smith,* Cassel & Company Ltd, 1959

". . . The greatest of all female blues singers"—Chris Albertson, Columbia album GP-33

References: Bessie, Chris Albertson, Stein & Day, 1972

Great American Popular Singers, Henry Pleasants, Simon & Schuster, 1974

Downbeat magazine, Aug 24, 1967, pp 22-3

SMITH, CARRIE

Born: Aug 25, 1941, Fort Gaines (Clay Co), GA

Father is George Smith; mother is Mattie Evans; interested in music early and sang in local church choir at 7 years of age; moved to Newark, NJ, where she was raised from 8 years of age; frequently sang in choir at Greater Harvest Baptist Church, Newark,

Carrie Smith
Photo by Guy Schoukroun

NJ, through 50s; worked w Back Home Choir, Newport Jazz Festival, Newport, RI, 1957 (por rel Verve label); app on Joe Bostic's GOSPEL TV TIME Show, WOR-TV, NYC, NY, 1957; worked outside music, Newark, NJ, into 60s; worked w Brother John Sellers, Gerde's Folk City, NYC, c1966; worked Juanita Hall's Club, NYC, c1967; worked outside music (as personal aide to Juanita Hall), Las Vegas, NV, c1967; worked (solo) gospel program, Town Hall, NYC, c1968; worked Ye Little Club, Beverly Hills, CA, c1968; app on ART LINKLETTER Show (HOUSE PARTY), CBS-TV, c1969; w Al Hirt's New Orleans Music Festival, Carnegie Hall, NYC, 1970; toured w Big Tiny Little working Western Hotel chain club dates across US c1970-2; worked USO package show, Guantanamo Bay, Cuba, c1972; worked extended residency w Big Tiny Little, Al Hirt's Club, New Orleans, LA, c1972; settled in Union, NJ, c1973; worked w Tyree Glenn Sextet, Royal Box, Americana Hotel, NYC, 1973; worked some club dates out of NYC area, 1974; worked w New York Jazz Repertory Company, Carnegie Hall, NYC, 1975 (por rel Atlantic label); w Jonah Jones Orch, Rainbow Room, NYC, 1975; Sonny's Place, Seaford, NY, 1975; Kennedy Center, Washington, DC, c1975; Smithsonian Institute concert, Washington, DC, 1975; toured w New York Jazz Repertory Company working concert dates through Soviet Union, 1975; worked Newport Jazz Festival, NYC, 1976; w Slam Stewart, The Forum, Binghamton, NY, 1976; The Nice Jazz Festival, Nice, France, 1976; toured Europe working concert dates, 1976; rec Black & Blue label, Barcelona, Spain, 1976; worked Ronnie Scott's Club, London, Eng, 1976-7; Basin Street, Toronto, Can, 1976; frequently worked Eddie Condon's Club, NYC, 1976-7; Storyville Club, NYC, 1976; worked Broadmoor Hotel, Beulah, CO, 1976 (por shown in film DICK GIBSON'S JAZZ PARTY); w Alvin Ailey American Dance Company, New York City Center, NYC, 1976; app on JOE FRANKLIN Show, WOR-TV, NYC, 1977; worked Rainbow Room, NYC, 1977-8; w New York Repertory Orch, The New School for Social Research, NYC, 1977; toured w Harlem on Parade Show working Nice Jazz Festival, Nice, France, then concerts in Tunisia/Switzerland/Holland, 1977; rec Black & Blue label, Bordeaux/Paris, France, 1977; worked Newport Jazz Festival Blues Picnic, Waterloo Village, Stanhope, NJ, 1977; toured w New All-Stars working concerts across US, 1977; worked Monterey Jazz Festival, Monterey, CA, 1977; Ronnie Scott's Club, London, Eng, 1978; Hotel Meridian, Paris, France, 1978; Fortune Garden, NYC, 1978

Infl by: Ella Fitzgerald/Billie Holiday/Peggy Lee/Miss Rhapsody/Bessie Smith/Victoria Spivey/Dinah Washington

Quotes: "She is blessed with a rich, vibrant, contralto voice and sings with great feeling and a compelling rhythmic swing at any tempo"—Eric Townley, *Jazz Journal* magazine (UK), Nov 1976, p 4

"Carrie Smith carries off Bessie Smith more convincingly than any other singer I've heard . . ."—Dan Morgenstern, *Jazz Journal* magazine (UK), Jun 1977, p 21

Reference: Jazz Journal magazine (UK), Nov 1976, pp 4-5

SMITH, CLARA

(aka: Violet Green)

Courtesy Sheldon Harris Collection

Born: c1894, Spartanburg (Spartanburg Co), SC
Died: Feb 2, 1935, Detroit, MI
Inst: Piano

Reportedly worked on many southern vaudeville theater circuits as youngster from c1910 through teens; worked as headline attraction, Lyric Theater, New Orleans, LA/Bijou Theater, Nashville, TN and other TOBA circuit theaters from 1918; toured w Al Well's Smart Set tent show working under canvas through South, 1920; worked Dream Theater, Columbus, GA, 1921; Booker T Washington Theater, St Louis, MO, 1923; settled in New York, NY, 1923, to work Harlem cellar clubs/speakeasies/cabarets; rec w

Bessie Smith/Lonnie Johnson/others, Columbia label, NYC, 1923-32; owned/operated/worked Clara Smith Theatrical Club, NYC, from 1924; toured West Coast working theater dates, 1924-5; worked Bijou Theater, Nashville, TN, 1925; Lafayette Theater, NYC, 1925; app in own BLACK BOTTOM Revue, Lincoln Theater, NYC, 1927; app in own CLARA SMITH REVUE, Lincoln Theater, NYC, 1927; worked Apollo Theater, Atlantic City, NJ, 1927; app in SWANEE CLUB REVUE, Lafayette Theater, NYC, 1928; app w Swanee Club Revue on local radio, NYC, 1928; app in OPHELIA SNOW FROM BALTIMO Revue, Lincoln Theater, NYC, 1928-9; app in DREAM GIRLS Revue, Alhambra Theater, NYC, 1929; app in CANDIED SWEETS Revue, Alhambra Theater, NYC, 1929; app in HELLO 1930 Revue, Alhambra Theater, NYC, 1929-30; app in HERE WE ARE Revue, Alhambra Theater, NYC, 1930; app in DUSTY LANE Revue, Alhambra Theater, NYC, 1930; app in show SWEET CHARIOT, Ambassador Theater, NYC, 1930; app in JANUARY JUBILEE Revue, Alhambra Theater, NYC, 1931; worked w Charlie Johnson's Paradise Band, Harlem Opera House, NYC, 1931; app in all-Negro musical Western show TROUBLE ON THE RANCH, Standard Theater, Philadelphia, PA, 1931; frequently worked club dates, Cleveland, OH, early 30s; worked Harlem Opera House, NYC, 1932; app in HARLEM MADNESS Revue, Harlem Fifth Avenue Theater, NYC, 1933; worked Orchestra Gardens, Detroit, MI, 1934-5; worked w Paul Barbarin, Strollers Club, NYC, 1935; entered Parkside Hospital where she died of heart disease; buried Lincoln Cemetery, Macomb County, MI

Personal: Married Charles Wesley (ex-baseball manager) (1926-). No relation to singers Bessie Smith/Mamie Smith

Billings: Jolly Clara Smith/The Queen of the Moaners/The World's Champion Moaner

Songs: Court House Blues/Deep Blue Sea Blues/Every Woman Blues/So Long Jim

Quotes: ". . . although Clara could be extremely moving with blues numbers, she was equally at home tackling a boisterous comedy routine or a conventional popular song"—Norman Stevens, VJM album 15

"Her voice is powerful or melancholy by turn. It tears the blood from one's heart"—Carl Van Vechten, *Vanity Fair* magazine, 1926

Reference: Jazz Monthly magazine (UK), Apr 1958, p 8

SMITH, CLARENCE *"Pine Top"*
Born: Jun 11, 1904, Troy (Pike Co), AL
Died: Mar 15, 1929, Chicago, IL
Inst: Piano

Father was Sam Smith; mother was Molly ———; one of 5 children; moved to Birmingham, AL, 1918, where he taught self piano; frequently worked East End Park, Birmingham, 1918-20; moved to Pittsburgh, PA, working local club/cabaret dates from 1920; frequently toured w Raymond Brothers/Whitman Sisters/Matty Dorsey's Pickaninnies/other road shows as pianist/comedian/dancer/monologist/singer out of Pittsburgh, into 20s; worked The Rathskeller, Pittsburgh, 1924; toured extensively w Ma Rainey/Butterbeans and Susie/Grant and Wilson/others in various vaudeville acts at Bailey's 81 Theater, Atlanta, GA/Monogram Theater, Chicago, IL/Grand Theater, Chicago, IL/Lyric Theater, New Orleans, LA/Koppin Theater, Detroit, MI/Barassos Theater, Memphis, TN/other theaters on TOBA circuit to 1928; frequently worked solo at rent parties/chittlin' suppers/whorehouses in Omaha, NE/St Louis, MO/Chicago, IL, to late 20s; settled in Chicago, IL, 1928; worked Forestville Tavern, Chicago, 1928; rec Vocalion/Brunswick labels, Chicago, 1928-9; while attending a dance at Masonic Lodge Hall was accidentally shot by one David Bell; taken to Henrotin Hospital where he died of hemorrhage; buried Restvale Cemetery, Worth, IL

Personal: Married Sarah Horton in 1924. 2 children. Named "Pine Top" during childhood as he often played in local pine trees (as reported by wife and refutes other references to his hair color and head shape). Not to be confused with pianist "Pinetop" (Aaron Sparks) or pianist Joe Willie "Pinetop" Perkins

Book: 5 Boogie Woogie Blues Piano Solos by Pine Top Smith, Frank Paparelli, Leeds Music Corporation, 1941

Songs: I Got More Sense Than That/I'm Sober Now/Jump Steady Blues/Now I Ain't Got Nothing at All/Pinetop's Blues/Pinetop's Boogie Woogie

Infl by: Jimmy Yancey

Infl to: Memphis Slim/Romeo Nelson/Pinetop Perkins

Quotes: "Pinetop, in his day, was the greatest of the boogie pianists and probably did more than any other individual to make the style practical and actually identify his mode of playing"—Sharon A Pease, *Downbeat* magazine, Oct 15, 1939, p 8

"As a blues singer, Pine Top was a folk artist

of rare distinction, in spite of a peculiar high-pitched voice"—(William Russell) Frederic Ramsey Jr/ Charles Edward Smith, *Jazzmen*, Harcourt, Brace & Company, 1939

Reference: Downbeat magazine, Oct 1/Oct 15, 1939

SMITH, DRIFTING
(see Mickle, Elmon)

SMITH, FUNNY PAPA/PAPER
(see Smith, John)

SMITH, *"Little"* GEORGE "Harmonica"
(aka: George Allen/Harmonica King/Little Walter Jr)
Born: Apr 22, 1924, Helena (Phillips Co), AR
Died: Oct 2, 1983, Los Angeles, CA
Inst: Harmonica

Father was James Smith; mother was Jessie ____ who played guitar/piano/harmonica; born Allen George Smith; one of 3 children; interesed in music early and learned harmonica from mother at 4 years of age; moved to Cairo, IL, where he was raised from childhood; frequently toured w Earley Woods Country Band working dances/picnics/honky-tonks/jukes through Illinois/Kentucky/Mississippi/ elsewhere, 1934-6; left home to hobo through South working outside music with frequent street singing (as "Hip-Cat"), late 30s into 40s; frequently worked outside music in various government work programs (as National Recovery Act [NRA]/Civilian Conservation Corps [CCC] and others) into early 40s; settled in Rock Island, IL, to work outside music with occasional local gigs, 1941-3; toured w The Jackson Jubilee singers working churches out of Jackson, MS, 1943-4; frequently worked streets for tips through Mississippi through 40s; worked outside music (as projectionist/ promoter/some-time performer), Dixie Theater, Itta Benna, MS, 1948-51; settled in Chicago, IL, to work outside music from 1951; worked w Otis Rush in local club dates, Chicago, 1951-2; worked Zanzibar Club, Chicago, 1953; Ader's Lounge, Chicago, 1953; worked w Muddy Waters Band in local club dates, Chicago, with tours through South working clubs/dances, 1954; worked Orchid Room, Kansas City, MO, 1954; rec RPM label, Kansas City, MO, 1954; rec w Otis Spann, Checker label, Chicago, 1955; rec (as "Little Walter Jr"/"Harmonica King"), Lapel label, Los Angeles, 1955; toured w Jack Dupree for Universal Attractions package show working clubs/concerts through Southwest, 1955; rec w Jack Dupree, King label, Cincinnati, OH, 1955; formed own trio to work as feature act (or as acc to Mama Thornton) in local club dates, Los Angeles, CA/Palm Springs, CA/ Phoenix, AZ, from 1955; rec J&M/Carolyn labels, Los Angeles (?), 1956; rec Sotoplay label (as "George Allen"), Oakland, CA, 1957; worked as single in Los Angeles/San Francisco areas through 50s into 60s; rec Sotoplay label, Oakland, CA, 1965; formed own Bacon Fat group working club dates on West Coast, mid-60s; replaced Jimmy Cotton in Muddy Waters Band working clubs in Chicago, 1966-7; rec Spivey label, Chicago (?), c1966; worked Univ of Southern California, Los Angeles, 1967; w Mama Thornton, Monterey Jazz Festival, Monterey, CA, 1968; rec World Pacific/Liberty labels, Los Angeles, 1968-9; worked Ash Grove, Los Angeles, 1968; Golden Bear, Los Angeles, 1969; w Mama Thornton, Thee Experience Club, Los Angeles (?), 1969 (por rel Mercury label); rec Blue Horizon label, Los Angeles, 1969; rec BluesWay label, Hollywood, CA, 1969; rec w Aaron "T-Bone" Walker, BluesTime label, NYC, 1969; worked Ungano's, NYC, 1969; Ann Arbor Blues Festival, Ann Arbor, MI, 1970; rec Deram label, London, Eng, 1970; worked w Muddy Waters Band, 1971; rec acc to Eddie Taylor, Advent label, Hollywood, CA/Glendale, CA, 1972; worked w own quintet, Ash Grove, Los Angeles, 1972; Shaboo Inn, Mansfield, CT, 1973; Academy of Music, NYC, 1973; Topanga Corral, Los Angeles, 1974; Golden Bear, Los Angeles, 1974; Berkeley Blues Festival, Berkeley, CA, 1975; T-Bone Walker Memorial Concert, Musicians Union Hall, Los Angeles, 1975; w Big Mama Thornton, Monroe State Prison, Monroe, WA, 1975 (por rel Vanguard label); Oregon State Reformatory, Eugene, OR, 1975 (por rel Vanguard label); Monterey Jazz Festival, Monterey, CA, 1975 (por heard KEST-radio, San Francisco); Kingston Mines, Chicago, IL, 1976; Midwest Blues Festival, Univ of Notre Dame, South Bend, IN, 1976; Eugene Blues Festival, Eugene, OR, 1977; Murphy's, Eugene, 1977; worked clubs/festivals on West Coast into 80s; toured Japan, 1979; toured Europe, 1980-2; toured US/Canada, 1983; died of heart disease; buried Compton, CA

Songs: As Long as I Live/Blowing the Blues/Blue Switch/Blues for Reverend King/Blue Fog/Brown Mule/Hey Mr Porter/I Found My Baby/If You Were a Rabbit/Juicy Harmonica/Look Out Victoria/Loose Screws/McComb Mississippi/Milk That Cow/Mississippi River Blues/No Time for Jive/Nobody Knows/ Old Ugly Man Like Me/Roaming/Sometime You Win When You Lose/Soul Feet/Tight Dress/Times Won't Be Hard Always/Trying to Hide the Things I Do

Infl by: Larry Adler/Little Walter

Quotes: ". . . a nonpareil blues singer and harmonica

George "Harmonica" Smith *Courtesy* Living Blues *Magazine*

player"—Pete Welding, World Pacific album 21887

"[He] has a strong sense of his musical individuality and independence and . . . cares very deeply about the music he plays"—Peter Hatch, *Coda* magazine (Canada), Feb 1971, p 12

References: Coda magazine (Canada), Feb 1971, pp 12-13

Blues Unlimited magazine (UK), Dec 1966, pp 5-8

SMITH, GUY
(see Erby, John)

SMITH, HONEY BOY
(see Whittaker, Hudson)

SMITH, HOWLIN'
(see Smith, John)

SMITH, JANE
(see Cox, Ida)

SMITH, JOHN T *"JT"/"Funny Papa (Paper)"/"Howlin' "*
(aka: The Howlin' Wolf)
Born: 1890, Texas (unconfirmed)
Died: (unknown)
Inst: Guitar

Reportedly worked outside music from childhood and became interested in music during youth; worked Lincoln Theater, NYC, NY, c1917; worked outside music (as overseer of plantation) with frequent work at picnics/local dances/other events, Wickoff's Store, OK, area through 20s/30s; frequently worked w Tom Shaw in Frederick, OK, area, 1930-1; rec Vocalion label, Chicago, IL, 1930-1; rec acc to Dessa Foster, Melotone label, Chicago, 1931; served time in local penitentiary in Texas c1931-5; rec Vocalion label, Ft Worth, TX, 1935; rec acc to Bernice Edwards, Vocalion label, Ft Worth, 1935; frequently toured w Texas Alexander working jukes through Texas 1939; whereabouts unknown thereafter

Personal: Married (during 20s). Took name "The Howlin' Wolf" from his 1930 record of same name. Not to be confused with Chester Burnett who also used pseudonym "Howlin' Wolf." Frequently known to have worn stovepipe hat with his name stitched thereon

Infl to: Willie Lane/Tom Shaw/JD Short/Josh White

Quotes: "Smith had a rare ability to create vocal melodies and accompaniment-patterns of subtle novelty . . ."—Tony Russell, *Jazz & Blues* magazine (UK), Apr 1971, p 41

"One of the few recorded bluesmen . . . who made a real art of blues composition"—Nick Perls, Yazoo album 1031

Reference: Yazoo album 1031

SMITH, MABEL LOUISE
(aka: Big Maybelle/Mamie Webster)
Born: May 1, 1924, Jackson (Madison Co), TN
Died: Jan 23, 1972, Cleveland, OH
Inst: Piano

Father was Frank W Smith; mother was Alice Easley; frequently sang in local Sanctified Church choir, Jackson, TN, c1932-6; won first prize in Memphis Cotton Carnival Singing Contest, Memphis, TN, 1932; worked w Dave Clark Band, Memphis, mid-30s; toured w Sweethearts of Rhythm (all girl) band working dances from Pineywood, MS, to Indianapolis, IN, from 1936 into 40s; worked dance dates w Christine Chatman Orch, 1944; rec w Christine Chatman, Decca label, NYC, NY, 1944; worked/toured w Tiny Bradshaw Orch, 1947-50; rec King label, Cincinnati, OH (?), 1947; worked w Jimmy Witherspoon, Flame Show Bar, Detroit, MI, 1951; rec w Leroy Kirkland Orch, OKeh label, NYC, 1952-4; frequently worked as single, Baby Grand Club and others, NYC, through 50s; worked w Roy Hamilton Show, Trianon Club, Chicago, IL, c1954; Royal Peacock, Atlanta, GA, 1954; rec w Danny Mendelsohn Orch, OKeh label, NYC (?), 1954; rec w Quincy Jones Orch, OKeh label, NYC, 1955; rec w Kelly Owens Orch/Ernie Wilkins Orch, Savoy label, NYC/elsewhere, 1956-9; worked Newport Jazz Festival, Newport, RI, 1958 (por shown in film JAZZ ON A SUMMER'S DAY); worked Mardi Gras Club, Kansas City, MO, 1959; Bud Billiken parade/concert, Chicago, IL, 1960; Connie's, NYC, NY, 1960; frequently worked Apollo Theater, NYC, 1960-7; Blues at Carnegie Show, Carnegie Hall, NYC, 1961; Branker's Club, NYC, 1961; w King Curtis group, Birdland, NYC, 1963; Town Hill Restaurant, Brooklyn, NY, c1964; rec Brunswick/Rojac labels (NYC?), mid-60s; worked Brevoort Theater, Brooklyn, NY, 1966; Baron's Lounge, NYC, 1967; mostly inactive in music due to illness from late 60s; settled in Cleveland, OH, c1967; worked Cleveland Arts Festival, Cleveland, 1967; Randalls Island Concert, NYC, 1968; Electric Lady, NYC, 1971; entered Cleveland Metropolitan General Hospital where she died of diabetic coma; buried Evergreen Cemetery, Bedford, OH

Mabel Smith (Big Maybelle) *Courtesy Sheldon Harris Collection*

Personal: Had one child. Was known to have sung in 4 languages

Quotes: "One of the great female blues shouters"—Mike Leadbitter, *Blues Unlimited* magazine (UK), Aug 1973, p 26

"When she sang she was possessed by a magic that could drive out her own personal devils . . ."—Dave Godin, *Black Music* magazine (UK), Feb 1974, p 44

SMITH, MAMIE

Born: May 26, 1883, Cincinnati (Hamilton Co), OH (unconfirmed)
Died: Sept 16, 1946, New York, NY (unconfirmed)
Inst: Piano

Left home to tour w The Four Dancing Mitchells (as dancer) working theater circuit from c1893; toured (as chorus dancer) in J Homer Tutt/Salem Tutt-Whitney's The Smart Set Company working theaters across US, 1912; frequently worked Barron's/Leroy's/Edmond's/Percy Brown's/William Banks/Goldgraben's and other clubs/cabarets/cafes, NYC, NY, area, 1913-20; app in Perry Bradford's musical revue MADE IN HARLEM, Lincoln Theater, NYC, 1918; frequently worked Lincoln Theater, NYC, 1918-20; The Orient, NYC, 1919; rec (unissued test) Victor label, NYC, 1920; worked Digg's Cafe, NYC, 1920; rec extensively, OKeh label, NYC, 1920-3; worked Gibson's Standard Theater, Philadelphia, PA, 1920; toured in Fanchon and Marco Revue working theater dates into 20s; worked w own Jazz Hounds, Dunbar Theater, Philadelphia, PA, 1920; Putnam Theater, Brooklyn, NY, 1920; Howard Theater, Washington, DC, 1920; 12th Street Theater, Kansas City, MO, 1921; Billy Sunday's Tabernacle, Norfolk, VA, c1921; Pershine Theater, Philadelphia, PA, 1921; Avenue Theater, Chicago, IL, 1921-2; Bal Tabarin Theater, Atlantic City, NJ, 1922; Proctor's, NYC, NY, 1922; Loew's Theater, Toronto, Can, 1922; Loew's Theater, Ottawa, Can, 1922; Metropolitan Theater, Brooklyn, NY, 1922; Lincoln Theater, NYC, 1922; w Bubber Miley/Sidney Bechet, Garden of Joy, NYC, 1922; app in musical comedy FOLLOW ME, Lafayette Theater, NYC, 1922; app w Jazz Hounds as headliner, Lafayette Theater, NYC, 1923; toured in own STRUTTIN' ALONG Revue working theaters on West Coast, 1923; worked Green Parrot Dance Hall, Dallas, TX, c1923; City Auditorium, Houston, TX, c1924; Chicago Auditorium, Chicago, 1924; Indiana Theater, Chicago, 1924; app as headliner, SYNCOPATIONLAND REVUE, Lafayette Theater, NYC, 1924; app in DIXIE REVUE, Lafayette Theater, NYC, 1924; rec Ajax label, NYC, 1924; worked w own Jazz Hounds, Lafayette Theater, NYC, 1924; frequently worked Lincoln Theater, NYC, 1924-5; app in own SYNCOPATED REVUE, Howard Theater, Washington, DC, 1925; frequently worked Entertainers Cabaret, New Orleans, LA, mid-20s; rec Victor label, NYC, 1926; worked Lafayette Theater, NYC, 1926; app in FROLICKING AROUND Revue, Lincoln Theater, NYC, 1926; worked Delancey Street Theater, NYC, 1926; toured in own Mamie Smith Company working theater dates on Loew's circuit through South, 1926-7; worked Orpheum Theater, Newark, NJ, 1927; Savoy Theater, Atlantic City, NJ, 1927; Carlton Theater, Red Bank, NJ, 1928; Capitol Theater, Trenton, NJ, 1928; app in musical comedy SUGAR CANE Revue, Lafayette Theater, NYC, 1928; app as Mamie Smith and Her Gang, A RIOT OF FUN Revue, Lincoln Theater, NYC, 1928; app in musical comedy SUN-TAN FROLICS, Lincoln Theater, NYC, 1929; app in film short JAILHOUSE BLUES, 1929; rec OKeh label, NYC, 1929; app w Fats Waller-Jimmie Johnson Syncopators in FIREWORKS OF 1930 Revue, Lafayette Theater, NYC, 1930; rec OKeh label, NYC, 1931; app in RHUMBALAND Revue, Lafayette Theater, NYC, 1931; toured w Fats Pichon Orch in own YELPING HOUNDS Revue working theater dates, 1932-4; worked Grand Theater, West Palm Beach, FL, 1932; app in (untitled) revue, Lafayette Theater, NYC, 1933; worked Harlem Opera House, NYC, 1935; toured Europe working theater dates c1936; worked w own Beale Street Boys, Town Casino, NYC, 1936; app w Lucky Millinder Orch in film PARADISE IN HARLEM, 1939; app in film MYSTERY IN SWING, 1940; toured Florida working club dates c1940; app in film MURDER ON LENOX AVE, 1941; app in film SUNDAY SINNERS, 1941; app w Lucky Millinder Orch in soundie film BECAUSE I LOVE YOU, c1943; worked Lido Ballroom, NYC, 1944; reportedly entered Harlem Hospital c1944 where she died after lengthy illness; buried Frederick Douglass Memorial Park Cemetery, Staten Island, NY

Note: Death dates have variously been reported as Sept 16, 1946/Oct 30, 1946/Nov 5, 1946/others. While a death certificate has been located only for the Sept 16 date, there is reason to believe that this may not be for the same person

Personal: Married William "Smitty" Smith, singer (c1912-); Sam Gardner, comedian (1920s); Jack Goldberg (c1929-). No relation to singers Bessie Smith/Clara Smith/Trixie Smith

Billing: Queen of the Blues

Mamie Smith *Courtesy Frank Driggs Collection*

Awards/Honors: Recognized as first Negro to record a vocal blues ("Crazy Blues," OKeh 4169, Aug 10, 1920)

Infl to: Monette Moore/Jimmy Rushing/Tampa Red/Sippie Wallace

Quotes: "It was her pioneering work that paved the way for every other blues artist, regardless of style"—Derrick Stewart-Baxter, *Ma Rainey and the Classic Blues Singers*, Studio Vista Ltd, 1970

"She was a very high-class entertainer, as well as being one of the best-looking women in the business . . ."—Willie "The Lion" Smith, *Music on My Mind*, Doubleday & Company, 1964

Reference: Jazz, A History of the New York Scene, Samuel B Charters/Leonard Kunstadt, Doubleday & Company, 1962

SMITH, MANDY
(see Miles, Elizabeth)

SMITH, MOSES *"Whispering"*

Photo by Norbert Hess. Courtesy Living Blues Magazine

Born: Jan 25, 1932, Union Church (Jefferson Co), MS
Died: Apr 28, 1984, Baton Rouge, LA
Inst: Harmonica

Began playing harmonica at 14 years of age; frequently worked in small local band in local jukes, Brookhaven, MS, through 50s; moved to Baton Rouge, LA, 1957; worked outside music with occasional bar/tavern work through 50s; teamed w Lightnin' Slim to work local clubs, Baton Rouge, 1960-2; formed own group to work local club dates, Baton Rouge/Monroe/Shreveport, LA, c1962-6; rec Excello label, Crowley, LA, 1963-4; worked mostly outside music in Baton Rouge from 1966; rec Excello/Arhoolie labels, Baton Rouge, 1970; rec Blue Horizon label, Baton Rouge, c1971; worked Montreux Jazz Festival, Montreux, Switzerland, 1972 (por rel Excello label); toured w American Folk Blues Festival working concerts through England/Europe, 1972; toured w American Blues Legends 73 working concert/TV/radio dates through England/Europe, 1973 (por shown in film BLUES LEGENDS 73/por rel Atlantic label); rec Big Bear-Polydor label, London, Eng, 1973; sit-in/pick-up jobs in Baton Rouge area through 70s; inactive due to illness early 80s

Songs: A Thousand Miles from Nowhere/Baton Rouge Breakdown/Cold Black Mare/I Know You Don't Love Me/It's All Over/Storm in Texas/Take Me Back Baby/Texas Flood/The Way You Treat Me/What in the World's Come Over You?/You Want Me to Do It Again?

Quote: "Don't let that name fool you about his style of singing. It's strictly a joke. Moses Smith shouts the blues in a hoarse, earthy voice"—Pierre Gonneau, Excello album 8020

Reference: Blues Unlimited (UK), Jul 1970, pp 4-5

SMITH, PINE TOP
(see Smith, Clarence)

SMITH, SUSIE
(see Moore, Monette)

SMITH, TRIXIE
(aka: Tessie Ames/Bessie Lee)
Born: 1895, Atlanta (Fulton Co), GA
Died: Sept 21, 1943, New York, NY

Attended Selma University, Selma, AL, as youth; moved to New York City, NY, working Edmond's Novelty Cafe, Brooklyn, NY/Lincoln Theater, NYC, from c1915; worked New Standard Theater, Philadelphia, PA, 1916; frequently toured as feature singer on TOBA circuit c1918 into 20s; worked w Edwards & Edwards (Butterbeans & Susie) in theater dates, Pittsburgh, PA, 1920; toured w Mabel Whitman troupe working theaters c1920; toured w Gonzell White Company working theaters, 1921; frequently worked Lincoln Theater, NYC, 1921-3; rec Black Swan label, NYC, 1921-3; worked Reisenweber's,

Courtesy Sheldon Harris Collection

NYC, 1922; toured in 7-11 Revue working theater dates, 1922; worked Manhattan Casino, NYC, 1922; reportedly app on WDT-radio, NYC, 1923; worked w Eddie Heywood Sr in theater dates, Philadelphia, PA, 1923; worked Lafayette Theater, NYC, 1923; rec w Fletcher Henderson Orch/Down Home Syncopators, Paramount label, NYC, 1923-4; rec Silvertone label, NYC, 1925; rec w Jimmy Blythe and His Ragmuffins, Paramount label, Chicago, IL, 1926; toured in MOONLIGHT FOLLIES Revue working theater dates, 1927; worked Keith's Prospect Theater, NYC, 1927; app in NEW YORK REVUE, Lincoln Theater, NYC, 1928; app in HIGH LIGHTS OF HARLEM Revue, Lincoln Theater, NYC, 1928; app in NEXT DOOR NEIGHBORS Revue, Lincoln Theater, NYC, 1928; toured (non-singing role) in show LILY WHITE, then at Majestic Theater, Brooklyn, NY, 1930; app in musical comedy SUNSHINE, Alhambra Theater, NYC, 1930; app in show BRASS ANKLE, Masque Theater, NYC, 1931; app w Mae West in show THE CONSTANT SINNER, Royale Theater, NYC, 1931; app in film THE BLACK KING, 1932; worked Harlem Opera House, NYC, 1933; app in Theater Guild Production of show LOUISIANA, 48th Street Theater, NYC, 1933; toured theater dates extensively across US, 1933-5; app in THE MAN FROM BALTIMORE Revue, Majestic Theater, Brooklyn, NY, 1934; rec Decca label, NYC, 1938-9; app (non-singing role) in show BIG WHITE FOG, Lincoln Theater, NYC, 1940; mostly inactive thereafter with some charity appearances into 40s; died after short illness

Billing: The Southern Nightingale

Songs: Mining Camp Blues/Railroad Blues/Trixie('s) Blues/The World's Jazz Crazy

Award/Honor: Won first prize (silver loving cup presented by Mrs Vernon Castle) in blues contest at Manhattan Casino, NYC, 1922

Quotes: "Trixie had depth, real warmth and appeal"—(Sam Price) Nat Shapiro/Nat Hentoff (ed), *Hear Me Talkin' to Ya*, Rinehart & Company, Inc, 1955

"One of the earliest of the vaudeville-styled blues singers to record . . ."—(Paul Oliver) Albert McCarthy/Alun Morgan/Paul Oliver/Max Harrison, *Jazz on Record*, Hanover Books Ltd, 1958

SMITH, WHISPERING
(see Smith, Moses)

SMOKEHOUSE CHARLEY
(see Dorsey, Thomas A)

SMOKY BABE
(see Brown, Robert)

SMOTHERS, OTIS *"Smokey"*

Photo by Jim O'Neal. Courtesy Living Blues Magazine

SMOTHERS

Born: Mar 21, 1929, Lexington (Holmes Co), MS
Died: Jul 23, 1993, Chicago, IL
Inst: Guitar

Raised in Tchula, MS, area; frequently sang in local Baptist church choir as youth; learned guitar and frequently worked school socials from c1942; moved to Chicago, IL, c1946; frequently worked w Bo Diddley/Henry Strong/others on streets for tips, Chicago, early 50s; worked w Big Boy Spires' Rocket Four group at Castle Rock/BeBop Inn/Stormy's Inn/Cotton Club/others, Chicago, through early 50s; worked w Bo Diddley, Sawdust Trail, Chicago, 1954; formed own combo working local club dates, Chicago, from 1955; rec acc w Howlin' Wolf Band, Chess label, Chicago, 1956; frequently worked as rec session man on local labels, Chicago, through 50s/60s; rec w Freddie King and others, Federal label, Cincinnati, OH, 1960-2; worked w Mojo Buford in Muddy Waters Jr Band, Smitty's Corner, Chicago, c1961; worked/toured w Muddy Waters group from c1961-2; worked frequently as sideman w Little Walter group/Willie Williams group/others in local club dates, Chicago, through 60s; worked Theresa's Tavern, Chicago, 1970; worked mostly outside music in Chicago from early 70s; worked Mr M's, Chicago, 1972; Louise's South Park Lounge, Chicago, 1974; worked North Side club dates, Chicago through 80s; rec Red Beans label, Chicago, (?), 1986; died of heart disease
Songs: Come Home Baby/Come On Rock Little Girl/Crying Tears/Midnight and Day/My Dog Can't Bark/Smokey's Lovesick Blues/What Am I Going to Do?

Infl by: Jimmy Reed

References: Nothing But the Blues, Mike Leadbitter, Hanover Books, 1971
Living Blues, Mar/Apr 1978, pp 18-20

SNOOKY
(see Pryor, James)

SON
(see Bonds, Son)

SON JOE
(see Lawlars, Ernest)

SONNY
(see Terry, Sonny)

SONNY T
(see Terry, Sonny)

SPANN, LUCILLE

Courtesy Sheldon Harris Collection

Born: Jun 23, 1938, Bolton (Hinds Co), MS

Father was Sherman Jenkins; mother was Gertrude ———; born Mahalia Lucille Jenkins; one of 9 children; moved to Chicago, IL, c1952; frequently sang gospel at Mt Eagle Baptist Church, Chicago, from mid-50s; worked outside music, Chicago, into 60s; teamed w Otis Spann to work college dates, mid-60s; rec w Otis Spann, BluesWay label, NYC, NY, 1967; worked Five Stages, Chicago, 1970; rec w Joe Young, BluesWay-Blues on Blues label, Chicago, 1971; worked Ann Arbor Blues Festival, Ann Arbor, MI, 1972-3 (por 1972 concert rel Atlantic label); worked Brown Shoe, Chicago, 1972; Sutherland Hotel, Chicago, 1972; Urban Blues Festival, Auditorium Theater, Chicago, 1974; Ratso's, Chicago, 1976

Personal: Married Otis Spann (c1967-died 1970), musician/blues singer

Songs: Dedicated to Otis/I'm a Fool/My Man/Queen Bee

Infl by: Billie Holiday/BB King/Bessie Smith

References: Jazz & Pop magazine, Mar 1968, pp 27-9
BluesWay album 6070

SPANN, OTIS

Born: Mar 21, 1930, Jackson (Hinds Co), MS
Died: Apr 24, 1970, Chicago, IL
Inst: Harmonica/Organ/Piano

Otis Spann *Courtesy Sheldon Harris Collection*

Reportedly son of Friday Ford, a piano player; stepfather was Frank Houston Spann, a preacher and musician; mother was Josephine Erby, a singing guitarist who had worked w Memphis Minnie/Bessie Smith/others; one of 5 children; taught self piano with some instructions by local musicians (Frank Spann/Friday Ford/Little Brother Montgomery) from age of 7; frequently played piano in father's church, Jackson, MS, late 30s; won first prize in talent contest, Alamo Theater, Jackson, 1938; frequently worked outside music with work w Johnny Jones at local house parties, Jackson area, late 30s to mid-40s; attended Campbell Jr Col, Jackson, mid-40s; worked outside music (as pro football player for Bells Team) with frequent work in local blues bands in bars/dives/clubs, Jackson area, c1944-6; active as Golden Gloves boxer, then turned pro, mid-40s; served in US Army in Japan/Germany, 1946-51; worked outside music with occasional work w Muddy Waters/Memphis Slim/Little Brother/Roosevelt Sykes/others at house parties/clubs/lounges in Chicago, IL, from 1951; formed own combo to work Tick Tock Lounge, Chicago, 1951-3; rec w Muddy Waters Band, Chess label, Chicago, 1952; worked w Louis Myers Band in local clubs, Chicago, 1953; replaced Big Maceo Merriweather in Muddy Waters Band to work/tour/rec with band almost regularly thereafter from 1953; worked Smitty's Corner, Chicago, 1953; rec w Howlin' Wolf, Chess label, Chicago, 1954; rec w Bo Diddley, Chess label, Chicago, 1955; worked/rec as house pianist for Chess label, Chicago, through 50s into 60s; rec under own name, Chess/Checker labels, Chicago, 1955-63; toured w Muddy Waters Band/Chris Barber Band working clubs/concerts through England, 1958; worked Leeds Festival, London, Eng, 1958; rec w Robert Jr Lockwood, Barnaby/Candid labels, NYC, NY, 1960; worked w Muddy Waters Band, Newport Jazz Festival, Newport, RI, 1960 (por shown in film THE SUBTERRANEANS/por shown in USIA film short series JAZZ-USA [#19]/por rel Chess label); rec Howlin' Wolf, Chess label, Chicago, 1960; rec Decca label, Chicago, 1960; frequently worked Smitty's Corner, Chicago, into early 60s; w Muddy Waters Band, Carnegie Hall, NYC, 1961; Copa Cabana Club, Chicago, 1963; toured w American Folk Blues Festival working concert dates through England/Europe, 1963 (por shown on I HEAR THE BLUES, Granada-TV, London, Eng); rec Fontana label, Bremen, Ger, 1963; rec Storyville label, Copenhagen, Den, 1963; w Muddy Waters, Chicago Folk Music Festival, Chicago, 1964; rec Testament label, Chicago, 1964-5; worked Hunter Col Blues Concert, NYC, 1964; toured w American Blues Caravan working concert dates through England, 1964 (por shown on BLUES & GOSPEL TRAIN Show, Granada-TV, London, Eng); rec Decca (Eng)/Ace of Clubs labels, London, Eng, 1964; toured France working concert dates, 1964; worked Pepper's Lounge, Chicago, 1964; Newport Folk Festival, Newport, RI, 1964; Downbeat Jazz Festival, Chicago, 1965; rec Prestige label, Chicago, 1965; rec acc to Johnny Young, Arhoolie label, Chicago, 1965; worked Slug's, NYC, 1966; Cafe A-Go-Go, NYC, 1966; rec Spivey label, NYC, 1966; rec Vanguard label, Chicago, 1966; rec BluesWay label, NYC, 1966-8; rec acc to Johnny Shines, Testament label, Chicago, 1966; worked Monterey Jazz Festival, Monterey, CA, 1968; rec acc to Buddy Guy, Vanguard label, Chicago, 1968; rec acc to Johnny Shines, Blue Horizon label, Chicago, 1968; toured w Muddy Waters Band working concert dates across US, 1968-9; worked Eagle's, Seattle, WA, 1969; Winterland, San Francisco, CA, 1969; Electric Circus, NYC, 1969; rec BluesTime label, NYC, 1969; worked w own combo, Chicago Blues Festival, Chicago, 1969; toured w American Folk Blues Festival working concert dates through England/Scotland, 1969; worked Ronnie Scott Club, London, Eng, 1969 (por shown JAZZ SCENE AT RONNIE SCOTT'S, BBC-2-TV, 1970); Jazz Expo 69, London, Eng, 1969; Fillmore East, NYC, 1969; Washington Square Methodist Church, NYC, 1969; rec acc to Johnny Young, Blue Horizon label, NYC, 1969; rec Blue Horizon label, Chicago, 1969; rec Spivey label, Brooklyn, NY, 1969; rec acc to Junior Wells/Buddy Guy, Delmark label, Chicago, c1970; rec ST for UK film BLUES LIKE SHOWERS OF RAIN, 1970; inactive due to illness, 1970; entered Cook County Hospital where he died of cancer; buried Burr Oak Cemetery, Worth, IL

Personal: Married Ola Marie ——— (mid-40s). 3 children. Married singer Mahalia Lucille Jenkins (c1967-1970). Was first cousin of singer Johnny Jones. Not related to Muddy Waters as had been reported

Songs: Beat Up Team/Bird in a Cage/Bloody Murder/The Blues Don't Like Nobody/Blues Is a Botheration/Blues Never Die/Burning Fire/Chicago Blues/Country Boy/Crack Your Head/Diving Duck Blues/Doctor Blues/Dollar Twenty-Five/Don't You Know?/Down on Sarah Street/Down to Earth/Everything's Gonna Be Alright/Great Northern Stomp/Half Ain't Been Told/The Hardway/Hey Baby/Home to Mississippi/Hungry Country Girl/I Came from Clarksdale/I Got a Feeling/I Wonder Why/Iced Nehi/I'm a Bad Boy/If I Could Hear My Mother/It Must Have Been the Devil/Jangle Boogie/Keep Your

Hand out of My Pocket/Lost Sheep in the Fold/Lucky So and So/Make Away/Marie/Natural Days/No Sense in Worrying/Nobody Knows Chicago Like I Do/Otis' Blues/Otis in the Dark/SP Blues/Sad Day in Texas/ Sellin' My Thing/Someday Soon Baby/Sometimes I Wonder/Spann Blues/Spann's Boogie/Spann's Stomp/Steel Mill Blues/This Is the Blues/Twisted Snake/Walking the Blues/What Will Become of Me?/Worried Life Blues

Awards/Honors: The Site of the Ann Arbor Blues Festival, Ann Arbor, MI, was formally dedicated "The Otis Spann Memorial Field," 1972

Won *Blues Unlimited* magazine (UK) Readers Poll as Best Blues Pianist, 1973

Infl by: Leroy Carr/Coot Davis/Friday Ford/Tommy Johnson/Big Maceo Merriweather/Little Brother Montgomery/Joe Montgomery/Roosevelt Sykes

Infl to: Little Johnny Jones

Quotes: "Along with Muddy Waters, Sunnyland Slim, Little Walter and Jimmy Rogers, Spann pioneered a percussive, explosive blues that became known as 'Chicago Style' "—Eric Kriss, *Six Blues-Roots Pianists*, Oak Publications, 1973

"There is no doubt about the talents of Otis Spann. He was a brilliant blues pianist and could sing with strength and emotion"—Mike Leadbitter, Sunnyland album KS-100

References: Chicago Breakdown, Mike Rowe, Eddison Press Ltd, 1973

Jazz & Pop magazine, Mar 1968, pp 27-9

SPECKLED RED
(see Perryman, Rufus)

SPIDER SAM
(see McGhee, Walter)

SPIRES, ARTHUR *"Big Boy"*
Born: 1912, Yazoo City (Yazoo Co), MS
Inst: Guitar

Courtesy Chess Records/Living Blues Magazine

One of 8 children; born/raised on farm; worked outside music in Yazoo City, MS, area through 30s; learned guitar, late 30s; worked w Lightnin' Hopkins at The Beer Garden, Yazoo City, 1939; frequently worked local house parties, Yazoo City, into 40s; moved to Chicago, IL, to work mostly outside music from 1943; studied guitar with George Burns of Lyon & Healy Music Studio, Chicago, mid-40s; worked w Eddie Ell/Earl Dranes in local club dates, Chicago, late 40s; worked H&T Club, Chicago, c1949; frequently worked w Louis Myers/David Myers at local house parties, Chicago, early 50s; rec Checker label, Chicago, 1952; formed own Rocket Four group working Castle Rock/BeBop Inn/Stormy's Inn/Cotton Club/others, Chicago, through 50s; rec Chance label, Chicago, 1953; worked outside music with occasional local club dates, Chicago, from 1959; worked w Clemmy Godfrey in local club dates, Chicago, early 60s; rec w Johnny Young, Testament/Storyville labels, Chicago, 1965; continued outside music work, Chicago, through 60s

Personal: Married. Has children. His son Benjamin "Bud" Spires (born 1931) is musician

Infl by: Lightnin' Hopkins/Louis Myers

Quote: "His [recordings are] of such a markedly high quality in terms of force, individuality and emotional intensity [that they] assure him a place in the history of modern blues"—Pete Welding, *Blues Unlimited* magazine (UK), Dec 1965, p 3

References: Blues Unlimited magazine (UK), Dec 1965, pp 3-5

Chicago Breakdown, Mike Rowe, Eddison Press Ltd, 1973

SPIVEY, ADDIE
(*aka:* Hannah May/Sweet Peas[e])

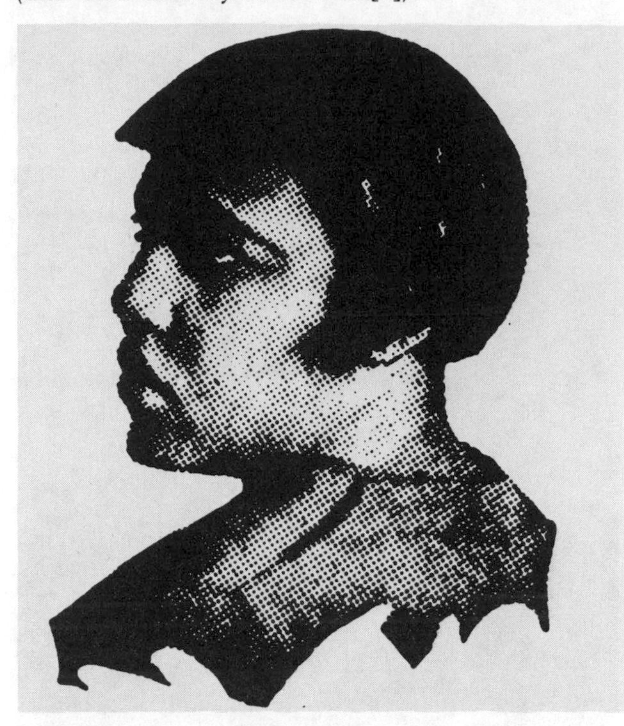

Courtesy Record Research Archives

Born: Aug 22, 1910, Houston (Harris Co), TX
Died: 1943, Detroit, MI
Inst: Piano

Father was Grant Spivey who worked in own family string band; mother was Addie Smith, a nurse; one of 8 children; interested in music early and frequently worked local shows/clubs, Houston, TX, late 20s; rec w Henry Allen Quartet, Victor label, NYC, 1929; frequently toured w sister Victoria Spivey working vaudeville houses/barrelhouses/theaters through Missouri/Texas/Michigan into 30s; rec w Dot Scott's Rhythm Dukes, Decca label, Chicago, IL, 1936; rec (as "Hannah May") w State Street Four, Vocalion label, Chicago, 1936; rec Bluebird label, Aurora, IL, 1937; reportedly settled in Detroit, MI, to work mostly outside music from late 30s

Personal: Married ——— McKesson (?). Was sister of singers Victoria Spivey/Elton Spivey

Songs: Double Dozens/Grievin' Me

Quote: "Besides having a fine voice she was a helluva pianist . . ."—Victoria Spivey, *Record Research* magazine, Nov 1969, p 6

Reference: Record Research magazine, Nov 1969, p 6

SPIVEY, ELTON ISLAND
(*aka:* The Za Zu Girl)
Born: Aug 12, 1900, Galveston (Galveston Co), TX
Died: Jun 25, 1971, East Meadow, NY

Father was Grant Spivey who worked in own family string band; mother was Addie Smith, a nurse; one of 8 children; moved to Mexico to live with husband who was in service, 1916-21; moved to Moberly, MO, 1921; worked mostly outside music with occasional local amateur shows in Moberly area through 20s; toured w sister Victoria Spivey working vaudeville houses/barrelhouses/theaters through Missouri/Texas/Michigan through 30s; rec ARC label group, Chicago, 1937; mostly inactive in music through 40s/50s and lived in Detroit, MI, from early 60s; lived in North Bellmore, NY, late 60s; entered Nassau County Medical Center Hospital where she died of cancer; buried Greenfield Cemetery, Hempstead, NY

Personal: Married ——— Harris. Had children. Was sister of singers Victoria Spivey/Addie Spivey

SPIVEY, VICTORIA REGINA *"Vicky"*
(*aka:* Jane Lucas)

Courtesy Frank Driggs Collection

Born: Oct 15, 1906, Houston (Harris Co), TX
Died: Oct 3, 1976, New York, NY
Inst: Organ/Piano/Ukulele

Father was Grant Spivey who worked in own family string band; mother was Addie Smith, a nurse; one of 8 children; interested in music early learning piano as child and occasionally worked local parties, Houston, TX, during teens; worked as pianist at Lincoln Theater, Dallas, TX, 1918; worked in Lazy Daddy's Fillmore Blues Band/LC Tolen's Band & Revue, Dallas, c1918; worked w Blind Lemon Jefferson and others in gambling/gay houses/clubs in Galveston/Houston, TX, area, early 20s; rec OKeh label, St Louis, MO, 1926; rec w John Erby/Lonnie Johnson/King Oliver/ Clarence Williams/Louis Armstrong/others, OKeh label, NYC, NY/St Louis, MO, 1926-9; worked as staff writer for St Louis Publishing Company, St Louis, 1927; toured as single working clubs/vaudeville houses from St Louis to NYC through 20s; worked Club Kentucky, NYC, 1927; app in HIT BITS FROM AFRICANA Revue, Lincoln Theater, NYC, 1927; worked Spider Web, Buffalo, NY, c1928; Metropolitan Theater, Chicago, IL, 1928; app in all-black musical film HALLELUJAH!, 1929; app w Dr Eva Jessye on (unknown) show, local radio, NYC, 1929; rec w Henry Allen Orch, Victor label, NYC, 1929; rec duets w Porter Grainger, Victor label, NYC, 1930; app w Eddie Hunter in revival of 4-11-44 musical comedy, Lafayette Theater, NYC, 1930; toured as director of Lloyd Hunter's Serenaders working colleges/dances/ pavilions/radio remotes through Midwest and Southwest, 1930-1; rec Vocalion label, Chicago, 1931; rec w Lloyd Hunter's Serenaders, Vocalion label, Chicago, 1931; toured w Jap Allen Band working dances through Midwest, 1931; toured w DALLAS TAN TOWN TOPICS Revue working shows through Texas/Oklahoma, 1933; frequently worked as single (or with sisters) in vaudeville houses/barrelhouses/theaters through mid-30s; toured w dancer Billy Adams working Minsky Burlesque circuit and other circuits through US/Canada from 1934; toured w Louis Armstrong through US, mid-30s; worked various revues, New Grand Terrace, Chicago, IL, mid-30s; rec Decca label, Chicago, 1936; rec (as "Jane Lucas") Vocalion label, Chicago, 1936; rec Vocalion label, NYC/ Chicago, 1937; worked Bill Robinson's Mimo Professional Club, NYC, c1938; app in musical revue HELLZAPOPPIN, RKO Palace/46th Street Theater/ Winter Garden Theater, NYC, 1938-9, then toured with show; worked Abe & Pappy Club, Dallas, TX, 1940; toured one-nighters w Billy Adams working Mike DeLisa Club, Chicago, IL/The Palladium, Cleveland, OH/Normandy Club, Cleveland/others across US, through 40s; briefly owned own club, East St Louis, IL, mid-40s; worked Small's Paradise, NYC, 1948; Apollo Theater, NYC, late 40s; app on local radio shows, NYC, early 50s; frequently worked Central Plaza/Stuyvesant Casino/Mayfair Lounge/ other jazz spots, NYC, from early 50s; worked mostly in church affairs, NYC area, mid to late 50s; worked Jimmy Ryan's Club/Cinderella Club/Nick's/others, NYC, 1960; w Don Lambert, Wallace's Lounge, East Orange, NJ, 1960; w Lonnie Johnson, Gerde's Folk City, NYC, 1961; formed/rec Queen Vee label, NYC, 1961; rec w Buster Bailey/Lonnie Johnson/others, Bluesville label, NYC, 1961; app on MUSIC USA, Voice of America-radio, 1961; rec Folkways label, NYC, 1962; app on BOB MAXWELL Show, CBS-radio, 1962; worked Jimmy Ryan's, NYC, 1962; Eddie Condon's, NYC, 1962; Cinderella Club, NYC, 1962; Central Plaza, NYC, 1962; formed own jazz/blues label, Spivey Record Company, Brooklyn, NY, 1962 (and frequently rec with many blues performers to 1976); worked Carnegie Hall, NYC, 1962; app w Butch Cage/Willie B Thomas, LYRICS AND LEGENDS (ep: The Blues), WNET-TV, NYC (syndicated), 1963; toured w American Folk-Blues Festival working concert dates through England/Europe, 1963 (por shown on I HEAR THE BLUES, Granada-TV, England); rec w Sonny Boy Williamson (Alex Miller), Spivey label, Baden-Baden, Ger, 1963; rec Fontana label, Bremen, Ger, 1963; contributed articles to *Record Research/Sounds & Fury* magazines, 1963-6; worked Celebrity Club, NYC, NY, 1964; Blues Alley Club, Washington, DC, 1965; Summer Arts Festival, Sterling Forest, Tuxedo Park, NY, 1965; rec w Easy Rider Jazz Band, GHB label, Connecticut, 1966; worked Half Note, NYC, 1969; Chicago Blues Festival, Chicago, 1969; w Turk Murphy Band/Woody Allen, Earthquake McGoon's, San Francisco, CA, 1970; app on local TV/radio shows, San Francisco, 1970; app on FREE TIME, PBS-TV, 1971; worked Univ of Pittsburgh Blues Festival, Pittsburgh, PA, 1971; frequently toured college circuit working concert dates, 1971-4; rec instructional cassettes for Conn Instrument Company of Chicago (and served as blues advisor), 1971; active in recording young talent (like Danny Russo/Ralph Rush/Ted Stilles/Sugar Blue/ Mark Ross/others), Spivey label, NYC area, from early 70s; worked Ann Arbor Blues Festival, Ann Arbor, MI, 1973; Philadelphia Folk Festival, Schwenksville, PA, 1973-4 (por 1974 concert shown PHILADELPHIA FOLK FESTIVAL, PBS-TV); Univ of Maine, Orono, ME, 1974; Upsala College, East Orange, NJ, 1974; New York Jazz Museum concert, NYC, 1974; Rutgers Institute of Jazz Studies concert, New Brunswick, NJ, 1974; app on local TV show, Paris, France, 1974; worked Chelsea House Cafe, Brattleboro, VT, 1975 (por rel Spivey label); w

Dicey-Ross Band, Max's Kansas City, NYC, 1976; The Fugue, NYC, 1976; Dr Generosity, NYC, 1976; Focus Coffeehouse, NYC, 1976; app on THE DEVIL'S MUSIC—A HISTORY OF THE BLUES (ep: Crazy Blues), BBC-1-TV, England, 1976; entered Beekman-Downtown Hospital where she died of internal hemorrhage; buried Greenfield Cemetery, Hempstead, NY; clip shown in ROOTS OF COUNTRY MUSIC & BLUES, KGO-TV, San Francisco, 1977

Personal: Married Reuben Floyd (c1928-early 30s); William "Billy" Adams (c1934-) who later served as manager, 1937. Married 2 other times. Her sisters Addie "Sweet Peas" Spivey/Elton "Za-Zu" Spivey/ Leona Spivey were singers

Billings: The Queen/Queen of the Blues

Songs: A Big One/A Bum Can't Do You No Good/The Alligator Pond Went Dry/Arkansas Road Blues/Beautiful World/Big Black Belt/Black Cat Blues/Black Snake Blues/Black Snake Swinger/Blood Hound Blues/Blood Thirsty Blues/By Yourself/Christmas Without Santa Claus/Closed Door/Detroit Moan/ Dirty Women's Blues/Don't Care/Don't Trust Nobody Blues/Don't Worry About It/Dope Head Blues/Dreaming of You/Eagle and the Hawk/Funny Feathers/Furniture Man Blues/Garter Snake Blues/ Go Tell My Other Man/Going Back Home/Going Blues/Good Sissages/Grant Spivey/Grow Old Together/Hoodoo Man Blues/How Do They Do It That Way?/I Can't Last Long/I Got Men All Over Town/I Got the Blues So Bad/I'll Never Fall in Love Again/I'm a Red Hot Mama/I'm Taking Over/Idle Hour Blues/It's a Mighty Poor Rat That Ain't Got But One Hole/It's Dangerous/Jet/Jook House Blues/Kazoo Papa Blues/Let Him Beat Me/Let's Ride Tonight/ Long Time Blues/Low Down Friends/Moaning the Blues/Mosquito Fly and Flea/Murder in the First Degree/My Head Is Bad/No Papa No/Number 12 Left Me Roam/Organ Grinder Blues/Red Lantern Blues/ Six Foot Daddy/Spider Web Blues/Sport Model Mama/Steady Grind/The Stevedore/TB Blues/TB's Got Me/Telephoning the Blues/That Man/Thursday Girl/Toothache Blues/(Can I) Wash Your Clothes/ What Is This Thing They're Talking About?/Won't Need/You Are My Man/You Done Lost Your Good Thing/You're Going to Miss Me When I'm Gone

Awards/Honor: Awarded BMI Commendation of Excellence "for long and outstanding contribution to the many worlds of music," 1970

Infl by: Robert Calvin/Sara Martin/Bessie Smith

Infl to: Edith Johnson/Mary Johnson/Alice Moore/ Carrie Smith

Quotes: "She's one of the last of a proud line of women classic blues singers whose vocal accomplishments have set the basic pattern for the singers of today"—Len Kunstadt, Bluesville album 1054

"... many of her blues were grim tales of death, despair, cruelty and agony, underscored by her somber piano and stark Texas blues moans"—Jim O'Neal, *Rolling Stone* magazine, Nov 18, 1976

"As performer, she was in turn joyous, somber, coy and showy, theatrically mirroring the moods of her composition"—Amy O'Neal, *Living Blues* magazine, Sept 1976, p 5

References: *Living Blues* magazine, Sept 1976, p 5
Record Research magazine, May 1956, pp 3-6

SPOON

(see Witherspoon, James)

SPROTT, HORACE

Courtesy Sing Out *Magazine*

Born: Feb 2, c1890, Sprott (Perry Co), AL
Died: (unknown)
Inst: Guitar/Harmonica

Mother was Bessie Ford, a slave on the Sprott Plantation where he was born/raised; took name from white owner; interested in music early and learned many religious hymns/jubilees/other songs from parents as child; ran away from home to work outside music in Dallas County, AL, from 11 years of age; served time in local county prison farm, Montgomery, AL, c1908;

hoboed across US working outside music with occasional work at local parties/picnics/dances into 30s; settled in Selma, AL, to work outside music with frequent work at local parties/breakdowns/picnics in area thereafter; rec Folkways label, Cahaba River/Marion, AL, 1954; app on ODYSSEY (ep: They Took a Blue Note), CBS-TV, 1956; occasional local party work, Selma, AL, thereafter

Personal: Married Marietta Waters (c1908-16); Ida Marner (c1924-7); Annie ——— (c1936-). 2 children

Infl by: Richard Bamburg/Will Harris

Quote: "To his singing, Sprott contributes a sombre 'straining voice,' a high degree of personal feeling, considerable skill in handling his voice, and a remarkable memory"—Frederic Ramsey Jr, Folkways album FA-2651

ST LOUIS JIMMY
(see Oden, James)

ST LOUIS MAC
(see Simmons, Mack)

STACKHOUSE, HOUSTON

Born: Sept 28, 1910, Wesson (Copiah Co), MS
Died: 1981, Crystal Springs, MS (unconfirmed)

Photo by Jim O'Neal. Courtesy Living Blues Magazine

Inst: Guitar/Harmonica/Mandolin/Violin

Born/raised on Randall Ford's Plantation; frequently worked outside music as child, Wesson, MS, area; moved to Crystal Springs, MS, mid-20s; learned guitar from Tommy Johnson/Mager Johnson/Clarence Johnson, Crystal Springs, MS, 1927; frequently worked w Tommy Johnson/Robert Nighthawk in local jukes/parties, Hollandale, MS, area, late 20s to 1932; worked w Jimmie Rodgers, Jackson, MS, 1931; frequently worked outside music with some party work w Robert Nighthawk, Crystal Springs, from early 30s; app w Robert Nighthawk on WJDX-radio, Jackson, early 30s; frequently worked w Mississippi Sheiks group (No 2) working white dances in Crystal Springs area through 30s into 40s; worked outside music in Wiggins, MS, area into 40s; app on WROX-radio, Clarksdale, MS, mid-40s; worked w Robert Jr Lockwood/Walter Jacobs, Helena, AR, c1944-7; app w Robert Nighthawk on MOTHER'S BEST FLOUR HOUR, KFFA-radio, Helena, AR, 1946; frequently app w Sonny Boy Williamson (Alex Miller) on KING BISCUIT TIME, KFFA-radio, Helena AR, 1946-7; teamed off/on w Peck Curtis to work clubs/cafes/jukes in Tunica, MS/Greenwood, MS/Forrest City, AR, and points south through 40s into 60s; worked Green Spot, Clarksdale, MS, 1947; Owl Cafe, Helena, AR, 1949; frequently worked dances/cafes in Belzoni, MS/Aberdeen, MS/Helena, AR/Little Rock, AR, from early to mid-50s; worked w Boyd Gilmore Trio, Pine Bluff, AR, early 60s; worked outside music with occasional club/radio work w Sonny Boy Williamson (Alex Miller)/Peck Curtis, Helena area, to 1965; frequently worked w Peck Curtis in Helena through 60s; rec Testament label, Dundee, MS, 1967; rec Flyright label, Crystal Springs, MS, 1967; lived in Crystal Springs, 1969 into 70s; worked Ann Brown's Club, Memphis, TN, 1970; worked Festival of American Folklife, Washington, DC, 1970-1; Ann Arbor Blues Recital, Ann Arbor, MI, 1971; River City Blues Festival, Ellis Auditorium, Memphis, 1971-3 (por 1973 concert heard MUSIC USA, VOA-radio); worked w Joe Willie Wilkins' King Biscuit Boys in local clubs, Memphis, c1972; worked Univ of Arkansas Delta Blues Festival, Fayetteville, AR, 1972; Boston Blues Society Concert, Boston, MA, 1972; toured w Hacksaw Harney working concert dates through New England, 1972; rec Adelphi label, 1972; worked Robinson's Cafe, Hughes, AR, 1972; Washington Square Church, NYC, 1972; Univ of Chicago Folk Festival, Chicago, IL, 1973; app on ATOMIC MAMA'S WANG DANG DOODLE BLUES Show,

WNIB-FM-radio, Chicago, c1973; worked Ann Arbor Blues Festival, Ann Arbor, MI, 1973; Festival of American Folklife, Washington, DC, 1973 (por shown on videotape BORN IN THE BLUES); toured w Joe Willie Wilkins' King Biscuit Boys on Memphis Blues Caravan show working concert circuit through Midwest, 1973; worked Univ of Miami, Coral Gables, FL, 1974; Quiet Knight, Chicago, 1974; film clip shown on OMNIBUS (ep: The Friendly Invasion), BBC-1-TV, Eng, 1975; toured Europe working concert dates, 1976; app on THE DEVIL'S MUSIC—A HISTORY OF THE BLUES (ep: Work and Mother Wit), BBC-1-TV, Eng, 1976; app on GOOD MORNIN' BLUES, PBS-TV, 1978; Delta Blues Fest, Greenville, MS, 1978-9

Personal: Cousin of Robert Nighthawk

Infl by: Clarence Johnson/Mager Johnson/Tommy Johnson

Infl to: Sammy Lawhorn/Robert Nighthawk/Jimmy Rogers/Houston Stovall

Quote: "As a country blues singer-guitarist Stack is one of the best around"—Jim O'Neal, *Living Blues* magazine, Summer 1974, p 20

Reference: Living Blues magazine, Summer 1974, pp 20-36

STAFFORD, MARY

Born: c1895, Missouri (unconfirmed)
Died: c1938, Atlantic City, NJ (unconfirmed)

Reportedly came east in early teens; worked w Eubie Blake, Goldfield Hotel, Baltimore, MD, c1915; worked w Bessie Smith, Paradise Cafe, Atlantic City, NJ, 1917; worked w Charlie Johnson, Barron Wilkins' Cabaret, NYC, 1920; frequently worked summer shows in clubs/hotels, Atlantic City, into 20s; worked w Charlie Johnson's Orch, Rafe's Paradise Cafe, Atlantic City, 1921; rec Columbia label, NYC, 1921; worked club dates in Harrisburg, PA, 1921; w Charlie Johnson's Orch, Nest Club, NYC, 1924-5 (frequent remotes on WHN-radio); Pod's and Jerry's (Catagonia Club), NYC, mid-20s; rec Pathe-Actuelle label, NYC, 1926; frequently worked Bill Landon's Club, Baltimore, MD, 1928-9; frequent local club dates in NYC through 20s; app in ROCKING CHAIR REVUE, Lafayette Theater, NYC, 1931; app in DEAR OLD SOUTHLAND musical comedy, Lafayette Theater, NYC, 1932; reportedly settled in Atlantic City to work outside music from early 30s; whereabouts unknown thereafter

Courtesy Frank Driggs Collection

Personal: Brother was George Stafford, jazz drummer (died 1936). True name reportedly Annie Burns but this is unconfirmed

Quote: "She had the hard-sounding, deep, speakeasy type of voice . . ."—John Godrich, VJM album LLP-30

STIDHAM, ARBEE

Born: Feb 9, 1917, De Valls Bluff (Prairie Co), AR
Inst: Alto Sax/Guitar/Harmonica

Father was Luddie Stidham, a musician who worked w Jimmie Lunceford Band; uncle was Ernest Stidham, leader of Memphis Jug Band; interested in music early and learned music as youngster; attended Prairie County Training School, then Dunbar HS, Little Rock, AR, late 20s; formed Southern Syncopators Band working local school dances/clubs in Little Rock area from c1930; toured w Southern Syncopators as acc to Bessie Smith c1930-1; app on KARK-radio, Little Rock, early 30s; frequently worked local clubs in Little Rock, AR/Memphis, TN, areas through 30s into 40s; rec Victor label, Chicago, IL, 1947; rec w Lucky Millinder Orch, Victor label, NYC, NY, 1948; rec Victor label, Chicago, 1949-50; rec Sittin In With label, Chicago, 1951; rec Checker label, Chicago, 1952; set-

Photo by Ray Flerlage (Kinnara Collection). Courtesy Living Blues Magazine

tled in Chicago where he learned guitar c1954; app on Studs Terkel's I COME FOR TO SING, local TV, Chicago, mid-50s; worked club dates, Atlanta, GA, mid-50s; rec Abco label, Chicago, 1956; rec w Lefty Bates Band, States label, Chicago, 1957; worked Zanzibar Club, Chicago, late 50s; frequently worked local club dates in Chicago and resort dates in Wisconsin, late 50s into 60s; rec w Memphis Slim, Folkways label, NYC, 1960-1; rec Prestige-Bluesville label, NYC, 1960; frequently worked outside music, Chicago, through 60s; moved to Cleveland, OH, to work outside music from late 60s into 70s; worked Casablanca Club, Youngstown, OH, early 70s; rec w Ernie Wilkins Orch, Mainstream label, Atlanta, GA, c1972; worked Royal Peacock Club, Atlanta, c1972; rec Folkways label, Cleveland, 1973; app in film THE BLUESMAN, 1973; occasionally lectured on blues at Cleveland State Univ, Cleveland, OH, through mid-70s

Personal: Married Geneva ———; Rose ———

Songs: Blue and Low/Come a Little Closer/Don't Look for Me Baby/Falling Blues/I Don't Want You Baby/I Stayed Away Too Long/I Want to Belong to You/I'm Tired of Wandering/I've Got to Forget You/(If) You Can't Live in This World by Yourself/If You Just Hold On/Let Me Love You/Let's Take the Long Way Home/Meet Me Halfway/Mr Texas and Pacific/My Baby Left Me/My Heart Belongs to You/My Lincoln Continental/(People) What Would You Do If You Were Me?/People's Blues/Please Let It Be Me/Standin' in My Window/Standing on the Corner/Take the Pain from My Heart/Take Your Hand off My Knee/There's Always Tomorrow/Walking Blues/Wee Hours/You Keep Me Yearning

Infl by: DeFord Bailey/John Lee "Sonny Boy" Williamson

Quotes: "Stidham is a powerful, deep-voiced jazz blues singer, in the Kansas City tradition of Joe Turner"—Joe Goldberg, Prestige album 1021

"Bedrock elements of blues are present in his singing, the down-to-earth tonality, insistent beat, vibrato and quaver of country blues style, sometimes blended with jump tempo and other characteristics associated with urban blues"—Charles Edward Smith, Folkways album FS-3824

Reference: Living Blues magazine, Nov 1975, pp 34-5

STOKES, FRANK

Courtesy Sheldon Harris Collection

Born: Jan 1, 1888, Whitehaven (Shelby Co), TN
Died: Sept 12, 1955, Memphis, TN
Inst: Guitar

Parents reportedly died early; was raised by stepfather Fred Carbin in Tutwiler, MS, area where he worked farm as child; worked outside music with occasional entertaining at local parties/suppers in area and Memphis, TN, from c1895; settled in Hernando, MS, to work outside music from c1900; frequently worked local streets/saloons for tips, Hernando, MS/Memphis, TN, areas to c1920; frequently toured w Garfield Akers (as black-face songster/buck dancer/comedian) in Doc Watts Medicine Show working through South through teens; settled in Oakville, TN, to work outside music (as blacksmith) with frequent work at parties/streets/saloons/picnics/suppers/fish fries in Memphis area from c1920; frequently returned to South to work local picnics/parties/tonks/jukes in northern Mississippi area through 20s into 30s; frequently worked w Dan Sain in Jack Kelly's Jug Busters in white country clubs/streets/parties/suppers in Memphis area from 1925; rec w Dan Sain as Beale Street Sheiks, Paramount label, Chicago, IL, 1927-9; rec Victor label, Memphis, 1928-9; worked frequently as street singer in Church's Park (WC Handy Park), Memphis, from mid-30s into 40s; often worked in various medicine shows/Ringling Brothers Circus/tent shows/others out of Memphis through 30s; frequently toured w Dan Sain working picnics/fairs/streets through Tennessee/Arkansas, mid-30s into late 40s; often worked Memphis Fair Grounds, Memphis, TN, mid-40s; often toured w Willie Borum/Roosevelt Stokes (son) working parties/jukes in Memphis/northern Mississippi area, mid- to late 40s; settled in Clarksdale, MS, area c1949; worked occasionally w Bukka White in small tonks in Clarksdale area, 1949-51; inactive due to poor health from 1951; entered John Gaston Hospital where he died of uremia; buried Hollywood Cemetery, Memphis, TN

Personal: Married Maggie Bannister (c1918-died 1952). 4 children (Curtis/Roosevelt/Georgia/Helen)

Songs: Ain't Goin' to Do Like I Used to Do/Beale Town Bound/Bunker Hill Blues/Downtown Blues/How Long?/Hunting Blues/Rockin' on the Hill Blues/South Memphis Blues/Wasn't That Doggin' Me?

Infl to: Garfield Akers/Joe Callicott/Jim Jackson

Quotes: "The stomping, pulsating, raggy sound of his guitar . . . contributed heavily to his popularity at jukes, country suppers, parties and shows; it was ideal for dancing. Add to that his rich distinctive voice and you have no problem seeing why he was one of the most talked about musicians in [Memphis] town"—Don Kent, Biograph album BLP-12041

"The greatest of [the] Memphis minstrels was Frank Stokes, a personable six footer who possessed the finest blues voice the city ever produced"—Steve Calt, Yazoo album L-1056

References: Blues Unlimited magazine (UK), Apr 1973, pp 25-7

Memphis Blues, Bengt Olsson, Studio Vista Ltd, 1970

Sweet as the Showers of Rain, Samuel B Charters, Oak Publications, 1977

STOVALL, JEWELL *"Babe"*

Born: Oct 14, 1907, Tylertown (Walthall Co), MS
Died: Sept 21, 1974, New Orleans, LA
Inst: Guitar

Father was sharecropper; one of 12 children; born/raised/worked on farm from childhood; taught self guitar as boy; dropped out of school to work outside music with frequent work w brother Tom Stovall at local parties/suppers/country breakdowns, Tylertown, MS, area through 20s into 30s; moved to Franklinton, LA, to work mostly outside music in area from early 30s into 50s; frequently hoboed through South working as itinerant musician in local streets/parks/jukes for tips through 40s/50s; worked streets of French Quarter, New Orleans, LA, 1957-8; worked Borenstein's Art Gallery, New Orleans, c1958; continued outside music work through 50s into 60s; frequently worked streets/parks for tips, New Orleans, from 1964; frequently worked Preservation Hall, New Orleans, from 1964; rec Verve label, New Orleans, 1964; worked Dream Castle Restaurant, New Orleans, 1964-5; Vaucresson's Club, New Orleans, mid-60s; Charles Street Coffeehouse, Boston, MA, 1965; Tet-A-Tete, Providence, MA, 1965; The Gaslight, NYC, 1965; Gerde's Folk City, NYC, 1965; rec Spivey label, Brooklyn, NY, 1965; Turk's Head, Boston, MA, 1965; toured West Coast working coffeehouses through California, 1965; frequently worked Intellect Club, New Orleans, 1966-7; rec w Roosevelt Holts, Blue Horizon label, Franklinton, LA, 1966; frequently worked streets and Jackson Square area, New Orleans, through 60s into 70s; worked Tulane Univ Jazz Festival, New Orleans, 1969; toured college circuit working concert dates from North Carolina to Florida c1969; worked New Orleans Jazz & Heritage Festival, New Orleans, 1970-4; rec Rounder label, Tylertown, MS, c1970; worked Univ of Arkansas Delta Blues Festival, Fayetteville, AR, 1972; JB's Club, New Orleans, LA, 1972; National Folk Festival, Wolf Trap Farm Park, Vienna, VA, 1973; continued occasional street singing for tips, New Orleans, LA, 1973-4; died of natural causes in sleep; buried Holt Cemetery, New Orleans, LA

Personal: Married Aretha Brown (c1939-). Had 10 children

Jewell "Babe" Stovall

Photo by Dan S Leyrer
Courtesy E L Borenstein Archives

Infl by: Tommy Johnson

Quotes: "Stovall is a 'roots' bluesman, a story teller minstrel with an earthy rasp in his voice"—Len Kunstadt, Spivey album LP-1009

"[Babe was] a songster in the tradition of Mance Lipscomb and Pink Anderson . . ."—Robert Tilling, *Blues Unlimited* magazine (UK), Jul 1976, p 29

Reference: Blues Unlimited magazine (UK), Jan/Feb/Mar 1966

STUCKEY, HENRY
Born: Apr 11, 1897, Bentonia (Yazoo Co), MS
Died: Mar 9, 1966, Jackson, MS
Inst: Guitar

Father was Will Stuckey; mother was Hattie Slader; taught self guitar 1905 and worked juke houses in Bentonia, MS, area from c1908; worked mostly outside music in Bentonia area to c1917; served in US Army c1917; teamed w Skip James working barrelhouses in Bentonia area through 20s; owned/operated barrelhouse in Bentonia area into 30s; continued outside music work with occasional local juke work, Bentonia area, into early 50s; worked briefly in local band in local clubs, Omaha, NE, early 50s; worked outside music in Yazoo City, MS, area into 60s; entered Veterans' Administration Hospital where he died of cancer; buried Old Pleasant Grove, MS

Personal: Married Ida Lee ———. His brother Shuke Stuckey was guitarist

Infl to: Skip James

Quote: " 'Father' of the Bentonia, Mississippi, 'school of blues' and teacher of young Skip James . . ."—Jacques Roche, *78 Quarterly* magazine, No 2 (1968), p 12

STUCKEY

Reference: *78 Quarterly* magazine, No 2 (1968), pp 12-14

SUDDOTH, J GUY

(see Erby, John)

SUGGS, JAMES DOUGLAS

Born: Mar 9, 1886, Kosciusko (Attala Co), MS
Died: Jun 19, 1955, Rural Jefferson Township, MI
Inst: Guitar

Father was Lee S Suggs, a preacher; mother was Belle Cottrell; frequently worked many farms from childhood while singing in local church choirs; frequently followed many black minstrel tent shows across US prior to c1917; served in US Army in Europe c1917; hoboed across US working outside music with frequent street work for tips through 20s/30s; moved to Chicago, IL, to work outside music from 1940; moved to Rural Jefferson Township, MI, where he frequently worked local parties/gatherings singing spirituals/minstrel songs/blues/ballads/folk songs; entered Cass County Hospital where he died of cancer; buried Coulters Chapel Cemetery, Cass County, MI

Personal: Married Sylvia ———. Had 12 children. Not to be confused with Doug Suggs, Chicago pianist (born Dec 3, 1894, St Louis, MO)

Quote: "[An] outstanding storyteller, JD Suggs also proved a fluent singer, with or without a guitar in his hands"—Richard M Dorson, *American Folklore*, Univ of Chicago Press, 1959

Reference: *American Folklore*, Richard M Dorson, Univ of Chicago Press, 1959

SUMLIN, HUBERT

Born: Nov 16, 1931, Greenwood (Leflore Co), MS
Inst: Drums/Guitar

One of 13 children; born/raised/worked outside music on farm from childhood; interested in music early and learned drums at about 10 years of age; learned guitar at 11 years of age; left home to form own band working local jukes in Greenwood, MS, area from c1943; toured w Jimmy Cotton Band working clubs/taverns through Arkansas/Tennessee, 1950-3; rec acc to Jimmy Cotton, Sun label, Memphis, TN, 1954; worked w Howlin' Wolf, Silkhairs Club, West Memphis, AR, c1954; moved to Chicago, IL, 1954; briefly attended Chicago Conservatory of Music, Chicago, c1954; worked/toured w Howlin' Wolf Band, 1954-6; toured w Muddy Waters Band, 1956; rejoined Howlin' Wolf Band working/touring almost continually in clubs/taverns/concerts out of Chicago, 1957 into 70s; toured w American Folk Blues Festival working concerts through England/Europe, 1964 (por of Musikhalle concert, Hamburg, Ger, rel Fontana label); rec Amiga label, Berlin, Ger, 1964; rec Blue Horizon label, Chicago (?), 1964; rec as sideman w Eddie Taylor Band, VJ label, Chicago, 1964; toured briefly w Muddy Waters Band, 1966; worked w Magic Sam group in local club dates, Chicago, mid-60s; worked Eddie Shaw's, Chicago, 1969; Key Largo Club, Chicago, 1969; Ann Arbor Blues Festival, Ann Arbor, MI, 1970; app w Howlin' Wolf in film short WOLF, 1971; worked Colonial Tavern, Toronto, Can, 1971; Flamingo Lounge, Chicago, 1971; Notre Dame Blues Festival, South Bend, IN, 1971; w Howlin' Wolf Band, Ann Arbor Blues Festival, Ann Arbor, 1971 (por rel Atlantic label); Univ of Waterloo, Waterloo, Can, 1972; continued working/touring/recording w Howlin' Wolf Band in clubs/concerts across US/Canada/Europe, 1972-6; worked Big Duke's Blue Flame, Chicago, 1974; Majestic "M," Chicago, 1974; Ann Arbor Blues & Jazz Festival, Windsor, Can, 1974; International Blues Festival, Louisville, KY, 1974; toured w Chicago Blues Festival working concert dates through Europe, 1975; worked w Howlin' Wolf Band, International Amphitheater, Chicago, 1975; El Mocambo Tavern, Toronto, Can, 1975; Eddie Shaw's Place, Chicago, 1975; assumed leadership of Howlin' Wolf Band, 1976-8; worked The New 1815 Club, Chicago, 1976; David & Thelma's

Photo by Len Kunstadt. Courtesy Record Research Archives

Lounge, Chicago, 1976; Antone's, Austin, TX, 1976; rec Black & Blue label, Paris, France, 1976; w Eddie Shaw & Wolf Gang, Red Creek, Rochester, NY, 1977; worked The Speakeasy Club, Cambridge, MA, 1977

Quote: "A killer guitar-picker"—Willie Leiser, *Blues Unlimited* magazine (UK), Jun 1973, p 17

References: *Cadence* magazine, Aug 1977, pp 11-12
Blues Unlimited magazine (UK), Jun 1973, pp 16-17

SUNNY JIM
(see Watson, Johnny)

SUNNY LAND/SUNNYLAND SLIM
(see Luandrew, Albert)

SUSIE
(see Edwards, Susie)

SWEET PEAS(E)
(see Spivey, Addie)

SWING BROTHER
(see Burns, Eddie)

SYKES, ROOSEVELT
(*aka:* The Blues Man/Dobby Bragg/The Honeydripper/Easy Papa Johnson/Willie Kelly)

Photo by Norbert Hess. Courtesy Living Blues Magazine

Born: Jan 31, 1906, Elmar (Phillips Co), AR
Died: Jul 11, 1983, New Orleans, LA
Inst: Guitar/Organ/Piano

Father was musician; mother was ——— Bragg; one of at least 4 children; moved to St Louis, MO, 1909; returned to Arkansas to frequently work outside music, West Helena area, from 1913; frequently played organ in local church, West Helena, c1916; taught self piano c1918; ran away from home to work local gambling houses/barrelhouses, West Helena area, from 1921; frequently worked w Lee Green in local dives/barrelhouses, Lake Providence, LA, mid-20s; moved to St Louis, MO, to work outside music from late 20s; frequently worked Jazzland Club/Cardinals' Nest/others, St Louis, from late 20s; rec OKeh label, NYC, NY/Chicago, IL, 1929; rec Victor label, Cincinnati, OH, 1930; frequently rec acc to many blues singers from 1930; rec Melotone label, Chicago, 1930; rec Victor label, Louisville, KY, 1931; rec w Curtis Mosby/Mary Johnson, Champion label, Richmond, IN, 1932; frequently worked local bars/dives, Memphis, TN, area into early 30s; frequently worked local clubs/bars in Chicago through 30s; rec Victor/Bluebird labels, Chicago, 1933; rec Decca label, Chicago/NYC, 1934-41; frequently worked (as talent scout) for Victor/Decca labels through 30s; teamed w St Louis Jimmy to tour one-nighters across US, late 30s; worked Nat Love's Club, East St Louis, IL, c1940; settled in Chicago, IL, c1941; rec OKeh label, Chicago, 1941-2; worked Tin Pan Alley Club, Chicago, 1943; formed own Honeydrippers group to tour club dates through South from 1943; frequently worked w Memphis Minnie/Son Joe in local club dates, Chicago, mid-40s; rec Bluebird label, Chicago, 1944-5; rec Cincinnati/B&W labels, Chicago, 1945; rec Victor label, Chicago, 1945-9; rec w Jump Jackson Band, Specialty label, Chicago, 1946-7; rec Bullet label, Chicago, 1947; app on own THE TOAST OF THE COAST Show, (unknown) TV, Mobile, AL, late 40s; toured one-nighters across US, 1947-9; worked The Rose Room, Dallas, TX, c1948; The Turk Club, Columbus, OH, c1948; rec Regal label, Chicago, 1949; worked w own trio, Hollywood Cafe, Chicago, 1949; frequently worked w Lonnie Johnson in local club dates, Chicago, 1950-1; toured (as single) working clubs in St Louis, MO/Chicago, IL/Texas and elsewhere, early 50s; rec United label, Chicago, 1951-4; moved to New Orleans, LA, to work outside music from c1954; rec Imperial label, New Orleans, 1954; worked P&E Club, East St Louis, IL, 1957; rec House of Sound label, Memphis, TN, 1957; worked w Henry Townsend, Beverly Lounge, Gulfport, MS, 1958-60; in residence, Golden Eagle Saloon, St Louis, MO, 1960; rec Decca label, Chicago, 1960; rec

Prestige-Bluesville label, Englewood Cliffs, NJ, 1960; toured concert dates through England/Europe, 1961; app in Belgian film ROOSEVELT SYKES "THE HONEYDRIPPER," 1961; rec Columbia label, London, Eng, 1961; worked Blind Pig, Chicago, 1961; Quid Club, Chicago, 1961; rec Folkways label, NYC, 1961; worked Gate of Horn, Chicago, 1962; Allegro Club, Chicago, 1962; Gerde's Folk City, NYC, 1962-3; Cinderella Club, NYC, 1962; rec Crown label, Chicago, 1962; rec Delmark label, Chicago, 1963; worked Fickle Pickle, Chicago, 1963; Room at the Bottom, NYC, 1963; rec Spivey label, NYC (?), 1963; worked Foxie's Floating Palace Riverboat, Houma, LA, 1964; toured w American Folk Blues Festival working concert dates through England/Europe, 1965-6 (por Berlin/Hamburg, Ger, concerts rel Fontana label); rec Storyville label, Copenhagen, Den, 1966; owned/operated Tiki Recording Studio, Houma, LA, 1966; worked George's, Kibitzeria, Toronto, Can, 1968; frequently worked w Smilin' Joe at Court of Two Sisters, New Orleans, LA, 1968-9; Ann Arbor Blues Festival, Ann Arbor, MI, 1969-70; rec Delmark label, Chicago, IL, 1969; worked Wisconsin Blues Festival, Beloit, WI, 1970; New Orleans Jazz & Heritage Festival, New Orleans, 1970-5; toured w Homesick James working concert dates through France/Spain, 1970; rec Black & Blue label, Bordeaux, France, 1970; rec w Memphis Slim, Barclay label, Paris, France, 1970; rec Spivey label, Brooklyn, NY, 1970; app in film ROOSEVELT SYKES, 1971; rec Southland label c1971; rec 77 label, New Orleans, 1971; worked Univ of Pittsburgh Blues Festival, Pittsburgh, PA, 1971; Festival of American Folklife, St Helen's Island, Montreal, Can, 1971; Univ of Chicago Folk Festival, Chicago, IL, 1972; Univ of Miami Blues Festival, Coral Gables, FL, 1972; Bourbon Street, Toronto, Can, 1972; Mariposa Folk Festival, Toronto, Can, 1972; clip shown in French film BLUES UNDER THE SKIN, 1972; toured w American Folk-Blues Festival working concert dates through England/Europe, 1972; app in French film OUT OF THE BLACKS INTO THE BLUES (pt 1: Along the Old Man River), 1972; rec Barclay label, France, c1972; worked Harpur Col, Binghamton, NY, 1973; rec Delmark label, Chicago, IL, 1973; rec BluesWay label, New Orleans, LA, 1973; worked Missouri Friends of Folk Arts Concert, St Louis, MO, 1973; Ann Arbor Blues Festival, Ann Arbor, MI, 1973; Sandy's, Beverly, MA, 1973; Kenny's Castaways, NYC, 1973; Univ of Miami, Coral Gables, FL, 1974; Richard's, Atlanta, GA, 1974; Academy of Music, Brooklyn, NY, 1974; app on BLUES PIANO ORGY, WLDC-radio, New Orleans, LA, 1975; worked Washington Univ, St Louis, MO, 1975; Art Park Theater, Lewiston, NY, 1975; Winnipeg Folk Festival, Birds Hill Park, Winnipeg, Can, 1975; Ambassador Hotel, Los Angeles, CA, 1976; Great American Music Hall, San Francisco, CA, 1976; Philadelphia Folk Festival, Schwenksville, PA, 1976; app on THE DEVIL'S MUSIC—A HISTORY OF THE BLUES (ep: The Movements of Providence/ep: Nothing But the Truth), BBC-1-TV, Eng, 1976; worked BB's Jazz, Blues & Soup Parlor, St Louis, MO, 1976; Rosy's Club, New Orleans, LA, 1976; New Orleans Jazz & Heritage Festival, New Orleans, 1976-9; Knickerbocker Cafe, Westerly, RI, 1977; Winnipeg Folk Festival, Winnipeg, Can, 1977; clip shown in ROOTS OF COUNTRY MUSIC & BLUES, KGO-TV, San Francisco, 1977; worked clubs/festivals across US into 80s; died of heart attack

Personal: Three brothers are musicians. Named "The Honeydripper" as youth for his reputation as a ladies' man. Muslim name was Roosevelt Sykes Bey

Billing: The Honeydripper

Songs: A Woman Is in Demand/Ace Boogie/All Days Are Good Days/All My Money Gone/Bicycle Riding Mama/Big Ben/Big Time Woman/Blue Bass/Blues Will Prank with Your Soul/Bop De Bip/Boogie Honky Tonky/Boot That Thing/BVD Blues/Coming Home/DBA Blues/Dangerous Man/Dirty Mother for You/Domestic Nurse Blues/Don't Push Me Around/Dookie Chase Boogie/Double Breasted Woman/Driving Wheel/Eagle-Rock Me Baby/Feel Like Blowing My Horn/Flames of Jive/47th Street Jive (Boogie)/Give Me Your Change/Gold Mine/Gulfport Boogie/Hangover/He's Just a Gravy Train/Henry Ford Blues/High as a Georgia Pine/High Price Blues/The Honeydripper/I Done You Wrong/I Hate to Be Alone/I Wanna Love/I'm a Dangerous Man/I'm a Nut/I'm Her Honeydripper/I'm the Sweet Root Man/Ice Cream Freezer/Jailbait/Jookin' in New Orleans/Jubilee Time/Kilroy's in Town/The Last Laugh/Life Is a Puzzle/Lonely Day/Long Lonesome Night/Look a Here/Mama Mama/Man Is in Trouble/May Be a Scandal/Mellow Queen/Mighty Men/Mislead Mother/Miss Dirty Gurty Blues/Miss Ida B/Mistake in Life/Moving Blues/Mr Sykes Blues/My Hamstring's Poppin'/Natch'l Go Getter/New 44 Blues/New Orleans Jump/Nighttime (Anytime) Is the Right Time/Number Nine/Peeping Tom/Persimmon Pie/Pocketful of Money/Put Up or Shut Up/Raining in My Heart/Red-Eye Jesse Bell/Rock-A-Bye Birdie/Roosevelt Daddy's Blues/Roosevelt's Mood/Runnin' the Boogie/Sad and Lonely Day/Safety Pin Blues/Satellite Baby/Set the Meat Out Doors/Shaking the Boogie/She Ain't for Nobody/Side Door Blues/Sleeping All Day Blues/Sneakin' and Dodgin'/Soft and Mellow/Southern Blues/Springfield Blues/Stompin' the Boogie/Sugar Cup/Sunny Road/Sweet Home Chicago/Sykes Gumboogie/Tall Heavy Mama/Thanks But No Thanks/Thanksgivin' Blues/32-20 Blues/Time Wasted on You/Tonight/Too Smart Too Soon/True Thing/Walkin' and Drinkin'/You Can't Be Lucky All the Time/You Understand

Infl by: "Red Eye" Jessie Bell/"Pork Chop" Lee Green

Infl to: Little Eddie Boyd/Detroit Jr/Fats Domino/ Henry Gray/Smiley Lewis/Willie Mabon/Memphis Slim/Pinetop Perkins/Otis Spann/Henry Townsend

Quotes: "Roosevelt Sykes is one of the most important urban bluesmen of all time"—Bob Koester, Delmark album DL-607

"[In the 40s] he recorded important transitional records that bridged the gap between southern rural blues and the modern, electric Chicago blues style"—Don Heckman, *BMI: The Many Worlds of Music*, 1969, p 26

". . . a truly immortal blues performer"—John Bentley, *Living Blues* magazine, Summer 1972, p 23

References: Delmark album DL-607
Living Blues magazine, Summer 1972, pp 21-3
Sing Out magazine, Sept/Oct 1977, pp 2-6

SYLVESTER, HANNAH/HANNA

(aka: Genevia Scott)
Born: c1900, Philadelphia (Philadelphia Co), PA
Died: Oct 15, 1973, New York, NY

Courtesy Frank Driggs Collection

Mother was Genevia Scott; began singing/dancing as child prodigy at 3 years of age; reportedly moved to New York City, NY, c1920; worked Paradise Cafe, Atlantic City, NJ, early 20s; rec w Fletcher Henderson Orch, Emerson/Paramount/Majestic/Pathe-Actuelle labels, NYC, 1923; long residency, Happy Rhone's Club, NYC, 1924; frequently toured theater circuits working vaudeville shows through 20s; worked Cotton Club/Club Harlem/others, NYC, late 20s; app in LOOK WHO'S HERE Revue, Drake-Walker Theater, NYC, 1928; app in CLUB HARLEM REVUE, Lincoln Theater, NYC, 1929; app in musical comedy JAZZOLA, Lafayette Theater, NYC, 1929; worked Nest Club, NYC, c1929; RKO Palace Theater, NYC, c1930; Hippodrome Theater, NYC, c1930; worked w Fletcher Henderson Orch, Howard Theater, Washington, DC, 1931 (remote WSJV-radio); app in INDIANOLA Revue, Alhambra Theater, NYC, 1931; app in BALLYHOO OF 1931 Revue, Lafayette Theater, NYC, 1931; app in HITS AND BITS Revue, Lafayette Theater, NYC, 1932; app in show HUMMIN' SAM, New Yorker Theater, NYC, 1933; app in SEVENTH AVENUE Revue, Lafayette Theater, NYC, 1933; app in Frank Montgomery's PARADISE CLUB REVUE, Lafayette Theater, NYC, 1933; app in Leonard Harper's ALL STAR REVUE, Harlem Opera House, NYC, 1933; app w Jimmie Lunceford Band, ADDISON CAREY'S REVUE, Lafayette Theater, NYC, 1933; worked Apollo Theater, NYC, 1934; Harlem Opera House, NYC, 1934; Dickie Well's Club, NYC, 1935; frequently toured w Snookum Russell Orch, 1940; worked mostly outside music (as bartender), Celebrity Club, NYC, from early 50s; occasionally worked w Buddy Tate Band, Celebrity Club, NYC, during 50s; app in X-GLAMOUR GIRLS Revue, Riverside Plaza Ballroom, NYC, 1962; rec w Lucille Hegamin, Spivey label, NYC, 1962; continued outside music work in NYC into 70s

SYLVESTER

Personal: Married Jeff Blunt, manager of Nest Club (late 20s-). Served as treasurer of New York X-Glamour Girls organization during 60s

Billing: Harlem's Mae West

Quote: "She was one of the least appreciated of all the lady performers"—Derrick Stewart-Baxter, *Jazz Journal* magazine (UK), Apr 1974, p 25

T

T V SLIM
(see Wills, Oscar)

TAMPA RED
(see Whittaker, Hudson)

TANGLE EYE
(see Horton, Walter)

TARHEEL SLIM
(see Bunn, Alden)

TATE, CHARLES HENRY *"Baby"*

Photo by Sudy L Bristol. Courtesy Peter B Lowry

Born: Jan 28, 1916, Elberton (Elbert Co), GA
Died: Aug 17, 1972, Columbia, SC
Inst: Guitar

Moved to Greenville, SC, where he was raised from 1926; frequently ran together w Blind Boy Fuller in Greenville area, late 20s; taught self guitar to work w Joe Walker/Roosevelt Brooks in Greenville area into 30s; app w Carolina Blackbirds on WFBC-radio, Greenville, 1932; frequently worked outside music with occasional local parties/picnics and passing medicine shows through 30s; served in US Army in North Africa/Italy/England/Europe (with occasional entertaining in local UK pubs/dances) c1942-6; worked outside music in Greenville, SC, with occasional local gigs from c1946 into 50s; rec Kapp label, Atlanta, GA, early 50s; moved to Spartanburg, SC, to work outside music with occasional work w Pink Anderson (or solo) at local parties/dances/jukes in area, 1954 into 70s; rec Bluesville label, Spartanburg, 1962; app in film documentary THE BLUES, 1963; rec w Peg Leg Sam, Trix label, Jonesville, SC, 1972; died of heart attack

Personal: Married Tillie ———. His brothers Isom/Ira Tate are musicians

Infl by: Blind Boy Fuller

Quote: Baby Tate is an outstanding performer in the old Carolina styles . . ."—Bob Groom, *Blues World* magazine (UK), Jul 1970, p 20

TAYLOR, ARTHUR *"Montana"*
Born: 1903, Butte (Silver Bow Co), MT
Died: (unknown)
Inst: Piano

Father was owner of Silver City Club, Butte, MT; moved briefly to Chicago, IL, c1910; moved to Indianapolis, IN, where he was raised from 1911; taught self piano, 1919; frequently worked rent parties in Indianapolis/Chicago from c1921; worked Hole In The Wall, Indianapolis, c1923; Goosie Lee's Rock House, Indianapolis, mid-20s; frequently worked residency at Golden West Cafe, Indianapolis, through 20s; frequently worked rent parties/music stores in Chicago, late 20s into 30s; rec Vocalion label, Chicago, 1929; moved to Cleveland, OH, working mostly outside music from 1936; rec w Bertha Chippie Hill, Circle label, Chicago, 1946; worked w Ber-

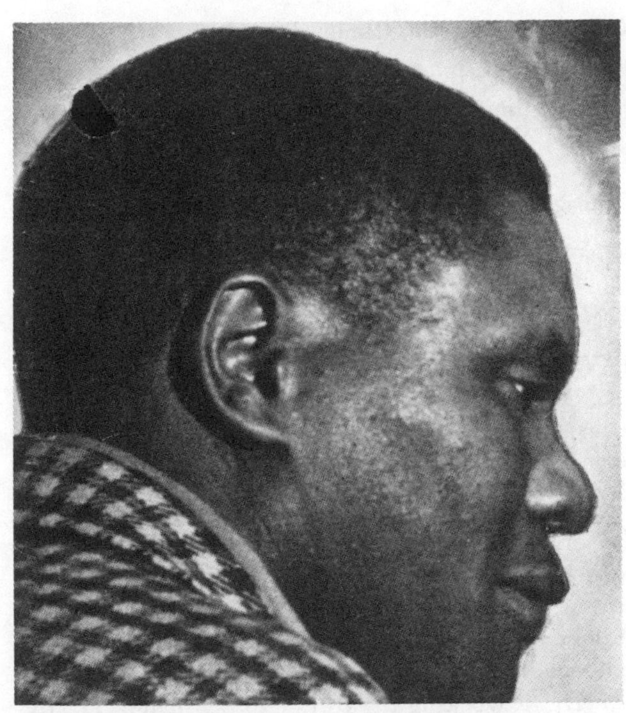

Courtesy Sheldon Harris Collection

tha Chippie Hill, Ziegfeld Theater, NYC, 1946; inactive in music thereafter

Songs: Detroit Rocks/Fo' Day/In the Bottom/Indiana Avenue Stomp/Rag Alley Drag

Infl by: Funky Five/Phil Harding/Tom Harding

Quote: "One of the greatest archaic singers"—Rudi Blesh, *Shining Trumpets*, Alfred A Knopf, 1946

Reference: The Jazz Record, Apr 1947, pp 8-10

TAYLOR, EDDIE *"Playboy"*
Born: Jan 29, 1923, Benoit (Bolivar Co), MS
Died: Dec 25, 1985, Chicago, IL
Inst: Guitar

Father was Joseph Taylor; mother Mamie Gaston; worked on farm as child; interested in music early; frequently followed Charley Patton to Stringtown/Leland, MS, early 30s; frequently worked local streets for tips, Stringtown, MS, late 30s; frequently worked w Big Joe Williams/Son House/Howlin' Wolf/Floyd Jones/Jimmy Reed/others in local jukes/bars/parties/suppers in Leland/Clarksdale, MS, areas, late 30s to c1943; moved to Memphis, TN, to work outside music from c1943; occasionally sat-in w Homesick James/Elmore James/Walter Horton/Johnny Shines/BB King/others with frequent solo work in local taverns/Church's Park (WC Handy Park), Memphis, c1943-9; moved to Chicago, IL, to work outside music with frequent work on Maxwell Street for tips from 1949; worked w Jimmy Lee Robinson, Jake's Tavern, Chicago, 1949; Club Alibi, Chicago, 1949; w Jimmy Reed at Club Jamboree, Chicago, 1949-52; Congo Lounge, Chicago, 1949; frequently rec acc to Jimmy Reed, Chance/VJ labels, Chicago, 1953 into 60s; worked w Muddy Waters Band, Zanzibar Club, Chicago, 1953; rec VJ label, Chicago, 1954-7; toured w John Lee Hooker working clubs/bars/concerts across US, mid-50s; worked 34 Club, Chicago, c1955; w Elmore James, Sylvio's, Chicago, 1955; toured extensively w Jimmy Reed working club dates through US/Mexico, 1955 into 60s; frequently worked w own group, Pepper's Lounge, Chicago, c1957 into 60s; app w Elmore James, BIG BILL HILL SHOW, WOPA-radio, Oak Park, IL, 1963; frequently worked w Floyd Jones in local clubs, Chicago, 1963-4; rec Vivid label, Chicago, 1964; worked w Paul Butterfield group, Sylvio's, Chicago, 1964; Big John's, Chicago, 1965; B&W Lounge, Chicago, 1966; rec Testament label, Chicago, 1966; rec w Jimmy Reed, BluesWay label, Chicago, 1966-8; toured w American Folk Blues Festival working concert dates through England/Europe,

Photo by Bill Greensmith. Courtesy *Living Blues Magazine*

1968 (por shown in UK film AMERICAN FOLK BLUES FESTIVAL); toured w John Lee Hooker working concert dates through England/Europe, 1969; worked w Carey Bell, Jo Jo's, Chicago, 1969; Wisconsin Blues Festival, Beloit, WI, 1970; toured w Carey Bell/Jimmy Dawkins working concerts through Europe, 1970; toured w Roosevelt Sykes working concert dates through France/Spain, 1970; rec w Roosevelt Sykes/Homesick James, Black & Blue label, Bordeaux, France, 1970; worked Flamingo Club, Chicago, 1970; Ann Arbor Blues Festival, Ann Arbor, MI, 1970; occasionally worked Maxwell Street area, Chicago, 1970; Tom's Musicians Club, Chicago, 1970; worked Big Duke's, Chicago, 1971; Notre Dame Blues Festival, South Bend, IN, 1971; frequently worked w Sam Lay Band in local clubs, Chicago, 1971; rec Advent label, Hollywood/Glendale, CA, 1972; worked Ann Arbor Blues Festival, Ann Arbor, MI, 1973; w Jimmy Dawkins, Univ of Vermont, Burlington, VT, 1973; toured w Chicago Blues Festival working concert dates through England/Europe, 1973; toured w American Blues Legends working concert dates through England/Europe, 1974 (por rel Big Bear label); app IN CONCERT Show, Radio-4, London, Eng, 1974; rec Munich/Big Bear labels, London, 1974; worked Teddy's Club, Milwaukee, WI, 1974; King's Club Waveland, Chicago, IL, 1974; Toronto Island Concert, Toronto Island, Can, 1974; Northwestern Univ, Evanston, IL, 1974; Eddie Shaw's Place, Chicago, 1975; Chicago Blues Festival, Jane Addams Theater, Chicago, 1975; Elsewhere Lounge, Chicago, 1976-7; w Jimmy Reed, The Savoy, San Francisco, CA, 1976; Orphans, Chicago, 1977; Pepper's, Chicago, 1977; toured Europe/Japan working concerts, 1977; worked Blues Festival, Holland, 1979; worked Chicago/NYC clubs/festivals into 80s; toured Europe w American Folk Blues Fest, 1980; worked Blues Festival, Chicago, 1984; died of pneumonia; buried Restvale Cemetery, Worth, IL

Songs: Bad Boy/Big Town Playboy/Blues in the Rain/Bullcow Blues/Do You Want Me to Cry?/Don't Knock at My Door/Gamblin' Man/I Feel So Bad/I Know My Baby/I Used to Have Some Friends/I'm a Country Boy/I'm Gonna Love You/I'm Sitting Here/Jackson Town/Playboy Boogie/Ready for Eddie/Ride 'em on Down/Seems Like a Million Years/Sittin' Here Thinkin'/Stop Breaking Down/Stroll Out West/Take Your Hand Down/There'll Be a Day/13 Highway/Too Late to Cry/Wreck on 83 Highway/You'll Always Have a Home

Infl by: Robert Johnson/Muddy Waters/Charley Patton/Jimmy Lee Robinson

Infl to: Freddy King/Jimmy Reed

Quotes: "An extremely moving singer and one of the most rhythmically propulsive guitarists in the modern blues"—Pete Welding, Testament album 2214

"One of the most experienced musicians in Chicago"—Keith Tillman, Python album PLP-KM6

References: Testament album 2214

Blues Unlimited magazine (UK), Nov 1964, pp 9-10

TAYLOR, EVA

(*aka:* Irene Gibbons/Catherine Henderson/Irene Williams)

Born: Jan 22, 1895, St Louis (St Louis Co), MO

Died: Oct 31, 1977, Mineola, NY

Father was ——— Gibbons; mother was Julia ———; born Irene Gibbons; one of 12 children; worked as pick w Josephine Gassman and Her Pickaninnies, Orpheum Theater, St Louis, MO, 1898; toured extensively w Josephine Gassman troupe on Orpheum circuit working theaters from Chicago, IL, to West Coast, 1898 to c1904; toured w Josephine Gassman troupe working theater dates through Hawaii/Australia/New Zealand from c1904-6; frequently toured w Josephine Gassman troupe working theater dates through US/England/Germany/France/Holland from 1906; worked Hippodrome Theater, London, Eng, 1906; app (as chorus girl) w Al Jolson in show VERA VIOLETTA, Winter Garden Theater, NYC, 1911; toured w Josephine Gassman Phina & Company Show working theaters through Australia/Tasmania/New Zealand, 1914-15; continued frequent tours (as ballad singer/dancer) w Josephine Gassman troupe working theaters across US from 1915; worked theater dates, Chicago, IL, c1919; settled in New York, NY, 1921; frequently worked (as blues/ballad singer) in Clarence Williams Trio in local clubs/theaters, NYC, from 1921; worked Lafayette Theater, NYC, 1921-2; w Happy Rhone's Orch, New Star Casino, NYC, 1922; Standard Theater, Philadelphia, PA, 1922; app w Florence Mills in musical comedy SHUFFLE ALONG, 63rd Street Theater, NYC, 1922; toured in Miller & Lyles variety show STEP ON IT working theaters on East Coast, 1922; worked Howard Theater, Washington, DC, 1922; app w Nora Bayes in show QUEEN O' HEARTS, George M Cohan Theater, NYC, 1922; rec w Clarence Williams group, Black Swan label, NYC, 1922; app w Clarence Williams Trio on Vaughn De Leath's MUSICAL PROGRAM Show, WEAF-radio, NYC, 1922; rec extensively w Clarence Williams and others, OKeh label, NYC, 1922-8; rec (as "Irene Gibbons") Colum-

Eva Taylor *Courtesy Spencer Williams*

bia label, NYC, 1922-3; rec duets w Sarah Martin/Lawrence Lomax, OKeh label, NYC, 1923; worked w Clarence Williams' Blue Five, Lincoln Theater, NYC, 1923; New Star Casino, NYC, 1923; Fox Terminal Theater, Newark, NJ, 1923 (por remote WAAM-radio); Madison Square Garden, NYC, 1924; app w Piron's New Orleans Orch, WJZ-radio, NYC, 1924; app frequently w Clarence Williams Radio Trio/Blue Three/Blue Five Orch on WHN-radio, NYC, 1924-8; app frequently w Clarence Williams/Clarence Todd, WGBS-radio, NYC, 1924-6; understudy to Florence Mills, DIXIE TO BROADWAY Revue, Broadhurst Theater, NYC, 1924; frequently worked w Clarence Williams at local music/department stores (promotional) and hotel gigs in NYC area from mid-20s; worked William Penn Hotel, Pittsburgh, PA, 1925; frequently toured Keith circuit working theater dates, 1925; app on KYW-radio, Chicago, IL, 1925; frequently worked Lincoln Theater, NYC, 1925-6; The Auditorium, Chicago, 1926 (por remote WGN-radio); The New Douglas Theater, NYC, 1926; w Clarence Williams, Sesqui-Centennial International Exposition, Philadelphia, PA, 1926; Harlem Casino, NYC, 1926; Lafayette Theater, NYC, 1926; Artist & Movie Ball, Renaissance Ballroom, NYC, 1926; app in CLARENCE WILLIAMS REVUE, Lincoln Theater, NYC, 1926; Savoy Ballroom, NYC, 1926; app w Clarence Williams in musical comedy BOTTOMLAND, Savoy Theater, Atlantic City, NJ, 1927/Princess Theater, NYC, 1927; frequently app in Clarence Williams Trio, WPAP/WPCH-radio, NYC, 1927-8; rec Columbia label, NYC, 1928-30; app on FLORENCE MILLS MEMORIAL HOUR, WABC-radio, NYC, 1928; app on BELOW THE MASON-DIXON LINE Show, WABC-radio, NYC, 1928; app on CLARENCE WILLIAMS & PALS SHOW, WOV-radio, NYC, 1929; rec Edison/Victor labels, NYC, 1929; rec w Charleston Chasers, Columbia label, NYC, 1929-30; app in Miller & Lyles musical show KEEP SHUFFLIN', Pearl Theater, Philadelphia, PA, 1929; worked as staff soloist for WEAF/WJZ-radio, NYC (NBC-Network), from 1929 into 30s; app on MAJOR BOWES CAPITOL FAMILY SHOW, WEAF-radio, NYC (NBC-Network), 1929; app on MORNING GLORIES Show, WEAF-radio, NYC (NBC-Network), 1929; app on THE RISE OF THE GOLDBERGS (The Goldbergs), WJZ-radio, NYC (NBC-Network), 1929; app w Nat Shilkret on THE EVEREADY HOUR, WEAF-radio, NYC (NBC-Network), 1929; app on ATWATER KENT HOUR, WEAF-radio, NYC, 1929; app w Kris Kringle Band, WEAF-radio, NYC, 1929; frequently app w Knickerbockers Orch, WJZ-radio, NYC, 1929; app first NBC coast-to-coast (untitled) show, WEAF/WJZ-radio, 1929 (also short-wave broadcast to England/Europe); app on SIXTY MINUTES OF BROADWAY ENTERTAINMENT, WGY-radio, Schenectady, NY, 1930 (also broadcast on General Electric short wave radio to Rear Admiral Richard E Byrd at the South Pole); app in black adaptation of Samson & Delilah on ALPHA & OMEGA OPERA COMPANY DELUXE INC Show, WEAF-radio, NYC (NBC-Network), 1930; rec (as "Catherine Henderson"), Velvetone label, NYC, 1930; rec w Clarence Williams Washboard Band and others, OKeh label, NYC, 1930; frequently app on BLUE STREAKS ORCH Show, WEAF-radio, NYC (NBC-Network), 1930-1; rec ARC label group, NYC, 1930; worked w Clarence Williams, Carnegie Hall, NYC, 1930; app on CLARENCE WILLIAMS TRIO Show, WOR-radio, NYC, 1930-1; app on CARELESS LOVE Show, WEAF-radio, NYC (NBC-Network), 1930-2; app on CLARENCE WILLIAMS AND HIS ENTERTAINING FOUR Show, WMCA/WPCH-radio, NYC, 1931; app on CLARENCE WILLIAMS QUARTET Show, WMCA-radio, NYC, 1931; app w Erno Rapee on GENERAL MOTORS Show, WEAF-radio, NYC (NBC-Network), 1931; app w Hugo Mariana's MARIONETTES ORCHESTRA Show, WEAF-radio, NYC (NBC-Network), 1931-2; app on DIXIE NIGHTINGALES Show, WOR-radio, NYC, 1932; app on own EVA TAYLOR, CROONER Show, WJZ-radio, NYC (NBC-Network), 1932-3/WEAF-radio, NYC (NBC-Network), 1932-3; app on CLUB VALSPAR Show, WEAF-radio, NYC, 1932; rec duet w Lil Armstrong (as "The Riffers"), Columbia label, NYC, 1932; app on HARLEM FANTASY Show, WEAF-radio, NYC (NBC-Network), 1932; app w Lil Armstrong/Clarence Williams Trio, SLOW RIVER SHOW, WEAF/WJZ-radio, NYC (NBC-Network), 1932-3; app in MELODIES OF 1933 Revue, Harlem Opera House, NYC, 1933; app on THE LOWLAND SINGERS/TRIO Show, WOR-radio, NYC, 1933; app on FOLKS FROM DIXIE Show, NBC-Network radio, 1933; rec w Clarence Williams Jug Band/Orch, Vocalion label, NYC, 1933-4; app w Paul Whiteman Orch, KRAFT MUSIC HALL Show, WEAF-radio, NYC (NBC-Network), 1933; rec w Clarence Williams Jug Band/Orch, Columbia label, NYC, 1933; app w Cab Calloway Orch, HARLEM Show, WJZ-radio, NYC (NBC-Network), 1933; app on GRANDMOTHER'S TRUNK SHOW, NBC-Network radio, 1934; app in Musical Life in Harlem Program, Little Theater of YMCA, NYC, 1934; headlined at Harlem Opera House, NYC, 1934; worked Lincoln Theater, Washington, DC, 1934; app on RYE CRISP Show, WJZ-radio, NYC, 1935; app on

MORNING GLORY Show, WEAF-radio, NYC (NBC-Network), 1935; app on SOFT LIGHTS AND SWEET MUSIC Show, WEAF-radio, NYC (NBC-Network), 1935; worked Apollo Theater, NYC, 1936; app on DROWSY RHYTHM Show, WENR-radio, Chicago, IL, 1936; app in show MR JIGGINS OF JIGGINSTOWN, Labor Stage Theater (Princess Theater), NYC, 1936; rec Bluebird label, NYC, 1937; worked w Clarence Williams, Carnegie Hall, NYC, 1939; app on YOUTH ON PARADE Show, local radio, NYC, 1939; app on THE SHEEP & GOAT CLUB Show, WOR-radio, NYC, 1940; rec Bluebird label, NYC, 1941; retired from active music work to frequently entertain for Hospital Reserve Corps in local hospitals, NYC, NY, area from c1942; worked Bessie Smith Memorial Concert, Town Hall, NYC, 1948; mostly inactive in music through 50s/60s; app w Anglo-American Alliance Jazz Groups, BBC-radio, London, Eng, 1967; rec w Anglo-American Boy Friends, Audubon label, Burnham, Eng, 1967; app on JOE FRANKLIN Show, WOR-TV, NYC, c1967; worked Overseas Press Club, Biltmore Hotel, NYC, 1974-5; worked w Sweet Peruna Jazz Band in concert, Copenhagen, Den, 1974 (por rel private label); worked w Maggie's Blue Five group in concert, Copenhagen, Den/Lund, Sweden, 1975-6; Stampen Club, Stockholm, Sweden, 1976 (por rel Kenneth label); app on national TV Show, Sweden, 1976; entered Nassau County Hospital where she died of cancer; buried St Charles Cemetery, Huntington, NY

Personal: Married Clarence Williams, pianist/leader/song writer/publisher, (1921-died 1965). 3 children. Daughter Irene Williams was singer. Katherine Henderson is niece. Actor Clarence Williams III may be distant cousin. Assumed stage name "Eva Taylor" in 1922 using sister's given name of "Eva" and "Taylor" from family she had lived with as youth

Billings: The Dixie Nightingale/The Queen of the Moaners

Song: May We Meet Again, Florence Mills

Infl to: Katherine Henderson/Sippie Wallace

Quote: "Though not possessed of a big voice like Bessie Smith or Sara Martin, her rich and thrilling contralto is nevertheless ideally suited to all kinds of songs, flexible, warm and human as its owner"—Brian Rust, Parlophone album PMC-7049

Reference: Storyville magazine (UK), Dec 1967/Feb 1968/Apr 1968

TAYLOR, HOUND DOG

(see Taylor, Theodore)

TAYLOR, *"Little"* JOHNNY LAMAR

Courtesy Living Blues *Magazine*

Born: Feb 11, 1943, Memphis (Shelby Co), TN
Inst: Harmonica

Born Johnny Young; moved to Los Angeles, CA, where he was raised from 1950; frequently sang in local gospel groups on West Coast from early 50s; toured w Clouds of Joy gospel group working churches/recitals/concerts across US, early 50s; rec w Mighty Clouds of Joy gospel group, Victor label, Hollywood, CA, mid-50s; rec w Stars of Bethel gospel group, Imperial label, mid-50s; frequently toured w Johnny Otis Blues Shows working concerts on West Coast, late 50s; frequently worked 109 Club/California Club/Ruthies Inn/The Cow Palace, Los Angeles area, late 50s into 60s; rec Swingin' label, Los Angeles, 1960; frequently worked club dates in Los Angeles, CA/Denver, CO, 1960-1; rec Galaxy label, San Francisco, CA, c1963-4; frequently toured as single working club dates through South, mid-60s; rec Ronn label, Muscle Shoals, AL, late 60s; frequently toured one-nighters across US/Canada, late 60s into 70s; worked Tenampa Ballroom, Chicago, IL, 1975; New 1815 Club, Chicago, 1975; Ruthie's Inn, Berkeley, CA, 1975; Ericson's Lounge, Buffalo, NY, 1976

Personal: Married. Has children. Not to be confused with Johnnie Harrison Taylor (born May 5, 1938), or

Koko Taylor *Photo by Doug Fulton. Courtesy Sheldon Harris Collection*

John/Johnny "Blues" Taylor, singers. No relation to Koko Taylor/Ted Taylor/Hound Dog Taylor

Songs: If You Love Me Like You Say/Looking at the Future/ Since I Found a New Love

Infl by: Bobby Bland/Little Willie John

Quote: "He really does preach the blues and is also one of the best blues balladeers"—Dick Shurman, *Living Blues* magazine, Mar 1976, p 15

Reference: Living Blues magazine, Mar 1975, pp 13-15

TAYLOR, KOKO
Born: Sept 28, 1935, Memphis (Shelby Co), TN

Born Cora Walton; was born/raised in Memphis, TN; was singing in local church choir from 15 years of age; moved to Chicago, IL, to work outside music from 1953; worked occasionally w Buddy Guy/Jr Wells in local club dates, Chicago, 1953 into 60s; rec w J B Lenoir, USA label, Chicago, 1963; rec Spivey label, Chicago, 1964; rec Checker label, Chicago, 1964-73; app on THE BEAT, WPIX-TV, NYC (syndicated), c1965; worked Western Hall, Chicago, 1965; Sylvio's, Chicago, 1966; toured w American Folk Blues Festival working concert dates through England/Europe, 1967; worked Chicago Blues Festival, Chicago, 1969; Grant Park Blues Festival, Chicago, 1969; toured one-nighters through South c1970; worked Pepper's Lounge, Chicago, 1970 (remote on WMAQ-TV); app in film THE BLUES IS ALIVE AND WELL IN CHICAGO, 1970; worked Salt & Pepper Lounge, Chicago, 1970 (remote on WOPA-radio); Five Stages, Chicago, 1970; Univ of Chicago, Chicago, 1970; frequently worked w Mighty Joe Young Band in local clubs, Chicago, 1970-1; app on BIG BILL HILL SHOW, WOPA-radio, Oak Park, IL, 1971; worked Alice's Revisited, Chicago, 1972; worked w Mighty Joe Young Band, Ann Arbor Blues Festival, Ann Arbor, MI, 1972 (por rel Atlantic label); w Muddy Waters, Montreux Jazz Festival, Montreux, Switzerland, 1972 (por rel Chess label); w Earl White's Revue, Cougar Show Club, Chicago, 1972; Joe's Place, Cambridge, MA, 1972; toured w Chicago Blues Festival working concert dates through Europe, 1973 (por rel Black & Blue label); Notre Dame Blues Festival, South Bend, IN, 1973; worked Hunter Col, NYC, 1974; Biddy Mulligan's, Chicago, 1974; Checkerboard Lounge, Chicago, 1974; Sandy's, Beverly, MA, 1974; frequently worked Wise Fools Pub, Chicago, 1974-8; app w Muddy Waters, SOUNDSTAGE, PBS-TV, 1974; rec Alligator label, Chicago, 1974; toured w own Blues Machine group working college circuit across US, 1975; worked Univ of Miami Blues Festival, Coral Gables, FL, 1975; Sheldon Art Gallery, Lincoln, NE, 1975; Theresa's, Chicago, 1975; Northern Illinois Univ, DeKalb, IL, 1976; Holmes Center Ballroom, DeKalb, IL, 1976; New England Blues Festival, Providence, RI, 1976; Silver Shadow, Chicago, 1977; Miller Theater, Houston, TX, 1977; Charlotte's Web, Rockford, IL, 1977; rec Alligator label, Chicago, 1977

Personal: Married Robert Taylor (1953-). 1 daughter, Joyce "Cookie" Taylor (born 1956). "Koko" is a childhood mispronunciation of her given name Cora

Songs: Be What You Want to Be/Honkey Tonkey/Nitty Gritty/ Voodoo Woman/ What Kind of Man Is This?

Quotes: "This talented artist is in the direct line of the great blues women like Bessie Smith, Memphis Minnie and Victoria Spivey"—Len Kunstadt, *Record Research* magazine, Dec 1972, p 5

"Chicago's premier blues growler"—Wesley Race, *Living Blues* magazine, May 1975, p 47

References: Living Blues, Winter 1971, pp 11-13
Cadence magazine, Nov 1979, pp 7-10

TAYLOR, MONTANA
(see Taylor, Arthur)

TAYLOR, THEODORE ROOSEVELT *"Hound Dog"*
Born: Apr 12, 1917, Natchez (Adams Co), MS
Died: Dec 17, 1975, Chicago, IL
Inst: Guitar/Piano

Father was Robert Taylor; mother was Della Herron; interested in music at early age and made first instrument from cigar box as child; frequently worked outside music (on farm) from childhood; ran away from home to hobo through South working outside music from 1926; frequently worked w Elmore James/Sonny Boy Williamson (Alex Miller)/Robert Jr Lockwood/ others or solo in jukes/barrelhouses/picnics/streets in Tchula, MS, area through 30s; app w Sonny Boy Williamson (Alex Miller) on KING BISCUIT TIME, KFFA-radio, Helena, AR, c1942; settled in Chicago, IL, to work outside music with occasional work on Maxwell Street for tips, 1942-57; worked Stormy's Club, Chicago, c1944; worked AT&T Club, Chicago, 1957; Three Brothers, Chicago, c1958; Wagon Wheel, Chicago, c1958; Ada's Tavern, Chicago, 1959; Cadillac Baby Club, Chicago, 1960; rec Bea & Baby label, Chicago, 1960; worked Blue Flame Lounge,

Theodore "Hound Dog" Taylor

Photo by Doug Fulton. Courtesy Living Blues *Magazine*

Chicago, 1961; rec Firma label, Chicago, 1962; formed own House Rockers group to work continuously from c1965; frequently app on BIG BILL HILL SHOW, WOPA-radio, Oak Park, IL, from mid-60s; worked Mr Kelly's, Chicago, 1966-70; Dodo Club, Chicago, 1966; toured w American Folk Blues Festival working concert dates through England/Europe, 1967; worked Florence's Lounge, Chicago, 1968-72; Theresa's Lounge, Chicago, 1969; Pepper's Lounge, Chicago, 1969-72; Big Duke's Flamingo Lounge, Chicago, 1969-70; Ann Arbor Blues Festival, Ann Arbor, MI, 1970; Farfield Club, Chicago, 1970; Expressway Lounge, Chicago, 1970-2; Notre Dame Blues Festival, South Bend, IN, 1970; Alice's Revisited, Chicago, 1970-2; The Kove, Kent, OH, 1971-3; rec Alligator label, Chicago, 1971; worked Copa Cabana Club, Chicago, 1971; Phoenix Club, Cicero, IL, 1971; Ann Arbor Blues Festival, Ann Arbor, MI, 1972-3 (por 1972 concert rel Atlantic label); app (unknown) show, WBCN-FM-radio, Boston, MA, early 70s; toured college circuit working concert dates, 1972; Univ of Miami Blues Festival, Coral Gables, FL, 1972; Smithsonian Blues Festival, Washington, DC, 1972; Psychedelic Shack, Chicago, 1972; El Mocambo, Toronto, Can, 1973-4; Joe's Place, Cambridge, MA, 1973; Shaboo Inn, Mansfield, CT, 1973; Checkerboard Lounge, Chicago, 1973-4; Univ of Vermont, Burlington, VT, 1973; Academy of Music, NYC, 1973; Avery Fisher Hall, NYC, 1973-4; Sandy's, Beverly, MA, 1973; Minstrel's, Chicago, 1974; Ivory's 604 Club, Chicago, 1974; Urban Blues Festival, Auditorium Theater, Chicago, 1974; rec Alligator label, Chicago, 1974; worked Northwestern Univ, Evanston, IL, 1974 (por rel Alligator label); Smiling Dog Saloon, Cleveland, OH, 1974 (por rel Alligator label); 1125 Club, Chicago, 1974; Florence's, Chicago, 1974; Louise's South Park Lounge, Chicago, 1974; Peyton Place, Chicago, 1974; Rat Trap,

Chicago, 1974; Willie's Inn, Chicago, 1974; toured w House Rockers group working concert dates through Australia/New Zealand, 1974-5; worked Grendel's Lair, Philadelphia, PA, 1975; Univ of Chicago Circle Campus, Chicago, 1975; Milwaukee Summerfest, Milwaukee, WI, 1975; entered Cook County Hospital where he died of cancer; buried Restvale Cemetery, Worth, IL

Personal: Married (c1951-). Had 5 children. Named "Hound Dog" as youth due to his reputation as a ladies' man

Songs: Buster's Boogie/Freddie's Blues/Give Me Back My Wig/Goodnight Boogie/Hideaway/It's Alright/ Kitchen Sink Boogie/Let's Get Funky/Sadie/Sarah Lee/See Me in the Evening/She's Gone/Sitting at Home Alone/Take Five/Taylor's Rock/Walking the Ceiling

Award/Honor: Won *Chicago Reader* magazine Readers Poll as No. 1 Chicago Blues Artist, 1975

Infl by: Lightnin' Hopkins/Elmore James/Sonny Boy Williamson (Alex Miller)

Infl to: Brewer Phillips

Quotes: ". . . he played and sang the blues, with serious, intense vocals and biting, dragged-out guitar lines"—Bruce Iglauer, *Living Blues* magazine, Jan 1976, p 7

"His was a 'good-time' music with a vengeance"—Mike Rowe, *Blues Unlimited* magazine (UK), Jan 1976, p 16

References: *Blues Unlimited* magazine (UK), Jul/Sept/ Oct 1972

Living Blues, Winter 1970, pp 4-7

Guitar Player, Aug 1975, pp 10, 28

TEMPLE, JOHNNY/JOHNNIE *"Geechie"*
Born: Oct 18, 1906, Canton (Madison Co), MS
Died: Nov 22, 1968, Jackson, MS
Inst: Guitar/Mandolin/Piano

Father was Tobe Temple; mother was Marimb Barte; born/raised on farm; moved to Jackson, MS, c1920; learned mandolin as youth and later was taught guitar by stepfather Slim Duckett; frequently worked w Horace Malcomb/Slim Duckett/Skip James/ others at local house parties, Jackson, MS, into 30s; moved to Chicago, IL, to work speakeasies/parties with frequent trips back to Jackson from c1932; frequently worked w McCoy Brothers (playing polkas/ Italian songs) in local club dates, Chicago, mid-30s; rec Vocalion label, Chicago, 1935; rec Decca label,

Photo by Yannick Bruynoghe. Courtesy Stanley Dance

Chicago, 1936-7; rec w Harlem Hamfats, Decca label, NYC, 1937-8; rec Decca label, NYC/Chicago, 1938-40; worked w Lil Armstrong/Sammy Price/Red Allen/ others in local club dates, NYC, c1939-40; rec Bluebird label, Chicago, 1941; frequently worked small club dates, Chicago, through 40s; rec King label, Chicago, 1946; worked Madison Ballroom, Chicago, 1949; rec Miracle label, Chicago, 1949; worked w Baby Face Leroy, The Spot, Chicago, c1952; worked w Billy Boy Arnold in one-nighters in local clubs, Chicago, from 1953; w Walter Horton, Cosy Inn, Chicago, 1954-5; formed own The Rolling Four working Club Hollywood, Chicago, 1956; returned to Jackson, MS, to work occasional club dates, mid-60s; worked Univ of Mississippi, Oxford, MS, c1967; mostly inactive in music due to illness, late 60s; died at home of cancer; buried Christian Valley Cemetery, Silver City, MS

Personal: Married Marion Collins

Songs: Big Leg Woman/Gimme Some of That Yum Yum Yum/Hoodoo Women/I'm Cuttin' Out/Louise Louise Blues/My Pony

Infl by: Skip James/Tommy Johnson

Reference: *Blues Unlimited* magazine (UK), Sept 1968, pp 7-8

TERRY, DOC

Photo by Sylvia Pitcher. Courtesy Living Blues Magazine

Born: 1921, Sunflower (Sunflower Co), MS
Inst: Harmonica

Father was Ralph Adail; mother was Ella Mae ———; born Terry Adail; was dancing and playing harmonica at 12 years of age; raised at Scott, MS, where he frequently worked outside music through 30s; served in US Army in Pacific Theater of Operations, 1944-6; returned to St Louis, MO, to work outside music c1946-71; frequent weekend work at Yukon Bar/Polka Dot Inn/Ned Love's Moonlight Inn/Red Top Club/The Early Bird/Clark's Bar/others, St Louis, MO, and Huff Gardens/Cotton Club, East St Louis, IL from late 40s into 70s; rec on own DTP label, Clayton, IL, 1971; worked Helen's Moonlight Lounge, St Louis, 1976

Personal: Married Nettie ———. His son Terry Jr is drummer

Song: Things Can't Stay the Same

Infl by: John Lee "Sonny Boy" Williamson

Reference: Blues Unlimited magazine (UK), Sept 1976, pp 18-19

TENNESSEE GABRIEL
(see McGhee, Walter)

TERRY, SANDERS
(see Terry, Sonny)

TERRY, SONNY
(*aka:* Sonny/Sonny T/Sanders Terry)

Courtesy Sheldon Harris Collection

Born: Oct 24, 1911, Greensboro (Greene Co), GA
Died: Mar 11, 1986, Mineola, LI, NY
Inst: Harmonica/Jaw Harp

Father was Reuben Terrell, harmonica player; mother, Mossiline Smith, was a singer; born Saunders Terrell; one of 8 children; raised on farm and interested in music at early age; frequently sang at local Baptist revival tent meets as child; taught self harmonica at 8 years of age; worked outside music with occasional work at local buck dances, Greensboro, GA, area into 20s; blinded in left eye, 1922, and the other, 1927, both due to accidents; moved to Shelby, NC, to work outside music, 1928; teamed w Bill Leach to hobo east working for tips on streets/tobacco warehouses through North Carolina, c1929; briefly toured as soloist w Doc Bizell medicine show through North Carolina, early 30s; frequently worked for tips on streets of Greensboro/Wadesboro, NC, early 30s; worked briefly w Blind Boy Fuller in Wadesboro, NC, 1934; teamed w Blind Boy Fuller (occasionally w Bull City Red) to work streets/tobacco warehouses/fish fries/house parties out of Durham, NC, 1934-8; frequently worked outside music, Durham, through late 30s; rec w Blind Boy Fuller, Vocalion/ARC label group, NYC, 1937-8; rec Library of Congress label, NYC, 1938; worked From Spirituals to Swing Concerts, Carnegie Hall, NYC, 1938-9 (por 1938 concert rel Vanguard label); rec w Blind Boy Fuller, OKeh/ Vocalion labels, Memphis, TN, 1939; rec w Sonny Jones, Vocalion label, Memphis, 1939; while working w Blind Boy Fuller in Burlington, NC, met Brownie McGhee and worked as team almost continuously thereafter from 1939; worked (as single) Cafe Society Downtown, NYC, 1939-40; worked w Brownie McGhee/Paul Robeson, Riverside Stadium, Washington, DC, 1940; worked w Brownie McGhee on streets of Durham, NC, 1940; rec w Blind Boy Fuller and others, OKeh/Vocalion labels, NYC/Chicago, 1940; worked w George "Oh Red" Washington in Greenwich Village clubs, NYC, c1940; rec w Brownie McGhee, OKeh label, NYC, 1941; rec w Buddy Moss, Columbia label, NYC, 1941; rec w Jordan Webb, OKeh label, NYC, 1941; frequently worked w Leadbelly/Brownie McGhee/Woody Guthrie/others (as "Headline Singers") on streets/house parties/ hootenannies/lofts, NYC, 1942; rec w Brownie McGhee/Leadbelly, Library of Congress label, Washington, DC, 1942; rec w Jack Dupree, Folkways label, NYC, 1942; frequently worked w Leadbelly at local folk concerts, NYC, early 40s; worked w Brownie McGhee, Stuyvesant Casino/Central Plaza, NYC, early 40s; rec w Jack Dupree, Solo label, NYC, 1943; rec w Leadbelly, Asch label, NYC, 1943; rec w Woody Guthrie, Asch label, NYC, 1944; rec Stinson/Savoy labels, NYC, 1944; rec w Brownie McGhee, Solo label, NYC, 1945; app on Office of War Information radio shows (frequently on BBC-radio, London, Eng), mid-40s; worked w Woody Guthrie/Brownie McGhee (as "Woody Guthrie Singers") at local hoots/concerts in NYC area c1946; rec w Brownie McGhee, Alert label, NYC, 1946; rec w Art Hodes Jazz Record Six, Jazz Record label, NYC, 1946; worked w Leadbelly, Town Hall, NYC, 1946; frequently worked Alan Lomax Blues at Midnight Concert Series, Town Hall, NYC, 1946; rec Capitol label, NYC, 1947; app w Brownie McGhee/Woody Guthrie in Alan Lomax OWI film short TO HEAR YOUR BANJO PLAY, 1947; app in musical show FINIAN'S RAINBOW, 46th Street Theater, NYC, 1947-8, then toured US/ Canada into 1949 (por rel Columbia label); app w Leadbelly on WNYC JAZZ FESTIVAL series, WNYC-FM radio, NYC, 1948; rec Savoy label, NYC, 1948; worked w Brownie McGhee, Leadbelly Memorial Concert, Town Hall, NYC, 1950; rec w Sticks McGhee, Atlantic label, NYC, 1950; worked w Brownie McGhee at local clubs/rent parties/lofts/barbecues, NYC, 1950-5; rec Capitol label, NYC, 1950; rec Gotham label, NYC, 1951-2; rec Gramercy/Folkways/Stinson/Verve/Archive of Folk Music labels, NYC, 1952; rec w Allen Bunn, Apollo label, NYC, 1952; rec w Bob Gaddy Alley Cats, Jackson label, NYC, c1952; rec w Brownie McGhee Jook Block Busters/Jook House Rockers, Sittin In With/Jax/ Mainstream/ Harlem labels, NYC, 1952; rec w Ralph Willis Country Boys, Prestige label, NYC, 1952; rec w Jack Dupree, Red Robin label, NYC, 1953; rec w Alex Seward, Elektra label, NYC, 1953; rec w Square Walton and others, Victor label, NYC, 1953; rec w Ralph Willis, King label, NYC, 1953; worked Latin Quarter, Montreal, Can, 1954; Tanglewood Festival, Lenox, MA, 1954; rec w Brownie McGhee, Savoy/ Groove labels, NYC, 1954-5; rec w Blind Gary Davis, Stinson label, NYC, 1954; rec w John Sellers, Vanguard label, NYC, 1954; rec w Billy Bland, Old Town label, NYC, 1955; rec w Alonzo Scales, Wing label, NYC, 1955; app w Brownie McGhee in show CAT ON A HOT TIN ROOF, Morosco Theater, NYC, 1955-7, then toured with show; rec Josie/Old Town labels, NYC, 1956; rec Fantasy label, San Francisco, CA, 1957; rec w Brownie McGhee/Bill Broonzy, Folkways/Xtra labels, Chicago, IL, 1957; rec w Brownie McGhee, Folkways label, NYC, 1957-8; worked Gate of Horn, Chicago, 1958; Ash Grove, Los Angeles, CA, 1958-62; toured w Brownie McGhee working concert dates through England/Europe, 1958; rec Nixa label, London, Eng, 1958; worked w Pete Seeger, Carnegie Hall, NYC, 1958; rec Old Town/Choice labels, NYC, 1959; toured w Brownie McGhee working concert dates through England, 1959; rec Columbia label, London, Eng, 1959; rec World Pacific label, Los Angeles, 1959-60; rec Fantasy label, San Francisco, 1959; app on TONIGHT WITH BELAFONTE Show, CBS-TV, 1959; worked Newport Folk Festival, Newport, RI, 1959 (por rel Vanguard/Folkways labels); toured w Brownie McGhee for US State Department working concert dates through India, 1959-60; worked Gerde's Folk City, NYC, 1960; Town Hall, NYC, 1960; One Sheridan Square, NYC, 1960; Fifth Peg, Toronto, Can, 1960-1; rec Prestige-Bluesville/Herald labels, NYC/ NJ, 1960; rec w Brownie McGhee, VJ/Verve/Archive of Folk Music labels, Los Angeles, CA, 1960; toured w Brownie McGhee working concert dates through Europe, 1960; toured w Brownie McGhee working concert dates through England, 1961; rec Folkways/ Choice labels, NYC, 1961; worked Berkshire Music Barn, Lenox, MA, 1961; rec w Luke Miles, Smash label, Los Angeles, 1961; worked Sugar Hill Club, San Francisco, 1961 (por rel Fantasy label); toured college circuit working concert dates across US, 1962; worked L'Hibou Coffeehouse, Ottawa, Can, 1962; app w Brownie McGhee on (unknown) show, CBC-

TV, Toronto, Can, 1962; worked Finjan Club, Montreal, Can, 1962; rec Prestige-Bluesville label, NYC, 1962; worked Second Fret, Philadelphia, PA, 1962 (por rel Prestige label); toured w Rhythm & Blues USA package group working concert dates through England/Europe, 1962; rec Polydor label, Hamburg, Ger, 1962; worked Raven Gallery, Detroit, MI, c1962; frequently toured w Harry Belafonte Show working theaters/concerts across US, 1962-5; worked Village Gate, NYC, 1963; Newport Folk Festival, Newport, RI, 1963 (por rel Vanguard label/por shown in film FESTIVAL); app on national TV commercial for Alka Seltzer, c1963; worked Hunter Col, NYC, 1964; app on A LA CARTE, CBC-TV, Toronto, Can, 1964; toured w American Blues Caravan working concert dates through England, 1964 (por shown on BLUES & GOSPEL TRAIN Show, Granada-TV, England); worked Folk City, NYC, 1964; app w Pete Seeger, ROOMFUL OF MUSIC, WNDT-TV, NYC, 1965; worked Fisher Theater, Detroit, MI, 1965; Apollo Theater, NYC, 1965-7; toured Australia working concert dates, 1965; worked Jordan Hall, Boston, MA, 1965; Riverboat Coffeehouse, Toronto, Can, 1965-73; Jazz Workshop, San Francisco, CA, 1966-7; Univ of Illinois, Urbana, IL, 1966; app on FESTIVAL PRESENTS THE BLUES, CBC-TV, Toronto, Can, 1966; worked Rheingold Central Park Music Festival, NYC, 1966; rec acc to Alec Seward, Blue Labor label, NYC, 1966; worked The Troubador, Los Angeles, CA, 1966; app on THE WORLD OF MUSIC, CBC-TV, Toronto, 1966; worked Mariposa Folk Festival, Toronto, 1966; Ash Grove, Los Angeles, 1967-73; New Penelope, Montreal, Can, 1967-8; toured w American Folk Blues Festival working concert dates through England/Europe, 1967; worked The Bitter End, NYC, NY, 1967; Arts Festival, Cleveland, OH, 1967; rec Fontana label, Chicago, IL, c1967; worked Woody Guthrie Memorial Concert, Carnegie Hall, NYC, 1968; app w Pete Seeger, RAINBOW QUEST, WNDT-TV, NYC, 1968; worked Riverqueen Coffeehouse, Vancouver, Can, 1968-9; Mandrake's, Berkeley, CA, 1969; El Matador, San Francisco, CA, 1969; rec BluesWay label, Los Angeles, CA, 1969; toured w Brownie McGhee/BB King working concert dates through England/Europe, 1969; app in film short WHOOPIN' THE BLUES, 1969; worked Newport Folk Festival, Newport, RI, 1969; Folk City, NYC, 1969; Berkeley Blues Festival, Univ of California, Berkeley, CA, 1969-70; Quiet Knight, Chicago, IL, 1970-1; toured w American Folk Blues Festival working concert dates through England/Europe, 1970 (por Frankfurt, Ger concert rel Scout label); worked Jazz Expo '70, London, Eng, 1970; app on THE HART & LORNE TERRIFIC HOUR, CBC-TV, Canada, 1970; worked The Gaslight, NYC, 1971; Four Muses, San Clemente, CA, 1971; Univ of British Columbia Student Union, Vancouver, Can, 1971; New Paltz Col, New Paltz, NY, 1971-2; app on VIRGINIA GRAHAM Show, WOR-TV, NYC (syndicated), 1971; app in film ROOTS OF AMERICAN MUSIC: COUNTRY & URBAN MUSIC (pt 2), 1971; worked Back Door Coffeehouse, Montreal, Can, 1971; toured Denmark working schools/clubs, 1971; rec Storyville label, Copenhagen, Den, 1971; rec ST for film CISCO PIKE, 1971; worked His Father's Mustache, Montreal, 1971; Funky Quarters, San Diego, CA, 1972; Esquire Showbar, Montreal, 1972; Univ of Waterloo, Waterloo, Can, 1972; app in French film BLUES UNDER THE SKIN, 1972; app in French film OUT OF THE BLACKS INTO THE BLUES (pt 1: Along the Old Man River/pt 2: A Way to Escape the Ghetto), 1972; app in UK film short PLAYING THE THING, 1972; rec ST for film BUCK AND THE PREACHER, 1972; rec ST for film BOOK OF NUMBERS, 1972; rec A&M/Impress labels, Hollywood, CA, 1972; worked Max's Kansas City, NYC, 1972-3; The Boarding House, San Francisco, CA, 1973; Mandrake's, Berkeley, CA, 1973; Lion's Share, San Anselmo, CA, 1973; Inn of the Beginning, Cotati, CA, 1973; app on ONE OF A KIND, PBS-TV, 1973; worked Joe's Place, Cambridge, MA, 1973; toured England/Europe working club/college/concert dates, 1973-5; worked Montreux Jazz Festival, Montreux, Switzerland, 1973; app in film BLUES FOR A BLACK FILM, 1973; worked Philadelphia Folk Festival, Schwenksville, PA, 1973; Great Southeast Music Hall, Atlanta, GA, 1973-4; Avery Fisher Hall, NYC, 1973; Michigan State Univ, East Lansing, MI, 1973; Liberty Hall, Houston, TX, 1973; frequently toured New Zealand/Australia working concert dates, 1973-6; Hunter Col, NYC, 1974; Academy of Music, Brooklyn, NY, 1974; Bottom Line, NYC, 1974; rec Blue Labor label, Queens, NY/NYC, 1974; app in film short SHOUTIN' THE BLUES, 1974; worked Univ of Louisville, Louisville, KY, 1974; McCabe's, Santa Monica, CA, 1974; Univ of North Carolina, Raleigh, NC, 1974; Frog & Nightgown Club, Raleigh, NC, 1974; Shaboo Inn, Mansfield, CT, 1974; Convocation Hall, Toronto, Can, 1975; Berkeley Blues Festival, Berkeley, CA, 1975; app on SOUNDSTAGE, PBS-TV, 1975; app in film SINCERELY THE BLUES, 1975; worked Juicy John Pink's Folk Center, DeKalb, IL, 1975; Good Karma Coffeehouse, Madison, WI, 1975; Milwaukee Summer Festival, Milwaukee, WI, 1975; Euphoria Tavern, Portland, OR, 1975; app on AM SAN

FRANCISCO, KGED-TV, San Francisco, CA, 1975; worked Sophie's, Palo Alto, CA, 1975; The Bodega, Campbell, CA, 1975; My Father's Place, Roslyn, NY, 1975; Egyptian Theater, DeKalb, IL, 1975; The Lighthouse, Los Angeles, CA, 1976; The Riverboat, Toronto, Can, 1976; rec ST for film LEADBELLY, 1976; app on national TV commercial for Blues Filter Cigarettes, Australia, 1976; worked Quiet Knight, Chicago, 1976-7; The Raven Gallery, Detroit, 1976-7; toured Europe working concert dates, 1977; worked Ivanhoe, Chicago, 1977; Charlotte's Web, Rockford, IL, 1977; Back Door, San Diego, CA, 1977; Lighthouse, Los Angeles, 1977; University of Toronto, Toronto, Can, 1977; The Rising Sun, Montreal, Can, 1978; app film THE JERK, 1979; festival in Eng, 1980; app FROM JUMP STREET (ep: City-Country Blues), PBS-TV, 1980; app HARD TRAVELIN', PBS-TV, 1984; app film THE COLOR PURPLE, 1985

Book: The Harp Styles of Sonny Terry, Sonny Terry, Oak Publications, 1975

Songs: Airplane Blues/All Alone Blues/Baby I Got My Mind Off You/Baby I Knocked on Your Door/Beer Garden Blues/Black Cat Bone/Blowin' The Fuses/Blues All Around My Bed/Blues for the Lowlands/Blues with a Whoop/Burnt Child Afraid of Fire/Callin' My Mama/Chasing the Fox/Climbing on Top of the Hill/Corn Bread, Peas and Black Molasses/Cousin John/Crazy Man Blues/Crow Jane Blues/Custard Pie Blues/Cut Off from My Baby/Dangerous Woman/Dirty Mistreater/Don't Mistreat Me/Early Morning Blues/Four O'Clock Blues/Fox Hunt/Freight Train/Great Tall Engine/Harmonica Blues/Harmonica Breakdown/Harmonica Rag/Harmonica with Slaps/High Powered Woman/Hooray Hooray/Hootin' Blues/Hot-Headed Woman/I Got a Little Girl/I Got My Eyes on You/I Woke Up with the Blues/I'm Afraid of Fire/I'm Crazy About Your Pie/I'm Gonna Get on My Feets Afterwhile/I'm in Love with You Baby/I'm Prison Bound/I've Been a Long Long Ways/Ida B/Just About Crazy/Leavin' Blues/Long Way from Home/Lost John/Louise (Blues)/Mean Old Woman/Mister Froggie/Motorcycle Blues/(My) Baby (Done) Changed the Lock on That Door/My Baby Done Gone/My Baby Leavin'/My Baby's So Fine/Night and Day/On the Road Again/Pepper Headed Woman/Pete's Jump/Playing with the Thing/Poor Man Blues/Poor Man But a Good Man/Pretty Little Girl/Riff and Harmonica Jump/Screamin' and Cryin' Blues/Sick Man/Sonny's Blues/Sonny's Jump/Sonny's Squall/Sonny's Thing/South Bound Express/Spread the News Around/Stranger Here/Sweet Little Girl/Sweet Lovin' Kind/Sweet Woman Blues/The Sweetest Girl I Know/Telephone Blues/Too Nicey Mama/Treated Wrong/Tryin' to Win/Wailin' and Whoopin'/Walkin' My Blues Away/When I Was Drinkin'/Whoee, Whoee/Whoopin' the Blues/Wine Headed Woman/The Woman Is Killin' Me/Worried Man Blues/You Keep Doggin' Me/You'd Better Mind

Infl by: DeFord Bailey/Leadbelly

Infl to: Carey Bell/Buster Brown/JC Burris/Taj Mahal/Johnny Mars/Jerry Portnoy/Alec Seward

Quotes: "Terry ranks among the original harmonica players in all blues"—Peter Hatch, *Coda* magazine (Canada), Apr 1971, p 31

"His vocal delivery is as rough, uncompromising and exhilarating as ever it was, embodying the raw essence of the country blues"—Ron Brown, Storyville album SLP-218

". . . Sonny is passing on to us a rich heritage from Africa, and hundreds of years of Afro-American life in the Southern states"—(Pete Seeger) Sonny Terry, *The Harp Styles of Sonny Terry*, Oak Publications, 1975

References: The Harp Styles of Sonny Terry, Sonny Terry, Oak Publications, 1975

Living Blues magazine, Summer 1973, pp 14-17

TEXAS GUITAR SLIM
(see Winter, Johnny)

TEXAS SLIM
(see Hooker, John Lee)

TEXAS TESSIE
(see Douglas, Lizzie)

TEXAS TOMMY
(see Dorsey, Thomas A)

THOMAS, BLANCHE

Born: Oct 16, 1922, New Orleans (Orleans Parish), LA
Died: Apr 21, 1977, New Orleans, LA

Father was Samuel Thomas who worked as trumpeter w Kid Howard/Big Jim Robinson Bands; mother was Malvina Stripling; interested in music early and worked as dancer in Kiddie Revue, Tick Tock Roof Garden, New Orleans, LA, mid-30s; worked outside music, New Orleans, late 30s into 40s; toured in USO package show working military camps through South, early 40s; worked w Six Brown Cats, Club Bali, New Orleans, mid-40s; toured w Dodison's World Circus working tent shows through South, late 40s; rec Pontchartrain label, New Orleans (?), early 50s; frequently worked w Alvin Alcorn/Joe Robichaux/others in local club dates, New Orleans, into 50s; rec w Dave Bartholomew Orch, Imperial label, New Orleans, c1953; app w Elvis Presley in film KING CREOLE, 1958; worked New Orleans Jazz Club Concert, New Orleans, 1959; w Bill Reinhardt Band, Jazz Ltd, Chicago, IL, 1960-1; Lee Roy Faulk's Annex Restaurant, New Orleans, 1961; app w Elvis Presley on Dave Garroway's TODAY Show, NBC-TV, 1961; worked w Franz Jackson Band, Jazz Ltd, Chicago, IL, 1962; w Franz Jackson Band, Red Arrow Club, Chicago, 1962; rec w Paul Barbarin Bourbon Street Beat Band, Southland label, New Orleans, c1962; worked Pick Collier Club, New Orleans, c1962; Skyline Night Club, Orlando, FL, 1963; Bourbon Street East, New Orleans, 1963; w Art Hodes, Showboat Sari-S, Chicago, 1964; rec w Papa French New Orleans Jazz Band, Nobility label, New Orleans, 1964; worked International Jazz Festival, New Orleans, 1965; frequently w Louis Cottrell Band, Dixieland Hall, New Orleans, from 1965; w Storyville Ramblers, War Memorial Auditorium, Boston, MA, 1966; toured w Louis Cottrell Band on USO circuit working US military bases in Vietnam/Thailand, 1967; frequently worked Royal Orleans Hotel, New Orleans, 1967-70; New Orleans Jazz Festival, New Orleans, 1968; The Hemisfair '68, San Antonio, TX, 1968; Dixieland at Disneyland Concert, Disneyland Park, Anaheim, CA, 1968; The Hidden Door, New Orleans, c1969; w own Dixieland Six, Roosevelt Hotel, New Orleans, 1969; w Al Hirt Band in local club dates, St Louis, MO, 1970; rec w Alvin Alcorn Band, Louisiana label, New Orleans, 1970; rec w Papa Albert French's Original Tuxedo Jazz Band, Capricorn label, New Orleans, c1971; worked *Delta Queen* Riverboat out of New Orleans, 1971; Kennedy Center, Washington, DC, 1971; Royal Sonesta Hotel, New Orleans, 1971-2; New Orleans Jazz & Heritage Festival, New Orleans, 1972; frequently w Heritage Hall Jazz Band, Heritage Hall, New Orleans, 1972; Court of Two Sisters, New Orleans, 1972; WC Handy Festival, Memphis, TN, 1973; New Orleans Jazz & Heritage Festival, New Orleans, 1974; w Louis Cottrell Jazz Band, Heritage Hall, New Orleans, 1974; rec w New Orleans Heritage Hall Jazz Band, Crescendo label, New Orleans, c1973; worked w Heritage Hall Jazz Band, Nice Jazz Festival, Nice, France, 1975; app in film short AMERICANS ALL, ABC-TV, 1975; toured w New York Jazz Repertory Company, working concert dates through Europe, 1975; mostly inactive due to illness from mid-70s; buried Holt Cemetery, New Orleans, LA

Personal: Married ——— Collins. Had children

Billing: Queen of the Blues

Award/Honor: Awarded certificate of appreciation from Gen William Westmoreland for her USO tour in Vietnam, 1967

Infl by: Ella Fitzgerald/Bessie Smith

Quote: "She was a perfectionist. Music was her life"—Pat Wyn, *New Orleans Times Picayune* newspaper, May 16, 1977

THOMAS, CHARLES

(*aka:* Jimmy [James] Davis/Maxwell Street Jimmy Davis/Maxwell Street Jimmy)

Courtesy Gerald Robs/Living Blues *Magazine*

Born: 1925, Clarksdale (Coahoma Co), MS
Inst: Guitar

Born/raised/worked outside music in Clarksdale, MS; first instrument was home-made guitar at 14 years of age; frequently toured w Silas Green from New Orleans minstrel show c1940; toured w Rabbit Foot Minstrels working as buck dancer, early 40s; moved to Detroit, MI, to work outside music from 1946; frequently worked local club dates w John Lee Hooker, Detroit, 1946-52; frequently hoboed through South working jukes/parties into 50s; frequently app on local radio shows, Greenville/Clarksdale, MS, mid-50s; settled in Chicago, IL, to work w drummer Porkchop

Eddie Hines on Maxwell Street for tips, from late 50s into 60s; worked some club dates, NYC, 1963; owned/operated The Knotty Pine Grill on Maxwell Street, Chicago (frequently also working out front on street for tips), from 1964; rec Testament label, Chicago, 1964-5; rec Elektra label, Chicago, 1965; continued working Maxwell Street area, Chicago, through 60s; worked clubs in Memphis, TN, area c1970-2; continued working Maxwell Street area, Chicago, into 70s; worked Univ of Chicago Folk Festival, Chicago, 1975

Infl by: John Lee Hooker

Quote: "An exciting, important artist who projects an almost fantastic degree of emotional intensity in both his singing and his guitar playing"—Pete Welding, *Jazz Journal* magazine (UK), Jul 1965, p 18

THOMAS, COTTON
(see Jaxon, Frankie)

THOMAS, HENRY
(see Johnson, Leslie)
(see Townsend, Henry)

THOMAS, HENRY *"Ragtime Texas"*
Born: 1874, Big Sandy (Upshur Co), TX (unconfirmed)
Died: (unknown)
Inst: Guitar/Harmonica/Quills (Panpipes)

One of at least 9 children; believed born/raised on farm near Big Sandy, TX; left home to hobo as itinerant singer/musician working country suppers/dances/parties/trains/streets/hobo camps/migrant farms out of Texas from c1890; reportedly worked Columbian Exposition, Chicago, IL, 1893; World's Fair, St Louis, MO, 1904; rec Vocalion label, Chicago, 1927-9; worked in Tyler, TX, area during 1950s; whereabouts unknown thereafter

Personal: Not to be confused with Leslie Johnson or Henry Townsend who used this name as pseudonym

Quotes: "Henry Thomas was a singular and important figure. He left behind a total of 23 issued (recording) selections which represent one of the richest contributions to our musical culture"—Mack McCormick, Herwin album 209

"For my money [he was] the best [songster] that ever recorded. Henry Thomas was a superb artist"—Derrick Stewart-Baxter, *Jazz Journal* magazine (UK), May 1975, p 44

References: Herwin album 209
The Bluesmen, Samuel B Charters, Oak Publications, 1967

THOMAS, HOCIEL

Courtesy Frank Driggs Collection

Born: Jul 10, 1904, Houston (Harris Co), TX
Died: Aug 22, 1952, Oakland, CA
Inst: Piano

Grandfather George Thomas Sr was deacon of Shiloh Baptist Church, Houston, TX; father was George W Thomas Jr, a musician/song writer/publisher; mother was Octavia Malone; moved to live with aunt Sippie Wallace, New Orleans, LA, from c1916; frequently worked w Sippie Wallace (or single) at local parties/Storyville houses, New Orleans, into 20s; moved to Chicago, IL, c1924; rec Gennett label, Richmond, IN, 1925; rec w Louis Armstrong and others, OKeh label, Chicago, 1925-6; worked Plantation Club, Chicago, mid-20s; Coliseum Theater, Chicago, 1926; frequently worked local theater dates in Chicago through 20s into early 30s; mostly inactive in music, Chicago, from early 30s; moved to Oakland, CA, c1942; worked mostly outside music, Oakland, through 40s; rec w Mutt Carey, Circle label, San Francisco, 1946; rec Riverside label, San Francisco, 1946; worked w Kid Ory Band, Swing Club, San Francisco, 1948; involved in fight with sister in which she lost her eyesight and sister died, Oakland, late

40s; tried and acquitted of manslaughter, Oakland, c1950; entered Highland-Alameda County Hospital where she died of heart disease; buried Greenlawn Cemetery, San Francisco

Personal: Married Arthur Tebo (1940s). 1 child, later raised by aunt, Sippie Wallace, a blues singer. Uncle Hersal Thomas was pianist

Songs: Shorty George Blues/Tebo's Texas Boogie

Quotes: "Hociel Thomas is a fairly straight-forward, earthy singer in the classic blues mould . . ."—Eddie Lambert, *Jazz & Blues* magazine (UK), Apr 1972, p 24

"She sang with a solemnity and majesty in a manner closely related to church singing"—Rudi Blesh, *Shining Trumpets*, Alfred A Knopf, 1946

Reference: Storyville magazine (UK), Jun 1968, pp 18-24

THOMAS, IRMA

Photo by Norbert Hess. Courtesy Living Blues *Magazine*

Born: Feb 18, 1941, Ponchatoula (Tangipahoa Parish), LA

Raised in New Orleans, LA, where she worked outside music through 50s; worked Doris Miller Theater, Austin, TX, 1956; rec Ron label, New Orleans, LA, 1958; worked Regal Theater, New Orleans, c1959; rec Minit label, New Orleans, c1960-3; worked The Germania Hall/The Safari Room/The F&M Patio/The Baby Grand/and other clubs, New Orleans, early 60s; rec Bandy label, New Orleans, early 60s; rec w HB Barnum's Orch, Imperial label, Los Angeles, 1963-4; toured Gulf Coast area working club dates into 60s; frequently worked dances, Union Hall, Chalmette, LA, mid-60s; worked Pussy Cat A-Go-Go, Birmingham, AL, 1966; Autocrat, New Orleans, 1966; The International Room, New Orleans, 1967; The Peacock, New Orleans, 1968; worked teen festival concert, New Orleans, 1968; moved to Oakland, CA, 1970; worked New Ruthie's Inn, Oakland, CA, 1971; rec w Dr John, Atlantic label, San Francisco, CA (?), 1972; worked w Dave Bartholomew Orch, Fontainebleau Hotel, New Orleans, 1973; Marriott Hotel, New Orleans, 1973-4; The Continental Club, Oakland, 1973; Uncle Sam's Club, New Orleans, early 70s; Ruthie's Inn, Berkeley, CA, 1974; Jed's University Inn, New Orleans, 1975; New Orleans Jazz & Heritage Festival, New Orleans, 1975-7 (por 1976 concert rel Island label); Sands club, New Orleans, 1976; worked The Steamboat *Natchez* out of New Orleans, 1976

Personal: Married. 4 children

Songs: Take a Look/Wish Someone Would Care

Infl by: Sam Cooke/Etta James

Quotes: "An outstanding singer in the same class as Esther Phillips . . ."—Michael Frank, *Living Blues* magazine, Jul 1975, p 39

"The undoubted queen-songstress of New Orleans"—Norbert Hess, *Blues Unlimited,* Jul 1976

THOMAS, JAMES *"Cairo"/"Son"/"Sonny Ford"*

Born: Oct 14, 1926, Eden (Yazoo Co), MS
Died: Jun 26, 1993. Greenville, MS
Inst: Guitar

Mother was Annie Mae Estes; born/raised on farm; moved to Leland, MS, as youth; worked mostly outside music with frequent work in local jukes/joints/barrelhouses in Leland/Greenville, MS, areas through 60s; rec Transatlantic label, Leland, c1968; rec Matchbox label, Leland, 1968; worked Memphis Blues Festival, Memphis, TN, 1969; app in film DELTA BLUES SINGER: JAMES "SONNY FORD" THOMAS, 1970; worked Jackson State College, Jackson, MS, 1971-2; Mississippi State Historical Museum, Jackson, 1972 (por rel Southern Folklore label); Univ of Maine, Orono, ME, 1972; app on MISSISSIPPI FOLKROOTS: DELTA BLUES, WMAB-TV (PBS), Jackson, 1972; app on CBS NEWS, CBS-TV, 1973; worked Tougaloo Col, Tougaloo, MS, c1973; Yale Univ, New Haven, CT, 1973-6; app in film short MISSISSIPPI DELTA

Photo by John R. Allison

BLUES, 1974; app in film GIVE MY POOR HEART EASE: MISSISSIPPI DELTA BLUESMEN, 1975; app w Sam Chatmon, TODAY Show, NBC-TV, 1976; app film GOT SOMETHING TO TELL YOU: SOUNDS OF THE DELTA BLUES, 1977; worked Delta Blues Festival, Greenville into 80s; worked concerts in Spain, 1982/86; toured concerts in US into 90s; died of heart attack; buried Bogue Cemetery, Leland, MS

Songs: Beef Stake Blues/Devil Blues/Fast Boogie

Award/Honor: The film DELTA BLUES SINGER: JAMES "SONNY FORD" THOMAS won Mississippi Arts Film Festival Award, 1972

Infl by: Arthur "Big Boy" Crudup/Elmore James

Quote: "The music of James Thomas emerges from the Delta musical tradition and is particularly important because it shows the blues in its most basic expression"—William R Ferris, Southern Folklore album 101

References: Southern Folklore album 101
Blues Unlimited, Apr 1970, pp 13-14

THOMAS, JOSEPHINE
(see Henderson, Rosa)

THOMAS, KID
(see Watts, Louis)

THOMAS, LAFAYETTE JERL *"The Thing"*

Courtesy Living Blues *Magazine*

Born: Jun 13, 1928, Shreveport (Caddo Parish), LA
Died: May 20, 1977, Brisbane, CA
Inst: Guitar/Piano

Father was Joe L Thomas; mother was Erylie Carter; encouraged to learn guitar by uncle Jesse "Baby Face" Thomas as child; frequently sang in local church choir as youth; moved to San Francisco, CA, 1945, where he was raised and frequently worked outside music through 40s; worked w Al Simmons Rhythm Rockers at Pago Pago Club/Arabian Nights Club/Slim Gaillard's Club/others, San Francisco, 1947-8; w Little Bob Young's Band, Bayview Theater, San Francisco, with frequent tours working clubs in Redwood City/Palo Alto, CA/elsewhere c1948; worked as single at House of Joy, Oakland, CA, 1948; toured (off and on) w Jimmy McCracklin's Band working club dates in Los Angeles area, 1948 into 60s; frequently rec as sideman w Jimmy McCracklin's Band on a variety of local labels on West Coast, late

40s into 70s; frequently rec as session guitarist for Jimmy Wilson and others on Big Town label and others, Oakland/Los Angeles areas, from late 40s into 50s; rec under own name, Jumping label, Oakland, 1955; rec Trilyte label, Oakland, mid-50s; frequently worked Ralph's Club/The Chi Chi Club/The Monterey/The Rhumboogie Club/Brown Derby, Oakland, CA, as well as other clubs in Richmond, CA, area from 1957; worked Rainbow Garden, NYC, NY, 1958; rec Savoy label, NYC, 1959; worked w Sammy Price at local club dates, NYC, 1959-60; rec acc to Little Brother Montgomery/Memphis Slim, Prestige-Bluesville label, NYC, 1960; continued local club work on West Coast from early 60s; frequently worked outside music in San Francisco area from 1966 into 70s; rec World Pacific label, Berkeley, CA, 1968; rec acc to Sugar Pie DeSanto, Jasman label, California, c1971; frequently worked w Candyman McGuirt's Band in local clubs, San Francisco/Oakland areas from 1973; worked Esther's Orbit Room, Oakland, 1974-5; West Dakota Club, Berkeley, 1975; Ralph's, Oakland, 1975; mostly inactive in music from mid-70s; suffered heart attack while at work on day job, DOA Kaiser Hospital; buried Olivet Memorial Park Cemetery, Colma, CA

Personal: Married Mary Sanders. His uncles Jesse "Baby Face" Thomas and (reportedly) Willard "Ramblin' " Thomas were musicians. Named "The Thing" due to his acrobatic style of playing

Infl by: Jesse "Baby Face" Thomas

Infl to: Little Joe Blue

Quotes: "Unquestionably the finest guitarist to emerge from the San Francisco-Oakland blues scene, there is hardly a guitarist around here today who doesn't owe a little something to Lafayette Thomas and that includes both Little Joe Blue and BB King"—Tom Mazzolini, *Living Blues* magazine, Jul 1977, p 6

"Thomas is a fine guitarist in the modern electric style . . . and an excellent vocalist in the contemporary soul-R&B idiom . . ."—Pete Welding, World Pacific album WPS-21893

Reference: Living Blues magazine, Jul 1977, pp 6-8

THOMAS, RUFUS

Born: Mar 26, 1917, Cayce (Marshall Co), MS

Moved to Memphis, TN, where he was raised from 1 year of age; began singing while attending Booker T Washington HS, Memphis, early 30s; frequently worked amateur shows at Palace Theater, Memphis, from 1931; toured briefly w Georgia Dixon travelling show (as comic) in Memphis, TN, area, 1936; frequently toured w Rabbit Foot Minstrels Show through South from 1936; frequently toured w Royal American Tent Shows through South from 1938; returned to Memphis to work as MC for amateur shows at Palace Theater from 1940; frequently worked outside music, Memphis, 1941-63; frequently worked w Robert Counts (as "Rufus & Bones") in tap dancing/scat singing act, Palace Theater, Memphis, 1941-51; worked Johnny Curry's Club, Memphis, 1950 (por rel Star Talent label); frequently worked w Robert Counts (as "Rufus & Bones") on various amateur shows, WC Handy Theater, Memphis, early 50s (remotes on WDIA-radio); frequently sat-in with local bands in club dates, Memphis, into 50s; rec Chess label, Memphis, 1951; rec Sun label, Memphis, 1953; frequently worked (as DJ) on own SEPIA SWING CLUB Show/HEEBIE JEEBIES Show/HOOT 'N' HOLLER Show, WDIA-radio, Memphis, 1953-74; rec Meteor label, Memphis, 1956; rec w daughter Carla Thomas, Satellite label, Memphis, 1960; rec Atco label, Memphis, 1961; rec Star Talent label, Dallas, TX, 1961; rec Stax label, Memphis, 1962-4; frequently toured in various package shows (and as single) working concerts/theaters across US from 1963; worked Apollo Theater, NYC, 1963 (por rel Atco label); frequently worked Apollo Theater, NYC, 1965-6; app on Dick Clark's AMERICAN BANDSTAND, ABC-TV, c1965; frequently toured England/Germany working concert dates from mid-60s into 70s; app on A SHADE OF SOUL, local TV, Washington, DC, c1968; worked Mid-South Coliseum, Memphis, 1968; Memphis Blues Festival, Memphis, 1969 (por shown on SOUNDS OF SUMMER, WNDT-TV, NYC); app on SOUL, PBS-TV, 1971; worked York Club, Los Angeles, 1971; Loser's Club, Dallas, TX, 1971; Memorial Auditorium, New Orleans, LA, 1971; PJ's Club, Los Angeles, c1972; Disneyland Park, Anaheim, CA, 1972; Wattstax 72 Concert, Memorial Coliseum, Los Angeles, 1972 (por shown in film WATTSTAX); River City Blues Festival, Memphis, 1972; app on BLACK OMNIBUS, WOR-TV, NYC, 1973; worked Disneyland Park, Anaheim, 1974; app IN CONCERT, BBC-2-TV, London, Eng, 1974; worked La Valbonne Discotheque, London 1975 (por shown DISCOMANIA, ABC-TV); worked Ed Howard's Club, San Francisco, 1976; toured South Africa c1976; worked Memphis Music Heritage Festival, Memphis, 1977 (remote on National Public Radio)

Rufus Thomas *Courtesy* Living Blues *Magazine*

Personal: Married (1940-). 3 children. His daughter Carla Thomas (born 1942) billed as "The Queen of Memphis Sound" is soul singer and son Marvell Thomas (born 1941) is musician

Songs: The Dog/The Funky Chicken/The Penguin/ Push and Pull/Walking in the Rain/Walking the Dog

Infl by: Louis Armstrong/Gatemouth Moore/Fats Waller

Quote: "While his background is different from most blues singers . . . his orientation and sense of tradition are very much the same"—Peter Guralnick, *Living Blues* magazine, Sept 1976, p 9

References: *Living Blues* magazine, Sept 1976, pp 9-12

Encyclopedia of Pop, Rock & Soul, Irwin Stambler, St Martin's Press, 1974

THOMAS, SIPPIE
(see Wallace, Beulah)

THOMAS, WILLIE B
Born: May 25, 1912, Lobdell (Bolivar Co), MS
Inst: Guitar/Kazoo

Parents were sharecroppers; born/raised/worked outside music on Bellemount Plantation from childhood; one of 7 children; frequently worked local parties/ picnics/get-togethers, Lobdell, MS, area from early 20s; suffered back injury and permanently crippled c1925; moved to Baton Rouge, LA, to work outside music from c1927; frequently worked w Butch Cage at local suppers/fish fries/dances, Baton Rouge area, into 30s/40s/50s; learned guitar, 1939; frequently worked streets (as singing preacher), Baton Rouge, late 40s into 50s; moved to Scotlandville, LA, to work outside music from late 50s; rec w Butch Cage, Folk-Lyric label, Zachary, LA, 1959-60; worked w Butch Cage, Newport Folk Festival, Newport, RI, 1959-61 (por 1959 concert rel Folkways label/por 1960 concert shown in USIA film short series JAZZ USA [Nos 20, 22]); rec Decca/Arhoolie labels, Zachary, LA, 1960; app in film THE BLUES, 1962; app w Butch Cage/ Victoria Spivey on LYRICS AND LEGENDS (ep: The Blues), WNET-TV, NYC (syndicated), 1963; worked Preservation Hall, New Orleans, LA, 1963; continued outside music work, Baton Rouge, through 60s into 70s; rec ST for UK film BLUES LIKE SHOWERS OF RAIN, 1970; worked Louisiana Heritage Festival, New Orleans, 1970; clip shown in PEOPLE'S MUSIC—AND ALL THAT JAZZ, BBC-2-TV, London, Eng, 1976

Personal: Married. Wife is drummer. Has 3 children

THORNTON, WILLIE MAE "*Big Mama*"
Born: Dec 11, 1926, Montgomery (Montgomery Co), AL
Died: Jul 25, 1984, Los Angeles, CA
Inst: Harmonica/Drums

Father was George Thornton, a minister; mother was Mattie Hughes a singer; interested in music at early age and won first prize in local amateur show, Montgomery, AL, c1939; after death of mother worked outside music to support family, 1940; toured w Sammy Green's Hot Harlem Revue working as singer/dancer/comedian in clubs/theaters through South, 1941-8; settled in Houston, TX, 1948; frequently worked Eldorado Club, Houston, from 1948; Bronze Peacock, Houston, c1950; rec w Harlem Stars, E&W label, Houston, c1951; rec Peacock label, Houston, TX/Los Angeles, CA, 1951-7; occasionally worked w Roy Milton Band/Joe Liggins Band in local clubs, Houston, early 50s; toured w Johnny Otis Rhythm & Blues Caravan package show working one-nighters in clubs/theaters/dance halls/auditoriums across US, 1952; worked Apollo Theater, NYC, NY, 1952; formed own trio working local club dates, Los Angeles, 1953; toured w Junior Parker/Johnny Ace package shows working theaters across US, 1953-4; worked as single in local clubs, Phoenix, AZ, 1955; toured w Gatemouth Brown, 1956; settled on West Coast to work local clubs/concerts in San Francisco Bay area from c1957; worked Rhumboogie Club, Oakland, CA, c1961; rec Baytone label, Oakland, CA, 1961; worked Beachcomber Club/Gate Way Club, Santa Cruz, CA, 1961; Basin Street West, San Francisco, CA, 1964; Monterey Jazz Festival, Monterey, CA, 1964; Moore's Swing Club, Los Angeles, 1964; Cabale Club, Berkeley, CA, 1964; Sportsman Club, Oakland, 1964; rec Sotoplay label, Los Angeles, 1965; rec w Johnny Talbot Band, Kent label, San Francisco (?), 1965; toured w American Folk Blues Festival working concert dates through England/Europe, 1965 (por Hamburg, Ger, concert rel Fontana label); Fairfield Hall, London, Eng, 1965; rec Arhoolie label, London, 1965; rec w Chicago Blues Band, Arhoolie label, San Francisco, 1966; worked Both/And Club, San Francisco, 1966-7; Monterey Jazz Festival, Monterey, CA, 1966; Pacific Jazz Festival, Costa Mesa, CA, 1966-7; The Troubadour, Los Angeles, 1966; Jazz Workshop, San Francisco, 1966-7; Ash Grove, Los Angeles, 1966-7; Univ of California, Berkeley, CA, 1967; Apollo Theater, NYC, NY, 1967; From Spirituals to Swing Concert, Carnegie Hall, NYC, 1967; app on BLACK, WHITE & BLUE, PBS-TV (syndicated), 1967; frequently worked R&B clubs in Los Angeles area, 1967; Monterey Jazz Festival, Monterey, CA, 1968; Shrine Expo Hall, Los

Willie Mae "Big Mama" Thornton
Photo by Julie Snow

Angeles, 1968; Sky River Rock Festival, Sultan, WA, 1968-9; Univ of California, Los Angeles, 1968; Hungry i, San Francisco, 1968; rec Arhoolie label, San Francisco, 1968; worked Ungano's, NYC, 1969; Electric Circus, NYC, 1969; rec Mercury label, Hollywood, CA, 1969; worked The Madrague, Oakland, CA, 1969; Newport Folk Festival, Newport, RI, 1969; Chicago Blues Festival, Chicago, 1969; Ann Arbor Blues Festival, Ann Arbor, MI, 1969-70; Magic Circus, Los Angeles, 1969; Plugged Nickel, Chicago, 1969; app on DELLA, WOR-TV (syndicated), NYC, 1969; worked Jazz Workshop, Boston, MA, 1969-70; Thee Experience Club, Los Angeles (?), 1969 (por rel Mercury label); The Colonial Tavern, Toronto, Can, 1969; app on ROCK 1, CBC-TV, Toronto, 1970; worked Berkeley Blues Festival, Berkeley, 1970; Jazz Workshop, San Francisco, 1970; The Berkley, Boston, 1970; Carnegie Hall, NYC, 1970; Apollo Theater, NYC, 1970; app on DICK CAVETT Show, ABC-TV, 1971; worked Museum of Modern Art Concert, NYC, 1971; Blues Festival, Liberty Hall, Dallas, TX, 1971; Liberty Hall, Houston, 1971; The Gaslight, NYC, 1971; Alice's Revisited, Chicago, 1971; Ash Grove, Los Angeles, 1971; rec ST in film VANISHING POINT, 1971; worked Univ of Waterloo, Waterloo, Can, 1972; toured w American Folk Blues Festival working concert dates through Europe, 1972; worked The Lighthouse, Los Angeles, 1972; The Parisian, Los Angeles, 1972; Continental Club, Oakland, CA, 1973; Newport Jazz Festival, Philharmonic Hall, NYC, 1973 (por rel Buddah label); Twelfth Gate Club, Atlanta, GA, 1973; Le Coq D'or Tavern, Toronto, Can, 1973; Academy of Music, NYC, 1973; Academy of Music, Brooklyn, NY, 1974; app on MIDNIGHT SPECIAL, NBC-TV, 1974; rec Vanguard label, NYC, 1975; Monroe State Prison, Monroe, WA, 1975 (por rel Vanguard label); Oregon State Reformatory, Eugene, OR, 1975 (por rel Vanguard label); worked Berkeley Blues Festival, Berkeley, 1975; California Club, Los Angeles, 1976; The Longbranch, San Francisco, 1976; The Palms, San Francisco, 1977; Wise Fools Pub, Chicago, 1977; The Starwood, Hollywood, CA, 1977; George Washington Univ, Washington, DC, 1977; worked blues/jazz clubs/festivals across US/Canada, 1978 into 80s; app OMNIBUS, ABC-TV, 1980; app THREE GENERATIONS OF THE BLUES, PBS-TV, 1984; died consequence of alcoholism; buried Inglewood Park, Inglewood, CA

Songs: Ball and Chain/Big Change/Big Mama's New Love/Don't Need No Doctor/Down-Home Shakedown/Everybody's Happy (But Me)/Everything Gonna Be Alright/Guide Me Home/I Feel the Way I Feel/I'm Feeling Alright/I'm Lost/Jail/Just Can't Help Myself/Lost City/Private Number/Sassy Mama/Session Blues/Sometimes I Have a Heartache/Swing It On Home/They Call Me Big Mama/Walking Blues/Willie Mae's Blues/Your Love Is Where It Ought To Be

Infl by: Memphis Minnie/Junior Parker/Ma Rainey/Bessie Smith

Infl to: Aretha Franklin/Janis Joplin

Quotes: "Her voice is gutsy, earthy and coarse but at the same time there is a beauty, sensitivity and control to everything she does"—John Norris, *Coda* magazine (Canada), Sept 1969, p 4

Reference: *Living Blues,* Nov-Dec 1992, pp 26-32

TOO TIGHT HENRY

(see Townsend, Henry)

TOWNSEND, HENRY

(*aka:* Henry Thomas/Too Tight Henry)

Photo by Hans Andreasson. Courtesy Living Blues Magazine

Born: Oct 27, 1909, Shelby (Bolivar Co), MS
Inst: Guitar/Piano

Father was Allen Townsend; mother Omeauly Blount; raised in Cairo, IL then St Louis, MO; taught self guitar and frequently worked house parties/picnics in area, late 20s into 30s; rec Columbia label, Chicago, IL, 1929; rec Paramount label, Grafton, WI, 1931; frequently worked w Henry Brown/Robert Nighthawk/Sonny Boy Williamson (Alex Miller)/Roosevelt Sykes/Alice Moore/others, St Louis, from early 30s; frequently toured w Walter Davis working club dates through South, early 30s; rec (as "Henry Thomas") Bluebird label, Chicago, 1933; worked w Robert Johnson, Ernest Walker's house party, St Louis, 1935; rec Bluebird label, Chicago, 1935; rec Bluebird label, Aurora, IL, 1937; frequent residence, Harlem Club, St Louis, late 30s; worked w Henry Spaulding, Golden Lily Club, St Louis, late 30s; rec Bullet label, Nashville, TN, c1939; frequently worked w Roosevelt Sykes in local clubs, St Louis, into 40s; frequently worked outside music with occasional work at local dances, St Louis, through 40s/50s; worked w Roosevelt Sykes, Beverly Lounge, Gulfport, MS, 1958-60; rec Decca label, St Louis, 1960; rec Prestige-Bluesville label, St Louis, 1961; continued outside music work, St Louis, through 60s/70s; rec Adelphi label, St Louis, 1969; rec Adelphi label, Potomac, MD, 1970-1; rec ST for UK film BLUES LIKE SHOWERS OF RAIN, 1970; rec Adelphi label, Silver Spring, MD, 1971; worked National Folk Festival, Wolf Trap Farm Park, Vienna, VA, 1971; Missouri Friends of Folk Arts Concert, St Louis, 1973; rec Adelphi label, St Louis, 1974; mostly inactive due to illness with occasional small gigs in St Louis through mid-70s; worked BB's Jazz, Blues & Soup Parlor, St Louis, 1976; app on THE DEVIL'S MUSIC—A HISTORY OF THE BLUES (ep: Nothing But the Truth/ep: Work and Mother Wit), BBC-1-TV, England, 1976; worked w wife Vernell Townsend, Univ of Chicago Folk Festival, Chicago, IL, 1977; National Folk Festival, Wolf Trap Farm Park, Vienna, VA, 1977

Personal: Married Vernell Perry who has also sung blues. Not to be confused with guitarist Henry Lee Castle who also used pseudonym "Too Tight Henry" (died 1971)

Songs: Biddle Street Blues/Buzz Buzz Buzz/Christmas Blues/Deep Morgan Stomp/Doing Better in Life/Don't You Remember Me?/Everyday of My Life/Heart Trouble/Henry's Jive/I Asked Her If She Loved Me/Mistreated Blues/My Baby Have Come

Back/My Home Ain't There/Now or Never/Rocks Have Been My Pillow/She Drove Me to Drinking/She Just Walked Away/Sloppy Drunk Again/Tears Came Rolling Down/Tired of Being Mistreated/The Train Is Coming/Why Do We Love Each Other?

Infl by: James "Steady Roll" Johnson/Lonnie Johnson/Roosevelt Sykes

Infl to: Walter Davis

Quotes: "A commanding genius of a musician"—Dick Spottswood, *Blues Unlimited* magazine (UK), Dec 1971, p 18

". . . an exciting blues artist"—Samuel B Charters, Prestige-Bluesville album 1041

Reference: *Blues Unlimited,* Jan/Feb 1979, pp 4-10

TRICE, RICHARD *"Rich"*
(aka: Little Boy Fuller)

Courtesy Peter B Lowry

Born: Nov 16, 1917, Hillsborough (Orange Co), NC
Inst: Guitar

Father was Reuben Trice, mother was Lula Mae ———, both musicians; interested in music early and learned guitar from uncle Albert Trice at about 13 years of age; frequently worked w brother Willie Trice at local parties/dances/streets in Durham, NC, area from early 30s; frequently toured w Blind Boy Fuller working tobacco plants/fairs/streets through North Carolina through 30s; rec w Willie Trice, Decca label, NYC, 1937; moved to Newark, NJ, area to work outside music with occasional gigs w Lester "Fats" Jackson in area from 1946; rec (as "Little Boy Fuller") Savoy label, NYC, 1949; returned to Hillsborough, NC, to work outside music with occasional work w Diamond Tone Gospel Quartet in local churches in Hillsborough/Durham, NC, areas from early 50s

Personal: Brother of William Augusta Trice, blues singer

Infl by: Blind Boy Fuller/Albert Trice

Reference: *Blues Unlimited* magazine (UK), Dec 1969, pp 7-8

TRICE, WILLIAM AUGUSTA *"Welly"/"Willie"*

Photo by Peter B Lowry

Born: Feb 10, 1910, Hillsborough (Orange Co), NC
Died: Dec 10, 1976, Durham, NC
Inst: Guitar

Father was Reuben Trice, mother was Lula Mae ———, both musicians; interest in music from early age and learned guitar from uncle Albert Trice; frequently worked outside music in area from mid-20s; frequently worked w brother Rich Trice/John Holman at local parties/dances/streets in Durham, NC, area from early 30s; app on WPTF-radio, Raleigh, NC, 1932; continued outside music work in area through 30s/40s/50s; rec w Rich Trice, Decca label, NYC, 1937; frequently worked local parties in Durham area into 60s; mostly inactive due to illness from c1963; both legs amputated due to diabetes, 1970; rec Trix label, Durham, 1971-3; rec Flyright label, Orange County, NC, 1972-3; worked Univ of North Carolina, Chapel Hill, NC, 1972-3 (por 1973 concert rel Flyright label); mostly inactive due to illness into 70s; rec Trix label, Durham, 1975; reportedly entered Chapel Hill Hospital where he died of cancer; buried Mt Sinai Baptist Church Cemetery, Orange County, NC

Personal: Brother of Richard "Rich" Trice, blues singer

Songs: Baby Baby/Goin' to the Country/Good Time Boogie/I love You Sweet Baby/I've Had Trouble/My Baby's Ways/New Diddey Wah Diddey/She's Coming on the C&O/Shine On/Three Little Kittens Rag/Trouble Some Mind/Trying to Find My Baby/You Have Mistreated Me

Infl by: Blind Boy Fuller/Albert Trice

Quote: "Willie Trice was a unique artist in many ways. A contemporary and true peer of Blind Boy Fuller . . ."—Pete Lowry, *Living Blues* magazine, Mar 1977, p 6

Reference: Trix album 3305

TUCKER, LUTHER

Photo by Doug Fulton. Courtesy Living Blues Magazine

Born: Jan 20, 1936, Memphis (Shelby Co), TN
Died: Jun 18, 1993, San Francisco, CA (unconfirmed)
Inst: Guitar

Mother was Alfrieda ________; lived in Chicago, IL from 1945; served time at St Charles Reformatory, Chicago, 1948; attended Drake HS, Chicago, early 50s; worked briefly w Jr Wells in local clubs, Chicago, 1952; frequently worked/toured w Little Walter's Jukes (with some recording as sideman) out of Chicago, 1952-8; worked Ricky's Show Lounge, Chicago, 1953; Bodega Club, Chicago, 1953; worked w Lòuis Myers/David Myers/Sunnyland Slim in west side clubs, Chicago, 1958; briefly worked w Muddy Waters/Sonny Boy Williamson (Alex Miller), Chicago, late 50s; frequently worked outside music, with occasional weekend club dates/streets/party work, Chicago, into 60s; worked w Otis Rush Band, Club Alibi, Chicago, c1965; rec (as sideman) w Otis Rush Band, Vanguard label, Chicago, 1965; frequently worked/rec w Jimmy Cotton Band, Los Angeles/Chicago/elsewhere, 1966-8; frequently worked as sideman/sit-in musician in various local blues groups, Chicago, late 60s; moved to Marin, CA, 1969; frequently worked w John Lee Hooker in San Francisco area, early 70s; worked Community Music Center, San Francisco, 1973; w Sunnyland Slim, Great American Music Hall, San Francisco, 1974; Monterey Jazz Festival, Monterey, CA, 1974; w John Lee's Band, Toronto Blues Festival, Olympic Island, Toronto, Can, 1974; Minnie's Can-Do Club, San Francisco, 1975; Cat's Cradle, San Francisco, 1975; frequently worked w Charlie Musselwhite's Band in local club dates, San Francisco, 1975; worked w own band, Yellow Brick Road Club, San Francisco, 1975; Family Light School of Music Blues Festival, Sausalito, CA, 1975; The Savoy, San Francisco, 1976; San Francisco Blues Festival, McLaren Park, San Francisco, 1976 (por rel Jefferson label); app on BLUES BY THE BAY, KPFA-FM-radio, Berkeley, CA, 1976; rec Messaround label, San Francisco, 1976; worked Green Earth Cafe, San Francisco, 1976; WOW Hall, Eugene, OR, 1977; worked w Louis Myers Band, Kingston Mines, Chicago, 1977

Personal: Married twice. 2 children

Songs: Fallin' Rain/Tuckerology

Infl by: Robert Jr Lockwood

Quote: "One of the most accessible figures from the heydey of Chicago's postwar blues scene is Luther Tucker"—Bob Eagle, *Blues Unlimited* magazine (UK), May 1973, p 9

Reference: Blues Unlimited magazine (UK), May 1973, pp 9-10

TUCKER, TOMMY *"Tee"*

Courtesy Living Blues Magazine

Born: Mar 5, 1933, Springfield (Clark Co), OH
Died: Jan 22, 1982, Newark, NJ
Inst: Bass/Drums/Clarinet/Organ/Piano

Father was Leroy Higginbotham; mother Mary Woods; born Robert Higginbotham; was playing family piano at about 7 years of age; studied music while in elementary/high schools, Springfield, OH, through 40s; rec Arc/Hudson labels, Cincinnati, OH, 1947; worked w Bobby Wood Orch in local clubs/bars in Dayton/Columbus/Springfield, OH, area, early 50s; was boxing contender in Golden Gloves c1950; renamed Bobby Wood Orch to The Cavaliers (or Dusters) working small bars in Springfield, OH, area through 50s; frequently worked Harris Bar, Dayton, OH, 1957-9; rec Atco label, Newark, NJ, 1960; toured club dates on East Coast, early 60s; rec Atlantic label, NYC, 1962; rec Checker label, NYC, NY/Chicago, IL, c1964; toured w Ray Charles and Dionne Warwick shows working theater dates, 1964-5; rec Jubilee label, NYC, 1964; app on SHINDIG, ABC-TV, 1965; toured w The Animals working concert dates through Europe, 1965; formed own organ trio working clubs/lounges in NYC area through 60s; worked mostly outside music w occasional gigs in NYC area into 80s; rec acc to Louisiana Red, Atco label, NYC, 1971; toured w American Blues Legends 75 working concert dates through England/Europe, 1975; worked 100 Club, London, Eng, 1975 (por rel Big Bear label); toured Europe working concert dates, 1977; app on BLUES AM DIENSTAG, NDR-radio, Hamburg, Ger, 1977; rec Ornament label, Berlin, Ger, 1977; worked 100 Club, London, 1977; toured Eng/Ger/Switzerland, 1978; toured Ger/Belgium, 1980; died of liver infection; buried Springfield, OH

Personal: Not to be confused with dance band leader Tommy Tucker (1908-1989)

Songs: Alimony/Hey Lawdy Mama Whose Old Funky Drawers Are These?/Hi-Heel Sneakers/In the Morning/Is that the Way God Planned It?

Infl by: Ray Charles

References: *Living Blues* magazine, Jan 1975, pp 24-5
Blues Unlimited, Nov 1975, pp 14-16
Jazz Journal, Nov 1977, pp 22-23, 31

TULSA RED
(see Fulson, Lowell)

TURNER, BABE KYRO LEMON *"BK"/"Buck"*
(aka: Black Ace)

Photo by Chris Strachwitz. Courtesy Living Blues Magazine

TURNER

Born: Dec 21, 1907, Hughes Springs (Cass Co), TX
Died: Nov 7, 1972, Ft Worth, TX
Inst: Guitar

Father was JT Turner, a farmer; mother was Della Lee Lewis; born/raised/worked farm from childhood; one of at least 3 children; frequently sang in local church choir as child; interested in music early and learned guitar on home-made instrument as child; frequently worked local parties/dances/picnics in Hughes Springs, TX, area, through 20s; frequently worked w Smokey Hogg at local country dances, Greenville, TX, early 30s; moved to Shreveport, LA, mid-30s; frequently worked w Buddy Woods at local house parties/joints/barrelhouses, Shreveport, from mid-30s; toured (frequently as solo) working one-nighters through Louisiana/Oklahoma/Texas, c1935-6; moved to Ft Worth, TX, to work outside music from c1936; rec ARC label group, Ft Worth, 1936; frequently app on KFJZ-radio, Ft Worth, 1936-41; rec Decca label, Chicago, 1937; app in film THE BLOOD OF JESUS, 1941; served in US Army from 1943; worked mostly outside music, Ft Worth, through 40s/50s/60s; app in film THE BLUES, 1962; entered St Joseph Hospital where he died of cancer; buried Stean Cemetery, Malakoff, TX

Personal: Married Minnie R ———. 1 child. Took name "Black Ace" from his 1936 recording of the same name

Infl by: Buddy Woods

Infl to: John Hogg

Quote: "His blues reflect his environment and his past life . . ."—Paul Oliver, Arhoolie album F-1003

Reference: Arhoolie album F-1003

TURNER, BLIND SQUIRE
(see Darby, Theodore)

TURNER, JOSEPH VERNON *"Big Joe"/"Joe"*
(aka: Big Vernon)
Born: May 18, 1911, Kansas City (Jackson Co), MO
Died: Nov 24, 1985, Inglewood, CA

Father Joseph Turner Sr; mother Georgie Herrington; frequently sang in streets as child; often led local blind man, sang in local church choirs and worked in small kids' street quartet on streets of Kansas City, MO, as youth; after death of father dropped out of school to work as part-time singer/bartender/cook/bouncer at Hole-in-the-Wall Club/The Backbiters Club/Black & Tan Club/The Cherry Blossom/Hawaiian Gardens/Piney Brown's Place/Subway Club/Reno Club and other clubs/beerjoints, Kansas City, MO, 1925-35; frequently worked w Pete Johnson at dances/club dates/breakfast parties at Sunset Club/Kingfish Club/The Lone Star, Kansas City and elsewhere, early 30s; frequently toured w Bennie Moten Band/George Lee Band/Andy Kirk Band/Count Basie Band working local dances in Kansas City area through 30s; worked Apollo Theater, NYC, NY, 1936; Famous Door Club, NYC, 1936; Spinning Wheel Club, Kansas City, MO, 1937; w Pete Johnson group, Sunset Crystal Palace, Kansas City, 1938 (remotes W9XBY-radio); worked Wolf's Buffet, Kansas City, 1937-8; Lone Star Club, Kansas City, 1938; app w Pete Johnson/Benny Goodman on CAMEL CARAVAN Show, CBS-radio (Network), 1938; worked From Spirituals to Swing Concert, Carnegie Hall, NYC, 1938-9 (por rel Vanguard label); frequently worked Cafe Society Uptown/Downtown, NYC, 1938-42; rec w Pete Johnson, Vocalion label, NYC, 1938-9; toured US working concert/club dates c1938-9; worked w Harry James Band, Panther Room, Chicago, IL, c1939; rec w Varsity Seven, Varsity label, NYC, 1940; app w Pete Johnson on THE CHAMBER MUSIC SOCIETY OF LOWER BASIN STREET Show, NBC-radio (Blue Network), 1940; rec w own Fly Cats, Decca label, NYC, 1940; rec w Willie "The Lion" Smith, Decca label, NYC, 1940; rec w Benny Carter Orch, OKeh label, NYC, 1940; rec w Joe Sullivan Cafe Society Orch, Vocalion label, NYC, 1940; app in Duke Ellington's JUMP FOR JOY Revue, Mayan Theater, Hollywood, CA, 1941, then tour on West Coast; frequently worked Swanee Inn, Hollywood, 1941-4; rec w Art Tatum Band/Sam Price Trio, Decca label, NYC, 1941; rec w Freddie Slack Trio, Decca label, Los Angeles, CA, 1941; toured w Meade Lux Lewis on Willie Bryant package show working theater dates across US, 1942; app on WILLIE BRYANT Show, NBC-radio (Network), 1942; worked w Meade Lux Lewis, Swanee Inn, Hollywood, 1943; toured w Little Beau's Orch working dances across US/Canada, 1944; worked Municipal Auditorium, Kansas City, MO, 1944; toured w Pete Johnson/Albert Ammons working one-nighters across US, 1944; rec w Pete Johnson, Decca label, Chicago, IL, 1944; rec w Pete Johnson, National label, NYC, NY, 1945; toured w Luis Russell Orch working dances across US, 1945; worked w Pete Johnson, The Blue Room, Los Angeles, 1945; Club DeLisa, Chicago, 1946; Brown Derby, Chattanooga, TN, c1946; rec National label, Los Angeles/Chicago, 1946-7; rec Stag label, San Francisco, 1947; worked Memo Cocktail Lounge, San Francisco, 1947-8; Harold Blackshear's

Joseph "Big Joe" Turner
Courtesy Sheldon Harris Collection

Supper Club, San Francisco, 1947-8; rec w Dootsie Williams, Deetone label, Los Angeles, 1948; rec extensively Swingtime and other labels, Los Angeles, 1948-9; toured club dates through South, 1949; worked Rhythm Club, New Orleans, LA, 1949; Dew Drop Inn, New Orleans, 1949; rec Freedom label, Houston, TX, 1949; rec Imperial/Bayou labels, New Orleans, 1950; frequently worked w Pee Wee Crayton/Lowell Fulson in local club dates, Saginaw, MI, 1950; w Count Basie, Apollo Theater, NYC, 1951; rec Atlantic label, NYC/Chicago/New Orleans, 1951-9; worked Slim Jenkins Club, Oakland, CA, 1951; app in HARLEM VARIETY Revue, Apollo Theater, NYC, 1954 (por shown SHOWTIME AT THE APOLLO, syndicated TV, 1955/por shown in films RHYTHM & BLUES REVUE, 1955; ROCK 'N' ROLL REVUE also titled HARLEM ROCK 'N' ROLL, 1955); worked Celebrity Club, Providence, RI, 1955; Flame Showbar, Detroit, MI, 1955; Newport Jazz Festival, Newport, RI, 1955 (por on MUSIC USA, VOA-radio); Berkshire Music Barn, Lenox, MA, 1955; app in film SHAKE, RATTLE AND ROCK, 1956; extensive tour w Red Prysock Rock 'N' Roll Orch in Biggest Rock 'N' Roll Show of 1956 package show working dances/concerts/theaters across US/Australia, 1956; worked Casino Royale, Washington, DC, 1957; toured in Alan Freed's Summer Festival package rock & roll show working concerts across US, 1957; worked w Pete Johnson, Newport Jazz Festival, Newport, RI, 1958 (por on CBS-radio); w Pete Johnson, Great South Bay Jazz Festival, Great River, NY, 1958; toured w Pete Johnson/Jazz at the Philharmonic group working concert dates through Europe, 1958; worked World's Fair, Brussels, Belgium, 1958; frequently worked club dates, New Orleans, LA, early 60s; Five-Four Ballroom, Los Angeles, 1961; rec Coral label, NYC, 1963; worked Birdland, NYC, 1964; Monterey Jazz Festival, Monterey, CA, 1964; The Showcase, Oakland, CA, 1964; toured w Humphrey Lyttelton Band working concert dates through England/Europe, 1965; worked Kleinhan's Music Hall, Buffalo, NY, 1966; toured w American Folk Blues Festival working concert dates through England/Europe, 1966 (por Berlin, Ger, concerts rel Amiga/Fontana labels); worked w Pete Johnson in From Spirituals to Swing '67 Concert, Carnegie Hall, NYC, 1967 (por rel CBS label); rec BluesWay label, NYC, 1967; toured w Johnny Otis Show working concerts on West Coast, late 60s; worked Tiki Island Club, Los Angeles, CA, 1969; rec BluesTime label, NYC, 1969; worked Basin Street West, San Francisco, 1970; app w Johnny Otis Revue on HOMEWOOD SHOW, PBS-TV, 1970; worked Carnegie Hall, NYC, 1970 (por rel BluesTime label); app on DELLA, WOR-TV, NYC (syndicated), 1970; worked Ash Grove, Los Angeles, 1970-3; worked w Johnny Otis Show, Monterey Jazz Festival, Monterey, CA, 1970-1 (por 1970 concert in film MONTEREY JAZZ/por rel Epic label); Ann Arbor Blues Festival, Ann Arbor, MI, 1970; Shelly's Manne Hole, Los Angeles, 1970; Palladium, Hollywood, CA, 1971; toured concert dates through Europe, 1971; rec Black & Blue label, Paris, France, 1971; worked Nite Life, Van Nuys, CA, 1971; Ebonee Ballroom, Seattle, WA, 1971; Esther's Orbit Room, Oakland, CA, 1972; toured w Count Basie Orch working concert dates through Europe, 1972; worked Continental Club, Oakland, 1973 (por shown ALL TOGETHER NOW, KPIX-TV); rec w Della Reese, Trojan label, Los Angeles (?), c1973; worked Topanga Corral, Los Angeles, 1973; The Parisian Room, Los Angeles, 1973; app w Count Basie in documentary film THE LAST OF THE BLUE DEVILS (The Kansas City Jazz Story), 1974 (rel 1979); rec w Basie, Pablo label, Los Angeles, 1973; worked Monterey Jazz Festival, Monterey, CA, 1974; Oldies But Goodies Club, Hollywood, CA, 1974 (por remote on ART LABOE'S Show, local radio); rec LMI label, Hollywood, 1974; app on OSCAR PETERSON PRESENTS, CBS-TV, 1974; toured w Count Basie Orch working concert dates through England/Europe, 1974; worked Golden Bear, Los Angeles, 1974; The Parisian Room, Los Angeles, 1975; T-Bone Walker Memorial Concert, Musician's Union Auditorium, Los Angeles, 1975; Civic Center, San Gabriel, CA, 1975; Cat's Cradle, San Francisco, 1975; rec w Pee Wee Crayton, Pablo label, Los Angeles, 1976; worked The Cookery, NYC, NY, 1976-7; Monterey Jazz Festival, Monterey, CA, 1976; rec ST for ROOTS, ABC-TV, 1977; worked The Palms, San Francisco, 1977; Jazz Showcase, Chicago, 1977; toured w Lloyd Glenn working concert dates across US, 1977; rec Spivey label, NYC, 1977; worked Tralfamadore Cafe, Buffalo, NY, 1977 (por remote WBFO-radio); Lee Magid's Cafe, Tarzana, CA, 1977; The Palms, San Francisco, CA, 1977; The Starwood, Hollywood, CA, 1977; Fox Venice Theater, Los Angeles, 1977; toured West/East Coast club dates through 70s/80s; worked long residency at Tramps, NYC into 80s; app SWINGIN' THE BLUES (ep: Goin' To Kansas City), PBS-TV, 1982; worked Kool Jazz Festival, NYC 1983; residency at The Cookery, NYC, 1983; suffered fatal stroke; buried Roosevelt Cemetery, Gardena, CA

Personal: Married Lou Willie Brown (1945-c1965); Pat Sims (1969-85). Not to be confused with jazz pianist Joe "Stride" Turner (1907-1990)

Billings: The Boss of the Blues/The World's Greatest Blues Shouter

Songs: Adam Bit the Apple/After While You Will Be Sorry/Baby Look at You/Back Breaking Blues/Big Joe's Lonesome Blues/Big Wheel/Bluer Than Blue/Blues on Central Avenue/Boss of the House/Can't Read Can't Write Blues/Cherry Red/Chewed Up Grass/Doggin' the Dog/Empty Pocket Blues/Feelin' Happy/Feelin' So Sad/Flip Flop and Fly/Good Morning Blues/Got a Gal/I Got Love for Sale/It's the Same Old Story/Joe's Blues/Jumpin' Down Blues/Just a Travelin' Man/Last Goodbye Blues/Let Me Be Your Dog/Life Is a Card Game/Little Birdie Tweet-Tweet-Tweet/Little Bitty Baby/Little Bittie Gal's Blues/Low Down Dog/Lucille, Lucille/Mad Blues/Messin' Around/Midnight Rockin'/Milk and Butter Blues/Moody Baby/Morning Glory/Mrs Geraldine/Nobody in Mind/Ooh-Wee Baby/Piney Brown Blues/Playboy Blues/Poor House/Rainy Day Blues/Rebecca/Roll 'em Pete/Sally Zu Zaz/Since I Was Your Man/So Many Women Blues/Still in the Dark/Story to Tell/The Sun Is Shining/Sun Risin' Blues/Sunday Morning Blues/TV Mama/Watch That Jive/Wee Baby Blues/Well Oh Well/When The Rooster Crows/You Know I Love You

Awards/Honors: Won *Esquire* magazine Silver Award as Male Vocalist in All-American Jazz Band, 1945

Won *Downbeat* magazine Critics Poll as Best New Male Singer, 1956

Won *Melody Maker* magazine (UK) Critics Poll as Top Male Singer, 1965

Won *Jazz Journal* magazine (UK) Poll for Best Blues Record, 1965

Infl by: Roy Brown/Jimmy Rushing/Bessie Smith/Aaron "T-Bone" Walker

Infl to: Ray Charles/Lowell Fulson/BB King/Big Miller/Little Milton/Eddie Vinson/Joe Williams/Jimmy Witherspoon

Quotes: "In my opinion, Joe is the greatest blues singer (or shouter, if you prefer) of them all"—(Pete Johnson) Hans J Mauerer, *The Pete Johnson Story*, 1965

"A superb blues shouter of impeccable intonation and infectious beat . . ."—Barry Ulanov, *A Handbook of Jazz*, Viking Press, 1957

References: Living Blues magazine, Autumn 1972, pp 20-6

Downbeat magazine, Nov 18, 1965, pp 16-17, 42

U

UKULELE KID
(see Burse, Charlie)

UNCLE SKIPPER
(see Jordan, Charles)

UNDERHILL, VIOLA
(see Wells, Viola)

V

VAN RONK, DAVID *"Dave"*

Courtesy Sing Out *Magazine*

Born: Jun 30, 1936, Brooklyn (Kings Co), NY
Inst: Guitar

Moved to Queens, NY, as youth and attended Richmond Hill HS; served in US Merchant Marine, early 50s; returned to NYC, NY, to work local gigs with traditional jazz bands, mid-50s; frequently worked Greenwich Village clubs/coffeehouses as single, NYC, from 1957; rec Lyrichord label, NYC, 1958; frequently toured folk festivals/clubs from 1958; rec Folkways label, NYC, c1959-60; worked Cafe Lena, Saratoga Springs, NY, 1960; Gaslight Cafe, NYC, 1961; City Col, NYC, 1962; formed own Ragtime Jug Stompers working Village Vanguard, NYC, 1963; Club 47, Cambridge, MA, 1963; Newport Folk Festival, Newport, RI, 1963 (por rel Vanguard label); rec Prestige label, NYC, 1963-4; rec w Ragtime Jug Stompers, Mercury label, NYC, 1964; worked Gaslight Cafe, NYC, 1964-5; app on FOLK MUSIC, USA, WGBH-TV, Boston, MA, 1964; worked Unicorn, Boston, 1964; Swarthmore Folk Festival, Swarthmore, PA, 1964; Newport Folk Festival, Newport, RI, 1964; Carnegie Hall, NYC, 1964; New York Folk Festival, Carnegie Hall, NYC, 1965; Town Hall, NYC, 1965; app on own folk show series, WBAI-FM-radio, NYC, 1966; worked Town Hall, Philadelphia, PA, 1966; rec Verve/Folkways labels, NYC, 1967-8; worked Folk/Rock concert, Village Theater, NYC, 1967; Cafe A-Go-Go, NYC, 1967-8; app on TWANG, ABC-TV, 1967; worked Fillmore East, NYC, 1968; Philadelphia Folk Festival, Schwenksville, PA, 1968-9; Woodstock Playhouse, Woodstock, NY, 1968; rec MGM label, NYC (?), 1968; worked The Riverboat, Toronto, Can, 1969; Main Point, Bryn Mawr,

PA, 1969; Gaslight Cafe, NYC, 1970; frequently worked clubs/colleges with occasional work as guitar teacher, NYC area, into 70s; rec Cadet/Fantasy labels, NYC, early 70s; Passim Coffeehouse, Cambridge, MA, early 70s; worked Carnegie Hall, NYC, NY, 1972; Great Folk Revival, Nassau Coliseum, Uniondale, NY, 1974; frequently worked South Street Seaport, NYC, 1976; rec Philo label, NYC, c1976; app on PHIL OCHS MEMORIAL CELEBRATION, PBS-TV, 1976; worked Philadelphia Folk Festival, Schwenksville, PA, 1977

Personal: Married Terri ———

Songs: Bad Dream Blues/Bamboo/Frankie's Blues/If You Leave Me/Pretty Mama/Sunday Street

Infl by: Gary Davis/Furry Lewis/Josh White

Quotes: "An integral part of the Village scene, Dave Van Ronk was one of its most colorful personalities, and, with his bawdy, raspy vocal style, he emerged as one of the [1960s] most distinctive folk performers"—Kristin Baggelaar/Donald Milton, *Folk Music:More Than a Song*, Thomas Y Crowell Company, 1976

"Van Ronk's approach . . . is one which is deeply indebted to the country blues, but is more of an interpretation than anything like an imitation"—Mike Goodwin, *Sing Out* magazine, Jan 1965, p 26

References: Folk Music: More Than a Song, Kristin Baggelaar/Donald Milton, Thomas Y Crowell Company, 1976

Sing Out magazine, Jan 1965, pp 26-30

VINCENT, MONROE
(*aka:* Mr Calhoun/Vince Monroe/Polka Dot Slim
Born: Dec 9, 1919, Woodville (Wilkinson Co), MS
Died: 1982, Oakland, CA (unconfirmed)
Inst: Drums/Harmonica

Born/raised in Woodville, MS, area with frequent moving through New Orleans, LA, then New York City, NY, through 30s; served in US Army, 1942-54; frequently worked local bars/streets for tips, New Orleans, c1954-8; moved to Baton Rouge, LA, to work occasionally w Lightnin' Slim in area from 1958; rec (as "Vince Monroe") Excello label, Baton Rouge (?), c1959; rec (as "Mr Calhoun") Zynn label, Baton Rouge (?), c1959; frequently worked w Guitar Joe Willis in local clubs, New Orleans, from 1960; rec Instant label, Detroit, MI, 1963; worked New Orleans Jazz & Heritage Festival, New Orleans, LA, 1974-6; reportedly died of heart attack

Infl by: John Lee "Sonny Boy" Williamson

Photo by Norbert Hess. Courtesy Living Blues *Magazine*

Quote: "His singing [is] as remarkable as his harp playing—a cross between Lightnin' Slim and Ike Turner"—Mark Humphrey, *Whiskey, Women And . . .* magazine, May 1975, p 14

VINCENT, WALTER
(see Vinson, Walter)

VINCSON, WALTER
(see Vinson, Walter)

VINSON, EDDIE *"Cleanhead"/"Mr Cleanhead"*
Born: Dec 18, 1917, Houston (Harris Co), TX
Died: Jul 2, 1988, Los Angeles, CA
Inst: Alto Saxophone

Grandfather was violinist; father "Piano" Sam Vinson and mother Arnella Sessions were musicians; interested in music early and frequently sang in local church quartets as child; attended Jack Yates HS where he studied sax, Houston, TX, 1934-6; toured w Chester Boone's Band working dances during summer vacation out of Houston, 1935; worked w Milton Larkins Band in local dances, Houston, from 1936 with frequent tours through South and Midwest to 1940; continued local work w Milton Larkin Band (fronted by Floyd Ray) in Houston area, 1940-1; toured w Bill Broonzy in Lil Green road show work-

Courtesy Sheldon Harris Collection

ing dance dates through South c1941; settled in NYC, NY, 1942; joined Cootie Williams Orch to work Grand Terrace Ballroom, Chicago, 1942 with frequent tours to 1945; rec w Cootie Williams Orch, OKeh label, NYC, 1942; worked w Cootie Williams Orch, Minton's, NYC, 1943; app w Cootie Williams Orch in film shorts FILM-VODVIL NO 2 (1943)/ COOTIE WILLIAMS AND HIS ORCHESTRA (1944); rec w Cootie Williams Orch, Hit label, NYC, 1944; toured w Cootie Williams Band in Ink Spots package show working theaters/dances on RKO circuit, 1944-5; w Cootie Williams Orch, Stanley Theater, Pittsburgh, PA, 1944; Savoy Ballroom, NYC, 1944 (w frequent remotes on WOR-radio); Apollo Theater, NYC, 1944; rec w Cootie Williams Orch, Capitol label, NYC, 1945; served briefly in US Army, 1945; formed own band to work Club Zanzibar, NYC, 1945-7 (with frequent remotes, NBC-radio); rec w own band, Mercury label, NYC/Chicago, 1945-6; w own band, Apollo Theater, NYC, 1946; rec Mercury label, St Louis, MO, 1947; frequently worked Riviera Club, St Louis, MO, 1947; frequently gigged in various small groups in local club dates, NYC, 1947; toured in own band working in Ink Spots package show at concerts/dances/theaters on RKO-Keith circuit across US into Canada, 1947-9; worked Club Alabam, Los Angeles, CA, 1947; Orpheum Theater, Los Angeles, 1947; rec King label, Cincinnati, OH, 1949-50; frequently worked in own (or other) small groups in local club dates, Chicago, IL, late 40s into early 50s; rec King label, NYC, NY, 1950-1; rec King label, Cincinnati, 1952; worked Majestic Hotel, Cleveland, OH, 1953; Basin Street Club, Chicago, 1954-5; toured w Cootie Williams group working club dates across US, 1954; resettled in Houston, TX, to work outside music (with some work as music teacher) with occasional local gigs, 1954 into 60s; rec Bethlehem label, NYC, 1957; worked club dates, Kansas City, MO, early 60s; rec w Cannonball Adderley, Riverside label, Chicago, IL, 1961/NYC, NY, 1962; worked McKie's Club, Chicago, 1962; w Arnett Cobb Orch, Cafe Hannibal/Club Ebony/other clubs, Houston, 1966; app on SOME OF THE PEOPLE, KUHF-FM-radio, Houston, 1966; rec BluesWay label, NYC, 1967; worked Stan's Pad, Chicago, 1967; toured w Jay McShann Orch working concert dates through England/Europe, 1968-70; rec Black & Blue label, Paris, France, 1968; rec BluesTime label, NYC, 1969; worked It Club, Los Angeles, 1970; Black Fox, Los Angeles, 1970; app w Johnny Otis Revue, HOMEWOOD Show, PBS-TV, 1970 (syndicated); worked Carnegie Hall, NYC, 1970 (por rel BluesTime label); Ann Arbor Blues Festival, Ann Arbor, MI, 1970; w Johnny Otis package show working Monterey Jazz Festival, Monterey, CA, 1970 (por shown in film MONTEREY JAZZ/por rel Epic label); toured w Johnny Otis package show working concert/college/ club dates across US, 1970-1; worked Shelly's Manne Hole, Los Angeles, 1970; Ash Grove, Los Angeles, 1970-1; Basin Street West, San Francisco, 1970; The Palladium, Hollywood, CA, 1971; rec Black & Blue label, Bordeaux, France, 1970; worked Montreux Jazz Festival, Montreux, Switzerland, 1971 (por rel Mega/Flying Dutchman labels); toured w Count Basie Orch working concert dates through England/Europe, 1972; frequent weekend residencies at Rubaiyat Lounge, Los Angeles, 1972-7; worked Off Plaza, San Francisco, 1972-4; Monterey Jazz Festival, Monterey, CA, 1972-4; Sandy's, Beverly, MA, 1973; Elks Hall, Los Angeles, 1973; Ann Arbor Blues Festival, Ann Arbor, MI, 1973; Newport Jazz Festival, Philharmonic Hall, NYC, 1973 (por rel Buddah label); Berlin Jazz Festival, Berlin, Ger, 1973; Twin Lounge Society Club, Gloucester City, NJ, 1973; Viking Lounge, Cincinnati, 1974; Kolbeh Club, Berlin, Ger, 1974; Montreux Blues Festival, Montreux, Switzerland, 1974 (por rel Black Lion label); San Sebastian Festival, San Sebastian, Spain, 1974; The Sting, Burlington, VT, 1975; Parisian Room, Los Angeles, 1975; T-Bone Walker Memorial Concert, Musicians Union Auditorium, Los Angeles, 1975; w Johnny Otis Package Show, El Mocambo, Toronto, Can, 1975; toured Europe working concert dates, 1977; worked Storyville Jazz Club, NYC, 1977; The Rising Sun, Montreal, Can, 1977; Lee Magid's Cafe, Tarzana, CA, 1977; rec w Johnny Otis Orch, Jazz World label, Los Angeles, 1977; toured jazz/blues festivals in Eng/Europe, 1978-9; worked clubs/festivals across US into 80s; app on videotape AMERICA'S MUSIC-BLUES #1, 1983; died of cancer; buried Lincoln Memorial Park, Compton, CA; app PLAYED IN THE USA (ep: Papa John Creach), PBS-TV, rel 1991

Personal: Not to be confused w Eddie Vinson, an early New Orleans trombonist. "Cleanhead" referred to his baldness

Songs: Alimony Blues/Arriving Soon/Back Door Blues/Cleanhead Blues/Cleanhead Is Back/Four/ Goodnight Baby Blues/Hold It Right There/I Needs to Be Be'd Wid/Juice Head Baby/Kidney Stew Blues/ Lazy Gal/Old Maid Boogie/Old Maid Got Married/ Person to Person/They Call Me Mr Cleanhead/ Tune Up

Infl by: Bill Broonzy/Leroy Carr/Johnny Hodges/ Lightnin' Hopkins/Charlie Parker/Joe Turner

Quote: "A marvelously potent combination of primitive bluesman and sophisticated jazzman."—Brian Case/Stan Britt, *Illustrated Encyclopedia of Jazz,* Harmony Books, 1978

References: *Jazz* magazine, Jul 1967, pp 13-15
Down Beat, May 8, 1975, pp 16, 29
Blues Unlimited, Jul 1975, pp 4-6

VINSON, WALTER JACOBS

(*aka:* Walter Jacobs/Walter Vincent/Walter Vincson)

Courtesy Walter & Alice Vinson/Living Blues Magazine

Born: Feb 2, 1901, Bolton (Hinds Co), MS
Died: Apr 22, 1975, Chicago, IL
Inst: Guitar/Violin

Father was Walter Vinson; mother was Mary Jacobs; born/raised on farm near Bolton, MS; interested in music early and learned guitar at 6 years of age; frequently entertained from back of wagon in Bolton area from 8 years of age; frequently worked local parties/picnics in Bolton area through teens; worked w Tommy Johnson/Ishmon Bracey in jukes, Crystal Springs, MS, area, from c1921; frequently worked w Rubin Lacy/Son Spand/CharlieMcCoy/others at local dances/parties/streets, Jackson, MS, area into 20s; teamed w Lonnie Chatmon working parties in Hollandale, MS, area from c1928; rec w Chatmon's Mississippi Hot Footers, Brunswick label, Memphis, TN, 1929-30; rec w Carter Brothers, OKeh label, San Antonio, TX, 1930; rec w Bo Chatmon, OKeh label, Atlanta, GA, 1930; rec w Mississippi Sheiks, OKeh label, Shreveport, LA, 1930; rec OKeh label, Atlanta, GA, 1930-2; mostly inactive in music due to illness, Jackson, MS, into 30s; rec Paramount label, Grafton, WI, 1932; rec OKeh label, NYC, 1933; rec Bluebird label, San Antonio, TX, 1934; rec Bluebird label, New Orleans, LA, 1935; rec acc to Tommy Griffin, Bluebird label, NYC, 1936; rec w Harry Chatmon, Decca label, New Orleans, 1936; continued to rec acc to other bluesmen through 30s; rec Bluebird label, Chicago, IL, 1941; moved to Chicago to work mostly outside music, 1941 through 60s; rec Riverside label, Chicago, 1961; worked Limelight Theater, Chicago, 1962; Univ of Chicago Folk Festival, Chicago, 1972; rec w New Mississippi Sheiks, Rounder label, Chicago, 1972; worked Smithsonian Festival of American Folklife, Washington, DC, 1972; mostly inactive due to illness, Chicago, from 1972; entered South Shore Nursing Center where he died of bronchopneumonia; buried Holy Sepulchre Cemetery, Worth, IL

Personal: Married Alice Jones (1965-). No relation to musician/singer Eddie Vinson. Not to be confused with musician/singer Marion "Little Walter" Jacobs

Songs: A Wonderful Thing/Don't Wake It Up/I Knew You Were Kiddin' All the Time/Isn't a Pain to Me/ She's Crazy About Her Lovin'/Sitting on Top of the World/Tell Me to Do Right

VIVIAN, LILA

(see Hicks, Edna)

VON SCHMIDT, ERIC

Photo by Diana Davies © 1978. Courtesy Sing Out Magazine

Born: May 29, 1930, Westport (Fairfield Co), CT
Inst: Guitar/Harmonica

Born/raised in Westport, CT, where he majored in art studies; served in US Army, late 40s; studied art on Fulbright grant, Florence, Italy, early 50s; worked outside music (as illustrator) with occasional work as folk singer in Cambridge/Boston, MA, areas through 50s into 60s; worked New York Folk Festival, Carnegie Hall, NYC, 1965; First Freedom Folk Festival, Cambridge, MA, 1965; Newport Folk Festival, Newport, RI, 1965; Club 47, Cambridge, 1965; The In, New Britain, CT, 1966; Newport Folk Festival, Newport, 1968; worked mostly outside music (as painter) from 1968

Personal: Married. 2 children

Book: Come for to Sing, Eric Von Schmidt, Houghton Mifflin, 1963

Award/Honor: Won major awards in painting and commercial design

Infl by: Leadbelly

WALKER, AARON THIBEAUX *"T-Bone"*

(aka: Oak Cliff T-Bone)
Born: May 28, 1910, Linden (Cass Co), TX
Died: Mar 16, 1975, Los Angeles, CA
Inst: Banjo/Guitar/Mandolin/Organ/Piano/Ukulele/Violin

Grandmother was Cherokee Indian; father Rance Walker and mother Movelia Jimerson were musicians; was an only child; moved to Dallas, TX, c1912 where he attended Holy Ghost Church as child; interested in music early and sang with stepfather Marco Washington at local drive-in soft drink stands in area as youth; frequently worked as lead-boy for Blind Lemon Jefferson along Central Avenue, Dallas, c1920; taught self guitar and worked local parties in area from 1923; toured w Dr Breeding's Big B Tonic Medicine Show working as singer/musician/comedian/dancer through Texas, mid-20s; toured w Ida Cox road show through South, late 20s; rec Columbia label, Dallas, 1929; won first prize in Cab Calloway's Amateur Show, Dallas, c1930; toured briefly w Cab Calloway Band in Dallas area c1930; worked w Coley Jones Dallas String Band in area, early 30s; w Lawson Brooks Band at dance one-nighters in Dallas/San Antonio, TX, area, early 30s; toured w Count Biloski Band working dance dates through South, 1933; toured w Milt Larkins Band working dances, 1933; worked w Ma Rainey, Colosseum, Ft Worth, TX, 1934; moved to West Coast, 1934; worked frequently Little Harlem Club, Los Angeles, CA, 1934-9; Trocadero, Hollywood, CA, 1936-7; toured w Les Hite Cotton Club Orch working dance halls/club dates mainly through Midwest, 1939-40; worked in residence w Les Hite Orch, Golden Gate Ballroom, NYC, NY, 1940; Apollo Theater, NYC, 1940; rec w Les Hite Orch, Varsity label, NYC, 1940; in residence w Les Hite Orch, Joe Louis' Hurricane Club, Chicago, IL, 1940; formed own band to tour one-nighters into 40s; frequently worked Little Harlem Club, Los Angeles, CA, 1941-3; rec Capitol label, Hollywood, CA, 1942-4; frequently worked Rhumboogie Club, Chicago, IL, 1942-5; toured US Army bases working concert dates across US, early 40s; worked Silver Slipper Playhouse, San Diego, CA,

Aaron "T-Bone" Walker *Courtesy Sheldon Harris Collection*

1943; Capri Club, Hollywood, CA, 1943; Trocadero, Hollywood, 1943; Casablanca Club, Los Angeles, CA, 1943-4; w Fletcher Henderson Orch, Club Plantation, Los Angeles, 1944; Circle Cafe, Hollywood, CA, 1944; Tappet Inn, Los Angeles, c1944; rec w Marl Young Orch, Rhumboogie label, Chicago, IL, 1945; worked Lincoln Theater, Los Angeles, mid-40s; rec w Jack McVea's All-Stars, B&W label, Hollywood, CA, 1946; formed own band working one-nighters across US from 1946 to early 50s; worked Avalon Grill, San Antonio, TX, 1946; rec w Al Killian Quintet, B&W label, Hollywood, CA, 1947; worked Bronze Peacock, Houston, TX, 1947; rec Comet label, Los Angeles, CA, 1947; opened WC Handy Theater, Memphis, TN, c1948; frequently worked Flame Show Bar/Twenty Grand Club/Frolic Show Bar/others, Detroit, MI, late 40s; rec Capitol label, Los Angeles, late 40s; rec Imperial label, Los Angeles, 1950-1; app on Ed Sullivan's TOAST OF THE TOWN Show, CBS-TV, early 50s; rec w Jim Wynn's Orch, Imperial label, Hollywood, CA, 1952-4; worked Celebrity Club, Providence, RI, 1953; Showboat Club, Philadelphia, PA, 1953; Flame Show Bar, Detroit, MI, 1954-6; Sportstown Club, Buffalo, NY, 1954; worked in Rhythm & Blues Jubilee package show in Los Angeles, CA, area, 1954; rec Atlantic label, Chicago, IL, 1955-9; worked The Chatterbox, Cleveland, OH, 1955; extensive residency at Blue Mirror Club, San Francisco, CA, 1956-60; app frequently on local West Coast TV, late 50s; worked Savoy Club, Richmond, CA, late 50s; Five-Four Ballroom, Los Angeles, 1960; Atmosphere Club, Dallas, TX, 1961; Longhorn Ranch Club, Dallas, 1961; Sugar Hill, San Francisco, 1961; Regal Theater, Chicago, c1962; toured w Rhythm & Blues USA package show working concerts/festivals through England/Europe, 1962; rec w Memphis Slim, Polydor label, Hamburg, Ger, 1962; rec w Jimmy Witherspoon, Prestige label, Los Angeles, 1963-4; worked McKie's, Chicago, 1964; Sportsman's Lounge, Los Angeles, 1964; rec Modern label, Chicago, 1964; toured England working clubs/shows, 1965; app on NOT ONLY . . . BUT ALSO Show, BBC-TV, London, Eng, 1965; worked Apollo Theater, NYC, 1965-7; Soul City Club, Buffalo, NY, 1965; Cafe A-Go-Go, NYC, 1965; toured w Jazz at the Philharmonic jazz show working concert dates through Europe, 1966 (some filmed concerts shown on BBC-2-TV, London, Eng); worked Ash Grove, Los Angeles, 1966; rec Jet Stream label, Pasadena, TX, 1966; worked Monterey Jazz Festival, Monterey, CA, 1967 (por shown on MONTEREY JAZZ FESTIVAL, PBS-TV [syndicated]/por shown in film MONTEREY JAZZ); Pacific Jazz Festival, Costa Mesa, CA, 1967; rec BluesWay label, NYC, 1967-8; worked UCLA concert, Los Angeles, 1968; Shelly's Manne Hole, Los Angeles, 1968-9; toured w American Folk Blues Festival working concert dates through England/Europe, 1968 (por shown in UK film AMERICAN FOLK BLUES FESTIVAL); rec Polydor label, Paris France, 1968; rec Black & Blue label, Paris, 1968-9; worked Trois Mailletz, Paris, 1968-9; Watts Summer Festival, Los Angeles, CA, 1968; Ann Arbor Blues Festival, Ann Arbor, MI, 1969; rec BluesTime label, NYC, 1969; worked Fillmore East, NYC, 1969; Berkeley Blues Festival, Univ of California, Berkeley, CA, 1970; frequently worked w Johnny Otis Revue from 1970; app w Johnny Otis Revue, HOMEWOOD Show, PBS-TV (syndicated), 1970; worked Carnegie Hall, NYC, NY, 1970 (por rel BluesTime label); rec Polydor label, Paris, France, 1970; worked Ash Grove, Los Angeles, CA, 1970; rec Wet Soul label, Nashville, TN, c1971; worked Jazz Workshop, Boston, MA, 1971; Nice Jazz Festival, Nice, France, 1971; Colonial Tavern, Toronto, Can, 1971-2; Parisian Room, Los Angeles, CA, 1972-3; London House, Chicago, IL, 1972; toured w American Folk Blues Festival working concert dates through Europe, 1972; app in French film L'AVENTURE DU JAZZ (UK title: JAZZ ODYSSEY), 1972; worked Montreux Jazz Festival 72, Montreux, Switzerland, 1972 (por rel Polydor label); La Bastille, Houston, TX, 1972-3; Callie's Place, Chicago, IL, 1972; Southern California Hot Jazz Society concert, Los Angeles, CA, 1972; Max's Kansas City, NYC, NY, 1972-3; app on MIKE DOUGLAS Show, CBS-TV, c1972; worked Viking Lounge, Cincinnati, OH, 1972; Topanga Corral, Los Angeles, CA, 1973; Sandy's, Beverly, MA, 1973-4; Le Hibou, Ottawa, Can, 1973; El Mocambo, Toronto, Can, 1973; Carnegie Hall, NYC, NY, 1973; rec Reprise label, Hollywood, CA/NYC, NY, 1973; worked Hanscom Airbase, Bedford, MA, 1973; Nixon Theater, Pittsburgh, PA, 1974; inactive in music due to illness from 1974; entered Vernon Convalescent Hospital where he died of bronchial pneumonia; buried Inglewood Cemetery, Inglewood, CA; a memorial concert was held at Musicians Union Auditorium, Los Angeles, CA, 1975

Personal: Married Vida Lee Lashley (1935-75). "T-Bone" was mothers' pet name for Thibeaux

Book: *Stormy Monday: The T-Bone Walker Story,* Helen Oakley Dance, LA State Univ Press, 1987

Billing: Daddy of the Blues

Songs: Ain't That Cold Baby/All Night Long/Baby You Broke My Heart/Blues for Marili/Blues Jam/Blues

Rock/Bye Bye Baby/Call It Stormy Monday/Don't Give Me the Runaround/Don't Go Back to New Orleans/Don't Leave Me Baby/Feeling the Blues/Flower Blues/Get These Blues off Me/Glamour Girl/Goin' to Funky Town/Going to Build Me a Playhouse/Good Boy/Good Feelin'/Got No Use for You/Got to Cross the Deep Blue Sea/I Get So Weary/I Gotta Break Baby/I Hate to See You Go/I Know Your Wig Is Gone/I Wish My Baby/I Wonder Why/I'll Understand/I'm in an Awful Mood/I'm Still in Love with You/Jealous Woman/Jot's Blues/Late Blues/Leaving You Behind/Left Home When I Was a Kid/Long Lost Lover/Long Skirt Baby Blues/Louisiana Bayou Drive/Mean Old World/My Baby Left Me/My Patience Keeps Running Out/No Do Right/No Worry Blues/Papa Ain't Salty/Paris Blues/Play On Little Girl/Poon Tang/Reconsider/Sail On/See You Next Time/Shake It Baby/She Is Going to Ruin Me/She's My Old Time Used to Be/Shufflin' the Blues/Someone Is Going to Mistreat You/T-Bone Blues Special/T-Bone Boogie/T-bone Jumps Again/T-Bone Shuffle/T-Bone's Way/That Evening Train/To Be a Slave Like Me/Treat Me So Low Down/Two Bones and a Pick/Vacation/Vida Lee/When I Grow Up/When We Were Schoolmates/Woman You Must Be Crazy

Award/Honor: Won National Academy of Recording Arts & Sciences "Grammy" Award for best ethnic/traditional recording, 1970 ("Good Feelin'," Polydor album 24-4502)

Infl by: Leroy Carr/Ida Cox/Blind Lemon Jefferson/Lonnie Johnson/Jimmy Rushing

Infl to: Duane Allman/Billy Boy Arnold/Jeff Beck/Chuck Berry/Bobby Bland/Mike Bloomfield/Lonnie Brooks/Andrew Brown/Gatemouth Brown/Little Jr Cannady/Eric Clapton/Albert Collins/Tom Courtney/Pee Wee Crayton/Lowell Fulson/Slim Green/Guitar Slim/Buddy Guy/Harmonica Slim/Jimi Hendrix/Earl Hooker/Bee Houston/JB Hutto/Albert King/BB King/Freddie King/Johnie Lewis/Little Milton/Little Walter/Big Miller/Johnny Moore/Willie Nix/Jimmy Page/RS Rankin/Fenton Robinson/Otis Rush/Doug Sahm/Joe Turner/Phillip Walker/Johnny "Guitar" Watson/Joe Willie Wilkins/Johnny Winter

Quotes: "One of the most striking of all modern blues guitarists possessing a matchless technique, impeccable taste and a flawless sense of rhythmic placement"—Pete Welding, BluesWay album 6008

"He was a figure of major importance . . . playing the kind of lean, biting guitar licks and solos which turned a generation of blues and R&B exponents around in new directions . . ."—Max Jones, *Melody Maker* magazine, Apr 5, 1975

"I believe it all comes originally from T-Bone Walker. BB King and I were talking about that not long ago and he thinks so, too"—Freddie King, *Melody Maker* magazine, Mar 8, 1969

References: Stormy Monday: The T-Bone Walker Story, Helen Oakley Dance, LA State Univ Press, 1987

Guitar Player, Mar 1977
Living Blues, Winter 1972-3
Living Blues, Spring 1973

WALKER, CHARLES

Photo by Fred Seibert. Courtesy Tom Pomposello

Born: Jul 26, 1922, Macon (Bibb Co), GA
Died: Jun 24, 1975, New York, NY
Inst: Guitar

Father was Freeman Walker, a musician; mother was Turine Birds; moved to Newark, NJ, to work outside music as youth; worked Ben 29 Club, Newark, 1955; frequently worked local clubs in Newark, NJ/NYC, NY, area from 1955 into early 60s; rec Holiday label, NYC, 1956; rec Vest label, NYC, 1958; rec Atlas label, NYC, 1963; worked Colonial House, Huntington Station, NY, c1963; continued outside music work through 60s into 70s; rec P&P/Fury labels, NYC, 1971; frequently worked small bars in Harlem area of NYC, early 70s; app w Larry Johnson on Tom Pomposello's SOMETHING INSIDE OF ME Show, WKCR-FM-radio, NYC, 1973; rec Oblivion label, NYC, 1973-4; worked Sweet Basil Club, NYC, 1975; entered Sydenham Hospital where he reportedly died of lung disease; buried Mt Holiness Cemetery, Butler, NJ

Personal: Married Teresa Harrison (1962-c1968); Josephine ——— (c1970-)

Songs: Gladly/Hard Working Man

Reference: Living Blues magazine, Autumn 1974, pp 14-15

WALKER, JAMES *"Jimmy"*

Courtesy Jimmy Walker/Living Blues Magazine

Born: Mar 8, 1905, Memphis (Shelby Co), TN
Inst: Piano

Father was John H Walker; mother Anna Brown; to Chicago c1908; learned piano c1921; worked w Lonnie Johnson/Lee Green/others in local rent parties/dances with frequent outside music work, Chicago, late 20s into early 30s; worked w Homesick James, The Square Deal Club, Chicago, 1934; worked mostly outside music, Chicago, through 30s/40s into 50s; toured w Big Joe Williams working club dates through Ohio/Pennsylvania, early 50s; worked w Billy Boy Arnold, Barrelhouse Lounge, Chicago, 1955-6; w Elmore James, Tuxedo Lounge/Square Deal Club, Chicago, c1955; w Billy Boy Arnold, 708 Club, Chicago, 1958; frequently worked local club dates with many live remote radio broadcasts, Chicago, through 50s into 60s; rec w Erwin Helfer, Testament label, Chicago, 1964; worked outside music, Chicago, through 60s/70s; worked w Erwin Helfer, Univ of Chicago Folk Festival, Chicago, 1973; The Quiet Knight, Chicago, 1973; rec w Erwin Helfer, Flying Fish label, Chicago, 1973; worked Univ of Chicago Folk Festival, Chicago, 1975; Univ of Miami Blues Festival, Coral Gables, FL, 1975; Elsewhere Lounge, Chicago, 1975-7; Eddie Shaw's Place, Chicago, 1975; Chicago Blues Festival, Jane Addams Theater, Chicago, 1975; rec Sirens label, Chicago, 1976

Personal: Married Lillian ———

Songs: Come In Here Baby/Getting Out of Town/I Just Want to Hold On/JW Boogie/Why Don't You Hurry Home?

Infl by: Lorenzo Murphy

Quote: "Jimmy is from the solid rocking school of piano players"—Erwin Helfer, Testament album 60690

Reference: Blues Unlimited magazine (UK), Nov 1975, pp 5-8

WALKER, JOHN MAYON *"Johnny"*
(*aka:* Big Moose/Moose John)
Born: Jun 27, 1927, Greenville (Bolivar Co), MS
Inst: Organ/Piano

Father was Rev TBF Walker; mother Berta _____; learned music from c1942; left home to travel as sideman w Cleanhead Love and others working jukes through South from 1947; app on KING BISCUIT TIME, KFFA-radio, Helena, AR, c1950; served in US Army, 1952-5; rec Ultra label, Los Angeles, CA, 1955; frequently worked/toured/rec as sideman w Lowell Fulson/Choker Campbell Bands, 1955-8; toured w Elmore James Band working one-nighters through South, late 50s; settled in Chicago, IL, c1959; frequently worked w Earl Hooker Band in local club work, Chicago, c1959 into 60s; rec w Earl Hooker, Bea & Baby label, Chicago, 1959; rec w Curtis Jones, Prestige label, NYC, NY, 1960; frequently

Courtesy Living Blues *Magazine*

WALKER, PHILLIP

Born: Feb 11, 1937, Welsh (Jefferson Parish), LA
Inst: Guitar/Harmonica/Piano

Moved to Port Arthur, TX, where he was raised from 8 years of age; interested in music early and made first instrument from cigar box at 13 years of age; frequently sat-in with local bluesmen in local jukes/taverns/dance halls while working outside music, Port Arthur, from 1952; rec (as sideman) w Roscoe Gordon Band, RPM (?) label, Memphis, TN, c1952; frequently worked w Lonesome Sundown Band/Long John Hunter Band in clubs/bars/halls, Port Arthur area, c1953; toured w Clifton Chenier Band working one-nighters through Texas coast area, 1954-7; frequently toured w Clifton Chenier's Band/Lloyd Price/Etta James/Lowell Fulson/Jimmy Reed/others on various R&B package shows working theater dates through South, mid-50s; frequently rec (as sideman) w Clifton Chenier, Specialty/Argo labels, Los Angeles, CA, mid-50s; worked w Clifton Chenier, Crown Propeller, Chicago, IL, c1955; formed The Blue Eagles Band to tour on Fats Domino/Little Richard Big 10 package shows across US from 1957; toured w Joe Young/Otis Rush/Magic Sam/others as sideman working club dates through 60s; rec w Earl Hooker Band, Age label, Chicago, 1963; rec w Al Benson, (unknown) label, Chicago, c1966; rec Blues label, Chicago, 1966; rec w Earl Hooker/Voice Odom/John Lee Hooker, BluesWay label, Los Angeles, 1969; worked Pepper's Lounge, Chicago, 1970; rec acc to Mighty Joe Young, Delmark label, Chicago, c1971; frequently worked w Jimmy Dawkins Band, 1972; worked Miami Blues Festival, Silver Springs, FL, 1972; Mr M's, Chicago, 1972; rec acc to Son Seals, Alligator label, Chicago, 1973; worked Theresa's, Chicago, 1974; Ma Bea's, Chicago, 1974; rec acc to Junior Wells, Delmark label, Chicago, 1974; rec acc to Otis Rush, Delmark label, Chicago, 1975; worked Kingston Mines, Chicago, 1976; Soul Queen, Chicago, 1976

Songs: Baby Talk/Chicken Shack/Footrace/Leave Me Alone/Moose Is on the Loose/Moose Huntin'/Rambling Woman/Rock Me Momma/Would You Baby?

Reference: *Living Blues* magazine, Sep/Oct 1992, pp 34-41

Courtesy Living Blues *Magazine*

worked Black & Tan Bar, El Paso, TX, 1957; The Lobby Inn, Juarez, Mexico, 1957; worked clubs in Farmington, NM, 1958; rec Elko label, Los Angeles, 1959; teamed w Ina Beatrice Walker to work Perkins Club and others, Los Angeles, from c1959; rec w Ina Beatrice Walker (as "Phil & Bea Bop"), AMC label, Los Angeles, 1963; frequently rec (as sideman) for Model T Slim/Eddie Taylor/Teddy Reynolds/others through 60s; toured w own band working club dates through Texas, 1966; rec Vault/Joliet labels, Los Angeles, c1969; rec acc to Johnny Shines/Eddie Taylor, Advent label, Hollywood/Glendale, CA, 1972; worked Ash Grove, Los Angeles, 1972; Topanga Corral, Los Angeles, 1973; frequently worked local club dates, Los Angeles area, into 70s; rec Playboy label, Los Angeles, 1973; worked Rick's Bar, Los Angeles, 1973; app on ATOMIC MAMA'S WANG DANG DOODLE BLUES Show, WNIB-FM-radio, Chicago, IL, 1973-4; worked Univ of California, Santa Barbara, CA, 1974; toured college circuit working concert dates, 1974; worked San Diego Univ Folk Festival, San Diego, CA, 1974 (por remote KPFK-FM-radio); The Palace Club, Los Angeles, 1974; frequently worked NCO Club, El Toro Marine Air Base, Los Angeles, 1974; rec Joliet label, Los Angeles, 1977; worked The Bluebird, Santa Barbara, CA, 1977; San Francisco Blues Festival, McLaren Park, San Francisco, CA, 1977; Eugene Blues Festival, Eugene, OR, 1977; Smilin' Faces, Santa Barbara, CA, 1977

Personal: Married Ina Beatrice "Bea Bop" ———, a singer. Second cousin of Gatemouth Brown. Not related to Dennis Walker, musician

Songs: All in Your Mind/Beaumont Blues/Do the Shovel/El Paso Blues/Hello My Darling/Hey Hey Baby's Gone/If We Can Find It/It Was You/It's All in Your Mind/Someday You'll Have These Blues/Sure Is Cold

Infl by: Guitar Jr/Long John Hunter/BB King/Lonesome Sundown/Aaron "T-Bone" Walker

Quote: ". . . one of the most versatile figures on the Los Angeles Rhythm & Blues circuit"—Roy Greenberg, *Living Blues* magazine, Sept/Oct 1977, p 39

References: Blues Unlimited magazine (UK), Dec 1974, pp 14-15

Living Blues magazine, Autumn 1973, p 8

WALKER, T-BONE
(see Walker, Aaron)

WALKER JR, T-BONE
(see Rankin, R S)

WALKER, *"Blind"* WILLIE
Born: 1896, South Carolina
Died: Mar 4, 1933, Greenville, SC
Inst: Guitar

Father was George Walker; mother was Lucy ———; born blind; reportedly raised in Greenville, SC, from c1911; believed to have worked local string band, Greenville, into teens; frequently worked as itinerant musician on streets in area led on occasion by Josh White during 20s; rec Columbia label, Atlanta, GA, 1930; died of congenital syphilis; buried Richland Cemetery

Infl to: Roosevelt "Baby" Brooks/Josh White

Quotes: "Walker was certainly sophisticated and his clear, almost minstrel-like vocal delivery went perfectly with his delicate yet strongly-structured guitar lines . . ."—Bruce Bastin, *Crying for the Carolines*, Studio Vista Ltd, 1971

"He was the best guitarist I've ever heard, even better than Blind Blake. Blake was fast but Walker was like Art Tatum"—Josh White, *Blues Unlimited* magazine (UK), Sept 1968, p 16

Reference: Crying for the Carolines, Bruce Bastin, Studio Vista Ltd, 1971

WALKIN' SLIM
(see Minter, Iverson)

WALLACE, BEULAH *"Sippie"*
(*aka:* Sippie Thomas)
Born: Nov 1, 1898, Houston (Harris Co), TX
Died: Nov 1, 1986, Detroit, MI
Inst: Organ/Piano

Father was George W Thomas Sr, deacon of Shiloh Baptist Church; mother was Fanny Bradley; born Beulah Thomas; one of 13 children; sang/played organ in father's church as child; moved to New Orleans, LA, to briefly live with brother George W Thomas Jr c1910; returned to Houston, TX, to attend local school into teens; frequently toured in local tent shows out of Houston, late teens into 20s; moved to Chicago, IL, 1923; rec w Eddie Heywood, OKeh label, Chicago, 1923; rec w Clarence Williams, OKeh label, NYC, NY, 1923; teamed w brother Hersal Thomas to tour TOBA circuit working theater dates through South, early 20s; rec w King Oliver (others), OKeh label, Chicago, 1925; worked Coliseum Theater, Chicago, 1926; rec w Louis Armstrong (others),

Beulah "Sippie" Wallace

Photo by Doug Fulton. Courtesy Living Blues *Magazine*

OKeh label, Chicago, 1926-7; teamed w Floyd Taylor to work theater dates from 1926; rec Victor label, Chicago, 1929; settled in Detroit, MI, to work mostly outside music while working as organist/singer w Leland Baptist church from 1929 into 70s; served as director of National Convention of Gospel Choirs and Choruses Inc, Chicago, from mid-30s; worked w Jimmie Noone Orch, Platinum Lounge, Vincennes Hotel, Chicago, 1937; rec w Albert Ammons, Mercury label, Chicago, 1945; rec w Fine Arts Trio, Fine Arts label, Detroit, MI, 1959; rec w James Cohen Trio, Bango label, Detroit, MI; 1962; worked Univ of Detroit, Detroit, 1966; toured w American Folk Blues Festival working concert dates through England/Europe, 1966 (por Berlin, Ger, concert rel Fontana label); rec Storyville label, Copenhagen, Den, 1966; worked Chicago Folk Festival, Chicago, 1967; Michigan State Univ, E Lansing, MI, 1967; w Kweskin Jug Band, Newport Folk Festival, Newport, RI, 1967; rec w Jim Kweskin Jug Band, Reprise label, NYC, NY, 1967; worked w Jim Kweskin Jug Band, Town Hall, NYC, 1967; Mariposa Folk Festival, Toronto, Can, 1967; rec Spivey label, Detroit, MI, 1970; worked Ann Arbor Blues Festival, Ann Arbor, MI, 1972 (por rel Atlantic label); Philadelphia Folk Festival, Schwenksville, PA, 1973; Ambassador Hotel, Los Angeles, CA, 1976; Great American Music Hall, San Francisco, CA, 1976; Compared to What Club, Detroit, MI, 1976; worked w Little Brother Montgomery, Avery Fisher Hall, NYC, 1977; worked clubs/concerts/festivals into 80s; app DAVID LETTERMAN Show, NBC-TV, 1980-2; app TODAY Show, NBC-TV, 1981; app THREE GENERATIONS OF THE BLUES, PBS-TV, 1984; died of natural causes; buried Trinity Cemetery, Detroit

Personal: "Sippie" was pet childhood name due to her habit of sipping food

Billing: The Texas Nightingale

Songs: Advice Blues/Baby I Can't Use You No More/Bedroom Blues/Caldonia Blues/Can Anybody Take Sweet Mama's Place?/Gambler's Dream/He's the Cause of My (Me) Being Blue/I'm a Mighty Tight Woman/Lonesome for Someone to Love/Lonesome Hours Blues/Murder Gonna Be My Crime/Off and On Blues/Oh Angel Eyes It's All for You/The Rocks/Special Delivery Blues/Stranger's Blues/Suitcase Blues/Then I Won't Feel Blue/Till the Honey Come Down/Trouble Everywhere I Roam/Underworld Blues/Until I Go to Sleep/Women Be Wise/You Got to Know How

Infl by: Mamie Smith/Eva Taylor/Hersal Thomas

Infl to: Bonnie Raitt

Quotes: "A voice of great richness in the lower range and power in the higher"—Ronald P Harwood, *Storyville* magazine (UK), Jun 1968, p 17

"Sippie Wallace had the qualities of shading and inflection in her singing that marked the classic blues artist"—(Paul Oliver) McCarthy/Morgan/Oliver/Harrison, *Jazz on Record,* Hanover Books Ltd, 1968

References: Storyville magazine (UK), Jun 1968, pp 17-24

Who's Who of Jazz, John Chilton, Bloomsbury Book Shop, 1970

Cadence magazine, Oct 1978, pp 14-19

WALTER
(see Horton, Walter)

WALTON, MERCY DEE
(aka: Mercy Dee)
Born: Aug 3, 1915, Waco (McLennan Co), TX
Died: Dec 2, 1962, Murphys, CA
Inst: Piano

Courtesy Sheldon Harris Collection

Father was Fred Walton; mother was Bessie Wade; worked outside music (on farm) in Brazos Bottom area of Texas as youth; taught self piano at 13 years of age and frequently worked local house parties, Waco, TX, area, into 30s; moved to West Coast to work outside music, late 30s; frequently worked local joints/clubs in San Francisco/Los Angeles/Oakland, CA, areas into 40s; frequently worked for migrant farm camps on West Coast through 40s; rec Spire label, Fresno, CA, 1949; rec Imperial/Bayou/Colony labels, Los Angeles, 1950; rec Heritage label, Oakland, CA, c1950; rec Rhythm label, Los Angeles, 1954; rec Flair label, Los Angeles, 1955; frequently toured in various R&B package shows working auditoriums/dance halls/concerts across US through 50s; toured w Big Jay McNeely Band working dance halls on West Coast, late 50s; frequently worked Sugar Hill Club, San Francisco, 1961; rec Arhoolie label, Stockton/Berkeley, CA, 1961; rec Prestige-Bluesville label, Berkeley, CA, 1961; frequently worked local club dates, Stockton, CA, area, 1961-2; rec Arhoolie label, Stockton, 1962; suffered cerebral hemorrhage and entered Bret Harte Hospital where he died; buried at rural cemetery, Stockton, CA

Songs: After the Fight/Betty Jean/Call the Asylum/Danger Zone/Dark Muddy Bottom/The Drunkard/Five Card Hand/Have You Ever Been Out in the Country?/Jack Engine/Lady Luck/Mercy's Party/Mercy's Troubles/My Little Angel/One Room Country Shack/Pity and a Shame/Red Light/Shady Lane/Troublesome Mind/Walked Down So Many Turnrows/Your Friend and Woman

Infl by: Delois Maxey

Infl to: Albert King

Quote: "Mercy Dee Walton is an artist of such sincerity, depth, simplicity, enthusiasm and feeling as to make criticism or attempt at written analysis almost an impertinence"—Ron Anger, *Coda* magazine (Canada), Oct 1963, p 25

Reference: Rhythm & Blues magazine, Jul 1963, pp 10-11

WALTON, WADE

Photo by Jim O'Neal. Courtesy Living Blues *Magazine*

Born: Oct 10, 1923, Lombardy (Sunflower Co), MS
Inst: Guitar/Harmonica/Organ

Born on Lemaise Plantation outside of Lombardy, MS; one of 17 children; moved to Head Plantation, Goldfield, MS, as infant; worked outside music (on farms) from childhood; interested in music from age of 12; frequently sang/danced for prisoners at Parchman State Farm, Parchman, MS, mid-30s; teamed w brother Honey Walton to follow minstrel shows working for tips through area, late 30s; frequently worked outside music in Goldfield, MS/Memphis, TN, into 40s; attended Martin Barber Col, early 40s; settled in Clarksdale, MS, to work outside music (as barber) from 1943; teamed w Ike Turner to form The Kings of Rhythm group working local jukes, Clarksdale area, through 40s into 50s; rec Arhoolie label, Clarksdale, 1960; rec Bluesville label, Bergenfield, NJ, 1962; continued working/entertaining in own barber shop-bar, Clarksdale, through 60s into 70s; rec ST for UK film BLUES LIKE SHOWERS OF RAIN, 1970; app in film MISSISSIPPI DELTA BLUES, 1974; app in film GIVE MY POOR HEART EASE: MISSISSIPPI DELTA BLUESMEN, 1975

Song: Razor Strop Boogie

Infl by: Horace Walton

Quote: "The music of Wade spans three generations of blues on the Mississippi Delta—from the very primitive style of singers like Charley Patton to modern rhythm & blues"—Dave Mangurian, Bluesville album 1060

References: Living Blues magazine, Sept 1976, pp 23-5

Bluesville album 1060

WARD, VERA HALL
(see Hall, Vera)

WARREN, ROBERT HENRY *"Baby Boy"*
(aka: Johnny Williams)

Courtesy Living Blues *Magazine*

Born: Aug 13, 1919, Lake Providence (East Carroll Parish), LA
Died: Jul 1, 1977, Detroit, MI
Inst: Guitar

Father was Lee Warren, a farmer; mother was Beulah Butler; one of 12 children; moved to Memphis, TN, where he was raised from 3 months of age; interested in music at early age and learned guitar from older brother at 8 years of age; worked Slick Collins' Roadhouse, West Memphis, AR, 1931; dropped out of school to work outside music with occasional local party work, Memphis, from c1931; frequently worked w Howlin' Wolf/Robert Jr Lockwood/Little Buddy Doyle/Black Bubba/others at Church's Park (WC Handy Park), Memphis, through 30s; frequently toured w Howlin' Wolf/Johnny Shines working parties/dances/honky tonks through Arkansas, late 30s; frequently worked w Johnny Shines (or single) in local dance halls/roadhouses in Helena/West Memphis/Hughes, AR areas and elsewhere, late 30s to 1942; app w Sonny Boy Williamson (Alex Miller), KING BISCUIT TIME, KFFA-radio, Helena, AR, c1941; moved to Detroit, MI, to work outside music, 1942-77; frequently worked w Willie Blackwell and others on night/weekend gigs at local bars/streets, Detroit, from mid-40s; formed own combo working Brown Derby, Detroit, 1949; rec Staff label, Detroit, 1949-50; rec Cadet label, Detroit, 1952; worked The Chicken Shack, Detroit, c1952; frequently worked w Sonny Boy Williamson (Alex Miller) in local clubs, Detroit, 1953-4; rec w Sonny Boy Williamson (Alex Miller), JVB label, Detroit, 1953-4; rec Excello/Blue Lake/Drummond/Sampson labels, Detroit, 1954; frequently worked Mary's Bar/Casbah Lounge/Tavern Lounge/Rage Showbar/Club Plantation/Sandy's Bar/Prince Royal Club/Flame Showbar/Paradise Club/others, Detroit, through 50s/60s; worked Black Velvet Club, Mt Clements, MI, late 50s; worked Detroit Blues Festival, Detroit, 1971; Blues Festival, Saginaw, MI, 1971; toured w Boogie Woogie Red working concert dates through England/Europe, 1972; worked Ann Arbor Blues Festival, Ann Arbor, MI, 1973; Windsor Concert, Windsor, Can, 1973; mostly inactive in music from 1974; suffered fatal heart attack at home; buried Detroit Memorial Park Cemetery, McComb County, MI

Personal: Married (1935-); Carrie Edwards (early 60s). Had 7 children. Named "Baby Boy" by older brothers as child. Not to be confused with musicians Johnny Williams or John Lee Hooker who also used name "Johnny Williams" as pseudonym

Infl by: Little Buddy Doyle/Robert Johnson

Quotes: "Warren was arguably the finest of the older breed of bluesmen remaining in Detroit . . ."—Jim O'Neal, *Living Blues* magazine, Jul 1977, p 5

"His songs, deftly performed, were magic—the brilliantly original lyrics, the truth, the humour and the beauty of his music all bore the hallmark of a major craftsman of the blues"—Mike Rowe, *Blues Unlimited* magazine (UK), Jul 1977, p 16

References: Blues Unlimited magazine (UK), Nov/Dec 1972, Jan 1973, p 16
Cadence magazine, Sept 1977, pp 3-6, 9

WASHBOARD SAM
(see Brown, Robert)

WASHBOARD WILLIE
(see Hensley, William)

WASHINGTON, ALBERT
Born: Aug 17, 1935, Rome (Floyd Co), GA
Inst: Guitar/Organ/Piano

Moved to Cincinnati, OH, 1945; dropped out of school to tour w Religious Gospelaires group working local churches with some local recordings, Cincinnati, through 50s; rec Peacock/Fence labels, Cincinnati, 1962; formed own The Kings group to work long residency at Vet's Lounge, Cincinnati, c1962-70; rec Bluestown label, Boston, MA, 1965; rec Fraternity label, Cincinnati, late 60s; worked w own Astro's group, Soul Lounge, Cincinnati, 1970; Satan's Den, Cincinnati, 1971; Viking Lounge, Cincinnati, 1972; worked w own Astro's group in residency, Vet's Lounge, Cincinnati, c1972-5; rec Eastbound label, Nashville, TN, 1973; app w own Astro's group, NIGHT LIFE Show, WLWT-TV, Cincinnati, 1975; frequently app on STEVE TRACY Show, WAIF-FM-radio, Cincinnati, 1975-6; worked Horoscope Lounge, Cincinnati, 1976 (por remote WAIF-FM-radio); Bogart's Cafe American, Cincinnati, 1977 (por remote WAIF-FM-radio)

Personal: Married. Has 6 children

Infl by: BB King

Reference: Blues Unlimited magazine (UK), Jul 1971, p 15

WASHINGTON, D C
(see Bender, D C)

Albert Washington *Photo by Jim O'Neal. Courtesy Living Blues Magazine*

WASHINGTON, DINAH
Born: Aug 29, 1924, Tuscaloosa (Tuscaloosa Co), AL
Died: Dec 14, 1963, Detroit, MI
Inst: Piano

Father was Ollie Jones; mother was Alice Williams; born Ruth Lee Jones; moved to Chicago, IL, 1927; mother taught her religious singing as child and frequently toured churches across US giving musical recitals into 30s; learned piano early and frequently played at St Luke's Baptist Church, Chicago, from 1935, later to work there as choir director; won amateur talent show, Regal Theater, Chicago, 1939; studied singing w Sallie Martin c1940; toured w Sallie Martin Gospel Singers working gospel circuit through Midwest/South, 1940-1; worked Dave's Rhumboogie Club, Chicago, 1941; w Fats Waller, Downbeat Room, Sherman Hotel, Chicago, 1942; Three Deuces, Chicago, 1942; Garrick Lounge, Chicago, 1942; toured extensively w Lionel Hampton Band working dances/theaters across US, 1943-6; rec w Lionel Hampton group, Keynote label, NYC, NY, 1943; rec w Lionel Hampton Orch, Decca label, Los Angeles, CA, 1944-5; worked w Lionel Hampton Orch, Strand Theater, NYC, 1944; Capitol Theater, NYC, 1944; Symphony Hall, Boston, MA, 1944; Apollo Theater, NYC, 1944; State Theater, Hartford, CT, 1944; Carnegie Hall, NYC, 1945 (por rel Decca label); rec w Lucky Thompson's All Stars, Apollo label, Los Angeles, 1945; frequently worked HARLEM VARIETY REVUE, Apollo Theater, NYC, 1945-55 (por shown SHOWTIME AT THE APOLLO, syndicated TV, 1955/por shown in films HARLEM JAZZ FESTIVAL, 1955; BASIN STREET REVUE, 1956; ROCK 'N' ROLL REVUE also titled HARLEM ROCK 'N' ROLL, 1955); rec w Gus Chappel's Orch/Tab Smith Orch/Chubby Jackson Orch, Mercury label, Chicago/NYC, 1946; toured extensively working one-nighters (as single) in clubs across US from 1946 into 50s; worked Dunes Club, Neptune, NJ, 1946; Kelly's Stable, NYC, 1946; w Eddie Vinson Band, Apollo Theater, NYC; 1946; w Louis Jordan Band, Regal Theater, Chicago, 1946; rec w Dave Young Orch/Cootie Williams Orch/Ike Carpenter/others, Mercury label, Chicago/NYC/Los Angeles, 1947-61; worked Foster's Rainbow Room,

Dinah Washington *Courtesy BMI Archives*

New Orleans, LA, c1947; Tiffany Club, Los Angeles, 1951; The Paradise Club, Detroit, MI, 1951; Harlem Club, Philadelphia, PA, 1951; Basin Street East, NYC, 1954; Club Oasis, Los Angeles, 1954; Newport Jazz Festival, Newport, RI, 1955-8 (por 1955 concert heard on MUSIC USA, VOA-radio/por 1958 concert shown in film JAZZ ON A SUMMER'S DAY and rel Mercury label); worked Alan Freed's Diddley Daddy R&B package show, Loew's State Theater, Boston, MA, 1955; Weeke's Tavern, Atlantic City, NJ, 1955; The Showboat, Philadelphia, 1955-6; Moulin Rouge, Las Vegas, NV, 1955; The Paramount Theater, Los Angeles, 1955; Sahara Hotel, Las Vegas, c1955; Club Calvert, Miami, FL, 1956; Safari Lounge, New Orleans, 1956; Flame Showbar, Detroit, 1956; Casino Royale, Washington, DC, 1957; The Blackhawk, San Francisco, 1957; Mr Kelly's, Chicago, 1957; Pep's Musical Showbar, Philadelphia, 1957-61; Zardi's Jazzland, Hollywood, CA, 1957; Robert's Show Lounge, Chicago, IL, 1957; Club Tijuana, Baltimore, MD, 1957; Graystone Ballroom, Detroit, MI, 1957; app on DU PONT SHOW OF THE MONTH (ep: Crescendo), CBS-TV, 1957; worked Cotton Club, Atlantic City, NJ, 1957; Club 53, San Francisco, CA, 1958; Birdland, NYC, NY, 1958; worked club dates in Toronto, Can, 1959; toured England/Europe working concert/TV/radio dates, 1959; worked w Red Garland Trio, Village Vanguard, NYC, 1959; Carnegie Hall, NYC, 1959; Randalls Island Jazz Festival, Randalls Island, NY, 1959; Westbury Music Fair, Westbury, NY, 1959; Basin Street East, NYC, NY, 1959-60; Berkeley Theater, Berkeley, CA, 1960; Masonic Temple, San Francisco, CA, 1960; Storyville, Boston, MA, 1960; Frolics Revere Beach, Boston, 1960; Indiana Jazz Festival, Evansville, IN, 1960; Paramount Theater, Brooklyn, NY, 1960; app on SINGING, SWINGING YEARS, (unknown) TV, 1960; worked Flame Showbar, Detroit, MI, 1960-1; Buffalo Jazz Festival, Buffalo, NY, 1960-1; worked gambling casinos, Newport, KY, 1960; Quaker City Jazz Festival, Connie Mack Stadium, Philadelphia, PA, 1960; worked Bud Billiken parade/concert, Chicago, IL, 1960; Robert's Show Lounge, Chicago, 1960, then managed/performed at club through 1961; worked Apollo Theater, NYC, 1961; Birdland, NYC, 1961-2; The Birdhouse, Chicago, 1962; International Jazz Festival, Washington, DC, 1962; The Flamingo Club, Oakland CA, 1962; worked outside music as owner/manager of restaurant, Detroit, MI, from c1962; rec Roulette label, NYC, 1962-3; worked Holiday House, Monroeville, PA, 1963; worked w own revue, Basin Street West, San Francisco, CA, 1963; Jazz Temple, Cleveland, OH, 1963; app on local TV shows, Cleveland, 1963; worked w Count Basie Orch, Ravinia Park Festival, Chicago, IL, 1963; w Duke Ellington Orch, Michigan State Fair, Detroit, MI, 1963; worked club/hotel dates, Las Vegas, NV, 1963; died at home from OD of sleeping pills; buried Burr Oak Cemetery, Worth, IL

Personal: Married John Young (1942-3)/George Jenkins (1946-8)/Robert Grayson (c1949)/Walter Buchanan (1950)/Eddie Chamblee (1957)/Raphael Campos (1957)/Horatio Maillard (1959-60)/Jackie Hayes (1960)/Richard Lane (1963). Not all confirmed. 2 children

Billing: Queen of the Blues

Book: *Queen of the Blues,* Jim Haskins, William Morrow Co, 1987

Songs: Fast Movin Mama/Fine Fat Daddy/Juice Head Man of Mine

Award/Honor: Won National Academy of Recording Arts & Sciences Grammy Award for Best R&B recording of 1959 ("What a Diff'rence a Day Makes," Mercury 71435)

Infl by: Billie Holiday/Ma Rainey/Bessie Smith

Infl to: Ruth Brown/Etta James/Barbara Morrisson/Esther Phillips/Irene Reid/Diana Ross/Diane Schuur/Carrie Smith/Dionne Warwick/Nancy Wilson

Quotes: "Dinah Washington brought to a blues song . . . pathos and melancholy . . ."—Jack Schiffman, *Uptown, The Story of Harlem's Apollo Theater,* Cowles Book Company Inc, 1971

"By restraining and a gradual revealing vocal intensity and building her emotional pattern, Miss Washington transforms a narrative into an individual's dramatic monologue . . ."—Martin Williams, Mercury album 20439

References: *Encyclopedia of Pop, Rock & Soul,* Irwin Stambler, St Martin's Press, 1974

Queen of the Blues, Jim Haskins, William Morrow Co, 1987

WATERS, ETHEL

(*aka:* Mamie Jones/Martha Pryor)
Born: Oct 31, 1896, Chester (Delaware Co), PA
Died: Sept 1, 1977, Chatsworth, CA

Father was John Wesley Waters, a pianist; mother Louise Tar Anderson; raised by grandmother Sally Anderson from infancy; began singing (as

Ethel Waters *Courtesy Frank Driggs Collection*

"Baby Star") in local church from 1901; frequently won many dance contests at Pop Grey's Dance Hall, Chester, from 1907; dropped out of school to work outside music, Chester, 1909-17; worked Jack's Rathskeller, Philadelphia, PA, 1917; worked as singer/dancer (billed as "Sweet Mama Stringbean") w Braxton & Nugent vaudeville unit, Lincoln Theater, Baltimore, MD, 1917; toured (as one of "The Hill Sisters" trio) working southern vaudeville circuit, 1917-18; worked Gibson's North Pole Theater, Philadelphia, 1917; Monogram Theater, Chicago, IL, 1917; toured w White's Greater Shows carnival working tent shows across US c1918; worked 81 Theater, Atlanta, GA, 1918; 91 Theater, Atlanta, 1918; Howard Theater, Washington, DC, 1918; Standard Theater, Philadelphia, 1918; frequently worked Barney Gordon's Saloon, Philadelphia, 1918-19; Leroy's Cabaret, NYC, 1919; app in musical comedy HELLO 1919!, Lafayette Theater, NYC, 1919, then toured; worked Lincoln Theater, NYC, 1920; Edmond's Cellar, NYC, 1920-1; frequently worked The Boathouse/Egg Harbor/Pekin Theater/Philadelphia House, Atlantic City, NJ, c1920; frequently worked Rafe's Paradise Theater, Atlantic City, NJ, c1920-2; William Banks Cafe, NYC, c1920; Libya Cafe, NYC, c1920; Lafayette Theater, NYC, c1920; rec w Albury's Blue and Jazz Seven, Cardinal label, NYC, 1921; rec w Cordy Williams' Jazz Masters, Black Swan label, NYC, 1921; rec w Jazz Masters, Black Swan label, NYC, 1921-3; toured w Fletcher Henderson's Jazz Masters in Black Swan Troubadours troupe working Standard Theater, Philadelphia, PA/Regent Theater, Philadelphia, PA/Douglass Theater, Baltimore, MD/Lafayette Theater, NYC, 1921; Lincoln Theater, Louisville, KY, 1922; Booker T Washington Theater, St Louis, MO, 1922; Washington Theater, Indianapolis, IN, 1922; Grand Theater, Chicago, IL, 1922; Emery Hall, Cincinnati, OH, 1922; Palace Theater, Memphis, TN, 1922; Bijou Theater, Nashville, TN, 1922; Lyric Theater, New Orleans, LA, 1922; app w Fletcher Henderson's Jazz Masters, WVG-radio, New Orleans, 1922; worked Academy of Music, Wilmington, NC, 1922; app in JUMP STEADY Revue, Lafayette Theater, NYC, 1922; toured in Tutt-Whitney's OH JOY Revue working theater dates, 1922; toured as single working theaters on TOBA circuit, 1922; toured briefly in musical comedy DUMB LUCK working theater dates in New England, 1922; toured as headliner w Rabbit Foot Minstrels tent show (including Big Joe Williams/Birmingham Jug Band) working through South c1923; worked Lafayette Theater, NYC, 1923; Alhambra Theater, NYC, 1923; app in Madame Mamie Hightower's Golden Brown Beauty Preparations national newspaper advertisement, 1923; toured as single (acc by Fletcher Henderson) working theater dates, 1923; rec Paramount/Vocalion labels, Chicago/NYC, 1924; toured w Earl Dancer working BF Keith Theater, Toledo, OH/Palace Theater, Chicago, IL/State Lake Theater, Chicago, IL/Palace Theater, Milwaukee, WI/Majestic Theater, Cedar Rapids, IA/Orpheum Theater, St Paul, MN/Orpheum Theater, Winnipeg, Can, and other Keith/Orpheum theaters, 1924-5; worked Everglades Club, NYC, 1925; Lincoln Theater, NYC, 1925; Lafayette Theater, NYC, 1925; Dunbar Theater, Philadelphia, PA, 1925; replaced Florence Mills in PLANTATION REVUE, Sam Selvin's Plantation Club, NYC, 1925, then toured; frequently worked vaudeville shows, Palace Theater, NYC, 1925-8; app in TAN TOWN TOPICS Revue, Lafayette Theater, NYC, 1925; app in TOO BAD Revue, Lafayette Theater, NYC, 1925; frequently rec Columbia label, NYC, 1925-31; frequently toured in own variously titled revues—ETHEL WATERS FLOOR SHOW/ETHEL WATERS VANITIES/ETHEL WATERS REVUE working theaters/auditoriums/one-nighters across US, 1926; worked Howard Theater, Washington, DC, 1926; National Theater, Wilmington, DE, 1926; Orpheum Theater, Newark, NJ, 1926; app in BLACK BOTTOM REVUE, Lafayette Theater, NYC, 1926; app in tab show MISS CALICO, Alhambra Theater, NYC/Lafayette Theater, NYC, 1926, then toured into 1927; app in BLACK CARGO Revue, Orpheum Theater, Newark, NJ/Lafayette Theater, NYC/Savoy Theater, Atlantic City, NJ, 1927; app in musical revue AFRICANA, Daly's 63rd Street Theater, NYC/National Theater, NYC/Lafayette Theater, NYC, 1927, then toured; app in PARIS BOUND Revue, Lafayette Theater, NYC, 1927; worked Palace Theater, Chicago, IL, 1927-8; Oriole Terrace Club, Detroit, MI, 1928; app in ETHEL WATERS BROADWAY REVUE, Standard Theater, Philadelphia, PA, 1928; app in revised AFRICANA Revue, Lafayette Theater, NYC, 1928; worked Cafe de Paris, Chicago, IL, 1928; toured as headliner working Keith-Albee Palace Theater, NYC, 1928; Proctor's 86th Street Theater, NYC, 1928; Proctor's Theater, Newark, NJ, 1928; Franklin Theater, NYC, 1928; Broadway Theater, NYC, 1928; Albee Theater, Brooklyn, NY, 1928; Riverside Theater, NYC, 1928; Fordham Theater, NYC, 1928; Keith Theater, Syracuse, NY, 1928; Shea's Theater, Buffalo, NY, 1928; Shea's Theater, Toronto, Can, 1928; Keith Theater, Youngstown, OH, 1928; Keith 104th Street Theater, Cleveland, OH, 1928; Keith Theater, Dayton, OH, 1928; Keith

Theater, Akron, OH, 1928; Orpheum Theater, Winnipeg, Can, 1928; Strand Theater, Calgary, Can, 1928; New Orpheum Theater, Seattle, WA, 1929; Orpheum Theater, San Francisco, CA, 1929; Orpheum Theater, Oakland, CA, 1929; Orpheum Theater, Los Angeles, CA, 1929; Hill Street Theater, Los Angeles, 1929; Palace Theater, Chicago, IL, 1929; St Louis Theater, St Louis, MO, 1929; State Theater, Chicago, 1929; Keith Theater, Rochester, NY, 1929; Earl Theater, Philadelphia, PA, 1929; Garden Theater, Baltimore, MD, 1929; Regent Theater, NYC, 1929; Keith Memorial Theater, Boston, MA, 1929; app in film ON WITH THE SHOW, 1929 (por heard in film short THE VOICE THAT THRILLED THE WORLD); app in BANJOLAND Revue, Lafayette Theater, NYC, 1929; worked The Palladium, London, Eng, 1929; Kit Kat Club, London, Eng, 1929; extensive residency, Cafe de Paris, London, Eng, 1929; Holborn Empire Theater, London, Eng, 1929; Loew's Victoria Theater, NYC, 1930; app in JAZZLAND IN 1930 Revue, Lafayette Theater, NYC, 1930; app in Lew Leslie's musical revue BLACKBIRDS OF 1930, Majestic Theater, Brooklyn, NY/Royale Theater, NYC, 1930, then toured; app in RHAPSODY IN BLACK Revue, Belasco Theater, Washington, DC, 1930/Paramount Theater, NYC/ Sam Harris Theater, NYC/Majestic Theater, Brooklyn, NY/New Brighton Theater, Brooklyn/Lafayette Theater, NYC, 1931/Chicago Theater, Chicago/ Apollo Theater, Chicago, elsewhere, 1932; worked Harlem Opera House, NYC, 1932; app in DIXIE TO BROADWAY Revue, Paramount Theater, NYC, 1932; Albee Theater, Cincinnati, OH, 1932; app in FROM BROADWAY BACK TO HARLEM Revue, Lafayette Theater, NYC, 1932; rec w Duke Ellington Orch, Brunswick label, NYC, 1932; rec Brunswick label, NYC, 1932-4; worked Shubert Theater, Newark, NJ, 1933; app in revised RHAPSODY IN BLACK Revue, Lafayette Theater, NYC, 1933; app w Duke Ellington Orch, COTTON CLUB PARADE Revue, Cotton Club, NYC, 1933 (with frequent remotes on WJZ-radio, NYC, NBC-Network); app in COTTON CLUB REVUE, Capitol Theater, NYC, 1933; app on Rudy Vallee FLEISCHMANN HOUR Show, WJZ-radio, NYC (NBC-Network), 1933; app w Jack Denny Orch as headliner on AMERICAN OIL REVUE weekly show (AMOCO SHOW), WABC-radio, NYC (CBS-Network), 1933, then continued on show w Dorsey Brothers Orch into 1934; app in STORMY WEATHER Revue, Loew's State Theater, NYC, 1933; rec w Benny Goodman Orch, Columbia label, NYC, 1933; app in Vitaphone film short RUFUS JONES FOR PRESIDENT, 1933; app w Hall Johnson Choir, HALL OF FAME SHOW, WEAF-radio, NYC, 1934; app in musical revue AS THOUSANDS CHEER, Music Box Theater, NYC, 1933-4, then toured into 1935; worked Palais Royale Club, NYC, 1934; app in film THE GIFT OF GAB, 1934; app in film short BUBBLING OVER, 1934; app in film short HOT 'N' BOTHERED, 1934; rec Decca label, NYC, 1934; app AT HOME ABROAD Revue, Winter Garden Theater/Majestic Theater, NYC, 1935-6, then toured; rec w Russell Wooding Orch, Liberty label, NYC, 1935; frequently toured w Eddie Mallory's Band in own revue working vaudeville circuit across US, 1935-7; worked Apollo Theater, NYC, 1936 (then annually into 40s); app on BEN BERNIE, THE OLD MAESTRO Show, WJZ-radio, NYC (NBC-Blue Network), 1936; worked The Trocadero, Hollywood, CA, 1936-7; app w Duke Ellington Orch, THE COTTON CLUB EXPRESS Revue, Cotton Club, NYC, 1937; toured w Eddie Mallory's Band in own SWING HARLEM SWING Revue working RKO-Theater circuit, 1937-8; worked w Hall Johnson Choir in concert recital, Carnegie Hall, NYC, 1938; app on CARNEGIE HALL Show, NBC-radio Network, 1938; worked RKO Palace Theater, NYC, 1938; Roxy Theater, NYC, 1938; app in CRAZY SHOW Revue, Casa Manana Club, NYC, 1938; rec w Eddie Mallory's Orch, Bluebird label, NYC, 1938-9; rec Decca label, NYC, 1938; app in Federal Theater Project (WPA) show, ANDROCLES AND THE LION, Seattle, WA, c1939; app in film short SOUTHERN BLUES, 1939; worked concert dates at New York World's Fair, Queens, NY, 1939-40; app on (untitled) variety show, W2XBS-TV, NYC (RCA/NBC), 1939; app in non-singing role in show MAMBA'S DAUGHTERS, Empire Theater, NYC, 1939, then toured into 1940 with a return to Broadway Theater, NYC, 1940; toured w Balaban & Katz vaudeville production company working theater dates, 1940; worked w Louis Armstrong Orch, Paramount Theater, NYC, 1940; rec w Max Meth Orch, Liberty label, NYC, 1940; app in show CABIN IN THE SKY, Martin Beck Theater, NYC, 1940-1, then toured to West Coast; worked Fefe's Monte Carlo Club, NYC, 1941; app on Bing Crosby's KRAFT MUSIC HALL Show, WEAF-radio, NYC (NBC-Network), 1941; worked Orpheum Theater, Los Angeles, CA, 1942; toured w Hattie McDaniel working military bases through California, 1942; frequently app for USO Camp Shows Inc on network-radio, 1942; worked Strand Theater, Brooklyn, NY, 1942; app in film CAIRO, 1942; app in film TALES OF MANHATTAN, 1942; app in film CABIN IN THE SKY, 1943; app in film STAGE DOOR CANTEEN, 1943; app in variety revue LAUGH TIME, Curran Theater, San Francisco, CA/Biltmore Theater, Los Angeles, CA/Shubert Theater, NYC/Ambassador Theater, NYC, 1943; worked RKO Theater, Boston, MA, 1943; together with Tommy Brookins owned Cabin in the Sky Club, Chicago, 1944; app on COMMAND PERFORMANCE Show, Armed Forces Radio Service (AFRS), Hollywood, CA (syndicated-radio), c1944; app as guest on AMOS 'N' ANDY Show, NBC-radio Network, 1944; worked Show of Shows benefit, Madison Square Garden, NYC, 1944; Club Zanzibar, NYC, 1944; app in all-Negro revue BLUE HOLIDAY, Belasco Theater, NYC, 1945; worked Embassy Club, NYC, 1945; rec w JC Heard's Orch, Continental label, NYC, 1946; worked Club Baron, NYC, 1946; rec Mercury label, Chicago, 1947; rec w Herman Chittison Trio, Victor label, NYC, 1947; worked Slapsie Maxie's Club, Hollywood, CA, 1948; The Click, Philadelphia, 1948; Tia Juana Club, Cleveland, OH, 1948; toured w Fletcher Henderson working one-woman recitals on West Coast, 1948-9; app on TEX AND JINX Show, NBC-radio Network, 1949; toured southern Canada working club dates, 1949; worked Three Sixes, Detroit, 1949; app in film PINKY, 1949; worked w Fletcher Henderson, Roxy Theater, NYC, 1949; app on Ed Sullivan's TOAST OF THE TOWN, CBS-TV, c1949; worked Blue Mirror Club, Washington, DC, 1949; app in show THE MEMBER OF THE WEDDING, Empire Theater, NYC, 1950-1, then toured into 1952; app as lead in series BEULAH, ABC-TV, 1950-1; app in command performance show ANTA ALBUM, Ziegfeld Theater, NYC, 1950; worked Capitol Theater, NYC, 1951; app in BLACK BOTTOM REVUE, unknown theater, NYC, 1952; app in HEAT WAVE Revue, unknown theater, NYC, 1952; worked Apollo Theater, NYC, 1952; La Vie en Rose, NYC, 1952; app in film THE MEMBER OF THE WEDDING, 1953; frequently toured in various stock companies of show THE MEMBER OF THE WEDDING working theaters across US from 1953; app on AMERICAN INVENTORY, NBC-TV, 1953; contributed article to *NY Herald Tribune* newspaper, 1953; app in one-woman recital AT HOME WITH ETHEL WATERS, 48th Street Theater, NYC, 1953 (later changing title to AN EVENING WITH ETHEL WATERS) then touring frequently across US/Canada working theater concerts into 60s; frequently app on Tex & Jinx CLOSE UP Show, WNBT-TV, NYC (NBC-Network), 1954-7; app in pre-Broadway tryout of show GENTLE FOLK, 1955; app in film CARIB GOLD, 1955; app in FAVORITE PLAYHOUSE (ep: Speaking to Hannah), CBS-TV, 1955; app on CLIMAX (ep: The Dance), CBS-TV, 1955; app on GENERAL ELECTRIC THEATER (ep: Winner by Decision), CBS-TV, 1955; app on PLAYWRIGHTS 56 (ep: Sound and the Fury), NBC-TV, 1955; app on Steve Allen's TONIGHT Show, NBC-TV, 1956; worked Le Ruban Bleu, NYC, 1956; The Boulevard, Queens, NY, 1956; app in film THE HEART IS A REBEL, 1956; app in summer stock show THE VOICE OF STRANGERS, Ivy Tower Playhouse, Spring Lake, NJ, 1956; app w Thornton Wilder in two one-act plays BERNICE/THE HAPPY JOURNEY TO TRENTON AND CAMDEN, Congress Hall Theater, Berlin, Ger, 1957; app on MATINEE THEATER (ep: Sing for Me), NBC-TV, 1957; rec in concert, Evergreen label, NYC, 1957; worked in choir of Billy Graham Youth for Christ Crusade (an Evangelist religious meet), Madison Square Garden, NYC, 1957 (por shown syndicated TV); rec w Paul Mickelson Orch/Choir, Word label, NYC, 1957; app on TENNESSEE ERNIE FORD Show, NBC-TV, 1957; frequently app on BREAK THE $250,000 BANK game show, NBC-TV, c1958; app in film THE SOUND AND THE FURY, 1959; app on MIKE WALLACE INTERVIEWS, WNTA-TV, NYC, 1959; app on ONE NIGHT STAND, WNTA-TV, NYC, 1959; app in own AN EVENING WITH ETHEL WATERS recital, Renata Theater, NYC, 1959; app on ROUTE 66 Show (ep: Goodnight Sweet Blues), CBS-TV, 1961; worked Crossroads Club, Detroit, MI, 1962; app on ED SULLIVAN SHOW, CBS-TV, 1963; app on GREAT ADVENTURES (ep: Go Down Moses), CBS-TV, 1963 (rel as film HARRIET TUBMAN AND THE UNDERGROUND RAILROAD); app in stock company show THE MEMBER OF THE WEDDING, Pasadena Playhouse, Pasadena, CA, 1964; worked New York World's Fair, Queens, NY, 1964; worked Billy Graham Hawaiian Crusade, Honolulu, HI, 1965 (por shown syndicated TV); w Billy Graham Greenville-Southern Piedmont Crusade, Greenville, SC, 1966 (por shown syndicated TV); w Billy Graham London Crusade, London, Eng, 1966 (por shown syndicated TV); app w Pearl Bailey, SOMETHING SPECIAL Show, WOR-TV, NYC (syndicated), 1966; app on VACATION PLAYHOUSE, CBS-TV, 1966; app on national TV commercial for Jello (dessert) products, 1967; worked Billy Graham Canadian Centennial Crusade, Winnipeg, Can, 1967 (por shown on syndicated TV); app on JOEY BISHOP Show, ABC-TV, 1967; clip shown in film THE NEGRO IN ENTERTAINMENT, 1968; app on HOLLYWOOD PALACE Show, ABC-TV, 1969; worked Billy Graham New York Crusade, Madison Square Garden, NYC, 1969 (por shown syndicated TV); w Billy

Graham Southern California Crusade, Anaheim, CA, 1969 (por shown syndicated TV); app in stock company show THE MEMBER OF THE WEDDING, Ivanhoe Theater, Chicago, IL, 1970, then brief tour; app on DANIEL BOONE SHOW (ep: Mama Cooper), NBC-TV, 1970; app on DELLA, WOR-TV, NYC (syndicated), 1970; worked w Billy Graham New York Crusade, Shea Stadium, NYC, 1970 (por shown syndicated TV); w Billy Graham Louisiana Crusade, Louisiana State Univ, Baton Rouge, LA, 1970 (por shown syndicated TV); w Billy Graham Kentucky Crusade, Lexington, KY, 1971 (por shown syndicated TV); sang at Sunday Worship Service for President Richard M Nixon at The White House, Washington, DC, 1971; worked w Billy Graham Northern California Crusade, The Coliseum, Oakland, CA, 1971 (por shown syndicated TV); app on PEARL BAILEY Show, ABC-TV, 1971; worked w Billy Graham Greater Chicago Crusade, McCormick Place, Chicago, IL, 1972 (por shown syndicated TV); app on DICK CAVETT Show, ABC-TV, 1972; app on MIKE DOUGLAS Show, CBS-TV, 1972; app on MERV GRIFFIN Show, WNEW-TV, NYC (syndicated), 1972; worked w Billy Graham Alabama Crusade, Birmingham, AL, 1972 (por shown syndicated TV); w Billy Graham Northern Ohio Crusade, Cleveland, OH, 1972 (por shown syndicated TV); app on Johnny Carson's TONIGHT Show, NBC-TV, 1972; app on OWEN MARSHALL, COUNSELOR AT LAW (ep: Run Carol Run), ABC-TV, 1972; mostly inactive due to poor health from 1972; worked w Billy Graham New York Crusade, NYC, 1974 (por shown syndicated TV); w Billy Graham Mississippi Crusade, Jackson, MS, 1975 (por shown syndicated TV); app on DINAH! Show, CBS-TV, 1976; worked w Billy Graham Southern California Crusade, San Diego, CA, 1976 (por shown syndicated TV); died at home of kidney failure and cancer; buried Forest Lawn Memorial Park Cemetery, Glendale, CA

Personal: Married Merritt "Buddy" Pernsley (c1909-10); Clyde Edward Matthews (c1928-34). Was VP of Negro Actors Guild of America (1942-43). Not to be confused with Martha Pryor, a white vaudeville singer of the 20s

Billings: America's Foremost Ebony Comedienne/The Ebony Nora Bayes/The Original Dinah/Sweet Mama Stringbean Direct from St Louis

Books: *His Eye Is on the Sparrow,* Ethel Waters/Charles Samuels, Doubleday & Company, Inc, 1951

Ethel Waters, Finally Home, Julian DeKorte, FH Revell Co, 1978

To Me It's Wonderful, Ethel Waters, Harper & Row, 1972

Songs: Chinese Blues/Ethel Sings 'Em/Go Back Where You Stayed Last Night/Kind Lovin' Blues/ Maybe Not at All/Satisfyin' Papa/Stop Myself from Worrying over You/Tell 'em 'Bout Me/You'll Want Me Back

Awards/Honors: Reportedly first professional Negro female singer to appear on radio, Apr 21, 1922

Was first Negro woman to star as single at Palace Theater, NYC, 1925

Appeared in "first dialogue motion picture in natural colors" (ON WITH THE SHOW), 1929

Was first Negro woman to star in commercial network radio show, 1933

Awarded Silver Loving Cup by Popular Song Association for first singer to introduce 50 songs that became hits, 1933

Was first Negro woman to star on Broadway in dramatic play (MAMBA'S DAUGHTERS), 1939

Reportedly first Negro singer to appear on television, 1939

Awarded Negro Actors Guild of America plaque for dramatic achievement for her performance in film PINKY, 1949

Nominated for Academy of Motion Picture Arts & Sciences Award for best supporting actress in film PINKY, 1949

The show THE MEMBER OF THE WEDDING won New York Drama Critics Award for Best American Play for 1949-50 season

Won New York Drama Critics Award for best actress in show THE MEMBER OF THE WEDDING, 1950

Honored by Chamber of Commerce, Boston, MA, as one of America's 20 most distinguished women of achievement, 1951

Awarded Tamiment Institute Award for outstanding literary work for book *His Eye Is On The Sparrow,* 1951

Awarded St Genesius Medal (Patron Saint of Actors) by American National Theater & Academy (ANTA), 1951

An Ethel Waters Day was proclaimed by Mayor Impelliteri, New York, NY, 1953

Nominated for Academy of Motion Picture Acts & Sciences Award for Best Supporting Actress in film THE MEMBER OF THE WEDDING, 1953

An Ethel Waters Day was proclaimed by The New York World's Fair, Queens, NY, 1964

Awarded The Joseph Jefferson Award for her performance in show THE MEMBER OF THE WEDDING, Chicago, IL, 1970

An Ethel Waters Day was proclaimed by her home town, Chester, PA, 1972

Introduced many songs including "St Louis Blues" (1917); "Dinah" (1924); "Am I Blue?" (1929); "Stormy Weather" (1933)

Infl by: Louis Armstrong

Infl to: Mildred Bailey/Thelma Carpenter/Lena Horne/Miss Rhapsody/Maxine Sullivan

Quotes: "Along with Bessie Smith and Louis Armstrong, she was a fountainhead of all that is finest and most distinctive in American popular singing"—Henry Pleasants, *The Great American Popular Singers*, Simon & Schuster, 1974

"Ethel Waters—in her time a blues singer, a jazz singer, a music hall singer and in 1938/9 probably the best band singer"—John Norris, *Coda* Magazine (Canada), Mar 1974, p 16

". . . Ethel Waters could pour all her own memories of grief, sorrow and loneliness [into her songs] and make them unforgettable vignettes of great dramatic intensity"—Langston Hughes, *Famous Negro Music Makers*, Dodd, Mead & Company, 1955

References: His Eye Is on the Sparrow, Ethel Waters/Charles Samuels, Doubleday & Company Inc, 1951

To Me It's Wonderful, Ethel Waters, Harper & Row, 1972

The Great American Popular Singers, Henry Pleasants, Simon & Schuster, 1974

WATERS, MUDDY
(see Morganfield, McKinley)

WATERS JR, MUDDY
(see Buford, George)

WATSON, JOHNNY *"Guitar"*
Born: Feb 3, 1935, Houston (Harris Co), TX
Inst: Alto Sax/Guitar/Piano

Father John Watson Sr was a pianist; mother was Wilma ———; born John Watson; interested in music early, learning piano from father as youth; moved to Los Angeles, CA, c1950, where he frequently entered

Photo by Norbert Hess. Courtesy Living Blues Magazine

many local talent shows/contests/shows in area into 50s; worked frequently as sideman in Chuck Higgins Band/Joe Houston Band/Jay McNeely Band/others in local club dates, Los Angeles, CA, area, early 50s; rec w Chuck Higgins and His Mellotones, Combo label, Los Angeles, c1952; rec (as "Young John Watson") w Amos Milburn Band, Federal label, Los Angeles, 1953-4; rec RPM label, Los Angeles, 1954-6; rec w Bumps Blackwell Orch, Keen label, Los Angeles, 1957; rec on small local labels in Los Angeles through late 50s; rec King label, Los Angeles, 1961; teamed w Larry Williams to tour club dates frequently from 1964; toured w Larry Williams on rock/soul package show working concerts through England, 1965; rec w Larry Williams, Decca label, London, Eng, 1965; frequently worked local gigs in Los Angeles area through 60s into 70s; T-Bone Walker Memorial Concert, Musicians Union Hall, Los Angeles, 1975; worked Howard's Place, Oakland, CA, 1975; toured w Rhythm & Blues: Roots of Rock Show working concerts through Europe, 1975; worked Ratso's, Chicago, 1976; The Place, Los Angeles, 1976; Community Center, Berkeley, CA, 1976; rec DJM label, Los Angeles, 1976; toured w own Watsonian Institute group on Euro-Tour 76 working concerts through England/Europe, 1976; app on HONKY TONK Show, BBC-radio, London, Eng, 1976; worked The Roxy, Los Angeles, 1977; app on MERV GRIFFIN Show,

WNEW-TV, NYC, 1977; worked Shea's Theater, Buffalo, NY, 1977; Music Hall, Houston, TX, 1977; The Amphitheater, Chicago, IL, 1977; Wings Stadium, Kalamazoo, MI, 1977; Cobo Arena, Detroit, MI, 1977

Personal: Not to be confused with Johnny Watson (Daddy Stovepipe). Cousin of Little Frankie Lee

Songs: Gangster of Love/Three Hours Past Midnight

Infl by: Aaron "T-Bone" Walker

Infl to: Jimi Hendrix

WATSON, JOHNNY *"Jimmy"*
(*aka:* Daddy Stovepipe/Rev Alfred Pitts/Sunny Jim)

Photo by Ray Flerlage (Kinnara Collection). Courtesy Sing Out Magazine

Born: Apr 12, 1867, Mobile (Mobile Co), AL
Died: Nov 1, 1963, Chicago, IL
Inst: Guitar/Harmonica/Jug/Kazoo

Born/raised in Mobile, AL, and frequently worked outside music as youth; frequently toured in Rabbit Foot Minstrels and other minstrel/medicine shows working as entertainer through South through 1910; formed one-man band to work streets for tips in Memphis, TN/Chicago, IL/elsewhere into 20s; rec Gennett label, Richmond, IN, 1924; rec w Whistlin' Pete, Gennett label, Birmingham, AL, 1927; continued working streets for tips through 20s into 30s; rec w Mississippi Sarah, Vocalion label, Chicago, 1931; rec Bluebird label, Chicago, 1935; worked outside music, Greenville, MS, 1935-7; continued working streets for tips through South/Southwest/Mexico through 30s; frequently worked in local Zydeco Bands in Galveston/Houston, TX, area into 40s; worked mostly outside music in Delta area, MS, through 40s; moved to Chicago, IL, 1948; worked outside music with frequent work on Maxwell Street for tips, Chicago, 1948 into 60s; rec Heritage label, Chicago, 1960; rec 77 label, Chicago, 1961; frequently worked as "Rev Alfred Pitts" (singing gospel music), Maxwell Street, Chicago, into 60s; worked Fickle Pickle, Chicago, 1963; entered Cook County Hospital where he was operated on for gall bladder problem but died of bronchopneumonia; buried Restvale Cemetery, Worth, IL

Personal: Married "Mississippi" Sarah ——— (late 20s?). Named "Daddy Stovepipe" due to his usual dress of embroidered waistcoat with gold epaulettes and a silk top hat. Not to be confused with "Sweet Papa Stovepipe" McKinley Peebles (born 1897), a New York street singer. Not to be confused with Johnny "Guitar" Watson, blues singer

Reference: Nothing But the Blues, Mike Leadbitter, Hanover Books, 1971

WATTS, LOUIS THOMAS *"Lou"*
(*aka:* Tommy Lewis/Tommy Louis/Kid Thomas)
Born: Jun 20, 1934, Sturgis (Oktibbeha Co), MS
Died: Apr 13, 1970, Beverly Hills, CA
Inst: Drums/Harmonica

Father was VT Watts; mother was Virgie Coleman; moved to Chicago, IL, to work outside music from 1941; learned harmonica from Little Willie Smith and frequently worked bars/clubs, Chicago, late 40s; frequently worked Cadillac Baby's, Chicago, 1949-55; frequently sat-in w Little Walter/Muddy Waters/Elmore James/Bo Diddley/others in local clubs, Chicago, through mid-50s; rec Federal label, Chicago, 1955; worked local club dates, Wichita, KS, 1956-8; rec TRC label, Los Angeles, CA, 1957; frequently toured small club dates from Denver, CO, through southern California, 1958-60; settled in Los Angeles, CA, to work outside music with frequent after-hour club dates/beer joints/private parties from

1960; rec w Rhythm Rockers, Muriel label, Los Angeles, c1962; worked Cozy Lounge, Los Angeles, 1969-70; rec Cenco label, Los Angeles, 1970; while driving through Beverly Hills, CA, was involved in accident that killed local boy; manslaughter charges were later dismissed and father of dead child shot him; DOA UCLA Medical Center, West Los Angeles; buried Woodlawn Memorial Park, Los Angeles, CA

Personal: Married Linda Dickson. Not to be confused with Kid Thomas Valentine, jazz musician

Quote: "He can make his harp sound like a horn one second and an organ the next; this, along with his flexible but strong vocal style make him one of the most promising blues artists on the Coast"—Darryl Stolper, *Blues Unlimited* magazine (UK), May 1970, p 9

References: Blues Unlimited magazine (UK), May 1970, pp 7-9
Blues Unlimited magazine (UK), Nov 1970, p 20

WEAVER, *"Blind"* CURLEY JAMES

(*aka:* Slim Gordon)
Born: Mar 25, 1906, Covington (Newton Co), GA
Died: Sept 20, 1962, Covington, GA
Inst: Guitar

Father was James Weaver; mother was Savanah Shepard, a musician; moved to Tom Brown's farm outside Porterdale, GA, where he was raised from childhood; learned guitar c1922; moved to Atlanta, GA, 1925; frequently worked outside music, Atlanta, from 1925; rec Columbia label, Atlanta, 1928; rec w Eddie Mapp, QRS label, Long Island City, NY, 1929; frequently worked w Buddy Moss/Eddie Anthony/Slim Kirkpatrick in local gigs, Atlanta area, into 30s; rec w Clarence Moore, OKeh label, Atlanta, 1931; rec Banner label, NYC, 1933; rec w Georgia Brown's group, Banner label, NYC, 1933; rec ARC label group, NYC, 1933; rec w Blind Willie McTell, Decca/Champion labels, Chicago, IL, 1935; frequently worked w Willie McTell at Pig 'n' Whistle food stand, Atlanta, late 30s; frequently toured w Willie McTell working clubs through Tennessee/Alabama, late 30s; continued outside music work, Atlanta, into 40s/50s; rec w Blind Willie McTell, Regal/Sittin' In With labels, Atlanta, 1949; frequently worked w Buddy Moss in local gigs, Atlanta, from 1951; due to childhood eye illness suffered complete blindness, 1959; moved to Almon, GA, late 50s; entered Newton County Hospital where he died of uremia; buried Springfield Baptist Church Cemetery, Covington, GA

Personal: Reportedly married. Had daughter

Infl by: Kokomo Arnold/Blind Boy Fuller/Charlie Hicks/Robert Hicks

Quote: "Curley James Weaver was one of the coterie of blues-singers from the Atlanta area who seemingly bridged the gap between the early and the more recent, more 'Piedmont' guitar styles"—Peter Lowry, *Blues Unlimited* magazine (UK), Jul 1972, p 13

Reference: Blues Unlimited magazine (UK), Jul 1972, p 13

WEBB, *"Boogie"* BILL

(*aka:* Boogie Bill)

Photo by Hans Andreasson. Courtesy John Broven

Born: 1924, Jackson (Hinds Co), MS
Died: Aug 23, 1990, New Orleans, LA
Inst: Guitar

Mother was Julia May ____ ; to New Orleans, LA as youth, learning guitar from Roosevelt Holts; returned to Jackson, MS, to work local jukes in area from 1942; frequently worked w Tommy Johnson/Ishmon Bracey/Bubba Brown/others in Jackson area through 40s; app in film short THE JACKSON JIVE, 1948; worked w Chuck Berry in local club dates, late 40s; returned to New Orleans, early 50s; worked w Fats Domino Band in local gigs, New Orleans, 1953;

rec Imperial label, New Orleans, 1953; worked outside music with occasional local gigs, New Orleans, late 50s; moved to Chicago, IL, to work local houseparties into 60s; frequently sat-in w Muddy Waters/John Lee Hooker/others in club dates, Chicago area, through early 60s; returned to New Orleans to work outside music with occasional local club dates from mid-60s; rec Decca-Rounder label, New Orleans, 1966; rec Flyright label, New Orleans, 1969; rec w Roosevelt Holts, Bluesman/Arhoolie labels, Bogalusa, LA; 1970-1; local gigs in New Orleans area into 80s; Jazz & Heritage Fest, New Orleans, 1984; rec Flying Fish label, New Orleans (?), 1989

Songs: I Ain't for It/Love Me Mama

Infl by: Bubba Brown/Tommy Johnson

Quote: "He has a fantastic repertoire, ranging from old Tommy Johnson numbers through R&B and rock"—David Evans, *Blues Unlimited* magazine (UK), Nov 1968, p 14

References: Blues Unlimited magazine (UK), Dec 1972/Jan 1973
Blues Unlimited (UK), Nov 1968, p 14

WEBSTER, KATIE
Born: Jan 9, 1939, Houston (Harris Co), TX
Inst: Harmonica/Organ/Piano

Father Cryus Thorne; mother Myrtle Connely; born Kathryn Thorne; worked Ruby's Club Vegas, Dallas, TX, 1957; Harmony Club, Dallas, 1957; Club Raven, Beaumont, TX, 1958; Manhattan Club, Houston, 1958; moved to Lake Charles, LA, 1959; worked w Ashton Savoy Band working local club dates, Lake Charles, from 1959; rec w Ashton Savoy Comb, Hollywood label, Lake Charles, c1959; rec w Ashton Savoy Combo, Storyville label, Lake Charles, 1959; rec w Ashton Savoy Combo, Kry label, Crowley, LA, 1959; frequently rec as session musician for Lonesome Sundown/Slim Harpo/others on local labels, Crowley, 1959 into 60s; rec under own name, Rocko/Action/Spot/Zynn labels, Crowley, c1961; toured w Otis Redding show working concerts through South, mid-60s; rec w Rockin' Sydney, Jin label, Ville Platte, LA, 1963-4; rec w Rockin' Sydney, Goldband label, Lake Charles, 1965-6; worked Casa Blanca Club, New Iberia, LA, 1966; formed own band working Bamboo Club, Lake Charles, c1968; Rico's Lounge, Baton Rouge, LA, c1968; King's Black & Gold Club, Monroe, LA, c1968; mostly inactive in music in Lake Charles into 70s; worked dates in Kinder, LA, 1974

Quote: "Katie Webster is an honest, well-piped singer whose tastes run to blues, Rhythm & Blues, rock and roll and country music."—Bill Shoemaker, *Cadence* magazine, Nov 1980, p 62

Reference: Nothing But the Blues, Mike Leadbitter, Hanover Books, 1971

WEBSTER, MAMIE
(see Smith, Mabel)

WELDON, WILL *"Casey Bill"/"Kansas City Bill"*
(*aka:* Levee Joe)
Born: Jul 10, 1909, Pine Bluff (Jefferson Co), AR
Died: (unknown)
Inst: Guitar

Reportedly frequently worked in various medicine shows through South during 20s; rec Victor label, Atlanta, GA, 1927; rec w Memphis Jug Band, Victor label, Memphis, TN, 1927; rec w Charlie Burse/Picaninny Jug Band, Champion label, Richmond, IN, 1932; reportedly worked outside music, Kansas City, MO, through 30s; rec Vocalion label, Chicago, IL, 1935-7; rec Bluebird label, Chicago, 1935-6; rec w Brown Bombers of Swing, Vocalion label, Chicago, 1937; rec Bluebird label, Aurora, IL, 1938; moved to West Coast where he reportedly rec ST for films through 40s; reportedly settled in Detroit, MI, to work outside music into 60s; whereabouts unknown thereafter; may be deceased

Personal: Married Lizzie Douglas (Memphis Minnie) (1920s). "Casey" is contraction of "KC" (Kansas City)

Billing: The Hawaiian Guitar Wizard

Songs: How Can You Love Me?/I'm Gonna Move to the Outskirts of Town/Somebody's Got to Go

Infl by: Peetie Wheatstraw

Quote: "Although Weldon's singing is in the familiar mode of Bill Broonzy, Jazz Gillum and Washboard Sam, his arrangements are unique in blues"—Stephen Calt, Yazoo album 1949

WELLS, AMOS *"Little Junior"/"Junior"*
Born: Dec 9, 1934, Memphis (Shelby Co), TN
Inst: Harmonica

Grandmother was gospel singer; born Amos Blackmore in John Gaston Hospital and raised in

Courtesy Sheldon Harris Collection

West Memphis/Marion, AR, area from infancy; interested in music early and taught self harmonica to work streets for tips, West Memphis, AR, from c1941; moved to Chicago, IL, to work outside music, 1946 through late 40s; sat-in w Tampa Red, C&T Lounge, Chicago, IL, 1948; together w Dave Myers/Louis Myers formed The Little Boys group working C&T Lounge, Chicago, 1948; renamed group The Three Deuces and worked local clubs, Chicago, 1948; w Muddy Waters, Ebony Lounge, Chicago, c1949; renamed group Three Aces to work local clubs, Chicago, c1949; renamed group The Four Aces working Brookmont Hotel/Miss King's/others, Chicago, 1949-52; replaced Little Walter in Muddy Waters Band working local club dates, Chicago, 1952-3; frequently w Memphis Slim Band in local clubs, Chicago, 1953; rec w Eagle Rockers, States label, Chicago, 1953-4; worked Bodega Club, Chicago, 1953; served in US Army, 1953-5; rec w Muddy Waters Band, Chess label, Chicago, c1954; worked briefly w Muddy Waters Band in local clubs, Chicago, 1955; reformed own The Three Aces working Du Drop Inn, Chicago, c1956; Brookmont Hotel, Chicago, c1957; toured w Three Aces working club dates across US, late 50s; worked Blue Flame Club, Chicago, 1958; frequently worked Pepper's Lounge, Chicago, 1958-72; w Buddy Guy, Theresa's Lounge, Chicago, 1958; toured almost continuously w Buddy Guy thereafter into 60s; worked State Univ of New York, Buffalo, NY, 1959; rec Shad/Profile labels, NYC/Chicago, 1959; rec Chief label, Chicago, 1959-61; worked McKie's Lounge, Chicago, 1959; rec w Buddy Guy, Chess label, Chicago, 1960-1; frequently worked Theresa's Lounge, Chicago, 1963-76 (por 1975 date remote on WXRT-radio); Mr Lee's Lounge, Chicago, 1963; rec USA label, Chicago, 1963; worked w own band, Univ of Chicago Folk Festival, Mandel Hall, Chicago, 1963; Swarthmore Col Folk Festival, Swarthmore, PA, 1965; Big John's, Chicago, 1965; Just Me Lounge, Chicago, 1965; rec w Buddy Guy, Vanguard label, Chicago, 1965; worked Univ of Chicago, Chicago, 1966; app on local TV shows, Chicago, 1966; toured w American Folk Blues Festival working concerts/one-nighters/TV dates through England/Europe, 1966 (por Berlin, Ger, date rel Fontana/Amiga labels); toured college circuit working concert dates through Midwest, 1966; worked Philadelphia Folk Festival, Schwenksville, PA, 1966-7; Second Fret, Philadelphia, 1966; Club 47, Boston, MA, 1966; Cafe A-Go-Go, NYC, 1966-8; Ash Grove, Los Angeles, CA, 1966; rec Delmark label, Chicago, 1966; worked w Buddy Guy, Pepper's Lounge, Chicago, 1966-8 (por rel Vanguard label); rec Vanguard label, Chicago, 1967; worked The Riverboat, Toronto, Can, 1967-8; Rheingold Central Park Music Festival, NYC, 1967; app on local TV shows, Boston, MA, 1967; worked New Penelope, Montreal, Can, 1967; Expo '67, Montreal, Can, 1967; toured for US State Department working concert dates through Africa, 1967-8; rec w Buddy Guy, Atlantic label, Chicago, c1968; worked Electric Factory, Philadelphia, PA, 1968; toured West Coast working club dates, 1968; worked Retinal Circus, Vancouver, Can, 1968; Newport Folk Festival, Newport, RI, 1968; Blue Flame Lounge, Chicago, 1968-70; Auditorium Theater, Chicago, 1969; toured for US State Department working concert dates through Far East, 1969; worked Kinetic Playground, Chicago, 1969; The Pavilion, NYC, 1969; Chicago Blues Festival, Chicago, 1969; Ann Arbor Blues Festival, Ann Arbor, MI, 1969-70; Main Point, Bryn Mawr, PA, 1969; worked w Canned Heat group, Bath Festival, Bristol, Eng, 1970; toured w The Rolling Stones group working concert dates through Europe, 1970; rec w Memphis Slim, Barclay label, Herouville, France, 1970; worked Palais des Sports, Paris, France, 1970; rec Atco label, Miami, FL, 1970; rec w Buddy Guy, Delmark label, Chicago, c1970; worked Fillmore East, NYC, 1970; Washington Blues

Festival, Howard Univ, Washington, DC, 1970; app in Harley Cokliss UK film CHICAGO BLUES, 1970 (shown on OMNIBUS, BBC-1-TV, London, Eng); worked Notre Dame Blues Festival, South Bend, IN, 1971; toured US working club/concert dates, 1971; worked Golden Bear, Huntington Beach, CA, c1971 (por rel Blue Rock label); Sweet Queen Bee's Lounge, Chicago, 1972-5; Mr M's, Chicago, 1972; film clip shown in French film BLUES UNDER THE SKIN, 1972; app in French film OUT OF THE BLACKS INTO THE BLUES (pt. 2: A Way to Escape the Ghetto), 1972; worked Univ of Vermont, Burlington, VT, 1972; toured w American Blues Festival working concert dates through Australia, 1972; worked Felt Forum, Madison Square Garden, NYC, 1973; El Mocambo Tavern, Toronto, Can, 1973; Keystone Korner, Berkeley, CA, 1973-4; Minnie's Can Do, San Francisco, c1973; Sandy's Club, Beverly, MA, 1973-4; Hunter Col, NYC, 1973-4; app on SOUNDSTAGE, PBS-TV, 1974-5; worked Montreux Blues Festival, Montreux, Switzerland, 1974; Newport Jazz Festival, NYC, 1974; Sports Arena, Toledo, OH, 1974; Toronto Blues Festival, Olympic Island, Toronto, Can, 1974; rec Delmark label, Chicago, 1974; worked Peyton Place Club, Chicago, 1974-6; Checkerboard Lounge, Chicago, 1974-6; Joint Bar, Minneapolis, MN, 1974; Vibes Lounge, Chicago, 1974; Univ of Miami Blues Festival, Coral Gables, FL, 1975; Univ of North Florida, Jacksonville, FL, 1975; toured w blues package show working concert dates through Japan, 1975; worked Yubin Chokin Hall, Tokyo, Japan, 1975 (por rel Bourbon label); worked Civic Auditorium, Portland, OR, 1975; Univ of Vermont, Burlington, VT, 1975; In Concert Club, Montreal, Can, 1975; Great American Music Hall, San Francisco, 1976; El Mocambo, Toronto, Can, 1976; Belle Star, Colden, NY, 1976-7; New England Blues Festival, Providence, RI, 1976; Jazz Life Festival, Dortmund, Ger, 1976; Bottom Line, NYC, 1976; Opry Club, Burlington, VT, 1977; Sandy's Jazz Revival, Beverly, MA, 1977; The Lighthouse, Los Angeles, CA, 1977; Theresa's, Chicago, IL, 1977; Nancy Jazz Festival, Nancy, France, 1977; Cafe Campus, Montreal, Can, 1978; Bottom Line, NYC, 1978

Personal: Married Zearline McBeck (1955-)

Billing: The Little Giant of the Blues

Songs: A Poor Man's Plea/All Night Long/Blues for Mayor Daley/Cha Cha Cha in Blue/Come On in This House/Country Girl/Everything's Going to Be Alright/Have Mercy Baby/Hoodoo Man/In the Wee Wee Hours/It's My Life Baby/It's So Sad to Be Lonely/Lawdy, Lawdy/Little by Little/Look How Baby/Shake It Baby/Ships on the Ocean/Slow Slow/Snatch It Back and Hold It/So Tired/Stomach Ache/Tomorrow Night/Vietcong Blues/We're Ready/You Lied to Me

Awards/Honors: Won JAY Award from *Jazz* magazine for best blues album of 1966 ("Hoodoo Man Blues," Delmark DL-612)

Won *Downbeat* magazine International Poll for Rock-Pop-Blues group deserving wider recognition, 1968

Infl by: Howlin' Wolf/Junior Parker/Muddy Waters/John Lee "Sonny Boy" Williamson/Sonny Boy Williamson (Alex Miller)

Infl to: Billy Boy Arnold/Paul Butterfield/Johnny Mars/Chicago Bob Nelson/Charles Musselwhite/Junior Parker/Piazza & Company/Fenton Robinson

Quotes: "Junior is a forceful singer with a resonant voice, whose declamatory style and complete involvement with his material translate into a commanding stage presence"—Roy Greenberg, *Living Blues* magazine, Mar 1977, p 29

"Junior Wells is a spunky little ball of energy who keeps the Chicago blues scene alive with his fiery harp . . . he is an excellent exponent of the funky Chicago blues sound"—Alex Cramer, *Coda* magazine (Canada), May 1975, p 6

References: *Coda* magazine (Canada), May 1975, pp 6-8

Delmark album DL-612

WELLS, VIOLA GERTRUDE

(aka: Miss Rhapsody/Viola Underhill)
Born: Dec 14, 1902, Newark (Essex Co), NJ
Died: Dec 22, 1984, Belleville, NJ

Father was Earl Henry Wells; mother was Roberta Olivia Simmons; moved to Surry, VA, c1906-10; returned to Newark, NJ, where she was raised from 1910; frequently sang in local church choirs, Newark area, into 20s; frequently worked local amateur shows/parties, Newark, from early 20s; worked theater dates in Washington, DC/Atlantic City, NJ, late 20s; worked Mack's, Atlantic City, 1932; Subway Grill, Chester, Pa, 1933-4; Liberty Club, South Chester, Pa, 1933-4; Mickey Mouse Club, Philadelphia, PA, 1934-5; Cotton Club, Trenton, NJ, 1935; Chinchilly Club, Scranton, PA, 1936; Ike Dixon's Comedy Club, Baltimore, MD, 1936; toured w Banjo Bernie group working

Courtesy Viola Wells

theaters/clubs through Southeast, 1936-7; toured w Mighty Sheesley Carnival show, 1937; toured w Ida Cox Harlem Strutters working theater dates on TOBA circuit, 1937; worked (as singer/producer) Sunset Crystal Palace/The Spinning Wheel, Kansas City, MO, 1937-8; frequently worked The Nest Club/ Fisher's Tavern/Boston Plaza/Kit Kat Club/Chantalier Club, Newark, NJ, 1938-9; w Bunny Berigan Orch, Apollo Theater, NYC, 1939; w Bill Doggett Orch, Club Sudan, NYC, 1939; frequently worked w Charlie Barnet Orch/Earl Robinson Orch/others, NYC area, 1939-40; w Claude Hopkins Orch, Apollo Theater, NYC, 1940; Cafe Society Downtown, NYC, 1940; Small's Paradise, NYC, 1940; app frequently on SHEEP & GOAT CLUB, WOR-radio series, NYC, 1940; worked New Deal Club, Asbury Park, NJ, 1940-1; Rockhead's Paradise, Montreal, Can, 1940; frequently worked w Art Tatum/Benny Carter/others, Kelly's Stable, NYC, 1940-3; w Count Basie Orch at President Franklin Roosevelt Inaugural Ball, Washington, DC, 1940; w Erskine Hawkins Orch, Apollo Theater, NYC, 1941-2; Kinney Club, Newark, NJ, 1941; Omega Bar, Roselle, NJ, 1942-3; Hide-A-Way, Newark, NJ, 1942; Crystal Caverns, Washington, DC, 1943; toured w Willie Bryant group on USO package show working US military bases through Europe, early 40s; worked Empire Theater, Newark, 1944; rec w Jay Cole Band, Savoy label, NYC, 1944-5; worked Brown Derby, Chattanooga, TN, 1945; Blue Grass Club, Cleveland, OH, 1945; Club 666, Detroit, MI, 1945; Melody Club, Newark, 1945; Twinlite Club, Newark, 1945; w own Sportsmen of Rhythm group in DIXIE TO HARLEM Revue, Fans Theater, Philadelphia, PA, 1945; worked Big Track Club, Norfolk, VA, 1945; Gamby's, Baltimore, MD, 1946; Dodgers Grill, Newark, 1946; Three Towers, South Somerville, NJ, 1946; app as DJ on MISS RHAPSODY & THREE SPORTSMEN OF RHYTHM, WFTC-radio, Kinston, NC, 1946-7; worked Cafe Superior, Newark, 1947; Baby Grand, NYC, 1947; worked mostly outside music (as owner/manager of restaurant), Newark, 1947 through 50s; worked Club Caravan, Newark, 1950; Pitt's Place, Newark, early 60s; Valley Inn, West Orange, NJ, early 60s; continued outside music work through 60s; rec unissued test, Columbia label, NYC, 1965; rec Spivey label, Brooklyn, NY, c1965; worked frequent concert dates, International Center, NYC, 1968-74; Golden Nugget, Elizabeth, NJ, 1968; occasional club/concert/benefit work in Newark/NYC area into 70s; rec Saydisc-Matchbox label, NYC, 1972; app on JOE FRANKLIN Show, WOR-TV, NYC, 1973; rec 400 W 150 label, NYC, 1973; app w Clyde Bernhardt Band, WBAI-FM-radio, NYC, 1975; app six-part bio TV documentary in Paris, France, 1975; w Bernhardt Band, Connecticut Traditional Jazz Club concert, Meriden, CT, 1975; Harbor Island Park, Mamaroneck, NY, 1975-6; rec 400 W 150 label, NYC, 1975; worked Jazz Vespers, United Presbyterian Church, Newark, 1975; rec w Clyde Bernhardt and the Harlem Blues and Jazz Band, Barron label, NYC, 1975; worked Emelin Theater, Mamaroneck, NY, 1976/8; Nassau Community Col, Garden City, NY, 1976-7; app on PHIL SCHAAP Show, WKCR-radio, NYC, 1976; toured w Harlem Blues and Jazz Band working concerts/ dances/clubs/radio through Eng/Europe, 1976-81; app THE GOOD DAY Show, WCVB-TV, Needham, MA, 1978; worked colleges/concerts/jazz clubs in NYC-NJ area into 80s; one-year residency at The Ginger Man, NYC, 1981-2; entered Clara Maass Hospital where she died of heart attack; buried Heavenly Rest Cemetery, E Hanover, NJ

Personal: Married Howard Nicholas; married Melvyn Evans. Had one daughter (1934-81). Named "Miss Rhapsody" early in career due to her frequent singing of "Rhapsody in Rhythm" and "Rhapsody in Song"

Songs: Bye Bye Baby/Don't Rush Me Baby/Grooving The Blues/I Fell for You/Long Tall Tan & Terrific/ My Lucky Day

Infl by: Ethel Waters

Infl to: Carrie Smith

Quotes: ". . . one of the finest singers of blues and sacred music in the US"—Albert Vollmer, 400 W 150 album 1

References: Swing City: Newark Night Life, 1925-50, Barbara J Kukla, Temple Univ Press, 1991
Past and Promise: Lives of New Jersey Women, Women's Project of NJ, Scarecrow, 1990

WEST, CHARLES *"Charlie"*
(aka: Poor Charlie)

Photo by Jim O'Neal. Courtesy Living Blues Magazine

Born: Sept 27, 1914, Andalusia (Covington Co), AL
Died: Apr 16, 1976, Chicago, IL
Inst: Piano

Father was Kendrick West; moved to Cincinnati, OH, where he was raised from 1923; frequently worked w Leroy Carr in local joints, Covington, KY, 1926; toured club dates through Ohio, late 20s; settled in Chicago, IL, 1929; frequently worked w Bill Broonzy and others in local club dates, Chicago, through 30s; rec Bluebird label, Aurora, IL, 1937; rec Vocalion label, Chicago, 1937; frequently worked local goodtime houses, Chicago, through 30s into 40s; served in US Army, early 40s; worked mostly outside music with occasional work at parties/gatherings, Chicago, 1947 into 70s; occasionally worked w Carey Bell's group, Chicago, late 60s; w Carey Bell's group, Jo Jo's, Chicago, 1969; suffered heart attack and DOA at Roseland Hospital, buried Burr Oak Cemetery, Worth, IL

Personal: Married. Had children. His daughter Dorothy West married Carey Bell, blues singer

Reference: Blues World magazine (UK), Autumn 1972, p 8

WHEATSTRAW, PEETIE *"Pete"*
(aka: Devil's Son-in-Law)

Courtesy Sheldon Harris Collection

Born: Dec 21, 1902, Ripley (Lauderdale Co), TN
Died: Dec 21, 1941, East St Louis, IL
Inst: Guitar/Piano

Father was James Bunch; mother was Mary Burns; born William Bunch; one of many children; believed raised in Cotton Plant, AR, from childhood; was playing piano/guitar as youth; left home to hobo through southern states from 1927; settled in East St Louis, IL, 1929; frequently worked Lovejoy Club and other clubs/bars, East St Louis area, into 30s; rec Vocalion label, Chicago, IL, 1930-1; rec Bluebird label, Chicago, 1931; rec Vocalion label, NYC, 1932; rec Vocalion label, Chicago, 1934-6; rec Decca label, Chicago/NYC, 1934-41; worked Cabin Inn, St Louis, MO, 1935; frequently worked w Harmon Ray in local clubs, St Louis, with frequent tours south through 30s; rec w Bumble Bee Slim, Decca label, Chicago, 1936; rec w Kokomo Arnold, Decca label, NYC, 1936-7; rec w Lonnie Johnson, Decca label, NYC, 1938-9; together w Big Joe Williams operated/performed at St Louis Club, St Louis, from c1939; suffered fatal injuries in auto accident; buried Growders Cemetery, Cotton Plant, AR

Personal: Married Lizzie ———. His son "Tango" was musician

Billings: Devil's Son-In-Law/High Sheriff from Hell

Books: The Devil's Son-In-Law, Paul Garon, Studio Vista Ltd, 1971

Songs: Bring Me Flowers While I'm Living/C and A Blues/Crazy with the Blues/Don't Hang My Clothes on No Barb Wire Line/Good Whiskey Blues/Jungle Man Blues/Peetie Wheatstraw Stomp/Possum Den Blues/Santa Fe Blues/Sleepness Nights Blues/Throw Me in the Alley

Infl by: Leroy Carr

Infl to: Bill Broonzy/Clarence "Gatemouth" Brown/ Floyd "Dipper Boy" Council/Teddy Darby/Jack Dupree/Jimmy "Peetie Wheatstraw's Brother" Gordon/Andrew "Smokey" Hogg/Robert Nighthawk/Harmon Ray/James Sherill/Johnny Shines/ Sunnyland Slim/Casey Bill Weldon

Quotes: "His style of blues singing was magnetically influential upon all those who came in contact with him or heard his records"—Paul Garon, *The Devil's Son-In-Law,* Studio Vista Ltd, 1971

"One of the most popular blues singers of the thirties . . ."—(Paul Oliver) McCarthy/Morgan/ Oliver/Harrison, *Jazz on Record,* Hanover Books Ltd, 1968

Reference: The Devil's Son-In-Law, Paul Garon, Studio Vista Ltd, 1971

WHITE, BOOKER T WASHINGTON *"Bucca"/ "Bukka"*
(aka: Washington White)

Photo by Julie Snow

Born: Nov 12, 1906, Houston (Chickawaw Co), MS
Died: Feb 26, 1977, Memphis, TN
Inst: Guitar/Harmonica/Piano

Father was John White, a railroad worker who was also a musician; mother was Lula Davison; born/ raised on grandfather Rev Punk Davison's farm outside Houston, MS; one of 7 children; interested in music early and learned guitar from father in 1915; moved to uncle Ben's farm where he worked outside music, Brazell, MS, 1915-20; learned piano c1917; left home to work outside music with frequent work in local honky tonks/pool rooms/barrelhouses, St Louis, MO, from c1921; frequently hoboed through South working local parties/dances/streets/bars through 20s; worked local jukes/bars, Memphis, TN, 1930; rec Victor label, Memphis, 1930; worked outside music with frequent gigs w George "Bullet" Williams at local barrelhouses, West Point, MS, area, 1934-5; frequently worked streets/houseparties, Aberdeen, MS, c1935-7; frequently worked outside music (as professional boxer/ballplayer in Negro leagues), mid-30s; rec Vocalion label, Chicago, 1937; served time for assault in Parchman Farm Prison, Parchman, MS, 1937-9; rec Library of Congress label, Parchman, MS, 1939; worked w Jack Kelly in local jug bands, Memphis,

1939; rec Vocalion/OKeh labels, Chicago, 1940; toured widely working club dates in Cleveland, OH/St Louis, MO/Detroit, MI/Baltimore, MD/Chicago, IL/elsewhere, c1940-2; served in US Navy frequently entertaining troups c1942-4; settled in Memphis, TN, to work outside music with occasional local roadhouse gigs, 1944-63; worked Cabale Club, Berkeley, CA, 1963; Ash Grove, Los Angeles, CA, 1963; rec Takoma-Sonet label, Memphis, 1963; rec Arhoolie label, Berkeley, 1963; rec Takoma label, Berkeley, 1964; worked Univ of California Folk concert, Los Angeles, 1964; Cafe A-Go-Go, NYC, 1965-6 (por 1966 date rel Verve label); Folk Song '65 Concert, Carnegie Hall, NYC, 1965; Club 47, Cambridge, MA, 1965; Brown Univ, Providence, RI, 1965; app on FESTIVAL PRESENTS THE BLUES, CBC-TV, Toronto, Can, 1966; worked Newport Folk Festival, Newport, RI, 1966; Memphis Blues Festival, Memphis, 1966-9 (por 1968 concert rel Sire-Blue Horizon label/por 1969 concert shown on SOUNDS OF SUMMER, WNDT-TV, NYC); toured w Memphis Blues Society Show working concert dates across US, 1966; worked Avant Garde Coffeehouse, Milwaukee, WI, 1967; toured w American Folk Blues Festival working concert dates through England/Europe, 1967; worked Ash Grove, Los Angeles, 1967; Quiet Knight, Chicago, 1968-70; Univ of Chicago Folk Festival, Chicago, 1968; rec Sire-Blue Horizon label, Memphis, 1968; rec w Furry Lewis, Asp label, Memphis, 1968; worked American Embassy, Mexico City, Mexico, 1968; Mariposa Folk Festival, Toronto, Can, 1968; Kibitzeria, Toronto, 1968; Guelph Univ, Toronto, 1969; The Onion, Toronto, 1969; WC Handy Blues Festival, Memphis, 1969; Ing Hall, Berkeley, CA, 1969; Matrix, San Francisco, 1969; rec Blue Thumb/Adelphi labels, Memphis, 1969; worked Festival of American Folklife, Washington, DC, 1970; toured w American Folk Blues Festival working concert dates through England/Europe, 1970 (por of Frankfurt, Ger, concert rel Scout label); worked Jazz Expo '70, London, Eng, 1970; River City Blues Festival, Memphis, 1971-2; Gaslight Club, NYC, 1971; Univ of Arkansas Delta Blues Festival, Fayetteville, AR, 1972; Mariposa Folk Festival, Toronto, Can, 1972; toured w American Folk-Blues Festival working concerts through England, 1972; rec Blues Beacon label, Munich, Ger, 1972; app on MR CRUMP'S BLUES, WKNO-TV, Memphis, TN, 1972; rec Albatross label, Memphis, 1972; film clip shown in French film BLUES UNDER THE SKIN, 1972; app in French film OUT OF THE BLACKS INTO THE BLUES (pt 1: Along the Old Man River), 1972; worked Tulane Univ, New Orleans, LA, 1973; rec Biograph label, West Memphis, AR, 1973; worked New Orleans Jazz & Heritage Festival, New Orleans, 1973; toured w Memphis Blues Caravan working concert/college dates through Midwest, 1973-4; worked Bethune Col, Toronto, Can, 1974; w Juke Boy Bonner in local club dates, Austin, TX, 1974; Centennial Folk Festival, Winnipeg, Can, 1974; Mariposa Folk Festival, Toronto Islands, Toronto, 1974; Berkeley Blues Festival, Berkeley, CA, 1975; toured Germany working concert dates, 1975 (por Bremen, Ger, concert rel Sparkasse in Concert label); app in film COCKSUCKERS BLUES, 1976; app in THE DEVIL'S MUSIC—A HISTORY OF THE BLUES (ep: Nothing But the Truth/ep: Work and Mother Wit), BBC-1-TV, England, 1976; inactive due to illness from mid-70s; entered City of Memphis Hospital where he died of cancer; buried New Park Cemetery, Memphis, TN; clip shown on GOOD MORNIN' BLUES, PBS-TV, 1978

Personal: Married Ruby ——— (1920s); Nancy Buchauney (1933-46); Leola ——— (1964-). Had 4 children. Named after Negro educator Booker T Washington. Was cousin of BB King

Billing: The Singing Preacher

Songs: Aberdeen Mississippi Blues/Alabama Blues/Army Blues/Atlanta Special/Bald Eagle Train/Bed Spring Blues/Big Boat Up the River/Black Cat Bone Blues/Black Crepe Blues/Black Train Blues/Bukka's Jitterbug Swing/Cool Operator/Cryin' Holy unto the Lord/Decoration Day/Don't Fuzz Blues/Drifting Blues/Drunk Man Blues/Fixin' to Die/Fried Chicken/Georgia Skin Game/Gibson Hill/Gibson Town/Give Me an Old Old Lady/Glory Bound Train/Good Gin Blues/Got Sick and Tired/High Fever Blues/Hot Springs Arkansas/I Am in the Heavenly Way/Jelly Roll Workin' Man/Magie Lee/Midnight Blues/Miss Mary/Mixed Water/My Baby/My Mother Died/My Wife Is Getting Old/New Orleans Streamline/1936 Triggertoe/Old Lady/Old Man Tom/Panama Limited/Parchman Farm Blues/Poor Boy a Long Way from Home/School Learning/Shake 'em On Down/Shake My Hand Blues/Sic 'em Dogs On/Single Man Blues/Sleepy Man Blues/Stone/Strange Place Blues/Stuttgart Arkansas/Sugar Hill/Tippin' In/Way Out West/When Can I Change My Clothes?/World Boogie

Infl by: Charley Patton

Infl to: Richie Havens/BB King

Quotes: "A phenomenal blues singer"—John Norris, *Coda* magazine (Canada), Sept 1958, p 40

"His records . . . testify to his genius for songwriting on an intensely personal level, while his guitar work, encompassing slide and brilliant, unconventional percussive action, maintained that high standard"—Amy O'Neal, *Living Blues* magazine, May 1977, p 6

"One of the great original talents and most successful revivalist"—Simon Napier, *Blues Unlimited* magazine (UK), Sept 1971, p 10

References: Blues magazine (Canada), Dec 1976, pp 6-13, 20-30, 38-44

The Bluesmen, Samuel B Charters, Oak Publications, 1967

The Legacy of the Blues, Samuel B Charters, Calder & Boyars Ltd, 1975

WHITE, CLARA
(see McCoy, Viola)

WHITE, CLEVE
(aka: Schoolboy Cleve)

Photo by Tom Mazzolini. Courtesy Living Blues Magazine

Born: Jun 10, 1928, Baton Rouge (East Baton Rouge Parish), LA
Inst: Guitar/Harmonica

Interested in music at early age and taught self harmonica at about 6 years of age; frequently worked w local groups in Baton Rouge/Port Allen, LA, areas from mid-40s; worked w Lloyd Reynaud Band in local club dates, Opelousas, LA, early 50s; rec w Lightnin' Slim, Feature label, Crowley, LA, 1954; worked w Lightnin' Slim in local clubs, Crowley/Baton Rouge, LA, areas, 1955-6; frequently toured as single working clubs through Louisiana from 1956; rec Ace label, Baton Rouge, 1957; moved to Los Angeles, CA, to work mostly outside music, 1960-70; moved to San Francisco, CA, to work mostly outside music from c1970; worked Univ of California Extension Center, San Francisco, 1973; San Francisco Bay Blues Festival, San Francisco, 1973; Nardi's, San Bruno, CA, 1973; rec Cherrie label, San Francisco, 1973; app on BLUES BY THE BAY, KPOO-FM-radio, San Francisco, 1974-5; worked Sand Dunes, San Francisco, 1974; Minnie's Can-Do Club, San Francisco, 1975; Club La Jolla, San Francisco, 1975; worked Green Earth Cafe, San Francisco, 1976; Univ of California, Berkeley, CA, 1977

Personal: Named "Schoolboy" early in career referring to his then young age

Songs: Here I Go Again/Really, I Apologize

Infl by: Sonny Boy Williamson (Alex Miller)

Reference: Blues Unlimited magazine (UK), Jan 1970, p 22

WHITE, ELLA
(see Crippen, Katie)

WHITE, GEORGIA

Courtesy Frank Driggs Collection

Born: Mar 9, 1903, Sandersville (Washington Co), GA
Died: c1980 (unconfirmed)
Inst: Piano

Moved to Chicago, IL, during 1920s; worked Apex Club, Chicago, IL, 1929; rec w Jimmie Noone Apex Club Orch, Vocalion label, Chicago, 1930; reportedly worked local clubs in Chicago through 30s; rec Decca label, Chicago/NYC, 1935-41; formed all-girl band to work dances in Chicago area, late 40s; worked w Bill Broonzy's Laughing Trio, The Bee Hive and other clubs, Chicago, 1949-50; worked club dates in Chicago area into 50s; worked Downer's Grove, Chicago, 1959; reportedly inactive in music thereafter

Quote: "She had a strong contralto voice with a keen edge to her intonation and was a capable pianist in the barrelhouse tradition"—(Paul Oliver) McCarthy/ Morgan/Oliver/Harrison, *Jazz on Record*, Hanover Books Ltd, 1968

WHITE, GLADYS
(see Henderson, Rosa)

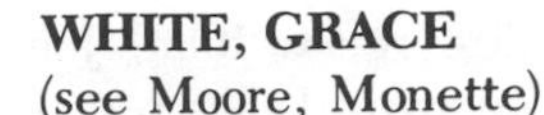

WHITE, GRACE
(see Moore, Monette)

WHITE, JOSHUA DANIEL *"Josh"*
(aka: Tippy Barton/Pinewood Tom/The Singing Christian)
Born: Feb 11, 1915, Greenville (Greenville Co), SC
Died: Sept 5, 1969, Manhasset, NY
Inst: Guitar

Father was Dennis White, a preacher; mother was Daisy Elizabeth Humphrey who frequently sang in local church choirs; one of 8 children; frequently sang in Church of God in the Saints of Christ choir as child, Greenville; frequently worked (as guide) for street singer Blind John Henry Arnold, Greenville, c1922; dropped out of school to guide/sing w Blind Joe Taggart/Blind Blake/Willie Walker/Joe Walker/Willie Johnson/Archie Jackson/Columbus Williams and other street singers working streets/picnics/resort areas mostly through southeastern US, 1922 into 30s; worked streets w John Henry Arnold, Chicago, IL, 1924; reportedly worked w Blind Lemon Jefferson

Joshua "Josh" White

Courtesy Frank Driggs Collection

through North Carolina, mid-20s; rec w Blind Joe Taggart, Paramount label, Chicago, 1928; rec w Carver Boys, Paramount label, Richmond, IN, 1929; returned to Greenville, SC, to complete Stirling HS, late 20s into 30s; moved to NYC, NY, 1932; app frequently w Clarence Williams Southernaires on HARLEM FANTASY Show and others, WEAF-radio, NYC (NBC-Network), 1932-5; rec Banner/ARC label group, NYC, 1932-6; worked mostly outside music, NYC, 1936-9; formed Josh White Singers working long residencies (also as single), Cafe Society Downtown, NYC, 1939-47; app w Paul Robeson in show JOHN HENRY, Erlanger Theater, Philadelphia, PA, 1939/44th Street Theater, NYC, 1940; rec w own The Carolinians, Columbia label, NYC, 1940; frequently worked w Leadbelly, Village Vanguard, NYC, 1940; app on BACK WHERE I COME FROM, CBS-radio Network, 1940; frequently worked w Sonny Terry/Brownie McGhee/Woody Guthrie/others at local houseparties/hootenannies/lofts in NYC area, early 40s; rec Keynote/Conqueror labels, NYC, 1941; frequently entertained for President Franklin D Roosevelt at White House Concerts, Washington, DC, early 40s; frequently worked Library of Congress concerts, Washington, early 40s; rec Library of Congress label, Washington, early 40s; app in weekly Office of War Information radio shows (frequently on BBC-radio, London, Eng), early 40s; app w Burl Ives in film short TALL TALES, 1941; coached/teamed w Libby Holman in Early American Blues and Other Songs program working long residency at La Vie Parisienne Club and others, NYC, c1941 with frequent tours across US to 1944; rec acc to Libby Holman, Decca label, NYC, 1942; toured w Golden Gate Quartet for US State Department working concert dates through Mexico, 1942; app w Paul Robeson in Langston Hughes operetta THE MAN WHO WENT TO WAR, OWI-radio, 1944; worked Salute to Fats Waller concert, Carnegie Hall, NYC, 1944; app on local show, WNEW-radio, NYC, 1944; app on NEW WORLD A-COMING Show, WMCA-radio, NYC, 1944; rec Asch/V-Disc/Disc labels, NYC, 1944; rec Decca label, NYC, 1944-7; worked President Franklin D Roosevelt Inaugural Ball, Washington, DC, 1945; app w Ethel Waters in BLUE HOLIDAY Revue, Belasco Theater, NYC, 1945; app in film CRIMSON CANARY, 1945; worked in concert w Elwood Smith, Town Hall, NYC, 1945; worked Cafe Society Uptown, NYC, 1945; extensive tours working concerts across US/Canada, 1946-7; worked Art Institute, Detroit, MI, 1946; Academy of Music, Philadelphia, PA, 1946; w Woody Guthrie, Town Hall, NYC, 1946; Orchestra Hall, NYC, 1946; Earl Theater, Philadelphia, PA, 1946; rec Keynote/Apollo labels, NYC, 1947; app w Sonny Terry/Brownie McGhee in film short TO HEAR YOUR BANJO PLAY, 1947; worked New York City Center, NYC, 1947-8; frequently worked Town Hall, NYC, 1947-51; app in show A LONG WAY FROM HOME, Maxine Elliott's Theater, NYC, 1948; worked Apollo Theater, NYC, 1948; app w Libby Holman in film DREAMS THAT MONEY CAN BUY, 1948; app on ADVENTURES IN JAZZ, CBS-TV, 1949; app in film THE WALKING HILLS, 1949; app in show HOW LONG TILL SUMMER?, Edward M Gilbert Playhouse, NYC, 1949; worked Village Vanguard, NYC, 1949; sang at Leadbelly's funeral, NYC, 1949; worked w Fletcher Henderson, Cafe Society Downtown, NYC, 1950 (por remote WOR-radio); app on ARTHUR GODFREY AND FRIENDS Show, CBS-TV, 1950; toured England/Europe working concert/BBC radio dates, 1950-1; rec Vogue label, Paris, France, 1950; rec London label, London, Eng, 1950-1; rec Columbia label, London, 1951; worked Kingsway Hall, London, 1951; rec Mayor label, Milan, Italy, 1951; worked Storyville Club, Boston, MA, 1952; Eaton Hall, Toronto, Can, 1952; The Blue Angel, NYC, 1952; frequently rec Elektra label, NYC, 1954-62; worked Storyville Club, Boston, MA, 1955; Hungry i, San Francisco, CA, 1955; frequently worked Gate of Horn, Chicago, from c1955; toured Europe working concert dates, 1955-6; rec Nixa label, London, 1956; worked Town Hall, NYC, 1956; rec Period label, NYC, 1956; rec ABC-Paramount label, NYC, 1956-7; worked Community Church Auditorium, NYC, 1956; Jordan Hall, Boston, MA, 1957; app on ART FORD'S GREENWICH VILLAGE PARTY, WNEW-TV, NYC, 1957; app on STEVE WERDENSCHLAG Show, WKCR-FM-radio, NYC, 1957; app on ART FORD'S JAZZ PARTY, WNTA-TV, NYC, 1958; worked Plateau Hall, Toronto, Can, 1958-9; Town Hall, NYC, 1959; One Sheridan Square, NYC, 1959; The Village Gate, NYC, 1960-1; Jordan Hall, Boston, MA, 1960; app on LOOK UP AND LIVE, CBS-TV, 1961; worked San Remo Coffeehouse, Schenectady, NY, 1961; The Roundtable, NYC, 1961; Town Hall, NYC, 1961 (por rel Mercury label); Royal Festival Hall, London, Eng, 1961 (por rel ABC-Paramount label); app in series of shows, Granada-TV, Eng, 1961; worked Dalton Saloon, Cleveland, OH, 1962; Hunter Col, NYC, 1962; Opera House, Seattle World's Fair, Seattle, WA, 1962; Purple Onion, Toronto, Can, c1962; Gate of Horn, Chicago, IL, 1962; rec Mercury label, Chicago, 1963; worked Vassar College, Poughkeepsie, NY, 1963; Town Hall, Philadelphia, PA, 1963; Sheraton Park

Hotel, Washington, DC, 1963 (por shown DINNER WITH THE PRESIDENT, CBS-TV); app on HOOTENANNY, ABC-TV, 1963-4; worked Regency Towers Hotel, Toronto, Can, 1963; Univ of British Columbia, Vancouver, Can, 1963; Emory Univ, Atlanta, GA, 1964; The Village Gate, NYC, 1964; toured England/Europe working concert dates, 1965; worked Newport Folk Festival, Newport, RI, 1965; The Bunkhouse, Vancouver, Can, 1965-7; Mother Blues, Chicago, 1965; The Troubadour, Los Angeles, CA, 1965; The Bitter End, NYC, 1965-7 (por shown FROM THE BITTER END, WOR-TV, NYC [syndicated]); Orchestra Hall, Chicago, 1966; The Cellar Door, Washington, DC, 1966; Berkshire Music Barn, Lenox, MA, 1966; app on THE WORLD OF MUSIC, CBC-TV, Toronto, Can, 1966; worked Penny Farthing, Toronto, 1966; toured Australia working concert dates c1966; worked Village Gate, NYC, 1967; toured England working concert dates, 1967; app on WOODY WOODBURY Show, KTTV-TV, Los Angeles (syndicated), 1967; app on DIMENSION Show, CBS-radio, 1968; worked The Riverqueen, Vancouver, Can, 1969; Berkeley Blues Festival, Berkeley, CA, 1969; entered North Shore Hospital where he died during open heart surgery; buried Cypress Hills Cemetery, Glendale, NY

Personal: Married Carol Carr (1934-). 5 children. His son Joshua Donald White (born 1940) and daughter Beverly White (born 1939) are singers

Books: The Josh White Guitar Method, Josh White/Ivor Maroints, 1956

The Josh White Song Book, Robert Shelton/Walter Raim, Quadrangle Books, 1963

Songs: Ball and Chain Blues/Can't Help But Crying Sometimes/Collins' Body Lies in Sound Cave/Delia/Hard Time Blues/I Had a Woman/I Know Moonlight/Jim Crow Train/Little Man Sittin' on a Fence/Silicosis Blues/Timber/Number 12 Train/Uncle Sam Says/Welfare Blues

Awards/Honors: Awarded Honorary Doctorate of Folk Anthology from Fisk University, Nashville, TN, 1949

Won *Cavalier* magazine readers folk poll as Best Blues Singer, 1965

Infl by: Blind Blake/Blind Lemon Jefferson/JT Smith/Willie Walker

Infl to: Harry Belafonte/Oscar Brown Jr/Dave Van Ronk

Quotes: ". . . he achieved his greatest renown through appearances in East Side in-group Manhattan clubs, where his good looks and slick showmanship made him a pre-Belafonte black sex idol. To folk singing, if not the blues, he brought matinee sexuality, bell-like diction, and pop appeal . . ."—Arnold Shaw, *The World of Soul*, Cowles Book Company Inc, 1970

"A leading popularizer of the blues, Mr White captivated audiences with his casual charm and his authoritatively sensual style"—Carter Horsley, *New York Times* newspaper, Sept 5, 1969

"He was one of the finest artists America has ever produced . . ."—Don McLean, *Sing Out* magazine, Winter 1969

References: Sing Out magazine, Winter 1969, pp 9-12

Blues Unlimited magazine (UK), Jul/Sept 1968

The Josh White Song Book, Robert Shelton/Walter Raim, Quadrangle Books, 1963

WHITE, PRINCESS

Courtesy Princess White

Born: Jan 14, 1881, Philadelphia (Philadelphia Co), PA
Died: Mar 21, 1976, Port Chester, NY
Inst: Piano

Father was George White, a free black; mother was

Helena ———, a full-blooded Indian; was one of three children; toured w Salica Bryan and Her Pickaninnies working as toe dancer-singing pick in shows through Europe/Australia, 1886-93; toured as comedian/chorus dancer/coon shouter in theaters/juke joints along the East Coast c1893-1900; frequently worked w Black Patti/Butterbeans and Susie/Ethel Waters/Ida Cox and others on Consolidated/TOBA circuits (as leading lady/male impersonator) in theaters/road shows/tent shows through South c1900-17; toured Europe working theater dates through teens; toured w Jim Europe Regiment Band working concert dates through Europe c1916; toured w Homer Tutt/Salem Tutt-Whitney's The Smart Set Company working shows across US c1916-17; toured w Charlie Gaines Carnival working tent shows across US, c1918-23; worked Dixieland Theater, Charleston, SC, c1918; Pecan Theater, Savannah, GA, c1918; Lafayette Theater, Winston-Salem, NC, 1919; Dreamland Theater, Badin, NC, 1920; toured SH Dudley Theater circuit out of Washington, DC, early 20s; toured w Wilbur Sweatman Band working club dates, early 20s; frequently worked nightspots, NYC area, early 20s; rec w Clarence Williams Band, OKeh label (unissued test), NYC, early 20s; worked Plantation Nightclub, St Louis, MO, early 20s; frequently toured w Silas Green from New Orleans minstrel tent show from early 20s to 1938; toured w Whitman Sisters working Lafayette Theater, NYC, and others c1930-3; worked w Noble Sissle Orch, Faye Theater, Philadelphia, PA, c1935; toured Europe working club dates mid-30s; toured w Irvin C Miller's BROWN SKIN MODELS Revue working shows through South/Southwest c1940-4; toured on USO package show working US military bases through England c1944; worked outside music as owner/manager of restaurants/bars/hotels and The LD Nightclub, Newport News, VA, through 40s into 60s; moved to Newark, NJ, and mostly active in local church work through 60s/70s; worked w Clyde Bernhardt Harlem Blues Band, Connecticut Traditional Jazz Club, Meriden, CT, 1975 (por rel Conn Trad label); w Clyde Bernhardt Band, Harbor Island Park, Mamaroneck, NY, 1975; rec Barron label, NYC, 1975; worked Overseas Press Club, Biltmore Hotel, NYC, 1975; while appearing in concert at Emelin Theater, Mamaroneck, NY, suffered heart attack and DOA at United Hospital; buried Graceland Memorial Park, Kenilworth, NJ

Personal: Married Edward Goodbar (c1894)/Baby Seals/Charles Whiting/Fred Durrah and others. Had 2 children

Billing: International Entertainer

Songs: Everywoman Blues/Keyhole Blues

Quotes: "She was one of the greatest blues singers and jazz singers . . . that I ever heard"—Clyde Bernhardt, *Storyville* magazine (UK), Dec 1974, p 47

"To those who come to her by her recording she will reveal herself as a vibrant artist of the highest order"—Al Vollmer, *Living Blues* magazine, Jul 1976, p 6

WHITE, WASHINGTON

(see White, Booker)

WHITMAN, ESSIE BARBARA

Born: Jul 4, 1882, Osceola (Mississippi Co), AR
Died: May 7, 1963, Chicago, IL

Father was Rev Albert A Whitman, a first cousin to poet Walt Whitman; mother was Caddie White; one of 4 children; won first prize in talent contest in local theater, Kansas City, MO, c1892; moved to Atlanta, GA, where she frequently worked local socials/benefits in area, late 90s; formed family act (with mother and sister May Whitman) singing jubilee and harmony songs in Atlanta area from c1900; toured Europe with family act working vaudeville circuit c1902; formed New Orleans Troubadours (with family and Tony Jackson, pianist) to tour vaudeville circuits across US, 1904-10; reorganized group as The Whitman Sisters to tour as road show in major theaters across US, 1910-18; toured w sister Alice Whitman (as duo) working as comedian/singer on vaudeville circuit into 20s; expanded act to include a wide variety of performers/acts to tour as a revue across US, early 20s; rec w Jazz Masters, Black Swan label, NYC, 1921; worked w Alice Whitman, Lafayette Theater, NYC, 1922; reportedly rec Paramount label (unissued) c1924-5; retired from music (while sisters continued touring as act) to settle in Chicago, IL, 1925; frequently worked as costume/scenic designer for sisters' productions through 20s; app with sisters in own revue, Lafayette Theater, NYC, 1930; founded Theatrical Cheer Club to aid show performers during 30s; active as evangelist in church affairs, Chicago, into 60s; suffered smoke inhalation in home fire; died at Provident Hospital; buried South View Cemetery, Atlanta, GA

Personal: Married Prince Ishmael/Johnnie Woods/Carter Hayes. Her sister Mabel (May) Whitman was manager/singer (died 1942); sister Alberta (Bert) Whitman was dancer/male impersonator (died 1964); sister Alice Whitman was dancer (died early 70s);

some references improperly list given name as "Elsie"

Quote: "The Whitman Sisters were the royalty of Negro vaudeville"—Marshall W Stearns/Jean Stearns, *Jazz Dance,* The Macmillan Company, 1968

WHITTAKER, HUDSON
(aka: Jimmy Eager/Honey Boy Smith/Tampa Red)

Courtesy Institute of Jazz Studies

Born: Jan 8, 1904, Smithville (Lee Co), GA
Died: Mar 19, 1981, Chicago, IL
Inst: Guitar/Kazoo/Piano

Father was John Woodbridge; mother was Elizabeth Whittaker; born Hudson Woodbridge; after death of parents moved to Tampa, FL, to live with grandmother Whittaker and assume family name; interested in music and taught self guitar as youth; frequently toured jukes/tonks from Tampa to St Augustine, FL, from early 20s; moved to Chicago, IL, c1925; frequently worked club dates and streets, Chicago, from c1925; rec w Georgia Tom/Hokum Boys/solo, Paramount label, Chicago, 1928-9; rec acc to Ma Rainey/Madlyn Davis/others, Paramount label, Chicago, 1928; rec w Georgia Tom/Tampa Red's Hokum Jug Band/solo, Vocalion label, Chicago, 1928-31; teamed w Georgia Tom working house rent parties/theaters/dance halls/juke joints/excursion boats in Chicago area with frequent tours as team on TOBA southern theater circuit, 1928-9; worked Palace Theater, Memphis, TN, 1929; rec w Georgia Tom, Brunswick label, Chicago, 1929; rec w Georgia Tom/Memphis Minnie/Hokum Jug Band, Vocalion/ARC label group, Chicago, IL/NYC, NY, 1932; rec solo or with own Chicago Five, Bluebird label, Chicago, 1934-6; frequently worked w Big Maceo/Bill Broonzy/others in local club dates, Chicago, through 30s into 40s; extended residency, C&T Club, Chicago, late 30s; rec Bluebird label, Aurora, IL, 1937-8; rec Bluebird label, Chicago, 1944-5; worked w Big Maceo, Flame Club, Chicago, 1945; worked w Sunnyland Slim at local clubs, Gary, IN, mid-40s; frequently worked Purple Cat Club/Sylvio's/Club Georgia/708 Club/The Zanzibar/The Peacock/others as well as jukes/rent parties, Chicago, from mid-40s to early 50s; rec Victor label, Chicago, 1945-7; worked C&T Lounge, Chicago, 1948-9; w Sunnyland Slim, 21 Club, Chicago, 1948; Peacock Lounge, Chicago, 1949; rec Victor label, Chicago, 1949-53; mostly inactive in music, Chicago, from c1953; rec Sabre label, Chicago, 1953-4; entered local hospitals where he was treated for alcoholism, Chicago, c1955-60; rec Prestige-Bluesville label, Chicago, 1960; worked w Barbara Dane, Sugar Hill Club, San Francisco, 1961; worked mostly outside music, Chicago, through 60s; retired and lived in various nursing homes, Chicago, from 1974; suffered fatal heart attack; buried Mt Glenwood Cemetery, Glenwood, IL

Personal: Married Francies ____ (died 1953). Pseudonym "Tampa Red" refers to city of his youth plus his red hair

Billing: The Guitar Wizard

Songs: Anna Lou Blues/Better Let My Gal Alone/Big Stars Falling Blues/Birmingham Bessemer Blues/Black Angel Blues/But I Forgive You/Crying Won't Help You/Detroit Blues/Don't You Lie to Me/The Duck's Yas Yas Yas/Give It Up Buddy and Get Goin'/Give Me Mine Now/Grievin' and Worryin' Blues/Hard Road Blues/If I Let You Get Away with It/I'll Kill Your Soul/I'm Bettin' on You/It's Tight Like That/It's Too Late Now/The Jitter Jump/Kingfish Blues/Let Me Play with Your Poodle/Love (Her) with a Feeling/Mean and Evil Woman/Mean Mistreater Blues/Mercy Mama (Blues)/Mr Rhythm Man/My First Love Blues/My Gal Is Gone/No Matter How She Done It/Nutty & Buggy Blues/Play Proof Woman/Please Try to See It My Way/Rambler's Blues/Rock It Rhythm/Seminole Blues/She Want to Sell My Monkey/She's Love Crazy/Shine On/So Crazy About You Baby/So Much Trouble/Somebody's

Been Doing That Thing/Stockyard Fire/Stranger Blues/That's the Way I Do It/Train Time Blues/Travel On/The Way to Get Lowdown/When I Take My Vacation in Harlem/When Things Go Wrong with You (It Hurts Me Too)/When You Were a Girl of Seven/Witching Hour Blues/You Gonna Miss Me When I'm Gone/You Got Me Worryin'/You Missed a Good Man

Infl by: Piccolo Pete/Ma Rainey/Bessie Smith/Mamie Smith

Infl to: John Brim/Frank Edwards/Little Walter Jacobs/Brownie McGhee/Robert Nighthawk

Quotes: "One of the blues most fluent, inventive and hence influential guitarists and . . . one of its foremost, perennially fertile original song writers"—Pete Welding, *Downbeat* magazine, Oct 9, 1975, p 29

"Tampa Red is one of the blues major artists"—Jim De Koster, *Living Blues* magazine, Mar 1975, p 26

Reference: Bluebird album AXM2-5501

WILBER, BILL
(see McCoy, Joe)

WILBORN, NELSON
(*aka:* Dirty Red/Red Devil/Red Nelson)
Born: Aug 31, 1907, Summer (Tallahatchie Co), MS
Inst: Piano

Born/raised on farm and frequently worked outside music through 20s; moved to Chicago, IL, to work outside music with some rent-party gigs from early 30s; rec Decca label, Chicago, 1934-6; rec Vocalion label, Chicago, 1935; rec Bluebird label, Aurora, IL, 1937; rec Vocalion label, Chicago, 1938; worked mostly outside music, Chicago, through 40s/50s; rec Aladdin label, Chicago, 1947; frequently worked outside music (as waiter), Trocadero Lounge Club, Chicago, into 60s; worked w Muddy Waters Band in local club dates, Chicago, during 60s

Song: Mother Fuyer

WILKINS, JOE WILLIE
Born: Jan 7, 1923, Davenport (Coahoma Co), MS
Died: Mar 28, 1979, Memphis, TN
Inst: Guitar/Harmonica

Father was Frank Wilkins; mother Parlee Holmes; was an only child; taught self harmonica as child; frequently worked in father's small band at local dances, Bobo, MS, from 1933; taught self guitar to work local churches in area from 1935; frequently hoboed w Sonny Boy Williamson (Alex Miller)/Robert Jr Lockwood working streets/jukes/barrelhouses in Sherard/Alligator/Duncan, MS, late 30s; served in US Navy, early 40s; frequently app w Sonny Boy Williamson (Alex Miller) on KING BISCUIT TIME, KFFA-radio, Helena, AR, from 1945; frequently app w Robert Nighthawk on BRIGHT STAR FLOUR Show/MOTHER'S BEST FLOUR HOUR Show, KFFA-radio, Helena, AR, 1946-7, with frequent local tours; frequently toured w Sonny Boy Williamson (Alex Miller)/Willie Love/Willie Nix (as "The Four Aces") working jukes through Arkansas/Tennessee/Mississippi, 1949-50; app w BB King on PEPTICON BOY Show, WDIA-radio, Memphis, TN, c1950; app w Willie Love Three Aces on BROADWAY FURNITURE STORE Show, KWEM-radio, West Memphis, AR, c1950; rec w Sonny Boy Williamson (Alex Miller), Trumpet label, Jackson, MS, 1951-3; worked w Willie Nix, Hippodrome Theater, Memphis, TN, early 50s; rec w Willie Love, Trumpet label, Jackson MS, 1952; frequently rec as sideman for Arthur Crudup/Willie Nix/Roosevelt Sykes/others through 50s/60s; worked King Solomon Bar, Detroit, MI, 1954; frequently toured w Roosevelt Sykes and others, late 50s into 60s; settled in Memphis to work outside music, 1959 into 70s; worked Festival of American Folklife, Washington, DC, 1970; formed Joe's King Biscuit Boys working local clubs, Memphis, c1972; worked River City Blues Festival, Ellis Auditorium, Memphis, 1972-3 (por 1973 concert on MUSIC USA, VOA-radio); w Houston Stackhouse, Robinson's Cafe, Hughes, AR, 1972; Hot Mama's Coffee House, Memphis, 1972; rec

Photo by Peter B Lowry

Mimosa label, Memphis, c1973; worked Ann Arbor Blues Festival, Ann Arbor, MI, 1973; toured w own Joe's King Biscuit Boys on Memphis Blues Caravan Show working concert dates through Midwest, 1973; film clip shown on OMNIBUS (ep: The Friendly Invasion), BBC-1-TV, England, 1975; worked Monterey Jazz Festival, Monterey, CA, 1976; app on THE DEVIL'S MUSIC—A HISTORY OF THE BLUES (ep: Work and Mother Wit), BBC-1-TV, England, 1976; residency at Birth of The Blues Club, Memphis, 1978; Delta Blues Fest, Greenville, MS, 1978; suffered fatal heart attack; buried Galilee Cemetery, Arlington, TN

Infl by: Aaron "T-Bone" Walker

Quote: "One of the greatest blues guitarists Memphis has ever known"—Jim O'Neal, *Living Blues* magazine, Winter 1972, p 13

Reference: Living Blues, Winter 1972, pp 13-17

WILKINS, Rev. **ROBERT TIMOTHY** *"Tim"*
(aka: Keghouse)
Born: Jan 16, 1896, Hernando (De Soto Co), MS
Died: May 26, 1987, Memphis, TN
Inst: Guitar

Father was George Wilkins; mother was Julia Starks; assumed stepfather's surname of Oliver at 2 years of age; raised on farm and learned some guitar from stepfather as youth; frequently worked w Gus Cannon/Jim Jackson/others at local dances/parties/picnics/fish fries in Hernando, MS, area, 1911-15; moved to Memphis, TN, to reassume true father's surname of Wilkins and work outside music, 1915-18; worked outside music, Hernando, MS, 1918; served in US Army, 1918-19; returned to Memphis to work outside music, 1919 into 30s; frequently worked w own jug band and Furry Lewis/Memphis Minnie/Son House/others in local sporting houses/hotels/dances/houseparties/streets, Memphis, c1927 into 30s; app on local radio show, Memphis, 1927; frequently toured with small

Rev Robert "Tim" Wilkins *Photo by Julie Snow*

vaudeville/minstrel shows working through South, late 20s into 30s; rec Victor label, Memphis, 1928; rec Brunswick label, Memphis, 1929-30; teamed w Son Joe to work local jukes/streets, Memphis, c1931-6; rec Vocalion label, Jackson, MS, 1935; worked outside music, Memphis, from 1936 through 40s; ordained a minister of Church of God in Christ Church, Memphis, 1950 and serving into 70s; worked Ontario Place, Washington, DC, 1964; rec (religious songs) Piedmont label, Washington, DC, 1964; worked Newport Folk Festival, Newport, RI, 1964 (por shown in film FESTIVAL); Univ of Chicago Folk Festival, Chicago, IL, 1965; toured w Memphis Blues Society working concerts out of Memphis, 1966; Memphis Blues Festival, Memphis, 1968-9 (por 1968 concert rel Sire-Blue Horizon label); Tyrone Guthrie Theater, Minneapolis, MN, 1970; Wisconsin Delta Blues Festival, Beloit, WI, 1970; Washington Blues Festival, Howard Univ, Washington, DC, 1970; National Folk Festival, Wolf Trap Farm Park, Vienna, VA, 1971; worked in music infrequently thereafter; died of pneumonia; buried National Cemetery, Memphis

Songs: Get Away Blues/Here Am I, Send Me/I'll Go with Her/I'm Going Home to My Heavenly King/In Heaven Sitting Down/Jail House Blues/Jesus Said If You Go/Jesus Will Fix It Alright/Kansas City Blues/ The Prodigal Son/Thank You Jesus

Infl by: Garfield Akers/Aaron "Buddy" Taylor

Quotes: ". . . one of the most important performers in folk music today"—Dick Spottswood, Piedmont album 13162

"Robert Wilkins' blues are of great interest for their unusual verse structure and very personal content . . ."—(Paul Oliver) McCarthy/Morgan/ Oliver/Harrison, *Jazz on Record*, Hanover Books, 1968

Reference: Blues Unlimited magazine (UK), Mar/ Apr/May/Jun/Jul/Sept 1968

WILLIAMS, ANDRE *"Bacon Fat"/"Mr Rhythm"*
Born: c1936, Chicago (Cook Co), IL

Interested in music early and frequently sang in CH Cobbs Baptist Church choir, Chicago, IL, through 40s; frequently worked local amateur shows, Chicago, late 40s; moved to Detroit, MI, to work local theaters from early 50s; formed own The Five Dollars to rec Fortune label, Detroit, 1955; toured w Five Dollars working club dates through South, 1956; rec w Five Dollars/Don Juans/Joe Weaver Combo, Fortune label, Detroit, 1956; rec Fortune label, Detroit, 1957-61

Personal: Took name "Bacon Fat" from his hit record of same name

Song: How to Do the Bacon Fat

Infl by: Walter Spriggs

Reference: Blues Unlimited magazine (UK), Aug 1964, pp 7-8

WILLIAMS, BESSIE
(see Henderson, Rosa)
(see McCoy, Viola)

WILLIAMS, *"Colonel"* **BILL**

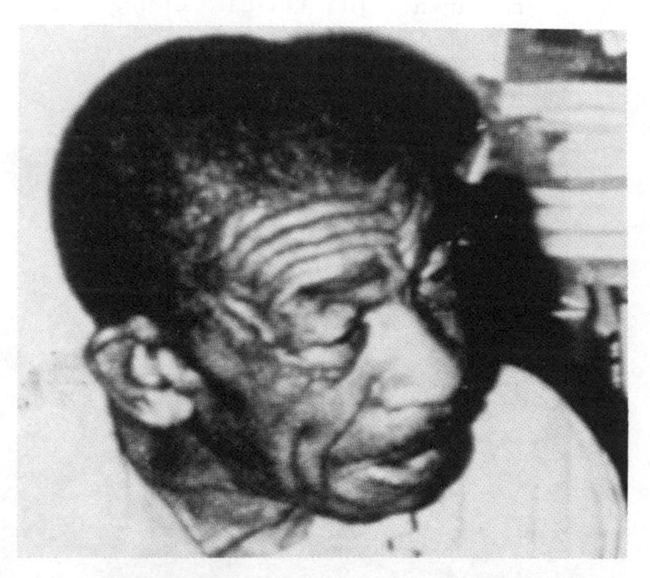

Courtesy Living Blues *Magazine*

Born: Feb 28, 1898, Richmond (Henrico Co), VA
Died: Oct 6, 1973, Greenup, KY
Inst: Guitar

Father was Emmett Williams; mother was Mary ———; born William Williams; one of a few children; taught self guitar at 10 years of age; frequently worked outside music, Richmond, VA, area as youth; left home to hobo across US to work outside music through teens; teamed w Blind Blake to entertain in road gang camps near Bristol, TN, 1921; settled in Greenup, KY, to work mostly outside music in area, 1922-58; frequently worked social parties, Greenup, from 1958; worked Mountain Heritage Folk Festival, Greenup, 1970 (por shown on Kentucky Educational TV network/por heard on COFFEE HOUSE Show, WIRO-radio, Ironton, OH); rec Blue Goose label,

Greenup, 1970; worked Community Col, Ashland, KY, 1970; Berea Col, Berea, KY, c1970; Univ of Louisville Folk Festival, Louisville, KY, c1970; Univ of Chicago Folklore Society Festival, Chicago, IL, 1970-1; app on CBS NEWS, CBS-TV, 1971; worked Festival of American Folklife, St Helen's Island, Montreal, Can, 1971; Festival of American Folklife, Washington, DC, 1971; Mariposa Folk Festival, Toronto, Can, c1971; Harpur Col, Binghamton, NY, 1972-3; Washington Square Church, NYC, 1972; app in film short THINKING OUT LOUD, 1972; toured college circuit/club dates on East Coast, 1972; rec Blue Goose label, NYC, 1972; suffered fatal heart attack at home; buried Riverview Cemetery, Greenup, KY

Personal: Married Margaret Martin

Songs: Banjo Rag/Bill's Rag/Blake's Rag/Bubblegum/The Chicken/Corn Liquor Blues/I'll Follow You/Low and Lonesome/Lucky Blues/My Girlfriend Left Me/Pocahontas/That's the Human Thing to Do/Total Rag/When the Roses Bloom Again

Infl by: Blind Blake

Quotes: "He is a find of outstanding importance . . . and who is, in his own right, a musician of outstanding ability"—Paul Oliver, *Jazz & Blues* magazine (UK), Aug 1971, p 10

"Bill Williams is incredible and his vast repertoire is a total delight"—Pete Lowry, *Blues Unlimited* magazine (UK), Oct 1972, p 18

References: *Living Blues* magazine, Winter 1973, p 5
Jazz & Blues magazine (UK), Dec 1971, pp 37-8

WILLIAMS, BLIND BOY
(see McGhee, Walter)

WILLIAMS, EMERY H *"Little Junior"*
(aka: Detroit Jr)
Born: Oct 26, 1931, Haynes (Lee Co), AR
Inst: Guitar/Piano

Father was Emery Williams Sr; moved to Forrest City, AR, as infant; moved to Memphis, TN, c1937; moved to Pulaski, IL, where he was raised by grandmother from c1943; took interest in music mid-40s; moved to Flint, MI, where he frequently worked houseparties/shows, 1947-50; worked outside music in Pontiac, MI, 1950, then Cleveland, OH, 1951; worked Mellowland Club, Pontiac, 1952; rec Great Lakes label (unissued), Pontiac, c1952; formed own

Courtesy Living Blues *Magazine*

The Blues Champs group working Club Cabana, Saginaw, MI, 1952; frequently worked local club dates, Flint/Lansing/Pontiac, MI, areas, 1952-3; frequently worked Circle Club, Flint, 1953-6; Plooze Bar, Flint, c1955; worked w JT Brown at Club 99, Joliet, IL, 1957; Squeeze Club, Chicago, IL, 1957; w Eddie Taylor, Pepper's Lounge, Chicago, c1957; Congo Lounge, Chicago, c1957; w Little Mack, Pepper's Lounge, Chicago, c1958; frequently worked Cadillac Baby Lounge, Chicago, through 50s; rec Bea & Baby/Chess/Foxy labels, Chicago, 1960; rec w Little Mac, Pacer label, Chicago, 1961; formed own band to work local club dates, Chicago, from c1961; rec with own Junior & The Troyettes group, Palos label, Chicago, early 60s; frequently worked w Little Mac's Band in local clubs, Chicago, through 60s into 70s; rec GJ label, Chicago, 1964; rec USA label, Chicago, 1965; rec Tip Top label, Chicago, 1967; worked w Howlin' Wolf Band, Key Largo Club and others, Chicago, 1969; app in film THE BLUES IS ALIVE AND WELL IN CHICAGO, 1970; toured w James Cotton Band working club/concert dates, 1970; worked Pepper's Lounge, Chicago, 1970-1; rec BluesWay label, Chicago, 1971; frequently worked as sideman w Sammy Lay/Eddie Taylor/Johnny Twist/

others, Chicago, into 70s; worked w Howlin' Wolf Band, Ann Arbor Blues Festival, Ann Arbor, MI, 1972 (por rel Atlantic label); frequently toured as sideman w Howlin' Wolf Band working clubs/concerts across US, 1972-6; worked International Blues Festival, Louisville, KY, 1974; In Concert Club, Montreal, Can, 1974; w Howlin' Wolf Band, El Mocambo Tavern, Toronto, Can, 1975; The New 1815 Club, Chicago, 1976; World Surrealist Exhibition, Chicago, 1976

Personal: Married twice

Songs: Money Tree/You Say You're Leaving

Infl by: Roosevelt Sykes

References: Blues Unlimited magazine (UK), Mar 1976, pp 21-2
Coda magazine (Canada), Jun/Aug 1970

WILLIAMS, HENRY *"Rubberlegs"*
Born: Jul 14, 1907, Atlanta (De Kalb Co), GA
Died: Oct 17, 1962, New York, NY

Father was John R Williamson; mother was Mattie Hopkins; born Henry Williamson; interested in music at early age and worked (as singer/dancer) in Lizzie Murphy's Sporting House, Atlanta, GA, c1918; toured w Bobby Grant's Female Impersonators Revue working shows through Atlanta, GA, area, 1919; won local Charleston dancing contest in Atlanta and toured (as single act) on TOBA circuit from 1920; worked local theater dates, Birmingham, AL, 1922; toured w Sunshine Exposition Show and Carnival working under canvas through South, 1922; toured w Naomi Thomas' Brazilian Nuts Show working Keith theater circuit, 1926; worked Cotton Club, NYC, late 20s; toured extensively as singer/comedian/strutter/trucking dancer on vaudeville/night club circuits across US through 20s into 30s; app in DREAMY MELODIES Revue, Lafayette Theater, NYC, 1933; worked Loew's State Theater, NYC, 1933; teamed w Cora La Redd to app in COTTON CLUB PARADE Revue, Cotton Club, NYC, 1933; worked King's Terrace, NYC, 1933; app in Lew Leslie's BLACKBIRDS OF 1933-4 Revue, Majestic Theater, Brooklyn, NY, 1933/42nd Street Apollo Theater, NYC, 1933-4; app in Vitaphone film short SMASH YOUR BAGGAGE, 1933; worked w Fletcher Henderson Band, Lafayette Theater, NYC, 1934; app w Chick Webb Band, GET TOGETHER Revue, Lafayette Theater, NYC, 1934; worked Ubangi Club, NYC, 1934; owned/operated/performed at Poosepahtuck Club, NYC, 1934; worked Harlem Opera House, NYC, 1934; Dickie Well's, NYC, 1934; sang at Bessie Smith's funeral service, OV Catto Elks Lodge, Philadelphia, PA, 1937; worked Washington House, Washington, DC, 1938; frequently worked as MC, Lincoln Theater, New Orleans, LA, 1941; worked LD Club, Newport News, VA, early 40s; Apollo Theater, NYC, 1943; rec w Clyde Hart All Stars, Continental label, NYC, 1945; rec w Oscar Pettiford All-Stars, Manor label, NYC, 1945; rec w Herbie Fields Band, Savoy label, NYC, 1945; rec Haven label, NYC, 1946; worked mostly outside music in NYC from mid-40s; suffered fatal heart attack at Hotel Braddock; buried Ferncliff Cemetery, Hartsdale, NY

Songs: Bring It on Home/Deep Sea Blues/Did You Ever Set Thinkin'?/Going Back to Washington Corner 7th and "T"/That's the Blues

WILLIAMS, IRENE
(see Taylor, Eva)

WILLIAMS, JO JO
(see Williams, Joseph)

WILLIAMS, JODY
(see Williams, Joseph Leon)

WILLIAMS, JOE
Born: Dec 12, 1918, Cordele (Crisp Co), GA
Inst: Piano

Father was Willie Goreed; mother Anne Gilbert was singer; born Joseph Goreed; to Chicago, IL c1922; afflicted by tuberculosis at 15; often worked as singer in local churches/weddings/funerals, Chicago, mid-30s; formed own The Jubilee Boys working local churches, Chicago, mid-30s; worked w Jimmie Noone Band at Cabin Inn and other clubs, Chicago, 1937-8; worked Savoy Ballroom, Chicago, c1938; toured w Les Hite Band working dance dates, 1939-40; worked w Coleman Hawkins Band, Cafe Society, Chicago, 1941; w Lionel Hampton Band in local clubs, Chicago, 1943; toured w Andy Kirk Band working dance dates c1944; worked briefly w Albert Ammons/Pete Johnson, early 40s; frequently worked w Red Saunders Band, Club De Lisa, Chicago, from 1945 into 50s; rec w Red Saunders Band, OKeh label, NYC, c1946; worked w Andy Kirk Band, Apollo Theater, NYC, 1946; w Jay Burkhart Orch, Blue Note Club, Chicago, c1949; w Count Basie Septet, Brass Rail, Chicago, 1950; Paris Club, Chicago, c1950; rec w Red Saunders Band (as "Jumpin' Joe Williams"), Columbia label, Chicago, 1950; rec w Red Saunders

Joe Williams *Courtesy Sheldon Harris Collection*

Orch, OKeh label, Chicago, 1951; rec w Red Saunders Band, Regent label, Chicago, 1954; joined Count Basie Band and toured extensively working clubs/concerts, 1954-61; frequently w Count Basie at Birdland, NYC, 1955-8; rec w Count Basie Orch, Clef label, NYC, 1955-6; worked Newport Jazz Festival, Newport, RI, 1955 (por on MUSIC USA, VOA-radio); rec w Count Basie Orch, Verve label, NYC, 1956; frequently w Count Basie Orch, Apollo Theater, NYC, 1956 into 60s (por of 1956 date rel Vanguard label); toured w Count Basie Orch working concert dates through England/Europe, 1956; rec Verve label, Gothenburg, Sweden, 1956; worked New York Jazz Festival, Randalls Island, NY, 1956-8; rec Verve label, Los Angeles, 1956-7; toured w Count Basie on Alan Freed & His Rock 'n' Roll Holiday Jubilee package show working theaters, 1956; rec w Count Basie Orch/Jimmy Mundy Orch, Roulette label, NYC, 1957; worked Birdland All-Stars Revue, Carnegie Hall, NYC, 1957, then toured with revue working concerts across US/Canada; worked Newport Jazz Festival, Newport, RI, 1957 (por rel Verve label/por on MUSIC USA, VOA-radio); app w Count Basie Orch in film JAMBOREE, 1957; worked Stratford Jazz Festival, Stratford, Can, 1957 (por on Trans-Canada radio network); app w Count Basie, PERRY COMO SHOW, CBS-TV, 1958; rec w Count Basie Orch, Roulette label, NYC, 1958; worked Bermuda Palms Ballroom, San Rafael, CA, 1958; app on ED SULLIVAN Show, CBS-TV, 1959; app on GEORGE HAMILTON IV Show, ABC-TV, 1959; worked Toronto Jazz Festival, Toronto, Can, 1959; Monterey Jazz Festival, Monterey, CA, 1959; Crescendo Club, Hollywood, CA, 1959; Newport Jazz Festival, Newport, RI, 1959; French Lick Jazz Festival, French Lick, IN, 1959; Playboy Jazz Festival, Chicago Stadium, Chicago, IL, 1959; Blue Note Club, Chicago, 1959; Festival of Music, Philadelphia, PA, 1959; rec Roulette label, NYC/Los Angeles, CA/Miami, FL, 1959-60; app w Count Basie Orch, FRED ASTAIRE Show, CBS-TV, 1960; worked Mosque Theater, Newark, NJ, 1960; Rockland Palace, NYC, 1960; Donnelly Theater, Boston, MA, 1960; Buffalo Jazz Festival, Buffalo, NY, 1960-1; app w Count Basie in film CINDERFELLA, 1960; worked Robert's Show Lounge, Chicago, 1960; extensively toured w Harry Edison Quintet working club dates, 1960-2; rec w Harry Edison, Roulette label, Los Angeles/NYC, 1961; worked Jazz Gallery, NYC, 1961; The Cloister, Los Angeles, 1961 (por rel Roulette label); worked Club Neve, San Francisco, 1961; Pep's, Philadelphia, PA, 1961; The Tivoli, Chicago, 1961; Impulse Club, Rochester, NY, 1961; New York Jazz Festival, Randalls Island, NY, 1961; The Roundtable, NYC, 1961; app on MOODS IN MELODY Show, unknown TV, 1961; worked New Fack's, San Francisco, 1961; frequently at Town Tavern, Toronto, Can, 1961-8; Sutherland Hotel, Chicago, 1961; Birdland, NYC, 1961-4 (por 1962 date rel Roulette label); Renaissance Club, Los Angeles, CA, 1962; Colonial Tavern, Toronto, 1962; Toronto Jazz Festival, Toronto, 1962; Newport Jazz Festival, Newport, RI, 1962 (por rel in film NEWPORT JAZZ FESTIVAL 1962); Village Vanguard, NYC, 1962; rec w Oliver Nelson's Orch, Victor label, NYC, 1962; toured w Junior Mance Trio working concert dates through England, 1962; worked Cinestage Theater, Chicago, IL, 1962; Sugar Hill Club, San Francisco, 1963; rec w Jimmy Jones Orch/Oliver Nelson Orch, Victor label, NYC, 1963; worked Basin Street East, NYC, 1963; Newport Jazz Festival, Newport, RI, 1963 (por rel Victor label); Pio's Lodge, Providence, RI, 1963; app on PARADE Show, CBC-TV, Toronto, Can, 1963; worked Jazz Villa, St Louis, MO, 1963; New Leo's Casino, Cleveland, OH, 1963; Le Bistro Club, Chicago, 1963; Basin Street South, Boston, MA, 1963; Grand Bar, Detroit, MI, 1963; Pep's, Philadelphia, PA, 1963-5; app on THE STEVE ALLEN SHOW, WABC-TV, NYC (syndicated), 1963; frequently app on Johnny Carson's TONIGHT Show, NBC-TV, 1963-7; worked Pittsburgh Jazz Festival, Pittsburgh, PA, 1964; Newport Jazz Festival, Newport, RI, 1964-7 (por 1966 concert heard on MUSIC USA, VOA-radio); Hootenanny Club, Los Angeles, CA, 1964; Bourbon Street, Chicago, IL, 1964; Monterey Jazz Festival, Monterey, CA, 1964; Diplomat Hotel, Hollywood, FL, 1965; Jazzville, San Diego, CA, 1965; app on SHINDIG, ABC-TV, 1965; Basin Street West, San Francisco, CA, 1965-7; The Bistro, Atlantic City, NJ, 1965; The Phone Booth, NYC, 1965; Downbeat Jazz Festival, Chicago, IL, 1965; Ohio Valley Jazz Festival, Cincinnati, OH, 1965; Shrine Auditorium, Los Angeles, CA, 1965; The Blue Angel, Chicago, IL, 1965; Al Hirt's Club, New Orleans, LA, 1965; w Count Basie Orch, Philharmonic Hall, NYC, 1965; toured England working club/concert dates, 1965; worked Versailles, Cleveland, OH, 1966; Fremont Theater, Las Vegas, NV, 1966; Baker's Keyboard Lounge, Detroit, MI, 1966-8; app on ARTHUR GODFREY TIME, CBS-radio, 1966; app on STROLLIN' 20s, CBS-TV, 1966; app on DIAL M FOR MUSIC, CBS-TV, 1966-7; worked Lennie's, Boston, MA, 1966-7; Ohio Valley Jazz Festival, Cincinnati, OH, 1966; Harry's American Showroom, Miami, FL, 1966; Half Note Club, NYC, 1966; app on MIKE DOUGLAS Show, WOR-TV, NYC, 1966-7; app on DANNY

KAYE Show, CBS-TV, 1966; worked extensive residencies at Hong Kong Bar, Century Plaza Hotel, Los Angeles, CA, 1966-72; The Showcase, Oakland, CA, 1966; Shelly's Manne Hole, Los Angeles, 1967; Rainbow Grill, NYC, 1967-8; app on BRUCE MORROW Show, ABC-TV, 1967; worked Plugged Nickel, Chicago, IL, 1967-8; Ad Lib Club, Milwaukee, WI, 1967; Rheingold Music Festival, Central Park, NYC, 1967-8; app on JOEY BISHOP Show, ABC-TV, 1967-8; worked Colonial Tavern, Toronto, Can, 1967-70; Watts Festival, Los Angeles, 1967; Olympic Hotel, Seattle, WA, 1967; Marty's, Los Angeles, 1967; The Living Room, Cincinnati, 1967; Opera House, Chicago, 1967; app on MIKE DOUGLAS Show, CBS-TV, 1968-71; worked Bay Area Jazz Festival, Berkeley, CA, 1968; The Cellar Door, Washington, DC, 1968; app on STEVE ALLEN Show, WOR-TV, NYC (syndicated), 1968; app w Count Basie, MIKE & MUSIC Show, CBS-TV, 1968; app on MERV GRIFFIN Show, WNEW-TV, NYC (syndicated), 1968; app on George Jessel's HERE COMES THE STARS, WOR-TV, NYC (syndicated), 1968; app on DONALD O'CONNOR SHOW, WNEW-TV, NYC (syndicated), 1968; toured West Germany working club/concert dates, 1969; worked Circle Star Theater, San Carlos, CA, 1969; app on PETER WOLF Show, CBS-TV, 1969; worked Club Baron, NYC, 1969; app on Hugh Hefner PLAYBOY AFTER DARK Show, WOR-TV, NYC, 1969; worked Hotel Tropicana, Las Vegas, NV, 1969-71; app at Awards Presentation for Duke Ellington hosted by President Richard Nixon at The White House, Washington, DC, 1969 (por shown in film DUKE ELLINGTON AT THE WHITE HOUSE); app in non-singing role in film THE MOONSHINE WAR, 1969; app on STEVE ALLEN Show, WPIX-TV, NYC (syndicated), 1970; app on DELLA Show, WOR-TV, NYC (syndicated), 1970; app on Johnny Carson's TONIGHT Show, NBC-TV, 1970-1; worked Paul's Mall, Boston, MA, 1970; Pittsburgh Jazz Festival, Pittsburgh, PA, 1970; Monterey Jazz Festival, Monterey, CA, 1970 (por shown in film MONTEREY JAZZ); worked Lennie's, Boston, MA, 1970; CYO Jazz Festival, Pittsburgh, PA, 1970; Apollo Theater, NYC, 1970-1; High Chaparral, Chicago, 1970; rec w George Shearing group, Sheba label, c1970; worked Disneyland Park, Anaheim, CA, 1971; Mr Henry's, Washington, DC, 1971; Palace Theater, Milwaukee, WI, 1971; app frequently as DJ, KVOV-radio, Las Vegas, NV, 1971; worked Kennedy Center Festival, Washington, DC, 1971; app on MERV GRIFFIN Show, CBS-TV, 1971; app on OUR AMERICAN MUSICAL HERITAGE, CBS-TV, 1971; worked Mill Run Theater, Niles, IL, 1971; University Club, Pasadena, CA, 1971; toured w Count Basie Orch working concert dates through England/Europe, 1972; worked w Count Basie Orch, Newport Jazz Festival, NYC, 1972; Monterey Jazz Festival, Monterey, CA, 1972; Philharmonic Hall, NYC, 1972 (por shown TIMEX ALL-STAR SWING FESTIVAL, NBC-TV); worked Half Note, NYC, 1972-4; app w US Air Force Band on SERENADE IN BLUE, syndicated radio, 1972-7; app on DUKE ELLINGTON SPECIAL, CBS-TV, 1973; worked extensive club/hotel/show work in Las Vegas, NV, 1973; Newport Jazz Festival, NYC, 1973 (por heard MUSIC USA, VOA-radio); Shrine Auditorium, Los Angeles, 1973; Concert by the Sea, Los Angeles, 1973-5; The Landmark, Kansas City, MO, 1973; La Casa Club, St Louis, MO, 1973-4; Just Jazz Club, Philadelphia, PA, 1973; rec w Cannonball Adderley, Fantasy label, Berkeley, CA, 1973; worked Jazz Showcase, Chicago, 1974; Playboy Club, Chicago, 1974; app on FEELING GOOD, PBS-TV, 1974; app on MERV GRIFFIN Show, WNEW-TV, NYC, 1974; app on MIDNIGHT SPECIAL, NBC-TV, 1974; worked Caribbean Cruise Ship SS *Rotterdam*, 1974; sang at Duke Ellington funeral, Cathedral Church of St John the Divine, NYC, 1974 (por remote WRVR-FM-radio/MUSIC USA, VOA-radio); app w Count Basie Orch, OSCAR PETERSON PRESENTS, CBS-TV, 1974; worked w Count Basie Orch, Newport Jazz Festival, NYC, 1974 (por on MUSIC USA, VOA-radio); app on AM AMERICA, ABC-TV, 1975; worked Winston Towers, Cliffside Park, NJ, 1975; app on SAMMY AND COMPANY, NBC-TV, 1975; worked w Buddy Rich Band, Buddy's Place, NYC, 1975; The Parisian Room, Los Angeles, 1975; app on MIKE DOUGLAS Show, CBS-TV, 1976; app on FESTIVAL OF LIVELY ARTS FOR YOUNG PEOPLE (ep: All Star Jazz Show), CBS-TV, 1976; worked Harrah's Club, Reno, NV, 1976; Newport Jazz Festival, NYC, 1976; Hopper's, NYC, 1976-8; app on AT THE TOP, PBS-TV, 1976; app on JOE FRANKLIN Show, WOR-TV, NYC, 1976; fronted Count Basie Band working local club dates through California, 1976; worked Plymouth Hilton, Detroit, MI, 1976; app on MERV GRIFFIN Show, WNEW-TV, NYC, 1977; w Count Basie Orch, Masonic Temple, Detroit, MI, 1977; Sandy's Jazz Revival, Beverly, MA, 1977; Newport Jazz Festival, Carnegie Hall, NYC, 1977; Basin Street, Toronto, Can, 1977; Jazz Showcase, Chicago, 1977; Nice Jazz Festival, Nice, France, 1977; Paul Gray's Place, Lawrence, KS, 1977; Monterey Jazz Festival, Monterey, CA, 1977; toured w Clark Terry group for US State Department working concert/TV dates through Egypt/Turkey/Afghanistan/Pakistan/

India, 1977; worked Rick's Cafe American, Chicago, 1978; app w Count Basie Orch, BIG BAND BASH, PBS-TV, 1978; app on CHUCK BARRIS RAH RAH SHOW, NBC-TV, 1978; worked w Count Basie Orch, Newport Jazz Festival, Avery Fisher Hall, NYC, 1978; app on Johnny Carson's TONIGHT Show, NBC-TV, 1978

Personal: Married 4 times. Not to be confused w "Big" Joe Lee Williams, blues singer/guitarist

Book: *Every Day: The Story of Joe Williams,* Leslie Gourse, Quartet Books, 1985

Songs: My Baby Upsets Me/Sho She Do

Awards/Honors: Won *Downbeat* magazine Readers Poll for Best Male Band Singer, 1955, 1956

Won *Downbeat* magazine International Critics Poll for Best New Star Male Singer, 1955

Won *Rhythm & Blues* magazine plaque for top song of 1956 ("Everyday I Have the Blues")

Won *Billboard* magazine DJ Poll for favorite male vocalist, 1959

Won *Downbeat* magazine International Critics Poll for Best Male Singer, 1974, 1975, 1976, 1977, 1978

Infl by: Joe Turner

Quotes: "His natural style is closer to the Kansas City urban blues shout of Rushing and Witherspoon"—Ray Townley, *Downbeat* magazine, Jan 17, 1974, p 19

". . . while his reputation was made on blues, Joe excels on ballads and jazz material"—Dan Morgenstern, *Jazz Journal* magazine (UK), Aug 1977, p 15

Reference: *Every Day: The Story of Joe Williams,* Leslie Gourse, Quartet Books, 1985

WILLIAMS, *"Big"/"Po"* JOE LEE

(aka: Big Joe)
Born: Oct 16, 1903, Crawford (Lowndes Co), MS
Died: Dec 17, 1982, Macon, MS
Inst: Accordion/Guitar/Harmonica/Kazoo

Father was John "Red Bone" Williams, a Cherokee Indian; mother was Carlee May; born Joseph Lee Williams on a farm on edge of Knoxford Swamp outside of Crawford, MS; one of 16 children; interested in music early and learned music on homemade guitar and flute at about 5 years of age; left home to hobo through Mississippi working outside music with frequent work as singer/dancer/guitarist at

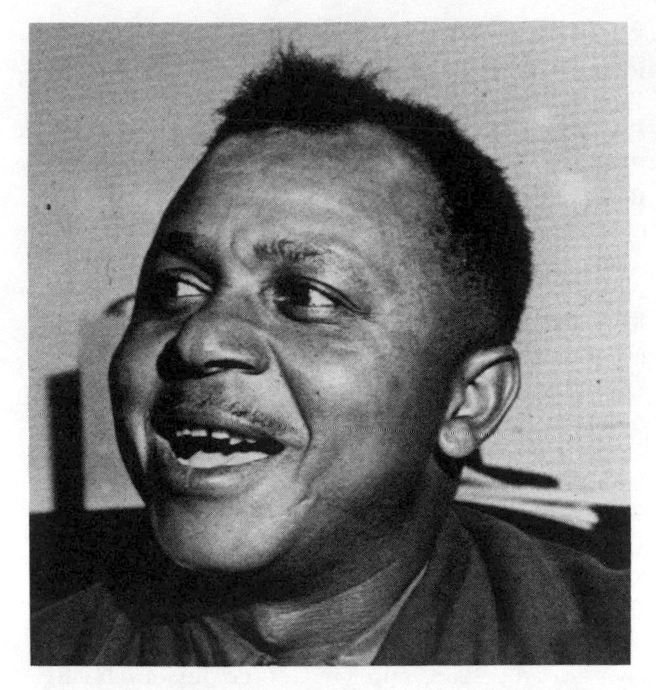

Courtesy Frank Driggs Collection

picnics/roadhouses/dances/fish fries/levee and railroad camps from c1915 into 20s; worked in Doc Bennett Medicine Show, Mobile, AL, c1918; reportedly rec on (unknown) label, New Orleans, LA, c1921; toured w Birmingham Jug Band on Rabbit Foot Minstrels tent show through South c1922-4; frequently toured w Little Brother Montgomery working brothel circuit through Mississippi/Louisiana through 20s; continued to hobo across US working outside music with frequent work at parties/picnics/suppers through 20s; rec Vocalion label, Memphis, TN, 1929; frequently worked w St Louis Jimmy at local house rent parties, St Louis, MO, c1929; frequently toured w Birmingham Jug Band working jukes/streets through Bessemer/Birmingham/Tuscaloosa, AL, areas, late 20s into 30s; rec w Birmingham Jug Band, OKeh label, Atlanta, GA, 1930; rec Paramount label, Grafton, WI, 1932; continued to hobo across US working outside music with frequent work at country suppers/picnics/turpentine camps/levee-lumber camps/brothels/streets through 30s; worked w Honeyboy Edwards at parties/dances through Mississippi/Louisiana into Gulf Coast areas, 1932-3; worked w Bogus Ben Covington at Century of Progress Exposition, Chicago, IL, 1934; frequently rec Bluebird label, Chicago, 1935-45; together w Peetie Wheatstraw operated/performed at St Louis Club, St Louis, MO, c1939 and frequently as single into 40s; frequently worked w Bill Lucas in local streets, St Louis, 1941; formed own group (including Muddy Waters) working local clubs/jukes, Clarksdale, MS, 1941; rec Chicago label, Chicago, 1945; frequently worked w Charley Jordan in local clubs, St Louis, through 40s; rec w John Lee "Sonny Boy" Williamson, Columbia label, Chicago, 1947; rec Bullet label, St Louis, 1949; rec Oldie Blues label, St Louis, 1951-2; app on Studs Terkel I COME FOR TO SING Show, local TV, Chicago, early 50s; rec Trumpet label, Jackson, MS, 1952; toured w Jimmy Walker working club dates through Ohio/Pennsylvania, early 50s; rec VJ label, Chicago, 1956; worked Westminster Col, Fulton, MO, 1957; rec Delmar(k) label, St Louis, 1957-8; rec Collector label, Chicago, 1957; rec Arhoolie label, Oakland, CA, 1959; rec Arhoolie label, Los Gatos, CA, 1960; rec w Sonny Terry/Brownie McGhee, World Pacific label, Los Angeles, CA, 1960; worked Ash Grove, Los Angeles, 1960; Gate of Horn, Chicago, 1960; Oxford Coffee House, Chicago, 1960; Blind Pig, Chicago, 1960-1; rec Delmar(k)/Folkways/Xtra labels, Chicago, 1961; worked Univ of Chicago Folk Festival, Chicago, 1962; Yale Univ, New Haven, CT, 1962; Univ of Illinois, Urbana, IL, 1962; Gerde's Folk City, NYC, 1962 (por rel Bluesville label); Carnegie Hall, NYC, 1962; rec Bluesville label, NYC, 1962; formed own trio to work local dance halls/clubs, St Louis, from 1962; worked Birdhouse, Chicago, 1963; Gate of Horn, Chicago, 1963; Limelight Cafe, Chicago, 1963; Paul's Roast Round, Chicago, 1963; Skylight Theater, Milwaukee, WI, 1963; Fickle Pickle, Chicago, 1963-4; toured w American Folk-Blues Festival working concert dates through England/Europe, 1963 (por on I HEAR THE BLUES, Granada-TV, London, Eng); rec Fontana label, Bremen, Ger, 1963; rec Storyville label, Copenhagen, Den, 1963; worked Ravisloe Country Club, Homewood, IL, 1963; rec Spivey label, Chicago, 1963; worked Grinnell Col Folk Festival, Grinnell, IA, 1963; rec w Yank Rachell, Delmark label, Chicago, 1963-4; rec Testament label, Chicago, 1964; rec Milestone label, Chicago, 1964-6; worked Univ of Chicago Folk Festival, Chicago, 1964; Big John's Club, Chicago, 1964; toured Midwest working small clubs/coffeehouses in Bloomington, IN/DeKalb, IL/Milwaukee, WI/elsewhere, 1964; worked Bard Col, Annandale-on-Hudson, NY, 1964; rec w Short Stuff Macon, Spivey/Folkways labels, Brooklyn, NY, 1964; worked Rockford Col Seminar, Rockford, IL, 1965; The Yellow Unicorn, Chicago, 1965; Downbeat Jazz Festival, Chicago, 1965; Cafe A-Go-Go, NYC, 1965-6 (por 1966 date rel Verve label); Folksong '65, Carnegie Hall, NYC, 1965; La Faim Foetale, Montreal, Can, 1965; app on FESTIVAL PRESENTS THE BLUES, CBC-TV, Toronto, Can, 1966; worked Electric Circus, NYC, 1968; toured w American Folk Blues Festival working concert dates through England/Europe, 1968 (por shown in UK film AMERICAN FOLK BLUES FESTIVAL); rec World Pacific label, London, 1968; worked United Disciple of Christ Church, Chicago, 1968; Univ of Wisconsin Blues Festival, Madison, WI, 1969; Chicago Blues Festival, Chicago, 1969; rec Adelphi label, Chicago, 1969; Ann Arbor Blues Festival, Ann Arbor, MI, 1969; rec Arhoolie label, Berkeley, CA, 1969; worked The Matrix, San Francisco, 1970; Roosevelt Univ, Chicago, 1970; Univ of Illinois, Urbana, IL, 1970; Wisconsin Delta Blues Festival, Beloit Col, Beloit, WI, 1970; Alice's Revisited, Chicago, 1970-2; rec Delmark label, Chicago, c1971; toured w Chicago Blues Festival working concert dates/TV appearances through Europe, 1971; rec Blues on Blues label, Chicago (?), c1971; worked Ash Grove, Los Angeles, CA, 1971; New Orleans Jazz & Heritage Fair, New Orleans, LA, 1972; toured w American Folk-Blues Festival working concert dates through Europe, 1972; rec Storyville label, Copenhagen, Den, 1972; rec Sonet label, Stockholm, Sweden, 1972; toured extensively working concert dates through Europe, 1973; worked Zodiac Club, Amstelveen, Holland, 1973 (por rel Oldie Blues label); mostly inactive in music due to illness from 1974; app on local blues show, WMAB-TV, Jackson, MS, 1974; worked State Historical Museum Concert, Jackson, 1974; toured w Blues Festival working concert dates through Japan, 1974; rec Blues on Blues label, Muscle Shoals, AL, 1974; worked Festival of American Folklife, Washington, DC, 1976 (por shown on GLORIOUS FOURTH, NBC-TV); John Henry Folk Festival, Camp Virgil Tate, Princeton, WV, 1976; app on THE DEVIL'S MUSIC—A HISTORY OF THE BLUES (ep: Work and Mother Wit/ep: The Movements of Providence), BBC-1-TV, England, 1976; toured concert dates through Germany, 1976; worked Quartier Latin, Berlin, Ger, 1977; app GOOD MORNIN' BLUES, PBS-TV, 1978; Delta Blues Fest, Greenville, MS, 1978-80 (por 1980 concert shown MISSISSIPPI DELTA BLUES, PBS-TV, 1981); New Orleans Jazz & Heritage Fest, New Orleans, LA, 1979; concerts in US into 80s; died of heart disease; buried Crigler Cemetery, Crawford, NJ

Book: Me and Big Joe, Michael Bloomfield/SE Summerville, RE/SEARCH Productions, 1980

Songs: A Change Gotta Be Made/A Man Against Men/Army Man in Vietnam/Baby Keeps On Breaking 'em Down/Back Home Blues/Back on My Feet/Bad Living/Big Fat Mama/Black Gal You're Sure Looking

Warm/Blues Around the World/Break 'em On Down/Bringin' My Baby Back Home/Brother James/Christmas Blues/Church Bells Ring/Crazin' the Blues/Creole Queen/The Death of Dr Martin Luther King/Delta Blues/Dirt Road Blues/Don't Your Plums Look Mellow Hanging on Your Tree/El Paso Blues/ Every Day Brings Out a Change/Everybody's Gonna Miss Me When I'm Gone/Four Corners of the World/Going Down Home/Got to Put You Down/ Greystone Blues/Hang It Up on the Wall/Highway 49/I Been Wrong But I'll Be Right/I Know You Gonna Miss Me/I Want to Know What My Baby's Puttin' Down/I Won't Be in Hard Luck No More/I Won't Do That No More/I'm Getting Wild About Her/If You Can't Shimmy-She-Wabble/Jefferson and Franklin Blues/Jinx Blues/Jockey Ride Blues/Juanita Blues/ Juanita Stomp/Jump Jump Julie/Keep-A-Walkin' Little Girl/King Jesus/Kingshighway Blues/Levee Break Blues/Little Annie Mae/Lone Wolf/Lookie Here Baby/Louisiana Bound/Mad Mad Blues/Mama Don't Allow No Doggin' All Night Long/Mama Don't Like Me Runnin' 'Round/Mean Stepfather/Meet Me Around the Corner/Mink Coat Blues/Miss Emma Lou Blues/Montreal Blues/My Baby Left Town/My Baby Won't Be Back No More/New Car Blues/Oh Baby/ Old Saw Mill Blues/Overhaul Your Machine/Peach Orchard Mama/Pearly Mae Blues/Pick a Pickle/Poor Beggar/President Roosevelt/Pretty Willie Done Me Wrong/Quit Draggin'/Ramblin' and Wanderin' Blues/Remember Way Back/Rollin' in Your Arms/ Rootin' Ground Hog/Saturday Night Jump/Scardie Mama/71 Cadillac Blues/Shady Grove/Shaggy Hound Blues/Shake 'em On Down/She Won't Do Right/ Sittin' 'n Thinkin'/So Glad/So Soon I'll Be Goin' My Way Back Home/Some Old Rainy Day/Somebody's Been Foolin'/Somebody's Been Worryin'/Someday Baby/Southern Whistle Blow/Sugar Hill/Take It All/ Take Me Out of the Bottom/Taylor Made Stomp/Tell Me Who's Been Telling You/Tell My Mother/That Thing's in Town/Things Gonna Come My Way/ Thinking of What They Did to Me/This Heavy Stuff of Mine/This Old London Town/Throw the Boogie Woogie/Tiajuana Blues/Trouble for Everybody/ Turnroad Blues/Vitamin A (Blues)/Vitamin B Blues/ Wanita/When I First Left Home/Whistling Pine Blues/Working on the Levy/Yo Yo Blues/You Done Me Wrong/You're an Old Lady

Award/Honor: Won Grand Prix du Disque de Jazz of The Hot Club of France, 1962 ("Blues on the Highway," Delmark album 604)

Infl by: Blind Lemon Jefferson

Infl to: Honeyboy Edwards/John Paul Hammond

Quotes: "Big Joe Williams is one of the very last of the great blues singers"—David Mangurian, Bluesville album 1083

"Over the decades, Big Joe's expressive powers have deepened into an extraordinarily refined and complete interaction of voice and guitar"—Pete Welding, Milestone album 63813

"Big Joe Williams' blues is a beautiful experience"—John B Litweiler, *Downbeat* magazine, Oct 31, 1968, p 28

References: *Downbeat* magazine, Feb 13, 1964, pp 23-5, 40

Jazz Journal magazine (UK), Jun 1963, pp 14-17

WILLIAMS, JOHNNY

(see Hooker, John Lee)
(see Warren, Robert)

WILLIAMS, Rev *"Uncle"* JOHNNY

Born: May 15, 1906, Alexandria (Rapides Parish), LA
Inst: Guitar

Parents were both musicians; moved to Houston, TX, as child; moved to Belzoni, MS, c1917; taught self guitar at 12 years of age; frequently worked outside music, Belzoni, to 1923; left home to hobo north working outside music, 1923-c30; returned to Belzoni to work outside music with occasional local work at parties/dances in area c1930-8; moved to Chicago, IL, 1938; frequently worked outside music with frequent work on Maxwell Street for tips, Chicago, from 1938; worked One Way Inn, Chicago, c1940; w Hound Dog Taylor, Stormy's Club, Chicago, c1944; suffered loss of finger in accident and inactive in music through mid-40s; worked w Johnny Young on Maxwell Street, Chicago, from 1947; rec w Johnny Young, Ora-Nelle label, Chicago, 1947; worked w Johnny Young, Square Deal Club, Chicago, 1947 into 50s; w Johnny Young, Millgate Club, Chicago, c1947; 24 Club, Chicago, c1947; rec w Johnny ("Man") Young, Planet label, Chicago, c1947; worked w Snooky Pryor, 24 Club, Chicago, c1947; w Little Walter, Purple Cat Club, Chicago, c1948; w Grayhaired Bill, Kitty Cat Club, Chicago, c1949; worked 520 Club, Chicago, 1951; worked w Big Boy Spires Rocket Four in local club dates, Chicago, early 50s; rec w Big Boy Spires, Chance label, Chicago, 1953; worked w Hound Dog Taylor and others, Square Deal Club/Cotton Club/ 708 Club/Ebony Lounge/620 Club/The Castle Rock/ Alibi Club/others, Chicago, through 50s; worked Turner's Blue Lounge, Chicago, late 50s; w Hound Dog Taylor, Ada's Tavern, Chicago, 1959; mostly active in church work, Chicago, from 1959; ordained pastor of New St Matthew's Baptist Church, Chicago, early 60s

Personal: Cousin of Johnny Young. Not to be confused with John Lee Hooker/Robert Warren who used this name as pseudonym

Infl by: Robert Foster

Quote: "Johnny Williams . . . recorded one of the first modern blues in Chicago ('Worried Man Blues,' Ora-Nelle 712, 1947)"—Sandy Sutherland, *Blues Unlimited* magazine (UK), Feb 1973, p 7

References: Blues Unlimited magazine (UK), Feb/Apr 1973

Jazz & Blues magazine (UK), Dec 1971/ Jan 1972

WILLIAMS, JOSEPH *"Jo Jo"*

Courtesy HH Hanington/Living Blues Magazine

Born: 1920, Coahoma (Coahoma Co), MS
Inst: Guitar

Father was a railroad man; moved to live on farm, Walls, MS, from 1923; learned guitar on home-made instrument as child; moved to Memphis, TN, where he was raised from a youth; worked occasional local parties, Memphis area, late 20s; worked Princess Theater, Memphis, c1942; worked mostly outside music, Memphis, through 40s; moved to Chicago, IL, c1953; formed own band to work club dates in Argo, IL/Chicago, IL, through mid-50s; worked w Bill Lucas in Earl Dranes Trio, Tuxedo Lounge, Chicago, 1956; w Mojo Buford Band (later renamed Muddy Waters Jr Band) working Smitty's Corner/Jamboree Club and others off and on, 1956-60; toured w Harmonica Slim working club dates through South, late 50s; rec Atomic-H label, Chicago, 1959; toured w Muddy Waters Band working road gigs, 1960-2; settled in Minneapolis, MN, to work outside music with frequent work w Mojo Buford and others in local clubs/bars from 1962; reportedly inactive in music, Minneapolis, into 70s

Personal: Not to be confused with singers Joe Williams (Joseph Goreed)/Big Joe Lee Williams/Joseph Leon Williams

Infl by: Jimmy Reed

Reference: Blues Unlimited magazine (UK), Jul/Sept 1969

WILLIAMS, JOSEPH LEON *"Jody"/"Joe"/"Sugar Boy"*
(aka: Little Papa Joe)
Born: Feb 3, 1935, Mobile (Mobile Co), AL
Inst: Bass/Drums/Guitar/Harmonica/Piano

Moved to Chicago, IL, 1941; frequently worked w Bo Diddley Washboard Trio in local streets/houseparties/amateur shows, Chicago, 1946-51; toured w Charles Brown Band in R&B package show working theater dates across US through early 50s; worked w Howlin' Wolf Band in local club dates, Chicago, 1954; w Bo Diddley, Howard Theater, Washington, DC, c1955; worked as house guitarist for VJ/Chess labels, Chicago, through 50s; worked Apollo Theater, NYC, mid-50s; frequently worked w Billy Boy Arnold Band in local clubs, Chicago, through 50s; rec w Billy Boy Arnold Band, VJ label, Chicago, mid-50s; rec Blue Lake label, Chicago, 1955; rec Argo label, Chicago, 1957; rec w Jimmy Rogers Band, Chess label, Chicago, c1959; toured w Otis Rush Band, late 50s; rec w Otis Rush Band, Cobra label, Chicago, late 50s; served in US Army in Germany, late 50s to early 60s; worked/recorded w Bobby Davis Big Three Trio in Chicago, early 60s; rec Herald label, Chicago, 1960; rec w The Daylighters, Jive label, Chicago, 1962; rec Raines label, Chicago, 1965; rec Yulando label, Chicago, 1966; worked mostly outside music, Chicago, through 60s into 70s; worked Ramada Inn, Chicago, early 70s

WILLIAMS

Personal: Not to be confused with singers Joe Williams (Joseph Goreed)/Big Joe Lee Williams/Joseph "Jo Jo" Williams

Songs: I Was Fooled/Lucky Lou

Infl by: BB King

Quote: "An outstanding blues, jazz and R&B guitarist, songwriter and vocalist"—Dick Shurman, *Living Blues* magazine, Spring 1974, p 24

Reference: Living Blues magazine, Spring 1974, pp 24-6

WILLIAMS, L C
(*aka:* Lightnin' Jr)
Born: Mar 12, 1930, Crockett (Houston Co), TX
Died: Oct 18, 1960, Houston, TX
Inst: Drums

Father was Sam Williams; mother was Oddie Bell Reece; moved to Mullican, TX, where he was raised; moved to Houston, TX, c1945; frequently worked local stage shows/dance halls (as singer/dancer), Houston, through 40s; frequently worked w Lightnin' Hopkins and local bands (as sideman) in dance halls/clubs/bars, Houston area, late 40s into 50s; rec w Lightnin' Hopkins and others, Gold Star label, Houston, 1947-8; rec w Connie's Combo (Conrad Johnson), Eddie's label, Houston, 1948; rec w Connie McBooker, Eddie's label, Houston, 1949; rec w JC Conney's Combo, Freedom label, Houston, 1949; rec w Elmore Nixon, Freedom label, Houston, 1949; rec w Lightnin' Hopkins, SIW/Jax label, Houston, 1951; rec Mercury label, Houston, 1951; frequently worked local gigs in Houston area through 50s; app on FOLKSAY, KUHF-FM-radio, Houston, 1959; app on MACK McCORMICK AND FRIENDS, KUHF-FM-radio, Houston, 1960; rec w Lightnin' Hopkins (unissued), Houston, 1960; worked w Lightnin' Hopkins, Sputnik Bar, Houston, 1960; entered TB Hospital where he died of lung disease; buried Bethel Grove, Navasota, TX

Personal: Married/divorced. Given names are initials only

Infl by: Lightnin' Hopkins

Reference: Jazz Monthly magazine (UK), Mar 1961, p 15

WILLIAMS, LEE *"Shot"*
Born: 1938, Lexington (Holmes Co), MS

Interested in music at early age and frequently sang at local parties as child; moved to Chicago, IL, mid-50s; frequently sat-in w Little Mac/Earl Hooker/others in local club dates, Chicago, into 60s; worked Regal Theater, Chicago, early 60s; worked w Oliver Sain's Band, East St Louis, IL, early 60s; rec Foxy label, Chicago (?), 1962; rec King-Federal label, Cincinnati, OH, 1963-4; frequently worked one-nighters in Detroit, MI, area with tours through South through 60s; frequently worked Pepper's Lounge/Blue Flame/The Checkmate/Burning Spear/Bonanza Club/High Chaparral/others, Chicago, through 60s into 70s; rec Palos label, Chicago, 1966; rec Gamma label, Chicago, 1968; rec Sussex label, Chicago (?), 1970; rec PM label, Chicago (?), 1972; worked Key Largo Club, Chicago, 1976; Majestic Lounge, Chicago, 1976; formed own Sweetback Band to tour club dates through South, 1976; worked Eddie Shaw's Place, Chicago, 1977; The Stingrey, Chicago, 1977

Quote: "A good example of a post BB King-Bobby Bland vocalist who mixes current pop styles with a basic blues delivery is Lee 'Shot' Williams"—Dick Shurman, *Blues Unlimited* magazine (UK), Jul 1975, p 16

Reference: Blues Unlimited magazine (UK), Jul 1975, pp 16-17

WILLIAMS, LESTER
Born: Jun 24, 1920, Groveton (Trinity Co), TX
Inst: Guitar

Raised in Houston, TX; worked local club dates with local groups, Houston, from c1945; worked w Smalley's Band in local club dates, Houston, through 40s; formed own combo working local club dates, Houston, from 1949; rec Macy's label, Houston, TX, 1949-50; rec Specialty label, Houston, 1951-2; rec Duke label, Houston, 1954; worked w own band on Dinah Washington Show, Carnegie Hall, NYC, NY, mid-50s; rec Imperial label, Los Angeles, CA, 1956; frequently app on local radio/TV shows in Houston area, late 50s; frequently toured one-nighters across US/Canada/Mexico through 50s into 60s; worked King's Inn, Houston, 1967; worked small clubs/lounges in Minneapolis, MN, 1974-5; worked as one man band in Houston, 1975

Personal: Married. 1 child

Award/Honor: Voted "King of the Blues" by *The Houston Courier* newspaper, Houston, TX, 1952

Quote: ". . . a popular and very well known local (Houston, TX) musician"—Mike Leadbitter, *Blues Unlimited* magazine (UK), Aug 1967, p 11

Reference: Blues Unlimited magazine (UK), Aug 1967, p 11

WILLIAMS, RABBIT'S FOOT
(see Coleman, Burl)

WILLIAMS, ROBERT PETE

Photo by Amy O'Neal. Courtesy Living Blues Magazine

Born: Mar 14, 1914, Zachary (East Baton Rouge Parish), LA
Died: Dec 31, 1980, Rosedale, LA
Inst: Guitar/Kazoo

Parents were sharecroppers; born on Mr Anderson's Place as Robert Williams (adding "Pete" as teenage nickname); one of 9 children; unschooled and worked outside music (as farm hand) from childhood; moved to Scotlandville, LA, working outside music from 1928; first instrument was home-made cigar box guitar, 1934; frequently worked local dances/country suppers/parties/fish fries while continuing outside music work in Zachary/Baton Rouge, LA, areas through 30s into 50s; served time for murder at Angola State Prison Farm, Angola, LA, 1956-9; rec Louisiana Folklore Society label, Angola, 1958; rec Folk-Lyric/Arhoolie labels, Angola/Scotlandville, 1959-61; worked outside music on servitude parole, Denham Springs, LA, 1959-64; rec Prestige-Bluesville label, Scotlandville (?), 1961; worked Preservation Hall, New Orleans, LA, 1963; Newport Folk Festival, Newport, RI, 1964 (por rel Vanguard label); Univ of Chicago Folk Festival, Chicago, IL, 1965; Club 47, Cambridge, MA, 1965; Beloit Lounge, Beloit, WI, 1965; Chumley's Club, Brandeis Univ, Waltham, MA, 1965; Berkeley Folk Festival, Berkeley, CA, 1966; rec Takoma label, Berkeley, 1966; toured w American Folk Blues Festival working concert dates through England/Europe, 1966 (por Berlin, Ger, concert rel Fontana label); rec Fontana label, Bremen, Ger, 1966; worked Ash Grove, Los Angeles, CA, 1966; settled in Maringouin, LA, to work outside music from 1968; rec Saydisc/Ahura Mazda labels, Maringouin, 1970; worked Univ of Notre Dame, South Bend, IN, 1970; San Diego Folk Festival, San Diego, CA, 1970; Tyrone Guthrie Theater, Minneapolis, MN, 1970; Berkeley Blues Festival, Berkeley, CA, 1970; Wisconsin Blues Festival, Beloit Col, Beloit, WI, 1970; Ann Arbor Blues Festival, Ann Arbor, MI, 1970; Univ of Chicago Folk Festival, Chicago, IL, 1971; Boston Blues Society Concert, Harvard Univ, Cambridge, MA, 1971; Festival of American Folklife, Montreal, Can, 1971; rec 77 label, New Orleans, 1971; worked New Orleans Jazz & Heritage Fair/Festival, New Orleans, 1971-8; app in film ROOTS OF AMERICAN MUSIC: COUNTRY & URBAN MUSIC (pt 1), 1971; toured w American Folk Blues Festival working concert dates through Europe, 1972; app in French film OUT OF THE BLACKS INTO THE BLUES (pt 1: Along the Old Man River), 1972; film clip shown in French film BLUES UNDER THE SKIN, 1972; rec Blues Beacon label, Munich, Ger, 1972; rec Storyville label, Copenhagen, Den, 1972; worked Newport Jazz Festival, Philharmonic Hall, NYC, NY 1972; Univ of Vermont, Burlington, VT, 1972; app in film short THINKING OUT LOUD, 1972; rec Sonet label, Baton Rouge, LA, 1973; worked Univ of Miami, Miami, FL, 1974; toured Europe working concert dates, 1974; worked Lewis & Clark Col, Portland, OR, 1974; worked outside music through 70s; rec Dischi Della Quercia label, Milan, Italy, 1977; app MUSIC OF MAN (ep: Parting of The Ways), PBS-TV, 1979; died of heart disease; buried local cemetery, Scotlandville, LA

Songs: Angola Penitentiary Blues/Broken Hearted Man/Come Here and Sit Down on My Knee/Death Blues/Doctor Blues/Farm Blues/Free Again/Freight Train Blues/Goin' Out Have Myself a Ball/Gonna Stand No Quittin'/Goodbye Baby/Goodbye Fay & John/Got Me Way Down Here/Got on His Mind/Graveyard Blues/Greyhound Bus/High as I Want to Be/I'm Lonesome Blues/It's a Long Old Road/It's Hard to Tell/Keep Your Bad Dog off Me/Late Night Boogie/Levee Camp Blues/Lord, Help Poor Me/Meet Him over in Paradise/Pardon Denied Again/Poor Girl out on the Mountain/Prisoner's Talking Blues/Railroad Blues/Rub Me Until My Love Come Down/Salty Woman/So Long Boogie/Some Got Six Months/Somebody Help Poor Me/Sweep My Floor/Talkin' Blues/Texas Blues/Tombstone Blues/Ugly/Up and Down Blues/Vietnam Blues/Whiskey Head Man/Woman You Ain't No Good/You Used to Be a Sweet

Cover Shaker Woman/You're My All Day Steady and My Midnight Dream

Infl by: Lacey Collins/Lightnin' Hopkins/Blind Lemon Jefferson/Guitar Welch

Quotes: "He is almost, in himself, a definition of the country bluesman—a poet of his own experience, his language and idiom coming from the hard country background that shaped him"—Samuel B Charters, *The Legacy of the Blues*, Calder & Boyars Ltd, 1975

"Robert Pete is a real rural bluesman, whose music is tough, mean and, above all, impassioned, like the man himself"—Pete Welding, *Downbeat* magazine, Nov 3, 1966, p 27

"The blues of Robert Pete Williams are more original, more directly personal, and more evocative in their expression of love, frustration, and despair"—Dr Harry Oster, Arhoolie album 2011

References: Takoma album B-1011

Feel Like Going Home, Peter Guralnick, Outerbridge & Dienstfrey, 1971

The Legacy of the Blues, Samuel B Charters, Calder & Boyars Ltd, 1975

WILLIAMS, RUBBERLEGS
(see Williams, Henry)

WILLIAMS, SUGAR BOY
(see Williams, Joseph Leon)

WILLIAMS, SUSAN
(see McCoy, Viola)

WILLIAMSON, *"James"* JOHN A
(*aka:* Homesick James/Jick [and His Trio])
Born: Apr 30, 1910, Somerville (Fayette Co), TN
Inst: Bass/Guitar/Harmonica

Born John William Henderson; parents were unmarried but given father's surname as child; one of at least 13 children; parents were musicians; taught self guitar at 10 years of age; ran away from home to work dances/suppers/fish fries/picnics/taverns/streets in area from 1920; hoboed widely working w Blind Boy Fuller/John Estes/Frank Stokes/others in streets/jukes/picnics through Tennessee/North Carolina/Mississippi through 20s; settled in Chicago, IL, c1930; frequently worked outside music with occasional houseparties, Chicago, into 30s; worked w Horace Henderson group, Circle Inn, Chicago, 1934; Square Deal Club, Chicago, 1934; rec Victor label, Memphis, TN, 1937; formed own The Dusters working jukes/taverns through South, 1938; frequently worked picnics/suppers in Memphis area, 1939; rec w Buddy Doyle, Vocalion label, Memphis, 1939; hoboed extensively across US into 40s; worked w Big Joe Williams in local clubs, St Louis, MO, c1941; worked w Othum Brown on streets/whiskey joints, Chicago, early 40s; worked w John Lee "Sonny Boy" Williamson, Purple Cat, Chicago, c1945; frequently worked club dates w Elmore James, Memphis, c1946; frequently worked/toured w Elmore James through 40s into 50s; worked w Floyd Jones, Club Jamboree, Chicago, late 40s into early 50s; w Lazy Bill, 1015 Club, Chicago, 1951; rec Chance label, Chicago, 1951; w Albert King working local club dates, South Bend, IN, 1953; frequently worked outside music in Chicago area through 50s into 60s; worked w Baby Face Leroy, Club Jamboree, Chicago, mid-50s; w Bill Broonzy, Johnson Lounge, Chicago, mid-50s; w Bill Lucas, Cotton Club, Chicago, c1954; toured w Elmore James working club dates in St Louis, MO, from mid-50s; rec w Elmore James, Flair label, c1955; worked Key Largo Club, Chicago, 1956; Club Alex, Chicago, 1956; Charlie's Lounge, Chicago, 1956; Sylvio's, Chicago, 1956; rec w Elmore James, Chief label, Chicago, 1957; rec w Elmore James, Fire/Chess labels, Chicago, 1959-61; worked Thelma's, Chicago, c1960; rec Atomic label, Chicago, 1960; rec Colt/USA labels, Chicago, 1962; rec w Roosevelt Sykes, Delmark label, Chicago, 1963; formed own band working Andrew's Lounge, Chicago, 1963; Fickle Pickle, Chicago, 1963; Shamrock Club, Chicago, 1963-4; Pride & Joy Club, Chicago, 1963-4; rec Spivey/Decca/Bluesville-Prestige labels, Chicago, 1964; worked

Photo by Peter B Lowry

Monterey Jazz Festival, Monterey, CA, 1964; rec Vanguard label, Chicago, 1965; worked Kansas City Red's, Chicago, 1969; Monterey Jazz Festival, Monterey, CA, 1969; Berkeley Festival, Berkeley, CA, 1969; Grant Park Blues Festival, Chicago, 1969; Rose & Kelly's, Chicago, 1970; toured w American Blues Festival working concert dates through England/Europe, 1970; rec Black & Blue label, Bordeaux, France, 1970; rec Chess label, Chicago, 1970; worked North Park Hotel, Chicago, 1971; Notre Dame Blues Festival, South Bend, IN, 1971; The Brown Shoe, Chicago, 1972; app on WNIB-FM-radio, Chicago, 1972; worked Digby's, Chicago, 1972; The Post, Chicago, 1972; Wise Fools Pub, Chicago, 1972; rec w Snooky Pryor, Today label, Chicago, 1972; app on ATOMIC MAMA'S WANG DANG DOODLE BLUES SHOW, WNIB-FM-radio, Chicago, 1972-3 (por 1973 date rel Advent label); toured w Snooky Pryor and American Blues Legends '73 working TV/radio/concert dates through England/Europe, 1973; rec w Snooky Pryor, Big Bear-Polydor label, London, Eng, 1973; worked Philadelphia Folk Festival, Schwenksville, Pa, 1973; rec BluesWay label, Chicago, 1973; worked Ann Arbor Blues Festival, Ann Arbor, MI, 1973; Univ of Chicago Folk Festival, Chicago, 1974; Otto's, Chicago, 1975; toured w American Blues Legends '75 working concert dates through England/Europe, 1975; worked 100 Club, London, 1975 (por rel Big Bear label); Elsewhere Club, Chicago, 1975-8; Chicago Blues Festival, Jane Addams Theater, Chicago, 1975; Kingston Mines, Chicago, 1976; Great American Coffee House, Chicago, 1976

Personal: Married. 1 child. Reportedly cousin of Elmore James. Named "Homesick James" (by Lazy Bill Lucas) after his 1951 record of "Homesick"

Songs: Alligator Man/Been 'round a Long Time/Can't Do It/Can't Hold Out/Go Away Go Away Blues/Homecoming Blues/Homesick (Blues)/Homesick's Blues/Homesick's Rock/Homesick's Shuffle/I Believe My Baby's Gone/I Need Love/I've Got to Move/If I Could Live My Life All Over Again/Johnny Mae/Kissing in the Dark/Lonesome Train/Mailman/My Baby's Gone/No More Lovin'/Set a Day/Sugar Mama/Tin Pan Alley/Unlucky/Woman I Love/Workin' with Homesick

Infl by: Blind Blake/Elmore James

Infl to: Magic Sam

Quotes: "There is a curiously powerful, strangely unique quality that marks Homesick's playing"—Pete Welding, Prestige album 7388

"His bottle neck guitar has that compound of mellifluous grace and power that characterises his work"—Mike Rowe, *Chicago Breakdown,* Eddison Press Ltd, 1973

References: Blues Unlimited magazine (UK), Sept/Oct/Nov 1971

Chicago Breakdown, Mike Rowe, Eddison Press Ltd, 1973

WILLIAMSON, JOHN LEE *"Sonny Boy"*

Courtesy Living Blues *Magazine*

Born: Mar 30, 1914, Jackson (Madison Co), TN
Died: Jun 1, 1948, Chicago, IL
Inst: Harmonica

Father was Ray Williamson; mother was Nancy Utley; taught self harmonica as child; left home to hobo with Yank Rachell/John Estes working juke joints/taverns/streets/picnics/parties through Tennessee/Arkansas, late 20s into 30s; worked w Sunnyland Slim in local clubs, Memphis, TN, early 30s; worked w Yank Rachell, Blue Flame Club, Jackson, TN, 1933; settled in Chicago, IL, 1934; frequently worked as sideman in many blues groups in local clubs, Chicago, 1934 into 40s; rec Bluebird label, Aurora, IL, 1937-8; rec Bluebird label, Chicago, 1939-45; frequently worked Maxwell Street area for tips, Chicago, through 30s into 40s; worked w Bill Broonzy, Ruby's Tavern, Chicago, 1940; frequently worked Triangle Inn, Chicago, 1942-5; frequently worked w Muddy Waters Band, Plantation Club and others, Chicago, from 1943; frequently worked Van's Hot Spot, Gary, IN, 1943-5; Chicken Shack, Chicago, IL, 1943; Sylvio's, Chicago, 1943; toured w Lazy Bill Lucas working club dates in Battle Creek, MI/South Bend, IN/Chicago, IL, through 40s; worked Kitty Kat Club, Chicago, c1945; rec Victor label, Chicago, 1945-7; worked Tempo Tap Club/Flame Club/Purple Cat/White Front/others, Chicago, 1945-8; worked club dates in Memphis, TN, 1946; w Baby Face Leroy working clubs/parties, Chicago, 1946; rec w Big Joe Williams, Columbia label, Chicago, 1947; worked Music at Midnight Concert, Town Hall, NYC, NY, 1947; frequently worked Club Georgia, Chicago, 1947-8; Plantation Club, Chicago, 1948; upon leaving Plantation Club was mugged and beaten; entered Michael Reese Hospital where he died of skull fracture and other injuries; buried local cemetery, Jackson, TN

Personal: Married Lacey Belle ——— (who co-wrote many of his songs). Not to be confused with Sonny Boy Williamson (Alex Miller) or others who have used this or similar names. This singer is generally considered to be the original "Sonny Boy" Williamson

Songs: Big Apple Blues/Biscuit Baking Woman/Black Panther Blues/Bluebird Blues/Blues That Made Me Drunk/Check Up On My Baby/Christmas Morning Blues/Come On Baby and Take a Walk/Dealing with the Devil/Decoration Day (Blues)/Deep Down in the Ground/Early in the Morning/Elevator Woman/Good Morning Little Schoolgirl/Goodbye Red/Honey Bee Blues/Hoo-doo Hoo-doo/Hoo-doo Man/Jiving the Blues/Little Girl Blues/Lord Oh Lord Blues/Love Me Baby/Low Down Ways/Mean Old Highway/Mellow Chick Swing/Miss Stella Brown Blues/My Black Name Ringing/Number Five Blues/Rainy Day Blues/The Right Kind of Life/Shake the Boogie/Shannon Street Blues/Shot Gun Blues/Stop Breaking Down/Susie Q/Train Fare Blues/Wartime Blues/Western Union Man/Whiskey Headed Blues/Win the War Blues/You Got to Step Back/You're an Old Lady/You've Been Foolin' 'round Downtown

Infl by: John Estes/Hammie Nixon

Infl to: Billy Boy Arnold/Little Eddie Burns/Frank Edwards/Julio Finn/Forest City Joe/Shakey Jake Harris/John Lee Henley/Big Walter Horton/Lightnin' Slim/Little Walter/Elmon Mickel/Luke Miles/Polka Dot Slim/Snooky Pryor/Yank Rachell/Dr Ross/Arbee Stidham/Doc Terry/Jr Wells/John Wrencher/Johnny Young

Quotes: "A forceful singer, popular recording artist and the first truly virtuosic blues harmonica player, whose richly imaginative solo flights resulted in completely re-shaping the playing approach and the role of this humble instrument in the blues"—Pete Welding, Blues Classics album 21

"The man who, more than anyone else, shaped the course of Chicago's classic blues of the 40s and 50s and brought the harmonica into prominence as a major blues instrument was John Lee 'Sonny Boy' Williamson"—Jim O'Neal, *Downbeat* magazine, Sept 12, 1974, p 26

". . . one of the grestest, most influential and best-loved blues artists of all time"—Mike Rowe, *Chicago Breakdown*, Eddison Press Ltd, 1973

References: Chicago Breakdown, Mike Rowe, Eddison Press Ltd, 1973

Blues Unlimited magazine (UK), Nov-Dec 1967, pp 14-15

WILLIAMSON, SONNY BOY
(see Williamson, John Lee)

WILLIAMSON, SONNY BOY
(*aka:* Little Boy Blue)

Courtesy Living Blues *Magazine*

Born: Dec 5, 1899, Glendora (Tallahatchie Co), MS
Died: May 25, 1965, Helena, AR
Inst: Drums/Guitar/Harmonica

Mother was Millie Ford; born Aleck Ford but later assumed stepfather Jim Miller's surname; one of many children; interested in music early and taught self harmonica at 5 years of age; frequently worked local parties for tips, Glendora, MS, from c1906; left home to hobo through South working as itinerant spiritual musician at courthouses/schools/streets, singing (as "Little Boy Blue") from early 20s; worked many juke joints/dives/picnics/parties (as a blues musician) in Arkansas/Mississippi and elsewhere through 20s; worked Delpee's Club, New Orleans, LA, late 20s; frequently w Sunnyland Slim working local clubs, Caruthersville, MO, early 30s; extensive hoboing as single or one-man band (harmonica/drums/zoothorn) working dance halls/ballparks/carnivals/plantations/lumber camps through Arkansas/Mississippi/Missouri/Tennessee through 30s; worked Grand Ole Opry, Nashville, TN, mid-30s; frequently worked w Elmore James/Big Boy Crudup/Robert Johnson/others in various jukes/parties through South, late 30s into 40s; frequently toured w Howlin' Wolf working jukes through Delta area of Mississippi, c1937-8; frequently w Robert Jr Lockwood working streets for tips, Clarksdale, MS, area, 1938-9; w Robert Jr Lockwood working streets, Helena, AR, 1941; app (as "Sonny Boy Williamson") w Robert Jr Lockwood on KING BISCUIT TIME, KFFA-radio, Helena, AR, 1941-5 (also heard on Delta network: WROX-radio, Clarksdale, MS/KXJK-radio, Forrest City, AR) with frequent tours working local theaters/jukes; app w own King Biscuit Entertainers (including Willie Love/Peck Curtis and others) on KING BISCUIT TIME, KFFA-radio, Helena, AR, 1942-7 (also heard on Delta network: WROX-radio, Clarksdale, MS/KXJK-radio, Forrest City, AR) with occasional appearances thereafter; worked New York Inn, New Orleans, LA, 1944; app on KNOE-radio, Monroe, LA, c1944; app on KARK-radio/KGHI-radio, Little Rock, AR, c1945; frequently worked w Boogie Woogie Red in clubs/bars, Detroit, MI, c1945-8; worked clubs/jukes in Cairo, IL, 1946; app w Elmore James on TALAHO SYRUP Show, WAZF-radio, Yazoo City, MS, 1947-8; worked Club Georgia, Chicago, IL, 1947; rec (as "Sib") United Artists label, NYC, NY, 1947; app on WGVM-radio, Greenville, MS, c1948; app w Howlin' Wolf on HADACOL Show, KWEM-radio, West Memphis, AR, 1949; toured w Willie Love/Willie Nix/Joe Willie Wilkins (as "Four Aces") working jukes through Arkansas/Tennessee/Mississippi, 1949-50; worked Be-Bop Hall, West Memphis, AR, 1950; extensive touring w Elmore James/as single/with own band working bars/tonks through South, early 50s; rec Trumpet label, Jackson, MS, 1951-4; frequently worked club dates in Chicago, IL/Detroit, MI/Philadelphia, PA, 1951; app on LASSES OF JEFFERSON, TEXAS Show, KFFA-radio, Helena, AR, 1952; toured w Willie Love working jukes/tonks through South, 1953; frequently worked w Baby Boy Warren Combo in local clubs/lounges, Detroit, MI, 1953-4; rec w Baby Boy Warren, JVB/Drummond/Excello labels, Detroit, c1953-4; worked w Willie Love, Tavern Lounge, Detroit, 1954; rec Ace label, Jackson, MS, 1954; rec Checker-Chess label, Chicago, IL, 1955-63; continued touring club dates in St Louis, MO/East St Louis, IL/Chicago, IL/Milwaukee, WI, areas, 1955 into 60s; worked club dates in Marvell, AR, 1962; rec acc to Josh White, Mercury label, Chicago, 1963; worked Sylvio's, Chicago, 1963; Twist City, Chicago, 1963; toured w American Folk Blues Festival working club/concert dates through England/Europe, 1963 (por shown I HEAR THE BLUES, Granada-TV, Eng); rec w Victoria Spivey, Spivey label, Baden-Baden, Ger, 1963; rec w Otis Spann, Fontana label, Bremen, Ger, 1963-4; toured w Memphis Slim working concert dates through Poland, 1963; worked w Chris Barber's Band in concert dates through England, 1963-4 (por 1964 concert rec Black Lion label); w Memphis Slim, Blues Bar, Paris, France, 1963 (por rel Vogue label); rec w Memphis Slim, Storyville label, Copenhagen, Den, 1963; rec Collectors Special label, Copenhagen, Den, 1963; app in Danish film short SONNY BOY WILLIAMSON c1963; worked w Yardbirds group, Crawdaddy Club, London, Eng, 1963 (por rel Mercury label); w Cyril Davies All-Stars, Marquee Club, London, Eng, 1963; New Marquee Club, London, Eng, 1964; toured w American Blues Festival working concert dates through Europe, 1964 (por Musikhalle Concert, Hamburg, Ger, rel Fontana label); rec w Brian Auger & The Trinity, Marmalade label, London, Eng, 1965; app on SOME OF THE PEOPLE, KUHF-FM-radio, Houston, TX, 1965; worked local club/juke dates and app on KING BISCUIT TIME, KFFA-radio, Helena, AR, 1965; died in sleep of natural causes; buried Whitfield Baptist Church Cemetery, Tutwiler, MS; gravestone erected 1977

Note: While this singer's true name was Aleck ("Alex") Miller he was also commonly known as "Rice" Miller, a childhood pet name

Personal: Married Mary ———, half-sister of Chester Burnett (Howlin' Wolf), during 1930s; married Mattie Lee Gordon (1949-). Was known to have used aliases Willie Williamson/Willie Williams/Willie Miller and others. (Willie Miller was his brother.) Not to be confused with John Lee "Sonny Boy" Williamson (who is generally considered to be the original "Sonny Boy") or others who have used this or similar names

Billing: King of the Harmonica

Songs: All My Love in Vain/Baby Don't Worry/Baby Stop Crying/Born Blind/Bye Bye Bird/Chicago Bound/Come On Back Home/Coming Home to You/Cool Disposition/Cool Cool Blues/Crazy About You Baby/Cross My Heart/Dissatisfied/Do It If You Wanna/Do the Weston/Don't Let Your Right Hand Know/Don't Lose Your Eye/Don't Start Me to Talking/Down and Out/Eyesight to the Blind/Fattening Frogs for Snakes/Getting Out of Town/Getting Together/Girl Friends/The Goat/Good Evening Everybody/Got to Move/Have You Ever Been in Love?/Help Me/The Hunt/I Can't Be Alone/I Can't Do Without You/I Can't Understand/I Cross My Heart/I Don't Care No More/I Don't Know/I Know What Love Is All About/I Never Do Wrong/I See a Man Downstairs/I Wonder Do I Have a Friend/I Wonder Why/I'm So Glad/It's a Bloody Life/Keep It to Yourself/Keep Your Hand Out of My Pocket/Key to Your Door/Let Me Explain/Let Your Conscience Be Your Guide/Like Wolf/Little Girl How Old Are You?/Little Village/Lonesome Cabin/Mighty Long Time/Movin' Down the River/Movin' Out/Mr Downchild/My Younger Days/Nine Below Zero/99/On My Way Back Home/Once upon a Time/One Way Out/Open Road/Out of Water Coast/Peach Tree/Pontiac Blues/Sad to Be Alone/Same Girl/Santa Claus/She Brought Life Back to the Dead/She Got Next to Me/She Was Dumb/She's My Baby/Slowly Walk Close to Me/Somebody Help Me/Sonny Boy's Christmas Blues/Stop Crying/Stop Now Baby/The Story of Sonny Boy Williamson/Take It Easy Baby/Temperature 110/This Is My Apartment/This Old Life/Too Close Together/Too Old to Think/Too Young to Die/Trust My Baby/Trying to Get Back on My Feet/23 Hours Too Long/Understand My Life/Unseeing Eye/Wake Up Baby/Walking/West Memphis Blues/When the Lights Went Out/Why Are You Crying?/Work with Me/You Killing Me/Your Imagination/Your Funeral and My Trial

Infl to: Clarence Anderson (Sonny Boy Williamson Jr)/Carey Bell/Mike Bloomfield/Juke Boy Bonner/Billy Branch/George Buford/Little Eddie Burns/George Butler/Paul Butterfield/Eric Clapton/Jimmy Cotton/Frank Frost/John Lee Henley/Howlin' Wolf/King David/Lightnin' Slim/Little Milton/Little Walter/Johnny Mars/John Mayall/Little Jr Parker/Snooky Pryor/Jimmy Reed/Charlie Sayles/Schoolboy Cleve/Hound Dog Taylor/Jr Wells/Little Sonny Willis

Quotes: "He was in fact one of the most genuinely creative, persuasive, strikingly individualistic performers the blues has ever seen"—Pete Welding, Chess album 417

"Sonny Boy was an original with a highly personal means of expression within the blues idiom and an artist of real stature"—Paul Oliver, Arhoolie album 2020

"Sonny Boy was a bad influence on my soul" —James Cotton, *Coda* magazine (Canada), Jun 1971, p 13

References: *Blues Unlimited* magazine (UK), Jan 1973, pp 4-13

Blues World magazine (UK), May 1970, pp 7-11

American Folk Music Occasional #2 (1970), pp 39-44

WILLIE B
(see Borum, William)

WILLIE C
(see Cobbs, Willie)

WILLIS, AARON *"Little Son"*
(aka: Little Sonny)
Born: Oct 6, 1932, Greensboro (Hale Co), AL
Inst: Guitar/Harmonica

Born/raised on farm; frequently played sandlot baseball as youth; frequently worked w local gospel groups in local churches into 50s; moved to Detroit, MI, 1954; worked mostly outside music while learning some harmonica from 1954; frequently worked w Washboard Willie Band, Good Time Bar, Detroit, 1955; worked outside music (as photographer), Club Plantation, Detroit, c1956; formed own combo working Bank Bar, Detroit, 1956-7; Congo Lounge, Detroit, 1957-9; rec Duke label, Detroit, 1958; rec JVB label, Detroit, 1959; worked w own group, Club Carribe, Detroit, 1960; rec on own Speedway label, Detroit, early 60s; worked Apex Club, Detroit, 1963-7; Univ of Detroit, Detroit, 1965; rec Revilot label, Detroit, 1966; worked Calumet Bar, Detroit, 1967 into 70s; worked Detroit Blues Festival, Detroit, 1970; Little Sam's, Detroit, 1970; rec Enterprise label, De-

Aaron "Little Son" Willis *Photo by Doug Fulton. Courtesy* Living Blues *Magazine*

troit, c1971-3; worked w own group, Ann Arbor Blues Festival, Ann Arbor, MI, 1972; Wattstax 72 Concert, Memorial Coliseum, Los Angeles, CA, 1972 (por shown in film WATTSTAX)

Personal: Married. His son Aaron Willis Jr (born c1957) is musician. Not to be confused w pianist, "Little Son" Malcolm Willis

Songs: Back Down Yonder/The Creeper Returns/The Day You Left Me/Do It Right Now/Don't Ask Me No Questions/Eli's Pork Chop/Hey Little Girl/I Want You/Memphis B-K/Sad Funk/Sonny's Fever/Sure Is Good/They Want Money/Tomorrow's Blues Today/ You Can Be Replaced/You Made Me Strong

Infl by: Little Walter Jacobs/Sonny Boy Williamson (Alex Miller)

WILLS, OSCAR
(*aka:* TV Slim)
Born: Feb 10, 1916, Houston (Harris Co), TX
Died: Oct 21, 1969, Kingman, AZ
Inst: Guitar/Harmonica

Interested in music early and learned on home-made guitar as youth; frequently worked local dances in Houston, TX, from late 30s; worked mostly outside music, Houston, from 30s; reportedly moved to Shreveport, LA, during 50s; rec Cliff label, Shreveport, 1957; rec w Fats Domino Band, Argo label, New Orleans, LA, 1957; formed/rec Speed Recording Company, Shreveport, LA/Los Angeles, CA, 1958-65; moved to Los Angeles, CA, 1959; frequently toured w Roy Hamilton/Faye Adams/others on various package shows, early 60s; worked mostly outside music (in own Ideal Music & TV Repair Shop), Los Angeles, from 1964; rec Excell/Timbre labels, Los Angeles, c1966; while returning from Chicago, IL, concert date suffered fatal automobile accident

Personal: Married. Had 11 children. Named "TV Slim" due to his outside music work

Songs: Ain't Got But 15c/Flat Foot Sam/Flat Foot Sam Meets Jim Dandy/Going to California/Hen Peck Joe/My Dolly B/To Prove My Love/TV Man/You Won't Treat Me Right

Infl by: De Ford Bailey

Quote: "Slim is an all 'round talented man, all his songs are originals and he is a good guitarist and harp player"—Darryl Stolper, *Blues Unlimited* magazine (UK), Jul 1968, p 6

Reference: Blues Unlimited magazine (UK), Jul 1968, pp 5-6

WILSON, EDITH
(*aka:* Aunt Jemima)

Courtesy Edith Wilson

Born: Sept 2, 1896, Louisville (Jefferson Co), KY
Died: Mar 30, 1981, Chicago, IL

Great-grandfather was John C Breckinridge, a VP of United States; father was Hundley Goodall, a school teacher; mother was Susan Jones; born Edith Goodall; one of 3 children; interested in music at early age and worked White City Park, Louisville, KY, 1909; to Chicago, IL, to work local cabarets/club dates, 1919-21; teamed w Danny Wilson/Lena Wilson to work as trio, Thomas' Club, Washington, DC/Rafe's Paradise Theater, Atlantic City, NJ, and elsewhere, 1921; replaced Mamie Smith in all black musical revue PUT AND TAKE, Town Hall, NYC, NY, 1921; rec w Johnny Dunn's Jazz Hounds, Columbia label, NYC, 1921-2; toured w Johnny Dunn group working theater dates on TOBA circuit, 1921; worked Lincoln Theater, NYC, 1921; toured with star billing on Keith/ Loew's circuits working theater dates across US, 1921; worked Connie's Inn, NYC, 1921; app in Lew Leslie's revue NIGHTIME IN DIXIELAND, Plantation Room, NYC, 1922; occasionally worked New Star Casino, NYC, 1922-3; app w Florence Mills in Lew Leslie's PLANTATION REVUE, Plantation Room, NYC, 1922; app in PLANTATION REVUE (expanded), Lafayette Theater, NYC/Brady's 48th Street Theater, NYC/Winter Garden Theater, NYC, 1922; app w Florence Mills in Plantation Revue Company in FROM DOVER STREET TO DIXIE Revue, The Pavilion, London, Eng, 1923; app in PLANTATION REVUE, Plantation Room, NYC, 1924; app w Fletcher Henderson Orch, CREOLE FOLLIES Revue, Club Alabam, NYC, 1924 (remotes WHN-radio); app in CLUB ALABAM REVUE, Lafayette Theater, NYC, 1924; worked w Alberta Hunter, 44th Street Theater, NYC, 1924; rec w own Jazz Band/Jazz Hounds/Alabama Joe, Columbia label, NYC, 1924; teamed w James "Doc" Straine to work Lincoln Theater, NYC/Nixon Grand Theater, Philadelphia, PA/ Lafayette Theater, NYC/Palace Theater, Pittsfield, MA/State Theater, Pawtucket, RI/Loew's American, NYC/Loew's Fulton Street Theater, Brooklyn, NY/ Greely Square Theater, NYC/State Theater, NYC/ Delancey Street Theater, NYC/Boulevard Theater, NYC/Metropolitan Theater, Brooklyn, NY, 1924; frequently w Doc Straine, Cotton Club, NYC, 1924-5; app w Florence Mills, DIXIE TO BROADWAY Revue, Broadhurst Theater, NYC, 1924, with tours into 1925; toured w Doc Straine working Orpheum Theater, Boston, MA/State Theater, Newark, NJ/Liberty Theater, Staten Island, NY/State Theater, NYC/Bedford Theater, Brooklyn, NY/Lincoln Theater, NYC/ Grand Theater, Chicago, IL/American Theater, NYC/Orpheum Theater, NYC/Fulton Theater, NYC, 1925; rec w Doc Straine, Columbia label, NYC, 1925; toured w Sam Wooding Orch in CHOCOLATE KIDDIES Revue working concert/theater dates through England/Europe/Russia/South America, 1925; app in Lew Leslie's BLACKBIRDS OF 1926 Revue, Alhambra Theater, NYC, 1926; app w Florence Mills in Lew Leslie's BLACKBIRDS REVUE, London Pavilion, London, Eng, 1926, then toured w show working theaters through Europe to 1927; frequently worked w Duke Ellington Orch, Cotton Club, NYC, 1927 (remote CBS-radio network); app w Duke Ellington Orch, JAZZMANIA Revue, Lafayette Theater, NYC, 1927; app w Sam Wooding's Band, ON THE AIR Revue, Lafayette Theater, NYC, 1928; app w Sam Wooding's Band, CREOLE REVELS musical comedy, Lafayette Theater, NYC, 1928; toured w Sam Wooding's Chocolate Kiddies in THE BLACK REVUE (Die Schwarze Revue) working theater dates in Germany/Austria/Romania and Turkey, 1928; worked extended solo residency, Chez Florence Jones Cabaret, Paris, France, 1928-9; rec Brunswick label, NYC, 1929; app w Louis Armstrong/Fats Waller (as "The Thousand Pounds of Harmony"), HOT CHOCOLATES Revue, Connie's Inn/Hudson Theater, NYC, 1929-30, with brief road tour and a return to Lafayette Theater, NYC, 1930; app w Louis Armstrong, Rudy Vallee's THE FLEISCHMANN HOUR, WJZ-radio, NYC (NBC-Network), c1930; app w Eddie Rector in all black HOT RHYTHM Revue, Times Square Theater, NYC, 1930; rec Victor label, NYC, 1930; app in own EDITH WILSON REVUE, Alhambra Theater, NYC, 1930; app in RED PASTURES Revue, Lafayette Theater, NYC, 1930; worked Connie's Inn, NYC, 1931; L'Ange Bleu Club and others, Paris, France, 1931-2; app w Sam Wooding Orch, MUSIC BOX REVUE, Lafayette Theater, NYC, 1932; app in BLACKBERRIES OF 1932 Revue, Liberty Theater, NYC, 1932; app in YEAH-MAN Revue, Park Lane Theater, NYC, 1932; app in HAPPY DAYS Revue, Lafayette Theater, NYC, 1932; app in musical comedy SHUFFLE ALONG OF 1933, Majestic Theater, Brooklyn, NY/Capitol Theater, NYC/Mansfield Theater, NYC, 1932-3/Lafayette Theater, NYC, 1933, then toured with show; app in show HUMMIN' SAM, New Yorker Theater, NYC, 1933; worked Savoy Ballroom, NYC, 1933; app in JIG-SAW Revue, Lafayette Theater, NYC, 1933; worked Harlem Opera House, NYC, 1933; app in HOT HARLEM Revue, Lafayette Theater, NYC, 1933; app w Bill Robinson in Lew Leslie's musical revue BLACKBIRDS OF 1933-34, Majestic Theater, Brooklyn, NY, 1933/42nd Street Apollo Theater, NYC, 1933-4; app in DANCE ROUNDUP Revue, Apollo Theater, NYC, 1934; app in Lew Leslie's BLACKBIRDS OF 1934, London Coliseum, London, Eng, 1934; frequently toured w Cab Calloway Band/Noble Sissle Band/Jimmie Lunceford Band/ Lucky Millinder Band working club dates across US from mid-30s; worked w Fess Williams Band in theater dates, NYC area, c1939; moved to West Coast, c1939; app (in non-singing role) in film I'M STILL ALIVE, 1940; toured as Edith Wilson Rockin' & Rhythm working theater dates on Burt Levy's vaudeville circuit on West Coast/Canada into early 40s; frequently toured on various USO package shows working military bases across US, early 40s; app frequently (in non-singing role) on AMOS 'N' ANDY Show, NBC-radio Network series, from early 40s; app (in non-singing role) in film TO HAVE AND HAVE NOT, 1944; app in SWEET 'N' HOT Revue, Mayan

Theater, Los Angeles, 1944; app w Todd Duncan in musical show revival SHOW BOAT, Philharmonic Auditorium, Los Angeles, 1944; app w Bill Robinson in show MEMPHIS BOUND, Broadway Theater, NYC, 1945, then toured with show; app in repertory theater shows ANOTHER PART OF THE FOREST/SPRINGFIELD COUPLE/others, Pasadena Playhouse, Pasadena, CA, mid-40s; rec w Irving Asby Sextet, Enterprise label, Los Angeles, 1946; app (in non-singing roles) on PRIZEFIGHT FIX/THE GREAT GILDERSLEEVE/others, NBC-radio, late 40s; toured promotionally for Quaker Oats Company (as "Aunt Jemima" personality) for civic/charity/youth activities with app on Don McNeill's BREAKFAST CLUB, NBC-radio/GARRY MOORE Show, CBS-TV/JACKIE GLEASON Show, CBS-TV and other radio/TV shows as well as schools/hospitals/charities/social clubs across US, 1947-65; app on live singing commercial for Quaker Oats on CLIFTON UTLEY Show, local radio, Chicago, IL, 1948; app on live singing commercial for Quaker Oats on LADIES BE SEATED, ABC-radio (Blue Network), 1949; worked Central Plaza, NYC, 1950; app on AUNT JEMIMA HOME FOLKS Show, local radio, Nashville, TN, mid-50s; worked Tivoli Theater, Chicago, 1963; retired from music to work as executive secretary of Negro Actors Guild from 1966 (elected VP c1970); associated with St James Church (helping talented children), Chicago, early 70s; contributed article to *Ebony Jr* magazine, 1972; rec w Eubie Blake, EBM label, NYC, 1972; worked WC Handy Festival, Florence, AL, 1973; rec w Little Brother Montgomery & State Street Ramblers, Delmark label, Chicago, 1973-6; worked w Little Brother, Northeastern Illinois Univ, Chicago, 1973; w Terry Waldo's Gut Bucket Syncopators, Ohio Theater, Columbus, OH, 1974 (por rel Blackbird label); worked Univ of Chicago Folk Festival, Chicago, 1974; app on local TV show, Paris, France, 1974; worked w Little Brother, National Folk Festival, Washington, DC, 1974; Philadelphia Folk Festival, Schwenksville, PA, 1974; Jazz Vespers, United Presbyterian Church, Newark, NJ, 1975; Nassau Community Col, Garden City, NY, 1975-7; Univ of Chicago Folk Festival, Chicago, 1976; Goodtime Jazz Club Concert, Babriolet, Libertyville, IL, 1976; app on THE DEVIL'S MUSIC—A HISTORY OF THE BLUES (ep: Crazy Blues), BBC-1-TV, England, 1976; worked Rochester Junior Col, Rochester, MN, 1977; app w Little Brother, MADE IN CHICAGO, WTTW-TV, Chicago, 1977; w Little Brother, Redford's Saloon, Chicago, 1979; Newport Jazz Festival, NYC, 1979 (por heard JAZZ ALIVE, NPR-radio); Chicago Jazz Fest, Chicago, 1979; app BLACK BROADWAY revue, Town Hall, NYC, 1980; suffered fatal cerebral hemorrhage; buried Mt Glenwood, Glenwood, IL

Note: "Aunt Jemima" was a true person who achieved some note as an expert cook after the Civil War. She was portrayed in vaudeville/shows by Tess Gardella and Ada Brown

Personal: Married pianist Danny Wilson (1920-28); Millard Wilson (1947-81); singer Lena Wilson was sister of Danny Wilson. Husbands were not related

Songs: Carrie/Daddy Change Your Mind/Let's Get Back to the Old Times/Put a Little Love in Everything You Do/Rainy Day Friend/She Knew All Along It Was Wrong/To Keep from Twiddling Your Thumbs

Infl by: Danny Wilson

Quotes: "Edith Wilson . . . is an artist firmly entrenched in the vaudeville-cabaret tradition . . ."—Derrick Stewart-Baxter, *Ma Rainey and the Classic Blues Singers*, Studio Vista Ltd, 1970

". . . a fine artist in the Ethel Waters tradition, able to sing a wide variety of material with complete competence . . ."—Chris Ellis, Fountain album FB-302

"Edith Wilson, one of the few surviving singers from the classic period of the 1920s . . ."—Paige Van Vorst, *The Mississippi Rag* magazine, Feb 1975, p 1

References: *The Mississippi Rag*, Feb 1975, pp 1-4
Cadence magazine, Aug 1979, pp 19-22
Ma Rainey and the Classic Blues Singers, Derrick Stewart-Baxter, Studio Vista Ltd, 1970

WILSON, HARDING *"Hop"*
(aka: Poppa "Poppy" Hop)
Born: Apr 27, 1921, Grapeland (Houston Co), TX
Died: Aug 27, 1975, Houston, TX
Inst: Guitar/Harmonica

Father was Charlie Wilson; mother was Alma B Johnson; one of about 13 children; moved to Crockett, TX, where he was raised from childhood; learned harmonica/guitar as boy; worked mostly outside music, Crockett, from mid-30s; served in US Army, 1942-6; continued outside music work in Crockett area into 50s; teamed w Ivory Lee Semien to tour club dates through Texas/Louisiana, 1956-60; rec Goldband label, Lake Charles, LA, 1958; rec Goldband label, Houston, TX, 1959; rec Ivory label, Houston,

Photo by Mack McCormick

1960-1; frequently worked outside music, Houston area, through 60s; app on SOME OF THE PEOPLE, KUHF-FM-radio, Houston, 1965; worked Sallie's Cafe, Houston, 1967; frequently worked w Ivory Semien, Irene's Bar, Houston, early 70s; worked in residence, Hayes Lounge, Houston, 1974-5; entered Veterans Administration Hospital where he died of brain disease; buried Mt Zion Cemetery, Grapeland, TX

Personal: Married Glendora ———, a musician. Name "Hop" is a derivation of childhood nickname "Harp" (a harmonica)

Infl by: Blind Lemon Jefferson

Quote: "When he sings, his voice is deep and full of melancholy, possessing a strength that is belied by his stature"—Mike Leadbitter, Flyright album LP-4700

Reference: Living Blues magazine, Mar 1976, pp 8-9

WILSON, LENA
(aka: Nelly Coleman)
Born: c1898, Charlotte (Mecklenburg Co), NC
Died: c1939, New York, NY (unconfirmed)

Was an adopted child; teamed w brother Danny Wilson to tour as vaudeville act on TOBA circuit working theater dates through South c1918-20; teamed w Edith Wilson/Danny Wilson to work as trio at Thomas' Club, Washington, DC/(unknown theater) Baltimore, MD/Rafe's Paradise Theater, Atlantic City, NJ, 1921; worked Shuffle Inn, NYC, NY, 1921; app in show THE FLAT BELOW, Lafayette Theater, NYC, 1922; app in BUZZIN' AROUND Revue, Club Maurice, NYC, 1922; rec w Nubian Five, Pathe label, NYC, 1923; rec w Johnny Dunn's Jazz Hounds, Columbia label, NYC, 1923; rec w Perry Bradford's Jazz Phools, Paramount label, NYC, 1923; rec Black Swan/Victor/Columbia/Vocalion/Brunswick/Pathe/Ajax labels, NYC, 1923; app on WDT-radio, NYC, 1923; worked w pianist Porter Grainger, Capitol Palace Cabaret, NYC, c1923; Happy Rhone's Orchestra Club, NYC, c1924; Standard Theater, Philadelphia, PA, 1924; rec Brunswick/Ajax/Emerson labels, NYC, 1924; app in ACES AND QUEENS Revue, Lafayette Theater, NYC, 1925; app in all Negro show LUCKY SAMBO, Colonial Theater, NYC, 1925; app in musical comedy SYNCOPATION, Lincoln Theater, NYC, 1926; app w Florence Mills in Lew Leslie's BLACKBIRDS REVUE, London Pavilion, London, Eng, 1926, then toured with show to Europe; app w Edith Wilson, JAZZMANIA Revue, Lafayette Theater, NYC, 1927; app w Rosa Henderson in SITTING PRETTY Revue, New Alhambra Theater, NYC, 1927; app w Rosa Henderson in THE SEVENTH AVENUE STROLLERS Revue, New Alhambra Theater, NYC, 1927; app in FLAMING FOLLIES Revue, New Alhambra Theater, NYC, 1927; app w Duke Ellington Band, DANCE MANIA Revue, Lafayette Theater, NYC, 1927; app in BRONZE BUDDIES Revue, Lincoln Theater, NYC, 1928; app in musical comedy CREOLE REVELS, Lafayette Theater, NYC, 1928; app in NIFTIES OF

Courtesy *Edith Wilson*/Living Blues *Magazine*

1928 Revue, Lafayette Theater, NYC, 1928; app in musical comedy ASHES AND BILO IN HARLEM, Lafayette Theater, NYC, 1928; frequently worked Lenox Club, NYC, 1929-31; app in LENOX CLUB REVUE, Lincoln Theater, NYC, 1929; app in show DEEP HARLEM, Biltmore Theater, NYC, 1929; rec Clarion/Diva labels, NYC, 1930; rec Columbia label, NYC, 1931; app in MAKE IT SNAPPY Revue, Lafayette Theater, NYC, 1931; app in BLACK & WHITE REVUE, Lafayette Theater, NYC, 1932; worked w Shrimp Jones in night club dates in upstate New York from mid-30s; worked Continental Hall (Lenox Club), NYC, late 30s; reportedly died of pneumonia in NYC area

Personal: Married Shrimp Jones, violinist. Was sister of pianist Danny Wilson and sister-in-law of singer Edith Wilson

Songs: I Need You to Drive the Blues Away/Sad 'n' Lonely Blues

WILSON, LEOLA B
(see Grant, Leola B)

WILSON, *"Kid"* WESLEY *"Sox"/"Socks"*
(aka: Jenkins/Pigmeat Pete)
Born: Oct 1, 1893, Jacksonville (Duval Co), FL
Died: Oct 10, 1958, Cape May Court House, NJ
Inst: Organ/Piano

Father was James Wilson; mother was Irene Davis; born/raised in Jacksonville, FL, and interested in music at early age; worked as pianist in pit band of local theater, Jacksonville, 1905-c12; teamed w Leola B Pettigrew (as "Coot Grant & Socks Wilson") touring on vaudeville circuit working theaters through Midwest/West/South c1912 into 20s; rec w Coot Grant, Paramount label, Chicago, IL, 1925-6; rec w Fletcher Henderson Orch, Paramount label, NYC, NY, 1925; rec w Coot Grant (as "Kid & Coot"), Columbia label, NYC, 1928; rec Cameo/Romeo and other labels, NYC, 1928; toured w Coot Grant in musical comedy THE CHOCOLATE SCANDALS working theaters on vaudeville circuit across US, 1928, then Lafayette Theater, NYC, 1928; app w Coot Grant, BACK HOME AGAIN Revue, Lincoln Theater, NYC, 1928; app (as single) in CREOLE VANITIES Revue, Lafayette Theater, NYC, 1928; app (as single) in PARISIANA Revue, Lincoln Theater, NYC, 1928; app w Coot Grant, PITTER PATTER Revue, Alhambra Theater, NYC, 1929; app in HONEY Revue, Lincoln Theater, NYC, 1929; rec QRS label, Long Island City, NY, 1929; rec (solo) OKeh label, NYC, 1929; app w Coot Grant/Louis Armstrong, LOUISIANA Revue, Lafayette Theater, NYC, 1929; rec w Harry McDaniel (as "Pigmeat Pete & Catjuice Charlie") or solo, Columbia label, NYC, 1929-31; continued extensive touring w Coot Grant on vaudeville circuit working theaters across US into 30s; app in MIDGET FOLLIES Revue, Lafayette Theater, NYC, 1930; app in JAZZ MINE Revue, Alhambra Theater, NYC, 1931; rec w Coot Grant, Columbia label, NYC, 1931-2; app w Coot Grant in film EMPEROR JONES, 1933; rec w Coot Grant, Banner label, NYC, 1933; rec w Coot Grant (as "Hunter & Jenkins"), Vocalion label, NYC, 1933; app w Coot Grant, HOLIDAY IN HARLEM Revue, Apollo Theater, NYC, 1934; mostly inactive in music from mid-30s; rec w Coot Grant, Decca label, NYC, 1938; rec w Mezzrow-Bechet Quintet, King Jazz label, NYC, 1946; worked w Mezz Mezzrow, Really the Blues Concert, Town Hall, NYC, 1947; app on THIS IS JAZZ, WOR-radio, NYC (Mutual Network), 1947; formed own HOLIDAY IN BLUES Revue working local theaters, Newark, NJ, 1948; worked Bessie Smith Memorial Concert, Town Hall, NYC, 1948; Stuyvesant Casino, NYC, 1949; mostly inactive due to illness from 1949; moved to Los Angeles, CA, 1951-5; moved to Whitesboro, NJ, from 1955; entered Burdette Tomlin Memorial Hospital where he suffered fatal stroke; buried in unmarked grave, Household of Ruth Cemetery, Whitesboro, NJ

Personal: Married Leola B Pettigrew ("Coot Grant") (c1912-58). 1 son. "Socks" refers to his song "Dem Socks My Daddy Used to Wear"

Songs: Ashley Street Blues/Blue Monday Up on Sugar Hill/Boodle Boo/Boop Poop a Doop/Dem Socks My Daddy Used to Wear/Dirty Spoon Blues/Dish Rag Blues/Do You Call That a Buddy?/Down in the Dumps/Ducks/Dying Blues/Gimme a Pigfoot/Have Your Chill/He's a Good Meat Cutter/I Ain't Going to Sell You None/I Can't Get Enough/I Don't Want That Stale Stuff/Jive Lover/Key Hole Blues/Mamma Didn't Do It/Rasslin' Till the Wagon Comes/Razor Totin' Mama/Rock Aunt Dinah Rock/Rollin' Mill Blues/Scoop It/Speak Now/Stevedore Man/Take Me for a Buggy Ride/Wilson Dam/You Can't Do That to Me/You Dirty Mistreater/You Need a Woman Like Me/Your Kitchen Floor Is Plenty Good for Me

Quote: "Sox Wilson was a genius"—Mezz Mezzrow, *Jazz & Blues* magazine (UK), Aug 1972, p 15

WINTER, JOHNNY
(aka: Texas Guitar Slim)

Courtesy Sheldon Harris Collection

Born: Feb 23, 1944, Beaumont (Jefferson Co), TX
Inst: Guitar/Harmonica/Ukulele

Both parents were musicians; interested in music early and learned clarinet at about 5 years of age and ukulele at about 8; taught self guitar at about 11 years of age; attended schools in Leland, MS/Beaumont, TX, as youth; teamed w brother Edgar Winter as uke duo to work local talent shows, Beaumont area, mid-50s; formed own Johnny & the Jammers rock band to work local talent contests, Beaumont, 1959; toured w Gene Terry & the Downbeats working gigs through Texas/Louisiana, late 50s; formed various rock groups as The Crystaliers/It & Them/The Black Plague/Traits to work local gigs into 60s; briefly attended Lamar State Col, Beaumont, c1962; worked club dates, Chicago, 1962-3; worked w Mike Bloomfield, Fickle Pickle Coffeehouse, Chicago, 1963; toured w brother Edgar Winter in own group working clubs/roadside bars/campus concerts through Southwest, 1964-6; worked Act III Club, Houston, TX, 1966; rec acc to Loudmouth Johnson, Avco label, Houston, 1966; rec Frolic label, Beaumont, TX, c1966; worked The Love Street Light Circus and other local clubs, Houston, c1967-8; formed Winter group to rec Sonobeat label, Austin, TX, 1968; worked club dates in London, Eng, 1968; worked Houston Country Club, Houston, 1968; Avalon Ballroom, San Francisco, CA, 1968; Fillmore West, San Francisco, 1968-70; Fillmore East, NYC, NY, 1968-9; The Scene, NYC, 1969; rec Columbia label, Nashville, TN/NYC, 1969-74; worked Texas International Pop Festival, Lewisville, TX, 1969; Memphis Blues Festival, Memphis, TN, 1969; Newport '69, Northridge, CA, 1969; Newport Jazz Festival, Newport, RI, 1969; Toronto Pop Festival, Toronto, 1969; Laurel Pop Festival, Laurel, MD, 1969; Woodstock Music & Art Fair, Bethel, NY, 1969; Ann Arbor Blues Festival, Ann Arbor, MI, 1970; toured Europe working concert dates, 1970; worked Painters Mill Theater, Baltimore, MD, 1971; app on national TV commercial for Tijuana Smalls Cigar c1971; toured w own Johnny Winter And group working concert dates across US, 1971; worked The Rock Pile, Island Park, NY, 1971; inactive in music spending year in River Oaks Hospital, New Orleans, LA, for drug addiction, 1972; worked Madison Square Garden, NYC, 1973; Maple Leaf Gardens, Toronto, Can, 1973; The Spectrum, Philadelphia, PA, 1973; Winterland, San Francisco, CA, 1973; app on FIRST ANNIVERSARY OF IN CONCERT Show, ABC-TV, 1974; app w Muddy Waters, SOUNDSTAGE, PBS-TV, 1974; worked Palace Theater, NYC, 1974 (por shown DON KIRSHNER'S ROCK CONCERT Show, WNEW-TV, NYC [syndicated]); Sports Arena, Long Beach, CA, 1974; The Arena, San Diego, CA, 1974; rec Blue Sky label, California (?), 1974; worked Winterland, San Francisco, 1975; toured US working concert dates, 1975; worked The Spectrum, Philadelphia, 1975; active as producer for Blue Sky Records from mid-70s; rec w Muddy Waters, Blue Sky label, Westport, CT, 1976-7; app on MIKE DOUGLAS Show, CBS-TV, 1977; worked w Foghat group, The Palladium, NYC, 1977 (por shown DON KIRSHNER'S ROCK CONCERT Show, NBC-TV, 1978); toured w Muddy Waters/James Cotton working concert/college dates, 1977

Personal: Singer is an albino and partially blind. His brother Edgar Winter is rock musician

Songs: Dallas/I'm Yours and I'm Hers/Leland Mississippi Blues/Rock & Roll/Too Much Seconal

Infl by: John Lee Hooker/Elmore James/Robert Johnson/Albert King/BB King/Johnny Shines/Aaron "T-Bone" Walker

Quotes: "Johnny Winter in the hollering tradition of Lemon and Patton has fine vocal style and authenticity . . ."—Carman Moore, *Village Voice* newspaper, Apr 24, 1969

"Winter is the best male white blues guitarist there ever was"—Mike Leadbitter, *Blues Unlimited* magazine (UK), Sept 1968, p 24

References: Rolling Stone magazine, Oct 15, 1970, pp 22-5

Encyclopedia of Pop, Rock & Soul, Irwin Stambler, St Martin's Press, 1974

WITHERSPOON, JAMES *"Jimmy"*
(aka: Spoon)
Born: Aug 18, 1923, Gurdon (Clark Co), AR
Inst: Bass

Father was Leonard Witherspoon; mother Eva Tatum; mother was pianist; one of 2 children; frequently sang in First Baptist Church choir, Gurdon, AR, at about 5 years of age; won first prize in Clark County singing contest as child; ran away from home to work outside music in Los Angeles, CA, area c1935-41; served in Merchant Marine in Pacific Theater of Operations, 1941-3; sat-in w Teddy Weatherford Band, Grand Hotel Winter Garden, Calcutta, India, 1943; app on Armed Forces Radio Service Show, Calcutta, 1943; returned to work Waterfront Cafe, Vallejo, CA, 1944; replaced Walter Brown in Jay McShann Band working club dates on West Coast, then toured clubs/ballrooms/dances across US, 1944-8; rec w Jay McShann Jazz Men, Philo-Aladdin label, Los Angeles, 1945; rec w Jay McShann Band, Mercury label, Los Angeles, 1946; rec Supreme label, Los Angeles, 1947; rec Downbeat-Swingtime label, Los Angeles, 1947-8; rec w Buddy Floyd/Roy Milton/Al Wichard/others, Modern label, Los Angeles, 1947-51; formed own group working one-nighters/R&B concerts/dances through California, then toured US, 1948-52; frequently worked Melody Club, Hollywood, CA, 1948-9; w Gene Gilbeaux Qt/Roy Milton's Band, Just Jazz Concert, Civic Auditorium, Pasadena, CA, 1949-50 (por rel Modern label); worked Apollo Theater, NYC, 1950; Flame Show Bar, Detroit, MI, 1951; rec w Trinity Baptist Church Choir, Modern label. Los Angeles, 1951; rec Crown label, Los Angeles, c1951; rec extensively Federal label, Los Angeles/Cincinnati, OH, 1952-3; worked occasional one-nighters mostly on West Coast through 50s; rec Checker label, Chicago, 1954-5; worked Dew Drop Inn, New Orleans, c1955; rec w Wilbur DeParis New Orleans Band, Atlantic label, NYC, 1956; rec Rip label, Los Angeles, 1957; rec w Jessie Stone Band/Jay McShann Band, Victor label, NYC, 1957; rec World Pacific label, Los Angeles, 1958; app on JOHNNY OTIS SHOW, KFOX-radio, Long Beach, CA, 1958; worked w Jay McShann Band, Johnny Baker's Club, Kansas City, MO, 1958; rec w Riley Hampton Orch, VJ label, Chicago, 1959; worked w Charles Brown in local gambling casinos, Newport, KY, 1959; Monterey Jazz Festival, Monterey, CA, 1959-63 (por 1959 concert rel HiFi label); rec (religious songs) w Randy van Horne Choir, HiFi label, Los Angeles, 1959; worked w Gerry Mulligan Quintet, Ben Shapiro's Renaissance Club, Hollywood, CA, 1959-61 (por 1959 gig rel HiFi label); rec Reprise label, Los Angeles, 1959; worked The Sundown, Los Angeles, 1960; rec w Jon Hendricks, Columbia label, Los Angeles, 1960; worked w Ben Webster group, Jazz Cellar, San Francisco, CA, 1960; Carnegie Hall, NYC, 1961; Copa City, NYC, 1961; toured w Buck Clayton All-Stars working concerts/festivals through Europe, 1961; worked Olympia Theater, Paris, France, 1961 (por rel Vogue label); German Jazz Festival, Essen, Ger, 1961; app in Belgian film short BUCK CLAYTON AND HIS ALL-STARS, 1961; worked Newport Jazz Festival, Newport, RI, 1961; w Ben Webster group, Jazz Workshop, San Francisco, 1961-2; rec w HB Barnum's Orch and others, Reprise label, Los Angeles, 1961-2; worked w Onzy Matthews Band, Virginia Club, Los Angeles, 1962; w Ben Webster group, Archway Club, Chicago, IL, 1962; rec Trio label, California (?), 1962; rec ST for THE PAUL CRUMP STORY, local TV, Chicago, 1962; worked It Club, Los Angeles, 1962; rec Prestige label, Los Angeles, CA/NYC, NY/Bergenfield, NJ, 1963-4; worked Town Tavern, Toronto, Can, 1963; app w Ralph Gleason, JAZZ CASUAL, PBS-TV, 1963; worked Sutherland Hotel, Chicago, 1963; app on STEVE ALLEN Show, WABC-TV, NYC (syndicated), 1963; toured w Count Basie Orch working concert dates through Japan, 1963; worked The Outrigger, Monterey, CA, 1963; The Side Door, Oakland, CA, 1963; Jazz Workshop, San Francisco, 1964; Basin Street South, Boston, MA, 1964; app w Dizzy Reece group, QUEST, CBC-TV, Toronto, Can, 1964; worked Cafe A-Go-Go, NYC, 1964; McKie's, Chicago, IL, 1964; frequently toured England/Europe working club/concert/radio/TV dates, 1964-9; worked The Showcase, Oakland, CA, 1964; w Cole-

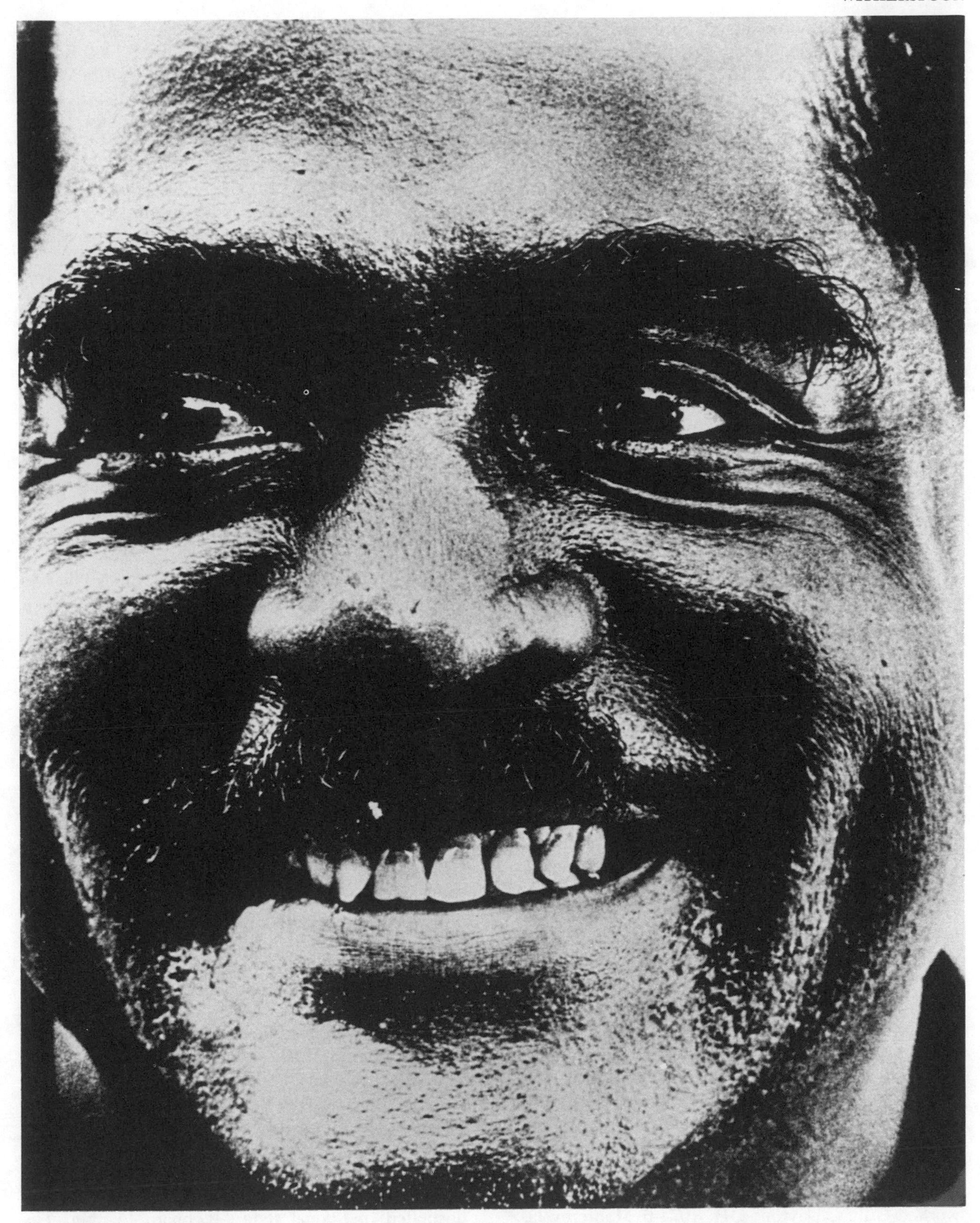

James "Jimmy" Witherspoon *Courtesy BMI Archives*

man Hawkins, Showboat, Washington, DC, 1964; rec w Benny Golson Orch, Prestige label, London, Eng, 1965; app on HOLLYWOOD A-GO-GO, (syndicated) TV, 1965; app on SHINDIG, ABC-TV, 1965; app on SHIVAREE, (syndicated) TV, 1965; worked The Half Note, NYC, 1965-6; Lennie's on the Turnpike, Boston, MA, 1965-6; The Club, Chicago, IL, 1965; Leo's Casino, Cleveland, OH, 1965; Apollo Theater, NYC, 1966-7; Univ of British Columbia, Vancouver, Can, 1966; Blue Horn, Vancouver, 1966; Jazz Workshop, San Francisco, 1966-7; Village Gate, NYC, 1966; Marty's, Los Angeles, 1967; Stan's Pad, Chicago, 1967; app on JAZZ SCENE USA, WGBH-TV, Boston, MA, 1967; worked Redd Foxx's Club, Los Angeles, 1967; rec Prestige label, Los Angeles (?), 1967; rec Verve label, Los Angeles, 1967-8; worked Robbin's Nest, Detroit, MI, 1968; Both/And Club, San Francisco, 1968; The Penthouse, Seattle, WA, 1968; The Living Room, Cincinnati, 1968; Randalls Island Jazz Festival, NYC, 1968; Village Vanguard, NYC, 1968; toured US military clubs in Tokyo, Japan, area, 1968; worked Basin Street West, San Francisco, 1969; Aqua Jazz Lounge, Philadelphia, PA, 1969; Jazz Workshop, San Francisco, 1969; Parisian Room, Los Angeles, 1969-70; rec BluesWay label, Los Angeles, 1969; rec ABC label, Los Angeles, 1970-1; worked Redd Foxx's Club, Los Angeles, 1970; Ash Grove, Los Angeles, 1970-2; Blue Gardenia, Oakland, CA, 1970; Monterey Jazz Festival, Monterey, CA, 1970-2; app on SOUL, PBS-TV (syndicated), 1971; worked Festival of American Folklife, St Helens Island, Montreal, Can, 1971; Mr Henry's, Washington, DC, 1971; Whiskey A-Go-Go, Los Angeles, 1971; toured w Eric Burdon working festivals across US, 1971; worked Shrine Auditorium, Los Angeles, 1971; Funky Quarters, San Diego, CA, 1972; Univ of California, Irvine, CA, 1972; Donte's, Los Angeles, 1972; The Lighthouse, Los Angeles, 1972; Keystone Korner, San Francisco, 1972; app on own JIMMY WITHERSPOON Show series (as DJ), KMET-FM-radio, Los Angeles, CA, from 1972; worked Continental Club, Oakland, CA, 1973; Ronnie Scott's Club, London, Eng, 1973; rec United Artists label, Chipping Norton, Eng, 1974; rec w Groove Holmes, Olympic label, c1974; worked Playboy Club, Los Angeles, 1974-7; app in film THE BLACK GODFATHER, 1974; rec Capitol label, Chipping Norton, Eng, 1974; worked Teddy's Club, Milwaukee, WI, 1974; Highland Park Community Col, Detroit, MI, 1974; app on Johnny Carson's TONIGHT Show, NBC-TV, 1974; app on MIDNIGHT SPECIAL, NBC-TV, 1974; worked Gilly's, Dayton, OH, 1974-6; Monterey Jazz Festival, Monterey, CA, 1974; Keystone, Berkeley, CA, 1975-6; Roxy Theater, Los Angeles, 1975-7; rec Blue Note label, c1975; worked Robert's 300 Room, Chicago, 1975-6; Playboy Club, Boston, 1975; Viking Lounge, Cincinnati, OH, 1976; Main Point, Bryn Mawr, PA, 1976; Encore II, Pittsburgh, PA, 1976; app on ANTHONY NAVARRO'S BLUES SHOW, WYEP-FM-radio, Pittsburgh, 1976; worked Basin Street, Toronto, Can, 1976; Jazz 200 Concert, Hamburg, Ger, 1976; Quartier Latin, Berlin, Ger, 1976; Montreux Music Festival, Montreux, Switzerland, 1976 (por on MUSIC FROM MONTREUX, BBC-2-TV, London, Eng); Boojum Tree, Phoenix, AZ, 1977; Ivanhoe, Chicago, IL, 1977; Cafe Concert, Tarzana, CA, 1977; The Improvisation, Los Angeles, CA, 1977

Personal: Married Rachel ——— (c1960); married Diane ——— (1962-). Has children

Songs: Bags Under My Eyes/Big Fine Girl/Blue Monday Blues/Blues and Trouble/Cane River/Don't Get Flakey with Me/Don't Gotta/Drinking Beer/Failing by Degrees/I Can't Hardly See/I Made a Lot of Mistakes/I Was Lost/I'll Go On Living/Late One Evening/Money's Getting Cheaper/No Rolling Blues/Part-Time Woman/Past Forty Blues/Pillar to Post/Rain Is Such a Lonesome Sound/Spoon's Beep Beep Blues/Testifying/Thoughts of Home/The Time Has Come/Time's Gettin' Tougher Than Tough/You Can't Do a Thing When You're Drunk

Awards/Honors: Won *Downbeat* magazine International Jazz Critics Poll for New Star Male Vocalist, 1961, 1968

Won *Melody Maker* magazine Readers/Critics Poll as top blues singer, 1965

Won NAACP Image Award, 1975

Won *Ebony* magazine Hall of Fame Award, 1977

Infl by: Bill Broonzy/Doc Clayton/Jimmy Rushing/Joe Turner

Infl to: Bobby Bland/Reuben Ford/Big Miller

Quotes: "Every great blues singer is a great story teller and Jimmy Witherspoon is one of the very best"—Billy Taylor, Verve album 5030

"Working with the right musicians, Spoon is a dynamic, shattering performer who creates his own special force-field"—Mack McCormick, *Montreal Gazette* newspaper, Jun 26, 1971

"A big voiced extroverted blues singer in an unspoiled traditional style"—Leonard Feather, *The New Encyclopedia of Jazz*, Horizon Press, 1960

References: Downbeat magazine, Jul 13, 1967, pp 23-5

Living Blues, Jul 1977, pp 15-24

Honkers and Shouters, Arnold Shaw, Collier Books, 1978

WITHERSPOON, MATILDA
(aka: Mississippi Matilda)
Born: Jan 27, 1914, Hattiesburg (Forrest Co), MS
Died: Nov 15, 1978, Chicago, IL

Father Dallas Witherspoon; moved to Clyde, MS, then Bogalusa, LA, as child; frequently sang in Mt Zion Church choir, Bogalusa, 1926; frequently worked outside music (as field hand) with frequent work in local cafes/jukes, Hollandale, MS, area into 30s; moved to Anguilla, MS, to work outside music through 30s; frequently toured w husband working local clubs/jukes/ dances through Mississippi, 1935-7; rec Bluebird label, New Orleans, LA, 1936; continued outside music work with rare local juke work through Mississippi into 50s; worked outside music in Scott, MS/Chicago into 70s; died of heart disease; buried Burr Oak Cemetery, Worth, IL

Personal: Married Calvin Bass (1928-early 30s); Eugene Powell (1935-52); Jasper Williams (1957-).

Reference: Living Blues magazine, Spring 1972, p 7

WOODFORK, ROBERT
(aka: Poor Bob)
Born: Mar 13, 1925, Lake Village (Chicot Co), AR
Died: c May, 1988 (unconfirmed)
Inst: Guitar

Father was King Woodfork, mother was Annie Mae ———; learned music on home-made guitar at age of 15; moved to Chicago, IL, to work outside music, 1941-3; served in US Army in England frequently entertaining at local USO shows, 1943-7; returned to Chicago, 1947; frequently worked w Otis Rush Band in local club dates, Chicago, from 1947; worked w Otis Rush Band, Bob's Tavern, Chicago, 1947; frequently worked/toured as sideman w Jimmy Rogers/Howlin' Wolf/George Smith/others, Chicago, through 50s; worked w Otis Rush, Club Alibi, Chicago, 1955; worked w Little Walter's group, local clubs, Chicago, into 60s; rec as sideman w George Smith/Sunnyland Slim, Chicago, into 60s; rec Decca label, Chicago, 1965; continued working as sideman in local bands, Chicago, into 70s; worked Rat Trap, Chicago, 1974

Reference: Blues Unlimited magazine (UK), Mar 1966, p 10

WOODS, BIG BOY
(see Collins, Sam)

WOODS, OSCAR *"Buddy"*
Born: 1900, Shreveport (Caddo Parish), LA (unconfirmed)
Died: c1956, Shreveport, LA (unconfirmed)
Inst: Guitar

Raised in Natchitoches, LA, area from childhood; frequently worked local houseparties, Shreveport, LA, area through 20s; frequently worked w Ed Schaffer in Shreveport area into 30s; rec w Ed Schaffer's Shreveport Home Wreckers, Victor label, Memphis, TN, 1930; worked local jukes in Memphis c1930; rec w Jimmie Davis, Victor label, Dallas, TX, 1932; rec w Ed Schaffer (as "Eddie & Oscar"), Victor label, Dallas, 1932; teamed w Black Ace working houseparties/ joints/barrelhouses in Shreveport from mid-30s; rec Decca label, New Orleans, LA, 1936; rec w Wampus Cats, Vocalion label, San Antonio, TX, 1937; rec Vocalion label, Dallas, TX, 1938; rec Library of Congress label, Shreveport, 1940; continued working local club dates, Shreveport, through 40s/50s; whereabouts unknown thereafter

Billings: The Lone Wolf/The Troubadour/Street Rustler

Song: Don't Sell It Blues

Infl to: Black Ace

WRENCHER, *"Big"* JOHN THOMAS
(aka: One-Armed John)
Born: Feb 12, 1923, Sunflower (Sunflower Co), MS
Died: Jul 15, 1977, Clarksdale, MS
Inst: Harmonica

Father was Jonah Wrencher, mother was Heneretta Calvin; one of 7 children; raised on Davis Plantation outside Clarksdale, MS; interested in music early and taught self harmonica as child; frequently worked outside music (as farmer) in area through 40s; left home to hobo as itinerant musician working streets/picnics/parties/jukes through Tennessee/Missouri/ Indiana /Illinois, 1947-55; moved to Detroit, MI, to work outside music from 1955; frequently worked as sideman w Baby Boy Warren/Little George Jackson, Detroit area, through late 50s; formed own trio to work clubs in Detroit, MI/Clarksdale, MS, areas from c1958; lost left arm in auto accident outside Memphis, TN, c1958; worked Cotton Club, East St Louis, IL, 1960; Red Top Club, St Louis, MO, 1960; frequently toured clubs into Arkansas to 1962; settled in

"Big" John Wrencher *Photo by Frank Nazareth. Courtesy* Living Blues *Magazine*

Chicago, IL, 1962; frequently worked outside music with work on Maxwell Street for tips, Chicago, from 1962 into 70s; app in film short AND THIS IS FREE, 1963; rec Testament label, Chicago, 1964; w Johnny Young at Kelly's Blue Lounge, Chicago, 1965; rec Testament label, Chicago, 1966; rec w Maxwell Street Boys, Barrelhouse label, Chicago, 1969; worked Mary's, Chicago, 1972; frequently worked w Pat Rushin's group on Maxwell Street for tips, Chicago, 1972-6; toured w Chicago Blues Festival working concerts through England/Europe, 1973; toured w American Blues Legends working concerts through England/Europe, 1974 (por rel Big Bear label); app on IN CONCERT Show, Radio 4, London, Eng, 1974; rec w Eddie Taylor & the Blueshounds, Big Bear label, London, Eng, 1974; worked Walton's Corner, Chicago, 1974; Univ of Chicago, Chicago, 1974; Smitty's Pig Trail Inn, Clarksdale, MS, 1974; toured Europe working concert dates, 1975; worked Kingston Mines, Chicago, 1976; Midwest Blues Festival, Univ of Notre Dame, South Bend, IN, 1976; residency at Elsewhere Club, Chicago, 1976-7; while on visit to father's home suffered heart failure; buried Shuffordville Cemetery, Lyon, MS

Personal: Married. 2 children

Songs: Big John's Boogie/Conductor Took My Baby to Tennessee/Come On Over/Don't Want No Special Rider/Dust My Bed/Gonna Bring Down All My Clothes/Ha Ha Baby/John's Moonshine Blues/Lonesome in My Cabin/Mama Here Come Your Root Man/Maxwell Street Alley Blues/No Good Weasel/Now Darling/Rockin' Chair Blues/Rubbin' My Root/Telephone Blues/Trouble Makin' Woman

Infl by: John Lee "Sonny Boy" Williamson

Quote: "His command of the harmonica, mellow voice, wide repertoire and sheer presence indicate a professionalism rarely witnessed in blues circles"—Mike Leadbitter, *Blues Unlimited* magazine (UK), Feb 1974, p 11

References: *Blues Unlimited* magazine (UK), Feb 1974, p 11

Nothing But the Blues, Mike Leadbitter, Hanover Books, 1971

Y

YANCEY, ESTELLA *"Mama"*
Born: Jan 1, 1896, Cairo (Alexander Co), IL
Died: May 4, 1986, Chicago, IL
Inst: Guitar/Piano

Father Elie Harris; mother Mary ——— ; born Estella Harris; moved to Chicago, IL, at 6 months; raised in Chicago where she took interest in music at early age; frequently sang in local church choir as child; learned guitar as youth; frequently worked w husband Jimmy Yancey at local private parties/house rent parties, Chicago, from 1919 through 30s; rec w Jimmy Yancey, Session label, Chicago, 1943; worked w Richard M Jones, Art Institute of Chicago concert, Chicago, c1945; frequently worked outside music (as Democratic ward precinct captain), Chicago, c1945 through 60s; worked w Jimmy Yancey/Kid Ory/others, Carnegie Hall, NYC, NY, 1948; w Jimmy Yancey, Orchestra Hall, Chicago, c1948; w Jimmy Yancey at local concert date, Minneapolis, MN, c1948; occasionally w Jimmy Yancey on weekend gigs, Bee Hive Club, Chicago, c1948-50; rec w Jimmy Yancey, Atlantic label, Chicago, 1951; mostly inactive in music, Chicago, from 1951; rec w Don Ewell, Windin' Ball label, Chicago, 1952; worked Sugar Hill Club, San Francisco, CA, 1961; rec w Little Brother Montgomery, Riverside label, Chicago, 1961; worked Limelight Club, Chicago, 1962; Red Lion Club, Chicago, 1962; Touch of Olde Club, Chicago, 1964; rec w Art Hodes, Verve-Folkways label, Chicago, 1965; app w Art Hodes, JAZZ ALLEY, PBS-TV, 1969; inactive in music, Chicago, into 80s; worked Elsewhere Club, Chicago, 1976; Univ of Chicago Folk Festival, Chicago, 1977-9; w Earl Hines, Northwestern Univ, Evanston, IL, 1977; Chicago Jazz Fest, Chicago, 1979; Kool Jazz Festival, Carnegie Hall, NYC, 1981; rec Red Beans label, Chicago, 1982-3; suffered fatal heart attack; buried Burr Oak Cemetery, Worth, IL

Personal: Married Jimmy Yancey, blues singer/pianist (1919-died 1951)

Songs: Cabbage Patch/Death Letter Blues/Everyday of the Week/Four O'Clock Blues/Get Him Out of Your System/Good Conductor/Good Package Blues/Mama Yancey's Blues/Monkey Woman Blues/Santa Fe Blues/Sweet Lovin' Daddy

Infl by: Lottie Grady/Memphis Minnie/Bessie Smith

Infl to: Barbara Dane

Estella "Mama" Yancey *Photo by Steve Tomashefsky. Courtesy Delmark Records*

Quote: "Estella 'Mama' Yancey is one of the world's great subterranean philosophers, blues singers, mother wits, and heroines"—Barbara Dane, Verve album 9015

Reference: *Cadence* magazine, Nov 1978, pp 3-5

YANCEY, JAMES EDWARD *"Jimmy"/"Papa"*
Born: Feb 20, 1898, Chicago (Cook Co), IL
Died: Sept 17, 1951, Chicago, IL
Inst: Harmonium/Piano

Father Mose Yancey was bass singer/guitarist and later travelled with son in vaudeville; mother was Irene Oulsey; one of 4 children; interested in music from early childhood; app as singer/dancer in MAN FROM BAM Revue, Pekin Theater, Chicago, IL, 1903-8; frequently toured (as buck & wing dancer/singer) w Jeannette Adler Company/Cozy Smith Troupe/Bert Earle Company/other touring troupes working vaudeville circuits across US, 1908-11; toured w Bert Earle Company working theater dates on Orpheum Circuit in US/Europe c1912-14; worked a command performance for King George V, Queen Mary and the Royal Family, Buckingham Palace, London, Eng, 1913; learned piano from brother Alonzo Yancey, 1915; frequently worked local rent parties/skiffles/gin mills/small clubs, Chicago, from 1915; frequently worked outside music (as baseball player for Chicago All-Americans), Chicago, IL, from c1919; frequently worked Cabaret Moonlight Inn/The Beartrap Inn and local houseparties/joints/dances, Chicago, c1919-25; worked outside music (as groundkeeper for Chicago White Sox baseball team), Comiskey Park, Chicago, 1925-50; continued occasional local party work, Chicago, through 20s/30s/40s; rec Solo Art label, Chicago, 1939; rec Victor label, Chicago, 1939-40; app on WE, THE PEOPLE, CBS-network radio, 1939; worked Ross Tavern, NYC, NY, 1939; rec Vocalion/Bluebird labels, Chicago, 1940; rec Session label, Chicago, 1943; worked w Mama Yancey, Carnegie Hall, NYC, 1948; w Albert Ammons, Orchestra Hall, Chicago, c1948; w Mama Yancey at local concert date, Minneapolis, MN, c1948; frequently worked as resident intermission pianist, Bee Hive Club, Chicago, c1948-50; rec Paramount label, Chicago, 1950; rec Atlantic label, Chicago, 1951; app at local boogie woogie concert, Chicago, 1951; suffered from diabetes and died in diabetic coma; buried Lincoln Cemetery, Worth, IL

Personal: Married blues singer Estella Harris (1919 until his death). His brother Alonzo Yancey was pianist

James "Jimmy" Yancey *Courtesy Institute of Jazz Studies*

Songs: Assembly Call Boogie/Barber Shop Rag/Blues for Albert/East St Louis Blues/Eternal Blues/Everlasting Blues/Four O'Clock Blues/I Received a Letter/Jimmy's Good Night Blues/Jimmy's Rocks/Keep a Knockin'/The Mellow Blues/Monkey Woman Blues/Mournful Blues/Salute to Pinetop/Santa Fe Blues/Shave 'em Dry/Slow and Easy Blues/35th & Dearborn/White Sox Stomp/Yancey Special/Yancey's Bugle Call/Yancey's Mixture

Infl by: Alonzo Yancey

Infl to: Dave Alexander/Albert Ammons/Roy Byrd/Don Ewell/Meade Lux Lewis/Clarence Lofton/Pine Top Smith/Charlie Spand

Quotes: "An archaic blues singer of the most touching accents . . ."—Rudi Blesh, *Shining Trumpets*, Alfred A Knopf, 1946

"With a deceptively simple [piano] style, the man was, quite simply, a genius"—Mike Rowe, *Blues Unlimited* magazine (UK), Aug 1974, p 22

References: Record Research magazine, Feb 1956, pp 3-6

The Art of Jazz, Martin T Williams, Oxford Univ Press, 1959

YANKEE, PAT

Photo by Andrew Wittenborn

Born: Jul 2, 1929, Lodi (San Joaquin Co), CA

Born Patricia Millicent Weigum; worked as tap dancer from age 14 and app in some films for Columbia Pictures during 40s; began singing locally in San Francisco, CA, area from 1951; app on local TV shows, San Francisco, from mid-50s; worked club dates, Anchorage, AK, c1957; toured/worked w Turk Murphy Band out of San Francisco, 1959 into 70s; worked w Turk Murphy Band, Village Vanguard, NYC, 1959; rec w Turk Murphy Band, Roulette label, NYC, 1959; worked The Metropole, NYC, 1960; extensive residency w Turk Murphy Band, Earthquake McGoon's, San Francisco, from 1960 into 70s; rec w Turk Murphy Band, Victor label, Los Angeles, 1961; worked w Turk Murphy Band, Santa Monica Civic Auditorium, Santa Monica, CA, c1961; Sheraton Palace, San Francisco, 1963; Wilshire Ebell Theater, Los Angeles, 1970; reportedly moved to Spain, early 70s

Infl by: Ma Rainey/Bessie Smith

YOUNG, JOHN OLIVER *"Johnny"/"Man"*

(*Born:* Jan 1, 1918, Vicksburg (Warren Co), MS
Died: Apr 18, 1974, Chicago, IL
Inst: Guitar/Harmonica/Mandolin

Father was Horace Young; mother was Nellie Williams a harmonica player; one of 7 children; dropped out of school to work outside music, Rolling Fork, MS, from 1929; taught self harmonica, 1930; learned guitar/mandolin from uncle Anthony Williams, 1931; frequently worked outside music (as professional boxer) with occasional work at local houseparties/dances/picnics, Rolling Fork area, c1933-40; worked Blue Room Club, Vicksburg, MS, c1939; moved to Chicago, IL, 1940; worked mostly outside music, Chicago, through 40s into 60s; worked w Muddy Waters/John Lee "Sonny Boy" Williamson, Plantation Club, Chicago, 1943; The Spot, Gary, IN, 1943; frequently worked w Snooky Pryor/Floyd Jones/Johnny Williams/others on Maxwell Street for tips, Chicago, from 1947 into 60s; worked Square Deal Club, Chicago, 1947; 24 Club, Chicago, 1947; Millgate Club, Chicago, c1947; rec w Johnny Williams, Ora-Nelle label, Chicago, 1947; rec Planet/Swingmaster labels, Chicago, 1948; frequently worked w Robert Nighthawk in local club dates, Chicago, early 50s; worked Purple Cat, Chicago, 1952; frequently worked/rec as sideman, Chicago, through 50s into 60s; rec Testament label, Chicago, 1962-6; app in film short AND THIS IS FREE, 1963; rec USA label, Chicago, c1963; formed own trio working Shirley's, Chicago, 1963; Mandel Hall concert, Chicago, 1963;

Photo by Chris Strachwitz. Courtesy Arhoolie Records

First Floor Club, Chicago, 1964; Cricket Lounge, Chicago, 1965; frequently worked Pete's Lounge/ I Spy Club/Pasa Tiempo/J&L Lounge/others, Chicago, mid-60s; Kelly's Blue Lounge, Chicago, 1965; Centaur Club, Chicago, 1965; rec Arhoolie label, Chicago, 1965; worked Mariposa Folk Festival, Toronto, Can, 1966; frequently worked 63rd Street club dates, Chicago, 1966-7; worked w Otis Spann, Cafe A-Go-Go, NYC, 1966; rec w Otis Spann, Spivey label, NYC, 1966; rec w Walter Horton, Arhoolie label, Chicago, 1967; worked Univ of Chicago R&B Festival, Chicago, 1968; Alex's 1815 Club, Chicago, 1968; Blues Festival, Madison, WI, 1968; Chicago Blues Festival, Chicago, 1969; frequently worked w Bob Riedy Chicago Blues Band working The Attic/ The Peanut Barrel/The Wise Fools Pub/Five Stages/others, Chicago, 1969-74; rec Blue Horizon label, NYC, 1969; Wisconsin Blues Festival, Beloit, WI, 1970; Kingston Mines Company Store Coffeehouse, Chicago, 1970; Sutherland Hotel, Chicago, 1970; Ann Arbor Blues Festival, Ann Arbor, MI, 1970; North Park Hotel, Chicago, 1971; toured w American Folk Blues Festival working concert dates through England/Europe, 1972; rec Decca (Eng)/Blue Horizon labels, London, Eng, 1972; rec Storyville label, Copenhagen, Den, 1972; worked The Post, Chicago, 1972; Ratso's, Chicago, 1972; rec w Bob Riedy Chicago Blues Band, Blues on Blues label, Chicago, 1972; rec ABC-BluesWay label, Chicago, 1973; rec w Bob Riedy Chicago Blues Band, Rounder label, Chicago, 1973; worked Uprising Tavern, DeKalb, IL, 1974; suffered heart attack at home; DOA at Osteopathic Hospital; buried Lincoln Cemetery, Urbana, IL

Personal: Married Ora-Nelle ——— (40s into 70s). Was cousin of Johnny Williams

Songs: All My Money Gone/Bad Blood/Blues and Trouble/Come Early in the Morning/Cross-Cut Saw/Deal the Cards/Did You Get That Letter?/Don't You Lie to Me/Drinking Straight Whiskey/Fumbling Around/Heard My Doorbell Ring/Hot Dog/Humpty Dumpty/I Can't Keep My Foot from Jumpin'/I Got It/I Tried Not to Cry/I'm Doing All Right/I'm Goin' I'm Goin'/I'm Having a Ball/I'm Leaving Baby/ Jackson Bound/Keep On Drinkin'/Keep Your Nose Out of My Business/Kid Mama Blues/Kid Man Blues/Lend Me Your Love/Let Me Ride Your Mule/ Little Girl Little Girl/Lorraine/Lula Mae/Mandolin Boogie/Mary Lou/Moaning and Groaning/My Baby Walked Out/My Home Ain't Here/My Trainfare Out of Town/On the Road Again/Prison Bound/Ring Around My Heart/Slam Hammer/Sleeping with the Devil/Sometimes I Cry/Trompin' at the Ballroom/ Walking Slow/Whoop It Up/Why Did You Break My Heart?/Wild Wild Woman/You Made Me Feel So Good

Infl by: Big Bill Broonzy/Bo Chatmon/Edgar Chatmon/Lonnie Chatmon/John Estes/Charlie McCoy/ John Lee "Sonny Boy" Williamson

Quotes: "A fine, expressive singer with a ringing, shouting delivery, an inventive, agile guitarist, and a fluent performer on the mandolin . . . a moving, individual interpreter of the modern blues style"—Pete Welding, Arhoolie album F-1029

"His warm, straightforward vocal style and his use of the mandolin made him popular"—Jim DeKoster, *Living Blues* magazine, May 1975, p 46

References: Living Blues magazine, Summer 1974, pp 6-7

Blues Unlimited magazine (UK), Sept 1965, pp 8-9

YOUNG, JOSEPH *"Mighty Joe"*

Courtesy Sheldon Harris Collection

Born: Sept 23, 1927, Shreveport (Caddo Parish), LA
Inst: Guitar

Father was Joseph Young Sr; mother Sallie Smith; was playing father's guitar at about 7 years of age; moved to Los Angeles, CA, early 40s; moved to Milwaukee, WI, c1945; received some private lessons from Columbia Musical Company, Milwaukee, WI, through 40s; frequently worked as amateur boxer in Milwaukee area, late 40s; worked in local blues band, Milwaukee area, 1953; formed own trio to work local gigs, Milwaukee, 1954; worked local club dates, Shreveport, LA, 1955-6; rec Jiffy label, Ruston, LA, 1956; moved to Chicago, IL, 1956; frequently sat-in w Howlin' Wolf Band in local clubs, Chicago, 1956; frequently worked w Joe Little and His Heart Breakers Band at Old Cermak Inn Lounge and others, Chicago, 1956; worked w Billy Boy Arnold at Columbian Club/Barrelhouse Lounge, Chicago, 1956; frequently worked w Jimmy Rogers Band in local club dates, Chicago, 1957; frequently w Billy Boy Arnold Band at The Rock 'n' Roll Club/Castle Rock Lounge/others, Chicago, 1958-9; rec Atomic-H label, Chicago, c1958; worked w own trio, Theresa's, Chicago, 1959; frequently worked w Otis Rush Band at Castle Rock Lounge/Alex Club/Mr Lee's/Pepper's/ others, Chicago, 1959-62; rec as sideman w Magic Sam/Willie Dixon/Albert King/others, Chicago, into 60s; rec acc to Otis Rush, Duke label, Chicago, 1962; rec acc to Billy Boy Arnold, Prestige label, Chicago, 1964; formed own group working local club dates, Chicago, from c1964; worked Rock's Tavern, Rockford, IL, 1968; Blue Flame Club, Chicago, 1969; L&A Lounge, Chicago, 1969; Chicago Blues Festival, Chicago, 1969; Don's Cedar Club, Chicago, 1969-70; Grant Park Blues Festival, Chicago, 1969; Sportsman's Lounge, Chicago, 1969; formed own Touch of Souls Band working Alex Club, Chicago, 1969-70; rec w Koko Taylor, Chess label, Chicago, c1970; worked Alice's Revisited, Chicago, 1970; Five Stages, Chicago, 1970; Riviera Lounge, Chicago, 1970-2; Ann Arbor Blues Festival, Ann Arbor, MI, 1970; rec Delmark label, Chicago, c1971; app on BIG BILL HILL Show, WOPA-radio, Oak Park, IL, 1971; worked Ann Arbor Blues Recital, Ann Arbor, MI, 1971; The Brown Shoe, Chicago, 1972; Esquire Showbar, Montreal, Can, 1972; Cougar Show Club, Chicago, 1972; Ma Bea's Lounge, Chicago, 1972; Joe's Place, Cambridge, MA, 1972-4; worked w own band, Ann Arbor Blues Festival, Ann Arbor, 1972-3 (por 1972 concert rel Atlantic label); Hawaii Club, Waukegan, IL, 1972; rec Sonet label, Chicago, 1972; worked The Kove, Kent, OH, 1973; El Mocambo Tavern, Toronto, Can, 1973; Pick-Congress Hotel, Chicago, 1973; Wise Fools Pub, Chicago, 1974-5; Sandy's Concert Club, Boston, MA, 1974; rec acc to Fenton Robinson/Koko Taylor, Alligator label, Chicago, 1974; rec Ovation label, Chicago, 1974; worked Majestic "M," Chicago, 1974; Rat Trap, Chicago, 1974; White Stallion, Chicago, 1974; Minstrel's, Chicago, 1974; Peanut Barrel, Chicago, 1974; The Orphanage, San Francisco, CA, 1974; toured club dates working through northwestern US into Canada, 1974; toured concert dates through France/Spain, 1975; worked Smiling Dog Saloon, Cleveland, OH, 1975; Foundation Tavern, Tacoma, WA, 1975; The New 1815 Club, Chicago, 1975; Shamrock Lounge, DeKalb, IL, 1975; rec acc to Otis Rush, Delmark label, Chicago, 1975; Biddy Mulligan's, Chicago, 1975-8; Zoo Bar, Lincoln, NE, 1976-7; rec Ovation label, Chicago, 1976; worked Second Chance, Ann Arbor, MI, 1977; Belle Star, Colden, NY, 1977; Wise Fools Pub, Chicago, 1977; app on

MADE IN CHICAGO, WTTW-TV, Chicago, 1977; clip shown in ROOTS OF COUNTRY MUSIC & BLUES, KGO-TV, San Francisco, CA, 1977

Songs: Big Talk/Early in the Morning/Flower Pot/ Green Light/I Give/Just a Minute/Lookin' for You/ Mama-in-Law Blues/Mighty Man/Move On Higher/ Need a Friend/New Orleans Women/Serve My Time/ Something on Your Mind/Take My Advice/ Take Over Chicago/Takes Money/Wishy Washy Woman

Infl by: BB King

Quotes: "Mighty Joe is practically the epitome of two-fisted but tasty urban bar blues . . ."—Rich Mangelsdorff, *Living Blues* magazine, Jan 1975, p 28

"Even his vocals . . . are all blues and his reliability, foresight in musical taste and talent make him a joy to deal with"—Dick Shurman, *Blues Unlimited* magazine (UK), Apr 1974, p 5

Reference: Blues Unlimited magazine (UK), Apr 1974, p 5

YOUNG WOLF, THE
(see Jenkins, Gus)

Z

ZA ZU GIRL, THE
(see Spivey, Elton)

Selected Bibliography

Books

During the course of research, a great many source books were consulted and most of the following are recommended. Without the searching insight and consuming interest of these many devoted scholars, this work could never have been as complete as it is.

Aaronson, Charles S., ed. *International Motion Picture Almanac for 1963.* New York, NY: Quigley Publishing Co., 1962

Agostinelli, Anthony J., ed. *The Newport Jazz Festival: Rhode Island (1954-71).* Providence, RI: Anthony J. Agostinelli, 1977

Albertson, Chris. *Bessie.* New York, NY: Stein & Day, 1972

———. *Bessie Smith, Empress of the Blues.* New York, NY: Walter Kane & Son Inc., 1975

Allen, Walter C. *Hendersonia.* Highland Park, NJ: Walter C. Allen, 1973

——— and Brian Rust. *King Joe Oliver.* Belleville, NJ: Walter C. Allen, 1955

Asch, Moses and Alan Lomax, eds. *The Leadbelly Songbook.* New York, NY: Oak Publications, 1962

Baggelaar, Kristin and Donald Milton. *Folk Music: More Than a Song.* New York, NY: Thomas Y. Crowell Co., 1976

Balliett, Whitney. *Dinosaurs in the Morning.* New York, NY: J. B. Lippincott Co., 1962

Bastin, Bruce. *Crying for the Carolines.* London, Eng.: Studio Vista Ltd., 1971

Bechet, Sidney. *Treat It Gentle.* London, Eng.: Cassell & Co., Ltd., 1960

Bell, Judy, ed. *Leadbelly.* New York, NY: TRO Folkways/The Big 3 Music Corp., 1976

Berendt, Joachim. *The New Jazz Book.* New York, NY: Hill & Wang, 1962

Blesh, Rudi. *Combo: USA.* New York, NY: Chilton Book Co., 1971

———. *Shining Trumpets.* New York, NY: Alfred A. Knopf, 1946

——— and Harriet Janis. *They All Played Ragtime.* New York, NY: Alfred A. Knopf, 1950

Bogle, Donald. *Toms, Coons, Mulattoes, Mammies and Bucks.* New York, NY: The Viking Press, 1973

Borenstein, Larry and Bill Russell. *Preservation Hall Portraits.* Baton Rouge, LA: Louisiana State University Press, 1968

Borneman, Ernest. *A Critic Looks at Jazz.* London, Eng.: Jazz Music Books, 1946

Botkin, B. B., ed. *Folk-Say: 1930.* Norman, OK: University of Oklahoma Press, 1930

Bradford, Perry. *Born with the Blues.* New York, NY: Oak Publications, 1965

Broven, John. *Walking to New Orleans.* Sussex, Eng.: Blues Unlimited, 1974

Brown, Len and Gary Friedrich. *Encyclopedia of Rock & Roll.* New York, NY: Tower Publications Inc., 1970

Bruynoghe, Yannick. *Big Bill Blues: Big Bill Broonzy's Story as Told to Yannick Bruynoghe.* London, Eng.: Cassell & Co., Ltd., 1955

Burton, Jack. *The Blue Book of Broadway Musicals.* Watkins Glen, NY: Century House, 1952

———. *The Blue Book of Hollywood Musicals.* Watkins Glen, NY: Century House, 1953

Buxton, Frank and Bill Owen. *The Big Broadcast, 1920-1950.* New York, NY: Viking Press Inc., 1972

Charles, Ray and David Ritz. *Brother Ray, Ray Charles' Own Story.* New York, NY: The Dial Press, 1978

Charters, Samuel B. *The Bluesmen.* New York, NY: Oak Publications, 1967

———. *The Country Blues.* New York, NY: Rinehart & Co., Inc., 1959

———, and Leonard Kunstadt. *Jazz: A History of the New York Scene.* Garden City, NY: Doubleday & Co., Inc., 1962

———. *Jazz: New Orleans (1885-1957).* Belleville, NJ: Walter C. Allen, 1958

———. *The Legacy of the Blues.* London, Eng.: Calder & Boyars Ltd., 1975

———. *The Poetry of the Blues.* New York, NY: Oak Publications Inc., 1963

———. *Robert Johnson.* New York, NY: Oak Publications Inc., 1973

Chase, Gilbert. *America's Music: From the Pilgrims to the Present.* New York, NY: McGraw-Hill Book Co., Inc., 1955

Chilton, John. *Who's Who of Jazz: Storyville to Swing Street.* London, Eng.: The Bloomsbury Book Shop, 1970

Condon, Eddie and Hank O'Neal. *The Eddie Condon Scrapbook of Jazz.* New York, NY: St. Martin's Press, 1973

Connor, D. Russell and Warren W. Hicks. *BG on the Record: A Bio-Discography of Benny Goodman.* New Rochelle, NY: Arlington House, 1969

Cook, Bruce. *Listen to the Blues.* New York, NY: Charles Scribner's Sons, 1973

Dalton, David. *Janis.* New York, NY: Simon & Schuster, 1971

Dance, Stanley, ed. *Jazz Era: The 'Forties.* London, Eng.: Jazz Book Club, 1961

———. *The World of Duke Ellington.* New York, NY: Charles Scribner's Sons, 1970

De Micheal, Don and Pete Welding., eds. *Down Beat's Jazz Record Reviews* (Vols. VI-VIII). Chicago, IL: Maher Publications, 1962

de Toledano, Ralph. *Frontiers of Jazz.* New York, NY: Oliver Durrell Inc., 1947

Dexter, Jr., Dave. *Jazz Cavalcade: The Inside Story of Jazz.* New York, NY: Criterion Music Corp., 1946

———. *The Jazz Story: From the '90s to the '60s.* Englewood Cliffs, NJ: Prentice Hall Inc., 1964

Dimmitt, Richard Bertrand. *A Title Guide to the Talkies* (2 Vols). New York, NY: The Scarecrow Press Inc., 1965

———. *An Actor's Guide to the Talkies* (2 Vols). Metuchen, NJ: The Scarecrow Press Inc., 1967

Dixon, Robert M. W. and John Godrich. *Blues & Gospel Records (1902-1942).* Middlesex, Eng.: Brian Rust, 1963

——— and ———. *Recording the Blues.* London, Eng.: Studio Vista Ltd., 1970

Dorson, Richard M. *American Folklore.* Chicago, IL: University of Chicago Press, 1959

Dunning, John. *Tune In Yesterday.* Englewood Cliffs, NJ: Prentice Hall Inc., 1976

Erlich, Lillian. *What Jazz Is All About.* New York, NY: Julian Messner Inc., 1962

Evans, David. *Tommy Johnson.* London, Eng.: Studio Vista Ltd., 1971

Ewen, David. *Complete Book of American Musical Theater.* New York, NY: Holt & Co., 1958

Feather, Leonard. *The Book of Jazz: From Then Till Now.* New York, NY: Horizon Press, 1965

———. *The Encyclopedia of Jazz in the Sixties.* New York, NY: Horizon Press, 1966

———. *The History of the Blues.* New York, NY: Charles Hansen Music & Books, 1972

———. *The New Edition of the Encyclopedia of Jazz.* New York, NY: Horizon Press, 1960

Fernett, Gene. *Swing Out: Great Negro Dance Bands.* Midland, MI: Pendell Publishing Co., 1970

Ferris, Bill and Judy Peiser, eds. *American Folklore Films & Videotapes: An Index.* Memphis, TN: Center for Southern Folklore, 1976

Ferris Jr., William. *Blues from the Delta.* London, Eng.: Studio Vista Ltd., 1970

Fletcher, Tom. *100 Years of the Negro in Show Business!* New York, NY: Burdge & Co. Ltd., 1954

Fox, Charles. *Fats Waller.* New York, NY: Barnes & Co., Inc., 1961

——— and Peter Gammond, Alun Morgan, Alexis Korner, eds. *Jazz on Record: A Critical Guide.* London, Eng.: Hutchinson of London Ltd., 1960

———. *The Jazz Scene.* Middlesex, Eng.: Hamlyn Publishing Group Ltd., 1972

Francis, Andre. *Jazz.* New York, NY: Grove Press, 1960

Fredericks, Vic. *Who's Who in Rock 'n' Roll.* New York, NY: Frederick Fell Inc., 1958

Gammond, Peter, ed. *The Decca Book of Jazz.* London, Eng.: The Jazz Book Club, 1960

Gara, Larry. *The Baby Dodds Story.* Los Angeles, CA: Contemporary Press, 1959

Garland, Phyl. *The Sound of Soul.* Chicago, IL: Henry Regnery Co., 1969

Garon, Paul. *The Devil's Son-In-Law: The Story of Peetie Wheatstraw and His Songs.* London, Eng.: Studio Vista Ltd., 1971

Garvin, Richard M. and Edmond G. Addeo. *The Midnight Special: The Legend of Leadbelly.* New York, NY: Bernard Geis Assoc., 1971

Gert zur Heide, Karl. *Deep South Piano.* London, Eng.: Studio Vista Ltd., 1970

Gillenson, Lewis W., ed. *Esquire's World of Jazz.* New York, NY: Esquire Inc. (n.d.), c1965

Gleason, Ralph, ed. *Jam Session: An Anthology of Jazz.* New York, NY: G.P. Putnam's Sons, 1958

Glover I, Tony "Little Sun." *Blues Harp.* New York, NY: Oak Publications, 1965

Goffin, Robert. *Jazz: From the Congo to the Metropolitan.* Garden City, NY: Doubleday, Doran & Co., 1944

Goldman, Albert. *Freakshow: The Rocksoulbluesjazzsickjewblackhumorsexpoppsych Gig and Other Scenes from the Counter-Culture.* New York, NY: Atheneum Publishers, 1971

Greenway, John. *American Folksongs of Protest.* Philadelphia, PA: University of Pennsylvania Press, 1953

Grossman, Stefan. *Ragtime Blues Guitarists.* New York, NY: Oak Publications, 1970

Gurnalnick, Peter. *Feel Like Going Home: Portraits in Blues and Rock 'n' Roll.* New York, NY: Outerbridge & Dienstfrey, 1971

Guthrie, Woody. *American Folksong.* New York, NY: Disc Co. of America, 1947

Hadlock, Richard. *Jazz Masters of the Twenties.* New York, NY: The Macmillan Co., 1965

Hammond, C. S. *Universal World Atlas.* Maplewood, NJ: C. S. Hammond, 1965

Handy, W. C., ed. *Blues: An Anthology.* New York, NY: Albert & Charles Boni, 1926

Haralambos, Michael. *Right On: From Blues to Soul in Black America.* London, Eng.: Eddison Press Ltd., 1974

Harris, Rex and Brian Rust. *Recorded Jazz: A Critical Guide.* Middlesex, Eng.: Penguin Books Ltd., 1958

Haskins, Jim. *The Cotton Club.* New York, NY: Random House, 1977

Heilbut, Tony. *The Gospel Sound: Good News and Bad Times.* New York, NY: Simon & Schuster, 1971

Hentoff, Nat and Albert J. McCarthy, eds. *Jazz: New Perspectives on the History of Jazz.* New York, NY: Rinehart & Co., Inc., 1959

———. *The Jazz Life.* New York, NY: The Dial Press, 1961

Herbert, Ian, ed. *Who's Who in the Theater: A Biographical Record of the Contemporary Stage.* Detroit, MI: Gale Research Co., 1977

Hippenmeyer, Jean-Roland. *Jazz Sur Films.* Yverdon, Switz.: De La Thiele, 1973

Hobson, Wilder. *American Jazz Music.* New York, NY: W. W. Norton & Co., Inc., 1939

Horricks, Raymond. *Count Basie & His Orchestra: Its Music and Its Musicians.* New York, NY: The Citadel Press, 1957

Hughes, Langston. *The Big Sea.* New York, NY: Alfred A. Knopf Inc., 1940

——— and Milton Meltzer. *Black Magic: A Pictorial History of the Negro in American Entertainment.* Englewood Cliffs, NJ: Prentice Hall Inc., 1967

———. *Famous Negro Music Makers.* New York, NY: Dodd, Mead & Co., 1955

Isaacs, Edith J. R. *The Negro in American Theater.* New York, NY: Theater Arts Inc., 1947

James, Edward J., ed. *Notable American Women 1607-1950: A Biographical Dictionary* (3 Vols). Cambridge, MA: Harvard University Press, 1971

Jenkinson, Philip and Alan Warner. *Celluloid Rock: Twenty Years of Movie Rock.* New York, NY: Warner Books Inc., 1976

Jepsen, Jorgen Grunnet, ed. *Jazz Records (1942-62/5/7/8/9)* (11 Vols). Copenhagen, Den.: Karl Emil Knudsen, 1963-70

Johnson, James Weldon. *Black Manhattan.* New York, NY: Alfred A. Knopf, 1930

Jones, Hettie. *Big Star Fallin' Mama: Five Women in Black Music.* New York, NY: The Viking Press, 1974

Jones, R. P. *Jazz.* London, Eng.: Metheun & Co., Ltd., 1963

Joseph, Bea and Charlotte Warren Squires, eds. *Biography Index: A Cumulative Index to Biographical Material in Books and Magazines* (3 Vols). New York, NY: H. W. Wilson Co., 1946-55

Kaminsky, Max and V. E. Hughes. *My Life in Jazz.* New York, NY: Harper & Row, 1963

Keepnews, Orrin and Bill Grauer Jr. *A Pictorial History of Jazz.* New York, NY: Crown Publishers Inc., 1955

Keil, Charles. *Urban Blues.* Chicago, IL: The University of Chicago Press, 1966

Kimball, Robert & William Bolcom. *Reminiscing with Sissle and Blake.* New York, NY: The Viking Press, 1973

Kinkle, Roger D. *The Complete Encyclopedia of Popular Music and Jazz, 1900-1950* (4 Vols). New Rochelle, NY: Arlington House Publishers, 1974

Kirkeby, Ed. *Ain't Misbehavin': The Story of Fats Waller.* New York, NY: Dodd, Mead & Co., 1966

Knight, Curtis. *Jimi: An Intimate Biography of Jimi Hendrix.* New York, NY: Praeger Publishers Inc., 1974

Kriss, Eric. *Six Blues-Roots Pianists.* New York, NY: Oak Publications, 1973

Lang, Iain. *Jazz in Perspective: The Background of the Blues.* London, Eng.: Jazz Book Club, 1957

Laurie, Joe, Jr. *Vaudeville: From the Honky-Tonks to the Palace.* New York, NY: Henry Holt & Co., 1953

Lawless, Ray M. *Folksingers and Folksongs in America.* New York, NY: Duel, Sloan and Pearce, 1960

Leadbitter, Mike and Neil Slaven. *Blues Records, Jan 1943 to Dec 1966.* London Eng.: Hanover Books Ltd., 1968

———. *Crowley, Louisiana Blues.* Sussex, Eng.: Blues Unlimited, 1968

———. *Nothing But the Blues.* London, Eng.: Hanover Books, 1971

Lees, Eugene, ed. *Down Beat Jazz Record Reviews, Vol IV.* Chicago, IL: Maher Publications, 1960

——— and Don De Micheal, eds. *Down Beat's Jazz Record Reviews, Vol V.* Chicago, IL: Maher Publications, 1961

Local 802 American Federation of Musicians Directory and Instrumentation, 1974-5. New York, NY: Associated Musicians of Greater New York, 1974

Logan, Nick and Bob Woffinden. *The Illustrated Encyclopedia of Rock.* London, Eng.: Hamlyn Publishing Group, 1976

Lomax, Alan. *The Rainbow Sign: A Southern Documentary.* New York, NY: Duell, Sloan & Pearce, 1959

Lomax, John A. *Adventures of a Ballad Hunter.* New York, NY: Macmillan Co., 1947

——— and Alan Lomax, eds. *Best Loved American Folk Songs (Folk Song: USA).* New York, NY: Grosset & Dunlap, 1947

——— and ———. *Negro Folk Songs as Sung by Lead Belly.* New York, NY: The Macmillan Co., 1936

Longstreet, Stephen. *Sportin' House: A History of the New Orleans Sinners and the Birth of Jazz.* Los Angeles, CA: Sherbourne Press Inc., 1965

Lord, Tom. *Clarence Williams.* Essex, Eng.: Storyville Publications & Co. Ltd., 1976

Lovell, John, Jr. *Black Song: The Forge and the Flame.* New York, NY: The Macmillan Co., 1972

Lucas, John. *Basic Jazz on Long Play.* Northfield, MN: Carleton College, 1954

Lydon, Michael. *Rock Folk: Portraits from the Rock 'n' Roll Pantheon.* New York, NY: The Dial Press, 1971

Lynn Farnol Group, Inc., ed. *The ASCAP Biographical Dictionary of Composers, Authors and Publishers.* New York, NY: The American Society of Composers, Authors and Publishers, 1966

Lyttelton, Humphrey. *Second Chorus.* London, Eng.: Macgibbon & Kee, 1958.

Mahony, Dan. *The Columbia 13/14000-D Series: A Numerical Listing.* Stanhope, NJ: Walter C. Allen, 1961

Mann, Woody. *Six Black Blues Guitarists.* New York, NY: Oak Publications, 1973.

Marshall, Jim and Baron Wolman, Jerry Hopkins. *Festival!: The Book of American Music Celebrations.* New York, NY: Macmillan Co., 1970

Mauerer, Hans J. *The Pete Johnson Story.* Frankfurt, Ger.: Hans J. Mauerer, 1965

May, Chris. *Rock 'n' Roll.* London, Eng.: Socion Books, 1973

McCarthy, Albert. *Big Band Jazz.* London, Eng.: G.P. Putnam's Sons, 1974

———, ed. *Jazz Book 1947.* London, Eng.: PL Editions Poetry, 1947

——— and Alun Morgan, Paul Oliver, Max Harrison, eds. *Jazz on Record: A Critical Guide to the First 50 Years, 1917-1967.* London, Eng.: Hanover Books Ltd., 1968

———, ed. *The PL Yearbook of Jazz, 1946.* London, Eng.: PL Editions Poetry, 1946

McGill, Raymond D., ed. *Notable Names in the American Theater.* New York, NY: James T. White & Co., 1976

McNamara, Daniel I., ed. *The ASCAP Biographical Dictionary of Composers, Authors, and Publishers.* New York, NY: Thomas Y. Crowell Co., 1948

Meeker, David. *Jazz in the Movies: A Guide to Jazz Musicians, 1917-1977.* New Rochelle, NY: Arlington House Publishers, 1977

Mezzrow, Milton "Mezz" and Bernard Wolfe. *Really the Blues.* New York, NY: Random House Inc., 1946

Michael, Paul. *The American Movies Reference Book: The Sound Era.* Englewood Cliffs, NJ: Prentice Hall, 1969

Miller, Paul Edward, ed. *Esquire's Jazz Book.* New York, NY: Smith & Durrell Inc., 1944

———. *Miller's Yearbook of Popular Music.* Chicago, IL: PEM Publications, 1943

Mitchell, George. *Blow My Blues Away.* Baton Rouge, LA: Louisiana State University Press, 1971

Mize, Dr. J. T. H., ed. *The International Who Is Who in Music.* Chicago, IL: Who Is Who In Music Inc., Ltd., 1951

Moore, Carman. *Somebody's Angel Child: The Story of Bessie Smith.* New York, NY: Thomas Y. Crowell Co., 1969

Moritz, Charles, ed. *Current Biography Yearbook* (36 Vols). New York, NY: H. W. Wilson Co., 1942-77

Morris, Lloyd. *Incredible New York: High Life and Low Life of the Last Hundred Years.* New York, NY: Random House, 1951

Murrells, Joseph. *Daily Mail Book of Golden Discs.* London, Eng.: McWhirter Twins Ltd., 1966

Myrus, Donald. *Ballads, Blues and the Big Beat.* New York, NY: The Macmillan Co., 1966

Napier, Simon A. *Back Woods Blues.* Sussex, Eng.: Blues Unlimited, 1968.

Neff, Robert and Anthony Connor. *Blues.* Boston, MA: David R. Godine Pub., 1975

Neihengen, Raymond M., ed. *Spot Radio Rates and Data.* Skokie, IL: Standard Rate & Data Service Inc., 1976

———, ed. *Spot Television Rates and Data.* Skokie, IL: Standard Rate & Data Service, 1976

The New York Times Directory of the Theater, New York, NY: Quadrangle/The New York Times Book Co., 1973

Nicholas, A. X., ed. *Woke Up This Mornin': Poetry of the Blues.* New York, NY: Bantam Books, Inc., 1973

Noble, Peter. *The Negro in Films.* London, Eng.: Skelton Robinson, (n.d.) c1949

Oakley, Giles. *The Devil's Music: A History of the Blues.* London, Eng.: British Broadcasting Corp., 1976

Oliver, Paul. *Bessie Smith.* New York, NY: A. S. Barnes & Co., Inc., 1961.

———. *Blues Fell This Morning: The Meaning of the Blues.* London, Eng.: Cassell & Co., Ltd., 1960

———. *Conversation with the Blues.* New York, NY: Horizon Press Pub., 1965.

———. *Savanah Syncopators: African Retentions in the Blues.* London, Eng.: Studio Vista Ltd., 1970

———. *Screening the Blues: Aspects of the Blues Tradition.* London, Eng.: Cassell & Co., Ltd., 1968

———. *The Story of the Blues.* New York, NY: Chilton Book Co., 1969.

Olsson, Bengt. *Memphis Blues and Jug Bands.* London, Eng.: Studio Vista Ltd., 1970

Oster, Harry. *Living Country Blues.* Detroit, MI: Folklore Associates, 1969

Ottley, Roi. *New World A-Coming: Inside Black America.* Boston, MA: Houghton Mifflin Co., 1943

Panassié, Hugues and Madeleine Gautier. *Guide to Jazz.* Boston, MA: Houghton Mifflin Co., 1956

———. *The Real Jazz.* New York, NY: Smith & Durrell Inc., 1942

Paparelli, Frank. *5 Boogie Woogie Blues Piano Solos by Pinetop Smith.* New York, NY: Leeds Music Corp., 1941

Parish, James Robert. *Actors' Television Credits, 1950-1972.* Metuchen, NJ: Scarecrow Press Inc., 1973

Petrie, Gavin, ed. *Black Music.* London, Eng.: Hamlyn Pub Group Ltd., 1974

Pleasants, Henry. *The Great American Popular Singers.* New York, NY: Simon and Schuster, 1974

Ragan, David. *Who's Who in Hollywood 1900-1976.* New Rochelle, NY: Arlington House Publishers, 1976

Ramsey Jr., Frederic. *Been Here and Gone.* New Brunswick, NJ: Rutgers University Press, 1960

———. *A Guide to Longplay Jazz Records.* New York, NY: Long Player Publications Inc., 1954

——— and Charles Edward Smith. *Jazzmen.* New York, NY: Harcourt, Brace & Co., 1939

Redd, Lawrence N. *Rock Is Rhythm and Blues: The Impact of Mass Media.* East Lansing, MI: Michigan State University Press, 1974

Rigdon, Walter, ed. *The Biographical Encyclopedia and Who's Who of the American Theater.* New York, NY: J. H. Heineman, 1966

Rodgers, Mrs. Jimmie. *My Husband Jimmie Rodgers.* San Antonio, TX: San Antonio Southern Literary Institute, 1935

Rooney, James. *Bossmen: Bill Monroe & Muddy Waters.* New York, NY: The Dial Press, 1971

Rose, Al and Edmond Souchon, M.D. *New Orleans Jazz: A Family Album.* Baton Rouge, LA: Louisiana State University Press, 1967

Rosenthal, George S. and Frank Zachary, eds. *Jazzways.* New York, NY: Greenberg Publishers, 1946

Rowe, Mike. *Chicago Breakdown.* London, Eng.: Eddison Press Ltd., 1973

Roxon, Lillian. *Rock Encyclopedia.* New York, NY: Grosset & Dunlap, 1969

Russell, Ross. *Jazz Style in Kansas City and the Southwest.* Berkeley, CA: University of California Press, 1971

Russell, Tony. *Blacks, Whites and Blues.* London, Eng.: Studio Vista Ltd., 1970

Rust, Brian. *The Dance Bands.* New Rochelle, NY: Arlington House Publishers, 1974

———. *Jazz Records 1897-1942* (2 Vols). London, Eng.: Storyville Publications & Co., 1969

Sandberg, Larry and Dick Weissman. *The Folk Music Sourcebook*. New York, NY: Alfred A. Knopf, 1976

Schiffman, Jack. *Uptown: The Story of Harlem's Apollo Theater*. New York, NY: Cowles Book Co., Inc., 1971

Scheuer, Steven H., ed. *TV Movie Almanac & Ratings, 1958-1959*. New York, NY: Bantam Books, 1958

———. *Movies on TV, 1975-76 Edition*. New York, NY: Bantam Books, 1974

———. *Movies on TV, 1978-79 Edition*. New York, NY: Bantam Books, 1977

Shapiro, Nat and Nat Hentoff, eds. *Hear Me Talkin' to Ya*. New York, NY: Rinehart & Co., Inc., 1955

——— and ———, eds. *The Jazz Makers*. New York, NY: Rinehart & Co., Inc., 1957

Shaw, Arnold. *Belafonte: An Unauthorized Biography*. Philadelphia, PA: Chilton Co., 1960

———. *The Street That Never Slept: New York's Fabled 52nd Street*. New York, NY: Coward, McCann & Geoghegan Inc., 1971

———. *The World of Soul: Black America's Contribution to the Pop Music Scene*. New York, NY: Cowles Book Co., Inc., 1970

———. *Honkers and Shouters*. New York, NY: Collier Books, 1978

Shaw, Charles G. *Night Life*. New York, NY: John Day Company, 1931

Shestack, Melvin. *The Country Music Encyclopedia*. New York, NY: Thomas Y. Crowell, Co., 1974

Shirley, Kay, ed. and Frank Driggs, annotator. *The Book of the Blues*. New York, NY: Crown Publishers Inc., 1963

Short, Bobby. *Black and White Baby*. New York, NY: Dodd, Mead & Co., 1971

Silverman, Jerry. *Folk Blues*. New York, NY: The Macmillan Co., 1958

Simon, George T. *The Big Bands*. New York, NY: The Macmillan Co., 1967

———. *Simon Says: The Sights and Sounds of the Swing Era 1935-1955*. New York, NY: Galahad Books, 1971

Smith, Willie the Lion and George Hoefer. *Music on My Mind: The Memoirs of an American Pianist*. Garden City, NY: Doubleday & Co., Inc., 1964

Southern, Eileen. *The Music of Black Americans: A History*. New York, NY: W. W. Norton & Co., Inc., 1971

Spradling, Mary Mace, ed. *In Black and White: Afro-Americans in Print*. Kalamazoo, MI: Kalamazoo Public Library, 1976

Stagg, Tom and Charlie Crump. *New Orleans, The Revival*. London, Eng.: Bashall Eaves, 1973

Stambler, Irwin. *Encyclopedia of Pop, Rock & Soul*. New York, NY: St. Martin's Press, 1977

Stearns, Marshall and Jean Stearns. *Jazz Dance: The Story of American Vernacular Dance*. New York, NY: The Macmillan Co., 1968

———. *The Story of Jazz*. New York, NY: Oxford University Press, 1956

Stewart-Baxter, Derrick. *Ma Rainey and the Classic Blues Singers*. London, Eng.: Studio Vista Ltd., 1970

Stoddard, Tom. *Pops Foster: An Autobiography of a New Orleans Jazzman*. Berkeley, CA: University of California Press, 1971

Surge, Frank. *Singers of the Blues*. Minneapolis, MN: Lerner Publications Co., 1969

Terrace, Vincent. *The Complete Encyclopedia of Television Programs 1947-1976* (2 Vols). Cranbury, NJ: A.S. Barnes & Co., Inc., 1976

Terry, Sonny. *The Harp Styles of Sonny Terry*. New York, NY: Oak Publications, 1975

Titon, Jeff Todd. *Early Downhome Blues: A Musical and Cultural Analysis*. Urbana, IL: University of Illinois Press, 1977

———. *From Blues to Pop: The Autobiography of Leonard "Baby Doo" Caston*. Los Angeles, CA: John Edwards Memorial Foundation Inc., 1974

Tracy, Jack, ed. *Down Beat Jazz Record Reviews, Vol II*. Chicago, IL: Maher Publications Inc., 1958

Traill, Sinclair, ed. *Concerning Jazz*. London, Eng.: The Jazz Book Club, 1958

——— and The Hon. Gerald Lascelles. *Just Jazz* (Nos. 1, 2). London, Eng.: Peter Davies Ltd., 1957/1958

———. *Just Jazz* (No. 3). London, Eng.: Landsborough Pub Ltd., 1959

———. *Just Jazz* (No. 4). London, Eng.: Souvenir Press Ltd., 1960

U.S. Copyright Office. *Catalogue of Copyright Entries, Motion Pictures* (1912-69). Washington, D.C.: Government Printing Office, c1970

Ulanov, Barry. *A Handbook of Jazz*. New York, NY: The Viking Press, 1957

———. *Duke Ellington*. New York, NY: Creative Age Press, Inc., 1946

Vreede, Max E. *Paramount 12000/13000 Series*. London, Eng.: Storyville Publications & Co., 1971

Waters, Ethel and Charles Samuels. *His Eye Is on the Sparrow*. Garden City, NY: Doubleday & Co., Inc., 1951

———. *To Me It's Wonderful.* New York, NY: Harper & Row Publishers, 1972

Weaver, John T. *Forty Years of Screen Credits, 1929-1969* (2 Vols). Metuchen, NJ: The Scarecrow Press Inc., 1970

Wells, Dicky. *The Night People.* Boston, MA: Crescendo Pub. Co., 1971

Whitburn, Joel. *Top Rhythm & Blues Records, 1949-1971.* Menomonee Falls, WI: Record Research, 1973

Williams, Clarence. *The "Boogie Woogie" Blues Folio.* New York, NY: Clarence Williams Publishing Co., Inc., 1940

Williams, Martin T., ed. *The Art of Jazz: Essays on the Nature and Development of Jazz.* New York, NY: Oxford University Press, 1959

———, ed. *Jazz Panorama: From the Pages of the Jazz Review.* New York, NY: The Crowell-Collier Press, 1962

Williamson, Ken, ed. *This Is Jazz.* London, Eng.: Newnes, 1960

Wilmer, Valerie. *Jazz People.* New York, NY: The Bobbs-Merrill Co., Inc., 1970

Yurchenco, Henrietta. *A Mighty Hard Road: The Woody Guthrie Story.* New York, NY: McGraw-Hill, 1970

Periodicals

The following periodicals were consulted in the preparation of this work. Since many are defunct and included unavailable or irrelevant issues, the use of complete runs were precluded in some cases.

ABC-TV Hootenanny
After Beat
Alley Music
American Folk Music Occasional
Arhoolie Occasional
Atlantic City Press
Big Beat/Blues Train
Billboard
Black Music
Blue Flame
Blue Sky Review
Blues
Blues & Soul
Blues News
Blues Research
Blues Unlimited
Blues Unlimited Collectors Classics
Blues Views
Blues World
Broadcast Music Inc: Rhythm & Blues
Broadside
Cadence
Chicago Defender
Chicago Tribune
Coda
Collier's
Come for to Sing
Crawdaddy
Crazy Music
Crescendo
Cue
Downbeat
Downbeat Yearbook/Music Annual
Ebony
Esquire
Essence
Eureka
Evergreen Review
Festival of American Folklife Festival Program
Figaro
Folk Music
Folk Music Occasional
Folk Music Yearbook
Folk Scene
Folkin' Around/Sounds
Foot Note
Guitar Player
Hit Parader Songs & Stories
Hootenanny
Jazz
Jazz and Blues
Jazz and Pop
Jazz Beat
Jazz Finder
Jazz Forum
Jazz Information
Jazz Journal (International)
Jazz Monthly
Jazz Quarterly
Jazz Record
Jazz Register
Jazz Report
Jazz Review
Jazz World
Jazzologist
Jet
Journal of Jazz Studies

Life
Lightning Express
Living Blues
Look
Mariposa Program
Matrix
Melody Maker
Metronome
Metronome Yearbook
Mississippi Rag
Music Memories
Music Reporter
New Musical Express
New York Age
New York Amsterdam News
New York News
New York Post
New York Times
New Yorker
Newark Star Ledger
Newport Jazz Festival Program
Newsweek
Orchestra World
Our World
Pierre Key's Radio Annual
Pick Up
Pittsburgh Courier
Planet Presents
Playback
Playbill
Playboy
Port Huron Times Herald
Record Changer
Record Research
Rhythm and Blues
Rolling Stone
San Francisco Examiner
Saturday Evening Post
Saturday Review
Schwann Long Playing Record Catalog
Second Line
Sepia
78 Quarterly
Shout
Show Business Illustrated
Sing Out
Sounds
Sounds and Fury
Soul Illustrated
Storyville
Tan
Time
Tune In
TV Guide
Vieux Carré Courier
Village Voice
Washington Star
What's on the Air
Whiskey, Women And . . .
Who's Who in Television & Radio

Magazines in Print

As of Summer 1993, the following blues magazines were in print. It should be pointed out that Living Blues magazine, whose masthead states it is "A Journal of The African-American Blues Tradition," has been the voice of blues since its inception in 1970. This fine American publication features biographies, discographies, news, reviews and a mass of other information presented professionally and most thoroughly. It is highly recommended and deserving of support.

Living Blues, Center for the Study of Southern Culture, Univ of Mississippi, University MS 38677

Blues Access, 1455 Chestnut Place, Boulder, CO, 80304

Blues & Rhythm, 16 Bank St, Cheadle, Cheshire, SK8 2AZ, England

Blues Life Journal, PO Box 33, A-1035, Vienna Austria

Blues Magazine, P.O. Box 585, Station P, Toronto, Canada M5S 2T1

Blues Research, 65 Grand Avenue, Brooklyn, NY 11205

Blues Revue Quarterly, Rt 2, Box 118, West Union, WV, 26456

Blues Unlimited, 36 Belmont Park, Lewisham, London SE13 5DB, England

Crazy Music, P.O. Box 1029, Canberra City, A.C.T. 2601, Australia

Il Blues, PO Box 1022, 20101, Milano, Italy

Jazz, Blues and Co., 1 rue Dalloz, 75013 Paris, France

Jefferson, c/o Tommy Lofgren, Skordevagen 5, S-186 00, Vallentuna, Sweden

Juke Blues, PO Box 148, London W91DY, Eng. (US address: 3S 321 Winfield Road, Warrenville, IL, 60555)

Lead Belly Letter, P.O. Box 6679, Ithaca, NY, 14851

Talking Blues, P.O. Box 226, London SW4 OEH, England

In addition, the following magazines feature blues articles or news of the field.

Black Music, Dorset House, Stamford Street, London SE1 9LU, England
The Black Perspective in Music, P.O. Drawer 1, Cambria Heights, NY 11411
Block, Persbureau Bossa Nova, Postbus 244, 7600 AE Almedo, Netherlands
Cadence, Cadence Bldg, Redwood, NY, 13679
Coda, P.O. Box 1002, Station 'O', Toronto, Ontario, Canada, M4A 2N4
Come for to Sing, 909 W. Armitage, Chicago, IL 60614
Contemporary Keyboard, Box 907, Saratoga, CA 95070
Downbeat, 222 W. Adams, Chicago, IL 60606
Guitar Player, Box 615, 12333 Saratoga/Sunnyvale Rd., Saratoga, CA 95070
Jazz Hot, 14, rue Chaptal, Paris 9, France
Jazz Journal International, Oakfield House, Perrymount Road, Haywards Heath, W. Sussex RH16 3DH, England
Jazz Report, P.O. Box 476, Ventura, CA 93001
JEMF Quarterly, Folklore & Mythology Center, UCLA, 11369 Bunche Hall, Los Angeles, CA 90024
Lightnin' Express, 10341 San Pablo Avenue, El Cerrito, CA 94530
Melody Maker, 24/34 Meymott St, London SE1, England
The Mississippi Rag, 5644 Morgan Avenue So., Minneapolis, MN 55419
Musician's News, P.O. Box 492, San Francisco, CA 94101
Old Time Music, 33 Brunswick Gardens, London W8 4AW, England
Record Exchanger, Box 6144, Orange, CA 92667
Record Research, 65 Grand Avenue, Brooklyn, NY 11205
Rolling Stone, 625 Third St., San Francisco, CA 94107
Shout, P.O. Box 226, London SW4, OEH, England
Sing Out!, PO Box 5253, Bethleham, PA, 18015
Soul Bag, 25, rue Trezel, 92-Levallois-Peret, France
Storyville, 66, Fairview Drive, Chigwell, Essex IG7 6HS, England
The Victory Music Folk & Jazz Review, Court C Possibilities, Box 36, Tillicum Br., Tacoma, WA 98492

Record Companies

As of Spring 1978, the following record companies reportedly issued and/or reissued blues recordings. An indebtedness is owed to these and others whose interest and concern helps to maintain the life flame of the blues.

ABC/Dunhill Records, 8255 Beverly Blvd., Los Angeles, CA 90048
Adelphi/Piedmont Records, P.O. Box 288, Silver Spring, MD 20907
Advent/Bullfrog/Muskadine Productions, P.O. Box 635, La Habra, CA 90631
Ahura Mazda Records, P.O. Box 15582, New Orleans, LA 70175
Airway Records, 368 E. 69th St., Chicago IL 60637
Alarm Records, 3316 Line Ave., Shreveport LA 71104
Alligator Records, P.O. Box 60234, Chicago, IL 60660
Antilles Records, 444 Madison Ave., NYC, NY 10022
Archive of Folk Song (see Everest Archive)
Argo, 115 Fulham Rd., London SW 1, England
Arhoolie/Blues Classics/Folklyric, 10341 San Pablo Ave., El Cerrito, CA 94530
Ariola-Eurodisc, Steinhauser Str. 3, 8000 Munich 90, W. Germany
Asch Records (see Folkways Records)
Atco Records (see Atlantic)
Atlantic Recording Corp/Atco Records, 75 Rockefeller Plaza, NYC, NY 10019
Baron Records, 11 Dell Ave., Melrose, MA 02176
Barrelhouse Records, 6512 S. Talman, Chicago, IL 60629
Barron (see 400 W. 150 Records)
Bear Family Records, Goethestrasse 9, 2800 Bremen, W. Germany
Bellaphon Records, GmbH & Co., KG, Mainzer Landstrasse 87-89, 6000 Frankfurt, W. Germany
Big-Star Records, 4228 Joy Rd., Detroit, MI 48204
Big Town (see Cadet)
Biograph Records Melodeon, 16 River St., Chatham, NY 12037
Birch Records, P.O. Box 92, Wilmette, IL 60091
Black & Blue Records, 15 Rue Doulong, 75017, Paris, France
Blind Pig Records, 208 S. First St., Ann Arbor, MI 48103
Blue Flame (see CJ Records)
Blue Fox (see Sun)
Blue Goose Records (see Yazoo)
Blue Horizon Records, Blue Horizon House, 165 W. 74th St., NYC, NY 10023
Blue Labor Records, P.O. Box 1262, Peter Stuyvesant Station, NYC, NY 10009
Blue Note (see United Artists)
Blue Rock (see Mercury)
Blue Sky Records, 745 Fifth Ave., Suite 1803, NYC, NY 10022
Bluebeat, c/o Hans Ewert, P.O. Box 1126, 5466 Neustadt, Germany

Blues Beacon, c/o Peter Gleissner Prod., Apt. 02-06, Tulpenstr, 28, 8192 Geretsried 1, W. Germany
Blues Classics (see Arhoolie)
Blues King, 1202 N.E. 105th Pl., Seattle, WA 98125
Blues Obscurities, 75 Charing Cross Rd., London WC 2, England
Blues Spectrum, 4218 W. Jefferson Blvd., Los Angeles, CA 90016
Broadsides (see Folkways Records)
Buddah Records Inc., 1350 Ave. of Americas, NYC, NY 10019
Bullfrog (see Advent Productions)
CBS/Columbia /Epic, 51 W. 52 St., NYC, NY 10019
CBS Schallplatten GmbH, Bleichstr, 64-662, 6000 Frankfurt, W. Germany
CJ Records/Blue Flame, 4827 S. Prairie Ave., Chicago, IL 60615
Cadet Records/Big Town/Crown/Custom/Flair/Grenade/Kent/Modern/United, 5810 S. Normandie Ave., Los Angeles, CA 90044
Columbia (see CBS)
Creed Taylor Inc. (CTI)/Kudu, 1 Rockefeller Plaza, NYC, NY 10020
Crescendo Records (see GNP)
Crown (see Cadet)
Custom (see Cadet)
DJM Records, 119 W. 57 St., Suite 400, NYC, NY 10019
Delmark/Pearl Records, 4243 N. Lincoln Ave., Chicago, IL 60618
Deutsche Grammophon GmbH (DGG), P.O. Box 301240, Hohe Bleichen 14-16, 2000 Hamburg 36, W. Germany
Dharma Records, P.O. Box 615, 117 W. Rockland Road, Libertyville, IL 60048
Dobell's/77 Records, 77 Charing Cross Rd., London WC2H OAB, England
Duke, 2809 Erastus St., Houston, TX 77026
Dunhill Records (see ABC Records)
Dusty Road Records, 340 Beach 12th St., Far Rockaway, NY 11691
EBM (Eubie Blake Music), 284-A Stuyvesant Ave., Brooklyn, NY 11221
EMI Electrola GmbH, Maarweg 149, 5000 Cologne 41, W. Germany
ENJA Records, Nymphen Burger Str., 209, 8000 Munich 19, W. Germany
Elektra, 962 La Cienega, Los Angeles, CA 90069
Epic (see CBS)
Esceha, Altenhof 3, D-5400 Koblenz, Germany
Euphonic, 357 Leighton Drive, Ventura, CA 93001
Eurodisc (see Ariola)
Everest Archive/Archive of Folk Song/Legacy/Tradition, 10920 Wilshire Blvd., Los Angeles, CA 90024
Excello (see Nashboro Records)
Fantasy/Milestone/Prestige/Stax, 10th & Parker Streets, Berkeley, CA 94710
Fat Cat's Jazz, P.O. Box 458, Manassas, VA 22110
Flair (see Cadet)
Flying Fish Records, 1304 W. Schubert, Chicago, IL 60614
Flyright/Magpie Records, 18 Endwell Rd., Bexhill-on-Sea, E. Sussex TN39 3EP, England
Folk-Legacy Records, Sharon Mountain Rd., Sharon, CT 06069
Folklyric (see Arhoolie)
Folkways/Asch/Broadsides/RBF, 43 W. 61 St., NYC, NY 10023
400 W. 150/Barron, 11 Dogwood Lane, Larchmont, NY 10538
GNP Crescendo Records, 8560 Sunset Blvd., Suite 603, Los Angeles, CA 90069
Goldband Recording, 313 Church St., Lake Charles, LA 70601
Grenade (see Cadet)
Groove Merchant, 515 Madison Ave., Suite 3701, NYC, NY 10022
Harlekin, Heidelberger Str., 6, 2800 Bremen 1, W. Germany
Heritage, Rt. 3, Box 278, Galax, VA 24333
Herwin Records, 45 First St., Glen Cove, NY 11542
Historical Records, P.O. Box 4204, Jersey City, NY 07304
Intercord Tongesellschaft mbH, Aixheimer Str. 26, 7000 Stuttgart 75, W. Germany
JSP Records, 112 Sunny Gardens Rd., London N.W. 4, England
Janus, GRT Corp., 1286 N. Lawrence Station Rd., Sunnyvale, CA 94086
Jazzology-GHB Records, 3008 Wadsworth Mill Place, Decatur, GA 30032
Jewel Records/Ronn, 728 Texas St., Shreveport, LA 71163
Jim Taylor Presents (JTP), 12311 Gratiot Ave., Detroit, MI 48205
John Edwards Memorial Foundation, c/o Center for Study of Folklore & Mythology, UCLA, Los Angeles, CA 90024
Joliet Record Co., P.O. Box 67201, Los Angeles, CA 90067
Kent (see Cadet)
Kicking Mule Records, P.O. Box 3233, Berkeley, CA 94703
King/Power Pak, 220 Boscobel St., Nashville, TN 37213
Kudu (see Creed Taylor Inc.)
Legacy (see Everest Archive)
Library of Congress, Music Division, Recorded Sound Section, Washington, DC 20540
London Records, 539 W. 25 St., NYC, NY 10001
M&M Records, Bruckhofstrasse 3, 6000 Frankfurt 1, W. Germany
MCA Records, 100 Universal City Plaza, Universal City, CA 91608
MCM, Marcelle Morgantini, "Les Bruyeres," 64290 Gan, France
Magpie Records (see Flyright Records)
Maison de Soul, Flat Town Music Co., 434 E. Main, Ville Platte, LA 70586
Mamlish, Box 417, Cathedral Station, NYC, NY 10025
Matchbox (see Saydisc)
Melodeon (see Biograph Records)
Mercury/Blue Rock, 1 IBM Plaza, Chicago, IL 60611
Metronome Musik GmbH, Ueberseering 21, 2000 Hamburg 60, W. Germany

Milestone (see Fantasy)
Mimosa Records, 4920 Maiden Lane, La Mesa, CA 92041
Modern (see Cadet)
Mr. Blues Records, 5216 S. Lockwood, Chicago, IL 60638
Muse Records, 160 W. 71 St., NYC, NY 10023
Muskadine Productions (see Advent Productions)
Nashboro/Excello Records, 1011 Woodland St., Nashville, TN 37206
Newgrape Records, Box 683, Haymarket N.S.W., Australia
Nighthawk, P.O. Box 15856, St. Louis, MO 63114
Oblivion, Box X, Roslyn Hts., NY 11577
Oldie Blues, Albert Schweitzerlarn 9, 6721 AW Bennekom, Holland
Origin Jazz Library (OJL), Box 863, Berkeley, CA 94701
Ornament, Goerresstrasse 3, 5400 Koblenz 1, W. Germany
Ovation Records, 1249 Waukegan Rd., Glenview, IL 60025
P-Vine Special, Blues Interactions Inc., 5-18-11-201, Daizawa, Setagaya-ku, Tokyo 155, Japan
Pearl Records (see Delmark Records)
Philo Records, The Barn, N. Ferrisburg, VT 05473
Phoenix Jazz Records, P.O. Box 3, Kingston, NJ 08528
Phonogram GmbH, Roedingsmarkt 14, 2000 Hamburg 11, W. Germany
Piedmont Records (see Adelphi Records)
Playboy Records, 8560 Sunset Blvd., Los Angeles, CA 90069
Power Pak (see King)
Prestige Records (see Fantasy)
RBF (see Folkways Records)
RCA Records (Victor), 1133 Avenue of Americas, NYC, NY 10036
RSO Records, 8335 Sunset Blvd., Los Angeles, CA 90069
Red Lightnin′ Records, 517 Eastern Ave., Ilford, Essex 1G2-6LT, England
Ronn (see Jewel Records)
Roots, Box 17, A-2345, Brunn a Geb, Austria
Rounder Records, 186 Willow Ave., Somerville, MA 02144
Route 66, Smokestack Records, P.O. Box 29005, S-100 52, Stockholm, Sweden
SSS International (see Sun)
Savoy Records, 342 Westminster Ave., Elizabeth, NJ 07208
Saydisc/Matchbox, The Barton, Inglestone Common, Badminton Glos, GL9-1BX, England
77 Records (see Dobell's)
Smithsonian Classic Jazz, P.O. Box 14196, Washington, DC 20044
Sonet, Sonet Productions, 121 Ledbury Rd., London W11, England
Sonet Grammofon AB, Atlasvaegen 1, S-181 20 Lidingoe, Sweden
Specialty, 8300 Santa Monica Blvd., Los Angeles, CA 90069
Specialty, Ember Records Ltd., Carlton Tower Pl., Suite 4, Sloane St., London SW1X 9P2 England
Spivey Records, 65 Grand Ave., Brooklyn, NY 11205
Stash Records, P.O. Box 390, Brooklyn, NY 11215
Stax Records Inc. (see Fantasy)
Storyville Records, Jydeholmen 15, DK-2720 Vanloese, Denmark
Styletone Records, 254 E. 29 St., Los Angeles, CA 90011
Sun/Blue Fox/SSS International, 3106 Belmont Blvd., Nashville, TN 37212
Swaggie Records, P.O. Box 125, S. Yarra, Victoria 3141, Australia
Takoma Records, P.O. Box 5369, 3105 Pico Blvd., Santa Monica, CA 90405
Tangerine Record Corp., 2107 W. Washington Blvd., Los Angeles, CA 90018
Testament Records, 507 Paco Verde Ave., Pasadena, CA 91107
Tomato Records, 611 Broadway, NYC, NY 10022
Tradition (see Everest Archive)
Transatlantic, 86 Marylebone High St., London 1 4AY, England
Trio Records, Houraiya Bldg., 5-2-1, Roppongi Minato-ku, Tokyo 106, Japan
Trip, 947 US Hwy. 1, Rahway, NJ 07065
Trix Records, Drawer AB, Rosendale, NY 12472
United (see Cadet)
United Artists/Blue Note, 6920 Sunset Blvd., Los Angeles, CA 90028
VJM (Vintage Jazz Music), 12 Slough Lane, London NW9 8QL, England
Vanguard Records, 71 W. 23 St., NYC, NY 10010
Victor Records (see RCA)
Vivid Sound, 2-23-8, Shimomeguro, Meguro-ku, Tokyo 153, Japan
Yazoo/Blue Goose Records, 245 Waverly Place, NYC, NY 10014

Film Index

This is an index of titled commercial films, shorts, soundies, telescriptions, videotapes and cartoons in which singers listed in this book participated. Participation may be a singing or non-singing appearance, including directorial, composing, scoring, voice-over, sound track recording or other work. A film about a singer without his participation is indicated by the singer's name in parentheses. Film lengths range from three minutes (soundies) to over three hours for commercial theater releases. For purposes of this book, telescriptions and videotapes are considered commercial film releases.

The year date of each film is shown in parentheses after the title when known, although there seems to be an inconsistency within the film industry regarding such dates. Generally, the year is either the copyright or release date, although on a rare occasion it may be a production or live performance date.

A film released only or originally as a television show will be found in the TV index. For further details regarding kind of participation, category of film, sub-title or part, and country of origin other than the United States, refer to the bio entry.

All titles beginning with the articles "A," "An" and "The" are indexed by the second word. My appreciation to Joseph G. Palladino for his work on this index.

A Nous Deux la France (1970). *Peter Chatman*
Affectionally Yours (1941). *Hattie McDaniel*
After Seben (1929). *Louis Jordan*
Air Mail Special (1941). *James Rushing*
Ali the Man (1975). *Richard Havens*
Alice Adams (1935). *Hattie McDaniel*
Along the Old Man River (see: Out of the Blacks into the Blues)
American Folk Blues Festival (1968): *John Lee Hooker; Walter Horton; Curtis Jones; Mathis Reed; Eddie Taylor; Aaron Walker; Joe Lee Williams*
American Graffiti (1973). *Antoine Domino*
American Hot Wax (1978): *Charles Berry; Jalacy Hawkins*
American Music: From Folk to Jazz and Pop (see TV show: Anatomy of Pop: The Music Explosion)
And This is Free (1963): *Carey Bell; Arvella Gray; Robert Nighthawk; John Wrencher; John Young*
Angel Angel Down We Go (see: The Cult of the Damned)
Anniversary Trouble (1935). *Hattie McDaniel*
Another Face (1935). *Hattie McDaniel*
Arbor Day (1936). *Hattie McDaniel*
Arthur Crudup: Born in the Blues (see TV show: Arthur Crudup: Born in the Blues)
Autobiography of Miss Jane Pittman, The (see TV show: The Autobiography of Miss Jane Pittman)

Babbitt (1934). *Hattie McDaniel*
Baby Doll (1956). *Smiley Lewis*
Ballad in Blue (1964) (Blues for Lovers—USA title) (Light out of Darkness—UK title). *Ray Charles*
Basin Street Revue (1956): *Helen Humes; Amos Milburn; Dinah Washington*
Battle of Broadway (1938). *Hattie McDaniel*
Because I Love You (c1943). *Mamie Smith*
Beginning, The (1970) (Evil Doing). *Clarence Miller*
Believe in Me (1971). *Louis Rawls*
Bessie Smith (1968). *Bessie Smith*
Beware (1946). *Louis Jordan*
Big Beat, The (1957). *Antoine Domino*
Big Bill Blues (1956). *William Broonzy*
Big Bill Broonzy (c1942). *William Broonzy*
Big Fat Mamas (c1943). *Benjamin Jackson*
Big Name Bands No. 1 (1941) *James Rushing*

Big T.N.T. Show, The (1966): *Ray Charles; Ellas McDaniel*
Big Wheel, The (1949). *Hattie McDaniel*
Black Godfather, The (1974). *James Witherspoon*
Black King, The (1932). *Trixie Smith*
Black Music in America—From Then Til Now (1970): *Riley King; Huddie Ledbetter; Bessie Smith*
Black Rodeo (1972): *Ray Charles; Riley King; Richard Penniman*
Black Roots (1970): *Gary Davis; Larry Johnson*
Blind Gary Davis (1972): *Gary Davis; Larry Johnson*
Blind Gary Davis in New York (1964). *Gary Davis*
Blonde Venus (1932). *Hattie McDaniel*
Blood of Jesus, The (1941). *Babe Turner*
Blues, The (1962): *Barbara Dane; Jesse Fuller; Lowell Fulson; Sam Hopkins; Mance Lipscomb; Alexander Moore; Edwin Pickens; Willie Thomas; Babe Turner*
Blues, The (1963): *Pink Anderson; William Borum; Gus Cannon; John Estes; Walter Lewis; J. D. Short; Henry Tate*
Blues Accordin' to Lightnin' Hopkins, The (1968): *George Butler; Joel Hopkins; Sam Hopkins; Mance Lipscomb*
Blues Between the Teeth (see: Blues Under the Skin)
Blues for a Black Film (1973): *Walter McGhee; Sonny Terry*
Blues for Lovers (see: Ballad in Blue)
Blues Is Alive and Well in Chicago, The (1970): *George Guy; McKinley Morganfield; Koko Taylor; Emery Williams*
Blues Legends 73 (1973): *Otis Hicks; Moses Smith*
Blues Like Showers of Rain (1970): *James Brewer; James Cage; Arvella Gray; Sam Hopkins; Alonzo Johnson; James Johnson; J. B. Lenoir; Mance Lipscomb; Robert Lockwood; Albert Luandrew; Eurreal Montgomery; James Oden; Rufus Perryman; Edwin Pickens; Billie Pierce; Otis Spann; Willie Thomas; Henry Townsend; Wade Walton*
Blues Maker, The (1968). *Fred McDowell*
Blues Under the Skin (1972) (Blues Between the Teeth): *George Guy; Riley King; Walter Lewis; Mance Lipscomb; Walter McGhee; Roosevelt Sykes; Sonny Terry; Amos Wells; Booker White; Robert Williams*
Bluesman, The (1973). *Arbee Stidham*
Boarding House Blues (1948). *Benjamin Jackson*
Body and Soul (part 2) (see TV show: Of Black America)
Bongo Wolf's Revenge (1970). *Michael Bloomfield*
Book of Numbers (1972): *Walter McGhee; Sonny Terry*
Born in the Blues (1975): *Carey Bell; James Dawkins; John Estes; Hammie Nixon; Houston Stackhouse*
Bound for Glory (1976). *(Woodrow Guthrie)*
Bride Walks Out, The (1936). *Hattie McDaniel*
Brothers (1977). *Taj Mahal*
Bubbling Over (1934). *Ethel Waters*
Buck and the Preacher (1972): *Walter McGhee; Sonny Terry*
Buck Clayton and His All Stars (1961). *James Witherspoon*
Buzz Me (1945). *Louis Jordan*

Cabin in the Sky (1943). *Ethel Waters*
Cairo (1942). *Ethel Waters*
Caldonia (Soundie) (1945). *Louis Jordan*
Caldonia (Filmshort) (1945). *Louis Jordan*
Can This Be Dixie? (1936). *Hattie McDaniel*
Carefree (1938). *Hattie McDaniel*
Carib Gold (1955). *Ethel Waters*
Carry It On (1970) (Joan). *Peter Chatman*
Catch My Soul (1973). *Richard Havens*
Catcher, The (1972). *William Perryman*
Chases of Pimple Street (1934). *Hattie McDaniel*
Chicago Blues (1970): *Willie Dixon; George Guy; Joseph Hutto; Floyd Jones; Johnie Lewis; McKinley Morganfield; Amos Wells*
China Seas (1935). *Hattie McDaniel*
Choo Choo Swing (1943). *James Rushing*
Chris Barber Bandstand (1962). *Ottilie Patterson*
Chris Barber's Jazz Band (1956). *Ottilie Patterson*
Cincinnati Kid (1965). *Ray Charles*
Cinderfella (1960). *Joe Williams*
Cinerama Holiday (1955). *Odetta Gordon*
Cisco Pike (1971). *Sonny Terry*
Citizen South—Citizen North (1962). *John Estes*
Clay Pigeon (1971) (Trip to Kill). *Taj Mahal*
Cocksuckers Blues (1976). *Booker White*
Coleman Hawkins Quartet (1961). *McHouston Baker*
Columbia, The (1948). *Woodrow Guthrie*
Conversations with Shakey Jake (1972). *James Harris*
Cooley High (1976). *Luther Allison*
Cootie Williams and His Orchestra (1944). *Eddie Vinson*
Cosmic Ray (1962). *Ray Charles*
Count Basie and His Orchestra (1951). *Helen Humes*
Crazy House (1943) (Funzapoppin'). *James Rushing*
Crime Nobody Saw, The (1937). *Hattie McDaniel*
Crimson Canary, The (1945). *Joshua White*
Crowfoot (early 70s). *Clarence Miller*
Cult of the Damned, The (1969) (Angel Angel Down We Go). *Louis Rawls*

Dedans le Sud Dela Louisiane (see: Within Southern Louisiana)
Delinquents, The (1957). *Julia Lee*
Delta Blues Singer: James "Sonny Ford" Thomas (1970) (Sonny Ford: Delta Artist). *James Thomas*
Dick Gibson's Jazz Party (1976). *Carrie Smith*
Disc Jockey Jamboree (see: Jamboree)
Disneyland After Dark (see TV Show: Wonderful World of Color)
Do Re Mi (see: The Girl Can't Help It)
$ (Dollars) (1971) (The Heist—UK title). *Richard Penniman*
Don't Cry and Say No (1944). *Louis Jordan*
Don't Knock the Rock (1957). *Richard Penniman*
Don't Look Back (1967). *John Mayall*
Don't Tell the Wife (1937). *Hattie McDaniel*

Double Trouble (1962) (Swinging Along—UK title). *Ray Charles*
Down Down Down (1942). *Louis Jordan*
Dreams That Money Can Buy (1948). *Joshua White*
Dry Wood and Hot Pepper (1973). *Clifton Chenier*
Duke Ellington at the White House (1969). *Joe Williams*
Dynamite Chicken (1971): *James Hendrix; Luther Johnson Jr.; McKinley Morganfield*

East of Suez (1924). *Jesse Fuller*
Easy Rider (1969). *James Hendrix*
Ee Baba Leba (1947). *Helen Humes*
Emperor Jones (1933): *Leola Grant; Wesley Wilson*
En Remontant le Mississippi (see: Out of the Blacks into the Blues)
End of the World (1929). *Jesse Fuller*
Ethnic Folk Songs of the Southland (1957). *John Sellers*
Everybody's Baby (1939). *Hattie McDaniel*
Evil Doing (see: The Beginning)
Experience (1969). *James Hendrix*

Face in the Crowd, A (1957). *Walter McGhee*
Family Honeymoon (1948). *Hattie McDaniel*
Fate's Fathead (1934). *Hattie McDaniel*
Festival (1967): *Michael Bloomfield; Chester Burnett; Paul Butterfield; Odetta Gordon; Eddie House; John Hurt; John Koerner; Fred McDowell; Walter McGhee; Sonny Terry; Robert Wilkins*
Fighting for Our Lives (1974). *Taj Mahal*
Film-Vodvil No. 2 (1943). *Eddie Vinson*
First Baby, The (1936). *Hattie McDaniel*
Five Guys Named Moe (1942). *Louis Jordan*
Flame, The (1947). *Hattie McDaniel*
Follow the Boys (1944). *Louis Jordan*
For the Love of Ivy (1968). *Riley King*
Forever Young, Forever Free (see: The Lolly Pop)
45 Fathers (1937). *Hattie McDaniel*
47th Street Jazz (1942). *Roy Milton*
Four-Star Boarder, The (1935). *Hattie McDaniel*
Fred McDowell (1969). *Fred McDowell*
Fritz the Cat (1971): *Riley King; Ellas McDaniel*
Funzapoppin' (see: Crazy House)
Fuzzy Wuzzy (1942). *Louis Jordan*

G.I. Jive (1943). *Louis Jordan*
Gather No Moss (see: The T.A.M.I. Show)
Gentle Julia (1936). *Hattie McDaniel*
George Washington Slept Here (1942). *Hattie McDaniel*
Gettin' Back (1974): *Clifton Chenier; John Lee Hooker*
Gift of Gab, The (1934). *Ethel Waters*
Girl Can't Help It, The (1956) (Do Re Mi): *Antoine Domino; Richard Penniman*
Give My Poor Heart Ease: Mississippi Delta Bluesmen (1975): *Riley King; James Thomas; Wade Walton*
Go Johnny Go (1959). *Charles Berry*
Golden West (1932). *Hattie McDaniel*
Gone with the Wind (1939). *Hattie McDaniel*
Grass Roots Series #1—Old Time Music (1974). *Elizabeth Cotten*
Greased Lightning (1977). *Richard Havens*
Great Lie, The (1941). *Hattie McDaniel*
Great White Hope, The (1970). *Jesse Fuller*

Hallelujah! (1929): *Gus Cannon; Jim Jackson; Victoria Spivey*
Harlem Jazz Festival (1955): *Helen Humes; Amos Milburn; Dinah Washington*
Harlem Rock 'n' Roll (see: Rock 'n' Roll Revue)
Harriet Tubman and the Underground Railroad (see TV Show: Great Adventures)
Heart Is a Rebel, The (1956). *Ethel Waters*
Hearts Divided (1936). *Hattie McDaniel*
Hearts in Dixie (1929). *Jesse Fuller*
Heavy Traffic (1973). *Charles Berry*
Heist, The (see $ [Dollars])
Hello Bill (c1927). *Sara Martin*
Het Compromis (1968). *Huddie Ledbetter*
Hey Lawdy Mama (c1942). *Roy Milton*
Hey Tojo Count Yo' Men (c1943). *Louis Jordan*
Hi Beautiful (1944). *Hattie McDaniel*
High Tension (1936). *Hattie McDaniel*
Highway Girl (see: Return to Macon County)
Hillbilly Music (1962). *James Campbell*
Hit Parade of 1943 (1943). *Wynonie Harris*
Hole in the Head (1959). *Joanne Horton*
Holiday (1957). *Ottilie Patterson*
Honey Chile (c1943). *Louis Jordan*
Hospital, The (1971). *Beulah Bryant*
Hot 'n' Bothered (1934). *Ethel Waters*
Hot Nasty (1975). *Michael Bloomfield*
Hypnotized (1932). *Hattie McDaniel*

I Cried for You (c1950). *Helen Humes*
If I Could Be with You (c1950). *Helen Humes*
If You Can't Smile and Say Yes (c1943). *Louis Jordan*
If You Got the Feelin' (1973). *William Dupree*
I'm No Angel (1933). *Hattie McDaniel*
I'm Still Alive (1940). *Edith Wilson*
Imitation of Life (1934). *Hattie McDaniel*
In the Heat of the Night (1967). *Ray Charles*
In This Our Life (1942). *Hattie McDaniel*
It's a Mad Mad Mad Mad World (1963). *Clarence Miller*
It's Trad, Dad (1962). *Ottilie Patterson*

Jackson Jive, The (1948). *Bill Webb*
Jailhouse Blues (1929). *Mamie Smith*
Jamboree (1957) (Disc Jockey Jamboree—UK Title). *Antoine Domino; Joe Williams*
Janie (1944). *Hattie McDaniel*
Janie Gets Married (1946). *Hattie McDaniel*
Janis (1974). *Janis Joplin*
Jazz Odyssey (see: L'Aventure du Jazz)
Jazz on a Summer's Day (1960): *Charles Berry; Beulah Bryant; Mabel Smith; Dinah Washington*

Jazz—U.S.A. (series) (1960): *James Cage; Ray Charles; John Lee Hooker; McKinley Morganfield; Otis Spann; Willie Thomas*
Jessie "Lone Cat" Fuller (1968). *Jesse Fuller*
Jimi Hendrix (1973): *James Hendrix; Richard Penniman*
Jimi Plays Berkeley (1970): *James Hendrix; Richard Penniman*
Jivin' in Bebop (1947). *Helen Humes*
Joan (see: Carry It On)
Johnny Come Lately (1943). *Hattie McDaniel*
Johnny Shines: Black and Blues (1973). *John Shines*
Jordan Jive (1944). *Louis Jordan*
Judge Priest (1934). *Hattie McDaniel*
Jumpin' at the Jubilee (1944). *Louis Jordan*

Kansas City Jazz Story, The (see: Last of the Blue Devils)
Keep On Rockin' (see: Sweet Toronto)
King Creole (1958). *Blanche Thomas*

Larry Johnson (1970). *John Paul Hammond; Larry Johnson*
Last of the Blue Devils, The (1974) (The Kansas City Jazz Story). *Joseph Turner*
Last Time I Saw Paris, The (1954). *Odetta Gordon*
Last Waltz, The (1978): *Michael Bloomfield; Paul Butterfield; McKinley Morganfield*
L'Aventure du Jazz (1972) (Jazz Odyssey—UK title): *Peter Chatman; John Lee Hooker; Aaron Walker*
Leadbelly (1976): *J. C. Burris; Hi Tide Harris; (Huddie Ledbetter); Walter McGhee; Sonny Terry*
Learning Tree, The (1969). *James Rushing*
Legend of Bo Diddley, The (1966). *Ellas McDaniel*
Leo the Last (c1968). *Ram Holder*
Let the Church Say Amen (1973). *Riley King*
Let the Good Times Roll (1973): *Charles Berry; Antoine Domino; Ellas McDaniel; Richard Penniman*
Libeled Lady (1936). *Hattie McDaniel*
Light out of Darkness (see: Ballad in Blue)
Lightnin' Sam Hopkins (see: A Program of Songs by Lightnin' Sam Hopkins)
Little Big Man (1970). *John Hammond*
Little Colonel, The (1935). *Hattie McDaniel*
Little Men (1934). *Hattie McDaniel*
Lolly Pop, The (c1975) (Forever Young, Forever Free). *Beulah Bryant*
Look Out Sister (1948). *Louis Jordan*
Lost in the Stratosphere (1934). *Hattie McDaniel*
Louis Jordan Medley No. 1 (c1944). *Louis Jordan*
Louis Jordan Medley No. 2 (c1944). *Louis Jordan*
Low Light and Blue Smoke (1956). *William Broonzy*

Mad Miss Manton, The (1938). *Hattie McDaniel*
Male Animal, The (1942). *Hattie McDaniel*
Mandingo (1975): *Hi Tide Harris; McKinley Morganfield*
March of Time Newsreel (1935). *Huddie Ledbetter*
Margie (1946). *Hattie McDaniel*
Maryland (1940). *Hattie McDaniel*
Medicine Ball Caravan (1971) (We Have Come for Your Daughters—UK Title). *Riley King*
Meet Miss Bobby Socks (Sox) (1944). *Louis Jordan*
Member of the Wedding, The (1953). *Ethel Waters*
Memphis Slim (1960). *Peter Chatman*
Merry-Go-Round of 1938 (1937). *Hattie McDaniel*
Mickey (1948). *Hattie McDaniel*
Mississippi Delta Blues (1974). *James Thomas; Wade Walton*
Mister Brown (1972). *John Lee Hooker*
Mister Rock and Roll (1957): *Charles Berry; Jalacy Hawkins; Richard Penniman*
Momma Don't Allow (1955). *Ottilie Patterson*
Monkey's Uncle (1977). *Beulah Bryant*
Monterey Jazz (1968): *Richard Havens; Riley King; Aaron Walker*
Monterey Jazz (1973): *Margie Evans; Don Harris; Esther Phillips; James Rushing; Joseph Turner; Eddie Vinson; Joe Williams*
Monterey Pop (1968): *James Hendrix; Janis Joplin*
Moonshine War, The (1969). *Joe Williams*
Murder on Lenox Ave (1941). *Mamie Smith*
Music Is Magic (1935). *Hattie McDaniel*
My Blue Heaven (1950). *Helen Humes*
Mystery in Swing (1940). *Mamie Smith*

Negro In Entertainment, The (1968). *Ethel Waters*
Never Say Goodbye (1946). *Hattie McDaniel*
Newport Jazz Festival 1962 (1962): *James Rushing; Joe Williams*
Next Time We Love (1936). *Hattie McDaniel*
Nothing Sacred (1937). *Hattie McDaniel*

Okay Toots! (1935). *Hattie McDaniel*
Old Man Mose (1942). *Louis Jordan*
On with the Show (1929). *Ethel Waters*
Operator Thirteen (1934). *Hattie McDaniel*
Out of the Blacks into the Blues (1972) (En Remontant le Mississippi) (Along the Old Man River—Part 1) (A Way to Escape the Ghetto—Part 2): *Arthur Crudup (2); Willie Dixon (2); George Guy (2); Riley King (2); Walter Lewis (1); Mance Lipscomb (2); Walter McGhee (1) (2); Roosevelt Sykes (1); Sonny Terry (1) (2); Amos Wells (2); Booker White (1); Robert Pete Williams (1)*
Outsider, The (1962). *Monette Moore*
Outskirts of Town, The (1942). *Louis Jordan*
Over the Goal (1937). *Hattie McDaniel*

Panic in the Streets (1950). *Helen Humes*
Paradise in Harlem (1939). *Mamie Smith*
Part II Sounder (1976). *Taj Mahal*
Pinky (1949). *Ethel Waters*
Playing the Thing (1972): *James Cotton; Sonny Terry*
Postal Inspector (1936). *Hattie McDaniel*
Program of Songs by Lightnin' Sam Hopkins, A (1971) (Lightnin' Sam Hopkins). *Sam Hopkins*

Racing Lady (1937). *Hattie McDaniel*
Radio Parade of 1935 (1934). *Alberta Hunter*
Rainbow Bridge (1970). *James Hendrix*
Ramblin' (1970): *Jack Elliott; Odetta Gordon*
Ration Blues (1944). *Louis Jordan*
Reet, Petite and Gone (1947). *Louis Jordan*
Return to Macon County (1975) (Highway Girl). *Antoine Domino*
Reunion (1936). *Hattie McDaniel*
Reverend Gary Davis (1967). *Gary Davis*
Rhythm and Blues Revue (1955): *Amos Milburn; Joseph Turner*
Ride On Ride On (1944). *Roy Milton*
Riot (1968). *Louis Rawls*
Riverboat 1988 (1976). *J. C. Burris*
Rock 'n' Roll Revue (1955) (Harlem Rock 'n' Roll): *Joseph Turner; Dinah Washington*
Rock Rock Rock (1956). *Charles Berry*
Roosevelt Story, The (1947). *Walter McGhee*
Roosevelt Sykes (1971). *Roosevelt Sykes*
Roosevelt Sykes "The Honeydripper" (1961). *Roosevelt Sykes*
Roots of American Music: Country & Urban Music (1971) (Parts 1/2/3): *Jessie Fuller (1) (2); John Lee Hooker (1); Eddie House (1); Walter Lewis (1); Mance Lipscomb (1); Fred McDowell (3); Walter McGhee (2); John Shines (2); Sonny Terry (2); Robert Williams (1)*
Rufus Jones for President (1933). *Ethel Waters*

St. Louis Blues (1929). *Bessie Smith*
Sam Lightnin' Hopkins (see TV Show: Artists in America)
Sanctuary (1960). *Odetta Gordon*
Saratoga (1937). *Hattie McDaniel*
Save the Children (1973). *Arvella Gray*
Scorpio Rising (1963). *Ray Charles*
Scott Joplin (1976). *Taj Mahal*
Sergeant, The (1968). *Peter Chatman*
Seven Minutes, The (1971). *Riley King*
Shake Rattle and Rock (1956): *Antoine Domino; Joseph Turner*
She's Got It (c1957). *Richard Penniman*
Shining Hour, The (1938). *Hattie McDaniel*
Shopworn Angel, The (1938). *Hattie McDaniel*
Shoutin' the Blues (1974). *Sonny Terry*
Show Boat (1936). *Hattie McDaniel*
Since You Went Away (1944). *Hattie McDaniel*
Sincerely the Blues (1975): *Carey Bell; James Dawkins; Benjamin Jackson; Walter McGhee; Sonny Terry*
Sing Sing Thanksgiving (1974). *Riley King*
Singing Brakeman, The (1929). *James Rodgers*
Singing Kid, The (1936). *Hattie McDaniel*
Smash Your Baggage (1933). *Henry Williams*
Son House (1969). *Eddie House*
Song of the South (1946). *Hattie McDaniel*
Sonny Boy Williamson (c1963). *Sonny Boy Williamson (Alex Miller)*
Sonny Ford: Delta Artist (see: Delta Blues Singer: James "Sonny Ford" Thomas)
Sound and the Fury, The (1959). *Ethel Waters*
Sound of Jazz, The (see TV show: Seven Lively Arts)
Sounder (1972): *Sam Hopkins; Taj Mahal*
Sounds of the Seventies (1971). *Taj Mahal*
Southern Blues (1939). *Ethel Waters*
Spanish Monastery, The (late 50s). *Joanne Horton*
Spooky Loot (c1956). *Alexander Lightfoot*
Stage Door Canteen (1943). *Ethel Waters*
Star for a Night (1936). *Hattie McDaniel*
Star Is Born, A (1954). *Monette Moore*
Stardust Ring, The (c1933). *Elizabeth Miles*
Steelyard Blues (1973): *Michael Bloomfield; Paul Butterfield*
Stormy Weather (1943). *Ada Brown*
Story of Temple Drake, The (1933). *Hattie McDaniel*
Street Music (1974). *McKinley Morganfield*
Subterraneans, The (1960): *James Cotton; McKinley Morganfield; James Rushing; Otis Spann*
Sunday Sinners (1941). *Mamie Smith*
Sun's Gonna Shine, The (1967). *Sam Hopkins*
Supershow (1970). *George Guy*
Sweet Toronto (1970) (Keep On Rockin'—short version): *Charles Berry; James Hendrix; Janis Joplin; Ellas McDaniel; Richard Penniman*
Swing Parade of 1946 (1946). *Louis Jordan*
Swingin' the Dream (1939): *William Broonzy; Louis Jordan*
Swinging Along (see: Double Trouble)

T.A.M.I. Show, The (1964) (Gather No Moss—UK title) (Teenage Command Performance—UK title). *Charles Berry*
Take a Girl Like You (1970). *Ram Holder*
Take Me Back Baby (1941). *James Rushing*
Taking of Pelham One-Two-Three, The (1974). *Beulah Bryant*
Tales of Manhattan (1942). *Ethel Waters*
Tall Tales (1941). *Joshua White*
Tan and Terrific (1947). *Helen Humes*
Teenage Command Performance (see: T.A.M.I. Show)
Thank Your Lucky Stars (1943). *Hattie McDaniel*
They Died with Their Boots On (1941). *Hattie McDaniel*
Thief of Bagdad, The (1924). *Jesse Fuller*
Thinking Out Loud (1972): *Scott Dunbar; John Estes; Walter Lewis; Bill Williams; Robert Williams*
This Train (1973). *William Broonzy*
Three Is a Family (1944). *Hattie McDaniel*
Three Songs by Leadbelly (1945). *Huddie Ledbetter*
Tick Tack Toe (c1933). *Elizabeth Miles*
Tillie (1945). *Louis Jordan*
To Have and Have Not (1944). *Edith Wilson*
To Hear Your Banjo Play (1947): *Woodrow Guthrie; Walter McGhee; Sonny Terry; Joshua White*
Top Man (1943). *James Rushing*
Traveling Saleslady (1935). *Hattie McDaniel*
Trip, The (1967). *Michael Bloomfield*
Trip to Kill (see: Clay Pigeon)
True Confession (1937). *Hattie McDaniel*

Two Gentlemen Sharing (c1968). *Ram Holder*

Valiant Is the Word for Carrie (1936). *Hattie McDaniel*
Vanishing Point (1971). *Willie Thornton*
Velvet Vampire (1971). *John Shines*
Visage des P.T.T. (1964). *Peter Chatman*
Voice That Thrilled The World, The (1943). *Ethel Waters*

W. W. & the Dixie Dancekings (1975). *Walter Lewis*
Walking Hills, The (1949). *Joshua White*
Warnung vor Einer Heiligen Nutte (1970). *Ray Charles*
Washington Masquerade (1932). *Hattie McDaniel*
Wattstax (1973): *Milton Campbell; Albert King; Rufus Thomas; Aaron Willis*
Way to Escape the Ghetto, A (see: Out of the Blacks into the Blues)
We Have Come for Your Daughters (see: Medicine Ball Caravan)
Well Spent Life, A (1971). *Mance Lipscomb*
Where Has Poor Mickey Gone? (1964). *Ottilie Patterson*
Whoopin' the Blues (1969). *Sonny Terry*
Wild Catter, The (1937). *Hattie McDaniel*
Within Southern Louisiana (1974) (Dedans le Sud de la Louisiane). *Clifton Chenier*
Wolf (1971): *Chester Burnett; Albert Luandrew; Hubert Sumlin.*
Wolfgang Van Tripps (1975). *Beulah Bryant*
Woodstock (1970): *Richard Havens; James Hendrix*

Yes Sir Mr. Bones (1951). *Monette Moore*
You Are What You Eat (1968). *Paul Butterfield*
Your Three Minutes Are Up (1972). *Carol Leigh*
You're in The Army Now (1941). *Hattie McDaniel*

Zenobia (1939). *Hattie McDaniel*

Radio Index

This is an index of titled commercial and public radio programs in which singers listed in this book participated. Participation may be a singing or non-singing appearance as an entertainer, actor, bandsman, host, or master of ceremonies or in other capacities. Programs are of an indeterminate length.

While many programs were one-time shows, others were continuous or episodic over a period of time. Consequently, the year date of a singer's participation is shown in parentheses after the name, when known. It should be noted that this date may cover more than one participation within the year.

For purposes of this book, American network shows (NBC-Red and Blue [1922–43] and NBC-Red and ABC-Blue [from 1943]) are considered national unless otherwise indicated in entry. Local programming is generally limited to a single outlet whereas syndicated and public radio shows are randomly spotted across the nation. While the bio entry lists a single station for local shows, this does not preclude the fact that the program may have appeared on other stations and at other times. Radio transcriptions (Armed Forces Radio Service/Office of War Information and others) are listed as syndicated radio.

For further details regarding the kind of participation, network and syndication specifics, station identification, location and other program facts, refer to bio entry.

All titles beginning with the articles "A," "An" and "The" are indexed by the second word. My appreciation to Joseph G. Palladino for his work on this index.

Adventures in Music. *Woodrow Guthrie (1940)*

African Vibrations. *Esther Phillips (1975)*

Alberta Hunter Show. *Alberta Hunter (1938–40)*

Alma John. *Beulah Bryant (1969)*

Alpha & Omega Opera Company Deluxe Inc. *Eva Taylor (1930)*

American Music Festivals. *Woodrow Guthrie (1940)*

American Oil Revue (Amoco Show). *Ethel Waters (1933–4)*

Amoco Show (see: American Oil Revue)

Amos 'n' Andy Show: *Hattie McDaniel (1945–7); Ethel Waters (1944); Edith Wilson (early 40s)*

Anthony Navarro's Blues Show. *James Witherspoon (1976)*

Arlene Francis Show. *Alberta Hunter (1977)*

Art Ford's New Sunday Swing Session. *Oran Page (1945)*

Art Hodes Show. *Charles Davenport (c1942)*

Art Laboe's Show. *Joseph Turner (1974)*

Arthur Godfrey's Talent Scouts. *Beulah Bryant (c1946)*

Arthur Godfrey Time. *Joe Williams (1966)*

Assignment: *John Estes (1964); Hammie Nixon (1964); James Rachell (1964)*

Atomic Mama's Wang Dang Doodle Blues Show: *Robert Bland (c1972); Lonnie Brooks (c1973); Eddie Clearwater (c1973); James Dawkins (1973); Joseph Hutto (c1973); Albert Luandrew (c1973); Andrew McMahon (c1973); McKinley Morganfield (1975); James Pryor (1972–3); Mathis Reed (c1973); Fention Robinson (c1973); Houston Stackhouse (c1973); Phillip Walker (1973–4); John A. Williamson (1972–3)*

Atwater Kent Hour. *Eva Taylor (1929)*

Aunt Jemima Home Folks Show. *Edith Wilson (mid-50s)*

Back Where I Come From: *Woodrow Guthrie (1940); Huddie Ledbetter (1940); Joshua White (1940)*

Ballads and Blues. *Irene Scruggs (1953)*

Barbara's Blues. *Barbara Dane (1960–1); Clarence Miller (1961)*

Below the Mason–Dixon Line. *Eva Taylor (1928)*

Ben Bernie, The Old Maestro. *Ethel Waters (1936)*

Beulah. *Hattie McDaniel (1947-50)*
Big Bill Hill Show: *William Broonzy (1952); Chester Burnett (60s); John Davis (1952); Elmore James (late 50s/early 60s); Luther Johnson Jr. (1971); William Lucas (early 50s); Samuel Maghett (mid 60s); McKinley Morganfield (1960); Otis Rush (1956-8); Mack Simmons (1972); Eddie Taylor (1963); Koko Taylor (1971); Theodore Taylor (from mid-60s); Joseph Young (1971)*
Billie Burke Show. *Hattie McDaniel (c1945)*
Bing Crosby Kraft Music Hall (see: Kraft Music Hall)
Blue Monday (see also: Johnny Otis Show). *Margie Evans (1971); Frank Patt (1970)*
Blue Streaks Orchestra Show. *Eva Taylor (1930-1)*
Blueberry Hill. *Hattie McDaniel (1943)*
Blues am Dienstag (Blues on Tuesday): *William Perryman (1977); Tommy Tucker (1977)*
Blues by the Bay: *Dave Alexander (1974); Joe Blue (1975); Charles Brown (1976); J. C. Burris (1975-7); James Dawkins (1977); Floyd Dixon (1974); K. C. Douglas (1973); Hi Tide Harris (1975); Matthew Jacobs (1974/77); Robert Lowery (1976); Jimmy McCracklin (1976); John Mars (1975); Mathis Reed (1976); Louis Robinson (1976); Otis Rush (1977); Luther Tucker (1976); Cleve White (1974-5)*
Blues for Monday Show. *Irene Scruggs (1953)*
Blues International Show. *Albert Luandrew (c1968)*
Blues Piano Orgy. *Roy Byrd (1975); Roosevelt Sykes (1975)*
Bob Fass Show: *Larry Johnson (1970); John Shines (1975)*
Bob Maxwell Show. *Victoria Spivey (1962)*
Bon-Ton Show. *Clarence Garlow (1955-61)*
Breakfast Club. *Edith Wilson (50s?)*
Bright Star Flour Show: *Robert Nighthawk (1943-7); Joe Perkins (c1943-5); Joe Wilkins (1946-7)*
Broadway Furniture Store: *James Cotton (c1950); Willie Love (1949-50); Willie Nix (1949-50); Joe Pugh (1949); Joe Wilkins (c1950)*

Camel Caravan. *Joseph Turner (1938)*
Careless Love. *Katherine Henderson (1931); Eva Taylor (1930-2)*
Carnegie Hall Show. *Ethel Waters (1938)*
Cavalcade of America. *Woodrow Guthrie (1940)*
Chamber Music Society of Lower Basin Street, The: *Huddie Ledbetter (1949); Joseph Turner (1940)*
Chesterfield Supper Club. *Alden Bunn (c1950)*
Clarence Williams & His Entertaining Four. *Eva Taylor (1931)*
Clarence Williams & Pals. *Eva Taylor (1929)*
Clarence Williams Quartet. *Eva Taylor (1931)*
Clarence Williams Trio. *Eva Taylor (1930-1)*
Clifton Utley Show. *Edith Wilson (1948)*
Club Valspar Show. *Eva Taylor (1932)*
Coffee House Show. *Bill Williams (1970)*
Command Performance: *Louis Jordan (1944); James Rushing (1943); Ethel Waters (c1944)*

Davis Avenue Blues Association. *Ike Darby (from 1963)*
Dimension. *Joshua White (1968)*
Dixie Nightingales. *Eva Taylor (1932)*
Doc Ross Show. *Charles Ross (1953-4)*
Donahue!. *Riley King (1977)*
Downbeat Derby. *Louis Jordan (1944)*
Drowsy Rhythm. *Eva Taylor (1936)*

Eddie Cantor Show (see: Time to Smile)
Eddie Condon's Jazz Concert. *Oran Page (1944)*
Elder Moten Hour: *Robert Johnson (1937); John Shines (1937)*
Esquire Swing Show. *Oran Page (1938-9)*
Eva Taylor, Crooner. *Eva Taylor (1932-3)*
Eveready Hour, The. *Eva Taylor (1929)*

Famous Coachman Show. *John Jenkins (early 70s)*
Fenner's Warehouse Show. *Arthur Jackson (1936-51)*
Fleischmann Hour (Rudy Vallee Show): *Ethel Waters (1933); Edith Wilson (c1930)*
Florence Mills Memorial Hour. *Eva Taylor (1928)*
Folk Songs of America: *Woodrow Guthrie (1940); Huddie Ledbetter (1940)*
Folks from Dixie: *Katherine Henderson (1933); Eva Taylor (1933)*
Folksay: *Sam Hopkins (1959); L. C. Williams (1959)*
Folksong Festival. *Woodrow Guthrie (late 50s)*

Gene Norman Show. *Floyd Dixon (mid-50s)*
General Motors Show. *Eva Taylor (1931)*
Goldbergs, The (see: The Rise of the Goldbergs).
Good Old Days. *Barbara Dane (c1949)*
Grandmothers Trunk Show. *Eva Taylor (1934)*
Great Gildersleeve, The. *Edith Wilson (late 40s)*

Hadacol Show: *Elmore James (1949); Riley King (1949); Willie Love (1949); Joe Pugh (1949); Sonny Boy Williamson (Alex Miller) (1949)*
Hall of Fame Show. *Ethel Waters (1934)*
Harlem. *Eva Taylor (1933)*
Harlem Fantasy: *Eva Taylor (1932); Joshua White (1932)*
Harts Bread: *James Cotton (c1952); Willie Nix (c1952)*
Heebie Jeebies. *Rufus Thomas (50/60s?)*
Hobby Lobby Show. *Ida Cox (1939)*
Honky Tonk Show: *James Booker (1976); Johnny Watson (1976)*
Hoot 'n' Holler. *Rufus Thomas (50/60s?)*
Hot Sauce Jazz. *Margie Evans (c1970)*

In Concert: *Pleasant Joseph (1974); Charles Ross (1974); John Wrencher (1974)*

Jack Brickhouse/Eddie Hubbard Show. *Barbara Dane (1962)*
Jack O'Brien Show. *Alberta Hunter (1978)*
Jazz Alive: *Helen Humes (1977); Alberta Hunter (1977)*

Jazz Alternatives. *Otis Rush (1978)*
Jazz Profiles. *Helen Humes (1978)*
Jazz Radio—Canada. *Clarence Miller (1977)*
Jimmy Mitchell Show. *Jeanne Carroll (1976)*
Jimmy Witherspoon Show: *Connie Crayton (1975); James Witherspoon (early 70s)*
Johnny Otis Show (see also: Blue Monday Show). *James Witherspoon (1958)*
Jubilee U.S.A.: *Walter Brown (c1943); Benjamin Jackson (1944); Louis Jordan (1944–5); James Rushing (1943)*

Katz Clothing Store Show: *Marion Walter Jacobs (1949); McKinley Morganfield (1949); James Rogers (1949); Charles Ross (1949)*
King Biscuit Time: *William Borum (late 40s); James Cotton (late 40s); Arthur Crudup (mid-40s); James Curtis (1942 into 50s); Frank Frost (early 60s); Earl Hooker (1949 to mid-50s); Marion Walter Jacobs (c1944); Elmore James (1947); John Jenkins (c1941); Robert Lockwood (1941–3); Willie Love (1942); Robert Nighthawk (1965); Joe Perkins (1943–8); Charles Ross (1950); Houston Stackhouse (1946–7); Theodore Taylor (c1942); John Walker (c1950); Robert Warren (c1941); Joe Wilkins (from 1945); Sonny Boy Williamson (Alex Miller) (1941–7/1965)*
Kraft Music Hall: *Eva Taylor (1933); Ethel Waters (1941)*

Ladies Be Seated. *Edith Wilson (1950)*
Lasses of Jefferson, Texas. *Sonny Boy Williamson (1952)*
Let's Chat. *Joanne Horton (1967–8)*
Light and Mellow. *Barbara Dane (1949)*
Lonnie Johnson, Recording Guitarist. *Alonzo Johnson (1929–30)*
Lowland Singers/Trio, The. *Eva Taylor (1933)*

Mack McCormick and Friends: *Clarence Brown (1961); Peppermint Harris (1961); Joel Hopkins (1960); Sam Hopkins (1960–61); Mance Lipscomb (1960–61); Alexander Moore (1961); Edwin Pickens (1960); Robert Shaw (1960); L. C. Williams (1960)*
Major Bowes Capitol Family Show. *Eva Taylor (1929)*
Major Bowes Original Amateur Hour: *Leroy Dallas (c1940); Frank Edwards (c1940)*
Man Who Went to War, The. *Joshua White (1944)*
Marindale Amateur Hour. *Beulah Bryant (1937)*
Marionettes Orchestra. *Eva Taylor (1931–2)*
Miss Rhapsody and the Three Sportsmen of Rhythm. *Viola Wells (1946–7)*
Monday Night Feature. *James Rodgers (1928)*
Morning Glories Show. *Eva Taylor (1929)*
Morning Glory Show. *Eva Taylor (1935)*
Mothers Best Flour Hour: *Marion Walter Jacobs (1945–6); Robert Lockwood (1943–4); Robert Nighthawk (1943–7); Joe Perkins (c1943–5); Houston Stackhouse (1946); Joe Wilkins (1946–7)*
Muscle-Tone Show. *Frankie Jaxon (1931–41)*
Music—U.S.A.: *Ray Charles (1958/72); Helen Humes (1973/5); Louis Jordan (1973); Riley King (1972/75); Elizabeth Miles (1957); James Rushing (c1955/c1957/66); Victoria Spivey (1961); Houston Stackhouse (1973); Joseph Turner (1955); Dinah Washington (1955); Joe Wilkins (1973); Joe Williams (1955/1957/1966/1973–4)*
Musical Program. *Eva Taylor (1922)*

Natch'l Blues. *John Shines (1974)*
National Negro Forum Hour. *Ada Brown (1932)*
Negro Achievement Hour: *Lucille Hegamin (1929); Alberta Hunter (1930)*
Negro Music in America. *Jean Kittrell (1968)*
New World a-Coming. *Joshua White (1944)*
Night in Harlem, A. *Monette Moore (1929)*

Optimistic Donut's. *Hattie McDaniel (1931)*

Pabst Blue Ribbon Show. *James Rushing (1942)*
Pepticon Boy Show: *Riley King (1949–50); Joe Hill Louis (1950); Willie Nix (1949–50); Joe Wilkins (c1950)*
Phil Schaap Show: *Clyde Bernhardt (1976); Viola Wells (1976)*
Philco Radio Time. *Hattie McDaniel (1949)*
Pipe Smoking Time. *Woodrow Guthrie (1940)*
Poppa Stoppa Show. *Elizabeth Miles (c1950)*
Prizefight Fix. *Edith Wilson (late 40s)*
Pursuit of Happiness. *Woodrow Guthrie (1940)*

Radio Caroline. *Michele Castell (1963–7)*
Radio Hall of Fame. *Louis Jordan (1944)*
Rise of the Goldbergs, The (The Goldbergs). *Eva Taylor (1929)*
Rudy Vallee Show (see also: Fleischmann Hour). *Hattie McDaniel (c1941)*
Rye Crisp Show. *Eva Taylor (1935)*

School of the Air. *Woodrow Guthrie (1940)*
Sepia Swing Club. *Rufus Thomas (50/60s?)*
Serenade in Blue. *Joe Williams (1972–7)*
Sheep & Goat Club: *Eva Taylor (1940); Viola Wells (1940)*
Show Boat. *Hattie McDaniel (1932–3)*
Sing Out. *Barbara Dane (1965)*
Sixty Minutes of Broadway Entertainment. *Eva Taylor (1930)*
Slow River. *Eva Taylor (1932–3)*
Soft Lights and Sweet Music. *Eva Taylor (1935)*
Some of the People: *John Lee Hooker (1965); Sam Hopkins (1966); Eddie House (1965); John Hurt (1965); Mance Lipscomb (1966); Robert Shaw (1966); Eddie Vinson (1966); Sonny Boy Williamson (Alex Miller) (1965); Harding Wilson (1965)*

RADIO INDEX

Something Inside of Me: *Alden Bunn (1975); Larry Johnson (1973); Eddie Kirkland (1976); Iverson Minter (1976); Charles Sayles (1975); Charles Walker (1973)*
Speaking of Blues. *Clarence Miller (1970)*
Standard School Broadcast. *Barbara Dane (1949)*
Steve Tracy Show. *Albert Washington (1975–6)*
Steve Werdenschlag Show. *Joshua White (1957)*

Talaho Syrup: *Elmore James (1947–8); Sonny Boy Williamson (Alex Miller) (1947–8)*
Ted Steele. *Alden Bunn (c1952)*
Tex and Jinx Show. *Ethel Waters (1949)*
This Is Jazz: *Leola Grant (1947); Bertha Hill (1947); Wesley Wilson (1947)*
Time to Smile (Eddie Cantor Show). *Hattie McDaniel (c1941)*
Tolerance thru Music. *Lemuel Johnson (1944)*
Traditional Music Collective Concert: *Robert Lowery (1976); Louis Robinson (1976)*

WNYC Jazz Festival: *Huddie Ledbetter (1948); Sonny Terry (1948)*
We the People: *Woodrow Guthrie (1940); James Yancey (1939)*
Welcome Travellers. *Beulah Bryant (early 50s)*
Willie Bryant Show. *Joseph Turner (1942)*
Woody and Lefty Lou Show. *Woodrow Guthrie (1937–8)*

Youth on Parade. *Eva Taylor (1939)*

Zeke Manners. *Alden Bunn (c1952)*

Television Index

This is an index of titled commercial and public television programs in which singers listed in this book participated. Participation may be a singing or non-singing appearance as an entertainer, actor, bandsman, host or as a member of a talk or game show as well as soundtrack recordings and other work. With one noted exception, untitled shows are not listed and may be found in the bio entries. Programs are from one minute ("Bicentennial Minute") to an indeterminate length.

While many TV programs were one-time shows, others were continuous or episodic over a period of time. Consequently, the year date of a singer's participation is shown in parentheses after the name. Generally, the indicated date represents the first commercial TV presentation of the show, although in the case of some live concerts it may be the actual time of the performance. Episodes are listed when known. It should be noted that a show date may cover more than one appearance within a calendar year for a continuous program. Repeat programs and clips or stills within a show are generally not listed when known.

For purposes of this book, principal American Network shows (ABC/CBS/NBC) are considered national unless otherwise indicated. Public Broadcast Service shows (PBS) are usually syndicated on the National Education Television Network. A local syndicated show station is noted in most cases although the show may have been aired locally elsewhere at other times.

For further details regarding the kind of participation, network and syndication specifics, station identification, location and other program facts, refer to the bio entry. A TV program originally released as a commercial film will be found in the Film Index.

All titles beginning with the articles "A," "An" and "The" are indexed by the second word. My appreciation to Joseph G. Palladino for his work on this index.

A La Carte: *Olive Brown (1964); Walter McGhee (1964); Sonny Terry (1964)*

A.M. America: *Esther Phillips (1975); Joe Williams (1975)*

A.M. San Francisco. *J. C. Burris (1975); Walter McGhee (1975); Sonny Terry (1975)*

Academy Awards Presentation. *Louis Rawls (1970)*

Adventures in Jazz: *Oran Page (1949); Joshua White (1949)*

Al Collins Show. *Carol Leigh (1963)*

Alan Burke Show. *Beulah Bryant (1967)*

Alan Lomax Folk Special. *Mable Hillery (1961)*

Alfred Hitchcock Presents (Ep: Captive Audience). *Barbara Dane (1962)*

All Star Jazz Show (see: Festival of Lively Arts for Young People)

All Star Swing Festival (see: Timex All Star Swing Festival)

All Together Now: *Lowell Fulson (1973); Riley King (1973); Jimmy McCracklin (1973); Joseph Turner (1973)*

America 2Night. *Louis Rawls (1978)*

American Bandstand: *Charles Berry (1958); Eddy Clearwater (c1959); Antoine Domino (1958); Albert King (1968); Jimmy McCracklin (c1957); Richard Penniman (1971–2); Frankie Sims (c1957); Rufus Thomas (c1965)*

American Bandstand 25th Anniversary. *Charles Berry (1977)*

American Bandstand 23rd Birthday. *Antoine Domino (1975)*

American Inventory. *Ethel Waters (1953)*

TELEVISION INDEX

American Music Awards: *Charles Berry (1978); Louis Rawls (1977–8)*
Americans All. *Blanche Thomas (1975)*
Amos 'n' Andy Show. *Monette Moore (1951–3)*
Anatomy of Pop: The Music Explosion (rel as film: American Music: From Folk to Jazz and Pop): *Scott Dunbar (1966); Billie Pierce (1966)*
Andy Williams Show. *Ray Charles (1967)*
Apollo. *Taj Mahal (1976)*
Armstrong Circle Theater. *Beulah Bryant (c1958)*
Art Ford's Greenwich Village Party. *Joshua White (1957)*
Art Ford's Jazz Party: *George Guesnon (1958); Clarence Miller (1958); Joshua White (1958)*
Art Linkletter Show (House Party): *Clarence Miller (1962); Carrie Smith (c1969)*
Arthur Crudup: Born in the Blues (rel as film: Arthur Crudup: Born in the Blues). *Arthur Crudup (1973)*
Arthur Godfrey and Friends. *Joshua White (1950)*
Arthur Godfrey Talent Scouts. *Alden Bunn (c1952)*
Artists in America (rel as film: Sam "Lightnin" Hopkins). *Sam Hopkins (1971)*
Arts Action. *Joanne Horton (1976–7)*
At the Top: *Taj Mahal (1976); Joe Williams (1976)*
Austin City Limits: *Clarence Brown (1977–8); Clifton Chenier (1976); Louis Rawls (1976)*
Autobiography of Miss Jane Pittman, The (rel as film: Autobiography of Miss Jane Pittman, The). *Odetta Gordon (1974)*

B. B. King Revisits Cook County Jail. *Riley King (1973)*
Barbara McNair Show: *Riley King (1969); Louis Rawls (1969)*
Barbra Streisand Show. *Ray Charles (1973)*
Beat, The: *Clarence Brown (1966); Freddie King (1966); Louis Rawls (1966); Koko Taylor (c1965)*
Beat of the Brass. *Billie Pierce (1968)*
Beatles Forever, The. *Ray Charles (1977)*
Beautiful Phyllis Diller Show. *Louis Rawls (1968)*
Beulah: *Hattie McDaniel (1951–2); Ethel Waters (1950–1)*
Bicentennial Minute. *Louis Rawls (1976)*
Big Band Bash: *Helen Humes (1978); Joe Williams (1978)*
Big Valley, The. *Louis Rawls (1969)*
Bill Cosby Show. *Ray Charles (1971)*
Black Conversations. *Odetta Gordon (1976)*
Black Omnibus. *Rufus Thomas (1973)*
Black Pride. *Beulah Bryant (c1975)*
Black White & Blue. *Willie Thornton (1967)*
Blackbook. *McKinley Morganfield (1969)*
Blues, The (see: Lyrics and Legends)
Blues & Gospel Train Show: *Pleasant Joseph (1964); Walter McGhee (1964); Otis Spann (1964); Sonny Terry (1964)*
Boarding House: *Taj Mahal (1973); Esther Phillips (1974)*
Bob Braun Show. *Carol Leigh (1971)*
Bob Hope Show. *Louis Rawls (1968)*
Bob Hope Special. *Ray Charles (1969)*
Boboquivari: *Jack Elliott (1971); Odetta Gordon (1971); Sam Hopkins (1971); Freddie King (1971)*
Bonnie Raitt & Paul Butterfield: *Paul Butterfield (1974); Bonnie Raitt (1974)*
Bourbon Street Beat. *Louis Rawls (1959)*
Break the $250,000 Bank. *Ethel Waters (c1958)*
Brooklyn College. *Richard Havens (1976)*
Bruce Morrow Show: *Jalacy Hawkins (1967); Joe Williams (1967)*

CBS News: *James Thomas (1973); Bill Williams (1971)*
CBS Television Playhouse. *Beulah Bryant (c1963)*
Callback. *Beulah Bryant (1969)*
Camera Three (Ep A: Really the Country Blues) (Ep B: One Hundred Years from Today). *George Guy (1968) (A); Eddie House (1968) (A); Alberta Hunter (1978) (B); John Sellers (1962)*
Captain & Tennille. *Louis Rawls (1977)*
Captain & Tennille in New Orleans. *Antoine Domino (1978)*
Captive Audience (see: Alfred Hitchcock Presents).
Carol Burnett. *Ray Charles (1972)*
Celebration: The American Spirit. *Ray Charles (1976)*
Charlie Smith and the Fritter Tree (see: Visions)
Checkmate. *Barbara Dane (1960)*
Cher. *Ray Charles (1975)*
Childer Hour, The. *Clarence Miller (1975)*
Chuck Barris Rah Rah Show, The: *Charles Berry (1978); Ray Charles (1978); Joe Williams (1978)*
City Limits (see: Austin City Limits).
Clay Cole R&B Show. *John Hammond (1965)*
Climax (Ep: The Dance). *Ethel Waters (1955)*
Close Up. *Ethel Waters (1954–7)*
Club 88 Show. *Rabbit Muse (c1950)*
Color Me Jazz. *Louis Rawls (1965)*
Comedy In America Report. *Ray Charles (1976)*
Contact. *Louis Rawls (1970)*
Cotton Club 75. *Ray Charles (1974)*
Cousin Brucie Show. *Richard Havens (1969)*
Crazy Blues (see: Devil's Music—A History of the Blues, The)
Crescendo (see: DuPont Show of the Month)
Cromie Circle Show. *McKinley Morganfield (1971)*

Dance, The (see: Climax).
Daniel Boone Show (Ep: Mama Cooper). *Ethel Waters (1970)*
Danny Kaye Show. *Joe Williams (1966)*
Dateline Boston. *McKinley Morganfield (1966)*
Dateline: Hollywood. *Louis Rawls (1967)*
Dave Garroway's Wide Wide World (see: Wide Wide World)
David Brinkley's Journal: *George Guesnon (1961); Billie Pierce (1961)*
David Frost Show. *Odetta Gordon (1970); Richard Havens (1969–70); Riley King (1970); McKinley Morganfield (1971); Louis Rawls (1972)*

Dean Martin Show. *Louis Rawls (1969–70)*
Della: *Ray Charles (1969); Odetta Gordon (1969); Louis Rawls (1969–70); Willie Thornton (1969); Joseph Turner (1970); Ethel Waters (1970); Joe Williams (1970)*
Devil's Music—A History of the Blues, The (Ep 1: Nothing but the Truth) (Ep 2: Crazy Blues) (Ep 3: Work and Mother Wit) (Ep 4: The Movements of Providence) (Ep 5: Sticking with the Blues): *William Arnold (1976) (5); Gus Cannon (1976) (3); Sam Chatmon (1976) (1,3); Thomas Dorsey (1976) (2,4); Laura Dukes (1976) (2); Eurreal Montgomery (1976) (1,2,3,4); Louis Myers (1976) (5); Fention Robinson (1976) (5); Victoria Spivey (1976) (2); Houston Stackhouse (1976) (3); Roosevelt Sykes (1976) (1,4); Henry Townsend (1976) (1,3); Booker White (1976) (1,3); Joe Wilkins (1976) (3); Joe Lee Williams (1976) (3,4); Edith Wilson (1976) (2)*
Dial M for Music: *James Cotton (1970); Riley King (1969); Joe Williams (1966–7)*
Dick Cavett Show: *Charles Berry (1970); Ray Charles (1972); James Hendrix (1969); John Lee Hooker (1969); Janis Joplin (1970); Riley King (1969/72); Willie Thornton (1971); Ethel Waters (1972)*
Dick Clark and a Cast of Thousands. *Louis Rawls (1978)*
Dick Clark Presents the Rock & Roll Years: *Charles Berry (1973); Riley King (1973); Ellas McDaniel (1973)*
Dick Clark's American Bandstand (see: American Bandstand)
Dick Clark's Good Old Days. *Ellas McDaniel (1977)*
Dick Clark's Live Wednesday: *Charles Berry (1978); Ellas McDaniel (1978)*
Dick Clark's Saturday Night Beechnut Show: *Charles Berry (c1959); Antoine Domino (1958)*
Dinah! *Charles Berry (1976); Ray Charles (1975/7); Taj Mahal (1976); Richard Penniman (1976); Esther Phillips (1976); Louis Rawls (1976–7); Ethel Waters (1976)*
Dinah Shore. *Ray Charles (1962)*
Dinner with the President. *Odetta Gordon (1963); Joshua White (1963)*
Disco '77. *Louis Rawls (1977)*
Discomania. *Rufus Thomas (1976)*
Disneyland After Dark (see: Wonderful World of Color)
Don Ho Show. *Clarence Miller (1962)*
Don Kirshner's Rock Concert: *Charles Berry (1975/7); Paul Butterfield (1978); David Edwards (1978); John Lee Hooker (1978); Eddie Kirkland (1978); McKinley Morganfield (1978); Esther Phillips (1976); Louis Rawls (1976–7); Johnny Winter (1974/8)*
Don Sherwood Show. *Jesse Fuller (early 50s)*
Donald O'Connor Show: *Louis Rawls (1968); Joe Williams (1968)*
Donny & Marie Show: *Charles Berry (1977); Ellas McDaniel (1976); Richard Penniman (1976)*
Dr. John. *Roy Byrd (1971)*
Dr. John's New Orleans Swamp. *Roy Byrd (1974)*
Du Pont Show of the Month (Ep: Crescendo): *Elizabeth Miles (1957); Dinah Washington (1957)*
Duke Ellington Special: *Ray Charles (1973); Joe Williams (1973)*
Earle Pudney Show. *Joanne Horton (1962–3)*
Easter Special. *Odetta Gordon (1965)*
Ebony Readers Music Poll Award Show. *Ray Charles (1975)*
Ed Sullivan Show (see also: Toast of the Town): *Ray Charles (c1962); Richard Havens (1969); Janis Joplin (1969); Riley King (1970); Louis Rawls (1966–8); Ethel Waters (1963); Joe Williams (1959)*
Ed Sullivan's Toast of the Town (see: Toast of the Town)
Engelbert Humperdinck Show: *Ray Charles (1970); Louis Rawls (1970)*
Evening Show. *J. C. Burris (1977)*
Faces in Jazz. *Alberta Hunter (1971–2)*
Fanfare. *Riley King (1971)*
Farewell to Fillmore East. *Albert King (1971)*
Favorite Playhouse (Ep: Speaking to Hannah). *Ethel Waters (1955)*
Feeling Good: *Riley King (1974); Joe Williams (1974)*
Festival of Lively Arts for Young People (Ep: All Star Jazz Show). *Joe Williams (1976)*
Festival Presents the Blues: *Olive Brown (1964); Willie Dixon (1966); Jesse Fuller (1966); Mable Hillery (1966); Albert Luandrew (1966); Walter McGhee (1966); McKinley Morganfield (1966); Sonny Terry (1966); Booker White (1966); Joe Lee Williams (1966)*
50 Years of Country Music. *Ray Charles (1978)*
First Anniversary of In Concert. *Johnny Winter (1974)*
Flip Wilson Show: *Ray Charles (1971); Riley King (1970–2); Taj Mahal (1973)*
Floor Show. *Oran Page (1949)*
Folk Music U.S.A. *David Van Ronk (1964)*
Folksville U.S.A. *Barbara Dane (1951)*
For Blacks Only: *Chester Burnett (c1968); McKinley Morganfield (c1968)*
Frankly Jazz. *Louis Rawls (1962)*
Fred Astaire Show. *Joe Williams (1960)*
Free Time: *Taj Mahal (1971); Victoria Spivey (1971)*
Friendly Invasion, The (see: Omnibus)
From The Bitter End: *Charles Berry (1968); Odetta Gordon (1967); Joshua White (c1967)*

Garry Moore Show. *Edith Wilson (50s?)*
General Electric Theater (Ep: Winner by Decision). *Ethel Waters (1955)*
George Carlin Monsanto Chemical Special. *Riley King (1973)*
George Hamilton IV Show. *Joe Williams (1959)*
Get Down. *Riley King (1976)*
Glen Campbell Goodtime Hour: *Ray Charles (1970); Richard Penniman (1971)*
Glorious Fourth. *Joe Lee Williams (1976)*
Go Down Moses (see: Great Adventures)
Going Thing, The. *Louis Rawls (1969)*
Good Day Show, The: *Clyde Bernhardt (1978); Viola Wells (1978)*
Good Mornin' Blues: *Gus Cannon (1978); Sam Chatmon (1978); David Edwards (1978); Walter Horton (1978); Riley King (1978); Walter Lewis (1978); John Shines*

(1978); Houston Stackhouse (1978); Booker White (1978); Joe Lee Williams (1978)
Goodnight Sweet Blues (see: Route 66)
Gospel TV Time. *Carrie Smith (1957)*
Grammy Awards. *Louis Rawls (1978)*
Great Adventures (Ep: Go Down Moses) (Ep rel as film: Harriet Tubman and the Underground Railroad). *Ethel Waters (1963)*
Great American Dream Machine, The. *Odetta Gordon (1972)*

Hanging of Aaron Gibbs, The (see: Have Gun Will Travel)
Harlem Cultural Festival. *Robert Bland (1967)*
Harry Belafonte Special. *Odetta Gordon (1962)*
Hart & Lorne Terrific Hour, The: *Walter McGhee (1970); Sonny Terry (1970)*
Have Gun Will Travel (Ep: The Hanging of Aaron Gibbs). *Odetta Gordon (1961)*
Hee Haw. *Ray Charles (1970)*
Helen Reddy Show. *Riley King (1973)*
Here Come the Stars. *Joe Williams (1968)*
History of Jazz, The. *Clarence Miller (1973)*
Hollywood A-Go-Go: *Charles Berry (1965); James Witherspoon (1965)*
Hollywood Palace: *Ray Charles (1966); Janis Joplin (1968); Louis Rawls (1968); Ethel Waters (1969)*
Hollywood Squares: *Ray Charles (1977); Louis Rawls (1970)*
Homewood Show: *Charles Brown (1970); Margie Evans (1970); Lowell Fulson (1970); Walter Lewis (1970); Esther Phillips (1970); Joseph Turner (1970); Eddie Vinson (1970); Aaron Walker (1970)*
Hootenanny. *Joshua White (1963–4)*
House Party (see: Art Linkletter Show)
Hugh Hefner Show (see: Playboy After Dark)
I Come for to Sing: *William Broonzy (early 50s); Rosetta Howard (late 40s); Major Merriweather (late 40s); Arbee Stidham (mid-50s); Joe Lee Williams (late 50s)*
I Hear the Blues: *Peter Chatman (1963); Willie Dixon (1963); Alonzo Johnson (1963); McKinley Morganfield (1963); Otis Spann (1963); Victoria Spivey (1963); Joe Lee Williams (1963); Sonny Boy Williamson (1963)*
In Concert (UK). *Rufus Thomas (1974)*
In Concert (US). *Riley King (1973)*
In Performance at Wolf Trap. *Bonnie Raitt (1976)*
Inaugural Evening at Ford's Theater. *Odetta Gordon (1968)*
International Hour. *McKinley Morganfield (1963)*
It's Happening Baby. *Ray Charles (1965)*

Jack Barry Show. *Louis Rawls (1963)*
Jack Benny Program. *Louis Rawls (1965)*
Jack Kane Show. *James Rushing (1959)*
Jackie Gleason Show. *Edith Wilson (50s?)*
Jamboree. *Louis Rawls (1965)*
Jazz Alley. *Estella Yancey (1969)*
Jazz at the Maltings. *McKinley Morganfield (1968)*
Jazz Casual: *James Rushing (1964); James Witherspoon (1963)*
Jazz Scene at Ronnie Scott's: *William Dupree (1970); Albert King (1970); Otis Spann (1970)*
Jazz Scene—U.S.A.: *Louis Rawls (1963); James Witherspoon (1967)*
Jazz 625. *William Dupree (1964)*
Jerry Blavat Show. *Richard Penniman (1967)*
Jerry Lewis Show. *Ray Charles (1968)*
Jimi Hendrix Experience at the Saville Theater, 1967. *James Hendrix (1968)*
Joe Franklin Show: *Beulah Bryant (1968–9/77); Odetta Gordon (1976); Jalacy Hawkins (1974); Helen Humes (1975); Natalie Lamb (1966); Carrie Smith (1977); Eva Taylor (c1967); Viola Wells (1973); Joe Williams (1976)*
Joey Bishop Show: *Ray Charles (1968–9); Odetta Gordon (1967/9); Louis Rawls (1968–9); Ethel Waters (1967); Joe Williams (1967–8)*
John Gary Show. *Louis Rawls (1966)*
John Gunther's High Road. *James Rushing (1959)*
Johnny Carson's Tonight Show (see: Tonight Show)
Johnny Cash Show: *Ray Charles (1970); Jack Elliott (1970)*
Johnny Cash: Spring Fever. *Ray Charles (1978)*

Kaleidoscope 4: *Odetta Gordon (1965); John Lee Hooker (1965); James Rushing (1965)*
Kraft Music Hall: *Ray Charles (1967); Louis Rawls (1970)*
Kraft Television Theater. *Beulah Bryant (c1958)*
Kup's Show. *Riley King (1972)*
Lamp Unto My Feet. *Odetta Gordon (1959)*
Late Night Line-Up: *Arthur Crudup (1970); Eddie House (1970)*
Les Crane Show. *Jesse Fuller (1965)*
Like It Is: *Gary Davis (1970); Odetta Gordon (1971)*
Like Young. *McKinley Morganfield (1967)*
Live Like a Millionaire. *Beulah Bryant (c1953)*
Lloyd Thaxton Show. *Odetta Gordon (1964)*
Look Up and Live. *Joshua White (1961)*
Lou Rawls on Ice. *Louis Rawls (1978)*
Lou Rawls Show. *Louis Rawls (1971)*
Lou Rawls . . . Special. *Louis Rawls (1977)*
Lyrics and Legends (Ep A: Singing Styles) (Ep B: The Blues): *James Cage (1963) (B); John Lee Hooker (1963) (A); Victoria Spivey (1963) (B); Willie Thomas (1963) (B)*

Mac Davis Show. *Walter Lewis (1977)*
Made in Chicago: *Carey Bell (c1970); James Brewer (c1970); John Davis (1977); Joseph Hutto (c1970); John Littlejohn (1970); Eurreal Montgomery (1977); Edith Wilson (1977); Joseph Young (1977)*
Mama Cooper (see: Daniel Boone Show)
Mark of Jazz. *Taj Mahal (c1971)*
Marty Faye Show. *Samuel Maghett (1969)*

Matinee Theater (Ep: Sing for Me). *Ethel Waters (1957)*
Me and Stella: *Elizabeth Cotten (1977); Taj Mahal (1977)*
Memphis Blues Festival (see: Sounds of Summer)
Merv Griffin Show: *Charles Berry (1977–8); Ray Charles (1968–70); Antoine Domino (1975–6); Odetta Gordon (1968); Albert King (1969); Riley King (1969/75–7); Richard Penniman (1971–2); Louis Rawls (1969–71/75–77); Ethel Waters (1972); Johnny Watson (1977); Joe Williams (1968/71/74/77)*
Midday Live. *Louis Rawls (1975/7)*
Midnight Special: *Charles Berry (1975); Robert Bland (1974); Paul Butterfield (1974); Ray Charles (1976); John Lee Hooker (1974); Riley King (1973–4/6); Ellas McDaniel (1975); Richard Penniman (1974/76–7); Bonnie Raitt (1977); Louis Rawls (1976–7); Willie Thornton (1974); Joe Williams (1974/76); James Witherspoon (1974)*
Mike & Music Show. *Joe Williams (1968)*
Mike Douglas Show: *Charles Berry (1971/8); Ray Charles (c1972/1977); Antoine Domino (1970); Odetta Gordon (1970); Richard Havens (1969/78); Alberta Hunter (1977–8); Riley King (1971); Taj Mahal (1978); Ellas McDaniel (1971); McKinley Morganfield (1977); Richard Penniman (1970–1); Louis Rawls (1963/67/70/72/76–8); James Rushing (1967); Aaron Walker (c1972); Ethel Waters (1972); Joe Williams (1968–71); Johnny Winter (1977)*
Mike Wallace Interviews. *Ethel Waters (1959)*
Miss U. S. Television. *Barbara Dane (1951)*
Mississippi Folkroots: Delta Blues. *James Thomas (1972)*
Monkees Special: *Antoine Domino (1969); Richard Penniman (1969)*
Monterey Jazz Festival: *Richard Havens (1968); Riley King (1968); Aaron Walker (1968)*
Moods in Melody. *Joe Williams (1961)*
More Folk Music. *Barbara Dane (1964)*
Movements of Providence, The (see: Devil's Music — A History of the Blues, The)
Mr. Crump's Blues. *Booker White (1972)*
Muppet Show. *Louis Rawls (1977)*
Music from Montreux: *Odetta Gordon (1976); James Witherspoon (1976)*
Music Hall America. *Ray Charles (1976)*
Music in America. *Louis Myers (1976)*
Music Scene: *Richard Havens (1969); Janis Joplin (1969); Riley King (1969); John Mayall (1969); Ellas McDaniel (1970); Louis Rawls (1969)*

NBC Follies. *Ray Charles (1973)*
NET Jazz. *Riley King (1968)*
NET Playhouse (Ep: Thoughts of the Artist on Leaving the Sixties). *Taj Mahal (1970)*
National Collegiate Cheerleading Championships. *Louis Rawls (1978)*
New Orleans Jazz: *George Guesnon (1964); Billie Pierce (1964)*
New Steve Allen Show (see also: Steve Allen Show). *Louis Rawls (1961)*
New Yorker Show: *Beulah Bryant (1968); Richard Havens (1968)*
Newark & Reality. *Clyde Bernhardt (1978)*
Newark Arts Festival. *Natalie Lamb (c1972)*
Night Life. *Albert Washington (1975)*
Nightlife. *Odetta Gordon (1965)*
90 Minutes Live. *Clarence Miller (1977–8)*
Not Only . . . But Also. *Aaron Walker (1965)*
Nothing but the Truth (see: Devil's Music — A History of the Blues, The)
Now Generation, The. *Louis Rawls (1968)*

Observer, The: *John Estes (1964); Hammie Nixon (1964); James Rachell (1964)*
Occult, The. *Clarence Miller (1969)*
Odyssey (Ep: They Took a Blue Note). *Horace Sprott (1956)*
Of Black America (rel as film: Body & Soul, Pt 2). *Ray Charles (1968)*
Old Grey Whistle Test Show: *Pleasant Joseph (1974); Iverson Minter (1977)*
Omnibus (Ep A: The Friendly Invasion): *Charles Berry (1975) (A); Walter Lewis (1975) (A); James Rushing (1953); Charles Sayles (1976); Houston Stackhouse (1975) (A); Joe Wilkins (1975) (A)*
One Hundred Years from Today (see: Camera Three)
One Night Stand: *Riley King (1971); Ethel Waters (1959)*
One of a Kind: *Walter McGhee (1973); Sonny Terry (1973)*
Open Studio. *J. C. Burris (1975)*
Operation: Entertainment. *Ray Charles (1968)*
Oscar Peterson Presents: *Joseph Turner (1974); Joe Williams (1974)*
Oscar Peterson: Very Special. *Ray Charles (1976)*
Our American Musical Heritage: *James Rushing (1971); Joe Williams (1971)*
Owen Marshall: Counselor At Law (Ep: Run Carol Run). *Ethel Waters (1972)*

P. M. East . . . P. M. West. *Barbara Dane (1960)*
Parable in the Park. *Odetta Gordon (1960)*
Parade. *Joe Williams (1963)*
Pattern of Words & Music, A. *Sam Hopkins (1960)*
Paul Crump Story, The. *James Witherspoon (1962)*
Pearl Bailey Show, The: *Riley King (1971); Ethel Waters (1971)*
People's Music . . . And All That Jazz: *James Cage (1976); Willie Thomas (1976)*
Perpetual People Puzzle. *Richard Havens (1972)*
Perry Como Show. *Joe Williams (1958)*
Perspective: *Dave Alexander (1975); Floyd Dixon (1975)*
Peter Appleyard Presents The Climax Jazz Band with Carol Leigh. *Carol Leigh (1978)*
Peter Martin Show: *John Hammond (1968); Richard Havens (1968–70)*

Peter Wolf. *Joe Williams (1969)*
Phil Ochs Memorial Celebration. *David Van Ronk (1976)*
Philadelphia Folk Festival: *Arthur Jackson (1975); Larry Johnson (1973); Fred McDowell (1971); Victoria Spivey (1974)*
Play It Again Sam. *Taj Mahal (1975)*
Playboy After Dark (Hugh Hefner Show): *James Cotton (1969); Louis Rawls (1969); Joe Williams (1969)*
Playboy's Penthouse. *Barbara Dane (1960)*
Playwrights 56 (Ep: Sound and the Fury). *Ethel Waters (1955)*
Positively Black: *Riley King (1973); Louis Rawls (1975)*

Quest. *James Witherspoon (1964)*

Rainbow City. *John Holder (c1968)*
Rainbow Quest: *Gary Davis (1967); Jack Elliott (c1965); John Hurt (c1966); Walter McGhee (1968); Sonny Terry (1968)*
Ready, Steady, Go: *James Hendrix (1966); Earl Hooker (1965); Esther Phillips (1965); Mathis Reed (1964)*
Really the Country Blues (see: Camera Three)
Red Skelton Show. *Louis Rawls (1968–9)*
Rhythm & Blues: *Riley King (1974); Louis Rawls (1974)*
Robert Q. Lewis Show. *Beulah Bryant (c1954)*
Robinson Crusoe. *John Holder (1974)*
Rock & Roll Revival. *Richard Penniman (1974)*
Rock Concert. *Richard Havens (1973)*
Rock 1. *Willie Thornton (1970)*
Roomful of Music: *Walter McGhee (1965); Sonny Terry (1965)*
Roots. *Joseph Turner (1977)*
Roots of Country Music & Blues: *Peter Chatman (1977); James Dawkins (1977); Eddie House (1977); Riley King (1977); Huddie Ledbetter (1977); McKinley Morganfield (1977); Victoria Spivey (1977); Roosevelt Sykes (1977); Joseph Young (1977)*
Route 66 (Ep: Goodnight Sweet Blues). *Ethel Waters (1961)*
Run Carol Run (see: Owen Marshall: Counselor At Law)

Salute to American Imagination, A. *Ray Charles (1978)*
Salute to The Beatles. *Charles Berry (1975)*
Sammy and Company: *Charles Berry (1975); Ray Charles (1975); Riley King (1976); Louis Rawls (1975); Joe Williams (1975)*
San Francisco Blues, The. *J. C. Burris (c1976)*
Sanford and Son. *Riley King (1977)*
Saturday Night (see also: Saturday Night Live): *Charles Berry (1977); Paul Butterfield (1977); Ray Charles (1977); Taj Mahal (1977); Esther Phillips (1975)*
Saturday Night Beechnut Show (see: Dick Clark's Saturday Night Beechnut Show)
Saturday Night Live (see also: Saturday Night): *Ray Charles (1978); Bonnie Raitt (1978)*
Say Brother. *Larry Johnson (c1970)*
Second Barry Manilow Special, The. *Ray Charles (1978)*
Sesame Street. *Louis Rawls (1970)*
Seven Lively Arts, The (Ep A: The Sound of Jazz) (Ep A rel as film: The Sound of Jazz): *William Caradine (1958); James Rushing (1957) (A)*
77 Sunset Strip. *Louis Rawls (1959)*
Sha Na Na. *Charles Berry (1978)*
Shade of Soul, A. *Rufus Thomas (c1968)*
Shindig: *Chester Burnett (1965); Ray Charles (1965); Ellas McDaniel (1965); Tommy Tucker (1965); Joe Williams (1965); James Witherspoon (1965)*
Shivaree. *James Witherspoon (1965)*
Show, The. *Taj Mahal (1970)*
Showtime at The Apollo: *Helen Humes (1955); Amos Milburn (1955); Joseph Turner (1955); Dinah Washington (1955)*
Sing for Me (see: Matinee Theater)
Singing Styles (see: Lyrics and Legends)
Singing, Swinging Years: *Louis Jordan (1960); Dinah Washington (1960)*
60 Minutes: *Alberta Hunter (1978); Janis Joplin (1969)*
Smothers Brothers Comedy Hour (see also: Smothers Brothers Show): *Ray Charles (1969)*
Smothers Brothers Show (see also: Smothers Brothers Comedy Hour): *Ray Charles (1975); Richard Penniman (1970)*
Something Special. *Ethel Waters (1966)*
Songs of Freedom. *Odetta Gordon (1963)*
Sonny and Cher Comedy Hour. *Charles Berry (1973)*
Soul: *Milton Campbell (1970); Riley King (1969–70); Taj Mahal (1972); Esther Phillips (1971); Rufus Thomas (1971); James Witherspoon (1971)*
Soul Special. *Louis Rawls (1968)*
Soul Train: *Robert Bland (c1975); Riley King (1972–3/5); Louis Rawls (1975)*
Sound and the Fury (see: Playwrights 56)
Sound of Jazz, The (see: Seven Lively Arts, The)
Sounds for Saturday. *Charles Berry (1972)*
Sounds of Summer (Ep: Memphis Blues Festival): *Rufus Thomas (1969); Booker White (1969)*
Soundstage (Ep A: Together in the Blues): *Luther Allison (1978); Robert Bland (1977) (A); Michael Bloomfield (1974); Willie Dixon (1974); George Guy (1975); John Hammond (1975); Helen Humes (1975); Albert King (1978); Riley King (1977) (A); McKinley Morganfield (1974); Joe Perkins (1978); Bonnie Raitt (1975); Koko Taylor (1974); Sonny Terry (1975); Amos Wells (1974–5); Johnny Winter (1974)*
Soupy Sales Show. *R. S. Rankin (c1960)*
Speaking to Hannah (see: Favorite Playhouse)
St. Louis Jazz. *Jean Kittrell (1967)*
Stars of Jazz: *Barbara Dane (1959); Jesse Fuller (1959)*
Steve Allen Comedy Hour (see also: Steve Allen Show). *Louis Rawls (1967)*
Steve Allen Show (see also: New Steve Allen Show/Steve Allen Comedy Hour/Tonight Show): *Barbara Dane (1963); Richard Havens (1968); Riley King (1968); Clarence Miller (1963); Joe Williams (1963/68/70); James Witherspoon (1963)*
Steve Allen's Tonight Show (see: Tonight Show)

Sticking with the Blues (see: Devil's Music — A History of the Blues, The).
Strollin' 20s: *Walter McGhee (1966); Joe Williams (1966)*
Subject Is Jazz. *James Rushing (1958)*
Sue Lee Show. *Clarence Miller (1962)*
Switched-On Symphony. *Ray Charles (1970)*

TV Critics Circle Awards. *Louis Rawls (1977)*
Talent Hunch Show. *Clarence Richardson (1973)*
Tennessee Ernie Ford Show. *Ethel Waters (1957)*
Thank You Rock 'n' Roll. *Ray Charles (1978)*
They Took a Blue Note (see: Odyssey)
This Hour Has Seven Days. *John Hurt (1965)*
Thoughts of the Artist on Leaving the Sixties (see: NET Playhouse)
Three Flames Show. *Oran Page (1948)*
Through the Eyes of Tomorrow. *James Hendrix (c1969)*
Tilmon Tempo Show: *Morris Holt (1975); Taj Mahal (1972)*
Timex All Star Jazz Show. *Barbara Dane (1959)*
Timex All Star Swing Festival. *Joe Williams (1972)*
To Tell the Truth. *Alberta Hunter (1978)*
Toast of the Coast, The. *Roosevelt Sykes (40s)*
Toast of the Town (see also: Ed Sullivan Show): *Louis Jordan (c1949); Ellas McDaniel (1955); Oran Page (1951); Aaron Walker (early 50s); Ethel Waters (c1949)*
Today Show: *Charles Berry (1978); Peter Chatman (1960); Sam Chatmon (1976); James Dawkins (1975); Willie Dixon (1960); Richard Havens (1968); Helen Humes (1975); Alberta Hunter (1977–8); Blanche Thomas (1961); James Thomas (1976)*
Together in the Blues (see: Soundstage).
Tom Jones Show: *Ray Charles (1970); Janis Joplin (1969); Richard Penniman (1972); Louis Rawls (1970)*
Tommy Banks Show. *Clarence Miller (1963)*
Tonight Show (Steve Allen's Tonight Show, 1954–7) (see also: Steve Allen Show) (Johnny Carson's Tonight Show, from 1962–): *Ray Charles (1972/76); Barbara Dane (c1962); John Hammond (1969); Richard Havens (1968/72/76); James Hendrix (1969); John Hurt (c1963); Riley King (1969–70); Walter Lewis (1974); Richard Penniman (1968–71); Esther Phillips (1969/72); Louis Rawls (1963/69–71/75–6); James Rushing (1954/56); Ethel Waters (1956/72); Joe Williams (1963–7/70–1/78); James Witherspoon (1974)*
Tonight with Belafonte: *Odetta Gordon (1959); Walter McGhee (1959); Sonny Terry (1959)*
Toughing It Out. *Larry Johnson (1976)*
Twang: *Odetta Gordon (1967); David Van Ronk (1967)*
24 Hours. *William Dupree (1971)*

Untitled Variety Program. *Ethel Waters (1939)*
Upbeat: *Charles Berry (1968); Albert King (1968); Riley King (1969); Taj Mahal (1969); Louis Rawls (1967)*

Vacation Playhouse. *Ethel Waters (1966)*
Virginia Graham Show: *Odetta Gordon (1971); Riley King (1971); Walter McGhee (1971); Louis Rawls (1971); Sonny Terry (1971)*
Visions (Ep: Charlie Smith and the Fritter Tree). *Robert Shaw (1978)*

Wake Up & Sing. *Barbara Dane (c1961)*
Weequahic Park Love Festival. *Robert Bland (1969)*
What's My Line. *Riley King (c1972)*
Wide Wide World (Dave Garroway's Wide Wide World). *Elizabeth Miles (1958)*
Winner by Decision (see: General Electric Theater)
With Pierre Salinger. *Odetta Gordon (1968)*
Wonderama. *Richard Havens (1976)*
Wonderful World of Color (Ep: Disneyland After Dark) (Ep rel as film: Disneyland After Dark). *Monette Moore (1962)*
Woody Woodbury Show. *Joshua White (1967)*
Work and Mother Wit (see: Devil's Music — A History of the Blues, The)
World of Music, The: *Odetta Gordon (1966); Walter McGhee (1966); Sonny Terry (1966); Joshua White (1966)*

You Bet Your Life. *Clarence Miller (1961)*
You're Never Too Old. *Jesse Fuller (early 50s)*

Theater Index

This is an index of titled theatrical shows, revues, musicals, dramatic and tab shows, stock companies, recitals, variety and other stage shows in which singers listed in this book participated. Participation may be a singing or non-singing appearance as an entertainer, actor, bandsman, understudy, or member of the chorus or in another capacity. For the purposes of this book, the shows listed here are theatrical presentations which may have been on or off Broadway, toured vaudeville and other circuits, appeared in clubs, picture houses, or auditoriums, or were simply a single command performance. A show about a singer without his participation is indicated by the singer's name in parentheses. Untitled shows are not indexed and may be found in bio entries.

The year date of a singer's appearance, when known, is shown in parentheses after each name.

Certain traveling blues, minstrel and medicine troupes or folk, jazz, rock and other concerts loosely termed "Shows" or "Revues" will be found in the Names and Places Index.

For further details regarding the kind of presentation, theater name, location and specific work of the singer and other theater facts, refer to the bio entry.

All titles beginning with the articles "A," "An" and "The" are indexed by the second word. My appreciation to Joseph G. Palladino for his work on this index.

ANTA Album. *Ethel Waters (1950)*
Aces and Queens. *Lena Wilson (1925)*
Addison Carey's Revue. *Hannah Sylvester (1933)*
Africana. *Ethel Waters (1927–8)*
Alabama Bound. *Ida Brown (1920)*
All Star Revue. *Hannah Sylvester (1933)*
And How. *Rosa Henderson (1928)*
Androcles and the Lion. *Ethel Waters (c1939)*
Another Part of the Forest. *Edith Wilson (mid-40s)*
Are We Happy. *Ida Brown (1928)*
Arkansas Swift Foot: *Albert Luandrew (1931); Gertrude Rainey (from 1930)*
As Thousands Cheer: *Monette Moore (1934); Ethel Waters (1933–5)*
Ashes and Bilo in Harlem. *Lena Wilson (1928)*
At Home Abroad: *Monette Moore (1936); Ethel Waters (1935–6)*
At Home with Ethel Waters. *Ethel Waters (1953)*
At the Barbecue: *Ida Brown (1930); Viola McCoy (1930)*
Autumn Frolics. *Ida Brown (1928)*
Baby Blues. *Ida Brown (1919)*
Baby Pompadour. *Lillian Brown (1934)*
Baby's Birthday. *Viola McCoy (1930)*
Back Home Again: *Leola Grant (1928); Wesley Wilson (1928)*
Ballyhoo of 1931. *Hannah Sylvester (1931)*
Bandanna Babies. *Gertrude Rainey (1930)*
Bandannaland. *Ada Brown (1928)*
Banjo Land. *Lillian Brown (1924)*
Banjoland. *Ethel Waters (1929)*
Be Yourself. *Rosa Henderson (1928)*
Bernice. *Ethel Waters (1957)*
Bessie, Billie & Bo. *Jeanne Carroll (1975)*
Bessie Smith Revue. *Bessie Smith (1930)*
Big Moments. *May Alix (1931)*
Big White Fog. *Trixie Smith (1940)*
Billy Banks Revue. *May Alix (1932)*
Black & White Revue. *Susie Edwards (1926–7)*
Black & White Revue. *Lena Wilson (1932)*
Black Beaux Belles. *Lucille Hegamin (early 20s)*

Black Bottom Revue. *Ethel Waters (1926)*
Black Bottom Revue. *Clara Smith (1927)*
Black Bottom Revue. *Ethel Waters (1952)*
Black Cargo. *Ethel Waters (1927)*
Black Revue, The. *Edith Wilson (1928)*
Blackberries. *Rosa Henderson (1930)*
Blackberries of 1932. *Edith Wilson (1932)*
Blackbirds of 1926. *Edith Wilson (1926)*
Blackbirds of 1928. *Maggie Jones (1928–9)*
Blackbirds of 1930. *Ethel Waters (1930)*
Blackbirds of 1933–4: *Ida Brown (1933–4); Henry Williams (1933–4); Edith Wilson (1933–4)*
Blackbirds of 1934. *Edith Wilson (1934)*
Blackbirds Revue: *Edith Wilson (1926–7); Lena Wilson (1926)*
Blackbirds Revue. *Bessie Smith (1935)*
Blackouts of 1929. *Rosa Henderson (1929)*
Blue Holiday: *Ethel Waters (1945); Joshua White (1945)*
Blues in the Night. *Olive Brown (1941)*
Bon-Bon Buddy Jr. *Lillian Brown (1922)*
Bottomland: *Katherine Henderson (1927); Sara Martin (1927); Eva Taylor (1927)*
Brass Ankle. *Trixie Smith (1931)*
Broadway Rastus: *Esther Bigeou (1917); Lillian Brown (1918)*
Broadway Rastus. *Ida Brown (1928)*
Broadway Rastus. *Bessie Smith (1937)*
Broadway Rastus of 1920. *Ida Brown (1920)*
Broadway Revue. *Bessie Smith (1931)*
Bronze Buddies. *Lena Wilson (1928)*
Brown Buddies: *Ada Brown (1930); Monette Moore (1930)*
Brown Pepper Revue. *Monette Moore (1930)*
Brown Skin Brevities. *Viola McCoy (1928)*
Brown Skin Models: *Clarence Brown (early 40s); Princess White (c1940–4)*
Brunettes Preferred. *Rosa Henderson (1927)*
Bunch of Blackberries, A. *Gertrude Rainey (1900)*
Butterbeans & Susie 1930 Revue. *Susie Edwards (1930)*
Butterbeans & Susie Revue. *Susie Edwards (1927)*
Buzzin' Around. *Lena Wilson (1922)*
By Moonlight: *Ida Brown (1930); Viola McCoy (1930)*

Cabin Club Follies. *Maude De Forrest (1929)*
Cabin in the Sky: *Susie Edwards (1940–1); Ethel Waters (1940–1)*
Candied Sweets. *Clara Smith (1929)*
Cat on a Hot Tin Roof: *Walter McGhee (1955–7); Sonny Terry (1955–7)*
Change Your Luck. *Alberta Hunter (1930)*
Cherry Lane Follies. *Alberta Hunter (1930)*
Chicago Steppers. *Charles Davenport (late 20s/early 30s)*
Chocolate Blondes. *Mattie Hite (1929)*
Chocolate Kiddies. *Edith Wilson (1925)*
Chocolate Music Box. *Rosa Henderson (1929)*
Chocolate Scandals, The: *Leola Grant (1928); Wesley Wilson (1928)*
Christmas Revels. *Bessie Smith (1933–4)*
Circus Showman, The. *Ida Brown (1929)*
Clara Smith Revue. *Clara Smith (1927)*
Clarence Williams Revue: *Lucille Hegamin (1926); Eva Taylor (1926)*
Club Alabam Revue. *Edith Wilson (1924)*
Club Harlem Revue. *Hannah Sylvester (1929)*
Conjure Man, The. *Viola McCoy (1929)*
Connie's Inn 1932 Revue. *May Alix (1932)*
Constant Sinner, The. *Trixie Smith (1931)*
Cool Rhythm. *Monette Moore (1931)*
Cotton Club Express, The. *Ethel Waters (1937)*
Cotton Club Parade: *Ethel Waters (1933); Henry Williams (1933)*
Cotton Club Revue. *Alberta Hunter (1937)*
Cotton Club Revue. *Ethel Waters (1933)*
Country Boy, The. *Lillian Brown (1916)*
Cow Cow's Chicago Steppers (see: Chicago Steppers)
Crazy Hotel, The. *Viola McCoy (1929)*
Crazy Quilt Revue. *Monette Moore (1929)*
Crazy Show. *Ethel Waters (1938)*
Creole Follies: *Lucille Hegamin (1923); Edith Wilson (1924)*
Creole Revels: *Edith Wilson (1928); Lena Wilson (1928)*
Creole Vanities. *Wesley Wilson (1928)*

Dallas Tan Town Topics. *Victoria Spivey (1933)*
Dance Mania. *Lena Wilson (1927)*
Dance Round Up. *Edith Wilson (1934)*
Dancing Dandies. *Ida Brown (1928)*
Darktown Follies. *Esther Bigeou (1918–20)*
Darktown Frolics. *Bessie Brown (original) (1926)*
Darktown Scandals: *Ida Cox (30s/40s); Arnold Moore (1930s)*
Dear Old Southland. *Mary Stafford (1932)*
Death of Bessie Smith. *(Bessie Smith) (1960–1)*
Debut. *Alberta Hunter (1956)*
Deep Harlem. *Lena Wilson (1929)*
Derby Day In Dixie: *Birleanna Blanks (1921); Edna Hicks (1921)*
Desires of 1928. *Ida Brown (1927)*
Desires of 1930. *Mattie Hite (1930)*
Dixie Magnolias. *Ida Brown (1927)*
Dixie Revue. *Mamie Smith (1924)*
Dixie to Broadway: *Lillian Brown (1924–5); Eva Taylor (1924); Edith Wilson (1924)*
Dixie to Broadway. *Ethel Waters (1932)*
Dixie to Harlem. *Viola Wells (1945)*
Dream Girls. *Clara Smith (1929)*
Dreamy Melodies. *Henry Williams (1933)*
Dumb Luck. *Ethel Waters (1922)*
Dusty Lane. *Clara Smith (1930)*

Ease On Down. *Susie Edwards (1930)*
Easter Parade Revue. *May Alix (1934)*
Edith Wilson Revue: *Viola McCoy (1930); Edith Wilson (1930)*

Egg Nog. *Viola McCoy (1929)*
Eliza Scandals. *Virginia Liston (1925)*
Ethel Waters Broadway Revue. *Ethel Waters (1928)*
Ethel Waters Floor Show. *Ethel Waters (1926)*
Ethel Waters Revue. *Ethel Waters (1926)*
Ethel Waters Vanities. *Ethel Waters (1926)*
Evening with Ethel Waters, An. *Ethel Waters (1959)*
Exploits in Africa. *Birleanna Blanks (1919)*

Fan Waves: *Ida Cox (1934); Bessie Smith (1934)*
Fashion Plate Frolics. *Viola McCoy (1930)*
Figity Feet. *Katie Crippen (1929)*
Finian's Rainbow. *Sonny Terry (1947–9)*
Finian's Rainbow. *Odetta Gordon (1949)*
Fireworks of 1930. *Mamie Smith (1930)*
Flaming Follies: *Rosa Henderson (1927); Lena Wilson (1927)*
Flat Below, The. *Lena Wilson (1922)*
Flying Colors. *Monette Moore (1932)*
Flying High. *Viola McCoy (1928)*
Follow Me. *Edna Hicks (1916)*
Follow Me. *Mamie Smith (1922)*
4-11-44. *Victoria Spivey (1930)*
Four Star Revue. *Alberta Hunter (1932)*
Frolicers: *Birleanna Blanks (1923); Viola McCoy (1923)*
Frolicking Around. *Mamie Smith (1926)*
Frolics of 1930. *Susie Edwards (1930)*
From Broadway Back to Harlem. *Ethel Waters (1932)*
From Dover Street to Dixie. *Edith Wilson (1923)*

Gentle Folk. *Ethel Waters (1955)*
Get Happy Follies. *Sara Martin (1928)*
Get Together. *Henry Williams (1934)*
Go Get It. *Rosa Henderson (c1923)*
God Bless America. *Ram Holder (1968)*
Going Strong. *Rosa Henderson (1928)*
Going to Town. *Ada Brown (1932/4)*
Going Up. *Ida Brown (1928)*
Gossiping Liza. *Bessie Smith (1931)*

Happiness Revue. *Viola McCoy (1928)*
Happy Days. *Edith Wilson (1932)*
Happy Go Lucky. *Arthur Phelps (c1930–1)*
Happy Go Lucky. *Monette Moore (1931)*
Happy Journey to Trenton and Camden. *Ethel Waters (1957)*
Happy Times. *Bessie Smith (1930)*
Harlem Bound. *Susie Edwards (1932)*
Harlem Frolics. *Bessie Smith (1925–9)*
Harlem Girl. *Lillian Brown (1929)*
Harlem High Steppers. *Viola McCoy (1932)*
Harlem Madness. *Clara Smith (1933)*
Harlem Pastimes. *Ida Brown (1928)*
Harlem Rounders, The: *Ida Brown (1927); Rosa Henderson (1927)*
Harlem to Hollywood. *Ada Brown (1943)*
Harlem Variety Revue: *Helen Humes (early 50s); Amos Milburn (early 50s); Joseph Turner (1954); Dinah Washington (1944–55)*
Harvest Moon. *Lillian Brown (c1910)*
Hawaiian Moon. Ada Brown (1934)
Headin' for Harlem. *Lillian Brown (1933)*
Heat Wave. *Ethel Waters (1952)*
Hello 1919! *Ethel Waters (1919)*
Hello 1930. *Clara Smith (1929–30)*
Hellzapoppin. *Victoria Spivey (1938–9)*
Here 'Tis: *Lillian Brown (1932); Susie Edwards (1932)*
Here We Are. *Clara Smith (1930)*
Hidden Treasure. *Viola McCoy (1924)*
High Jinks. *Susie Edwards (1928)*
High Lights of Harlem. *Trixie Smith (1928)*
High Spots. *Monette Moore (1929)*
Hit Bits from Africana. *Victoria Spivey (1927)*
Hits and Bits. *Hannah Sylvester (1932)*
Holiday in Blues: *Leola Grant (1948); Wesley Wilson (1948)*
Holiday in Harlem: *Leola Grant (1934); Wesley Wilson (1934)*
Honey. *Ida Brown (1929); Wesley Wilson (1929)*
Hop Off. *Viola McCoy (1929)*
Hot Chocolates. *Edith Wilson (1929–30)*
Hot Feet. *Mattie Hite (1928)*
Hot from Harlem. *Bessie Smith (1934)*
Hot Harlem. *Edith Wilson (1933)*
Hot Rhythm. *Edith Wilson (1930)*
Hot Stuff. *Lillian Brown (1930)*
Hot Stuff of 1933: *Susie Edwards (1932); Bessie Smith (1932)*
Hot Town. *Bessie Brown (1930)*
How Come: *Alberta Hunter (1923); Bessie Smith (1923)*
How Long Till Summer. *Joshua White (1949)*
Huckle Buck. *Olive Brown (c1945)*
Hummin' Sam: *Hannah Sylvester (1933); Edith Wilson (1933)*
Hurry On. *Lucille Hegamin (1922)*

In the Swim. *Viola McCoy (1930)*
Indianola. *Hannah Sylvester (1931)*
It's Great To Be Alive. *Helen Humes (1957)*

Jangleland. *Ada Brown (1931)*
January Jubilee. *Clara Smith (1931)*
Jazz Jubilee. *Lucille Hegamin (1922)*
Jazz Mine. *Wesley Wilson (1931)*
Jazz Regiment, The. *Bessie Smith (1929)*
Jazzland in 1930. *Ethel Waters (1930)*
Jazzmania: *Edith Wilson (1927); Lena Wilson (1927)*
Jazzola. *Hannah Sylvester (1929)*
Jezebel. *Ida Brown (1933)*
Jig-Saw. *Edith Wilson (1933)*
Jimmie Cooper's Revue. *Susie Edwards (1927)*
John Henry. *Joshua White (1939–40)*
Joyland. *Viola McCoy (1928)*
Jump for Joy. *Joseph Turner (1941)*

Jump Steady: *Sara Martin (1922); Ethel Waters (1922)*
Jungle Drums. *Ada Brown (1934)*
Jungle Jive Revue. *Calvin Frazier (1946)*

Keep Shufflin': *Katherine Henderson (1929); Eva Taylor (1929)*
Kings Terrace Revue. *Gladys Bentley (1934)*
Kiss Me Kate. *Lillian Brown (1952)*
Knockouts of 1933 Revue. *May Alix (1933)*

Last Round-Up, The. *Monette Moore (1933)*
Late Hour Dancers. *Bessie Smith (1929)*
Laugh Time. *Ethel Waters (1943)*
Laughing Lightning. *Susie Edwards (1929)*
Laughing Through. *Viola McCoy (1928)*
League of Rhythm. *Bessie Smith (1936)*
Lenox Club Revue. *Lena Wilson (1929)*
Liberty Belles. *Bessie Smith (1918–9)*
Lily White. *Trixie Smith (1930)*
Lincoln Frolics. *Lucille Hegamin (1926)*
Long Way from Home, A. *Joshua White (1948)*
Look Who's Here. *Hannah Sylvester (1928)*
Louisiana: *Leola Grant (1929); Wesley Wilson (1929)*
Louisiana. *Trixie Smith (1933)*
Louisiana Blackbirds. *Gertrude Rainey (1927)*
Lucky Numbers. *Ida Brown (1927)*
Lucky Sambo: *Birleanna Blanks (1925–7); Monette Moore (1925); Lena Wilson (1925)*
Lucky Stars. *Monette Moore (1929)*

Made in Harlem. *Mamie Smith (1918)*
Make It Snappy. *Lena Wilson (1931)*
Mamba's Daughters: *Alberta Hunter (1939–40); Ethel Waters (1939–40)*
Mamba's Daughters. *Lillian Brown (1953)*
Man from Baltimore, The. *Trixie Smith (1934)*
Man from Bam. *James Yancey (1903–8)*
Manhattan Frolics: *Lillian Brown (1932); Maude De Forrest (1932)*
Me and Bessie. *(Bessie Smith) (1975–6)*
Melodies of 1933. *Eva Taylor (1933)*
Member of the Wedding, The. *Ethel Waters (1950–into 70s)*
Memphis Bound: *Ada Brown (1945); Edith Wilson (1945)*
Messin' Around. *Monette Moore (1929)*
Midget Follies. *Wesley Wilson (1930)*
Midnight Steppers: *Alonzo Johnson (1929); Bessie Smith (1929)*
Midnight Steppers, The. *Lucille Hegamin (1928)*
Misleading Lady, The. *Lillian Brown (1916)*
Miss Calico. *Ethel Waters (1926–7)*
Mississippi Days. *Bessie Smith (1928)*
Moanin' Low. *Bessie Smith (1930)*
Moonlight Follies. *Trixie Smith (1927)*
Moonshine: *Bessie Brown (1922); Viola McCoy (1922)*
Mr. Jiggins of Jigginstown. *Eva Taylor (1936)*
Mrs. Patterson. *Alberta Hunter (1954–5)*

Music and Laughter. *James Rushing (1931)*
Music Box Revue. *Edith Wilson (1932)*

New American, The: *Birleanna Blanks (1921); Edna Hicks (1921)*
New Revue of Stars. *Helen Humes (1946)*
New Year's Revels. *Lucille Hegamin (1930–1)*
New York Revue: *Viola McCoy (1928); Trixie Smith (1928)*
Next Door Neighbors. *Trixie Smith (1928)*
Nifties of 1928. *Lena Wilson (1928)*
Night Guitar. *Ram Holder (1970)*
Nightime in Dixieland. *Edith Wilson (1922)*
1928 Revue. *Susie Edwards (1927)*
North Ain't South. *Maude De Forrest (1923)*
Notorieties. *Susie Edwards (1931)*

Oh Joy. *Ethel Waters (1922)*
Okeh Revue. *Susie Edwards (1927)*
On the Air. *Edith Wilson (1928)*
On the Avenue. *Ida Brown (1928)*
Ophelia Snow from Baltimo. *Clara Smith (1928–9)*
Over the Top: *Birleanna Blanks (1919); Edna Hicks (1919)*

Pansy. *Bessie Smith (1929)*
Paradise Club Revue: *Lucille Hegamin (1933); Hannah Sylvester (1933)*
Paris Bound. *Ethel Waters (1927)*
Parisiana. *Wesley Wilson (1928)*
Parks Big Revue. *Bessie Smith (1914)*
Pearls of India. *Viola McCoy (1929)*
Peter and the Wolf. *Richard Havens (1969)*
Pitter Patter: *Leola Grant (1929); Wesley Wilson (1929)*
Plantation Days. *Maude De Forrest (1923)*
Plantation Days. *Ada Brown (1927)*
Plantation Revue: *Edith Wilson (1922/4); Ethel Waters (1925)*
Plenty of It. *Viola McCoy (1932)*
Policy Kings. *Frankie Jaxon (1938–9)*
Priceless Funny Revue: *Lillian Brown (1924); Rosa Henderson (1924)*
Prodigal Singer. *Lillian Brown (1965)*
Pullman Dandies. *Ida Brown (1927)*
Put and Take. *Edith Wilson (1921)*

Quakertown Scandals. *Ida Brown (1929)*
Queen at Home. *Lillian Brown (1930)*
Queen o' Hearts. *Eva Taylor (1922)*
Quintard Miller's Revue. *Rosa Henderson (1926)*

Radio Follies. *Susie Edwards (1929)*
Raisin' Cain: *Ida Cox (1929–early 30s); Jesse Crump (1929–early 30s)*
Ramblin' Around. *Rosa Henderson (1927)*
Rarin' to Go: *Katie Crippen (1927); Viola McCoy (1927)*
Ready Money. *Viola McCoy (1929)*

Red Pastures. *Edith Wilson (1930)*
Regina. *Lillian Brown (1949)*
Revue Negre. *Maude De Forrest (1925–9)*
Rhapsody in Black. *Ethel Waters (1930–3)*
Rhapsody in Black. *Edith Wilson (1935)*
Rhumbaland. *Mamie Smith (1931)*
Riot of Fun, A. *Mamie Smith (1928)*
Riverboat Follies of 1959. *Susie Edwards (1959)*
Rocking Chair Revue. *Mary Stafford (1931)*
Rodeo Girls Revue. *Rosa Henderson (1927)*
Roll On. *Lillian Brown (1926)*
Rolling Thunder. *Jack Elliott (1976)*
Roseanna. *Lillian Brown (1924)*
Runnin' Wild. *Josephine Miles (1923)*

Sam from Bam. *Lillian Brown (1929)*
Saratoga Frolics Revue. *Monette Moore (1931)*
Say It with Girls. *Lillian Brown (1930)*
Scramblin' Roun'. *Viola McCoy (1930)*
Setting the Pace. *Viola McCoy (1927)*
7–11 Revue. *Trixie Smith (1922)*
Seventh Avenue. *Hannah Sylvester (1933)*
Seventh Avenue Affairs. *Rosa Henderson (1927)*
Seventh Avenue Strollers: *Rosa Henderson (1927); Lena Wilson (1927)*
Showboat. *Alberta Hunter (1928–9)*
Showboat. *Hattie McDaniel (1929–30)*
Showboat. *Edith Wilson (1944)*
Shuffle Along. *Eva Taylor (1922)*
Shuffle Along (#2): *Lucille Hegamin (1922); Josephine Miles (c1922)*
Shuffle Along Jr. *Katie Crippen (1928–9)*
Shuffle Along of 1933. *Edith Wilson (1932–3)*
Shufflin' Feet. *Lucille Hegamin (1927)*
Simply Heavenly. *Helen Humes (1955)*
Simply Heavenly. *Walter McGhee (1957)*
Sitting Pretty: *Rosa Henderson (1927–8); Lena Wilson (1927)*
Small's Paradise Revue. *Ida Brown (1929)*
Smart Affairs. *Benjamin Jackson (1954)*
Snake Hips Revue. *Viola McCoy (1930)*
Southbound. *Viola McCoy (1928)*
Southern Syncopation. *Ada Brown (1932)*
Spirit of 1929. *Clyde Bernhardt (1928)*
Springfield Couple. *Edith Wilson (mid-40s)*
S'prise Me. *Bessie Brown (1930)*
Stars over Broadway. *Bessie Smith (1936)*
Steamboat Days. *Bessie Smith (1929)*
Step on It: *Ada Brown (1922); Eva Taylor (1922)*
Stormy Weather. *Ethel Waters (1933)*
Struttin' Along. *Mamie Smith (1923)*
Struttin' Time. *Alberta Hunter (1933)*
Sugar Cane. *Mamie Smith (1928)*
Sugar Hill. *Monette Moore (1949)*
Sultan Sam. *Ida Brown (1920)*
Sun-Tan Frolics: *Sara Martin (1929); Mamie Smith (1929)*
Sunshine. *Trixie Smith (1930)*
Surprise Party, The. *Viola McCoy (1929)*
Swanee Club Revue. *Clara Smith (1928)*
Sweet Chariot. *Clara Smith (1930)*
Sweet 'n' Hot. *Edith Wilson (1944)*
Sweet Papa Garbage. *Viola McCoy (1931)*
Sweethearts on Parade. *Viola McCoy (1929)*
Swing Harlem Swing. *Ethel Waters (1937–8)*
Syncopated Revue. *Mamie Smith (1925)*
Syncopation. *Lena Wilson (1926)*
Syncopationland. *Mamie Smith (1924)*

Tambourines to Glory: *Beulah Bryant (1963); John Sellers (1963)*
Tan Town Tomales. *Ada Brown (1930)*
Tan Town Topics. *Ethel Waters (1925)*
Temple of Jazz, The. *Mattie Hite (1929)*
Thanksgiving Revels. *Alberta Hunter (1930)*
That Gets It. *Mattie Hite (1932)*
They're Off. *Birleanna Blanks (1919)*
This and That. *Ida Brown (1919–20)*
Tip-Top Revue. *Mattie Hite (1928)*
Tommy. *Richard Havens (1972)*
Too Bad. *Ethel Waters (1925)*
Trip Around the World, A: *Birleanna Blanks (1921); Edna Hicks (1921)*
Troubadours Revue, The. *Ida Brown (1927)*
Trouble on the Ranch. *Clara Smith (1931)*
Tunes and Topics. *Bessie Smith (1923)*

Ubangi Club Revue: *Gladys Bentley (1934); Viola McCoy (1934)*
Up and Down. *Sara Martin (1922)*

Varieties of 1934 Revue. *May Alix (1933)*
Vera Violetta. *Eva Taylor (1911)*
Voice of Strangers, The. *Ethel Waters (1956)*

Walking on Air. *Viola McCoy (1934)*
Whirl of Joy, The. *Bessie Brown (1922)*
Whitman Sisters Revue. *James Rushing (1931)*
Who Stole the Money. *Viola McCoy (1924)*
Winners All. *Ida Brown (1928)*

X-Glamour Girls Revue. *Hannah Sylvester (1962)*

Yeah-Man: *Rosa Henderson (1932); Edith Wilson (1932)*
Yellow Girl Revue. *Bessie Smith (1927–9)*
Yelping Hounds: *Walter Pichon (1932–4); Mamie Smith (1932–4)*

Song Index

This is an index of over 6,800 blues and non-blues songs credited as having been written by the singers in this book. Co-authors are not noted unless they too are singers herein, in which case they are coupled.

Sources are from standard reference indices, sheet music, phonograph records, personal interviews, articles, books, correspondence and other material.

The subject of blues authorship is, at the very least, a controversial one due mainly to the nature of the art form. Some of this music has been drawn from the public domain of black folk roots or old melodies and phrases within the oral tradition. Songs frequently were not legally copyrighted, while the copyrights of others were incorrect or had long expired. Some held wrong or assumptive composer credits or no credit at all. Others were multiple versions of the same song, often with different titles and as many authors. And to add to the confusion, apparently some identical or variant songs are occasionally credited to present-day singers.

Certainly, most songs listed in this index are true originals and copyright holders are acknowledged when known, but due to the large number of similar titles, lyrics, melodies and themes, aural comparisons were not always possible to ascertain duplicates. My apologies to any holder whose song may be unintentionally mistitled or miscredited, and substantiated corrections and additions are welcome.

It is suggested that all spelling, punctuation, language idioms and other title variants be checked when locating a song. All titles beginning with the articles "A," "An" and "The" are indexed by the second word.

My appreciation to Joseph G. Palladino and Maria Dostis for their work on this index.

A&V Railroad Blues. *Eurreal Montgomery*
ABC's. *Pleasant Joseph*
"A" Jump: *John Tyler Adams/Shirley Griffith*
Aberdeen Mississippi Blues. *Booker White*
Abide My Wish. *John Shines*
Abilene. *Sam Hopkins*
Absent Minded Blues. *Thomas Delaney*
Ace Boogie. *Roosevelt Sykes*
Ace's Blues. *Luther Johnson*
Ace's Shuffle. *Louis Myers*
Across the Atlantic Ocean. *Alexander Moore*
Across the Bay Blues. *Louis Robinson*
Across the Hall Blues *Albert Luandrew*
Act Like You Love Me. *James Rogers*
Adam. *Richard Havens*
Adam Bit the Apple. *Joseph Turner*
Advice Blues. *Beulah Wallace*
Afraid to Trust Them. *Ernest Lawlars*
After Dinner Blues. *Rufus Perryman*
After Five Long Years. *Willie Dixon*
After Hours. *Vernon Harrison*
After It's Over. *Charles Berry*
After the Fight. *Mercy Dee Walton*
After While You Will Be Sorry. *Joseph Turner*
After You There Won't Be Nobody Else. *James Pryor*
Ah Come On Honey. *Alexander Lightfoot*
Ah'w Baby. *Marion Walter Jacobs*
Aimlessly Driftin'. *Charles Berry*
Ain't a Gonna Do. *Woodrow Guthrie*
Ain't Doing Bad Doin' Nothing. *Ted Bogan*
Ain't Doin' Too Bad. *Edward Boyd*
Ain't Goin' Let You Worry My Life No More. *Huddie Ledbetter*
Ain't Goin' to Do Like I Used to Do. *Frank Stokes*

Ain't Gonna Cry No More. *Rufus Perryman*
Ain't Gonna Drink No More. *Peter Clayton*
Ain't Gonna Worry Any More. *Clifton Chenier*
Ain't Gonna Worry My Life Anymore. *Riley King*
Ain't Got But 15¢. *Oscar Wills*
Ain't It Crazy? *Sam Hopkins*
Ain't It Sad? *Edward Harris*
Ain't Never Had Nothing. *James Dawkins*
Ain't No Big Deal. *Mathis James Reed*
Ain't No Big Deal on You. *Milton Campbell*
Ain't No Business We Can Do. *Peter Clayton*
Ain't No Time for a Fussin'. *Mathis James Reed*
Ain't Nothing But a Texas Boogie on a Harpsichord. *Peter Chatman*
Ain't Superstitious. *Chester Burnett*
Ain't That a Shame? *Antoine Domino*
Ain't That a Shame? *William Dupree*
Ain't That Cold Baby? *Aaron Walker*
Ain't That Dandy Chicken Shift? *Clarence Brown*
Ain't That Love? *Ray Charles*
Ain't That Lovin' You Baby? *Mathis James Reed*
Ain't You Sorry? *Mance Lipscomb*
Airplane Blues: *John Estes/Hammie Nixon*
Airplane Blues. *Sam Hopkins*
Airplane Blues. *Sonny Terry*
Airport Blues. *Silas Hogan*
Airy Man Blues. *Charlie Jackson*
Alabama Blues. *Booker White*
Alabama Boogie. *John Lee*
Alberta. *Peter Chatman*
Alberta. *Huddie Ledbetter*
Alcatraz Blues. *Frank Edwards*
Alex Thinking. *Alexander Moore*
Alimonia Blues. *John Lee Hooker*
Alimony. *Tommy Tucker*
Alimony Blues. *Joe Johnson*
Alimony Blues. *Eddie Vinson*
Alki Blues. *Leroy Carr*
All Aboard. *Charles Berry*
All Aboard. *McKinley Morganfield*
All Alone Blues. *Sonny Terry*
All Around Man. *Lee Jackson*
All by Myself. *William Broonzy*
All by Myself. *Peter Chatman*
All by Myself. *Antoine Domino*
All Day Long. *Clifton Chenier*
All Days Are Good Days. *Roosevelt Sykes*
All Down Blues. *Wilbert Ellis*
All for Business. *James Dawkins*
All I Got Is Gone. *Sam Hopkins*
All in Your Mind. *Phillip Walker*
All Is Forgiven. *Charles Brown*
All Is Well. *Amos Milburn*
All My Friends Are Gone. *Gary Davis*
All My Love in Vain. *Sonny Boy Williamson (Alex Miller)*
All My Money Gone. *Roosevelt Sykes*
All My Money Gone. *John Young*
All My Whole Life. *Samuel Maghett*
All Night Long. *Clifton Chenier*
All Night Long. *Nehemiah James*
All Night Long. *Samuel Maghett*
All Night Long. *Aaron Walker*
All Night Long. *Amos Wells*
All of My Life. *Lonnie Brooks*
All on Account of You. *Rufus Perryman*
All Over Again. *Riley King*
All She Wants to Do Is Rock. *Wynonie Harris*
All the Way. *Edward Boyd*
All Walks of Life. *James Cotton*
All Your Love. *Samuel Maghett*
All Your Love. *Otis Rush*
Alley Boogie. *Lucille Bogan*
Alley Bound Blues. *Curtis Jones*
Alligator Man. *John Williamson*
Alligator Pond Went Dry, The. *Victoria Spivey*
Almost Gone. *Charles Sayles*
Almost Grown. *Charles Berry*
Alone. *Willie Dixon*
Along About Midnight. *Eddie Jones*
Alphonsia Blues: *Ida Cox/Jesse Crump*
Angel. *James Hendrix*
Angel Child. *Peter Chatman*
Angels in Harlem. *Peter Clayton*
Angola Penitentiary Blues. *Robert Pete Williams*
Animal Farm. *McHouston Baker*
Animal in Me, The. *Peter Chatman*
Anna Lou Blues. *Albert Luandrew*
Anna Lou Blues. *Hudson Whittaker*
Annie Lee. *Robert Nighthawk*
Annie Mae Blues. *Fred McDowell*
Anniversary Blue Yodel. *James Rodgers*
Another Mule Kickin' in My Stall. *Roosevelt Holts*
Another Night to Cry. *Alonzo Johnson*
Anthony Boy. *Charles Berry*
Any Kind of a Man Would Be Better Than You. *Hattie McDaniel*
Any Old Time. *James Rodgers*
Anytime for You. *Major Merriweather*
Anytime Is the Right Time (see: Nighttime Is the Right Time)
Apologize. *John Lee Hooker*
Appealing Blues. *McKinley Morganfield*
Are You Experienced? *James Hendrix*
Arguing and Boodling. *John Shines*
Arkansas Boogie. *Charles Musselwhite*
Arkansas Road Blues. *Victoria Spivey*
Army Blues. *Booker White*
Army Camp Harmony Blues. *Gertrude Rainey*
Army Man in Vietnam. *Joe Lee Williams*
Around and Around. *Charles Berry*
Arriving Soon. *Eddie Vinson*
As Long as I Live. *George Smith*
As Long as the World Stands. *John Shines*
Ash Tray Taxi. *Sam Chatmon*
Ashes in My Whiskey. *Walter Davis*
Ashes on My Pillow. *Oran Page*

Ashley Street Blues. *Wesley Wilson*
Ask Me No Questions. *Riley King*
Assembly Call Boogie. *James Yancey*
At Home Blues. *Sam Hopkins*
At My Window. *Woodrow Guthrie*
At the Golden Jubilee. *Thomas Dorsey*
At the (New) Jump Steady Ball. *Thomas Delaney*
Atlanta Boogie. *Charles Sayles*
Atlanta Bounce. *William Perryman*
Atlanta Rag. *Charles Davenport*
Atlanta Special. *Booker White*
Atlanta Strut. *Willie McTell*
Atomic Blues. *Bertha Hill*
Avalon Blues. *John Hurt*
Aw Shucks Hush Your Mouth. *Mathis James Reed*
Away from You. *Charles Berry*
Awful Moaning Blues. *Alger Alexander*
Axe and the Wind. *Willie Dixon*

B&O Blues (see: New B&O Blues)
B&O Blues. *Sam Chatmon*
BB's Gibson Guitar Blues. *Riley King*
BM Special. *Walter Brown McGhee*
BVD Blues. *Roosevelt Sykes*
Babe I'm Leavin'. *Richard Havens*
Baby B Blues. *James Johnson*
Baby Baby. *William Trice*
Baby Be a Boy Child Named After Me. *Thomas Shaw*
Baby Be Strong. *John Lee Hooker*
Baby Blues. *John Lee*
Baby Can't You See? *Arthur Gunter*
(My) Baby (Done) Changed the Lock on That Door. *Sonny Terry*
Baby Child. *Andrew McMahon*
Baby Come Back to Me. *Leroy Carr*
Baby Do Liddle. *Tommy Ridgley*
Baby Doll. *Peter Chatman*
Baby Doll. *Bessie Smith*
Baby Don't Be So Mean. *Charlie Jackson*
Baby Don't Tell on Me. *James Rushing*
Baby Don't Worry. *Sonny Boy Williamson (Alex Miller)*
Baby Don't You Tear My Clothes. *William Broonzy*
Baby How Long. *Walter Brown McGhee*
Baby I Can't Use You No More. *Beulah Wallace*
Baby I Done Got Wise. *William Broonzy*
Baby I Got My Mind Off You. *Sonny Terry*
Baby I Knocked on Your Door. *Sonny Terry*
Baby I Love You. *John Lee Hooker*
Baby I'm Going to Throw You Out. *Alden Bunn*
Baby Keeps On Breaking 'em Down. *Joe Lee Williams*
Baby Let Me Hold Your Hand. *Ray Charles*
Baby Let Me Lay Down. *Fred McDowell*
Baby Let Me Lay It on You. *Gary Davis*
Baby Let's Play House. *Arthur Gunter*
Baby Listen to Me Howl. *Johnie Lewis*
Baby Look at You. *Joseph Turner*
Baby Lou Blues. *Arthur Phelps*
Baby Please Come Back to Me. *Silas Hogan*
Baby Please Don't Go. *Mary Johnson*
Baby Please Loan Me Your Heart. *Charlie Jackson*
Baby Please Set a Date. *Elmore James*
Baby Scratch My Back. *James Moore*
Baby Stop Crying. *Sonny Boy Williamson (Alex Miller)*
Baby Talk. *John Walker*
Baby What You Want Me to Do? *Mathis James Reed*
Baby What's Wrong with You? *Edward Boyd*
Baby Why Don't You Write Me? *Willie Mabon*
Baby Will You Please Help Me? *Charles Musselwhite*
Baby Won't You Tell Me? *John Paul Hammond*
Baby You Broke My Heart. *Aaron Walker*
Baby You Done Wrecked My Life. *Charles Sayles*
Baby You Don't Know. *Pleasant Joseph*
Baby You Just Don't Know. *Woodrow Adams*
Baby You Know It's True. *Eddie Kirkland*
Baby You're Not Going to Make a Fool out of Me. *Sam Hopkins*
Baby's So Sweet. *Mathis James Reed*
Bachelor's Blues. *Pleasant Joseph*
Back Beat. *Edward Boyd*
Back Breaking Blues. *Joseph Turner*
Back Door. *Robert Brown (Washboard Sam)*
Back Door Blues. *James Arnold*
Back Door Blues. *Eddie Vinson*
Back Door Friend. *James Rogers*
Back Door Man. *Willie Dixon*
Back Down Yonder. *Aaron Willis*
Back Home. *Johnny Fuller*
Back Home Blues. *Joe Lee Williams*
Back in the USA. *Charles Berry*
Back on My Feet. *Joe Lee Williams*
Back on the Road Again. *Iverson Minter*
Back Slider Fare You Well. *Huddie Ledbetter*
Back Step Blues. *Francis Blackwell*
Back to Arkansas. *William Broonzy*
Back to Memphis. *Charles Berry*
Back to New Orleans. *Walter Brown McGhee*
Back to the Steel Mill. *John Shines*
Back to the Wall. *Irene Scruggs*
Back Track. *Marion Walter Jacobs*
Back Yard Back Talk. *Albert Collins*
Backslap. *Edward Boyd*
Backwater Blues. *Bessie Smith*
Bad Acting Woman. *William Broonzy*
Bad Blood. *William Dupree*
Bad Blood. *John Young*
Bad Boy. *Eddie Taylor*
Bad Case of the Blues. *Iverson Minter*
Bad Condition. *James Oden*
Bad Dream Blues. *David Van Ronk*
Bad Feeling Blues. *Arthur Phelps*
Bad Life. *William Dupree*
Bad Living. *Joe Lee Williams*
Bad Love. *Gabriel Brown*
Bad Luck. *Riley King*
Bad Luck. *Luke Miles*
Bad Luck and Trouble. *Clifton Chenier*

SONG INDEX

Bad Luck and Trouble. *John Jenkins*
Bad Luck Blues. *James Arnold*
Bad Luck Blues. *Shirley Griffith*
Bad Luck Blues. *Otis Hicks*
Bad Luck Blues. *Lemon Jefferson*
Bad Luck Blues. *Eddie Jones*
Bad Luck Blues. *Pleasant Joseph*
Bad Luck Dice. *Clifford Gibson*
Bad Luck Man. *William Broonzy*
Bad Luck Overtook Me. *Johnny Fuller*
Bad Luck Time. *James Harris*
Bad News Is Coming. *Luther Allison*
Bad Whiskey. *Robert Brown (Smokey Babe)*
Bad Whiskey Bad Women. *Charles Ross*
Bags Under My Eyes. *James Witherspoon*
Baker Shop Boogie. *Willie Nix*
Baker's Dozen. *McHouston Baker*
Bakershop Blues. *Lemon Jefferson*
Bald Eagle Train. *Booker White*
Bald Head. *Roy Byrd*
Bald Headed Woman. *Sam Hopkins*
Ball and Chain. *Willie Mae Thornton*
Ball and Chain Blues. *Joshua Howell*
Ball and Chain Blues. *Joshua White*
Ball of Twine. *Sam Hopkins*
Ballad of Harriet Tubman. *Woodrow Guthrie*
Ballad of Harry Bridges. *Woodrow Guthrie*
Ballad to Abraham Lincoln. *John Lee Hooker*
Ballin' with Archie. *Leon T. Gross*
Bama Bound Blues. *Ida Cox*
Bamboo. *David Van Ronk*
Bang Bang Bang Bang. *John Lee Hooker*
Banjo. *Charles Sayles*
Banjo Rag. *Bill Williams*
Banty Rooster Blues. *Charley Patton*
Baptize Me in Wine. *Jalacy Hawkins*
Barber Shop Rag. *James Yancey*
Bare Foot Rock. *Herman Parker*
Barefoot Boy. *Pleasant Joseph*
Barking Bull Dog. *Walter Brown McGhee*
Barnyard Dance. *Carl Martin*
Barrelhouse Blues. *Roosevelt Holts*
Barrelhouse Flat Blues. *Mary Johnson*
Barron Boogie. *Clyde Bernhardt*
Bass Key Boogie. *Eurreal Montgomery*
Bassology. *Albert Luandrew*
Baton Rouge Breakdown. *Moses Smith*
Bayou Drive. *Clifton Chenier*
Be Careful. *Edward Boyd*
Be Careful. *John Brim*
Be Careful. *Alonzo Johnson*
Be My Baby. *Albert Luandrew*
Be My Guest. *Antoine Domino*
Be Ready When He Comes. *Nehemiah James*
Be What You Want to Be. *Koko Taylor*
Beale Street Sugar. *John Estes*
Beale Town Bound. *Frank Stokes*
Beans Beans Beans. *Sam Hopkins*
Bear-Mash Blues: *IdaCox/Jesse Crump*
Beat from Rampart Street. *Larry Johnson*
Beat It on Down the Line. *Jesse Fuller*
Beat Up Team. *Otis Spann*
Beat You Doing It. *Edith North Johnson*
Beaumont Blues. *Phillip Walker*
Beautician Blues. *Riley King*
Beautiful Delilah. *Charles Berry*
Beautiful World. *Victoria Spivey*
Becky Deem. *Huddie Ledbetter*
Bed Sitter Girl. *John Holder*
Bed Spring Blues. *Booker White*
Bed Springs Blues. *Lemon Jefferson*
Bed Time Blues. *Virginia Liston*
Bedroom Blues. *Beulah Wallace*
Beedle Um Bum. *Thomas Dorsey*
Beef Stake Blues. *James Thomas*
Been Around the World. *John Littlejohn*
Been in Jail. *Woodrow Guthrie*
Been Mistreated Blues. *Thomas Dorsey*
Been 'round a Long Time. *John Williamson*
Beer Drinkin' Woman. *Vernon Harrison*
Beer Drinking Woman. *Peter Chatman*
Beer Garden Blues. *Sonny Terry*
Beggin' and Cryin'. *Walter Brown McGhee*
Beggin' Back. *Lemon Jefferson*
Beggin' My Baby. *Milton Campbell*
Begging Woman. *Pleasant Joseph*
Behind the Plow. *John Lee Hooker*
Believe I'll Make a Change. *Robert Brown (Washboard Sam)*
Believe In Me. *Milton Campbell*
Bell Cow Blues. *Alger Alexander*
Bellevue Blues. *Leroy Dallas*
Bells Are Ringing, The. *Smiley Lewis*
Bertha. *Earl Hooker*
Bertha May. *Peter Chatman*
Bessemer Bound Blues. *Thomas Dorsey*
Best Wishes. *Roy Milton*
Better Cut That Out. *Thomas Dorsey*
Better Let My Gal Alone. *Hudson Whittaker*
Better to Be by Yourself. *Al King*
Betty Jean. *Charles Berry*
Betty Jean. *Mercy Dee Walton*
Between Midnight and Dawn. *Peter Chatman*
Bicycle Riding Mama. *Roosevelt Sykes*
Biddle Street Blues: *Walter Davis/Henry Townsend*
Big Apple Blues. *John Lee Williamson*
Big Beat, The. *Antoine Domino*
Big Bell, The. *Edward Boyd*
Big Ben. *Roosevelt Sykes*
Big Bill Blues. *William Broonzy*
Big Bill's Boogie. *William Broonzy*
Big Black Belt. *Victoria Spivey*
Big Blues, The. *Taj Mahal*
Big Boat. *Willie Dixon*
Big Boat up the River. *Booker White*
Big Boss Man. *Willie Dixon*

Big Boy Blues. *Gertrude Rainey*
Big Car Blues. *Sam Hopkins*
Big Change. *Willie Mae Thornton*
Big City Blues. *Wynonie Harris*
Big City Blues. *Major Merriweather*
Big City Girl. *Peter Chatman*
Big "D" Blues. *Oran Page*
Big Fat Mama. *Joe Lee Williams*
Big Fat Mama Blues. *Tommy Johnson*
Big Fine Girl. *James Witherspoon*
Big Fine Thing. *Norman Green*
Big Four Blues. *Leroy Carr*
Big Hip Mama. *Alexander Seward*
Big Joe's Lonesome Blues. *Joseph Turner*
Big John's Boogie. *John Wrencher*
Big Leg Blues. *John Hurt*
Big Leg Mama. *James Arnold*
Big Leg Woman. *Johnny Temple*
Big Mama's New Love. *Willie Mae Thornton*
Big Momma Little Momma. *Willie Dixon*
Big Night Blues. *Lemon Jefferson*
Big One, A. *Victoria Spivey*
Big Question, The. *Edward Boyd*
Big Question, The. *Clayton Love*
Big Question. *Walter Brown McGhee*
Big Road Blues. *Tommy Johnson*
Big Ship Blues. *James Arnold*
Big Stars Falling Blues. *Hudson Whittaker*
Big Talk. *Joseph Young*
Big Time Girl. *Peter Chatman*
Big Time Woman. *Roosevelt Sykes*
Big Town Playboy. *John Jones*
Big Town Playboy. *Eddie Taylor*
Big Walter's Boogie. *Walter Horton*
Big Wheel. *Joseph Turner*
Big World. *Floyd Jones*
Biggest Thing That Man Has Ever Done, The. *Woodrow Guthrie*
Bill Draw. *Virginia Liston*
Billie's Gumbo Blues. *Billie Pierce*
Bill's Rag. *Bill Williams*
Billy Boy's Blues. *William Arnold*
Billy's Boogie. *William Branch*
Bingo. *Lonnie Brooks*
Bio. *Charles Berry*
Bird in a Cage. *Otis Spann*
Bird Nest Bound. *Charley Patton*
Birmingham Bessemer Blues. *Hudson Whittaker*
Birmingham Blues. *John Lee Hooker*
Biscuit Bakin' Mama. *Eddie Burns*
Biscuit Baking Woman. *John Lee Williamson*
Biscuit Roller Blues. *James Arnold*
Bite Again, Bite Again. *Wynonie Harris*
Black and Evil. *Sam Hopkins*
Black Angel Blues. *Hudson Whittaker*
Black Brown and White. *William Broonzy*
Black Cat Blues. *Victoria Spivey*
Black Cat Bone. *Sam Hopkins*
Black Cat Bone: *Walter Brown McGhee/Sonny Terry*
Black Cat Bone Blues. *Booker White*
Black Cat Cross My Trail. *Peter Chatman*
Black Cat Hoot Owl Blues. *Thomas Dorsey*
Black Cat Trail. *Edward Harris*
Black Cow Blues. *Charley Patton*
Black Crepe Blues. *Jesse Crump*
Black Crepe Blues. *Booker White*
Black Dog Blues. *Arthur Phelps*
Black Eyed Peas and Hog Jowls. *Alexander Moore*
Black Gal. *Walter Horton*
Black Gal. *Mance Lipscomb*
Black Gal. *Robert Shaw*
Black Gal Blues. *Mary Johnson*
Black Gal Gets There Just the Same. *Charles Davenport*
Black Gal You're Sure Looking Warm. *Joe Lee Williams*
Black Ghost. *Robert Brown (Smokey Babe)*
Black Ghost Blues. *Sam Hopkins*
Black Girl. *Huddie Ledbetter*
Black Horse Blues. *Lemon Jefferson*
Black Jack Blues. *Gabriel Brown*
Black London Blues. *John Holder*
Black Man Blues. *Mary Johnson*
Black Mare Blues. *Tommy Johnson*
Black Mattie. *John Estes*
Black Minnie. *Fred McDowell*
Black Panther Blues. *John Lee Williamson*
Black Pony Blues. *Arthur Crudup*
Black Snake Blues. *Victoria Spivey*
Black Snake Moan (see: That Black Snake Moan)
Black Snake Swinger. *Victoria Spivey*
Black Spatch Blues. *John Erby*
Black Train Blues. *Booker White*
Black Wolf Blues. *William Dupree*
Blackjack. *Ray Charles*
Blackmarket Blues. *Bertha Hill*
Blacksnake. *John Lee Hooker*
Blake's Rag. *Bill Williams*
Blake's Worried Blues. *Arthur Phelps*
Blame It on the Blues. *Thomas Dorsey*
Bless You My Darling. *Alden Bunn*
Blind Boy Blues. *Henry Brown*
Blind Lemon. *Huddie Ledbetter*
Blind Lemon's Penitentiary. *Lemon Jefferson*
Blind Love. *Riley King*
Blind Man. *Pernell Charity*
Blind Man. *McKinley Morganfield*
Block and Tackle. *Robert Brown (Washboard Sam)*
Blood Hound Blues. *Victoria Spivey*
Blood Ran Like Wine. *John Shines*
Blood Thirsty Blues. *Victoria Spivey*
Bloodstain's on the Wall. *Gus Jenkins*
Bloody Murder. *Otis Spann*
Bloomington Closer. *Luther Allison*
Blow Wind Blow. *McKinley Morganfield*
Blowin' the Fuses: *Walter Brown McGhee/Sonny Terry*
Blowin' to California. *Wynonie Harris*
Blowing Down This Old Dusty Road. *Woodrow Guthrie*

SONG INDEX

Blowing the Blues. *George Smith*
Blue and Disgusted. *Peter Chatman*
Blue and Lonesome. *Peter Chatman*
Blue and Low. *Arbee Stidham*
Blue Bass. *Roosevelt Sykes*
Blue Blues. *Walter Davis*
Blue Blues. *Bessie Smith*
Blue Brew. *Peter Chatman*
Blue Carnegie. *Mathis James Reed*
Blue Coat Man. *Edward Boyd*
Blue Devil Blues. *Alger Alexander*
Blue Feeling. *Walter Brown McGhee*
Blue Feeling Today. *Charles Musselwhite*
Blue Fog. *George Smith*
Blue Ghost Blues. *Walter Davis*
Blue Ghost Blues. *Alonzo Johnson*
Blue Guitar. *Earl Hooker*
Blue Horizon, The. *John Shines*
Blue in the Morning. *Joe Hill Louis*
Blue Lights. *Marion Walter Jacobs*
Blue Monday. *John Lee Hooker*
Blue Monday. *Smiley Lewis*
Blue Monday Blues. *Edward Boyd*
Blue Monday Blues. *Charlie Jackson*
Blue Monday Blues. *James Witherspoon*
Blue Monday up on Sugar Hill: *Leola B Grant/Wesley Wilson*
Blue 'n' Whistling: *Francis Blackwell/Leroy Carr*
Blue Piano in Bordeaux. *Willie Mabon*
Blue Shadows Fall. *Earl Hooker*
Blue Shadows Falling. *Herman Parker*
Blue Soul. *Lowell Fulson*
Blue Switch. *George Smith*
Blue This Evening. *Peter Chatman*
Blue Tumbleweeds. *Dave Alexander*
Blue Yodel (12 versions). *James Rodgers*
Bluebird. *John Lee Hooker*
Bluebird Blues. *John Lee Williamson*
Bluer Than Blue. *Joseph Turner*
Blues, A. *Francis Blackwell*
Blues After Hours. *Connie Crayton*
Blues After Hours. *Arthur Gunter*
Blues Ain't Nothin' Else But. *Ida Cox*
Blues All Around My Bed. *Sonny Terry*
Blues All the Time. *Clifton Chenier*
Blues and Trouble. *Sidney Maiden*
Blues and Trouble. *James Witherspoon*
Blues and Trouble. *John Young*
Blues Around Midnight. *Willie McTell*
Blues Around the World. *Joe Lee Williams*
Blues at Midnight. *Leonard Caston*
Blues at Sunrise. *Albert King*
Blues Before Sunrise: *Francis Blackwell/Leroy Carr*
Blues, Blues. *David Edwards*
Blues Blues Blues. *William Perryman*
Blues City Shake Down. *John Mayall*
Blues Do Me a Favor. *Joseph Hutto*
Blues Don't Like Nobody, The. *Otis Spann*
Blues for Albert. *James Yancey*
Blues for Chantel. *Willie Mabon*
Blues for Charlie O'Brien. *Henry Brown*
Blues for Fonessa. *Joseph Hutto*
Blues for Marcelle. *Louis Myers*
Blues for Marili. *Aaron Walker*
Blues for Mayor Daley. *Amos Wells*
Blues for Moot. *Wilbert Ellis*
Blues for My Baby. *Peter Chatman*
Blues for My Baby. *Connie Crayton*
Blues for My Baby. *John Lee Hooker*
Blues for Queen Elizabeth. *Sam Hopkins*
Blues for Rampart Street. *Ida Cox*
Blues for Reverend King. *George Smith*
Blues for the Lowlands: *Walter Brown McGhee/Sonny Terry*
Blues Got Me Rockin', The. *William Dupree*
Blues Had a Baby, The. *Walter Brown McGhee*
Blues Had a Baby and They Named It Rock and Roll, The. *McKinley Morganfield*
Blues in E. *Sam Chatmon*
Blues in G. *Mance Lipscomb*
Blues in Moscow. *John Holder*
Blues in the Bottle. *Mance Lipscomb*
Blues in the Dark. *James Rushing*
Blues in the Ghetto. *Connie Crayton*
Blues in the Ghetto. *James Dawkins*
Blues in the Morning. *Walter Horton*
Blues in the Rain. *Eddie Taylor*
Blues Is a Botheration. *Otis Spann*
Blues Is a Feeling. *Sam Hopkins*
Blues Is Everywhere, The. *Peter Chatman*
Blues Is Here To Stay. *Edward Boyd*
Blues Is Troubles. *Peter Chatman*
Blues Jam. *Aaron Walker*
Blues Knock at My Door. *Edward Harris*
Blues Leave Me Alone. *James Rogers*
Blues Never Die. *Otis Spann*
Blues of Happiness. *Walter Brown McGhee*
Blues Oh Blues. *Gertrude Rainey*
Blues on Blues. *William Arnold*
Blues on Central Avenue. *Joseph Turner*
Blues on My Brain. *Rufus Perryman*
Blues over Europe. *John Holder*
Blues Power. *Albert King*
Blues Rock. *Aaron Walker*
Blues 'round My Door. *Alonzo Johnson*
Blues Stay Away from Me. *Joseph Hutto*
Blues Stomp. *Henry Brown*
Blues That Made Me Drunk. *John Lee Williamson*
Blues What Am, The. *Robert Brown (Washboard Sam)*
Blues When It Rains. *Buster Brown*
Blues Will Prank with Your Soul. *Roosevelt Sykes*
Blues with a Feeling. *Marion Walter Jacobs*
Blues with a Whoop. *Sonny Terry*
Blues Won't Let Me Take My Rest, The. *Henry Gray*
Blues You Can't Lose. *Willie Dixon*
Bluesingly Yours. *Peter Chatman*

Bo Diddley. *Ellas McDaniel*
Bo Diddley Is Loose. *Ellas McDaniel*
Bo Diddley's a Gun Slinger. *Ellas McDaniel*
Bo Weavil Blues. *James Arnold*
Bo Weavil Blues. *Gertrude Rainey*
Bo's a Lumberjack. *Ellas McDaniel*
Bo's Blues. *Ellas McDaniel*
Bob Martin Blues. *Albert Luandrew*
Bobby Sox Baby. *James Moore*
Bobby's Rock. *Elmore James*
Bobo Stomp. *Leroy Carr*
Boe Hog Blues. *Alger Alexander*
Bogalusa Boogie. *Clifton Chenier*
Boll Weevil, The. *Huddie Ledbetter*
Bon Ton Roulay (see: New Bon Ton Roulay)
Bon Ton Roule. *Clarence Garlow*
Bones Blues. *J. C. Burris*
Bones Blues. *Granville McGhee*
Boodie Bum Bum. *Will Shade*
Boodle Boo: *Leola B. Grant/Wesley Wilson*
Booger Rooger Blues. *Lemon Jefferson*
Boogie at Midnight. *Roy Brown*
Boogie Chillun. *John Lee Hooker*
Boogie Cross the Country. *Frankie Lee Sims*
Boogie Disease. *Charles Ross*
Boogie Duo. *Peter Chatman*
Boogie Everywhere I Go. *John Lee Hooker*
Boogie Honky Tonky. *Roosevelt Sykes*
Boogie in the Barrel. *Alexander Moore*
Boogie in the Dark. *Mathis James Reed*
Boogie in the Mud. *Sidney Semien*
Boogie Right-On. *Joseph Hutto*
Boogie Rock. *Riley King*
Boogie with the Hook. *John Lee Hooker*
Boogie Woogie Baby. *Eddy Clearwater*
Boogie Woogie Baby. *Cecil Gant*
Boogie Woogie Blue Plate. *Louis Jordan*
Booker T Blues. *Robert Brown (Washboard Sam)*
Boom Boom Boom Boom. *John Lee Hooker*
Boomtown Bill. *Woodrow Guthrie*
Boop Poop a Doop. *Wesley Wilson*
Booster Blues. *Lemon Jefferson*
Boot That Thing. *Roosevelt Sykes*
Bootleg Whiskey. *Arthur Phelps*
Bootleggin' Ain't Good No More. *Theodore Darby*
Bop De Bip. *Roosevelt Sykes*
Bordeaux in My Pirough. *Charles Berry*
Born Blind. *Sonny Boy Williamson (Alex Miller)*
Born Dead. *J. B. Lenoir*
Born in Georgia. *Luther Johnson*
Born in Poverty. *James Dawkins*
Born in Texas. *Silas Hogan*
Born in the Bottoms. *Sam Hopkins*
Born in the Country. *K. C. Douglas*
Born in This Time. *Hi Tide Harris*
Born to Live the Blues. *Walter Brown McGhee*
Born to Love Me. *Willie Dixon*
Born with the Blues. *Peter Chatman*
Borrowed Love. *Irene Scruggs*
Boss of the House. *Joseph Turner*
Bossy Woman. *William Broonzy*
Bottle (Shake) It Up and Go. *Tommy McClennan*
Bottled in Bond. *Henry Brown*
Bound to Lose. *Charles Berry*
Bound to Lose My Mind. *Clarence Garlow*
Bourgeois Blues, The. *Huddie Ledbetter*
'Bout a Spoonful. *Mance Lipscomb*
Bow-Legged Mamma. *Thomas Delaney*
Box Car Shorty. *Pleasant Joseph*
Boy and Girl Thing. *Raymond Agee*
Brakeman's Blues. *James Rodgers*
Bran' New Wagon. *James Rushing*
Brand New Day Blues. *Charlie Burse*
Break 'em On Down. *Joe Lee Williams*
Break It On Down. *James Pryor*
Break It Up. *Marion Walter Jacobs*
Breaking My Back. *Louis Rawls*
Brenda. *Peter Chatman*
Brenda Lee. *Charles Berry*
Bricks in My Pillow. *Robert Nighthawk*
Bright Eyes. *Robert Brown (Washboard Sam)*
Bright Eyes. *Charlie Jackson*
Bright Lights, Big City. *Mathis James Reed*
Bright Lights in the City. *Richard Havens*
Bright Street Jump: *John Tyler Adams/Shirley Griffith*
Bring It On Home. *Willie Dixon*
Bring It On Home. *John Mars*
Bring It On Home. *Henry Williams*
Bring It to Jerome. *Ellas McDaniel*
Bring Me a Little Water, Silvy. *Huddie Ledbetter*
Bring Me Flowers While I'm Living. *Peetie Wheatstraw*
Bringin' My Baby Back Home. *Joe Lee Williams*
Brixton Blues. *John Holder*
Broadway Boogie. *Peter Chatman*
Broke and Hungry. *Walter Davis*
Broke and Hungry. *John Estes*
Broke and Hungry. *Lemon Jefferson*
Broke and Hungry. *Albert Luandrew*
Broke and Hungry Blues. *Major Merriweather*
Broke Down Engine Blues. *Willie McTell*
Broke Man Blues. *James Arnold*
Broken Arrow. *Charles Berry*
Broken Heart. *K. C. Douglas*
Broken Heart Blues. *William Dupree*
Broken Hearted Blues. *Willie Dixon*
Broken Hearted Blues. *Gertrude Rainey*
Broken Hearted Blues. *James Rogers*
Broken Hearted Man. *Robert Pete Williams*
Broken Hearted Ragged and Dirty Too. *John Estes*
Broken Hearted Rollin' Tears. *Lonnie Brooks*
Broken Yo-Yo. *Alger Alexander*
Brother James. *Joe Lee Williams*
Brotherhood. *Edward Boyd*
Brother's Boogie. *Eurreal Montgomery*
Brought It All on Myself. *Raymond Agee*
Brown-Eyed Handsome Man. *Charles Berry*

SONG INDEX

Brown Mule. *George Smith*
Brown Skin Gals. *Clarence Lofton*
Brown Skin Woman. *Albert Luandrew*
Brown Skin Woman. *Harmon Ray.*
Brown Skin Women. *Clifton Chenier*
Brown Skin Women Blues. *Sam Chatmon*
Brown Skinned Woman. *James Rogers*
Brownie's (New) Blues. *Walter Brown McGhee*
Brownskin Gal I Got My Eyes on You. *Jesse Fuller*
Brownsville. *Walter Lewis*
Brownsville Blues. *John Estes*
Bubblegum. *Bill Williams*
Buck and Wing. *Jesse Fuller*
Buck-Town Blues. *Arthur Phelps*
Buckwheat Cakes. *Charles Davenport*
Bud Russell Blues. *Sam Hopkins*
Buddy. *Johnny Fuller*
Buddy Brown Blues. *James Arnold*
Build Myself a Cage. *David Edwards*
Built for Comfort. *Willie Dixon*
Built Right on the Ground. *Theodore Darby*
Bukka's Jitterbug Swing. *Booker White*
Bull Cow. *Huddie Ledbetter*
Bull Cow Blues. *William Broonzy*
Bull Head, Go Ahead Angie. *Eddie Burns*
Bull Headed Woman. *James Arnold*
Bullcow Blues. *Eddie Taylor*
Bum Can't Do You No Good, A. *Victoria Spivey*
Bumble Bee. *Lizzie Douglas*
Bumble Bee Blues. *Norman Green*
Bumblebee Bumblebee. *John Lee Hooker*
Bunker Hill Blues. *Frank Stokes*
Burnin' in L. A. *Sam Hopkins*
Burnin' Love. *Eddie Kirkland*
Burning Fire. *Otis Spann*
Burning Hell. *John Lee Hooker*
Burnt Child Afraid of Fire. *Sonny Terry*
Bury Me Back in the USA. *Eddie Burns*
Bus Driver. *McKinley Morganfield*
Bus Station Blues. *John Lee Hooker*
Business Man. *Willie Dixon*
Business You're Doin'. *Sam Hopkins*
Bust Up Blues. *Ishmon Bracey*
Busters Boogie. *Theodore Taylor*
But I Forgive You. *Hudson Whittaker*
But I'll Be Back. *Louis Jordan*
But on the Other Hand, Baby. *Percy Mayfield*
Butterscotch. *Charles Berry*
Buttin' in other Folks Buzzness. *Thomas Delaney*
Buy Me an Airplane. *Sidney Maiden*
Buzz Buzz Buzz. *Henry Townsend*
Buzz Me Baby. *James Moore*
Buzzin'. *James Moore*
By Myself. *Jimmy McCracklin*
By Myself. *William Broonzy*
By the Spoonful. *J. D. Short*
By Yourself. *Victoria Spivey*
Bye Bye Baby. *James Rushing*
Bye Bye Baby. *Aaron Walker*
Bye Bye Baby. *Viola Wells*
Bye Bye Baby Blues. *Roy Milton*
Bye Bye Bird. *Sonny Boy Williamson (Alex Miller)*
Bye Bye Bird. *Willie Dixon*
Bye Bye Blues. *Tommy Johnson*
Bye Bye Johnny. *Charles Berry*

C and A Blues. *Peetie Wheatstraw*
CB Blues. *John Shines*
CC and O Blues, The. *Walter Brown McGhee*
CCC Blues. *Robert Brown (Washboard Sam)*
CC Woman. *McKinley Morganfield*
C Rocker. *Peter Chatman*
CV Wine Blues. *Chester Burnett*
Cabbage Greens. *William Dupree*
Cabbage Patch. *Estella Yancey*
Cage of Apes. *Sara Martin*
Caldonia. *James Cotton*
Caldonia. *Louis Jordan*
Caldonia Blues. *Beulah Wallace*
California. *Albert King*
California Blues. *Chester Burnett*
California Boogie. *Chester Burnett*
California Showers. *Sam Hopkins*
Calinda. *Clifton Chenier*
Call It Stormy Monday. *Aaron Walker*
Call Me the Wolf. *Chester Burnett*
Call Me When You Need Me. *James Harris*
Call the Asylum. *Mercy Dee Walton*
Call the Doctor. *James Pryor*
Callin' Corrine. *Frankie Jaxon*
Callin' My Mama. *Sonny Terry*
Camille. *William Dupree*
Can Anybody Take Sweet Mama's Place? *Beulah Wallace*
Can Be Your Friend. *James Pryor*
Can I Be Your Man a Little While? *James Pryor*
Can I Wash Your Clothes? (see: Wash Your Clothes)
Can You Hear Me? *James Hendrix*
Canadian Walk. *Albert Luandrew*
Canary Bird. *McKinley Morganfield*
Candy Kitchen. *Charles Musselwhite*
Candy Man Blues. *John Hurt*
Candyman. *Gary Davis*
Cane River. *James Witherspoon*
Canned Heat Blues. *Tommy Johnson*
Cannonball. *Edward Boyd*
Can't Be Successful. *Sam Hopkins*
Can't Do It. *John Williamson*
Can't Find My Way. *Raymond Agee*
Can't Find Nobody to Do Like My Old Daddy Do. *Sara Martin*
Can't Get Along with You. *John Shines*
Can't Get No Grindin'. *McKinley Morganfield*
Can't Get That Woman off My Mind. *Sam Hopkins*
Can't Hardly Get Along. *Johnie Lewis*
Can't Help But Crying Sometimes. *Joshua White*
Can't Hold Back the Tears. *Milton Campbell*

Can't Hold Out. *John Williamson*
Can't Hold Out Much Longer. *Marion Walter Jacobs*
Can't Last Too Long. *Henry Gray*
Can't Make Another Day. *Edith North Johnson*
Can't Read Can't Write Blues. *Joseph Turner*
Can't Stop Loving My Baby. *Elmore James*
Can't Wait No Longer. *Michael Bloomfield*
Can't You Hear Me Talking to You? *Riley King*
Canton Mississippi Breakdown. *Elmore James*
Captain, Captain. *Mance Lipscomb*
Car Machine Blues. *William Borum*
Caress Me Baby. *Mathis James Reed*
Carnegie Boogie. *Vernon Harrison*
Carol. *Charles Berry*
Carrie. *Edith Wilson*
Carrie Lee. *J. B. Lenoir*
Carried Water for the Elephant. *Leroy Carr*
Casino Trick Stick. *James Dawkins*
Castles Are Made of Sand. *James Hendrix*
Cat Squirrel (see: Mississippi Blues)
Catfish Blues. *K. C. Douglas*
Caught Him Doing It. *Thomas Dorsey*
Caught My Man and Gone. *Iverson Minter*
Cecil Boogie. *Cecil Gant*
Cecil's Jam Session. *Cecil Gant*
Cell Bound Blues. *Gertrude Rainey*
Cell No. 13 Blues. *William Broonzy*
Cha Cha Cha in Blue. *Amos Wells*
Chain Gang. *Richard Havens*
Chain Gang Blues. *James Arnold*
Chain Gang Blues. *Thomas Dorsey*
Chain Gang Bound. *Amos Easton*
Chains and Things. *Riley King*
Change Gotta Be Made, A. *Joe Lee Williams*
Change My Way. *Chester Burnett*
Change Your Way. *Sam Hopkins*
Charlie Cherry. *Melvin Jackson*
Charlie Stone. *Larry Johnson*
Chasing the Fox. *Sonny Terry*
Chattanooga Woman. *Clyde Bernhardt*
Chauffeur Blues. *Robert Brown (Washboard Sam)*
Cheater Can't Win, A. *Walter Brown McGhee*
Cheatin'. *Antoine Domino*
Check Up on My Baby. *Harmon Ray*
Check Up on My Baby. *John Lee Williamson*
Check Yourself. *Lowell Fulson*
Checking on My Woman. *Fention Robinson*
Cherry Ball Blues. *Nehemiah James*
Cherry Hill Blues. *Irene Scruggs*
Cherry Picking Blues: *Ida Cox/Jesse Crump*
Cherry Red. *Joseph Turner*
Chewed Up Grass. *Joseph Turner*
Chicago Blues (see: New Chicago Blues).
Chicago Blues. *John Jones*
Chicago Blues. *Otis Spann*
Chicago Boogie. *Joseph Hutto*
Chicago Bound. *James Rogers*
Chicago Bound. *Sonny Boy Williamson (Alex Miller)*
Chicago Bound Blues. *Ida Cox*
Chicago Breakdown. *Major Merriweather*
Chicago Breakdown. *Charles Ross*
Chicago Hop. *John Sellers*
Chicago Is Just That Way. *Edward Boyd*
Chicago Monkey Man Blues. *Ida Cox*
Chicago on My Mind. *James Dawkins*
Chicken, The. *Bill Williams*
Chicken a la Blues. *Pleasant Joseph*
Chicken Ain't Nothin' but a Bird, A. *Walter Lewis*
Chicken Raid. *Frank Edwards*
Chicken Shack. *William Dupree*
Chicken Shack. *John Walker*
Chicken Shack Boogie. *Amos Milburn*
Chief Tuscaloosa. *John Shines*
Chief's E-Flat Blues. *Wilbert Ellis*
Childhood Sweetheart. *Charles Berry*
Chimes Blues. *Charles Davenport*
Chinch Bug Blues. *Lemon Jefferson*
Chinese Blues. *Ethel Waters*
Chinese Man Blues. *Eurreal Montgomery*
Chirping the Blues. *Alberta Hunter*
Chock House Blues. *Lemon Jefferson*
Choo Choo. *Peter Chatman*
Christina. *Peter Chatman*
Christine. *Walter Horton*
Christmas. *Charles Berry*
Christmas Blues. *Henry Townsend*
Christmas Blues. *Joe Lee Williams*
Christmas Morning Blues. *John Lee Williamson*
Christmas Time Blues. *Roy Milton*
Christmas Time Is Coming. *Sam Hopkins*
Christmas Without Santa Claus. *Victoria Spivey*
Chuck's Beat. *Charles Berry*
Chump Man Blues. *Arthur Phelps*
Church Bell Tone. *John Lee Hooker*
Church Bells Ring. *Joe Lee Williams*
Churnin' Man Blues. *Peter Chatman*
Cigarette Blues. *Willie McTell*
Cincinnati Blues. *Jesse Fuller*
Cincinnati Flow Rag. *Gary Davis*
Cincinnati Shout. *Lewis Muse*
Circle Around the Sun. *John Lee*
Circle Round the Moon. *Charley Patton*
City Girl. *Michael Bloomfield*
Clap Your Hands. *Peter Chatman*
Cleanhead Blues. *Eddie Vinson*
Cleanhead Is Back. *Eddie Vinson*
Clementine Blues. *Alonzo Johnson*
Climbing on Top of the Hill. *Sonny Terry*
Close Down Boogie. *James Dawkins*
Close to You. *Alden Bunn*
Close to You. *Willie Dixon*
Close Together. *Mathis James Reed*
Closed Door. *Victoria Spivey*
Cloud Sailin'. *Freddie King*
Cloudy Day. *Lowell Fulson*
Club Nitty Gritty. *Charles Berry*

SONG INDEX

C'mon If You're Comin'. *Walter Brown McGhee*
Coal Black Mare. *Arthur Crudup*
Coal Man Blues. *Joshua Howell*
Coalman Blues. *Charlie Jackson*
Cocaine Blues. *Gary Davis*
Coffee Blues. *Sam Hopkins*
Coffee Blues. *John Hurt*
Coffee Pot Blues. *Charlie Jackson*
Cold Black Mare. *Moses Smith*
Cold Blooded Woman. *Roy Milton*
Cold Chills. *Henry Gray*
Cold Chills. *John Lee Hooker*
Cold Chilly Woman. *Willie Mabon*
Cold Feeling. *Dave Alexander*
Cold Feeling. *Iverson Minter*
Cold Feet. *Albert King*
Cold Hearted Blues. *John Jenkins*
Cold Hearted Mama Blues. *Arthur Phelps*
Cold Love. *Gabriel Brown*
Cold Love Blues. *Arthur Phelps*
Cold Sweat Blues. *James Dawkins*
Cold White Sheet. *Iverson Minter*
Cold Winter Blues. *James Arnold*
Collin's Body Lies in Sound Cave. *Joshua White*
Collin's Mix. *Albert Collins*
Come a Little Closer. *Arbee Stidham*
Come and Get Me. *Alexander Moore*
Come Back Baby. *Ray Charles*
Come Back Baby. *William Dupree*
Come Back Baby. *Sam Hopkins*
Come Back Baby. *Charles Ross*
Come Back Home. *Son Bonds*
Come Back to Me Baby. *Mack Simmons*
Come by Here. *Riley King*
Come Day, Go Day. *James Oden*
Come Early in the Morning. *John Young*
Come Go Along with Me. *Clifton Chenier*
Come Here and Sit Down on My Knee. *Robert Pete Williams*
Come Home Baby. *Otis Smothers*
Come Home Early. *William Broonzy*
Come Home This Morning. *Edward Boyd*
Come Home This Morning. *Lee Jackson*
Come in Here Baby. *James Walker*
Come On. *Charles Berry*
Come On Around to My House Mama. *Willie McTell*
Come On Baby. *Willie Mabon*
Come On Baby and Take a Walk. *John Lee Williamson*
Come On Back Home. *Sonny Boy Williamson (Alex Miller)*
Come On Boys Let's Do That Messin' Around. *Arthur Phelps*
Come On Coot Do That Thing. *Leola B Grant*
Come On Home. *Edward Boyd*
Come On In. *Thomas Dorsey*
Come On in My Kitchen. *Robert Johnson*
Come On in This House. *Amos Wells*
Come On Over. *John Wrencher*
Come On Over to My House. *Julia Lee*
Come On Rock Little Girl. *Otis Smothers*
Come On Sock It to Me. *Syl Johnson*
Come Over and See Me. *Harmon Ray*
Come Right In. *Ida Cox*
Come See About Me. *George Guy*
Come to Me. *Andrew Odom*
Comeback, The. *Peter Chatman*
Comin' Home. *Janis Joplin*
Comin' Home Someday. *Lowell Fulson*
Coming Back to You Again. *Andrew Hogg*
Coming Home. *Edward Boyd*
Coming Home. *Elmore James*
Coming Home. *Roosevelt Sykes*
Coming Home to You. *Sonny Boy Williamson (Alex Miller)*
Coming Up Fast. *James Oden*
Competition Bed Blues. *Lemon Jefferson*
Concerto in "B Goode". *Charles Berry*
Conductor Took My Baby to Tennessee. *John Wrencher*
Confessin' the Blues. *Walter Brown*
Confession Blues. *Ray Charles*
Contribution Box. *Charles Davenport*
Conversion Blues. *Earl Hooker*
Cool About My Living. *Sam Chatmon*
Cool Cool Blues. *Sonny Boy Williamson (Alex Miller)*
Cool Disposition. *Sonny Boy Williamson (Alex Miller)*
Cool Kind Papa from New Orleans. *Shirley Griffith*
Cool Kind Treatment. *Edward Boyd*
Cool Operator. *Booker White*
Cool Water. *Eddy Clearwater*
Cool Water Blues. *Tommy Johnson*
Cooney Vaughn's Tremblin' Blues. *Eurreal Montgomery*
Cootie for Your Tootie. *Thomas Delaney*
Corinna Blues. *Lemon Jefferson*
Corinne Corinna (see: Corrine Corrina)
Corn-Bread Blues. *Alger Alexander*
Corn Bread, Peas and Black Molasses: *Walter Brown McGhee/Sonny Terry*
Corn Bread Rough. *Huddie Ledbetter*
Corn Likker Blues. *Leroy Carr*
Corn Liquor Blues. *Charlie Jackson*
Corn Liquor Blues. *Bill Williams*
Cornet Pleading Blues. *Edith North Johnson*
Corrine (see: New Corrine)
Corrine. *Walter Davis*
Corrine Corrina: *Armenter Chatmon/Sam Chatmon*
Cotton Crop Blues. *James Cotton*
Cotton Fields. *Huddie Ledbetter*
Cotton Patch Hot Foots. *Walter Horton*
Cotton Picking Blues. *Frank Seals*
Cotton Song, The (see: Cotton Fields)
Couldn't Find a Mule. *Albert Luandrew*
Count the Days I'm Gone. *Raymond Agee*
Count the Days I'm Gone. *Thomas Dorsey*
Count the Days I'm Gone. *Arthur Kelley*
Count the Days I'm Gone. *William Perryman*
Countin' the Blues. *Gertrude Rainey*

Country, The. *Percy Mayfield*
Country & Western. *Earl Hooker*
Country Boogie. *Elmore James*
Country Boy. *William Broonzy*
Country Boy. *John Lee Hooker*
Country Boy: McKinley Morganfield/Otis Spann
Country Boy Blues. *Lowell Fulson*
Country Clown. *Charles Ross*
Country Girl. *K. C. Douglas*
Country Girl. *Lee Jackson*
Country Girl. *Riley King*
Country Girl. *Amos Wells*
Country Jail Blues. *Major Merriweather*
Country Playboy. *Iverson Minter*
Country Style. *Willie Dixon*
County Jail. *McKinley Morganfield*
Court House Blues. *Clara Smith*
Courtroom Blues (see: Take a Walk Around the Corner)
Cousin John. *Sonny Terry*
Cow Cow Blues. *Charles Davenport*
Cow Cow Boogie. *Charles Davenport*
Cow Hooking. *John Hurt*
Crack Your Head. *Otis Spann*
Crackin' Up. *Ellas McDaniel*
Cracklin' Bread. *Clyde Bernhardt*
Crawfishin'. *Clarence Garlow*
Crawlin' King Snake (see: New Crawlin' King Snake)
Crawlin' King Snake. *Tony Hollins*
Crawling King Snake. *John Lee Hooker*
Crazin' the Blues. *Joe Lee Williams*
Crazy About Oklahoma. *Mathis James Reed*
Crazy About You Baby. *Sonny Boy Williamson (Alex Miller)*
Crazy 'bout a Woman. *Jesse Fuller*
Crazy for My Baby. *Willie Dixon*
Crazy Legs. *Marion Walter Jacobs*
Crazy Man Blues. *Sonny Terry*
Crazy Mixed Up World. *Willie Dixon*
Crazy With the Blues. *Peetie Wheatstraw*
Creeper, The. *James Cotton*
Creeper Creeps Again, The. *James Cotton*
Creeper Returns, The. *Aaron Willis*
Creepin' Blues. *Alexander Seward*
Creole Queen. *Joe Lee Williams*
Cross and Evil Woman Blues. *Gary Davis*
Cross Cut Saw. *Albert King*
Cross-Cut Saw. *John Young*
Cross Cut Saw Blues. *Sam Chatmon*
Cross My Heart. *Sonny Boy Williamson (Alex Miller)*
Cross Town. *James Pryor*
Crosseyed Cat. *McKinley Morganfield*
Crossroads Blues. *Robert Johnson*
Crosstown Traffic. *James Hendrix*
Crow Jane. *Nehemiah James*
Crow Jane Blues. *Sonny Terry*
Crow Jane Woman. *Ida Cox*
Crowing Rooster Blues. *Alonzo Johnson*
Cruel Little Baby. *John Lee Hooker*
Cruel Papa But a Good Man to Have Around. *Irene Scruggs*
Cruisin'. *John Mars*
Cry On! Cry On! *Amos Easton*
Cry Pretty Baby. *Roy Byrd*
Cryin' Holy unto the Lord. *Booker White*
Cryin' in My Sleep. *Rufus Perryman*
Cryin' the Blues. *Ike Darby*
Cryin' the Blues. *Floyd Jones*
Cryin' with the Blues. *Roy Brown*
Cryin' Woman Blues. *William Dupree*
Cryin' Won't Help You. *Frankie Lee Sims*
Crying Blues. *James Arnold*
Crying for Bread. *Sam Hopkins*
Crying Tears. *Otis Smothers*
Crying Won't Help. *Lowell Fulson*
Crying Won't Help You. *Hudson Whittaker*
Crying Won't Help You Now. *Riley King*
Crying Won't Make Him Stay. *Leola B. Grant*
Crying Won't Make Me Stay. *Johnny Fuller*
Curtis Jones Boogie. *Curtis Jones*
Custard Pie Blues. *Sonny Terry*
Cut Me Out Baby. *Sam Hopkins*
Cut Off from My Baby. *Sonny Terry*
Cuttin' Off My Days. *Walter Davis*
Cuttin' Out Blues. *Albert Luandrew*
Cypress Grove Blues. *Nehemiah James*

DBA Blues. *Roosevelt Sykes*
DT Moan. *Eddie House*
Daddy and Home. *James Rodgers*
Daddy Change Your Mind. *Edith Wilson*
Daddy Ease This Pain of Mine. *Sara Martin*
Daddy Please Don't Cry. *Eddie Kirkland*
Daddy Roll 'em. *Richard Havens*
Daisy Mae. *Clyde Bernhardt*
Dallas. *Johnny Winter*
Dallas Blues. *Floyd Dixon*
Damper Down Blues. *Gertrude Rainey*
Dance of the Tambourine. *Oran Page*
Dance with Me. *Riley King*
Danger Zone. *Percy Mayfield*
Danger Zone. *Mercy Dee Walton*
Dangerous Blues. *Eurreal Montgomery*
Dangerous Man. *Roosevelt Sykes*
Dangerous Woman. *James Pryor*
Dangerous Woman. *Sonny Terry*
Dark and Cloudy. *Sam Hopkins*
Dark Clouds. *Silas Hogan*
Dark Muddy Bottom. *Mercy Dee Walton*
Dark Road. *Floyd Jones*
Dark Shadows. *Alden Bunn*
Darlin' You Know I Love You. *Riley King*
Darling I Miss You. *Peter Chatman*
Davis Boogie. *John Davis*
Day Is Past and Gone, The. *Thomas Dorsey*
Day You Left Me, The. *Aaron Willis*
Dead Drunk Blues. *Gertrude Rainey*

Dead from the Dust. *Woodrow Guthrie*
Dead Shrimp Blues. *Robert Johnson*
Dead Stray Dog. *Iverson Minter*
Deal the Cards. *John Young*
Deal Yourself Another Hand. *Cecil Gant*
Dealin' from the Bottom. *Granville McGhee*
Dealing with the Devil. *John Lee Williamson*
Dear Abby and Ann. *Peter Chatman*
Dear Dad. *Charles Berry*
Dearest Darling. *Ellas McDaniel*
Death Bed Blues. *Alger Alexander*
Death Bells. *Sam Hopkins*
Death Blues. *Robert Pete Williams*
Death Call. *Larry Johnson*
Death-Call Blues. *Willie McTell*
Death Cell Rounder Blues. *Michael Bloomfield*
Death Don't Have No Mercy. *Gary Davis*
Death House Blues. *Thomas Delaney*
Death House Blues. *Pleasant Joseph*
Death in My Family. *Michael Bloomfield*
Death Letter Blues. *Jesse Crump*
Death Letter Blues. *Eddie House*
Death Letter Blues. *Huddie Ledbetter*
Death Letter Blues. *Estella Yancey*
Death of Big Bill Broonzy, The. *William Dupree*
Death of Blind Boy Fuller, The. *Walter Brown McGhee*
Death of Dr. Martin Luther King, The. *Joe Lee Williams*
Death of Ealase. *Iverson Minter*
Death of Louis, The. *William Dupree*
Death of Luther King, The. *William Dupree*
Death Sting Me Blues. *Sara Martin*
Death Valley Blues. *Arthur Crudup*
Death Valley Blues. *John Estes*
Death Valley Is Just Half-Way to My Home. *Alonzo Johnson*
Death Valley Moan. *Bessie Smith*
Deceitful Brownskin Blues. *Lemon Jefferson*
Deceiving Blues. *Theodore Darby*
Deceiving Man Blues. *Leola B. Grant*
December 7, 1941. *Sam Hopkins*
Decoration Day. *Booker White*
Decoration Day (Blues). *John Lee Williamson*
Decoration Day Blues. *Curtis Jones*
Dedicated to Otis. *Lucille Spann*
Dedication to My Baby. *Edward Boyd*
Deep Blue Sea Blues. *Clara Smith*
Deep Down in Florida. *McKinley Morganfield*
Deep Down in My Heart. *John Lee Hooker*
Deep Down in My Soul. *Roy Brown*
Deep Down in the Ground. *John Lee Williamson*
Deep Feeling. *Charles Berry*
Deep Freeze. *John Shines*
Deep Fried. *Eurreal Montgomery*
Deep in the Wilderness. *John Mars*
Deep Morgan Blues. *Henry Brown*
Deep Morgan Is Delmar Now. *Henry Brown*
Deep Morgan Stomp. *Henry Townsend*
Deep Sea Blues. *Henry Williams*
Deep Sea Diver. *George Buford*
Deep Water Blues. *Robert Brown*
Definition Blues. *John Holder*
DeKalb Blues. *Huddie Ledbetter*
Delia. *Joshua White*
Delia. *Gary Davis*
Delta Blues. *Joe Lee Williams*
Delta Haze Blues. *Shirley Griffith*
Delta Pine. *John Shines*
Dem Socks My Daddy Used to Wear. *Wesley Wilson*
Democrat Blues. *John Jenkins*
Democrat Man. *John Lee Hooker*
Denmark. *Edward Boyd*
Dentist Blues. *Walter Davis*
Deportee. *Woodrow Guthrie*
Depot Blues. *John Lee*
Depression Blues. *Clarence Brown*
Depression Blues. *Albert Luandrew*
Desert Blues. *James Rodgers*
Detroit Black Bottom. *Eddie Burns*
Detroit Blues. *Hudson Whittaker*
Detroit Bound. *Arthur Phelps*
Detroit City Blues. *Antoine Domino*
Detroit Moan. *Victoria Spivey*
Detroit Rocks. *Arthur Taylor*
Deuce, A. *Charles Berry*
Devil, The. *Eddie Kirkland*
Devil Blues. *James Thomas*
Devil Got My Woman. *Nehemiah James*
Devil Is a Busy Man. *Albert Luandrew*
Devil Is Going to Get You. *Leroy Foster*
Devil Sent the Rain Blues. *Charley Patton*
Devil's Daughter. *John Shines*
Devil's Gonna Get You, The. *Walter Brown McGhee*
Devil's Got the Blues. *Alonzo Johnson*
Devil's Jump. *John Lee Hooker*
Dewey's Walkin' Blues. *Dewey Corley*
Diamond Ring. *Walter Brown McGhee*
Dices Oh Dices. *Wilbert Ellis*
Did You Ever? *James Rushing*
Did You Ever Love a Woman? *Riley King*
Did You Ever Love a Woman? *Arnold Moore*
Did You Ever Set Thinkin'? *Henry Williams*
Did You Get That Letter? *John Young*
Diddey Wah Diddey (see: New Diddey Wah Diddey)
Diddie Wa Diddie. *Arthur Phelps*
Diddley Daddy. *William Arnold*
Diddley Daddy. *Ellas McDaniel*
Diggin' My Potatoes: *William Broonzy/Robert Brown*
Diggin' the Boogie. *William Perryman*
Dimples. *John Lee Hooker*
Diploma for Two. *Charles Berry*
Direct South. *Amos Easton*
Directly from My Heart to You. *Richard Penniman*
Dirt on the Ground. *Dave Alexander*
Dirt Road Blues. *Joe Lee Williams*
Dirty Mistreater. *Sonny Terry*
Dirty Mother for You. *Roosevelt Sykes*

Dirty News. *James Pryor*
Dirty No-Gooder's Blues. *Bessie Smith*
Dirty Spoon Blues. *Wesley Wilson*
Dirty Woman Blues. *Joe Johnson*
Dirty Women's Blues. *Victoria Spivey*
Discotheque Special. *Willie Mabon*
Discouraged. *Alden Bunn*
Dish Rag Blues: *Leola B Grant/Wesley Wilson*
Dissatisfied. *Sonny Boy Williamson (Alex Miller)*
Dissatisfied Blues. *Walter Brown McGhee*
Diving Duck Blues. *John Estes*
Diving Duck Blues. *Otis Spann*
Dixie Flyer Blues. *Bessie Smith*
Do It If You Wanna. *Eddie Burns*
Do It If You Wanna. *Sonny Boy Williamson (Alex Miller)*
Do It If You Want To. *James Pryor*
Do It Right Now. *Aaron Willis*
Do Lawd Do. *Jesse Crump*
Do Me Right. *Willie Dixon*
Do My Baby Ever Think of Me? *Fred McDowell*
Do-Re-Mi, The. *Woodrow Guthrie*
Do Right Blues. *William Broonzy*
Do She Love Me? *William Perryman*
Do Something Baby. *Willie Dixon*
Do the Boogie Woogie. *Charles Ross*
Do the Do. *Willie Dixon*
Do the Shovel. *Phillip Walker*
Do the Weston. *Sonny Boy Williamson (Alex Miller)*
Do What You Did. *Cornelius Green*
Do What You Do. *McHouston Baker*
Do What You Want to Do. *Travis Blaylock*
Do What You Want to Do. *Albert Collins*
Do What You Want to Do, Be What You Want to Be. *Willie Dixon*
Do You Believe? *Raymond Agee*
Do You Call That a Buddy? *Leola B. Grant/Wesley Wilson*
Do You Call That Religion? *Charles Davenport*
Do You Feel Good? *Richard Havens*
Do You Love Me? *Lowell Fulson*
Do You Remember? *Major Merriweather*
Do You Remember Me? *John Lee Hooker*
Do You Want Me to Cry? *Eddie Taylor*
Do Yourself a Favor. *Edward Boyd*
Doctor Blues. *Walter Davis*
Doctor Blues. *Otis Spann*
Doctor Blues. *Robert Pete Williams*
Doctor Brown. *Buster Brown*
Doctor Clayton Blues. *Peter Clayton*
Doctor Professor Longhair. *Roy Byrd*
Doctor (Dr.) Ross Breakdown. *Charles Ross*
Doctor Ross Rockin'. *Charles Ross*
Dog, The. *Rufus Thomas*
Dog House Blues. *James Oden*
Doggin' the Dog. *Joseph Turner*
Doin' It. *Roy Byrd*
Doin' the Shout. *John Lee Hooker*
Doing a Stretch. *Arthur Phelps*
Doing Better in Life. *Henry Townsend*
Dollar Twenty-Five. *Otis Spann*
Domestic Nurse Blues. *Roosevelt Sykes*
Done Changed My Way of Living. *Taj Mahal*
Done Somebody Wrong. *Elmore James*
Done Somebody Wrong. *Eddie Kirkland*
Don't Agitate Me Blues. *Virginia Liston*
Don't Ask Me No Questions. *Aaron Willis*
Don't Be Messing with My Bread (see: Messing with My Bread)
Don't Be Messin' with My Bread. *John Lee Hooker*
Don't Be So Evil. *Lowell Fulson*
Don't Bother Me. *Frank Seals*
Don't Break Down on Me. *Charlie Jackson*
Don't Care. *Victoria Spivey*
Don't Come Knockin'. *Antoine Domino*
Don't Cry. *Iverson Minter*
Don't Destroy Me. *Lowell Fulson*
Don't Do It. *Clarence Richardson*
Don't Dog Your Woman (When You Ain't Doing Right Yourself). *Buster Brown*
Don't Dog Your Woman. *J. B. Lenoir*
Don't Doubt Me. *Peter Chatman*
Don't Drive Me from Your Door. *Alonzo Johnson*
Don't Embarrass Me Baby. *Sam Hopkins*
Don't Ever Leave Me All Alone. *Andrew Odom*
Don't Ever Love. *Alonzo Johnson*
Don't Fish in My Sea: *Gertrude Rainey/Bessie Smith*
Don't Fool with My Baby. *Frank Seals*
Don't Forget to Close the Door. *Connie Crayton*
Don't Fuzz Blues. *Booker White*
Don't Get Flakey with Me. *James Witherspoon*
Don't Give Me the Runaround. *Aaron Walker*
Don't Go Baby. *John Lee Hooker*
Don't Go Back to New Orleans. *Aaron Walker*
Don't Go No Further. *Willie Dixon*
Don't Gotta. *James Witherspoon*
Don't Hang My Clothes on No Barb Wire Line. *Peetie Wheatstraw*
Don't Have to Cry. *Riley King*
Don't Have to Worry. *Earl Hooker*
Don't Irritate Me Blues. *Virginia Liston*
Don't Knock at My Door. *Eddie Taylor*
Don't Laugh at Me. *Chester Burnett*
Don't Leave Me Baby. *Aaron Walker*
Don't Leave No News. *Fird Eaglin*
Don't Let That Music Die. *Willie Dixon*
Don't Let Your Right Hand Know. *Sonny Boy Williamson (Alex Miller)*
Don't Lie Buddy. *Huddie Ledbetter*
Don't Lie to Me. *Antoine Domino*
Don't Listen to Me. *Richard Havens*
Don't Look Back. *John Lee Hooker*
Don't Look for Me Baby. *Arbee Stidham*
Don't Lose Your Cool. *Albert Collins*
Don't Lose Your Eye. *Sonny Boy Williamson (Alex Miller)*
Don't Love Nobody. *Roy Brown*

Don't Mean You No Good Blues. *Lucille Bogan*
Don't Mess with the Messer. *Willie Dixon*
Don't Mistreat Me: *Walter Brown McGhee/Sonny Terry*
Don't Need No Doctor. *Willie Mae Thornton*
Don't Pity Me. *Walter Brown McGhee*
Don't Push Me Around. *Roosevelt Sykes*
Don't Ration My Love. *Peter Chatman*
Don't Rush Me Baby. *Viola Wells*
Don't Sell It Blues. *Oscar Woods*
Don't Sell It Give It Away. *Sam Chatmon*
Don't Shake It No More. *Thomas Dorsey*
Don't Start Crying Now. *James Moore*
Don't Start Me to Talking. *Sonny Boy Williamson (Alex Miller)*
Don't Stay Out All Night. *William Arnold*
Don't Take It Out on Me. *Frankie Lee Sims*
Don't Take My Heart. *Eddie Kirkland*
Don't Tell It. *Clyde Bernhardt*
Don't Tell Me Your Troubles. *Ray Charles*
Don't Think You're Smart. *Peter Chatman*
Don't Throw Your Love on Me. *Albert King*
Don't Touch My Head. *J. B. Lenoir*
Don't Treat That Man the Way You Treat Me. *Sam Hopkins*
Don't Trust Nobody Blues. *Victoria Spivey*
Don't Turn Me Away from Your Door. *John Lee Hooker*
Don't Wait for Me. *Walter Brown McGhee*
Don't Wake It Up. *Walter Jacobs Vinson*
Don't Want No Special Rider. *John Wrencher*
Don't Worry About It. *Gabriel Brown*
Don't Worry About it. *Victoria Spivey*
Don't Worry 'bout the Bear. *Charles Ross*
Don't You Be No Fool. *William Broonzy*
Don't You Know. *Ray Charles*
Don't You Know. *Otis Spann*
Don't You Lie to Me. *Walter Brown McGhee*
Don't You Lie to Me. *Hudson Whittaker*
Don't You Lie to Me. *John Young*
Don't You Love Your Daddy No More? *Huddie Ledbetter*
Don't You Make Me High. *Louisa Barker*
Don't You Miss Your Baby? *James Rushing*
Don't You Quit Me Daddy. *Sara Martin*
Don't You Remember Me? *Henry Townsend*
Don't You Want a Man Like Me? *James Rushing*
Don't You Want to Go? *Walter Davis*
Don't You Want to Ride? *William Broonzy*
Don't Your Plums Look Mellow Hanging on Your Tree. *Joe Lee Williams*
Dookie Chase Boogie. *Roosevelt Sykes*
Door to Success. *Walter Brown McGhee*
Dope Head Blues. *Victoria Spivey*
Double Breasted Woman. *Roosevelt Sykes*
Double Crossin' Mamma. *Peter Chatman*
Double Dozens. *Addie Spivey*
Double Eye Whammy. *Tommy Ridgley*
Double Eyed Whammy. *Freddie King*
Double Trouble. *Otis Rush*
Double Trouble Blues. *Thomas Dorsey*
Doug the Jitterbug. *Louis Jordan*
Down and Lost My Mind. *William Broonzy*
Down and Out. *Walter Davis*
Down and Out. *Sonny Boy Williamson (Alex Miller)*
Down and Out Blues. *James Arnold*
Down at the Landing. *John Lee Hooker*
Down at the Razor Ball. *Sara Martin*
Down at Your Buryin'. *James Cotton*
Down Baby. *Sam Hopkins*
Down Don't Bother Me. *Albert King*
Down Home Blues. *Peter Chatman*
Down Home Blues. *Thomas Delaney*
Down Home Blues. *Thomas Dorsey*
Down-Home Shakedown. *Willie Mae Thornton*
Down Home Special. *Ellas McDaniel*
Down Home Waltz. *Jesse Fuller*
Down in Boogie Alley. *Lucille Bogan*
Down in Spirit. *John Shines*
Down in the Bottom. *Gabriel Brown*
Down in the Bottom. *Willie Dixon*
Down in the Country. *Leola B Grant*
Down in the Dumps: *Leola B Grant/Wesley Wilson*
Down on Me. *Janis Joplin*
Down on My Bended Knee. *Joe Holmes*
Down on My Knees. *Eddie Kirkland*
Down on Pennsylvania Avenue. *Thomas Delaney*
Down on Sarah Street. *Otis Spann*
Down South Blues: *John Estes/Hammie Nixon*
Down South Blues. *Alberta Hunter*
Down South Blues. *McKinley Morganfield*
Down That Big Road. *Peter Chatman*
Down the Dirt Road Blues. *Charley Patton*
Down the Line Blues. *William Broonzy*
Down the Road. *Smiley Lewis*
Down the Road. *Mathis James Reed*
Down the Staff, A. *Eddie House*
Down to Earth. *Otis Spann*
Down Yonder We Go Ballin'. *Smiley Lewis*
Downbound Train. *Charles Berry*
Downfall of the Lion. *Richard Brown*
Downhearted Blues. *Alberta Hunter*
Downtown Blues. *Frank Stokes*
Drafted Mama. *J. D. Short*
Dream. *John Littlejohn*
Dream Blues. *Gertrude Rainey*
Dream Daddy Blues. *Mary Johnson*
Dream Lucky Blues. *Julia Lee*
Dream of Mine, A. *Gabriel Brown*
Dreamin' Blues. *John Lee Hooker*
Dreaming. *Clarence Garlow*
Dreaming of You. *Victoria Spivey*
Dreamy Eyed Baby. *William Broonzy*
Driftin' Blues. *Charles Brown*
Drifting. *Edward Boyd*
Drifting Apart. *Raymond Agee*
Drifting Blues. *Booker White*
Drifting from Town to Town. *Robert Bland*
Drifting Heart. *Charles Berry*

Drink of Wine, Mop Mop. *Granville McGhee*
Drinkin' Wine. *John Fortescue*
Drinkin' Wine Spo-Dee-O-Dee. *Granville McGhee*
Drinking. *Albert Luandrew*
Drinking Beer. *James Witherspoon*
Drinking by Myself. *Wynonie Harris*
Drinking Straight Whiskey. *John Young*
Drive My Blues Away. *McKinley Morganfield*
Driving Me Mad. *Roy Brown*
Driving Wheel. *Roosevelt Sykes*
Driving Sideways. *Freddie King*
Drop Anchor. *Travis Blaylock*
Drop Down Mama. *John Estes*
Drop Out Song. *Jesse Fuller*
Drop That Sack. *Charlie Jackson*
Drunk Man Blues. *Booker White*
Drunkard, The. *Mercy Dee Walton*
Drunken-Hearted Man. *Robert Johnson*
Drunken Spree. *Nehemiah James*
Dry Chemical Blues. *Silas Hogan*
Dry Southern Blues. *Lemon Jefferson*
Dry Spell Blues. *Eddie House*
Dry Well Blues. *Charley Patton*
Dryburg Drive. *Curtis Jones*
Ducks. *Wesley Wilson*
Duck's Yas Yas. *James Johnson*
Duck's Yas Yas Yas, The. *Hudson Whittaker*
Dud Low Joe. *Eurreal Montgomery*
Dun Goin' Down. *Gary Davis*
Dupree's Special. *William Dupree*
Dust Bowl Refugee. *Woodrow Guthrie*
Dust My Bed. *John Wrencher*
Dust My Broom (see: I Believe I'll Dust My Broom)
Dust Pneumonia Blues. *Woodrow Guthrie*
Dusty Road. *John Lee Hooker*
Dyin' Flu. *Albert Collins*
Dying Blues. *Wesley Wilson*
Dying Crapshooter's Blues. *Willie McTell*
Dying Miner, The. *Woodrow Guthrie*
Dying Mother Blues. *William Borum*
Dying Rider. *Iromeio Nelson*
Dyna Flow. *Albert King*
Dynamite Blues. *Lemon Jefferson*

E Blues: *Francis Blackwell/Leroy Carr*
Eagle and the Hawk. *Victoria Spivey*
Eagle Eyed Mama. *Lemon Jefferson*
Eagle-Rock Me Baby. *Roosevelt Sykes*
Eagle Rock Me Papa. *Thomas Dorsey*
Earl Hooker Blues. *Earl Hooker*
Early Grave. *Edward Boyd*
Early in the Mornin'. *Louis Jordan*
Early in the Morning. *John Lee Williamson*
Early in the Morning. *Joseph Young*
Early (in the) Morning Blues. *John Henry Barbee*
Early Morning Blues. *McKinley Morganfield*
Early Morning Blues. *Rufus Perryman*
Early Morning Blues. *Arthur Phelps*
Early Morning Blues. *Sonny Terry*
Early One Morning. *Thomas Courtney*
Early One Morning. *Richard Penniman*
Early This Morning. *Walter Davis*
Earth Quake and Hurricane. *Willie Dixon*
East Coast Blues. *Walter Brown McGhee*
East of the Sun. *Jerry McCain*
East St. Louis. *Walter Lewis*
East St. Louis. *J. D. Short*
East St. Louis Blues. *James Yancey*
Eastern Chimes Blues. *Henry Brown*
Easy. *Walter Horton*
Easy Baby. *Willie Dixon*
Easy Baby. *James Harris*
Easy Baby. *Samuel Maghett*
Easy Go. *Otis Rush*
Easy Listening. *Vernon Harrison*
Eddie's Blues. *Edward Boyd*
Eddie's Boogie Chillen. *Eddie Kirkland*
Eight Hour Woman. *Edith North Johnson*
Eighteen Hammers. *Taj Mahal*
1839 Blues. *Elmore James*
80 Highway. *John Estes*
88 Boogie. *Peter Chatman*
Eisenhower Blues. *J. B. Lenoir*
El Paso Blues. *Phillip Walker*
El Paso Blues. *Joe Lee Williams*
Elder Greene Blues. *Charley Patton*
Electric Chair. *John Estes*
Electric Church. *James Hendrix*
Elevator Woman. *John Lee Williamson*
Elim Stole My Baby. *Don Harris*
Eli's Pork Chop. *Aaron Willis*
Ella Speed. *Huddie Ledbetter*
Elmore Jumps One. *Elmore James*
Elmo's Shuffle. *Elmore James*
Empire State Express. *Eddie House*
Empty Arms. *Edward Boyd*
Empty Pocket Blues. *Joseph Turner*
End It All. *Alonzo Johnson*
End of the Blues. *Earl Hooker*
Endless Boogie. *John Lee Hooker*
Ends and Odds. *Mathis James Reed*
Eternal Blues. *James Yancey*
Ethel May. *Arthur Crudup*
Ethel Sings 'Em. *Ethel Waters*
European Blues. *Peter Chatman*
Evaleena. *William Arnold*
Evening Shadows. *Willie Mabon*
Evening Sun. *John Shines*
Everlasting Blues. *James Yancey*
Every Day Brings Out a Change. *Joe Lee Williams*
Every Day I Have the Blues. *Peter Chatman*
Every Day We Rock & Roll. *Charles Berry*
Every Girl I See. *Willie Dixon*
Every Hour. *Richard Penniman*
Every Jug Stands on its Own Bottom. *Eddie Burns*
Every Night About This Time. *Antoine Domino*

Every Night and Every Day. *Jimmy McCracklin*
Every Second a Fool Is Born. *Lowell Fulson*
Every Time I Gets to Drinking. *Albert Luandrew*
Every Time My Heart Beats. *Ernest Lawlars*
Every Tub Stands on Its Own Bottom. *Robert Brown (Washboard Sam)*
Every Woman Blues. *Clara Smith*
Every Woman Needs a Man. *Sara Martin*
Everybody Got a Mojo. *George Butler*
Everybody Lies a Little. *Riley King*
Everybody Needs Somebody. *Silas Hogan*
Everybody Wants to Go to Heaven But Nobody Wants to Die. *Thomas Delaney*
Everybody's Blues. *Thomas Delaney*
Everybody's Blues. *William Dupree*
Everybody's Blues. *Melvin Jackson*
Everybody's Blues. *Irene Scruggs*
Everybody's Boogie. *John Davis*
Everybody's Gonna Miss Me When I'm Gone. *Joe Lee Williams*
Everybody's Happy (But Me). *Willie Mae Thornton*
Everyday of My Life. *Henry Townsend*
Everyday of the Week. *Estella Yancey*
Everything Gonna Be All Right. *Samuel Maghett*
Everything Gonna Be Alright. *Marion Walter Jacobs*
Everything Gonna Be Alright. *Willie Mae Thornton*
Everything I Do Is Wrong. *Peter Chatman*
Everything I Get Ahold To. *Roy Dunn*
Everything I Had Is Gone. *Walter Brown McGhee*
Everything Is OK. *Walter Davis*
Everything's Going to Be Alright. *Amos Wells*
Everything's Gonna Be Alright. *William Dupree*
Everything's Gonna Be Alright. *Otis Spann*
Everywoman Blues. *Princess White*
Evil. *McKinley Morganfield*
Evil Blues. *Robert Brown (Washboard Sam)*
Evil Blues. *James Rushing*
Evil Hearted Me. *Walter Brown McGhee*
Evil Hearted Women Blues. *John Shines*
Evil Is Going On. *Willie Dixon*
Evil Ways. *James Oden*
Evil Woman. *William Dupree*
Evil Woman. *Alonzo Johnson*
Evil Woman Blues. *Alger Alexander*
Evil Woman Blues. *Alexander Seward*
Evolution Blues. *Pleasant Joseph*
Excuse Me Baby. *Luther Johnson*
Experience Blues. *Alberta Hunter*
Explainin' the Blues. *Thomas Dorsey*
Eyes Like an Eagle. *Fred McDowell*
Eyesight to the Blind. *Sonny Boy Williamson (Alex Miller)*

FBI Blues. *John Fortescue*
FDR Blues. *William Dupree*
Fables Aren't Nothing But Doggone Lies. *Jesse Fuller*
Failing by Degrees. *James Witherspoon*
Faith. *Raymond Agee*
Faking Blues, The. *Charlie Jackson*
Fallin' Rain. *Luther Tucker*
Falling Blues. *Arbee Stidham*
Falling Rain. *Walter Davis*
Falling Rain Blues. *Floyd Jones*
Family Blues. *James Harris*
Famous Cornfield Blues (see: Those Dogs of Mine)
Family Rules. *Lonnie Brooks*
Fan It. *Frankie Jaxon*
Fannie Mae. *Buster Brown*
Fannie Mae. *Roy Brown*
Fannie Mae's Place. *Buster Brown*
Fannin' Street (see: Mr. Tom Hughes Town)
Fanny Lou. *K. C. Douglas*
Fare Thee Well Poor Gal. *Jesse Crump*
Farewell Daddy Blues. *Gertrude Rainey*
Farewell Sweet Man of Mine. *Jesse Crump*
Farish Street Jive. *Eurreal Montgomery*
Farm Blues. *Robert Pete Williams*
Farm Hand Blues. *Alger Alexander*
Fast and Free. *Peter Chatman*
Fast as My Legs Can Go. *Andrew McMahon*
Fast Boogie. *James Thomas*
Fast Life Woman. *Sam Hopkins*
Fast Movin' Mama. *Dinah Washington*
Fast Woman Blues. *Robert Brown (Washboard Sam)*
Fat and Forty. *Peter Chatman*
Fat Mama. *John Shines*
Fat Man, The. *Antoine Domino*
Fat Mouth Blues. *Charlie Jackson*
Fats Frenzy. *Antoine Domino*
Fattening Frogs for Snakes. *Sonny Boy Williamson (Alex Miller)*
'Fatuation. *James Cotton*
Feast in the Mau Mau. *Jalacy Hawkins*
Fed Up. *Lowell Fulson*
Feel Like Balling the Jack. *Sam Hopkins*
Feel Like Blowing My Horn. *Roosevelt Sykes*
Feel Like Screamin' and Cryin'. *Peter Chatman*
Feel So Bad. *John Lee Hooker*
Feel So Bad. *Sam Hopkins*
Feel So Bad. *Robert Nighthawk*
Feel So Good. *Andrew Odom*
Feelin' Good. *James Cotton*
Feelin' Happy. *Joseph Turner*
Feelin' It. *Charles Berry*
Feelin' Is Gone, The. *John Lee Hooker*
Feelin' So Sad. *Joseph Turner*
Feeling Good. *JB Lenoir*
Feeling the Blues. *Peter Chatman*
Feeling the Blues. *Aaron Walker*
Feelings from the Fingers. *Alonzo Johnson*
Ferguson Brother's Killing. *Woodrow Guthrie*
Festival. *Charles Berry*
Fifteen Cents. *Frankie Jaxon*
Fifteen Years. *Mathis James Reed*
Fifth Street Alley Blues. *Norman Green*

Fifth Street Blues. *Charles Davenport*
51st Anniversary. *James Hendrix*
Fightin' the Jug. *Arthur Phelps*
Fillmore Blues. *Charles Berry*
Fillmore Street. *Dave Alexander*
Find Yourself Another Fool. *McKinley Morganfield*
Fine Booze and Heavy Dues. *Alonzo Johnson*
Fine Fat Daddy. *Dinah Washington*
Fine Little Mama. *Elmore James*
Fine Looking Woman. *Riley King*
Finger Lickin' Good. *Charles Musselwhite*
Fire. *Willie Dixon*
Fire Department. *John Estes*
First Degree. *Iverson Minter*
First Look Around the Corner. *James Hendrix*
First Time I Met You, The. *Eurreal Montgomery*
Fish and Chips. *Charles Berry*
Fisherman's Blues. *William Dupree*
Fishing in the Dark. *Dewey Corley*
Five Card Hand. *Mercy Dee Walton*
Five Feet Four. *William Broonzy*
Five Long years. *Edward Boyd*
Five Years in Prison. *Charles Edwards*
Fix It. *Thomas Dorsey*
Fixin' to Die. *Booker White*
Flames of Jive. *Roosevelt Sykes*
Flat Foot Sam. *Oscar Wills*
Flat Foot Sam Meets Jim Dandy. *Oscar Wills*
Flip, The. *Lonnie Brooks*
Flip Flop and Fly. *Joseph Turner*
Floating Bridge: *John Estes/Hammie Nixon*
Flood Water Blues. *Alonzo Johnson*
Florida Blues. *Oran Page*
Florida Bound Blues. *Leroy Carr*
Flossie Mae. *Alexander Moore*
Flower Blues. *Aaron Walker*
Flower Pot. *Joseph Young*
Floyd's Blues. *Floyd Dixon*
Fly Hen Blues. *Pleasant Joseph*
Fly Right Baby. *Alonzo Johnson*
Flyin' Home. *Charles Berry*
Flying Crow Blues. *Ernest Lawlars*
Flying Eagle Blues. *Shirley Griffith*
Flying Saucer. *Marion Walter Jacobs*
Fo' Day. *Arthur Taylor*
Fo' Day Blues. *Joshua Howell*
Fogyism: *Ida Cox/Jesse Crump*
Follow the Deal On Down. *Thomas Delaney*
Fool About That Woman. *Robert Brown (Washboard Sam)*
Fool for You, A. *Ray Charles*
Fool Too Long, A. *Riley King*
Fooling Around. *Willie Mabon*
Foolish Heart. *James Harris*
Foolish Man Blues. *Bessie Smith*
Footrace. *John Walker*
Footrace Is On. *Sam Hopkins*
For Heaven's Sake. *Richard Havens*
For Now, So Long. *Clarence Brown*
For the Love of Mike. *John Shines*
For You. *Floyd Dixon*
'Fore Day Blues. *Louis Jordan*
'Fore Day Creep. *Alden Bunn*
'Fore Day Creep. *Jesse Crump*
Fore day in the Morning. *Roy Brown*
Forever I'll Be Yours. *Alden Bunn*
Fort Worth and Dallas Blues. *Huddie Ledbetter*
Forty Days and Forty Nights. *McKinley Morganfield*
Forty-Four. *Chester Burnett*
44 Blues (see: New 44 Blues)
47th Street Jive (Boogie). *Roosevelt Sykes*
Forty Years or More. *Peter Chatman*
Found Love. *Mathis James Reed*
Found My Baby Gone. *Mathis James Reed*
Four. *Eddie Vinson*
Four Corners of the World. *Joe Lee Williams*
Four Day Honory Scat. *Gertrude Rainey*
Four Day Worry Blues. *Huddie Ledbetter*
Four Full Seasons of Love. *Frank Seals*
Four Leaf Clover. *Edward Boyd*
Four O'Clock Blues. *Nehemiah James*
Four O'Clock Blues. *Sonny Terry*
Four O'Clock Blues: *Estella Yancey/James Yancey*
Four O'Clock Boogie. *Peter Chatman*
Four Walls and Me. *Alonzo Johnson*
Fox Hunt. *Sonny Terry*
Foxy Lady. *James Hendrix*
Frankie's Blues. *Frankie Lee Sims*
Frankie's Blues. *David Van Ronk*
Freddie's Blues. *Theodore Taylor*
Fred's Worried Life Blues. *Fred McDowell*
Free Again. *Robert Pete Williams*
Free and Equal. *William Dupree*
Freedom. *Peter Chatman*
Freedom Blues. *Richard Penniman*
Freedom I'm Ready. *John Holder*
Freedom Loan. *John Estes*
Freeway 75. *Freddie King*
Freight Train. *Elizabeth Cotten*
Freight Train: *Walter Brown McGhee/Sonny Terry*
Freight Train. *Charles Ross*
Freight Train. *John Shines*
Freight Train Blues. *Thomas Dorsey*
Freight Train Blues. *Robert Pete Williams*
Freight Train Moanin' Blues. *Billie Pierce*
Freight Train to Ride. *Iverson Minter*
French Woman. *Peter Chatman*
Frenzy. *Jalacy Hawkins*
Fried Chicken. *Booker White*
Friendless and Blue. *Alonzo Johnson*
Friendless Blues. *William Broonzy*
Friends. *Riley King*
Frisco Blues. *Walter Davis*
Frisco Hi-Ball Blues. *Eurreal Montgomery*
Frisco Line. *Fred McDowell*
'Frisco Train Blues. *Alger Alexander*

SONG INDEX

Frisky Gal. *Alexander Moore*
Frog. *Lonnie Brooks*
From Four till Late. *Robert Johnson*
From Memphis to New Orleans. *Frank Floyd*
From North Dallas to the East Side. *Alexander Moore*
Front Door Blues (32–20 Blues). *James Arnold*
Frosty. *Albert Collins*
Fumbling Around. *John Young*
Funk and Wagner. *Don Harris*
Funk-Shun. *Albert King*
Funky. *Freddie King*
Funky Butt. *McKinley Morganfield*
Funky Butt Lover. *George Butler*
Funky Chicken, The. *Rufus Thomas*
Funky Down Easy. *Jerry McCain*
Funny Bone. *Freddie King*
Funny But I Still Love You. *Ray Charles*
Funny Caper Blues. *William Borum*
Funny Feathers. *Victoria Spivey*
Funny Feelin'. *Amos Easton*
Furniture Man Blues. *Victoria Spivey*
Furry's (Worried) Blues. *Walter Lewis*
Future Blues. *Willie Lee Brown*

GI Slim. *Otis Hicks*
Gallis Pole, The. *Huddie Ledbetter*
Galveston. *Clarence Green*
Gambler's Blues. *Peter Chatman*
Gambler's Blues. *Riley King*
Gambler's Dream. *Beulah Wallace*
Gamblin' Man. *Eddie Taylor*
Gangster of Love. *Johnny Watson*
Garter Snake Blues. *Victoria Spivey*
Gasoline Rationing Blues. *Robert Jeffery*
Gate Walks to Board. *Clarence Brown*
Gate You Swing Me Down. *Clyde Bernhardt*
Gay Cattin'. *Charlie Jackson*
Gee But It's Hard. *Thomas Dorsey*
Gee Pretty Baby. *Curtis Jones*
General Motors Blues. *Charles Ross*
George Street Blues. *Francis Blackwell*
Georgia Bound. *Arthur Phelps*
Georgia Skin Game. *Booker White*
Georgia Stockade Blues. *Thomas Delaney*
Georgia Stockade Blues. *Thomas Dorsey*
Georgia Woman. *Eddie Kirkland*
Get Away Blues. *William Broonzy*
Get Away Blues. *Robert Wilkins*
Get Back. *William Broonzy*
Get Back Home to the USA. *John Lee Hooker*
Get Down Brother. *Robert Brown*
Get Him out of Your System. *Estella Yancey*
Get Hip to Yourself. *Albert Luandrew*
Get Off My Back Woman. *Riley King*
Get Off My Toe. *Sam Hopkins*
Get Off with Me. *Leola B Grant*
Get on the Right Track Baby. *Ray Charles*
Get out of Here. *Riley King*
Get These Blues off Me. *Aaron Walker*
Get to My Baby. *Willie Dixon*
Get with It. *William Dupree*
Get Your Mind out of the Gutter. *Granville McGhee*
Get Yourself Together. *Alonzo Johnson*
Getaway, The. *Fention Robinson*
Gettin' It Fixed (see: You Should Not A' Done It)
Getting Dirty Just Shaking That Thing. *Iromeio Nelson*
Getting out of Town. *James Walker*
Getting out of Town. *Sonny Boy Williamson (Alex Miller)*
Getting Together. *Sonny Boy Williamson (Alex Miller)*
Ghetto Woman. *Riley King*
Gibson Hill. *Booker White*
Gibson Town. *Booker White*
Gimme a Pigfoot: *Leola B. Grant/Wesley Wilson*
Gimme a Smile. *James Harris*
Gimme Some of That Yum Yum Yum. *Johnny Temple*
Girl Across the Street, The. *Tommy Ridgley*
Girl at the Bottom. *John Lee Granderson*
Girl Friends. *Sonny Boy Williamson (Alex Miller)*
Girl from Kooka Monga, The. *Tommy Ridgley*
Give It Up. *Bonnie Raitt*
Give It Up Buddy and Get Goin'. *Hudson Whittaker*
Give Me a Break Blues. *Ida Cox*
Give Me an Old Old Lady. *Booker White*
Give Me Back My Wig. *Theodore Taylor*
Give Me Mine Now. *Hudson Whittaker*
Give Me That Old Slow Drag. *Thomas Delaney*
Give Me Time to Think. *Sam Hopkins*
Give Me Your Change. *Roosevelt Sykes*
Give My Heart a Break. *John Shines*
Give You Some Air. *Fention Robinson*
Give Your Mama One Smile. *William Broonzy*
Gladly. *Charles Walker*
Gladrags. *John Shines*
Glamour Girl. *Aaron Walker*
Glory Bound Train. *Booker White*
Glory for Me. *Thomas Dorsey*
Go Ahead. *Sam Hopkins*
Go and Leave Me. *Woodrow Guthrie*
Go Away Go Away Blues. *John Williamson*
Go Back Old Devil. *Sam Chatmon*
Go Back to the Country. *Robert Brown*
Go Back Where You Stayed Last Night. *Ethel Waters*
Go Bobby Soxer. *Charles Berry*
Go Down Ol' Hannah. *Huddie Ledbetter*
Go Get Some More You Fool. *James Rushing*
Go Go Go. *Charles Berry*
Go On to School. *Mathis James Reed*
Go Tell My Other Man. *Victoria Spivey*
Go to the Mardi Gras. *Roy Byrd*
Go Underground. *Riley King*
Goat, The. *Sonny Boy Williamson (Alex Miller)*
God Knows I Can't Help It. *John Henry Barbee*
God's Gift. *Willie Dixon*
Goin' Away. *Sam Hopkins*
Goin' Away Baby. *James Rogers*
Goin' Back to Mississippi. *Eddie Kirkland*

Goin' Down in Georgia. *John Fortescue*
Goin' Down Slow. *James Oden*
Goin' Down to the River. *Fred McDowell*
Goin' Home. *Willie Dixon*
Goin' Home. *Antoine Domino*
Goin' Home. *Otis Hicks*
Goin' Home Blues. *Charles Davenport*
Goin' Out Have Myself a Ball. *Robert Pete Williams*
Goin' South. *John Lee Hooker*
Goin' to Chicago. *James Rushing*
Goin' to Dallas. *Sam Hopkins*
Goin' to Funky Town. *Aaron Walker*
Goin' to Jail About Her. *Francis Blackwell*
Goin' to Louisiana. *John Lee Hooker*
Goin' to Paris. *William Dupree*
Goin' to the Country. *William Trice*
Goin' Up, Goin' Down. *Charles Sayles*
Going Away Baby. *Charles Ross*
Going Away Blues. *Shirley Griffith*
Going Back Home. *Travis Blaylock*
Going Back Home. *Robert Brown (Smokey Babe)*
Going Back Home. *Frank Seals*
Going Back Home. *Victoria Spivey*
Going Back South. *Charles Ross*
Going Back to Arkansas. *Robert Brown (Washboard Sam)*
Going Back to Florida. *Billie Pierce*
Going (Back) to Louisiana. *William Dupree*
Going Back to Memphis. *Albert Luandrew*
Going Back to Memphis. *Will Shade*
Going Back to Washington Corner 7th & "T." *Henry Williams*
Going Blues. *Victoria Spivey*
Going by the River. *Mathis James Reed*
Going Down Home. *Joe Lee Williams*
Going Fishing. *Mathis James Reed*
Going Home. *Iverson Minter*
Going My Way. *Gabriel Brown*
Going 'round the World. *John Lee Granderson*
Going to Build Me a Playhouse. *Aaron Walker*
Going to California. *Oscar Wills*
Going to Chicago. *William Broonzy*
Going to Get You. *Willie Mabon*
Going to Louisiana (see: Going Back to Louisiana)
Going to Move to Alabama. *Charley Patton*
Going to New York. *Mathis James Reed*
Going to the River. *Antoine Domino*
Going to the River. *Charles Ross*
Going Up and Down. *Earl Hooker*
Going Up to the Country. *Taj Mahal*
Gold Mine. *Roosevelt Sykes*
Gold Tailed Bird. *James Rogers*
Gold Teeth. *Andrew McMahon*
Gold Tooth Blues. *Alger Alexander*
Golden Rule Blues. *Bessie Smith*
Gone Again. *Peter Chatman*
Gone Baby Gone. *Walter Brown McGhee*
Gone But Not Forgotten. *Walter Brown McGhee*
Gone Daddy Blues. *Gertrude Rainey*
Gone Dead on You Blues. *Lemon Jefferson*
Gone Gal. *Walter Brown McGhee*
Gone So Long. *Roy Byrd*
Gonna Be a Lovin' Old Soul. *Sara Martin*
Gonna Be My Baby. *Albert Luandrew*
Gonna Bring Down All My Clothes. *John Wrencher*
Gonna Hit the Highway. *Robert Brown (Washboard Sam)*
Gonna Keep On Lovin' You. *Riley King*
Gonna Love My Baby. *Buster Brown*
Gonna Need My Help. *McKinley Morganfield*
Gonna Stand No Quittin'. *Robert Pete Williams*
Gonna Stick to You Baby. *Cornelius Green*
Gonna Take My Rap. *Robert Brown (Washboard Sam)*
Good Boy. *Aaron Walker*
Good Bye Blues. *Sara Martin*
Good Chib Blues. *Edith Johnson*
Good Conductor. *Estella Yancey*
Good Evening Everybody. *Sonny Boy Williamson (Alex Miller)*
Good Feelin'. *Aaron Walker*
Good Gin Blues. *Booker White*
Good Good Whiskey. *Amos Milburn*
Good Home Cooking. *Dave Alexander*
Good Jelly. *William Broonzy*
Good Letting Alone, A. *Johnny Fuller*
Good Liquor Gonna Carry Me Down. *William Broonzy*
Good Livin' Good Lovin' Blues. *Riley King*
Good Looking Woman. *Charles Berry*
Good Looking Women. *K. C. Douglas*
Good Lover. *Mathis James Reed*
Good Lovin'. *Robert Bland*
Good Luck Blues. *Robert Brown (Washboard Sam)*
Good Luck Darling. *Alonzo Johnson*
Good Mornin' Blues. *Huddie Ledbetter*
Good Morning Blues. *James Rushing*
Good Morning Blues. *Joseph Turner*
Good Morning Corrine. *Wynonie Harris*
Good Morning Little Schoolgirl. *John Lee Williamson*
Good Morning Miss Brown. *Taj Mahal*
Good Night Little Arlo. *Woodrow Guthrie*
Good Old Cabbage Greens. *William Broonzy*
Good Old Easy Street. *Robert Brown (Washboard Sam)*
Good Old Union Feeling. *Woodrow Guthrie*
Good Package Blues. *Estella Yancey*
Good Potatoes. *William Borum*
Good Rockin' Man. *Roy Brown*
Good Rockin' Tonight. *Roy Brown*
Good Sissages. *Victoria Spivey*
Good Soul Lovin'. *Lonnie Brooks*
Good Soul Music. *Dave Alexander*
Good Thing Blues. *Charles Ross*
Good Things Come to My Mind. *Charles Ross*
Good Time Boogie. *William Trice*
Good Time Charlie. *Peter Chatman*
Good Time Special. *Curtis Jones*
Good Time Tonight: *William Broonzy/Robert Brown*

Good Times. *James Harris*
Good Times Here. *Sam Hopkins*
Good Times up in Harlem. *Thomas Delaney*
Good Tonk Blues. *Billie Pierce*
Good Whiskey Blues. *Peetie Wheatstraw*
Good Woman Blues. *Clyde Bernhardt*
Good Woman Blues. *Curtis Jones*
Good Woman Is Hard to Find, A. *William Dupree*
Good Women's Blues. *Charles Davenport*
Goodby Baby Blues. *William Broonzy*
Goodby Mama Moan. *Arthur Phelps*
Goodbye. *John Shines*
Goodbye Baby. *Robert Williams*
Goodbye Daddy Blues. *Gertrude Rainey*
Goodbye Fay & John. *Robert Pete Williams*
Goodbye Good Luck to You. *George Guesnon*
Goodbye Kitten. *Alonzo Johnson*
Goodbye Red. *John Lee Williamson*
Goodnight Baby Blues. *Eddie Vinson*
Goodnight Boogie. *Theodore Taylor*
Goodnight Irene. *Huddie Ledbetter*
Goody Goody Goody. *James Oden*
Got a Bad Break. *Albert Luandrew*
Got a Gal. *Joseph Turner*
Got a Good Thing Goin'. *Albert Collins*
Got a Little Old Mama. *Peter Chatman*
(She's) Got a Thing Going On. *Albert Luandrew*
Got It and Can't Quit It. *Henry Brown*
Got It and Gone. *Charles Berry*
Got Love If You Want It. *James Moore*
Got Me Way Down Here. *Robert Pete Williams*
Got My Mojo Working. *McKinley Morganfield*
Got No Use For You. *Aaron Walker*
Got No Walking Shoes (see: Made a Date with an Angel)
Got Nowhere to Go. *Mathis James Reed*
Got on His Mind. *Robert Pete Williams*
Got Sick and Tired. *Booker White*
Got the Blues. *Lemon Jefferson*
Got the Blues, Can't Be Satisfied. *John Hurt*
Got the Blues for the West End. *Alonzo Johnson*
Got the Blues So Bad. *Bonnie Jefferson*
Got to Be a Reason. *Mathis James Reed*
Got to Cross the Deep Blue Sea. *Aaron Walker*
Got to Get to My Baby. *Albert Luandrew*
Got to Have Some. *Willie Mabon*
Got to Know. *Edward Boyd*
Got to Leave My Home Blues. *Sara Martin*
Got to Love My Baby. *Eddie Kirkland*
Got to Move. *Sonny Boy Williamson (Alex Miller)*
Got to Move You Baby. *Sam Hopkins*
Got to Put You Down. *Joe Lee Williams*
Got to Reap What You Sow. *William Gillum*
Got to See Her Every Night. *Walter Davis*
Gotta Find My Baby. *Riley King*
Gotta Get to Boston. *Woodrow Guthrie*
Gotta Gimme Whatcha Got. *Julia Lee*
Gotta Go Baby. *Joe Hill Louis*
Gotta See My Lawyer. *Albert Luandrew*
Gotta Wake Up. *Fention Robinson*
Government Money. *Hammie Nixon*
Governor OK Allen. *Huddie Ledbetter*
Governor Pat Neff. *Huddie Ledbetter*
Grand Central Station. *Walter Lewis*
Grand Coulee Dam. *Woodrow Guthrie*
Grandma. *William Dupree*
Grandma Plays the Numbers. *Wynonie Harris*
Grandma Told Grandpa. *Sam Hopkins*
Grant Spivey. *Victoria Spivey*
Gravedigger Cried, The. *Willie Dixon*
Gravel Road Blues. *Fred McDowell*
Gravel Road Woman. *James Rachell*
Graveyard Blues. *John Lee Hooker*
Graveyard Blues. *Robert Pete Williams*
Graveyard Bound Blues. *John Erby*
Graveyard Dream Blues. *Ida Cox*
Graveyard Love. *Thomas Delaney*
Gravy Child. *George Butler*
Gray's Bounce. *Henry Gray*
Greasy Spoon. *McHouston Baker*
Great Dust Storm, The. *Woodrow Guthrie*
Great Historical Bum, The. *Woodrow Guthrie*
Great Long Ways from Home. *Joe Callicott*
Great Medical Menagerist, The. *Frank Floyd*
Great Northern Stomp. *Otis Spann*
Great Tall Engine. *Sonny Terry*
Green Corn. *Huddie Ledbetter*
Green Country Gal. *Charles Edwards*
Green Flowers. *McKinley Morganfield*
Green Gal Can't Catch On. *Sara Martin*
Green Grass Blues. *William Broonzy*
Green Light. *Joseph Young*
Green River Blues. *Charley Patton*
Green's Bounce. *Clarence Green*
Grey Goose, The. *Huddie Ledbetter*
Greyhound Bus. *Robert Pete Williams*
Greyhound Bus Blues. *Arthur Crudup*
Greystone Blues. *Joe Lee Williams*
Grievin' and Worryin' Blues. *Hudson Whittaker*
Grievin' Me. *Addie Spivey*
Grieving Blues. *Thomas Dorsey*
Grinder Man. *John Lee Hooker*
Grinder Man Blues. *Peter Chatman*
Groaning the Blues. *Willie Dixon*
Grooving the Blues. *Viola Wells*
Grosebeck Blues. *Sam Hopkins*
Grow Old Together. *Victoria Spivey*
Gruff. *Edward Boyd*
Guess I'd Better Knock on Wood. *John Erby*
Guide Me Home. *Willie Mae Thornton*
Guilty Blues. *Willie Mabon*
Guitar Blues. *Sara Martin*
Guitar Boogie. *Charles Berry*
Guitar King. *Andrew McMahon*
Guitar Lovin' Man. *John Lee Hooker*
Guitar Mambo. *McHouston Baker*
Guitar Pete's Blues. *Edward Franklin*

Guitar Rag. *Earl Hooker*
Guitar Rag. *Sara Martin*
Guitar Slim. *Eddie Jones*
Gulfport Boogie. *Roosevelt Sykes*
Gun. *Charles Berry*
Guy with the .45, The. *Alden Bunn*
Gwine Dig a Hole. *Huddie Ledbetter*
Gyp, the Blood. *Richard Brown*
Gypsy Glass Blues. *Jesse Crump*
Gypsy Woman. *McKinley Morganfield*

Ha Ha Baby. *John Wrencher*
Ha, Ha Thisaway. *Huddie Ledbetter*
Had a Date with Barbara Last Night. *Iverson Minter*
Had a Little Woman. *Henry Johnson*
Hadicol Bounce. *Roy Byrd*
Half a Stranger. *John Lee Hooker*
Half Ain't Been Told. *James Oden*
Half Ain't Been Told. *Otis Spann*
Hallelujah I Love Her So. *Ray Charles*
Hammer Blues. *Charley Patton*
Hampstead Blues. *John Holder*
Hampstead to Lose the Blues. *John Holder*
Hand in Hand. *Elmore James*
Hand in Hand. *Walter Brown McGhee*
Hand Me Down Baby. *Sidney Maiden*
Hand Me Down My Walking Cane. *Arthur Crudup*
Hand Reader Blues. *Robert Brown (Washboard Sam)*
Handsome Johnny. *Richard Havens*
Handy Man Blues. *Henry Brown*
Hang It Up on the Wall. *Joe Lee Williams*
Hang Knot. *Woodrow Guthrie*
Hang Loose Baby. *Willie Mabon*
Hang Man's Blues. *Lemon Jefferson*
Hangover. *Roosevelt Sykes*
Happy Blues for John Glenn. *Sam Hopkins*
Happy Shout. *Virginia Liston*
Hard Boiled Papa. *Thomas Delaney*
Hard Days. *McKinley Morganfield*
Hard Feelings Blues. *William Dupree*
Hard Headed Blues. *Clifford Gibson*
Hard Headed Woman. *John Lee Hooker*
Hard Hearted Woman. *William Broonzy*
Hard Hearted Woman. *Eddie Burns*
Hard Hearted Woman. *Walter Horton*
Hard Loving Woman. *Raymond Agee*
Hard Luck Blues. *Roy Brown*
Hard Luck Blues. *Edna Hicks*
Hard-Luck Child. *Nehemiah James*
Hard Oh Lawd: *Ida Cox/Jesse Crump*
Hard Pill to Swallow, A. *Son Bonds*
Hard Pushing Papa. *Arthur Phelps*
Hard Road Blues. *Arthur Phelps*
Hard Road Blues. *Hudson Whittaker*
Hard Road to Travel, A. *James Harris*
Hard Time Blues. *Bessie Smith*
Hard Time Blues. *Joshua White*
Hard Time Killin' Floor Blues. *Nehemiah James*
Hard Times. *Travis Blaylock*
Hard Times. *Roy Brown*
Hard Times. *Johnny Fuller*
Hard Times. *Floyd Jones*
Hard Times Ain't Gone Nowhere. *Alonzo Johnson*
Hard Times Blues. *Ida Cox*
Hard to Love a Woman. *Sam Hopkins*
Hard to Raise a Family Today. *Eddie Kirkland*
Hard Travelling. *Woodrow Guthrie*
Hard Working Man. *Raymond Agee*
Hard Working Man. *Charles Walker*
Hard Working Man Blues. *William Borum*
Hardway, The. *Otis Spann*
Hare Lip Blues. *William Dupree*
Harlem Bound. *Peter Chatman*
Harlem Can't Be Heaven. *Albert Luandrew*
Harmonica Blues. *Sonny Terry*
Harmonica Boogie. *Charles Ross*
Harmonica Breakdown. *Sonny Terry*
Harmonica Rag. *Sonny Terry*
Harmonica Special. *Willie Mabon*
Harmonica with Slaps. *Sonny Terry*
Harp and Soul. *Frank Frost*
Harpo's Blues. *James Moore*
Harris County Line-Up. *Albert Collins*
Hattie Green. *Robert Shaw*
Haunted House, The. *Johnny Fuller*
Havana Moon. *Charles Berry*
Have Mercy Baby. *Amos Wells*
Have Mercy Judge. *Charles Berry*
Have Mercy on Me. *Eddie Kirkland*
Have Mercy on My Soul. *John Lee Hooker*
Have You Changed Your Mind? *Lowell Fulson*
Have you Ever Been in Love? *Sonny Boy Williamson (Alex Miller)*
Have You Ever Been Out in the Country? *Mercy Dee Walton*
Have You Ever Loved a Woman? *Sam Hopkins*
Have You Heard the News? *John Jenkins*
Have You Seen That Lonesome Train? *Eddie Kirkland*
Have Your Chill. *Wesley Wilson*
Havin' Fun. *Peter Chatman*
Having Fun Here and There. *Alexander Moore*
Having My Say. *Riley King*
Hawaiian Boogie. *Elmore James*
Hawk Squat. *Joseph Hutto*
He Caught That B&O. *Amos Easton*
He Don't Love You. *Dusty Brown*
He Knows How Much You Can Bear. *Thomas Dorsey*
He May Be Yours But He Ain't Yours All Alone. *John Erby*
He Sho' Don't Mean No Harm. *Charles Davenport*
He Was More Than a Friend of Mine. *Mable Hillery*
Head Rag Hop (Hop Head Rag). *Iromeio Nelson*
Headed for Nashville. *Peter Chatman*
Hear Me Howlin'. *KC Douglas*
Hear Me Talking to You. *Gertrude Rainey*
Heard My Doorbell Ring. *John Young*

Hearseman Blues. *Harmon Ray*
Heart Like Railroad Steel. *Charley Patton*
Heart Trouble. *Henry Townsend*
Heart Trouble Blues. *Theodore Darby*
Heartache. *Albert Luandrew*
Heartaches and Trouble. *Mathis James Reed*
Heartbreaker. *Riley King*
Held Up in One Town. *Iverson Minter*
Hell Hound on My Trail. *Robert Johnson*
Hell Is a Name for All Sinners. *Alonzo Johnson*
Hello and Goodbye. *Walter Brown*
Hello Baby. *Walter Davis*
Hello Central. *Sam Hopkins*
Hello Little Girl. *Clarence Miller*
Hello Little Girl, Goodbye. *Charles Berry*
Hello Miss Jessie Lee. *Eddie Burns*
Hello My Darling. *Phillip Walker*
Hello Stranger. *William Arnold*
Hello Stranger. *Edward Boyd*
Help Me. *Sonny Boy Williamson (Alex Miller)*
Help Me Some. *Peter Chatman*
Help Me Some. *J. D. Short*
Help Me Spend My Gold. *Otis Hicks*
Help Yourself. *Mathis James Reed*
Hen House Blues. *K. C. Douglas*
Hen Peck Joe. *Oscar Wills*
Henry Brown Blues. *Henry Brown*
Henry Ford Blues. *Huddie Ledbetter*
Henry Ford Blues. *Roosevelt Sykes*
Henry's Jive. *Henry Brown*
Henry's Jive. *Henry Townsend*
Here Am I, Send Me. *Robert Wilkins*
Here Come the Blues. *Wynonie Harris*
Here Comes the Train. *Charles Sayles*
Here I Am a Fool in Love Again. *John Jenkins*
Here I Go Again. *Cleve White*
Here Rattler Here (see: Old Riley)
Here's My Picture. *William Arnold*
Here's Where You Get It. *Jerry McCain*
He's a Creepin' Man. *Robert Brown (Washboard Sam)*
He's a Good Meat Cutter: *Leola B Grant/Wesley Wilson*
He's Gone Blues. *Bessie Smith*
He's Just a Gravy Train. *Roosevelt Sykes*
He's the Cause of My (Me) Being Blue. *Beulah Wallace*
Hey Baby. *John Henry Barbee*
Hey Baby. *Otis Spann*
Hey Bo Diddley. *Ellas McDaniel*
Hey Bud Blues. *William Broonzy*
Hey Fat Man. *Antoine Domino*
Hey Foreman. *Michael Bloomfield*
Hey Girl. *Willie Mabon*
Hey Good Lookin'. *Charles Berry*
Hey Hey. *William Broonzy*
Hey Hey. *Jesse Fuller*
Hey Hey Baby's Gone. *Phillip Walker*
Hey Lawdy Mama Whose Old Funky Drawers Are These? *Tommy Tucker*
Hey Little Girl. *McHouston Baker*
Hey Little Girl. *Aaron Willis*
Hey Little Lee. *James Moore*
Hey Miss Bertha. *Clyde Bernhardt*
Hey Mr. Nixon. *Thomas Shaw*
Hey Mr. Porter. *George Smith*
Hey Now Baby. *Roy Byrd*
Hey Pedro. *Charles Berry*
Hey Slim. *Peter Chatman*
Hi-Heel Sneakers. *Tommy Tucker*
Hidden Charms. *Willie Dixon*
Hide Away. *Freddie King*
Hide Away Blues. *Antoine Domino*
Hide Me in Thy Bosom. *Thomas Dorsey*
Hide nor Hair. *Percy Mayfield*
Hideaway. *Theodore Taylor*
High and Lonesome. *Mathis James Reed*
High as a Georgia Pine. *Roosevelt Sykes*
High as I Want to Be. *Robert Pete Williams*
High Fever Blues. *Booker White*
High Powered Woman. *Sonny Terry*
High Price Blues. *Roosevelt Sykes*
High Priced Woman. *John Lee Hooker*
High Rise. *Freddie King*
High Sheriff Blues. *Charley Patton*
High Water Everywhere. *Charley Patton*
High Water Rising. *K. C. Douglas*
Higher and Higher. *Roy Brown*
Highway Blues. *J. C. Burris*
Highway Blues. *Charles Musselwhite*
Highway Bound. *Riley King*
Highway 59. *Dave Alexander*
Highway 51 Blues. *Curtis Jones*
Highway 49. *Chester Burnett*
Highway 49. *Joe Lee Williams*
Highway Is Like a Woman, The. *Percy Mayfield*
Highway 99. *Joe Hill Louis*
Hijack Blues. *Walter Davis*
Hindenburg Disaster. *Huddie Ledbetter*
Hip Shakin'. *Joseph Hutto*
Hip Shakin' Strut. *Thomas Dorsey*
His Daughter Caroline. *Charles Berry*
Hit or Miss. *Odetta Gordon*
Hit the Floor. *John Lee Hooker*
Hit the Right Lick. *William Broonzy*
Hit the Road. *John Lee Hooker*
Hit the Road, Jack. *Percy Mayfield*
Hobo. *Eddie House*
Hobo Blues. *John Lee Hooker*
Hobo Blues. *Joshua Howell*
Hobo Blues. *Johnie Lewis*
Hobo Blues. *James Rachell*
Hobo's Meditation. *Louis Robinson*
Hobson City Stomp. *Charles Davenport*
Hoist Your Window and Let Your Curtain Down. *Joe Callicott*
Hold It. *John Lee Hooker*
Hold It Right There. *Eddie Vinson*
Hold Me Baby. *Willie Dixon*

Hold Me Baby. *Amos Milburn*
Hold Me in Your Arms. *James Cotton*
Hold Me in Your Arms. *Walter Brown McGhee*
Hold Me Tight. *J. C. Burris*
Hold On Baby. *John Fortescue*
Hold On I'm Comin'. *Earl Hooker*
Hold That Bus, Conductor. *James Harris*
Hold That Plane. *George Guy*
Hold That Train. *Riley King*
Hold That Train Conductor. *Peter Clayton*
Hole in the Wall. *Walter Brown McGhee*
Hollerin' (and Cryin') the Blues. *William Broonzy*
Home Call. *James Rodgers*
Home to Mamma. *Willie Dixon*
Home to Mississippi. *Otis Spann*
Home Town Blues. *Irene Scruggs*
Home Wrecker's Blues. *Alonzo Johnson*
Homecoming Blues. *John Williamson*
Homesick. *Walter Davis*
Homesick (Blues). *John Williamson*
Homesick Blues. *Floyd Dixon*
Homesick's Blues. *John Williamson*
Homesick's Rock. *John Williamson*
Homesick's Shuffle. *John Williamson*
Homogenized Love. *Jerry McCain*
Honest I Do. *Mathis James Reed*
Honey Babe. *Sam Hopkins*
Honey Bee. *John Mars*
Honey Bee. *McKinley Morganfield*
Honey Bee Blues. *Silas Hogan*
Honey Bee Blues. *John Lee Williamson*
Honey Dripper Blues. *Edith North Johnson*
Honey in the Bee Ball. *Louis Jordan*
Honey Maker Blues. *William Borum*
Honey Where You Been So Long? *Thomas Delaney*
Honeydripper, The. *Roosevelt Sykes*
Honeymoon Blues. *Robert Johnson*
Honeysucker Blues. *Charles Jordan*
Honkey Tonkey. *Koko Taylor*
Hoo Doo Blues. *Willie Dixon*
Hoo-doo Hoo-doo. *John Lee Williamson*
Hoo-doo Man. *John Lee Williamson*
Hoochie Coochie Man (see: I'm Your Hoochie Coochie Man)
Hoodoo Man, The. *Dave Alexander*
Hoodoo Man. *Amos Wells*
Hoodoo Man Blues. *Victoria Spivey*
Hoodoo Woman Blues. *Cornelius Green*
Hoodoo Women. *Johnny Temple*
Hoogle-De-Doo. *John Fortescue*
Hook, Line and Sinker. *Smiley Lewis*
Hooker 'n' Steve. *Earl Hooker*
Hooker Special. *Earl Hooker*
Hookin'. *Earl Hooker*
Hooray Hooray. *Sonny Terry*
Hootie Blues. *Walter Brown*
Hootin' Blues. *Sonny Terry*
Hooversville. *Woodrow Guthrie*
Hop Head Rag (see: Head Rag Hop)
Hop Stroll. *Jerry McCain*
Horseshoe over the Door. *Robert Brown (Washboard Sam)*
Hoss. *Lonnie Brooks*
Hot & Heavy. *Earl Hooker*
Hot Club Drive. *Clarence Brown*
Hot Dog. *John Young*
Hot-Headed Woman. *Sonny Terry*
Hot 'n' Cold. *Albert Collins*
Hot Pappa Blues. *Charlie Jackson*
Hot Sauce. *Frank Seals*
Hot Springs Arkansas. *Booker White*
Hot Springs Blues. *David Edwards*
Hot Springs Blues. *Bessie Smith*
Hotel Blues. *Edward Boyd*
House Cleanin' Blues. *Louis Robinson*
House Cleaning. *Peter Chatman*
House Lady. *Walter Brown McGhee*
House Party. *Amos Milburn*
House Rent Boogie. *John Lee Hooker*
House Rent Party. *William Dupree*
House Rocker. *James Rogers*
How About That? *Jimmy McCracklin*
How About You? *Thomas Dorsey*
How Can I Play Fair? *Robert Brown (Washboard Sam)*
How Can I Stay When All I Have Is Gone? *Arthur Kelley*
How Can You Love Me? *Will Weldon*
How Could She Leave Me? *Frank Seals*
How Do They Do It That Way? *Victoria Spivey*
How Do You Want Your Lovin' Done? *James Rushing*
How Have You Been? *Sam Hopkins*
How Long? *Frank Stokes*
How Long Blues. *Leroy Carr*
How Long Brother? *Eurreal Montgomery*
How Long Buck? *Nehemiah James*
How Long Can a Fool Go Wrong? *James Cotton*
How Long Can This Go On? *Herman Parker*
How Long Has That Train Been Gone? *Roy Byrd*
How May More Years? *Chester Burnett*
How Much More Long? *Charles Ross*
How to Do the Bacon Fat. *Andre Williams*
Howdy Blues. *Walter Brown McGhee*
Howlin' Blues. *Chester Burnett*
Howlin' for My Baby. *Willie Dixon*
Howling Wind. *David Edwards*
Howling Wind Blues. *Walter Davis*
Hoy Hoy. *John Jones*
Huffin' and Puffin'. *James Harris*
Humble Blues. *William Broonzy*
Hump in Your Back. *Jesse Fuller*
Humpty Dumpty. *John Young*
Hungry Country Girl. *Otis Spann*
Hunt, The. *Willie Dixon*
Hunt, The. *Sonny Boy Williamson (Alex Miller)*
Hunting Blues. *Frank Stokes*
Hurry and Bring It Home Blues. *Charles Davenport*
Hurry Down Sunshine. *Arthur Kelley*

Hurry Down Sunshine (see: What Tomorrow Bring). *Will Shade*
Hush Baby Don't You Cry. *Edward Boyd*
Hush Hush. *Mathis James Reed*
Hush Your Mouth. *Ellas McDaniel*
Hustlin' Blues. *Gertrude Rainey*

I Ain't for It. *Bill Webb*
I Ain't from Chicago. *Mathis James Reed*
I Ain't Going to Sell You None: *Leola B. Grant/Wesley Wilson*
I Ain't Gonna. *Cecil Gant*
I Ain't Gonna Be Bad No More. *Fred McDowell*
I Ain't Gonna Be Worried No More. *Hammie Nixon*
I Ain't Gonna Be Your Fool. *Alonzo Johnson*
I Ain't Gonna Pick No More Cotton. *John Henry Barbee*
I Ain't Gonna Scold You. *Walter Brown McGhee*
I Ain't Gonna Suffer. *Louis Bo Collins*
I Ain't Got No Home in This World Anymore. *Woodrow Guthrie*
I Ain't Got No Money. *William Arnold*
I Ain't Got You. *Mathis James Reed*
I Ain't No Ice Man. *Charles Davenport*
I Ain't Superstitious. *Willie Dixon*
I Am in the Heavenly Way. *Booker White*
I Am Not Dead. *Charles Ross*
I Am the Blues. *Peter Chatman*
I Am the Blues. *Willie Dixon*
I Am the Gambler. *Raymond Agee*
I Am the Light of This World. *Gary Davis*
I Asked for Water. *Chester Burnett*
I Asked Her If She Loved Me. *Henry Townsend*
I Asked the Bossman. *Sam Hopkins*
I Ate the Wrong Part. *Gus Jenkins*
I Been Wrong But I'll Be Right. *Joe Lee Williams*
I Believe. *Elmore James*
I Believe I Make a Change. *John Shines*
I Believe I'll Dust My Broom. *Robert Johnson*
I Believe My Baby's Gone. *John Williamson*
I Better Go Now. *Chester Burnett*
I. C. Blues. *William Broonzy*
I. C. Blues, The. *Peter Chatman*
I Call It Love. *Eddie Burns*
I Called You Up Daddy. *Clarence Garlow*
I Came from Clarksdale. *Otis Spann*
I Can Always Tell When (My/a) Man Is Treatin' Me Cool. *Sara Martin*
I Can Fix It. *William Broonzy*
I Can Tell by the Way You Smell. *Walter Davis*
I Can't Be Alone. *Sonny Boy Williamson (Alex Miller)*
I Can't Be Satisfied. *McKinley Morganfield*
I Can't Do Nothing But Boogie. *John Lee Granderson*
I Can't Do Without You. *Sonny Boy Williamson (Alex Miller)*
I Can't Explain. *Riley King*
I Can't Get Enough. *Wesley Wilson*
I Can't Hardly See. *James Witherspoon*
I Can't Keep My Foot from Jumpin'. *John Young*
I Can't Last Long. *Victoria Spivey*
I Can't Lose with the Stuff I Use. *Pleasant Joseph*
I Can't Quit the Blues. *George Guy*
I Can't Quit You Baby. *Willie Dixon*
I Can't Sleep at Night. *Walter Brown McGhee*
I Can't Stand. *Clifton Chenier*
I Can't Stay Here. *Andrew McMahon*
I Can't Stop Loving You (see: I'll Never Stop)
I Can't Understand. *Sonny Boy Williamson (Alex Miller)*
I Couldn't Believe My Eyes. *Walter Brown McGhee*
I Couldn't Take It. *John Erby*
I Cried. *Edward Boyd*
I Cross My Heart. *Sonny Boy Williamson (Alex Miller)*
I Cry. *Edward Boyd*
I Cry I Cry. *John Shines*
I Didn't Know. *Chester Burnett*
I Didn't Tell Her to Leave. *Silas Hogan*
I Do Really Love You. *Charles Berry*
I Done Got Wise. *Riley King*
I Done Got Wise. *McKinley Morganfield*
I Done Talked and I Done Talked. *Frankie Lee Sims*
I Done You Wrong. *Albert Luandrew*
I Done You Wrong. *Roosevelt Sykes*
I Don't Care No More. *Sonny Boy Williamson (Alex Miller)*
I Don't Care Where You Take It. *Thomas Delaney*
I Don't Care Who Knows. *Willie Dixon*
I Don't Hurt Anymore. *Alonzo Johnson*
I Don't Know. *Clarence Lofton*
I Don't Know. *Willie Mabon*
I Don't Know. *Sonny Boy Williamson (Alex Miller)*
I Don't Know It. *Arthur Crudup*
I Don't Know the Reason. *Walter Brown McGhee*
I Don't Know Why. *William Broonzy*
I Don't Know Why. *Thomas Dorsey*
I Don't Live Today. *James Hendrix*
I Don't Need No Heater. *Fred McDowell*
I Don't Need No Steam Heat. *John Lee Hooker*
I Don't Need You Woman. *Sam Hopkins*
I Don't Wanna Go to Vietnam. *John Lee Hooker*
I Don't Want a Woman to Stay Out All Night Long. *Nehemiah James*
I Don't Want Maybe. *Willie Dixon*
I Don't Want No Woman If She Got Hair Like Drops of Rain. *James Brewer*
I Don't Want That Stale Stuff. *Wesley Wilson*
I Don't Want You Baby. *Arbee Stidham*
I Don't Want Your Money. *John Lee Hooker*
I Enjoy Myself in Pau. *Willie Mabon*
I Feel All Right. *Walter Davis*
I Feel All Right. *Luke Miles*
I Feel Alright. *James Pryor*
I Feel Alright, Now. *Walter Brown McGhee*
I Feel Bad, Bad, Bad. *Carey Bell*
I Feel Like Ballin' the Jack. *Peter Chatman*
I Feel Like Calling You. *Clarence Garlow*
I Feel So Bad. *Eddie Taylor*
I Feel So Fine. *William Hensley*

I Feel So Good. *Raymond Agee*
I Feel So Good. *William Broonzy*
I Feel the Way I Feel. *Willie Mae Thornton*
I Fell for You. *Viola Wells*
I Found a True Love. *George Guy*
I Found My Baby. *George Smith*
I Found My Way to Wine. *Jalacy Hawkins*
I Get a Strange Feeling. *Willie Dixon*
I Get Evil. *Albert King*
I Get Evil When My Love Comes Down. *Gabriel Brown*
I Get So Weary. *Aaron Walker*
I Give. *Joseph Young*
I Got a Feelin'. *James Cotton*
I Got a Feeling. *Otis Spann*
I Got a Funny Feeling. *Arthur Kelley*
I Got a Little Girl. *Sonny Terry*
I Got a Little Woman. *Otis Hicks*
I Got a Mind to Ramble. *Jesse Fuller*
I Got a Mind to Ramble. *Alberta Hunter*
I Got a Whole Lot of Talk for You. *Curtis Jones*
I Got a Woman. *Edward Boyd*
I Got a Woman. *Ray Charles*
I Got It. *John Young*
I Got Love for Sale. *Joseph Turner*
I Got Men All Over Town. *Victoria Spivey*
I Got More Sense Than That. *Clarence Smith*
I Got My Brand on You. *McKinley Morganfield*
I Got My Eyes on You. *George Guy*
I Got My Eyes on You. *Sonny Terry*
I Got Myself a Working Man. *Alberta Hunter*
I Got News for You Baby. *Alonzo Johnson*
I Got Some Help I Don't Need. *Riley King*
I Got Somebody Else. *William Gillum*
I Got Somebody Else. *Joe McCoy*
I Got Something to Tell You. *Charles Ross*
I Got Sumpin' for You. *Eddie Jones*
I Got the Blues. *Edward Boyd*
I Got the Blues. *Walter Horton*
I Got the Blues About My Baby. *Albert Luandrew*
I Got the Blues at Bedtime. *William Broonzy*
I Got the Blues Everywhere. *Peter Chatman*
I Got the Blues So Bad. *Victoria Spivey*
I Got the Feelin'. *Andrew Odom*
I Got Tired. *Sam Hopkins*
I Got to Find My Baby. *Marion Walter Jacobs*
I Got to Go. *Marion Walter Jacobs*
I Got to Keep Rolling. *Mathis James Reed*
I Got What It Takes But It Breaks My Heart to Give It Away. *Charlie Jackson*
I Got You Covered. *Alden Bunn*
I Got Your Bath Water On. *Susie Edwards*
I Gotta Break Baby. *Aaron Walker*
I Gotta Find My Baby. *Peter Clayton*
I Gotta Go Now. *Elmore James*
I Gotta Look Under Your Hood. *Walter Brown McGhee*
I Guess I'm a Fool. *Peter Chatman*
I Had a Dream. *William Broonzy*
I Had a Dream. *Ray Charles*
I Had a Dream. *William Dupree*
I Had a Dream. *William Lucas*
I Had a Dream Last Night. *Cornelius Green*
I Had a Dream Last Night. *George Guy*
I Had a Dream Last Night. *Lee Jackson*
I Had a Woman. *Joshua White*
I Had It Hard. *Albert Luandrew*
I Had My Fun. *Rufus Perryman*
I Had to Get with It. *Jimmy McCracklin*
I Had to Give Up Gym. *Thomas Dorsey*
I Had to Let Her Go. *Edward Boyd*
I Had to Stop to Conquer You Baby. *Pleasant Joseph*
I Hate to Be Alone. *Roosevelt Sykes*
I Hate to See You Go. *Aaron Walker*
I Have a Right to Love My Baby. *Elmore James*
I Have Found Somebody. *William Borum*
I Have Made Up My Mind. *James Oden*
I Have the Blues Every Day. *John Sellers*
I Hear Some Blues Downstairs. *Fention Robinson*
I Hear You Knockin'. *Smiley Lewis*
I Hear Voices. *Jalacy Hawkins*
I Heard My Baby. *John Barbee*
I Heard My Children Crying. *Sam Hopkins*
I Heard Somebody Call. *Fred McDowell*
I Heard Somebody Cryin'. *Alexander Lightfoot*
I Heard the Angels Singing. *Gary Davis*
I Held My Baby Last Night. *Elmore James*
I Just Can't Hold On Much Longer. *John Lee Hooker*
I Just Can't Leave You. *James Moore*
I Just Don't Know. *John Lee Hooker*
I Just Got to Know. *Jimmy McCracklin*
I Just Keep Loving Her. *Marion Walter Jacobs*
I Just Want a Daddy I Can Call My Own. *Thomas Dorsey*
I Just Want to Hold On. *James Walker*
I Keep On Aching (see: Pneumonia Blues)
I Keep Rollin' On. *Oran Page*
I Knew You Were Kiddin' All the Time. *Walter Jacobs Vinson*
I Know Better. *Walter Brown McGhee*
I Know It's a Sin. *Mathis James Reed*
I Know Moonlight. *Joshua White*
I Know My Baby. *Eddie Taylor*
I Know She Will. *William Broonzy*
I Know the Price. *Riley King*
I Know the Winds Are Blowing. *John Shines*
I Know What Love Is All About. *Sonny Boy Williamson (Alex Miller)*
I Know What You're Puttin' Down. *Louis Jordan*
I Know You Don't Love Me. *Moses Smith*
I Know You Gonna Miss Me. *Joe Lee Williams*
I Know Your Wig Is Gone. *Aaron Walker*
I Laid My Cards on the Table. *Robert Brown (Washboard Sam)*
I Left My Baby. *James Rushing*
I Like 'em Fat Like That. *Louis Jordan*
I Like the Way You Spread Your Wings. *Walter Davis*
I Like to See You Walk. *John Lee Hooker*

I Looked at the Sun. *Fred McDowell*
I Lost My Appetite. *William Lucas*
I Lost the Good Woman. *James Rogers*
I Love My Baby. *Robert Brown (Washboard Sam)*
I Love My Baby. *Milton Campbell*
I Love My Baby. *Joe Hill Louis*
I Love My Baby. *Tommy McClennan*
I Love My Man Better Than I Love Myself. *Ida Cox*
I Love That Woman. *John Jenkins*
I Love the Life I'm Living. *James Moore*
I Love You. *Edward Boyd*
I Love You Baby. *David Edwards*
I Love You Baby. *Mathis James Reed*
I Love You Daddy But You Don't Mean Me No Good. *Thomas Delaney*
I Love You Only. *William Arnold*
I Love You So. *William Dupree*
I Love You Sweet Baby. *William Trice*
I Made a Lot of Mistakes. *James Witherspoon*
I Need a Little Spirit. *Dave Alexander*
I Need a Lover Not Just a Friend. *Eddie Kirkland*
I Need a Man to Love. *Janis Joplin*
I Need Love. *John Williamson*
I Need More and More. *Willie Dixon*
I Need My Baby. *Peter Clayton*
I Need Some Money. *John Lee Hooker*
I Need You. *John Lee Hooker*
I Need You. *Elmore James*
I Need You to Drive the Blues Away. *Edith Wilson*
I Need Your Love. *Walter Horton*
I Needs to Be Be'd Wid. *Eddie Vinson*
I Never Do Wrong. *Sonny Boy Williamson (Alex Miller)*
I Offer You. *John Erby*
I Put a Spell on You. *Jalacy Hawkins*
I Received a Letter. *James Yancey*
I See a Man Downstairs. *Sonny Boy Williamson (Alex Miller)*
I See My Baby. *Elmore James*
I Should Have Known. *Haskell Sadler*
I Stayed Away Too Long. *John Estes*
I Stayed Away Too Long. *Arbee Stidham*
I Still Don't Know. *Willie Mabon*
I Still Love You Baby. *Lowell Fulson*
I Submit to You. *Alden Bunn*
I Surely Know There's Been a Change in Me. *Thomas Dorsey*
I Thank God for My Song. *Thomas Dorsey*
I Tried. *Eddie Kirkland*
I Tried Not to Cry. *John Young*
I Tried to Be a Friend. *Eddie Kirkland*
I Used to Have a Woman. *James Rogers*
I Used to Have Some Friends. *Eddie Taylor*
I Walked All Night Long. *Albert King*
I Walked All the Way from E. St. Louis. *Fred McDowell*
I Walked from Dallas. *Chester Burnett*
I Walked Twelve Miles. *Eddie Kirkland*
I Wanna Be Loved. *Mathis James Reed*
I Wanna Dance. *Peter Chatman*
I Wanna Love. *Roosevelt Sykes*
I Wanna Trade with You. *Eddie Burns*
I Wanna Walk You Home. *Antoine Domino*
I Want a True Lover. *John Sellers*
I Want a Two-Fisted, Double-Jointed, Rough-and-Ready Man. *Alberta Hunter*
I Want All My Friends to Know. *Charles Ross*
I Want Her Back. *Arthur Gunter*
I Want to Be Loved. *McKinley Morganfield*
I Want to Be Your Driver. *Charles Berry*
I Want to Belong to You. *Arbee Stidham*
I Want My Fanny Brown. *Roy Brown*
I Want My Hands on It. *William Broonzy*
I Want to Do Something for You. *Lizzie Douglas*
I Want to Go Fishin'. *James Pryor*
I Want to Have a Word with You. *Chester Burnett*
I Want to Go Home. *Charles Brown*
I Want to Know. *Ray Charles*
I Want to Know. *James Dawkins*
I Want to Know. *Antoine Domino*
I Want to Know. *Lowell Fulson*
I Want to Know What My Baby's Puttin' Down. *Joe Lee Williams*
I Want to Know Why. *James Brewer*
I Want to Shout. *John Lee Hooker*
I Want to Tear It All the Time. *Hammie Nixon*
I Want to Thank You Lord for My Blessings. *Alberta Hunter*
I Want to Warn You Baby. *John Shines*
I Want You. *Aaron Willis*
I Want You by My Side. *William Broonzy*
I Want You So Bad. *Riley King*
I Want You to Love Me. *McKinley Morganfield*
I Was Fooled. *Joseph Leon Williams*
I Was Lost. *James Witherspoon*
I Was Out Walking. *Iverson Minter*
I Was So in Love with You. *Eurreal Montgomery*
I Was So Wrong. *Mathis James Reed*
I Was Standing by the Wayside. *John Lee Hooker*
I Went to Louisiana. *Sam Hopkins*
I Will Always Love You. *James Harris*
I Will Do My Last Singing in This Land Somewhere. *Gary Davis*
I Will Never Forget That Floating Bridge (see: Floating Bridge)
I Will Not Let You Go. *Charles Berry*
I Will Trust in the Lord. *Thomas Dorsey*
I Will Turn Your Money Green. *Walter Lewis*
I Wish I Had Somebody. *Hattie McDaniel*
I Wish I Was a Baby. *Sam Hopkins*
I Wish My Baby. *Aaron Walker*
I Wish You Would. *William Arnold*
I Woke Up Cryin'. *Cornelius Green*
I Woke Up One Morning and I Could Hardly See. *Walter Brown McGhee*
I Woke Up This Morning. *Clifton Chenier*
I Woke Up with the Blues. *Sonny Terry*
I Wonder. *Cecil Gant*

I Wonder. *Willie Mabon*
I Wonder Do I Have a Friend. *Sonny Boy Williamson (Alex Miller)*
I Wonder to Myself. *Tommy Johnson*
I Wonder Where She Can Be Tonight. *Sam Hopkins*
I Wonder Who. *Iverson Minter*
I Wonder Why. *John Lee Hooker*
I Wonder Why. *Otis Spann*
I Wonder Why. *Aaron Walker*
I Wonder Why. *Sonny Boy Williamson (Alex Miller)*
I Won't Be Back If I Don't Find My Brown at All. *Sara Martin*
I Won't Be Here Long. *Oran Page*
I Won't Be in Hard Luck No More. *Joe Lee Williams*
I Won't Be Sober Long. *Robert Brown (Washboard Sam)*
I Won't Do That No More. *Joe Lee Williams*
I Would Hate to Hate You (Like I Love You). *Walter Davis*
Iberville and Franklin. *George Guesnon*
Ice and Snow Blues. *Clifford Gibson*
Ice Cream Freezer. *Roosevelt Sykes*
Ice Cream Man. *John Brim*
Ice Man. *Louis Jordan*
Ice Man Blues. *Arthur Phelps*
Ice Storm Blues. *Sam Hopkins*
Iced Nehi. *Otis Spann*
I'd Been Well Warned. *John Estes*
I'd Give My Life for You. *Willie Dixon*
I'd Love to Love You. *Walter Brown McGhee*
I'd Rather Be an Old Woman's Baby Than a Young Woman's Slave. *Charles Ross*
Ida B. *Sonny Terry*
Ida Mae. *Sam Hopkins*
Idle Hour Blues. *Victoria Spivey*
If Crying Would Help Me. *Milton Campbell*
If I Could Hear My Mother. *Otis Spann*
If I Could I Would. *Sidney Semien*
If I Could Live My Life All Over Again. *John Williamson*
If I Didn't Love You. *Joe McCoy*
If I Ever Get Back Home. *Arthur Kelley*
If I Get Lucky. *Arthur Crudup*
If I Had a Listen. *John Davis*
If I Had a Woman. *John Mars*
If I Keep On Worrying. *Clarence Garlow*
If I Let You Get Away with It. *Hudson Whittaker*
If I Lose Let Me Lose. *Thomas Delaney*
If I Only Knew. *Roy Byrd*
If It Hadn't Been for You. *Walter Davis*
If It's True. *Cecil Gant*
If This Ain't the Blues. *James Rushing*
If Trouble Was Money. *Louis Bo Collins*
If We Can Find It. *Phillip Walker*
If You Can't Live in This World by Yourself (see: You Can't Live in This World by Yourself)
If You Can't Shimmy-She-Wabble. *Joe Lee Williams*
If You Change Your Mind. *Joseph Hutto*
If You Ever Been Down. *Rufus Perryman*
If You Got a Dollar. *John Lee Hooker*
If You Haven't Any Hay Get On Down the Road. *Nehemiah James*
If You Just Hold On. *Arbee Stidham*
If You Leave Me. *David Van Ronk*
If You Love Me. *Milton Campbell*
If You Love Me Like You Say. *Johnny Taylor*
If You Love These Blues. *Michael Bloomfield*
If You Need Me. *Antoine Domino*
If You See My Baby. *Cornelius Green*
If You See My Saviour. *Thomas Dorsey*
If You Sing a Gospel Song. *Thomas Dorsey*
If You Treat Me Right. *Walter Davis*
If You Were a Rabbit. *George Smith*
If You Were Mine. *Willie Dixon*
If You'll Only Understand. *Walter Davis*
I'll Be Anything. *Walter Brown McGhee*
I'll Be Glad When You're Dead You Rascal You. *Charles Davenport*
I'll Be Gone. *Antoine Domino*
I'll Be Gone Babe. *Charlie Jackson*
I'll Be Up Some Day. *James Arnold*
I'll Catch the Train and Ride. *Roosevelt Holts*
I'll Follow You. *Bill Williams*
I'll Forget About You. *Herman Parker*
I'll Forget You Blues. *Sara Martin*
I'll Get Along Somehow. *William Gillum*
I'll Go On Living. *James Witherspoon*
I'll Go with Her. *Robert Wilkins*
I'll Keep On Hurtin'. *Willie Mabon*
I'll Kill Your Soul. *Hudson Whittaker*
I'll Know Tonight. *John Lee Hooker*
I'll Meet You in the Bottom. *Amos Easton*
I'll Never Fall in Love Again. *Victoria Spivey*
I'll Never Stop (I Can't Stop Loving You). *Edward Boyd*
I'll Never Turn Back. *Thomas Dorsey*
I'll Never Walk in Your Door. *Edward Harris*
I'll Rock You Baby. *Al King*
I'll Take Love. *Travis Blaylock*
I'll Tell It Wherever I Go. *Thomas Dorsey*
I'll Try. *William Dupree*
I'll Understand. *Aaron Walker*
Illinois Blues. *Nehemiah James*
Illinois Central. *Albert Luandrew*
I'm a Back-Bitin' Mama. *Thomas Delaney*
I'm a Bad Boy. *Otis Spann*
I'm a Country Boy. *Eddie Taylor*
I'm a Dangerous Man. *Roosevelt Sykes*
I'm a Fool. *Edward Boyd*
I'm a Fool. *Joe McCoy*
I'm a Fool. *Lucille Spann*
I'm a Good Hearted Mama. *Thomas Delaney*
I'm a Hog for You. *Clifton Chenier*
I'm a King Bee. *James Moore*
I'm a Lonely Man. *Robert Brown (Washboard Sam)*
I'm a Man (Manish Boy). *Ellas McDaniel*
I'm a Mighty Tight Woman. *Beulah Wallace*
I'm a Mojo Man. *Cornelius Green*
I'm a Nut. *Roosevelt Sykes*

I'm a One Man Woman But I Never Found My Man. *Jean Kittrell*
I'm a Prisoner. *Edward Boyd*
I'm a Prowlin' Ground Hog. *Robert Brown (Washboard Sam)*
I'm a Red Hot Mama. *Victoria Spivey*
I'm a Roaming Stranger. *Iverson Minter*
I'm a Rocker. *Charles Berry*
I'm a Steady Rollin' Man. *Robert Johnson*
I'm a Tearing Little Daddy. *John Estes*
I'm Afraid of Fire. *Sonny Terry*
I'm Alabama Bound. *Charlie Jackson*
I'm Bad. *Ellas McDaniel*
I'm Bad Like Jesse James. *John Lee Hooker*
I'm Bettin' on You. *Hudson Whittaker*
I'm Black. *Walter Lewis*
I'm Broke and I'm Hungry. *Robert Brown (Smokey Babe)*
I'm Coming Home. *Edward Boyd*
I'm Cracking Up over You. *Riley King*
I'm Crazy About You Baby. *Fred McDowell*
I'm Crazy About Your Pie. *Sonny Terry*
I'm Crying. *Peter Chatman*
I'm Cuttin' Out. *Johnny Temple*
I'm Doing All Right. *John Young*
I'm Feeling Alright. *Willie Mae Thornton*
I'm Feeling Low Down. *Curtis Jones*
I'm Getting Old. *John Shines*
I'm Getting Wild About Her. *Joe Lee Williams*
I'm Glad She's Mine. *Cornelius Green*
I'm Goin' Home. *John Fortescue*
I'm Goin' Home. *Charley Patton*
I'm Goin' I'm Goin'. *John Young*
I'm Goin' to Build a Heaven of My Own. *Sam Hopkins*
I'm Goin' to Keep Lovin' You. *Eddie Kirkland*
I'm Goin' to Quit Saying Goodbye. *Jean Kittrell*
I'm Going Away. *Elizabeth Cotten*
I'm Going Back to Georgia. *Iverson Minter*
I'm Going — But I'll Be Back. *Buster Brown*
I'm Going Home. *John Estes*
I'm Going Home to My Heavenly King. *Robert Wilkins*
I'm Going to Get You. *Willie Mabon*
I'm Going to St. Louis. *Joe McCoy*
I'm Going to Wait for You. *Eddie Kirkland*
I'm Going Upstairs. *John Lee Hooker*
I'm Gonna Be a Wheel Someday. *Antoine Domino*
I'm Gonna Do What They Do to Me. *Riley King*
I'm Gonna Fight for You J. B. *John Mayall*
I'm Gonna Forget You. *Eddie Kirkland*
I'm Gonna Get on My Feets Afterwhile. *Sonny Terry*
I'm Gonna Hoodoo You. *Sara Martin*
I'm Gonna Keep What I've Got. *James Moore*
I'm Gonna Live the Life I Sing About in My Song. *Thomas Dorsey*
I'm Gonna Love You. *Eddie Taylor*
I'm Gonna Make You Glad. *Richard Havens*
I'm Gonna Meet My Baby Somewhere. *Sam Hopkins*
I'm Gonna Move. *William Arnold*
I'm (We) Gonna Move to the Outskirts of Town (Outskirts of Town). *Will Weldon*
I'm Gonna Quit My Baby. *Riley King*
I'm Gonna Quit My Baby. *Johnie Lewis*
I'm Gonna Quit You Baby. *Silas Hogan*
I'm Gonna Steal Somebody's Man. *Charles Davenport*
I'm Gonna Take It Easy. *Gabriel Brown*
I'm Gonna Train My Baby. *Robert Brown (Washboard Sam)*
I'm Gonna Walk Your Log. *Leonard Caston*
I'm Happy to Be Free. *William Dupree*
I'm Having a Ball. *John Young*
I'm Having Fun. *William Dupree*
I'm Her Honeydripper. *Roosevelt Sykes*
I'm Hungry. *Willie Mabon*
I'm in an Awful Mood. *Aaron Walker*
I'm in Korea. *J. B. Lenoir*
I'm in Love Again. *Antoine Domino*
I'm in Love with You Baby. *Sonny Terry*
I'm in the Mood. *John Lee Hooker*
I'm in Trouble. *Jerry McCain*
I'm Just a Bum. *William Broonzy*
I'm Just a Drifter. *John Lee Hooker*
I'm Just a Name. *Charles Berry*
I'm Just Wastin' My Time. *JD Short*
I'm Leavin' Just to Ease My Worried Mind. *Thomas Delaney*
I'm Leaving Just to Ease My Worried Mind. *Thomas Dorsey*
I'm Leaving. *John Lee Hooker*
I'm Leaving. *Mathis James Reed*
I'm Leaving Baby. *John Young*
I'm Leaving Here Blues. *Ida Cox*
I'm Lonesome Blues. *Robert Pete Williams*
I'm Lonesome Too. *James Rodgers*
I'm Looking for a Woman. *Ellas McDaniel*
I'm Looking for My Jesus. *Mance Lipscomb*
I'm Lost. *Willie Mae Thornton*
I'm Louisiana Red. *Iverson Minter*
I'm Mad. *Willie Mabon*
I'm Mad with You. *Charles Sayles*
I'm Mr. Luck. *Mathis James Reed*
I'm Nervous. *Mathis James Reed*
I'm Not Looking Back. *Raymond Agee*
I'm Not the Best. *George Guy*
I'm Not the Lad. *Ernest Lawlars*
I'm Not Wanted Any More. *Riley King*
I'm Nuts over You. *Alonzo Johnson*
I'm on My Way. *Richard Havens*
I'm on My Way Blues. *Robert Brown (Washboard Sam)*
I'm Out to Get You Baby. *Raymond Agee*
I'm Pleading. *Edward Boyd*
I'm Prison Bound. *John Lee Hooker*
I'm Prison Bound: *Walter Brown McGhee/Sonny Terry*
I'm Ready. *Willie Dixon*
I'm Shorty. *Willie Dixon*
I'm Sitting Here. *Eddie Taylor*

I'm So All Alone. *Peter Chatman*
I'm So Glad. *Nehemiah James*
I'm So Glad. *Sonny Boy Williamson (Alex Miller)*
I'm So Sorry. *James Moore*
I'm Sober Now. *Clarence Smith*
I'm Sorry Blues. *Sara Martin*
I'm St. Louis Bound. *James Oden*
I'm Still a Fool for You. *Amos Milburn*
I'm Still In Love with You. *Aaron Walker*
I'm Taking a Devil of a Chance. *Sam Hopkins*
I'm Taking Over. *Victoria Spivey*
I'm Talking About you. *Charles Berry*
I'm the One. *Amos Easton*
I'm the Sweet Root Man. *Roosevelt Sykes*
I'm the Wolf. *Chester Burnett*
I'm Throwing Up My Hand. *Gary Davis*
I'm Tired of Wandering. *Arbee Stidham*
I'm Trying to Please You. *Mathis James Reed*
I'm Walking. *Antoine Domino*
I'm Walking Out. *Sidney Semien*
I'm with You. *Riley King*
I'm Woke Up Now. *William Broonzy*
I'm Worried. *Willie Dixon*
I'm Worried. *Elmore James*
I'm Your Bread Maker Baby. *James Moore*
I'm Your Hoochie Coochie Man. *Willie Dixon*
I'm Your Part Time Love. *Al King*
I'm Yours and I'm Hers. *Johnny Winter*
Impressions from France. *Luther Johnson*
In a Boogie Mood. *Clarence Garlow*
In Heaven Sitting Down. *Robert Wilkins*
In My Own Dream. *Paul Butterfield*
In the Bottom. *Arthur Taylor*
In the Evenin'. *Connie Crayton*
In the Evening When the Sun Goes Down. *Leroy Carr*
In the House Blues. *Bessie Smith*
In the Jailhouse Now. *James Rodgers*
In the Moonlight. *James Rushing*
In the Morning. *Tommy Tucker*
In the Night. *Roy Byrd*
In the Racket. *Billie Pierce*
In the Same Old Way. *Tommy Ridgley*
In the Wee Wee Hours: *George Guy/Amos Wells*
Indian Rope Man. *Richard Havens*
Indiana Avenue Blues. *John Tyler Adams*
Indiana Avenue Blues. *Shirley Griffith*
Indiana Avenue Stomp. *Arthur Taylor*
Industrial Blues. *Charles Ross*
Inflation Blues. *J. C. Burris*
Inform Me Baby. *Walter Brown*
Information Blues. *Roy Milton*
Insane Asylum. *Willie Dixon*
Inside of Him. *Richard Havens*
Instrumental. *Charles Berry*
Insurance Man Blues. *James Rachell*
Into My Life. *Luther Allison*
Is That the Way God Planned It? *Tommy Tucker*
Is You Is or Is You Ain't My Baby? *Louis Jordan*
Isn't a Pain to Me. *Walter Jacobs Vinson*
It Ain't Like That. *Oran Page*
It Ain't Right. *Marion Walter Jacobs*
It Don't Take But a Few Minutes. *Charles Berry*
It Hurts Me. *Richard Havens*
It Hurts Me Too. *Elmore James*
It Hurts So Good. *Henry Brown*
It Looks Bad for You. *Joe McCoy*
It Looks Too Bad for You. *William Gillum*
It Makes My Love Come Down. *Bessie Smith*
It Must Have Been the Devil. *Otis Spann*
It Really Is a Hurtin' Thing. *Sidney Semien*
It Seem Like a Dream. *Charles Ross*
It Serves You Right to Suffer. *James Dawkins*
It Takes Time. *Otis Rush*
It Was You. *Phillip Walker*
It Was Your Love. *Raymond Agee*
It Wasn't Me. *Charles Berry*
It Won't Act Right. *Will Shade*
It Won't Be Long. *Charley Patton*
It Won't Happen Again. *James Harris*
It's a Bloody Life. *Sonny Boy Williamson (Alex Miller)*
It's a Crazy Mixed Up World. *John Lee Hooker*
It's a Hard Pill to Swallow. *William Dupree*
It's a Helluva Thing. *Raymond Agee*
It's a Long Old Road. *Robert Pete Williams*
It's a Long Time. *Lowell Fulson*
It's a Mellow Day. *Edward Boyd*
It's a Mean World Till You Die. *Gary Davis*
It's a Mighty Poor Rat That Ain't Got But One Hole. *Victoria Spivey*
It's All in Your Mind. *Phillip Walker*
It's All Over. *McKinley Morganfield*
It's All Over. *Moses Smith*
It's All Over Now. *William Gillum*
It's All Right. *Ray Charles*
It's Alright. *Clarence Brown*
It's Alright. *Theodore Taylor*
It's Been a Long Time Baby. *Clyde Bernhardt*
It's Been So Long. *Walter Davis*
It's Dangerous. *Victoria Spivey*
It's Dangerous to Be a Husband. *Pleasant Joseph*
It's Getting Soft. *Gabriel Brown*
It's Hard to Explain. *Raymond Agee*
It's Hard to Tell. *Robert Pete Williams*
It's in the News. *Willie Dixon*
It's Later Than You Think. *Roy Milton*
It's Miserable to Be Alone. *Edward Boyd*
It's My Desire. *Thomas Dorsey*
It's My Life Baby. *Amos Wells*
It's My Own Business. *Charles Berry*
It's My Own Fault. *John Lee Hooker*
It's 1984. *Dave Alexander*
It's Not Killing Me. *Michael Bloomfield*
It's So Good This Morning Blues. *Clyde Bernhardt*
It's So Sad to Be Lonely. *Amos Wells*

It's the Same Old Story. *Joseph Turner*
It's Tight Like That: *Thomas Dorsey/Hudson Whittaker*
It's Too Bad. *Edward Boyd*
It's Too Bad Things Are Going So Tough. *Freddie King*
It's Too Dark in There. *Charles Berry*
It's Too Late. *Alden Bunn*
It's Too Late. *Roy Milton*
It's Too Late Now. *Robert Brown (Washboard Sam)*
It's Too Late Now. *Hudson Whittaker*
It's Too Late Now to Get Your Baby Back. *Sara Martin*
It's You. *Clayton Love*
It's You Baby. *Albert Luandrew*
It's You I Love. *Antoine Domino*
It's You I Love Baby. *John Lee Hooker*
It's Your Life. *Johnny Fuller*
It's Your Own Fault. *Lowell Fulson*
It's Your Time Now. *William Broonzy*
I've Been a Good Thing for You. *James Moore*
I've Been a Long Long Ways. *Sonny Terry*
I've Been Abused. *Chester Burnett*
I've Been Blue Too Long. *Riley King*
I've Been Crying Since You Been Gone. *John Hurt*
I've Been Deceived. *Edward Boyd*
I've Been Down So Long. *John Mars*
I've Been Mistreated. *William Dupree*
I've Been Treated Wrong. *Robert Brown (Washboard Sam)*
I've Changed. *Fention Robinson*
I've Cried My Last Time Over You. *Thomas Delaney*
I've Done Stopped Gambling. *Gabriel Brown*
I've Got a Bird to Whistle. *Walter Lewis*
I've Got a Lot of Respect. *Eddie Burns*
I've Got an Evil Woman. *Eddie Kirkland*
I've Got to Be with You Tonight. *James Moore*
I've Got to Forget You. *Arbee Stidham*
I've Got to Get Rid of You. *Alonzo Johnson*
I've Got to Go. *Louis Robinson*
I've Got to (Go and) Leave My Daddy Behind. *Sara Martin*
I've Got to Move. *John Williamson*
I've Got to Stop Drinkin'. *Gabriel Brown*
I've Had My Fun. *Sam Hopkins*
I've Had Trouble. *William Trice*
I've Made Nights by Myself. *Albert King*

JW Boogie. *James Walker*
Jack and Jill Blues. *Hammie Nixon*
Jack Engine. *Mercy Dee Walton*
Jock o' Diamond Blues. *Lemon Jefferson*
Jackson Bound. *John Young*
Jackson Tennessee. *John Lee Hooker*
Jackson Town. *Eddie Taylor*
Jackson's Blues. *Charlie Jackson*
Jacqueline. *William Broonzy*
Jaguar and the Thunderbird. *Charles Berry*
Jail. *Willie Mae Thornton*
Jail House Blues. *Robert Wilkins*
Jail House Junkers Blues. *William Dupree*
Jailbait. *Roosevelt Sykes*
Jailhouse Blues. *John Estes*
Jailhouse Blues. *Granville McGhee*
Jailhouse Blues. *Bessie Smith*
Jake's Blues. *James Harris*
Jake's Cha Cha. *James Harris*
Jam It Up. *Albert Collins*
Jam on a Monday Morning. *George Guy*
Jangle Boogie. *Otis Spann*
Jaspers Gal. *Peter Chatman*
Jawing. *Albert Collins*
Jaybird. *Scott Dunbar*
Jazz Gillum's Blues. *Robert Brown (Washboard Sam)*
Jazz Me Blues. *Thomas Delaney*
Jealous Hearted Blues. *Virginia Liston*
Jealous Hearted Man. *McKinley Morganfield*
Jealous Man. *Walter Brown McGhee*
Jealous Woman. *Aaron Walker*
Jefferson and Franklin Blues. *Joe Lee Williams*
Jefferson County Blues. *Peter Chatman*
Jelly Bean Blues. *Gertrude Rainey*
Jelly Jam. *Willie Dixon*
Jelly Jelly. *Alonzo Johnson*
Jelly Roll Baker. *Alonzo Johnson*
Jelly Roll Baker. *Frankie Lee Sims*
Jelly Roll Workin' Man. *Booker White*
Jenny. *John Mayall*
Jenny Jenny. *Richard Penniman*
Jerdine. *Eddie Kirkland*
Jersey Bull Blues. *Charley Patton*
Jerusalem. *Peter Chatman*
Jesus Christ. *Woodrow Guthrie*
Jesus Said If You Go. *Robert Wilkins*
Jesus Will Fix It Alright. *Robert Wilkins*
Jet, The. *Sam Hopkins*
Jet. *Victoria Spivey*
Jet Stream. *Jerry McCain*
Jilted. *Charles Brown*
Jim Crow Train. *Joshua White*
Jim Jam Blues. *Eurreal Montgomery*
Jim Lee Blues. *Charley Patton*
Jim String. *John Shines*
Jim Tampa Blues. *Lucille Bogan*
Jimmy's Blues. *James Rushing*
Jimmy's Good Night Blues. *James Yancey*
Jimmy's Rocks. *James Yancey*
Jimmy's Round the Clock Blues. *James Rushing*
Jinx Blues (see: Old Black Cat Blues)
Jinx Blues. *Jo-Ann Kelly*
Jinx Blues. *Joe Lee Williams*
Jitter Jump, The. *Hudson Whittaker*
Jitterbug Rag. *Alden Bunn*
Jive Lover. *Wesley Wilson*
Jivin' Mr. Fuller Blues. *William Broonzy*
Jiving the Blues. *John Lee Williamson*
Jo Jo Gunne. *Charles Berry*
Jockey Ride Blues. *Joe Lee Williams*

Joe Chicago. *Walter Horton*
Joe Louis Blues. *Carl Martin*
Joe's Blues. *Joseph Turner*
Joe's Troubled Blues. *Joe Callicott*
John Jackson Breakdown. *John Jackson*
John Lee's Dirty Dozen. *John Lee Granderson*
Johnny Ace's Last Letter. *Johnny Fuller*
Johnny B. Goode. *Charles Berry*
Johnny Mae. *William Lucas*
Johnny Mae. *John Williamson*
Johnny's Jive. *John Littlejohn*
Johnny's Lowdown Blues. *Johnny Fuller*
John's Moonshine Blues. *John Wrencher*
Johnson Machine Gun. *Albert Luandrew*
Join the Army. *Henry Johnson*
Jook House Blues. *Victoria Spivey*
Jookin' in New Orleans. *Roosevelt Sykes*
Jot 'em Down Blues. *Bessie Smith*
Jot's Blues. *Aaron Walker*
Journey, The. *John Lee Hooker*
Juanita. *Lee Jackson*
Juanita Blues. *Joe Lee Williams*
Juanita Stomp. *Joe Lee Williams*
Jubilee Time. *Roosevelt Sykes*
Judge Boyshoy Blues. *Walter Lewis*
Judgment, The. *Dave Alexander*
Jug Band Waltz. *Will Shade*
Juice Head Baby. *Eddie Vinson*
Juice Head Man of Mine. *Dinah Washington*
Juicy Harmonica. *George Smith*
Juicy Lucy. *Jerry McCain*
Juke. *Marion Walter Jacobs*
Juke Box Boogie. *Charles Ross*
Julee Boogie. *Julia Lee*
Julia's Blues. *Julia Lee*
July Boogie. *Alexander Moore*
Jump Jack. *Cecil Gant*
Jump Jump Julie. *Joe Lee Williams*
Jump Little Children. *Walter Brown McGhee*
Jump Little Jitterbug. *Charles Davenport*
Jump Sister Bessie. *Willie Dixon*
Jump Steady Blues. *Clarence Smith*
Jumpin' Blues. *Walter Horton*
Jumpin' Down Blues. *Joseph Turner*
Jumpin' for Joy. *Clarence Garlow*
Jumpin' in the Morning. *Ray Charles*
Jumping the Blues. *Walter Brown*
Jungle Juice. *Granville McGhee*
Jungle Man Blues. *Peetie Wheatstraw*
Just a Blues. *Alexander Moore*
Just a Dream. *William Broonzy*
Just a Feeling. *Marion Walter Jacobs*
Just a Fool. *Edward Riley Boyd*
Just a Kiss. *Lowell Fulson*
Just a Little Love. *Riley King*
Just a Little Tenderness. *John Shines*
Just a Lonely Boy. *Clifton Chenier*
Just a Minute. *Joseph Young*
Just a Poor Country Boy. *Mathis James Reed*
Just a Travelin' Man. *Joseph Turner*
Just About Crazy. *Sonny Terry*
Just Above My Hobby Horse's Head. *Richard Havens*
Just Before Dawn. *Clarence Brown*
Just Blues. *Peter Chatman*
Just Call Me. *John Shines*
Just Can't Help Myself. *Willie Mae Thornton*
Just Can't Make It by Myself. *Barbara Dane*
Just for You. *James Moore*
Just Give Me a Chance. *Silas Hogan*
Just Goes to Show You. *Thomas Courtney*
Just Got Lucky. *Clarence Brown*
Just Got to Hold You. *William Broonzy*
Just Like I Treat You. *Willie Dixon*
Just Made Twenty-One. *Otis Hicks*
Just Make Love to Me. *Willie Dixon*
Just One More Time. *Walter Davis*
Just One Step. *Thomas Dorsey*
Just Passing By. *Chester Burnett*
Just Pickin'. *Freddie King*
Just Playing My Axe. *George Guy*
Just Rockin' Love Me. *Joe McCoy*
Just Rocking. *William Broonzy*
Just Shakey. *James Harris*
Just Stopped By to Get a Cup of Coffee. *Jack Elliott*
Just the Blues. *Edward Boyd*
Just Want to Make Love to You (see: Want to Make Love to You)
Just Whaling. *Louis Myers*
Just Your Fool. *Marion Walter Jacobs*

K. C. Bound. *Lowell Fulson*
KC's Doctor Blues. *K. C. Douglas*
Kansas City. *Willie Littlefield*
Kansas City. *Robert Nighthawk*
Kansas City Baby. *Mathis James Reed*
Kansas City Blues. *Jim Jackson*
Kansas City Blues. *Will Shade*
Kansas City Blues. *Robert Wilkins*
Kansas City Papa. *Huddie Ledbetter*
Katie. *McKinley Morganfield*
Katie Mae. *Sam Hopkins*
Kazoo Papa Blues. *Victoria Spivey*
Keep A-Knockin'. *Richard Penniman*
Keep A Knockin'. *James Yancey*
Keep A-Loving Me Baby. *James Harris*
Keep-A-Walkin' Little Girl. *Joe Lee Williams*
Keep It to Yourself. *Sonny Boy Williamson (Alex Miller)*
Keep Movin' On. *Riley King*
Keep My Lover with Me. *Willie Mabon*
Keep On Drinkin'. *John Young*
Keep On Loving Me Baby. *Otis Rush*
Keep On Pushing. *Sidney Semien*
Keep On Running. *Willie Dixon*
Keep On Sailing. *Amos Easton*
Keep On Walkin'. *Walter Brown McGhee*
Keep Praying All the Time. *Thomas Dorsey*

SONG INDEX

Keep Smiling. *Raymond Agee*
Keep the Faith. *Mathis James Reed*
Keep Your Arms Round Me. *Arthur Crudup*
Keep Your Bad Dog off Me. *Robert Pete Williams*
Keep Your Fat Mouth out of My Business. *James Pryor*
Keep Your Hand out of My Pocket. *Otis Spann*
Keep Your Hand out of My Pocket. *Sonny Boy Williamson (Alex Miller)*
Keep Your Hands off Her. *William Broonzy*
Keep Your Hands off Her. *Huddie Ledbetter*
Keep Your Hands off My Woman. *Iverson Minter*
Keep Your Hands off That Woman. *Arthur Crudup*
Keep Your Nose out of My Business. *John Young*
Kelly's Killer. *Arthur Kelley*
Key Hole Blues. *Wesley Wilson*
Key to the Highway. *William Broonzy*
Key to the Mountain Blues. *Mary Johnson*
Key to Your Door. *Sonny Boy Williamson (Alex Miller)*
Keyhole Blues. *Princess White*
Kick Hit 4 Hit Kix U. *John Lee Hooker*
Kid Mama Blues. *John Young*
Kid Man Blues. *John Young*
Kidney Stew Blues. *Eddie Vinson*
Kill It Kid. *Willie McTell*
Killing Floor, The. *Chester Burnett*
Kilroy Won't Be Back. *Edward Boyd*
Kilroy's in Town. *Roosevelt Sykes*
Kind Hearted Blues. *William Broonzy*
Kind Hearted Woman. *Robert Johnson*
Kind Hearted Woman. *McKinley Morganfield*
Kind Lovin' Blues. *Ethel Waters*
Kind of Lonesome. *Mathis James Reed*
Kind Treatment. *Alberta Hunter*
Kindness for Weakness. *Edward Boyd*
Kinfolk's Blues. *McKinley Morganfield*
King-A-Ling. *Freddie King*
King Jesus. *Joe Lee Williams*
King of Spades. *Shirley Griffith*
King Zulu. *George Guesnon*
Kingfish Blues. *Hudson Whittaker*
King's Special. *Riley King*
Kingshighway Blues. *Joe Lee Williams*
Kissing at Midnight. *William Arnold*
Kissing in the Dark. *John Williamson*
Kitchen Sink Boogie. *Theodore Taylor*
Klickety Klock. *Willie Mabon*
Knockin' Myself Out. *Lillian Green*
Knocking Down Windows. *Mance Lipscomb*
Knocking on Your Door. *Elmore James*
Knocking on Your Door. *Mathis James Reed*
Knocks Me Out. *Lonnie Brooks*
Kokomo Blues (see: Old Original Kokomo Blues)
Kokomo Blues. *Fred McDowell*
Korea Blues. *J. B. Lenoir*
Kozmic Blues. *Janis Joplin*
L & N Blues. *Walter Davis*
L & N Blues. *William Borum*
LM Blues. *Louis Myers*
La La. *Antoine Domino*
La Salle Street Boogie. *Albert Luandrew*
Ladbroke Grove Blues. *John Holder*
Lady in the Raw. *Lowell Fulson*
Lady Luck. *Mercy Dee Walton*
Lake Cormorant Blues. *Eddie House*
Lakeshore Blues. *Eurreal Montgomery*
Lament to Love. *Clarence Miller*
Last Call. *Alonzo Johnson*
Last Dime Blues. *Willie McTell*
Last Fair Deal Gone Down. *Robert Johnson*
Last Go-Round Blues. *George Guesnon*
Last Goodbye Blues. *Joseph Turner*
Last Laugh, The. *Roosevelt Sykes*
Last Mile Blues. *Jesse Crump*
Last Minute Blues. *Thomas Dorsey*
Last Night. *Marion Walter Jacobs*
Last Night Blues. *Sam Hopkins*
Last Time. *James Rogers*
Late Blues. *Aaron Walker*
Late Hours at Midnight. *Elmore James*
Late Last Night. *John Lee Hooker*
Late Last Night. *James Moore*
Late Night Boogie. *Robert Pete Williams*
Late One Evening. *James Witherspoon*
Late One Saturday Evening. *Alexander Seward*
Laugh and Cry. *Charles Berry*
Laugh and Grin Blues. *James Arnold*
Laughing at the Blues. *Mathis James Reed*
Laundromat Blues. *Albert King*
Laura. *Huddie Ledbetter*
Lawd Send Me a Man Blues. *Gertrude Rainey*
Lawdy, Lawdy. *Amos Wells*
Lawdy Lawdy Blues. *Ida Cox*
Lawdy Lawdy Worried Blues. *Theodore Darby*
Laws Must Change, The. *John Mayall*
Lawyer Clark. *John Estes*
Lay Some Flowers on My Grave. *Willie McTell*
Lay Your Habits Down. *Clyde Bernhardt*
Layin' in My Cell Sleepin'. *Albert Luandrew*
Lazy Blues. *John Hurt*
Lazy Daisy. *McHouston Baker*
Lazy Gal. *Eddie Vinson*
Leading Brand, The. *Earl Hooker*
Leap Year Blues. *William Broonzy*
Learn to Treat Me Better. *Cornelius Green*
Leave Jike Mary Alone. *Sam Hopkins*
Leave Me. *James Rushing*
Leave Me Alone. *Raymond Agee*
Leave Me Alone. *John Walker*
Leave Me or Love Me. *Alonzo Johnson*
Leave My Girl Alone. *George Guy*

Leave My Man Alone. *Thomas Dorsey*
Leave My Money Alone. *Cornelius Green*
Leave My Wife Alone. *John Lee Hooker*
Leave My Woman Alone. *Ray Charles*
Leavin' Blues. *Huddie Ledbetter*
Leavin' Blues. *Sonny Terry*
Leavin' Day. *William Broonzy*
Leavin' It All Up to You. *Don Harris*
Leavin' Memphis. *Jesse Fuller*
Leaving in the Morning. *Marion Walter Jacobs*
Leaving This Morning. *Gertrude Rainey*
Leaving This Town, Won't Be Back to Fall. *Roosevelt Holts*
Leaving Town Blues. *Eurreal Montgomery*
Leaving You Behind. *Aaron Walker*
Leaving You Blues: *Francis Blackwell/Leroy Carr*
Left Alone Blues. *Ishmon Bracey*
Left Handed Woman. *Mathis James Reed*
Left Home When I Was a Kid. *Aaron Walker*
Left My Wife and My Baby. *John Lee Hooker*
Left Overs. *Albert Collins*
Leftover Blues. *Clarence Brown*
Lela. *Gus Cannon*
Leland Mississippi Blues. *Johnny Winter*
Lemon's Cannon Ball Moan. *Lemon Jefferson*
Lemon's Worried Blues. *Lemon Jefferson*
Lend Me Your Love. *Peter Chatman*
Lend Me Your Love. *John Young*
Let a Good Thing Do. *Alexander Seward*
Let Everybody Boogie. *Willie Dixon*
Let Her Go. *William Broonzy*
Let Him Beat Me. *Victoria Spivey*
Let It All Hang Out. *Lonnie Brooks*
Let It Be Me. *Edward Boyd*
Let It Rock. *Charles Berry*
Let Me Be Your Big Dog. *Walter McGhee*
Let Me Be Your Dog. *Joseph Turner*
Let Me Be Your Hatchet. *Silas Hogan*
Let Me Be Your Santa. *Clarence Garlow*
Let Me Be Your Winder. *William Broonzy*
Let Me Dig It. *Joe McCoy*
Let Me Explain. *Sonny Boy Williamson (Alex Miller)*
Let Me Have My Way. *James Dawkins*
Let Me Hold You in Your Arms Tonight. *Jesse Fuller*
Let Me in Your Saddle. *Walter Davis*
Let Me Love You. *Riley King*
Let Me Love You. *Arbee Stidham*
Let Me Love You Baby. *Willie Dixon*
Let Me Play with Your Poodle. *Hudson Whittaker*
Let Me Play Your Vendor. *Peter Clayton*
Let Me Ride Your Mule. *John Young*
Let Me Stand Next to Your Fire. *James Hendrix*
Let the Four Winds Blow. *Antoine Domino*
Let the Good Times Roll. *Thomas Delaney*
Let the Mermaids Flirt with Me. *John Hurt*
Let Us Get Together Right Down Here. *Gary Davis*
Let Your Conscience Be Your Guide. *Sonny Boy Williamson (Alex Miller)*
Let Your Hair Down. *Curtis Jones*
Let Your Money Talk. *Amos Easton*
Let's Boogie. *Charles Berry*
Let's Boogie All Night Long. *Charles Ross*
Let's Do Our Thing Together. *Charles Berry*
Let's Do the Boogie. *Riley King*
Let's Get Back to the Old Times. *Edith Wilson*
Let's Get Down to Business. *Riley King*
Let's Get Funky. *Theodore Taylor*
Let's Get It On. *William Perryman*
Let's Get It Together. *Albert Collins*
Let's Get with It. *Peter Chatman*
Let's Have a Little Talk. *Luther Allison*
Let's Have a Natural Ball. *Albert King*
Let's Have a Party. *Amos Milburn*
Let's Make It. *John Lee Hooker*
Let's Ride Tonight. *Victoria Spivey*
Let's Shake Hand in Hand. *Walter Lewis*
Let's Take the Long Way Home. *Arbee Stidham*
Let's Talk About Love. *Raymond Agee*
Let's Try and Talk It Over. *Tommy Ridgley*
Letter from My Baby. *Joseph Hutto*
Letter Home. *Peter Chatman*
Letter Missin' Blues. *Edward Boyd*
Letter to My Baby. *William Broonzy*
Letter to My Baby. *John Lee Hooker*
Levee Bound Blues. *Thomas Dorsey*
Levee Break Blues. *Joe Lee Williams*
Levee Camp (Blues). *Ernest Lawlars*
Levee Camp Blues. *Robert Pete Williams*
Levee Camp Moan. *Eddie House*
Levee Camp Moan Blues. *Alger Alexander*
Liberty Bill. *James Brewer*
Lick for Licks. *James Dawkins*
Life Get to Be a Burden. *Edward Boyd*
Life Is a Card Game. *Joseph Turner*
Life Is a Gamble. *Walter Brown McGhee*
Life Is a Mean Mistreater. *James Dawkins*
Life Is a Puzzle. *Roosevelt Sykes*
Life Is Just a Book. *Ernest Lawlars*
Life Is Like That. *Milton Campbell*
Life Is Like That. *Peter Chatman*
Life Is Suicide. *Percy Mayfield*
Light out of Darkness. *Ray Charles*
Lightnin' Don't Feel Well. *Sam Hopkins*
Lightnin' Struck the Poorhouse. *Pleasant Joseph*
Lightnin's Love. *Sam Hopkins*
Lights Out. *Marion Walter Jacobs*
Like Wolf. *Sonny Boy Williamson (Alex Miller)*
Limited Love. *Clayton Love*
Lines in My Face. *Alonzo Johnson*
Little and Low. *Sam Hopkins*

Little Annie Mae. *Joe Lee Williams*
Little Antoinette. *Sam Hopkins*
Little Baby. *Willie Dixon*
Little Birdie Tweet-Tweet-Tweet. *Joseph Turner*
Little Bitty Baby. *Joseph Turner*
Little Bittie Gal's Blues. *Joseph Turner*
Little Black Engine. *Walter Brown McGhee*
Little Black Train. *Jesse Fuller*
Little Boy Blue. *Robert Lockwood*
Little Boy Blue. *Roy Milton*
Little Boy Blues. *Walter Horton*
Little by Little. *Amos Wells*
Little Children's Blues. *Huddie Ledbetter*
Little City Woman. *William Broonzy*
Little Cow and Calf Is Gonna Die Blues. *Nehemiah James*
Little Delia. *Willie McTell*
Little Eva. *Pleasant Joseph*
Little Every Day, A. *John Davis*
Little Geneva. *McKinley Morganfield*
Little Girl. *McKinley Morganfield*
Little Girl. *Rufus Perryman*
Little Girl Blues. *Albert Luandrew*
Little Girl Blues. *John Lee Williamson*
Little Girl How Old Are You? *Sonny Boy Williamson (Alex Miller)*
Little Girl Little Girl. *John Young*
Little Lonely Girl. *Peter Chatman*
Little Mama Blues. *Sam Hopkins*
Little Man Sittin' on a Fence. *Joshua White*
Little Marie. *Charles Berry*
Little Miss Muffet. *Leon T. Gross*
Little Piece of Dying. *Paul Butterfield*
Little Queen of Spades. *Robert Johnson*
Little Queenie. *Charles Berry*
Little Red Rooster. *Willie Dixon*
Little Sisters Boogie. *Sam Hopkins*
Little Soldier Boy. *Charles Ross*
Little Soul Food, A. *Don Harris*
Little Star. *Charles Berry*
Little Talk with Jesus, A. *Thomas Dorsey*
Little Turch. *Fention Robinson*
Little Village. *Sonny Boy Williamson (Alex Miller)*
Little Wheel. *John Lee Hooker*
Little Willie's Boogie. *Willie Littlefield*
Little Wolf. *John Shines*
Live at Ma Bea's. *James Rogers*
Live Today Like the Day Before. *Percy Mayfield*
Lo, I'll Be with You Always. *Gary Davis*
Lock Me in Your Heart (and Throw Away the Key). *Alden Bunn*
Log Cabin Blues. *Thomas Delaney*
Log Camp Blues: *Thomas Dorsey/Gertrude Rainey*
Lollipop Mama. *Roy Brown*
London Berry Blues. *Charles Berry*
London Paris Rome Blues Express. *John Holder*
London Shout. *Eurreal Montgomery*
Lone Wolf. *Joe Lee Williams*
Loneliness. *J. C. Burris*
Lonely Blues. *Willie Mabon*
Lonely Boy Blues. *Walter Brown*
Lonely Day. *Roosevelt Sykes*
Lonely Girl. *Lee Jackson*
Lonely Hours. *Travis Blaylock*
Lonely Hours. *Lowell Fulson*
Lonely School Days. *Charles Berry*
Lonely Without Love. *Lee Jackson*
Lonesome. *William Broonzy*
Lonesome Bedroom Blues. *Curtis Jones*
Lonesome Blues. *Ida Cox*
Lonesome Blues. *James Rogers*
Lonesome Cabin. *Sonny Boy Williamson (Alex Miller)*
Lonesome Cabin Blues. *Otis Hicks*
Lonesome Daddy Blues. *Lucille Bogan*
Lonesome Day. *Walter Brown McGhee*
Lonesome Desert Blues. *Bessie Smith*
Lonesome for My Baby. *Milton Campbell*
Lonesome for Someone to Love. *Beulah Wallace*
Lonesome Graveyard. *Sam Hopkins*
Lonesome Home Blues. *William Borum*
Lonesome Home Blues. *Tommy Johnson*
Lonesome Hours Blues. *Beulah Wallace*
Lonesome in My Cabin. *John Wrencher*
Lonesome La La. *Silas Hogan*
Lonesome Lonely Blues. *Cornelius Green*
Lonesome Mama Blues. *Eurreal Montgomery*
Lonesome Man Blues. *Pleasant Joseph*
Lonesome Monday Mornin'. *Lucille Hegamin*
Lonesome Old Feeling. *Amos Easton*
Lonesome Road Blues. *James Arnold*
Lonesome Road Blues. *McKinley Morganfield*
Lonesome Swamp Rattlesnake. *J. D. Short*
Lonesome Talkin' Blues. *Eddie Kirkland*
Lonesome Trail Blues. *Amos Easton*
Lonesome Train. *John Williamson*
Lonesome Train Blues. *Dave Alexander*
Lonesome Traveler. *Peter Chatman*
Long About Midnight. *Roy Brown*
Long About Sunrise. *Andrew Odom*
Long as I Have You. *Charles Musselwhite*
Long Distance Blues. *Jesse Crump*
Long Distance Call. *McKinley Morganfield*
Long Distance Moan. *Lemon Jefferson*
Long Gone. *Sam Hopkins*
Long Gone. *Luke Miles*
Long Lonesome Blues. *Lemon Jefferson*
Long Lonesome Day Blues. *Alger Alexander*
Long Lonesome Night. *Roosevelt Sykes*
Long Lost Lover. *Aaron Walker*
Long Old Road. *Bessie Smith*
Long Razor Blues. *Robert Brown*
Long Skirt Baby Blues. *Aaron Walker*
Long Tall Girl Got Stuck on Me. *Mance Lipscomb*
Long Tall Sally. *Richard Penniman*
Long Tall Tan and Terrific. *Viola Wells*
Long Tall Woman. *Elmore James*

Long Time Baby, A. *Peter Chatman*
Long Time Blues. *Victoria Spivey*
Long Way from Home. *Sonny Terry*
Long Way Home, A. *Clarence Brown*
Longest Train I've Ever Seen. *Robert Brown*
Longing for Daddy Blues. *Sara Martin*
Lonnie's Traveling Light. *Alonzo Johnson*
Look A Here. *Roosevelt Sykes*
Look A-Here Baby. *Chester Burnett*
Look at the Rain. *John Lee Hooker*
Look down the Road. *Nehemiah James*
Look How Baby. *Amos Wells*
Look in Your Eyes Pretty Mama. *Andrew Hogg*
Look Now Baby. *Frank Seals*
Look on Yonder(s) Wall. *Arthur Crudup*
Look Out. *Louis Jordan*
Look Out. *Albert King*
Look Out Papa Don't Tear Your Pants. *Charlie Jackson*
Look Out Victoria. *George Smith*
Look What You Are Today. *Robert Brown*
Look Whatcha Done. *Samuel Maghett*
Lookie Here Baby. *Joe Lee Williams*
Lookin' for You. *Joseph Young*
Looking at the Future. *Johnny Taylor*
Looking for My Baby. *Luther Johnson*
Looking Good. *Samuel Maghett*
Looking Up at Down. *William Broonzy*
Loose as a Goose. *Cecil Gant*
Loose Screws. *George Smith*
Lord Has Laid His Hands on Me, The. *Thomas Dorsey*
Lord Have Mercy on Me. *Peter Chatman*
Lord, Help Poor Me. *Robert Pete Williams*
Lord I'm Discouraged. *Charley Patton*
Lord Oh Lord Blues. *John Lee Williamson*
Lord Search My Heart (see: Search My Heart)
Lorraine. *John Young*
Loser. *Edward Boyd*
Losers Weepers. *Peter Chatman*
Losing Faith in You. *Riley King*
Lost City. *Willie Mae Thornton*
Lost in a Dream. *Buster Brown*
Lost John. *Sonny Terry*
Lost Love. *Percy Mayfield*
Lost Love Affair. *Louis Bo Collins*
Lost Love Letter Blues. *John Shines*
Lost Man Blues. *Ida Cox*
Lost My Job. *John Lee Hooker*
Lost Sheep in the Fold. *Otis Spann*
Lost Wandering Blues. *Gertrude Rainey*
Lost Without Love. *Cornelius Green*
Lost Your Head Blues. *Bessie Smith*
Lots of Luck to You. *John Erby*
Louis Collins. *John Hurt*
Louise. *Robert Brown (Washboard Sam)*
Louise. *Chester Burnett*
Louise (Blues). *Sonny Terry*
Louise Louise Blues: *William Broonzy/Johnny Temple*
Louise McGhee. *Eddie House*
Louisiana Bayou Drive. *Aaron Walker*
Louisiana Blues. *Clifton Chenier*
Louisiana Blues. *Clarence Garlow*
Louisiana Blues. *Tommy Johnson*
Louisiana Blues. *Eurreal Montgomery*
Louisiana Blues. *McKinley Morganfield*
Louisiana Bound. *Joe Lee Williams*
Louisiana Hoo Doo Blues. *Gertrude Rainey*
Louisiana Women. *Margie Evans*
Love. *Travis Blaylock*
Love. *Roy Brown*
Love Ain't Nothing to Play With. *Jerry McCain*
Love and Confusion. *James Hendrix*
Love Bug. *Raymond Agee*
Love Bug. *Otis Hicks*
Love Cry Shadows Calling Me Home. *Alonzo Johnson*
Love Grow Cold. *Lowell Fulson*
Love (Her) with a Feeling. *Hudson Whittaker*
Love Hides All Fault. *Leroy Carr*
Love I Have for You, The. *Alberta Hunter*
Love in Vain. *Robert Johnson*
Love Is a Burning Thing. *John Lee Hooker*
Love Is a Cold Shot. *Raymond Agee*
Love Is a Gamble. *Raymond Agee*
Love Is a Story. *John Sellers*
Love Is a Wonderful Thing. *John Mars*
Love Is Just for Fools. *Dave Alexander*
Love Is My Stuff. *Charley Patton*
Love Is Strange. *McHouston Baker*
Love Like a Butterfly. *George Butler*
Love Me All Night Long. *K. C. Douglas*
Love Me Baby. *John Lee Williamson*
Love Me Darlin'. *Chester Burnett*
Love Me Love Me. *Lonnie Brooks*
Love Me Mama. *Luther Allison*
Love Me Mama. *Bill Webb*
Love Me Now. *Cornelius Green*
Love Me Right. *Jerry McCain*
Love Me This Way. *Samuel Maghett*
Love Me to Death. *Willie Dixon*
Love Me with a Feeling. *Samuel Maghett*
Love My Baby. *Robert Bland*
Love My Baby. *Frank Edwards*
Love My Baby. *John Lee Hooker*
Love My Baby. *Alexander Lightfoot*
Love My Baby. *Herman Parker*
Love 'n' Things. *Lowell Fulson*
Love of Life, The. *Raymond Agee*
Love Season Blues. *Curtis Jones*
Love Sick. *John Erby*
Love Speaks Louder Than Words. *Riley King*
Love Truth and Confidence. *Walter Brown McGhee*
Love Weapon. *McKinley Morganfield*
Love with a Feeling (see: Love Her with a Feeling)
Love You Baby. *McHouston Baker*
Love You from Now On. *George Butler*
Love You, Yes I Do (see: Good Lovin')
Lover Girl. *Willie Mabon*

Lover's Lane Blues. *Robert Brown (Washboard Sam)*
Love's a Disease. *Walter Brown McGhee*
Lovesick Soul. *Edward Boyd*
Lovin' Blues, The. *Fred McDowell*
Lovin' Is the Thing I'm Wild About. *Ida Cox*
Lovin' Man. *McKinley Morganfield*
Lovin' My Baby. *Walter Horton*
Lovin' You. *Lowell Fulson*
Low and Lonesome. *Bill Williams*
Low Down Dirty Shame. *Curtis Jones*
Low Down Dog. *Joseph Turner*
Low Down Friends. *Victoria Spivey*
Low Down in Paris. *John Holder*
Low Down Mama Blues. *Thomas Delaney*
Low Down Man Blues. *Charles Davenport*
Low Down Ways. *John Lee Williamson*
Low Down Worried Blues. *Curtis Jones*
Low Society. *Lowell Fulson*
Lowland Blues: *William Broonzy/Robert Brown (Washboard Sam)*
Lowland Blues. *Albert Luandrew*
Lucille. *Riley King*
Lucille. *Richard Penniman*
Lucille Blues. *Larry Johnson*
Lucille, Lucille. *Joseph Turner*
Lucille Talks Back. *Riley King*
Lucille's Granny. *Riley King*
Lucinda. *Willie Mabon*
Lucky Blues. *Bill Williams*
Lucky Lou. *Joseph Leon Williams*
Lucky Lucky Man. *Henry Gray*
Lucky So and So. *Otis Spann*
Lucky to Be Living. *Frank Frost*
Lucy Mae Blues. *John Sellers*
Lucy Mae Blues. *Frankie Lee Sims*
Ludella. *Arthur Gunter*
Ludella. *James Rogers*
Ludlow Massacre, The. *Woodrow Guthrie*
Lula Mae. *John Young*
Lullaby Yodel. *James Rodgers*
Lula Belle's Here. *Joseph Hutto*
Lu's Blues. *Louisa Barker*
Luther's Blues. *Luther Allison*
Lying Signifying. *Riley King*
Lying Woman, A. *Percy Mayfield*

M & O Blues. *Willie Lee Brown*
M & O Blues. *Walter Davis*
M & O Blues. *Floyd Jones*
M & S Boogie. *Peter Chatman*
MJR Blues. *James Rushing*
Ma Grinder, The. *Robert Shaw*
Mabon's Boogie. *Willie Mabon*
Maceo's 32–20. *Major Merriweather*
Mad Blues. *Joseph Turner*
Mad Mad Blues. *Joe Lee Williams*
Mad with You Baby. *John Lee Hooker*
Made a Date with an Angel (Got No Walking Shoes). *William Broonzy*
Madison Blues. *Elmore James*
Madison Shuffle. *Buster Brown*
Maggie Campbell. *Robert Nighthawk*
Maggie Campbell Blues. *Tommy Johnson*
Magic Rocker. *Samuel Maghett*
Magie Lee. *Booker White*
Magnolia Blues. *Charley Patton*
Mailbox Blues. *James Moore*
Mailman. *John Williamson*
Make Away. *Otis Spann*
Make Love All Night. *Norman Green*
Make Love to Me Baby. *Alonzo Johnson*
Make Me Down a Pallet. *J. D. Short*
Make Me Know It. *Roy Milton*
Make My Dreams Come True. *Elmore James*
Make My Getaway. *William Broonzy*
Makin' Love to Music. *Charles Sayles*
Making Friends. *McKinley Morganfield*
Malted Milk. *Robert Johnson*
Mama Can't Lose. *Lottie Beaman*
Mama Don't Allow. *Charles Davenport*
Mama Don't Allow No Doggin' All Night Long. *Joe Lee Williams*
Mama Don't Dog Me. *Mance Lipscomb*
Mama Don't Like Me Runnin' Round. *Joe Lee Williams*
Mama Doo Shee Blues. *Ida Cox*
Mama Here Come Your Root Man. *John Wrencher*
Mama, I Heard You Brought It Right Back Home. *Alger Alexander*
Mama-In-Law Blues. *Joseph Young*
Mama Mama. *Roosevelt Sykes*
Mama Yancey's Blues. *Estella Yancey*
Mama You Don't Mean Me No Good. *Eurreal Montgomery*
Mama's Baby Child. *Sam Hopkins*
Mama's Bad Luck Child. *Alger Alexander*
Mama's Got the Blues. *Sara Martin*
Mamma Cookie's Blues. *Ann Cook*
Mamma Didn't Do It. *Wesley Wilson*
Man Against Men, A. *Joe Lee Williams*
Man and His Environment. *Clarence Brown*
Man and the Blues, A. *George Guy*
Man and the Donkey. *Charles Berry*
Man for the Nation, A. *John Lee Granderson*
Man I'm Lovin'. *Jo-Ann Kelly*
Man in Trouble Blues. *Roy Brown*
Man Is Crying, A. *James Moore*
Man Is in Trouble. *Roosevelt Sykes*
Man Killing Broad. *Alonzo Johnson*
Man Like Me Is Hard to Find, A. *Sam Hopkins*
Man of Many Words, A. *George Guy*
Man of Stone. *Eddie Kirkland*
Man on the Run. *Lowell Fulson*
Man or Mouse. *Herman Parker*
Mance's Blues. *Mance Lipscomb*

Mandolin Boogie. *John Young*
Manhattan Slide. *Elmore James*
Manhole. *Freddie King*
Manic Depression. *James Hendrix*
Manish Boy (see: I'm a Man)
Many Hard Years. *Riley King*
Marcelle Jacques et Luc. *James Dawkins*
Marack. *Peter Chatman*
Marble Stone Blues. *Ida Cox*
Mardi Gras in New Orleans. *Roy Byrd*
Marie. *Otis Spann*
Market Street Blues. *Lowell Fulson*
Married Life's a Pain. *Willie McTell*
Married Man's Blues. *Frank Floyd*
Married Woman. *Frankie Lee Sims*
Married Woman Blues. *Alden Bunn*
Married Woman Blues. *John Estes*
Married Woman Blues. *Tony Hollins*
Married Woman Blues. *Joseph Hutto*
Martha Blues. *William Broonzy*
Martin Luther King. *Thomas Shaw*
Mary Ann. *Ray Charles*
Mary Helen. *Travis Blaylock*
Mary Johnson Blues. *Mary Johnson*
Mary Lou. *John Young*
Mary Mary. *Mathis James Reed*
Match Box Blues. *Lemon Jefferson*
Maxwell Street Alley Blues. *John Wrencher*
Maxwell Street Blues. *Charlie Jackson*
May Be a Scandal. *Roosevelt Sykes*
May This Be Love. *James Hendrix*
May We Meet Again, Florence Mills. *Eva Taylor*
Maybe It's the Blues. *Thomas Dorsey*
Maybe Not at All. *Ethel Waters*
Maybellene. *Charles Berry*
McComb Mississippi. *George Smith*
McCoy Boogie. *Robert McCoy*
Me. *Michael Bloomfield*
Me and My Buddy. *William Gillum*
Me and My Dog. *Henry Johnson*
Me and My Dog. *Walter Brown McGhee*
Me and My Mule. *William Dupree*
Me and Sonny. *Walter Brown McGhee*
Me and the Devil Blues. *Robert Johnson*
Me Myself and I. *Peter Chatman*
Mean and Evil (Baby). *Eddie Burns*
Mean and Evil Woman. *Hudson Whittaker*
Mean Atlantic Ocean. *James Dawkins*
Mean Black Cat Blues. *Charley Patton*
Mean Black Gobbler. *John Shines*
Mean Black Man Blues. *Mary Johnson*
Mean Black Moan. *Charley Patton*
Mean Black Snake. *Louis Rawls*
Mean Disposition. *McKinley Morganfield*
Mean Little Woman. *Thomas Shaw*
Mean Mean Woman. *John Lee Hooker*
Mean Mistreater. *McKinley Morganfield*
Mean Mistreater Blues. *Hudson Whittaker*
Mean Mistreater Mama. *Leroy Carr*
Mean Mistreatin' Mama. *Peter Chatman*
Mean Mistreatin' Mama. *Elmore James*
Mean Ol' World. *Roy Byrd*
Mean Old Highway. *John Lee Williamson*
Mean Old Train (see: New Mean Old Train)
Mean Old Woman. *Sonny Terry*
Mean Old World. *Marion Walter Jacobs*
Mean Old World. *Aaron Walker*
Mean Ole Frisco Blues. *Arthur Crudup*
Mean Papa Turn Your Key. *Ida Cox*
Mean Stepfather. *Joe Lee Williams*
Medicine Man, The. *Huddie Ledbetter*
Medicine Man Blues. *William Broonzy*
Meet Him over in Paradise. *Robert Pete Williams*
Meet Me. *Mathis James Reed*
Meet Me Around the Corner. *Joe Lee Williams*
Meet Me Halfway. *Arbee Stidham*
Meet Me in the Bottom. *Amos Easton*
Meet Me Tomorrow. *Roy Byrd*
Meet Me up in Harlem. *Thomas Delaney*
Meet My Happiness. *Riley King*
Meet You at the Chicken Shack. *Sam Hopkins*
Mellow Blues, The. *James Yancey*
Mellow Chick Swing. *John Lee Williamson*
Mellow Queen. *Roosevelt Sykes*
Memories of My Trip. *Walter Brown McGhee*
Memphis B–K. *Aaron Willis*
Memphis Boogie. *Jesse Fuller*
Memphis Boogie. *Charles Ross*
Memphis Bound Blues. *Thomas Dorsey*
Memphis Jug Blues. *Will Shade*
Memphis on the Mississippi. *Peter Chatman*
Memphis Slim USA. *Peter Chatman*
Memphis Tennessee. *Charles Berry*
Men Get Wise to Yourself. *Alonzo Johnson*
Meningitis Blues. *Lizzie Douglas*
Mercury Boogie. *K. C. Douglas*
Mercy. *Fred McDowell*
Mercy Blues. *Ida Cox*
Mercy Blues. *Walter Davis*
Mercy Blues. *Clarence Lofton*
Mercy Mama (Blues). *Hudson Whittaker*
Mercy Mercy. *Johnny Fuller*
Mercy on Me. *William Dupree*
Mercy's Party. *Mercy Dee Walton*
Mercy's Troubles. *Mercy Dee Walton*
Merrily We Rock & Roll. *Charles Berry*
Merry Christmas Baby. *Charles Brown*
Merry-Go-Round Blues. *William Broonzy*
Merry Way. *Albert King*
Mess Up. *Vernon Harrison*
Messed Up in Love. *William Broonzy*
Messin' Around. *Joseph Turner*
Messin' with the Hook. *John Lee Hooker*
Messing Around. *Peter Chatman*

(Don't Be) Messing with My Bread. *Eddie Burns*
Met My Mule. *William Dupree*
Michelle. *Willie Mabon*
Midnight. *Riley King*
Midnight and Day. *Otis Smothers*
Midnight Bells. *R. S. Rankin*
Midnight Blues. *Booker White*
Midnight Cold. *Jesse Fuller*
Midnight Hour. *Clarence Brown*
Midnight Hour Blues. *Leroy Carr*
Midnight Hour Blues. *Ida Cox*
Midnight Jump. *Albert Luandrew*
Midnight Midnight. *McHouston Baker*
Midnight Rockin'. *Joseph Turner*
Midnight Special, The. *Huddie Ledbetter*
Might as Well Say We're Through. *John Lee Hooker*
Mighty Long Time. *Sonny Boy Williamson (Alex Miller)*
Mighty Man. *Joseph Young*
Mighty Men. *Roosevelt Sykes*
Miles Davis Blues. *Eurreal Montgomery*
Milk and Butter Blues. *Joseph Turner*
Milk Cow Blues. *James Arnold*
Milk Cow Blues. *John Estes*
Milk That Cow. *George Smith*
Milk Train. *McHouston Baker*
Milkcow's Calf Blues. *Robert Johnson*
Mill Man Blues. *William Broonzy*
Milton's Boogie. *Roy Milton*
Mindin' My Own Business: *William Broonzy/ Robert Brown (Washboard Sam)*
Minglewood Blues. *Noah Lewis*
Mini Dress Wearer. *Frank Edwards*
Mini Skirts. *John Lee Hooker*
Mining Camp Blues. *Trixie Smith*
Mink Coat Blues. *Joe Lee Williams*
Mink Hollow Slide. *Eddie Kirkland*
Minnie's Blues. *Hammie Nixon*
Minute Man Blues. *Walter Davis*
Misbelieving Baby. *John Lee Hooker*
Misery. *Peter Chatman*
Misery Blues. *Ida Cox*
Misery Blues. *Gertrude Rainey*
Mislead Mother. *Roosevelt Sykes*
Misled Blues. *Eurreal Montgomery*
Miss Ada Blues. *William Dupree*
Miss Anna Brown. *Thomas Dorsey*
Miss Baker's Blues. *Thomas Dorsey*
Miss Bessie Mae. *Albert Luandrew*
Miss Dirty Gurty Blues. *Roosevelt Sykes*
Miss Elvira. *Charles Ross*
Miss Emma Lou Blues. *Joe Lee Williams*
Miss Fanny Brown. *Roy Brown*
Miss Hazel Mae. *Luke Miles*
Miss Ida B. *Roosevelt Sykes*
Miss Ledora Blues. *Charles Ross*
Miss Lillie Brown. *Lowell Fulson*
Miss Lizzie Can't Strut No More. *Thomas Delaney*
Miss Loretta. *Sam Hopkins*
Miss Mary. *Booker White*
Miss Matie Mae. *James Pryor*
Miss Nellie Gray (Nellie Gray). *John Henry Barbee*
Miss No Good Weed. *Alexander Moore*
Miss Sarah's a Good Girl. *Otis Hicks*
Miss Stella Brown Blues. *John Lee Williamson*
Mississippi Blues. *Lucille Hegamin*
Mississippi Blues (Cat Squirrel). *Charles Ross*
Mississippi Bound. *James Dawkins*
Mississippi County Farm. *Eddie Burns*
Mississippi County Farm Blues. *Eddie House*
Mississippi Heavy Water Blues. *Robert Hicks*
Mississippi Moon. *James Rodgers*
Mississippi River. *Robert Brown (Smokey Babe)*
Mississippi River Blues. *William Broonzy*
Mississippi River Blues. *George Smith*
Mistake in Life. *Peter Chatman*
Mistake in Life. *Roosevelt Sykes*
Mistake in My Life. *Johnie Lewis*
Mistaken Blues. *Clarence Lofton*
Mister (see also Mr.)
Mister Charlie. *James Arnold*
Mister Charlie. *Sam Hopkins*
Mister Freddie. *Peter Chatman*
Mister Froggie. *Sonny Terry*
Mister Man. *Charlie Jackson*
Mistreat Me Woman. *Joe Hill Louis*
Mistreated Blues. *Sam Hopkins*
Mistreated Blues. *Alberta Hunter*
Mistreated Blues. *Henry Townsend*
Mistreatin' Daddy Blues. *Ida Cox*
Mistreatin' Woman Blues. *Eurreal Montgomery*
Mistreating Man Blues. *Sara Martin*
Mixed Water. *Booker White*
Moanin' at Midnight. *Chester Burnett*
Moanin' for My Baby. *Chester Burnett*
Moanin' Groanin'. *Joshua Howell*
Moanin' Groanin' Blues. *John Erby*
Moaning and Groaning. *John Shines*
Moaning and Groaning. *John Young*
Moaning Blues. *John Lee Hooker*
Moaning Blues. *Alonzo Johnson*
Moaning Groaning Blues. *Ida Cox*
Moaning the Blues. *Victoria Spivey*
Mojo Blues. *Walter Davis*
Mojo Hand. *Sam Hopkins*
Mojo Hand. *McKinley Morganfield*
Mojo Hand Blues: *Ida Cox/Jesse Crump*
Mojo in My Hand. *Louis Robinson*
Mona. *Ellas McDaniel*
Monday Morning Blues. *James Arnold*
Monday Morning Blues. *John Hurt*
Money Marbles and Chalk. *James Rogers*
Money Tree. *Emery Williams*
Money's Getting Cheaper. *James Witherspoon*
Monkey and the Engineer, The. *Jesse Fuller*
Monkey Faced Woman. *James Oden*
Monkey Not for Sale. *John Jenkins*

Monkey on My Back, The. *Raymond Agee*
Monkey on My Back. *Olive Brown*
Monkey Woman Blues: *Estella Yancey/James Yancey*
Monterey Story. *Clarence Miller*
Montreal Blues. *Joe Lee Williams*
Moody Baby. *Joseph Turner*
Moody Blues. *James Moore*
Moon Going Down. *Charley Patton*
Moon Is Rising. *Earl Hooker*
Moon Is Rising, The. *Robert Nighthawk*
Moon Is Rising, The. *Mathis James Reed*
Moonlight Is My Spread. *Walter Davis*
Moonshine Blues. *Marion Walter Jacobs*
Moonshine Blues. *Gertrude Rainey*
Moonshine Woman Blues. *Peter Clayton*
Moose Huntin'. *John Walker*
Moose Is on the Loose. *John Walker*
Moppers Blues. *William Broonzy*
Morning Blues. *Jesse Fuller*
Morning Blues. *Sam Hopkins*
Morning Glory. *Joseph Turner*
Morning Hour Blues. *Gertrude Rainey*
Morocco Blues. *Curtis Jones*
Mortgage on My Soul. *Fred McDowell*
Mosquito Fly and Flea. *Victoria Spivey*
Mosquito Moan. *Lemon Jefferson*
Mother Before This Time Another Year. *Charles Ross*
Mother Earth. *Peter Chatman*
Mother Fuyer. *Nelson Wilborn*
Mother Had a Sick Child. *Mance Lipscomb*
Mother-in-Law. *Eddie Kirkland*
Mother-in-Law Blues. *William Dupree*
Mother's Bad Luck Child. *McKinley Morganfield*
Mother's Day. *James Oden*
Mother's Place. *John Shines*
Motorcycle Blues. *Sonny Terry*
Mound of Your Grave, The. *Woodrow Guthrie*
Mournful Blues. *Thomas Delaney*
Mournful Blues. *James Yancey*
Move Back to the Woods. *Walter Davis*
Move It on out of Here. *Thomas Delaney*
Move On Down the Line. *Jesse Fuller*
Move On Higher. *Joseph Young*
Move Over. *Janis Joplin*
Movin' down the River. *Sonny Boy Williamson (Alex Miller)*
Movin' Out. *Sam Hopkins*
Movin' Out. *Sonny Boy Williamson (Alex Miller)*
Moving. *Chester Burnett*
Moving Blues. *Roosevelt Sykes*
Mr. (see also Mister)
Mr. Airplaneman. *Chester Burnett*
Mr. Blues. *Melvin Jackson*
Mr. Charlie Mule. *James Pryor*
Mr. Clean. *Raymond Agee*
Mr. Cool. *Albert Luandrew*
Mr. Cover Shaker. *John Shines*
Mr. Downchild. *Sonny Boy Williamson (Alex Miller)*
Mr. Dupree Blues. *William Dupree*
Mr. Highway Man. *Edward Boyd*
Mr. Highway Man. *Chester Burnett*
Mr. Jack's Dance. *J. C. Burris*
Mr. James. *John Mayall*
Mr. Johnson Swing. *Alonzo Johnson*
Mr. Khrushchev. *Ellas McDaniel*
Mr. Leader Man Swing That Band. *Thomas Delaney*
Mr. Longfingers. *Peter Chatman*
Mr. Rhythm Man. *Hudson Whittaker*
Mr. Shoe Man Blues. *Jean Kittrell*
Mr. Sykes Blues. *Roosevelt Sykes*
Mr. Texas and Pacific. *Arbee Stidham*
Mr. Tom. *Mance Lipscomb*
Mr. Tom Hughes Town (Fannin' Street). *Huddie Ledbetter*
Mrs. Geraldine. *Joseph Turner*
Much Too Late. *Alden Bunn*
Mud in Your Ear. *McKinley Morganfield*
Muddy Water Blues. *Thomas Dorsey*
Muddy Waters Shuffle. *McKinley Morganfield*
Mule Gallop. *Gus Cannon*
Mule Kicking in My Stall. *McKinley Morganfield*
Mumsy Mumsy Blues. *Charlie Jackson*
Murder. *Albert King*
Murder Gonna Be My Crime. *Beulah Wallace*
Murder in th First Degree. *Victoria Spivey*
Muskadine. *Marion Walter Jacobs*
My Airplane Chick. *Charles Ross*
My Babe. *Willie Dixon*
My Baby. *James Cotton*
My Baby. *Willie Dixon*
My Baby. *Booker White*
My Baby Business. *James Rushing*
My Baby Done Changed the Lock (see: Baby Changed the Lock on That Door)
My Baby Done Gone. *Sonny Terry*
My Baby Don't Love Me. *John Lee Hooker*
My Baby Gone Home. *Granville McGhee*
My Baby Got Another Man. *George Butler*
My Baby Have Come Back. *Henry Townsend*
My Baby Leavin'. *Sonny Terry*
My Baby Left Me. *Peter Chatman*
My Baby Left Me. *Arthur Crudup*
My Baby Left Me. *William Perryman*
My Baby Left Me. *Arbee Stidham*
My Baby Left Me. *Aaron Walker*
My Baby Left Town. *Joe Lee Williams*
My Baby Put Me Down. *Robert Brown (Smokey Babe)*
My Baby Put Me Down. *John Lee Hooker*
My Baby She Told Me. *Robert Brown (Smokey Babe)*
My Baby She's Got It. *James Moore*
My Baby Told Me. *Mathis James Reed*
My Baby Upsets Me. *Joe Williams*
My Baby Walked Out. *John Young*
My Baby Won't Be Back No More. *Joe Lee Williams*
My Baby Won't Write to Me. *Willie Mabon*
My Baby's Comin' Home. *Riley King*

My Baby's Coming Home. *Iverson Minter*
My Baby's Gone. *Alden Bunn*
My Baby's Gone. *John Williamson*
My Baby's House. *Henry Johnson*
My Baby's on the Line. *Connie Crayton*
My Baby's So Fine. *Sonny Terry*
My Baby's Sweater. *Willie Dixon*
My Baby's Ways. *William Trice*
My Back Scratcher. *Frank Frost*
My Be Bop Gal. *Charles Ross*
My Best Friend. *John Lee Hooker*
My Best Friend. *Elmore James*
My Best Friend. *John Shines*
My Best Friend's Blues. *William Lucas*
My Big Money. *Robert Brown (Washboard Sam)*
My Bitter Seed. *Mathis James Reed*
My Black and White Dog. *William Dupree*
My Black Mama. *Eddie House*
My Black Name Ringing. *John Lee Williamson*
My Bleeding Heart. *Elmore James*
My Blues Is in the Bottle. *Henry Brown*
My Buddy Blind Papa Lemon. *Joe Holmes*
My Castle's Rocking. *Alberta Hunter*
My Country Sugar Mama. *Chester Burnett*
My Daddy Told Me. *Luther Johnson*
My Daddy's Calling Me. *Irene Scruggs*
My Daily Wish. *Robert Lockwood*
My Ding-A-Ling. *Charles Berry*
My Dog. *McHouston Baker*
My Dog Can't Bark. *Otis Smothers*
My Dog Got the Measles. *Walter Lewis*
My Dog Is Mean. *Peter Chatman*
My Dolly B. *Oscar Wills*
My Dream. *John Mars*
My Dream (Poem). *Charles Berry*
My Electrical Invention Blues. *Eurreal Montgomery*
My Error. *Percy Mayfield*
My Fault. *Walter Brown McGhee*
My Feeling for the Blues. *Freddie King*
My Feet Jumped Salty. *Ernest Lawlars*
My First Love Blues. *Hudson Whittaker*
My First Wife Left Me. *John Lee Hooker*
My 40 Year Old Woman. *George Butler*
My Friend. *Percy Mayfield*
My Friends. *Chester Burnett*
My Friends Don't Know Me. *Walter Davis*
My Gal. *Nehemiah James*
My Gal Is Gone. *Hudson Whittaker*
My Game Blues. *Larry Johnson*
My Girl Won't Quit Me. *Travis Blaylock*
My Girlfriend Left Me. *Bill Williams*
My Grandpa Is Old Too. *Sam Hopkins*
My Hamstring's Poppin'. *Roosevelt Sykes*
My Happiness Depends on You. *Amos Milburn*
My Head Is Bad. *Victoria Spivey*
My Heart Beats for You. *William Dupree*
My Heart Beats Like a Drum. *Joe Blue*
My Heart Belongs to You. *Arbee Stidham*
My Heart Is Loaded with Trouble. *James Oden*
My Heart Is Out. *William Arnold*
My Home Ain't Here. *John Young*
My Home Ain't There. *Henry Townsend*
My Home Is in the Delta. *McKinley Morganfield*
My Home's in Hell. *William Dupree*
My Hoodoo Doctor. *Willie Dixon*
My Idea. *Edward Boyd*
My John the Conquer Root. *Willie Dixon*
My Kind of Woman. *Joseph Hutto*
My Kinda Woman. *Alden Bunn*
My Lady. *Edward Boyd*
My Laona Blues. *Theodore Darby*
My Last Affair. *Chester Burnett*
My Last Goodbye to You. *William Broonzy*
My Last Letter. *Al King*
My Last Suit. *Walter Brown McGhee*
My Life Is Ruined. *McKinley Morganfield*
My Lincoln Continental. *Arbee Stidham*
My Little Angel. *Mercy Dee Walton*
My Little Angel Child. *Norman Green*
My Little Flower. *William Broonzy*
My Little Gal. *Johnie Lewis*
My Little Kitten Susie. *Alonzo Johnson*
My Little Love-Light. *Charles Berry*
My Love Can't Hide. *John Shines*
My Love Don't Belong to You. *Alonzo Johnson*
My Love Is Down. *Alonzo Johnson*
My Love Will Never Die. *Willie Dixon*
My Love Will Never Die. *Otis Rush*
My Luck Is Bound to Change. *Amos Milburn*
My Lucky Day. *Viola Wells*
My Mama Told Me. *Clifton Chenier*
My Man. *Lucille Spann*
My Man Blues. *Bessie Smith*
My Mellow Man. *William Broonzy*
My Mind Is Ramblin'. *Chester Burnett*
My Mind Never Changed. *John Fortescue*
My Mood. *Riley King*
My Mother Died. *Booker White*
My Mother Often Told Me. *Johnie Lewis*
My Mustang Ford. *Charles Berry*
My Old Lady. *Michael Bloomfield*
My Old Lizzie. *William Broonzy*
My Old Pal. *James Rodgers*
My Own Blues. *Peter Clayton*
My Own Boogie. *John Davis*
My Own Fault. *Riley King*
My Own Life to Live. *Riley King*
My Past Life. *Albert Luandrew*
My Patience Keeps Running Out. *Aaron Walker*
My Plan. *Walter McGhee*
My Playful Baby's Gone. *Wynonie Harris*
My Pony. *Johnny Temple*
My Rare Dog. *J. D. Short*
My Second Mind. *Fred McDowell*
My Silent Prayer. *Riley King*
My So Called Friends. *Raymond Agee*

My Starter Won't Work. *Otis Hicks*
My Tight Woman. *Pleasant Joseph*
My Trainfare out of Town. *John Young*
My Trouble Blues. *Fred McDowell*
My Troubles and Me. *Chester Burnett*
My Well Is Dry. *James Arnold*
My Wife Is Getting Old. *Booker White*
My Woman. *Charles Berry*
My Woman Is Tired of Me Lyin'. *Alexander Lightfoot*
My Younger Days. *Sonny Boy Williamson (Alex Miller)*

Nadine. *Charles Berry*
Name of the Game. *Lowell Fulson*
Nappy Head Woman. *William Broonzy*
Nappy Head Woman. *Joe Hill Louis*
Naptown Blues: *Francis Blackwell/Leroy Carr*
Naptown Boogie. *John Tyler Adams*
Nashville Jump. *Cecil Gant*
Natchez Burnin'. *Chester Burnett*
Natch'l Go Getter. *Roosevelt Sykes*
Natural Days. *Otis Spann*
Natural Man. *J. B. Lenoir*
Natural Wig. *Luther Johnson*
Nature. *Chester Burnett*
Neck Bones. *Lee Jackson*
Need a Friend. *Joseph Young*
Need More Baby. *Willie Dixon*
Need More Blues: *John Estes/Hammie Nixon*
Need My Baby. *Walter Horton*
Need Somebody's Help. *J. B. Lenoir*
Neglected Woman. *Alexander Moore*
Neighborhood Affair. *Riley King*
Nellie Gray (see: Miss Nellie Gray)
Nelson Street Blues. *Willie Love*
Nervous. *Willie Dixon*
Never Drive a Beggar from Your Door. *Thomas Delaney*
Never Get out of the Blues Alive. *John Lee Hooker*
Never Go Wrong Blues. *Eurreal Montgomery*
Never Love Again. *Louis Bo Collins*
Never, Never. *Robert Brown (Washboard Sam)*
Never No Mo' Blues. *James Rodgers*
Never Will Forget Your Love. *Hi Tide Harris*
New Auto Blues. *Armenter Chatmon*
New B&O Blues. *Walter Davis*
New B&O Blues. *Amos Easton*
New Bon Ton Roulay. *Clarence Garlow*
New Car Blues. *Joe Lee Williams*
New Chicago Blues. *Mathis James Reed*
New Corrine. *Jesse Fuller*
New Crawlin' King Snake. *Chester Burnett*
New Deal Blues. *Carl Martin*
New Diddey Wah Diddey. *William Augusta Trice*
New 44 Blues. *Roosevelt Sykes*
New Jersey Women. *Iverson Minter*
New Leaf, A. *Mathis James Reed*
New Mean Old Train. *Alexander Lightfoot*
New Orleans. *Walter Davis*
New Orleans Blues. *Alonzo Johnson*
New Orleans Jump. *Roosevelt Sykes*
New Orleans Streamline. *Booker White*
New Orleans Woman. *Roy Brown*
New Orleans Women. *Joseph Young*
New Satellite Blues (see: Satellite Blues)
New Style of Loving. *Arthur Phelps*
New Way Blues. *Lucille Bogan*
New Year's Blues. *Alonzo Johnson*
New York Glide. *Thomas Delaney*
New York — St. Louis. *Charles Sayles*
Newport News Blues. *Will Shade*
Nickle's Worth of Liver Blues. *Edith North Johnson*
Night and Day: *Walter Brown McGhee/Sonny Terry*
Night Beat. *Charles Berry*
Night Blue. *McHouston Baker*
Night Latch Key Blues. *Virginia Liston*
Night Mare Blues. *John Lee Hooker*
Night Time. *Alexander Lightfoot*
Night Time Blues. *Thomas Dorsey*
Night Watchman Blues. *William Broonzy*
Nighthawk Boogie. *Robert Nighthawk*
Nightmare Is Over. *Edward Boyd*
Nighttime (Anytime) Is the Right Time. *Roosevelt Sykes*
Nine Below Zero. *Sonny Boy Williamson (Alex Miller)*
1913 Massacre, The. *Woodrow Guthrie*
1937 Flood. *Carl Martin*
1936 Triggertoe. *Booker White*
Ninety-Eight Degree Blues. *Alger Alexander*
99. *Sonny Boy Williamson (Alex Miller)*
99 Blues. *Robert Brown (Washboard Sam)*
99 Years and One Dark Day. *Jesse Fuller*
Nitty Gritty. *Koko Taylor*
No. *Peter Chatman*
No Buts, No Maybes. *Roy Byrd*
No Do Right. *Aaron Walker*
No Dough Blues. *Arthur Phelps*
No Good. *Riley King*
No Good Weasel. *John Wrencher*
No Good Woman. *Sidney Semien*
No Good Woman Blues: *Francis Blackwell/ Leroy Carr*
No Lie. *George Guy*
No Love for Sale. *Alonzo Johnson*
No Matter How She Done It. *Hudson Whittaker*
No Money Down. *Charles Berry*
No Money No Honey. *Luke Miles*
No More Cryin'. *K. C. Douglas*
No More Cryin'. *Alonzo Johnson*
No More Lovin'. *John Williamson*
No More Trouble. *James Dawkins*
No More Troubles. *Andrew Odom*
No Naggin' No Draggin'. *Arthur Gunter*
No No Baby. *Clarence Garlow*
No No Baby. *Frank Seals*
No One Knows. *Herman Parker*
No Papa No. *Victoria Spivey*
No Particular Place to Go. *Charles Berry*
No Pickin' No Pullin'. *John Henry Barbee*
No Place to Go. *Chester Burnett*

No Rolling Blues. *James Witherspoon*
No Sense in Worrying. *Otis Spann*
No Shoes. *John Lee Hooker*
No Special Boogie. *Eurreal Montgomery*
No Special Rider. *Albert Luandrew*
No Special Rider Blues. *Eurreal Montgomery*
No Strain. *Peter Chatman*
No Time at All. *Alden Bunn*
No Time for Jive. *George Smith*
No Whiskey Blues. *Albert Luandrew*
No Women No Nickel. *Amos Easton*
No Worry Blues. *Aaron Walker*
Nobody Cares for Me. *John Hurt*
Nobody in Mind. *Joseph Turner*
Nobody Knows. *James Rushing*
Nobody Knows. *George Smith*
Nobody Knows Chicago Like I Do. *Otis Spann*
Nobody Knows the Way I Feel This Mornin'. *Thomas Delaney*
Nobody Love You. *Cecil Gant*
Nobody Loves Me But My Mother. *Otis Hicks*
Nobody Loves Me But My Mother. *Riley King*
Nobody Wants You When You're Old & Grey. *Arthur Crudup*
Nobody's Dirty Business. *John Hurt*
Nobody's Fault But Mine. *John Shines*
None of Nothing. *George Butler*
Nora. *Eddie Kirkland*
Nora's Dove. *Richard Havens*
North Carolina Blues. *Johnie Lewis*
Northbound Blues. *Maggie Jones*
Nothin' but Trouble. *John Lee Hooker*
Nothing. *Edward Boyd*
Nothing but the Blues. *James Oden*
Nothing but the Blues. *Walter Price*
Nothing but Trouble. *Edward Boyd*
Nothing but Trouble. *James Pryor*
Nothing in Rambling. *Lizzie Douglas*
Notoriety Woman Blues. *Arthur Phelps*
Notting Hill Eviction Blues. *John Holder*
Now Darling. *John Wrencher*
Now I Ain't Got Nothing at All. *Clarence Smith*
Now I Got the Blues. *Peter Chatman*
Now I'm Satisfied. *Alberta Hunter*
Now Now, I'll Tell You When. *Gabriel Brown*
Now or Never. *Henry Townsend*
Now That I'm Down. *Frank Seals*
Now That You've Lost Me. *Riley King*
Now What Do You Think. *Lillian Green*
Now You Know. *Lonnie Brooks*
Number Five Blues. *John Lee Williamson*
Number Nine. *Roosevelt Sykes*
Number Nine Train. *Alden Bunn*
Number Ten at the Station and Number Twelve Is on the Road. *Arthur Kelley*
Number 12 Is at the Station. *Amos Milburn*
Number 12 Left Me Roam. *Victoria Spivey*
Number 12 Train. *Joshua White*
Number's Blues, The. *Roy Milton*
Nuts About That Gal. *Alonzo Johnson*
Nutty & Buggy Blues. *Hudson Whittaker*

O, Glory How Happy I Am. *Gary Davis*
O'Fallon Blues. *Henry Brown*
Off and On Blues. *Beulah Wallace*
Off Business. *James Dawkins*
Off the Hook. *Earl Hooker*
Off the Wall. *Marion Walter Jacobs*
Off the Wall. *Louis Myers*
Oh Angel Eyes It's All for You. *Beulah Wallace*
Oh Babe. *Walter Lewis*
Oh Baby. *William Arnold*
Oh Baby. *Marion Walter Jacobs*
Oh Baby. *Joe McCoy*
Oh Baby. *Joe Lee Williams*
Oh Baby Doll. *Charles Berry*
Oh Baby Hold Me. *Chester Burnett*
Oh Carol. *Charles Berry*
Oh Joe. *Joe McCoy*
Oh John. *Mathis James Reed*
Oh Lawdy. *William Dupree*
Oh Little Girl. *John Sellers*
Oh Lord, Search My Heart (see: Search My Heart)
Oh Louisiana. *Charles Berry*
Oh Mama How I Love You. *William Broonzy*
Oh Me Oh My Blues. *Walter Davis*
Oh My Babe Blues. *Gertrude Rainey*
Oh My Soul. *Richard Penniman*
Oh Papa Blues. *Gertrude Rainey*
Oh Red. *Chester Burnett*
Oh Red. *Joe McCoy*
Oh Red! *Rufus Perryman*
Oh Susannah. *Taj Mahal*
Oh What a Time. *Virginia Liston*
Oh What Kind of Woman. *John Sellers*
Oh Yea. *Ellas McDaniel*
Oh Yes. *William Broonzy*
Oh Yes Baby. *Alonzo Johnson*
Oklahoma Hills. *Woodrow Guthrie*
Old and Grey. *William Dupree*
Old Army Mule. *Woodrow Guthrie*
Old Aunt Jane. *Lee Jackson*
Old Black Cat Blues (Jinx Blues). *James Arnold*
Old Cotton Fields at Home (see: Cotton Fields)
Old Fashioned Baby. *Connie Crayton*
Old Folks Boogie. *Norman Green*
Old Grey Mule, You Ain't What You Used to Be. *Sam Chatmon*
Old Lady. *Booker White*
Old Maid Boogie. *Eddie Vinson*
Old Maid Got Married. *Eddie Vinson*
Old Man. *Sam Hopkins*
Old Man Blues. *William Broonzy*
Old Man Tom. *Booker White*
Old Original Kokomo Blues. *James Arnold*
Old Riley (Here Rattler Here). *Huddie Ledbetter*

Old Rounders Blues. *Lemon Jefferson*
Old Saw Mill Blues. *Joe Lee Williams*
Old Ship of Zion. *Thomas Dorsey*
Old Taylor. *Peter Chatman*
Old Time Shuffle. *Vernon Harrison*
Old Ugly Man Like Me. *George Smith*
Old Woman Blues. *Sam Hopkins*
Old Women Blues. *William Dupree*
Olie Blues. *John Estes*
On My Knees. *Frank Seals*
On My Last Go Round. *Joe Callicott*
On My Way. *Woodrow Guthrie*
On My Way. *Al King*
On My Way Back Home. *Sonny Boy Williamson (Alex Miller)*
On My Way to School. *Charles Ross*
On the Cooling Board. *Willie McTell*
On the Road Again. *Luther Johnson*
On the Road Again. *Floyd Jones*
On the Road Again: *Walter Brown McGhee/Sonny Terry*
On the Road Again. *John Young*
Once upon a Time. *Sonny Boy Williamson (Alex Miller)*
Once Was a Gambler. *Sam Hopkins*
One Day You're Going to Get Lucky. *Willie Dixon*
One Good Man. *Janis Joplin*
180 Days. *Alden Bunn*
One I Crave, The. *James Pryor*
One Letter Home. *William Gillum*
One More Chance with You. *Marion Walter Jacobs*
One More Mile. *James Cotton*
One More Time. *Willie Dixon*
One More Time. *Edward Harris*
One Night of Sin. *Smiley Lewis*
One of These Mornings. *J. C. Burris*
One Room Country Shack. *Mercy Dee Walton*
One Scotch, One Bourbon, One Beer. *William Dupree*
One Step at a Time. *Clifton Chenier*
One Sweet Letter from You. *Walter Davis*
One Thing for Sure. *Walter Brown McGhee*
1011 Woodland. *James Dawkins*
1009 Blues. *Johnny Fuller*
One Time Blues. *Arthur Phelps*
One Way Out. *Willie Dixon*
One Way Out. *Sonny Boy Williamson (Alex Miller)*
One Way Ticket. *John Lee Hooker*
One Woman's Man. *Walter Brown*
Only Fools Have Fun. *Peter Chatman*
Only Woman, The. Walter Davis
Ooh Baby. *Ellas McDaniel*
Ooh-ee Baby. *Albert King*
Ooh-Wee Baby. *Joseph Turner*
Open Nose. *Alden Bunn*
Open Road. *Sonny Boy Williamson (Alex Miller)*
Open Up Baby. *George Butler*
Open Up Your Door. *Sam Hopkins*
Operator. *Edward Boyd*
Operator 210. *Floyd Dixon*
Orange Driver. *Eddie Burns*
Organ Grinder Blues. *Victoria Spivey*
Orphan Home Blues. *Andrew McMahon*
Otis' Blues. *Otis Spann*
Otis in the Dark. *Otis Spann*
Our Only Child. *Eddie Jones*
Out of Business. *James Dawkins*
Out of Water Coast. *Sonny Boy Williamson (Alex Miller)*
Out on the Ocean. *Gary Davis*
Out on the Road. *James Rogers*
Out West Blues. *Eurreal Montgomery*
Out with the Wrong Woman. *Robert Brown (Washboard Sam)*
Outside Help. *Riley King*
Outskirts of Town (see: I'm Gonna Move to the Outskirts of Town)
Over the Hill. *Fred McDowell*
Overall Junction. *Albert King*
Overhaul Your Machine. *Joe Lee Williams*

P-38 Blues. *William Borum*
Pack My Clothes. *James Rachell*
Packin' Trunk Blues. *Huddie Ledbetter*
Packin' Up, Gettin' Ready. *Walter Brown McGhee*
Packing Up Her Trunk to Leave. *Roosevelt Holts*
Paer Lee. *Walter Lewis*
Painful Party. *Percy Mayfield*
Paint My Mailbox Blues. *Taj Mahal*
Panama Limited. *Booker White*
Panama Limited Blues. *Esther Bigeou*
Panther Squall Blues. *Arthur Phelps*
Papa Ain't Salty. *Aaron Walker*
Papa Do Do Do Blues. *Charlie Jackson*
Papa Papa Blues. *Sara Martin*
Papa Slick Head. *Henry Brown*
Papa's Lawdy Lawdy Blues. *Charlie Jackson*
Parable of Ramon, The. *Richard Havens*
Parcel Post Blues. *Walter Brown McGhee*
Parchman Farm Blues. *Booker White*
Pardon Denied Again. *Robert Pete Williams*
Paris Blues. *Aaron Walker*
Paris Scene. *Peter Chatman*
Parson Jones. *Thomas Delaney*
Part-Time Woman. *James Witherspoon*
Past Bedtime. *Sidney Semien*
Past Forty Blues. *James Witherspoon*
Pastures of Plenty. *Woodrow Guthrie*
Pat-a-Foot Blues. *Thomas Dorsey*
Pawn Show. *Walter Brown McGhee*
Pay Day Blues. *Lowell Fulson*
Pay Me No Mind. *Ishmon Bracey*
Pay Roll Blues. *Lucille Bogan*
Payday. *John Hurt*
Paying the Cost to Be the Boss. *Riley King*
Pea Vine Blues. *Charley Patton*
Peace. *Willie Dixon*
Peace in the Valley. *Thomas Dorsey*
Peace Lovin' Man. *John Lee Hooker*
Peace of Mind. *Raymond Agee*

Peach Orchard Mama. *Joe Lee Williams*
Peach Tree. *Sonny Boy Williamson*
Peach Tree Blues. *James Rachell*
Pearl Harbor Blues. *Peter Clayton*
Pearline. *Eddie House*
Pearly Mae Blues. *Joe Lee Williams*
Pee Pa Pobble. *Eddie Burns*
Pee Wee's Boogie. *Connie Crayton*
Peepin' and Hidin'. *Mathis James Reed*
Peeping Tom. *Roosevelt Sykes*
Peetie Wheatstraw Stomp. *Peetie Wheatstraw*
Peg Leg. *Joshua Howell*
Penguin, The. *Rufus Thomas*
Penitentiary Moan Blues. *Alger Alexander*
Penny Pinching Blues. *Jeanne Carroll*
People People. *Peter Chatman*
People What Would You Do If You Were Me? (see: What Would You Do If You Were Me?)
People's Blues. *Arbee Stidham*
Pepper Headed Woman. *Sonny Terry*
Pera Lee. *John Hurt*
Persimmon Pie. *Roosevelt Sykes*
Person to Person. *Eddie Vinson*
Pet Cream Man. *Joseph Hutto*
Pet Rabbit. *John Shines*
Pete's Jump. *Sonny Terry*
Philadelphia Lawyer. *Woodrow Guthrie*
Phone Call from My Baby. *Connie Crayton*
Phoney Women Blues. *Pleasant Joseph*
Phonograph Blues. *Robert Johnson*
Picadilly Circus Blues. *John Holder*
Piccolo Man. *Blind Boy Fuller*
Pick a Bale o' Cotton. *Huddie Ledbetter*
Pick a Pickle. *Joe Lee Williams*
Pickin' 'em Out Again. *Henry Brown*
Pickpocket Blues. *Bessie Smith*
Picture in the Frame. *Edward Boyd*
Pig Meat Blues. *Thomas Dorsey*
Pig Meat Mama. *Pernell Charity*
Pigalle and Love. *Peter Chatman*
Pillar to Post. *James Witherspoon*
Pinch Backs, Take 'em Away. *Bessie Smith*
Pinetop's Blues. *Clarence Smith*
Pinetop's Boogie Woogie: *Joe Willie Perkins/Clarence Smith*
Piney Brown Blues. *Joseph Turner*
Pitchin' Boogie. *Clarence Lofton*
Pity and a Shame. *Mercy Dee Walton*
Pity on Me. *Eddie Kirkland*
Plane Wreck at Los Gatos. *Woodrow Guthrie*
Play It Cool. *Freddie King*
Play My Baby's Blues. *John Erby*
Play On Little Girl. *Norman Green*
Play On Little Girl. *Aaron Walker*
Play Proof Woman. *Hudson Whittaker*
Play Your Hand. *William Broonzy*
Playboy Blues. *John Jenkins*
Playboy Blues. *Joseph Turner*
Playboy Boogie. *Eddie Taylor*
Playin' Myself the Blues. *Cecil Gant*
Playing with the Thing. *Sonny Terry*
Pleading Blues. *Ida Cox*
Pleading Blues. *Eurreal Montgomery*
Please. *Lonnie Brooks*
Please Accept My Love. *Clarence Garlow*
Please Accept My Love. *Riley King*
Please Baby. *Alonzo Johnson*
Please Baby Come Home to Me. *Harmon Ray*
Please Be on That 519. *Cornelius Green*
Please Believe Me. *William Broonzy*
Please Believe Me. *Curtis Jones*
Please Come Back. *James Rushing*
Please Come Home for Christmas. *Charles Brown*
Please Don't Dog Your Woman. *Walter Brown McGhee*
Please Don't Go. *Dusty Brown*
Please Don't Leave Me. *Antoine Domino*
Please Don't Turn Me Down. *James Moore*
Please Find My Baby. *Elmore James*
Please Help. *Joseph Hutto*
Please Help Me. *Alonzo Johnson*
Please Help Me. *Riley King*
Please Help Me Get Him Off My Mind. *Bessie Smith*
Please Let It Be Me. *Arbee Stidham*
Please Love Me. *Riley King*
Please Ma'am. *Joshua Howell*
Please Mr. Nixon. *Clarence Brown*
Please Remember Me. *Walter Davis*
Please Send Me Someone to Love. *Percy Mayfield*
Please Tell Me Baby. *Clarence Brown*
Please Try to See It My Way. *Hudson Whittaker*
Pleasing You. *Alonzo Johnson*
Plough (Plow) Hand Blues. *William Broonzy*
Pneumonia Blues (I Keep On Aching). *William Broonzy*
Po' Howard. *Huddie Ledbetter*
Pocahontas. *Bill Williams*
Pocket Full of Money. *Frank Frost*
Pocket Full of Shells. *Frank Frost*
Pocketful of Money. *Roosevelt Sykes*
Poison Ivy. *Willie Mabon*
Poker Woman Blues. *Arthur Phelps*
Pokey. *Jerry McCain*
Police Blues. *Thomas Delaney*
Police Dog Blues. *Arthur Phelps*
Policy Blues. *Armenter Chatmon*
Policy Wheel Blues. *James Arnold*
Polly Wee. *Huddie Ledbetter*
Pontiac Blues. *Sonny Boy Williamson (Alex Miller)*
Pony Blues. *Eddie House*
Pony Blues. *Charley Patton*
Poon Tang. *Thomas Delaney*
Poon Tang. *Aaron Walker*
Poor Beggar. *Joe Lee Williams*
Poor Boy. *Chester Burnett*
Poor Boy. *John Jackson*
Poor Boy a Long Way from Home. *Booker White*
Poor Boy Blues. *Joe Callicott*

Poor Boy Blues. *William Dupree*
Poor Boy Blues. *Lowell Fulson*
Poor Boy Blues. *James Oden*
Poor Girl out on the Mountain. *Robert Pete Williams*
Poor House. *Joseph Turner*
Poor Kelly Blues. *Major Merriweather*
Poor Man Blues. *Sonny Terry*
Poor Man but a Good Man. *Sonny Terry*
Poor Man's Blues. *Bessie Smith*
Poor Man's Friend. *Hammie Nixon*
Poor Man's Plea, A. *Amos Wells*
Poor Man's Tonic. *John Shines*
Poor Me. *John Lee Hooker*
Poor Me. *Charley Patton*
Poor Me Blues. *Edna Hicks*
Poor Poor Me. *Antoine Domino*
Popcorn. *Jerry McCain*
Possum Den Blues. *Peetie Wheatstraw*
Postwar Future Blues. *Pleasant Joseph*
Pots On, Gas On High. *John Lee Hooker*
Pouring Down Rain. *John Lee Hooker*
Praise to Helsinki. *Edward Boyd*
Praise to My Baby. *Edward Boyd*
Pratt City Blues. *Bertha Hill*
Praying Blues. *John Erby*
Praying to the Lord. *Riley King*
Preachin' Blues. *Robert Johnson*
Preachin' the Blues. *Eddie House*
Precious Lord Take My Hand. *Thomas Dorsey*
Precious Stone. *Joseph Hutto*
President Kennedy Blues. *William Dupree*
President Roosevelt. *Joe Lee Williams*
Presidents Blues. *Harmon Ray*
Pretty Baby. *Herman Parker*
Pretty Baby Blues. *Woodrow Adams*
Pretty Boy Floyd. *Woodrow Guthrie*
Pretty Little Girl. *Sonny Terry*
Pretty Mama. *David Van Ronk*
Pretty Papa. *Huddie Ledbetter*
Pretty Thing. *Ellas McDaniel*
Pretty Willie Done Me Wrong. *Joe Lee Williams*
Pretty Woman with a Sack Dress On. *Alexander Moore*
Prison Bound. *Wilbert Ellis*
Prison Bound. *John Young*
Prison Bound Blues. *Leroy Carr*
Prison Cell Blues. *Lemon Jefferson*
Prison Cell Blues. *Mary Johnson*
Prisoner's Talking Blues. *Robert Pete Williams*
Private Number. *Willie Mae Thornton*
Prodigal Son, The. *Robert Wilkins*
Promised Land. *Charles Berry*
Prove It on Me Blues. *Gertrude Rainey*
Prowling Blues. *Johnny Fuller*
Prowling Ground Hog. *Thomas Shaw*
Pub Crawling Blues. *John Holder*
Pulp Wood. *Freddie King*
Puppy Love. *Amos Easton*
Pure Religion. *Gary Davis*
Purple Haze. *James Hendrix*
Push and Pull. *Rufus Thomas*
Push Ka Pee Shee Pie. *Louis Jordan*
Pushing That Thing. *William Perryman*
Put a Little Love in Everything You Do. *Edith Wilson*
Put Her Down. *Charles Berry*
Put It All in There. *Willie Dixon*
Put It Where I Can Get It. *Jerry McCain*
Put Up or Shut Up. *Roosevelt Sykes*
Put Your Arms Around Me. *Frank Edwards*
Put Your Mind on No One Man. *Virginia Liston*
Putting Out the Vibrations and Hoping It Comes Home. *Richard Havens*

Quarter past Nine. *Elmore James*
Quarter to Twelve. *Marion Walter Jacobs*
Queen Bee. *Lizzie Douglas*
Queen Bee. *John Lee Hooker*
Queen Bee. *Taj Mahal*
Queen Bee. *Lucille Spann*
Queen of Diamonds. *Roy Brown*
Quiet Whiskey. *Wynonie Harris*
Quit Draggin'. *Joe Lee Williams*

RM Blues. *Roy Milton*
Rabbit Blues. *Robert Brown (Smokey Babe)*
Rabbit Foot Blues. *Lemon Jefferson*
Racehorse Called Mae, A. *William Dupree*
Rack 'em Back. *Edward Boyd*
Rack 'em Back Jack. *Peter Chatman*
Rag Alley Drag. *Arthur Taylor*
Rag in G. *Mance Lipscomb*
Rag Mama. *Edward Harris*
Ragged and Dirty. *Luther Allison*
Raggedy and Dirty. *Frankie Lee Sims*
Raidin' the Joint (see: They Raided the Joint)
Railroad Blues. *Jesse Fuller*
Railroad Blues. *Trixie Smith*
Railroad Blues. *Robert Pete Williams*
Rain Eyes. *Charles Berry*
Rain Is Such a Lonesome Sound. *James Witherspoon*
Rainin' All the Time. *Riley King*
Rainin' in My Heart. *Peter Chatman*
Rainin' in My Heart. *James Moore*
Raining in My Heart. *Riley King*
Raining in My Heart. *Roosevelt Sykes*
Raining on the Cold Cold Ground. *Alonzo Johnson*
Raining the Blues. *Peter Chatman*
Rainy Day Blues. *James Rachell*
Rainy Day Blues. *Joseph Turner*
Rainy Day Blues. *John Lee Williamson*
Rainy Day Friend. *Edith Wilson*
Rainy Rainy Day. *Walter Brown McGhee*
Ramble This Highway. *Peter Chatman*
Rambler's Blues. *Hudson Whittaker*
Ramblin'. *John Shines*
Ramblin' and Wanderin' Blues. *Joe Lee Williams*
Ramblin' Bill. *William Broonzy*

Ramblin' by Myself. *John Lee Hooker*
Ramblin' Mama Blues. *Arthur Phelps*
Ramblin' on My Mind. *Robert Johnson*
Rambling Blues. *Ida Cox*
Rambling Woman. *John Walker*
Ramona Say Yes. *Charles Berry*
Rampart Street Special. *William Dupree*
Range in My Kitchen Blues. *Alger Alexander*
Rap. *Fred McDowell*
Rasslin' Till the Wagon Comes. *Wesley Wilson*
Ration Blues. *Louis Jordan*
Rats in My Kitchen. *John Estes*
Rattle Snake Blues. *Charley Patton*
Rattler, The. *Dave Alexander*
Rattlesnake. *John Brim*
Rattlesnake Blues. *Mary Johnson*
Razor Ball, The. *Willie McTell*
Razor Strop Boogie. *Wade Walton*
Razor Totin' Mama. *Wesley Wilson*
Ready for Eddie. *Eddie Taylor*
Real Gone Lover. *Smiley Lewis*
Real Good Feeling. *Edward Boyd*
Real Real Love. *Raymond Agee*
Really Got the Blues. *Peter Chatman*
Really, I Apologize. *Cleve White*
Reap What You Sow. *Edward Boyd*
Rebecca. *Joseph Turner*
Reckless Blues. *Bessie Smith*
Reckless Rider Blues. *Robert Brown (Washboard Sam)*
Reconsider. *Aaron Walker*
Reconsider Baby. *Lowell Fulson*
Red Beans and Rice. *James Arnold*
Red Cross Store. *Huddie Ledbetter*
Red-Eye Jesse Bell. *Roosevelt Sykes*
Red Lantern Blues. *Victoria Spivey*
Red Light. *Mercy Dee Walton*
Red River. *Huddie Ledbetter*
Red River Blues. *Clyde Bernhardt*
Red River Blues. *Blind Boy Fuller*
Red River Dam Blues. *Larry Johnson*
Red River Run, The. *J. D. Short*
Redbird. *Huddie Ledbetter*
Red's "A" Train. *Vernon Harrison*
Red's Boogie. *William Perryman*
Red's Boogie Woogie. *Rufus Perryman*
Red's Dream. *Iverson Minter*
Red's Own Blues. *Rufus Perryman*
Red's Rhumba. *Vernon Harrison*
Reelin' and Rockin'. *Charles Berry*
Reelin' and Rockin'. *John Littlejohn*
Reeling and Rocking. *John Jenkins*
Reet Petite and Gone. *Louis Jordan*
Relaxin'. *Vernon Harrison*
Release Me. *Gus Jenkins*
Remember. *James Hendrix*
Remember Me. *McKinley Morganfield*
Remember My Name. *Alberta Hunter*
Remember Way Back. *Joe Lee Williams*
Restless Blues. *Melvin Jackson*
Reuben Blues. *Woodrow Guthrie*
Revenue Man Blues. *Charley Patton*
Reverend Bounce. *Peter Chatman*
Rice, Salmon and Black-Eyed Peas. *Albert Luandrew*
Richland Women Blues. *John Hurt*
Ride and Roll. *Walter Brown McGhee*
Ride 'em On Down. *Eddie Taylor*
Ride with Your Daddy Tonight. *Frank Frost*
Riff and Harmonica Jump. *Sonny Terry*
Right Kind of Life, The. *John Lee Williamson*
Right Now. *Gary Davis*
Right Now. *William Dupree*
Right off Rampart Street. *Charles Berry*
Right Place Wrong Time. *Otis Rush*
Right String But the Wrong Yo Yo, The. *Rufus Perryman*
Riley Springs. *William Gillum*
Ring Around My Heart. *John Young*
Ring Tailed Tom. *Frank Floyd*
Rising Wind. *Floyd Jones*
River Hip Mama. *Robert Brown (Washboard Sam)*
River Line Blues. *Shirley Griffith*
River of Life. *J. C. Burris*
Riverboat. *McHouston Baker*
Riverboat. *Willie Mabon*
Riverside. *Taj Mahal*
Riverside Blues. *Thomas Dorsey*
Road House. *James Hendrix*
Road Runner. *Ellas McDaniel*
Roamin' Blues. *Sara Martin*
Roamin' Rambler. *Alonzo Johnson*
Roaming. *George Smith*
Roberta. *Huddie Ledbetter*
Rochester Blues. *Eddie House*
Rock. *Thomas Shaw*
Rock-a-Bye Birdie. *Roosevelt Sykes*
Rock and Roll. *James Rushing*
Rock and Roll. *Johnny Winter*
Rock and Roll Bed Blues. *Alexander Moore*
Rock Aunt Dinah Rock. *Wesley Wilson*
Rock Bottom. *Marion Walter Jacobs*
Rock 'em Dead. *Lowell Fulson*
Rock Island Line. *Huddie Ledbetter*
Rock It Rhythm. *Hudson Whittaker*
Rock Me. *Thomas Dorsey*
Rock Me Baby. *Riley King*
Rock Me Baby. *McKinley Morganfield*
Rock Me Mama. *Arthur Crudup*
Rock Me Momma. *John Walker*
Rock Me Woman. *Peter Chatman*
Rock My Baby Tonight. *Elmore James*
Rock 'n' Roll Music. *Charles Berry*
Rock the Rock. *Edward Boyd*
Rock This Morning. *Lowell Fulson*
Rocker. *Marion Walter Jacobs*
Rockhouse. *Ray Charles*
Rockin' after Midnight. *Charles Ross*
Rockin' and Rollin'. *Charles Berry*

Rockin' and Rollin'. *Melvin Jackson*
Rockin' at Midnight. *Charles Edwards*
Rockin' at the Fillmore. *Charles Berry*
Rockin' at the Philharmonic. *Charles Berry*
Rockin' Chair Blues. *William Broonzy*
Rockin' Chair Blues. *Ray Charles*
Rockin' Chair Blues. *John Wrencher*
Rockin' Chair Boogie. *John Davis*
Rockin' Chair Daddy. *Frank Floyd*
Rockin' on the Hill Blues. *Frank Stokes*
Rockin' the Pad. *Peter Chatman*
Rockin' with Peggy. *Louis Robinson*
Rockin' with Red. *William Perryman*
Rocking Chair Blues. *Bessie Smith*
Rocking Daddy. *Chester Burnett*
Rocking on the Railroad. *Charles Berry*
Rocking with Chromanica. *Carey Bell*
Rocks, The. *Beulah Wallace*
Rocks and Gravel. *Joshua Howell*
Rocks Have Been My Pillow. *Henry Townsend*
Rocks in My Bed. *Leroy Carr*
Rocky Mountain. *James Brewer*
Rocky Road. *Melvin Jackson*
Rocky Road Blues. *James Arnold*
Rode That Train All Night Long. *Milton Campbell*
Roe Buck Man. *Arthur Crudup*
Roll Dem Bones. *William Broonzy*
Roll 'em Pete. *Joseph Turner*
Roll On, Baby. *Raymond Agee*
Roll On Columbia. *Woodrow Guthrie*
Roll Over Beethoven. *Charles Berry*
Roll Roll Roll. *Lonnie Brooks*
Roll Your Money Maker. *James Harris*
Rollin' and Rollin'. *Sam Hopkins*
Rollin' and Tumblin'. *McKinley Morganfield*
Rollin' Blues. *Lowell Fulson*
Rollin' in Your Arms. *Joe Lee Williams*
Rollin' Mill Blues: *Leola B Grant/Wesley Wilson*
Rollin' Stone. *McKinley Morganfield*
Rollin' Stone Man. *Eddie Kirkland*
Rollin' Woman Blues. *Sam Hopkins*
Rolling. *Silas Hogan*
Rolling and Stumbling Blues. *Alger Alexander*
Rolling Around Dallas. *Alexander Moore*
Romance in the Dark. *Lillian Green*
Romance without Finance. *William Broonzy*
Room to Move. *John Mayall*
Roosevelt Daddy's Blues. *Roosevelt Sykes*
Roosevelt Song. *Huddie Ledbetter*
Roosevelt's Mood. *Roosevelt Sykes*
Rooster Song. *Antoine Domino*
Root Man Blues. *Walter Davis*
Rootin' Ground Hog. *Joe Lee Williams*
Rope Stretching Blues. *Arthur Phelps*
Rosa Lee Swing. *Edward Boyd*
Rose Mary. *Antoine Domino*
Rough and Tumble Blues. *Gertrude Rainey*
Rough Treatment. *Hudson Shower*
'Round and 'Round. *Charles Berry*
Round and Round. *J. B. Lenoir*
Round for You. *Willie Mabon*
Round Round Hitler's Grave. *Woodrow Guthrie*
Route 90. *Clarence Garlow*
Rub Me Until My Love Come Down. *Robert Pete Williams*
Rub My Root. *Willie Dixon*
Rubber Tyred Hack. *Alexander Moore*
Rubbin' My Root. *John Wrencher*
Ruby, Ruby. *Willie Littlefield*
Ruby's Monkey. *Willie Mabon*
Ruff Stuff. *Jerry McCain*
Rumba Negro. *Oran Page*
Run Around. *Charles Berry*
Run Away Blues. *Gertrude Rainey*
Run Away Boogie. *John Davis*
Run Joe. *Louis Jordan*
Run On Babe. *John Lee Hooker*
Run Rudolph Run. *Charles Berry*
Run, Shaker Life. *Richard Havens*
Run Sinner Run. *Mance Lipscomb*
Run Uncle John Run. *Jerry McCain*
Runnin' the Boogie. *Roosevelt Sykes*
Runnin' Wild Blues. *Milton Campbell*
Runnin' Wild Blues. *Charley Patton*

S. P. Blues. *Otis Spann*
Sabine River Blues. *Alger Alexander*
Sad and Lonely Day. *Roosevelt Sykes*
Sad and Lonesome. *Amos Easton*
Sad and Lonesome Blues. *Walter Davis*
Sad and Lonesome Blues. *Albert Luandrew*
Sad and Sorrow Blues. *Sara Martin*
Sad Day in Texas. *Otis Spann*
Sad Day Uptown. *Luther Johnson*
Sad Funk. *Aaron Willis*
Sad Hours. *Marion Walter Jacobs*
Sad Letter. *McKinley Morganfield*
Sad 'n' Lonely Blues. *Edith Wilson*
Sad News. *Iverson Minter*
Sad News Blues. *Lemon Jefferson*
Sad News from Korea. *Sam Hopkins*
Sad Sad Day. *McKinley Morganfield*
Sad to Be Alone. *Sonny Boy Williamson (Alex Miller)*
Saddle My Pony. *Chester Burnett*
Sadie. *Theodore Taylor*
Safety Mama. *Bessie Smith*
Safety Pin Blues. *Roosevelt Sykes*
Sail On. *Aaron Walker*
Sail On Blues. *Peter Chatman*
Sail On Little Girl. *Amos Easton*
Sailing. *Gary Davis*
Sales Tax. *Sam Chatmon*
Sally in the Alley Blues: *Francis Blackwell/Leroy Carr*
Sally Long Blues. *Virginia Liston*
Sally Where'd You Get the Liquor From? *Gary Davis*
Sally Zu Zaz. *Joseph Turner*

SONG INDEX

Salty Dog. *John Hurt*
Salty Dog (Blues). *Charlie Jackson*
Salty Woman. *Robert Pete Williams*
Salute to Pinetop. *James Yancey*
Same Girl. *Sonny Boy Williamson (Alex Miller)*
Same Mistake Twice. *Joseph Hutto*
Same Thing, The. *Willie Dixon*
Samson & Delilah. *Gary Davis*
San Antonio Blues. *William Broonzy*
San Francisco Bay Blues. *Jesse Fuller*
San Francisco Breakdown. *Charles Ross*
San Francisco Dues. *Charles Berry*
San Quentin Blues. *Sidney Maiden*
Santa Claus. *Sonny Boy Williamson (Alex Miller)*
Santa Claus Blues. *Walter Davis*
Santa Fe Blues. *Sam Hopkins*
Santa Fe Blues. *Eurreal Montgomery*
Santa Fe Blues. *Peetie Wheatstraw*
Santa Fe Blues: *Estella Yancey/James Yancey*
Sara Jane. *William Lucas*
Sarah Lee. *Theodore Taylor*
Sassy Mae. *Peter Chatman*
Sassy Mama. *Willie Mae Thornton*
Satellite Baby. *Roosevelt Sykes*
(New) Satellite Blues. *Eurreal Montgomery*
Satisfyin' Papa. *Ethel Waters*
Saturday Blues. *Ishmon Bracey*
Saturday Evening Blues. *William Broonzy*
Saturday Night Fish Fry. *Louis Jordan*
Saturday Night Jump. *Joe Lee Williams*
Saturday Night Spender Blues. *Lemon Jefferson*
Saturday Night Stomp. *Eddie Kirkland*
Saturday's Child. *John Holder*
Save Her Doctor. *Edward Boyd*
Save Your Money Baby. *James Harris*
Say Man. *Ellas McDaniel*
Say No to the Devil. *Gary Davis*
Scardie Mama. *Joe Lee Williams*
Scat Boogie. *John Fortescue*
Scattered Everywhere. *Leon T. Gross*
School Day. *William Dupree*
School Days. *Charles Berry*
School Days. *Floyd Jones*
School Learning. *Booker White*
School Time. *William Arnold*
Scoop It: *Leola B. Grant/Wesley Wilson*
Scottsboro Blues. *Huddie Ledbetter*
Screamin' and Cryin' Blues. *Sonny Terry*
Screamin' and Crying. *McKinley Morganfield*
Screamin' and Hollerin' the Blues. *Charley Patton*
Screamin' the Blues. *Maggie Jones*
Screaming and Crying. *Alden Bunn*
Screech Owl Blues. *Gertrude Rainey*
Screwdriver. *Sam Chatmon*
Screwy Boogie. *Cecil Gant*
Scufflin' Boogie. *Henry Brown*
Sea Board Stomp. *Arthur Phelps*
Seaboard and Southern. *Walter Brown McGhee*
Search Me Lord. *Thomas Dorsey*
Search My Heart (Lord Search My Heart/Oh Lord, Search My Heart). *Gary Davis*
Search Warrant Blues. *Arthur Phelps*
Second Hand Women Blues. *Thomas Dorsey*
Security. *Alden Bunn*
See Me in the Evening. *Theodore Taylor*
See See Rider Blues. *Gertrude Rainey*
See That My Grave Is Kept Clean. *Lemon Jefferson*
See You Next Time. *Aaron Walker*
Seems Like a Million Years. *Willie Nix*
Seems Like a Million Years. *Eddie Taylor*
Seety Cat. *McHouston Baker*
Self Experience. *Charlie Jackson*
Sellin' My Thing. *Otis Spann*
Selling That Stuff. *Thomas Dorsey*
Seminole Blues. *Hudson Whittaker*
Sen-Sa-Shun. *Freddie King*
Send Me Your Pillow. *John Lee Hooker*
Send My Child Home to Me. *Sam Hopkins*
Sent for You Yesterday. *James Rushing*
Separated Blues. *Ida Cox*
Separation Blues. *Louis Robinson*
Serve Me Right to Suffer. *John Lee Hooker*
Serve My Time. *Joseph Young*
Session Blues. *Willie Mae Thornton*
Set a Day. *John Williamson*
Set the Meat Out Doors. *Roosevelt Sykes*
Seven Days and Seven Nights. *John Lee Hooker*
7-8-9-10 Blues. *Oran Page*
728 Texas. *Jerry McCain*
Seventh Son, The. *Willie Dixon*
75 Highway. *Sam Hopkins*
Seventy-Four. *Robert Nighthawk*
71 Cadillac Blues. *Joe Lee Williams*
73 Hop. *Robert Jeffery*
Sex Appeal. *Willie Dixon*
Shady Grove. *Joe Lee Williams*
Shady Lane. *Mercy Dee Walton*
Shady Lane Blues: *Francis Blackwell/Leroy Carr*
Shaggy Hound Blues. *Shirley Griffith*
Shaggy Hound Blues. *Joe Lee Williams*
Shake-A My Hand. *Charles Ross*
Shake Baby Shake. *Leon T. Gross*
Shake Boogie. *Edward Harris*
Shake Dancer. *Marion Walter Jacobs*
Shake 'em On Down. *John Jenkins*
Shake 'em On Down. *Booker White*
Shake 'em On Down. *Joe Lee Williams*
Shake 'em Up. *Norman Green*
Shake for Me. *Willie Dixon*
Shake It and Break It But Don't Let It Fall Mama. *Charley Patton*
Shake It Baby: *George Guy/Amos Wells*
Shake It Baby. *Curtis Jones*
Shake It Baby. *Aaron Walker*
Shake It Up and Go (see: Bottle It Up and Go)
Shake My Hand Blues. *Booker White*

Shake Shake Mama. *Mance Lipscomb*
Shake That Thing. *Charlie Jackson*
Shake the Boogie. *John Lee Williamson*
Shake Walkin'. *McHouston Baker*
Shake Your Hips. *James Moore*
Shake Your Money Maker. *Elmore James*
Shakin' the Boogie. *Willie Mabon*
Shaking the Boogie. *Roosevelt Sykes*
Shaky. *Willie Dixon*
Shame Shame Shame. *Jimmy McCracklin*
Shame Shame Shame. *Mathis James Reed*
Shannon Street Blues. *John Lee Williamson*
Share Cropper Song. *Woodrow Guthrie*
Sharecroppers Blues. *John Jenkins*
Shave 'em Dry. *James Yancey*
Shave 'em Dry Blues. *Gertrude Rainey*
She Ain't for Nobody. *Roosevelt Sykes*
She Belongs to Me Blues. *Charlie Jackson*
She Belongs to the Devil. *Ernest Lawlars*
She Brought Life Back to the Dead. *Sonny Boy Williamson (Alex Miller)*
She Can't Be Right Always Doin' Wrong. *J. C. Burris*
She Cook Corn Bread for Her Husband. *Roy Dunn*
She Devil. *Alonzo Johnson*
She Don't Know Who She Wants. *Alonzo Johnson*
She Drove Me to Drinking. *Henry Townsend*
She Fooled Me. *Robert Brown (Washboard Sam)*
She Got It from the Start. *Louis Robinson*
She Got Me Walkin'. *William Lucas*
She Got Next to Me. *Sonny Boy Williamson (Alex Miller)*
She Is Going to Ruin Me. *Aaron Walker*
She Is Real. *Edward Boyd*
She Just Walked Away. *Henry Townsend*
She Knew All Along It Was Wrong. *Edith Wilson*
She Knows How to Love Me. *James Pryor*
She Knows How to Rock. *Richard Penniman*
She Moves Me. *Luther Johnson*
She Moves Me. *McKinley Morganfield*
She Never. *William Broonzy*
She Once Was Mine. *Charles Berry*
She Put Me Outdoors. *Roosevelt Holts*
She Put the Whammee on Me. *Jalacy Hawkins*
She Put the Whammy on Me. *Freddie King*
She Suits Me to a Tee. *George Guy*
She Used to Love Me. *Albert Luandrew*
She Want to Sell My Monkey. *Hudson Whittaker*
She Wants to Boogie. *James Brewer*
She Was Born in New Orleans. *Lemoine Nash*
She Was Dumb. *Sonny Boy Williamson (Alex Miller)*
She Won't Do Right. *Joe Lee Williams*
She Won't Treat Me Kind. *William Gillum*
Shed No Tears. *Lowell Fulson*
Sheep out on the Foam, A. *John Lee Hooker*
Sheik of Displaines Street. *Charlie Jackson*
Shelby County. *James Rogers*
Shelby County Blues. *John Jones*
Shelby County Work House Blues. *John Estes*
She'll Be Sorry. *Alden Bunn*
She's All My Life. *Peter Chatman*
She's All Right. *McKinley Morganfield*
She's Coming On the C&O. *William Trice*
She's Crazy About Her Lovin'. *Walter Jacobs Vinson*
She's Crazy 'bout Entertainers. *Jerry McCain*
She's Drunk Again. *Alonzo Johnson*
She's Gone. *Edward Boyd*
She's Gone. *Theodore Taylor*
She's Gone with the Wind. *William Broonzy*
She's Got a Thing Going On (see: Got a Thing Going On)
She's Got It. *Richard Penniman*
She's in L. A. *Eddie Burns*
She's Just My Size. *Robert Brown (Washboard Sam)*
She's Long She's Tall (Weeping Willow). *John Lee Hooker*
She's Love Crazy. *Hudson Whittaker*
She's Mine All Mine. *Arthur Gunter*
She's Mine She's Yours. *James Rushing*
She's My Baby. *Sam Chatmon*
She's My Baby. *Antoine Domino*
She's My Baby. *Sonny Boy Williamson (Alex Miller)*
She's My Old Time Used to Be. *Aaron Walker*
She's Nineteen Years Old. *McKinley Morganfield*
She's So Far. *Alger Alexander*
She's So Fine. *Clarence Garlow*
She's So Mellow. *Albert Luandrew*
She's So Pretty. *McKinley Morganfield*
She's So Sweet. *Joseph Hutto*
She's the King. *Freddie King*
She's the One. *Edward Boyd*
She's Tough. *Jerry McCain*
Shewsberry Blues. *Tommy Ridgley*
Shine On. *William Trice*
Shine On. *Hudson Whittaker*
Shine On Shine On. *William Broonzy*
Shinin' Moon. *Sam Hopkins*
Ships on the Ocean. *Amos Wells*
Shipwreck Blues. *Bessie Smith*
Shirley Jean. *Walter Price*
Shirley Mae. *William Dupree*
Shirt Tail. *Robert Brown (Washboard Sam)*
Shiver and Shake. *Albert Collins*
Sho Nuff I Do. *Elmore James*
Sho She Do. *Joe Williams*
Shoo Blues. *William Broonzy*
Shopping Instead. *Joe Blue*
Short Haired Woman. *Sam Hopkins*
Shorty George Blues. *Hociel Thomas*
Shot Gun Blues. *Riley King*
Shot Gun Blues. *James Rachell*
Shot Gun Blues. *John Lee Williamson*
Shotgun. *Sam Hopkins*
Shotgun Whupin'. *John Shines*
Shouldn't Have Left Me. *Riley King*
Show Girl Blues: *John Erby/Monette Moore*
Showers of Rain. *Henry Gray*
Shreveport Farewell. *Eurreal Montgomery*

Shuckin' Sugar Cane Blues. *Lemon Jefferson*
Shufflin' the Blues. *Aaron Walker*
Shy Voice. *Joseph Hutto*
Sic 'em Dogs On. *Booker White*
Sick Bed Blues. *Nehemiah James*
Sick Man. *Sonny Terry*
Side Door Blues. *Roosevelt Sykes*
Side Show. *McHouston Baker*
Side Tracked. *Freddie King*
Sidewalk Boogie. *Edward Harris*
Sidney's Worried Life Blues. *Sidney Maiden*
Silicosis Blues. *Joshua White*
Silver City Bound. *Huddie Ledbetter*
Since I Found a New Love. *Johnny Taylor*
Since I Seen Your Smiling Face. *Edward Harris*
Since I Was Your Man. *Joseph Turner*
Since You Been Gone. *Major Merriweather*
Sinful Woman. *Elmore James*
Singing in My Soul. *Thomas Dorsey*
Single Man Blues. *Booker White*
Single Woman Blues. *Maggie Jones*
Sinner's Prayer. *Lowell Fulson*
Sinner's Prayer. *Sam Hopkins*
Sissy Blues. *Gertrude Rainey*
Sissy Man Blues. *James Arnold*
Sisterly Love. *Vernon Harrison*
Sit Down on My Knee. *Jo-Ann Kelly*
Sittin' and Cryin' the Blues. *Willie Dixon*
Sittin' Down Thinkin'. *Henry Johnson*
Sittin' Here Thinkin'. *Eddie Taylor*
Sittin' Here Thinking. *John Lee Hooker*
Sittin' Here Wondering. *James Moore*
Sittin' in My Dark Room. *John Lee Hooker*
Sittin' 'n' Thinkin'. *Joe Lee Williams*
Sittin' Pretty. *Walter Brown McGhee*
Sitting at Home Alone. *Theodore Taylor*
Sitting at My Window. *Frank Seals*
Sitting Down Thinking Blues. *James Oden*
Sitting in the Rain. *John Mayall*
Sitting on Top of the World: *Armenter Chatmon/Walter Jacobs Vinson*
Six Cold Feet in the Ground. *Leroy Carr*
Six Foot Daddy. *Victoria Spivey*
Six Weeks Old Blues. *John Henry Barbee*
Skeedle Loo Doo Blues. *Arthur Phelps*
Skeleton Key Blues. *John Erby*
Skid Row. *Curtis Jones*
Skin Game Blues. *Joshua Howell*
Skinny Minnie. *Riley King*
Skinny Woman. *Walter Lewis*
Skinny Woman. *Charles Musselwhite*
Skinny Woman Blues. *James Rachell*
Skoodle Um Skoo. *Charlie Jackson*
Skrontch. *Leola B. Grant*
Skull and Crossbone Blues. *John Shines*
Sky Above, The. *Lee Jackson*
Sky Is Crying, The. *Elmore James*
Sky's the Limit, The. *Andrew McMahon*
Slam Hammer. *John Young*
Slave to Love. *Willie Dixon*
Slave to the Blues. *Thomas Dorsey*
Slavery. *Sam Hopkins*
Slavery Time Breakdown. *John Shines*
Sleep Talking Blues. *Gertrude Rainey*
Sleeper. *Lowell Fulson*
Sleeping All Day Blues. *Roosevelt Sykes*
Sleeping Alone Tonight Blues. *John Holder*
Sleeping with the Devil. *John Young*
Sleepness Nights Blues. *Peetie Wheatstraw*
Sleepy Man Blues. *Booker White*
Slide Winder. *Joseph Hutto*
Slidin' Delta. *Tommy Johnson*
Slidin' Home. *John Littlejohn*
Sliding Delta. *John Hurt*
Sliding Delta. *J. D. Short*
Slim's Blues. *Peter Chatman*
Slim's Shout. *Albert Luandrew*
Slippin' 'n' Slidin'. *Richard Penniman*
Sloppy Drunk. *Walter Brown*
Sloppy Drunk. *Joseph Hutto*
Sloppy Drunk. *James Pryor*
Sloppy Drunk. *James Rogers*
Sloppy Drunk Again. *Henry Townsend*
Sloppy Joe's. *Cecil Gant*
Slow and Easy. *Alonzo Johnson*
Slow and Easy Blues. *James Yancey*
Slow and Steady. *Thomas Delaney*
Slow Down. *J. B. Lenoir*
Slow Drag. *William Dupree*
Slow Driving Moan. *Gertrude Rainey*
Slow Freight Blues. *Edward Harris*
Slow Slow: *George Guy/Amos Wells*
Slowdrag. *Charles Davenport*
Slowly Walk Close to Me. *Sonny Boy Williamson (Alex Miller)*
Smile on My Face. *Albert Luandrew*
Smokestack Lightning. *Chester Burnett*
Smokey's Lovesick Blues. *Otis Smothers*
Snake. *Luther Johnson*
Snaps Drinking Woman. *William Dupree*
Snatch It Back and Hold It. *Amos Wells*
Sneakin' and Dodgin'. *Roosevelt Sykes*
Sneakin' Around. *Riley King*
Sneaky Pete. *William Dupree*
Snitcher's Blues, The. *James Johnson*
Snoopin' Around. *James Moore*
Snow Is Falling, The. *Ray Charles*
So Bad Glad. *Granville McGhee*
So Close. *Otis Rush*
So Cold in Vietnam. *John Shines*
So Crazy About You Baby. *Hudson Whittaker*
So Different Blues. *Mance Lipscomb*
So Excited. *Riley King*
So Glad. *Chester Burnett*
So Glad. *Joe Lee Williams*
So Glad I'm Livin'. *Arthur Crudup*

So Hard to Share. *John Mayall*
So Lonely. *Peter Chatman*
So Long Baby. *Sam Hopkins*
So Long Blues. *Clyde Bernhardt*
So Long Blues. *Silas Hogan*
So Long Boogie. *Robert Pete Williams*
So Long It's Been Good to Know You. *Woodrow Guthrie*
So Long Jim. *Clara Smith*
So Long So Long. *Lowell Fulson*
So Long Woman. *Walter Horton*
So Many Tears. *Lowell Fulson*
So Many Women Blues. *Joseph Turner*
So Mean to Me. *Elmore James*
So Much Trouble. *Walter Brown McGhee*
So Much Trouble. *Hudson Whittaker*
So Much Wine. *J. D. Short*
So Soon I'll Be Goin' My Way Back Home. *Joe Lee Williams*
So Sweet, So Sweet. *Alden Bunn*
So Tired. *Roy Milton*
So Tired. *Amos Wells*
So Tired of Living by Myself. *Frank Frost*
Soaking Wet Blues. *James Johnson*
Soap and Water Blues. *Robert Brown (Washboard Sam)*
Sobbing Tears Blues. *Ida Cox*
Soft and Mellow. *Roosevelt Sykes*
Soft Blues: *Francis Blackwell/Leroy Carr*
Soft Pedal Blues. *Bessie Smith*
Solid Gold. *John Jenkins*
Some Cold Rainy Day. *Alden Bunn*
Some Day. *Iverson Minter*
Some Day Baby. *Alonzo Johnson*
Some Got Six Months. *Robert Pete Williams*
Some Happy Day. *Charley Patton*
Some of These Days I'll Be Gone. *Charley Patton*
Some Old Rainy Day. *Joe Lee Williams*
Some People. *Charles Berry*
Some People Say. *Alexander Seward*
Some Summer Day. *Charley Patton*
Some Sweet Day. *James Oden*
Somebody All My Own. *John Erby*
Somebody Been Ramblin' in My Drawers. *James Pryor*
Somebody Been Talkin'. *John Jenkins*
Somebody Changed That Lock on My Door (see: Baby Changed That Lock on My Door)
Somebody Changed That Lock on My Door. *William Broonzy*
Somebody Got to Pay. *Willie Mabon*
Somebody Help Me. *Sonny Boy Williamson (Alex Miller)*
Somebody Help Poor Me. *Robert Pete Williams*
Somebody Keeps Calling Me. *Fred McDowell*
Somebody Loan Me a Dime. *Luther Johnson*
Somebody Loan Me a Dime. *Fention Robinson*
Somebody Messed Up. *Raymond Agee*
Somebody Please Play the Blues. *Willie Dixon*
Somebody Stole My Baby and Gone. *Arthur Kelley*
Somebody Told Me. *Milton Campbell*
Somebody's Been Doing That Thing. *Hudson Whittaker*
Somebody's Been Foolin'. *Joe Lee Williams*
Somebody's Been Fooling You. *John Lee*
Somebody's Been Knockin'. *Thomas Courtney*
Somebody's Been Talking. *Jerry McCain*
Somebody's Been Worryin'. *Joe Lee Williams*
Somebody's Got to Go. *William Broonzy*
Somebody's Got to Go. *Sam Hopkins*
Somebody's Got to Go. *Will Weldon*
Somebody's Spoiling These Women. *James Rushing*
Someday. *Smiley Lewis*
Someday. *Fred McDowell*
Someday After a While. *Freddie King*
Someday Baby. *Joe Lee Williams*
Someday Baby (Blues): *John Estes/Hammie Nixon*
Someday Blues. *Jesse Crump*
Someday I'm Gonna Ketch You. *McKinley Morganfield*
Someday Somewhere. *Thomas Dorsey*
Someday Soon Baby. *Otis Spann*
Someday You'll Have These Blues. *Phillip Walker*
Someone Is Going to Mistreat You. *Aaron Walker*
Somethin' Else Again. *Richard Havens*
Somethin' Goin' On Wrong. *Thomas Delaney*
Something Fishy. *Alonzo Johnson*
Something Inside Me. *James Moore*
Something Inside of Me. *Elmore James*
Something Keeps A-Worryin' Me. *Eurreal Montgomery*
Something on My Mind. *Clifton Chenier*
Something on Your Mind. *Joseph Young*
Something to Remember You By. *Eddie Jones*
Something You Ate. *Earl Hooker*
Something's Gone Wrong in My Life. *Eddie Kirkland*
Something's Wrong. *Lowell Fulson*
Sometime You Win When You Lose. *George Smith*
Sometimes I Cry. *John Young*
Sometimes I Have a Heartache. *Willie Mae Thornton*
Sometimes I Think I Do. *James Rushing*
Sometimes I Wonder. *Otis Spann*
Sometimes You Made Me Feel So Bad. *John Lee Hooker*
Song of My Lover. *Charles Berry*
Sonny Boy's Christmas Blues. *Sonny Boy Williamson (Alex Miller)*
Sonny's Blues. *Sonny Terry*
Sonny's Fever. *Aaron Willis*
Sonny's Jump. *Sonny Terry*
Sonny's Squall: *Walter Brown McGhee/Sonny Terry*
Sonny's Thing. *Sonny Terry*
Son's Blues. *Eddie House*
Soon Forgotten. *James Oden*
Soon in the Morning. *Eddie House*
Soon My Work Will All Be Done. *Gary Davis*
Soon This Morning. *Gertrude Rainey*
Sorrow Valley Blues. *Irene Scruggs*
Sorrowful Blues. *Eurreal Montgomery*
Sorrowful Blues. *Bessie Smith*
Soul Brother Blues. *Curtis Jones*
Soul Feet. *George Smith*
Soul Food. *Albert Collins*
Soul Lover. *Roy Brown*

Soul of a Man. *Raymond Agee*
Soul Spasm. *Jerry McCain*
Sound the Bell. *Clarence Garlow*
South Bound Blues. *Thomas Delaney*
South Bound Express. *Sonny Terry*
South Forest Boogie. *Pink Anderson*
South Indiana. *Walter Horton*
South Memphis Blues. *Frank Stokes*
Southbound Backwater. *Alonzo Johnson*
Southbound Train. *William Broonzy*
Southbound with the Hammer Down. *Taj Mahal*
Southern Blues. *William Broonzy*
Southern Blues. *Joe McCoy*
Southern Blues. *Gertrude Rainey*
Southern Blues. *Roosevelt Sykes*
Southern Bound. *Louis Robinson*
Southern Can Is Mine. *Willie McTell*
Southern Flood Blues. *William Broonzy*
Southern House Blues. *Alexander Moore*
Southern Rag. *Arthur Phelps*
Southern Train. *Walter Brown McGhee*
Southern Whistle Blow. *Joe Lee Williams*
Southern Woman Blues. *Lemon Jefferson*
Southern Women. *Willie Dixon*
Spanish Fandango. *John Hurt*
Spank the Butterfly. *Eddie Kirkland*
Spann Blues. *Otis Spann*
Spann's Boogie. *Otis Spann*
Spann's Stomp. *Otis Spann*
Speak My Mind. *Joseph Hutto*
Speak Now. *Wesley Wilson*
Speak Now Woman. *James Oden*
Speakeasy Days. *William Dupree*
Special Agent. *John Estes*
Special Delivery. *Cecil Gant*
Special Delivery Blues. *Beulah Wallace*
Special Rider Blues. *Nehemiah James*
Spider in the Web. *Vernon Harrison*
Spider Man Blues. *Bessie Smith*
Spider Web Blues. *Victoria Spivey*
Spike Driver. *Theodore Darby*
Spike Driver Blues. *John Hurt*
Spoonful. *Willie Dixon*
Spoonful Blues. *Charley Patton*
Spoon's Beep Beep Blues. *James Witherspoon*
Sport Model Mama. *Victoria Spivey*
Sporting Life Blues. *William Dupree*
Sporting Life Blues. *Walter Brown McGhee*
Spread the News Around. *Sonny Terry*
Springfield Blues. *Roosevelt Sykes*
Squabbling Blues. *Sara Martin*
St. Juan Blues. *Peter Chatman*
St. Louis Fair Blues. *Alger Alexander*
St. Louis Stomp. *Rufus Perryman*
Stack O'Dollars Blues. *James Rachell*
Stack-O-Lee. *Leon T. Gross*
Stand by Me. *Herman Parker*
Stand by Me. *John Shines*
Standin' in Line. *Louis Robinson*
Standin' in My Window. *Arbee Stidham*
Standin' in the Rain Blues. *Bessie Smith*
Standin' 'round Crying. *McKinley Morganfield*
Standing at My Window. *Arthur Crudup*
Standing at the Crossroads. *Elmore James*
Standing on Broadway. *Roy Brown*
Standing on the Corner. *Arbee Stidham*
Starry Crown Blues. *J. D. Short*
State of Tennessee Blues. *Will Shade*
State Street Jive. *Charles Davenport*
Statesboro Blues. *Willie McTell*
Steady. *Jerry McCain*
Steady Grind. *Victoria Spivey*
Steady Rolling Blues. *Peter Chatman*
Steak House Rock. *Edward Boyd*
Stealin' Blues. *Charles Davenport*
Steam Roller. *McHouston Baker*
Steel Mill Blues. *Otis Spann*
Stella Mae. *John Lee Hooker*
Stella Mae. *Albert Luandrew*
Step at a Time. *Lowell Fulson*
Stepmother. *Albert Luandrew*
Stevedore, The. *Victoria Spivey*
Stevedore Man: *Leola B. Grant/ Wesley Wilson*
Stick with Me. *Gabriel Brown*
Still a Fool. *McKinley Morganfield*
Still Got the Blues. *Charles Berry*
Still in the Dark. *Joseph Turner*
Still Your Fool. *James Harris*
Sting It. *Luther Johnson*
Stocking Feet Blues. *Lemon Jefferson*
Stockyard Blues. *Floyd Jones*
Stockyard Fire. *Hudson Whittaker*
Stomach Ache: *George Guy/Amos Wells*
Stomp Blues. *William Broonzy*
Stompin' the Boogie. *Roosevelt Sykes*
Stone. *Booker White*
Stone Crazy. *George Guy*
Stoned Dead. *James Dawkins*
Stoned to the Bone. *Lowell Fulson*
Stones in My Passway. *Robert Johnson*
Stool Pigeon Blues. *Sam Hopkins*
Stop and Fix It: *William Broonzy/Robert Brown (Washboard Sam)*
Stop and Jump. *Louis Robinson*
Stop and Listen. *Charles Berry*
Stop Breakin' Down Blues. *Robert Johnson*
Stop Breaking Down. *Eddie Taylor*
Stop Breaking Down. *John Lee Williamson*
Stop Cryin'. *John Shines*
Stop Crying. *Charles Ross*
Stop Crying. *Sonny Boy Williamson*
Stop Ducking Me Baby. *Willie Dixon*
Stop in the Valley. *Thomas Shaw*
Stop Myself from Worrying over You. *Ethel Waters*
Stop Now. *Louis Robinson*
Stop Now Baby. *Sonny Boy Williamson (Alex Miller)*

Stop Pulling and Pushing Me. *Richard Havens*
Stop Putting the Hurt on Me. *Riley King*
Stop Teasing Me. *James Pryor*
Stop That Thing: *John Estes/Hammie Nixon*
Stop Using Me. *Chester Burnett*
Storm in Texas. *Moses Smith*
Stormy Sea Blues: *Thomas Dorsey/Gertrude Rainey*
Story of Bill. *Edward Boyd*
Story of My Life, The. *Eddie Jones*
Story of Sonny Boy Williamson, The. *Sonny Boy Williamson (Alex Miller)*
Story to Tell. *Joseph Turner*
Straighten Up Baby. *James Cotton*
Strange Angel. *Amos Easton*
Strange Kinda Feeling. *Elmore James*
Strange Land. *Charles Musselwhite*
Strange Love. *James Moore*
Strange Lovin' Blues. *Sara Martin*
Strange Place Blues. *Booker White*
Strange Things Are Happening. *Percy Mayfield*
Strange Woman. *Dave Alexander*
Strange Woman. *McKinley Morganfield*
Stranger. *Charles Musselwhite*
Stranger Blues. *Joseph Hutto*
Stranger Blues. *Walter Brown McGhee*
Stranger Blues. *Hudson Whittaker*
Stranger Here. *Sam Hopkins*
Stranger Here: *Walter Brown McGhee/Sonny Terry*
Strangers Blues. *Beulah Wallace*
Streamline Train. *Clarence Lofton*
Street Wailing Woman. *William Dupree*
Streets Paved with Gold. *Alberta Hunter*
Stroll Out West. *Eddie Taylor*
Strollin' down Pennsylvania Ave. *Thomas Delaney*
Strollin' down State Street. *Vernon Harrison*
Strollin' on the Strip. *James Harris*
Strollin' T. B. Blues. *William Dupree*
Strollin' thru the Park. *Peter Chatman*
Strung Out Woman. *Frank Seals*
Stumble. *Freddie King*
Stuttering Blues. *John Lee Hooker*
Stuttgart Arkansas. *Booker White*
Su Garee. *Edward Harris*
Substitute Woman. *Albert Luandrew*
Sue Answer. *Charles Berry*
Sue Cow. *Armenter Chatmon*
Sufferin' Mind. *Eddie Jones*
Sugar Babe It's All Over Now. *Mance Lipscomb*
Sugar Baby. *Jerry McCain*
Sugar Cup. *Roosevelt Sykes*
Sugar Farm Blues. *James Rachell*
Sugar Gal. *Charles Ross*
Sugar Hill. *Booker White*
Sugar Hill. *Joe Lee Williams*
Sugar Hips. *Iverson Minter*
Sugar Mama. *John Lee Hooker*
Sugar Mama. *John Williamson*
Sugar Sweet. *McKinley Morganfield*
Suicide Blues. *Curtis Jones*
Suitcase Blues. *Beulah Wallace*
Suitcase Full of Blues. *Ishmon Bracey*
Summerville Blues. *Louis Robinson*
Sun Brimmer's Blues. *Will Shade*
Sun Gonna Shine in My Door Someday, The. *William Broonzy*
Sun Is Rising, The. *Chester Burnett*
Sun Is Shining, The. *Elmore James*
Sun Is Shining, The. *Joseph Turner*
Sun Risin' Blues. *Joseph Turner*
Sunday Morning Blues. *Joseph Turner*
Sunday Street. *David Van Ronk*
Sundown. *Eddie House*
Sunflower Country Blues. *George Guesnon*
Sunny Road. *Roosevelt Sykes*
Sunnyland. *Elmore James*
Sunnyland Special. *Albert Luandrew*
Sunnyland Train. *Peter Chatman*
Sunset Blues. *James Harris*
Superstitious. *Alden Bunn*
Sure Is Cold. *Phillip Walker*
Sure Is Fun. *Willie Dixon*
Sure Is Good. *Aaron Willis*
Surfin' USA. *Charles Berry*
Surfing Steel. *Charles Berry*
Surpressin' the Blues. *Walter Brown*
Susie Q. *John Lee Williamson*
Sweep My Floor. *Robert Pete Williams*
Sweet Alesse. *Iverson Minter*
Sweet as an Apple in a Tree. *James Pryor*
Sweet as She Can Be. *James Oden*
Sweet Black Angel. *Robert Nighthawk*
Sweet Black Angel. *Charles Ross*
Sweet Bye and Bye. *Thomas Dorsey*
Sweet Home Chicago. *Robert Johnson*
Sweet Home Chicago. *Roosevelt Sykes*
Sweet Honey Bee. *William Broonzy*
Sweet Laura. *Andrew Odom*
Sweet Little Angel. *Riley King*
Sweet Little Girl. *Sonny Terry*
Sweet Little Rock and Roller. *Charles Berry*
Sweet Little Sixteen. *Charles Berry*
Sweet Lovin' Daddy. *Estella Yancey*
Sweet Lovin' Kind: *Walter Brown McGhee/Sonny Terry*
Sweet Lucy Blues. *Albert Luandrew*
Sweet Mama Janisse. *Taj Mahal*
Sweet Man, Sweet Man. *Lucille Bogan*
Sweet Man's the Cause of It All. *Sara Martin*
Sweet Momma. *Eurreal Montgomery*
Sweet Papa Low Down. *Arthur Phelps*
Sweet Potato Blues. *Bessie Smith*
Sweet Root Man. *Peter Chatman*
Sweet Sixteen. *Walter Davis*
Sweet Sixteen. *Riley King*
Sweet Sixteen Bars. *Ray Charles*
Sweet Thing. *Riley King*
Sweet Woman. *Alexander Seward*

Sweet Woman Blues. *Sonny Terry*
Sweetblood Call. *Iverson Minter*
Sweetest Girl I Know, The. *Sonny Terry*
Swing It on Home. *Willie Mae Thornton*
Swing Out Rhythm. *Alonzo Johnson*
Swingin' Party. *Lowell Fulson*
Swingin' the Gate. *Clarence Brown*
Swinging with Lonnie. *Alonzo Johnson*
Sykes Gumboogie. *Roosevelt Sykes*
Syl-vous Play Blues. *Curtis Jones*

T. B. Blues. *James Rodgers*
T. B. Blues. *Victoria Spivey*
T. B. Is Killing Me. *John Lee Hooker*
T. B. Sheets. *John Lee Hooker*
T. B.'s Got Me. *Victoria Spivey*
T-Bone Blues Special. *Aaron Walker*
T-Bone Boogie. *Aaron Walker*
T-Bone Jumps Again. *Aaron Walker*
T-Bone Shuffle. *Aaron Walker*
T-Bone's Way. *Aaron Walker*
T for Texas. *James Rodgers*
T-Model Blues. *Sam Hopkins*
TV Mama. *Joseph Turner*
TV Man. *Oscar Wills*
Tail Dragger. *Willie Dixon*
Take a Chance. *Jimmy McCracklin*
Take a Little Walk with Me. *Robert Johnson*
Take a Look. *Irma Thomas*
Take a Look Behind. *Otis Rush*
Take a Look Inside. *McHouston Baker*
Take a Walk. *Sam Hopkins*
Take a Walk Around the Corner (Courtroom Blues). *Leroy Carr*
Take a Whiff on Me. *Huddie Ledbetter*
Take Enough of Him. *Luther Johnson*
Take Five. *Vernon Harrison*
Take Five. *Theodore Taylor*
Take It All. *Joe Lee Williams*
Take It All Off. *Don Harris*
Take It Easy, Baby. *Robert Nighthawk*
Take It Easy, Baby. *Sonny Boy Williamson (Alex Miller)*
Take It If You Want It. *Sam Hopkins*
Take It Kind of Easy. *James Pryor*
Take It Slow. *Mathis James Reed*
Take It Slow an' Easy. *Jesse Fuller*
Take It Witcha. *Alexander Lightfoot*
Take Me as I Am. *John Lee Hooker*
Take Me Back. *Marion Walter Jacobs*
Take Me Back. *Bonnie Jefferson*
Take Me Back. *Huddie Ledbetter*
Take Me Back Babe. *Mance Lipscomb*
Take Me Back Baby. *William Dupree*
Take Me Back Baby. *James Rushing*
Take Me Back Baby. *Moses Smith*
Take Me Back Blues. *Charlie Jackson*
Take Me for a Buggy Ride: *Leola B. Grant/Wesley Wilson*
Take Me in Your Arms. *David Edwards*
Take Me out of the Bottom. *Joe Lee Williams*
Take Me Where You Go. *Elmore James*
Take My Advice. *Joseph Young*
Take Out Some Insurance. *Mathis James Reed*
Take Over Chicago. *Joseph Young*
Take the Pain from My Heart. *Arbee Stidham*
Take Your Hand Down. *Eddie Taylor*
Take Your Hand off My Knee. *Arbee Stidham*
Take Your Picture Darling. *Fred McDowell*
Take Your Time Rag. *Walter Lewis*
Takes Money. *Joseph Young*
Takin' My Time. *Charles Musselwhite*
Talk About Me. *Jalacy Hawkins*
Talk About Your Baby. *John Lee Hooker*
Talk to Me Baby. *Leroy Dallas*
Talk to Me Baby. *William Dupree*
Talk to Me Baby. *Elmore James*
Talk to Me Baby. *Arthur Kelley*
Talkin' About My Buddy. *Charles Berry*
Talkin' Blues. *Robert Pete Williams*
Talkin' Boogie. *Eurreal Montgomery*
Talkin' 'bout You. *Ray Charles*
Talkin' Casey. *John Hurt*
Talkin' out of My Head. *William Dupree*
Talkin' the Blues. *Riley King*
Talkin' to the Operator. *Edward Boyd*
Talking Colombia (Blues). *Woodrow Guthrie*
Talking Dust Bowl Blues. *Woodrow Guthrie*
Talking Miner. *Woodrow Guthrie*
Talking Slim Blues. *Albert Collins*
Talking Subway Blues. *Woodrow Guthrie*
Tall Heavy Mama. *Roosevelt Sykes*
Tampa Bound. *Arthur Phelps*
Tantalizing Blues. *Eurreal Montgomery*
Tappin' That Thing. *James Rachell*
Tasty Blues. *Eurreal Montgomery*
Taylor Made Stomp. *Joe Lee Williams*
Taylor's Arkansas. *Charles Musselwhite*
Taylor's Rock. *Theodore Taylor*
Te-Ni-Nee-Ni-Nu. *James Moore*
Teach Me. *Lowell Fulson*
Teachin' the Blues. *John Lee Hooker*
Tear Drops. *James Harris*
Tears Came Rolling Down. *Henry Townsend*
Tears of Sorrow. *Larry Davis*
Teasin' Brown Skin. *Walter Davis*
Tebo's Texas Boogie. *Hociel Thomas*
Tee-Nah-Nah. *Smiley Lewis*
Tee Pee Valley Blues. *Esther Bigeou*
Teenage Beat. *Marion Walter Jacobs*
Telephone Arguin' Blues. *J. D. Short*
Telephone Blues. *Bessie Smith*
Telephone Blues. *Sonny Terry*
Telephone Blues. *John Wrencher*
Telephoning the Blues. *Victoria Spivey*
Tell All the World About You. *Ray Charles*
Tell 'em 'bout Me. *Ethel Waters*

Tell Jesus Everything. *Thomas Dorsey*
Tell Me Baby. *Lonnie Brooks*
Tell Me Baby. *William Broonzy*
Tell Me Baby. *Walter Horton*
Tell Me Baby. *Eddie Kirkland*
Tell Me How Do You Feel. *Ray Charles*
Tell Me Mama. *Marion Walter Jacobs*
Tell Me to Do Right. *Walter Jacobs Vinson*
Tell Me What I've Done. *Chester Burnett*
Tell Me What More Can Jesus Do. *Clarence Richardson*
Tell Me What You Want Me to Do. *Mathis James Reed*
Tell Me When. *William Dupree*
Tell Me Who. *John Jenkins*
Tell Me Who's Been Telling You. *Joe Lee Williams*
Tell Me Woman. *Andrew Odom*
Tell Me Why. *Walter Brown McGhee*
Tell Me Woman Blues. *Alger Alexander*
Tell Me You'll Wait for Me. *Charles Brown*
Tell My Mother. *Joe Lee Williams*
Tell the Truth. *Edward Boyd*
Tell the Truth. *Ray Charles*
Tell the World I Do. *Mathis James Reed*
Temperature 110. *Sonny Boy Williamson (Alex Miller)*
Ten Cent Shot. *William Perryman*
Ten Long Years. *Riley King*
Ten to One. *Edward Boyd*
Ten Years Ago. *George Guy*
Terraplane Blues. *Robert Johnson*
Terrible Operation Blues. *Thomas Dorsey*
Testifying. *James Witherspoon*
Texas Blues. *Charlie Jackson*
Texas Blues. *Mance Lipscomb*
Texas Blues. *Major Merriweather*
Texas Blues. *Louis Robinson*
Texas Blues. *Robert Pete Williams*
Texas Flood. *Larry Davis*
Texas Flood. *Fention Robinson*
Texas Flood. *Moses Smith*
Texas Flyer. *Freddie King*
Texas Hop. *Connie Crayton*
Texas Oil. *Freddie King*
Texas Stomp. *Major Merriweather*
Texas Tony. *James Rachell*
Texas Tornado. *William Broonzy*
Thank You Baby. *Edward Boyd*
Thank You Jesus. *Robert Wilkins*
Thanks but No Thanks. *Roosevelt Sykes*
Thanksgivin' Blues. *Roosevelt Sykes*
That Ain't It. *Walter Horton*
That Black Snake Moan. *Lemon Jefferson*
That Crawlin' Baby Blues. *Lemon Jefferson*
That Evening Train. *Aaron Walker*
That Evil Child. *Riley King*
That Girl I Love. *John Estes*
That Man. *Victoria Spivey*
That New Love Maker of Mine. *Hattie McDaniel*
That Same Old Train. *Fird Eaglin*
That Stuff You Sell Ain't No Good. *Walter Davis*
That Thing's In Town. *Joe Lee Williams*
That Was Yesterday. *Haskell Sadler*
That Will Never Happen No More. *Arthur Phelps*
That's a Married Man's Weakness. *Jesse Crump*
That's All I Want. *Willie Dixon*
That's All Right. *Arthur Crudup*
That's All Right. *Robert Lockwood*
That's All Right. *Albert Luandrew*
That's All Right. *James Rogers*
That's All Right for You. *Leroy Carr*
That's Enough. *Ray Charles*
That's Good News. *Thomas Dorsey*
That's How I Feel. *Walter Brown McGhee*
That's My Man. *Edith North Johnson*
That's My Specialty. *John Erby*
That's the Blues. *Henry Williams*
That's the Human Thing to Do. *Bill Williams*
That's the Stuff You Got to Watch. *Wynonie Harris*
That's the Truth. *Joseph Hutto*
That's the Way I Do It. *Hudson Whittaker*
That's the Way It Is. *Raymond Agee*
That's What I Like. *Julia Lee*
That's What I've Been Thru. *Amos Milburn*
That's When I Miss You. *Edward Boyd*
That's Why I Keep Drinkin'. *Eurreal Montgomery*
That's Why I Love You. *James Moore*
That's Wrong Little Mama. *Riley King*
Thaw Out. *Albert Collins*
Then I Won't Feel Blue. *Beulah Wallace*
There Ought to Be a Law. *Dave Alexander*
There Was a Time When I Went Blind. *Gary Davis*
There You Stand. *Amos Easton*
There'll Be a Day. *Eddie Taylor*
There's a Fool in Town. *Peter Chatman*
There's Always Tomorrow. *Arbee Stidham*
There's Something Wrong with You. *Jalacy Hawkins*
There's Too Many Teardrops. *Jalacy Hawkins*
These Things Are True. *Raymond Agee*
They Call Me a Blind Man. *John Sellers*
They Call Me Big Mama. *Willie Mae Thornton*
They Call Me Big Walter. *Walter Horton*
They Call Me Crazy. *Clifton Chenier*
They Call Me Mr. Cleanhead. *Eddie Vinson*
They Call Me Muddy Waters. *McKinley Morganfield*
They Call Me Rockin'. *Sidney Semien*
They Raided the Joint (Raidin' the Joint). *Oran Page*
They Want Money. *Aaron Willis*
Thing Called Love's Done Made a Fool out of Me. *Thomas Delaney*
Thing to Do, The. *Eddie Burns*
Things Ain't Like They Used to Be. *Walter Davis*
Things Ain't Right. *Jerry McCain*
Things Are So Slow. *Joseph Hutto*
Things Can't Stay the Same. *Doc Terry*
Things Gonna Come My Way. *Joe Lee Williams*
Things I Used to Do. *Charles Berry*
Things Is Alright. *James Harris*
Things That I Used to Do, The. *Eddie Jones*

Things You Do. *Frank Frost*
Think It Over. *Riley King*
Think You Need a Shot. *Walter Davis*
Thinkin' 'bout My Mother. *Richard Penniman*
Thinking About You. *Willie Mabon*
Thinking Blues. *John Lee Hooker*
Thinking Blues. *Bessie Smith*
Thinking of What They Did to Me. *Joe Lee Williams*
Third Degree. *Edward Boyd*
Third Stone from the Sun. *James Hendrix*
13 Highway. *Eddie Taylor*
13 Is My Number. *Dave Alexander*
Thirteen Question Method. *Charles Berry*
Thirty Days. *Charles Berry*
Thirty Dirty Women. *Iverson Minter*
35th & Dearborn. *James Yancey*
34 Blues. *James Rachell*
39th and Indiana. *Charles Musselwhite*
32-20 Blues (see: Front Door Blues)
32-20 Blues. *Robert Johnson*
32-20 Blues. *Roosevelt Sykes*
This Christmas I Give Love. *John Erby*
This Heavy Stuff of Mine. *Joe Lee Williams*
This Is My Apartment. *Sonny Boy Williamson (Alex Miller)*
This Is the Blues. *Otis Spann*
This Land Is Your Land. *Woodrow Guthrie*
This Little Girl of Mine. *Ray Charles*
This Little Woman. *Peter Chatman*
This Morning. *Albert King*
This Morning. *John Shines*
This Old Fool. *George Guy*
This Old Life. *Sonny Boy Williamson (Alex Miller)*
This Old London Town. *Joe Lee Williams*
This Thing Called Love. *Al King*
This Time Is My Time. *Robert Brown (Washboard Sam)*
This Time You Suffer Too. *Percy Mayfield*
This War Will Last You for Years. *Eddie House*
Those Dogs of Mine (Famous Cornfield Blues). *Gertrude Rainey*
Thought I Didn't Love You. *Travis Blaylock*
Thoughts of Home. *James Witherspoon*
Thousand Miles from Nowhere, A. *Moses Smith*
Three and One Boogie. *Peter Chatman*
Three Day Eternity. *Richard Havens*
Three Hours past Midnight. *Johnny Watson*
300 Pounds of Joy. *Willie Dixon*
Three Little Kittens Rag. *William Trice*
Three O'Clock Blues. *Lowell Fulson*
Three O'Clock Blues. *Riley King*
Three Times a Fool. *Otis Rush*
Three Times Seven. *James Harris*
Three Women Blues. *Peter Chatman*
Thrill Me Baby. *Melvin Jackson*
Throw Me in the Alley. *Peetie Wheatstraw*
Throw the Boogie Woogie. *Joe Lee Williams*
Throw Your Time Away. *Frank Edwards*
Thunder and Lightning. *Clarence Green*
Thunderbird. *Marion Walter Jacobs*
Thursday Blues. *James Rushing*
Thursday Girl. *Victoria Spivey*
Thy Kingdom Come. *Thomas Dorsey*
Tia Juana. *Peter Chatman*
Tiajuana Blues. *Joe Lee Williams*
Ticket Agent Blues. *Willie McTell*
Tickler. *Edward Boyd*
Tiger in Your Tank. *Willie Dixon*
Tight Dress. *George Smith*
'Til Death Do Us Part. *Raymond Agee*
Till I Made My Tonsils Sore. *John Shines*
Till the End of Never. *Roy Brown*
Till the Honey Come Down. *Beulah Wallace*
Tim Moore's Farm (Blues). *Sam Hopkins*
Timber. *Joshua White*
Time Changes Things. *Melvin Jackson*
Time Has Come, The. *James Witherspoon*
Time Waits on No One. *James Pryor*
Time Wasted on You. *Roosevelt Sykes*
Time's Gettin' Tougher Than Tough. *James Witherspoon*
Times Won't Be Hard Always. *George Smith*
Tin Cup Blues. *Lemon Jefferson*
Tin Pan Alley. *Albert Luandrew*
Tin Pan Alley. *John Williamson*
Tin Pan Alley Blues. *Curtis Jones*
Ting-Tang-Tigalu. *Jerry McCain*
Tip On In. *James Moore*
Tipitina. *Roy Byrd*
Tippin' In. *Booker White*
Tired of Being Mistreated. *Clifford Gibson*
Tired of Being Mistreated. *Henry Townsend*
Tired of Living a Bachelor. *Roy Dunn*
Titanic Man Blues. *Gertrude Rainey*
To Be a Slave Like Me. *Aaron Walker*
To Claim It's Love. *Percy Mayfield*
To Keep from Twiddling Your Thumbs. *Edith Wilson*
To Live the Past. *Percy Mayfield*
To Prove My Love. *Oscar Wills*
Toad Frog Blues. *John Erby*
Today. *Thomas Dorsey*
Toddle, The. *Marion Walter Jacobs*
Together We Will Always Be. *Charles Berry*
Tollin' Bells. *Willie Dixon*
Tom Green's Farm. *John Shines*
Tom Joad. *Woodrow Guthrie*
Tom Rushen Blues. *Charley Patton*
Tombstone Blues. *Robert Pete Williams*
Tomorrow. *William Broonzy*
Tomorrow Is Another Day. *Riley King*
Tomorrow Night. *Amos Wells*
Tomorrow's Blues Today. *Aaron Willis*
Tongue Tied Blues. *William Dupree*
Toni Louise. *Eddie Burns*
Tonight. *Roosevelt Sykes*
Too Bad. *Edward Boyd*
Too Close Together. *Sonny Boy Williamson (Alex Miller)*
Too Evil to Cry. *William Dupree*

Too Hot to Hold. *James Harris*
Too Late. *Charles Berry*
Too Late. *Peter Chatman*
Too Late. *Willie Dixon*
Too Late. *Joseph Hutto*
Too Late to Cry. *Alonzo Johnson*
Too Late to Cry. *Eddie Taylor*
Too Lazy. *John Shines*
Too Long Freight Trains. *John Shines*
Too Many Drivers. *Sam Hopkins*
Too Many Drivers. *Smiley Lewis*
Too Many Ways. *Willie Dixon*
Too Many Women. *Robert Brown (Smokey Babe)*
Too Much Alcohol. *Joseph Hutto*
Too Much Beef. *Charlie Burse*
Too Much Blues. *John Holder*
Too Much Competition. *Alden Bunn*
Too Much Monkey Business. *Charles Berry*
Too Much Pride. *Joseph Hutto*
Too Much Seconal. *Johnny Winter*
Too Nicey Mama: *Walter Brown McGhee/Sonny Terry*
Too Old to Think. *Sonny Boy Williamson (Alex Miller)*
Too Poor to Die. *Iverson Minter*
Too Smart Too Soon. *Roosevelt Sykes*
Too Tight. *Joshua Howell*
Too Tight Blues. *Arthur Phelps*
Too Tight to Walk Loose. *Pleasant Joseph*
Too Young to Die. *Sonny Boy Williamson (Alex Miller)*
Too Young to Know. *McKinley Morganfield*
Took a Long Time. *Lowell Fulson*
Tool Bag Boogie. *Elmore James*
Toothache Blues. *Victoria Spivey*
Top of the Boogaloo. *Luther Johnson*
Tore Down. *Freddie King*
Torn to Pieces. *Walter Price*
Tornado Blues. *Mary Johnson*
Tortured Soul. *Edward Boyd*
Total Rag. *Bill Williams*
Touch Me. *Pleasant Joseph*
Tough Luck Blues. *Gertrude Rainey*
Tough Times. *John Brim*
Tra La La. *Tommy Ridgley*
Tragedy. *Raymond Agee*
Trailing My Baby. *Louis Robinson*
Train, The. *Lonnie Brooks*
Train Bring My Baby Back. *J. D. Short*
Train Done Gone. *Eddie Kirkland*
Train Fare Blues. *McKinley Morganfield*
Train Fare Blues. *John Lee Williamson*
Train Fare Home. *Clarence Garlow*
Train Fare Home. *Charles Ross*
Train I Ride, The. *Fred McDowell*
Train Is Coming. *Woodrow Adams*
Train Is Coming. *Edward Boyd*
Train Is Coming, The. *Henry Townsend*
Train Is Gone. *Michael Bloomfield*
Train Time. *Walter Horton*
Train Time. *Louis Robinson*
Train Time Blues. *Cecil Gant*
Train Time Blues. *Hudson Whittaker*
Train Whistle Boogie. *Frank Floyd*
Tramp. *Lowell Fulson*
Tramp. *Jimmy McCracklin*
Transome Blues. *James Johnson*
Travel On. *Hudson Whittaker*
Travelin' Man. *Pink Anderson*
Travelin' Man. *Roy Brown*
Travelin' Man. *Albert King*
Travelin' Man Blues. *Paul Bookbinder*
Travelin' to California. *Albert King*
Travelin' Woman. *Melvin Jackson*
Traveling On. *Thomas Dorsey*
Traveling Riverside Blues. *Robert Johnson*
Travellin' This Lonesome Road. *Walter Davis*
Travelling Blues. *Clarence Lofton*
Treat Me So Low Down. *Aaron Walker*
Treat Me Wrong. *John Littlejohn*
Treated Wrong: *Walter Brown McGhee/Sonny Terry*
Treated Wrong Blues. *Monette Moore*
Tree Top Tall Papa. *Ida Cox*
Tremblin' Blues. *Eurreal Montgomery*
Trembling Blues. *Albert Luandrew*
Tribute to a Friend. *Mathis James Reed*
Tribute to Orang. *James Dawkins*
Trick or Treat. *Charles Berry*
Tricks, The. *William Dupree*
Tricks Ain't Walking No More. *Lucille Bogan*
Tricky. *Gus Jenkins*
Tricky Woman. *James Rogers*
Triflin' Woman Blues. *Clyde Bernhardt*
Trixie(s) Blues. *Trixie Smith*
Trompin' at the Ballroom. *John Young*
Trouble and Lying Woman. *William Broonzy*
Trouble at Home Blues. *Silas Hogan*
Trouble at Midnight. *Roy Brown*
Trouble Blues. *Charles Brown*
Trouble Blues. *Sam Hopkins*
Trouble Blues. *Eddie House*
Trouble Blues. *Willie Mabon*
Trouble Don't Last. *Eddie Jones*
Trouble Everywhere. *Lowell Fulson*
Trouble Everywhere I Go. *Peter Chatman*
Trouble Everywhere I Roam. *Beulah Wallace*
Trouble for Everybody. *Joe Lee Williams*
Trouble-Hearted Blues. *Ishmon Bracey*
Trouble Is a Woman. *McHouston Baker*
Trouble I've Had It All My Days. *John Hurt*
Trouble Makin' Woman. *John Wrencher*
Trouble No More. *McKinley Morganfield*
Trouble Some Mind. *William Trice*
Trouble Trouble. *William Dupree*
Trouble Trouble. *Lowell Fulson*
Trouble Trouble Blues. *Ida Cox*
Trouble with the Blues. *Lowell Fulson*
Troubled Blues. *Sara Martin*
Troubles. *William Arnold*

Troubles Don't Last. *Riley King*
Troubles Troubles Troubles. *Riley King*
Troublesome Blues. *Thomas Delaney*
Troublesome Mind. *Mercy Dee Walton*
Trucking Little Woman. *William Broonzy*
True Blues. *Roy Milton*
True Thing. *Roosevelt Sykes*
Trust My Baby. *Sonny Boy Williamson (Alex Miller)*
Truth About the Thing, The: *Francis Blackwell/Leroy Carr*
Truthful Blues. *Leroy Carr*
Try Me One More Time. *Willie Nix*
Tryin' to Win: *Walter Brown McGhee/Sonny Terry*
Trying to Deceive Me. *Walter Brown McGhee*
Trying to Find My Baby. *William Trice*
Trying to Get Back on My Feet. *Sonny Boy Williamson (Alex Miller)*
Trying to Hide the Things I Do. *George Smith*
Trying to Sell My Monkey. *James Pryor*
Tuckerology. *Luther Tucker*
Tulane. *Charles Berry*
Tune Up. *Eddie Vinson*
Tunnel of Love. *Edward Boyd*
Turkey Leg Woman. *Charles Ross*
Turn Me On Like a TV. *Mathis James Reed*
Turn the Lights on Popeye. *Jerry McCain*
Turn Your Radio On. *Huddie Ledbetter*
Turnroad Blues. *Joe Lee Williams*
Turnup Greens. *Sam Chatmon*
Turtle Blues. *Janis Joplin*
Tutti Frutti. *Richard Penniman*
21st Street Stomp. *Henry Brown*
24 Hours. *William Dupree*
24 Hours. *Edward Boyd*
24 Hours of Fear. *Edward Boyd*
24 Years. *John Jenkins*
29 Ways. *Willie Dixon*
29th and Dearborn. *Thomas Dorsey*
21 Days in Jail. *Samuel Maghett*
20% Alcohol. *Joseph Hutto*
22nd Day of November. *Bill Jackson*
23 Hours Too Long. *Sonny Boy Williamson (Alex Miller)*
22-20 Blues. *Nehemiah James*
Twist "62." *Jerry McCain*
Twisted Snake. *Otis Spann*
Two Bones and a Pick. *Aaron Walker*
Two Bugs and a Roach. *Earl Hooker*
Two Drinks of Wine. *William Arnold*
Two Fifty Three. *Iverson Minter*
Two of a Kind. *Peter Chatman*
Two Piano Blues. *Floyd Dixon*
Two Steps Forward. *McKinley Morganfield*
Two Timin' Women. *Melvin Jackson*
Two Wings. *Robert Brown (Smokey Babe)*
Two Women. *Buster Brown*
Two Years of Torture. *Percy Mayfield*
U.S. Boogie. *Robert Nighthawk*
Ugly. *Robert Pete Williams*
Ugly Woman. *William Dupree*
Uh Huh My Baby. *Willie Dixon*
Uncle Sam. *Johnie Lewis*
Uncle Sam Blues. *William Borum*
Uncle Sam Blues. *Sara Martin*
Uncle Sam Blues. *Oran Page*
Uncle Sam Says. *Joshua White*
Undecided Blues. *James Rushing*
Understand Me. *Walter Brown McGhee*
Understand My Life. *Sonny Boy Williamson (Alex Miller)*
Undertaker's Blues. *Maggie Jones*
Underworld Blues. *Beulah Wallace*
Unfair Lovers. *Edward Boyd*
Union County Slide. *Henry Johnson*
Union Maid. *Woodrow Guthrie*
Universal Rock. *Earl Hooker*
Unlucky. *John Williamson*
Unlucky One. *Albert Luandrew*
Unseeing Eye. *Sonny Boy Williamson (Alex Miller)*
Unselfish Love. *Alonzo Johnson*
Until I Found You. *Riley King*
Until I Go to Sleep. *Beulah Wallace*
Until I'm Dead and Cold. *Riley King*
Up and Down Blues. *Robert Pete Williams*
Up and Down the Avenue. *Charles Musselwhite*
Up on Telegraph Avenue. *Sam Hopkins*
Up Side the Wall. *Mathis James Reed*
Up, Sometimes Down. *Walter Brown McGhee*
Up the Line. *Marion Walter Jacobs*
Up the Line. *John Jones*
Up the Way Bound. *Lillian Brown*
Up Tight. *Mathis James Reed*
Ups and Downs. *Louis Robinson*
Use What You Got. *Freddie King*

V-8 Ford. *Eugene Moss*
Vacation. *Aaron Walker*
Vacation from the Blues. *Edward Boyd*
Vacation Time. *Charles Berry*
Valley of Tears. *Antoine Domino*
Vallie Lee. *John Shines*
Vanado Anderson Blues. *Eureal Montgomery*
Vernita (Blues): *John Estes/Hammie Nixon*
Vicksburg Blues. *Eurreal Montgomery*
Victim of the Blues: *Thomas Dorsey/Gertrude Rainey*
Vida Lee. *Aaron Walker*
Vietcong Blues. *Amos Wells*
Vietnam. *Charles Sayles*
Vietnam Blues. *J. B. Lenoir*
Vietnam Blues. *Robert Pete Williams*
Violent Love. *Willie Dixon*
Viper Song. *Vernon Harrison*
Vitamin A (Blues). *Joe Lee Williams*
Vitamin B Blues. *Joe Lee Williams*

Viva Rock & Roll. *Charles Berry*
Voodoo Blues. *Otis Hicks*
Voodoo Child. *James Hendrix*
Voodoo Woman. *Koko Taylor*

W. B. Blues. *Walter Brown*
WDIA. *Michael Bloomfield*
WPA Blues. *Thomas Shaw*
Wadie Green. *James Rachell*
Wah Wah Blues. *Earl Hooker*
Wailin' and Whoopin'. *Sonny Terry*
Wailing the Blues. *William Dupree*
Wait Baby. *John Jones*
Waitin' on You. *Riley King*
Waiting at the Gate. *Woodrow Guthrie*
Waiting for a Train. *James Rodgers*
Waiting Game. *Peter Chatman*
Wake Me Up in the Morning. *Mathis James Reed*
Wake Up at Daybreak. *Mathis James Reed*
Wake Up Baby. *Sonny Boy Williamson (Alex Miller)*
Wake Up Bright Eye Mama. *J. D. Short*
Wake Up Cecil Wake Up. *Cecil Gant*
Wake Up in the Mornin'. *Amos Easton*
Wake Up Old Lady. *Sam Hopkins*
Wake Up Workin' Women. *K. C. Douglas*
Walk Down That Aisle. *Freddie King*
Walk On. *Lowell Fulson*
Walk On. *Walter Brown McGhee*
Walk Right In. *Gus Cannon*
Walk That Broad. *Thomas Delaney*
Walk Your Blues Away. *Roy Byrd*
Walked Down So Many Turnrows. *Mercy Dee Walton*
Walkin' Across the Country. *Arthur Phelps*
Walkin' and Drinkin'. *Roosevelt Sykes*
Walkin' Blues. *Shirley Griffith*
Walkin' Blues. *Sam Hopkins*
Walkin' Blues. *Robert Johnson*
Walkin' Dr. Bill. *Riley King*
Walkin' in a Daze. *Oran Page*
Walkin' My Blues Away: *Walter Brown McGhee/Sonny Terry*
Walkin' the Boogie. *Peter Chatman*
Walkin' the Lonesome Road. *William Broonzy*
Walkin' to New Orleans. *Antoine Domino*
Walkin' Upside Your Head. *William Dupree*
Walking. *Alden Bunn*
Walking. *Sonny Boy Williamson (Alex Miller)*
Walking Blues. *Willie Dixon*
Walking Blues. *Gertrude Rainey*
Walking Blues. *Arbee Stidham*
Walking Blues. *Willie Mae Thornton*
Walking by Myself. *James Rogers*
Walking in the Rain. *Rufus Thomas*
Walking Slow. *John Young*
Walking the Blues. *William Dupree*
Walking the Blues. *Otis Spann*
Walking the Ceiling. *Theodore Taylor*
Walking the Dog. *Rufus Thomas*
Walking This Road. *Sam Hopkins*
Walking Thru the Park. *McKinley Morganfield*
Walter's Blues. *Walter Horton*
Wang Dang Doodle. *Willie Dixon*
Wanita. *Joe Lee Williams*
(Just) Want to Make Love to You. *Willie Dixon*
War Blues. *Pernell Charity*
War Is Over, The. *Sam Hopkins*
War News Blues. *Sam Hopkins*
War Time Man Blues. *Lucille Bogan*
Warehouse Blues. *Robert Brown (Washboard Sam)*
Wartime Blues. *Lemon Jefferson*
Wartime Blues. *John Lee Williamson*
Wash Out. *Freddie King*
(Can I) Wash Your Clothes. *Victoria Spivey*
Washington Blues. *Elizabeth Cotten*
Washington D. C. Hospital Center Blues. *Nehemiah James*
Wasn't He Bad. *Robert Brown (Washboard Sam)*
Wasn't That Doggin' Me. *Frank Stokes*
Wasted Life Blues. *Bessie Smith*
Watch Dog Blues. *K. C. Douglas*
Watch Out Baby. *Peter Chatman*
Watch That Jive. *Joseph Turner*
Watch Where You Step. *Raymond Agee*
Watch Yourself. *George Guy*
Watcha Say. *Albert Collins*
Watching and Waiting. *Thomas Dorsey*
Watergate Blues. *Robert Jeffery*
Watergate Blues. *John Jenkins*
Watergate Boogie Woogie. *Robert Jeffery*
Way Down. *Cecil Gant*
Way Down in Bam. *Thomas Delaney*
Way I Feel, The. *Walter Brown McGhee*
Way I Feel, The. *James Rushing*
Way I Love You, The. *Walter Davis*
Way It Was Before, The. *Charles Berry*
Way Out on the Mountain. *James Rodgers*
Way Out West. *Booker White*
Way She Walks, The. *James Dawkins*
Way to Get Lowdown, The. *Hudson Whittaker*
Way Up High. *John Holder*
Way You Treat Me, The. *Jesse Fuller*
Way You Treat Me, The. *Moses Smith*
Waycross Georgia Blues. *Robert Hicks*
Wayward Girl Blues. *Lottie Beaman*
We Can't Buy It No More. *Charlie Jackson*
We Can't Make It. *Riley King*
We Gonna Move (see: I'm Gonna Move to the Outskirts of Town)
We Gonna Pitch a Boogie Woogie. *Joe McCoy*
We Have No Friends. *Walter Brown McGhee*
We Shall Be Free. *Huddie Ledbetter*
Wear Something Green. *Mathis James Reed*

Weary Way Blues. *Ida Cox*
Webster's Blues. *Henry Brown*
Wedding Day Blues. *Pleasant Joseph*
Wednesday Evening Blues. *John Lee Hooker*
Wee Baby Blues. *Joseph Turner*
Wee Hours. *Arbee Stidham*
Wee (Wee) Hours (Blues). *Charles Berry*
Weekend Blues. *Curtis Jones*
Weepin' Woman Blues. *Gertrude Rainey*
Weeping and Wailing. *John Hurt*
Welcome Back Pretty Baby. *Charles Berry*
Welfare Blues. *Joshua White*
Welfare Line. *James Dawkins*
Well, I Done Got Over It. *Eddie Jones*
Well I Tried. *Jalacy Hawkins*
Well Oh Well. *Joseph Turner*
Well That's All Right. *Chester Burnett*
Well Well Baby. *William Perryman*
We're Drifting Apart. *Raymond Agee*
We're Ready: *George Guy/Amos Wells*
West Coast Blues. *Arthur Phelps*
West Memphis Blues. *Sonny Boy Williamson (Alex Miller)*
West Texas Blues. *Eurreal Montgomery*
West Texas Woman. *Alexander Moore*
Western Union Man. *Joe Hill Louis*
Western Union Man. *John Lee Williamson*
What a Woman. *James Oden*
What About You? *Jerry McCain*
What Am I Going to Do? *Otis Smothers*
What Can I Do to Change Your Mind? *Albert King*
What Could I Do? *Thomas Dorsey*
What Ever I Am You Made Me. *Willie Dixon*
What Evil Have I Done? *Walter Brown*
What Happened? *Riley King*
What Have I Done? *J. B. Lenoir*
What Have I Done Wrong? *Walter Davis*
What in the World You Goin' to Do? *Willie Dixon*
What in the World's Come Over You? *Moses Smith*
What Is That She Got? *William Broonzy*
What Is That She Got? *McKinley Morganfield*
What Is the Blues? *Peter Chatman*
What Is This Thing They're Talking About? *Victoria Spivey*
What Kind of Man Are You? *Ray Charles*
What Kind of Man Is This? *Koko Taylor*
What Makes These Things Happen to Me? *Edward Boyd*
What More Can a Monkey Woman Do? *Sara Martin*
What More Can I Say John? *Richard Havens*
What Shall It Profit a Man? *Woodrow Guthrie*
What Will Become of Me? *Otis Spann*
What Would I Do Without You? *Ray Charles*
(People) What Would You Do If You Were Me? *Arbee Stidham*
What You Gonna Do? *Joe McCoy*
What You Gonna Do When Death Comes Creepin' at Your Room? *Mance Lipscomb*
What'd I Say? *Ray Charles*
What's Goin' On Baby? *James Moore*
What's Going On? *Jimmy McCracklin*
What's on Your Worried Mind? *Cecil Gant*
What's the Matter Baby? *John Lee Hooker*
What's the Matter Baby? *Alberta Hunter*
What's the Name of That Thing? *Sam Chatmon*
When a Young Girl Is 18. *William Dupree*
When Buddy Come to Town. *Peter Chatman*
When Can I Change My Clothes? *Booker White*
When I Been Drinking. *William Broonzy*
When I First Came to Chicago. *Lee Jackson*
When I First Left Home. *John Jenkins*
When I First Left Home. *Joe Lee Williams*
When I First Started Hoboing. *Eddie Kirkland*
When I Get Blues. *Thomas Delaney*
When I Get Lucky. *Floyd Dixon*
When I Grow Up. *Aaron Walker*
When I Had I Didn't Need. *Cornelius Green*
When I Laid Down I Was Troubled. *Chester Burnett*
When I Leave This Time Baby. *Thomas Delaney*
When I Make Love. *Willie Dixon*
When I Meet My Girl. *Tommy Ridgley*
When I Take My Vacation in Harlem. *Hudson Whittaker*
When I Was a Cowboy. *Huddie Ledbetter*
When I Was Drinkin'. *Sonny Terry*
When I Was Young. *Peter Chatman*
When I Was Young. *Vernon Harrison*
When I Woke Up This Morning. *Mathis James Reed*
When I'm Dead and Gone. *Eugene Moss*
When I'm Gone. *Clyde Bernhardt*
When I'm Wrong. *Riley King*
When It's Love Time. *Walter Brown McGhee*
When I've Done the Best I Can. *Thomas Dorsey*
When My Heart Beats Like a Hammer. *Riley King*
When My Left Eye Jumps. *Willie Dixon*
When My Man Shimmies. *Susie Edwards*
When the Cuckoo... *Edward Boyd*
When the Eagle Flies. *Willie Dixon*
When the Gates Swing Open. *Thomas Dorsey*
When the Last Mile Is Finished. *Thomas Dorsey*
When the Lights Went Out. *Sonny Boy Williamson (Alex Miller)*
When the Rooster Crows. *Joseph Turner*
When the Roses Bloom Again. *Bill Williams*
When Things Go Wrong with You (It Hurts Me Too). *Hudson Whittaker*
When We Were Schoolmates. *Aaron Walker*
When Will I Get to Be Called a Man? *William Broonzy*
When You Get Lonesome. *David Edwards*
When You Got a Good Friend. *Robert Johnson*
When You Need My Help. *Walter Davis*
When You Were a Girl of Seven. *Hudson Whittaker*
When Your Dough Roller Is Gone. *Peter Chatman*
When Your Mama Quit Your Papa. *Albert Luandrew*
When Your Man Is Going to Put You Down. *Leola B. Grant*
When Your Way Gets Dark. *Charley Patton*
Where Can My Baby Be? *Elmore James*

Where Can You Be? *Mathis James Reed*
Where Did You Stay Last Night? *Thomas Dorsey*
Where Has Poor Mickey Gone? *Ottilie Patterson*
Where Is My Friend? *Iverson Minter*
Where My Money Goes. *John Lee*
Where You Belong. *Edward Boyd*
Where's My Woman Been? *McKinley Morganfield*
While in Korea. *Willie Cobbs*
Whiskey Ain't No Good. *McKinley Morganfield*
Whiskey and Gin Blues. *Peter Chatman*
Whiskey and Wimmen. *John Lee Hooker*
Whiskey Blues. *Mance Lipscomb*
Whiskey Blues. *McKinley Morganfield*
Whiskey Drinking Man. *Peter Chatman*
Whiskey Head Man. *Robert Pete Williams*
Whiskey Head Woman. *William Dupree*
Whiskey Headed Blues. *John Lee Williamson*
Whiskey, Women and Loaded Dice. *Granville McGhee*
Whispering to My Man. *Edith North Johnson*
Whistle Stop. *McHouston Baker*
Whistlin' Blues. *Gary Davis*
Whistling Alex Moore's Blues. *Alexander Moore*
Whistling Pine Blues. *Joe Lee Williams*
White Lightnin'. *Fred McDowell*
White Sox Stomp. *James Yancey*
Whizzle Wham. *Peter Chatman*
Who Am I and Who Are You? *Mable Hillery*
Who Been Fooling You? *Iverson Minter*
Who Do You Love? *Ellas McDaniel*
Who Was That Here a While Ago? *William Broonzy*
Whoa, Back, Buck. *Huddie Ledbetter*
Whoee, Whoee. *Sonny Terry*
Whole Lot of Lovin'. *Riley King*
Whole Lotta Lovin'. *Antoine Domino*
Whole World, The. *Iverson Minter*
Wholesale Dealin' Papa. *Walter Brown McGhee*
Whoop It Up. *John Young*
Whoopee Blues. *Joe Holmes*
Whoopin' the Blues. *Sonny Terry*
Who's Been Fooling You? *Roy Byrd*
Who's Been Fooling You? *Arthur Crudup*
Who's Been Here? *Armenter Chatmon*
Who's Been Talkin'? *Chester Burnett*
Who's Been Telling You Buddy Brown Eyes? *Hammie Nixon*
Who's Gonna Be Your Sweet Man When I'm Gone? *McKinley Morganfield*
Who's Gonna Do Your Jelly Rollin'? *Jesse Crump*
Whose Muddy Shoes. *Elmore James*
Why Are You Crying? *Sonny Boy Williamson (Alex Miller)*
Why Did He Have To Go? *James Brewer*
Why Did It Happen to Me? *Willie Mabon*
Why Did She Leave Me? *Edward Boyd*
Why Did You Break My Heart? *John Young*
Why Did You Do That to Me? *William Broonzy*
Why Do We Love Each Other? *Henry Townsend*
Why Don't You Come Home Blues. *Walter Lewis*
Why Don't You Do Right? *Joe McCoy*
Why Don't You Hurry Home? *James Walker*
Why Don't You Leave Me Alone? *Luther Johnson*
Why Don't You Write Me? *Lowell Fulson*
Why I Love the Blues. *Luther Allison*
Why I Sing the Blues. *Riley King*
Why Should I Be Lonely? *James Rodgers*
Why Should I Spend Money? *William Broonzy*
Why Should We End This Way? *Charles Berry*
Wide Open. *Freddie King*
Wig Wearing Woman. *Eddie Burns*
Wiggling Worm, The. *Willie Dixon*
Wild About You Baby. *Elmore James*
Wild Cat Blues. *Barbara Dane*
Wild Fire. *William Perryman*
Wild Water Blues. *James Arnold*
Wild Wild Woman. *John Young*
Wild Woman. *Albert King*
Wild Women Don't Have the Blues. *Ida Cox*
Wildcat Tamer. *Alden Bunn*
Wilkin's Street Stomp. *Rufus Perryman*
Will the Day Ever Come When I Can Rest? *Alberta Hunter*
Willie Anderson's Blues. *Eurreal Montgomery*
Willie Mae. *William Broonzy*
Willie Mae. *Roy Byrd*
Willie Mae's Blues. *Willie Mae Thornton*
Willie Poor Boy. *Mance Lipscomb*
Wilson Dam: *Leola B Grant/Wesley Wilson*
Wimpy Bar Blues. *John Holder*
Win the War Blues. *John Lee Williamson*
Wine. *Alden Bunn*
Wine Drinking Woman. *William Borum*
Wine Head Woman. *Woodrow Adams*
Wine Headed Woman. *Sonny Terry*
Wine-O-Wine. *Jerry McCain*
Wine-O-Woman. *Tony Hollins*
Wine, Woman, Whiskey. *Alexander Lightfoot*
Winehead Baby. *Edward Harris*
Wings over Jordan. *Thomas Dorsey*
Winter Time Blues. *Sam Chatmon*
Wish Me Well. *Peter Chatman*
Wish Someone Would Care. *Irma Thomas*
Wishy Washy Woman. *Joseph Young*
Witching Hour Blues. *Hudson Whittaker*
Without You. *Clyde Bernhardt*
Wobblin' Baby. *John Lee Hooker*
Woke Up Cold in Hand. *William Gillum*
Woke Up This Morning. *K. C. Douglas*
Woke Up This Morning. *Riley King*
Woke Up This Morning. *Lee Semien*
Wolf Is at Your Door. *Chester Burnett*
Woman Don't Lie. *Luther Johnson*
Woman I Ain't Gonna Drink No More Whiskey. *Albert Luandrew*
Woman I Love. *John Williamson*
Woman I Love Blues, The. *Eurreal Montgomery*
Woman Is in Demand, A. *Roosevelt Sykes*

Woman Is Killin' Me, The. *Sonny Terry*
Woman Trouble Blues. *Roy Brown*
Woman Woman Blues. *Ishmon Bracey*
Woman You Ain't No Good. *Robert Pete Williams*
Woman You Must Be Crazy. *Aaron Walker*
Women and Money. *John Lee Hooker*
Women Be Wise. *Beulah Wallace*
Women Blues Boogie. *Peter Chatman*
Women Won't Need No Man. *Lucille Bogan*
Women's Lament, A. *Olive Brown*
Wonder What I'm Doing Wrong. *Walter Davis*
Wonderful Thing, A. *Walter Jacobs Vinson*
Wondering and Worryin'. *James Moore*
Won't Be Hanging Around. *Albert King*
Won't Do That No More. *Albert Luandrew*
Won't Need. *Victoria Spivey*
Woodpecker. *Charles Berry*
Work for Your Money. *Chester Burnett*
Work with Me. *Sonny Boy Williamson (Alex Miller)*
Workin' with Homesick. *John Williamson*
Working Class Woman. *Barbara Dane*
Working for My Baby. *Arthur Gunter*
Working Man. *Michael Bloomfield*
Working Man Blues. *Thomas Delaney*
Working Man Blues. *John Estes*
Working Man Blues. *Blind Boy Fuller*
Working Man Blues. *Alonzo Johnson*
Working Man Blues. *Iverson Minter*
Working on the Levy. *Joe Lee Williams*
World Boogie. *Booker White*
World of Trouble. *Willie Mabon*
World's in a Tangle, The. *Sam Hopkins*
World's Jazz Crazy, The. *Trixie Smith*
Worn Down Daddy. *Ida Cox*
Worried About My Baby. *Chester Burnett*
Worried About My Baby. *Elmore James*
Worried All the Time. *Chester Burnett*
Worried Any How Blues. *Ida Cox*
Worried Blues (see: Furry's Worried Blues)
Worried Blues. *James Harris*
Worried Blues Ain't Bad. *John Shines*
Worried Dream. *Riley King*
Worried Head. *John Littlejohn*
Worried Life Blues. *Roy Brown*
Worried Life Blues. *Clifton Chenier*
Worried Life Blues: *Walter Brown McGhee/Sonny Terry*
Worried Life Blues. *Major Merriweather*
Worried Life Blues. *Otis Spann*
Worry Blues. *Willie Mabon*
Worry Worry. *Lowell Fulson*
Worry Worry Worry. *Walter Brown McGhee*
Worst Thing in My Life. *Riley King*
Would You Baby? *John Walker*
Wrapped in Sin. *James Pryor*
Wrapped, Tied and Tangled. *Alden Bunn*
Wrapped Up in Love Again. *Albert King*
Wreck on 83 Highway. *Eddie Taylor*
Write Me a Few Lines. *Fred McDowell*
Wrong Man Blues. *Leroy Carr*
Wrong Track. *Walter Brown McGhee*
Wrong Woman Blues. *Roy Brown*
Wynonie's Boogie. *Wynonie Harris*

Yancey Special. *James Yancey*
Yancey's Bugle Call. *James Yancey*
Yancey's Mixture. *James Yancey*
Yellow Bee Blues. *Jo-Ann Kelly*
Yellow, Black and Brown. *Robert Brown (Washboard Sam)*
Yellow Gal. *Huddie Ledbetter*
Yes, I Got Your Woman. *Joe McCoy*
Yes, It's Good for You. *Willie Dixon*
Yes My Darling. *Antoine Domino*
Yes Yes Yes. *Mathis James Reed*
Yes, You'll Play. *Percy Mayfield*
Yo Yo Blues. *Lemon Jefferson*
Yo Yo Blues. *Joe Lee Williams*
Yodeling Cowboy. *James Rodgers*
Yonder Come the Blues. *Gertrude Rainey*
You. *Travis Blaylock*
You Ain't Got a Chance. *William Perryman*
You Ain't No Good. *Gabriel Brown*
You Ain't Nothin' but Fine. *Sidney Semien*
You Ain't Nothing but a Devil. *Jimmy McCracklin*
You Ain't Nowhere. *Louis Jordan*
You Ain't (So) Such-a-Much. *Pleasant Joseph*
You Ain't Treatin' Me Right. *Esther Bigeou*
You and My Old Guitar. *James Rodgers*
You Are My Life. *Alonzo Johnson*
You Are My Love. *Edward Boyd*
You Are My Man. *Victoria Spivey*
You Are My Trophy. *Raymond Agee*
You Are So Sweet. *James Rogers*
You Be My Baby. *Ray Charles*
You Been Dealin' with the Devil. *John Lee Hooker*
You Better Believe It. *Travis Blaylock*
You Better Change Your Way of Livin'. *Alberta Hunter*
You Better Cut That Out. *William Arnold*
You Better Stop Her. *Sam Hopkins*
You Better Watch Yourself. *Marion Walter Jacobs*
You Buzzard You. *James Johnson*
You Cain' Lose-a Me Cholly. *Huddie Ledbetter*
You Called Me at Last. *Peter Chatman*
You Can Be Replaced. *Aaron Willis*
You Can Pack Your Suitcase. *Antoine Domino*
You Can Run But You Can't Hide. *Paul Butterfield*
You Can't Be Lucky All the Time. *Roosevelt Sykes*
You Can't Catch Me. *Charles Berry*
You Can't Do a Thing When You're Drunk. *James Witherspoon*
You Can't Do That to Me. *Wesley Wilson*
You Can't Judge a Book by Its Cover. *Willie Dixon*
You Can't Keep a Good Man Down. *Jesse Fuller*
(If) You Can't Live in This World by Yourself. *Arbee Stidham*

You Can't Lose What You Ain't Never Had. *McKinley Morganfield*
You Can't Run Around. *James Rushing*
You Changed. *William Broonzy*
You Didn't Want Me. *Riley King*
You Dirty Mistreater. *Wesley Wilson*
You Do Me Any Old Way. *William Broonzy*
You Done Lost Your Good Thing. *Victoria Spivey*
You Done Me Wrong. *Joe Lee Williams*
You Don't Have to Go. *Mathis James Reed*
You Don't Have to Go. *John Shines*
You Don't Know. *Riley King*
You Don't Know. *Walter Brown McGhee*
You Don't Know My Mind. *Peter Chatman*
You Don't Know My Mind Blues. *Virginia Liston*
You Don't Love Me. *Ellas McDaniel*
You Don't Love Me No More. *William Arnold*
You Don't Move Me. *Alonzo Johnson*
You Don't Want Me. *Earl Hooker*
You Don't Want Me Honey. *Sara Martin*
You Drink Too Much Whiskey. *William Gillum*
You Gonna Be Sorry. *Fred McDowell*
You Gonna Miss Me. *John Lee Hooker*
You Gonna Miss Me When I'm Gone. *Hudson Whittaker*
You Gonna Need My Help. *McKinley Morganfield*
You Gonna Quit Me Baby. *Mance Lipscomb*
You Got Me. *John Brim*
You Got Me Crying. *Mathis James Reed*
You Got Me Dizzy. *Mathis James Reed*
You Got Me Running. *Mathis James Reed*
You Got Me Worryin'. *Hudson Whittaker*
You Got That Wrong. *Charlie Jackson*
You Got the Best Go. *William Broonzy*
You Got to Go. *John Estes*
You Got to Go Down. *Gary Davis*
You Got to Have Soul. *Luther Johnson Jr.*
You Got to Help Me Some. *Peter Chatman*
You Got to Know How. *Beulah Wallace*
You Got to Lose. *Earl Hooker*
You Got to Love Her with a Feeling. *Freddie King*
You Got to Move (You've Got to Move). *Fred McDowell*
You Got to Play Your Hand. *William Broonzy*
You Got to Reap! *Edward Boyd*
You Got to Reap Just What You Sow. *Alberta Hunter*
You Got to Reap What You Sow (see: You've Got to Reap What You Sow)
You Got to Reap What You Sow. *Leroy Carr*
You Got to Roam. *J. C. Burris*
You Got to Run Me Down. *Robert Brown (Washboard Sam)*
You Got to Step Back. *John Lee Williamson*
You Got What I Want. *Irene Scruggs*
You Have Mistreated Me. *William Trice*
You Have No Love in Your Heart. *Alonzo Johnson*
You Hit Me Where It Hurts. *Raymond Agee*
You Just Using Me for a Convenience. *Walter Brown McGhee*
You Keep Doggin' Me: *J. C. Burris/Sonny Terry*
You Keep Me Yearning. *Arbee Stidham*
You Keep On Spending My Change. *Armenter Chatmon*
You Killing Me. *Sonny Boy Williamson (Alex Miller)*
You Know I Got a Reason. *William Broonzy*
You Know I Love You. *Riley King*
You Know I Love You. *Joseph Turner*
You Know My Love. *Willie Dixon*
You Know That You Love Me. *Freddie King*
You Know What Love Is. *Fention Robinson*
You Know Who to Turn to. *Jimmy McCracklin*
You Know You Don't Love Me Baby. *Luther Johnson*
You Know You're Looking Good. *Mathis James Reed*
You Lied to Me. *Amos Wells*
You Lost a Good Man. *John Lee Hooker*
You Make Me Feel So Good. *Norman Green*
You Made Me Feel So Good. *John Young*
You Made Me Strong. *Aaron Willis*
You May Go But You'll Come Back Some Day. *Thomas Delaney*
You May Go But You'll Come Back Some Day. *Thomas Dorsey*
You Messed Up My Mind. *Raymond Agee*
You Might Pizen Me. *Charles Davenport*
You Missed a Good Man. *Robert Nighthawk*
You Missed a Good Man. *Hudson Whittaker*
You Move Me. *Luther Johnson*
You Move Me So. *Riley King*
You Need a Woman Like Me. *Wesley Wilson*
You Never Can Tell. *Charles Berry*
You One Black Rat. *Sam Hopkins*
You Oughtn't Do That. *John Estes*
You Said You Love Me. *Antoine Domino*
You Say I'm a Bad Feller. *Alexander Moore*
You Say That You're Leaving. *Eddie Burns*
You Say You're Leaving. *Emery Williams*
You Shook Me. *Willie Dixon*
You Should Give Some Away. *Robert Brown (Washboard Sam)*
You Should Not a' Done It (Gettin' It Fixed). *James Arnold*
You Spoiled Your Baby. *James Harris*
You Stole My Love. *Robert Brown (Washboard Sam)*
You Stole My Man. *Ida Cox*
You Thought I Was Blind But Now I Can See. *Virginia Liston*
You Threw Your Love on Me Too Strong. *Albert King*
You Told Me. *Gus Jenkins*
You Told Me You Love Me. *Luther Johnson*
You Treat Po' Lightnin' Wrong. *Sam Hopkins*
You Two. *Charles Berry*
You Understand. *Roosevelt Sykes*
You Upset Me Baby. *Riley King*
You Used to Be a Sweet Cover Shaker Woman. *Robert Pete Williams*
You Used to Love Me. *Albert Luandrew*
You Wait Too Long. *James Pryor*
You Want Me to Do It Again. *Moses Smith*
You Was Wrong. *Freddie King*

You Wear Your Hair Too Long. *Percy Mayfield*
You Were Wrong. *George Guy*
You Will Always Have a Friend. *Louis Jordan*
You Will Need Me. *Alonzo Johnson*
You Will Never Understand. *John Jenkins*
You Won't Let Me Go. *Alonzo Johnson*
You Won't Treat Me Right. *Oscar Wills*
You'd Better Mind: *Walter Brown McGhee/Sonny Terry*
You'll Always Have a Home. *Eddie Taylor*
You'll Be Mine. *Willie Dixon*
You'll Want Me Back. *Ethel Waters*
Young Dreamers. *Riley King*
Young Fashioned Ways. *Willie Dixon*
Young Generation Blues. *Curtis Jones*
Young Girl Blues. *William Dupree*
Young Hawks Crawl. *Joseph Hutto*
Young Woman Blues. *Melvin Jackson*
Young Woman's Blues. *Bessie Smith*
Your Baby Ain't Sweet Like Mine. *Charlie Jackson*
Your Fine Brown Frame. *Albert Luandrew*
Your Friend and Woman. *Mercy Dee Walton*
Your Funeral and My Trial. *Sonny Boy Williamson (Alex Miller)*
Your Going Ain't Giving Me the Blues. *Sara Martin*
Your Imagination. *Sonny Boy Williamson (Alex Miller)*
Your Kitchen Floor Is Plenty Good for Me: *Leola B. Grant/Wesley Wilson*
Your Lick. *Charles Berry*
Your Love. *John Lee Hooker*
Your Love Is Like a Cancer. *Frank Seals*
Your Love Is Like a Checker Game. *Ike Darby*
Your Love Is Where It Ought to Be. *Willie Mae Thornton*
Your Picture Done Faded. *Edward Harris*
Your Precious Love. *Raymond Agee*
Your So Called Friends. *Raymond Agee*
Your Thingerma-do. *Raymond Agee*
Your Time Is Coming. *Walter Davis*
Your Time Now. *William Broonzy*
Yours Eternally. *Don Harris*
You're an Old Lady. *Joe Lee Williams*
You're an Old Lady. *John Lee Williamson*
You're Going to Miss Me When I'm Gone. *Victoria Spivey*
You're Gonna Miss me. *Riley King*
You're Gonna Need Me. *Albert King*
You're Gonna Need My Help One Day. *Peter Chatman*
You're Gonna Need Somebody When You Die. *Charley Patton*
You're Gonna Reap (Everything You Sow). *Alden Bunn*
You're in My Book First. *Jimmy McCracklin*
You're Killing My Love. *Michael Bloomfield*
You're Laughing Now. *William Gillum*
You're Looking Good Tonight. *John Lee Hooker*
You're Losing Me. *Riley King*
You're Mean. *Riley King*
You're My All Day Steady and My Midnight Dream. *Robert Pete Williams*
You're My Baby. *Mathis James Reed*
You're My Girl. *William Arnold*
You're My Midnight Dream. *Henry Gray*
You're No Good. *Jesse Fuller*
You're So Fine. *Marion Walter Jacobs*
You're So Hard to Please. *Willie Cobbs*
You're So Kind. *Frank Frost*
You're Something Else. *Mathis James Reed*
You're Still My Woman. *Riley King*
You're Tempting Me. *J. D. Short*
You're the One. *Peter Chatman*
You're the One. *James Rogers*
You're the One I Love. *John Shines*
You're Too Late Baby. *Silas Hogan*
You're Worrying Me. *Roy Dunn*
Youth Wants to Know. *Peter Chatman*
You've Been Foolin' 'round Downtown. *John Lee Williamson*
You've Been Gone Too Long. *John Sellers*
You've Done Tore Your Playhouse Down. *Clarence Lofton*
You've Got Me Licked. *Jimmy McCracklin*
You've Got Something There. *Blind Boy Fuller*
You've Got to Keep On Trying. *James Dawkins*
You've Got to Move (see: You Got to Move)
You've Got to Move. *Gary Davis*
You've Got to Reap What You Sow. *Walter Davis*

Zip Code. *Edward Boyd*

Names & Places Index

This is an index of all identifiable names, places and other subjects listed in the text. Titles of songs and films, as well as radio, television (TV) and theater shows may be found in the preceding individual indices. Film and show titles are listed in the text in capital letters for easy reference.

Pseudonyms have been cross-referenced with proper names when known. Places have been located and further identified when identification is not part of the subject name. Page numbers of biographical entries are listed in bold type and photographs in italic type. Names and places beginning with articles "A," "An" and "The" are indexed by second word and apparent textual inconsistencies have been unified.

My appreciation to Joseph G. Palladino for his work on this index.

A&M (label), 367, 504
ABC (label), 113, 240, 308, 309, 310, 311, 588
ABC-Blue Thumb (label), 352
ABC-BluesWay (label) (see also: BluesWay [label]), 240, 308, 311, 312, 435, 447, 595
ABC-Dunhill (label), 51, 309, 310, 346, 393
ABC-Impulse (label), 51, 310
ABC-Paramount (label), 113, 157, 308, 556
AFRS (Armed Forces Radio Service) (label), 137, 406
A.M. Billings Hospital (Chicago, IL), 69, 181
AMC (label), 531
ARC (label group), 56, 68, 127, 133, 146, 159, 169, 184, 193, 263, 288, 297, 317, 336, 355, 356, 386, 391, 426, 480, 496, 502, 518, 546, 556, 559
ARC Music Corporation (organization) (Chicago, IL), 155
ARC Music Publishers Company (Chicago, IL), 359
AT&T Club (Chicago, IL), 499
A-Bet (label), 283
Abbey Sutton Show (tour), 264
Abco (label), 155, 394, 485
Abe & Pappy Club (Dallas, TX), 481
Abernathy, Marion, 406
Abramson, Herb, 379
Absinthe House (bar/lounge) (New Orleans, LA), 300, 396, 419, 420
Abyssinian Baptist Church (New York, NY), 83
Academie Charles Cros Award, 225
Academy of Motion Picture Arts & Sciences Award, 362, 543
Academy of Music (Brooklyn Academy of Music) (theater) (Brooklyn, NY), 46, 113, 194, 195, 218, 240, 253, 261, 304, 367, 378, 490, 504, 513
Academy of Music (theater) (New York, NY), 158, 220, 310, 352, 468, 500, 513
Academy of Music (theater) (Philadelphia, PA), 113, 347, 431, 432, 556
Academy of Music (theater) (Wilmington, NC), 152, 540
Ace, Johnny, 50, 51, 74, 76, 188, 308, 407, 512
Ace (label), 60, 76, 137, 227, 334, 337, 372, 395, 461, 554, 577
Ace of Clubs (label), 165, 478
Aces (group), The (see also: Four Aces), 336, 394, 395
Aces Club (Los Angeles, CA), 114
Acorn (label), 212, 238
Act III Club (Houston, TX), 585
Action (label), 96, 547
Actors Equity Association (organization), 543
Ad Lib Club (Milwaukee, WI), 567
Adail, Ralph, 502
Adail, Terry, 502
Adail, Terry, Jr. (Terry Jr.), 502
Adams, Billy, 481
Adams, Faye, 580
Adams, John Tyler "J.T.," **27**, *27*, 276
Adams, Johnny, 27
Adams, Will, 231
Adams, William "Billy," 482
Adams, Woodrow Wilson, **27**, *28*, 95, 349, 350
Adams Theater (Newark, NJ), 281, 298
Adams West (club) (Los Angeles, CA), 431
Ada's Tavern (Chicago, IL), 499, 570
Addeo, Edmond, 319
Adderley, Cannonball, 523, 567
Addison, Little, 291
Adell (label), 91
Adelphi (label), 59, 79, 106, 107, 108, 109, 130, 147, 169, 177, 179, 197, 246, 252, 283, 327, 340, 381, 457, 483, 514, 553, 569
Adelphi College (Garden City, NY), 173
Ader's Lounge (Chicago, IL), 468
Adins, George, 402
Adkins, Henry, 283
Adler, Larry, 468
Admiral Steamship (see: S.S. Admiral)
Admiral Streckfuss Riverboat (see: S.S. Admiral Streckfuss)

Adnopoz, Elliott Charles, 173
Advent (label), 120, 134, 233, 274, 276, 315, 336, 394, 456, 457, 468, 494, 531, 575
Afquest (label), 234
African Methodist Church (Cedartown, GA), 134
African Methodist Church (Pelahatchie, MS), 315
Africana Club (Zurich, Switz.), 165
Afro-American Hospital (Clarksdale, MS), 464
Age (label), 237, 530
Agee, Raymond (Little Ray), **28**, *28*
Agee Brothers Gospel Quartet, 28
Agora Club (Cleveland, OH), 307
Agorilla (label), 117
Ahlstrand, Clas, 66, 197
Ahmanson Theater (Los Angeles, CA), 346
Ahura Mazda (label), 163, 573
Ailey, Alvin, 453, 466
Airdrome Theater (Columbus, GA?), 428
Airport Hilton Inn (St. Louis, MO), 314
Airport Inn (Camden, NJ), 44
Airway (label), 340, 341
Airways Lounge (New York, NY), 90
Ajax (label), 223, 227, 356, 357, 374, 385, 472, 583
Akers, Garfield, 62, 104, 486, 562
Akins, Ollie, 107
Al Foxes Den (club) (Astoria, NY), 90
Al Gaines Carnival Show (tour), 428
Al Hammer Club (Charleston, WV), 436
Al Hirt's Club (New Orleans, LA), 157, 230, 466, 566
Alabama Joe (pseudonym), 581
Alabama Minstrels (tour), 373
Alabama State Troupers Show (tour), 327
Alabama Theological Seminary (Selma, AL), 144
Alabamians (band), 44
Aladdin (hotel) (Las Vegas, NV), 352, 411
Aladdin (label), 28, 37, 53, 74, 76, 92, 136, 154, 187, 188, 191, 200, 214, 216, 243, 253, 279, 298, 328, 329, 338, 372, 398, 560
Aladdin Chicken Shackers (band), 372
Alameda (label), 453
Alamo Ballroom (New Orleans, LA), 203
Alamo Theater (Jackson, MS), 478
Alan Freed Presents the Big Beat Show (tour), 45
Alan Freed Rock & Roll Extravaganzas (tour), 38
Alan Freed's R&B Package Show (tour), 281
Albany Hotel (St. Louis, MO), 150
Albany Symphony Orchestra (Albany, NY), 245
Albatross (label), 120, 130, 163, 177, 401, 553
Albee, Edward, 464
Albee Circuit, 222
Albee Theater (Brooklyn, NY), 540
Albee Theater (Cincinnati, OH), 541
Albee Theater (Providence, RI), 71
Albert Hall (London, Eng.), 224
Albertson, Chris, 222, 244, 316, 464, 465
Albury's Blue and Jazz Seven (band), 540
Alcorn, Alvin, 506
Alcorn A&M College (Lorman, MS), 338
Aldwych Theater (London, Eng.), 234
Alert (label), 164, 365, 503
Alex Club (Club Alex) (Chicago, IL) (see also: New Alex Club), 208, 238, 271, 388, 444, 574, 596
Alexander, Alger "Texas," **29**, *29*, 93, 120, 188, 190, 233, 243, 244, 267, 327, 461, 470
Alexander, Bob, 381
Alexander, Dave, **29-31**, *30*, 76, 116, 154, 594
Alexander, Dave (Black Ivory King), 31
Alexander, David (Little David), 31
Alexander, Lux, 405
Alexander, Michael, 287
Alexander, Texas (see: Alexander, Alger)
Alexander Shargenski Troupe (tour), 373
Alexandria Lounge (Miami, FL), 104
Alex's 1815 Club (see: 1815 Club)
Alf Bonner's Place (juke) (Gill, AR), 266, 274
Algiers Stompers (band), 203
Alhambra Theater (New York), (see also: New Alhambra Theater), 31, 74, 80, 82, 197, 256, 357, 385, 463, 464, 467, 475, 491, 540, 581, 584
Ali, Bardu, 74
Alibi Club (see: Club Alibi)
Alibi Inn (Chicago, IL), 266
Alice's Revisited (club) (Chicago, IL), 33, 65, 91, 93, 150, 156, 169, 190, 197, 198, 211, 247, 260, 334, 341, 352, 381, 389, 404, 412, 437, 442, 444, 499, 500, 513, 569, 596
Aliomar, Latif, 439
Alix, Liza May, 31
Alix, May (see Hicks, Edna) (see: Hunter, Alberta)
Alix, May "Mae," **31**
Alka Seltzer (product), 366, 504
All American Cabaret (Ft. Worth, TX), 295
All Boy (label), 199
All-Girl Band, 268
All Hallows Church (San Francisco, CA), 121
All National Independents (group), 164
All Night Jack (pseudonym), 455
All Souls Unitarian Church (Washington, DC), 142
All Star Band (Oran Page), 405
All Star Club (Chicago, IL), 200
All Stars (band), The (Dixon), 155
All Stars (band), The (Nicholson), 398
Allegro Club (Chicago, IL), 490
Allen, ______, 222
Allen, Annisteen, 452
Allen, Bessie, 252
Allen, Calvin, 184
Allen, Dick, 384
Allen, Ella, 427
Allen, Fulton, 184
Allen, George (see: Smith, George)
Allen, Henry "Red," 480, 481, 501
Allen, Ivora, 267
Allen, Jap, 481
Allen, Lillian, 251
Allen, Maybelle (see: Johnson, Edith North)
Allen, Othum "Sonny," 110
Allen, Rickey, 237
Allen, Steve, 447, 542
Allen, Walter C., 229
Allen, Woody, 481
Allentown Fair (Allentown, PA), 114
Alley (club), The (Ann Arbor, MI), 364
Alley Cats (band), 503
Alley Music (magazine), 79, 293, 326
Alley Theater (Houston, TX), 243
Alligator (label), 41, 68, 247, 437, 438, 450, 451, 499, 500, 530, 596
Allison, Grant, 32
Allison, Luther, **31-33**, *32*, 150, 305, 307, 311, 345, 445
Allison, Mose, 344, 353, 390
Allison, Ollie Lee, 32, 33
Allman, Duane, 528
Allmen, Diane, 144
Allums, Roberta, 235
Almanac (label), 455
Almanac Singers (group), 206
Almerico, Tony, 373
Alpert, Herb, 420
Al's Starlight Inn (New Orleans, LA), 157
Alternative Center of International Arts (gallery) (New York, NY), 169
Altheimer, Joshua, 118
Amazingrace (club) (Evanston, IL), 33, 195, 445
Ambassador Hotel (Los Angeles, CA), 114, 310, 429, 490, 532
Ambassador Theater (New York, NY), 464, 467, 542
Ambrose, Lena, 374
America (label), 343
American Academy of Achievement (organization), 115
American Association of University Women (organization), 245
American Blues Caravan (tour), 300, 366, 478, 504
American Blues Festival (tour), 93, 138, 208, 266, 340, 549, 575, 577
American Blues Legends (tour), 36, 55, 63, 96, 217, 225, 228, 300, 424, 439, 443, 474, 494, 517, 575, 591
American Club, The (Denver, CO), 133
American Dance Company (tour), 453, 466
American Embassy (government office) (Mexico City, Mex.), 553
American Festival of Music (Boston, MA), 239
American Folk Blues Festival (tour), 39, 41, 57, 63, 117, 121, 151, 156, 165, 176, 177, 208, 228, 238, 239,

243, 246, 249, 265, 269, 272, 280, 292, 304, 322, 345, 363, 366, 381, 382, 388, 401, 404, 427, 435, 439, 442, 443, 444, 474, 478, 481, 488, 490, 493, 499, 500, 504, 512, 513, 520, 527, 532, 548, 553, 569, 573, 577, 595
American Folk Music Festival (Wilmington, CA), 120
American Folk Music Occasional (magazine), 578
American Folklife Festival (see: Festival of American Folklife)
American Folklore (book), 488
American Folksong: Woody Guthrie (book), 206
American Folksongs of Protest (book), 207
American Friends Service Committee (organization) (Philadelphia, PA), 429
American Jazz Festival (Detroit, MI), 141
American Music (label), 128, 203, 288, 420
American Music Conference (organization), 47, 114, 160, 207, 289, 441, 464
American National Theater & Academy (ANTA) (organization), 543
American Negro Commemorative Society (organization), 464
American Recording Society (label), 139
American River College (Sacramento, CA), 30, 98, 339, 440
American Society of African Culture Center (Lagos, Nigeria), 195
American Telephone & Telegraph (product), 308
American Theater (see: Loew's American Theater)
Americana Hotel (New York, NY), 309, 431, 466
America's Blue Yodeler (billing), 441
America's Foremost Brown Blues Singer (billing), 257
America's Foremost Ebony Comedienne (billing), 543
Amerson, Richard "Rich," **33**, 209
Ames, Tessie (see: Smith, Trixie)
Amiga (label), 60, 155, 340, 381, 444, 488, 520, 548
Amigo (label), 260
Ammons, Albert, 31, 406, 518, 532, 564, 592, 594
Ammons, Gene, 84
Amos (see: Easton, Amos)
Ampex (label), 327
Amphitheater, The (Chicago, IL), 461, 545
Amvets (hall) (Oakland, CA), 190, 449
Anchorage Club (W. Baton Rouge, LA), 292
Anchorage Jazz Festival (Anchorage, AK), 393
Anderson, Clarence, 578
Anderson, Earl, 436
Anderson, Eric, 207
Anderson, Ian A., 302
Anderson, Joe, 111
Anderson, John, 33
Anderson, Louise Tar, 538
Anderson, Lucille, 56
Anderson, Milton, 104
Anderson, Pink, **33-34**, *34*, 59, 158, 261, 487, 492
Anderson Theater (New York, NY), 46, 296, 308
Andrade, Vernon, 44, 252
Andreasson, Hans, 514, 546
Andrews Gospel Singers (group), 72
Andrew's Lounge (Chicago, IL), 574
Angeleo's Steak House (San Jose, CA), 332
Angeles Abbey Cemetery (Los Angeles, CA), 201
Angelo's Speakeasy Lounge (Stone Park, IL), 123
Anger, Ron, 534
Anglish Lounge (Chicago, IL), 169
Anglo-American Alliance Jazz Group (band), 497
Anglo-American Boy Friends (band), 497
Angola State Prison Farm (see: Louisiana State Penitentiary)
Animals (band), The, 360, 517
Anka, Paul, 187
Ann Arbor Blues & Jazz Festival (Windsor, Can.), 33, 151, 217, 240, 310, 336, 341, 488
Ann Arbor Blues Festival (Ann Arbor, MI), 30, 32, 33, 41, 51, 55, 57, 91, 93, 96, 114, 121, 127, 132, 136, 138, 150, 151, 156, 177, 190, 202, 204, 208, 217, 226, 228, 240, 243, 247, 249, 260, 266, 278, 304, 305, 309, 312, 329, 330, 334, 336, 341, 342, 345, 363, 368, 381, 389, 393, 394, 403, 407, 412, 427, 429, 435, 443, 444, 445, 457, 468, 476, 479, 481, 484, 488, 490, 494, 499, 500, 513, 520, 523, 527, 532, 535, 548, 561, 564, 569, 573, 575, 580, 585, 595, 596
Ann Arbor Blues Recital (Ann Arbor, MI), 183, 483, 596
Ann Brown's Club (Memphis, TN), 483
Annex (club), The (Chicago, IL), 385
Annex Buffet (club) (Chicago, IL), 229
Annex Restaurant (New Orleans, LA), 506
Anthony, Eddie, 251, 546
Antibes Jazz Festival (Antibes, Fr.), 113, 157, 305, 389
Antibes Jazz Festival (Paris, Fr.), 240, 340
Antilles (label), 343, 344, 363
Antioch Baptist Church (St. Louis, MO), 45
Antioch College (Yellow Springs, OH), 210
Antone's (club) (Austin, TX), 33, 122, 240, 304, 310, 390, 435, 489
Antwine, Della Beatrice, 115
Apache Club/Inn (Dayton, OH), 74, 378
Apartment (club), The (Chicago, IL), 417
Apex (label), 164
Apex Bar (Omaha, NE), 215
Apex Chateau (club) (Robbins, IL), 457
Apex Club (Baton Rouge, LA), 270
Apex Club (Chicago, IL), 555
Apex Club (Detroit, MI), 55, 238, 312, 434, 578
Apex Club (La Grange, IL), 460
Apex Club Orchestra, 555
Apex Grill (bar) (Robbins, IL), 251
Apollo (label), 39, 61, 91, 92, 164, 216, 219, 340, 343, 403, 406, 454, 503, 536, 556
Apollo Theater (Atlantic City, NJ), 467
Apollo Theater (Brooklyn, NY), 188
Apollo Theater (Chicago, IL), 541
Apollo Theater (42nd Street, New York, NY), 80, 254, 564, 581
Apollo Theater (125th Street, New York, NY), 31, 35, 44, 51, 68, 71, 74, 86, 88, 90, 104, 111, 113, 134, 136, 140, 157, 165, 171, 173, 188, 194, 195, 197, 200, 215, 216, 219, 220, 239, 252, 253, 256, 263, 268, 274, 279, 281, 289, 293, 298, 299, 308, 309, 310, 357, 359, 366, 372, 378, 383, 388, 393, 406, 407, 411, 415, 417, 418, 430, 431, 435, 444, 446, 447, 452, 464, 470, 481, 491, 497, 504, 510, 512, 513, 518, 519, 520, 523, 525, 527, 536, 538, 541, 542, 550, 556, 564, 566, 567, 571, 581, 584, 586, 588
Apostolic Church (Opelousas, LA), 200
Aqua Jazz Lounge (Philadelphia, PA), 588
Aquarius Tavern (Seattle, WA), 132, 389
Arabian Nights Club (San Francisco, CA), 509
Arabian Sands (club) (Chicago, IL), 236
Aragon Ballroom (Chicago, IL), 93, 219, 345, 352
Aragon Ballroom (Dallas, TX), 305
Arc (label), 517
Archer, Don, 452
Archey, Jimmy, 256
Archibald (see: Gross, Leon T.)
Archie Boy (see: Gross, Leon T.)
Archive of Folk Music (label), 206, 366, 454, 503
Archway Club (Chicago, IL), 586
Arena (club), The (Long Beach, CA), 46, 113
Arena (club), The (San Diego, CA), 585
Arena (club), The (Seattle, WA), 431
Aretha King's Club (Baton Rouge, LA), 232, 301
Argo (label), 121, 208, 246, 388, 530, 571, 580
Argyle (club) (London, Eng.), 256
Argyle (label), 332
Arhoolie (label), 29, 30, 41, 57, 58, 59, 63, 98, 103, 104, 120, 121, 122, 130, 132, 139, 141, 150, 161, 167, 199, 203, 208, 230, 232, 236, 238, 241, 242, 243, 244, 246, 249, 250, 265,

266, 267, 268, 301, 324, 329, 330, 333, 334, 347, 363, 364, 382, 393, 397, 404, 412, 415, 420, 439, 455, 462, 474, 478, 512, 513, 514, 518, 533, 534, 547, 553, 569, 573, 574, 578, 595
Arie Crown Theater (Chicago, IL), 113, 352, 431
Ariola-Ember (label), 224
Aristocrat (label), 62, 155, 181, 294, 339-40, 343, 388, 398, 403, 412, 425
Aristocrat Club (New Orleans, LA), 437
Ark (club), The (Boston, MA), 137
Ark (club), The (Vancouver, Can.), 141, 147
Arkansas Baptist College (Little Rock, AR), 298
Arlington Street Church (Boston, MA), 389
Armadillo World Headquarters (Austin, TX), 307
Armed Forces Radio Service (label) (see: AFRS label)
Armory (hall), The (Akron, OH), 269
Armory (hall), The (Flint, MI), 86
Armory (hall), The (New York, NY), 281
Armstrong, Howard, 57, 348
Armstrong, Lil, 496, 501
Armstrong, Louis, 31, 60, 141, 142, 229, 254, 256, 276, 279, 295, 298, 331, 373, 385, 406, 438, 465, 481, 507, 512, 531, 541, 544, 581, 584
Armstrong, Shelley (see: Easton, Amos)
Arnold, Augustus "Gus" (Julio Finn), 36, 247, 576
Arnold, Betty, 181
Arnold, Billy Boy (see: Arnold, William)
Arnold, James "Kokomo," **34-35**, 271, 289, 546, 552
Arnold, Jerome, 36
Arnold, John, 441
Arnold, John Henry, 555
Arnold, Kokomo (see: Arnold, James)
Arnold, William "Billy Boy," **35-36**, *35*, 199, 269, 289, 501, 528, 529, 549, 571, 576, 596
Arnold's Club (Cincinnati, OH), 37
Art Institute (Detroit, MI), 556
Art Institute of Chicago (Chicago, IL), 430, 591
Art of Jazz, The (book), 371, 594
Art Park Theater (Lewiston, NY), 57, 349, 490
Art-Tone (label), 63, 357
Artesan Hall (New Orleans, LA), 300, 373
Arthur P. Williams Elementary School (New Orleans, LA), 101
Artist & Movie Ball (New York, NY), 221, 496
Artistic (label), 208, 213, 345
Arto (label), 221
Art's Cafe (Philadelphia, PA), 464
Arts Festival (Cleveland, OH), 366, 504
Arts Festival (London, Eng.), 302
Arts Society (Phoenix, AZ), 363
Asby, Irving, 582
Asch, Moses, 318, 147, 164, 206, 317, 503, 556
Ascot Club (Toronto, Can.), 239
Ash Grove (club) (Hollywood/Los Angeles, CA), 54, 57, 93, 117, 121, 125, 136, 138, 141, 142, 147, 155, 156, 161, 174, 177, 178, 185, 188, 194, 210, 211, 230, 240, 243, 246, 257, 260, 272, 304, 305, 314, 330, 345, 363, 364, 366, 371, 375, 378, 389, 393, 397, 417, 427, 442, 448, 457, 461, 468, 503, 504, 512, 513, 520, 523, 527, 531, 548, 553, 569, 573, 588
Ashland Auditorium (Chicago, IL), 51, 305, 308, 407
Asp (label), 327, 553
Astoria Club (Indianapolis, IN), 164
Astoria Hotel (New Orleans, LA), 292
Astrodome (stadium), The (Houston, TX), 51, 174, 219, 310
Astrodome Holiday Inn (Houston, TX), 199
Astrodome Jazz Festival (Houston, TX), 114, 432
Astrodome Jazzfest (Houston, TX), 309
Astro's (group), 535
Asylum (label), 100
Atco (label), 92, 208, 216, 239, 293, 378, 510, 517, 548
Atkinson, Bob, 174
Atlanta Blues Festival (Atlanta, GA), 164, 171, 244, 261, 379, 389, 391, 435
Atlanta Jazz Festival (Atlanta, GA), 391
Atlantic (label), 33, 37, 38, 51, 91, 95, 101, 103, 111, 113, 114, 151, 155, 158, 165, 166, 200, 203, 208, 209, 210, 217, 219, 230, 271, 288, 294, 295, 304, 305, 353, 363, 364, 365, 368, 369, 370, 389, 394, 411, 412, 417, 420, 425, 429, 430, 436, 445, 447, 457, 466, 474, 476, 488, 499, 500, 503, 508, 517, 519, 521, 527, 532, 548, 564, 586, 591, 592, 596
Atlantic Blues Band, 286
Atlantic Hotel (Belmar, NJ), 418
Atlas (label), 74, 378, 528
Atmosphere Club (Dallas, TX), 527
Atomic (label), 123, 574
Atomic-H (label), 123, 571, 596
Attic (club/lounge), The (Chicago, IL), 99, 123, 334, 360, 595
Attic (club), The (Vancouver, Can.), 141
Attuck Grammar School (Kansas City, MO), 273
Audiophile (label), 423
Auditorium, The (Galveston, TX), 53
Auditorium, The (Long Beach, CA), 54, 211, 346
Auditorium, The (Oakland, CA), 113
Auditorium, The (Richmond, CA), 51
Auditorium, The (Santa Monica, CA), 190, 304
Auditorium Theater, The (Chicago, IL), 42, 46, 54, 95, 100, 114, 123, 132, 208, 240, 247, 334, 359, 389, 476, 496, 500, 548
Audubon (label), 497
Auger, Brian, 577
Aunt Jemima (see: Brown, Ada)
Aunt Jemima (see: Wilson, Edith)
Austin, Chuck, 36, 37
Austin, Claire, **36-37**, *36*, 423
Austin, Lovie, 229, 256, 360, 428
Autocrat (club) (New Orleans, LA), 508
Autry, Gene, 174
Avalon, Frankie, 187
Avalon Ballroom (San Francisco, CA), 121, 188, 208, 249, 263, 296, 345, 585
Avalon Grill (bar) (San Antonio, TX), 76, 527
Avant Garde Coffeehouse (Milwaukee, WI), 137, 177, 363, 427, 553
Avco (label), 243, 585
Avenue Lounge (Chicago, IL), 67, 334, 445
Avenue Theater (Chicago, IL), 79, 221, 463, 472
Avery Church Junior Choir (group), 261
Avery Fisher Hall (New York, NY) (see also: Philharmonic Hall, NYC, NY) (see also: Lincoln Center, NYC, NY), 95, 115, 132, 346, 367, 381, 389, 412, 429, 500, 504, 532, 568
Avodon Ballroom (Los Angeles, CA), 446
Avon Theater (Poughkeepsie, NY), 70
Avon Theater (Watertown, NY), 70
Axion Soap (product), 308

B&B Center (Dallas, TX), 382
B&W (label), 253, 403, 439, 489, 527
B&W Lounge (Chicago, IL), 493
BB (label), 67
B.B. Anderson's (club) (Memphis, TN), 264, 326-327
B.B. Jr. (see: Odom, Andrew)
B.B. King Songbook (book), 310
B.B.'s Jazz, Blues & Soup Parlor (club) (St. Louis, MO), 490, 514
BBC Dance Orchestra, 256
B.F. Keith's Theaters (see: Keith Theaters)
B.J.'s Buffeteria (club) (Bay City, MI), 96, 217, 443
B.M. Studio (music school) (New York, NY), 365
BMI Archives (organization) (New York, NY), 45, 106, 224, 303, 318, 359, 537, 587
BMI: The Many Worlds of Music (magazine), 70, 241, 280, 337, 491
Babriolet (club) (Libertyville, IL), 582
Baby Blues (see: Brown, Ida G.)
Baby Doo (see: Caston, Leonard)
Baby Duke (see: Caston, Leonard)
Baby Face (see: Foster, Leroy)
Baby Face Leroy (see: Foster, Leroy)
Baby Grand (club) (Canton, OH), 90
Baby Grand (club) (New Orleans, LA), 508
Baby Grand (club) (New York, NY), 219, 279, 375, 417, 470, 550

Baby Snooks (Fanny Brice), 167
Baby Star (pseudonym), 540
Back Bay Theater (Boston, MA), 431
Back Door (club), The (San Diego, CA), 51, 367, 505
Back Door Club (Ventura, CA), 32
Back Door Coffeehouse (Montreal, Can.), 147, 367, 504
Back Home Choir (group), 466
Back Woods Blues (book), 125
Back Yard Bandstand (club) (Elmont, NY), 114
Backbiters Club, The (Kansas City, MO), 518
Backporch Boys (group), The, 454
Bacon Fat (band), 398, 468
Bad Sign (club) (Chicago, IL), 389
Baez, Joan, 207
Bag O'Nails Club (London, Eng.), 224
Baggelaar, Kristin, 59, 130, 142, 174, 196, 210, 219, 430, 522
Bailey, Buster, 256, 481
Bailey, DeFord, 67, 180, 444, 485, 505, 580
Bailey, Dorphy, 305
Bailey, Junior Daddy, 313
Bailey, Kid, 89, 409
Bailey, Mildred, 254, 465, 544
Bailey, Pearl, 406, 542
Bailey's 81 Theater (Atlanta, GA) (see: 81 Theater)
Bailey's Theater, (Atlanta, GA), 274
Bajes Club (Amsterdam, Holland), 381
Bajes Cooper Station (club) (Amsterdam, Holland), 389
Baker, Cary, 198
Baker, Fannie/Fanny (see: Brown, Lillian) (see: Hegamin, Lucille)
Baker, Josephine, 152, 256
Baker, Lee, Jr., 67, 163
Baker, Lee, Sr., 67
Baker, McHouston "Mickey," **37-38**, *37*, 165, 166, 311, 343
Bakers Keyboard Lounge (Detroit, MI), 84, 423, 431, 566
Bal Tabarin Theater (Atlantic City, NJ), 472
Balaban & Katz Company (tour), 541
Balcony Hall (Scottsdale, AZ), 240, 346
Ballads of Sacco and Vanzetti (book), 206
Balliett, Whitney, 521
Balloy Club (New Orleans, LA), 300
Balmoral Racetrack (Chicago, IL), 51, 304
Baltabaris Club, The (The Hague, Neth.), 256
Bamboo Club (Lake Charles, LA), 547
Bamboo Inn (New York, NY), 44, 137
Bambu Club (Chicago, IL), 380-381
Bamburg, Richard, 483
Band, Ray, 45
Band, Tommy, 377
Band Box (club) (Chicago, IL), 88
Band of Gypsies (band), The, 224
Bandanna Girls (tour), 428
Bandera (label), 79, 438
Bandy (label), 508
Banff Centre School of Fine Arts (Banff, Can.), 377
Bangar (label), 91
Bango (label), 532
Banjo Bernie (pseudonym), 549
Banjo Boy (see: Nash, Lemoine)
Banjo Boy, The (billing), 396
Banjo Joe (see: Cannon, Gus)
Banjo King of the Southland (billing), 204
Bank Bar (Detroit, MI), 96, 578
Bank Street College of Education (New York, NY), 231
Banks, Andrew, 230
Banks, Charlie, 163
Banks, Classie, 274
Banks, Hobart, 284
Bankston, Ben, 38
Bankston, Dick, **38-39**, *38*, 89, 290, 409
Banner (label), 40, 56, 68, 73, 80, 223, 357, 373, 374, 546, 556, 584
Banner Show Lounge (Chicago, IL), 461
Bannister, Maggie, 486
Bantley, Charley, 175
Baptist Congress Band, 359
Baptist Hospital (Jackson, MS), 338
Baptist Hospital (Memphis, TN), 364
Barassos Theater (Memphis, TN), 467
Barbarin, Paul, 48, 373, 467, 506
Barbary Coast (label), 141
Barbecue Bob (see: Hicks, Robert)
Barbee, John Henry, **39**, *39*, 70
Barber, Chris, 165, 185, 292, 299, 388, *408*, 408, 409, 478, 577
Barclay (label), 78, 117, 208, 490, 548
Bard College (Annandale-on-Hudson, NY), 344, 569
Barefoot Bill (pseudonym), 43
Barker, Danny, 39, 40, 380
Barker, Louisa "Blue Lu," **39-40**, *40*
Barkoot's Travelling Carnival (tour), 144
Barn (club), The (Tunica, MS), 183
Barnaby (label), 118, 244, 478
Barnaby-Candid (label), 403
Barnaby's (club) (Chicago, IL), 304, 359
Barner, Juke Boy (see: Bonner, Weldon)
Barnes, Adam, 196
Barnes, Emile, 203, 420
Barnes, Fae/Faye (see: Jones, Maggie)
Barnes, George, 70
Barnes, Mae, 52, 385
Barnes, Paul, 420
Barnes, Walter, 383
Barnet, Charlie, 550
Barney Gallant's Club (New York, NY), 281
Barney Gordon's Saloon (Philadelphia, PA), 540
Barnum, H.B., 508, 586
Baron's Lounge (New York, NY), 470
Barrelhouse (club) (Burdette, MS), 107
Barrelhouse (label), 65, 110, 180, 182, 183, 225, 591
Barrelhouse Club (Watts/Los Angeles, CA), 136, 154, 372, 417, 439
Barrelhouse Lounge (Chicago, IL) (see also: Kid Riverar's Barrelhouse Lounge), 269, 529, 596
Barrelhouse Revue Show (tour), 417
Barrelhouse Rockers (band), 175
Barrelhouse Sammy (see: McTell, Willie)
Barrelhouse Tommy (see: Dorsey, Thomas)
Barron, Ed (see: Bernhardt, Clyde)
Barron (label), 44, 550, 558
Barron Wilkin's Cafe (New York, NY), 231, 484
Barron's (club) (New York, NY), 472
Barrons Exclusive Club (New York, NY), 137
Barte, Marimb, 501
Bartholomew, Dave, 101, 157, 506, 508
Barton, Tippy (see: White, Joshua)
Bascomb, Dud, 44, 216
Basement Coffee House, The (College Station, TX), 330
Basic Jazz on Long Play (book), 319
Basie, Count, 194, 252, 253, 362, 375, 405, 406, 445, 446, 447, 518, 519, 520, 523, 538, 550, 564, 566, 567, 568, 586
Basin Street Bar (Casablanca, Morocco), 292
Basin Street Club (Chicago, IL), 523
Basin Street Club (Toronto, Can.), 117, 210, 466, 567, 588
Basin Street East (club) (New York, NY), 299, 359, 447, 538, 566
Basin Street South (club) (Boston, MA), 566, 586
Basin Street West (club) (San Francisco, CA), 211, 239, 309, 411, 435, 512, 520, 523, 538, 566, 588
Basiuk, Bo, 349
Bass, Calvin, 589
Bassins (club) (Washington, DC), 174
Bastin, Bruce, 34, 185, 250, 370, 391, 531
Bat Man Club, The (Chicago, IL), 236
Bat the Hummingbird, (see: Davenport, Charles), (see: Robinson, James)
Bates, Deacon, L. J. (see: Jefferson, Lemon)
Bates, Lefty, 485
Bates, Otha Ellas, 359
Bath Festival (Bristol, Eng.), 548
Bath Jazz Festival (Bath, Eng.), 409
Battle, Billy, 175
Battle Club (New Orleans, LA), 300
Battleaxe (pseudonym), 300
Batts, Miles, 40
Batts, Will, **40**, 163
Batts, Will, Jr., 40
Batts South Memphis Jug Band, 40
Baum, Allen (see: Bunn, Alden)
Baxter, Bob, 330
Baxters Beer Garden (Florida), 81
Bay Area Jazz Festival (Berkeley, CA), 567
Bayes, Nora, 494
Bayou (club), The (Washington, DC), 42, 152, 260, 437, 445
Bayou (label), 519, 533
Bayou Boys (group), 322
Bayshore Inn (Vancouver, Can.), 377
Baytone (label), 512

Bayview Theater (San Francisco, CA), 509
Bea & Baby (label), 63, 150, 237, 266, 340, 368, 401, 460, 499, 529, 563
Beach Boys (band), 47
Beach House (club), The (Venice, CA), 304
Beach Walk Ebbtide Hotel (Honolulu, HI), 254
Beachcomber (club), The (Omaha, NE), 298, 321
Beachcomber (club), The (Providence, RI), 406
Beachcomber Club (Santa Cruz, CA), 339, 512
Beacon (label), 117, 234
Beacon-Philips (label), 234
Beacon Theater (New York, NY), 51, 310
Beal, Maggie, 405
Beale Street Blues Boy (billing), 308, 310
Beale Street Blues Festival (Memphis, TN), 310
Beale Street Boys (duo) (Cannon & Woods), 106
Beale Street Boys (band) (Mamie Smith), 472
Beale Street Jug Band, 145, 161, 355
Beale Street Originals (band), 163
Beale Street Palace Theater (Memphis, TN) (see also: Palace Theater), 463
Beale Street Rounders (band), 145
Beale Street Sheiks (band), 40, 486
Beale Streeters (band), The, 50, 308, 334, 400, 407
Beaman, Lottie, **40-41**, *41*
Beaman, William, 41
Bear (club), The (Chicago, IL), 388
Bearcats Band, 141
Beartrap Inn, The (Chicago, IL), 592
Beat City (club) (London, Eng.), 46
Beatles (band), The, 47, 219, 238, 390, 411, 412, 417
Beatty, Josephine (see: Hunter, Alberta)
Beatty, Josephine, 257
Be-Bop Boy (billing), The, 337
Be-Bop Hall (W. Memphis, AR), 130, 577
BeBop Inn (Chicago, IL), 476, 479
Bechet, Sidney, 197, 285, 300, 406, 463, 472, 584
Beck, Jeff, 528
Beckman & Garrity Carnival (tour), 382
Beck's Restaurant (New Orleans, LA), 326
Becky Thatcher Riverboat (see: S.S. Becky Thatcher)
Bedford Ballroom (Brooklyn, NY), 405
Bedford Theater (Brooklyn, NY), 581
Bee Hive (club), The (Chicago, IL), 69, 116, 213, 555, 591, 592
Bee Kelly's Floor Show (tour), 133
Beekman-Downtown Hospital (New York, NY), 482
Been Here and Gone (book), 163
Beer Garden, The (Yazoo City, MS), 243, 479
Belafonte, Harry, 366, 504, 557
Belasco Theater (New York, NY), 542, 556
Belasco Theater (Washington, DC), 541
Belcher, Jerry, 68, 70
Belcher, Mittie, 68
Bell, Carey, **41-42**, *42*, 150, 240, 247, 269, 393, 412, 494, 505, 551, 578
Bell, David, 467
Bell, Edward "Ed," **42-43**
Bell, Elmon "Shorty," 261
Bell, Jessie, 491
Bell, Judy, 319
Bell, Lurrie, 42
Bell, Viola, 199
Bell (label), 231
Belle, Ida, 460
Belle Star (club) (Colden, NY), 209, 247, 450, 459, 549, 596
Belle Starr (club) (Buffalo, NY), 132, 240, 304, 389, 390, 413
Bellemount Plantation (Lobdell, MS), 512
Bellerive, Carol, 124
Bellevue Hospital (New York, NY), 318
Bellevue Theater (Niagara Falls, NY), 82
Bell's Bar (Kenner, LA), 57
Bell's Cafe (Vicksburg, MS), 379
Bells of Joy (group), 426
Bells Team (football team), 478
Bellson, Louis, 431
Belmont High School (Los Angeles, CA), 193
Belmont Racing Park (Elmont, NY), 114
Belmont Theater (New York, NY), 463, 464
Belmont Theater (Pensacola, FL), 420
Beloit College (Beloit, WI), 41, 150, 327, 341, 363, 569, 573
Below, Fred, 393
Belvedere Orchestra, 298
Ben Franklin Hotel (Philadelphia, PA), 280
Ben 29 Club (Newark, NJ), 528
Benbow, Edna, 373, 374
Benbow, William "Will," 76, 227, 351, 373
Benbow Stock Company (tour), 373
Bender, D. C., **43**
Benford, Aldora, 251
Bennett, Wayne, 73
Benny Star's Club (Tallulah, LA), 379
Benson, Al, 530
Bentley, George, 43
Bentley, Gladys, **43**, *43*, 357
Bentley, John, 491
Bentley, William, 180
Benton, Emma, 456
Benton's Busy Bees (band), 29, 419
Berea College (Berea, KY), 563
Berigan, Bunny, 550
Berk, Chuck, 305
Berkeley Blues Festival (Berkeley, CA), 30, 32, 55, 57, 98, 121, 147, 161, 174, 187, 243, 249, 266, 327, 330, 366, 367, 388, 439, 468, 504, 513, 527, 553, 557, 573
Berkeley Community Center (Berkeley, CA), 411, 417, 544
Berkeley Festival (Berkeley, CA), 575
Berkeley Folk Festival (Berkeley, CA), 187, 230, 330, 363, 573
Berkeley Jazz Festival (Berkeley, CA), 346
Berkeley Music Festival (Berkeley, CA), 449
Berkeley Square (park) (Berkeley, CA), 30
Berkeley Theater (Berkeley, CA), 538
Berkley (club), The (Boston, MA), 208, 513
Berkshire Music Barn (theater) (Lenox, MA), 194, 195, 366, 447, 503, 519, 557
Berkshire Music Festival (Lenox, MA), 308
Berlin Jazz Days Festival (Berlin, Ger.), 156, 211, 246, 457
Berlin Jazz Festival (Berlin, Ger.), 65, 195, 336, 341, 343, 381, 455, 523
Berlin Jazztage Festival (Berlin, Ger.), 156
Bermuda Palms Ballroom (San Rafael, CA), 566
Bernard Graff Plantation (Rolling Fork, MS), 290
Bernhardt, Clyde, 43, **43-45**, *44*, 550, 558
Bernhardt, Washington Michael, 43
Berry, Brooks, 49
Berry, Charles "Chuck," **45-47**, *45*, 89, 124, 158, 225, 299, 528, 546
Berry, Chu, 405, 406
Berry, Connie, 254
Berry, Henry, 45
Berry Park (Wentzville, MO), 45
Bert Earle Company (tour), 592
Bertrand, Robert, 103
Bessie (book), 464, 465
Bessie Smith (book), 464, 465
Bessie Smith, Empress of the Blues (book), 464
Bessie Smith Memorial Concert (New York, NY), 197, 464, 497, 584
Best of Harlem Club (Stockholm, Swed.), 195
Bethel College (McKenzie, TN), 313
Bethel Grove (cemetery) (Navasota, TX), 572
Bethel Missionary Baptist Church (Oakland, CA), 29
Bethlehem (label), 523
Bethune College (Toronto, Can.), 341, 553
Better Days (band), 100
Betty Lou's Package Goods (club) (Chicago, IL), 343
Beverly Caverns (club) (Los Angeles, CA), 385
Beverly Lounge (Gulfport, MS), 489, 514
Bey, Iverson (see: Minter, Iverson)
Bey, Roosevelt Sykes, 490
Biddy Mulligan's (bar) (Chicago, IL). 42, 65, 68, 123, 151, 236, 260, 276, 334, 369, 445, 499, 596
Bidwell, Maggie, 290
Big Apple Tavern, The (Chicago, IL), 336
Big Bear (label), 36, 38, 55, 96, 300, 343, 348, 394, 439, 443, 494, 517, 575, 591

Big Bear Concert (London, Eng.), 38
Big Bear-Munich (label), 443
Big Bear-Polydor (label), 217, 225, 228, 424, 443, 474, 575
Big Beat (label), 287
Big Beat Package Show (tour), 359
Big Bill (see: Broonzy, William)
Big Bill Blues (book), 69, 70, 86
Big Bloke (see: Oden, James)
Big Brother & The Holding Company (band), 296
Big Chief (see: Ellis, Wilbert)
Big Chief Indian & Western Cowboy Medicine Show (tour), 396
Big D (label), 127
Big Duke's (club) (Chicago, IL), 334, 435, 442, 494
Big Duke's Blue Flame Lounge (Blue Flame Lounge) (Chicago, IL), 93, 132, 266, 341, 437, 488, 499-500, 548
Big Duke's Flamingo Lounge (Chicago, IL), 41, 42, 500
Big Ed (see: Burns, Eddie)
Big Foot (see: Burnett, Chester)
Big Four (club), The (Memphis, TN), 62
Big Four Club (Dallas, TX), 317
Big George's Club Carribe (see: Club Carribe)
Big Grundy's (club) (Memphis, TN), 264, 326
Big Horn Jazz Festival (Mundelein, IL), 84, 108, 313, 316, 322
Big Ike's Record Sales Music Store (Mobile, AL), 142
Big Jerry Johnson's Cozy Corner Club (Chicago, IL), 62
Big Joe (see: McCoy, Joe) (see: Williams, Joe Lee)
Big Joe and His Rhythm (band), 355, 433
Big John's (club) (Chicago, IL), 35, 53, 93, 99, 208, 345, 388, 444, 493, 548, 569
Big John's Plantation (Belzoni, MS), 252
Big Maceo (see: Merriweather, Major)
Big Mama Bev (see: Hill, Beverly)
Big Mama Showboat Theater (Pittsburgh, PA), 173
Big Maybelle (see: Smith, Mabel)
Big Moose (see: Walker, John)
Big Poppa's Band, 227
Big Sea, The (book), 43
Big Six (band), The, 238
Big Squeeze Club (Chicago, IL), 93, 150
Big Star (label), 278, 336
Big Star Recording Studio (Detroit, MI), 278
Big Stella (pseudonym), 185
Big Sur Folk Festival (Big Sur, CA), 346
Big T. Lounge (Chicago, IL), 151, 404
Big Ten (R&B) Show (tour), 76, 157, 411, 530
Big Three Trio (Bobby Davis), 571
Big Three Trio (Willie Dixon), 110, 155, *155*, 251
Big Town (label), 188, 510
Big Track Club (Norfolk, VA), 550
Big Vernon (see: Turner, Joseph)
Big Voice (see: Odom, Andrew)
Big Walter (see: Horton, Walter) (see: Price, Walter)
Big Walter (pseudonym), 468
Big Willie (see: Mabon, Willie)
Bigeou, Esther, **48**, *48*, 81
Biggest Rock 'n' Roll Show (tour), 359, 519
Bigtown (label), 337
Bijou (club), The (Bangor, ME), 82
Bijou Cafe (Philadelphia, PA), 51, 347
Bijou Theater (Nashville, TN), 134, 350, 428, 463, 466, 467, 540
Bijou Theater (Woonsocket, RI), 82
Bill (see: Broonzy, William)
Bill, Casey, 297
Bill Broonzy Benefit Concert (Chicago, IL), 194, 322, 340, 380
Bill Brown's Club (Los Angeles, CA), 221
Bill Johnson's Jug Band, 274
Bill Landon's Club (Baltimore, MD), 484
Bill of Fare (club) (Los Angeles, CA), 431
Bill Street Club (Chicago, IL), 334
Billboard (magazine), 47, 76, 158, 225, 352, 390, 456, 568
Billings Hospital (see: A. M. Billings Hospital)
Billups, Amanda, 52
Billy & Jesse (duo), 139
Billy Berg's Swing Club (Hollywood, CA), 298
Billy King Company (tour), 48, 445
Billy Riley's Palace Park (Shreveport, LA), 86
Billy Sunday's Tabernacle (Norfolk, VA), 472
Billy Terrell's Comedians (tour), 440
Billy's Night Club (Elizabeth, NJ), 92
Biloski, Count, 525
Biltmore Hotel (New York, NY), 497, 558
Biltmore Theater (Los Angeles, CA), 542, 584
Bimbo's (club) (Ann Arbor, MI), 421, 423
Bims, Hamilton, 152
Binghamton Folk Festival (Binghamton, NY), 56, 130, 349
Biograph (label), 107, 147, 161, 206, 210, 229, 276, 283, 316, 317, 327, 363, 369, 391, 392, 416, 428, 457, 486, 553
Biography of a Phantom (book), 289
Birch (label), 198
Bird Lounge (Houston, TX), 243
Bird S. Coler Hospital (Welfare Island, NY), 223
Birdhouse (club), The (Chicago, IL), 292, 538, 569
Birdland (club) (New York, NY), 375, 406, 447, 470, 519, 538, 566
Birdland (club) (Peoria, IL), 32
Birdland All-Stars Revue (show) (New York, NY), 566
Birds, Turine, 528
Birds Hill Park (Winnipeg, Can.), 120
Birmingham, Wright, 291
Birmingham Jug Band, 125, 264, 540, 568
Birmingham Sam (see: Hooker, John Lee)
Birmingham Theater (Birmingham, AL), 74
Birtian Club (Chicago, IL), 195
Biscayne (label), 302
Bishop, Elvin, 46, 238, 311
Bistro (club), The (Atlantic City, NJ), 566
Bitter End (club), The (New York, NY), 195, 314, 346, 366, 504, 557
Bitter Lemon Coffeehouse (Memphis, TN), 272, 327
Bix Beiderbecke Memorial Jazz Festival (Davenport, IA), 423
Bix Beiderbecke Memorial Society (label), 423
Bizarre (label), 211
Blache, Marie, 203
Black, Frankie (see: Blackwell, Francis)
Black Ace (see: Turner, Babe)
Black Aces (band), 284
Black & Blue (label), 38, 68, 78, 151, 254, 286, 299, 300, 343, 379, 394, 404, 442, 445, 457, 466, 489, 490, 494, 499, 520, 523, 527, 575
Black & Tan Bar (El Paso, TX), 531
Black & Tan Club (Chicago Heights, IL), 434
Black & Tan Club (Kansas City, MO), 518
Black & Tan Club (Seattle, WA), 111
Black Bear Series (label), 305
Black Bob (pseudonym), 161
Black Boy Shine (see: Holiday, Harold)
Black Bubba (pseudonym), 535
Black Cat Drug Store (Hollandale, MS), 398
Black Dome (club) (Cincinnati, OH), 345
Black Elks Club (Waterloo, IA), 95
Black Fox (club), The (Clarksdale, MS), 183
Black Fox (club) (Los Angeles, CA), 523
Black Gladiator, The (pseudonym), 360
Black Gold Club (New Orleans, LA), 299
Black Hillbillies (group), 159, 274
Black Ivory King (see: Alexander, Dave)
Black Jr. (see: Johnson, Luther, Jr.)
Black Lion (label), 254, 299, 363, 415, 523, 577
Black Music (magazine), 31, 116, 290, 301, 347, 348, 418, 472
Black Muslims (organization), 378
Black Nightingale (billing), 428
Black Orange Cafe (Kansas City, MO), 455
Black Patti (label), 125, 274
Black Patti (pseudonym), 558
Black Plague (band) The, 585
Black Rose of Paris, The (pseudonym), 374
Black Swan (club) (Ottawa, Can.), 42
Black Swan (label), 137, 152, 233, 254, 295, 374, 463, 474, 494, 540, 558, 583

Black Swan Troubadours (troupe), 152, 374, 540
Black Velvet Club (Mt. Clements, MI), 535
Blackbeard's (club) (Santa Barbara, CA), 240
Blackbird (label), 381, 582
Blackburn College (Carlinville, IL), 314
Blackhawk (hotel), The (San Francisco, CA), 538
Blackman, "Tee Wee," 454, 455
Blackmore, Amos, 547
Blackmouth (pseudonym), 79
Blacks, Whites and Blues (book), 441
Blackwell, Bumps, 544
Blackwell, Francis "Scrapper," 27, **48-50**, *49*, 107, 110, 202, 459
Blackwell, Payton, 48
Blackwell, R. A, 136
Blackwell, Willie, 535
Blaise's Club (London, Eng.), 224
Blake, Eubie, 484, 582
Blake's Carnival (tour), 436
Blakey, Anna Blye, 421
Blanchard, Edgar, 300
Blanche Thomas Memorial Concert (New Orleans, LA), 40
Blanche's Lounge (Chicago, IL), 291
Bland, Billy, 503
Bland, Robert "Bobby Blue," 28, **50-51**, *50*, 60, 88, 104, 190, 211, 249, 250, 291, 294, 308, 310, 311, 404, 407, 437, 499, 528, 572, 588
Blank, Les, 121, 243, 330
Blanks, Addison, 52
Blanks, Arsceola, 52
Blanks, Birleanna, **52**, *52*
Blanks Sisters (duo), 52
Blare, Mary, 237
Blaylock, Travis (Harmonica Slim), **52-3**, *52*, 398, 528, 571
Blesh, Rudi, 229, 397, 493, 508, 591, 594
Blevins, Kinky, 238
Blevins, Leo, 238
Blevins, Mary, 303
Blind Arthur (see: Phelps, Arthur)
Blind Blake (see: Higgs, Blake)
Blind Blake (see: Phelps, Arthur)
Blind Boy Fuller No. 2 (see: McGhee, Walter)
Blind Boy Fuller's Buddy (billing), 133
Blind Boys of Jackson Mississippi (group), The, 421
Blind Doggie (see: McTell, Willie)
Blind Gary (see: Davis, Gary)
Blind Joe (pseudonym), 327
Blind Lemon Jefferson (book), 276
Blind Lemon Jefferson Club (New York, NY), 276
Blind Lemon Jefferson Club (San Pablo, CA), 185, 276
Blind Lemon's Buddy (billing), 235
Blind Murphy (pseudonym), 312, 313
Blind Percy (pseudonym), 438
Blind Pig (club) (Ann Arbor, MI), 217
Blind Pig (club) (Chicago, IL), 65, 117, 292, 340, 490, 569
Blind Pig (label), 217
Blind Sammy/Sammie (see: McTell, Willie)
Blind Willie (see: McTell, Willie)
Block, Martin, 446
Bloomfield, Michael "Mike," **53-54**, *53*, 210, 311, 390, 393, 528, 578, 585
Bloomfield's Gambling Joint (Vance, MS), 193
Blossom Music Center (Cleveland, OH), 243, 308, 309, 420
Blow My Blues Away (book), 153, 230
Blue, Joe (Little Joe), **54-55**, *54*, 127, 299, 311, 378, 510
Blue, Lu (see: Barker, Louisa)
Blue Angel (club), The (Chicago, IL), 566
Blue Angel (club) (New York, NY), 194, 556
Blue Angel Club (Cincinnati, OH), 76, 372
Blue Angel Club (London, Eng.), 174
Blue Beat (label), 63
Blue Blazers (band), The, 44
Blue Bonnet (label), 232, 461
Blue Butterfly Inn (New York, NY), 385
Blue Devils (band), 284, 385, 405, 445
Blue Dolphin (club) (San Francisco, CA), 30
Blue Eagle Four Spiritual Group, 267
Blue Eagles Band, The, 530
Blue Five (band), 222, 496
Blue Flame Club (Chicago, IL), 99, 208, 238, 345, 444, 461, 548, 572, 596
Blue Flame Club (Jackson, TN), 426, 575
Blue Flame Club (St. Louis, MO), 79
Blue Flame Lounge (see: Big Duke's Blue Flame Lounge)
Blue Flame Syncopators (band), 221
Blue Flames (band), The, 224, 283, 348, 407
Blue Gardenia (club) (Birmingham, AL), 188
Blue Gardenia (club) (Oakland, CA), 588
Blue Goose (label), 59, 120, 182, 202, 247, 274, 283, 302, 427, 456, 562, 563
Blue Goose Club (Osceola, AR), 450
Blue Grass Club (Cleveland, OH), 550
Blue Heaven Club (Memphis, TN), 176, 401
Blue Horizon (label), 63, 74, 104, 156, 165, 169, 228, 236, 246, 283, 285, 292, 322, 331, 340, 341, 371, 443, 444, 457, 468, 474, 478, 486, 488, 595
Blue Horn (club) (Vancouver, Can.), 588
Blue Jay Club (New Orleans, LA), 420
Blue Labor (label), 261, 366, 367, 378, 454, 457, 504
Blue Lake (label), 181, 216, 340, 342, 424, 535, 571
Blue Lantern Drive-In Restaurant (Atlanta, GA), 369
Blue Light (label) (Chicago, IL), 461
Blue Light Club (Memphis, TN), 337
Blue Mirror Club (San Francisco, CA), 98, 430, 527
Blue Mirror Club (Washington, DC), 542
Blue Monday Club (New Orleans, LA), 157
Blue Moon Ballroom (Elgin, IL), 304
Blue Moon Club (Port Arthur, TX), 120, 200
Blue Morocco (club) (Port Arthur, TX), 121
Blue Mountain College (Blue Mountain, MS), 313
Blue Nebulae Revue (band), 32
Blue Note (club) (Chicago, IL), 69, 157, 229, 373, 447, 452, 564, 566
Blue Note (label), 44, 203, 588
Blue Note Concert (New York, NY), 145
Blue Rhythms (band), 342
Blue Rock (label), 549
Blue Room (club), The (Los Angeles, CA), 518
Blue Room (club) (New York, NY), 446
Blue Room Club (Vicksburg, MS), 594
Blue Rhythms (band), 394
Blue Sky (label), 132, 247, 390, 413, 442, 585
Blue Smitty (see: Smith, Claude)
Blue Star (label), 38, 78, 101, 117
Blue Three (group), 496
Blue Thumb (label), 177, 238, 393, 553
Blue Yodel (book), 441
Bluebeat (label), 63, 199
Bluebird (label), 49, 57, 62, 68, 84, 110, 116, 119, 120, 122, 137, 144, 148, 150, 154, 161, 167, 176, 193, 200, 203, 256, 279, 282, 292, 317, 325, 334, 348, 354, 355, 370, 380, 386, 398, 403, 405, 406, 414, 426, 433, 480, 497, 501, 514, 524, 541, 545, 547, 551, 552, 559, 560, 568, 575, 589, 592
Bluebird Cafe (Santa Barbara, CA), 200, 439, 531
Bluejay (label), 436
Blues (label), 530
Blues Alley (club) (Washington, DC), 254, 447, 448, 481
Blues & Rhythm (label), 59
Blues & Soul (magazine), 60
Blues at Carnegie Show (New York, NY), 470
Blues at Midnight Concert (New York, NY), 69, 365, 503
Blues Ball (concert) (Toronto, Can.), 375
Blues Bar (Paris, Fr.), 117, 577
Blues Beacon (label), 381, 389, 456, 553, 573
Blues Blasters (band), 357
Blues Blowers (band), 313
Blues Boy (see: Odom, Andrew) (see: Seward, Alec)
Blues Boy (billing), 308, 310
Blues Boy Bill (see: Broonzy, William)
Blues Boy From Beale Street (billing), 308, 310
Blues Boys (duo), 127, 454
Blues Boys Kingdom (label), 308

Blues Busters (band), 256
Blues Caravan (tour), 147, 388
Blues Cats (band), 305, 410
Blues Champs (band), The, 563
Blues Chasers (band), 84
Blues Classics (label), 162, 185, 576
Blues Connoisseur (label), 270, 339
Blues Consolidated Show (tour), 50, 407
Blues Doctor, The (billing), 122
Blues Dusters (band), The, 134
Blues Factory/Soul Productions (organization) (Chicago, IL), 156
Blues Filter Cigarettes (product), 367, 505
Blues Guitar Method (book), 310
Blues Jubilee Concert (Los Angeles, CA), 253, 378
Blues Jumpers (band), 101
Blues King (see: Seward, Alec)
Blues Machine (band), 499
Blues Magazine (Canada), 148, 210, 266, 349, 554
Blues Magazine (Japan), 289
Blues Man, The (see: Sykes, Roosevelt)
Blues Man (billing), 312
Blues On Blues (label), 435, 569, 595
Blues Rockers (band), 342, 343
Blues Room (club) (Los Angeles, CA), 213
Blues Scene 69 (tour), 165, 240, 302, 363
Blues Sensation from the West (billing), 351
Blues Serenaders (band), 229, 251, 256, 428
Blues Singer Supreme (billing), 221
Blues Society Concert (Santa Barbara, CA), 456
Blues Soul (label), 283
Blues Spectacle (label), 84
Blues Spectrum (label), 76, 136, 299, 372
Blues Syndicate Band, 352
Blues Twins (duo), 86
Blues Unlimited (magazine), 28, 33, 35, 36, 39, 47, 55, 57, 59, 60, 63, 66, 67, 68, 78, 79, 88, 91, 95, 96, 99, 101, 103, 120, 122, 125, 127, 132, 133, 137, 139, 140, 149, 156, 157, 161, 162, 163, 167, 169, 172, 180, 181, 185, 188, 192, 193, 197, 199, 200, 202, 204, 211, 213, 220, 226, 228, 229, 232, 233, 235, 236, 238, 247, 260, 269, 272, 278, 283, 285, 289, 290, 291, 299, 301, 302, 303, 307, 311, 313, 315, 316, 320, 324, 326, 329, 332, 334, 336, 337, 338, 342, 344, 345, 348, 353, 354, 360, 364, 370, 371, 372, 378, 379, 382, 383, 384, 390, 392, 395, 396, 397, 398, 399, 400, 404, 408, 410, 413, 415, 417, 421, 424, 425, 430, 435, 439, 444, 449, 451, 453, 455, 460, 461, 470, 472, 474, 479, 486, 487, 489, 494, 501, 502, 508, 509, 515, 516, 517, 524, 529, 530, 531, 535, 546, 547, 554, 557, 562, 563, 564, 571, 572, 575, 576, 578, 580, 586, 589, 591, 594, 595, 597
Blues Unlimited Club (Detroit, MI), 239, 388, 435
Blues World (magazine), 33, 70, 80, 96, 108, 144, 148, 163, 187, 233, 276, 280, 289, 324, 345, 382, 410, 459, 492, 551, 578
Bluesbreakers (band), 63, 239, 352
Bluesettes (group), The, 378
Blueshounds (group), The 591
Bluesmaker (label), 188
Bluesman (label), 69, 236, 547
Bluesmen (book), The, 29, 125, 127, 249, 273, 276, 354, 410, 507, 554
BluesTime (label), 53, 127, 468, 478, 520, 523, 527
Bluestown (label), 211, 535
Bluesville (label), 27, 34, 49, 62, 86, 117, 118, 155, 161, 181, 182, 185, 202, 283, 285, 403, 426, 438, 481, 482, 492, 534, 569, 570
Bluesville-Prestige (label) (see also: Prestige-Bluesville label), 35, 147, 574
BluesWay (label) (see also: ABC-BluesWay label), 41, 54, 76, 88, 238, 239, 240, 243, 266, 286, 300, 312, 334, 341, 366, 383, 404, 424, 439, 468, 476, 478, 490, 493, 504, 520, 523, 527, 528, 530, 563, 575, 588
BluesWay-Blues on Blues (label), 476
Blunt, Jeff, 492
Blythe, Jimmy, 475
B'nai B'rith (organization) (New York, NY), 311
Bo Diddley (see: McDaniel, Ellas)
Boarding House (club), The (San Francisco, CA), 30, 51, 98, 101, 122, 243, 346, 360, 367, 418, 457, 504
Boat Club (Norfolk, VA), 313
Boat House (club), The (San Francisco, CA), 439
Boathouse (club), The (Atlantic City, NJ), 540
Bob Slaters Minstrel Maids (group), 48
Bobbin (label), 104, 192, 304, 338
Bobby Dee (see: Bender, D.C.)
Bobby McGhee's (club) (Cleveland, OH), 57, 349
Bobby Shore's Tavern (Meridian, MS), 41
Bob's Tavern (Chicago, IL), 589
Bodega (club) (Campbell, CA), 339, 367, 505
Bodega Club (Chicago, IL), 516, 548
Body Politic (club) (Chicago, IL), 389
Bogan, Cornelia, 56
Bogan, Lucille, **55-56,** *55,* 263
Bogan, Nazareth, 56
Bogan, Ted, **56-57,** *56,* 348, 349
Bogan's Birmingham Busters (band), 56, 356
Bogart's Cafe American (Cincinnati, OH), 322, 535
Bogle, Donald, 219, 362
Bohanna, Scott, 386
Bohemian Caverns Club (Washington, DC), 388, 431
Bohemian Embassy Coffee House (Toronto, Can.), 147
Boines, Houston, 59
Bokelman, Marina, 28, 38, 81, 349
Boll Weenie Bill (see: Moore, Willie C.)
Boll Weevil Bill (see: Moore, Willie C.)
Boll Weevil Jazz Band, 313
Bolling, Billie, 42
Bombay (label), 108
Bon Ran (label), 192
Bon Soir Club (New York, NY), 256
Bon Ton Boys (band), 191
Bon-Ton Cavern (club) (Buffalo, NY), 388
Bon Ton Drive-In, The (Beaumont, TX), 120, 191
Bon Ton Roulet (club) (Lafayette, LA), 121
Bona Vista (club) (Buffalo, NY), 260
Bonano, Joseph "Sharkey", 373
Bonanza Club (Chicago, IL), 572
Bond, Johnny, 441
Bonds, Aaron, 57
Bonds, Son, **57,** 401
Bonner, Alf, 266
Bonner, Emanuel, 57
Bonner, Weldon "Juke Boy", **57-59,** *58,* 435, 553, 578
Boogie Bill (see: Webb, Bill)
Boogie Blues Blasters (band), 28
Boogie Jake (see: Jacobs, Matthew)
Boogie Man (see: Hooker, John Lee)
Boogie Ramblers (band), 193
Boogie Woogie Blues Folio (book), 128
Boogie Woogie Festival (Cologne, Ger.), 302
Boogie Woogie Inn (Chicago, IL), 181, 268, 388, 442
Boogie Woogie Red (see: Harrison, Vernon)
Boojum Tree (club) (Phoenix, AZ), 588
Bookbinder, Paul Roy, 34, **59,** *59,* 147
Booker, Betty Jean, 60
Booker, Charlie, **59**
Booker, James, **60,** *60,* 103, 202
Booker, James Carroll, II, 60
Booker, John Lee (see: Hooker, John Lee)
Booker, Lucius, 59
Booker Boy and The Rhythmaires (band), 60
Booker T. Washington Community Center (Louisville, KY), 252
Booker T. Washington High School (Memphis, TN), 510
Booker T. Washington Theater (St Louis, MO), 48, 49, 107, 172, 276, 279, 288, 450, 463, 466, 540
Books, Strings & Things Coffeehouse (Blacksburg, VA), 187
Boone, Chester, 522
Booze, Beatrice "Wee Bea", **60-1,** *61*
Bop City (club) (New York, NY), 298
Borenstein, E. Lorenz (E.L.) "Larry", 421, 487
Borenstein's Art Gallery (New Orleans, LA), 420, 486
Born to Win (book), 206
Borneman, Ernest, 56
Borum, William (Willie B.), *61,* **62,** 89, 106, 288, 327, 337, 454, 486

NAMES & PLACES INDEX

Boss of the Blues (billing), 520
Bossman of the Blues (billing), 310
Bossmen: Bill Monroe & Muddy Waters (book), 390, 391
Bostic, Earl, 83, 300
Bostic, Joe, 466
Boston-American Festival of Music (Boston, MA), 388
Boston Arts Festival (Boston, MA), 174, 447
Boston Blues Society Concert (Cambridge/Boston, MA), 260, 364, 457, 483, 573
Boston Club, The (Cambridge, MA), 132, 286, 389
Boston Club (Sacramento, CA), 55
Boston Folk Festival (Boston, MA), 249, 388
Boston Folksong Society (Boston, MA), 348
Boston Garden (club) (Boston, MA), 224
Boston Globe Jazz Festival (Boston, MA), 308
Boston Jazz Festival (Boston, MA), 375
Boston Plaza (club) (Newark, NJ), 550
Boston Tea Party (club) (Boston, MA), 346
Boston University (Boston, MA), 32-3, 240, 330, 348
Boswell, Connie, 465
Both/And Club (San Francisco, CA), 51, 117, 512, 588
Bottom Line (club), The (New York, NY), 33, 42, 54, 132, 150, 174, 209, 210, 304, 307, 352, 367, 379, 389, 390, 418, 429, 449, 450, 504, 549
Boues Sur Tois Club (Paris, Fr.), 256
Boulevard (club), The (Queens, NY), 542
Boulevard Lounge (Chicago, IL), 279
Boulevard Theater (New York, NY), 221, 581
Bound for Glory (book), 206, 207
Bourbon (label), 208, 457, 549
Bourbon Street (club) (Chicago, IL), 148, 566
Bourbon Street (club) (Toronto, Can.), 490
Bourbon Street Banana Factory (club) (Toronto, Can.), 108
Bourbon Street Beat Band, 506
Bourbon Street Club (Hollywood, CA), 414
Bourbon Street East (club) (New Orleans, LA), 506
Bourne, Mike, 352
Bowery (club), The (Chicago, IL), 132
Bowie, David, 220
Boxer (label), 278
Boy Friends (group), 321
Boyd, Edward "Little Eddie", **62-63**, *62*, 66, 107, 117, 188, 289, 334, 357, 370, 371, 388, 390, 403, 491
Boyd, Ernie (see: Boyd, Edward "Little Eddie")
Boyd, Julia, 444
Boyd, Robert (see: Byrd, Roy)
Boyd, Walter, 317
Boyd, William, 62
Boyd, Willie, 212
Bozeman, Eliza, 440
Bracey, Ishmon, **64**, *64*, 202, 290, 315, 354, 355, 524, 546
Bracey, Richard, 64
Bradford, Alex, 116, 383, 412
Bradford, Perry, 472, 583
Bradley, Jack, 285, 347, 452
Bradley, Tom, 520
Bradley, Velma (see: Cox, Ida)
Bradley University (Alton, IL), 314
Bradshaw, Tiny, 83, 200, 263, 357, 470
Brady's 48th Street Theater (New York, NY) (see also: 48th Street Theater), 581
Bragg, ______, 489
Bragg, Doby (see: Sykes, Roosevelt)
Branch, William "Billy", **64-65**, *64*, 269, 578
Brand, Oscar, 206
Brandeis University (Waltham, MA), 185, 330, 573
Brandin (label), 28
Branker's Club (New York, NY), 470
Branning, Don, 393
Brantley, Charlie, 111
Brass Rail (club) (Chicago, IL), 110, 154, 380, 406, 564
Bratskellar (club), The (San Francisco, CA), 30
Brave (label), 72
Braxton & Nugent (duo), 540
Brazilian Nuts Show (tour), 564
Bread & Roses Coffeehouse (Baltimore, MD), 142
Breckinridge, John C., 580
Breckow, John, 137
Breda Jazz Festival (Breda, Holland), 316
Brenham Cemetery (Hempstead, TX), 419
Brenner, Harold, 341
Brentwood Lounge (San Francisco, CA), 439
Bret Harte Hospital (Murphys, CA), 533
Brevoort Theater (Brooklyn, NY), 378, 411, 434, 470
Brewer, Fannie, 65
Brewer, James "Jimmy", **65-66**, *65*, 70, 290
Brick Club (New York, NY), 406
Brickseller (club), The (Washington, DC), 257
Briggs, J.T., 282
Brim, Ernest, 66, 67
Brim, Grace, **66**, *66*
Brim, John, **66-67**, *66*, 70, 181, 332, 370, 424, 434, 560
Brim, John, Jr., 66, 67
Brim, Mrs. John (see: Brim, Grace)
Brimmer, Annie, 454, 455
Brimmer, Mary, 454
Brimmer, Son (see: Shade, Will)
Briscoli's Grenada Cafe (Peoria, IL), 110
Bristol, Sudy L., 492
British Beaulieu Jazz Festival (London, Eng.), 132
Brittwood Grill (New York, NY), 385
Broadhurst Theater (New York, NY), 82, 496, 581
Broadmoor (label), 157
Broadmoor Hotel (Beulah, CO), 466
Broadmoor Hotel (Colorado Springs, CO), 254
Broadway (label), 380
Broadway Theater (New York, NY), 70, 71, 82, 256, 540, 541, 582
Broadway Theater (Washington, DC), 221
Broadway's Queen of Song & Jazz (billing), 43
Brockton Theater (Brockton, MA), 82
Broken Drum (club) (Minneapolis, MN), 342
Bromberg, Bruce, 200, 371
Bromberg, Michael, 272
Bronks, Ella, 80
Bronx Bar (Detroit, MI), 216
Bronze Peacock (club) (Houston, TX), 76, 512, 527
Brookins, Tommy, 542
Brooklyn Academy of Music (see: Academy of Music, Brooklyn, NY)
Brooklyn Blowers (band), 300
Brooklyn College (Brooklyn, NY), 206, 218
Brooklyn Hospital (Brooklyn, NY), 74
Brookmeyer, Bob, 375
Brookmont Hotel (Chicago, IL), 393, 548
Brooks, Jennie (see: Beaman, Lottie)
Brooks, Junior, 371
Brooks, Lawson, 525
Brooks, Leola, 270
Brooks, Lonnie (Guitar Jr.), **67-68**, *67*, 78, 158, 208, 287, 311, 412, 435, 528, 531
Brooks, Roosevelt, 492, 531
Brooks, Shelton, 350
Broom, Alonzo, 175
Broomcorn Festival (Arcola, IL), 313
Broomdusters (band), 155, 271, 294, 395
Broomsley, Big Bill (see: Broonzy, William)
Broonzy, Bill (see: Broonzy, William)
Broonzy, Frank, 68, 84
Broonzy, William "Big Bill", 39, 65, 67, **68-70**, *68*, 84, 85, 86, 93, 116, 118, 138, 148, 161, 174, 178, 193, 200, 215, 233, 263, 264, 268, 269, 276, 280, 313, 322, 324, 342, 348, 355, 365, 366, 368, 370, 380, 386, 393, 403, 416, 424, 442, 452, 453, 503, 522, 524, 547, 551, 552, 555, 559, 574, 576, 588, 595
Brother Blues (see: Dupree, William)
Brother George (see: Fuller, Blind Boy) (see: McGhee, Walter)
Brother John (see: Sellers, John)
Brother Johnny (pseudonym), 234
Brother Joshua (see: Joseph, Pleasant)
Brother Ray, Ray Charles' Own Story (book), 114, 116
Broussard, Ophelia, 191
Broven, John, 88, 95, 158, 202, 301, 326, 344, 546
Brown, Ada, **70-72**, *71*, 385, 582
Brown, Amanda (see: McCoy, Viola)
Brown, Andrew, **72-73**, *72*, 305, 311, 528

Brown, Arelean, 402
Brown, Aretha, 486
Brown, Arthur, 220
Brown, B.B., 448
Brown, B. Daniel, 74
Brown, Bessie, #1 ("The Original"), **73,** *73,* 74
Brown, Bessie, #2, **73-74,** *73*
Brown, Bubba, 349, 546, 547
Brown, Buster, **74,** *74,* 158, 505
Brown, Charles, 31, 60, **74-76,** *75,* 116, 154, 158, 188, 199, 250, 311, 332, 372, 571, 586
Brown, Chocolate (see: Scruggs, Irene)
Brown, Clarence "Gatemouth", 68, **76-78,** *77,* 101, 125, 127, 136, 250, 293, 299, 305, 353, 383, 512, 528, 531, 552
Brown, Clarence, Sr., 76
Brown, Dewey, 137
Brown, Dusty, **78-79,** *78,* 199, 269, 299, 390
Brown, Eliza, 74
Brown, Gabriel, **79**
Brown, Gatemouth (see: Brown, Clarence)
Brown, Georgia, 546
Brown, Henry "Hi Henry," 79
Brown, Henry "Papa Henry," **79,** 514
Brown, Honey, 44
Brown, Ida G., **79-80,** *80*
Brown, Ike, 396
Brown, J.C. (see: Jefferson, Lemon)
Brown, J.T., 62, 150, 291, 563
Brown, James, 55, 353, 383, 412
Brown, James "Jim," 80
Brown, James "Widemouth," 78
Brown, John Henry "Bubba," **80,** *81*
Brown, Lee, 180
Brown, Lil, 83
Brown, Lillian "Lillyn," **80-83,** *81*
Brown, Lottie (see: Beaman, Lottie)
Brown, Mel, 80
Brown, Nappy, 37, 165, 270
Brown, Olive, **83-84,** *83,* 465
Brown, Oscar, Jr., 65, 557
Brown, Othum, 574
Brown, Percy "Fast Black," 413
Brown, Pete, 252, 300
Brown, Piney, 125
Brown, Richard "Rabbit," **84**
Brown, Robert (Smoky Babe), 85, **86**
Brown, Robert (Washboard Sam), 69, 70, **84-86,** *85,* 86, 393, 547
Brown, Ron, 368, 505
Brown, Roy, 51, **86-88,** *87,* 104, 149, 157, 216, 407, 412, 437, 448, 520
Brown, Ruth, 37, 111, 538
Brown, Sammy, 336
Brown, Tommy (see: Brown, Roy)
Brown, Troy "Bear," 357
Brown, Walter, 47, **88-89,** *88,* 377, 586
Brown, Willie, 38, 39, 62, **89,** 95, 247, 249, 288, 289, 290, 349, 409
Brown, Willie "Little Willie," 89
Brown, Yancy, 86
Brown & DeMont (duo), 81
Brown & Straine (duo), 73
Brown Bombers of Swing (band), 547
Brown Buddies (band), The, 154
Brown Chapel Church (Sumter, SC), 436
Brown Derby (club) (Chatanooga, TN), 383, 518, 550
Brown Derby (club) (Chicago, IL), 168
Brown Derby (club), The (Dallas, TX), 382
Brown Derby (club) (Detroit, MI), 535
Brown Derby (club) (Los Angeles, CA), 398
Brown Derby (club) (Oakland, CA), 510
Brown Jug (club) (W. Memphis, AR), 337
Brown Shoe (club) (Chicago, IL), 424, 476, 575, 596
Brown Skin Syncopators (band), 350
Brown University (Providence, RI), 553
Brownie McGhee's Home of the Blues Music School (see: Home of the Blues Music School)
Brown's Bar (Detroit, MI), 370
Brown's Lounge (Chicago, IL), 404
Brubeck, Dave, 447
Bruce, Lennie, 141
Bruce's Log Cabin (club) (Wyandanch, NY), 90
Brunner, Ruby Lee, 277
Brunswick (label), 41, 56, 73, 79, 104, 106, 118, 134, 139, 155, 159, 222, 223, 227, 252, 281, 282, 288, 298, 321, 355, 357, 406, 411, 414, 467, 470, 524, 541, 559, 562, 581, 583
Brussels World's Fair (Brussels, Bel.), 174, 447, 519
Bruynoghe, Yannick, 69, 70, 86, 173, 299, 501, 524
Bryan, Salica, 558
Bryant, Beulah, **89-90,** *89*
Bryant, Otis, 90
Bryant, Paul, 78
Bryant, Willie, 518, 550
Buchanan, Celia, 193
Buchanan, Ed, 193
Buchauney, Nancy, 553
Buck, Dennis, 119
Buck, George, Jr., 37, 322
Buckingham Club (Chicago, IL), 334, 340
Buckingham Palace (government office) (London, Eng.), 592
Buckner, Teddy, 83
Bud Billiken Parade/Concert (Chicago, IL), 470, 538
Buddah (label), 78, 114, 132, 138, 178, 224, 241, 309, 389, 513, 523
Buddie's Club (Chicago, IL), 208
Buddy Boy (see: Guy, George)
Buddy's Place (club) (New York, NY), 418, 432, 567
Budweiser Beer (product), 108, 432
Buffalo Bearcats (band), 263
Buffalo Folk Festival (Buffalo, NY), 378, 538, 566
Buffalo Nickel (club) (Buffalo Grove, IL), 322
Buford, George "Mojo" (Muddy Waters Jr.), **90-91,** *91,* 101, 269, 311, 342, 390, 435, 476, 571, 578
Bull, Frank, 154
Bull City Red (see: Washington, George)
Bull Cow (see: Burnett, Chester)
Bullet (label), 110, 150, 155, 191, 216, 232, 308, 403, 489, 514, 569
Bulls (club) (Chicago, IL), 106
Bumble Bee Slim (see: Easton, Amos)
Bunch, James, 551
Bunch, William, 551
Bungalow (club), The (Chicago, IL), 32, 250
Bunk House (club), The (San Francisco, CA), 440
Bunkhouse (club), The (Vancouver, Can.), 557
Bunn, Alden (Tarheel Slim), 70, **91-93,** *92,* 148, 185, 368, 391, 503
Bunn, Ann, 92
Bunn, Henry, 91
Bunn, Teddy, 385
Burdette Tomlin Memorial Hospital (Cape May Court House, NJ), 584
Burdon, Eric, 116, 224, 588
Buried Alive (book), 296, 297
Burkhart, Jay, 564
Burks, John, 225
Burley, Dan, 364
Burne, Jerry, 116
Burnett, Chester (Howlin' Wolf), 27, 28, 29, 35, 72, **93-95,** *94,* 101, 130, 139, 199, 246, 276, 289, 290, 291, 294, 334, 341, 343, 345, 349, 360, 368, 396, 397, 407, 409, 425, 442, 453, 459, 470, 476, 478, 488, 493, 535, 549, 563, 564, 571, 577, 578, 589, 596
Burnett, Dock, 93
Burning Bush Band, The, 348
Burning Eight (band), 418
Burning Spear (club), The (Chicago, IL) (see also: New Burning Spear), 51, 104, 115, 304, 308, 309, 389, 407, 572
Burns, Annie, 484
Burns, Eddie, **95-96,** *96,* 225, 354, 576, 578
Burns, George, 479
Burns, Mary, 551
Burr Oak Cemetery (Worth, IL), 35, 127, 478, 538, 551
Burrell, Kenny, 445
Burris, J.C., **96-98,** *97,* 184, 505
Burse, Charlie, **98,** *98,* 454, 455, 547
Burse, Robert, 98
Burse, Robert, 98
Burt Levy's Circuit, 581
Burton, Buzzin', 274, 462
Bush, Josie, 89
Butch's Club (La Honda, CA), 439
Butler, Beulah, 535
Butler, George "Wild Child," **99,** *99,* 150, 244, 578
Butlin Holiday Camps (England), 245
Butterbeans & Susie (duo) (see also: Edwards, Jody) (see also: Edwards, Susie), 172, 173, 467, 474, 558
Butterfield, Erskine, 39
Butterfield, Paul, 54, **99-101,** *100,* 269, 390, 393, 395, 493, 549, 578
Butterfield Blues Band, 95, 99

Byas, Don, 253
Byrd, Henry Roeland, 101
Bryd, James Lucius, 101
Bryd, John, 290
Bryd, Richard E., 496
Byrd, Robert, 101
Byrd, Roy (Professor Longhair), **101-103**, *102*, 158, 167, 594
Byrd's Nest (club) (Washington, DC), 447

C&F (label), 125
C&J Lounge (Chicago, IL), 393
C&P Lounge (Houston, TX), 43, 57, 453
C&T Lounge (Chicago, IL), 294, 393, 548, 559
CBS (label), 41, 57, 70, 121, 210, 238, 266, 322, 345, 382, 432
C.H. Cobbs Baptist Church (Chicago, IL), 562
CJ (label), 237, 238, 266
C.J.K. Medicine Show (tour), 101
CTI (label), 417
C.W. Parks Minstrels (tour), 427-8
CYO Jazz Festival (Pittsburgh, PA), 567
Cab-A-Bob Club (Toronto, Can.), 84
Cabale Club/Coffeehouse (Berkeley, CA), 98, 141, 147, 161, 185, 243, 330, 461, 512, 553
Cabaret Moonlight Inn (Chicago, IL), 592
Cabin Club (New York, NY), 152
Cabin In the Sky Club (Chicago, IL), 542
Cabin Inn (Chicago, IL), 229, 564
Cabin Inn (St. Louis, MO), 433, 552
Cabo-Verdi Cafe (San Francisco, CA), 185
Cabooze (club), The (Minneapolis, MN), 156
Cabrera, Felix, 393
Cabriolet (club), The (Libertyville, IL), 381
Cadence (magazine), 27, 59, 116, 175, 217, 286, 287, 342, 349, 392, 402, 413, 427, 489, 533, 535
Cadet (label), 216, 522, 535
Cadillac Baby('s) Bar/Club/Lounge (Chicago, IL), 41, 123, 169, 271, 286, 305, 340, 368, 438, 460, 499, 545, 563
Cadillac Baby Specials (group), 266
Cadillac Bob's Toast of the Town Club (Chicago, IL), 125, 343, 383
Cadillac Club (Chicago, IL), 188
Cadillac Hotel (Detroit, MI), 423
Cadillac Jake (see: Harris, James D.)
Caesar's Palace (hotel) (Las Vegas, NV), 309
Caesar's Roman Theater (Las Vegas, NV), 411
Cafe A Go-Go (New York, NY), 46, 93, 99, 100, 132, 142, 210, 218, 224, 230, 239, 249, 257, 272, 286, 304, 308, 327, 388, 478, 521, 527, 548, 553, 569, 586, 595
Cafe Bizarre (New York, NY), 217
Cafe Campus (Montreal, Can.), 33, 151, 209, 260, 549
Cafe Concert (club) (Tarzana, CA), 588
Cafe Continentale (Chicago, IL), 141
Cafe de Paris (Chicago, IL), 540
Cafe de Paris (London, Eng.), 541
Cafe Galerie (Detroit, MI), 280
Cafe Hannibal (Houston, TX), 523
Cafe Lena (Saratoga Springs, NY), 521
Cafe Nostalgique (Detroit, MI), 84
Cafe Rafio (New York, NY), 234
Cafe Society (Chicago, IL), 110, 154, 564
Cafe Society (New York, NY) (see also: Cafe Society Downtown/Uptown), 200, 406, 419, 446
Cafe Society Downtown (New York, NY), 68, 134, 252, 405, 503, 518, 550, 556
Cafe Society Orchestra, 518
Cafe Society Uptown (New York, NY), 518, 556
Cafe Superior (Newark, NJ), 550
Cafe Wha? (New York, NY), 217, 224
Cafe Yana (Boston, MA), 147, 257
Cage, James "Butch," **103**, 231, 481, 512
Cahn, Nick, 142
Cahn, Rolf, 142
Cahoon, Franz, 452
Cain, Perry, **103**
Cain Raisers (band), 139
Cakehouse, Gordon, 63
Calamity Jane (pseudonym), 296
Caldonia Inn (New Orleans, LA), 101
Caldonia Lounge (Chicago, IL), 213
Calicott, Joe (see: Callicott, Joe)
California Blues Band, 439
California Club (Los Angeles, CA), 497, 513
California Hotel (Oakland, CA), 308
California State Polytechnic College (San Luis Obispo, CA), 114, 456
California to the New York Island (book), 206
Californians (band), 203
Callender, Howard, 200
Callender, Red, 136
Callicott, Joe, **103-104**, 486
Callicutt, Joe (see: Callicott, Joe)
Callie's Place (club) (Chicago, IL), 527
Calliope Street Cafe (New Orleans, LA), 128
Calloway, Cab, 392, 496, 525, 581
Cal's Corner (club) (Chicago, IL), 345
Calt, Stephen "Steve," 118, 120, 160, 192, 229, 486, 547
Calumet Bar (Detroit, MI), 578
Calumet Hotel (St. Louis, MO), 150
Calumet Show Club (Detroit, MI), 225
Calvin, Heneretta, 589
Calvin, Robert, 482
Calypso Club (New York, NY), 82
Camay (label), 253
Cambridge Folk Festival (Cambridge, Eng.), 147
Camelot Club (Chicago, IL), 381
Camelot Club (Jackson, MS), 395
Cameo (label), 221, 357, 584
Cameo Club (Rochester, NY), 285
Cameo Girl (billing), 221
Camil Productions (organization), 104
Camp, Red, 373
Camp Virgil Tate (Princeton, WV), 175, 177, 195
Campaign for Nuclear Disarmament (organization), 142
Campbell, Charlie, 356
Campbell, Chocker, 188, 529
Campbell, David, 178
Campbell, James, 104
Campbell, Milton (Little Milton), 51, 88, **104-106**, *105*, 152, 183, 299, 311, 338, 349, 412, 520, 528, 578
Campbell, Milton, Sr., 104
Campbell Jr. College (Jackson, MS), 478
Canadian Festival Express Show (tour), 208, 296
Canadian National Exhibition (show) (Toronto, Can.), 84, 208
Candid (label), 117, 193, 241, 243, 334, 478
Candle Lit Club (Dallas, TX), 283
Candlelight Club, The (Muncie, IN), 139
Cannady, Little, Jr., 528
Canned Heat (band), 117, 240, 241, 339, 548
Canned Heat Electric Band, 345
Cannon, Gus, 62, **106-107**, *106*, 264, 325, *325*, 326, 327, 561
Cannon, John, 106
Cannon & Woods (duo), 106
Cannon's Jug Stompers (trio), *325*
Canterbury House (club) (Ann Arbor, MI), 218
Canton (label), 201
Cantor, Eddie, 362
Capitol (label), 39, 67, 89, 132, 141, 175, 224, 317, 321, 363, 365, 366, 373, 393, 407, 431, 503, 523, 525, 527, 588
Capitol-Bullfrog (label), 444
Capitol Lounge (Chicago, IL), 110, 154, 298
Capitol Palace Cabaret (New York, NY), 373, 583
Capitol Palace Cafe (New York, NY), 373
Capitol Theater (Chicago, IL), 310
Capitol Theater (Dunkirk, NY), 82
Capitol Theater (Flint, MI), 70
Capitol Theater (Hartford, CT), 82
Capitol Theater (Montreal, Can.), 33, 210, 240, 305, 310
Capitol Theater (New Britain, CT), 82
Capitol Theater (New York, NY), 536, 541, 542, 581
Capitol Theater (Passaic, NJ), 100, 309
Capitol Theater (Trenton, NJ), 82, 472
Capitol Theater (Union Hill, NJ), 70
Capitol-Track (label), 224
Cappuccio, Robert, 345
Capri Club (Hollywood, CA), 527
Capricorn (label), 506
Captain's Table (club) (St. Louis, MO), 414
Caravan Hotel (Edmonton, Can.), 377
Carbin, Fred, 485
Cardinal (label), 540
Cardinals' Nest (club) (St. Louis, MO), 489

Carey, Mutt, 507
Caribbean Lounge (Los Angeles, CA), 137
Caribe Hilton Hotel (San Juan, PR), 310
Carioca Club (Cleveland, OH), 145
Carlson, Jeff, 334
Carlton Theater (Red Bank, NJ), 472
Carnegie Hall (New York, NY), 45, 68, 84, 100, 113, 114, 117, 130, 132, 134, 142, 147, 158, 174, 194, 195, 206, 210, 218, 219, 229, 240, 243, 245, 249, 252, 253, 257, 272, 279, 304, 309, 352, 359, 366, 375, 380, 388, 389, 406, 429, 431, 434, 446, 453, 466, 470, 478, 481, 496, 497, 503, 504, 512, 513, 518, 520, 521, 522, 523, 525, 527, 536, 538, 541, 553, 556, 566, 567, 569, 572, 586, 591, 592
Carnegie Recital Hall (New York, NY), 388
Carnival (label), 99
Carnival of Swing Show (New York, NY), 446
Carolina Blackbirds (band), 492
Carolina Cotton Pickers (band), 383
Carolina Slim (see: Harris, Edward)
Carolinians (band), The, 556
Carolyn (label), 468
Carousel Club (Oakland, CA), 125
Carousel Motor Hotel (St. Louis, MO), 338
Carousel Theater (Framingham, MA), 309
Carousel Theater (Los Angeles, CA), 431
Carpenter, Ike, 536
Carpenter, Thelma, 544
Carr, Carol, 557
Carr, Dora, 144, 145
Carr, Gunter Lee (see: Gant, Cecil)
Carr, John, 107
Carr, Leroy, 48, 49, 63, **107-108**, *107*, 150, 161, 166, 168, 182, 191, 233, 322, 348, 356, 413, 448, 479, 524, 528, 551, 552
Carr, Sam, 183, 399
Carradine, William (Cat-Iron), **108**
Carriage House (club) (Rochester, NY), 322
Carroll, Albertha, 108
Carroll, Jeanne, **108-109**, *108*
Carr's Beach Club (Annapolis, MD), 263
Carson, Johnny, 114, 141, 210, 218, 219, 224, 257, 308, 327, 411, 417, 431, 432, 543, 566, 567, 568, 588
Carson, Nelson, **109**
Carter, Benny, 436, 518, 550
Carter, Bo (see: Chatmon, Armenter)
Carter, Bunny (see: Collins, Sam)
Carter, Charlie (see: Jackson, Charlie)
Carter, Erylie, 509
Carter, Goree, 78
Carter, Joe, **109-110**, *109*, 271
Carter, Nelson (see: Carson, Nelson)
Carter Barron Amphitheater (Washington, DC), 431
Carter Brothers (band), 524
Carumet (label), 117
Carver Boys (group), 556
Cary, Clara (see: Beaman, Lottie)
Casa Blanca Club (Greenville, MS), 59, 338
Casa Blanca Club (New Iberia, LA), 453, 547
Casa de las Americas (label), 142
Casa Fiesta Club (Kansas City, MO), 88
Casa Madrid (club) (Chicago, IL), 123
Casa Madrid (club) (Louisville, KY), 89
Casa Manana Club (New York, NY), 541
Casablanca Club (Chicago, IL), 380
Casablanca Club (Los Angeles, CA), 385, 527
Casablanca Club (Youngstown, OH), 485
Casba Bar (Houston, TX), 103
Casbah Club/Lounge (Detroit, MI), 84, 535
Casbah Lounge (Chicago, IL), 78, 305
Cascais Jazz Festival (Cascais, Portugal), 195
Caserta, Peggy, 296, 297
Casey Bill (see: Weldon, Will), 355
Cash (label), 28, 154, 277, 353
Cashbox (magazine), 51, 76, 296
Casino (club), The (Bern, Switz.), 379
Casino de Paris (Paris, Fr.), 256
Casino Royale (Washington, DC), 519, 538
Casino Theater (Brooklyn, NY), 173
Casino Theater (New York, NY), 227
Casper, Jazz, 374
Cass County Hospital (Rural Jefferson Township, MI), 488
Cassell's Lounge (Long Island City, NY), 316
Cassidy Hotel (Richmond, CA), 358
Castell, Michele, **110**
Castell, Robb, 110
Castle, Henry Lee, 514
Castle, Lee, 84
Castle, Vernon (Mrs.), 475
Castle Creek (club) (Austin, TX), 244
Castle Farm (club) (Cincinnati, OH), 434
Castle Frank (club) (Toronto, Can.), 453
Castle, George (club) (Toronto, Can.), 280
Castle Rock Lounge (Chicago, IL) (see also: New Castle Rock), 35, 359, 442, 444, 476, 479, 570, 596
Caston, Leonard "Baby Doo," 50, **110-111**, *155*
Castro, Fidel, 142
Casuals on the Square (club) (Oakland, CA), 322
Caswell Cemetery (Kimball, MI), 204
Cat (label), 37, 154
Cat and the Fiddle Club (New Orleans, LA), 420
Cat Iron (see: Carradine, William)
Catacombs (club), The (Boston, MA), 345
Catagonia Club (Pod's & Jerry's) (New York, NY), 231, 484
Catalina (label), 278
Cathedral Church of St. John the Divine (New York, NY), 567
Catjuice Charlie (see: McDaniel, Harry)
Catjuice Charley (see: Hicks, Charlie)
Cats (band), The, 199
Cat's Cradle (club) (San Francisco, CA), 154, 190, 439-440, 516, 520
Cavalcade of Jazz (concert) (Los Angeles, CA), 86
Cavalcade of Jazz (concert) (Philadelphia, PA), 113
Cavalier (label), 185
Cavalier Club (Little Rock, AR), 149
Cavalier Club (Port Chester, NY), 90
Cavalier Magazine, 557
Cavalier Show Lounge (Chicago, IL), 123
Cavaliers (band), The, 517
Cavatone (label), 357
Cave Supper Club, The (Vancouver, Can.), 90, 375
Caverns (club), The (Washington, DC), 90
Cedar Club (see: Don's Cedar Club)
Cedar Gardens Club (Cleveland, OH), 263
Cedar Springs School for Blind People (Spartanburg, SC), 146
Celebrity (label), 164
Celebrity Club (Freeport, NY), 165
Celebrity Club (New York, NY), 39, 83, 221, 481, 491
Celebrity Club (Providence, RI), 298, 519, 527
Celeste (label), 28
Celestin, Papa, 145, 164, 203
Cellar (club), The (Chicago, IL), 93
Cellar (club), The (Philadelphia, PA), 280
Cellar Door (club), The (Washington, DC), 304, 557, 567
Cellar Dwellers (band), 230
Cemetery of the Evergreens (Brooklyn, NY), 221
Cenco (label), 546
Centaur (club), The (Montreal, Can.), 195
Centaur Club (Chicago, IL), 41, 595
Centennial Folk Festival (Winnipeg, Can.), 553
Center (label), 420
Center (club), The (Philadelphia, PA), 280
Center Arena (Seattle, WA), 113
Center for New Music (New York, NY), 92
Center for Southern Folklore (organization) (Memphis, TN), 163, 509
Center Raven Baptist Church (Gray Court, SC), 145
Centerville Cemetery (Centerville, TX), 241
Central High School (Cleveland, OH), 261
Central High School (Omaha, NE), 215
Central Illinois Jazz Festival (Decatur, IL), 314, 322
Central Park Music Festival (New York, NY) (see also: Rheingold Music Festival) (see also: Dr. Pepper's Central Park Music

Festival), 46, 113, 114, 132, 137, 157, 195, 208, 218, 224, 240, 308, 309, 388, 389, 411, 431
Central Plaza (hall) (New York, NY), 39, 90, 164, 206, 229, 318, 365, 385, 406, 408, 481, 503, 582
Central Theater (Dallas, TX), 464
Century (label), 380
Century of Progress (World's Fair) (Chicago, IL), 134, 274, 568
Century Plaza Hotel (Los Angeles, CA), 432, 567
Century Room (club) (Kansas City, MO), 88
Century Theater (New York, NY), 254
Cham Fields (club) (Memphis, TN), 264, 326
Chambers Brothers (group), 142, 330
Chamblee, Eddie, 538
Champion (label), 49, 68, 98, 137, 159, 176, 288, 348, 355, 401, 403, 438, 450, 454, 489, 546, 547
Champion Bar (Detroit, MI), 83
Champion-Decca (label), 49
Champion Theater (Birmingham, AL), 405, 445
Champs-Elysees Theater (Paris, Fr.), 152
Chance (label), 225, 238, 259, 340, 342, 394, 400, 434, 452, 479, 493, 570, 574
Chancellor (label), 220
Chances Are Club (Chicago, IL), 65
Chandler, Len, 207
Chaney's Club (Beaumont, TX), 353
Channel Gardens (walkway) (New York, NY), 254
Chantalier Club (Newark, NJ), 550
Chantilly's Lace Club (Los Angeles, CA), 137, 179, 213, 353
Chapel Hill Hospital (Durham, NC), 516
Chappel, Gus, 536
Charisse Lounge (Chicago, IL), 155
Charity, Pernell, **111**, *111*, 184, 244
Charity Gospel Singers (group), 425
Charles, Antoinette, 244
Charles, Henry (see: Brown, Henry)
Charles, Maceo, 371
Charles, Ray, 31, 37, 38, 76, **111-116**, *112*, 136, 138, 154, 167, 190, 211, 219, 278, 293, 299, 353, 390, 517, 520
Charles, Ray, 115
Charles Hotel (Washington, DC), 153
Charles Street Coffeehouse (Boston, MA), 486
Charleston Chasers (band), 496
Charley Patton (book), 409, 494
Charlie Douglas Theater (Macon, GA), 172
Charlie Letts Cafe (Chicago, IL), 221
Charlie Palooka's (club) (New Orleans, LA), 420
Charlie's Lounge (Chicago, IL), 79, 271, 574
Charlotte's Web (Rockford, IL), 33, 57, 349, 367, 499, 505
Charly (label), 28
Charters, Samuel B. "Sam," 29, 34, 57, 59, 86, 107, 108, 125, 127, 162, 166, 167, 176, 178, 226, 229, 244, 249, 252, 259, 273, 276, 289, 327, 328, 341, 354, 368, 370, 391, 392, 410, 417, 419, 455, 460, 474, 486, 507, 515, 554, 574
Chase, Charley, 362
Chateau Club (Houston, TX), 125
Chateau de Count et Eve Club (Indianapolis, IN), 388
Chateau Restaurant (Denver, CO), 195
Chatman, Bo (see: Chatmon, Armenter)
Chatman, Christine, 470
Chatman, John Len, 116
Chatman, Peter (Memphis Slim), 38, 62, 63, 68, 70, 108, **116-118**, *116*, 141, 145, 155, 193, 208, 268, 342, 461, 467, 478, 485, 490, 491, 510, 527, 548, 577
Chatman, Peter, Sr., 116
Chatman, Sam (see: Chatmon, Sam)
Chatman Brothers (group) (see also: Chatmon Brothers), 120
Chatmon, Armenter "Bo," **118-119**, *118*, 119, 120, 355, 524, 595
Chatmon, Burt, 119
Chatmon, Charlie, 119
Chatmon, Edgar, 119, 595
Chatmon, Harry, 119, 524
Chatmon, Henderson, 118, 119
Chatmon, Lamar, 119
Chatmon, Larry, 119
Chatmon, Lonnie, 119, 120, 524, 595
Chatmon, Sam, 119, **119-120**, *119*, 276, 280, 509
Chatmon, Sam "Singing Sam," 120
Chatmon, Ty, 119
Chatmon, Willie, 119
Chatmon Brothers (group) (see also: Chatman Brothers), 80, 350, 409
Chatmon's Mississippi Hot Footers (band), 524
Chatta-Hoo-Chie (label), 154
Chatterbox (club), The (Cleveland, OH), 527
Chatterbox Room (club) (Pittsburgh, PA), 446
Chauffeurs Club (St. Louis, MO), 288
Check (label), 28
Checker, Chubby, 158
Checker (label), 27, 55, 74, 96, 104, 121, 137, 154, 155, 162, 188, 199, 237, 269, 271, 286, 291, 317, 322, 334, 337, 350, 357, 359, 378, 388, 393, 400, 460, 468, 478, 479, 484, 499, 517, 586
Checker-Chess (label), 67, 268, 359, 577
Checkerboard Lounge (Chicago, IL), 132, 208, 404, 429, 437, 499, 500, 549
Checkmate (club), The (Chicago, IL), 572
Cheetah (club) (Chicago, IL), 93, 99
Chelsea House Cafe (Brattleboro, VT), 481
Chenier, Cleveland, 120, 122
Chenier, Clifton, 67, **120-122**, *121*, 188, 192, 200, 243, 435, 530
Chenier, Joseph, 120
Chenier, Morris, 122
Cherrie (label), 554
Cherry Blossom Club (Kansas City, MO), 321, 382, 518
Cherry Lane Theater (New York, NY), 256
Cherry Red (label), 393
Cherryland (club) (Los Angeles, CA), 377
Chesapeake Bay Jazz Band, 313
Chess (label), 45, 46, 50, 54, 60, 63, 66, 67, 69, 85, 88, 93, 95, 100, 116, 132, 155, 169, 175, 179, 181, 199, 208, 238, 239, 246, 266, 269, 271, 277, 278, 291, 294, 322, 343, 353, 360, 378, 388, 389, 390, 398, 413, 442, 443, 444, 445, 457, 476, 478, 499, 510, 548, 563, 571, 574, 575, 578, 596
Chess Record Company (Chicago, IL), 277, 479
Chessmate (club) (Detroit, MI), 99, 187
Chestnut Hill Cemetery (Atlanta, GA), 251
Chez Florence Jones Cabaret (Paris, Fr.), 256, 581
Chez Mitchell Club (Paris, Fr.), 373
Chez Paree (club) (Chicago, IL), 200
Chez Paree Club (see: Gilmore's Chez Paree Club)
Chez Paris Club (Little Rock, AR), 450
Chi Chi Club, The (Oakland, CA), 510
Chicago (label), 569
Chicago All-Americans (baseball team), 592
Chicago All-Stars (band), 42, 155, 156, 178, 340, 341, 457
Chicago Auditorium (Chicago, IL), 461, 472
Chicago Bill (see: Broonzy, William)
Chicago Blues All-Stars (band), 41, 42, 156, 246, 266, 393
Chicago Blues Band, 389, 412, 512, 595
Chicago Blues Festival (Chicago, IL), 32, 67, 99, 104, 108, 148, 155, 177, 238, 246, 294, 334, 340, 341, 359, 381, 389, 404, 427, 461, 478, 481, 494, 499, 513, 529, 548, 569, 575, 595, 596
Chicago Blues Festival (tour), 68, 78, 151, 286, 300, 343, 394, 442, 457, 461, 488, 494, 499, 569, 591
Chicago Blues Stars (see: Chicago Blues All-Stars)
Chicago Bob (see: Nelson, Bob)
Chicago Bob Blues Band, 396
Chicago Breakdown (book), 67, 122, 138, 150, 181, 247, 272, 324, 371, 479, 575, 576
Chicago Broomdusters (band), 110
Chicago Conservatory of Music (Chicago, IL), 488
Chicago Cyclone (billing), 221
Chicago Film Festival (Chicago, IL), 244
Chicago Five (band), 559
Chicago Folk (Music) Festival (Chicago, IL), 272, 327, 478, 532
Chicago Hound Dogs (band), 294
Chicago Music Company (publisher) (Chicago, IL), 159, 175

Chicago Reader (magazine), 451, 501
Chicago Roadhouse Restaurant (Detroit, MI), 84
Chicago School of Music (Chicago, IL), 438
Chicago Stadium (Chicago, IL), 447, 566
Chicago Stompers (band), 313
Chicago String Band, 197
Chicago Sunny Boy (see: Louis, Joe Hill)
Chicago Theater (Chicago, IL), 541
Chicago Tribune (newspaper), 108
Chicago White Sox (baseball team), 592
Chickawaw Country Club (Memphis, TN), 454
Chicken Hawks (band), 220
Chicken Shack (club) (Chicago, IL), 388, 576
Chicken Shack (club) (Detroit, MI), 535
Chief (label), 237, 271, 345, 405, 548, 574
Chief Thundercloud Medicine Show (tour), 34, 261
Childe Harold (club), The (Washington, DC), 450
Childs Restaurant (New York, NY), 203
Chili Parlor (Dallas, TX), 382
Chilton, John, 31, 45, 257, 288, 299, 374, 386, 419, 448, 533
Chilton Inn (St. Louis, MO), 313
Chinchilly Club (Scranton, PA), 549
Chirrup (label), 67
Chitter-Chatter Club (Atlanta, GA), 415
Chittison, Herman, 542
Chittlins, Papa, 292
Chocolate Brown (see: Scruggs, Irene)
Chocolate Dandies (band), 279
Chocolate Kiddies (band), 581
Choice, Harriette, 108
Choice (label), 366, 503
Choo Choo Jazzers (band), 357, 385
Chrischaa (label), 148, 379
Christian, Charlie, 38, 137, 280, 336
Christian, J. T., 305
Christian Club (Houston, TX), 125
Christian Valley Cemetery (Silver City, MS), 501
Chuck's Club (Chicago, IL), 271
Chumley's Club (Waltham, MA), 573
Church of God & Christ (Hernando, MS), 91
Church of God in Christ (group), The, 65
Church of God in Christ Church (Memphis, TN), 383, 562
Church of God in the Saints of Christ (Greenville, SC), 555
Church's Park (W. C. Handy Park) (Memphis, TN), 62, 93, 106, 128, 161, 169, 246, 288, 327, 334, 454, 457, 486, 493, 535
Cincinnati (label), 452, 489
Cincinnati Gardens (club) (Cincinnati, OH), 224
Cinder Club (Houston, TX), 353
Cinderella Club (New York, NY), 481, 490
Cinderella Dance Palace (Little Rock, AR), 405, 445
Cinestage Theater (Chicago, IL), 566
Circle (label), 145, 229, 364, 365, 373, 406, 464, 492, 507
Circle Ballroom (Cleveland, OH), 308
Circle Cafe (Hollywood, CA), 527
Circle Club (Flint, MI), 63, 238, 372, 563
Circle Club (Vinton, LA), 78
Circle Inn (Chicago, IL), 574
Circle Star Theater (San Carlos, CA), 113, 114, 567
Ciro's (club) (Los Angeles, CA), 321
City Auditorium (Clarksdale, MS), 183
City Auditorium (Houston, TX), 308, 472
City Auditorium (Memphis, TN), 113
City Cemetery (E. Spartanburg, SC), 158
City Center Casino (New York, NY), 298
City Center Theater (New York City Center) (New York, NY), 218, 453, 466, 556
City College (New York, NY), 521
City College (Los Angeles, CA), 194
City College (San Francisco, CA), 98
City Hospital (Columbus, GA), 428
City of Memphis Hospital (Memphis, TN), 130, 553
City Opera House (Chicago, IL), 411, 444
City University of New York (New York, NY), 231
Civic Arena (Pittsburgh, PA), 309
Civic Auditorium (Albuquerque, NM), 434
Civic Auditorium (Atlanta, GA), 417
Civic Auditorium (Chicago, IL), 305, 407
Civic Auditorium (Jacksonville, FL), 307
Civic Auditorium (Pasadena, CA), 141, 373, 586
Civic Auditorium (Portland, OR), 208, 429, 549
Civic Auditorium (Santa Monica, CA), 45, 99, 114, 125, 141, 218, 219, 243, 352, 594
Civic Auditorium Music Hall (Omaha, NE), 51, 310
Civic Center (Atlanta, GA), 231, 457
Civic Center (Baltimore, MD), 100, 224, 296, 308, 309, 346, 431
Civic Center (San Francisco, CA), 346
Civic Center (San Gabriel, CA), 310, 520
Civic Center (Santa Monica, CA), 100
Civic Light Opera Theater (Glendale, CA), 179
Civic Opera House (Chicago, IL), 359, 417, 383, 388
Clairol Hair Products (product), 256
Clam House (club), The (New York, NY), 43, 256
Clamdiggers Piano Bar (Detroit, MI), 423
Clapton, Eric, 54, 269, 305, 307, 311, 528, 578
Clara Smith Theatrical Club (New York, NY), 467
Clarence Muse Vaudeville Company (tour), 295
Clarence Williams Music Publishing Company (New York, NY), 222
Clarence Williams Washboard Band, 331
Clarion (label), 584
Clark, Dave, 470
Clark, Dick, 45, 123, 157, 304, 357, 411, 431, 461, 510
Clark, Dorothy Ethel, 313
Clark, Jim, 266
Clark's Bar (St. Louis, MO), 502
Clayton, Buck, 194, 253, 447, 586
Clayton, Doc (see: Clayton, Peter)
Clayton, Jennie "Jenny," 454, 455
Clayton, Kid, 203
Clayton, Peter "Doc," 110, **122**, *123*, 148, 187, 311, 336, 339, 388, 588
Clayton, Peter, Sr., 122
Cleanhead (see: James, Elmore) (see: Vinson, Eddie)
Clearwater, Eddy, 47, **122-124**, *124*, 291, 345
Clearwater Saloon (Chicago, IL), 266
Clef (label), 566
Clef Club, The (Oakland, CA), 136
Cleighton, Peter (see: Clayton, Peter)
Clemens, Albert (see: Lofton, Clarence)
Clenn & Jenkins (duo), 279
Cleveland Arts Festival (Cleveland, OH), 470
Cleveland Metropolitan General Hospital (Cleveland, OH), 470
Cleveland State University (Cleveland, OH), 485
Click (club), The (Philadelphia, PA), 542
Cliff, Daisy (see: McCoy, Viola)
Cliff (label), 580
Climax Jazz Band, 165, 245, 322
Clock Lounge, The (Chicago, IL), 175, 343
Cloister (club), The (Los Angeles, CA), 113, 566
Cloister Club, The (Chicago, IL), 375
Cloisters (club), The (Chicago, IL), 141
Clouds Club, The (Honolulu, HI), 375
Clouds of Joy (group), 497
Clover Club (Portland, OR), 36
Club, The (Chicago, IL), 304, 308, 588
Club (label), 340
Club Alabam (Birmingham, AL), 53
Club Alabam (Los Angeles, CA), 215, 385, 523
Club Alabam (New York, NY), 82, 581
Club Alabam (Philadelphia, PA), 221, 357
Club Alex (Chicago, IL) (see: Alex Club)
Club Alibi (Chicago, IL), 35, 410, 438, 444, 460, 493, 516, 570, 589
Club Alley Cat (Toronto, Can.), 280
Club Aquarius (Chicago, IL), 404
Club Arden (Chicago, IL), 35, 343
Club Bali (New Orleans, LA), 505
Club Bali (Washington, DC), 298
Club Bamville (New York, NY), 373
Club Bandstand (St. Louis, MO), 45
Club Baron (New York, NY), 542, 567

Club Basin (Detroit, MI), 238
Club Bizarre (Canton, MS), 271
Club Cabana (Saginaw, MI), 563
Club Calvert (Miami, FL), 299, 538
Club Caravan (Newark, NJ), 550
Club Carribe (Detroit, MI), 96, 217, 238, 278, 578
Club Cheetah (New York, NY), 224
Club Claremont (Chicago, IL), 35
Club Columbia (Chicago, IL), 35
Club Copacabana (Honolulu, HI), 375
Club DeLisa (Chicago, IL), 72, 90, 200, 229, 308, 375, 383, 434, 457, 518, 564
Club DeLisa (Houston, TX), 235
Club DeLuxe (New York, NY), 373
Club des Rhythms Africans (Tangier, Morocco), 195
Club Desire (New Orleans, LA), 76
Club Ebony (Houston, TX), 523
Club 845 (see: 845 Club)
Club 53 (San Francisco, CA), 299, 538
Club Fortune (Reno, NV), 90
Club 47 (Cambridge/Boston, MA), 93, 99, 147, 208, 210, 211, 218, 239, 249, 272, 314, 388, 444, 521, 525, 548, 553, 573
Club Georgia (Chicago, IL), 62, 279, 559, 576, 577
Club Grenada (Galveston, TX), 86
Club H. (Bowling Green, OH), 151
Club Harlem (New York, NY), 491
Club Harlem (Winstonville, MS), 104
Club Haven (Westbury, NY), 90
Club Hello (Chicago, IL), 123
Club Hello Dolly (Chicago, IL), 381
Club Hollywood (Chicago, IL), 269, 501
Club Jakovac (St. Louis, MO), 414
Club Jamaica (Columbus, OH), 308
Club Jamboree (Chicago, IL), 66, 91, 181, 246, 294, 342, 393, 424, 434, 493, 571, 574
Club Jetty (Maui, HI), 78
Club Karen (Detroit, MI), 378
Club Kentucky (New York, NY), 481
Club Key Largo (see: Key Largo Club)
Club La Commedia (New York, NY), 256
Club La Jolla (San Francisco, CA), 358, 439, 554
Club La Veek (Houston, TX), 55, 190
Club Lolease (Chicago, IL), 322
Club Long Island (San Francisco, CA), 55, 190
Club Madrid (Cleveland, OH), 73
Club Matinee (Houston, TX), 50-51, 53
Club Maurice (New York, NY), 583
Club Miami (Hamilton, Can.), 263
Club Montmartre (Copenhagen, Den.), 69
Club Moonglow (Buffalo, NY), 84
Club Morocco (Little Rock, AR), 149, 308
Club Morocco (Winnipeg, Can.), 375
Club Neve (San Francisco, CA), 566
Club 99 (Joliet, IL), 67, 236, 332, 345, 388, 434, 563
Club Oasis (Los Angeles, CA), 538
Club Paradise (Memphis, TN), 304, 308
Club Peacock (see: Royal Peacock Club)
Club Pig Pen (New Orleans, LA), 420
Club Plantation (Detroit, MI), 96, 535, 578
Club Plantation (Los Angeles, CA), 89, 446, 527
Club Platmond (Chicago, IL), 460
Club Playtime (Bunkie, LA), 420
Club Playtime (Chicago, IL), 259
Club Ramonaga (London, Eng.), 256
Club Raven (Beaumont, TX), 547
Club Renaissance (see: Renaissance Club)
Club Rhumboogie (see: Rhumboogie Club)
Club Riviera (see: Riviera Club)
Club Robin Hood (New Orleans, LA), 86
Club Savoy (see: Savoy Club)
Club 77 (New Orleans, LA), 300
Club 76 (Toronto, Can.), 84, 420
Club Shalimar (Berkeley, CA), 55, 439
Club 68 (Hamilton, Can.), 176, 401, 427
Club 666 (Detroit, MI), 550
Club Streamline (Port Allen, LA), 308
Club Sudan (New York, NY), 550
Club Sue-B-Rue (Chicago, IL), 104
Club Sunset (Jackson, MS), 395
Club Supreme (Elizabeth, NJ), 90
Club Tay May (see: Tay May Club)
Club 34 (see: 34 Club)
Club Three Deuces (see: Three Deuces)
Club Three Sixes (see: Three Sixes Club)
Club Tijuana (Baltimore, MD), 538
Club Tijuana (New Orleans, LA), 293, 411
Club Troubadour (New York, NY) (see also: Troubadour Club), 298
Club Vegas (Dallas, TX), 547
Club Walahuje (Atlanta, GA), 293
Club Yana (Boston, MA), 210
Club Zanzibar (Chicago, IL) (see: Zanzibar Club)
Club Zanzibar (Nashville, TN), 191
Club Zanzibar (New York, NY), 44, 71, 523, 542
Club Zayante (Felton, CA), 121, 339
Club Zircon (Cambridge, MA), 379
Club Zodiac (Chicago, IL), 108, 124, 341, 461
Club Zombi (Detroit, MI), 83
Coach House (club) (Cleveland, OH), 336
Coach Stop (club) (Detroit, MI), 230
Coast to Coast Blues Band, 240
Cobb, Arnett, 78, 523
Cobb, Oliver, 281
Cobblestone (label), 309
Cobbs, Buddy, 225
Cobbs, Willie, **124-125**, 400, 425
Cobo Arena (Detroit, MI), 545
Cobo Hall (Detroit, MI), 431
Cobra (label), 155, 180, 181, 208, 246, 266, 269, 305, 340, 342, 345, 380, 394, 444, 571
Cobra Room (club) (Los Angeles, CA), 377
Coca Cola (product), 113
Cocker, Joe, 116
Cocoanut Grove (club) (Hollywood/Los Angeles, CA), 113, 114, 411, 431
Coda (magazine), 31, 33, 122, 149, 152, 166, 180, 185, 209, 217, 238, 347, 377, 442, 444, 470, 505, 514, 534, 544, 549, 553, 564, 578
Coffee & Confusion Coffeehouse (San Francisco, CA), 96-97
Coffee Gallery (club) (San Francisco, CA), 78, 98, 190, 260, 296, 393, 445
Coffey, Ira, 44
Cohen, A. M., 65
Cohen, Andy, 34, 147
Cohen, Dave, 330
Cohen, James, 532
Cohn, Lawrence "Larry," 70, 161, 276, 319, 347, 428
Cohn, Zinky, 385
Cokliss, Harley, 549
Cola, Kid Sheik, 203
Cole, Jay, 44, 550
Cole, Nat, 47, 76, 116, 383, 433, 436
Cole Brothers Carnival/Circus (tour), 179, 373
Coleman, Burl "Jaybird," **125**, 402
Coleman, Earthy Anne, 33
Coleman, Jaybird (see: Coleman, Burl)
Coleman, Joe, 86
Coleman, Lizzie, 125
Coleman, Margaret, 318
Coleman, Nelly (see: Wilson, Lena)
Coleman, Virgie, 545
Coleman (label), 288
Coleman Club, The (Lubbock, TX), 133
Colgate University (Hamilton, NY), 420
Coliseum, The (see also: Coliseum Theater/Colosseum, The)
Coliseum (Austin, TX), 84
Coliseum (Jackson, MS), 104
Coliseum, The (New Orleans, LA), 298
Coliseum, The (Oakland, CA), 431, 543
Coliseum, The (Seattle, WA), 224
Coliseum, The (Washington, DC), 435
Coliseum Theater (Chicago, IL), 145, 173, 229, 256, 279, 350, 507, 531
Coliseum Theater (New York, NY) (see: Keith Coliseum Theater)
Collector (label), 117, 569
Collectors Special (label), 577
College of Art (Manchester, Eng.), 351-352
College of Composition & Arranging (Chicago, IL), 159
College of Marin (Kentfield, CA), 30
Collegiate Ramblers (band), 380
Collins, ______, 506
Collins, Albert, 78, **125-127**, *126*, 244, 287, 311, 528
Collins, Annie Mae, 364
Collins, Jimmy, 401
Collins, John, 137
Collins, Judy, 207
Collins, Lacey, 574
Collins, Lee, 292
Collins, Little Mack (see: Collins, Mack)

Collins, Louis Bo (Mr. Bo), 55, **127**, *127*, 311
Collins, Mack (Little Mack), 127, 461
Collins, Marion, 501
Collins, Roger, 213
Collins, Samuel "Sam," **127-128**, 235
Collins, Samuel, Sr., 127
Collins, Tom (see: Dupree, William) (see: McGhee, Walter)
Colonial House (club) (Huntington Station, NY), 528-529
Colonial Park (club) (New York, NY), 447
Colonial Tavern (Toronto, Can.), 33, 51, 84, 93, 132, 219, 304, 310, 334, 341, 389, 390, 418, 447, 488, 513, 527, 566, 567
Colonial Theater (Allentown, PA), 70
Colonial Theater (New York, NY), 52, 374, 385, 583
Colonial Theater (Newport, RI), 82
Colony (label), 202, 533
Colony (club), The (Oakland, CA), 136
Colored Methodist Episcopal Church (Lyon, MS?), 247
Colored Sophie Tucker, The (billing), 362
Colored Waifs' Home for Boys (New Orleans, LA), 164
Colosseum (Ft. Worth, TX), 525
Colt (label), 574
Columbia (label), 33, 42, 53, 54, 68, 69, 73, 106, 108, 110, 118, 119, 125, 132, 153, 155, 156, 157, 158, 161, 174, 175, 195, 197, 210, 218, 221, 223, 226, 227, 228, 231, 246, 247, 251, 252, 254, 256, 279, 295, 296, 302, 315, 316, 317, 337, 345, 346, 347, 350, 355, 356, 357, 366, 369, 370, 373, 375, 381, 382, 385, 391, 403, 406, 408, 446, 447, 452, 463, 464, 465, 467, 484, 490, 494, 496, 503, 514, 525, 531, 540, 541, 546, 550, 556, 564, 569, 576, 580, 581, 583, 584, 585, 586
Columbia-CBS (label), 54
Columbia College (Chicago, IL), 95
Columbia Musical Company (Milwaukee, WI), 596
Columbia-Pix (label), 447
Columbia-Testament (label), 388, 457
Columbia Theater (New York, NY), 52, 173
Columbia Theater (Sharon, PA), 256
Columbia University (New York, NY), 209, 257, 317
Columbian Club (Chicago, IL), 596
Columbian Exposition (World's Fair) (Chicago, IL), 507
Comber, Chris, 441
Combo (label), 277, 302, 407, 544
Combo Boys (group), 439
Come For to Sing (book), 525
Comedy Club (Baltimore, MD), 549
Comet (label), 145, 527
Comiskey Park (ball park) (Chicago, IL), 592
Committee for US-Vietnamese Friendship (organization), 142
Commodore (label), 406
Community Center (see: Berkeley Community Center)
Community Church Auditorium (New York, NY), 556
Community College (Ashland, KY), 563
Community Hospital of San Diego (San Diego, CA), 277
Community Music Center (San Francisco, CA), 30, 120, 161, 439, 456, 516
Community Playhouse (Atlanta, GA), 420
Community Theater (Berkeley, CA), 224, 239, 304, 435, 439
Compared to What Club (Detroit, MI), 532
Compos, Rafael, 538
Compton, Clover, 373
Concert by the Sea (club) (Los Angeles, CA), 418, 567
Concert by the Sea (club) (Redondo Beach, CA), 254
Concert Hall (Stockholm, Swed.), 165, 408
Concerts at the Grove (club) (Los Angeles, CA), 51, 310, 418
Concord Club (Southampton, Eng.), 228
Concord's Coliseum (San Francisco, CA), 411
Condon, Eddie, 406, 447
Congo Club/Lounge (Detroit, MI), 88, 578
Congo Lounge (Chicago, IL), 563, 493
Congresge Bouw (club), The (The Hague, Holland), 310
Congress Centre (club) (The Hague, Holland), 33, 63, 114, 117, 240
Congress Hall Theater (Berlin, Ger.), 542
Congress Theater (Saratoga, NY), 82
Conn Instrument Company of Chicago (Chicago, IL), 481
Conn Trad (label), 558
Connecticut Traditional Jazz Club (Meriden, CT), 44, 108, 316, 550, 558
Conney, J. C., 572
Connie Mack Stadium (Philadelphia, PA), 538
Connies (label), 88
Connie's Combo (band), 572
Connie's Inn (club) (New York, NY), 31, 43, 256, 385, 464, 580, 581
Connie's On Lenox (club) (New York, NY), 84, 470
Connors Club (New York, NY), 221
Conqueror (label), 373, 556
Conservation Service Award, 207
Consolidated Cigar Corporation (product), 309
Consolidated circuit, 558
Constellation (label), 340
Constitution Hall (Washington, DC), 310, 431, 432
Contemporary (label), 36, 254
Contemporary Art Festival (Houston, TX), 420
Contemporary Arts Museum (Houston, TX), 122
Continental (hotel), The (Cairo, UAR), 256
Continental (label), 91, 164, 354, 406, 542, 564
Continental Club (Los Angeles, CA), 243
Continental Club (Oakland, CA) 55, 161, 188, 190, 213, 303, 357, 439, 508, 513, 520, 588
Continental Hall (Lenox Club) (New York, NY), 584
Continental Showcase (club) (Houston, TX), 51, 104, 121, 304, 310
Convention Center (Dallas, TX), 132
Convention Center (Louisville, KY), 431
Convention Center Auditorium (Pine Bluff, AR), 149
Convention Hall (Anaheim, CA), 224
Convention Hall (Asbury, NJ), 113
Convention Hall (Atlantic City, NJ), 44
Convention Hall (Miami, FL), 310
Conversation with the Blues (book), 288
Convocation Hall (Toronto, Can.), 367, 504
Conway Hall (London, Eng.), 165, 292, 302
Cooder, Ry, 147, 345
Cook, Ann, **128**, *128*
Cook, Bruce, 266, 396
Cook, Carl, 128
Cook, Gillian, 148
Cook, Otis, 419
Cook (label), 161, 373
Cook County Hospital (Chicago, IL), 39, 85, 122, 294, 336, 478, 501, 545
Cook County Jail (Chicago, IL), 309, 389, 402, 438
Cooke, Sam, 223, 402, 421, 431, 433, 508
Cooker, John Lee (see: Hooker, John Lee)
Cookery (restaurant), The (New York, NY), 195, 254, 256, 453, 520
Cool (label), 35
Cool Papa (see: Sadler, Haskell)
Cooper, Alice, 220
Cooper, Jimmie/Jimmy, 73, 173
Cooper, Ralph, 71, 231
Cooper, Rob, 455
Cooper, Sonny, 305, 438
Coot(s) (see: Grant, Leola B.)
Copa Cabana Club (Chicago, IL), 93, 150, 213, 239, 271, 345, 388, 478, 500
Copa City (club) (Jamaica, NY), 375
Copa City (club) (Los Angeles, CA), 74
Copa City (club) (Monterey, CA), 139
Copa City (club) (New York, NY), 586
Copacabana (club) (New York, NY), 113
Copacabana Club (Chicago, IL) (see: Copa Cabana Club)
Copley Square Hotel (Boston, MA), 141
Copper Penny Club (Farmington, NM), 78
Coq D'or (club) (Toronto, Can.), 33, 99, 132
Coral (label), 79, 519
Cork 'n' Fork Restaurant (Minneapolis, MN), 110

Corley, Dewey, **128-130**, *128*
Cornell Folk Festival (Ithaca, NY), 327, 459
Cornell University (Ithaca, NY), 427
Corner Tavern (Cleveland, OH), 308
Correctional Training Facility (prison) (Soledad, CA), 240
Cosby, Bill, 322
Cosimo Studio Band, 60
Cosmo Alley (club) (Hollywood, CA), 141
Cosmopolitan Club (E. St. Louis, IL), 45
Cosy Inn (Chicago, IL), 246, 501
Cotillion (label), 100, 219, 224, 305, 444
Cotillion Ballroom (Wichita, KS), 51
Cotten, Elizabeth "Libba," **129**, *130*
Cotten, Frank, 130
Cotton, James "Jimmy," 54, **130-132**, *131*, 390, 400, 468, 488, 516, 563, 578, 585
Cotton Bowl (club) (Edwardsville, IL), 314
Cotton Brothers (band), 348
Cotton Carnival (concert) (Memphis, TN), 106, 420
Cotton Club (Argo, IL), 305
Cotton Club (Atlantic City, NJ), 538
Cotton Club (Carteret, NJ), 92
Cotton Club (Chicago, IL), 168, 342, 344, 375, 388, 410, 460, 476, 479, 570, 574
Cotton Club (Cincinnati, OH), 252
Cotton Club (E. St. Louis, IL), 502, 589
Cotton Club (Indianapolis, IN), 49, 107, 164, 300
Cotton Club (Los Angeles, CA?), 398
Cotton Club (New Orleans, LA), 101
Cotton Club (New York, NY), 31, 43, 44, 82, 173, 221, 373, 464, 491, 541, 564, 581
Cotton Club, The (Paris, Fr.), 256
Cotton Club (Portland, OR), 30
Cotton Club (Trenton, NJ), 549
Cotton Club Orchestra, 525
Cotton Club Syncopators (band), 221
Cotton Festival (concert) (Memphis, TN), 84
Cotton Top Mountain Sanctified Singers (group), 274
Cottrell, Belle, 488
Cottrell, Louis, 506
Cougar Show Club (Chicago, IL), 499, 596
Coulters Chapel Cemetery (Cass County, MI), 488
Council, Floyd, **133**, *133*, 184, 552
Council of Foods and Nutrition (organization), 309
Count Basie and His Orchestra (book), 448, 568
Count Rockin' Sydney (see: Semien, Sidney)
Counterpoint (club) (Chicago, IL), 239
Countess Willie Piazza House (sporting house), 128
Coun-Tree (label), 304
Country Blues (book), The, 86, 107, 108, 244, 259, 276, 368, 410, 455
Country Boys (band), 366, 503
Country Music Encyclopedia (book), 441
Country Music Hall of Fame (museum) (Nashville, TN), 441
Country Paul (see: Harris, Edward)
Counts, Robert, 510
Court of Two Sisters (club) (New Orleans, LA), 202, 300, 326, 490, 506
Court Tavern (New Orleans, LA), 99
Courtney, Thomas "Tom," **133-134**, *133*, 528
Courtney (label), 398
Cousin Joe/Joseph (see: Joseph, Pleasant)
Covan's Club Morocco (New York, NY), 385
Covington, Ben (Bogus Ben), **134**, 568
Cow Palace (auditorium/hall) (Los Angeles, CA), 497
Cow Palace (hall) (San Francisco, CA), 113
Cowens, Herb, 44
Cowtown Ballroom (Kansas City, MO), 100
Cox, Adler, 134
Cox, Geraldine "Jerri," 407
Cox, Ida, 84, **134-136**, *135*, 139, 142, 263, 382, 406, 420, 421, 450, 464, 525, 528, 550, 558
Coy, Carol, 130
Coy, Gene, 284
Cozy Bar (Minneapolis, MN), 91, 342, 389, 407
Cozy Corner Club (Chicago, IL), 62, 68, 116, 457
Cozy Inn (Chicago, IL), 169
Cozy Lounge (Los Angeles, CA), 546
Cozy Smith Troupe (tour), 592
Crab Tree Brothers Club (Richmond, CA), 188
Crabtree, Will, 273
Craig Corporation (product), 114
Cramer, Alex, 442, 549
Crank Lounge (St. Louis, MO), 45
Crash (label), 345
Crawdaddy Club (London, Eng.), 577
Crawdaddy Magazine, 138
Crawford, James Lloyd, 362
Crawford, Ollie, 110
Crawford, Pete, 336
Crayton, Connie "Pee Wee," **136-137**, *136*, 188, 233, 407, 519, 520, 528
Crazy Al's (club) (Indianapolis, IN), 427
Crazy Cajun (label), 121
Crazy Music (magazine), 38, 42, 98, 213, 236, 287, 438
Cream (band), 95
Creath, Charlie, 279, 282
Creation (club), The (Encino, CA), 304
Creedence Clearwater (band), 359
Creedmore State Hospital (Queens, NY), 206
Creighton University (Omaha, NE), 215
Creole Jazz Band, 203
Creole Jazz Hounds (band), 373
Creole Songbird (billing), 48, 374
Crescendo (label), 38, 166, 506
Crescendo Club (Hollywood, CA), 566
Crescent City Joymakers (band), 203
Cricket Lounge (Chicago, IL), 595
Crippen, Catherine, 137
Crippen, John, 137
Crippen, Katie, 137
Crippen & Brown (duo), 137
Crispus Attucks High School (Indianapolis, IN), 181
Crissman, Lefty Lou, 205
Critic Looks at Jazz (book), A, 56
Crocket, Ida, 200
Cromwell, Odie, 43
Cromwell's Restaurant (San Francisco, CA), 30
Crosby, Bing, 362, 541
Cross, Joe, 79
Cross Keys Theater (Philadelphia, PA), 70
Cross Road Cemetery (Starkville, MS), 344
Crossover (label), 114
Crossroads Club (Detroit, MI), 542
Crossroads Productions Company, 432
Crowley Louisiana Blues (book), 228, 384
Crown (label), 232, 308, 490, 586
Crown Hill Cemetery (Indianapolis, IN), 182, 202
Crown Lounge (Chicago, IL), 188
Crown Propeller (club) (Chicago, IL), 53, 120, 375, 378, 530
Crudup, Arthur "Big Boy," 59, 70, 116, **137-139**, *138*, 178, 271, 313, 324, 426, 429, 444, 509, 560, 577
Crudup, Percy Lee (see: Crudup, Arthur)
Crudux, Art (see: Crudup, Arthur)
Crump, Arthur (see: Crudup, Arthur)
Crump, Georgianna, 271
Crump, Jesse, 134, **139**
Crusoe, Mary, 294
Crutchfield, Jimmy, 438
Cry (label), 283
Cryin' Red (see: Minter, Iverson)
Crying for the Carolines (book), 34, 185, 370, 391, 531
Crystal Bar (Detroit, MI), 370
Crystal Caverns (club) (Washington, DC), 550
Crystal Gazers Club (New Orleans, LA), 157
Crystal Grill (Oakland, CA), 439
Crystal Lake Ballroom (Ellington, CT), 389
Crystal Saloon, The (Juneau, AK), 367, 505
Crystaliers (band), The, 585
Cuban Room, The (Kansas City, MO), 321
Cuca (label), 238
Cue (label), 78
Cuesta, Henry, 84
Cullen, Thomas J., III, 132, 157
Culley, Frank, 447
Cummings, Tony, 74, 116, 290, 301, 348
Cunningham, Chesley, 52
Cureay, Ida, 363

Curley's Bar (Chicago, IL), 208, 444
Curran Theater (San Francisco, CA), 542
Current Biography (book), 196, 207, 363
Curtis, James "Peck," **139-140,** *139,* 371, 483, 577
Curtis, John, 139
Curtis, King, 60, 223, 312, 470
Curtis, Peck (see: Curtis, James)
Curtis Coleman Club (Gulfport, MS), 379
Curtis Hixon Hall (Tampa, FL), 296
Curtiss, Lou, 120, 274
Curtiss, Virginia, 133, 277
Cypress Hills Cemetery (Glendale, NY), 557
Cypress Lawn Memorial Park (Colma, CA), 440
Cypress View Cemetery (San Diego, CA), 277

DIR (label), 443
DJ's Bar/Tavern (Toronto, Can.), 245, 322
DJM (label), 74, 544
DRA (label), 88
DRC Dixielanders (band), 230
DRC Racetrack (Detroit, MI), 230
DTP (label), 502
Daddy Deep Throat (see: Cain, Perry)
Daddy of the Blues (billing), 527
Daddy Stovepipe (see: Watson, Johnny)
Dago Frank's Cafe (Chicago, IL), 254
Dailey Brothers Circus (tour), 133
Daily Worker (newspaper), The, 205
Daisy Maes (club) (Los Angeles, CA), 53
Dakota Inn (Detroit, MI), 423
Dale, Flora (see: Brown, Ida G.) (see: Henderson, Rosa)
Dalio's (club) (New Orleans, LA), 326
Dallas, Leroy, **140,** 171, 172, 365
Dallas Art Museum (Dallas, TX), 319
Dallas Cemetery (Dallas, TX), 406
Dallas Jamboree Jug Band, 145
Dallas String Band, 525
Dallas Texas Jubilee Singers, The, 272
Dallas Theater (Dallas, TX), 134
Dalton, David, 296, 297
Dalton Saloon (Cleveland, OH), 556
Daly's 63rd Street Theater (see: 63rd Street Theater)
Damen (label), 383
Dance, Stanley, 299, 501, 524
Dance Bands (book), The, 257
Dancer, Earl, 540
Dandridge, Putney, 279
Dane, Barbara, 136, **140-142,** *140,* 231, 319, 330, 374, 428, 465, 559, 591, 592
Danger Bar (New Orleans, LA), 418
Danny Boy's (club) (Houston, TX), 199
Darby, Ike, **142,** *143*
Darby, Theodore "Teddy," **142, 144,** *144,* 552
Darby (label), 142
Darensbourg, Joe, 373
Darin, Bobby, 116
Darnell, Larry, 216
Dart (label), 215
Davenport, Charles "Cow Cow," 117, **144-145,** *144,* 356, 438
Davenport, Clement, 144
Davenport, Cow Cow (see: Davenport, Charles)
Davenport, Jed, **145,** 161, 355
Davenport & Company (tour), 144
Davenport & Smith (duo), 145
Davenport Hotel (Spokane, WA), 36
Dave's Rhumboogie Club (Chicago, IL), 536
David & Mason's Club (Chicago, IL), 388
David & Thelma's Lounge (Chicago, IL), 488-489
Davies, Cyril, 269, 577
Davies, Diana, 138, 174, 525
Davis, ______, 401
Davis, Bob, 145
Davis, Bobby, 571
Davis, Carl, **145,** 280
Davis, Charlie, 355
Davis, Coot, 479
Davis, Gary, 59, 93, 141, **146-148,** *146,* 184, 283, 347, 368, 386, 416, 454, 503, 522
Davis, Hammie, 401
Davis, Henrietta, 74
Davis, Irene, 584
Davis, Jasper, 373
Davis, Jimmie, 589
Davis, Jimmy (see: Thomas, Charles)
Davis, John, 146
Davis, John, 149
Davis, John "Johnny," 149
Davis, John H. (Blind John Davis), 69, **148-149,** *148,* 166
Davis, John Henry, Jr., 149
Davis, John Wesley, 148
Davis, Larry, 88, **149,** *149,* 311, 437
Davis, Madlyn, 559
Davis, Mary Lee "Mama," 435
Davis, Maxwell, 76, 136
Davis, Miles, 211
Davis, Sister, 147
Davis, Tyrone, 445
Davis, Walter, 107, **149-150,** *149,* 278, 403, 514, 515
Davis, Walter, Jr., 150
Davis Plantation (Clarksdale, MS), 589
Davis Theater (Pittsburgh, PA), 70
Davison, Lula, 552
Davison, Rev. Punk, 552
Davison, Wild Bill, 141, 245
Dawkins, James "Jimmy," 32, 38, 41, 106, **150-152,** *151,* 326, 341, 343, 404, 444, 445, 494, 530
Dawn Club (label), 373
Dawson, Mary, 386
Day, Bobby, 101
Day, Edith, 256
Day, Odell, 281
Daybreak Plantation (Belzoni, MS), 271
Daylighters (band), The, 571
Daynes-Wood, Bill, 223
De Forrest, Maude, **152**
DeGaston, Gallie, 273
DeJean, Harold, 300
DeKoster, Jim, 78, 326, 459, 560, 595
De Leath, Vaughn, 73, 494
DeLegge, Boisy, 428
DeLuxe (label), 86, 96, 238, 300, 326, 419
De Luxe Cafe (Chicago, IL), 221, 254, 373
DeLuxe Club (see: Hughes DeLuxe Club)
DeLuxe Music Shop (St. Louis, MO), 281
DeLuxe Restaurant (St. Louis, MO), 281, 283
DeMont, William "Billy," 81, 82, 83
DeParis, Wilbur, 586
DeSanto, Sugar Pie, 510
DeWitt Clinton Community Center (New York, NY), 82
Dead End Productions (organization), 432
Dean, Joe, 42
Decca (label), 35, 39, 44, 57, 60, 63, 79, 88, 91, 103, 110, 144, 145, 161, 165, 167, 176, 184, 191, 197, 198, 203, 215, 217, 220, 232, 234, 239, 243, 246, 251, 252, 253, 256, 263, 267, 274, 279, 281, 284, 285, 288, 292, 297, 298, 300, 322, 330, 334, 348, 355, 364, 365, 369, 381, 382, 385, 398, 401, 403, 405, 406, 408, 417, 419, 433, 436, 446, 452, 453, 454, 470, 475, 478, 480, 481, 489, 501, 512, 514, 515-516, 518, 524, 536, 541, 544, 546, 552, 555, 556, 560, 574, 584, 589, 595
Decca-Ace of Clubs (label), 292
Decca-Champion (label), 57
Decca-London (label), 452
Decca-Rounder (label), 236, 547
Dee, Bobby, 43
Dee, Mercy (see: Walton, Mercy Dee)
Deep South Piano (book), 128, 381, 382
Deer Park Plantation (Deer Park Plantation, MS), 163
Deetone (label), 519
Degand, Virgile, 191, 372
Delancey Street Theater (New York, NY), 472, 581
Delaney, Abral, 152
Delaney, Thomas "Tom," **152-153,** *152*
Delehant, Jim, 407
Delmar (label) (see: Delmark label)
Delmark (label), 32, 41, 53, 138, 150, 151, 152, 169, 176, 177, 208, 260, 266, 292, 336, 340, 345, 381, 394, 401, 403, 404, 412, 413, 414, 426, 444, 445, 460, 478, 490, 491, 530, 548, 549, 569, 570, 574, 582, 592, 596
Delpee's Club (New Orleans, LA), 164, 577
Delta (label), 246, 294
Delta Bell (club) (Bethel Island, CA), 332
Delta Big Four (group), 238
Delta Blues Festival (Fayetteville, AR), 327

Delta Boys (group), 57
Delta Joe (see: Luandrew, Albert)
Delta John (see: Hooker, John Lee)
Delta Queen Riverboat (see: S.S. Delta Queen Riverboat)
Democratic National Committee (organization), 239
Den (club), The (New York, NY), 141
Denim, Joe (see: Cotton, James)
Dennis, Bernardo, *155*
Denny, Jack, 541
Denver Festival (Denver, CO), 224
Deram (label), 468
Derby (label), 44
Deschamps, Rosa, 222
Desdunes, Clarence, 380
Desvigne, Sidney, 418, 419
Detroit Athletic Club (organization) (Detroit, MI), 423
Detroit Blues Club (Detroit, MI), 278
Detroit Blues Festival (Detroit, MI), 96, 127, 168, 225, 278, 535, 578
Detroit Hot Jazz Society (Detroit, MI), 84, 316
Detroit Hot Jazz Society (South Gate, MI), 423
Detroit Institute of Art (Detroit, MI), 141
Detroit Jr. (see: Williams, Emery, Jr.)
Detroit Memorial Park Cemetery (McComb County, MI), 535
Detroit Red (see: Perryman, Rufus)
Detroit-Windsor Jazz/Ragtime Festival (Detroit, MI), 230, 423
Devereaux, Wesley, 216
Devil's Daddy-in-Law (see: Council, Floyd)
Devil's Music—A History of the Blues, The (book), 252, 264, 416
Devil's Son-in-Law (see: Wheatstraw, Peetie)
Devil's Son-in-Law (billing), 552
Devil's Son-in-Law (book), 552
Dew Drop Inn (New Orleans, LA), 76, 191, 293, 326, 519, 586
Dharma (label), 369
Diabolo Valley College (Concord, CA), 113
Diamond, Billy, 157
Diamond, William, **153**
Diamond Jim (label), 127
Diamond Lounge (Chicago, IL), 380
Diamond Tone Gospel Quartet (group), 515
Diamond's Den (club) (Chicago, IL), 334
Dicey, Bill, 286
Dicey-Ross Band, 482
Dick Saunders Memorial Concert (Royal Oak, MI), 230, 423
Dickerson, Carroll, 31
Dickie Well's Club (New York, NY), 491, 564
Dickson, Linda, 546
Diddley, Bo (see: McDaniel, Ellas)
Diddley Daddy R & B Show (tour), 359, 538
Diddley Daddy Show (tour), 269
Dig (label), 201, 347
Digby's (club) (Chicago, IL), 575
Digg's Cafe (New York, NY), 472
Dillard, Bill, 318
Dillard University (New Orleans, LA), 300
Dingle, Carrie, 92
Dinkler Motor Inn (Syracuse, NY), 322
Dinner Key Auditorium (Miami, FL), 113, 431
Diplomat Hotel (Hollywood, CA), 566
Dipsy Doodle Club (Osceola, AR), 450
Dirty Girty Club (Chicago, IL), 289
Dirty Red (see: Wilborn, Nelson)
Disc (label), 117, 279, 365, 556
Disc-Delmark (label), 380
Disc Magazine, 225
Disciples (group), 443
Disciples of Christ Church (Chicago, IL), 389
Discovery (label), 253, 378
Disneyland Park (Anaheim, CA), 385, 386, 432, 506, 510, 567
Diva (label), 584
Dix, Mae, 274
Dixie Flyers (group), 417
Dixie Nightingale (billing), 497
Dixie Park (New Orleans, LA), 372
Dixie Rhythm Boys (band), 62
Dixie Stompers (band), 414
Dixie Theater (Atlanta, GA), 462
Dixie Theater (Itta Benna, MS), 468
Dixie Theater (Memphis, TN), 81
Dixieland at Disneyland (concert) (Anaheim, CA), 506
Dixieland Hall (New Orleans, LA), 506
Dixieland Jazz Quintet, 420
Dixieland Jubilee (concert) (Hollywood, CA), 408
Dixieland Rhythm Kings (band), 414
Dixieland Six (band), 506
Dixieland Theater (Charleston, SC), 558
Dixon, Charlie, 154
Dixon, Floyd, 31, 76, 116, **153-154**, *154*, 299, 308, 372
Dixon, Floyd, 154
Dixon, Freddie, 156
Dixon, Georgia, 510
Dixon, Ike, 549
Dixon, James (see: Dixon, Willie James)
Dixon, Stewart, 250
Dixon, Willie James, 41, 42, 65, 110, 116, 117, **154-157**, *155*, 178, 208, 246, 381, 596
Diz's Club (Chicago, IL), 197, 398
Djon Ballroom (Los Angeles, CA), 309
Do-Kay-Lo (label), 90
Doc (see also: Doctor/Dr.)
Doc Bennett Medicine Show (tour), 568
Doc Clayton (see: Clayton, Peter)
Doc Ross (see: Ross, Charles)
Doc Sugar's Medicine Show (tour), 419
Doc Terry (see: Terry, Doc)
Doc Thompson Carnival (tour), 261
Doc W.R. Kerr's Indian Remedy Company Medicine Show (tour), 33, 158, 261
Doc Watts Medicine Show (tour), 486
Doctor (see also: Doc/Dr.)
Doctor Clayton's Buddy (see: Luandrew, Albert)
Doctor Willie Lewis Medicine Show (tour), 106, 264, 327
Dodds, Baby, 279, 321
Dodds, Charles, 288
Dodge (label), 154
Dodgers Grill (bar) (Newark, NJ), 550
Dodison's World Circus (tour), 505
Dodo Club (Chicago, IL), 500
DoDo's Club (New Orleans, LA), 379
Doerflinger, William, 206
Doggett, Bill, 86, 253, 550
Doherty, Kevin R., 378, 449
Dollar Bill (group), 438
Dollettes (group), The, 212
Dolphin Cafe (New York, NY), 221
Domino, Antoine "Fats," 47, 60, 68, 74, 76, 103, **157-158**, *157*, 166, 202, 219, 270, 299, 329, 332, 372, 412, 491, 530, 546, 580
Domino (label), 73
Domino's Lounge (Eunice, LA), 200
Don & Dewey (duo), 211
Don Juans (group), 562
Donald MacGregor's Carnival Show (tour), 427
Donald Sharp Memorial Hospital (San Diego, CA), 456
Donaldson, Marie, 328
Donnelly Theater (Boston, MA), 113, 566
Donovan (pseudonym), 147
Donovan's Pub Ltd. (Wheeling, IL), 108, 381
Don's Cedar Club (Chicago, IL), 236, 444, 461, 596
Don's Den (club) (Chicago, IL), 161, 292, 457
Donte's (club) (Los Angeles, CA), 588
Dooley, Simmie, 33, 34, **158**
Dooley Square (club) (Tunica, MS), 93, 291
Dooley's (club) (Phoenix, AZ), 347
Dootone (label), 378
Dorchester Hotel (London, Eng.), 256
Dore (label), 178
Doris Miller Auditorium (Austin, TX), 120, 434
Doris Miller Theater (Austin, TX), 508
Dorsey, Court, 65
Dorsey, Lee, 116
Dorsey, Lee, 158
Dorsey, Thomas A. "Tom" (Georgia Tom), 49, **158-160**, *159*, 229, 251, 264, 274, 351, 428, 559
Dorsey, Thomas, Madison, 159
Dorsey, Thomas "Tommy," 159
Dorsey Brothers Orchestra, 541
Dorsey's Book of Poems (book), 160
Dorson, Richard M., 488
Dortmund Jazz Life Festival (Dortmund, Ger.), 60, 244
Dot (label), 141, 326
Dottie's Stardust Lounge/Club (San Francisco, CA), 55, 76, 190, 418, 439
Douglas, Abe, 161
Douglas, John, 160
Douglas, K.C., 107, **160-161**, *160*, 276, 280, 290, 347

Douglas, Kid, 161
Douglas, Lizzie (Memphis Minnie), 68, 145, 159, **161-162**, *162*, 197, 297, 302, 317, 322, 327, 330, 349, 355, 403, 424, 478, 489, 499, 514, 547, 559, 561, 591
Douglas, Tommy, 321
Douglas (label), 224, 286, 388
Douglas Gilmore Theater (Baltimore, MD), 462
Douglas International-Transatlantic (label), 217
Douglass High School (Oklahoma City, OK), 284, 445
Douglass Hotel (Macon, GA), 134
Douglass Theater (Baltimore, MD), 152, 463, 540
Douzier, Gene, 232
Dowling Convalescent Hospital (Oakland, CA), 187
Down East Festival (Cambridge, MA), 320
Down Home Syncopators (band), 475
Down Under Club (Houston, TX), 58
Down Under Coffeehouse (Holt, AL), 457
Downbeat (label), 191
Downbeat Club (Houston, TX), 53
Downbeat Club (New Orleans, LA), 86
Downbeat Club (New York, NY), 89, 300, 448
Downbeat Club (San Francisco, CA), 447
Downbeat Jazz Festival (Chicago, IL), 132, 388, 478, 566, 569
Downbeat Magazine, 31, 51, 95, 103, 114, 116, 118, 122, 138, 141, 145, 152, 157, 158, 178, 211, 225, 238, 241, 244, 247, 254, 260, 266, 269, 301, 305, 311, 312, 313, 316, 319, 321, 328, 347, 352, 371, 377, 390, 391, 406, 418, 421, 432, 445, 448, 451, 464, 465, 467, 468, 520, 521, 524, 538, 549, 560, 568, 570, 574, 576, 588, 589
Downbeat Music: 1968 (magazine), 178, 249, 410
Downbeat Music: 1973 (magazine), 148
Downbeat Room (club) (Chicago, IL), 256, 321, 536
Downbeat-Swingtime (label), 586
Downbeats (group), 395, 585
Downer's Grove (club) (Chicago, IL), 555
Downes, Emma, 290
Downey Brothers (tour), 396
Downstairs Club (Hamilton, Can.), 280
Downtown (label), 161, 188, 347, 357
Downtown Theater (Detroit, MI), 71
Doyle, Buddy, 246, 535, 574
Dozier, Katie, 107
Dr. (see also: Doc/Doctor)
Dr. Benson Medicine Show (tour), 106, 264
Dr. Breeding's Big B. Tonic Medicine Show (tour), 525
Dr. C. Hankenson's Medicine Show (tour), 106, 264
Dr. Dupress' Plantation (Bolton, MS), 118
Dr. Generosity (club) (New York, NY), 379, 482
Dr. Grim(m)'s Medicine Show (tour), 176, 401
Dr. Hood's Medicine Show (tour), 179
Dr. Hudson's Medicine Show (tour), 410
Dr. Jive's R&B Revue (concert) (New York, NY), 359
Dr. John (see: Rebennack, Mac)
Dr. McFadden's Medicine Show (tour), 247
Dr. Mine's Medicine Show (tour), 56
Dr. Pepper's Central Park Music Festival, 219
Dr. Simpson's Medicine Show (tour), 64, 290
Dr. Stokey Medicine Show (tour), 106
Dr. Streak's Medicine Show (tour), 106, 264
Dr. W.B. Miller Medicine Show (tour), 106, 264
Drake High School (Chicago, IL), 344, 516
Drake-Walker Theater (New York, NY), 491
Dranes, Arizona, 350
Dranes, Earl, 342, 343, 479, 571
Draper, Florence Amelia, 244-245
Dream Castle Restaurant (New Orleans, LA), 486
Dream Club (Scotlandville, LA), 396
Dream Theater (Columbus, GA), 466
Dreamland Ballroom (Omaha, NE), 74
Dreamland Cabaret/Cafe (Chicago, IL), 31, 229, 254, 373
Dreamland Inn (Kilgore, TX), 29
Dreamland Theater (Badin, NC), 558
Driftin' Slim/Smith (see: Mickle, Elmon)
Driggs, Frank, 40, 43, 48, 49, 68, 71, 88, 107, 123, 135, 149, 155, 168, 172, 192, 201, 205, 216, 220, 228, 229, 251, 255, 257, 262, 275, 281, 287, 320, 337, 356, 374, 385, 405, 411, 418, 440, 446, 448, 463, 473, 480, 484, 491, 507, 539, 554, 555, 568
Drive 'em Down (see: Hall, Willie)
Drops of Joy (group), The, 266
Druid City Hospital (Tuscaloosa, AL), 209
Drummer's Lounge (Chicago, IL), 41, 246
Drummond (label), 216, 535, 577
Drury Lane Theater (London, Eng.), 256
Du Drop Inn (Chicago, IL), 181, 268, 388, 410, 442, 460, 548
Duckett, Slim, 402, 501
Dudley, Jimmy, 56
Duke (label), 51, 149, 199, 215, 403, 407, 437, 444, 572, 578, 596
Duke University (Durham, NC), 261, 282, 420
Dukes, Laura, **163**, 398
Dukes (group), The, 437, 453
Dukes of Swing (band), 457
Duke's Place (club) (Chicago, IL), 41
Duling, Vincent, 379
Dumine, Louis, 128
Dumbarton Club (E. Palo Alto, CA), 439
Dump (club), The (Detroit, MI), 334
Dunbar, Scott, **163**, *163*
Dunbar High School (Chicago, IL), 430
Dunbar High School (Little Rock, AR), 484
Dunbar Theater (Columbus, OH), 350
Dunbar Theater (Philadelphia, PA), 463, 472, 540
Duncan, Adolph, 50
Duncan, Harry C., 31
Duncan, Todd, 582
Duncan, Willie, 434
Dunes Club (Neptune, NJ), 536
Dunkirk Jazz Festival (Dunkirk, Fr.), 110
Dunlap, Frances M., 183
Dunn, Johnny, 221, 580, 583
Dunn, Roy, **164**, *164*
Dunn, Sara, 350
Dunn, William, 350
Dunn, Willie, 164
Dunn Brothers (group), The, 164
Duo (label), 436
Dupree, William "Champion Jack," 37, 38, 49, 101, 107, 149, 158, **164-166**, *165*, 328, 329, 352, 365, 366, 368, 468, 503, 552
Durbin, Mary, 78
Durham, Eddie, 166, 285
Durham, Edward Lee, **166**
Durhamville Baptist Church Cemetery (Durhamville, TN), 177-178
Durrah, Fred, 558
Dusky Stevedores (band), 418
Dusters (band), The, 517, 574
Dustin, Father Joseph, 229
Dusty Road (label), 449
Dylan, Bob, 53, 141, 147, 174, 195, 207, 219, 330, 352
Dymally, Senator, 179
Dyson, Joe, 72

E&W (label), 512
EBM (label), 582
E.M. (label), 371
Eager, Jimmy (see: Whittaker, Hudson)
Eagle, Bob, 28, 79, 176, 295, 326, 353, 516
Eagle Rockers (band), 198, 394, 548
Eagle Theater (Asheville, NC), 396
Eagles (club), The (Seattle, WA), 99, 100, 132, 296, 308, 389, 478
Eaglin, Fird "Snooks," 101, 116, **167**, *167*
Eaglin, Fird, Sr., 167
Earbenders (group), The, 404
Earl of Old Town (club) (Chicago, IL), 56, 349
Earl Theater (Philadelphia, PA), 541, 556
Earl White's Revue (tour), 499
Earle Theater (Atlantic City, NJ), 82
Earl's Place (club) (Argo, IL), 32
Earl's Shangri-La Lounge (Chicago,

IL) (see also: Shangri-la Lounge), 175, 343
Early American Blues and Other Songs (program), 556
Early Bird (label), 421
Early Bird (club), The (St. Louis, MO), 502
Early Downhome Blues (book), 111
Earth Breeze (club) (Vancouver, Can.), 156
Earthquake McGoon's (club) (San Francisco, CA), 322, 481, 594
Easley, Alice, 470
East, Dorothy Bonita, 296
East Denver High School (Denver, CO), 360
East End Park (Birmingham, AL), 467
East Harlem Plaza (club) (New York, NY), 453
East Tennessee Baptist Hospital (Knoxville, TN), 134
East-West (label), 76
Eastbound (label), 535
Easter Concert (Cocoa Beach, FL), 95, 132
Easter Jubilee Show (tour), 359
Eastern Airlines (organization), 432
Easton, Amos (Bumble Bee Slim), 107, 161, **167-168,** *168*, 348, 552
Eastwood Country Club (San Antonio, TX), 90, 353
Easy Eddie's (club) (New Orleans, LA), 300
Easy Guitar (book), 46
Easy 9 Chord Guitar System (book), 38
Easy Rider Jazz Band, 481
Easy Street Club (Chicago, IL), 148
Easy Street Club (San Francisco, CA), 141, 299, 373
Eaton Auditorium/Hall (Toronto, Can.), 194, 556
Ebb (label), 28, 101, 154, 232
Ebbet's Field (club) (Denver, CO), 346
Ebenezer Baptist Church (Chicago, IL), 359
Ebonee Ballroom (Seattle, WA), 346, 520
Ebony (label), 291, 380
Ebony Club (Cleveland, OH), 293, 378
Ebony Club (Houston, TX), 235
Ebony Club (New York, NY), 373
Ebony Jr. Magazine, 582
Ebony Lounge (Chicago, IL), 388, 393, 442, 548, 570
Ebony Magazine, 152, 219, 241, 311, 390, 418, 588
Ebony Nora Bayes (billing), The, 543
Echo Club (Mexico City, Mex.), 199
Ed Howard's Club (San Francisco, CA), 51, 510
Eddie & Oscar (duo), 589
Eddie Condon Presents Show (concert), 406
Eddie Condon's (club) (New York, NY), 406, 466, 481
Eddie Shaw & Wolf Gang (band), 489
Eddie Shaw's (see: Eddie Shaw's Place)
Eddie Shaw's New 1815 Club (see: Eddie Shaw's Place)
Eddie Shaw's Place (club) (Chicago, IL) (Eddie Shaw's/Eddie's Place/ New 1815 Club) (see also: 1815 Club), 36, 42, 95, 123, 151, 278, 291, 334, 345, 394, 404, 435, 437, 445, 488, 494, 497, 529, 564, 572, 596
Eddie's (label), 199, 332, 572
Eddie's Place (see: Eddie Shaw's Place)
Edelweiss Club (Chicago, IL), 31
Eden Roc Hotel (Miami Beach, FL), 431
Eden Rock (hotel) (Las Vegas, NV), 411
Edge Lounge (Chicago, IL), 108, 381
Edison, Harry, 566
Edison (label), 223, 357, 374, 496
Edith Wilson Rockin & Rhythm (band), 581
Edmond's (see: Edmond's Cellar)
Edmond's Cellar (club) (New York, NY), 137, 229, 231, 472, 540
Edmond's Novelty Cafe (Brooklyn, NY), 474
Eduardo's (club) (Buffalo, NY), 114
Edward M. Gilbert Playhouse (New York, NY), 556
Edwards, Bernice, 455, 470
Edwards, Carrie, 535
Edwards, Charles (Good Rockin' Charles), **168-169,** *169*, 394
Edwards, David "Honeyboy," **169-170,** *170*, 246, 289, 354, 408, 409, 460, 568, 570
Edwards, Frank, 140, **171-172,** *171*, 560, 576
Edwards, Henry, 169
Edwards, Honeyboy (see: Edwards, David)
Edwards, Jody "Butterbeans," 172, *172*, 173
Edwards, Susie (see also: Butterbeans & Susie), **172-173,** *172*
Edwards, Teddy, 299
Edwards & Edwards (duo), 172, 474
Edwards & Hawthorn (duo), 172
Effie's Go-Go (club) (Beaumont, TX), 243
Egerton's (club) (Toronto, Can.), 341
Egg Harbor (club) (Atlantic City, NJ), 540
Egge, Ray (see: Agee, Raymond)
Ego's Penthouse Lounge (Chicago, IL), 67
Egremont Inn (S. Egremont, MA), 245
Egress (club), The (Vancouver, Can.), 95, 389
Egyptian Theater (DeKalb, IL), 367, 505
845 Club (Bronx, NY), 216, 256, 383
1815 Club (Chicago, IL) (Alex's 1815 Club) (see also: Eddie Shaw's Place), 32, 41, 345, 437, 442, 444, 595
8th Street Theater (Chicago, IL), 116
85th Street Playhouse (New York, NY), 366
81 Theater (Atlanta, GA) (Bailey's 81 Theater), 74, 134, 159, 167, 172, 369, 383, 405, 411, 450, 462, 463, 467, 540
Eisenhower, Dwight, 110, 256
El-Bee (label), 305, 410
El Cafe (New York, NY) 449
El Camino Real (club) (Mexico City, Mex.), 114
El Dorado Ballroom (Houston, TX), 332
El Grotto Room (club) (Chicago, IL), 83
El Lobby Cafe (Juarez, Mex.), 90
El Macombo Lounge (Chicago, IL), 117
El Matador (club) (San Francisco, CA), 254, 366, 504
El Mocambo Tavern (Toronto, Can.), 33, 41, 51, 95, 125, 156, 158, 209, 240, 247, 260, 360, 379, 389, 488, 500, 523, 527, 549, 564, 596
El Morocco (club) (Chicago, IL), 123
El Morocco Club (New Orleans, LA), 326
El Rancho (club) (Chester, PA), 298
El Ray (club) (Los Angeles, CA), 190
El Toro Marine Air Base (Los Angeles, CA), 531
El Vido's (club) (Detroit, MI), 370
Elam, Dave Alexander, 29
Elbrown (see: Brown, Lillian)
Eldo (label), 211
Eldorado Club (Houston, TX), 512
Eldorado Room (Houston, TX) 375
Eldorados (group), 72
Eldridge, Jesse, 182
Eldridge Club (Chicago, IL), 345
Electric Ballroom (Atlanta, GA), 51, 132, 305, 310
Electric Circus (club) (New York, NY), 93, 137, 147, 155, 187, 190, 240, 246, 249, 260, 266, 283, 286, 305, 327, 340, 383, 388, 391, 411, 412, 457, 478, 513, 569
Electric Dust Band, 238
Electric Factory (hall) (Philadelphia, PA), 296, 308, 389, 548
Electric Flag (band), The, 54
Electric Lady Studios (New York, NY), 224, 470
Electric Theater (Chicago, IL), 296
Elektra (label), 54, 99, 173, 314, 319, 327, 454, 503, 507, 556
Eleven Aces (group), 418
1100 Club (Muncie, IN), 139
1125 Club (Chicago, IL), 169, 236, 247, 500
Eleventh Hour Coffee House (Indianapolis, IN), 181-182
Eli's Mile High Club (San Francisco, CA), 358, 440
Elite Arabian Sands (club) (Chicago, IL), 169
Elite Club (Dallas, TX), 372
Elite #2 Club (Chicago, IL), 221, 229, 254
Elkhorn Singers (group), 307
Elko (label), 28, 43, 120, 371, 531
Elks (club), The (Oakland, CA), 136
Elks Ball (Pittsburg, PA), 200
Elks Club (Los Angeles, CA), 76
Elks Club (Montgomery, AL), 308

Elks Club (Seattle, WA), 111
Elks Hall (Los Angeles, CA), 523
Elks Rendezvous Band, 298
Elks Rendezvous Club (New York, NY), 44, 71, 298
Ell, Eddie, 479
Ella B. Moore Theater (Dallas, TX), 29, 279, 295, 428
Ellen Cemetery (St. Bernard, LA), 128
Ellington, Duke, 31, 279, 375, 431, 518, 538, 541, 567, 581, 583
Elliott, Jack, 70, **173-174**, *174*, 207, 368
Elliott, John "Jack," 174
Elliot's Nest (club) (Rochester, NY), 279, 390
Ellis, Chris, 582
Ellis, Lem, 174
Ellis, Lena, 180
Ellis, Wilbert "Big Chief," 92, **174-175**, *175*, 364, 367
Ellis Auditorium (Memphis, TN), 327, 483, 560
Ellison, Ralph, 448
Elmore Theater (Pittsburgh, PA), 173, 331
Elmwood Cemetery (Jackson, MS), 338
Elmwood Hills Cemetery (Troy, NY), 386
Elsewhere Club/Lounge (Chicago, IL), 36, 63, 65, 66, 67, 108, 149, 168, 169, 217, 266, 294, 336, 341, 343, 395, 427, 494, 529, 575, 591
Elston, Natalie, 316
Elston, Norman, 316
Eltinge Theater (New York, NY), 295
Elwood, Philip, 297
Embassey (club), The (Paris, Fr.), 82
Embassy Club (New York, NY), 542
Embassy Hall (Los Angeles, CA), 122, 156
Ember (label), 96
Ember (club), The (Edmonton, Can.), 375
Embria, Guitrue, 69
Emelin Theater (Mamaroneck, NY), 550, 558
Emerson, N. T., 175
Emerson, William "Billy the Kid," **175**
Emerson (label), 81, 223, 373, 463, 491, 583
Emery, Pete, 302
Emery Hall (Cincinnati, OH), 540
Emmet Smith Medicine Show (tour), 33, 261
Emory University (Atlanta, GA), 557
Empire Room (club) (Dallas, TX), 232, 434, 461
Empire Room (club) (New York, NY), 114
Empire State College (Albany, NY), 166, 245
Empire Theater (Brooklyn, NY), 173
Empire Theater (New York, NY), 256, 541, 542
Empire Theater (Newark, NJ), 52, 550
Empire Theater (Red Bank, NJ), 82
Emporium of Jazz (club) (Mendota, MN), 322
Empress of the Blues (billing), 464
Encore (club), The (Los Angeles, CA), 375
Encore II (club) (Pittsburgh, PA), 588
Encyclopedia of Folk, Country and Western Music (book), 142, 196
Encyclopedia of Pop, Rock & Soul (book), 47, 54, 118, 158, 201, 209, 219, 305, 331, 345, 347, 352, 360, 412, 433, 512, 538, 586
Enrica (label), 220
Enterprise (label), 578, 582
Entertainers (cabaret), The (New Orleans, LA), 379, 472
Entertainers Club, The (Chicago, IL), 373
Environ (club), The (New York, NY), 92
Epic (label), 88, 136, 178, 211, 219, 302, 378, 415, 417, 520, 523
Epitaph (label), 322
Epperson, Nora, 375
Epworth Bar (Detroit, MI), 225
Equite Hall (New Orleans, LA), 373
Equity Library Community Theater (production company), 82
Erasmus Hall High School (Brooklyn, NY), 173
Erby, Jack (see: Erby, John)
Erby, John, **175-176**, *176*, 362, 386, 481
Erby, Josephine, 478
Ericson's Lounge (Buffalo, NY), 497
Erlanger Theater (Philadelphia, PA), 556
Ernie's Club (Irwinville, LA), 396
Esceha (label), 343, 443
Eshew, Colonel Jim, 173
Esoteric (label), 406
Esquire (label), 63
Esquire Jazz Concert (New York, NY), 298
Esquire Magazine, 520
Esquire Showbar (Montreal, Can.), 95, 125, 132, 240, 359, 367, 389, 504, 596
Essex (label), 199, 364
Essex County College (Newark, NJ), 550
Essex Hunt Club (Peapack, NJ), 316
Establishment (club), The (Toronto, Can.), 239
Estes, Annie Mae, 508
Estes, Daniel, 176
Estes, Dorothy, 326
Estes, John, 53, 70, 84, **176-178**, *177*, 196, 325, 401, 402, 426, 427, 574, 575, 576, 595
Estes, Virginia, 178, 401
Esther's Orbit Room (club) (Oakland, CA), 188, 510, 520
Ethel Barrymore Theater (New York, NY), 80
Ethel's (lounge) (Detroit, MI), 278, 304, 435
Etting, Ruth, 222
Eugene Blues Festival (Eugene, OR), 270, 468, 531
Euphonic (label), 79, 283, 288
Euphoria Tavern (Portland, OR), 130, 247, 367, 504
Eureka (magazine), 233
Euro-Tour 76 (tour), 544
Europe, Jim, 558
Evans, Cheryl, 414
Evans, David "Dave," 28, 38, 81, 89, 236, 290, 315, 349, 414, 547
Evans, Delmar, 179
Evans, James, 179
Evans, Margie, **178-179**, *178*, 465
Evans, Mattie, 465
Evans, Melvyn, 550
Evansville Jazz Festival (Evansville, IN), 84
Evening Melody Boys of St. Louis (group), The, 421
Evening with Dorsey (tour), An, 159
Everglades Club (New York, NY), 540
Evergreen (label), 542
Evergreen Cemetery (Bedford, OH), 470
Evergreen Cemetery (Cleveland, OH), 145
Evergreen Cemetery (Oakland, CA), 187
Evergreen Club (Chicago, IL), 460
Evergreen Review (magazine), 448
Everson, Lottie (see: Beaman, Lottie)
Every Hour Blues Boys (band), 305, 438
Ewell, Don, 84, 591, 594
Ewins, Ernest, 250
Excell (label), 580
Excello (label), 90, 151, 199, 200, 204, 216, 227, 228, 232, 270, 285, 301, 342, 354, 383, 384, 394, 405, 443, 474, 522, 535, 577
Excello-Flyright (label), 270
Excelsior (label), 43, 357, 446
Excelsior Club (Alexandria, Egypt), 256
Excelsior Jazz Band, 37
Exclusive (label), 74, 232
Exclusive Club (New York, NY), 43
Exhibition Hall (Columbus, GA), 447
Exodus (label), 435
Experience (band), The, 224
Exploratorium (club), The (San Francisco, CA), 30, 98, 154
Expo 67 (fair) (Montreal, Can.), 91, 218, 388, 548
Expressway Lounge (Chicago, IL), 450, 500

F&J Lounge (Gary, IN), 388, 444
F&L (label), 179
F&M Patio (club), The (New Orleans, LA), 508
FAIRR (organization), 309
FBS (label), 63
FM (label), 108, 381
F.S. Wolcott's Rabbit Foot Minstrels (tour) (see also: Rabbit Foot Minstrels), 203, 450
Fabian's Fox Theater (Brooklyn, NY), 86, 157
Fahey, John, 302, 409
Fair, Archie, 311
Fairbanks, Douglas, 185
Fairfield Four (group), The, 238
Fairfield Hall (London, Eng.), 63, 512

Fairfield Lounge (Chicago, IL), 279
Fairlawn Cemetery (Fairlawn, NJ), 92
Fairmont Hotel (Dallas, TX), 432
Fairmont Hotel (New Orleans, LA), 158
Fairmont Hotel (San Francisco, CA), 431
Falconer, Jim, 151
Fallen Angel Club (San Francisco, CA), 141
Fame (label), 453
Family Circle (club) (Dallas, TX), 389
Family Inn (Houston, TX), 57
Family Light School of Music (Sausalito, CA), 30, 54, 98, 347, 393, 516
Famous Club (Birmingham, AL), 356
Famous Door (club) (New York, NY), 252, 406, 446, 464, 518
Famous Door Lounge (New Orleans, LA), 300
Famous Hokum Boys (group), 159
Famous Negro Music Makers (book), 544
Famous Southern Stompers (band), 110
Fanchon & Marco Revue (tour), 472
Fans Theater (Philadelphia, PA), 406, 550
Fantasy (label), 78, 141, 161, 239, 264, 328, 366, 503, 522, 567
Fantasy Lounge (Jackson Heights, NY), 90
Faragher's Back Room (club) (Cleveland, OH), 336
Farandole (label), 117
Faren, Johnny, 322
Farfield Club (Chicago, IL), 500
Farmdell Club (Dayton, OH), 372
Farragut High School (Chicago, IL), 31
Fast Black (see: Brown, Percy)
Fast Twice Together (band), 448
Fat Black Pussy Cat (club) (New York, NY), 217
Fat Black Pussycat (club) (Lansing, MI), 210
Fat Cat (label) (see: Fat Cat's Jazz label)
Fat Cat's Jazz (label), 245, 316, 423
Fat Chance Saloon (Chicago, IL), 168, 395
Fat Chappelle's Rabbit Foot Minstrels (tour) (see also: Rabbit Foot Minstrels), 427, 462
Father Blues (club) (Chicago, IL), 304, 345
Father of British Blues (billing), 352
Faulk, Lee Roy, 506
Faye Theater (Philadelphia, PA), 558
Feather, Leonard, 37, 44, 142, 253, 281, 300, 377, 409, 524, 538, 568, 588
Feature (label), 191, 192, 227, 554
Federal (label), 101, 123, 232, 305, 320, 332, 338, 343, 406, 417, 476, 544, 545, 586
Federal Theater (Salem, MA), 82
Federal Theater Project (production company), 541
Fed's Chicken & Barbecue Place (New York, NY?), 74
Feel Like Going Home (book), 95, 273, 289, 391, 459, 574
Feeley's Theater (Hazelton, PA), 82
Feelgood, Doctor (see: Perryman, William)
Fefe's Monte Carlo Club (New York, NY), 541
Feldman, Martin, 287
Felious, Odetta, 193
Felt Forum (stadium) (New York, NY), 132, 174, 208, 411, 417, 418, 549
Felters, Frank, 103
Female Bert Williams (billing), The, 362
Female Impersonators Revue (tour), 564
Fence (label), 535
Fention (see: Robinson, Fention)
Fergie's (club) (Goleta, CA), 55, 125, 136, 178, 190
Ferguson, Johnny, 259
Fern Oak Cemetery (Griffith, IN), 181
Fernandez, Mildred (see: Brown, Lillian)
Ferncliff Cemetery (Hartsdale, NY), 564
Ferris, William "Bill," 163, 509
Festival (label), 173
Festival for Peace (concert) (New York, NY), 100, 219, 296
Festival of American Folklife (Montreal, Can.), 32, 246-7, 266, 334, 341, 381, 455, 490, 563, 573, 588
Festival of American Folklife (Washington, DC) (American Folk-Life Festival/Folk Life Festival) (see also: Smithsonian Festival of American Folklife/Smithsonian Folk Festival), 41, 56, 101, 130, 138, 147, 151, 177, 187, 243, 265, 266, 273, 276, 278, 300, 330, 349, 389, 401, 427, 440, 449, 455, 457, 483, 484, 553, 560, 563, 569
Festival of American Folklife Program, 140
Festival of Arts Concert (Chicago, IL), 67, 154, 343, 381
Festival of L'Unita (Florence, It.), 142
Festival of L'Unita (Turin, It.), 142, 231
Festival of Music (Philadelphia, PA), 566
Festival on the Strand (concert) (Galveston, TX), 455
Fickle Pickle (club/coffeehouse) (Chicago, IL), 35, 54, 85, 148, 176, 193, 225, 246, 294, 322, 340, 342, 401, 426, 460, 490, 545, 569, 574, 585
Fiddler's Green (club) (Toronto, Can.), 148
Fidelity (label), 167, 232
Fields, Ernie, 216, 252, 377
Fields, Herbie, 564
Fifth Dimension (club) (Montreal, Can.), 147
Fifth Peg (club) (New York, NY), 453
Fifth Peg (club) (Toronto, Can.), 239, 366, 503
50 Grand Club (Detroit, MI), 137
Figaro's (club) (Chicago, IL), 32
Figi, J. B., 51
Figueroa Ballroom (Los Angeles, CA), 359
Fillmore Auditorium (San Francisco, CA), 46, 53, 54, 132, 218, 296, 304, 305, 308, 353, 359, 439
Fillmore East (club) (New York, NY), 32, 46, 51, 54, 100, 114, 132, 157, 195, 208, 210, 218, 219, 224, 272, 296, 304, 305, 308, 346, 352, 383, 411, 420, 478, 521, 527, 548, 585
Fillmore West (club) (San Francisco, CA), 30, 32, 46, 54, 55, 100, 114, 125, 132, 208, 224, 243, 296, 304, 305, 308, 345, 346, 352, 420, 444, 450, 585
Fine Arts (label), 532
Fine Arts Trio, 532
Finjan Club (Montreal, Can.), 366, 504
Finn, Julio (see: Arnold, Augustus)
Fiofori, Tom, 157
Fire (label), 74, 137, 243, 271, 574
Fire-Fury (label), 92
Fireworks Station (see: Ned Love's Club)
Firma (label), 500
First African Baptist Church (Columbus, GA), 427
First Baptist Church (Gurdon, AR), 586
First Bass Club (New Orleans, LA), 101
First Birmingham Boogie Convention (Birmingham, Eng.), 348
First Church Congregational (Cambridge, MA), 179
First Floor Club (Chicago, IL), 595
First Floor Club (Toronto, Can.), 176, 388, 398, 401, 427
First Freedom Folk Festival (Cambridge, MA), 525
First International Jazz Festival (Washington, DC), 93
First Step (club) (Tucson, AZ), 147
First World Youth Festival (Prague, Czech.), 141
Fisher, Cora, 465
Fisher Theater (Detroit, MI), 366, 504
Fisher's Tavern (Newark, NJ), 550
Fisk Unieversity (Nashville, TN), 557
Fitzgerald, Ella, 90, 254, 298, 466, 506
5 Boogie Woogie Blues Piano Solos by Pine Top Smith (book), 467
Five Breezes (group), The, 110, 154
Five College Folk Festival (Amherst, MA), 266
Five Dollars (group), The, 562
Five-Four Ballroom (5-4 Ballroom) (Los Angeles, CA), 45, 51, 53, 86, 120, 157, 188, 200, 309, 388, 407, 430, 519, 527
Five Hounds of Jazz (band), 288
500% More Man (billing), 360
501 Club (New Orleans, LA), 101, 167
Five Pennies (band), 375
Five Royales (group), 353
Five Stages (club) (Chicago, IL), 99, 150, 156, 208, 304, 334, 389, 476, 499, 595, 596
Five Star Playhouse (New Orleans, LA), 158
520 Club (Chicago, IL), 181, 570

Flag (label), 302
Flair (label), 192, 271, 294, 533, 574
Flame (label), 38, 117
Flame Club (Chicago, IL), 62, 213, 279, 339, 343, 370, 388, 559, 576
Flame Show Bar/Flame Showbar (Detroit, MI), 108, 154, 299, 375, 430, 470, 519, 527, 535, 538, 586
Flames (group), The, 223
Flames of Rhythm (group), 398
Flamingo (club), The (Kansas City, MO), 375
Flamingo Club/Lounge (Chicago, IL), 36, 79, 93, 236, 334, 341, 450, 488, 494
Flamingo Club (London, Eng.), 239, 352
Flamingo Hotel (Las Vegas, NV), 157, 158, 309, 310, 373
Flamingo Hotel (Memphis, TN), 145
Flamingo Steer Club (Oakland, CA), 188, 538
Flamingoes (group), The, 167
Flangan, Georgia, 345
Flash (label), 277, 347, 407, 448
Flash Back (label), 338
Flat Rock Society Orchestra, 230
Flerlage, Iola, 193
Flerlage, Ray, 65, 193, 196, 259, 344, 403, 485, 545
Fletcher, Tom, 415
Fletcher Theater (Danville, IL), 70
Flipside (Club), The (Cleveland, OH), 336
Floberg, Janet, 381
Flohil, Dick, 209
Floral Park, (Indianapolis, IN), 107
Florence Mills Memorial Benefit (New York, NY), 31
Florence Nightingale Nursing Home (New York, NY), 52
Florence's Lounge (Chicago, IL), 41, 42, 91, 169, 236, 247, 260, 266, 334, 394, 404, 437, 442, 450, 500
Florida A&M University (Tallahassee, FL), 114
Florida Club (London, Eng.), 256
Florida Cotton Blossom Minstrels (tour) (see also: Pete Werley's Florida Blossom Minstrels), 134, 427, 462
Florida Playboys (band), 111
Flower & Fifth Avenue Hospital (New York, NY), 448, 454
Flowers, Mary (see: Miles, Josephine)
Floyd, Bud, 179
Floyd, Buddy, 586
Floyd, Frank, **179-180**, *179*, 276, 441
Floyd, Papa, 138
Floyd, Reuben, 482
Floyd, Troy, 405
Fly Cats (band), 79, 518
Flying Clouds of Detroit (group), The, 421
Flying Dutchman (label), 523
Flying Dutchman Club (Harbor Springs, MI), 230
Flying Eagle (billing), 443
Flying Fish (label), 42, 56, 123, 349, 529
Flyright (label), 28, 40, 57, 80, 92, 96, 163, 164, 166, 171, 180, 191, 217, 250, 260, 261, 282, 312, 350, 424, 453, 483, 516, 547, 583
Flyright-Matchbox (label), 74
Focus Coffeehouse (New York, NY), 482
Fogerty, John, 95
Foghat (group), 100, 169, 240, 312, 390, 585
Foghorn (club) (Baltimore, MD), 210
Foley, Red, 123
Folk Arts Store (San Diego, CA), 134, 277
Folk Blues (book), 207
Folk Blues Festival (tour), 155
Folk City (see: Gerde's Folk City)
Folk City (Mike Porco) (club) (New York, NY) (see also: Gerde's Folk City), 142, 261, 378, 379, 449, 453
Folk Festival (John's Island, SC), 141
Folk Festival (Sun Valley, ID), 185
Folk Life Festival (see: Festival of American Folklife)
Folk-Lyric (label), 86, 103, 147, 167, 185, 348, 420, 512, 573
Folk Music Festival (Berkeley, CA), 132
Folk Music Festival (San Diego, CA), 371
Folk Music: More Than a Song (book), 59, 130, 142, 174, 196, 210, 219, 430, 522
Folk Review (magazine), 302
Folk Scene (magazine), 57, 130
Folk Song 65 Concert (New York, NY), 174, 210, 249, 272, 553, 569
Folk Star (label), 192
Folkart (label), 91
Folklore Center (store) (New York, NY), 34, 120, 231, 249
Folklore Society of Greater Washington (Washington, DC), 391
Folkmasters (group), The, 366
Folkways (label), 33, 69, 96, 98, 103, 106, 108, 117, 118, 130, 141, 142, 147, 155, 163, 164, 167, 193, 203, 209, 243, 256, 317, 318, 327, 344, 364, 365, 366, 368, 381, 414, 420, 454, 460, 481, 483, 485, 490, 503, 512, 521, 569
Fondation des Etats-Unis Concert (Paris, Fr.), 318
Fontainebleau Hotel (New Orleans, LA), 158, 508
Fontana (label), 39, 63, 93, 117, 136, 147, 155, 177, 187, 208, 239, 243, 246, 280, 322, 340, 363, 366, 381, 388, 401, 427, 439, 443, 444, 478, 481, 488, 490, 504, 512, 520, 532, 548, 569, 573, 577
Fool's Mate (club) (Westport, CT), 249, 272
Forbidden City (club) (Honolulu, HI), 219, 375
Ford, Aleck, 577
Ford, Bessie, 482
Ford, Friday, 478, 479
Ford, Ledella, 252
Ford, Millie, 577
Ford, Reuben, 588
Ford Chapel Cemetery (W. Junction, TN), 337
Ford Hotel (Toronto, Can.), 84
Ford Motor Company Show (tour), 217
Fordham Theater (see: Keith-Albee Fordham Theater)
Fordham University (Bronx, NY), 447
Ford's Theater (Washington, DC), 195
Foreman, Rufus, 208
Foremost (label), 321
Forest/Forrest City Joe (see: Pugh, Joe)
Forest Hills Music Festival (New York, NY), 113
Forest Inn (Detroit, MI), 238
Forest Inn Cafe (Chicago, IL), 221
Forest Lawn Memorial Park Cemetery (Glendale, CA), 543
Foresters State Service, 114
Forestville Tavern (Chicago, IL), 467
Formal (label), 343, 438
Forrest, Earl, 308
Forrest Theater (Philadelphia, PA), 464
Fort, Bill, 149
Fort Boulevard Recreation Bowling Alley/Bar (Detroit, MI), 278
Fort Monmouth Concert (Fort Monmouth, NJ), 406
Fort Valley State College (Fort Valley, GA), 74
Fortescue, Bud E., 180
Fortescue, John Henry, **180**, *180*
Fortune (label), 66, 238, 239, 278, 312, 370, 443, 562
Fortune Garden (club) (New York, NY), 466
48th Street Theater (New York, NY) (see also: Brady's 48th Street Theater), 475, 542
4400 Club (Brentwood, MD), 263
44th Street Theater (New York, NY), 254, 556, 581
49 Club (Drew, MS), 59
42nd Street Apollo Theater (see: Apollo Theater, 42nd Street)
46th Street Theater (New York, NY), 82, 481, 503
Forum (club), The (Binghamton, NY), 466
Forum (club), The (Los Angeles, CA), 96, 309, 359, 411
Forum (club), The (Toronto, Can), 114
Forward Times (newspaper), 57
Foster, Dessa, 470
Foster, Jim (see: Collins, Sam)
Foster, Leroy (Baby Face Leroy), **180-181**, *181*, 289, 294, 339, 388, 424, 501, 574, 576
Foster, Robert, 181, 571
Foster, Sadie, 421
Foster, Tony, 180
Foster, Will, 181
Foster, Willie/Willy, 181, **181**, 247, 342
Foster Vocational High School (Chicago, IL), 359
Foster's Club (Jackson, MS), 395
Foster's Rainbow Room (club) (New Orleans, LA), 216, 536-538
Fouche, Sam, 134
Foundation for the Advancement of Inmate Rehabilitation and Recreation (organization), 309

Foundation Tavern (Tacoma, WA), 156, 596
Fountain (label), 582
Four Aces (group) (Louis Myers) (see also: Aces, The), 268, 393, 548
Four Aces (group) (Willie Love), 338, 399, 560, 577
Four Barrons (group), 91
Four Brothers (label), 72
Four Dancing Mitchells (group), 472
Four H's Gospel Group, 250
400 Club (Dallas, TX), 382
400 Club (Denver, CO), 76, 78
400 Club (Hollywood/Los Angeles, CA), 141, 373
400 Club (New York, NY), 298
400 Club (South River, NJ), 90
400 W. 150 (label), 44, 550, 551
Four Jivers (group), 32
Four Jumps of Jive (group), 155
Four Keys String Band, 56, 348
Four Kings (group), 400
Four Leaf Clover (label), 195
Four Locks (club) (Westmont, IL), 124
Four Muses (club) (San Clemente, CA), 125, 346, 367, 504
4-Star (label), 136, 191
1444 Gallery (club) (Indianapolis, IN), 49
1410 Club (Chicago, IL), 68, 116
Fowler, Billie, 44
Fowler, Craig, 147
Fowler, T. J., 84, 182
Fox, Brother, 150
Fox, Charles, 145, 276
Fox (label), 136
Fox Head Tavern (Cedar Rapids, IA), 298
Fox Hole (see: Hill's Fox Hole)
Fox Terminal Theater (Newark, NJ), 496
Fox Theater (see: Fabian's Fox Theater)
Fox Theater (Detroit, MI), 113
Fox Venice Theater (Los Angeles, CA), 520
Foxboro Raceway (Boston, MA), 352
Foxie's Floating Palace Riverboat (Houma, LA), 490
Foxy (label), 563, 572
Foxy GGM (billing), 84
France, Iva, 145
Frances Amis Hall (New Orleans, LA), 373
Francis, Cletha, 175
Francis, Elizabeth, 48
Francis Delafield Hospital (New York, NY), 364
Frank, Johnny (see: Sellers, John)
Frank, Michael, 508
Frank, Virginia, 76
Frank Curry Show (tour), 33
Frank Moore's Plantation (Stovall, MS), 62
Frank Pineri's Place (club) (New Orleans, LA), 279, 282
Frank Wiggins Trade School (Los Angeles, CA), 277
Franklin, Aretha, 60, 113, 114, 415
Franklin, Edward "Pete," 107, **181-182,** *182*
Franklin, Flossie Woods, 182
Franklin, Julius, 181
Franklin, Minnie, 409
Franklin, Pete (see: Franklin, Edward)
Franklin, Sarah, 276
Franklin K. Lane High School (Brooklyn, NY), 217
Franklin Theater (Birmingham, AL), 463
Franklin Theater (New York, NY) (see: Keith-Albee Franklin Theater)
Franks, Jay, 109
Fraternity (label), 535
Frazier, Calvin, **182-183,** *183*, 279, 289, 459
Frazier, Dan, 182
Freakshow (book), 101
Frederick, Professor O. W., 359
Frederick Douglass Memorial Park Cemetery (Staten Island, NY), 83, 223, 472
Fredericks, Henry, 345
Free Baptist Connection Church (Washington, NC), 146
Free Methodist God's Bible School (Cincinnati, OH), 234
Freeberg, Ron, 314
Freed, Alan, 45, 219, 269, 281, 359, 388, 519, 538, 566
Freedom (label), 29, 103, 419, 519, 572
Freedom Hall (Louisville, KY), 296
Freeman, Bud, 406
Freeman, Cora, 445
Freeman, Sonny, 309
Freemont Hotel (Las Vegas, NV), 431
Fremont Theater (Las Vegas, NV), 566
French, Albert, 506
French Academie du Jazz (organization), 70, 118, 241, 311, 418
French Lick Jazz Festival (French Lick, IN), 254, 447, 566
French Market Coffee Shop (New Orleans, LA), 396
Frenchy's Orchestra, 405
Fresh (label), 65
Fresh Air Tavern (Seattle, WA), 389
Fresno State University (Fresno, CA), 187
Friday Club, The (New York, NY), 406
Friedhof am Perlacher Forst Cemetery (Munich, Ger.), 292
Friedman, Myra, 296, 297
Friendly Brothers (group), The, 95
Friendly Brothers of Dallas (group), The, 421
Friendship (label), 88, 166
Friendship Baptist Church (Columbus, GA), 428
Frishberg, Dave, 322
Frog & Nightgown Club (Raleigh, NC), 367, 504
Frogs (club), The (Detroit, MI), 385
Frolic (label), 585
Frolic Show Bar (Detroit, MI), 527
Frolic Theater (Bessemer, AL), 463
Frolic Theater (Birmingham, AL), 48, 277, 428, 463
Frolics Revere Beach (club) (Boston, MA), 538
From Blues to Pop: The Autobiography of Leonard "Baby Doo" Caston (book), 110, 111
From Spirituals to Swing (concert) (New York, NY), 68, 134, 252, 405-406, 446, 502-503, 512, 518, 520
Front Room (club) (Newark, NJ), 447
Frontier (club), The (Las Vegas, NV), 114
Frost, Frank, **183-184,** *184*, 399, 435, 578
Frosty Corner (club) (Chicago, IL), 246, 266, 400, 457
Fugue (club), The (New York, NY), 247, 482
Full Note (club) (Chicago, IL), 437
Full Tilt Boogie Group, 296
Fuller, Blind Boy, 93, 98, 111, 133, 147, **184-185,** *185*, 204, 211, 212, 368, 386, 393, 416, 426, 436, 492, 502, 503, 515, 516, 546, 574
Fuller, Blind Boy, #2 (see: McGhee, Walter)
Fuller, Jesse, 141, 161, 174, **185-187,** *186*, 219, 314, 392
Fuller, Jim, 263
Fuller, Johnny, 76, **187-188,** *187*
Fuller, Little Boy (see: Trice, Richard)
Fuller, Major, 187
Fuller, Playboy (see: Minter, Iverson)
Fuller, Richard (see: Minter, Iverson)
Fuller, Rocky (see: Minter, Iverson)
Fulsom, Lowell (see: Fulson, Lowell)
Fulsome Steak Club (Brooklyn, NY), 90
Fulson, Lowell, 29, 51, 53, 111, 136, **188-190,** *189*, 212, 276, 280, 303, 311, 345, 448, 519, 520, 528, 529, 530
Fulson, Martin, 53, 188, 190
Fulton, Doug, 94, 227, 306, 335, 394, 412, 458, 498, 500, 516, 532, 579
Fulton, Robert, 172
Fulton Theater (New York, NY), 581
Fun with Guitar Chords (book), 38
Funchess, John, 332
Funky Five (pseudonym), 493
Funky Quarters (club) (San Diego, CA), 240, 304, 367, 504, 588
Fury (label), 283, 395, 529

GHB (label), 37, 203, 421, 481
GHB-Jazzology (label), 322
G.I. Sing-Sation (billing), The, 191
GJ (label), 563
GRT (label), 377
Gable, Clark, 360
Gabriel Brothers Band, 84
Gackscraggle Coffeehouse, The (San Francisco, CA), 213
Gaddy, Bob, 503
Gage, Bessie, 419
Gaillard, Slim, 322, 509
Gaines, Al, 428
Gaines, Charlie, 298, 558
Gaines, Henry, 231
Gaines, Roy, 430
Gaither, Bill, 107, 378
Galatin, Wiley, 443

Galaxy (label), 239, 497
Galveston College (Galveston, TX), 199
Galveston High School (Galveston, TX), 74
Gamby's (club) (Baltimore, MD), 550
Gamma (label), 572
Gammond, Peter, 145
Gant, Cecil, 107, **191**
Gardella, Tess, 582
Garden, Catherine, 137
Garden of Joy (club) (New York, NY), 472
Garden Theater (Baltimore, MD), 541
Gardens (club), The (Pittsburgh, PA), 200
Gardner, Sam, 472
Garfield High School (Seattle, WA), 223
Garfield Park Hospital (Chicago, IL), 193
Garland, Joe, 44
Garland, Red, 538
Garlow, Clarence "Bon Ton," 120, 122, **191-192,** *191*
Garlow, Compton, 191
Garon, Paul, 297, 427, 552
Garrett (label), 91
Garrick Bar/Lounge (Chicago, IL), 256, 298, 406, 536
Garroway, Dave, 117, 155, 373, 506
Garvin, Richard M., 319
Gary Kings (band), 66, 67, 434
Gaslight (club) (S. Miami, FL), 195
Gaslight (club) (Toronto, Can.), 280
Gaslight A Go-Go (club) (New York, NY), 305
Gaslight Auditorium (Washington, DC), 391
Gaslight Cafe/Club (New York, NY) (see also: Village Gaslight), 147, 174, 210, 243, 249, 257, 272, 280, 283, 302, 327, 344, 367, 429, 486, 504, 513, 521, 522, 553
Gaslight Club (Chicago, IL), 322
Gaslight Square (club) (St. Louis, MO), 192
Gaslighters (group), The, 421
Gassman, Josephine, 222, 494
Gasson, Roxanna, 152
Gassy Jack's Place (club) (Vancouver, Can.), 211, 359, 393, 437
Gaster, Gilbert, 45
Gate (club), The (Chicago, IL), 279
Gate of Horn (club) (Chicago, IL), 35, 69, 117, 141, 155, 194, 292, 322, 366, 381, 414, 453, 490, 503, 556, 569
Gate Way Club (Santa Cruz, CA), 339, 512
Gates Avenue Theater (Brooklyn, NY), 221
Gates Express (group), 76
Gatewoods Club (Chicago, IL), 370
Gatewood's Tavern (see: Ruby Gatewood's Tavern)
Gay Nineties (club), The (Dallas, TX), 382
Gayety Theater (Toronto, Can.), 173
Gayety Theater (Utica, NY), 82
Gayles, Billy, 149, 437
Gayno, Creole (see: Guesnon, George)
Gayten, Paul, 86, 300, 381
Gazzarri's (club) (Los Angeles, CA), 308
Gear, Robert, 320
Geddins, Bob, Jr., 213
Gee, Jack, 464
Gee, Jack, Jr., 464
Geenote (label), 201
Geer, Will, 205
Gene & Eunice (duo), 277
Gene Norman (label), 253, 378
Gene Norman's Blues Jubilee (tour), 154
General Artist (label), 278
General Hospital (Baton Rouge, LA), 383
General Hospital (Spartanburg, SC), 158
General Records (label), 206
Generation (club), The (New York, NY), 46, 208
Genesee Theater (Waukegan, IL), 70
Genius (billing), The, 114
Gennett (label), 41, 49, 68, 125, 127, 139, 144, 145, 159, 227, 254, 274, 282, 336, 356, 374, 402, 450, 507, 545
Gentlemen of Swing (band), 285
George V, King of England, 592
George M. Cohan Theater (New York, NY), 256, 494
George Miller Plantation (Terry, MS), 290
George Washington Carver High School (Baytown, TX), 74
George Washington University (Washington, DC), 266, 513
George York Cafe (Osceola, AR), 303
George's (club) (Houston, TX), 43
George's Club-20 (Hackensack, NJ), 224
George's Kibitzeria (club) (Toronto, Can.), 155, 280, 340, 490, 553
George's Log Cabin (club) (San Francisco, CA), 334
Georgetown University (Washington, DC), 347
Georgia Band, 428
Georgia Bill (see: McTell, Willie)
Georgia Colored Strollers (tour), The, 292
Georgia Cotton Pickers (band), 228, 391
Georgia Festival of Folkmusic (Atlantia, GA), 265
Georgia Grass Roots Music Festival (Atlanta, GA), 171, 391
Georgia Grinder (see: Davenport, Charles)
Georgia Hotel, The (Vancouver, Can.), 377
Georgia Jazz Band (see: Georgia Wild Cats Jazz Band)
Georgia Peach (pseudonym), 221
Georgia Peach (billing), 221
Georgia Pine (see: Harris, Edward)
Georgia Pine Boy (see: McCoy, Joe)
Georgia Sea Island Singers (group), 149, 230
Georgia Slim (see: Seward, Alexander)
Georgia Slim (pseudonym), 140
Georgia Smart Set Minstrels (tour) (see also: Smart Set), 386, 428
Georgia Tom (see: Dorsey, Thomas A.)
Georgia Wild Cats Jazz Band, 428
Georgian Inn (Roseville, MI), 423
Gerde's Folk City (club) (New York, NY) (see also: Folk City), 142, 147, 174, 176, 185, 239, 280, 300, 366, 379, 381, 401, 426, 427, 453, 466, 481, 486, 490, 503, 504, 569
Geremia, Paul, 34, 319
German Jazz Festival (Essen, Ger.), 586
Germania Hall, The (New Orleans, LA), 508
Gert (label), 88
Gert zur Heide, Karl, 128, 381, 382
Ghana Music Publishing Company (Chicago, IL), 155
Ghetto Club, The (Austin, TX), 296
Giant (label), 437
Giant Step Club, A (New Rochelle, NY), 90
Gibbons, ______, 494
Gibbons, Carroll, 245
Gibbons, Irene (see: Taylor, Eva)
Gibbons, Kitty, 222
Gibson, Clifford (Sluefoot Joe), **192,** 280
Gibson, Hardy, 43
Gibson, Ingrid, 46
Gibson, P. R., 341
Gibson, William, 192
Gibson Guitar (product), 310
Gibson Theater (Philadelphia, PA), 274
Gibson's Dunbar Theater (New York, NY), 82
Gibson's North Pole Theater (Philadelphia, PA), 540
Gibson's Standard Theater (see: Standard Theater, Philadelphia, PA)
Gilbeaux, Gene, 586
Gilded Cage (club) (Boston, MA), 263
Gillespie, Dizzy, 243, 452
Gilliam, Earl, 78
Gillis, Irene, 40
Gillum, Irving, 193
Gillum, William "Jazz," 84, 110, **192-193,** *192*, 547
Gilly's (club) (Dayton, OH), 588
Gilmore, Boyd, **193,** 271, 412, 483
Gilmore, Martha, 328
Gilmore's Chez Paree (label), 383
Gilmore's Chez Paree Club (Kansas City, MO), 215, 383
Gilt Edge (label), 191, 385
Gilton, Cora, 39
Gingerbread House (club) (Little Rock, AR), 149
Girl of Smiles (billing), The, 386
Girl with the Million Dollar Smile (billing), The, 48
Gitfiddle Jim (see: Arnold, James)
Gitry, Willie, 212
Glass Pavilion (amusement center) (Brooklyn, NY), 153
Glaze, Red Hot Willie (see: McTell, Willie)

Gleason, Ralph, 216, 297, 312, 514, 586
Gleason's (lounge) (Cleveland, OH), 45, 113, 293, 359, 372
Glenn, Lloyd, 116, 190, 520
Glenn, Tyree, 466
Glimpse Farm (Henning, TN), 325
Glinn, Lillian, 279, 465
Globe (label), 357, 398
Globe Theater (Cleveland, OH), 463
Globetrotter Lounge (Chicago, IL), 259, 271, 287
Glossen, Lonnie, 444
Glove Theater (Gloversville, NY), 82
Glover, Henry, 88, 216
Glover, Lilian, 428
Glover, Sammy, 111
Go-Go Club, The (Bakersfield, CA), 398
Godfrey, Clemmy, 479
Godin, Dave, 472
Godrich, John, 484
Going Down with Janis (book), 296, 297
Gold Coast (club), The (Chicago, IL), 123
Gold Coast Jazz Band, 381
Gold Hugo Award, 244
Gold Star (label), 43, 86, 103, 214, 235, 241, 243, 267, 572
Gold Top (label), 127
Goldband (label), 57, 67, 192, 424, 453, 547, 582
Goldberg, Jack, 472
Goldberg, Barry, 54, 393
Goldberg, Joe, 484
Golddigger Lounge (Chicago, IL), 334
Golden Bear Club (Huntington Beach, CA), 54, 239, 296, 435, 549
Golden Bear Club (Los Angeles, CA), 32, 53, 398, 468, 520
Golden Bell (club) (Detroit, MI), 216, 225
Golden Checkmate (club) (Chicago, IL), 304, 435
Golden Club (Reno, NV), 298
Golden Crowns Gospel Singers (group), The, 259
Golden Eagle Saloon (St. Louis, MO), 489
Golden Elephant (club) (Bronx, NY), 90
Golden Gate Ballroom (New York, NY), 406, 525
Golden Gate Park (San Francisco, CA), 30, 270, 296
Golden Gate Quartet (group), 317, 556
Golden Gate Theater (San Francisco, CA), 70, 446
Golden Gloves (boxing organization), 154, 478
Golden Gospel Singers (group), 164
Golden Grommet (club) (San Francisco, CA), 30-31
Golden Lantern (club) (Marksville, LA), 270
Golden Lily Club (St. Louis, MO), 514
Golden Necklace of the Blues (billing), The, 428
Golden Nugget (club) (Elizabeth, NJ), 550
Golden Nugget (club) (Toronto, Can.), 37, 84, 280
Golden Nugget Saloon (Houston, TX), 78
Golden Ram (club) (Chicago, IL), 42
Golden Slipper (club) (Çhicago, IL), 410, 437
Golden Slipper (club) (Newark, NJ), 407
Golden Slipper Club (Durango, CO), 78
Golden Stars Gospel Group, 250
Golden State Country Bluegrass Special (concert) (Sausalito, CA), 174
Golden 20s Club (Detroit, MI), 278
Golden Vanity (club) (Boston, MA), 147, 239, 366
Golden Voices Gospel Quartet (group), 365
Golden West Cafe (Indianapolis, IN), 139, 492
Golden West Gospel Singers (group), 187
Goldenrod Riverboat (see: S.S. Goldenrod Riverboat/Showboat)
Goldfield Hotel (Baltimore, MD), 484
Goldgraben's (club) (New York, NY), 472
Goldie's Saloon (Burlingame, CA), 270
Goldman, Albert, 101
Goldstein, Kenneth S., 34, 148
Goliard Club (Forest Hills, NY), 174
Golson, Benny, 588
Gondoliers (group), The, 328
Gone (label), 238
Gonneau, Pierre, 474
Gonzales, Anita, 288
Good Buddy (club), The (San Francisco, CA), 243
Good Karma Coffeehouse (Madison, WI), 367, 504
Good Rockin' Charles (see: Edwards, Charles)
Good Rockin' Lounge (Chicago, IL), 132
Good Rocking Sam (see: Maghett, Samuel)
Good Shepherd Cemetery (Prichard, MS), 89
Good Time Bar (Detroit, MI), 127, 225, 578
Good Time Jazz (label), 36, 139, 185
Goodall, Edith, 580
Goodall, Hundley, 580
Goodbar, Edward, 558
Goodman, Benny, 446, 447, 464, 518, 541
Goodman, Jerry, 211
Goodson, Edna, 420
Goodson, Madison, H., 419
Goodson, Wilhelmina Madison, 419
Goodtime Jazz Club (Libertyville, IL), 381, 582
Goodtime Louisiana & New Orleans Jazz (label), 39
Goodwin, Mike, 522
Goosie Lee's Rock House (club) (Indianapolis, IN), 492
Gordon, Dan, 195
Gordon, Dexter, 253
Gordon, Jimmy (Peetie Wheatstraw's Brother), 552
Gordon, Mattie, 578
Gordon, Odetta, **193-196,** *194*, 296, 379, 465
Gordon, Roscoe, 50, 51, 291, 437, 530
Gordon, Slim (see: Weaver, Curley)
Gordy (label), 33
Goreau, Laurraine, 374
Goreed, Joseph, 564
Gorgeous Weed (see: Phelps, Arthur)
Goshorn Quarters (club) (Memphis, TN), 339
Gospel Choral Union (organization), 159
Gospel Four (group), The, 91
Gospel Keys (group), 384
Gospel Minnie (see: Douglas, Lizzie)
Gospel Sound (book), The, 160
Gotham (label), 164, 219, 235, 238, 281, 300, 366, 426, 447, 452, 503
Gower, Walter "Walt," 423
Graceland Memorial Park (Kenilworth, NJ), 558
Grady, Guitar, 283
Grady, Learless, 176
Grady, Lottie, 591
Grady Memorial Hospital (Atlanta, GA), 251
Graham, ______, 63
Graham, Billy, 542, 543
Graham, Elnora, 349
Graham, Lonnie, 63
Grainger, Porter, 481, 583
Grambling College (Grambling, LA), 178
Gramercy (label), 366, 503
Granada Theater (Dallas, TX), 244, 390
Granada Theater (Waltham, MA), 82
Grand (label), 219
Grand Ballroom (Chicago, IL), 72, 123
Grand Ballroom (Detroit, MI), 132, 228, 308
Grand Bar/Lounge (Detroit, MI), 431, 566
Grand Central Discotheque (club) (Houston, TX), 58
Grand Central Theater (Chicago, IL), 173, 246, 454
Grand Hotel Winter Garden (Calcutta, Ind.), 586
Grand Ole Opry (theater) (Nashville, TN), 577
Grand Prix du Disque de Jazz (award), 114, 152, 464, 570
Grand Terrace (club) (New Orleans, LA), 299
Grand Terrace Ballroom (Birmingham, AL), 188, 356
Grand Terrace Ballroom (Chicago, IL) (see also: New Grand Terrace), 256, 271, 445, 523
Grand Terrace Cafe (Chicago, IL), 71
Grand Theater (Chicago, IL), 48, 134, 159, 173, 350, 428, 450, 463, 464, 467, 540, 581
Grand Theater (Long Beach, CA), 205
Grand Theater (W. Palm Beach, FL), 472
Grand Valley State College (Allendale, MI), 33, 217, 437, 450

Grande Carte (club) (Paris, Fr.), 256
Granderson, John Lee, 162, **196-197,** *196*, 276, 393
Grandview Inn (Columbus, OH), 141
Granite (label), 190
Grant, Bobby, 564
Grant, Leola B. "Coot," **197,** *197*, 584
Grant & Wilson (duo), 197, 467
Grant Park Blues Festival (Chicago, IL), 499, 575, 596
Granz, Norman, 253
Grapes of Wrath (club), The (Cleveland, OH), 336
Grateful Dead (band), The, 330
Gray, Arvella, 65, **197-198,** *198*
Gray, Henry, **198-199,** *198*, 371, 491
Gray, Sam, 48, 331
Gray (label), 198
Grayhaired Bill (pseudonym), 570
Grayson, ______, 538
Graystone Ballroom (Detroit, MI), 308, 388, 538
Grear, Charles C., 44
Greasy Spoon (club), The (Lubbock, TX), 133
Great American Coffee House (Chicago, IL), 575
Great American Music Hall (San Francisco, CA), 51, 98, 114, 130, 208, 304, 307, 310, 341, 360, 429, 490, 516, 532, 549
Great American Popular Singers (book), The, 116, 312, 441, 465, 544
Great Dame (label), 154
Great Folk Revival (Uniondale, NY), 522
Great Lakes (label), 563
Great Scott (label), 125
Great South Bay Jazz Festival (Great River, NY), 375, 447, 519
Great Southeast Music Hall (Atlanta, GA), 243, 244, 261, 346, 367, 379, 389, 435, 504
Great Stars of Jazz Show (tour), 108
Greater Harvest Baptist Church (Newark, NJ), 465
Greater St. Matthew #2 Baptist Church (New Orleans, LA), 128
Greek Theater (Los Angeles, CA), 194
Greely Square Theater (New York, NY), 221, 581
Green, Al, 402
Green, Cal, 78, 199
Green, Clarence, 199
Green, Clarence "Candy," 76, **199-200,** *199*
Green, Cornelius (Lonesome Sundown), **200,** *200*, 530, 531, 547
Green, Eli, 201, 364
Green, Hazel, 462
Green, L. C., 27
Green, Lee, 489, 491, 529
Green, Lillian "Lil," 44, 61, 68, **200-201,** *201*, 522
Green, Mary Lee, 371
Green, Norman "Slim," **201-202,** *202*, 293, 454, 528
Green, Peter, 307
Green, Rosa (see: Henderson, Rosa)
Green, Sadie (see: Brown, Bessie)
Green, Sammy, 277, 512
Green, Slim (see: Green, Norman)
Green, T. Baby, 192
Green, Tuff, 308
Green, Violet (see: Smith, Clara)
Green Bull (club) (Hermosa Beach, CA), 385
Green Bunny Lounge (Chicago, IL), 67, 461
Green Door (club), The (Chicago, IL), 35, 116
Green Earth Cafe (San Francisco, CA), 30, 55, 98, 125, 151, 213, 270, 332, 358, 440, 516, 554
Green Gables Club (Hot Springs, AR), 298
Green Park Hotel (London, Eng.), 256
Green Parrot (hall) (Dallas, TX), 382, 472
Green Planet (club) (Chicago, IL), 65
Green Spot (club) (Clarksdale, MS), 412, 483
Greenberg, Roy, 451, 531, 549
Greenblatt, Marjorie, 206
Greenbriar Country/Golf Club (WV), 423
Greenbrier Jr. College (Lewisburg, WV), 141
Greenfield, Adam, 250
Greenfield Cemetery (Hempstead, NY), 480, 482
Greenlawn Cemetery (San Francisco, CA), 508
Greensmith, Bill, 307, 347, 443, 493
Greentree Inn (Wichita, KS), 375
Greenway, John, 207
Greenwood Cemetery (Brooklyn, NY), 206
Greenwood Cemetery (Portland, OR), 288
Greenwood Cemetery (Renton, WA), 224
Greenwood Inn (Portland, OR), 360
Gregory, Jim, 270
Grenada County Hospital (Grenada, MS), 257
Grenade (label), 213
Grendel's Lair (coffeehouse) (Philadelphia, PA), 41, 95, 132, 156, 501
Grey, Al, 375
Greymore Hotel (Portland, ME), 44
Griffin, Tommy, 524
Griffith, Rich, 273
Griffith, Shirley, 27, 50, 64, **202,** 290, 427
Griffith, Willie, 202
Griffiths, David, 373
Griggs, Dave, 334
Grimes, Tiny, 89, 219, 300, 383
Grimes Memorial Hospital (Navasota, TX), 330
Grinnell College (Grinnell, IA), 249, 569
Grinnell Folk Festival (Grinnell, IA), 246, 340
Gritzbach, George, 147
Groom, Bob, 70, 276, 280, 289, 492
Groove (label), 37, 38, 137, 165, 338, 364, 366, 415, 503
Groove Merchant (label), 407
Groove Yard (club) (Vancouver, Can.), 51
Gross, Leon, 60, 158, **202**
Grossman, Stefan, 147, 249
Ground Hogs (group), 239
Group (group), The, 53
Grove (club), The (Los Angeles, CA), 114
Grove Hill Cemetery (Durham, NC), 184
Growders Cemetery (Cotton Plant, AR), 552
Guelph Folk Festival (Toronto, Can.), 210
Guelph University (Toronto, Can.), 553
Guesnon, George, **203-204,** *203*
Guesnon, George Sr., 203
Guest Star (label), 243
Guida, Louis, 149
Guide to Jazz (book), 35
Guide to Longplay Jazz Records (book), A, 33
Guild Theater (Louisville, KY), 345
Guilford College (Greensboro, NC), 420
Guitar Eddy (see: Clearwater, Eddy)
Guitar Jr. (see: Brooks, Lonnie) (see: Johnson, Luther, Jr.)
Guitar Nubbitt (see: Hankerson, Alvin)
Guitar Pete (see: Franklin, Edward)
Guitar Player (label), 54
Guitar Player (magazine), 311
Guitar Red (see: Minter, Iverson)
Guitar Shorty (see: Fortescue, John Henry)
Guitar Slim (see: Green, Norman) (see: Jones, Eddie) (see: Seward, Alexander)
Guitar Slim (pseudonym), 356
Guitar Slim Jr. (pseudonym), 293
Guitar Wizard (billing), The, 559
Gulliver's (club) (W. Paterson, NJ), 254
Gunter, Al, 204
Gunter, Arthur, 184, **204,** *204* 311, 435
Gunter, Larry, 204
Gunter, William, 204
Gunter Brothers (group), The, 204
Guralnick, Peter, 273, 289, 391, 459, 512, 574
Gut Bucket Syncopators (band), 582
Guthrie, Arlo, 206, 207
Guthrie, Charles Edward, 205
Guthrie, Jack, 205
Guthrie, Jeff, 205, 207
Guthrie, Marjorie, 206
Guthrie, Noralee, 206
Guthrie, Woodrow "Woody," 173, 174, **204-207,** *205*, 317, 319, 365, 503, 556
Guy, George "Buddy," **207-209,** *207*, 228, 241, 244, 280, 285, 308, 311, 394, 397, 438, 478, 499, 528, 548
Guy, Philip "Phil," 209
Guyden (label), 136
Guyton, Kathy, 445
Gwenn (label), 74
Gym Theater (Kingsport, TN), 365
Gypsy Tea Room (New Orleans, LA), 61, 89, 281, 299

H&T Club (Chicago, IL), 370, 479
HMV (label), 256

Haarlem Music Festival (Haarlem, Holland), 117
Hackensack Cemetery (Hacksensack, NJ), 454
Hadacol Boys (band), 400
Haeg's Circus (tour), 144
Hafford, Charlie, 456
Hagenbeck Wallace Circus (tour), 185
Haggard, Merle, 441
Hague, Douglas, 386
Haight Street Barbeque Club (San Francisco, CA), 185
Half Note (club) (New York, NY), 155, 246, 254, 340, 447, 448, 457, 481, 566, 567, 588
Hall, Adelaide, 71, 221
Hall, Alan, 321
Hall, Bob, 337
Hall, Henry, 256
Hall, Juanita, 466
Hall, Louvenia, 344
Hall, Skip, 89
Hall, Vera, 33, **209**, *209*
Hall, Willie (Drive 'em Down), 164, 166
Hall (label), 125
Hall Brothers Jazz Band, 322
Hall Johnson Choir (group), 541
Hallelujah Joe (see: McCoy, Joe)
Halsey Theater (Brooklyn, NY), 81, 254-256
Ham Gravy (see: Brown, Robert)
Hamfoot Ham (see: McCoy, Joe)
Hamilton, George (see: Davenport, Charles)
Hamilton, Roy, 60, 434, 470, 580
Hammersmith Odeon (theater) (London, Eng.), 310, 450
Hammerstein, June, 174
Hammie (see: Nixon, Hammie)
Hammie & Son (duo), 57
Hammond, John, Jr. (see: Hammond, John Paul)
Hammond, John Henry, Jr., 209, 254
Hammond, John Paul, 54, **209-210**, *210*, 241, 244, 276, 283, 289, 390, 429, 570
Hammond, Johnny, 210
Hammond, Merrill M., 152
Hammond Hill Church Cemetery (Como, MS), 364
Hampton, Lionel, 60, 216, 348, 375, 536, 564
Hampton, Riley, 586
Hampton, Slide. 417
Hampton Institute Jazz Festival (Hampton, VA), 272, 388
Hamp-Tone (label), 216, 377
Hamp-Tone All Stars (band), 216
Handbook of Jazz (book), A, 89, 229, 257, 521
Handley, Lillie, 95
Handy, W. C., 98, 163, 175, 326, 350, 454
Hanen, R. T., 192
Hangover Club (San Francisco, CA), 373, 447
Hanington, H. H., 571
Hankerson, Alvin, 184, **210-211**
Hanscom Airbase (Bedford, MA), 527
Hansen, Barret, 293, 311
Hanshaw, Annette, 110, 222
Happy (pseudonym), 266
Happy Bird (label), 148
Happy Home Club/Lounge (Chicago, IL), 35, 123, 259, 322
Happy Pals (band), 203
Happy Phillipson's Medicine Show (tour), 179
Happy Rhone's All Star Show (tour), 221
Happy Rhone's Orchestra Club (New York, NY), 254, 491, 583
Harbor College (see: Los Angeles Harbor College)
Harbor Island Park (Mamaroneck, NY), 44, 550, 558
Hard Knob Club (Chicago, IL), 460
Hardge, Johnny (Johnny Hodges), 450
Harding, Buster, 285
Harding, Phil, 493
Harding, Tom, 493
Hardwick, Otto, 419
Hardy, Marion, 44
Hare, Pat, 241
Harlem (label), 61, 164, 364, 365, 503
Harlem Blues & Jazz Band, 44, 45, 550
Harlem Blues Band, 558
Harlem Casino (club) (New York, NY), 496
Harlem Club (Arcola, MS), 59
Harlem Club (Brooklyn, NY), 282
Harlem Club (New York, NY), 164
Harlem Club (Osceola, AR), 304, 450
Harlem Club (Philadelphia, PA), 538
Harlem Club (St. Louis, MO), 514
Harlem Cultural Festival (New York, NY), 51, 308
Harlem Fifth Avenue Theater (New York, NY), 467
Harlem Gospel Singers (group), 426
Harlem Hamfats (band), 227, 250, 274, 355, 501
Harlem Hospital (New York, NY), 221, 229, 406, 472
Harlem Hotshots (band), 261
Harlem Inn (Detroit, MI), 95, 96, 217, 238, 338, 378
Harlem Night Club (Memphis, TN), 339
Harlem On Parade Show (tour), 466
Harlem Opera House (theater) (New York, NY), 31, 43, 71, 82, 152, 173, 256, 274, 298, 357, 385, 464, 467, 472, 475, 491, 496, 541, 564, 581
Harlem Square Club, The (Miami, FL), 434
Harlem Stars (band), 512
Harlem Strutters (band), 550
Harlem Syncopators Orchestra, 444
Harlem Tavern (Belzoni, MS), 271
Harlem's Favorite (billing), 221
Harlem's Mae West (billing), 492
Harmonia Hotel (Chicago, IL), 63, 69, 370
Harmonica Fats (pseudonym), 53
Harmonica Frank (see: Floyd, Frank)
Harmonica Harry (see: Mickle, Elmon)
Harmonica King (see: Smith, George)
Harmonica Slim (see: Blaylock, Travis) (see: Moore, James)
Harmonium Lounge (Chicago, IL), 444
Harmonizing Four (group), 137
Harmony (label), 373, 391, 406
Harmony Club (Dallas, TX), 547
Harmony Girls (group), 385
Harmony Inn (New Orleans, LA), 420
Harmony Kings Gospel Quartet (group), 303
Harmony Lounge (Chicago, IL), 343
Harney, Hacksaw, 483
Harold Blackshear's Supper Club (San Francisco, CA), 518-519
Harold Hopkins Plantation (Clarksdale, MS), 412
Harp Styles of Sonny Terry (book), The, 505
Harper, Leonard, 52, 220, 491
Harper, Nettie, 159
Harper & Blanks (duo), 52
Harpo, Slim (see: Moore, James)
Harpur College (Binghamton, NY), 34, 457, 490, 563
Harrah's (club) (Lake Tahoe, NV), 157, 299
Harrah's Club (Reno, NV), 113, 567
Harrigan's (club) (Houston, TX), 199
Harrington, Carey Bell, 41
Harrington, Eddy, 123
Harris, ______, 480
Harris, Coot, 241
Harris, Don "Sugarcane," 51, 116, **211**, *211*, 269, 311, 440
Harris, Edward (Carolina Slim), 184, **212**, 244
Harris, Estella, 591, 592
Harris, Hi Tide, **212-213**, *212*, 271
Harris, Homer, **213**
Harris, James (Shakey Jake), 32, 72, 213, **213-214**, *214*, 236, 269, 289, 345, 438, 576
Harris, Jesse, 209
Harris, Josephine, 271
Harris, Luther, 215
Harris, Mae (see: Henderson, Rosa)
Harris, Mamie (see: Henderson, Rosa)
Harris, Manzy, 111, 175
Harris, Mary, 226, 228
Harris, Pearl (see: Miles, Josephine)
Harris, Peppermint, **214-215**, *215*
Harris, Rex, 110
Harris, Scrap, 320-1
Harris, Shakey Jake (see: Harris, James)
Harris, Sheldon, 41, 50, 52, 55, 64, 73, 74, 80, 81, 87, 112, 148, 149, 151, 157, 179, 185, 197, 207, 232, 234, 239, 263, 264, 273, 278, 285, 290, 292, 297, 325, 327, 331, 336, 338, 346, 354, 355, 361, 365, 370, 372, 383, 387, 399, 401, 409, 425, 427, 429, 430, 444, 451, 461, 466, 471, 475, 476, 477, 485, 493, 498, 502, 523, 526, 533, 548, 551, 565, 585, 596
Harris, Son, 460
Harris, Sugarcane (see: Harris, Don)
Harris, Will, 483
Harris, Wynonie, 88, **215-216**, *216*, 220, 299, 406, 448
Harris, Zoolenia, 230

Harris Bar (Dayton, OH), 517
Harris' Blues & Jazz Seven (band), 221
Harris' Cabaret (Seattle, WA), 221
Harris Theater (McKeesport, PA), 70
Harris Theater (Pittsburgh, PA), 71, 81
Harrison, Dave, 35
Harrison, Max, 41, 64, 158, 162, 351, 354, 360, 410, 475, 533, 552, 555, 562
Harrison, Teresa, 529
Harrison, Vernon (Boogie Woogie Red), **216-217**, *217*, 371, 415, 535, 577
Harrison, Wilbert, 158
Harrison County Prison (Harrison County, TX), 317
Harry's American Showroom (club) (Miami, FL), 566
Hart, Clyde, 564
Hart, Genevieve, 316
Harvard Stadium (Cambridge, MA), 296
Harvard University (Cambridge, MA), 147, 176, 260, 415, 445, 457, 573
Harvest (label), 101
Harvey, Alex, 117
Harvey, Bill, 199, 308
Harvey (label), 96
Harwood, Ronald P., 533
Hatch, Peter, 238, 470, 505
Hatch, Provine, Jr., **217**
Haussler, Jerry, 187
Haven (label), 564
Havens, Dan, 313, 314
Havens, Richard "Richie," 116, **217-219**, *218*, 553
Hawaii Club (Waukegan, IL), 596
Hawaiian Gardens (club) (Kansas City, MO), 518
Hawaiian Guitar Wizard (billing), The, 547
Hawketts (group), 60
Hawkins, Coleman, 134, 564, 586-588
Hawkins, Erskine, 550
Hawkins, Jalacy J. "Screamin' Jay," 216, **219-220**, *220*, 299, 412, 448
Hawks (band), The, 259, 266
Hawthorn, George, 172
Hawthorn, Susie, 172
Hawthorne, Gladys, 381
Hayes, Carter, 558
Hayes, Dobby, 299
Hayes, Edgar, 44, 285
Hayes, Henry, 103, 400
Hayes, Louis, 454
Hayes Lounge (Houston, TX), 57, 583
Hayloft Dinner Theater (Manassas, VA), 245, 313
Haywood Park General Hospital (Brownsville, TN), 177
Haze Quartet of Lake City, South Carolina (group), 425
Hazeley, Jimmy, 56
Head Plantation (Goldfield, MS), 534
Headhunters (group), 442
Headline Singers (group), 206, 317, 365, 503
Hear Me Talkin' to Ya (book), 31, 475
Heard, J. C., 542
Heart Breakers (group), 596
Heavenly Kings Gospel Quartet (group), 397
Hebb, Bobby, 29
Heckman, Don, 70, 241, 280, 337, 491
Heco (label), 63
Hefner, Hugh, 132, 432, 567
Hegamin, Bill, 221
Hegamin, Lucille, 48, **220-222**, *221*, 491
Heidt, Horace, 329
Heilbut, Tony, 160
Helena Hospital (Helena, AR), 399
Helen's Moonlight Lounge (St. Louis, MO), 502
Helfer, Erwin, 337, 529
Hemisfair (World's Fair) (San Antonio, TX), 313, 506
Hemphill, Jack, 415
Hemphill, Rosa Lee, 230
Hemphill, Sidney "Sid", 230, 364
Henderson, Catherine (see: Taylor, Eva)
Henderson, Catherine, 456
Henderson, Clarence, 230
Henderson, Douglas "Slim", 223
Henderson, Edmonia, 31, 223
Henderson, Eletha, 318
Henderson, Fletcher, 52, 71, 134, 137, 152, 197, 221, 222, 223, 231, 254, 295, 357, 475, 491, 527, 540, 542, 556, 564, 581, 584
Henderson, Griffin, 222
Henderson, Hetha Anna, 344
Henderson, Horace, 44, 574
Henderson, John Henry, 139
Henderson, John William, 574
Henderson, Katherine, **222**, *222*, 223, 497
Henderson, Rosa "Rose", 222, **222-223**, *223*, 357, 583
Henderson, Rose, 128
Henderson Newell's Plantation (Red Banks, MS), 106
Henderson's Royal Garden (club) (Ferriday, LA), 379
Hendricks, Jon, 586
Hendrix, George "Crow Jane", 315
Hendrix, James Allen, 223
Hendrix, James Marshall "Jimi", 47, 54, **223-225**, *224*, 238, 271, 289, 293, 305, 311, 391, 528, 545
Hendrix (book), 224, 225
Henley, John Lee, 169, **225**, 576, 578
Hennepin Theater (Minneapolis, MN), 70
Henrotin Hospital (Chicago, IL), 467
Henry, Clarence, 103, 158
Henry, Ernie, 385
Henry, Jeannetta, 407
Henry, Lou, 137
Henry, Thelma, 348
Henry, Willie, 348
Henry Ford Hospital (Detroit, MI), 228
Henry Ford Museum (Detroit, MI), 423
Henry's Swing Club (Detroit, MI), 217, 238
Hensley, William (Washboard Willie), 127, 182, 216, **225-226**, *226*, 578
Hentoff, Nat, 31, 259, 455, 475
Herald (label), 63, 96, 243, 364, 403, 436, 452, 503, 571
Herculon (label), 225
Here Coffeehouse (Minneapolis, MN), 147
Heritage (label), 65, 167, 187, 198, 419, 533, 545
Heritage Hall (New Orleans, LA), 506
Heritage Hall Jazz Band, 506
Heritage House Nightclub (Seattle, WA), 310
Herman Park (St. Louis, MO), 314
Herman's Inn (New York, NY), 373
Hermitage (club), The (St. Louis, MO), 314
Hermitage (label), 78
Hernando's Hideaway (club) (Chicago, IL), 269
Herrick Memorial Hospital (Berkeley, CA), 440
Herron, Della, 499
Herwin (label), 272, 507
Hess, Norbert, 39, 54, 60, 64, 77, 96, 102, 136, 154, 167, 198, 204, 211, 220, 237, 261, 300, 301, 352, 408, 417, 423, 430, 474, 489, 508, 522, 544
Hey Rube Club (Chicago, IL), 381
Heywood, Eddie, Jr., 252, 256
Heywood, Eddie, Sr., 475, 531
Hi (label), 289
Hi-Ball Bar (Kansas City, MO), 321
HiFi (label), 586
HiFi/Stereo Review (magazine), 455
Hi-Hat Hattie (see: McDaniel, Hattie)
Hi-Q (label), 443
Hibbler, Al, 89, 311, 448
Hickory House (club) (New York, NY), 406
Hicks, Charlie, **226**, 228, 546
Hicks, Charlie, Sr., 226, 228
Hicks, Edna, 31, **226-227**, 374
Hicks, John, 227
Hicks, Layfield, 227
Hicks, Minnie, 380
Hicks, Otis (Lightnin' Slim), 208, 209, **227-228**, *227*, 232, 244, 270, 285, 301, 383, 384, 391, 474, 522, 554, 576, 578
Hicks, Robert (Barbecue Bob), 226, **228-229**, *228*, 266, 391, 546
Hidden Door (club), The (New Orleans, LA), 506
Hide-A-Way (club) (Newark, NJ), 550
Hideaway Club (Chicago, IL), 393
Hideaway Club (New Orleans, LA), 157, 326
Higgenbotham, Robert, 517
Higgins, Chuck, 407, 544
Higgs, Blake, 415
High Chaparral (club) (Chicago, IL), 51, 95, 104, 190, 304, 310, 407, 435, 567, 572
High Sheriff from Hell (billing), 552
Highland (label), 28
Highland-Alameda County Hospital (Oakland, CA), 508
Highland Cemetery (Kansas City, MO), 321
Highland Park Community College (Detroit, MI), 84, 96, 217, 226, 278, 588

Highway (label), 382
Hill, Bertha "Chippie", 49, **229**, *229*, 406, 438, 492, 493
Hill, Beverly Jean (Big Mama Bev), **229-230**, *230*, 374, 465
Hill, Chippie (see: Hill, Bertha)
Hill, Eddie, 179
Hill, Ella, 290
Hill, Emma, 98
Hill, Gary, 235
Hill, Jessie, 103, 158
Hill, Jim, 251
Hill, Joe, 435
Hill, John, 229
Hill, King Solomon (see: Holmes, Joe)
Hill, King Solomon (pseudonym), 569
Hill, Lester, 337
Hill, Lockhart, 337
Hill, Ray, 338
Hill, Robert, 337
Hill, Rosa Lee, **230**
Hill, Ruffan, 230
Hill, Teddy, 256
Hill, Tom, 164
Hill, Z. Z., 154
Hill Sisters (group), The, 540
Hill Street Theater (Los Angeles, CA), 70, 541
Hillcrest Memorial Park Cemetery (Dallas, TX), 307
Hillery, Mable, **230-231**, *231*
Hillman, Chris, 136, 362
Hill's Fox Hole (club) (Chicago, IL), 437, 461
Hilltop (club), The (Little Rock, AR), 204
Hilltop (club), The (Pine Bluff, AR), 86
Hilton Hotel (Las Vegas, NV), 158, 310
Hine, Graham, 289
Hines, Earl "Fatha", 89, 108, 141, 256, 284, 447, 591
Hines, Eddie, 506-507
Hinton, Joe, 238
Hinton, Lester, 150
Hip-Cat (pseudonym), 468
Hippodrome Ballroom (Memphis, TN), 93, 269, 388
Hippodrome Theater (London, Eng.), 494
Hippodrome Theater (Memphis, TN), 400, 560
Hippodrome Theater (New York, NY), 71, 491
Hirt, Al, 157, 230, 466, 506
His Eye Is on the Sparrow (book), 543, 544
His Father's Mustache (club) (Montreal, Can.), 367, 504
Hit (label), 523
Hite, Bob, 127
Hite, Les, 231, 525, 564
Hite, Little, 236
Hite, Mattie/Matie, **231**
Hite, Nellie (see: Hite, Mattie)
Hite's Cabaret (Los Angeles, CA), 221
Ho-Ti Supper Club (Portland, OR), 30
Hob Nob Club (Chicago, IL), 213
Hodes, Art, 108, 141, 145, 229, 503, 506, 591
Hodges, Jay, 408
Hodges, Johnny (see: Hardge, Johnny)
Hodges, Johnny, 524
Hodges, Will, 233
Hoefer, George, 145
Hogan, Samuel, 232
Hogan, Silas, 228, **231-232**, *232*, 301, 435
Hogg, Anderson, 233
Hogg, Andrew "Smokey", 43, 70, 133, 134, 215, **232-233**, *232*, 234, 398, 461, 518, 552
Hogg, Frank, 232
Hogg, Isaac Andrew, 233
Hogg, John, 29, 134, **233**, *233*, 271, 276, 416, 518
Hogg, Willie Anderson "Smokey", 233, **233-234**
Hokum Boys (group), 159, 559
Hokum Jug Band, 159, 559
Holbert, Susan, 360
Holborn Empire Theater (London, Eng.), 541
Holder, "Ram" John, **234**, *234*
Hole (club), The (E. St. Louis, IL), 76
Hole in the Wall (club) (Atlanta, GA), 415
Hole in the Wall (club) (Helena, AR), 443
Hole in the Wall (club) (Indianapolis, IN), 492
Hole in the Wall (club) (Kansas City, MO), 518
Hole in the Wall (club) (Memphis, TN), 339
Holiday, Billie, 179, 251, 252, 406, 418, 465, 466, 476, 538
Holiday, Harold (Black Boy Shine), 455
Holiday (label), 95, 528
Holiday Ball (Akron, OH), 269
Holiday Club (Denver, CO), 133
Holiday House (club) (Monroeville, PA), 538
Holiday Inn (club) (Chicago, IL), 254
Holiday Inn (club) (Los Angeles, CA), 398
Holiday Inn (club) (Memphis, TN), 106
Holiday Inn (club) (Mission, TX), 84
Holiday Inn Bar (Saginaw, MI), 443
Holiday Inn Circuit, 322
Holiday Theater (New York, NY), 256
Holiness Church (Tyler, TX), 267
Hollins, Tony, **234**
Holloway, Hugh, 149
Holloway, Jim, 38
Hollywood (label), 28, 136, 357, 398, 547
Hollywood Bar (Muncie, IN), 139
Hollywood Bowl (stadium) (Hollywood/Los Angeles, CA), 113, 141, 157, 174, 195, 206, 219, 224, 309, 310, 408, 417, 431, 447
Hollywood Cafe (Chicago, IL), 489
Hollywood Canteen (Hollywood, CA), 298
Hollywood Cemetery (Memphis, TN), 486
Hollywood Club (New York, NY), 31
Hollywood Flames (group), 101
Hollywood Landmark Motor Hotel (Hollywood, CA), 209
Hollywood Lounge (Houston, TX), 43, 453
Hollywood Palladium (see: Palladium, The)
Hollywood Radio/TV Society (organization), 114
Hollywood Rendezvous (club) (Chicago, IL), 68, 246, 268, 393
Hollywood Show Lounge (Chicago, IL), 380
Hollywood Theater (Detroit, MI), 70
Holman, John, 515
Holman, Libby, 556
Holmes, Cap, 38
Holmes, Groove, 588
Holmes, Joe (King Solomon Hill), 127, **235**
Holmes, Odetta, 193
Holmes, Reuben, 193
Holmes, Robert, 384
Holmes, Wright, **235**
Holmes Center Ballroom (DeKalb, IL), 389, 450, 499
Holt, Douglas, 236
Holt, John, 324
Holt, Morris (Magic Slim), 169, **235-236**, *235*, 344
Holt, Nick, 236
Holt Cemetery (New Orleans, LA), 486, 506
Holts, Roosevelt, **236**, *236*, 290, 486, 546, 547
Holy Blues (book), The, 147
Holy Cross Cemetery (Los Angeles, CA), 386
Holy Ghost Church (Dallas, TX), 525
Holy Sepulchre Cemetery (Worth, IL), 227, 524
Holy Trinity Church (Blackville, SC), 259
Home Cooking (label), 58, 243
Home of the Blues (label), 28, 86, 350
Home of the Blues Club (Toronto, Can.), 280
Home of the Blues Music School (New York, NY), 147, 365, 454
Homer G. Phillips Hospital (St. Louis, MO), 297, 414, 460
Homer the Great (see: Crayton, Connie)
Homesick James (see: Williamson, John A.)
Honey Eddie (see: Edwards, David)
Honeyboy (see: Patt, Frank)
Honeydripper, The (see: Sykes, Roosevelt)
Honeydrippers (group), The, 489
Hong Kong Bar (Los Angeles, CA), 567
Honkers and Shouters (book), 190, 191, 299, 528, 538, 589
Hood, Mallie, 215
Hook & Ladder (club) (Toronto, Can.), 310
Hooker, Earl, 35, 41, 225, **237-238**, *237*, 240, 359, 396, 399, 404, 405, 412, 450, 528, 529, 530, 572
Hooker, Earl, Sr., 237

Hooker, John, Jr., 240
Hooker, John Lee, 41, 95, 150, 209, 210, 217, **238-241,** *239*, 269, 312, 313, 339, 352, 378, 388, 393, 396, 398, 407, 424, 434, 439, 453, 493, 494, 506, 507, 516, 530, 535, 547, 571, 586
Hooker, Robert, 240
Hooker Joe (see: Davis, Walter)
Hoolies Club (Chicago, IL), 292
Hoot Night (concert) (Los Angeles, CA), 428
Hootenanny Club (Los Angeles, CA), 141, 566
Hootenanny-in-the-Round (club) (Houston, TX), 243
Hopes Hall (New Orleans, LA), 373
Hopkins, Abbie, 244
Hopkins, Abe, 241, 242
Hopkins, Alice Mae, 244
Hopkins, Claude, 44, 221, 285, 550
Hopkins, Dailey, 244
Hopkins, Joel, **241**, 242, 243, 244
Hopkins, John Henry, **242**, 244
Hopkins, Lightnin' (see: Hopkins, Sam)
Hopkins, Linda, 464
Hopkins, Mattie, 564
Hopkins, Miriam, 80
Hopkins, Sam "Lightnin' ", 29, 43, 99 111, 127, 138, 141, 166, 209, 210, 212, 215, 228, 233, 241, **242-244,** *242*, 276, 280, 283, 301, 313, 324, 339, 375, 379, 419, 440, 461, 479, 501, 524, 572, 574
Hopper's (club) (New York, NY), 567
Horan's Madhouse Club (Philadelphia, PA), 463
Horizon (label), 141
Horne, Lena, 263, 544
Horoscope Lounge (Cincinnati, OH), 535
Horricks, Raymond, 448, 568
Horsley, Carter, 557
Horton, Big Walter (see: Horton, Walter)
Horton, Joanne Barbara "Pug", **245,** *245*, 374, 465
Horton, John, 245
Horton, Pug (see: Horton, Joanne)
Horton, Sarah, 467
Horton, Walter "Big Walter", 41, 42, 169, 181, **246-7,** *246*, 266, 269, 294, 337, 340, 424, 425, 493, 501, 576, 595
Hoskins Juke, The (Clarksdale, MS), 62
Hospital Reserve Corps (organization), 497
Hot Club of Cleveland (Cleveland, OH), 145
Hot Club of France (Paris, Fr.), 38, 117, 152, 254, 570
Hot Cottage (group), 247
Hot Five (band), 279
Hot Harlem Revue (tour), 277, 512
Hot Jazz Concert (Hamburg, Ger.), 166
Hot Line (label), 220
Hot Mama's (coffeehouse) (Memphis, TN), 179, 560
Hot Shot Willie (see: McTell, Willie)
Hot Shots (band), 274
Hot Shot's Club (Vance, MS), 339
Hot Sizzling Band, 120
Hot Tuna (group), 147
Hotel American (New York, NY), 405
Hotel Americana (see: Americana Hotel)
Hotel Braddock (New York, NY), 564
Hotel Meridian (Paris, Fr.), 466
Hotel Peabody (see: Peabody Hotel)
Hotel Pontchartrain (Detroit, MI), 84, 163, 230, 327, 423
Hotel Sherman (Chicago, IL), 406, 446, 536
Hotel Taft (New York, NY), 441
Hotel Tropicana (see: Tropicana Hotel)
Hotfeet Club, The (New York, NY), 256
Hotsy-Totsy Club, The (San Francisco, CA), 321
Hound Dogs (band), 404, 412
House, Eddie "Son", 89, **247-249,** *248*, 288, 289, 315, 349, 390, 409, 429, 493, 561
House, Eddie, Sr., 247
House, Eugene, 249
House, Son (see: House, Eddie)
House of Joy (club) (Oakland, CA), 188, 439, 449, 509
House of Sound (label), 337, 489
House Rockers (band) (Houndog Taylor), 500, 501
House Rockers (band) (Memphis Slim), 116, 155
House Rockers (band) (Mickey Baker), 37
Household of Ruth Cemetery (Whitesboro, NJ), 584
Houston, Bee (see: Houston, Edward)
Houston, Cisco, 174, 205, 206
Houston, Edward "Bee", 51, 76, 78, **249-250,** 311, 528
Houston, Joe, 544
Houston Country Club (Houston, TX), 585
Houston County Prison Farm (Houston, TX?), 243
Houston Courier (newspaper), 572
Houston Symphony Orchestra, 114
Hovel (club), The (Edmonton, Can.), 377
Hovington, Franklin "Frank", **250**
Howard, Kid, 203, 505
Howard, Rosetta, **250-251,** *251*, 355
Howard Street Tavern (Omaha, NE), 156
Howard Theater (Boston, MA), 81, 221
Howard Theater (Washington, DC), 44, 73, 82, 86, 88, 113, 154, 173, 298, 350, 359, 417, 463, 472, 491, 494, 540, 571
Howard University (Washington, DC), 32, 93, 130, 138, 177, 208, 219, 260, 266, 309, 327, 330, 363, 389, 401, 427, 549, 562
Howard's Place (club) (Oakland, CA), 544
Howell, Joshua "Peg Leg", 226, 228, **251-252,** *251*
Howell, Thomas, 251
Howlin' Wolf (see: Burnett, Chester) (see: Smith, John T.)
Hoy, Ophelia, 164
Hub (label), 68, 406
Hub City (label), 149
Hubbard, Freddie, 417
Hubbard, Roger, 289, 416
Hubbard Hospital (Nashville, TN), 191
Hubers Seafood Restaurant (Houston, TX), 78
Hucklebones (pseudonym), 454
Huddy Color Bar (Detroit, MI), 238
Hudson, Joe, 270
Hudson, Little, 198, 342
Hudson (label), 517
Hudson Theater (New York, NY), 385, 581
Huff, John, 252
Huff, Luther, **252,** *252*, 355
Huff, Percy, 252
Huff, Willie, 252
Huff Gardens (club) (E. St. Louis, IL), 45, 502
Hugh Hoskins Club (Chicago, IL), 254
Hughes, Hart, 76
Hughes, Langston, 43, 194, 366, 377, 453, 544, 556
Hughes DeLuxe Club (Chicago, IL), (see also: Joe's Deluxe Club), 279
Humes, Helen, 176, **252-254,** *253*, 256
Humes, John Henry, 252
Hummingbird Cabaret (New Orleans, LA), 203
Humphrey, Daisy Elizabeth, 555
Humphrey, Earl, 128
Humphrey, Mark, 522
Humphrey, Percy, 203
Hungry Eye Club (Dallas, TX), 382
Hungry i (club) (San Francisco, CA), 141, 194, 513, 556
Hunter, Alberta, 31, 231, **254-257,** *255*, 581
Hunter, Charles, 254
Hunter, Eddie, 481
Hunter, Ivory Joe, 136, 188
Hunter, Long John, 530, 531
Hunter, Patsy (see: Grant, Leola B.)
Hunter, Slim (see: Broonzy, William)
Hunter, Slim, 420
Hunter & Jenkins (duo), 584
Hunter College (New York, NY), 46, 93, 138, 147, 155, 194, 208, 240, 246, 257, 283, 300, 304, 305, 309, 316, 340, 341, 366, 367, 383, 388, 457, 478, 499, 504, 549, 556
Huntington Folk Society Concert (Huntington, NY), 283
Hurricane Bar (Pittsburgh, PA), 78
Hurricane Club (Chicago, IL), 525
Hurricane Lounge (Detroit, MI), 278
Hurt, Isom, 257
Hurt, John, 219, **257-259,** *258*, 266, 272, 392, 441
Hurtig & Seamon's (New) Theater (New York, NY), 52, 173
Hutto, Joseph Benjamin "J. B.", **259-260,** *259*, 266, 271, 294, 340, 391, 393, 396, 528

Hy Tone (label), 116, 340, 433
Hyatt Regency Hotel (Dearborn, MI), 115
Hyatt Regency Hotel (Houston, TX), 199
Hyder, George "Doc", 221
Hyers, Tom, 37

I Dischi Del Sole (label), 142
I Spy Club (Chicago, IL), 41, 393, 444, 595
Ice Palace (Las Vegas, NV), 359, 432
Icon (label), 203, 204, 420
Idaho, Bertha, 153
Ideal Music & TV Repair Shop (Los Angeles, CA), 580
Idle Hour Lounge (Detroit, MI), 278
Iglauer, Bruce, 266, 501
Ike, Rev., 378
Illinois Governor's Ball (concert) (Oak Brook, IL), 388
Illustrated Encyclopedia of Rock (book), The, 47, 101, 225, 312, 352
Imbroglio (club) (Boston, MA), 147
Immediate (label), 302
Impelliteri, Vincent, 543
Imperial (label), 60, 86, 125, 127, 136, 157, 167, 191, 202, 232, 267, 293, 300, 326, 329, 347, 353, 383, 400, 430, 436, 489, 497, 506, 508, 519, 527, 533, 547, 572
Imperial Hotel (Honolulu, HI), 431
Imperial Serenaders (band), 298
Imperial Theater (Montreal, Can.), 70, 82
Imperial Theater (New York, NY), 385
Impress (label), 367, 504
Improvisation (club), The (Los Angeles, CA), 588
Impulse (label), 165, 239, 292
Impulse Club (Rochester, NY), 566
In (club), The (New Britain, CT), 525
In Concert Club (Montreal, Can.), 33, 95, 156, 208, 240, 307, 360, 389, 418, 549, 564
In the Groove Boys (band), 303, 304
Independent (label), 232
Indian Princess (billing), The, 81, 83
Indiana Jazz Festival (Evansville, IN), 447, 538
Indiana Theater (Chicago, IL), 68, 137, 161, 317, 410, 472
Indiana University (Bloomington, IN), 187, 247, 421
Indianapolis Blues Band, 427
Indianapolis Jazz Club (Indianapolis, IN), 49
Indianhead Lounge (Lemont, IL), 322
Ing Hall (Berkeley, CA), 553
Inglewood Cemetery (Inglewood, CA), 527
Ingram, Connie, 448
Ingram, Hallie, 84
Ink Spots (group), 523
Inkwell (club), The (Chicago, IL), 322
Inn of the Beginning (club) (Cotati, CA), 98, 367, 504
Inner-Section (club) (Grand Rapids, MI), 217
Insomniac Club (Hermosa Beach, CA), 375
Inspirational Thoughts (book), 159
Instant (label), 522
Institute of Jazz Studies (organization) (see also: Rutger's Institute of Jazz Studies), 85, 128, 144, 214, 215, 269, 293, 326, 559, 593
Instrumental Folio (book), 114
Intellect Club (New Orleans, LA), 486
Interdependent Learning Model's Follow-Thru Program (organization), 231
International (label), 117
International Amphitheater, The (Chicago, IL), 33, 51, 68, 95, 104, 304, 310, 488
International Art of Jazz Festival (New York, NY), 359
International Artists (label), 243
International Blues Festival (Louisville, KY), 51, 95, 304, 310, 488, 564
International Center (organization) (New York, NY), 316, 550
International Club (Los Angeles, CA), 141
International Commander (label), 277
International Entertainer (billing), 558
International Festival of Song (concert) (Rio de Janeiro, Braz.), 219
International House (club) (Berkeley, CA), 74
International Jazz Festival (Comblain-la-Tour, Belg.), 46
International Jazz Festival (New Orleans, LA), 300, 506
International Jazz Festival (Washington, DC), 408, 538
International Jazz Jamboree (concert) (Warsaw, Pol.), 93
International People's Appeal Blues Concert (Chicago, IL), 260
International-Polydor (label), 38, 168, 190, 233, 363
International Pop Festival (Lewisville, TX), 132
International Pop Festival (Monterey, CA), 54, 99, 224, 296, 431
International Ragtime Festival (Minneapolis, MN), 423
International Room (club), The (New Orleans, LA), 508
Interns (group), The, 415, 443
Intersection Club/Tavern (Grand Rapids, MI), 152, 437, 450
Invaders (group), The, 238
Iowa State University (Ames, IA), 69, 437
Iowa Theater (Cedar Rapids, IA), 70-71
Irby, Evelene, 33
Irene's (bar/club) (Houston, TX), 43, 243, 453, 583
Irma (label), 57, 357
Iroquois Theater (New Orleans, LA), 279, 282
Irvin C. Miller's Show (tour) (see also: Miller, Irvin C.), 462
Ishmael, Prince, 558
Ish's (club) (Vancouver, Can.), 411
Isidore's Bar (Helena, AR), 443
Island (label), 60, 101, 243, 508
Isle of Wight Festival (Isle of Wight, Eng.), 219, 224
Isley Brothers (group), 224, 234
Isy's Club (Vancouver, Can.), 375
It & Them (group), 585
It Club (Chicago, IL), 31
It Club (Los Angeles, CA), 523, 586
Italian Franks (club) (New York, NY), 164
Ivanhoe (theater) (Chicago, IL), 132, 158, 219, 352, 367, 505, 543, 588
Ives, Burl, 130, 556
Ivie's Chicken Shack (club) (Los Angeles, CA), 74
Ivory, Nat, 216
Ivory (label), 453, 582
Ivory Lee (see: Semien, Lee)
Ivory Theater (Chattanooga, TN), 427, 462
Ivory's 604 Club (Chicago, IL), 500
Ivy Tower Playhouse (Spring Lake, NJ), 542

J&C Club (Chicago, IL), 41
J&J Lounge (Chicago, IL), 123
J&L Lounge (Chicago, IL), 393, 595
J&M (label), 468
J&M Fulbright (label), 201, 357
J&P Lounge (Chicago, IL), 150, 341
JATP (see: Jazz at the Philharmonic)
JAY Award, 549
J. B. (see: Hutto, Joseph) (see: Lenoir, J. B.)
JB (label), 293
J. B. and the Hawks (band), 259
JB Bar (Detroit, MI), 238
J. B.'s Club (New Orleans, LA), 486
JC (label), 460
J. C. Nightclub (E. St. Louis, IL), 150
J. C. O'Brien's Georgia Minstrels (tour), 233
J. Doug Morgan Show (tour), 441
J. E. Ranch Rodeo (tour), 173
J. F. Sligh Farm (Yazoo City, MS), 354
J. Gems (label), 371
J. J. Collins Medicine Show (tour), 276
JOB (label), 63, 66, 67, 125, 162, 181, 225, 246, 294, 304, 317, 322, 334, 403, 424, 457, 460
JP's House of Steaks (club) (Houston, TX), 84
JTP (label) (see: Jim Taylor Presents label)
JVB (label), 96, 182, 216, 225, 238, 535, 577, 578
Ja-Wes (label), 236
Jabberwock (club) (Berkeley, CA), 272
Jack Kelly's Jug Busters (band), 62
Jack Yates High School (Houston, TX), 522
Jack's (club) (Modesto, CA), 161
Jack's Cabaret (New York, NY), 357
Jack's Rathskeller (Philadelphia, PA), 540
Jack's Waterfront Hangout (San Francisco, CA), 141
Jackson, Al, 145
Jackson, Archie, 555
Jackson, Arthur (Peg Leg Sam), 34, **261**, *261*, 282, 492

Jackson, Benjamin "Bullmoose", 188, **261-263**, *262*
Jackson, Bessie (see: Bogan, Lucille)
Jackson, Bill, **263**
Jackson, Bruce, 273
Jackson, Bud, 106
Jackson, Bullmoose (see: Jackson, Benjamin)
Jackson, Charles, 145
Jackson, Charlie "Papa Charlie," 68, 70, **263-264**, *263*, 355, 415, 428
Jackson, Charlie, 263
Jackson, Chubby, 536
Jackson, Chuck, 223
Jackson, Cliff, 231
Jackson, Eliza, 118, 119
Jackson, Emma, 452
Jackson, Franz, 44, 108, 380, 381, 506
Jackson, George P., 443, 444
Jackson, Graham L., 445
Jackson, Jack, 256
Jackson, Jim, 62, 106, **264**, *264*, 324, 326, 414, 486, 561
Jackson, John, 228, 259, **264-266**, *265*, 276, 416
Jackson, John, 222
Jackson, Johnny, 267
Jackson, Jump, 110, 339, 403, 489
Jackson, Lee, 168, **266-267**, *267*
Jackson, Lester "Fats," 515
Jackson, "Lil/Little Son" (see: Jackson, Melvin)
Jackson, Little George, 589
Jackson, Mahalia, 109, 116, 196, 314, 452, 453, 465
Jackson, Melvin "Lil Son," 29, **267**, *268*, 280, 339
Jackson, Tommy, 315
Jackson, Tony, 221, 254, 558
Jackson, Warren, 266
Jackson (label), 187, 503
Jackson Jubilee Singers, The, 468
Jackson Park Hospital (Chicago, IL), 419
Jackson State College (Jackson, MS), 508
Jacobs, Adams, 268
Jacobs, Little Walter (see: Jacobs, Marion Walter)
Jacobs, Marion Walter (Little Walter), 35, 36, 41, 42, 63, 65, 67, 70, 72, 78, 79, 91, 101, 124, 169, 181, 198, 211, 213, 214, 247, **268-269**, *269*, 270, 277, 285, 294, 334, 339, 342, 345, 348, 354, 371, 388, 393, 395, 396, 398, 438, 461, 468, 476, 479, 483, 516, 524, 528, 545, 548, 560, 570, 576, 578, 580, 589
Jacobs, Mary, 524
Jacobs, Matthew (Boogie Jake), 158, 228, 269, **270**, *270*
Jacobs, Queen Victoria, 144
Jacobs, Walter (see: Jacobs, Marion Walter) (see: Vinson, Walter Jacobs)
Jacquet, Illinois, 216
Jake's Tavern (Chicago, IL), 438, 493
Jam With Sam Show (Chicago, IL), 269
Jamboree Club (see: Club Jamboree)
Jamboree Club (Barcelona, Spain), 117
James, Billy (see: Phelps, Arthur)
James, Eddie, 272
James, Elmer (see: Crudup, Arthur)
James, Elmore "Elmo," 35, 110, 137, 155, 193, 213, 225, 233, 260, 266, **270-271**, *270*, 286, 289, 291, 294, 307, 311, 322, 334, 338, 395, 399, 400, 435, 438, 493, 499, 501, 509, 529, 545, 574, 575, 577, 586
James, Elmore, Jr., 271
James, Elmore, Jr. (see: Minter, Iverson)
James, Etta, 353, 508, 530, 538
James, Harry, 252, 362, 447, 518
James, Homesick (see: Williamson, John A.)
James, Jimmy (see: Hendrix, James)
James, Joe Willie, 270
James, Nehemiah "Skip," **272-273**, *272*, 289, 381, 487, 501
James, Skip (see: James, Nehemiah)
James, Willie B., 70
James Lick Jr. High School (San Francisco, CA), 270
Jamie (label), 136
Jammers (group), The, 585
Jammin' Jim (see: Harris, Edward)
Jan & Dill (label), 57
Jane Addams Theater (Chicago, IL), 67, 148, 294, 341, 494, 529, 575
Janis (book), 296, 297
Janis Revue (band), 296
Jarahal School of Music (New York, NY), 83
Jardins des Petits Champs (club) (Istanbul, Turk.), 256
Jarvis, Al, 298
Jasman (label), 510
Jaspers (club) (Chicago, IL), 124
Java Lanes (bowling alley) (Long Beach, CA), 299
Javors, Bob, 92, 312, 379, 449
Jax (label), 415, 503, 572
Jaxon, Frankie "Half-Pint," **273-274**, *273*, 355
Jaxson, Frankie (see: Jaxon, Frankie)
Jazz, A History of the New York Scene (book), 474
Jazz & Blues (magazine), 33, 96, 104, 122, 138, 283, 355, 470, 508, 563, 571, 584
Jazz & Folk Music Festival (Toronto, Can.), 453
Jazz & Heritage Festival (see: New Orleans Jazz & Heritage Festival)
Jazz & Pop (magazine), 211, 225, 241, 296, 311, 352, 448, 476, 479, 551
Jazz Artdur (club) (Gothenburg, Swed.), 63
Jazz at Noon (concert) (Chicago, IL), 381
Jazz at the Philharmonic (JATP) (band/tour), 253, 519, 527
Jazz Beat (magazine), 178
Jazz/Blues Fusion (band), 352
Jazz by the Bay Concert (San Diego, CA), 195
Jazz Cardinals (band), 263
Jazz Cats (band), 313
Jazz Cellar (club) (San Francisco, CA), 586
Jazz Cellar Six (band), 245
Jazz Crusade (label), 203
Jazz Dance (book), 559
Jazz Ensemble (band), 406
Jazz Era: The 'Forties (book), 299, 524
Jazz Expo (concert) (London, Eng.), 114, 156, 165, 246, 266, 304, 367, 388-389, 478, 504, 553
Jazz Festival (Krizanke, Yugo.), 38
Jazz Festival (Mattoon, IL), 313
Jazz Festival Baden 73 (Baden, Switz.), 254
Jazz Five (band), 357
Jazz Gallery (club) (New York, NY), 566
Jazz Hounds (band) (Danny Barker), 40
Jazz Hounds (band) (Connie Berry), 254
Jazz Hounds (band) (Johnny Dunn), 580, 583
Jazz Hounds (band) (Mamie Smith), 472
Jazz Hounds (band) (Edith Wilson), 581
Jazz Institute of Chicago (school) (Chicago, IL), 260
Jazz Interlude (club) (San Francisco, CA), 141
Jazz Jamboree '76 (concert) (Warsaw, Pol.), 390
Jazz Jesters (band), 300
Jazz Journal (International) (magazine), 45, 59, 79, 84, 93, 107, 109, 120, 145, 148, 160, 178, 187, 200, 201, 222, 223, 234, 259, 282, 285, 312, 321, 325, 345, 374, 381, 386, 402, 406, 414, 418, 419, 445, 453, 466, 492, 507, 520, 568, 570
Jazz Life Festival (Dortmund, Ger.), 209, 390, 549, 569
Jazz Ltd. (club) (Chicago, IL), 506
Jazz Magazine, 297, 524, 549
Jazz Masters (band), 152, 540, 558
Jazz Men (band), 586
Jazz Monthly (magazine), 35, 467, 572
Jazz: New Orleans (1885-1957) (book), 419
Jazz Night (concert) (Hollywood, CA), 447
Jazz-O-Maniacs Band, 279, 282
Jazz Odyssey (label), 117, 240
Jazz on an Island Festival (Yvoir, Belg.), 117
Jazz on Record: A Critical Guide (book), 41, 64, 145, 158, 162, 351, 354, 360, 410, 475, 533, 552, 555, 562
Jazz Phools (band), 583
Jazz Podium (magazine), 70, 448
Jazz Record (label), 145, 365, 503
Jazz Record (magazine), 145, 493
Jazz Record Six (band), 145, 503
Jazz Review (magazine), 231
Jazz Showcase (club) (Chicago, IL), 152, 520, 567
Jazz Society (label), 69
Jazz Temple (club) (Cleveland, OH), 538
Jazz 200 Concert/Festival (Hamburg, Ger.), 117, 588
Jazz Villa (club) (St. Louis, MO), 566
Jazz Wizards (band), 229, 360
Jazz Workshop (club) (Boston, MA),

132, 240, 341, 388, 389, 447, 513, 527
Jazz Workshop (club) (San Francisco, CA), 366, 375, 388, 431, 447, 504, 512, 513, 586, 588
Jazz World (label), 524
Jazz Zoo (club) (Hamburg, Ger.), 166
Jazzbo Serenaders (band), 81
Jazzie Jeanie (billing), 314
Jazzland Club (St. Louis, MO), 49, 107, 288, 489
Jazzland Club (Vienna, Austria), 302
Jazzlife Festival (Dortmund, Ger.), 217
Jazzman (label), 385
Jazzmen (book), 468
Jazzola Eight (band), 128
Jazzology (label), 37, 230, 254, 313, 420
Jazzville (club) (Chicago, IL), 394, 444
Jazzville (club) (San Diego, CA), 308, 566
Jeannette Adler Company (tour), 592
Jean's Royal Sportsman's Lounge (Phoenix, IL), 72
Jed's Univeristy Inn (New Orleans, LA), 78, 100, 101, 122, 244, 307, 508
Jefferson, Alec, 274
Jefferson, Blind Lemon (see: Jefferson, Lemon)
Jefferson, Bonnie, **274**
Jefferson, Calvin, 274
Jefferson, Lemon (Blind Lemon), 27, 29, 64, 70, 95, 120, 161, 180, 190, 197, 210, 233, 235, 241, 244, 266, **274-276**, *275*, 292, 305, 311, 317, 319, 320, 324, 327, 330, 368, 390, 391, 440, 441, 454, 456, 459, 465, 481, 525, 528, 555, 557, 570, 574, 583, 586
Jefferson, Mabel, 276
Jefferson, Miles, 276
Jefferson, Thomas, 326
Jefferson (label), 54, 76, 213, 339, 516
Jefferson Airplane (band), 276
Jefferson Barracks Cemetery (St. Louis, MO), 460
Jefferson Theater (Auburn, NY), 70
Jefferson Theater (New York, NY), 70, 82
Jeffery, Bob (see: Jeffery, Robert)
Jeffery, George, 276
Jeffery, Robert "Bob," **276-277**, *277*, 456
Jeffrey's Plantation (Lula, MS), 247, 409
Jeffries, ______, 61
Jello (product), 542
Jenkins, Bobo (see: Jenkins, John)
Jenkins, Dub, 145
Jenkins, George, 538
Jenkins, Gus, 150, **277-278**, *278*, 407
Jenkins, John "Bobo," 183, **278-279**, *278*
Jenkins, Mahalia Lucille, 476, 478
Jenkins, Sarah, 419
Jenkins, Sherman, 476
Jenkins, Slim, 439
Jenkins (see: Wilson, Wesley)
Jenkins Orphanage (Charleston, SC), 152, 153
Jennings, Mary Esta, 206
Jeremy, John, 402
Jesse, Joe, 420
Jessel, George, 567
Jessye, Eva, 481
Jet Star Club (Chicago, IL), 260
Jet Stream (label), 527
Jeter, Claude, 421
Jeter Plantation (Mooringsport, LA), 317
Jett, Freddie, 417
Jewel (label), 55, 76, 99, 117, 154, 183, 190, 215, 243, 341, 354
Jewish Community Center (Houston, TX), 43
Jick and His Trio (see: Williamson, John A.)
Jiffy (label), 596
Jim (label), 453, 547
Jim Bell's Harlem Club (Omaha, NE), 215
Jim Hotel Dance Hall (Ft. Worth, TX), 455
Jim Taylor Presents (label) (JTP), 314
Jim Yeager's Plantation (Drew, MS), 89
Jimerson, Movelia, 525
Jimi (book), 224, 225
Jimi Hendrix Experience (band), The, 224
Jimmie Rodgers Entertainers (band), 440
Jimmie the Kid (book), 441
Jimmy Ryan's (club) (New York, NY), 61, 229, 300, 406, 481
Jim's Place (club) (St. Louis, MO), 79
Jinkins, Gus (see: Jenkins, Gus)
Jive (label), 571
Jive Club (Lawton, OK), 35
Jiving Five (band), The, 398
Jo Jo's (club) (Chicago, IL), 41, 494, 551
Joanne B. Horton Fashion Enterprises Inc. (organization) (Albany, NY), 245
Jocko & his Rocketship Rock 'n' Roll Stars (tour), 35, 281
Jody Farney's (club) (Memphis, TN), 62
Joe & Rose Beer Garden (Queens, NY), 222
Joe Davis (label), 79, 164
Joe's Bierhaus Club (Berlin, Ger.), 65, 156
Joe's Club (Chicago, IL), 110
Joe's Deluxe Club (Chicago, IL), (see also: Hughes DeLuxe Club), 277
Joe's East West (club) (New Paltz, NY), 312, 450
Joe's King Biscuit Boys (see also: King Biscuit Boys), 560, 561
Joe's Melody Club/Room (Vallejo, CA), 55, 190, 358, 448-449
Joe's Place (club) (Cambridge/Boston, MA), 41, 95, 125, 132, 151, 156, 190, 240, 247, 260, 305, 336, 367, 378, 393, 445, 499, 500, 504, 596
John, Little Willie, 90, 149, 213, 249, 499
John, Mike, 302
John F. Kennedy Center for the Performing Arts (theater) (Washington, DC), 389, 466, 506, 567
John Caston Hospital (Memphis, TN), 40, 317, 337, 455, 486, 547
John Gettis' Plantation (Bolton, MS), 119
John Henry Folk Festival (Princeton, WV), 57, 148, 175, 177, 195, 336, 349, 379, 401, 427, 436, 459, 569
John Henry Memorial Concert (Beckley, WV), 391, 436, 457
John Henry Memorial Concert (Clifftop, WV), 261, 346, 391, 436, 449, 457
John Lee's Ground Hogs (band), 239
John Roberts Plantation Show (tour), 369
John Robinson Circus (tour), 396
Johnny & the Jammers (band), 585
Johnny Baker's Club (Kansas City, MO), 586
Johnny Curry's Club (Memphis, TN), 510
Johnny Davis Duo, 148
Johnny Davis' Original Music Masters (band), 148
Johnny Winter And (band), 585
Johnny's Cafe (Baton Rouge, LA), 227
John's Lounge (Chicago, IL), 41
Johnson, Al Budd, 383
Johnson, Albert, 85
Johnson, Alec, 355
Johnson, Alma B., 582
Johnson, Alonzo "Lonnie," 29, 70, 120, 145, 148, 161, 175, 190, 192, 208, 244, 267, **279-280**, *279*, 282, 288, 289, 290, 305, 307, 311, 369, 450, 454, 459, 460, 464, 467, 481, 489, 515, 528, 529, 552
Johnson, Arthur, 286
Johnson, Big Bill (see: Broonzy, William)
Johnson, Big Jerry, 457
Johnson, Bill, 274, 288
Johnson, Blind Boy (see: Dupree, William)
Johnson, Blind Willie, 369, 440, 460, 555
Johnson, Blues (see: Carr, Leroy)
Johnson, Budd, 375
Johnson, Buddy (see: Johnson, Woodrow)
Johnson, Bunk, 276, 321, 372
Johnson, Charles "Charlie," 385, 463, 467
Johnson, Clarence, 280, 290, 483, 484
Johnson, Conrad, 572
Johnson, Daisy, 162
Johnson, Dink (see: Johnson, Oliver)
Johnson, Easy Papa (see: Sykes, Roosevelt)
Johnson, Edith, **281**, 283, 482
Johnson, Elias, 200
Johnson, Ella, **281**, *281*
Johnson, Ella Mae, 427
Johnson, Emma, 252
Johnson, Ernest "44," 413
Johnson, Fannie (see: McCoy, Viola)
Johnson, Gertrude, 187
Johnson, Gladys (see: McCoy, Viola)
Johnson, Hall, 295, 541
Johnson, Henry (see: McGhee, Walter Brown)
Johnson, Henry "Rufe," 261, **282**, *282*, 416
Johnson, Hopson "Hot Box," 70

Johnson, Idell, 280, 290
Johnson, Jack, 373
Johnson, James P. "Jimmie," 223, 229, 231, 274, 385, 472
Johnson, James "Steady Roll," 279, 280, **282**, 283, 515
Johnson, James "Stump," 281, **282-283**
Johnson, Jeff, 288
Johnson, Jessie, 281, 283
Johnson, Jimmie (see: Johnson, James P.)
Johnson, Jimmy, 289, 445
Johnson, Joe, **283**
Johnson, Joe "Smokey," 283
Johnson, Larry, 59, 147, 210, 244, **283**, *284*, 391, 454, 529
Johnson, Larry, 61
Johnson LeDell, 290
Johnson, Lemuel Charles, **284-285**, *285*
Johnson, Leslie (Lazy Lester), 208, 269, **285**, *285*, 435, 507
Johnson, Lilly, 326
Johnson, Little Arthur, 442
Johnson, Lonnie (see: Johnson, Alonzo)
Johnson, Lou, 203
Johnson, Loudmouth, 585
Johnson, Lucius Brinson, 285
Johnson, Luther "Georgia Boy," **285-286**, *286*, 287, 391
Johnson, Luther, Jr. "Guitar Jr.," 68, **286-287**, *287*, 305, 311, 391
Johnson, Luther, Sr., 286
Johnson, Mager, 290, 483, 484
Johnson, Margaret (see: Martin, Sara)
Johnson, Margaret, 351
Johnson, Margurite, 175
Johnson, Marjorie Ann, 178
Johnson, Martha (see: Beaman, Lottie)
Johnson, Martha, 453
Johnson, Mary, 79, **287-288**, *287*, 482, 489
Johnson, Meathead (see: Dupree, William)
Johnson, Morrison "Red," 289
Johnson, Noah, 288
Johnson, Noon, 396
Johnson, Oliver "Dink," **288**
Johnson, Paul, 379
Johnson, Pete, 406, 518, 519, 520, 521, 564
Johnson, Robert, 35, 62, 89, 93, 169, 181, 182, 183, 210, 225, 249, 271, 273, 280, **288-289**, 294, 334, 336, 338, 339, 347, 390, 399, 410, 429, 457, 459, 494, 514, 535, 577, 586
Johnson, Roosevelt, 282
Johnson, Rufe (see: Johnson, Henry)
Johnson, Sara (see: Henderson, Rosa)
Johnson, Stump (see: Johnson, James)
Johnson, Syl, **289-290**, *294*, 345
Johnson, Thelmon, 282
Johnson, Tillie, 374
Johnson, Tommy, 38, 39, 64, 65, 80, 89, 95, 160, 161, 202, 236, 280, **290**, *290*, 294, 315, 354, 409-410, 479, 483, 484, 487, 501, 524, 546, 547
Johnson, Willie (see: Johnson, Blind Willie)
Johnson, Willie, 128
Johnson, Willie Lee, 181, **291**
Johnson, Willis, 285
Johnson, Woodrow "Buddy," 281
Johnson Lounge (Chicago, IL), 69, 574
Johnson's Tavern (Chicago, IL), 68
Joint Bar (Minneapolis, MN), 33, 125, 208, 445, 549
Joliet (label), 200, 531
Joliet Penitentiary (Joliet, IL), 437
Jolly Clara Smith (billing), 467
Jolly Harmony Boys (band), The, 284
Jolson, Al, 360, 494
Jones, Alice, 524
Jones, Annie, 90
Jones, Arthur, 417
Jones, Augusta (see: Miles, Josephine)
Jones, B. B. (see: Nichols, Alvin)
Jones, Bertha, 386
Jones, Birmingham, 95, **291**, *291*
Jones, Caroline, 199
Jones, Clarence, 385
Jones, Coley, 525
Jones, Curtis, 276, **291-292**, *292*, 529
Jones, Eddie (Guitar Slim), 78, 111, 116, 201, 225, **293**, *293*, 454, 528
Jones, Esther Mae, 417
Jones, Floyd, 95, 181, 246, 247, 289, 290, **293-294**, *293*, 410, 424, 459, 493, 574, 594
Jones, George, 294
Jones, Hank, 406
Jones, Ida, 229
Jones, Jab, 176, 426, 454
Jones, James (The Tail Dragger), 95
Jones, Jimmy, 566
Jones, John "Johnnie"/"Little Johnny," 181, 213, 271, **294-295**, *294*, 371, 388, 478, 479
Jones, Johnny, 294
Jones, Jonah, 252, 466
Jones, Julius, 353
Jones, LeRoy, 118
Jones, Letha, 294
Jones, Maggie, **295**, *295*
Jones, Mamie (see: Waters, Ethel)
Jones, Maude (see: Brown, Lillian)
Jones, Max, 307, 318, 528
Jones, Moody, 39, 198, 269, 276, 294
Jones, Ollie, 536
Jones, Phyllis, 272
Jones, Quincy, 470
Jones, Richard M., 229, 360, 591
Jones, Ruth Lee, 536
Jones, Sadie (see: Brown, Ida G.)
Jones, Sam, 111
Jones, Shrimp, 584
Jones, Sonny, 185, 503
Jones, Susan, 580
Jones, Willie, 291
Jones Brothers & Wilson Circus (tour), 373
Jones Grove Church Cemetery (Thomson, GA), 369
Jones Hall (Houston, TX), 51, 114
Jones-Smith Inc. (band), 445
Jook Block Busters (band), 366, 503
Jook House Rockers (band), 503
Joplin, Janis, 100, 195, **295-297**, *295*, 319, 330, 465, 514
Joplin, Seth Ward, 296
Jordan, Charles "Charley," **297**, *297*, 569
Jordan, Jim, 289
Jordan, Jimmy (see: Johnson, Alonzo)
Jordan, Louis, 47, 55, 78, 79, 104, 116, 154, 158, 216, 220, 284, **297-299**, *297*, 307, 360, 406, 536
Jordan, Tom (see: Johnson, Alonzo)
Jordan, Willie (see: Dupree, William)
Jordan Hall (Boston, MA), 147, 194, 366, 504, 556
Jordon, Charley (see: Jordan, Charles)
Joseph, Pleasant (Cousin Joe/Smilin' Joe), 103, 202, **299-301**, *300*, 490
Joseph Jefferson Award, 544
Josephine Gassman and Her Pickaninnies (tour), 222, 494
Josephine Gassman Phina & Company (tour), 222, 494
Josephine's (club) (Chicago, IL), 236
Josh White Guitar Method (book), The, 557
Josh White Singers (group), 556
Josh White Song Book (book), The, 557
Josie (label), 503
Joyce, Mike, 59, 348, 437
Joyland Revellers (band), 380
Juanita Hall's Club (New York, NY), 466
Jubilee (label), 92, 517
Jubilee Boys (group), The, 564
Jubilee Four (group), 250
Jubilee Jazz Hall (Memphis, TN), 177, 327
Judge Wood's Plantation (Mt. Willing, AL), 319
Judson Memorial Church (New York, NY), 283
Jug Busters (band), 40, 486
Jug Stompers (band), 106, 325
Juicy John Pink's Club/Coffeehouse/Folk Center (DeKalb, IL), 57, 65, 198, 349, 367, 504
Juke Box (label), 256
Juke House Rockers (band), 366
Jukes (band), The, 268, 269, 393, 516
Jump and Jive Boys (band), 443
Jump Steady Club (Los Angeles, CA), 445
Jumping (label), 510
Jumps of Jive (band), 154
Junior & The Troyettes (group), 563
Jungle Band, 298
Jungle Lounge (Houston, TX), 57
Just Angels (club) (Harvey, IL), 42
Just Jazz (club) (Philadelphia, PA), 418, 567
Just Jazz/Blues Jubilee Concert (Los Angeles, CA), 253
Just Jazz Concert (Pasadena, CA), 586
Just Me Lounge (Chicago, IL), 289, 345, 548
Just Sunshine (label), 363

KAM Temple (Chicago, IL), 194, 322, 340, 380
K-Doe, Ernie, 103, 158
KGB (group), 54
KKK (organization), 378
Kabuki Theater (San Francisco, CA), 240, 439
Kaiser Hospital (Brisbane, LA), 510

Kaleidoscope (club) (Philadelphia, PA), 132, 195
Kaminsky, Max, 406
Kangaroo (label), 125
Kansas City Buddies (band), 44
Kansas City Butterball (billing), The, 41
Kansas City Five (band), 357
Kansas City Jazz Festival (Kansas City, MO), 431, 448
Kansas City Orchestra, 405, 445
Kansas City Red (pseudonym), 148, 238, 271, 294
Kansas City Red Band, 434
Kansas City Red's (club) (Chicago, IL), 575
Kansas City Seven (band), 375
Kansas City Stompers (band), 321
Kansas Joe (see: McCoy, Joe)
Kaplan, Fats, 59
Kapp (label), 492
Karney, Carol Ann, 321
Kate Crippen and Her Kids Revue (tour), 137
Kate Smith of Harlem (billing), The, 83
Kathleen Kirkwood Underground Theater (New York, NY), 222
Katy Red's Club (E. St. Louis, IL), 79, 279, 282
Katzman, Nick, 147
Kaz, Fred, 194
Kearney, David William, 180
Keen (label), 544
Keeney's Bay Ridge Theater (Brooklyn, NY), 256
Keepnews, Peter, 347
Keith-Albee (theater circuit) (see also: Albee Theaters)
Keith-Albee Fordham Theater (New York, NY), 70, 540
Keith-Albee Franklin Theater (New York, NY), 70, 540
Keith-Albee-Orpheum circuit, 137
Keith-Albee Palace Theater (New York, NY) (see also: RKO-Palace Theater, New York, NY), 540, 543
Keith circuit (see also: RKO-Keith circuit), 221, 222, 496, 540, 564, 580
Keith Coliseum Theater (New York, NY), 70
Keith Memorial Theater (Boston, MA), 541
Keith 104th Street Theater (Cleveland, OH), 540
Keith-Orpheum-Interstate circuit, 440-441
Keith Theater (Akron, OH), 540-1
Keith Theater (Boston, MA) (see also: RKO Theater, Boston, MA), 71
Keith Theater (Dayton, OH), 540
Keith Theater (Jersey City, NJ), 81
Keith Theater (Lowell, MA), 82
Keith Theater (Ottawa, Can.), 82
Keith Theater (Portland, ME), 82
Keith Theater (Rochester, NY), 541
Keith Theater (Syracuse, NY), 540
Keith Theater (Toledo, OH), 540
Keith Theater (Yonkers, NY), 256
Keith Theater (Youngstown, OH), 540
Keith's Orpheum Theater (Brooklyn, NY) (see also: Orpheum Theater, Brooklyn, NY), 82
Keith's Prospect Theater (New York, NY), 475
Keith's State Theater (Jersey City, NJ) (see also: State Theater, Jersey City, NJ), 256
Kelley, Arthur "Guitar," 232, 244, **301**, *301*
Kelley, Levi, 320
Kelly, Chris, 164, 203
Kelly, Dave, 302
Kelly, Jack, 40, 62, 128, 486, 552
Kelly, Jo-Ann, 162, **301-302**, *301*
Kelly, Stella, 441
Kelly, Willie (see: Sykes, Roosevelt)
Kelly Drew's Plantation (Hollandale, MS), 118
Kelly's Blue Lounge (Chicago, IL), 41, 246, 393, 591, 595
Kelly's Stable (club) (Chicago, IL), 450
Kelly's Stable (club) (New York, NY), 60, 285, 406, 536, 550
Ken Hawkins Club (Cleveland, OH), 308
Kennedy, Beno, 406
Kennedy Center (see: John F. Kennedy Center for the Performing Arts)
Kennerly Sanctified Temple (St. Louis, MO), 83
Kenneth (label), 302, 497
Kenny Lester's Sporting House (Chicago, IL), 181
Kenny's Castaways (club) (New York, NY), 101, 156, 283, 381, 490
Ken's Afterglow (club) (Portland, OR), 260
Kent, Don, 86, 297, 486
Kent (label), 55, 149, 154, 188, 201, 292, 308, 311, 371, 378, 382, 512
Kent State (Kent, OH), 57, 151, 349
Kenton, Stan, 431
Kentucky Derby (event) (Louisville, KY), 198
Kentucky State Fair (Lexington, KY), 263
Keppard, Freddie, 263, 274, 288, 373
Kersey's Lounge (Chicago, IL), 109
Kessee, Carrie, 57
Kewpie Doll (club) (San Francisco, CA), 139
Key Club (Minneapolis, MN), 91, 342
Key Hole Club (San Antonio, TX), 84, 372
Key Largo Club (Chicago, IL), 93, 271, 488, 563, 572, 574
Keyhole (label), 63, 266
Keymen's Club (Chicago, IL), 104, 289
Keynote (label), 536, 556
Keystone, The (see: Keystone Korner)
Keystone (club), The (Palo Alto, CA), 240
Keystone Korner (club) (Berkeley, CA), 30, 98, 132, 156, 208, 240, 244, 247, 304, 305, 336, 341, 389, 418, 439, 549, 588
Keystone Korner (club) (San Francisco, CA), 54, 393, 588
Khayyam, Omar Hakim, 31
Kibitzeria, The (see: George's Kibitzeria)
Kicking Mule (label), 38, 147
Kid & Coot (duo), 584
Kid Riverar's Barrelhouse Lounge (Chicago, IL) (see also: Barrelhouse Lounge), 35
Kid Stormy Weather (pseudonym), 103
Kid Thomas (see: Watts, Louis)
Kidd, Claude, 302
Kidd, Kenneth, **302**
Kiddie Revue (tour), 505
Kids Revue (tour), 137
Killian, Al, 527
Kimbrough, Lena (see: Beaman, Lottie)
Kimbrough, Lottie (see: Beaman, Lottie)
Kimbrough, Sylvester, 41
Kincaid Plantation (Belzoni, MS), 271
Kinetic Playground (club) (Chicago, IL), 100, 208, 238, 296, 304, 308, 389, 548
King, Al (Al K. Smith), 190, 302, **302-303**, *302*, 304, 358
King, Albert, 33, 73, 149, 183, 225, 276, 280, 287, 294, **303-305**, *303*, 307, 310, 311, 347, 402, 404, 412, 434, 445, 450, 451, 528, 533, 574, 586, 596
King, Albert, 307
King, Aretha, 232
King, B. B. (see: King, Riley)
King, Billy, 52, 227
King, Earl, 103, 448
King, Ella Mae, 305
King, Freddie "Freddy," 32, 33, 72, 271, 280, 299, 304, **305-307**, *306*, 310, 311, 345, 391, 410, 438, 442, 476, 494, 528
King, Freddie, 307
King, Kid, 35, 204
King, Leon, 305
King, Luther (see: Johnson, Luther)
King, Riley "B. B.," 33, 38, 50, 51, 53, 54, 55, 60, 68, 73, 76, 91, 95, 106, 122, 127, 149, 183, 190, 204, 208, 209, 211, 223, 225, 250, 271, 276, 280, 304, 305, 307, **307-312**, *307*, 322, 334, 337, 345, 346, 348, 366, 391, 397, 400, 402, 404, 407, 432, 435, 438, 445, 448, 450, 451, 461, 476, 493, 504, 510, 520, 528, 531, 535, 553, 560, 572, 586, 597
King, Shirley, 310
King (label) (see also: King Record Company), 37, 76, 86, 116, 164, 165, 191, 212, 216, 237, 238, 263, 279, 304, 305, 312, 329, 364, 366, 372, 378, 383, 406, 412, 415, 447, 452, 468, 470, 501, 503, 523, 544
King Arthur's Court (club) (San Antonio, TX), 353
King Arthur's Roundtable (club) (Hempstead, NY), 90
King Biscuit Boys (band) (see also: Joe's King Biscuit Boys), 443, 483, 484
King Biscuit Entertainers (band), 140, 577

King Biscuit Time Boys (band), 334, 338
King David (pseudonym), 578
King-Federal (label), 572
King Hall (Berkeley, CA), 243, 249, 330
King Ivory Lee (see: Semien, Lee)
King Jazz (label), 197, 300, 406, 584
King of the Blues (billing), 310
King of the Harmonica (billing), 578
King of the Jukeboxes (billing), 299
King of the South (billing), 122
King of the 12 String Guitar Players of the World (billing), 318
King of the Zydeco (billing), 122
King Record Company (Cincinnati, OH) (see also: King label), 88
King Solomon Bar (Detroit, MI), 216, 560
King Solomon Holy House of Prayer (E. St. Louis, IL), 144
King Tut's Tomb (club) (Chicago, IL), 379-380
Kingfish Club (Kansas City, MO), 518
Kingfish Club (New Orleans, LA), 300, 420
Kings (group), The, 535
Kings Ballroom (Lincoln, NE), 88
King's Black & Gold Club (Monroe, LA), 547
King's Castle (club) (Lake Tahoe, NV), 309
King's Club Waveland (Chicago, IL), 151, 247, 294, 494
King's Hall (club), (Bournemouth, Eng.), 256
King's Inn (club) (Houston, TX), 572
King's Motor Court (Panama City, FL), 420
Kings of Dixieland (band), 373
Kings of Rhythm (band) (Clayton Love), 338
Kings of Rhythm (band) (Ike Turner), 534
King's Terrace (club) (New York, NY), 43, 564
Kingston Mines Company Store (coffeehouse) (Chicago, IL), 36, 67, 123-124, 175, 266, 294, 322, 334, 342, 395, 410, 435, 468, 516, 530, 575, 591, 595
Kingston Theater (Kingston, NY), 82
Kingsway Hall (London, Eng.), 556
Kinnara Collection, 65, 196, 259, 403, 485, 545
Kinney Club (Newark, NJ), 550
Kirby, Fred, 352
Kirk, Andy, 61, 405, 518, 564
Kirk, Eddie (see: Kirkland, Eddie)
Kirkland, Eddie, 70, 138, 241, 244, **312-313,** *312*
Kirkland, Leroy, 219, 470
Kirkland College (Clinton, NY), 34
Kirkland College (N. Ferrisburg, VT), 65
Kirkpatrick, Slim, 546
Kirksey's Lounge (Chicago, IL), 123, 345
Kirkwood, Edward Allen, 230
Kirkwood, Kathleen, 222
Kismet Club (Los Angeles, CA), 375
Kit Kat Club (London, Eng.), 541
Kit Kat Club (New York, NY), 464
Kit Kat Club (Newark, NJ), 550
Kitcheman, Herbert, 245
Kitcheman, Joanne Barbara, 245
Kitt, Eartha, 256
Kittleson, Barry, 210
Kittrell, Edward, 314
Kittrell, Jean, **313-314,** *313*, 428, 465
Kitty Cat Club (see: Purple Cat)
Kiwanis Carnival (Johnson City, TN), 440
Klassic Kitten (club) (El Sobrante, CA), 449
Klay Folk Festival (New York, NY), 187
Kleinhans Music Hall (Buffalo, NY), 113, 132, 431, 520
Klip Joint (club) (Detroit, MI), 423
Klook's Kleek (club) (London, Eng.), 352
Knight, Curtis, 224, 225
Knickerbocker Cafe (Westerly, RI), 247, 459, 490
Knickerbocker Hotel (Monte Carlo, Monaco), 256
Knickerbockers Orchestra, 496
Knotty Pine Grill (club), The (Chicago, IL), 507
Knox College (Galesburg, IL), 246, 249
Ko Ko Club (Phoenix, AZ), 299
Koerner, John, 187, **314,** *314*, 319
Koester, Robert "Bob," 33, 260, 292, 491
Kohl, Paul, 339
Kohlman, Freddie "Freddy," 300, 373
Kola Shannah Club (San Bernadino, CA), 51
Kolax, King, 383
Kolbeh Club (Berlin, Ger.), 178, 523
Kool Jazz Festival (Houston, TX), 51, 310
Kooper, Al, 54, 305
Koppin Theater (Detroit, MI), 172, 385, 463, 467
Koret's Lounge (Houston, TX), 57
Kossoff, Paul, 307
Kove (club), The (Kent, OH), 33, 260, 336, 450, 500, 596
Kozmic Blues (band), 296
Krafton (label), 28
Kringle, Kris, 496
Kriss, Eric, 381, 414, 479
Kry (label), 547
Kudu (label), 417
Kunstadt, Leonard "Len," 42, 222, 223, 234, 286, 344, 474, 482, 487, 488, 499
Kusick, Eddie, 104
Kweskin, Jim, 532

L&A Lounge (Chicago, IL), 32, 289, 345, 444, 596
L&D Lounge (Chicago, IL), 123
L&H Club (Chicago, IL), 269
LC (label) (see: Library of Congress label)
L. C. Tolen's Band & Revue (tour), 481
LD Nightclub, The (Newport News, VA), 558, 564
LMI (label), 520
La Bastille (club) (Houston, TX), 132, 158, 243, 389, 435, 527
La Casa Club (St. Louis, MO), 567
La Cave (club) (Cleveland, OH), 99, 132, 195
La Faim Foetale (club) (Montreal, Can.), 249, 569
La Femina Club (Athens, Greece), 256
La Fiesta Cafe (Manitowoc, WI), 176
La Gaite Cabaret (Amsterdam, Holland), 256
La Hora del Pueblo (club) (Cuernavaca, Mex.), 322
La Jolla Club (see: Club La Jolla)
La Louisianne (label), 396
La Pena (club) (Berkeley, CA), 213
La Redd, Cora, 564
La Rose Noire de Paris (billing), 374
La Salle (label), 63, 123
La Strada Club (New Orleans, LA), 300
La Valbonne Discotheque (London, Eng.), 510
La Vere, Steve, 107, 130, 162, 328, 329, 400
La Vie en Rose (club) (New York, NY), 542
La Vie Parisienne Club (New York, NY), 556
Labor Stage Theater (New York, NY), 497
Lacy, Rubin, 64, 249, 276, 290, **315-316,** *315*, 354, 355, 524
Lacy, Rubin (Mrs.), *315*
Lafayette Stock Company (tour), 79
Lafayette Theater (Cleveland, OH), 73
Lafayette Theater (New York, NY), 31, 43, 44, 48, 52, 70, 71, 73, 74, 79, 80, 81, 82, 137, 152, 173, 197, 221, 223, 227, 231, 254, 256, 317, 350, 356, 357, 385, 445, 463, 464, 467, 472, 475, 481, 484, 491, 494, 496, 540, 541, 558, 564, 581, 583, 584
Lafayette Theater (Winston-Salem, NC), 558
Lafton Catholic Old Folks Home (New Orleans, LA), 374
Laidlaw, Frank, 245
Laine, Cleo, 114
Laine, Frankie, 74
Lake Forest College (Lake Forest, IL), 65, 249
Lake Meadows Park (Chicago, IL), 381
Lake View Inn (Los Angeles, CA), 398
Lakefront Jazz Festival (Milwaukee, WI), 313
Lakota's Lounge (Milwaukee, WI), 298
Lamar State College (Beaumont, TX), 296, 585
Lamare, Nappy, 385
Lamb, Natalie, **316,,** *316*, 428
Lambert, Don, 481
Lambert, Eddie, 508
Lambert, Lloyd, 293

Lambertville Music Circus (Lambertville, NJ), 114
Lamp (label), 92
Lamp Post (club), The (Syosset, NY), 375
Lampell, ______, 206
Lampertville Concert (Philadelphia, PA), 309
Lanchester Arts Festival (Lanchester, Eng.), 46
Landmark (hotel) (Dallas, TX), 283
Landmark Hotel (Kansas City, MO), 389, 567
Landon, Grelun, 142, 196
Landreaux, Edna, 227
Landreaux, Elizabeth Mary, 372
Landreaux, Victor, 227
Landskrona Jazz Festival (Landskrona, Swed.), 447
Lane, James A., 442
Lane, Richard "Night Train," 538
Lane, Steve, 110
Lane, Willie, 470
Lang, Little Eddie, 396
L'Ange Bleu Club (Paris, Fr.), 581
Langford, Sam, 254
Langille, Doug, 33, 149, 152, 180, 217, 279, 444
Langley Avenue Jive Cats (group), The, 359
Lapel (label), 468
Largo Theater (Los Angeles, CA), 417
Larkins, Milton "Milt," 254, 522, 525
Larks (group), The, 91
Larman, Allen, 57
Larry & Hank (duo), 283
Las Palmas Theater (Los Angeles, CA), 385
Last Chance Saloon (Poughkeepsie, NY), 132, 415
Last Mile Band, The, 348
Latin Casino (Philadelphia, PA), 113, 432
Latin Quarter (Montreal, Can.), 256, 263, 503
Latino Americano (club) (Juarez, Mex.), 360
Lauderdale Hospital (Ripley, TN), 326
Laughing Charley (see: Hicks, Charlie)
Laughing Trio (group), 69, 555
Laurel Garden (club) (New York, NY), 157
Laurel Pop Festival (Laurel, MD), 208, 585
Lauren (label), 239
Laurita's Club (London, Eng.), 199
Lawhorn, Sammy, 484
Lawlars, Ernest (Little Son Joe), 62, 162, **316-317,** 424, 489, 562
Lawrence Opera House (Lawrence, KS), 450
Laws of London (club) (San Francisco, CA), 449
Lawson, Georgia, 555
Lay, Sam "Sammy," 99, 269, 494, 563
Lazy (label), 342
Lazy Bill (see: Lucas, William)
Lazy Daddy's Fillmore Blues Band, 481
Lazy Lester (see: Johnson, Leslie)
Lazy Slim Jim (see: Harris, Edward)
Le Bistro Club (Chicago, IL), 566
Le Caberett (club) (Toronto, Can.), 84
Le Coq D'or (tavern) (Toronto, Can.), 210, 359, 435, 513
Le Gallerie Flambeau (club) (Baltimore, MD), 176, 427
Le Hibou (club) (Ottawa, Can.), 147, 527
LeRoy's (see: Leroy's Cabaret)
Le Ruban Bleu (club) (New York, NY), 542
Leach, Bill, 502
Leadbelly (see: Ledbetter, Huddie)
Leadbelly (book), 319
Leadbelly Memorial Concert (New York, NY), 141, 147, 206, 318, 366, 406, 503
Leadbelly Songbook (book), The, 318
Leadbitter, Mike, 36, 55, 60, 95, 96, 99, 140, 190, 200, 225, 228, 241, 252, 259, 267, 269, 285, 299, 316, 326, 338, 344, 365, 378, 384, 399, 424, 427, 453, 472, 476, 479, 545, 547, 572, 583, 586, 591
Leapfrogs (group), The, 204
Leary, Timothy, 224
Leatherman Plantation (Commerce, MS), 288
Ledbetter, Huddie (Leadbelly), 142, 185, 196, 205, 206, 207, 276, 296, 314, **317-319,** *318,* 365, 368, 454, 503, 505, 525, 556
Ledbetter, Terrell, 317, 319
Ledbetter, Wesley "Wes," 317
Lee, Bertha, 410
Lee, Bessie (see: Smith, Trixie)
Lee, Caroline (see: Brown, Bessie)
Lee Castles Dorsey Band, 84
Lee, Climon, 319
Lee, Ellie, 320
Lee, Frankie, 407, 461, 545
Lee, Freddie, 341
Lee, George, 518
Lee, George E., 321
Lee, George, Sr., 320
Lee, Goosie, 492
Lee, Helen, 274
Lee, Jimmy (see: Robinson, Jimmy Lee)
Lee, John (see: Henley, John Lee)
Lee, John Arthur, 276, **319-320,** *319,* 516
Lee, Johnny (see: Hooker, John Lee)
Lee, Julia, **320-321,** *320*
Lee, King Ivory (see: Semien, Lee)
Lee, Lillian, 285
Lee, Lonesome (see: Robinson, Jimmy Lee)
Lee, Lovey, 41, 42
Lee Magid's Cafe (Tarzana, CA), 76, 520, 524
Lee, Peggy, 116, 466
Lee Roy's Club (New Orleans, LA), 420
Lee, Warren (see: Jackson, Lee)
Leeds Festival (London, Eng.), 478
Lee's Imperial Jazz Band, 316
Lee's Lounge (Chicago, IL), 123
Lee's Sensation (club) (Detroit, MI), 84
Lefty Lou (see: Crissman, Lefty Lou)
Legacy of the Blues (book), The, 59, 166, 167, 341, 554, 574
Leigh, Carol, 107, 311, **321-322,** *321,* 428, 465
Leigh, James, 322
Leimbacher, Ed, 122
Leiser, Willie, 395, 489
LeJeune, Jean-Claude, 380
Leland Baptist Church (Detroit, MI), 532
Lemaise Plantation (Lombardy, MS), 534
Lemon Tree (club) (Chicago, IL), 123
Lemons, Amos, 326
Lemons, Overton Amos, 326
Lennie's (on the Turnpike) (club) (Boston, MA), 100, 132, 208, 304, 309, 389, 447, 566, 567, 588
Lenoir, Dewitt, 322
Lenoir, J. B., 70, 138, 244, 264, 276, 291, **322-324,** *323,* 340, 499
Lenore, J. B. (see: Lenoir, J. B.)
Lenox (label), 147, 164, 175, 417
Lenox Club (New York, NY), 584
Leonard Harper Minstrel Stock Company (tour), 220
Leo's Casino (Cleveland, OH) (see also: New Leo's Casino), 308, 431, 588
Leroy (see: Chatman, Peter)
Leroy, Baby Face (see: Foster, Leroy)
Leroy Percy Park (Jackson, MS), 120
Leroy's Cabaret (New York, NY), 229, 231, 472, 540
Les Trois Mailletz Club (see: Trois Mailletz Club)
Leslie, Lew, 80, 295, 541, 564, 580, 581, 583
Leslie E. Kell Shows (tour), 441
Lester, Julius, 249, 319
Lester High School (Memphis, TN), 116
Levee House (club) (Minneapolis MN), 414
Levee House (club) (St. Louis, MO), 313
Levee Joe (see: Weldon, Will)
Leventhal, Harold, 206
Leviege, Beatrice, 268
Levine, Henry, 256
Lewis, Agnes, 180
Lewis, Bill, 221
Lewis, Bonnie, 274
Lewis, Clark A., 274
Lewis, Daniel, 325
Lewis, Della Lee, 518
Lewis, Denis, 302
Lewis, Furry (see: Lewis, Walter)
Lewis, George, 141, 203, 373, 385, 420
Lewis, Ham, 454
Lewis, Jerry Lee, 158, 412
Lewis, Johnie, **324-325,** *324,* 393, 528
Lewis, Johnny (see: Louis, Joe Hill)
Lewis, Kate (see: Cox, Ida)
Lewis, Meade Lux, 31, 337, 518, 594
Lewis, Noah, 62, 106, **325-326,** *325*
Lewis, Smiley, 152, **326,** *326,* 329, 491
Lewis, Tommy (see: Watts, Louis)
Lewis, Walter "Furry," 62, 106, 264, **326-328,** *327,* 454, 522, 553, 561

Lewis & Clark College (Portland, OR), 573
Lewisohn Stadium (New York, NY), 195
Leyrer, Dan S., 487
L'Hibou Coffeehouse (Ottawa, Can.), 366, 503
Liberty (label), 57, 138, 240, 243, 249, 340, 439, 468, 541
Liberty Club (S. Chester, PA), 549
Liberty Hall (Dallas, TX), 156, 210, 330, 513
Liberty Hall (Houston, TX), 33, 57, 58, 78, 101, 122, 132, 190, 240, 244, 304, 305, 346, 364, 367, 435, 442, 504, 513
Liberty Inn Club (Monroe, LA), 268
Liberty Theater (Chattanooga, TN), 463
Liberty Theater (New York, NY), 71, 295, 581
Liberty Theater (Staten Island, NY), 581
Library of Congress (concert) (Washington, DC), 556
Library of Congress (label) (LC label), 33, 74, 79, 89, 169, 182, 206, 209, 247, 257, 317, 349, 365, 369, 386, 502, 503, 552, 556, 589
Libya Cafe (New York, NY), 221, 540
Licking Stick (club), The (Chicago, IL), 304
Lido Ballroom (New York, NY), 200, 472
Lieberman, Frank, 433
Lieberson, Dave, 147
Life and Works of Thomas Andrew Dorsey (book), 160
Life Board Baptist Church (Aberdeen, MS), 93
Liggins, Joe, 55, 512
Lightfoot, Alexander, **328-329,** *328*
Lightfoot, Andrew, 328
Lightfoot, Gordon, 219
Lighthouse (club), The (Hermosa Beach/Los Angeles, CA), 125, 209, 240, 244, 254, 359, 367, 375, 417, 431, 445, 447, 505, 513, 549, 588
Lighthouse (club), The (Lake Minnetonka, MN), 342
Lighthouse (club), The (New York, NY), 224
Lightnin' Express (magazine), 31, 330, 364
Lightnin' Jr. (see: Dupree, William) (see: Williams, L. C.)
Lightnin' Slim (see: Hicks, Otis)
Limelight (club), The (Los Angeles, CA), 141
Limelight Cafe/Club (Chicago, IL), 569, 591
Limelight Theater (Chicago, IL), 53, 176, 198, 524
Lincoln, Charley (see: Hicks, Charlie)
Lincoln Cafe (Durham, NC), 184
Lincoln Cemetery (Atlanta, GA), 226
Lincoln Cemetery (Blue Island, IL), 435
Lincoln Cemetery (Chicago, IL), 229
Lincoln Cemetery (Macomb County, MI), 467
Lincoln Cemetery (Urbana, IL), 595
Lincoln Cemetery (Worth, IL), 69, 592
Lincoln Center (New York, NY) (see also: Avery Fisher Hall/ Philharmonic Hall), 156, 240, 243, 346, 389, 417
Lincoln Gardens (club) (Los Angeles, CA), 398
Lincoln Hall (Kansas City, MO), 88
Lincoln Hotel (New York, NY), 446
Lincoln Memorial Cemetery (Drayton, SC), 34
Lincoln Memorial Gardens (Bessemer, AL), 125
Lincoln Memorial Park (Los Angeles, CA), 43, 56
Lincoln Memorial Park (Macomb County, MI), 252
Lincoln Memorial Park Cemetery (Dallas, TX), 267, 461
Lincoln Park (New Orleans, LA), 372
Lincoln Square Theater (New York, NY), 221
Lincoln Theater (Baltimore, MD), 540
Lincoln Theater (Dallas, TX), 481
Lincoln Theater (Houston, TX), 57
Lincoln Theater (Kansas City, MO), 463
Lincoln Theater (Los Angeles, CA), 74, 191, 215, 446, 527
Lincoln Theater (Louisville, KY), 540
Lincoln Theater (New Orleans, LA), 86, 101, 164, 464, 564
Lincoln Theater (New York, NY), 48, 80, 81, 82, 144, 172, 173, 197, 221, 223, 231, 256, 351, 356, 357, 405, 428, 450, 463, 464, 467, 470, 472, 474, 475, 481, 491, 496, 540, 580, 581, 583, 584
Lincoln Theater (Philadelphia, PA), 173, 256, 464
Lincoln Theater (Pittsburgh, PA), 428, 463
Lincoln Theater (Union City, PA), 70
Lincoln Theater (Washington, DC), 496
Lindahl, Erik, 384, 402
Linden Circle Theater (Memphis, TN), 179
Linnear, Prince, 175
Lion's Share (club) (San Anselmo, CA), 30, 210, 211, 367, 504
Lipscomb, Charlie, 330
Lipscomb, Mance, 142, 162, 276, 296, **329-331,** *329*, 375, 456, 487
Lisner Auditorium (Washington, DC), 420
Lissen (label), 203
Listen to the Blues (book), 266, 396
Liston, Virginia, **331,** *331*
Liston & Liston (duo), 331
Little, Big Tiny, 322, 466
Little, Joe, 596
Little Ann (see: Bunn, Ann)
Little Beau (pseudonym), 518
Little Boy Blue (see: Williamson, Sonny Boy)
Little Boys (group), The, 393, 548
Little Brother (see: Montgomery, Eurreal)
Little Club, The (Paris, Fr.), 256
Little David (see: Alexander, David)
Little Esther (see: Phillips, Esther)
Little Giant of the Blues (billing), 549
Little Harlem Chicken Shack (club) (San Diego, CA), 276, 456
Little Harlem Club (Buffalo, NY), 263
Little Harlem Club (Los Angeles, CA), 425
Little Hatchet Band, 217
Little Henry (see: Gray, Henry)
Little Hudson (see: Shower, Hudson)
Little Joe (see: Louis, Joe Hill)
Little Joe's Bar (Newark, NJ), 378-379
Little Johnny (see: Jones, John)
Little Junior/Jr. (see: Johnson, Luther) (see: Parker, Herman)
Little Laura (see: Dukes, Laura)
Little Lovin' Henry (see: Byrd, Roy)
Little Luther (see: Johnson, Luther)
Little Mac (see: Simmons, Mack)
Little Maceo (see: Merriweather, Rozier)
Little Mack (see: Simmons, Mack)
Little Man (see: Johnson, James)
Little Milton (see: Campbell, Milton)
Little Mt. Moriah Baptist Church (New York, NY), 147
Little Otis (see: Rush, Otis)
Little Papa Joe (see: Williams, Joseph Leon)
Little Papa Walter (see: Lightfoot, Alexander)
Little Peetie Wheatstraw (billing), 233
Little Rabbit Night Club (Pine Bluff, AR), 193
Little Ray (see: Agee, Raymond)
Little Richard (see: Penniman, Richard)
Little Sam (see: Broonzy, William)
Little Sam (club) (Detroit, MI), 578
Little Sister (see: Scruggs, Irene)
Little Son (see: Broonzy, William)
Little Son Joe (see: Lawlars, Ernest)
Little Sonny (see: Willis, Aaron)
Little Star (label), 411
Little Strand Theater (Chicago, IL), 81
Little T-Bone (see: Rankin, R. S.)
Little Temple (see: Jenkins, Gus)
Little Theater (New York, NY), 90, 453
Little Theater of YMCA (New York, NY), 496
Little Walter (see: Jacobs, Marion Walter)
Little Walter J. (see: Jacobs, Marion Walter)
Little Walter Jr. (see: Smith, George)
Little Wolf (see: Shines, John)
Little Wolf (pseudonym), 95
Littlefield, Willie, 76, 158, **332,** *333*, 417
Littlejohn, John "Johnny," 95, 271, 311, **332-334,** *333*, 391, 397, 442
Littricebey, Clara Alma Allen, 198
Litweiler, John B., 570
Living Blues (magazine), 29, 30, 31, 32, 33, 34, 35, 37, 38, 42, 43, 51, 60, 62, 63, 65, 66, 67, 72, 73, 75, 76, 77, 78, 91, 93, 94, 95, 97, 99, 102, 103, 105, 106, 108, 109, 111, 119, 124,

127, 128, 130, 131, 132, 133, 134, 136, 138, 142, 143, 144, 149, 152, 154, 157, 159, 160, 161, 162, 165, 166, 169, 170, 175, 178, 180, 181, 182, 184, 189, 190, 198, 199, 204, 209, 211, 212, 213, 214, 226, 227, 228, 232, 235, 248, 249, 250, 252, 253, 259, 260, 261, 265, 266, 267, 269, 270, 274, 277, 278, 279, 282, 283, 286, 287, 294, 295, 297, 300, 301, 302, 306, 307, 320, 323, 326, 328, 329, 330, 333, 335, 336, 339, 340, 343, 344, 345, 347, 350, 351, 353, 358, 368, 369, 371, 377, 378, 379, 380, 382, 384, 386, 392, 394, 395, 397, 398, 400, 402, 404, 407, 410, 412, 414, 417, 418, 422, 424, 425, 427, 428, 430, 433, 434, 435, 436, 438, 439, 440, 441, 442, 443, 445, 449, 451, 456, 458, 459, 469, 474, 475, 476, 479, 482, 483, 484, 485, 489, 491, 493, 497, 499, 500, 501, 502, 505, 506, 508, 509, 510, 511, 512, 514, 516, 517, 521, 522, 524, 528, 529, 530, 531, 532, 534, 535, 536, 544, 549, 551, 554, 558, 560, 561, 562, 563, 571, 572, 573, 575, 576, 579, 583, 589, 590, 595, 597
Living End (club), The (Detroit, MI), 132, 388
Living Legend (billing), The, 390
Living Room (club), The (Cincinnati, OH), 76, 308, 567, 588
Living Room (club) (Los Angeles, CA), 431
Livingston Negro Cemetery (Livingston, AL), 209
Liza and Her Shuffling Sextet Revue (tour), 137
Lizzie Murphy's Sporting House (Atlanta, GA), 564
Lloyd's Club (Hayward, CA), 188
Lobby Inn, The (Juarez, Mex.), 531
Lock & Key Club (Astoria, NY), 90
Lockwood, Ester, 289
Lockwood, Robert, 334
Lockwood, Robert "Jr.," 27, 63, 93, 122, 289, **334-336**, *335*, 343, 399, 442, 478, 483, 499, 516, 535, 560, 577
Loeb Student Center (school) (New York, NY), 240, 254, 286
Loew's American Theater (New York, NY), 581
Loew's circuit, 221, 440, 472, 580
Loew's Fulton Street Theater (Brooklyn, NY), 581
Loew's King Theater (Brooklyn, NY), 132
Loew's Prospect Theater (Brooklyn, NY), 82
Loew's State (theater) (Boston, MA), 269, 281, 359, 538
Loew's State Theater (Montreal, Can.), 82
Loew's State Theater (New York, NY) (see also: State Theater, New York, NY), 215, 541, 564
Loew's Theater (Ottawa, Can.), 472
Loew's Theater (Toronto, Can.), 472
Loew's Victoria Theater (New York, NY), 541
Loft (club), The (Boston, MA), 314
Lofton, Clarence, **336-337**, *336*, 352, 594
Lofton, Walter, 336
Log Cabin (club), The (San Francisco, CA), 345
Log Cabin Wranglers (band), 179
Logan, Agnes, 291
Logan, Nick, 47, 101, 225, 312, 352
Loma (label), 132, 326
Lomax, Alan, 206, 207, 209, 318, 319, 365, 503
Lomax, John A., 317, 318, 319
Lomax, Lawrence, 496
London (label), 165, 364, 556
London Blues Society Convention (London, Eng.), 302
London Coliseum (London, Eng.), 581
London-Decca (label), 63, 352
London House (club) (Chicago, IL), 51, 310, 527
London Pavilion (see: Pavilion, The)
Lone Star Beer Company of Texas (product), 78
Lone Star Club (Kansas City, MO), 518
Lone Wolf (billing), The, 589
Lonesome Lee (see: Robinson, Jimmy Lee)
Lonesome Sundown (see: Green, Cornelius)
Long, Son, 283
Long Beach Arena (Los Angeles, CA), 359
Long Beach Auditorium (Los Angeles, CA), 113, 352
Long Beach Civic Auditorium (Long Beach, CA), 327
Long Island National Cemetery (Pinelawn, NY), 364
Long Island Traditional Jazz Club (Babylon, NY), 316
Longbranch (club), The (San Francisco, CA), 513
Longhorn Jazz Festival (Austin, TX), 243
Longhorn Jazz Festival (Houston, TX), 308
Longhorn Ranch (club) (Dallas, TX), 51, 76, 113, 308, 461, 527
Longview Cemetery (Knoxville, TN), 134
Lookout House (club) (Cincinnati, OH), 432
Loop Inc. (club), The (Chicago, IL), 375
Lord Liquor Club (Chicago, IL), 380
Lornell, Kip, 34, 107, 111, 133, 261
Lorraine Gardens #2 (club), (Chicago, IL), 254
Los Angeles Broadway Theater (Los Angeles, CA), 221
Los Angeles Harbor College (Wilmington, CA), 120
Los Angeles Herald Examiner (newspaper), 433
Los Angeles Philharmonic (orchestra), 114
Los Angeles Six (band), 288
Los Angeles Times (newspaper), 433
Loser's Club, The (Dallas, TX), 51, 309, 352, 510
Lou Terrassi's (club) (New York, NY), 406
Louann's Club (Dallas, TX), 431
Louie's Lounge (Boston, MA), 396
Louis, Joe, 337, 525
Louis, Joe Hill, 62, **337**, *337*, 400, 454
Louis, Tommy (see: Watts, Louis)
Louis Armstrong Memorial Concert, (New York, NY), 254
Louis' Cafe (Los Angeles, CA), 377
Louise, Ella, 322
Louise's (club) (Chicago, IL), 36, 450
Louise's Palace (club) (Chicago, IL), 341
Louise's South Park Lounge (Chicago, IL), 110, 394, 476, 500
Louisiana (label), 506
Louisiana Club (San Francisco, CA), 439
Louisiana Folklore Society (label), 573
Louisiana Heritage Festival (New Orleans, LA), 512
Louisiana Red (see: Minter, Iverson)
Louisiana Six (band), 288, 312
Louisiana State Penitentiary (Angola, LA) (Angola State Prison Farm), 60, 317, 573
Louisiana State University (Baton Rouge, LA), 543
Louisville Cemetery (Louisville, KY), 351
Louisville Gardens (club) (Louisville, KY), 51, 310
Louisville General Hospital (Louisville, KY), 351
Lou's Rickshaw Room (club) (Houston, TX), 243
Love, Billy, 337, 338
Love, Clarence, 253
Love, Clayton, 289, **338**, 338
Love, Cleanhead, 529
Love, Earl, 464
Love, Eddie, 238, 338
Love, Jasper, 338
Love, Paul, 199
Love, Willie, 59, 104, 106, 271, 291, 317, 338, **338-339**, *338*, 399, 400, 412, 425, 443, 560, 577
Love, Willie, Sr., 338
Love (label), 63
Love Street Light Circus (club), The (Houston, TX), 585
Lovejoy Club (E. St. Louis, IL), 552
Lover Boys (group), 291
Lovers (duo), The, 92
Lover's Lounge (Chicago, IL), 78
Lovett, Baby, 321
Lovia's Lounge (Chicago, IL), 150
Lowery, Robert "Bob," 241, 244, 267, 289, **339**, *339*, 391
Lowry, Peter "Pete," 28, 92, 93, 111, 164, 171, 172, 180, 226, 228, 261, 293, 295, 312, 313, 319, 353, 364, 454, 492, 515, 516, 546, 560, 563, 574
Loyola University (Chicago, IL), 381

Loyola's Auditorium (New Orleans, LA), 113
Lt. Robert E. Lee Riverboat (see: S.S. Lt. Robert E. Lee Riverboat)
Luandrew, Albert (Sunnyland Slim), 39, 63, 66, 67, 122, 161, 180, 234, 260, 294, 334, **339-341**, *340*, 342, 343, 381, 388, 394, 400, 424, 439, 442, 479, 516, 552, 559, 575, 577, 589
Luandrew, T. W., 339
Lubzik, Wally, 83
Lucas, Bill (see: Lucas, William)
Lucas, Jane (see: Spivey, Victoria)
Lucas, John, 319
Lucas, William "Lazy Bill," 70, 118, 181, 341, **342**, *342*, 343, 394, 460, 568, 571, 574, 575, 576
Lucifer's (club) (Boston, MA), 310
Lucille's Place (club) (Los Angeles, CA), 136
Lucky Seven (label), 400
Lucky's Paradise (club) (Montreal, Can.), 90
Lucky's Plantation (Clarksdale, MS), 234
Ludlow Garage (club) (Cincinnati, OH), 346
Lulu's Storyville Saloon (Ann Arbor, MI), 421
Lumberjacks (group), The, 160
Lunceford, Jimmie, 484, 491, 581
Lupo's (club) (Providence, RI), 247, 450
Luthjen's Dance Hall (New Orleans, LA), 420
Lyceum Theater (Chicago, IL), 254
Lyceum Theater (Cincinnati, OH), 227
Lydon, Michael, 47, 225
Lyon & Healy Music School/Studio (Chicago, IL), 237, 479
Lyons Club (Detroit, MI), 230
Lyric (label), 191
Lyric Auditorium (Baltimore, MD), 431
Lyric Hall (Kansas City, MO), 321
Lyric Theater (Indianapolis, IN), 82
Lyric Theater (New Orleans, LA), 152, 331, 350, 463, 466, 467, 540
Lyric Theater (Rome, GA?), 428
Lyrichord (label), 521
Lyseng Studios (organization), 376
Lyttelton, Humphrey, 520

M&M (label), 217
M&O Gospel Singers (group), 91
MC Lounge (Gary, IN), 308
MCA (label), 54
MCM (label), 151, 394, 404
MGM (label), 79, 90, 113, 148, 285, 287, 432, 454, 521
MGM Grand Hotel (Las Vegas, NV), 432
MJR (label), 447
MPS (label), 155, 211, 246, 341, 457
M-Pac (label), 175
Ma Bea's Lounge (Chicago, IL), 151, 287, 334, 394, 404, 437, 442, 530, 596
Ma Cumba (label), 378
Ma Rainey and the Classic Blues Singers (book), 72, 222, 357, 374, 474, 582
Mabon, Willie, 38, 66, 334, 336, 341, 342, **343-344**, *343*, 371, 391, 438, 439, 460, 491
Mack, Mary, 420
Mackinac Jack's (club) (Ann Arbor, MI), 225
Mack's (club) (Atlantic City, NJ), 549
Mack's Merrymakers (group), 420
Macon, Albert, 344
Macon, John "Short Stuff," **344**, *344*, 569
Mac's Old House (club) (Antioch, CA), 332
Macy's (label), 191, 232, 572
Mad (label), 175, 334, 343
Madame Mamie Hightower's Golden Brown Beauty Preparations (product), 540
Madison Ballroom (Chicago, IL), 501
Madison Rink (Chicago, IL), 269
Madison Square Garden (stadium) (New York, NY), 46, 100, 114, 158, 219, 224, 231, 296, 304, 359, 383, 411, 417, 418, 496, 542, 549, 585
Madison Theater (Brooklyn, NY), 70, 82
Madrague (club), The (Oakland, CA), 513
Maggie's Blue Five (band), 497
Maggie's Opera House (Cincinnati, OH), 37
Maghett, Jessie, 344
Maghett, Samuel (Magic Sam), 32, 33, 72, 124, 150, 190, 208, 213, 235, 236, 269, 286, 289, 294, 307, 311, **344-345**, *344*, 348, 391, 438, 442, 488, 530, 575, 596
Magic (label), 435
Magic Circus (club) (Los Angeles, CA), 513
Magic Sam (see: Maghett, Samuel)
Magic Singing Sam (see: Maghett, Samuel)
Magic Slim (see: Holt, Morris)
Magic Touch (label), 397
Magnolia (label), 247, 294
Magnolia Ballroom (Atlanta, GA), 415
Magnolia Cemetery (Helena, AR), 140, 399
Magnum (label), 371
Magoo's (club) (Chicago, IL), 53
Mahal, Taj, 148, 289, 305, **345-347**, *346*, 401, 505
Maheu, Jack, 322
Maiden, Sidney, **347**, 448
Main Cafe (Muncie, IN), 139
Main Point (club), The (Bryn Mawr, PA), 32, 132, 195, 208, 210, 240, 345, 389, 429, 521, 548, 588
Main Squeeze (band), 296
Main Street Theater (Kansas City, MO), 70
Mainliner Club (San Francisco, CA), 122
Mainstream (label), 76, 243, 296, 485, 503
Maisonette (club), The (New York, NY), 389, 432
Majestic (label), 491
Majestic Hotel (Cleveland, OH), 523
Majestic Lounge (Chicago, IL), 572
Majestic "M" (club) (Chicago, IL), 123, 384, 445, 488, 596
Majestic Theater (Brooklyn, NY), 475, 541, 564, 581
Majestic Theater (Butler, PA), 70
Majestic Theater (Cedar Rapids, IO), 540
Majestic Theater (Elmira, NY), 82
Majestic Theater (Jersey City, NJ), 52
Majestic Theater (Johnstown, PA), 82
Majestic Theater (New York, NY), 541
Majestic Theater (San Antonio, TX), 440
Major-Minor (label), 110
Makers Nightclub (Pensacola, FL), 420
Malcomb, Horace, 501
Malibus Family (group), 137
Mallard, Horatio "Rusty", 538
Mallory, Eddie, 541
Malone, Mae, 49
Malone, Octavia, 507
Mama Can Can (see: Rainey, Gertrude)
Mama Lou's (club) (New Orleans, LA), 84
Mamie Smith and her Gang (band), 472
Mamie Smith Benefit Concert (New York, NY), 83, 221
Mamie Smith Company (tour), 472
Mamlish (label), 229, 280
Man and his World Concert (Montreal, Can.), 46, 309
Man and his World Exhibit (Montreal, Can.), 51, 359
Manassa Street Grade School (Memphis, TN), 457
Manassas Jazz Festival (Manassas, VA), 245, 313, 316, 423
Mance, Junior, 566
Manchester Grill (club) (Chicago, IL), 200
Manchester Junior School of Art (Manchester, Eng.), 351
Mandel, Johnny, 372
Mandel Hall (Chicago, IL), 65, 269, 398, 548, 594
Mandrake's (club) (Berkeley, CA), 98, 243, 366, 367, 389, 504
Manetta, Manuel, 373
Mangelsdorff, Rich, 103, 597
Mangurian, David "Dave," 534, 570
Manhattan Bar & Grill (New York, NY), 175
Manhattan Casino (Club) (New York, NY), 221, 475
Manhattan Center (theater) (New York, NY), 346
Manhattan Club, The (E. St. Louis, IL), 304
Manhattan Club (Galveston, TX), 125
Manhattan Club (Houston, TX), 547
Manhattan Club (Newport, KY), 191
Manhattan Community College (New York, NY), 231
Mann, Woody, 148
Manne, Shelly, 375

Manning, Wesley, 445, 448
Manny Greenhill's (club) (Boston, MA), 174
Manor (label), 564
Manor Plaza Hotel (San Francisco, CA), 372
Mansfield Theater (New York, NY), 581
Manson, Charlie, 297
Manual Arts High School (Los Angeles, CA), 211
Maple Grove Cemetery (Kew Gardens, Queens, NY), 448
Maple Leaf Club (Denver, CO), 360
Maple Leaf Gardens (stadium) (Toronto, Can.), 224, 585
Mapp, Eddie, 546
Marable, Fate, 279
Marco Polo Club (Vancouver, Can.), 431
Marco Polo Hotel (Miami, FL), 310
Mardi Gras (club) (Kansas City, MO), 308, 470
Mardi Gras (event), The (New Orleans, LA), 62, 454
Mardi Gras Lounge (New Orleans, LA), 203, 300, 373
Maree, Ben, 39, 290
Margaret (label), 331
Marian Anderson of the Blues (billing), 257
Mariana, Hugo, 496
Marigold (label), 167
Marina City Towers (Chicago, IL), 381
Marine World (aquarium) (Redwood City, CA), 30
Mariposa Folk Festival (Toronto Island/Toronto, Can.), 56, 57, 59, 93, 120, 130, 138, 147, 148, 174, 187, 208, 210, 246, 249, 257, 260, 261, 266, 272, 283, 340, 346, 347, 349, 363, 366, 443, 457, 490, 504, 532, 553, 563, 573, 595
Mar-Jan (label), 28
Mark Hellinger Theater (New York, NY), 432
Mark Scott Pub (club) (Dover, NJ), 550
Mark Twain Riverboat (see S.S. Mark Twain)
Markham, Pigmeat, 431
Marmalade (label), 577
Marner, Ida, 483
Maroints, Ivor, 557
Marquee Club (London, Eng.) (see also: New Marquee Club), 228, 234, 260, 352, 577
Marrero, John, 203
Marriott Hotel (New Orleans, LA), 40, 299, 316, 436, 508
Mars, John "Johnny," 269, 311, **347-348**, *347*, 435, 505, 549, 578
Mars, Jules, 348
Mars, Sylvia, **348**
Mars Club (Paris, Fr.), 117
Marsala, Joe, 406
Marsala, Marty, 139, 185
Marshall, Jim, 329
Marshall, Kaiser, 298
Marshall, Ron, 178
Martin, Carl, 56, 57, **348-349**, *348*
Martin, Carrie, 249
Martin, Carter, 349
Martin, Cora Mae, 184
Martin, "Fiddlin' " Joe (see: Martin, Joe)
Martin, Frank "Fiddlin'," 348
Martin, George (see: Phelps, Arthur)
Martin, Henry, 334
Martin, Jake, 350
Martin, Joe, 27, 28
Martin, Joe (Fiddlin' Joe), 161, **349-350**, *349*
Martin, Lawrence, 420
Martin, Margaret, 563
Martin, Melvyn, 103
Martin, Roland, 348, 349
Martin, Sallie, 159, 536
Martin, Sara "Sarah," **350-351**, *350*, 482, 496, 497
Martin & Walker Show (tour), 175
Martin Beck Theater (New York, NY), 173, 541
Martin Block Carnival of Swing Show (concert) (New York, NY), 446
Martin, Bogan and The Armstrongs (group), 56, 349
Martin Luther King Jr. General Hospital (Los Angeles, CA), 201
Martin's Cabaret (New Orleans, LA), 373
Martin's Corner (club) (Chicago, IL), 110, 154, 161, 279, 339, 355, 433
Martinsville Inn (Martinsville, NJ), 316
Marty's (club) (Los Angeles, CA), 567, 588
Marvel (label), 294
Marx, Groucho, 375
Mary Johnson Davis Gospel Singers (group), 288
Mary, Queen of England, 592
Maryland Inn (Annapolis, MD), 322
Mary's (club) (Chicago, IL), 591
Mary's Bar (Detroit, MI), 535
Ma's Place (club) (Chicago, IL), 457
Masked Marvel, The (see: Patton, Charley)
Mason, John, 223
Mason, Pearl, 153
Mason-Henderson Troupe (tour), 223
Masonic Auditorium/Hall (San Francisco, CA), 113, 141
Masonic Lodge Hall (Chicago, IL), 467
Masonic Temple (Detroit, MI), 431, 567
Masonic Temple (San Francisco, CA), 538
Mason's Lounge (New Orleans, LA), 101
Masque Theater (New York, NY), 475
Massey Hall (Toronto, Can.), 51, 84, 114, 208, 210, 257, 280, 308, 309, 388
Master (label), 116
Matchbox (label), 163, 327, 381, 508
Matinee, The (see: Club Matinee)
Matinee Club (Drew, MS), 59
Matrix (club), The (San Francisco, CA), 32, 54, 98, 174, 210, 243, 553, 569
Mattes, Al, 148
Matthews, Clyde Edward, 543
Mathews, Inzy, 375
Matthews, Onzy, 586
Matty Dorsey's Pickaninnies (tour), 467
Mauerer, Hans J., 521
Mauney, Elizabeth, 43
Maxey, Delois, 533
Maxim Trio (see: McSon Trio)
Maxine Elliott's Theater (New York, NY), 556
Max's Kansas City (club) (New York, NY), 33, 51, 95, 132, 195, 283, 367, 389, 482, 504, 527
Maxwell Street Boys (group), 591
Maxwell Street Jimmy (see: Thomas, Charles)
May, Butler "Stringbeans," 172
May, Chris, 360
May, Hannah, 159
Mayall, John, 63, 165, 211, 213, 239, 241, 337, **351-352**, *351*, 578
Mayan Theater (Hollywood/Los Angeles, CA), 518, 582
Mayes, Ethel (see: Moore, Monette)
Mayes, Ethel, 386
Mayfair Club (Boston, MA), 256
Mayfair Club/Lounge (New York, NY), 164, 481
Mayfair Grill (Cleveland, OH), 145
Mayfair Park (Edmonton, Can.), 377
Mayfield, Percy, 53, 91, 116, 277, **352-353**, *352*
Mayl, Gene, 37, 414
Mayme Remington's Pickaninnies (tour), 197
Mayor (label), 556
Mays, Curley, **353**
Mazzolini, Tom, 31, 53, 76, 98, 126, 154, 160, 161, 187, 339, 440, 510, 554
McAbee, Palmer, 180
McAuliffe, Leon, 440
McBeck, Zearline, 549
McBooker, Connie, 572
McCabe's (club) (Santa Monica, CA), 130, 174, 190, 210, 367, 459, 504
McCain, Jerry, 269, **353-354**, *353*
McCain, Mary Jan, 257
McCann, Les, 431
McCarthy, Albert, 41, 64, 158, 162, 318, 351, 354, 360, 410, 475, 533, 552, 555, 562
McCartney, Paul, 224
McCarty, David, 313
McCarty, Ethel Jean, 313
McClain, Henry, 44
McClennan, Tommy, 96, 138, 169, 315, **354**, *354*
McClennon, George, 152
McCollum, ______, 398
McCollum, Percy, 398, 399
McCollum, Robert Lee, 398
McCormick, Mack, 29, 244, 289, 330, 455, 507, 583, 588
McCormick Place (hall) (Chicago, IL), 113, 543
McCoy, ______, 398
McCoy, Charles "Charlie," 252, 290, 315, **354-355**, 355, 399, 524, 595
McCoy, Charlie, 355
McCoy, James "Jim," 249

McCoy, Joe, 161, 162, 355, **355-356,** *355,* 399, 433
McCoy, Minnie (see: Douglas, Lizzie)
McCoy, Patrick, 354, 355
McCoy, Robert "Cyclone," 399
McCoy, Robert Edward "Bob," **356**
McCoy, Robert Jesse, 356
McCoy, Robert Lee (see: Nighthawk, Robert)
McCoy, Viola "Violet," 223, **356-357,** *356*
McCoy, Wilber, 355
McCoy Brothers (duo), 501
McCracklin, Jimmy, 29, 63, 188, 212, 213, 302, 303, **357-358,** *358,* 398, 421, 461, 509
McCrea Gospel Singers (group), 217
McDaniel, Ellas (Bo Diddley), 35, 90, 237, 299, **359-360,** *359,* 390, 476, 478, 545, 571
McDaniel, Harry, 584
McDaniel, Hattie, 176, **360-363,** *361,* 541
McDaniel, Henry, 273, 360
McDaniel, Otis, 360
McDaniel, Sam "Deacon," 362
McDaniel Company (tour), 273, 360
McDaniel's Lounge (Houston, TX), 201
McDonald, Maggie, 202
McDonough, John, 254
McDowell, Annie Mae, 363
McDowell, Fred, **363-364,** *363,* 410, 429
McDowell, Jimmy, 363
McEwen, Joe, 397
McGhee, Brownie (see: McGhee, Walter Brown)
McGhee, George Duffield, 364, 365
McGhee, Granville "Stick," 96, **364-365,** *364,* 365, 367, 503
McGhee, Stick (see: McGhee, Granville)
McGhee, Walter Brown "Brownie," 70, 93, 140, 147, 147-148, 164, 166, 174, 175, 185, 206, 215, 276, 317, 319, 364, **365-368,** *365,* 375, 454, 503, 504, 556, 560, 569
McGill's Blue Room (club) (Omaha, NE), 215
McGowan, Charles, 438
McGriff, Jimmy, 407
McGuirt, Candyman, 510
McHouston, Ed (see: Baker, McHouston)
McKenna, Vandy, 364
McKenzie, Billy, 139
McKenzie, Daisy, 154
McKenzie & Crump (duo), 139
McKesson, ______, 480
McKie's Ballroom (Chicago, IL), 63
McKie's Club/Lounge (Chicago, IL), 35, 353, 388, 523, 527, 548, 586
McKinley, Bill (see: Gillum, William)
McKinney, E. Andrew, 333
McLaren Park (amphitheater) (San Francisco, CA), 30, 54, 76, 98, 125, 154, 270, 358
McLaurin, Annie, 64
McLean, Cy, 84
McLean, Don, 557
McLeese, Richard, 451
McMahon, Andrew "Blueblood," **368-369,** *368*
McMillan, James, 140
McMillan's Bar (St. Louis, MO), 414
McMullen, Fred, 35
McNeely, Jay, 533, 544
McNeill, Don, 582
McPartland, Marion, 406
McPartlan's Lounge (Chicago, IL), 381
McQuery, Sam, 311
McShann, Jay, 44, 88, 89, 321, 375, 436, 423, 586
McSon Trio (Maxim Trio), 111
McTell, Eddie, 369
McTell, Ralph, 148
McTell, Willie "Blind Willie," 164, 280, **369-370,** *369,* 391, 415, 546
McTier, Eddie, 369
McVea, Jack, 76, 216, 527
Meadowbrook (ballroom) (Cedar Grove, NJ), 316, 446
Meadowbrook Club (Savannah, GA), 86
Meadowbrook Jazz Festival (Detroit, MI), 114
Mean Mistreater (label), 236
Mecca Temple (New York, NY), 205
Medgar Evers Memorial Festival (Jackson, MS), 104, 156, 309
Mega (label), 523
Melhardt, Axel, 302
Mellodeers (group), The, 86
Mellotones (group), 544
Mellow Fellows (group), 51
Mellow Tones Blues Band, 448
Mellowland Club (Pontiac, MI), 563
Melodeon (label), 272, 273
Melodisc (label), 69, 234
Melody Club (Hollywood, CA), 586
Melody Club (Newark, NJ), 550
Melody Fair (club) (Buffalo, NY), 51, 310
Melody Land (club) (Anaheim, CA), 113
Melody Land Theater (Los Angeles, CA), 432
Melody Maker (magazine), 180, 225, 307, 311, 352, 409, 448, 520, 528, 588
Melody Show Bar (St. Louis, MO), 110, 115
Melotone (label), 159, 380, 406, 470, 489
Melrose Stompers (band), 373
Mel's Hideaway (lounge) (Chicago, IL), 213, 305
Memo Cocktail Lounge (San Francisco, CA), 518
Memorial Auditorium (Burlington, VA), 310
Memorial Auditorium (Dallas, TX), 46, 113, 431
Memorial Auditorium (Kansas City, MO), 113
Memorial Auditorium (New Orleans, LA), 51, 309, 510
Memorial Auditorium (Sacramento, CA), 36-37
Memorial Coliseum (Los Angeles, CA), 104, 304, 510, 580
Memory Lane Club (Los Angeles, CA), 417
Memory Lane Supper Lounge (W. Santa Barbara, CA), 418
Memphis Blues (book), 40, 264, 326, 328, 337, 455, 486
Memphis Blues Boy (see: Nix, Willie)
Memphis Blues Caravan (concert) (Milwaukee, WI), 327
Memphis Blues Caravan (tour), 177, 180, 327, 401, 484, 553, 561
Memphis Blues Festival (Memphis, TN), 99, 130, 177, 302, 327, 363, 427, 457, 508, 510, 553, 562, 585
Memphis Blues Society Show (tour), 327, 363, 553, 562
Memphis Cotton Carnival (concert) (Memphis, TN), 313, 470
Memphis Fair Grounds (Memphis, TN), 486
Memphis Folk Blues Festival (Memphis, TN), 104
Memphis Jim (see: Dorsey, Thomas A.)
Memphis Jimmy (pseudonym), 213
Memphis Jug Band, 40, 62, 98, 128, 161, 169, 246, 325, 327, 398, 454, 455, 484, 547
Memphis Mid-South Coliseum (Memphis, TN), 296
Memphis Minnie (see: Douglas, Lizzie)
Memphis Mose (see: Dorsey, Thomas A.)
Memphis Mudcats (band), 98
Memphis Music Heritage Festival (Memphis, TN), 510
Memphis Piano Red (see: Williams, John)
Memphis Queen (see S.S. Memphis Queen)
Memphis Riverfront Festival (Memphis, TN), 163
Memphis Slim (see: Chatman, Peter) (see: Davenport, Charles)
Memphis Willie B. (see: Borum, William)
Mendelsohn, Danny, 470
Mendota Jazz Festival (Minneapolis, MN), 56, 349
Menendez, Byron, 142
Menendez, Nina, 142
Menendez, Paul, 142
Mercon Cemetery (Bala-Cynwyd, PA), 273
Mercury (label), 46, 67, 69, 88, 89, 99, 101, 116, 155, 157, 219, 232, 233, 243, 253, 281, 299, 334, 340, 348, 357, 400, 403, 407, 411, 468, 513, 521, 523, 532, 536, 538, 542, 556, 572, 577, 586
Mercury-Blue Rock (label), 407
Mercy Dee (see: Walton, Mercy Dee)
Mercy Hospital (Urbana, IL), 322
Meridian 8 (label), 314
Meritt (label), 41, 321, 360
Meriwether, Roy, 371
Merriweather, Christopher "Kit," 370
Merriweather, Major "Maceo" (Big Maceo), 63, 66, 67, 110, 199, 217, 269, 295, 322, 343, **370-371,** *370,* 478, 479, 559
Merriweather, Rozier "Bob" (Little Maceo), 371

Merry Makers (band), 39
Mesner, Henry, 191
Messaround (label), 213, 339, 516
Metcalf, Louis, 405
Meteor (label), 28, 104, 271, 337, 350, 437, 510
Meth, Max, 541
Metro (club), The (New York, NY), 305
Metro Jazz (label), 366
Metronome (magazine), 89
Metropole (club), The (New York, NY), 299, 594
Metropolitan Museum (New York, NY), 195
Metropolitan Opera Guild Choir, 108
Metropolitan Theater (Brooklyn, NY), 221, 472, 581
Metropolitan Theater (Chicago, IL), 481
Meyers, Louis (see: Myers, Louis)
Mezzrow, Mezz, 197, 406, 584
Mezzrow-Bechet Quintet, 197, 584
Mezzrow-Bechet Septet, 300, 406
Miami Blues Festival (Silver Springs, FL), 530
Miami Pop Festival (Hallandale, FL), 46, 100, 132, 218
Michael Reese Hospital (Chicago, IL), 173, 576
Michaelson's (club) (Cincinnati, OH), 256
Michele (see: Castell, Michele)
Michigan Cafe Society (club) (Chicago, IL), 266
Michigan Inn (Detroit, MI), 423
Michigan State Fair (Detroit, MI), 538
Michigan State University (E. Lansing, MI), 147, 367, 504, 532
Michigan Theater (Ann Arbor, MI), 390
Michigan Theater (Detroit, MI), 88
Mickell's (club) (New York, NY), 33
Mickelson, Paul, 542
Mickey (see: Baker, McHouston)
Mickey & Sylvia (duo), 37, 38
Mickey Baker's Analysis of the Blues for Guitar (book), 38
Mickey Baker's Guitar Method (book), 38
Mickey Baker's Jazz Guitar (book), 38
Mickey Mouse Club (Philadelphia, PA), 549
Mickle, Elmon (Driftin' Slim/Model T. Slim) **371**, *371*, 531, 576
Mickle, William, 371
Mid-Drifs (group), 101
Mid-South Coliseum (Memphis, TN), 304, 510
Mid-South Jamboree (concert) (Memphis, TN), 179
Mid-Town North (club) (St. Louis, MO), 338
Midas (label), 67
Midnight (label), 430
Midnight Special (book), The 319
Midway Cafe (Memphis, TN), 116
Midway Club (Cleveland, OH), 372
Midway Stadium (St. Paul, MN), 100, 389
Midwest Blues Festival (South Bend, IN), 148, 236, 247, 294, 304, 336, 341, 342, 437, 445, 450, 459, 468, 591
Mighty Clouds of Joy (group), 497
Mighty Hagg Carnival (tour), 365
Mighty Hard Road (book), A, 206, 207
Mighty House Rockers (band), The, 365
Mighty Men (band), 86
Mighty Sheesley Carnival (tour), 550
Mighty Wiggle Carnival (tour), 420
Mike DeLisa Club (Chicago, IL), 161, 355, 481
Mike White Club (Toronto, Can.), 447
Mike's Bar (Minneapolis, MN), 91, 342
Mil-Lon (label), 238
Mil-Smi (label), 142
Milburn, Amos, 37, 76, 154, 158, 278, **372**, *372*, 544
Miles, Elizabeth "Lizzie," 142, 227, 230, 245, 300, **372-374**, *373*
Miles, J. C., 372
Miles, Josephine, "Josie," **374**, *374*
Miles, Lizzie (see: Miles, Elizabeth)
Miles, Luke, 244, 330, 366, **375**, 503, 576
Miles Ahead (label), 55
Miles College (Birmingham, AL), 113
Milestone (label), 136, 140, 169, 363, 371, 428, 569, 570
Milestone Inn (Derbyshire, Eng.), 245
Miley, Bubber, 472
Mill Run Theater (Niles, IL), 114, 158, 309, 390, 567
Milledgeville State Hospital (Milledgeville, GA), 369
Miller, Aleck "Alex" (see: Williamson, Sonny Boy)
Miller, Clarence "Big," 89, **375-377**, *376*, 448, 520, 528, 588
Miller, Henry, 375
Miller, Irvin C., 48, 79, 81, 462, 558
Miller, Jim (see: Moss, Eugene)
Miller, Jim, 577
Miller, John, 119
Miller, Mandie, 180
Miller, Punch, 279
Miller, Rice (see: Williamson, Sonny Boy)
Miller, Robert, 395
Miller, Willie, 378
Miller & Lyles (team), 70, 494, 496
Miller Beer (product), 158, 304
Miller Outdoor Theater (Houston, TX), 58
Miller Theater (Dallas, TX), 149, 390
Miller Theater (Houston, TX), 78, 240, 244, 287, 413, 424, 499
Miller's Grand Theater (Chicago, IL), 274
Millgate Club (Chicago, IL), 570, 594
Millinder, Lucky, 215, 216, 263, 285, 385, 419, 472, 484, 581
Million Dollar Theater (Los Angeles, CA), 68, 86, 154, 372, 446
Mills, Florence, 82, 231, 494, 496, 540, 581, 583
Mills, Grayson, 204
Milro Productions Ltd. (organization) (Edmonton, Can.), 377
Milton, Donald, 59, 130, 142, 174, 196, 210, 219, 430, 522
Milton, Roy, 55, 136, 253, **377-378**, *377*, 512, 586
Milton (label), 430
Milton Moore's Farm (Evergreen, AL), 319
Milton Starr's Negro Vaudeville Circuit, 463
Miltone (label), 235, 430
Miltonettes (group), The, 104
Milton's Taproom (club) (Kansas City, MO), 321
Milwaukee Jazz Festival (Milwaukee, WI), 148
Milwaukee Lakefront Festival (Milwaukee, WI), 254
Milwaukee Summer Festival (Milwaukee, WI), 65, 367, 504
Milwaukee Summerfest (Milwaukee, WI), 442, 501
Milwaukee Supreme Angels Gospel Group, 286
Mimo Professional Club (New York, NY), 31, 481
Mimosa (label), 561
Miner, J. W., 135
Mineral Cafe (Chicago, IL), 221
Miner's Theater (Bronx, NY), 173
Miniatures (group), The, 50
Minit (label), 270, 407, 508
Minneapolis Auditorium (Minneapolis, MN), 113
Minneapolis State Fair (Minneapolis, MN), 305
Minnie Lou's Club (Richmond, CA), 190
Minnie's Can-Do Club (San Francisco, CA), 30, 98, 154, 188, 208, 213, 270, 332, 393, 439, 516, 549, 554
Minnie's Club (Chicago, IL), 402
Minsky Burlesque Circuit, 481
Minstrel's (club) (Chicago, IL), 33, 99, 151, 260, 369, 445, 450, 500, 596
Minter, Iverson (Louisiana Red), 96, 195, 244, 261, **378-379**, *378*, 435, 457, 517
Minton's (club) (New York, NY), 253, 406, 523
Miracle (label), 116, 155, 403, 452, 501
Mirage (label), 65
Misiewicz, Roger, 122
Miss (label), 340, 461
Miss Bessie Allen's Junior Band, 252
Miss King's (club) (Chicago, IL), 69, 393, 548
Miss Rhapsody (see: Wells, Viola)
Missionary Baptist Church (Birmingham, AL), 272
Missionary Baptist Church (Jackson, MS?), 315
Missionary Baptist Connection Church (New York, NY), 147
Mississippi Arts Film Festival (Jackson, MS?), 509
Mississippi Black Snakes (band), 355
Mississippi Blues Band, 161
Mississippi Homecoming Festival (Fayette, MS), 309
Mississippi Hot Footers (band), 355, 524

Mississippi Matilda (see: Witherspoon, Matilda)
Mississippi Mockingbird (billing), The, 216
Mississippi Mudcats (band), 313, 314
Mississippi Mudder (see: McCoy, Charles) (see: McCoy, Joe)
Mississippi Rag Magazine, 57, 382, 423, 582
Mississippi Sarah (pseudonym), 545
Mississippi Sheiks (band), 29, 118, 119, 120, 398, 524
Mississippi Sheiks #2 (band), 483
Mississippi State Historical Museum (Jackson, MS), 508
Missouri Friends of Folk Arts (concert) (St. Louis, MO), 490, 514
Missouri Training School for Boys (Boonville, MO), 142
Mister (see: Mr.)
Misty Lounge (Dallas, TX), 382
Mitchell, Charles, 225
Mitchell, George, 153, 171, 230
Mitchell, Henderson, 153
Mitchell & Delaney (duo), 153
Moan, Eppie, 438
Mobile (label), 88
Model T. Slim (see: Mickle, Elmon)
Modern (label), 28, 50, 59, 96, 136, 140, 154, 193, 214, 232, 238, 246, 253, 303, 332, 337, 338, 357, 371, 378, 398, 407, 411, 417, 527, 586
Modern-Crown (label), 357
Modern Music (label), 74
Mojo (see: Buford, George)
Mojo (label), 63, 125
Molde Jazz Festival (Oslo, Norway), 117, 447
Mole, Miff, 464
Monarch (label), 199
Mondavi Winery Summer Festival (Oakville, CA), 132, 341
Monette's Place (club) (New York, NY), 385
Money (label), 116, 214
Mongin Club (Honolulu, HI), 375
Monitor (label), 453
Monk, Thelonious, 447
Monkees (group), The, 224
Monkey's Bottom (club) Portland, OR), 125
Monogram Theater (Chicago, IL), 350, 467, 540
Monogram Theater (Philadelphia, PA), 331
Monroe, Vince (see: Vincent, Monroe)
Monroe State Prison (Monroe, WA), 468, 513
Monroe's (club) (New York, NY), 406
Monte Carlo Club (Detroit, MI), 95, 238
Montefiore Hospital (Bronx, NY), 92
Monterey (club), The (Oakland, CA), 510
Monterey Jazz Festival (Monterey, CA), 30, 51, 78, 88, 99, 101, 117, 132, 136, 178, 179, 185, 194, 208, 211, 217, 225, 246, 247, 249, 254, 296, 308, 330, 336, 341, 359, 373, 375, 378, 388, 408, 417, 431, 447, 459, 466, 468, 478, 512, 516, 519, 520, 523, 527, 561, 566, 567, 575, 586, 588
Montgomery, E. (see: Montgomery, Eurreal)
Montgomery, Eurreal "Little Brother", 108, 141, 156, 200-201, 203, 272, 340, 341, **379-382,** *380,* 450, 478, 479, 510, 532, 568, 582, 591
Montgomery, Frank, 221, 491
Montgomery, Harper, 379
Montgomery, Huey Lee, 381
Montgomery, Joe, 381, 479
Montgomery, Little Brother (see: Montgomery, Eurreal)
Montgomery, Sam, 35
Montgomery, Tollie, 381
Montgomery Junior College (Takoma Park, MD), 272
Montreal Gazette (newspaper), 588
Montreal Jazz Festival (Montreal, Can.), 453
Montreux Blues Festival (Montreux, Switz.), 208, 254, 389, 412, 415, 523, 549
Montreux Jazz Festival (Montreux, Switz.), 46, 78, 91, 101, 104, 117, 125, 151, 156, 158, 166, 228, 249, 300, 304, 305, 343, 359, 367, 389, 394, 443, 455, 464, 474, 499, 504, 523, 527
Montreux Music Festival (Montreux, Switz.), 195, 588
Montreux Rock/Blues Festival (Montreux, Switz.), 58, 122, 190, 304, 379
Moon Glo Club (Buffalo, NY), 263
Moon Man Club (Los Angeles, CA), 430
Mooncusser (club) (Martha's Vineyard, MA), 99, 210, 314
Moondial (club) (Boston, MA), 195
Moondog Coronation Ball (concert) (Newark, NJ), 388
Moonlight Bar (E. St. Louis, IL), 412
Moonlight Bar (St. Louis, MO), 45
Moonlight Club (San Francisco, CA), 213, 439, 449
Moonlight Inn (New Orleans, LA), 293
Moonlight Inn (see: Ned Love's Moonlight Inn)
Moore, Alexander "Alex," 292, **382,** *382*
Moore, Alice, 482, 514
Moore, Arnold "Gatemouth," 78, **382-383,** 512
Moore, Bob, 110
Moore, Carman, 464, 586
Moore, Clarence, 546
Moore, Fleecie Ernestine, 299
Moore, Floyd, 384
Moore, Gatemouth (see: Moore, Arnold)
Moore, Grant, 284
Moore, James (Slim Harpo), 208, 227, 228, 270, **383-384,** *383,* 391, 396, 435, 547
Moore, Johnny, 74, 76, 154, 384, 528
Moore, Johnny B., **384,** *384*
Moore, Malcolm, 125
Moore, Monette, 176, 321, **385-386,** *385,* 474
Moore, William, 238, 241, 416
Moore, Willie "Wild Willie," 386
Moore, Willie C., **386,** *386*
Moore's Swing Club (Los Angeles, CA), 512
Moose Club (Atlanta, GA), 415
Moose Hall (Chicago, IL), 380
Moose John (see: Walker, John)
Moran, Mae (see: Beamon, Lottie)
Morand, Herbert "Herb," 227, 250, 374
Morand, Maurice, 374
Morehouse College (Atlanta, GA), 159
Morgan, Alun, 41, 64, 145, 158, 162, 351, 354, 360, 410, 415, 475, 533, 552, 555, 562
Morgan, John P., 441
Morgan, Sam, 203, 379, 418
Morganfield, McKinley (Muddy Waters), 35, 41, 45, 54, 62, 63, 65, 66, 72, 78, 79, 91, 99, 100, 101, 116, 124, 130, 132, 181, 210, 213, 225, 228, 238, 246, 247, 249, 260, 268, 269, 276, 283, 286, 287, 289, 291, 294, 307, 322, 334, 339, 343, 345, 359, 360, 368, 378, 384, **386-391,** *387,* 393, 394, 396, 399, 403, 410, 412, 413, 435, 439, 442, 444, 445, 453, 468, 476, 478, 479, 488, 493, 494, 499, 516, 545, 547, 548, 549, 560, 568, 571, 576, 585, 594
Morganfield, Ollie, 386
Morgantini, Marcelle, 404
Morgenstern, Dan, 406, 448, 465, 466, 568
Morning View Special (group), 344
Moroccos (group), 72
Morosco Theater (New York, NY), 366, 503
Morris, Anna, 70
Morris, Ed, 273
Morris, Jeff, 341
Morris, Robert, 423
Morris, Willie, 35
Morris Music Company (organization) (New Orleans, LA), 396
Morrison, George, 360
Morrison, Fannie, 204
Morrisson, Barbara, 538
Morrow Cemetery (Henning, TN), 326
Morson Hotel (Chicago, IL), 68
Morton, Jelly Roll, 82, 103, 134, 221, 276, 288, 373, 445
Mo's Swing Club (Los Angeles, CA), 55
Mosby, Curtis, 489
Mose, King, 395
Moseley, Bob, 37
Moses Stokes Show (tour), 427, 462
Mosley, Kathryn, 159
Mosque Theater (Newark, NJ), 447, 566
Moss, Eugene "Buddy," 93, 164, 228, 276, 369, **391-392,** *391,* 416, 503, 546
Moss, Teddy, 49
Moten, Bennie, 70, 274, 382, 405, 445, 518

Moten, Etta, 321
Mother Blues (club) (Chicago, IL), 93, 132, 147, 195, 296, 345, 381, 389, 444, 557
Mother Blues (club) (Dallas, TX), 243, 305, 330, 382, 435
Mother of the Blues (billing), 428
Mother's Boys (band), 230, 423
Motion Picture Home & Hospital (Hollywood, CA), 362
Motley, Julian, 231
Motor Inn (Fairfield, CT), 239
Motown (label), 33, 372
Mott, Bob, 70
Moulin Rouge (club) (Chicago, IL), 380
Moulin Rouge (club) (Las Vegas, NV), 538
Mound City All-Stars (band), 314
Mount (see also: Mt.)
Mount Glenwood Cemetery (Bloom, IL), 173, 336
Mount Lawn Cemetery (Sharon Hill, PA), 464
Mount Morris Park (New York, NY), 51
Mount Sinai Hospital Medical Center (Chicago, IL), 397
Mountain Heritage Folk Festival (Greenup, KY), 562
Mountain Park Casino (Holyoke, MA), 82
Mouth Piece Coffee House (Providence, RI), 59
Movin' (label), 55, 188
Mr. Anderson's Place (plantation) (Zachary, LA), 573
Mr. Blues (billing), 383
Mr. Blues (label), 168, 440
Mr. Bo (see: Collins, Louis)
Mr. Boogie 'n' Blues (billing), 415
Mr. Calhoun (see: Vincent, Monroe)
Mr. Five by Five (billing), 448
Mr. Henry's (club) (Washington, DC), 260, 417, 567, 588
Mr. Honey (see: Edwards, David)
Mr. Johnny Collier's Plantation (Dunleith, MS), 433
Mr. Jones Pub (Venice, CA), 154
Mr. Kelly's (club) (Chicago, IL), 108, 309, 381, 389, 432, 500, 538
Mr. Lee's (lounge) (Chicago, IL), 343, 439, 444, 461, 548, 596
Mr. M's (club) (Chicago, IL), 404, 476, 530, 549
Mr. P's Club (Jackson, MS), 271, 395
Mr. Shortstuff (see: Macon, John)
Mt. (see also: Mount)
Mt. Auburn Cemetery (Baltimore, MD), 153
Mt. Carmel Cemetery (Memphis, TN), 40
Mt. Eagle Baptist Church (Chicago, IL), 476
Mt. Holiness Cemetery (Butler, NJ), 529
Mt. Hope Cemetery (Mattapan, MA), 286
Mt. Hope Cemetery (San Diego, CA), 456
Mt. Olive Cemetery (St. Louis, MO), 299
Mt. Olivet Cemetery (New Orleans, LA), 396
Mt. Sinai Baptist Church Cemetery (Orange County, NC), 516
Mt. Zion Baptist Church (Atlanta, GA), 369
Mt. Zion Cemetery (Grapeland, TX), 583
Mt. Zion Church (Bogalusa, LA), 589
Mud Dauber Joe (see: McCoy, Joe)
Muddy Waters (see: Morganfield, McKinley)
Muddy Waters Jr. (see: Buford, George)
Muddy Waters Productions (organization) (Chicago, IL), 389
Mugar, Carolyn, 140
Muhlenbrink's Saloon (Underground Atlanta) (Atlanta, GA), 415
Mulligan, Gerry, 586
Mullins Cemetery (Clock, MS), 350
Multnomah Hospital (Portland, OR), 288
Mumbles (see: Horton, Walter)
Mumma's Worry (club) (Beaumont, TX), 78
Mundy, Jimmy, 447, 566
Munich (label), 494
Municipal Auditorium (Kansas City, MO), 89, 224, 518
Municipal Auditorium (Kerrville, TX), 84
Municipal Auditorium (New Orleans, LA), 51, 95, 304, 310, 346, 408, 431, 436
Municipal Tuberculosis Sanitarium (Chicago, IL), 238
Muriel (label), 546
Murphy, Lorenzo, 529
Murphy, Matt, 291
Murphy, Turk, 36, 141, 481, 594
Murphy & Me Club/Tavern (Eugene, OR), 122, 125, 240, 468
Murphy's (see: Murphy & Me Club)
Murray, Charles Sharr, 360
Murray, Doug, 409
Murray (label), 201
Muse, Clarence, 295
Muse, Lewis Anderson "Rabbit," **392,** *392*
Museum of Modern Art (New York, NY), 388, 389, 447, 513
Museum of the City of New York (New York, NY), 104
Music at Midnight Concert (New York, NY), 69, 116, 576
Music Box (club) (Chicago, IL), 110, 161, 355
Music Box Club (Paris, Fr.), 31
Music Box Theater (New York, NY), 541
Music City (label), 302
Music for Groups (book), 390
Music Hall, The (Atlanta, GA), 156
Music Hall (Boston, MA), 296
Music Hall, The (Cincinnati, OH), 431
Music Hall (Cleveland, OH), 113
Music Hall (Houston, TX), 545
Music Hall (Memphis, TN), 420
Music Hall Theater (Lewiston, ME), 70, 81, 82
Music Inn (club) (Lenox, MA), 238
Music of New Orleans (label), 203, 420
Music of the People—USA (tour), 56, 349
Music on My Mind (book), 474
Musical Bar (Cleveland, OH), 145
Musical Life in Harlem (concert) (New York, NY), 496
Musicalaires (group), The, 426
Musicians Union Auditorium/Hall (Los Angeles, CA), 137, 190, 430, 468, 520, 523, 527, 544
Musicraft (label), 44, 317
Musikhalle (theater) (Hamburg, Ger.), 39, 93, 155, 177, 243, 340, 401, 488, 577
Musselwhite, Charles "Charlie," 42, 213, 269, **392-393,** *392*, 395, 437, 455, 516, 549
Musselwhite, Charles, II, 393
My Club (Oakland, CA), 439
My Father's Place (club) (Roslyn, NY), 33, 42, 132, 156, 240, 304, 310, 352, 367, 505
My Husband, Jimmie Rodgers (book), 441
My Ups and Downs (book), 160
Myers, Bob, 395
Myers, David "Dave," 393, 395, 479, 516, 548
Myers, Louis, 36, 101, 168, 268, 269, 393, **393-395,** *394*, 425, 478, 479, 516, 548
Myers, Sammy "Sam," **395,** *395*
Myles, Big Boy, 103
Myrick, Ruthie, 251
Myrl (label), 424
Mystic Theater (Malden, MA), 82

NAACP (organization), 51, 311, 418, 588
NAIRD Convention (Chicago, IL), 57, 260, 349
NATRA Award, 311, 433
NFJO Jazz Band Ball (concert) (London, Eng.), 450
Nanc (label), 55
Nancy Jazz Festival (Nancy, Fr.). 209, 310, 379, 445, 450, 549
Napier, Bill, 322
Napier, Simon, 125, 167, 272, 290, 370, 554
Nardi's (club) (San Bruno, CA), 554
Nash, Frank, 350
Nash, Lemoine "Lemon," **396**
Nash General Hospital (Rocky Mount, NC), 180
Nashville Washboard Band, 104
Nassau Coliseum (Uniondale, NY), 522
Nassau Community College (Garden City, NY), 336, 381, 550, 582
Nassau County Hospital (Mineola, NY), 497
Nassau County Medical Center Hospital (East Meadow, NY), 480
Nat Ivory's Playground Club (see: Playground Club)
Nat Love's Club (E. St. Louis, IL), 150, 442, 489

Nat Phillips' Plantation (Twist, AR), 93
Natchez (see: Broonzy, William)
Natchez Charity Hospital (Natchez, MS), 329
Natchez Colored Cemetery (Natchez, MS), 329
Nate's Club (Kansas City, MO), 292
Nation (label), 404
National (label), 383, 406, 518
National Academy of Recording Arts & Sciences (organization), 114, 311, 390, 432, 433, 528, 538
National Cemetery (Memphis, TN), 425
National Convention of Gospel Choirs and Choruses Inc. (organization) (Chicago, IL), 159, 532
National Folk Festival (Vienna, VA), 130, 175, 182, 261, 266, 283, 320, 346, 354, 427, 449, 457, 486, 514, 562
National Folk Festival (Washington, DC), 56, 130, 175, 349, 381, 582
National Folk Festival Association (organization), 130
National Jazz & Blues Festival (London, Eng.), 117, 409
National Scala (club), The (Copenhagen, Den.), 256
National Theater (Havana, Cuba), 300
National Theater (New York, NY), 256, 540
National Theater (Wilmington, DE), 540
Natural Hit (label), A, 176, 385
Nazareth, Frank, 590
Neal, Raful, 269, **396**
Neckbones (pseudonym), 460
Ned Love's Fireworks Station (club) (E. St. Louis, IL), 104, 193
Ned Love's Moonlight Inn (St. Louis, MO), 398, 502
Negri, Pola, 185
Negro Actors Guild of America (organization), 72, 543, 582
Negro Folk Songs as Sung by Lead Belly (book), 318, 319
Nelson, ______, 303
Nelson, Albert, 303
Nelson, Bob (Chicago Bob), 209, 311, **396-397**, 549
Nelson, Dave, 44
Nelson, Emmett, 445
Nelson, Harrison, 214
Nelson, Iromeio "Romeo," **397**, *397*, 467
Nelson, John, 220
Nelson, Louisiana Earl, 396
Nelson, Lucille, 220
Nelson, Oliver, 566
Nelson, Red (see: Wilborn, Nelson)
Nelson, Romeo (see: Nelson, Iromeio)
Nelson, Versie, 396
Nero, Rose, 396
Nero's Club (Chicago, IL), 202
Nest Club (New York, NY), 137, 231, 256, 373, 463, 484, 491, 492
Nest Club (Newark, NJ), 550
New Alex Club (Chicago, IL) (see also: Alex Club) 155, 213, 345
New Alhambra Theater (New York, NY) (see also: Alhambra Theater), 80, 223, 583
New All-Stars (band), 466
New Black Eagle Hall (Hopkinton, MA), 322
New Boston Theater (Boston, MA), 82
New Brighton Theater (Brooklyn, NY), 541
New Burning Spear (club) (Chicago, IL) (see also: Burning Spear), 310, 461
New Cabaret (Atlantic City, NJ), 274
New Castle Rock (club) (Chicago, IL) (see also: Castle Rock Lounge), 394
New Cocoanut Club (New Orleans, LA), 420
New Crown Cemetery (Indianapolis, IN), 49
New Deal Club (Asbury Park, NJ), 550
New Douglas Theater (New York, NY), 222, 496
New 1815 Club (see: Eddie Shaw's Place/ 1815 Club)
New Empress of the Blues (billing), 84
New Encyclopedia of Jazz (book), 37, 281, 409, 524, 588
New England Blues Festival (Providence, RI), 156, 209, 307, 310, 389-390, 499, 549
New England Conservatory of Music (Boston, MA), 418
New Fack's (San Francisco, CA), 566
New Gate of Cleve (club) (Toronto, Can.), 177, 195, 239, 249, 257, 280, 427
New Generation Club (New York, NY), 296, 308
New Generation of Chicago Blues Show (concert) (Berlin, Ger.), 156
New Grand Terrace (Chicago, IL) (see also: Grand Terrace Ballroom), 481
New Hope Baptist Church (Minter City, MS), 286
New Hope Cemetery (Walls, MS), 162, 317
New Jazz Castle Rock Club (Chicago, IL), 394
New Jersey Folk Music Society Festival (NJ), 59
New Leo's Casino (Cleveland, OH) (see also: Leo's Casino), 566
New London Theater (London, Eng.), 88, 101
New Marquee Club (London, Eng.) (see also: Marquee Club), 117, 165, 409, 577
New McKinney's Cotton Pickers (band), 84
New Mississippi Sheiks (band), 120, 524
New Mount Pilgrim Church (Chicago, IL), 397
New Musical Express (newspaper), 360
New Old Waldorf (hotel) (San Francisco, CA) (see also: Old Waldorf), 213, 304
New Olympia Club (Detroit, MI), 238
New Orleans Band, 203, 420
New Orleans Bier Bar (Dusseldorf, Ger.), 313
New Orleans Boys (band), 373
New Orleans Club (Los Angeles, CA), 378
New Orleans Creole Jazz Band, 373
New Orleans Heritage Hall Jazz Band, 506
New Orleans House (club) (Berkeley, CA), 208
New Orleans House (club) (Los Angeles, CA), 457
New Orleans International Jazz Festival (New Orleans, LA), 39
New Orleans Jazz & Heritage Fair/ Festival (New Orleans, LA), 40, 51, 54, 60, 78, 95, 101, 120, 121, 158, 167, 199, 232, 240, 243, 261, 300, 301, 304, 309, 310, 346, 381, 389, 420, 429, 437, 457, 459, 486, 490, 506, 508, 522, 553, 569, 573
New Orleans Jazz Band, 203
New Orleans Jazz Club (New Orleans, LA), 374, 408, 423, 506
New Orleans Jazz Club of North California (San Francisco, CA), 316
New Orleans Jazz Festival (New Orleans, LA), 40, 195, 300, 423, 506
New Orleans Jazz Society (label), 203
New Orleans Louisiana (label), 288
New Orleans Music Festival (New York, NY), 466
New Orleans Pop Festival (Baton Rouge, LA), 296
New Orleans Rarities (label), 203
New Orleans Sextet, 300
New Orleans Stompers (band), 203
New Orleans Swing Club (San Francisco, CA), 136, 139
New Orleans Times Picayune (newspaper), 506
New Orleans Train Jazz Band, 45
New Orleans Troubadours (band), 558
New Orpheum Theater (Seattle, WA), 541
New Paltz College (New Paltz, NY), 367, 504
New Park Cemetery (Memphis, TN), 553
New Party Time Lounge (Chicago, IL), 123, 291
New Penelope (club) (Montreal, Can.), 99, 366, 388, 504, 548
New Penthouse (club), The (Vancouver, Can.), 375
New Ruthie's Inn (Oakland, CA) (see also: Ruthie's Inn), 305, 417, 508
New Salem Baptist Church Cemetery (Senatobia, MS), 230
New School for Social Research (New York, NY), 363, 449, 466
New St. Matthew's Baptist Church (Chicago, IL), 571
New Standard Theater (Philadelphia, PA), 474
New Star Casino (New York, NY), 82, 221, 227, 350, 373, 464, 494, 496, 581
New State Theater (Harrisburg, PA), 70

New Thing (club), The (Washington, DC), 208
New Victoria Theater (London, Eng.), 158, 390
New Westminster Hotel (Vancouver, Can.), 375
New World Cafe (Atlantic City, NJ), 274
New York City Center (see: City Center Theater)
New York City Head Start Program (organization), 231
New York Drama Critics Award, 543
New York Folk Festival (New York, NY), 46, 257, 388, 521, 525
New York Herald Tribune (newspaper), 542
New York Inn, The (New Orleans, LA), 101, 271, 322, 577
New York Jazz Festival (Randalls Island, NY), 431, 566
New York Jazz Museum (New York, NY), 254, 481
New York Jazz Repertory Company (tour), 466, 506
New York Post (newspaper), 216, 305
New York Repertory Orchestra, 466
New York State Prison (Rikers Island, NY), 317
New York State Public Service (government office), 431
New York Summer Festival (concert) (New York, NY), 234
New York Times (newspaper), 101, 120, 169, 196, 206, 209, 245, 302, 448, 557
New York University (New York, NY), 62, 106, 254, 286, 327
New York World's Fair (Queens, NY), 541, 542, 544
New Yorker Theater (New York, NY), 491, 581
New Yorker Theater (Toronto, Can.), 210, 244, 347
Newbern, Hambone (see: Newbern, Willie)
Newbern, Hattie, 57
Newbern, Willie (Hambone Willie), 178, 349, 426
Newborn, Calvin, 291
Newborn, Pat, 220
Newhart, Bob, 141
Newman, Jack, 398
Newman, Joe, 447
Newport All-Stars (band), 245
Newport Folk Festival (Newport, RI), 54, 93, 99, 103, 117, 121, 130, 141, 147, 148, 174, 176, 177, 185, 187, 194, 195, 208, 210, 217, 239, 243, 247, 249, 257, 265, 272, 296, 308, 314, 330, 346, 363, 366, 375, 388, 389, 391, 401, 420, 427, 478, 503, 504, 512, 513, 521, 525, 532, 548, 553, 557, 562, 573
Newport Hotel (Miami Beach, FL), 432
Newport Jazz Festival (New York, NY), 51, 54, 78, 101, 114, 138, 158, 177, 208, 245, 254, 257, 299, 309, 310, 352, 389, 401, 412, 432, 457, 466, 513, 523, 549, 567, 568, 573
Newport Jazz Festival (Newport RI), 45, 90, 113, 117, 132, 155, 194, 239, 254, 304, 352, 375, 381, 388, 417, 420, 447, 466, 470, 478, 519, 538, 566, 585, 586
Newport Jazz Festival (Stanhope, NJ), 78, 195, 287, 316, 379, 390, 413, 466
Newport Resort Motel (Miami Beach, FL), 309
Newport 69 (festival) (Northridge, CA), 125, 224, 296, 346, 585
Newton, Edmund, 305
Newton County Hospital (Covington, GA), 546
Nic Nacs (group), 417
Nice Jazz Festival (Nice, Fr.), 78, 245, 254, 287, 390, 413, 466, 506, 527, 567
Nicholas, Howard, 550
Nicholas, "Wooden" Joe, 128
Nicholas Brothers (dance team), 173
Nicholls, Muriel, 60
Nichols, Alvin (B. B. Jones), 311, **397-398**, *397*
Nichols, Jimmy (see: Nicholson, James)
Nicholson, James David "J. D.," 357, **398**
Nickelodeon Band, The, 230
Nickerson, Hammie (see: Nixon, Hammie)
Nick's (club) (New York, NY), 481
Night Cats (band), 268, 393
Night in New Orleans Revue/Show (tour), 44, 101
Nighthawk, Robert, 27, 163, 183, 197, 237, 238, 271, 289, 356, 390, 393, **398-399**, *399*, 412, 441, 450, 451, 460, 483, 484, 514, 552, 560, 561, 594
Nighthawks (band) (Robert Nighthawk), 183, 398, 399
Nighthawks (band) (James Wayne), 378
Nighthawks Orchestra, 420
Nimmons, Phil, 377
908 Club (Seattle, WA), 111
9-0-5 Club (St. Louis, MO), 79
91 Theater (Atlanta, GA), 463, 540
Nite Life (club) (Van Nuys, CA), 520
Nittayuma Cemetery (Sharkey, MS), 119
Nitty Gritty Club (Madison, WI), 32
Nix, Don, 327
Nix, Malissa, 428
Nix, Patty, 400
Nix, Willie, 50, 104, 130, 271, 291, 338, **399-400**, *400*, 528, 560, 577
Nixa (label), 69, 366, 408, 503, 556
Nixon, Bertha, 238
Nixon, Elmore, 353
Nixon Elmore, **400**, 572
Nixon, Hammie, 57, 84, 176, 178, 196, 347, **401-402**, *401*, 576
Nixon, Richard M., 431, 543, 567
Nixon Grand Theater (Philadelphia, PA), 581
Nixon Theater (Pittsburg, PA), 71, 240, 527
No Exit Cafe (Chicago, IL), 65
Noah's Temple of The Apostolic Faith (San Diego, CA), 456
Nobility (label), 203, 506
Noble, Kitty, 38
Noblett, Richard, 337
Nocturn (label), 74
Nolan, Bill, 321
Nolan, Dixie (see: Scruggs, Irene)
Nolan, Herb, 418
Nola's (club) (Houston, TX), 201
Nonie's Lounge (Chicago, IL), 402
Noone, Jimmie, 31, 229, 251, 532, 555, 564
Nora Bayes Theater (New York, NY), 274
Nordskog (label), 288
Norfolk Yacht Club (Norfolk, VA), 313
Normandy Club (Cleveland, OH), 481
Norman's (club) (New York, NY), 254
Norris, John, 31, 178, 185, 514, 544, 553
Norris, Roosevelt, 402
Norris, William, 305, 311, **402**, *402*
North, Edith (see: Johnson, Edith)
North, Hattie (see: Johnson, Edith)
North, Hattie, 281
North Carolina Baptist Convention, 147
North East Community Center (San Francisco, CA), 98
North Eastern Cemetery (Rocky Mount, NC), 180
North Memphis Cafe (Memphis, TN), 161, 355
North Park Hotel (Chicago, IL), 32, 343, 424, 435, 575, 595
North Sea Jazz Festival (Holland), 78, 166, 390
North Sea Jazz Festival 76 (The Hague, Holland), 33, 63, 114, 117, 240
North Shore Hospital (Manhasset, NY), 557
North Street Baptist Church (Louisville, KY), 252
Northampton-Accomac Memorial Hospital (Nassawadox, VA), 138
Northampton Jazz Festival (Northampton, Eng.), 165
Northeastern Illinois University (Chicago, IL), 381, 582
Northeastern University (Boston, MA), 447
Northern Illinois University (DeKalb, IL), 57, 148, 349, 389, 437, 450, 499
Northern Wonders (group), 423
Northside Armory (Indianapolis, IN), 104
Northwestern University (Evanston, IL), 57, 65, 69, 349, 494, 500, 591
Norvo, Red, 253
Norwood, Pig (see: Norwood, Sam)
Norwood, Sam "Peg Leg," 80, 261, **402**
Notable American Women (1607-1950) (book), 428
Nothing But the Blues (book), 36, 55, 95, 140, 225, 241, 252, 259, 267, 269, 316, 339, 344, 365, 427, 453, 476, 545, 547, 591
Notre Dame Blues Festival (South Bend, IN) (see also: University of Notre Dame), 41, 93, 150, 202, 208,

243, 330, 334, 363, 381, 389, 412, 442, 444, 488, 494, 499, 500, 549
Notre Dame University (see: University of Notre Dame)
Nottingham Blues & Jazz Festival (Nottingham, Eng.), 110
Novelty Band, 163
Novelty Club (Kansas City, MO), 321, 405
Novelty Singing Orchestra, 321
Now Grove (club) (Los Angeles, CA), 114
Noxubee County Hospital (Macon, MS), 344
Nubian Five (band), 583
Nugget (club), The (Carson City, NV), 78
Nutcracker Lounge (New Orleans, LA), 101, 240, 435

O.V. Catto Elks Lodge (Philadelphia, PA), 564
Oak Cliff T-Bone (see: Walker, Aaron)
Oak Grove Cemetery (Meridian, MS), 441
Oak Hill Cemetery (Gary, IN), 200
Oak Hill Cemetery (Pontiac, MI), 228
Oakdale Cemetery (Lemay, MO), 438
Oakdale Cemetery (St Louis, MO), 297, 414
Oakdale Musical Theater (Wallingford, CT), 366
Oakland Museum (Oakland, CA), 187
Oakland University (Rochester, MI), 309
Oakley, Giles, 252, 264, 416
Oakridge Cemetery (Hillside, IL), 95
Oakwood College Seminary (Huntsville, AL), 411
Oasis Ballroom (Michigan City, IN), 44
Oasis Club (Seattle, WA), 36
Oberlin College (Oberlin, OH), 32, 249, 257, 427
Oblivion (label), 283, 363, 529
O'Brien, J. C., 233
O'Brien, Justin, 266
Ocampo (label), 421
Ochs, Phil, 207
O'Connor's Ale House (Watchung, NJ), 316
Octive (label), 233
O'Dells Club (Miami, FL), 111
Oden, Henry, 403
Oden, James (St. Louis Jimmy), 150, 161, **403-404**, *403*, 438, 489, 568
Odeon (label), 117
Odeon Theater (Ipswich, Eng.), 224
Odetta (see: Gordon, Odetta)
Odom, Andrew "Voice," 51, 311, 395, **404**, *404*, 530
Odom, Guy, 404
Odom, King, 404
Odom, Voice (see: Odom, Andrew)
Odyssey Club/Coffeehouse (Boston, MA), 174, 187, 210
Off Beat Club (Chicago, IL), 321
Off Plaza (club) (San Francisco, CA), 523
Offett, John, 229
Officer's Club (Cherry Point, NC), 313
Offitt, Lillian, 237, **404-405**
Ogden, Bob, 86
O'Hare Motor Inn (Chicago, IL), 57, 260, 349
Ohio State University (Columbus, OH), 234
Ohio Theater (Columbus, OH), 582
Ohio Valley Jazz Festival (Cincinnati, OH), 46, 114, 309, 431, 432, 566
Oil Can Harry's (club) (Vancouver, Can.), 377
O'Keefe Center (Toronto, Can.), 113, 310
OKeh (label), 29, 31, 43, 48, 56, 68, 70, 98, 110, 116, 118, 119, 120, 122, 125, 128, 134, 144, 155, 161, 164, 166, 171, 172, 175, 184, 197, 219, 221, 229, 234, 246, 252, 256, 257, 263, 276, 279, 281, 282, 292, 317, 321, 326, 331, 348, 350, 354, 355, 360, 365, 366, 369, 373, 391, 402, 411, 415, 418, 446, 447, 450, 454, 463, 464, 470, 472, 474, 481, 489, 494, 496, 503, 507, 518, 523, 524, 531, 532, 546, 553, 558, 564, 566, 568, 584
Old Barrelhouse Honkeytonk (Honey Island, MS), 412
Old Cellar (club) (Vancouver, Can.), 211, 457
Old Cermak Inn Lounge (Chicago, IL), 596
Old Dixie Ballroom (Los Angeles, CA), 53, 190
Old Guys Jazz Band, 314
Old Keyhole (club) (San Antonio, TX), 76
Old Laurie (club) (Copenhagen, Den.), 256
Old Reliable Bar (New York, NY), 378
Old Town (label), 366, 503
Old Town North (club) (Chicago, IL), 106
Old Town School of Folk Music (Chicago, IL), 177, 401
Old Waldorf (hotel) (San Francisco, CA) (see also: New Old Waldorf), 51, 54, 125, 352
Oldie Blues (label), 148, 149, 356, 569
Oldies But Goodies Club (Hollywood, CA), 520
Olin Hotel (Denver, CO), 195
Olive C. School (Austin, TX), 136
Oliver, Joe "King," 29, 44, 134, 229, 254, 274, 288, 372, 373, 418, 450, 481, 531
Oliver, Kine (see: Alexander, Alger)
Oliver, King (see: Oliver, Joe)
Oliver, Paul, 41, 43, 56, 64, 79, 89, 104, 107, 125, 139, 158, 162, 168, 173, 185, 190, 233, 264, 274, 280, 288, 292, 325, 331, 341, 344, 351, 354, 356, 360, 382, 403, 410, 438, 464, 465, 475, 518, 533, 552, 555, 562, 563, 578
Oliver, Robert, 561
Olivet Memorial Park Cemetery (Colma, CA), 510
Olsson, Bengt, 40, 264, 326, 328, 337, 455, 486
Olympia Beer (product), 114
Olympia Theater (Haverhill, MA), 82
Olympia Theater (Lynn, MA), 70
Olympia Theater (New Bedford, MA), 70
Olympia Theater (Paris, Fr.), 46, 224, 586
Olympic (label), 588
Olympic Auditorium (Los Angeles, CA), 210, 304, 411
Olympic Hotel (Chicago, IL), 292, 380
Olympic Hotel (Seattle, WA), 567
Omega Bar (Roselle, NJ), 550
Ondines Club (New York, NY), 224
One-Armed John (see: Wrencher, John)
One-der-ful (label), 67
One Fifth Avenue Club (New York, NY), 316
100 Club (London, Eng.), 36, 55, 60, 96, 249, 260, 283, 302, 439, 517, 575
105th Street Theater (Cleveland, OH), 71
104th Street Theater (see: Keith 104th Street Theater)
109 Club (Los Angeles, CA), 497
101 Ranch Show (tour), 284
One Man Trio (billing), 58
One Sheridan Square (club) (New York, NY), 194, 366, 503, 556
161 Club (Buffalo, NY), 182
126 Club (Vallejo, CA), 439
One Way Inn (Chicago, IL), 424, 570
O'Neal, Amy, 66, 72, 91, 95, 148, 180, 282, 425, 436, 482, 554, 573
O'Neal, Jim, 51, 63, 66, 93, 109, 119, 127, 128, 138, 170, 183, 184, 204, 286, 313, 330, 395, 398, 399, 404, 410, 434, 435, 438, 475, 482, 483, 484, 534, 535, 536, 551, 561, 576
O'Neal, Johnny, 404, 412
Onion (club), The (Toronto, Can.), 147, 553
Onion Festival (Chicago, IL), 582
Only Me (billing), 222
Onondaga Community College (Syracuse, NY), 420
Onondaga Memorial Concert (Syracuse, NY), 46
Ontario Place (club) (Washington, DC), 247, 257, 265, 272, 562
Onyx (label), 253, 406
Onyx Club (New York, NY), 145, 285, 300, 405, 406
Opera (label), 340, 403
Opera House (theater) (Chicago, IL), 567
Opera House (theater) (Jamestown, NY), 82
Opera House (theater) (Sayville, NY), 48
Opera House (theater) (Seattle, WA), 359, 556
Operation Breadbasket Blues Festival (Chicago, IL), 104
Opry Club (Burlington, VT), 209, 549
Ora Nelle (label), 176, 268, 401, 442, 570, 571, 594
Orchard Lounge (Chicago, IL), 388
Orchestra Gardens (club) (Detroit, MI), 467

Orchestra Hall (Chicago, IL), 194, 195, 557, 591, 592
Orchestra Hall (New York, NY), 556
Orchid Club (Kansas City, MO), 299
Orchid Room (club) (Kansas City, MO), 76, 136, 468
Oregon State Reformatory (Eugene, OR), 468, 513
Oregon State University (Corvallis, OR), 57, 349
Orient (club), The (New York, NY), 472
Oriental Theater (Chicago, IL), 298, 411
Origin (label), 144, 397
Original Bessie Brown (billing), The, 73
Original Creole Orchestra, 288
Original Dinah (billing), The, 543
Original Four Hairs Combo (band), 101
Original Gay 90s Gal (billing), The, 83
Original Mid-Nite Ramblers Band, 44
Original Music Masters (band), 148
Original Paradise Ten (band), 385
Original Salty Dogs (band), 322, 423
Original Tuxedo Jazz Band, 506
Oriole (label), 63, 73
Oriole Terrace Club (Detroit, MI), 173, 540
Orleans (club) (Boston, MA), 249, 272
Orleans Mardi Gras Lounge (see: Mardi Gras Lounge)
Orphanage (club), The (San Francisco, CA), 418, 596
Orphans (club) (Chicago, IL), 142, 148, 494
Orpheum Circuit, 288, 494, 540, 592
Orpheum Theater (Baltimore, MD), 48
Orpheum Theater (Boston, MA), 581
Orpheum Theater (Brooklyn, NY), (see also: Keith's Orpheum Theater, Brooklyn, NY), 70
Orpheum Theater (Denver, CO), 70
Orpheum Theater (Germantown, PA), 82
Orpheum Theater (Hollywood, CA), 298
Orpheum Theater (Los Angeles, CA), 446, 523, 541
Orpheum Theater (Nashville, TN), 463
Orpheum Theater (New York, NY), 70, 82, 581
Orpheum Theater (Newark, NJ), 82, 173, 463, 472, 540
Orpheum Theater (Oakland, CA), 541
Orpheum Theater (San Francisco, CA), 541
Orpheum Theater (Seattle, WA), 70
Orpheum Theater (Sioux City, IO), 70
Orpheum Theater (St. Louis, MO), 494
Orpheum Theater (St. Paul, MN), 540
Orpheum Theater (Vancouver, Can.), 70
Orpheum Theater (Winnipeg, Can.), 540, 541
Ory, Kid, 36, 141, 229, 279, 288, 372, 380, 507, 591
Osaka Rascals (band), 322
Oscars Chicago Swingers (band), 35
Oshkosh Theater (Oshkosh, WI), 134
Osteopathic Hospital (Chicago, IL), 595
Oster, Harry, 86, 103, 574
Other End (club), The (New York, NY), 418
Otis, Johnny, 76, 88, 136, 178, 201, 211, 215, 277, 302, 372, 378, 408, 417, 439, 446, 497, 512, 520, 523, 524, 527
Otis Spann Memorial Field (Ann Arbor, MI), 479
Otto's (club) (Chicago, IL), 424, 575
Oude Stijl Jazz Festival (Breda, Holland), 45, 550
Oulsey, Irene, 592
Our Lady of Peace R.C. Church (New York, NY), 457
Our World (label), 84
Outlet (label), 392
Outrigger (club), The (Monterey, CA), 586
Outside Inn (Buffalo, NY), 132
Ovation (label), 156, 596
Overseas Press Club (New York, NY), 44, 254, 497, 558
Overton Park (Memphis, TN), 257
Owens, Herbert, 212
Owens, Kelly, 470
Owens, Leonia, 91
Owl (club), The (New York, NY), 280
Owl Cafe (Helena, AR), 388, 443, 483
Ox Club (Los Angeles, CA), 86
Oxford Coffee House (Chicago, IL), 569
Oxtot, Dick, 141
Ozark Mountain Folk Fair (AR), 121, 240

P&E Club (E. St. Louis, IL), 489
P&P (label), 529
P.J.'s Club (Los Angeles, CA), 510
PM (label), 461, 572
Pablo (label), 137, 520
Pacer (label), 460-461, 563
Pacific (label), 136
Pacific Jazz (label), 167, 168
Pacific Jazz Festival (Costa Mesa, CA), 243, 388, 512, 527
Paddock Club (Yonkers, NY), 316
Paddock Lounge, The (New Orleans, LA), 373
Page, Greene, 405
Page, Hot Lips (see: Page, Oran)
Page, Jimmy, 305, 528
Page, Oran "Hot Lips," 44, 134, 188, **405-406,** *405*
Page, Walter, 284, 385, 405, 445
Pago Pago Club (San Francisco, CA), 509
Paines-Deadman Plantation (Honey Island, MS), 193, 412
Painters Mill Theater (Baltimore, MD), 219, 352, 585
Pajaud, August, 374
Pajeaud, Willie, 203, 374
Palace Club, The (Los Angeles, CA), 531
Palace Hotel (Nice, Fr.), 256
Palace Theater (Albany, NY), 114
Palace Theater (Bridgeport, CT), 82
Palace Theater (Chicago, IL), 71, 540, 541
Palace Theater (Columbus, OH), 447
Palace Theater (Hartford, CT), 70
Palace Theater (Louisville, KY), 252
Palace Theater (Memphis, TN) (see also: Beale Street Palace Theater), 50, 308, 400, 510, 540, 559
Palace Theater (Milwaukee, WI), 540, 567
Palace Theater (New Haven, CT), 70
Palace Theater (New Orleans, LA), 101
Palace Theater (New York, NY) (see Keith-Albee Palace Theater/RKO-Palace Theater)
Palace Theater (Pittsfield, MA), 82, 581
Palace Theater (Springfield, MA), 82
Palace Theater (Worcester, MA), 82
Paladium Ballroom (Houston, TX), 51, 424
Palais des Sports (stadium) (Paris, Fr.), 113, 117, 208, 548
Palais Royale Club (New York, NY), 541
Palazetto Dello Sport (stadium) (Turin, It.), 390
Palladium (hall), The (Cleveland, OH), 481
Palladium (hall), The (Hollywood Palladium) (Hollywood, CA), 46, 113, 346, 378, 411, 417, 431, 520, 523
Palladium (hall), The (New York, NY), 100, 132, 169, 240, 312, 390, 585
Palladium (hall), The (San Diego, CA), 76
Palladium (theater), The (London, Eng.), 71, 256, 541
Palladium Dance Hall (Chicago, IL), 229
Palm Harbor General Hospital (Garden Grove, CA), 386
Palmer, Robert, 103, 169, 305
Palmer House (hotel) (Chicago, IL), 432
Palmer House (hotel) (Detroit, MI), 182
Palms (club), The (San Francisco, CA), 54, 513, 520
Palms Club, The (Hallandale, FL), 157, 293, 343
Palms Garden (club) (Jackson, MS), 395
Palomar Gardens (club) (San Jose, CA), 157
Palooka Washboard Band, 355
Palos (label), 63, 67, 437, 563, 572
Pam's Striptease Bar & Dance Lounge (Dallas, TX), 382
Panama Cafe/Club (Chicago, IL), 31, 221, 231, 254
Panama Club, The (Kansas City, MO), 292
Panama Club (Memphis, TN), 339
Panassié, Hugues, 35
Pandora's Box (club) (Hollywood, CA), 431

Panhandle Park (San Francisco, CA), 296
Pantages Circuit, 80, 360
Pantages Theater (Edmonton, Can.), 82
Pantages Theater (Fresno, CA), 82
Pantages Theater (Kansas City, MO), 82
Pantages Theater (Long Beach, CA), 82
Pantages Theater (Los Angeles, CA), 82
Pantages Theater (Minneapolis, MN), 82
Pantages Theater (Ogden, UT), 82
Pantages Theater (Portland, OR), 82
Pantages Theater (San Diego, CA), 82
Pantages Theater (San Francisco, CA), 82
Pantages Theater (Tacoma, WA), 82
Panther Room (club) (Chicago, IL), 518
Papa Charlie (see: McCoy, Charles)
Papa Charlie's Boys (band), 355
Papa Chittlins (see: Moore, Alexander)
Papa French New Orleans Jazz Band, 506
Papa George (see: Lightfoot, Alexander)
Papa Snow White (see: Page, Oran)
Paparelli, Frank, 467
Parade (label), 280
Paradise (label), 280
Paradise Band, 385, 467
Paradise Cabaret/Cafe (Atlantic City, NJ) (see: Rafe's Paradise Cafe)
Paradise Cafe (Chicago, IL), 52
Paradise Cemetery (Los Angeles, CA), 371
Paradise Club (Detroit, MI), 535, 538
Paradise Garden (club) (Los Angeles, CA), 288
Paradise Gardens (club) (Atlantic City, NJ)
Paradise Gardens (club) (Chicago, IL), 254, 463
Paradise Inn (club) (Montgomery, AL), 356
Paradise Theater (Atlantic City, NJ) (see: Rafe's Paradise Theater)
Paradise Theater (Detroit, MI), 88, 191, 281, 298, 377, 417
Paramount (label), 41, 42, 52, 56, 64, 68, 79, 89, 106, 119, 134, 139, 144, 145, 150, 152, 159, 167, 175, 197, 221, 222, 223, 227, 235, 247, 254, 263, 272, 276, 281, 282, 288, 290, 295, 315, 360, 380, 385, 393, 409, 415, 428, 450, 460, 475, 486, 491, 514, 524, 540, 556, 558, 559, 568, 583, 584, 592
Paramount Singers of Oakland (group), 421
Paramount Theater (Brooklyn, NY), 45, 157, 538
Paramount Theater (Los Angeles, CA), 538
Paramount Theater (New York, NY), 298, 362, 411, 446, 541
Paramount Trio, 385
Paramount Wildcat (billing), The, 428
Parchman State Farm Prison (Parchman Farm, MS), 236, 247, 534, 552
Paredon (label), 142
Parenti, Tony, 90, 313
Parham, Tiny, 263
Parham, Truck, 322
Paris, Geraldine, 78
Paris, Mike, 441
Paris Blues Festival (Paris, Fr.), 117
Paris Club (Chicago, IL), 564
Paris-Henry County Arts Council Concert (Paris, TN), 313
Paris Jazz Fair (Paris, Fr.), 318
Paris Qui Chante Supper Club (New York, NY), 256
Parish Prison (New Orleans, LA), 60
Parisian Room (club) (Los Angeles, CA), 88, 137, 179, 211, 431, 513, 520, 523, 527, 567, 588
Parisian Room (club) (New Orleans, LA), 373
Parisian Room Band, 373
Park Lane Hotel (New York, NY), 406
Park Lane Theater (New York, NY), 223, 581
Park 100 Restaurant (New York, NY), 316
Park Theater (Bridgeport, CT), 357
Park Theater (Louisville, KY), 580
Parker, Barber, 338, 443
Parker, Charlie, 524
Parker, Herman "Little Junior," 50, 51, 60, 88, 237, 241, 249, 291, **407**, *407*, 461, 512, 514, 549, 578
Parker, Herman, Sr., 407
Parker, Jr./Junior (see: Parker, Herman)
Parker, Knocky, 84
Parker, Leonard, 379
Parker, Little Junior (see: Parker, Herman)
Parker, Ray, 44
Parkside Hospital (Detroit, MI), 467
Parkway (label), 181, 268, 388
Parlophone (label), 224, 497
Parran (see: Garlow, Clarence)
Parrell, Cecelia, 418
Parrot (label), 66, 67, 78, 181, 199, 292, 304, 305, 322, 342, 410, 424, 434, 438, 447
Parson, Skip, 245
Pasa Tiempo (club) (Chicago, IL), 393, 595
Pasadena Auditorium (Los Angeles, CA), 253
Pasadena Civic Auditorium (Pasadena, CA), 327
Pasadena Playhouse (Pasadena, CA), 542, 582
Passim Coffeehouse (Cambridge, MA), 522
Pat O'Brien's (club) (New Orleans, LA), 396
Pathe (label), 73, 231, 295, 357, 583
Pathe-Actuelle (label), 223, 484, 491
Pathe-Marconi (label), 452
Patrick, Dave, 212, 358, 392, 422
Patt, Frank, 169, **407-408**, *408*
Patterson, Anna-Ottilie, 408
Patterson, Lila (see: Rainey, Gertrude)
Patterson, Ottilie, **408-409**, *408*
Patterson, Vance, 415
Pattison, Terry, 232, 301
Patton, "Big" Amos, 400
Patton, Bill, 409
Patton, Charley/Charlie, 38, 39, 89, 95, 119, 120, 169, 229, 247, 249, 289, 290, 294, 349, 364, 390, 393, **409-410**, *409*, 459, 493, 534, 553, 586
Paul, Les, 56
Paul, Steve, 149
Paul English Players (tour), 440
Paul Gray's Place (club) (Lawrence, KS), 567
Pauley Pavilion (Los Angeles, CA), 114
Paul's Club (Flushing, NY), 90
Paul's Mall (club) (Boston, MA), 132, 389, 418, 567
Paul's Roast Round (club) (Chicago, IL), 569
Paul's Sidewalk Cafe (Houston, TX), 417
Paulus, George, 110
Pavilion (theater), The (London, Eng.), 256, 581, 583
Pavilion (hall), The (New York, NY), 100, 208, 219, 304, 389, 548
Pavilion Folk Festival (New York, NY), 195
Pax (label), 336
Paxton, Tom, 207
Payne, Raymond, 364
Payton, Earl (see: Payton, Earlee)
Payton, Earlee, 305, **410**, *410*
Peabody Hotel (Memphis, TN), 106, 128, 145, 264, 337, 454
Peace Methodist Church (New York, NY), 92
Peacock (club) (Atlanta, GA) (see: Royal Peacock)
Peacock (club), The (New Orleans, LA), 508
Peacock (label), 60, 76, 89, 116, 199, 328, 357, 396, 400, 411, 424, 426, 512, 535
Peacock (lounge) (Chicago, IL), 559
Peacock Alley (club) (Minneapolis, MN), 289
Peanut Barrel (club) (Chicago, IL), 151, 236, 260, 369, 445, 595, 596
Peanut Cellar (club) (Union Lake, MI), 229
Peanut the Kidnapper (pseudonym), 356
Peanut's Pub (club) (Memphis, TN), 327
Pearl, Bernard, 330
Pearl (label), 203, 399
Pearl Theater (Philadelphia, PA), 222, 405, 445, 464, 496
Pease, Sharon A., 467
Pecan Theater (Savannah, GA), 558
Pee Wee Russell Memorial Stomp (concert) (Martinsville, NJ), 316
Pee Wee's (club) (Memphis, TN), 62, 264, 326, 339, 454
Peebles, McKinley (Sweet Papa Stovepipe), 545

Peetie Wheatstraw's Brother (see: Gordon, Jimmy)
Peetie Wheatstraw's Buddy (see: Ray, Harmon)
Peetie's Boy (see: Nighthawk, Robert)
Peg Leg Howell and His Band, 251
Peg-Leg Sam (see: Jackson, Arthur)
Peg Pete (see: Jackson, Arthur)
Pejoe, Morris, 198, 199
Pekin Theater (Atlantic City, NJ), 540
Pekin Theater (Chicago, IL), 70, 592
Pekin Theater Cabaret (Chicago, IL), 254
Pelican Cafe (New Orleans, LA), 418
Pemberton High School (Marshall, TX), 29
Penniman, Richard (Little Richard), 68, 88, 158, 211, 220, 223, 278, **410-412**, *411*, 424, 444, 530
Pennington, Mattie Lee, 175
Penny Farthing (club) (Toronto, Can.), 84, 280, 557
Penthouse (club), The (Seattle, WA), 588
Penthouse Supper Club (Cleveland, OH), 431
Peoples, Joe, 420
Peoples Club (Ocean Beach/San Diego, CA), 134
People's Daily World (newspaper), 205
Peoples Songs Inc. (organization/tour), 206, 318
Pepper Pot (club) (Gretna, LA), 101
Peppermint Cane (billing), 216
Peppermint Lounge (Chicago, IL), 32
Pepper's (lounge) (Chicago, IL), (see: Pepper's Lounge)
Pepper's Hideout (club) (Chicago, IL), 67, 95, 132, 305, 461
Pepper's Lounge (Chicago, IL), 35, 53, 93, 99, 109, 132, 188, 208, 213, 236, 238, 243, 285, 289, 309, 322, 341, 345, 388, 389, 395, 397, 404, 435, 437, 444, 460, 461, 478, 493, 494, 499, 500, 530, 548, 563, 572, 596
Pep's Musical Show Bar (Philadelphia, PA), 263, 298, 309, 375, 431, 447, 538, 566
Pepsi Cola (product), 308
Percy Brown's (club) (New York, NY), 472
Perfect (label), 68, 73
Performing Arts Center (Milwaukee, WI), 327
Perin & Henderson's Show (tour), 48
Period (label), 556
Perkins, Carl, 183
Perkins, Joe Willie "Pinetop," 95, 107, 193, 338, **412-413**, *412*, 467, 491
Perkins, O. C., 302
Perkins, Pinetop (see: Perkins, Joe Willie)
Perkins Club (Los Angeles, CA), 55, 531
Perlina, Hilda, 52
Perls, Nick, 470
Pernell, Ruth Mae, 384
Pernsley, Merritt "Buddy," 543
Perry Theater (Erie, PA), 70
Perryman, Gus, 414
Perryman, Henry, 413, 414
Perryman, Rufus (Speckled Red), 264, 398, **413-414**, *413*, 415
Perryman, William "Willie" (Piano Red), 369, 414, **414-415**, *414*
Pershine Theater (Philadelphia, PA), 472
Pershing Hotel (Chicago, IL), 83
Pershing Lounge (Chicago, IL), 345
Persian Room (club) (Little Rock, AR), 149
Personal Instructor (book), The, 310
Perspective (label), 404
Pete Johnson Story (book), The, 521
Pete Werley's Florida Blossom Minstrels (tour) (see also: Florida Cotton Blossom Minstrels), 134
Peters, Charley (see: Patton, Charley)
Peterson, Laura, 254
Pete's Lounge (Chicago, IL), 41, 595
Pete's Place (club) (Chicago, IL), 460
Pete's Tavern (Chicago, IL), 334
Petit, Buddy, 203, 379, 420
Pettiford, Oscar, 216, 564
Pettigrew, Leola B. (see: Grant, Leola)
Petway, Robert, 354
Peyton, Dave, 450
Peyton Place (club) (Chicago, IL), 132, 500, 549
Pharoah, Jaarone, 278
Pheasant Run (club) (St. Charles, IL), 108, 381
Phelps, Arthur (Blind Blake), 70, 147, 184, 197, 233, 266, 282, 391, **415-417**, *416*, 531, 555, 557, 562, 563, 575
Phelps Lounge (Detroit, MI), 90
Phil & Bea Bop (duo), 531
Philadelphia Folk Festival (Paoli, PA), 147, 174, 247, 257, 280
Philadelphia Folk Festival (Schwenksville, PA), 32, 44, 56, 57, 65, 78, 92, 101, 130, 138, 147, 175, 187, 195, 208, 249, 261, 265, 266, 283, 330, 349, 363, 367, 378, 379, 381, 429, 445, 449, 481, 490, 504, 521, 522, 532, 548, 575, 582
Philadelphia Folk Festival (Spring Mount, PA), 147, 230, 257, 272
Philadelphia House (club) (Atlantic City, NJ), 540
Philadelphia International (label), 432
Philharmonic Auditorium (Los Angeles, CA), 582
Philharmonic Hall (Hamilton, Can.), 310
Philharmonic Hall (New York, NY) (see also: Lincoln Center, New York, NY), 78, 114, 138, 218, 224, 305, 346, 352, 359-360, 389, 417, 420, 513, 523, 566, 567, 573
Philharmonic Hall (Warsaw, Poland), 93
Philips (label), 63, 69, 220
Phillips, Brewer, 435, 501
Phillips, Esther "Little Esther," **417-418**, *417*, 508, 538
Phillips, Pearl, 169
Phillips (label), 381
Phillips International (label), 183
Philo (label), 65, 253, 300, 342, 522
Philo-Aladdin (label), 586
Phina & Company (tour), 222, 494
Phinx Inn (New York, NY), 44
Phipps Auditorium (Denver, CO), 142
Phoenix Club (Chicago, IL), 254
Phoenix Club (Cicero, IL), 500
Phone Booth (club), The (New York, NY), 566
Physical World (club), The (Cambridge, MA), 320
Piano Red (see: Harrison, Vernon) (see: Perryman, William)
Piazza & Company (band), 549
Picaninny (Jug) Band, 454, 547
Piccolo Pete (pseudonym), 560
Pichon, Walter "Fats," **418-419**, *418*, 472
Pichon, Walter, Sr., 418
Pick, Sam, 360
Pick Collier Club (New Orleans, LA), 506
Pick-Congress Hotel (Chicago, IL), 596
Pickens, Edwin "Buster," 103, **419**
Pickens, Eli, 419
Pickens, Slim (see: Burns, Eddie)
Pickett, Charlie, 178
Pickett, Willie, 424
Pickett, Wilson, 60
Picou, Alphonse, 420
Pied Piper Club (Los Angeles, CA), 417, 431
Piedmont (label), 257, 259, 562
Pier 23 Cafe (San Francisco, CA), 322
Pierce, Billie, 134, 136, 299, **419-421**, *419*, 465
Pierce, Charlie, 454
Pierce, Joseph "Dede," 134, 299-300, 420, 421
Pierce, Nat, 375
Pig 'n' Whistle (foodstand) (Atlanta, GA), 369, 546
Pig 'n' Whistle Red (see: McTell, Willie)
Pigmeat Pete (see: Wilson, Wesley)
Pigrest Baptist Church (Greenville, AL), 43
Pilgrim Baptist Church (Chicago, IL), 159, 251
Pilgrim Congregational Church (Birmingham, MI), 423
Pilgrim Rest Baptist Church (Meltonia, MS), 433
Pilgrim Travelers (group), The, 421, 431
Pilgrimage Theater (Hollywood, CA), 346
Pimloco Club (New Orleans, LA), 436
Pin Wheel Club (Cleveland, OH), 145
Pine Lounge (Bronx, NY), 90
Pine Woods Folk Festival, 283
Pinetop (see: Sparks, Aaron)
Pinewood Tom (see: White, Joshua)
Pinewoods Society Concert (New York, NY), 120
Piney Brown's Place (club) (Kansas City, MO), 518

Pink Poodle (club) (Chicago, IL), 110, 150, 154
Pioneer (label), 277
Pio's Lodge (Providence, RI), 566
Pirates Den (club) (Jacksonville, FL), 432
Piron, Armand J. "A.J.," 80, 300, 372, 373, 419, 420
Piron's New Orleans Orchestra, 496
Pitcher, Sylvia, 323, 502
Pitt Theater (Pittsburg, PA), 82
Pittman, Sampson, 182
Pitts, Rev. Alfred (see: Watson, Johnny)
Pitts's Place (club) (Newark, NJ), 550
Pittsburgh Jazz Festival (Pittsburgh, PA), 113, 566, 567
Pizza Express (club) (London, Eng.), 245
Place (club), The (Los Angeles, CA), 544
Place (club), The (New York, NY), 285
Place des Arts (club) (Montreal, Can.), 309
Planet (label), 220, 424, 570, 594
Plant, Etta, 159
Plantation, The (see: Club Plantation)
Plantation Cabaret (Paris, Fr.), 31
Plantation Cabaret/Cafe/Club (Chicago, IL), 31, 70, 116, 134, 229, 274, 279, 342, 388, 460, 507, 576, 594
Plantation Club (Nashville, TN), 145
Plantation Club (New York, NY), 405, 540
Plantation Club (St. Louis, MO), 200, 558
Plantation Revue Company (tour), 581
Plantation Room (club) (New York, NY), 581
Plateau Hall (Toronto, Can.), 556
Platinum Lounge (Chicago, IL), 532
Playa Del Ray (club) (Los Angeles, CA), 32, 213
Playback (magazine), 229
Playboy (label), 318, 531
Playboy Club (Boston, MA), 588
Playboy Club (Chicago, IL), 254, 280, 353, 421, 435, 447, 567
Playboy Club (Los Angeles, CA), 588
Playboy Club (New Orleans, LA), 167
Playboy Club (Richmond, CA), 55, 270, 449
Playboy Club (San Francisco, CA), 449
Playboy Jazz Festival (Chicago, IL), 447, 566
Playboy Magazine, 116, 142, 225, 328
Playgirl Club (Denver, CO), 76
Playground Club (Chicago, IL), 216
Playhouse (theater), The (Passaic, NJ), 81
Playhouse in the Park (theater) (Boston, MA), 195
Playmate Club (Chicago, IL), 388
Playmates of Rhythm (band), The, 104
Playpen (club), The (Cliffside Park, NJ), 90
Plaza Theater (Bridgeport, CT), 81
Pleasant, Cousin Joe (see: Joseph, Pleasant)
Pleasant Green Cemetery (Sharon, MS), 161
Pleasant Joe (see: Joseph, Pleasant)
Pleasants, Henry, 116, 312, 441, 465, 544
Plooze Bar (Flint, MI), 563
Plugged Nickel (club) (Chicago, IL), 51, 157, 308, 381, 389, 513, 567
Plymouth Hilton (hotel) (Detroit, MI), 567
Pod's and Jerry's (see: Catagonia Club)
Pokempner, Marc, 451
Policy Wheel (label), 79
Political Song Festival (Berlin, Ger.), 142
Poljazz (label), 390
Polka Dot Inn (St. Louis, MO), 502
Polka Dot Slim (see: Vincent, Monroe)
Polydor (label), 117, 155, 190, 211, 213, 216, 224, 239, 276, 299, 322, 337, 348, 352, 364, 366, 381, 394, 400, 504, 527, 528
Polydor-Reprise (label), 224
Pomposello, Tom, 283, 528, 529
Ponderosa Club (Houston, TX), 125
Pontchartrain (label), 506
Poodle Patio Club (New Orleans, LA), 202
Poor Bob (see: Woodfork, Robert)
Poor Boy (see: Oden, James)
Poor Charlie (see: West, Charles)
Poor Jim (see: Rachell, James)
Poor Richard's (club) (Chicago, IL), 65
Poosepahtuck Club (New York, NY), 385, 564
Pop Grey's Dance Hall (Chester, PA), 540
Pope, Katie, 350
Popeye's (club) (New Orleans, LA), 420
Poppa/Poppy Hop (see: Wilson, Harding)
Pop's Place (Houston, TX), 243
Popular Song Association (organization), 543
Porco, Mike, 379
Pori Jazz Festival (Pori, Finland), 334
Pork Chop Chapman's Show (tour), 382
Poro School of Beauty Culture (St. Louis, MO), 45
Port Arthur College (Port Arthur, TX), 296
Portable Folk Festival (tour), 459
Porterdale Cemetery (Columbus, GA), 428
Porters Inn (New Orleans, LA), 101
Portland State College (Portland, OR), 57, 260, 349
Portnoy, Jerry, 247, 269, 505
Post (club), The (Chicago, IL), 41, 123, 266, 334, 442, 575, 595
Post (label), 400
Post-Bulletin (newspaper), 314
Post Club, The (Detroit, MI), 370
Pot Pourri (club) (Montreal, Can.), 147
Potter, Nettie (see: Moore, Monette)
Powell, Eugene, 589
Powell, Vance "Tiny," **421,** *422*
Powell Symphony Hall (St. Louis, MO), 304
Powerhouse Four (band), 352
Powers, Julia/Julius (see: Cox, Ida)
Powers, Ollie, 31
Powers Theater (Camden, NJ), 81
Prairie County Training School (Little Rock, AR), 484
Prairie View A&M College (Prairie View, TX), 74
Prather, Ida, 134
Pratt, Janie, 330
Preager, Lou, 256
Preer, Andy, 221
Premium (label), 92, 116, 321
Prentice Alley (club) (Nashville, TN), 76
Presbyterian Hospital (Dallas, TX), 307
Preservation Hall (New Orleans, LA), 39, 203, 300, 327, 420, 486, 512, 573
Preservation Hall (label), 420
Preservation Hall Jazz Band, 420
Preservation Hall Portraits (book), 421
Presidential Inn (South Gate, MI), 423
Presidents (group), The, 384
Presley, Elvis, 138, 360, 412, 506
Press Club (New Orleans, LA), 420
Prestige (label), 161, 185, 209, 239, 243, 283, 363, 366, 404, 478, 485, 503, 504, 521, 527, 529, 575, 586, 588, 596
Prestige-Bluesville (label) (see also: Bluesville-Prestige label), 34, 36, 49, 50, 117, 167, 213, 221, 222, 243, 256, 280, 283, 292, 327, 340, 347, 364, 366, 369, 370, 381, 419, 426, 454, 485, 490, 503, 504, 510, 514, 515, 533, 559, 573
Prestige-International (label), 147, 174
Prestige-Tru Sound (label), 312
Preston, Billy, 412
Preview Lounge (Chicago, IL), 380
Price, A. C., 111
Price, Kerry, 37, **421, 423,** *423*, 428, 465
Price, Lloyd, 60, 530
Price, Sam "Sammy," 61, 139, 145, 195, 284, 285, 300, 316, 385, 475, 501, 510, 518
Price, Walter (Big Walter), 247, **423-424,** *423*
Price, William Albert, 421
Pride & Joy Club (Chicago, IL), 269, 574
Pridgett, Gertrude, 427
Pridgett, Thomas, Jr., 428
Pridgett, Thomas, Sr., 427
Primalon (club) (San Francisco, CA), 154
Primrose Country Club (Cincinnati, OH), 36
Prince Hall (Detroit, MI), 434
Prince James Jazz Combo, 437
Prince Royal Club (Detroit, MI), 535
Princess of the Blues (billing), The, 84
Princess Theater (Harrisburg, PA), 295, 350
Princess Theater (Memphis, TN), 571

Princess Theater (New York, NY), 222, 351, 496, 497
Princess Theater (Vicksburg, MS), 379
Princeton University (Princeton, NJ), 316
Probe (label), 309, 346
Proctor's (theater) (Elizabeth, NJ), 81
Proctor's (theater) (New York, NY), 472
Proctor's (theater) (Schenectady, NY), 81
Proctor's 86th Street Theater (New York, NY), 70, 82, 540
Proctor's 5th Avenue Theater (New York, NY), 70
Proctor's 58th Street Theater (New York, NY), 70, 82
Proctor's 125th Street Theater (New York, NY), 82
Proctor's Theater (Albany, NY), 82, 256
Proctor's Theater (Mt. Vernon, NY), 70
Proctor's Theater (Newark, NJ), 82, 540
Proctor's Theater (Yonkers, NY), 82
Proctor's 25th Street Theater (New York, NY), 82
Professor Longhair (see: Byrd, Roy)
Professor Longhair and his Shuffling Hungarians (band), 101
Professor Longhair and The Four Hairs (band), 101
Profile (label), 548
Program of Blues and Ballads (concert), A, 431
Project Bar (Natchez, MS), 328
Promise, Martha, 318
Providence (label), 220
Provident Hospital (Baltimore, MD), 153
Provident Hospital (Chicago, IL), 35, 227, 269, 558
Prowlin' (label), 28
Pryor, James "Snooky," 181, 294, 342, **424-425**, *424*, 442, 570, 575, 576, 578, 594
Pryor, Jimmy, 298
Pryor, Martha (see: Waters, Ethel)
Pryor, Martha, 543
Pryor, Snooky (see: Pryor, James)
Prysock, Red, 359, 519
Psychedelic Shack (club) (Chicago, IL), 151, 450, 500
Psychedelic Super Market (club) (Boston, MA), 296
Psychopathic Hospital (Chicago, IL), 355
Public Hall (Cleveland, OH), 309
Public Theater (New York, NY), 357
Puerto Rican Solidarity Day (concert) (New York, NY), 231
Puerto Rico Music Festival (San Juan, PR), 309
Pug Horton's All-Stars (band), 245
Pugh, Joe (Forest City Joe), 247, **425**, 576
Pugh, Moses, 425
Pugh, Sally, 317
Pulaski Hall (Gary, IN), 304, 332-334, 434
Pulaski Lounge (Gary, IN), 66, 434
Pull (label), 180
Pully, Nora Ella, 307
Pu'o'Oro Plage Club (Papeete, Tahiti), 322
Purdue University (Lafayette, IN), 176
Pure Food & Drug Act (group), 211
Pure Gold (label), 125
Purple Cat (club) (Chicago, IL) (Kitty Cat Club), 68, 225, 246, 268, 305, 342, 388, 424, 442, 559, 570, 574, 576, 594
Purple Onion (club) (Hollywood, CA), 431
Purple Onion (club) (New York, NY), 224
Purple Onion (club) (Toronto, Can.), 147, 426, 556
Push (label), 63
Push & Pull Club (Lula, MS), 395
Pussy Cat-A-Go-Go (club) (Birmingham, AL), 435, 508
Pussy Cat A-Go-Go (club) (Uniontown, AL), 90
Putnam Theater (Brooklyn, NY), 73, 472
Pythian Temple Roof Garden (club) (New Orleans, LA), 373
Pythian Theater (Columbus, OH), 463
Python (label), 442, 494
Pzazz (label), 299

QRS (label), 175, 192, 197, 222, 281, 282, 351, 418, 546, 584
QRS Boys (band), 418
Quaker City Jazz Festival (Philadelphia, PA), 417, 538
Quaker City Rock Festival (Philadelphia, PA), 296, 308
Quaker Oats Company (product), 582
Qualiton (label), 408
Quality Night Club (Los Angeles, CA), 445
Quartier Latin (club) (Berlin, Ger.), 166, 302, 569, 588
Quarts of Joy (band), 274
Quasimodo Club (Berlin, Ger.), 65, 156
Quattlebaum, Douglas "Doug," 185, **425-426**, *425*
Queen (label), 28, 285
Queen (billing), The, 482
Queen Bea of Blues Singers (billing), 61
Queen City Minstrels Show (tour), 81
Queen Elizabeth Hall (London, Eng.), 117
Queen Elizabeth Theater (Vancouver, Can.), 113, 309, 388
Queen Elleezee (billing), 374
Queen-King (label), 89
Queen of Blues (billing), 72
Queen of Memphis Sound (Billing), The, 512
Queen of the Blues (billing), 173, 351, 472, 482, 506, 538
Queen of the Moaners (billing), The, 467, 497
Queen of the Night Clubs (billing), The, 31
Queen Vee (label), 481
Queens College (Queens, NY), 176, 401, 427
Quid Club (Chicago, IL), 490
Quiet Knight (club) (Chicago, IL), 33, 65, 93, 117, 147, 174, 177, 243, 366, 367, 389, 427, 429, 484, 504, 505, 529, 553
Quigley, John J., 153
Quogue Inn (Quogue, NY), 44

R&B Festival (Groningen, Neth.), 38, 154
RCA (label), 86
RCA-International (label), 150, 193
RCA Victor (label) (see also: Victor label), 114, 122, 220, 360, 448
RGA (label), 28
RIC (label), 354
RIH (label), 136
RK (label), 28
RKO Bushwick Theater (Brooklyn, NY), 256
RKO Circuit, 137, 279, 357, 523, 541
RKO-Keith Circuit, 523
RKO-Palace Theater (New York, NY) (see also: Keith-Albee Palace Theater, New York, NY), 71, 91, 113, 385, 481, 491, 541, 585
RKO Theater (Boston, MA) (see also: Keith Theater, Boston, MA), 542
RKO Theater (St. Louis, MO), 70
R. L. Shurden Plantation (Drew, MS), 193
RPM (label), 93, 114, 246, 291, 308, 312, 357, 371, 382, 400, 417, 468, 530, 544
RSO (label), 305, 307
Rabbit Foot Minstrels (tour) (see also: F. S. Wolcott's Rabbit Foot Minstrels/Fat Chappelle's Rabbit Foot Minstrels), 125, 134, 173, 176, 229, 230, 237, 264, 298, 365, 373, 382, 399, 401, 428, 450, 462, 506, 510, 540, 545, 568
Race, Wesley, 499
Racer Music Company (organization), 113
Rachell, George, 426
Rachell, J. C., 427
Rachell, James "Yank," 54, 176, 202, 401, **426-427**, *426*, 569, 575, 576
Radcliffe College (Cambridge, MA), 429
Radio City Music Hall (theater) (New York, NY), 51, 299, 304, 310, 360, 390, 411
Radio Trio (group), 496
Radio Stars Jamboree (show) (Los Angeles, CA), 205
Rafe's Paradise Cabaret/Cafe (Atlantic City, NJ), 137, 221, 350, 462, 484, 491
Rafe's Paradise Theater (Atlantic City, NJ), 231, 274, 331, 540, 580, 583
Rage Showbar (Detroit, MI), 535
Ragmuffins (band), 475
Ragtime Band, 385
Ragtime Bash of Toronto Ragtime Society (organization) (Toronto, Can.), 423

Ragtime Festival (Kerrville, TX), 84
Ragtime Jug Stompers (band), 521
Ragtime Society Concert (Toronto, Can.), 84
Railroad Bill (see: Dorsey, Thomas A.)
Raim, Walter, 557
Rainbow (label), 37
Rainbow Garden (club) (New York, NY), 510
Rainbow Gospel Four (group), 164
Rainbow Grill (club), The (New York, NY), 254, 567
Rainbow Inn (Woodbridge, NJ), 90
Rainbow Lake Club (Memphis, TN), 179
Rainbow Room (club) (Dallas, TX), 243
Rainbow Room (club) (Detroit, MI), 125, 132, 240
Rainbow Room (club) (New York, NY), 466
Rainbow Sign (book), The, 209
Rainbow Sign (club), The (Los Angeles, CA), 449
Rainbow Tavern (Seattle, WA), 240
Rainbow Theater, (Houston, TX), 29, 243
Raines (label), 571
Rainey, Danny, 428
Rainey, Gertrude "Ma," 56, 142, 159, 246, 295, 298, 314, 316, 322, 339, 362, 405, 415, 420, 423, **427-428**, *427*, 454, 462, 465, 467, 514, 525, 538, 559, 560, 594
Rainey, Memphis Ma, 428
Rainey, William "Pa," 427, 428
Rainey and Rainey, Assassinators of the Blues (billing), 428
Rainier Brewing Company (product), 420
Raitt, Bonnie, 138, 249, 289, 346, 364, **428-430**, *429*, 533
Raitt, John, 428
Ralph Theater (Reading, PA), 82
Ralph's Club (Chicago, IL), 116, 343
Ralph's Club (Oakland, CA), 510
Ralph's Lounge (Hazel Park, MI), 229
Rama (label), 280
Ramada Inn (Chicago, IL), 571
Ramada Inn (Mundelein, IL), 322
Ramada Inn (San Jacinto, CA), 229
Ramada Inn (Springfield, IL), 314
Ramada Inn and Jazz Emporium (Rochester, MN), 313
Ramada Inn Circuit, 76
Ramblers (group), The, 364
Ramblin' Bob (see: Nighthawk, Robert)
Ramey, Ben, 454
Ramsey, Frederick "Fred," Jr., 33, 163, 468, 483
Ramsey, George (see: Dorsey, Thomas A.)
Ramsey, Yvonne, 78
Rand, Odell, 250
Randall Ford's Plantation (Wesson, MS), 483
Randalls Island Jazz Festival (Randalls Island/New York, NY), 113, 308, 431, 470, 538, 588
Randolph, Amanda, 52
Random (label), 66
Randy van Horne Choir (group), 586
Raney, Wayne, 42
Rankin, R. S., **430**, *430*, 527, 528
Rap Club (Chicago, IL), 116
Rapa House (Detroit, MI), 240
Rapee, Erno, 496
Rarities (label), 298
Rat Trap (lounge/inn) (Chicago, IL), 439, 500-501, 589, 596
Rathskeller (club), The (Pittsburgh, PA), 467
Ratliff, Roberta, 322
Ratso's (club) (Chicago, IL), 65, 68, 108, 117, 132, 148, 151, 254, 304, 307, 343, 418, 450, 476, 544, 595
Rattler, Henry, 440
Raven & Rose Tavern (Los Angeles, CA), 36
Raven Gallery (Detroit, MI), 239, 366, 367, 379, 504, 505
Raven Oyster Bar (Beaumont, TX), 121, 243
Ravinia (club) (Los Angeles, CA), 296
Ravinia Folk Festival (Chicago, IL), 141, 148, 380, 453
Ravinia Park Festival (Chicago, IL), 100, 108, 194, 308, 538
Ravinia Theater (Chicago, IL), 431
Ravisloe Country Club (Homewood, IL), 569
Rawls, Louis "Lou," **430-433**, *430*
Ray, Floyd, 522
Ray, Harmon, **433**, *433*, 552
Ray, Isom (see: Agee, Raymond)
Ray Charles Enterprises (organization), 113
Ray Charles Show (tour), 114
Ray Charles Singers (group), 76, 115
Raye, Martha, 279
Raymond Brothers (duo), 467
Raynac (label), 419
Ray's Lounge (Chicago, IL), 236, 344
Ray's Place (Chicago, IL), 41
Rays Record (label), 232
Reader (newspaper), The, 156
Really the Blues Concert (New York, NY), 197, 406, 584
Rebel (label), 257
Rebennack, Mac (Dr. John), 54, 60, 103, 202, 210, 220, 415, 508
Record Changer (magazine), 139, 464
Record Research (magazine), 83, 99, 176, 222, 223, 286, 291, 453, 480, 481, 482, 499, 594
Record Research Archives, 118, 176, 221, 223, 291, 295, 344, 480, 488
Recordings of Jimmie Rodgers (book), The, 441
Rector, Eddie, 581
Red Arrow Club (Osaka, Japan), 423
Red Arrow Club (Stickney/Chicago, IL), 108, 313, 381, 506
Red Barn (club), The (Houston, TX), 424
Red Bob's Place (New Orleans, LA), 379
Red Carpet Club (San Jose, CA), 332
Red Carpet Lounge (Cleveland, OH), 90
Red Creek Bar/Club (Rochester, NY), 33, 240, 247, 459, 489
Red Devil (see: Milborn, Nelson)
Red Devil Trio (group), 198, 342, 460
Red Garter (club) (New Orleans, LA), 396
Red Garter Band, 423
Red Garter Banjo Band, 230
Red Garter Club (Detroit, MI), 230
Red Hot Louisiana Band, 121
Red Hot Willie (see: McTell, Willie)
Red Lightnin' (label), 36, 99, 106, 238, 247
Red Lion Club (Chicago, IL), 591
Red Nelson (see: Wilborn, Nelson)
Red Onion (club) (Memphis, TN), 454
Red Onion Cafe (New Orleans, LA), 128
Red Onion Jazz Babies (band), 254
Red Onion Jazz Band, 316
Red Peppers (band), 356
Red Rag (label), 302
Red Robin (label), 92, 164, 364, 366, 503
Red Rose Minstrel/Medicine Show (tour), 264, 414
Red Stag Club (San Jose, CA), 332
Red Top (label), 219
Red Top Club (St. Louis, MO), 502, 589
Red Velvet Club (Los Angeles, CA), 32
Redd, Lawrence N., 391
Redd Foxx Club (Los Angeles, CA), 254, 431, 588
Redding, Otis, 296, 312, 412, 547
Reddlery, Climmie, 174
Redman, Don, 71, 406, 464
Redmond, Katie, 320
Red's Playmore Lounge (Chicago, Il), 305
Red's Upstairs Lounge (Chicago, IL), 259
Reece, Dizzy, 586
Reece, Oddie Bell, 572
Reed, Aaron Corthen "A.C." 435
Reed, Al, 116
Reed, Doc, 209
Reed, Jesse, 435
Reed, Jimmy (see: Reed, Mathis)
Reed, Jimmy, Jr., 435
Reed, Joseph, 433
Reed, Malinda, 435
Reed, Mathis "Jimmy," 58, 66, 67, 68, 91, 121, 183, 199, 204, 232, 271, 285, 289, 304, 332, 348, 378, 379, 384, 391, **433-435**, *434*, 438, 444, 461, 476, 493, 494, 530, 571, 578
Reed, Nora (see: Hall, Vera)
Reed, Willie, 280, 459
Reed College (Portland, OR), 130, 247
Reese, Della, 520
Reese, Esther, 334
Reeves, Jimmy, Jr., 435
Reeves, Nina, 139
Refectory (club), The (Dublin, CA), 161
Regal (label), 63, 91, 161, 238, 256, 268, 317, 340, 369, 442, 489, 546
Regal Club (Chicago, IL), 405
Regal Tavern (Minneapolis, MN), 91
Regal Theater (Chicago, IL), 28, 51, 68, 104, 113, 116, 154, 200, 216, 219,

263, 269, 277, 281, 298, 304, 308, 388, 407, 444, 461, 527, 536, 572
Regal Theater (New Orleans, LA), 508
Regency Towers Hotel (Toronto, Can.), 557
Regent (label), 91, 238, 566
Regent Ballroom (Chicago, IL), 342, 460
Regent Theater (Baltimore, MD), 153, 350
Regent Theater (New York, NY), 541
Regent Theater (Paterson, NJ), 82
Regent Theater (Philadelphia, PA), 540
Reid, Irene, 538
Reinhardt, Bill, 506
Reisenwebers (club) (New York, NY), 474-475
Religious Gospelaires (group), 535
Rena, Kid, 164, 203
Renaissance (club) (Hollywood/Los Angeles, CA), 174, 194, 254, 566, 586
Renaissance Ballroom (New York, NY), 221, 252, 496
Renaissance Casino (New York, NY), 44, 74, 405
Renaissance Theater (New York, NY), 48
Renata Theater (New York, NY), 542
Reno Club (Kansas City, MO), 321, 405, 445, 518
Reno Sweeney (club) (New York, NY), 195, 254
Reprise (label), 76, 157, 224, 225, 330, 411, 527, 532, 586
Reprise-Atlantic (label), 224
Rest Haven Cemetery (Navasota, TX), 330
Rest Lawn Cemetery (Houston, TX), 58
Restvale Cemetery (Worth, IL), 39, 122, 193, 238, 294, 345, 355, 397, 403, 467, 501, 545
Retinal Circus (club) (Vancouver, Can.), 389, 548
Retort Club (Detroit, MI), 147, 243, 257
Reunion Club (San Francisco, CA), 30
Reuss, Richard, 206
Rev. Gary Davis/Blues Guitar (book), 147
Revilot (label), 578
Revival (label), 104, 153, 363
Reweliotty, Andre, 406
Rex (label), 354
Reynaud, Lloyd, 200, 554
Reynaud-Flyright (label), 232
Reynolds, Teddy, 531
Rheingold Music Festival (New York, NY) (see also: Central Park Music Festival, New York, NY), 99, 147, 187, 239, 249, 366, 504, 548, 567
Rhoades, Todd, 83
Rhodes, Sonny, 213
Rhone, Happy, 221, 494
Rhumboogie (label), 527
Rhumboogie Club (Chicago, IL) (see also: Dave's Rhumboogie Club), 215, 383, 525
Rhumboogie Club (Oakland, CA), 29-30, 188, 510, 512
Rhythm (label), 161, 187, 332, 439, 533
Rhythm Aces (band), 379
Rhythm & Blues (label), 28
Rhythm & Blues Caravan (tour), 417, 512
Rhythm & Blues Jubilee (tour), 417, 527
Rhythm & Blues King (billing), The, 183
Rhythm & Blues Magazine, 292, 534, 568
Rhythm & Blues: Roots of Rock Show (tour), 36, 178-179, 220, 360, 439, 544
Rhythm & Blues Show (tour), 308
Rhythm & Blues USA (tour), 117, 155, 213, 239, 254, 269, 366, 504, 527
Rhythm & Sounds Concert 73 Show (tour), 211
Rhythm Club (Baton Rouge, LA), 270
Rhythm Club (New Orleans, LA), 519
Rhythm Dukes (band), 480
Rhythm Kings (band) (Albert Ammons), 406
Rhythm Kings (band) (Oliver Cobb), 281
Rhythm Kings (band) (Henry Hayes), 400
Rhythm 'n Motion Festival (Alameda, CA), 30
Rhythm Rascals Trio (group), 110
Rhythm Rockers (band), The, 125, 285, 509, 546
Rialto Nightclub (New Orleans, LA), 420
Rialto Theater (Chicago, IL), 173
Rialto Theater (Glens Falls, NY), 70, 82
Rialto Theater (Poughkeepsie, NY), 82
Ric (label), 436
Rice, Eli, 284
Riceland (label), 400
Rich, Buddy, 567
Richard, John, 438
Richard's (club) (Atlanta, GA), 95, 247, 304, 310, 336, 389, 490
Richard's Playhouse (Jackson, MS), 395
Richardson, Clarence Clifford "C.C.," **436**, *436*
Richardson, James, 168
Richardson, Peg, 185
Richardson (label), 436
Richie Havens Anthology (book), 219
Richland Cemetery (Greenville, SC?), 531
Richmond Auditorium (Los Angeles, CA), 86
Richmond Hill High School (Queens, NY), 521
Richmond Jazz Festival (Richmond, Eng.), 408
Rick's Bar (Los Angeles, CA), 213, 531
Rick's Cafe American (Chicago, IL), 568
Ricky's Show Lounge (Chicago, IL), 35, 41, 109, 268, 269, 305, 410, 516
Ricordi (label), 69
Rico's Lounge (Baton Rouge, LA), 547
Riddle, Leslie, 365
Riddle, Nelson, 298
Ridgley, Tommy, 88, **436-437**, *436*
Riedy, Bob, 41, 42, 123, 276, 334, 442, 595
Riffers (duo), The, 496
Riley, Amos, 418
Riley, Judge, 148
Riley, Myrtle, 167
Ringling Brothers Circus (tour), 161, 198, 349, 486
Ringside Ball (New York, NY), 164
Rip (label), 101, 586
Rip's Playhouse (New Orleans, LA), 86
Rising Sons (group), 345
Rising Sun (club), The (Montreal, Can.), 149, 156, 240, 244, 341, 367, 450, 505, 524
Ritz, David, 114, 116
Ritz, Sally (see: Henderson, Rosa)
Ritz Barbeque Club (Richmond, CA), 393
Ritz Cafe (club) (Philadelphia, PA), 73
Ritz Carlton Hotel (Boston, MA), 446
Ritz Lounge, The (Chicago, IL), 76
Ritz Theater (Austin, TX), 120, 151, 360
River Bell (tavern) (New Orleans, LA), 420
River Camp Prison (Atlanta, GA), 251
River City Blues Festival (Memphis, TN), 120, 130, 163, 177, 179, 327, 364, 401, 483, 510, 553, 560
River Oaks Hospital (New Orleans, LA), 585
Riverboat (label), 191, 372
Riverboat (coffeehouse), The (Toronto, Can.), 132, 148, 195, 208, 210, 261, 366, 367, 379, 504, 505, 521, 548
Riverboat Jazz Band, 245
Riverqueen Club/Coffeehouse (Vancouver, Can.), 366, 504, 557
Rivers, Helen, 145
Riverside (label), 34, 134, 147, 148, 160, 194, 203, 239, 256, 288, 336, 381, 403, 420, 438, 507, 523, 524, 591
Riverside Plaza Ballroom (New York, NY), 491
Riverside Stadium (Washington, DC), 317, 365, 503
Riverside Theater (Milwaukee, WI), 298
Riverside Theater (New York, NY), 70, 540
Riverview Cemetery (Greenup, KY), 563
Riviera (club/lounge), The (Chicago, IL), 93, 334, 596
Riviera Civic Center (St. Louis, MO), 431
Riviera Club (New York, NY), 229, 406
Riviera Club, The (St. Louis, MO), 74, 90, 154, 263, 281, 299, 523
Riviera Theater (Brooklyn, NY), 82

Riviera Theater (Chicago, IL), 70
Riviera Theater (New York, NY), 82
Rivieras (group), The, 353
Rivoli Theater (Toledo, OH), 82
Roadmasters (band), 237, 450
Roaring '20s Cafe (Los Angeles, CA), 249
Roaring Twenties Club (Cincinnati, OH), 76
Rob Michael's Club (Chicago, IL), 168, 395
Robbin's Nest (club) (Detroit, MI), 588
Robert Johnson (book) (Sam Charters), 289
Robert Johnson (book) (Bob Groom), 289
Robert Jr. (see: Lockwood, Robert Jr.)
Robert Motel (Chicago, IL), 304
Roberts, Greg, 413
Roberts, Helen (see: Hunter, Alberta)
Roberts, Luckey, 44
Roberts, Sally (see: Martin, Sara)
Roberts, Snitcher (see: Johnson, James "Stump")
Robert's Motel 500 Room (club) (Chicago, IL), 338
Robert's Show Lounge (Chicago, IL), 237, 299, 308, 405, 538, 566
Robert's 300 Room (club) (Chicago, IL), 418, 588
Robertson, Robbie, 305
Robeson, Paul, 256, 365, 503, 556
Robichaux, Joseph "Joe," 300, 506
Robinson, A. C., 439
Robinson, Alvin, 116
Robinson, Arthur C. "A. C.," 439, 440
Robinson, Bailey, 111
Robinson, Bessie, 438
Robinson, Bill, 71, 80, 295, 360, 385, 481, 581, 582
Robinson, Bobby, 283
Robinson, Earl, 550
Robinson, Elzadie, 438
Robinson, Fention/Fenton, 149, 209, 311, **437-438**, *437*, 528, 549, 596
Robinson, Ikey, 274, 381
Robinson, James "Bat," **438**
Robinson, Jim, 203, 505
Robinson, Jimmy Lee, 305, **438-439**, *438*, 493, 494
Robinson, Little Jr., 286
Robinson, Louis Charles "L. C.," 29, 30, 211, 244, 276, **439-440**, *439*
Robinson, Ray Charles, 111
Robinson Brothers (duo), The, 439
Robinson's Cafe (Hughes, AR), 483, 560
Robinson's Knights of Rest (band), 49
Robs, Gerard, 506
Roby, L. C., 384
Roche, Jacques, 487
Rochester Junior College (Rochester, MN), 582
Rochester Philharmonic Orchestra, 195
Rock, Sullivan, 103
Rock and Roll (see also: Rock 'n' Roll)
Rock & Roll Revival Show (New York, NY), 46, 158, 359, 411
Rock and Roll Show of 1967 (Chicago, IL), 343
Rock & Roll Spectacular Show (New York, NY), 46, 158
Rock Bottom Club (Chicago, IL), 93
Rock Encyclopedia (book), 54
Rock Folk (book), 47, 225
Rock Garden (club), The (Jamaica, West Indies), 90
Rock House (club) (Indianapolis, IN), 492
Rock Is Rhythm and Blues (book), 391
Rock 'n' Roll (see also: Rock & Roll)
Rock 'n' Roll (book), 360
Rock 'n' Roll Club (Chicago, IL), 35, 596
Rock 'n' Roll Holiday Jubilee Show (tour), 566
Rock 'n' Roll Revival Spectacular (show) (New York, NY), 411
Rock Pile (club), The (Island Park, NY), 585
Rock Pile (club) (Toronto, Can.), 304, 389
Rockefeller Center (building) (New York, NY), 254
Rocket Four (group), 225, 479, 570
Rockets of Rhythm (group), 109
Rockford College (Rockford, IL), 177, 569
Rockhead's Paradise (club) (Montreal, Can.), 550
Rockin' (label), 237, 337
Rockin' & Rhythm (tour), 581
Rockin' Red (see: Minter, Iverson)
Rockin' Sydney (see: Semien, Sidney)
Rocking Chair Club (Seattle, WA), 111
Rocking Four (group), 442
Rockland Palace (ballroom) (New York, NY), 43, 434, 566
Rocko (label), 547
Rock's Tavern (Rockford, IL), 238, 340, 439, 596
Rockville Cemetery (Lynbrook, NY), 147
Rocky Road (label), 56
Rodgers, Aaron, 440
Rodgers, James "Jimmie," 180, 192, 259, 276, 398, **440-441**, *440*, 483
Rodgers, Jimmie (Mrs.), 441
Rodgers, John, 386
Rod's Outdoor Theater (Cool Valley, TX), 84
Rogers, Ike, 79
Rogers, James "Jimmy," 70, 150, 168, 198, 246, 247, 307, 334, 336, 345, 388, 394, 424, **441-442**, *441*, 479, 484, 571, 589, 596
Rogers, Will, 441
Roger's Club (Helena, AR), 443
Rogers Roost (club) (Warren, MI), 229, 230
Rojac (label), 470
Roker (label), 435
Roland, Walter, 280
Roleson, Dorothy, 141
Rolling Four (group), The, 501
Rolling Stone (magazine), 54, 122, 225, 297, 312, 418, 482, 586
Rolling Stones (band), 47, 95, 208, 269, 309, 360, 391, 411, 412, 548
Rolling Stones (band), 32
Romark (label), 28
Romeo (label), 584
Romeo's Place (club) (Chicago, IL), 268, 388, 442
Romulus (label), 354
Ron (label), 101, 508
Ronn (label), 497
Ronnie Scott's Club (London, Eng.), 165, 224, 304, 417, 466, 478, 588
Rookie Four Gospel Quartet (group), 86
Rookmaaker, Hans, Dr., 416
Room at the Bottom (club) (New York, NY), 141, 490
Rooney, James, 390, 391
Roosevelt, Franklin D., 550, 556
Roosevelt Grill (club) (New York, NY), 316
Roosevelt Hotel (New Orleans, LA), 506
Roosevelt Theater (Cincinnati, OH), 463
Roosevelt Theater (New York, NY), 351
Roosevelt Theater (Pittsburgh, PA), 464
Roosevelt University (Chicago, IL), 569
Roots (label), 38, 99, 169, 249
Rose, Al, 203
Rose, Wally, 373
Rose & Kelly's (club) (Chicago, IL), 67, 246, 260, 575
Rose Hill Cemetery (Memphis, TN), 98
Rose Room (club), The (Dallas, TX), 489
Rosedale Cemetery (Los Angeles, CA), 362
Roseland Ballroom (New York, NY), 44, 446
Roseland Hospital (Chicago, IL), 551
Rosenbaum, Arthur "Art," 27, 50, 182, 202
Roseroom Club (Los Angeles, CA), 43
Ross, Charles "Doc," 138, 338, 391, **442-444**, *443*, 576
Ross, Diana, 538
Ross, Jake, 442
Ross, Mark, 481
Ross, Virginia, 433
Ross Tavern (New York, NY), 592
Rossonian Club (Denver, CO), 321
Rosy's (club) (New Orleans, LA), 51, 78, 122, 307, 490
Rotterdam Jazz Festival "3-3" (Rotterdam, Neth.), 244
Roulette (label), 216, 220, 281, 378, 417, 538, 566, 594
Rounder (label), 41, 54, 56, 98, 120, 130, 320, 327, 334, 349, 442, 454, 486, 524, 595
Roundhouse (pseudonym), 454
Roundhouse Club (London, Eng.), 414
Roundtable (club), The (New York, NY), 417, 556, 566
Rouse, Rod, 386
Rowe, Mike, 67, 122, 138, 150, 181, 247, 270, 272, 324, 341, 371, 435, 460, 479, 501, 535, 575, 576, 594

Roy Flowers Plantation (Mattson, MS), 315
Roy Hamilton R&B Show (tour), 434
Roy Milton (label), 377
Royal, Marshall, 253
Royal, Money, 232
Royal (club), The (Baltimore, MD), 298
Royal Aces (group), 461
Royal Albert Hall (London, Eng.), 41, 57, 121, 238, 266, 345, 346, 382
Royal American (label), 354
Royal American Show (tour), 399, 510
Royal Box (club) (New York, NY), 309, 431, 466
Royal Festival Hall (London, Eng.), 408, 556
Royal Gardens Club (Flint, MI), 84
Royal Oak Musicale Chorus (group) (Royal Oak, MI), 423
Royal Orleans (hotel), The (New Orleans, LA), 420, 506
Royal Palace Hotel (London, Eng.), 256
Royal Peacock (club) (Atlanta, GA), 53, 86, 90, 269, 356, 434, 470, 485
Royal Rockers (band), 395
Royal Room (club) (Los Angeles, CA), 377
Royal Shakespeare Company (tour), 234
Royal Sonesta Hotel (New Orleans, LA), 40, 506
Royal Tahitian (club) (Ontario, CA), 113, 431
Royal Theater (Baltimore, MD), 44, 86, 88, 154, 200, 219, 298
Royale Theater (New York, NY), 70, 475, 541
Roy's Night Spot (club) (Los Angeles, CA), 377
Roy's Rib Inn (club) (Compton, CA), 137
Roxon, Lillian, 54
Roxy (theater) (Hollywood/Los Angeles, CA), 346-347, 390, 418, 544, 588
Roxy Theater (New York, NY), 295, 446, 541, 542
Rubaiyat Lounge (Los Angeles, CA), 523
Ruby, Jack, 547
Ruby (label), 44
Ruby (Lee) Gatewood's Tavern (Ruby's) (Chicago, IL), 35, 68, 69, 116, 161, 355, 576
Rudolf's Roaring 20s Club (Saginaw, MI), 217
Rufus & Bones (duo), 510
Ruggles (club) (Chicago, IL), 309
Ruler (label), 125
Rusch, Robert "Bob," 247, 392
Rush, Bobby, 287, 445
Rush, O. C., 444
Rush, Otis, 33, 35, 151, 155, 168, 208, 237, 246, 269, 305, 311, 340, 345, 380, 391, 394, 410, 437, **444-445**, *444*, 468, 516, 528, 530, 571, 589, 596
Rush, Ralph, 481
Rush Presbyterian—St. Lukes Medical Center Hospital (Chicago, IL), 403
Rushin, Pat, 591
Rushing, Andrew, 445
Rushing, James "Jimmy," 45, 107, 190, 216, 220, 311, 377, **445-448**, *446*, 465, 474, 520, 528, 568, 588
Russell, Bill, 371
Russell, Bill, 421
Russell, Luis, 31, 44, 200, 285, 418, 518
Russell, Ross, 319
Russell, Saul, 106
Russell, Snookum, 491
Russell, Tony, 122, 138, 191, 283, 355, 433, 441, 470
Russell, William, 468
Russo, Danny, 481
Rust, Brian, 257, 351, 497
Rutgers Institute of Jazz Studies (organization) (New Brunswick, NJ/ Newark, NJ) (see also: Institute of Jazz Studies), 481
Rutgers University (New Brunswick, NJ), 308
Ruthie's Inn (Berkeley, CA), 51, 55, 76, 122, 154, 188, 190, 439, 497, 508
Ruthie's Inn (Los Angeles, CA), 497
Ruthie's Inn (Oakland, CA) (see also: New Ruthie's Inn), 76, 439
Ruthie's Inn (Richmond, CA), 439
Ryerson Concert (Toronto, Can.), 84
Ryman Auditorium (Nashville, TN), 86

S&R Room (club) (Oakland, CA), 190
S. H. Dudley Theater Circuit, 558
SIW (label) (see: Sittin In With Label)
S.S. Admiral, 431
S.S. Admiral Streckfuss, 84
S.S. Becky Thatcher Riverboat, 79
S.S. Capitol Riverboat, 279
S.S. Delta Queen Riverboat, 506
S.S. Dixie, 300
S.S. Goldenrod Riverboat/Showboat, 84, 313, 322
S.S. Independence Cruise Ship, 90
S.S. Inland Queen Riverboat, 418
S.S. Lt. Robert E. Lee Riverboat, 314
S.S. Madison, 420
S.S. Mark Twain Riverboat, 385
S.S. Memphis Queen Steamer, 106
S.S. Natchez, 437, 508
S.S. Pennsylvania, 113
S.S. President, 373, 420
S.S. Rotterdam, 114, 567
S.S. St. Paul Riverboat, 279, 282
S.S. Viking Sea Cruise Ship, 40
Sabella's (club) (San Francisco, CA), 322
Sable High School (Chicago, IL), 343
Sabre (label), 400, 559
Sackedelic Shack (club) (Chicago, IL), 404
Sacramento Blues Festival (Sacramento, CA), 76, 190, 213, 303, 421
Sacre, Robert B., 38, 199
Sacred Heart Nursing Home (Chicago, IL), 559
Sadler, Haskell (Cool Papa), **448-449**, *449*
Safari Lounge (New Orleans, LA), 538
Safari Room, The (New Orleans, LA), 508
Sahara (label), 302
Sahara Hotel (Las Vegas, NV), 538
Sahm, Doug, 528
Sail'n Club (San Francisco, CA), 185
Sain, Dan, 486
Sain, Oliver, 572
Saint (see: St.)
Salem Church Cemetery (Monticello, MS), 322
Salem Methodist Church (New York, NY), 281
Salica Bryan and her Pickaninnies (tour), 558
Salle Pleyel (club) (Paris, Fr.), 69, 114, 447
Salle Pleyel Jazz Festival (Paris, Fr.), 406
Sallie Martin Gospel Singers (group), 536
Sallie's Cafe (Houston, TX), 583
Salt & Pepper Ballroom (Chicago, IL), 461
Salt & Pepper Lounge (Chicago, IL), 499
Salt City Six (band), 322
Salt Coffeehouse (Newport, RI), 34, 59
Salty Dog Sam (see: Collins, Sam)
Salty Dog's Band, 108
Salute to Fats Waller Concert (New York, NY), 406, 446, 556
Salute to W. C. Handy (concert) (Henderson, KY), 163, 327
Salvation Club (New York, NY), 224, 346
Salvo, Patrick William, 347
Sam Dale's Circus (tour), 382
Sam Ferrera's Lounge (Chicago, IL), 381
Sam Harris Theater (New York, NY), 541
Samarkand Hotel (London, Eng.), 224
Sammy Green's Down in Dixie Minstrels (tour), 382
Sampson, Sammy (see: Broonzy, William)
Sampson (label), 217, 535
Sam's Barbecue (Richmond, CA), 136
Samson & Delilah (show), 496
Samuel B. and Lemuel C. (duo), 284
Samuel Dent Memorial Jazz Band, 381
Samuels, Charles, 543, 544
Samuels, Clarence, 86
San Diego Folk Festival (San Diego, CA), 57, 233, 274, 573
San Diego State College (San Diego, CA), 134, 456
San Diego University (San Diego, CA), 57, 120, 180, 276, 349, 531
San Francisco Bay Blues Festival (San Francisco, CA), 161, 188, 332, 393, 439, 554

San Francisco Blues Festival (San Francisco, CA), 30, 54, 55, 76, 125, 154, 187, 213, 270, 303, 332, 339, 358, 393, 421, 448, 516, 531
San Francisco Chronicle (newspaper), 514
San Francisco Examiner (newspaper), 393
San Jacinto (label), 203
San Jacinto Hall (New Orleans, LA), 203
San Jose State College (San Jose, CA), 30, 321
San Remo Coffeehouse (Schenectady, NY), 556
San Roc Club (Hastings-on-Hudson, NY), 316
San Sebastian Festival (San Sebastian, Spain), 523
Sanctified Church (Jackson, TN), 470
Sand Dunes (club) (San Francisco, CA), 240, 270, 341, 554
Sanders, Flora, 193
Sanders, Mary, 510
Sanford, Anna, 92
Sands (hotel), The (Las Vegas, NV), 298
Sands Club (New Orleans, LA), 157, 508
Sandy's (club) (Beverly, MA), 132, 208, 286, 389, 490, 499, 500, 523, 527, 549
Sandy's Bar (Detroit, MI), 535
Sandy's Concert Club (Boston, MA), 33, 95, 240, 596
Sandy's Jazz Revival (club) (Beverly, MA), 209, 254, 322, 549, 567
Santa Barbara Blues Society Concert (Santa Barbara, CA), 137
Santa Cruz Blues Festival (Santa Cruz, CA), 30
Santa Monica Civic Auditorium (see: Civic Auditorium, Santa Monica, CA)
Santa Rosa Folk Festival (Santa Rosa, CA), 98, 120, 339
Santiago, Burnell, 202
Sara Mayo Hospital (New Orleans, LA), 420-421
Saratoga Club (New York, NY), 385
Satan's Den (club) (Cincinnati, OH), 372, 535
Satellite (label), 510
Saugatuck Jazz Festival (Saugatuck, MI), 447
Saunders, Red, 564, 566
Saunders, Robert "Dusty," 288
Sautter, C. Chris, 427
Savage Boys (group), The, 91
Saville Theater (London, Eng.), 157, 224
Savoy, Ashton, 547
Savoy (label), 37, 38, 164, 171, 181, 182, 212, 238, 253, 300, 329, 364, 365, 366, 375, 400, 403, 406, 417, 470, 503, 510, 515, 550, 564
Savoy Ballroom (Chicago, IL), 383, 564
Savoy Ballroom (Los Angeles, CA), 86, 215
Savoy Ballroom (New York, NY), 44, 88, 136, 200, 281, 298, 385, 405, 446, 447, 464, 496, 523, 581
Savoy Ballroom Band, 298
Savoy Ballroom Five (band), 279
Savoy Bohemians (band), 221
Savoy Club (Boston, MA), 300, 406
Savoy Club (Chicago, IL), 251
Savoy Club (Los Angeles, CA), 372
Savoy Club (Richmond, CA), 55, 188, 357, 439, 527
Savoy Club (San Francisco, CA), 76, 98, 213, 240, 339, 393, 435, 440, 494, 516
Savoy Eight (band), 298
Savoy Hotel (London, Eng.), 245
Savoy Theater (Atlantic City, NJ), 222, 351, 472, 496, 540
Savoy Theater (Chicago, IL), 68
Savoys (group), The, 302
Sawdust Trail (club) (Chicago, IL), 359, 476
Sax, Dave, 449
Saxes Lounge (Chicago, IL), 169
Saxony Motor Inn (Edmonton, Can.), 375
Saydisc (label), 35, 44, 382, 573
Saydisc-Matchbox (label), 550
Sayles, Charles "Charlie," **449**, *449*, 578
Scales, Alonzo, 503
Scandinavian Blues Association Concert (Orebro, Swed.), 154, 439
Scene (club), The (New York, NY), 90, 93, 149, 208, 210, 224, 228, 304, 308, 383, 585
Schaffer, Ed, 58, 589
Scheir, Bob, 106
Schiedt, Duncan, 50, 166
Schiffman, Jack, 216, 538
Schlitz Beer (product), 390
Scholar Coffeehouse (Minneapolis, MN), 342
School for the Blind (New York, NY), 369
Schoolboy Cleve (see: White, Cleve)
Schoukroun, Guy, 37, 165, 286, 465
Schubert Theater (Los Angeles, CA), 459
Schuss Mountain Jazz Symposium (Mancelona, MI), 423
Schuur, Diane, 538
Schwabinger Krankenhaus Hospital (Munich, Ger.), 292
Scobey, Bob, 36, 139, 148, 373
Scolly Square Theater (Boston, MA), 70, 82
Score (label), 141
Scotch Brand Recording Tape (product), 114
Scotch Mist (club) (Chicago, IL), 157
Scott, Ada, 70
Scott, Cecil, 44, 83
Scott, Dot, 480
Scott, Frank, 200, 202, 233, 371, 396, 456
Scott, Genevia (see: Sylvester, Hannah)
Scott, Genevia, 491
Scott, H. W., 70
Scott, Hammond, 301
Scott, James, 71, 424
Scott, Mabel, 76
Scott, Mamie, 274
Scott, Ray, 286
Scotty's (club) (Chicago, IL), 294
Scotty's Rock 'n' Roll Inn (Chicago, IL), 286
Scout (label), 156, 165, 166, 246, 266, 366, 504, 553
Scruggs, Irene, 136, 380, **450**, 465
Scruggs, Leazar "Baby," 450
Seals, Baby, 558
Seals, Frank "Son," 305, 311, 399 **450-451**, *451*, 530, 532
Seals, Jim "Son," 450
Seaport Museum (New York, NY), 283
Searles Gospel Singers (group), 378
Sears, Al, 252
Seattle Pop Festival (Duvall, WA), 46, 125, 359
Seattle World's Fair (Seattle, WA), 556
Second Chance (club) (Ann Arbor, MI), 33, 596
Second Fret (club) (Philadelphia, PA), 132, 141, 147, 177, 210, 218, 239, 243, 257, 260, 272, 366, 429, 504, 548
See See Rider Blues Girl (billing), 61
Seeds of Man (book), 206
Seeger, Charles, 130
Seeger, Pete, 69, 141, 147, 174, 194, 206, 231, 257, 319, 348, 365, 366, 503, 504, 505
Segal Theater (Philadelphia, PA), 331
Seibert, Fred, 528
Selah Jubilee Singers (group), 91
Sellers, "Brother" John, 69, 70, 110, **452-453**, *452*, 466, 503
Sells-Eloto (tour), 396
Selma University (Selma, AL), 144, 474
Selvin, Sam, 540
Semaine du Jazz Concert (Paris, Fr.), 229
Semien, "Ivory" Lee, 43, **453**, 582, 583
Semien, Sidney (Rockin' Sydney), 95, 241, 391, **453**, 547
Seminole, Paul, 414
Sensation (label), 95, 238
Sensation Club (Detroit, MI), 238
Sepia Mae West (billing), The 134
Serenaders (band) (Lovie Austin), 360
Serenaders (band) (Lloyd Hunter), 481
Serenaders (band) (Eugene Watt), 379
Serock (label), 74
Sesqui-Centennial International Exposition (Philadelphia, PA), 496
Sesserly, Willie B., 395
Session, Arnella, 522
Session (label), 336, 591, 592
Seven Black Aces (band), 439
7-11 Club (St. Louis, MO), 313
708 Club (Chicago, IL), 32, 35, 93, 130, 161, 169, 181, 208, 268, 269, 271, 289, 294, 317, 343, 344, 359, 388, 393, 394, 424, 442, 444, 529, 559, 570

721 Club (New York, NY), 385
Seventh Day Adventist Church (Alabama?), 411
78 Quarterly (magazine), 235, 297, 410, 487
77 (label), 49, 50, 79, 203, 243, 330, 340, 381, 420, 437, 490, 545, 573
Seward, Alexander "Alec," 148, 201, 276, 280, 283, 293, 366, 368, **453-454**, *454*, 503, 504, 505
Seward, Isaac, 453
Seymour, George (see: Erby, John)
Shaboo Inn (Mansfield, CT), 33, 132, 240, 367, 412, 468, 500, 504
Shad, Bob, 215
Shad (label), 322, 548
Shade, Will (Son Brimmer), 62, 98, 264, 326, 327, 337, 393, 398, **454-455**
Shade, Will, Sr., 454
Shadow Lawn Cemetery (Birmingham, AL), 175
Shadowland Ballroom (New York, NY), 44
Shadowland Ballroom (St. Joseph, MI), 405
Shadows Club (Washington, DC), 195
Shakespeare Theater (Liverpool, Eng.), 256
Shakespeare Theater (Stratford, CT), 346
Shakey Jake (see: Harris, James)
Shakey Walter (see: Horton, Walter)
Shaleey's Pizza Parlour (Vancouver, Can.), 375
Shalimar Club (Oakland, CA), 213
Shamrock Club (Chicago, IL), 574
Shamrock Lounge (DeKalb, IL), 334, 596
Shangri-la Lounge (Chicago, IL) (see also: Earl's Shangri-La Lounge), 294, 340, 405
Shapiro, Ben, 586
Shapiro, Nat, 31, 475
Sharkey's Kings of Dixieland (band), 373
Sharp (label), 99, 212
Shavers, Charlie, 256
Shaw, Arnold, 47, 158, 190, 191, 299, 528, 538, 557, 589
Shaw, Artie, 406
Shaw, Clarence, 73
Shaw, Louis, 456
Shaw, Robert "Fud," **455**, *455*
Shaw, Thomas Edgar "Tom," 276, **456**, *456*, 470
Shaw, Willie, Jr., 456
Shaw State Prison Farm (Huntsville, TX), 317
Shaw University (Raleigh, NC), 116
Shaw's Food Market (store) (Austin, TX), 455
Shea Stadium (New York, NY), 100, 219, 254, 296, 543
Shead, Gary, 195
Sheardeforee, Ann, 338
Shearing, George, 567
Shea's Hippodrome Theater (Buffalo, NY), 71
Shea's Theater (Buffalo, NY), 51, 310, 540, 545
Shea's Theater (Toronto, Can.), 540
Sheba (label), 567
Shed Club, The (Robbins, IL), 460
Sheftell, Joe, 80
Sheftell's Creole Fashion Revue Company (tour), 80
Sheid's Plaza (club), (Lindenhurst, NY), 385
Shelby, James "Son," **456**
Shelby County Cemetery (Memphis, TN), 455
Shelby County Hospital (Memphis, TN), 119
Sheldon Art Gallery (Lincoln, NE), 499
Shelly's Manne-Hole (club) (Hollywood/Los Angeles, CA), 53, 188, 254, 375, 389, 520, 523, 527, 567
Shelter (label), 305, 394, 442
Shelter Saloon (club) (San Jose, CA), 393
Shelton, Robert, 101, 206, 557
Shepard, Savanah, 546
Shepheard's Hotel (Cairo, UAR), 256
Sheppards (group), 302
Sheraton Cadillac (hotel) (Detroit, MI), 230
Sheraton Caravan Penthouse (club), The (Edmonton, Can.), 375
Sheraton Motor Cavalier (club) (Saskatoon, Can.), 375
Sheraton Palace (hotel) (San Francisco, CA), 594
Sheraton Park Hotel (Washington, DC), 195, 556-557
Sheraton-Tenny Club (Queens, NY), 316
Sheridan Square Theater (Pittsburgh, PA), 70
Sherill, James, 552
Sherman, Robert, 196
Sherman Blackwell Club (Chicago, IL), 221
Sherman Hotel (see: Hotel Sherman)
Shertser, Peter, 106
Shestack, Melvin, 441
Shigley, D., 42
Shiers Coffee House (Toronto, Can.), 148
Shilkret, Nat, 496
Shiloh Baptist Church (Greenville, FL), 111
Shiloh Baptist Church (Houston, TX), 507, 531
Shiloh Baptist Church Cemetery (Blanchard/Mooringsport, LA), 318
Shines, John "Johnny," 35, 50, 62, 95, 183, 246, 266, 276, 280, 288, 289, 292, 294, 340, 396, 400, 410, **457-459**, *458*, 478, 493, 531, 535, 552, 586
Shines, John, Sr., 457
Shining Trumpets (book), 229, 397, 493, 508, 591, 594
Ship Shore Lounge (Chicago, IL), 110
Shirley (label), 28, 302
Shirley & Lee (duo), 60
Shirley's (club) (Chicago, IL), 594
Sho-Bar (New Orleans, LA), 158
Sho Biz Restaurant (Houston, TX), 84
Shoe Shine Johnny (see: Shines, John)
Shook, W. D., III, M.D., 191
Short, J. D., 169, **459-460**, *459*, 470, 569
Short, Preston, 459
Shorty George (see: Johnson, James "Stump")
Show & Tell (club) (Chicago, IL), 404
Show Boat (club), The (Los Angeles, CA), 308
Show Boat (club) (Oakland, CA), 373
Show of Shows (concert) (New York, NY), 542
Show Time (label), 232
Showboat (club), The (Houston, TX), 243
Showboat (club), The (Philadelphia, PA), 113, 157, 388, 527, 538
Showboat (club), The (Vallejo, CA), 188
Showboat (club), The (Washington, DC), 257, 588
Showboat Lounge (Silver Spring, MD), 254
Showboat Sari-S (club) (Chicago, IL), 108, 148, 506
Showcase (club), The (Oakland, CA), 308, 431, 519-520, 567, 586
Shower, Elijah, 460
Shower, Hudson (Little Hudson), 280, 342, **460**
Shreveport Home Wreckers (band), 589
Shrimp Walk (club) (Chicago, IL), 381
Shrine & Elks Indoor Circuses (tour), 360
Shrine Auditorium (Los Angeles, CA), 113, 205, 216, 253, 304, 309, 345, 378, 435, 566, 567, 588
Shrine Exposition Hall (Los Angeles, CA), 100, 512-513
Shriners Auditorium (Dallas, TX), 243
Shubert Theater (New York, NY), 542
Shubert Theater (Newark, NJ), 254, 541
Shuffle Inn (New York, NY), 221, 583
Shufflers (group), The, 338
Shufflin' Sam (see: Brown, Robert)
Shuffordville Cemetery (Lyon, MS), 591
Shug's Cozy Spot (club) (Newark, NJ), 378
Shurman, Dick, 36, 73, 76, 154, 168, 236, 499, 572, 597
Sib (see: Williamson, Sonny Boy)
Siber, Paul, 342
Sibi Club (New York, NY), 254
Side Door (club), The (Oakland, CA), 586
Siena College (Memphis, TN), 33, 132, 138, 240, 389
Sierra Club (Stockton, CA), 154
Sievert, Jon, 97
Sign of the Sun (club) (San Diego, CA), 272
Signature (label), 89, 300
Silas Green From New Orleans (tour), 134, 264, 382, 386, 428, 436, 462, 506, 558
Silas Green Minstrel Show (see: Silas Green From New Orleans)
Silber, Irwin, 142

Silkhairs Club (W. Memphis, AR), 93, 488
Silly Kid, The (see: Floyd, Frank)
Silver City Club (Butte, MT), 492
Silver Creek Plantation (Belzoni, MS), 271
Silver Dollar Cafe (Greenville, MS), 338
Silver Dollar Cafe/Club (Minneapolis, MN), 33, 342, 389
Silver Dollar #2 (club) (Houston, TX), 243
Silver Frolics (club) (Chicago, IL), 321
Silver Kings Band, 338, 443
Silver Moon (club) (Chicago, IL), 437
Silver Shadow Show Lounge (Chicago, IL), 304, 499
Silver Slipper (club), (Dallas, TX), 382
Silver Slipper Club (New Orleans, LA), 300
Silver Slipper Playhouse (San Diego, CA), 298, 525
Silver Star Quartet (group), 282
Silverman, Jerry, 207
Silvertone (label), 125, 475
Silvio's (see: Sylvio's)
Simmons, Al, 509
Simmons, Cary Lee, 80
Simmons, Mack "Little Mac/Mack," 68, 269, 311, 402, 407, 435, **460-461**, *461*, 563, 572
Simmons, Roberta Olivia, 549
Simmons Grade School (St. Louis, MO), 45
Simmons Institute of South Carolina (school), The, 160
Simon Fraser University (Burnaby, Can.), 244
Simone, Nina, 30, 217, 219
Sims, Frances, 242
Sims, Frankie Lee, 232, 244, 357, **461**, *462*
Sims, Henry, 410, 461
Sims, Mac (see: Simmons, Mack)
Sing-In for Peace Concert (New York, NY), 142
Sing Out (magazine), 61, 65, 98, 116, 120, 138, 142, 146, 148, 162, 174, 196, 209, 231, 249, 273, 279, 283, 284, 403, 416, 459, 482, 491, 521, 522, 525, 545, 557
Sing Sing Prison (Ossining, NY), 309
Singer Bowl (Stadium) (New York, NY), 224, 296, 447
Singing Brakeman (billing), The, 441
Singing Christian, The (see: White, Joshua)
Singing Pianist (billing), The, 176
Singing Preacher (billing), The, 553
Singleton, Marge, 52
Singleton's (club) (Houston, TX), 358
Sinkkasten Club (Frankfurt, Ger.), 58
Sire (label), 104, 165, 246, 363
Sire-Blue Horizon (label), 104, 327, 553, 562
Sirens (label), 148, 341, 343, 529
Sissle, Noble, 89, 221, 558, 581
Sisters of Holy Family Chapel & Jesuit Church (New Orleans, LA), 374
Sittin' In With (label) (SIW label), 103, 109, 140, 175, 214, 232, 365, 400, 484, 503, 546, 572
Sitzmark (club) (Chicago, IL), 345
Six Blues-Roots Pianists (book), 381, 414, 479
Six Brown Cats (group), 505
Six O'Clock Club (Scotlandville, LA), 396
606 Club (Chicago, IL), 36
633 Club (Chicago, IL), 444
620 Club (Chicago, IL), 570
1623 Club (Evanston, IL), 369
16th Street Grill (bar) (Memphis, TN), 308
61 Club (Holt, AL), 457
63rd Street Theater (New York, NY), 494, 540
Skin & Cancer Hospital (New York, NY), 137
Skogg, Larry, 59
Sky River Rock Festival (Sultan, WA), 132, 513
Sky River Rock Festival (Tenino, WA), 132, 208, 363
Skylight Theater (Milwaukee, WI), 569
Skyline Club (Pittsburgh, PA), 378, 388
Skyline Night Club (Orlando, FL), 506
Skylock Club (Los Angeles, CA), 55
Skyway Lounge (Chicago, IL), 123
Slack, Freddie, 518
Slader, Hattie, 487
Slapsie Maxie's Club (Hollywood, CA), 542
Slat's (club) (San Francisco, CA), 30, 31, 358, 393, 440
Slaven, Neil, 150, 193
Slick Collins Roadhouse (club) (W. Memphis, AR), 535
Slim Gaillard's Club (San Francisco, CA), 509
Slim Harpo (see: Moore, James)
Slim Jenkins Club (Oakland, CA), 136, 299, 519
Slim Pickens (see: Burns, Eddie)
Sloan, Henry, 409
Slone's Lounge (Los Angeles, CA), 137
Sloppy Joe's (club) (Chicago, IL), 108, 381, 423
Sluefoot Joe (see: Gibson, Clifford)
Slug's (club) (New York, NY), 478
Smalley's Band, 572
Small's Paradise (club) (New York, NY), 31, 44, 83, 113, 157, 253, 300, 385, 405, 481, 550
Small's Paradise West (Los Angeles, CA), 431
Smart Set Company (tour) (Tutt-Whitney) (see also: Georgia Smart Set Minstrels), 472, 558
Smart Set Show (tour), 427
Smart Set Show (tour) (Al Well), 466
Smash (label), 136, 366, 375, 503
Smilin' Faces (club) (Santa Barbara, CA), 468, 531
Smiling Dog Saloon (club) (Cleveland, OH), 33, 336, 500, 596
Smiling Joe (see: Joseph, Pleasant)
Smiling Joe's Blues Trio, 300
Smith, Addie, 480, 481
Smith, Allen George, 468
Smith, Alvin "Al" K. (see: King, Al)
Smith, Anne (see: Rainey, Gertrude)
Smith, Bessie, 37, 56, 84, 109, 110, 134, 142, 144, 173, 179, 195, 196, 230, 245, 254, 274, 276, 279, 295, 296, 314, 322, 392, 420, 421, 423, 427, 428, 448, 450, **462-465**, *463*, 466, 467, 472, 476, 478, 482, 484, 497, 499, 506, 514, 520, 538, 544, 560, 564, 591, 594
Smith, Bessie Mae, 464
Smith, Cal, 280
Smith, Carrie, 465, **465-466**, *465*, 482, 538, 551
Smith, Charles Edward, 368, 428, 468, 485
Smith, Charles Harry Lee, 331
Smith, Clara, 295, 385, 464, **466-467**, *466*, 472
Smith, Clarence "Pinetop," 118, 356, 397, 413, **467-468**, 594
Smith, Claude (Blue Smitty), 427, 442
Smith, Dan, 426
Smith, Drifting (see: Mickle, Elmon)
Smith, Eddie, 251
Smith, Elwood, 556
Smith, Ethel Mae, 360
Smith, Frank W., 470
Smith, Funny Papa/Paper (see: Smith, John)
Smith, George, 465
Smith, George "Harmonica," 53, 91, 269, 398, 407, **468-470**, *469*, 589
Smith, George, Sr., 468
Smith, Gus, 152
Smith, Guy (see: Erby, John)
Smith, Harry, 406
Smith, Harrison, 61
Smith, Harrison, 236
Smith, Hobart, 276
Smith, Honey Boy (see: Whittaker, Hudson)
Smith, Howlin' (see: Smith, John)
Smith, Huey, 60, 103, 202, 293
Smith, Ivy, 145
Smith, James, 241
Smith, Jane (see: Cox, Ida)
Smith, Jimmy, 445
Smith, John T. ("J. T.") "Funny Papa," 95, 456, 460, **470**, 557
Smith, Keith, 165, 203
Smith, Laura, 163
Smith, Leroy, 298, 357
Smith, Mabel (Big Maybelle), 38, 136, 366, **470-472**, *471*
Smith, Mamie, 351, 386, 419, 448, 464, 467, **472-474**, *473*, 533, 560, 580
Smith, Mandy (see: Miles, Elizabeth)
Smith, Mary, 280, 288
Smith, Michael P., 121
Smith, Moses "Whispering," 228, **474**, *474*
Smith, Mossiline, 502
Smith, Pine Top (see: Smith, Clarence)
Smith, Ruby Walker, 464
Smith, Ruth A., 160

Smith, Sam, 467
Smith, Son, 163
Smith, Stan, 270
Smith, Stuff, 44
Smith, Susie (see: Moore, Monette)
Smith, Tab, 536
Smith, Thunder, 243, 244
Smith, Trixie, 172, 464, 472, **474-475**, *475*
Smith, Virginia, 152
Smith, Whispering (see: Smith, Moses)
Smith, William, 462
Smith, William "Smitty," 472
Smith, Willie (Little Willie), 545
Smith, Willie "Long Time," 168
Smith, Willie "The Lion," 221, 474, 518
Smith & Burton (duo), 462
Smithsonian Blues Festival (Washington, DC), 56, 341, 349, 500
Smithsonian Festival of American Folklife (Washington, DC) (see also: Festival of American Folklife), 120, 247, 334, 524
Smithsonian Folk Festival (Washington, DC) (see also: Festival of American Folklife), 230, 250
Smithsonian Folklife Conference (Washington, DC), 265
Smithsonian Institute (government office) (Washington, DC), 466
Smitty & Sadie's Club (Chicago, IL), 402
Smitty's Corner (club) (Chicago, IL), 91, 271, 340, 388, 400, 476, 478, 571
Smitty's Pig Trail Inn (Clarksdale, MS), 591
Smokehouse Charley (see: Dorsey, Thomas A.)
Smoky Babe (see: Brown, Robert)
Smoky Mountain Folk Festival (Gatlinburg, TN), 130
Smoot's (club) (Chicago, IL), 444
Smothers, Abraham "Little Smokey," 476
Smothers, Otis "Smokey," 168, **475-476**, *475*
Sneeze, Bud, 221
Snooks Dillehunt's Plantation (Ashport, TN), 106
Snooky (see: Pryor, James)
Snow, Julie, 100, 129, 146, 177, 186, 194, 210, 218, 231, 258, 272, 295, 363, 391, 426, 513, 552, 561
Snow Flakes Club (New Orleans, LA), 375
Snowden, Elmer, 418
Snyder, Bob, 230
Soap Creek Saloon (Austin, TX), 151
Society Entertainers (band), 221
Sold on Soul Concert (New York, NY), 114, 219
Solid Senders (group), 377
Solid Soul (label), 28
Solo (label), 164, 365, 454, 503
Solo Art (label), 336, 592
Somebody's Angel Child (book), 464
Son (see: Bonds, Son)
Son Joe (see: Lawlars, Ernest)
Sonet (label), 57, 59, 63, 117, 165, 166, 167, 243, 341, 445, 460, 569, 573, 596
Songbird of the South (billing), 428
Songwriters Hall of Fame (organization) (New York, NY), 114
Sonny (see: Terry, Sonny)
Sonny & Jaycee (duo), 96
Sonny T. (see: Terry, Sonny)
Sonny's Place (club) (Seaford, NY), 466
Sonobeat (label), 585
Sonoma State College (Rohnert Park, CA), 330
Sonora (label), 44
Sophie's (club) (Palo Alto, CA), 132, 244, 339, 367, 505
Sotoplay (label), 468, 512
Soul-Blue (group), 312
Soul Bowl (club), The (Dallas, TX), 114
Soul City Club (Buffalo, NY), 527
Soul Lounge (Cincinnati, OH), 535
Soul Man (billing), The, 51
Soul-O (label), 356
Soul Queen (club) (Chicago, IL), 530
Soul Revival Gospel Group, 384
Soul Set (label), 55
Soul Sisters (group), 453
Soulful Mary's Band, 287
Sound Corporation (group), 395
Sound Stage (label), 437
Sound Track Night Club (New Haven, CT), 447
Sounds & Fury (magazine), 249, 481
Sounds Magazine, 310
Sounds of Hawaii (label), 219
Soundtrack (club), The (Denver, CO), 346
South, Eddie, 31
South Bay Jazz Band, 385
South Memphis Jug Band, 128, 139, 163
South Park Lounge (see: Louise's South Park Lounge)
South Shore Nursing Center (Chicago, IL), 524
South Street Seaport (New York, NY), 522
South Texas State Fair (Beaumont, TX), 456
South View Cemetery (Atlanta, GA), 558
Southern (label), 452
Southern Baptist Church (Birmingham, AL), 313
Southern California Hot Jazz Society (Los Angeles, CA), 322, 527
Southern Folk Cultural Group (tour), 142
Southern Folk Cultural Revival Project (organization), 231
Southern Folk Festival (tour), 230, 457
Southern Folklore (label), 508, 509
Southern Harmoneers (group), 91
Southern Illinois University (Carbondale, IL), 39, 313
Southern Illinois University (Edwardsville, IL), 33, 389
Southern Methodist University (Dallas, TX), 113, 195
Southern Nightingale (billing), The, 475
Southern Steak House (club) (Dallas, TX), 382
Southern Students Organizing Committee (organization), 142
Southern Syncopators (band), 484
Southern Travellers (group), The, 31
Southern University (Baton Rouge, LA), 60
Southernaires (band) (Doc Hyder), 221
Southernaires (band) (Clarence Williams), 556
Southland (label), 490, 506
Southland Cafe (Boston, MA), 252
Southland Troubadors (band), 203, 380
Space (label), 55
Spaghettery (club) (Redwood City, CA), 161
Spaghetti Factory (club) (San Francisco, CA), 98
Spand, Charlie, 594
Spand, Son, 64, 290, 315, 354, 524
Spanier, Muggsy, 36
Spanish War Relief Concert (New York, NY), 229
Spann, Frank Houston, 478
Spann, Lucille, 311, 465, **476**, *476*
Spann, Otis, 107, 132, 142, 208, 280, 286, 290, 294, 295, 334, 371, 381, 388, 390, 394, 412, 425, 468, 476, **476-479**, *477*, 491, 547, 577, 595
Spann, Purvis, 407
Spare Rib (group), 302
Spark (label), 28
Sparkasse in Concert (label), 553
Sparkle Paradise Club (Bridge City, TX), 121
Sparks, Aaron ("Pinetop"), 467
Spartanburg General Hospital (Spartanburg, SC), 34
Spaulding, Henry, 460, 514
Spaulding's Club (Santa Cruz, CA), 339
Speakeasy Club, The (Cambridge, MA), 247, 442, 459, 489
Specialty (label), 110, 111, 120, 154, 167, 200, 211, 232, 238, 241, 277, 293, 339, 353, 370, 378, 407, 411, 461, 489, 530, 572
Speckled Red (see: Perryman, Rufus)
Spectrum (club), The (Philadelphia, PA), 132, 219, 352, 585
Speed (label), 580
Speedway (label), 578
Spencer, James, 56
Spencer Memorial Church (New York, NY), 453
Spider Sam (see: McGhee, Walter)
Spider Web (club) (Buffalo, NY), 252, 481
Spider's Web (club) (Oakland, CA), 270
Spiers, Charles, 384
Spikes Brothers Comedy Stars (tour), 360
Spillman, Barbara Jean, 141
Spillman, Gilbert, 141
Spinelli's Club (New Paltz, NY), 348

Spinning Wheel (club) (Kansas City, MO), 518, 550
Spire (label), 533
Spires, Arthur "Big Boy," 168, 225, 244, 395, 476, **479,** *479,* 570
Spires, Benjamin "Bud," 479
Spirit of Minter City (group), The, 286
Spiritual Harmonism Gospel Group, 384
Spirituals to Swing Concert (see: From Spirituals to Swing Concert)
Spivey, Addie (Sweet Peas), 480, **480,** *480,* 482
Spivey, Elton (The Za Zu Girl), 480, **480,** 482
Spivey, Grant, 480, 481
Spivey, Leona, 482
Spivey, Victoria, 103, 175, 280, 281, 288, 295, 351, 465, 466, 480, **480-482,** *480,* 499, 512, 577
Spivey (label), 39, 42, 84, 85, 117, 155, 156, 210, 221, 233, 234, 280, 283, 286, 340, 344, 381, 388, 403, 468, 478, 481, 486, 487, 490, 491, 499, 520, 532, 550, 569, 574, 577, 595
Spolestra, Mark, 207, 330
Spoon (see: Witherspoon, James)
Spooners Club (Irwinville, LA), 396
Spoonful (label), 156
Sportree Musical Bar (Detroit, MI), 279
Sports Arena (Copenhagen, Den.), 224
Sports Arena (Dallas, TX), 179
Sports Arena (Long Beach, CA), 585
Sports Arena (Toledo, OH), 208, 260, 278, 389, 549
Sports Guild (club) (Manchester, Eng.), 283
Sportsman Club (Oakland, CA), 353, 431, 512
Sportsman's Club/Lounge (Chicago, IL), 123, 334, 397, 437, 461, 596
Sportsman's Lounge (Los Angeles, CA), 527
Sportsman's Park (Chicago, IL), 46, 310
Sportsmen of Rhythm (group), 550
Sportstown Club (Buffalo, NY), 527
Spot (club), The (Chicago, IL), 65, 181, 501
Spot (club), The (Gary, IN), 388, 594
Spot (label), 547
Spotlight Club, The (New York, NY), 164, 300, 406
Spottswood, Richard "Dick," 109, 175, 259, 515, 562
Spradley, Bernice, 524
Sprecher, Muggsy, 314
Spriggs, Walter, 562
Springer Opera House (Columbus, GA), 427
Springfield Baptist Church Cemetery (Covington, GA), 546
Springfield Minstrels (tour), 153
Sprott, Horace, **482-483,** *482*
Sprott Plantation (Sprott, AL), 482
Spruel, Rossell Hattie Bell, 371
Spry (label), 53
Sputnik Bar (Houston, TX), 243, 572
Square Deal Cafe (W. Memphis, AR), 308
Square Deal Club (Chicago, IL), 271, 529, 570, 574, 594
Square Rigger (club), The (Napa, CA), 161
Squeeze Club (Chicago, IL), 208, 305, 563
Squire Girshback's Dixieland Jubilee (concert) (Sacramento, CA), 36
Squires (group), The, 211, 224
Squires Lounge (Chicago, IL), 110
Squyres Club (Chicago, IL), 297
St. Anthony Hospital (Chicago, IL), 345
St. Bernard Civic Auditorium (New Orleans, LA), 437
St. Bridget's of Erin Church (St. Louis, MO), 313
St. Charles Cemetery (Huntington, NY), 497
St. Charles Reformatory (Chicago, IL), 516
St. Elizabeth's Hospital (Boston, MA), 286
St. Francis Church (Houston, TX), 122
St. Francis Hospital (Blue Island, IL), 407
St. Francis of Assisi Parish Hall (Houston, TX), 122
St. Francis Parish Hall (E. Palo Alto, CA), 439
St. Genesius Medal (award), 543
St. James AMH Cemetery (Convent, LA), 326
St. James Cemetery (Avalon, MS), 257
St. James Church (Chicago, IL), 582
St. James Hospital (Newark, NJ), 212
St. James Theater (Ashbury Park, NJ), 82
St. John Gospel Singers (group), 307
St. John's Catholic School for Boys (Leavenworth, KS), 375
St. Joseph Hospital (Detroit, MI), 252
St. Joseph Hospital (Ft. Worth, TX), 518
St. Lawrence Centre (club) (Toronto, Can.), 278, 336
St. Louis All-Stars (band), 84
St. Louis City Hospital (St. Louis, MO), 438
St. Louis Club (St. Louis, MO), 297, 552, 568
St. Louis Combo (band), 338
St. Louis Country Club (St. Louis, MO), 313
St. Louis Jazz Club Concert (St. Louis, MO), 414
St. Louis Jimmy (see: Oden, James)
St. Louis Mac (see: Simmons, Mack)
St. Louis #2 Cemetery (New Orleans, LA), 204, 419, 421
St. Louis Publishing Company (organization) (St. Louis, MO), 481
St. Louis Ragfest (concert) (St. Louis, MO), 313, 322
St. Louis Ragtime & Jazz Festival (St. Louis, MO), 313
St. Louis Ragtime Festival (St. Louis, MO), 84, 230, 316, 423
St. Louis Symphony Orchestra, 304
St. Louis Theater (St. Louis, MO), 541
St. Louis University (St. Louis, MO), 304
St. Louis World's Fair (St. Louis, MO), 507
St. Luke's Baptist Church (Chicago,IL), 536
St. Luke's Hospital (New York, NY), 231
St. Marks Hall (Richmond, CA), 121
St. Mary Abbot's Hospital (London, Eng.), 224
St. Mary's Cemetery (Evergreen, IL), 269
St. Michele Club (Montreal, Can.), 182
St. Peter Cemetery (Brownsville, TN), 57
St. Peter's (club) (New York, NY), 187
St. Peter's Hospital (Albany, NY), 386
St. Peter's Lutheran Church (New York, NY), 256
St. Regis Hotel (New York, NY), 405
St. Rose Graduate School (Albany, NY), 245
St. Rose's Home (nursing home) (New York, NY), 83
Stackhouse, Houston, 140, 268, 290, 398, 399, 412, 442, **483-484,** *483,* 560
Staff (label), 216, 238, 535
Stafford, George, 484
Stafford, Mary, **484,** *484*
Stag (label), 518
Stage Lounge (Chicago, IL), 45, 108
Stage Number One Club (Los Angeles, CA), 137
Stambler, Irwin, 47, 54, 118, 142, 158, 196, 201, 209, 219, 305, 331, 345, 347, 352, 360, 412, 433, 512, 538, 586
Stampen Club (Stockholm, Swed.), 497
Standard Theater (Philadelphia, PA), 48, 81, 152, 298, 357, 463, 464, 467, 472, 494, 540, 583
Standish, Tony, 414
Stanford University (Stanford, CA), 249, 393, 420
Stanley Theater (Pittsburgh, PA), 523
Stan's Pad (club) (Chicago, IL), 523, 588
Stanton Theater (Philadelphia, PA), 279
Staples, Roebuck, 70, 410
Star Casino (club) (Reno, NV), 78
Star Dust (club) (Chicago, IL), 93
Star Talent (label), 101, 510
Star Theater (Philadelphia, PA), 463
Star Theater (Pittsburgh, PA), 144
Star Theater (Streveport, LA), 172, 350
Stardust (label), 61
Stardust Club/Lounge (Chicago, IL), 36, 41, 123
Stardust Inn (Chester, PA), 308
Stardust Inn (Waldorf, MD), 158
Stardust Inn (Washington, DC), 383
Stardust Lounge (see: Dottie's Stardust Lounge)
Stardust Trail Lounge (Chicago, IL), 35
Starkey Brothers (duo), 334
Starlight Club (Chicago, IL), 123

Starlight Club (New Orleans, LA), 86, 436
Starlight Club (Seffner, FL), 104
Starlite Grill (Cleveland, OH), 145
Starr, Milton, 463
Stars of Alabama (group), 457
Stars of Bethel (group), 497
Starwood (club), The (Hollywood/Los Angeles, CA), 190, 307, 513, 520
State Fair Music Hall (Dallas, TX), 352, 431
State Historical Museum (Jackson, MS), 569
State Lake Theater (Chicago, IL), 70, 540
State Line (club) (Lake Tahoe, NV), 298
State Penitentiary (Walla Walla, WA), 346
State School for Deaf and Blind Children (St. Augustine, FL), 111
State School for the Blind (Macon, GA), 369
State Street Four (band), 480
State Street Ramblers (band), 582
State Street Swingers (band), 84
State Theater (Chicago, IL), 541
State Theater (Hartford, CT), 298, 536
State Theater (Harrisburg, PA), 43, 82
State Theater (Jersey City, NJ) (see also: Keith's State Theater, Jersey City, NJ), 71
State Theater (New Brunswick, NJ), 82
State Theater (New York, NY) (see also: Loew's State Theater, New York, NY), 221, 581
State Theater (Newark, NJ), 581
State Theater (Pawtucket, RI), 581
State University of New York at Albany (Albany, NY), 32, 388
State University of New York at Buffalo (Buffalo, NY), 93, 117, 132, 187, 208, 218, 296, 322, 336, 389, 548
States (label), 199, 246, 394, 398, 484, 548
Statler Hilton Downtown Room (club) (Buffalo, NY), 254
Stax (label), 60, 104, 106, 240, 304, 327, 357, 450, 510
Steamboat Exchange (club) (Vicksburg, MS), 379
Steamboat Natchez (see: S. S. Natchez)
Stean Cemetery (Malakoff, TX), 518
Stearns, Genevieve, 139
Stearns, Jean, 559
Stearns, Marshall W., 559
Steele, Buster, 179
Steele's Tavern (Toronto, Can.), 280
Steeplechase Park (amusement center) (Brooklyn, NY), 153
Steig, Jeremy, 218
Steil's Wiggling Wagon (club) (New Orleans, LA), 420
Stemp Hall (St. Paul, MN), 434
Stern Grove Concert (San Francisco, CA), 420
Stevens, Norman, 467
Stevens, Vol, 454
Steve's Chicken Shack (club) (Gary, IN), 35
Stewart, Alan, 213
Stewart, Billy, 250
Stewart, Jack, 245
Stewart, Rex, 375
Stewart, Slam, 466
Stewart-Baxter, Derrick, 61, 72, 79, 84, 93, 109, 136, 178, 200, 222, 234, 282, 295, 357, 374, 382, 419, 474, 492, 507, 582
Sticks McGhee and his Buddies, 364
Sticky Wicket Pub (Hopkinton, MA), 45, 550
Stidham, Arbee, **484-485**, *485*, 576
Stidham, Ernest, 484
Stidham, Luddie, 484
Stiff, John, 160
Stiggars, Lula, 292
Stilles, Ted, 481
Sting (club), The (Burlington, VT), 33, 286, 523
Stingrey (Stingray) (club) (Chicago, IL), 51, 95, 104, 289, 304, 310, 435, 572
Stinson (label), 147, 206, 317, 503
Stirling High School (Greenville, SC), 556
Stoat, Joe C., 460
Stockbridge Inn (Stockbridge, MA), 245
Stokes, Carl B., 311
Stokes, Curtis, 486
Stokes, Frank, 62, 104, 247, 264, **485-486**, *485*, 574
Stokes, Georgia, 486
Stokes, Helen, 486
Stokes, Moses, 427, 462
Stokes, Roosevelt, 486
Stolper, Darryl, 28, 252, 546, 580
Stomp (label), 110
Stompers (band), 66, 67
Stompy Stevedores (band), 405
Stone, Gerry, 448
Stone, Jessie, 586
Stone, Joe C., 460
Stone Park (Chicago, IL), 46
Stone Steps Bar (Encinitas, CA), 134
Stoneman, Luther, 43
Stormy Forest (label), 219
Stormy Forest Production Company (organization) (Chicago, IL), 218
Stormy's Club (Chicago, IL), 499, 570
Stormy's Inn (Chicago, IL), 476, 479
Story of the Blues (book), 43, 56, 79, 89, 107, 125, 139, 173, 264, 274, 344, 356
Storyville (label), 39, 57, 63, 69, 79, 86, 117, 140, 165, 167, 177, 263, 280, 340, 341, 367, 368, 396, 401, 414, 426, 478, 479, 490, 504, 505, 532, 547, 569, 573, 577, 595
Storyville Club (Boston, MA), 116, 155, 194, 348, 375, 538, 556
Storyville Club (Frankfort, Ger.), 313
Storyville Club (New York, NY), 254, 466, 523-524, 550
Storyville Magazine, 45, 84, 136, 204, 254, 257, 362, 409, 428, 497, 508, 533, 551, 558
Storyville Ramblers (band), 203, 506
Stouffer's Inn (Indianapolis, IN), 316
Stouffer's Riverfront Inn (St. Louis, MO), 304
Stovall, Houston, 484
Stovall, Jewell "Babe," 236, 290, **486-487**, *487*
Stovall, Tom, 486
Stovall Plantation (Stovall, MS), 62
Strachwitz, Chris/C., 29, 30, 58, 121, 139, 162, 242, 244, 246, 250, 268, 324, 329, 333, 382, 455, 462, 514, 517, 595
Straight Theater (San Francisco, CA), 296
Straine, James "Doc," 73, 351, 581
Strand (label), 117
Strand Theater (Brooklyn, NY), 541
Strand Theater (Calgary, Can.), 541
Strand Theater (E. Liverpool, OH), 82
Strand Theater (Halifax, NC), 81
Strand Theater (New York, NY), 362, 536
Strangers Cemetery (St. Simons Island, GA), 231
Stratford (Jazz) Festival (Stratford, Can.), 447, 566
Streakers Rated-X Revue (show), 405
Street Rustler (billing), 589
Streetmonders (group), The, 197
Streets of Paris Club (Hollywood, CA), 253, 385
Strings of Rhythm (band), 283
Stripling, Malvina, 505
Strollers Club (New York, NY), 373, 467
Strong, Henry, 269, 476
Strowd, Leo, 133
Strowd, Thomas, 133
Strozier, Dorothy, 42
Stuckey, Henry, 272, 273, **487-488**
Stuckey, Shuke, 487
Stuckey, Will, 487
Stuckey's Candy Store (Como, MS), 363
Student Non-Violent Coordinating Committee (organization), 142
Stuyvesant Casino (hall) (New York, NY), 39, 90, 145, 197, 229, 365, 406, 447, 481, 503, 584
Suburban Inn (Milwaukee, WI), 360
Subway (club), The (Chicago, IL), 397
Subway Club (Kansas City, MO), 518
Subway Grill (Chester, PA), 549
Subway Lounge (Jackson, MS), 395
Suddoth, J. Guy (see: Erby, John)
Suds of Rhythm (band), 225
Sue (label), 272
Sugar Blue (pseudonym), 481
Sugar Foot Sam From Alabam (tour), 410
Sugar Foot Stompers (band), 405
Sugar Girls Medicine Show (tour), 312
Sugar Hill Club (New York, NY), 173
Sugar Hill Club (San Francisco, CA), 96, 141, 161, 185, 239, 243, 280, 330, 366, 375, 447, 503, 527, 533, 559, 566, 591
Sugar Lou (pseudonym), 405
Sugar Shack (club) (Boston, MA), 114
Sugarmen (group), 366
Suggs, Doug, 488

Suggs, James Douglas, 488
Suggs, Lee S., 488
Sullivan, Ed, 298, 359, 406, 527, 542
Sullivan, Joe, 518
Sullivan, Maxine, 544
Sulton (label), 328
Sumlin, Hubert, **488-489**, *488*
Summer Arts Festival (Tuxedo Park, NY), 481
Summer Festival (Milwaukee, WI), 114, 158, 309
Summer Festival Show (tour), 219, 519
Summers, Lynn, 106
Summerthing Concert (Boston, MA), 210
Summit (club), The (Hollywood, CA), 375
Summit (label), 88
Summuel, Virginia, 461
Sumner High School (St. Louis, MO), 45
Sun (label), 93, 104, 130, 175, 176, 179, 246, 291, 337, 400, 401, 407, 443, 488, 510
Sun Valley Motor Motel (Harlingen, TX), 84
Sunday, Billy, 472
Sundown (club), The (Los Angeles, CA), 586
Sunny Jim (see: Watson, Johnny)
Sunny South Singers (group), The, 53
Sunnyland (label), 479
Sunnyland Cotton Pickers (band), 221
Sunnyland Slim (see: Luandrew, Albert)
Sunset (label), 302, 400
Sunset Beer Garden (New York, NY), 385
Sunset Cafe/Club (Chicago, IL), 31, 254, 274, 438
Sunset Club (Kansas City, MO), 405, 518
Sunset Club (New York, NY), 385
Sunset Crystal Palace (hall) (Kansas City, MO), 88, 518, 550
Sunset Inn (Jackson, MS), 395
Sunset Royal Band, 252
Sunset Series Concert (Boston, MA), 100, 309, 432
Sunshine Club (Orlando, FL), 111
Sunshine Exposition Show and Carnival (tour), 564
Sunshine Lounge (Lawrence, NY), 90
Sunshine Orchestra, 288
Sunshine Record Company (organization), 424
Sunshine Sammy Troupe (tour), 385
Super Attractions Big Show of Stars (tour), 45
Super Cosmic Joy-Scout Jamboree (concert) (Chicago, IL), 54, 100, 389
Super Suds of Rhythm (band), 225
Superdisc (label), 263, 454
Supraphon (label), 199, 408
Supreme (label), 154, 353, 586
Supreme Blues (label), 412
Supreme Edition (book), 441
Supremes (group), The, 114
Susie (see: Edwards, Susie)
Sussex (label), 572
Sussex University (Brighton, Eng.), 234
Sutch, Screamin' Lord, 220
Sutherland, Sandy, 571
Sutherland Hotel (Chicago, IL), 93, 389, 476, 566, 586, 595
Suzie-Q Club (Hollywood, CA), 377
Swaggie (label), 351
Swain's Hollywood Follies (tour), 441
Swan (label), 406
Swan Club (Chicago, IL), 397
Swanee Club Revue (group), 467
Swanee Inn (Hollywood, CA), 518
Swann's Paradise Bar (Grand Rapids, MI), 312
Swarthmore College (Swarthmore, PA), 147, 548
Swarthmore Folk Festival (Swarthmore, PA), 187, 249, 521
Sweatman, Wilbur, 558
Sweet as the Showers of Rain (book), 57, 107, 162, 178, 226, 229, 252, 328, 370, 391, 392, 417, 455, 486
Sweet Basil Club (New York, NY), 529
Sweet Lips Club (Chicago, IL), 260
Sweet Mama Stringbean Direct from St. Louis (billing), 543
Sweet Papa Stovepipe (see: Peebles, McKinley)
Sweet Pea (club), The (Chicago, IL), 260, 340
Sweet Pea (club) (Santa Monica, CA), 154
Sweet Peas(e) (see: Spivey, Addie)
Sweet Peruna Jazz Band, 497
Sweet Queen Bee's Lounge (Chicago, IL), 91, 132, 287, 404, 412, 450, 549
Sweet Stavin' Chain Band, 429
Sweetback Band, 572
Sweethearts of Rhythm (band), 470
Sweet's Ballroom (Los Angeles, CA), 308
Sweets Mill Folk Festival (San Diego, CA), 276
Swing Auditorium (San Bernardino, CA), 346
Swing Brother (see: Burns, Eddie)
Swing Club (Hollywood, CA), 74, 298
Swing Club (San Francisco, CA), 507
Swing Journal (magazine), 114, 448
Swing Shop Boys (band), 385
Swinger's Lounge (Miami, FL), 310
Swingin' (label), 154, 497
Swinging Door Club, The (San Mateo, CA), 321
Swingland Club (Chicago, IL), 31, 110
Swingmaster (label), 594
Swingtime (label), 188, 191, 357, 519
Swingtime-Downbeat (label), 111
Swoon (label), 456
Sydenham Hospital (New York, NY), 529
Sykes, Johnny, 490
Sykes, Roosevelt, 63, 66, 67, 110, 118, 158, 199, 297, 326, 334, 336, 343, 403, 413, 478, 479, **489-491**, *489*, 494, 514, 515, 560, 564, 574
Sykes, Wallie, 490
Sykes, Walter, 339, 490
Sylvania Award, 195
Sylvester, Hannah, **491-492**, *491*
Sylvester's (club) (Chicago, IL), 57, 349
Sylvio's (Silvio's) (club/lounge) (Chicago, IL), 35, 69, 69-70, 91, 93, 99, 122, 132, 148, 155, 188, 213, 239, 243, 259, 271, 294, 305, 322, 334, 341, 342, 343, 345, 370, 388, 389, 442, 460, 493, 499, 559, 574, 576, 577
Symphony Hall (Boston, MA), 113, 253, 536
Symphony Hall (Newark, NJ), 114, 431
Synanon Drug Treatment Center (Santa Monica, CA), 417
Syncopators (band), 472
Syphen, Rosie, 69

TB Hospital (Houston, TX), 572
T-Bone Walker Memorial Concert (Los Angeles, CA), 137, 190, 430, 468, 520, 523, 544
T.D.S. (label), 334
TK (label), 42, 68, 266
T-99 Club (Osceola, AR), 303
TNT (label), 423
TOBA Circuit, 48, 73, 80, 139, 144, 145, 159, 172, 227, 229, 279, 295, 298, 331, 350, 357, 380, 405, 428, 450, 463, 464, 466, 467, 474, 531, 540, 550, 558, 559, 564, 580, 583
TRCT (label), 545
T. V. Slim (see: Wills, Oscar)
Taborian Park (Waco, TX), 274
Taggart, Blind Joe, 555, 556
Tail Dragger, The (see: Jones, James)
Tail Dragger Band, 410
Tailgate Ramblers (band), 229, 230
Take Three Coffee House (New York, NY), 300
Takoma (label), 54, 553, 573, 574
Takoma-Sonet (label), 553
Talbot, Johnny, 421, 512
Talisman (club), The (New Orleans, LA), 101
Talk of the Town (club) (St. Louis, MO), 338
Talk of the Town Club (Beverly Hills, CA), 74
Tallahassee Tight (pseudonym), 280
Tally Ho Club (Highwood, IL), 388
Tally Ho Club (Philadelphia, PA), 447
Tambo Lounge (Chicago, IL), 345
Tamiment Institute (organization), 543
Tampa Red (see: Whittaker, Hudson)
Tangerine (label), 113, 299
Tangerine Music Inc. (organization), 113
Tangiers 72 Jazz Festival (Tangier, Morocco), 195
Tangle Eye (see: Horton, Walter)
Tanglewood Festival (Lenox, MA), 452, 503
Tanglewood Jazz Concert (Tanglewood, MA), 309
Tango (pseudonym), 552
Tanner, Nora Belle, 205
Tappet Inn (Los Angeles, CA), 527
Tarheel Slim (see: Bunn, Alden)
Tarpon (label), 175

Tate, Baby (see: Tate, Charles)
Tate, Buddy, 447, 491
Tate, Charles "Baby," 185, **492,** *492*
Tate, Erskine, 383, 450
Tate, Ira, 492
Tate, Isom, 492
Tatum, Art, 116, 518, 531, 550
Tavern Lounge (Detroit, MI), 96, 535, 577
Tay May Club (Chicago, IL), 208, 271, 322, 345, 388
Taylor, Aaron "Buddy," 562
Taylor, Arthur "Montana," 229, **492-493,** *493*
Taylor, Billy, 588
Taylor, Carrie, 145
Taylor, Charley, 463
Taylor, Daniel, 426
Taylor, Dudlow, 268
Taylor, Eddie, 41, 150, 246, 271, 289, 294, 307, 337, 391, 410, 433, 434, 435, 438, 439, 468, 488, **493-494,** *493*, 531, 563, 591
Taylor, Emma, 505
Taylor, Eva, 222, 350, 351, **494-497,** *495*, 533
Taylor, Floyd, 532
Taylor, Hound Dog (see: Taylor, Theodore)
Taylor, Jim, 83
Taylor, John/Johnny "Blues," 499
Taylor, Johnnie Harrison, 497
Taylor, Johnny Lamar, 51, 133, 212, **497-499,** *497*
Taylor, Joyce, 499
Taylor, Koko, *498*, 499, **499,** 596
Taylor, Larry, 494
Taylor, Lizzie, 252
Taylor, Lula, 426
Taylor, Mick, 307
Taylor, Milton, 494
Taylor, Montana (see: Taylor, Arthur)
Taylor, Robert, 499
Taylor, Robert, 499
Taylor, Ted, 311, 499
Taylor, Theodore "Hound Dog," 41, 244, 271, 412, 450, 499, **499-501,** *500*, 570, 578
Taylor & Mack Troupe (tour), 396
Teagarden, Jack, 141, 465
Tebo, Arthur, 508
Technical High School (Omaha, NE), 215
Teddy's Club (Milwaukee, WI), 151, 156, 494, 588
Tee, Willie, 437
Teenage Gospel Singers (group), 187
Temple, Johnnie/Johnny, 35, 80, 181, 272, 273, 290, 349, 354, 355, **501,** *501*
Temple, Shirley, 360
Temple, Tobe, 501
Temple Hall, The (New Orleans, LA), 101, 167, 243
Temple Music Festival (Ambler, PA), 240
Temple Room (club) (Baton Rouge, LA), 269
Temple Theater (Cleveland, OH), 428
Temple Theater (Saginaw, MI), 70
Temple University (Ambler, PA), 51, 240
Temple University (Philadelphia, PA), 147, 389, 420
Tempo Tap Club (Chicago, IL), 216, 343, 576
Tempo-Tone (label), 181, 268, 294, 340
Tempo Toppers (group), 411
1015 Club (Chicago, IL), 99, 259, 342, 574
1049 Club (Chicago, IL), 394
Tenampa Ballroom (Chicago, IL), 104, 497
Tennessee Agricultural & Industrial State University (Nashville, TN), 404
Tennessee Chocolate Drops (band), 56, 348
Tennessee Gabriel (see: McGhee, Walter)
Tennessee House (club) (W. Memphis, AR), 337
Tenth Street Inn (club) (Berkeley, CA), 213, 393
Ter-Drops (group), 236
Terkel, Studs, 69, 251, 370, 485, 569
Terrace Ballroom (Salt Lake City, UT), 310
Terrace Lounge (Norwalk, CT), 90
Terrace Room (club) (Jacksonville, FL), 432
Terrell, Pha, 76
Terrell, Reuben, 502
Terrell, Saunders, 502
Terry, Clark, 567
Terry, Doc, **502,** *502*, 576
Terry, Dewey, 211
Terry, Gene, 585
Terry, Sanders (see: Terry, Sonny)
Terry, Sonny, 37, 38, 42, 74, 92, 96, 98, 166, 175, 184, 194, 206, 317, 318, 319, 347, 348, 364, 365, 366, 375, 386, 452, 454, **502-505,** *502*, 556, 569
Terry Jr. (see: Adail, Terry, Jr.)
Testament (label), 65, 140, 197, 213, 225, 246, 251, 260, 263, 266, 290, 294, 349, 363, 398, 399, 443, 444, 457, 459, 478, 479, 483, 493, 494, 507, 529, 569, 591, 594
Tet-A-Tete (club) (Providence, MA), 486
Tex, Joe, 60
Tex & Jinx (team), 542
Texas Blues Festival (Houston, TX), 364
Texas College (Tyler, TX), 405
Texas Guitar Slim (see: Winter, Johnny)
Texas Heritage Festival (Houston, TX), 330
Texas International Pop Festival (Lewisville, TX), 296, 305, 308, 585
Texas Lady (club) (Chicago, IL), 150, 444
Texas Nightingale (billing), 295, 533
Texas Opry House (Houston, TX), 78
Texas Rose Cafe (Houston, TX), 330
Texas Slim (see: Hooker, John Lee)
Texas Southern University (see: University of Texas)
Texas State Fair (Dallas, TX), 313
Texas Tessie (see: Douglas, Lizzie)
Texas Tommy (see: Dorsey, Thomas A.)
Texas Trio (group), 385
Theater Atlanta (Atlanta, GA), 420
Theater 1839 (San Francisco, CA), 152, 210, 390
Theater Guild (organization), 475
Theater Lounge (club) (Denver, CO), 321
Theater Royal (Edinburgh, Scotland), 256
Theatrical Cheer Club (Chicago, IL), 558
Theatrical Club (New York, NY), 385, 467
Theatrical Grill (see: Tyler's Theatrical Grill)
Thee Experience Club (Los Angeles, CA?), 468, 513
Thelma's Lounge (Chicago, IL), 271, 574
Theresa's Bar/Lounge/Tavern (Chicago, IL), 36, 91, 99, 132, 208, 238, 269, 294, 340, 343, 389, 394, 404, 435, 437, 476, 499, 500, 530, 548, 549, 596
38 Colt Club (New Orleans, LA), 437
3525 Club (Dallas, TX), 141
34 Club (Chicago, IL), 213, 294, 493
33rd Street Club (Chicago, IL), 35
This Is It Club (Dallas, TX), 382
This Way Inn (Franklin Park, IL), 123
Thomas, Annie, 226
Thomas, Ben, 80
Thomas, Beulah, 531
Thomas, Blanche, 465, **505-506**
Thomas, Carla, 510, 512
Thomas, Charles (Maxwell Street Jimmy), 241, **506-507,** *506*
Thomas, Cotton (see: Jaxon, Frankie)
Thomas, Ella, 212
Thomas, George "Fat Head," 373, 448
Thomas, George W., Jr., 507, 531, 532
Thomas, George W., Sr., 507, 531
Thomas, Henry (see: Johnson, Leslie) (see: Townsend, Henry)
Thomas, Henry "Ragtime Texas," **507**
Thomas, Hersal, 508, 531, 532, 533
Thomas, Hociel, **507-508,** *507*, 532
Thomas, Irma, 436, **508,** *508*
Thomas, James "Son"/"Sonny Ford," 138, 271, **508-509,** *509*
Thomas, Jesse "Baby Face," 509, 510
Thomas, Joe L., 509
Thomas, Johnny, 321
Thomas, Josephine (see: Henderson, Rosa)
Thomas, Kid (see: Watts, Louis)
Thomas, Lafayette, 29, 55, **509-510,** *509*
Thomas, Lillian, 80
Thomas, Marvell, 512
Thomas, Naomi, 564
Thomas, Ramblin' (see: Thomas, Willard)
Thomas, Rufus, 383, **510-512,** *511*
Thomas, Samuel, 505
Thomas, Sippie (see: Wallace, Beulah)
Thomas, Willard "Ramblin'," 235, 280, 456, 510
Thomas, Willie B., 103, 231, 481, **512**

Thomas A. Dorsey Gospel Songs Music Publishing Company (organization), 159
Thomas' Club (Washington, DC), 580, 583
Thomas Jefferson High School (Port Arthur, TX), 296
Thompson, Ashley, *325*
Thompson, Bob, 316
Thompson, Don, 375
Thompson, Lucky, 536
Thompson, Mack, 289
Thompson, Sam, 289
Thompson, Sonny, 60, 150, 251
Thompson, Sylvester, 289
Thompson, Wally, 178
Thornton, Millie, 176
Thornton, Willie Mae "Big Mama," 29, 63, 76, 162, 208, 213, 246, 249, 277, 296, 339, 363, 407, 428, 465, 468, **512-514,** *513*
Thousand Pounds of Harmony (billing), 581
Threadgill, Kenneth, 441
Threadgill's Bar (Austin, TX), 296
Three Aces (group) (Willie Love), 271, 317, 338, 400, 425, 560
Three Aces (group) (Louis Myers), 393, 548
Three B's (club) (Dallas, TX), 382
Three B's (group), 27, 365
Three Blazers (group), 74, 76, 154
Three Brothers (club) (Chicago, IL), 499
Three Deuces (club) (Chicago, IL), 279, 321, 536
Three Deuces (club) (New York, NY), 252
Three Deuces (group), 393, 548
Three Dixie Songbirds (group), 52
Three Flames (group), 90
Three Forks Cemetery (Greenwood, MS), 289
Three Forks Store (juke) (Greenwood, MS), 289
Three Hot Brown Boys (group), 439
Three J's Jug Band, 176, 426
III Kings (club) (DeKalb, IL), 369
308 Club (Chicago, IL), 200
Three Sisters (club) (West Paterson, NJ), 316
Three Sixes Club (Detroit, MI), 83, 279, 542
3 Star Package Revue (tour), 200
333 Club (Chicago, IL), 251
Three Towers (club) (South Somerville, NJ), 550
Thunder Bird (club), The (Jacksonville, FL), 432
Thunderbird from Coast to Coast (billing), The, 424
Thunderbirds (band), The, 423, 424
Tia Juana Club (Cleveland, OH), 372, 542
Tibble Theater (Stockholm, Sweden), 166
Tibbs, Leroy, 152
Tibet's Walkathon (dance hall) (Atlantic City, NJ), 44
Tic Toc Club (Boston, MA), 44, 200, 215, 298
Tick Tock Club (Macon, GA), 410
Tick Tock Lounge (Chicago, IL), 425, 478
Tick Tock Roof Garden (club) (New Orleans, LA), 505
Tide Family (group), 392
Tidwell's Barbecue Place (Atlanta, GA), 228
Tiebiro's Lounge (Chicago, IL), 123
Tiffany Club (Los Angeles, CA), 298, 321, 538
Tijuana Brass (band), 420
Tijuana Smalls Cigar (product), 309, 585
Tiki Island Club (Los Angeles, CA), 520
Tiki Recording Studio (Houma, LA), 490
Tiki's (club) (Monterey Park, LA), 178
Tilley, Big Poppa John, 208
Tillie & Her Toilers Band, 43
Tilling, Robert, 148, 187, 487
Tillis, Big Son, 43
Tillman, Curtis, 430
Tillman, Keith, 55, 442, 494
Tilyou Theater (Brooklyn, NY), 70
Timber Tap Club/Room (Chicago, IL), 116, 216
Timbre (label), 580
Time (label), 214, 215
Time (magazine), 142
Timely (label), 219
Times Hall (New York, NY), 318
Times-Picayune Newspaper Guild (organization) (Detroit, MI), 230
Times Square Theater (New York, NY), 82, 581
Timm, Robert, 330
Tin Angel (club) (San Francisco, CA), 36, 141, 194, 373
Tin Lizzie Club (Lansing, MI), 230
Tin Pan Alley Band, 65
Tin Pan Alley Club (Chicago, IL), 380, 489
Tindley, C. H., 160
Tip Top (label), 563
Tip Top Club (Chicago, IL), 397
Tipitina Club (New Orleans, LA), 101
Titanic (club), The (Picayune, MS), 379
Titon, Jeff, 56, 110, 111, 248, 342
Tivol Theater (Aberdeen, Scot.), 256
Tivoli, The (Stockholm, Swed.), 224
Tivoli Theater (Chicago, IL), 113, 173, 566, 582
Tmp-Ting (label), 289
To Me It's Wonderful (book), 543, 544
Toad's Place (club) (New Haven, CT), 156
Toast of the Town Club (see: Cadillac Bob's Toast of the Town Club)
Today (label), 424, 575
Todd, Clarence, 85, 496
Todd, Eva, 371
Tolbert, Skeets, 285
Tolen, L. C., 481
Tolliver's Circus and Musical Extravaganza Show (tour), 172, 428
Tom Anderson's Cafe/Saloon (New Orleans, LA), 84, 134
Tom Brown's Farm (Porterdale, GA), 546
Tom George's Country Club (Juneau, AK), 90
Tom Kirby Club (Plaquemine, LA), 379
Tom Lee Park (Memphis, TN), 163
Tom Sander Plantation (Drew, MS), 290
Tomashefsky, Steve, 169, 336, 592
Tomato (label), 240
Tomcat & The Blues Dusters (group), 134
Tommy Johnson (book), 89, 290
Tommy's 250 Club (Richmond, CA), 76, 188
Tomorrow Club (Youngstown, OH), 33, 307
Toms, Coons, Mulattoes, Mammies and Bucks (book), 362
Tom's Lounge/Tavern (see: Walton's Corner)
Tom's Musicians Club/Lounge (see: Walton's Corner)
Tone (label), 414, 420, 438
Tony's Cellar (club) (Chicago, IL), 148
Tony's Steak House (Houston, TX), 84
Tony's Upstairs (club) (Chicago, IL), 148
Too Tight Henry (see: Townsend, Henry)
Top & Lanes (club) (Helena, AR), 183
Top Hat (club) (Toronto, Can.), 298
Top Hat (label), 43
Top Hat Club (Chicago, IL), 110
Top of the Gate (club) (New York, NY), 300
Topanga Canyon Fiddlers Convention (concert) (Topanga, CA), 345
Topanga Corral (club) (Los Angeles, CA), 55, 136, 178, 190, 240, 249, 305, 346, 378, 442, 468, 520, 527, 531
Tornados (group), The, 32
Toronto Blues Festival (Olympic Island/Toronto, Can.), 33, 42, 51, 156, 208, 240, 320, 341, 516, 549
Toronto Globe (newspaper), 84
Toronto Island Blues Festival (Toronto Island/Toronto, Can.), 99, 249, 494
Toronto Jazz Festival (Toronto, Can.), 447, 566
Toronto Pop Festival (Toronto, Can.), 46, 224, 296, 359, 411, 585
Toronto Symphony Orchestra, 84
Tote's Place (club) (New Haven, CT), 240
Touch of Olde Club (Chicago, IL), 381, 591
Touch of Souls Band, 596
Tougaloo College (Tougaloo, MS), 311, 508
Toussaint, Allen, 60, 103, 116, 158, 202
Tower Theater (Kansas City, MO), 90
Town Casino (New York, NY), 472
Town Club (Cicero, IL), 450
Town Crier Cafe (Poughkeepsie, NY), 130
Town Hall (Birmingham, Eng.), 408
Town Hall (London, Eng.), 302

Town Hall (New York, NY), 68, 69, 99, 116, 117, 132, 142, 145, 147, 174, 194, 195, 197, 206, 229, 239, 257, 280, 316, 318, 330, 365, 366, 406, 408, 447, 448, 453, 464, 466, 497, 503, 521, 532, 556, 576, 580, 584
Town Hall (Philadelphia, PA), 383, 431, 521, 556
Town Hall Ballroom (Philadelphia, PA), 113
Town Hill Restaurant (Brooklyn, NY), 470
Town House (club) (Dearborn, MI), 127
Town Tavern (club) (Toronto, Can.), 84, 375, 448, 566, 586
Townley, Eric, 84, 466
Townley, John, 148
Townley, Ray, 568
Townsend, Henry, 150, 280, 282, 288, 398, 489, 491, 507, **514-515,** *514*
Townsend, Vernell, 514
Townsend, Willis Saxbe, 257
Toy, Minnie, 409
Track II Lounge (Grand Rapids, MI), 397
Tradition (label), 194, 243, 244, 375
Traditional Jazz Club Concert (Montreal, Can.), 453
Train Riders Band, The, 348
Traits (group), The, 585
Tralfamadore Cafe (Buffalo, NY), 520
Tramor Hotel (Chicago, IL), 161
Transatlantic (label), 96, 147, 247, 249, 363, 508
Travel Lodge (Montgomery, AL), 320
Travers, Tony, 79
Trey (label), 141
Tri-State Inn (Gary, IN), 238
Triangle Bar (Minneapolis, MN), 96, 314, 342
Triangle Inn (Chicago, IL), 62, 576
Trianon Ballroom (Chicago, IL), 208, 308
Trianon Club (Chicago, IL), 434, 470
Tribute to Huddie Ledbetter (book), A, 318
Tribute to Woody Guthrie (book), A, 206
Trice, Albert, 515, 516
Trice, Reuben, 515
Trice, Richard "Rich," 185, 515, **515,** *515,* 516
Trice, William "Welly"/"Willie," 185, 515, **515-516,** *515*
Trilon (label), 188, 357
Trilyte (label), 510
Trimbel, Raymond, 453
Trinity (group), The, 577
Trinity Baptist Church (Los Angeles, CA), 586
Trio (label), 336, 445, 586
Trio-Delmark (label), 177, 401
Trip (label), 117
Trix (label) 92, 93, 111, 164, 171, 172, 175, 180, 217, 261, 282, 312, 313, 336, 367, 492, 516
Trocadero (club) (Hollywood, CA), 298, 525, 527, 541
Trocadero Lounge (Chicago, IL), 286, 560
Trois Mailletz Club (Les Trois Mailletz) (Paris, Fr.), 63, 117, 155, 165, 292, 343, 453, 527
Trojan (label), 520
Trojan Horse (club) (Seattle, WA), 51
Tropicana (club) (Los Angeles, CA), 55
Tropicana Hotel (Las Vegas, NV), 310, 567
Troubado(u)r (club), The (Hollywood/ Los Angeles, CA) (see also: Club Troubadour), 30, 96, 132, 141, 185, 195, 218, 243, 366, 388, 428, 504, 512, 557
Troubadour (billing), The, 589
Troup, Bobby, 141, 185
Troy Hilton (hotel) (Detroit, MI), 230
Troyettes (group), The, 563
Tru Blue (label), 44, 454
Tru-Love (label), 88
True Heart Baptist Church (Bronx, NY), 147
Truman, Harry, 321
Trummy Cain's Show (tour), 57
Trumpet (label), 137, 252, 271, 308, 338, 354, 560, 569, 577
Tub Jug Washboard Band, 428
Tubb, Ernest, 441
Tucker, Becker, 39
Tucker, Ira, 51
Tucker, Luther, 336, 394, **516-517,** *516*
Tucker, Sophie, 257, 374
Tucker, Tommy, 517
Tucker, Tommy "Tee," 116, **517,** *517*
Tucker, William George, 39
Tudor, Dean, 166
Tufts University (Medford, MA), 346
Tulagi's (club) (Boulder, CO), 100, 389
Tulane University (New Orleans, LA), 101, 113, 167, 203, 420, 486, 553
Tulsa Red (see: Fulson, Lowell)
Tumble Inn (New Orleans, LA), 396
Tumbleweed (label), 125
Turk Club, The (Columbus, OH), 489
Turks Club (Chicago, IL), 99
Turk's Head (club) (Boston, MA), 486
Turnabout Theater (Hollywood, CA), 193, 194
Turner, Babe "Buck" (Black Ace), 232, 233, **517-518,** *517,* 589
Turner, Baby Face, 371
Turner, Ben, 103
Turner, Benny, 307
Turner, Bez, 307
Turner, Blind Squire (see: Darby, Theodore)
Turner, Bobby, 307
Turner, Ike, 104, 175, 193, 223, 237, 238, 309, 338, 522, 534
Turner, J. T., 518
Turner, Joe "Stride," 520
Turner, Joseph "Big Joe," 38, 45, 54, 88, 106, 116, 136, 137, 188, 190, 216, 271, 294, 305, 311, 377, 448, 465, 485, **518-521,** *519,* 524, 528, 568, 588
Turner, Tina, 223, 309, 353, 418
Turner Brothers Plantation (Belzoni, MS), 271
Turner's Blue Lounge (Chicago, IL), 246, 260, 266, 393, 570
Turner's Club (see: Turner's Blue Lounge)
Tutt, J. Homer, 472, 558
Tutt-Whitney, Salem, 472, 540, 558
Tuxedo Lounge (Chicago, IL), 181, 266, 271, 342, 343, 529, 571
Tuxedo Orchestra, 203
Twelfth Gate Club (Atlanta, GA), 513
12th Street Theater (Kansas City, MO), 472
12 String Guitar as Played by Leadbelly (book), 319
20th Century Fox (label), 61, 71, 125, 411
24 Club, The (Chicago, IL), 424, 570, 594
Twenty Grand Club (Detroit, MI), 308, 431, 527
21 Club (Chicago, IL), 181, 300, 339, 340, 442, 559
27-28 Club (Birmingham, AL), 356
Twilight-Twinight (label), 289
Twin Lounge Society Club (Gloucester City, NJ), 523
Twin Town (label), 91
Twinlite Club (Newark, NJ), 550
Twist, Johnny, 311, 404, 563
Twist City Club (Chicago, IL), 200, 332, 444, 577
Twisters (group), 259
Twitty, Conway, 183
Two Charlies (duo), The, 297
Two Fools Club (DeKalb, IL), 198
Two Kings (label), 375
270 Garden Restaurant (St. Louis, MO), 432
Two Spot Nite Club (Jacksonville, FL), 89, 111
230 Club (Chicago, IL), 161
Tyler's Theatrical Grill (New York, NY), 43, 385
Tympany Five (band), 298, 299
Tyrone Guthrie Theater (Minneapolis, MN), 296, 308, 389, 562, 573
Tyson, Jeffrey, 227

UCLA (see: University of California, Los Angeles, CA)
UCLA Medical Center (Los Angeles, CA), 546
US Air Force Band, 567
US Department of Interior (government office) (Washington, DC), 207
US House of Representatives (government office) (Washington, DC), 114
US State Department (government office) (Washington, DC), 78
USA (label), 67, 72, 123, 175, 322, 343, 437, 499, 548, 563, 574, 594
USC Medical Center (Los Angeles, CA), 216
USO Camp Shows, Inc. (tour), 90, 108, 110, 188, 256, 257, 466, 504, 506, 541, 550, 589
UTA Theater (Berlin, Ger.), 581

Ubangi Club (New York, NY), 43, 44, 298, 564
Ukulele Kid (see: Burse, Charlie)
Ulanov, Barry, 89, 229, 257, 521
Ultimates of Soul (group), 137
Ultra (label), 529
Umea Jazz Festival (Stockholm, Sweden), 166
Uncle Po's Club (Hamburg, Ger.), 245
Uncle Sam's Club (Macon, GA), 389
Uncle Sam's Club (New Orleans, LA), 508
Uncle Skipper (see: Jordan, Charles)
Uncle Tom's Plantation Club (Detroit, MI), 83
Uncrowned Queen of the Blues (billing), 134
Underground Pop Festival (Miami, FL), 224
Underground Theater (New York, NY), 222
Underhill, Viola (see: Wells, Viola)
Ungano's (club) (New York, NY), 93, 132, 240, 309, 346, 352, 389, 468, 513
Unicorn (club), The (Boston, MA), 99, 240, 272, 396, 521
Unicorn Club (Rochester, NY), 347
Union Baptist Church (Ridgecrest, CA), 315
Union Club (Madison, WI), 32
Union Hall (Chalmette, LA), 508
Union Theater (Chicago, IL), 150
United (label), 116, 398, 489
United Artists (label), 69, 113, 116, 117, 132, 158, 178, 375, 377, 388, 407, 577, 588
United Auto Workers (organization), 141
United Bar (Santa Cruz, CA), 339
United Black Artists Booking Agency (organization) (Paris, Fr.), 117
United Disciple of Christ Church (Chicago, IL), 569
United Hospital (Port Chester, NY), 558
United Memorial Gardens Cemetery (Plymouth, MI), 182
United Mine Workers (organization), 142
United Negro College Fund (organization), 114
United Presbyterian Church (Newark, NJ), 550, 582
Universal Attractions Show (tour), 165, 468
Universal Attractions Rock & Roll Show (tour), 38, 86, 113
University Club (Pasadena, CA), 567
University Gospel Singers (group), 159
University High School (Hollywood, CA), 428
University Hospital (Birmingham, AL), 175
University Hospital (Jackson, MS), 64
University of Arkansas (Fayetteville, AR), 177, 327, 401, 483, 486, 553
University of British Columbia (Vancouver, Can.), 367, 375, 504, 557, 588
University of Buffalo (see: State University of New York at Buffalo)
University of California (Berkeley, CA), 55, 121, 138, 185, 213, 243, 266, 304, 309, 327, 330, 366, 388, 420, 504, 512, 527, 554
University of California (Irvine, CA), 156, 588
University of California (Los Angeles, CA), 114, 125, 141, 147, 247, 330, 363, 420, 513, 527, 553
University of California (San Francisco, CA), 30, 161, 188, 330, 332, 357-358, 439, 554
University of California (Santa Barbara, CA), 180, 278, 309, 330, 531
University of California (Santa Cruz, CA), 98, 339
University of Chicago (Chicago, IL), 56, 57-58, 65, 67, 91, 93, 95, 99, 101, 120, 138, 147, 148, 154, 169, 179, 185, 190, 198, 208, 228, 246, 247, 257, 260, 261, 265, 272, 285, 286, 292, 294, 305, 313, 324, 327, 330, 339, 340, 341, 343, 345, 349, 363, 381, 388, 398, 414, 426-427, 457, 483, 490, 499, 501, 507, 514, 524, 529, 548, 553, 562, 563, 569, 573, 575, 582, 591, 595
University of Cincinnati (Cincinnati, OH), 249, 257
University of Connecticut (Storrs, CT), 173
University of Detroit (Detroit, MI), 132, 225, 309, 389, 443, 532, 578
University of Florida (Gainesville, FL), 434
University of Georgia (Athens, GA), 415
University of Houston (Houston, TX), 132
University of Illinois (Urbana, IL), 142, 176, 179, 292, 366, 443, 504, 569
University of Illinois, Chicago Circle Campus (Chicago, IL), 65
University of Illinois Press (organization) (Urbana, IL), 56, 342
University of Iowa (Iowa City, IA), 27, 202, 427
University of Kansas (Lawrence, KS), 432
University of Louisville (Louisville, KY), 367, 504, 563
University of Maine (Orono, ME), 481, 508
University of Massachusetts (Amherst, MA), 345
University of Miami (Coral Gables, FL), 33, 208, 231, 336, 450, 457, 484, 490, 499, 500, 529, 549
University of Miami (Miami, FL), 247, 573
University of Miami (Silver Springs, FL), 41, 151, 404, 457
University of Michigan (Ann Arbor, MI), 32, 185, 421
University of Minnesota (Minneapolis, MN), 32, 150, 249, 305, 314, 342
University of Mississippi (Oxford, MS), 501
University of Missouri (Columbia, MO), 88
University of Nebraska (Lincoln, NE), 33, 247
University of North Carolina (Chapel Hill, NC), 92, 96, 164, 171, 180, 217, 260, 261, 266, 282, 312, 516
University of North Carolina (Greensboro, NC), 420
University of North Carolina (Raleigh, NC), 367, 504
University of North Florida (Jacksonville, FL), 208, 457, 549
University of Notre Dame (South Bend, IN) (see also: Notre Dame Blues Festival), 57, 148, 236, 247, 249, 260, 294, 304, 336, 341, 342, 349, 437, 445, 450, 459, 468, 573, 575, 591
University of Oregon (Eugene, OR), 42, 54, 57, 156, 349, 390, 429, 445
University of Pennsylvania Hospital (Philadelphia, PA), 273
University of Pittsburgh (Pittsburgh, PA), 147, 283, 330, 364, 481, 490
University of San Francisco (San Francisco, CA), 185
University of Saskatchewan (Saskatoon, Can.), 244
University of Southern California (Los Angeles, CA), 371, 468
University of Tennessee (Knoxville, TN), 313
University of Texas (Austin, TX), 296, 318, 377, 456
University of Texas (Texas Southern University) (Houston, TX), 330
University of Texas Medical Branch Hospital (Galveston, TX), 241
University of Toronto, (Toronto, Can.), 367, 505
University of Utah (Salt Lake City, UT), 330
University of Vermont (Burlington, VT), 33, 138, 151, 208, 219, 243, 249, 286, 330, 336, 429, 450, 494, 500, 549, 573
University of Washington (Seattle, WA), 243
University of Waterloo (Waterloo, Can.), 95, 305, 341, 367, 488, 504, 513
University of Wisconsin (Madison, WI), 32, 151, 198, 260, 345, 404, 444, 569
University of Wisconsin (Milwaukee, WI), 294, 340, 381
University of Wyoming (Laramie, WY), 30
Untouchables (group), The, 436
Unusuals (group), The, 309
Upchurch, Phil, 60
Upper Haight Street Club (San Francisco, CA), 190
Uprising Tavern (DeKalb, IL), 151, 595
Upsala College (E. Orange, NJ), 481
Upsetters (group), The, 411
Upstairs Lounge (Chicago, IL), 198, 460

Upstarts (group), The, 353
Uptight Club (San Francisco, CA), 55
Uptown House Cafe (New York, NY), 385
Uptown, The Story of Harlem's Apollo Theater (book) 216, 538
Urban Blues Festival (Chicago, IL), 42, 95, 247, 334, 476, 500
Utley, Nancy, 575
Utopia (label), 190, 304, 305, 379
Utopia Club (W. Oakland, CA), 304

V-Disc (label), 71, 298, 406, 446, 556
VJ (label), 35, 67, 116, 136, 175, 211, 238, 239, 243, 266, 291, 294, 322, 340, 366, 411, 424, 434, 435, 488, 493, 503, 569, 571, 586
VJM (label), 295, 414, 467, 484
VJM Washboard Band, 110
Valentine, Kid Thomas, 546
Valery, Joseph, Jr., 54
Valery, Joseph, Sr., 54
Vallee, Rudy, 541, 581
Valley Inn (W. Orange, NJ), 550
Valley Music Theater (Woodland Hills, CA), 114, 309
van Horne, Randy, 586
Van Kirk, Anneka, 206
Van Olderen, Martin, 149
Van Ronk, David "Dave," 148, 327, **521-522**, *521*, 557
Van Sickle, Kurt, 330
Van Vechten, Carl, 467
Van Vorst, Paige, 421, 582
Vancouver Hotel (Vancouver, Can.), 377
Vanderbilt Theater (New York, NY), 82
Vanderbilt University (Nashville, TN), 104
Vanderpool Sylvia, 37, 38
Vandy Cobb's Place (juke) (Hughes, AR), 93
Vanguard (label), 68, 130, 132, 134, 136, 141, 147, 174, 176, 194, 208, 210, 239, 246, 247, 249, 252, 257, 259, 272, 273, 314, 358, 363, 366, 393, 401, 406, 427, 444, 447, 452, 457, 468, 478, 503, 504, 513, 516, 518, 521, 548, 566, 573, 575
Vanity Fair (magazine), 467
Van's Hot Spot (club) (Gary, IN), 62, 576
Varadero Pop Song Festival (Havana, Cuba), 142
Variety (label), 405
Varsity (label), 518, 525
Varsity Seven (band), 518
Vassar College (Poughkeepsie, NY), 556
Vaucresson's Club (New Orleans, LA), 486
Vaudeville Comedy Club Presentation (show), 173
Vaughan, Sarah, 113, 418
Vaughn, Cooney, 381
Vault (label), 329, 531
Vegetable Buddies Club (South Bend, IN), 57, 247, 349
Velma's Tavern (Chicago, IL), 434
Veltone (label), 28
Velvetone (label), 496
Vendome Hotel (Buffalo, NY), 252
Vendome Orchestra, 450
Vendome Theater (Chicago, IL), 450
Venetian Room at Italian Village (club) (San Francisco, CA), 36
Vennie, Joe, 43
Verbum Dei Auditorium (Los Angeles, CA), 122
Vernon, Mike, 63, 104
Vernon (label), 91
Vernon Convalescent Hospital (Los Angeles, CA), 527
Verrett, Harrison, 158
Versa (label), 123
Versailles (club) (Cleveland, OH), 566
Versailles (label), 38
Verve (label), 54, 69, 117, 132, 155, 239, 243, 249, 272, 366, 373, 447, 466, 486, 503, 521, 553, 566, 569, 588, 592
Verve-Folkways (label), 217, 239, 591
Verve-Forecast (label), 218
Vest (label), 528
Veteran's Administration Hospital (Columbia, SC), 492
Veteran's Administration Hospital (Dallas, TX), 267
Veteran's Administration Hospital (Hines, IL), 95
Veteran's Administration Hospital (Houston, TX), 583
Veteran's Administration Hospital (Jackson, MS), 487
Veteran's Administration Hospital (McKinney, TX), 232
Veteran's Administration Hospital (Tuskegee, AL), 125
Vet's Lounge, (Cincinnati, OH), 535
Vibes Lounge, The (Chicago, IL), 33, 208, 549
Victor (label) (see also: RCA-Victor label), 35, 37, 38, 40, 43, 62, 63, 64, 69, 84, 85, 98, 106, 122, 128, 137, 144, 150, 161, 176, 181, 192, 193, 194, 196, 200, 206, 221, 223, 227, 231, 233, 246, 253, 256, 264, 279, 282, 290, 294, 295, 298, 317, 325, 327, 339, 353, 355, 369, 370, 373, 385, 403, 405, 406, 411, 415, 418, 419, 426, 440, 441, 445, 446, 447, 450, 452, 454, 472, 480, 481, 484, 486, 489, 496, 497, 503, 532, 542, 547, 552, 559, 562, 566, 574, 576, 581, 583, 586, 589, 592, 594
Victory Bond Spiritual Singers (group), 164
Victory Club (Chicago, IL), 292, 380
Victory Theater (Holyoke, MA), 82
Vietnam Songbook (book), 142
Vietnamese Tet Celebration (concert) (Paris, Fr.), 142
Vieux Carre Club (Holt, AL), 457
Vik (label), 38, 165
Viking Lounge (Cincinnati, OH), 76, 372, 418, 523, 527, 535, 588
Viking Sea Cruise Ship (see: S.S. Viking Sea)
Villa Motor Hotel (Vancouver, Can.), 377
Village Corner (club) (Toronto, Can.), 147, 187
Village Gaslight (club) (New York, NY) (see also: Gaslight), 363, 389
Village Gate (club) (New York, NY), 46, 99, 117, 155, 157, 169, 194, 195, 208, 210, 219, 239, 243, 244, 286, 300, 304, 308, 366, 417, 418, 431, 445, 504, 556, 557, 588
Village Rest (club) (Modesto, CA), 161
Village Theater (New York, NY), 46, 142, 521
Village Vanguard (club) (New York, NY), 68, 117, 155, 210, 229, 252, 317, 375, 388, 406, 521, 538, 556, 566, 588, 594
Village Voice (newspaper), 586
Villageast (club) (New York, NY), 46, 359
Vincennes Hotel (Chicago, IL), 532
Vincent, Monroe (Polka Dot Slim), **522**, *522*, 576
Vincent, Walter (see: Vinson, Walter Jacobs)
Vincson, Walter (see: Vinson, Walter Jacobs)
Vinson, Alice, 524
Vinson, Eddie, 524
Vinson, Eddie "Cleanhead," 54, 70, 107, 240, 244, 520, **522-524**, *523*, 524, 536
Vinson, Sam, 522
Vinson, Walter, 524
Vinson, Walter Jacobs, 64, 118, 269, 290, 354, 524, **524**, *524*
Vintage (club) (Memphis, TN), 454
Viper Girl (billing), The, 251
Virginia Beach Jazz Festival (Virginia Beach, VA), 447
Virginia Club (Los Angeles, CA), 375, 586
Virginia Theater (Alexandria, VA), 220
Virgo (label), 149
Vi's Lounge (Chicago, IL), 181, 294, 438
Vita (label), 53
Vivian, Lila (see: Hicks, Edna)
Vivid (label), 291, 294, 435, 493
Vocalion (label), 29, 31, 39, 40, 48, 49, 56, 62, 68, 70, 73, 84, 98, 107, 133, 134, 144, 145, 148, 159, 161, 167, 184, 193, 223, 227, 229, 246, 252, 264, 274, 281, 288, 292, 297, 298, 317, 327, 331, 336, 348, 355, 356, 357, 369, 373, 385, 397, 398, 405, 406, 409, 414, 415, 445, 446, 450, 460, 467, 470, 480, 481, 492, 496, 501, 502, 503, 507, 518, 540, 545, 547, 551, 552, 553, 555, 559, 560, 562, 568, 574, 583, 584, 589, 592
Vocalion-Brunswick (label), 145
Vocal-style (label), 145
Voce, Steve, 418
Vo-De-Do Club (New York, NY), 137
Vogue (label), 36, 38, 69, 117, 148, 151, 165, 394, 395, 556, 577, 586
Vogue Lounge (Detroit, MI), 238
Vollmer, Albert "Al," 551, 558
Volt (label), 312
Von (label), 96, 225
Von Schmidt, Eric, 319, **525**, *525*

Von Tersch, Gary, 88, 345
Voyager Lounge (St. Louis MO), 338
Vulcan (label) 356

W. A. Blair Show, 33
WASP (label), 395, 404
W. C. Handy Blues Festival (Memphis, TN), 304, 506, 553
W. C. Handy Festival (Florence, AL), 582
W. C. Handy Park (see: Church's Park)
W. C. Handy Presentations (organization) (St. Louis, MO), 175
W. C. Handy Theater (Memphis, TN), 308, 510, 527
W. E. West's Motorized Show (tour), 179
W.O.W. Hall (Eugene, OR), 125, 339, 358, 393, 516
Wade, Bessie, 533
Wades Club (Cairo, IL), 237
Wagon Wheel (club) (Chicago, IL), 213, 345, 499
Wainwright, London, III, 174
Waldo, Terry, 582
Waldorf-Astoria Hotel (New York, NY), 114
Walker, Aaron "T-Bone," 36, 47, 51, 53, 54, 60, 68, 73, 76, 78, 106, 107, 127, 134, 136, 137, 190, 192, 202, 209, 225, 238, 250, 260, 269, 276, 277, 280, 293, 305, 307, 311, 325, 377, 400, 430, 438, 444, 445, 448, 461, 468, 520, **525-528,** *526,* 531, 545, 561, 586
Walker, Charles, 283, **528-529,** *528*
Walker, Dennis, 531
Walker, Ernest, 288, 514
Walker, Freeman, 528
Walker, George, 531
Walker, Hamp, 330
Walker, Ina, 531
Walker, James "Jimmy," 65, 421, **529,** *529,* 569
Walker, Joe, 492, 555
Walker, John "Johnny," **529-530,** *530*
Walker, Mary, 425
Walker, Mary Jane, 184
Walker, Mel, 76, 417
Walker, Moose, 36
Walker, Phillip, 68, 200, 276, 311, 353, 528, **530-531,** *530*
Walker, Rance, 525
Walker, T-Bone (see: Walker, Aaron)
Walker, T-Bone, Jr. (see: Rankin, R. S.)
Walker, Will, 159
Walker, William, 250
Walker, Willie, **531,** 555, 557
Walkin' Slim (see: Minter, Iverson)
Walking to New Orleans (book), 88, 158, 202, 301
Wallace, Beulah "Sippie," 295, 429, 430, 474, 497, 507, 508, **531-533,** *532*
Wallace, Matt, 532
Wallace, Minnie, 220
Wallace, Sippie (see: Wallace, Beulah)
Wallace Theater (Indianapolis, IN), 464
Wallace's Lounge (East Orange, NJ), 481
Waller, Bill, 311
Waller, Thomas "Fats," 44, 71, 73, 137, 350, 373, 406, 415, 472, 512, 536, 581
Waller Creek Boys (band), 296
Walter (see: Horton, Walter)
Walters Show Lounge (Chicago, IL), 91
Walton, Austin, 90
Walton, Beulah, 90
Walton, Cora, 499
Walton, Fred, 533
Walton, Honey, 534
Walton, Horace, 534
Walton, Mercy Dee, 305, 347, 439, **533-534,** *533*
Walton, Square, 503
Walton, Wade, **534,** *534*
Walton's Corner (club) (Chicago, IL) (Tom's Lounge/Tavern) (Tom's Musicians Club/Lounge),32, 41, 78, 305, 334, 388, 437, 442, 444, 457, 461, 494, 591
Wampus Cats (band), 589
Wander Inn (Philadelphia, PA), 464
Wandering Troubadors (band), 348
War (band), 224
War Memorial Auditorium (Boston, MA), 506
Ward, Billy, 178
Ward, Vera Hall (see: Hall, Vera)
Ward Singers (group), The, 426
Ward's Jazzville (club) (San Diego, CA), 431
Ware, Hayes, 181
Warehouse (club), The (Denver, CO), 310, 432
Ware's Tonk (juke) (Vicksburg, MS), 379
Warfield, William, 194
Warm Springs Methodist Church Cemetery (Crystal Spring, MS), 290
Warner Brothers (label), 54, 100, 117, 174, 190, 195, 219, 346, 390, 429
Warner Brothers-Bearsville (label), 100
Warners (club) (Galveston, TX), 199
Warped (label), 415
Warren, Baby Boy (see: Warren, Robert)
Warren, Earl, 37
Warren, Lee, 535
Warren, Robert "Baby Boy," 93, 216, 217, 240, 289, 334, 338, 457, **534-535,** *534,* 571, 577, 589
Warren, William, 398
Warwick, Dionne, 517, 538
Warwick (label), 378, 417
Warwick Hotel (Toronto, Can.), 84
Warwick Theater (Brooklyn, NY), 221
Wasco (label), 101
Washboard Band, 496
Washboard Sam (see: Brown, Robert)
Washboard Serenaders (band), 43
Washboard Willie (see: Hensley, William)
Washburne Lounge (Chicago, IL), 181, 291, 341
Washington, Albert, 311, **535,** *536*
Washington, Annie, 336
Washington, Booker T., 553
Washington, D.C. (see: Bender, D.C.)
Washington, Dinah, 109, 136, 329, 418, 428, 464, 466, **536-538,** *537,* 572
Washington, George "Oh Red" (Bull City Red), 147, 184, 502, 503
Washington, Henry, 111
Washington, Isidoe "Tuts," 103, 202, 326
Washington, Janie, 241
Washington, Lucille, 417
Washington, Marco, 525
Washington, Mary Jane, 439
Washington, Tuts (see: Washington, Isidoe)
Washington Blues Festival (Washington, DC), 32, 93, 130, 138, 177, 208, 219, 260, 266, 309, 327, 330, 363, 389, 401, 427, 457, 548-549, 562
Washington Folk Festival (Washington, DC), 265
Washington House (Club) (Washington, DC), 564
Washington Jazz Club (Washington, DC), 153
Washington Memorial Cemetery (Homewood, IL), 85
Washington Square Church (see: Washington Square United Methodist Church)
Washington Square Park (New York, NY), 173, 206
Washington Square United Methodist Church (New York, NY), 65, 120, 130, 142, 169, 260, 283, 478, 483, 563
Washington Star (newspaper), 142
Washington Street Theater (Boston, MA), 82
Washington Theater (Indianapolis, IN), 540
Washington University (St. Louis, MO), 100, 445, 490
Watch (label), 101
Waterfront Cafe (Vallejo, CA), 586
Waterfront Club (Newport, IL), 282
Waters, Ethel, 152, 153, 172, 173, 222, 229, 256, 274, 282, 362, 385, **538-544,** *539,* 550, 556, 558, 582
Waters, John Wesley, 538
Waters, Johnny, 543
Waters, Marietta, 483
Waters, Muddy (see: Morganfield, McKinley)
Waters, Muddy, Jr. (see; Buford, George)
Watertoons Music (organization) (Chicago, IL), 389
Watkins, Minnie, 369
Watson, Doc, 283
Watson, John (see: Watson, Johnny "Guitar")
Watson, John, Sr., 544
Watson, Johnny "Guitar," 152, 225, 528, **544-545,** *544*
Watson, Johnny "Jimmy" (Daddy Stovepipe), 349, 442, 545, **545,** *545*

Watsonian Institute (group), 544
Watt, Eugene, 379
Watters, Lu, 141
Watts, Louis (Kid Thomas), 203, **545-546**
Watts, V. T., 545
Watts Festival (Los Angeles, CA), 567
Watts Summer Festival (Los Angeles, CA), 527
Watts Way (label), 28
Wattstax 72 Concert (Los Angeles, CA), 104, 304, 510, 580
Waverley Hotel (Toronto, Can.), 84
Wax (label), 421
Wayne, James, 378
Wayne State University (Detroit, MI), 141, 247
Weatherford, Teddy, 586
Weathersby, Alan, 110
Weaver, Curley James, 35, 164, 185, 226, 228, 369, 391, **546**
Weaver, James, 546
Weaver, Joe, 562
Weaver, Martha, 299
Weaver, Savannah, 226
Weaver, Sylvester, 350
Weavers (group), The, 174, 319
Webb, Boogie Bill, 80, 290, **546-547**, *546*
Webb, Chick, 31, 298, 419, 564
Webb, Jordan, 503
Webb, Percy, 312
Webb, Stan, 307
Webb Jennings Plantation (Drew, MS), 38, 89, 290, 409
Webber's Inn (Belzoni, MS), 271
Webster, Ben, 406, 586
Webster, Freddie, 261
Webster, Katie, **547**
Webster, Mamie (see: Smith, Mabel)
Webster, Sherman, 547
Webster Hall (New York, NY), 447
Weekes Club/Tavern (Atlantic City, NJ), 263, 538
Weequahic Park Love Festival (Newark, NJ), 51
Weigum, Patricia Millicent, 594
Weinstock, Ronald, 293
Weintraug, Boris, 142
Weird Guitar Player (billing), The, 43
Weis (label), 331
Weiss, John, 148
Welch, Chris, 224, 225
Welch, Guitar, 574
Welding, Peter "Pete," 36, 47, 67, 95, 116, 118, 122, 127, 144, 157, 168, 178, 188, 214, 238, 241, 249, 251, 260, 263, 264, 267, 269, 290, 294, 328, 344, 364, 371, 391, 399, 410, 426, 435, 444, 445, 459, 470, 479, 494, 507, 510, 528, 560, 570, 574, 575, 576, 578, 595
Weldon, Will "Casey Bill," 162, 355, 454, **547**, 552
Well, Al, 466
Wellington, Marguerite, 172
Wells, Amos "Junior"/"Jr.," 36, 72, 95, 99, 101, 198, 208, 238, 285, 289, 348, 391, 393, 394, 397, 407, 437, 438, 478, 499, 516, 530, **547-549**, *548*, 576, 578
Wells, Dickie, 252
Wells, Earl, 549
Wells, Gertrude, 161
Wells, Jr. (see: Wells, Amos)
Wells, Viola (Miss Rhapsody), 466, 544, **549-551**, *550*
Wembley Jazz Club (London, Eng.), 110
Wembley Stadium (London, Eng.), 411
Wendell Phillips High School (Chicago, IL), 213
Wenner, Jann, 54
Wequasset Inn (E. Harwich, MA), 245
Werley, Pete, 134, 462
Wesley, Charles, 467
Wesley Chapel Community Church (Chicago, IL), 383
West, Charles "Charlie," 42, **551**, *551*
West, Dorothy, 42, 551
West, Kendrick, 551
West, Leana, 403
West, Mae, 360, 475
West Coast Carnival (tour), 439
West Dakota Club (Berkeley, CA), 30, 98, 358, 393, 435, 440, 510
West End Theater Club (New York, NY), 406
West Roosevelt Club (Chicago, IL), 271
West Spring Friendly Four (group), 282
Westbrook, Walter, J., 269
Westbury Music Fair (Westbury, NY), 113, 114, 218, 432, 538
Western Bicentennial Folk Festival (Berkeley, CA), 161
Western Hall (Chicago, IL), 239, 243, 322, 340, 343, 499
Western Hotels (circuit), 466
Westlawn Cemetery (Kansas City, KS), 71
Westminster College (Fulton, MO), 176, 414, 569
Westmoreland, William, 506
Westover Hotel (Toronto, Can.), 84, 254, 447
Wet Soul (label), 527
Wheatstraw, Peetie, 70, 78, 107, 133, 144, 166, 233, 297, 341, 399, 426, 433, 459, 547, **551-552**, *551*, 568
Wheeler, Doc, 252
Wheels (group), The, 92
Whidby, Lulu, 137
Whirl-A-Way (label), 125
Whiskey A-Go-Go (club) (Hollywood/Los Angeles, CA), 32, 46, 51, 99, 211, 296, 304, 305, 309, 352, 383, 393, 398, 411, 588
Whiskey, Women, And. . . . (magazine), 137, 211, 278, 334, 436, 522
Whispering Pine (club) (Houston, TX), 235
Whispering Syncopators (band), 159
Whistlin' Pete (pseudonym), 545
Whit (label), 396
White, Beverly, 557
White, Booker T. Washington "Bukka," 58, 84, 106, 219, 310, 311, 327, 410, 486, **552-554**, *552*
White, Caddie, 558
White, Clara (see: McCoy, Viola)
White, Cleve (Schoolboy Cleve), 227, **554**, *554*, 578
White, Dennis, 555
White, Earl, 499
White, Ella (see: Crippen, Katie)
White, George, 557
White, Georgia, *168*, **554-555**, *554*
White, Gladys (see: Henderson, Rosa)
White, Gonzell, 474
White, Grace (see: Moore, Monette)
White, John, 552
White, Joshua Daniel "Josh," 206, 276, 317, 319, 365, 416, 417, 470, 522, 531, **555-557**, *555*, 577
White, Joshua Donald, 557
White, Princess, **557-558**, *557*
White, Washington (see: White, Booker)
White & Clark Black & Tan Minstrels (tour), 134
White Elephant Club (Chicago, IL), 161
White Front (club) (Chicago, IL), 576
White Horse Club (Chicago, IL), 404
White Horse Inn (Chicago, IL), 238
White House (government office), The (Washington, DC), 321, 431, 543, 556, 567
White Rose Cafe/Club/Tavern (Phoenix/Chicago, IL), 41, 72, 322, 389
White Stable Club (E. Lansing, MI), 287, 389
White Stallion (club) (Chicago, IL), 67, 123, 445, 596
White Swan Club (Helena, AR), 183
White Women's Christian Temperence Association (organization) (Wichita, KS), 362
Whitehead, Colin, 245
Whiteman, Paul, 496
White's Greater Shows (tour), 540
White's Road House (club) (Dallas, TX), 382
Whitey's Tavern (New York, NY), 449
Whitfield Baptist Church Cemetery (Tutwiler, MS), 577
Whiting, Charles, 558
Whitley Brothers Show (Philadelphia, PA), 274
Whitman, Albert A., 558
Whitman, Alberta "Bert," 558
Whitman, Alice, 558
Whitman, Essie Barbara, **558-559**
Whitman, Elsie (see: Whitman, Essie)
Whitman, Mabel "May," 474, 558
Whitman, Russ, 322
Whitman, Walt, 234, 558
Whitman Sisters (group), 44, 467, 558, 559
Whitmire Studio (school) (Seattle, WA), 36
Whittaker, Elizabeth, 559
Whittaker, Hudson (Tampa Red), 67, 159, 171, 172, 229, 264, 268, 269, 274, 294, 339, 340, 348, 349, 368, 370, 388, 399, 414, 428, 465, 474, 548, **559-560**, *559*
Who's Who of Jazz (book), 31, 45, 257, 288, 299, 374, 386, 419, 448, 533

Why Not? (club) (New York, NY), 217
Wichard, Al, 586
Wiesand, Stephanie, 39
Wigges, John, 35
Wiggins, Gerald, 253
Wilber, Bill (see: McCoy, Joe)
Wilber, Bob, 245
Wilberforce University (Wilberforce, OH), 175, 445
Wilborn, Nelson (Red Nelson), 355, **560**
Wild (label), 342
Wild Fire Band, 402
Wildcats Jazz Band, 159
Wilder, Thornton, 542
Wiley College (Marshall, TX), 461
Wilkins, Ernie, 470, 485
Wilkins, Frank, 560
Wilkins, Joe Willie, 338, 399, 400, 483, 484, 528, **560-561,** *560*
Wilkins, Robert Timothy "Tim," 264, 316, 317, **561-562,** *561*
Wilkins, Tim (see: Wilkins, Robert)
Wilkins, Willie, 44, 412
Will Batts Novelty Band, 40
Will Dockery's Plantation (Dockery/Ruleville, MS), 89, 169, 409
Will Smith's Place (juke) (Hughes, AR), 93
Will Thomas' Place (juke) (Giles Corner, MS), 379
Will Weiler's Place (juke) (Hughes, AR), 93
Willard, Joe, 238
William Banks Cafe (New York, NY), 229, 472, 540
William Kessler Memorial Hospital (Hammonton, NJ), 147
William Land Park (Sacramento, CA), 76
William Penn Hotel (Pittsburgh, PA), 446, 496
William Penn Theater (Philadelphia, PA), 82
Williams, Alice, 536
Williams, Andre "Bacon Fat," **562**
Williams, Anthony, 594
Williams, Bessie (see: Henderson, Rosa) (see: McCoy, Viola)
Williams, Big Joe (see: Williams, Joe Lee)
Williams, Bill, 415, 416, **562-563,** *562*
Williams, Blind Boy (see: McGhee, Walter)
Williams, Carol, 103
Williams, Charles, 321
Williams, Clarence, 128, 221, 222, 295, 298, 331, 350, 351, 373, 397, 420, 450, 481, 494, 496, 497, 531, 556, 558
Williams, Clarence, III, 497
Williams, Columbus, 555
Williams, Cootie, 523, 536
Williams, Cordy, 540
Williams, Devonia, 220
Williams, Dootsie, 519
Williams, Douglas, 460
Williams, Eddie, 154
Williams, Edward, 260
Williams, Emery, Jr. (Detroit Jr.), 438, 491, **563-564,** *563*
Williams, Emery, Sr., 563
Williams, Emma, 288
Williams, Emmett, 562
Williams, Fat Head, 145
Williams, Fess, 71, 173, 284, 385, 419, 581
Williams, George "Bullet," 552
Williams, George W., 73, *73*, 74
Williams, Hank, 123
Williams, Henry "Rubberlegs," 251, **564**
Williams, Irene (see: Taylor, Eva)
Williams, Irene, 497
Williams, Jasper, 589
Williams, Jo Jo (see: Williams, Joseph)
Williams, Jody (see: Williams, Joseph Leon)
Williams, Joe, 116, 520, **564-568,** *565*, 569, 571, 572
Williams, Joe Lee "Big Joe," 54, 125, 134, 141, 169, 210, 225, 276, 283, 288, 297, 342, 344, 355, 379, 393, 398, 403, 412, 425, 460, 493, 529, 540, 552, **568-570,** *568*, 571, 572, 574, 576
Williams, John (Memphis Piano Red), 415
Williams, John "Red Bone," 568
Williams, Johnny (see: Hooker, John Lee) (see: Warren, Robert)
Williams, Johnny, 240, 535, 595
Williams, Rev. Johnny, **570-571,** 594
Williams, Joseph "Jo Jo," 91, 342, 435, **571,** *571*, 572
Williams, Joseph Lee (see: Williams, Joe Lee)
Williams, Joseph Leon, 311, 571, **571-572**
Williams, Juanita, 402
Williams, L. C., 244, **572**
Williams, Larry, 544
Williams, Larry C., 362
Williams, Lee "Shot," **572**
Williams, Lester, **572**
Williams, Martin T., 371, 538, 594
Williams, Neal, 149
Williams, Nellie, 594
Williams, Paul, 84
Williams, Peter, 396
Williams, Rabbit's Foot (see: Coleman, Burl)
Williams, Robert Pete, 244, 276, 429, **573-574,** *573*
Williams, Rubberlegs (see: Williams, Henry)
Williams, Ruby "Tuna Boy," 298
Williams, Ruthy Kate, 369
Williams, Sam, 572
Williams, Spencer, 222, 350, 495
Williams, Sugar Boy (see: Williams, Joseph Leon)
Williams, Susan (see: McCoy, Viola)
Williams, William, 562
Williams, Willie, 476
Williams, Willie, 578
Williams & Brown (duo), 73
Williams Bar (Buffalo, NY), 84
Williams Lounge (Chicago, IL), 341
Williamson, Carrie Cecil, 441
Williamson, Henry, 564
Williamson, John A. (Homesick James), 59, 181, 246, 271, 294, 304, 342, 344, 345, 393, 416, 424, 490, 493, 494, 529, **574-575,** 574
Williamson, John Lee "Sonny Boy," 36, 39, 62, 66, 68, 69, 96, 148, 172, 178, 180, 196, 214, 225, 228, 247, 269, 279, 342, 355, 370, 371, 375, 388, 401, 424, 425, 426, 427, 444, 485, 502, 522, 549, 569, 574, **575-576,** *575*, 578, 591, 594, 595
Williamson, John R., 564
Williamson, Ray, 575
Williamson, Sonny Boy (see also: Williamson, John Lee)
Williamson, Sonny Boy (Aleck/Alex Miller), 27, 42, 54, 58, 62, 65, 91, 93, 95, 96, 99, 101, 106, 109, 117, 130, 132, 137, 139, 140, 181, 183, 216, 225, 228, 237, 246, 261, 269, 271, 288-289, 291, 308, 322, 329, 334, 338, 339, 348, 352, 371, 399, 400, 407, 412, 425, 435, 437, 442, 443, 449, 450, 457, 481, 483, 499, 501, 514, 516, 535, 549, 554, 560, 576, **576-578,** *576*, 580
Williamson, Sonny Boy, Jr. (see: Anderson, Clarence)
Williamson, Willie, 578
Willie, Joe, 336
Willie B. (see: Borum, William)
Willie C. (see: Cobbs, Willie)
Willie the Lion and His Cubs (band), 221
Willie's Inn (Chicago, IL), 501
Willis, Aaron "Little Son/Sonny," 96, 269, 578, **578-580,** *579*
Willis, Aaron, Jr., 580
Willis, Guitar Joe, 522
Willis, Lee, 109
Willis, Little Son/Sonny (see: Willis, Aaron)
Willis, Malcolm, 122, 580
Willis, Ralph, 185, 366, 503
Willow (label), 38
Wills, Bob, 440
Wills, Oscar, **580**
Willy's Inn (Chicago, IL), 104
Wilmer, Valerie, 180
Wilshire Ebell Theater (Los Angeles, CA), 125, 190, 194, 300, 341, 381, 594
Wilson, Alan, 241
Wilson, Charlie, 582
Wilson, Danny, 580, 582, 583, 584
Wilson, Edith, 254, 381, **580-582,** *580*, 583, 584
Wilson, Harding "Hop," 276, 453, **582-583,** *583*
Wilson, Jackie, 84, 88, 308
Wilson, James, 584
Wilson, Jimmy, 510
Wilson, John S., 120, 245
Wilson, Kellogg, 377
Wilson, Lena, 580, 582, **583-584,** *583*
Wilson, Leo, 402
Wilson, Leola B. (see: Grant, Leola B.)
Wilson, Marjorie, 153
Wilson, Mary, 337
Wilson, Mary Ella, 290

Wilson, Millard, 582
Wilson, Nancy, 538
Wilson, Teddy, 83
Wilson, Teddy, 84
Wilson, Wesley "Socks," 197, **584**
Wilson, Willie, 249
Windin' Ball (label), 380, 591
Windsor Concert (Windsor, Can.), 278, 535
Wing (label), 219, 503
Wings Stadium (Kalamazoo, MI), 545
Winners Inn (Reno, NV), 78
Winnipeg Folk Festival (Winnipeg, Can.), 57, 120, 148, 174, 210, 266, 349, 459, 490
Winslow, Wilson, 212
Winston Towers (club) (Cliffside Park, NJ), 567
Winter (band), 585
Winter, Edgar, 585
Winter, Johnny, 54, 132, 241, 246, 271, 289, 305, 311, 390, 459, 528, **585-586**, *585*
Winter Erlich & Hearst Carnival (tour), 382
Winter Garden Theater (New York, NY), 481, 494, 541, 581
Winterland Auditorium (San Francisco, CA), 30, 51, 54, 100, 151-152, 296, 304, 305, 310, 345, 346, 359, 389, 390, 478, 585
Winters, Jim, 298
Wisconsin Blues Festival (Beloit, WI), 41, 249, 260, 266, 291, 330, 341, 342, 457, 490, 494, 573, 595
Wisconsin Delta Blues Festival (Beloit, WI), 363, 562, 569
Wise Fools Pub (club) (Chicago, IL), 42, 68, 123, 151, 156, 236, 240, 246, 260, 334, 369, 389, 395, 435, 437, 442, 444, 445, 450, 499, 513, 575, 595, 596
Witches Cauldron (club) (Hampstead, Eng.), 234
Withers, Hayes, 351
Witherspoon, Albert, 279
Witherspoon, James "Jimmy," 51, 70, 76, 122, 377, 448, 470, 520, 527, 568, **586-589**, *587*
Witherspoon, Matilda, **589**
Wittenborn, Andrew, 36, 419, 594
Woffinden, Bob, 47, 101, 225, 312, 352
Wolf Trap Farm Park (Vienna, VA), 130, 175, 182, 429
Wolfe, Karl Michael, 163
Wolf's Buffet (club) (Kansas City, MO), 518
Wolfson, Sylvester, 222
Wolverine Nighthawks (band), 414
Women Strike for Peace (label), 142
Women's Music Festival (Urbana, IL), 142
Wonder (label), 371
Wonder Bar Club (Cleveland, OH), 334
Wonder Garden (club) (Atlantic City, NJ), 308
Wood, ______, 206
Wood, Bobby, 517
Wood, George, 116, 216
Woodbine Plantation (Bentonia, MS), 272
Woodbridge, Hudson, 559
Woodbridge, John, 559
Woodfork, King, 589
Woodfork, Robert, **589**
Wooding, Russell, 541
Wooding, Sam, 221, 373, 581
Woodland Club (Birmingham, AL),
Woodlawn Cemetery (Bronx, NY), 52
Woodlawn Cemetery (Los Angeles, CA), 216
Woodlawn Hospital (Dallas, TX), 461
Woodlawn Memorial Park (Los Angeles, CA), 546
Woods, Big Boy (see: Collins, Sam)
Woods, Buddy (see: Woods, Oscar)
Woods, Earley, 468
Woods, Flossie, 181
Woods, Hosea, 106
Woods, Johnnie, 558
Woods, Johnny, 363
Woods, Oscar "Buddy," 518, **589**
Woodstock Music & Art Fair (concert) (Bethel, NY), 100, 219, 224, 296, 585
Woodstock Playhouse (Woodstock, NY), 521
Woody Guthrie Bibliography 1912-1967 (book), 206
Woody Guthrie Folk Songs: A Collection of Songs by America's Foremost Balladeer (book), 206
Woody Guthrie Memorial Concert (Hollywood, CA), 174, 195, 219
Woody Guthrie Memorial Concert (New York, NY), 174, 195, 218, 366, 504
Woody Guthrie Singers (group), 206, 365, 503
Woody Guthrie Songbook (book), 206
Woody Sez (book), 206
Word (label), 542
World Champions of Jazz Jam Session (concert) (Indianapolis, IN), 316
World Folk Song (label), 185
World of Soul (book), 47, 158, 299, 557
World Pacific (label), 30, 32, 141, 168, 213, 243, 366, 375, 439, 468, 470, 503, 510, 569, 586
World Surrealist Exhibition (Chicago, IL), 169, 564
World Transcription (label), 406
World's Champion Moaner (billing), The, 467
World's Fair (see: Brussels WF/ Chicago WF/Hemisfair/New York WF/St. Louis WF/Seattle WF)
World's Fair Bar (St. Louis, MO), 414
World's Greatest Blues Shouter (billing), 520
World's Greatest Blues Singer (billing), 280
Worsfold, Sally Ann, 321
Wortham Negro Cemetery (Wortham, TX), 276
Wrencher, John Thomas, 197, 576, **589-591**, *590*
Wrencher, Jonah, 589
Wright, Annie Bell, 147
Wright, Dan, 188
Wright, Leo, 199
Wright, Sister Annie (see: Wright, Annie Bell)
Wrigley Field (stadium) (Los Angeles, CA), 86, 136
Wyn, Pat, 506
Wynn, Al, 148, 380
Wynn, Jim, 527

X (label), 215
X-Glamour Girls (organization), 492
Xanadu Ballroom (Memphis, TN), 177, 401
Xtra (label), 117, 148, 231, 247, 318, 366, 443, 457, 503, 569

Yale University (New Haven, CT), 34, 194, 283, 311, 447, 508, 569
Y'alls Club (Chicago, IL), 79
Yambo (label), 156, 178, 246
Yancey, Alonzo, 592, 594
Yancey, Estella "Mama," 142, 162, 465, **591-592**, *592*, 592
Yancey, James "Jimmy," 31, 103, 337, 467, 591, **592-594**, *593*
Yancey, Mama (see: Yancey, Estella)
Yancey, Mose, 592
Yankee, Pat, 428, 465, **594**, *594*
Yardbirds (band), The, 95, 360, 577
Yazoo (label), 119, 160, 192, 264, 297, 336, 470, 486, 547
Yazoo City High School (Bentonia, MS), 272
Ye Little Club (Beverly Hills, CA), 466
Yellow Brick Road Club (San Francisco, CA), 516
Yellow Front Cafe (Kansas City, MO), 321
Yellow Unicorn (club), The (Chicago, IL), 569
York, Tiny, 111
York Club (Los Angeles, CA), 417, 510
York Opera House (York, PA), 70
York University (Toronto, Can.), 420
Young, Bob, 509
Young, Dave, 536
Young, Gene, 250
Young, Horace, 594
Young, John O. "Johnny," 41, 70, 119, 132, 150, 168, 178, 246, 291, 355, 393, 424, 478, 479, 570, 571, 576, 591, **594-595**, *595*
Young, Johnny, 497
Young, Joseph "Mighty Joe", 35, 311, 442, 476, 499, 530, **596-597**, *596*
Young, Lester, 291
Young, Marl, 527
Young, Robert, 365
Young & Myers Plantation (Ruleville, MS), 93
Young Men From New Orleans Band, 385
Young Wolf, The (see: Jenkins, Gus)
Youngblood, Rosa, 290
Youngest Interlocutor in the World (billing), 81, 83
Youth for Christ Crusades (religious program) 542-543
Yubin Chokin Hall (Tokyo, Japan), 177, 208, 336, 394, 401, 457, 549
Yugoslav Hall (New York, NY), 194

Yukon Bar (St. Louis, MO), 502
Yulando (label), 571
Yurchenco, Henrietta, 206, 207

Za Zu Girl (see: Spivey, Elton)
Zachery, Mamie, 230
Zachron (label), 289
Zack Lewis Club (Vicksburg, MS), 379
Zanzibar Club (see: Club Zanzibar, New York, NY)
Zanzibar Club (Buffalo, NY), 263
Zanzibar Club (Chicago, IL), 35, 41, 93, 109, 181, 268, 269, 305, 334, 388, 410, 442, 460, 468, 485, 493, 559
Zapot Coffee House (Louisville, KY), 426
Zappa, Frank, 211
Zardi's Jazzland (Hollywood, CA), 299, 373, 538
Zebra Club (San Diego, CA), 134
Zebra Lounge (Los Angeles, CA), 113
Zieger Osteopathic Hospital (Detroit, MI), 182
Ziegfeld Theater (New York, NY), 229, 493, 542
Zip (label), 89
Zodiac Club (see also: Club Zodiac)
Zodiac Club (Amstelveen, Holland), 569
Zonta Organization for Business & Professional Women, 245
Zoo Bar (Lincoln, NE), 33, 42, 68, 123, 124, 151, 236, 334, 450, 596
Zorba's (club) (Cicero, IL), 68, 124, 334
Zorita's 606 Club (New York, NY), 285
Zynn (label), 121, 522, 547